S0-ARC-229

THIRD EDITION

BUSINESS LAW PRINCIPLES AND CASES

UNIFORM COMMERCIAL CODE VOLUME

Ronald A. Anderson

Professor of Law and Government,
Drexel Institute of Technology

Member of the Pennsylvania and Philadelphia Bars

Coauthor of *Business Law*, Sixth Edition

Author of *Anderson's Uniform Commercial Code;*
Government and Business, Second Edition;
Anderson's Pennsylvania Civil Practice;
Couch's Cyclopedia of Insurance Law (2nd Edition);
Wharton's Criminal Law, Procedure, and Evidence;
Consulting Editor of the *Pennsylvania Law Encyclopedia*

Walter A. Kumpf

Editor in Chief,
South-Western Publishing Company

Coauthor of *Business Law*, Sixth Edition

SOUTH-WESTERN PUBLISHING CO.

Cincinnati   Chicago   Burlingame, Calif.   Dallas   New Rochelle, N.Y.

L39

Copyright, © 1963

by

SOUTH-WESTERN PUBLISHING COMPANY

Cincinnati, Ohio

All Rights Reserved

The text of this publication, or any part thereof, may not be reproduced in any manner whatsoever without permission in writing from the publisher.

Library of Congress Catalog Card Number: 63-10711

H263

Printed in the United States of America

PREFACE

Only once in several decades does the law of business seem to quicken its usual pace of gradual evolutionary development. Such a time is now, as society modernizes the rules that govern commercial transactions. We, as authors of this new edition of BUSINESS LAW PRINCIPLES AND CASES, are happy to share with instructors and students the excitement and challenge of this period of change by presenting this Uniform Commercial Code Volume.

In a very real sense, this is a fifth edition, not the third, of BUSINESS LAW PRINCIPLES AND CASES because this textbook has evolved, like the law, from the original CASES ON BUSINESS LAW by Dwight L. Pomeroy. That book appeared in two editions before it was transformed into a combination textbook-casebook. Now an even more significant change takes place as the materials on sales, negotiable instruments, secured transactions, and documents of title are based upon the Code, rather than upon the former uniform statutes.

The purpose of BUSINESS LAW PRINCIPLES AND CASES, Uniform Commercial Code Volume, is to present the fundamental principles of the important areas of subject matter through text matter and carefully edited extracts from the opinions in representative cases. The materials are organized into 12 parts. Part I, Law and Society, with its emphasis on social forces in the first two chapters and the introductory treatment of agencies for enforcing legal rights and court procedure in the third chapter, provides a solid foundation for the meaningful study of the more specific topics that follow.

Beginning with Part II, Contracts, each chapter includes three types of material—text, cases, and questions and case problems.

Text

1. The first part of each chapter presents the basic principles of the subject with quotations from and references to the Restatements of the American Law Institute and the uniform statutes. The Restatements deal with such subjects as contracts, agency, property, security, and torts. The Uniform Commercial Code and other uniform statutes or model acts pertain to such subjects as commercial paper, sales, secured transactions, documents of title, gifts to minors, aeronautics, fraudulent conveyances, partnerships, and business corporations.

2. The material in this edition has been brought up to date through an examination of all professional publications in the field, of federal legislation, and of every reported decision of the federal courts, the state supreme courts, and the important intermediate state courts.

3. Although every statement in the text has been carefully researched and documented, relatively few footnotes are used. In the areas affected by the Uniform Commercial Code, however, the subject matter is extensively footnoted for the convenience of instructors and students who may wish to check the provisions of the Code.

4. The materials are organized on a psychological, as well as a logical, basis. For example, notes, drafts, and checks are discussed in separate chapters.

5. The text material is written in a clear, concise manner for students who are studying this field for the first time. Unnecessary technicalities are omitted. Important new terms are carefully defined and explained when they are used for the first time. A glossary provides additional assistance.

6. The principles are presented in a self-outlining form. The importance of each heading is indicated by its position or indention, the style of type, and an identifying number or letter.

7. Each main topic is identified with a section heading, such as Sec. 4-C, which indicates that this is the third main topic in Chapter 4. These section headings, together with the numbers and letters that identify subtopics, provide a convenient means of reference to the text.

8. State variations in the law are indicated in the text, in special tables, and by means of footnotes for the uniform statutes.

9. The text is keyed to the cases that follow in each chapter. Instructors and students may turn immediately to each case for study if that method is preferred.

10. Illustrations of legal forms are limited to the simpler types of commercial paper. The value of illustrating other legal forms is doubtful because the wording and provisions vary in different states. Those forms in local use are best for instructional purposes in collegiate courses in business law.

Cases

1. Each case applies one or more principles of business law to a particular set of facts. In this way the cases give substance and enriched meaning to the principles.

2. The nature, purpose, and use of the cases are explained in Chapter 1 just preceding the first case and using that case as an example.

3. The first paragraph of each case contains a concise summary of the facts pertinent to the case, a statement of the issues involved, and a review of that portion of the procedure that is essential to an understanding of the case. The purpose of this paragraph is to provide the student with a background that is adequate for his analysis of the case but not so detailed and technical that he is confused when he reads the opinion.

4. The opinions have been carefully edited so that students can concentrate on the important legal principles and the business relations involved. Obsolete and technical terms and procedures have been omitted. Citations and statements that are of little value to beginning students have been dropped. The emphasis is upon substantive law. The cases have not been unduly simplified, however, because students should become familiar with the processes of judicial reasoning.

5. Emphasis has been placed on recent interesting cases that show the judicial process and the social forces at work. Selection has also been governed by the importance, clarity, organization, and geographical distribution of the cases.

6. The cases vary in length and difficulty. A number of longer cases are included. In a number of cases, extracts from dissenting opinions have been retained.

7. For the areas of subject matter based upon the Code, relatively few cases have been decided by courts of final jurisdiction. Under the circumstances, cases decided under the prior law have been used but they are followed by a Code comment, which indicates how the court would have ruled under the Code.

Questions and Case Problems

Beginning with Part II, two types of questions and problems are provided at the end of each chapter.

1. The questions in the first group require the student to determine the specific social objectives of selected rules or principles of law. These questions provide a continuous correlation with, and development of, Chapter 1, Social Forces and the Law.

2. The remaining items in the end-of-chapter section consist of problems that are adapted from adjudicated cases. The purpose of these is to challenge the student's understanding by presenting unfamiliar sets of facts to which the appropriate principles must be applied. In some problems the answer is not based directly on the text and case material in the chapter and the student must apply principles studied in earlier chapters. In this cumulative treatment, the student becomes increasingly aware that court cases seldom involve isolated points of law.

Appendix

The Appendix, Law and Its Enforcement, supplements Chapter 3. It is provided for those instructors who prefer a more detailed discussion of the following subjects before students embark upon the study of contracts: (a) Law and Sources of Law, (b) The Court System, and (c) Court Procedure.

Glossary

A new feature of this Third Edition is an extensive glossary. Terms that have been included have been selected on the basis of their helpfulness to the beginning student of business law. The glossary supplements the terms that are defined, explained, and illustrated in the text and which can be located by reference to the index.

Uniform Commercial Code Supplement

A Uniform Commercial Code Supplement is available. It is an analysis of the latest (1957) official text of the Code and the 1958 amendments. The 1962 amendments to the Code do not affect the coverage of this supplement.

Acknowledgments

Many instructors of business law have contributed to the production of a textbook that is truly a composite of a variety of teaching experiences. To them the authors are greatly indebted. More specific contributions to the current edition were made by Scott Hovey, Occidental College; Sister Frances Catherine, College of Mount St. Joseph on the Ohio; and Glen Wing, University of Arkansas.

R.A.A.

W.A.K.

CONTENTS

* The Appendix (page 949) is a supplement to Chapter 3.

Contents

PART I

LAW and SOCIETY

CHAPTER 1

Social Forces and the Law

Law has developed because man and society have wanted relationships between men, and between men and government, to conform to certain standards. Each person has desired to know what conduct he could reasonably expect from others as well as what conduct others could reasonably expect from him so that he could make decisions intelligently in terms of his legal rights and obligations. The rules adopted for this purpose have expressed the social, economic, and moral desires, standards, and aspirations of society. As democracy has expanded with the passing centuries, law has more truly expressed these desires of the community.

Today *law* consists of the entire body of principles that govern conduct and the observance of which can be enforced in courts. The expression, "a law," is ordinarily used in connection with a statute enacted by a state legislature or the Congress of the United States, such as an act by the federal Congress to extend the benefits of old-age insurance. All of the principles that make up "law," however, are not "laws" adopted by legislative bodies. Legal principles are also found in national and state constitutions, local ordinances, court decisions, and rules of administrative agencies, such as the National Labor Relations Board.

If there were no man-made law, no doubt many persons would be guided by principles of moral or natural law and choose to live and act much as they do today. Man would conduct himself in accordance with the dictates of his conscience, the precepts of right living that are a part of his religion, and the ethical concepts that are generally accepted in his community. Those who would choose to act otherwise, however, would constitute a serious problem for society. Man-made law is necessary to provide not only rules of conduct but also the machinery and procedures for enforcing right conduct, for punishing wrongful acts, and for settling disputes that arise even when both parties are motivated by good intentions.

Sec. 1-A. Law as Social Justice. The purpose of law in its broadest sense is to provide order, stability, and justice. Thus viewed, the law is the crystallization into relatively fixed rules of those patterns of conduct which society believes desirable. That is, according to the social morality of the community, certain conduct is proper and should be allowed or required and certain conduct is improper and should be prohibited. In short, law is a social institution; it is not an end unto itself but is an instrumentality of obtaining social justice.

Many factors and institutions have made their contribution in the molding of concepts of justice. Home and school training, religion, enlightened self-interest, social and business groups, and the various media of modern communication and entertainment all play a part. For example, various organizations such as chambers of commerce, better business bureaus, informal groups of businessmen, trade groups, and conferences have gradually changed the concept of what is ethical in business by stressing fair competition and service to the community. In turn, these organizations and groups have helped to bring about the adoption of statutes that modify the law to reflect the changed business ethics.

It would be a mistake, however, to assume that justice is a universal value which means the same to all people in all ages. Each individual's conception of justice varies in terms of his personality, his training, and his social and economic position. Justice has different meanings to the employer and the employee, to the millionaire and the pauper, to the industrial worker and the farmer, to the retired person and the young married adult, to the progressive and the conservative, or to the professor and the student! For this reason special interest groups attempt to modify the law so that it will be more favorable to the members of those groups. To the extent that such modifications are gained at the expense of the rights of the members of other groups, the law fails in its purpose of achieving justice for all. This is but one evidence of the fact that the law is no better than the human beings who make it, interpret it, and enforce it. Absolute justice is unattainable by human beings, but that is no reason why society should ever relent in its efforts to attain as high a level of substantial justice as is humanly possible.

When we consider a rule of law only as it exists today, it may appear just as arbitrary as the rule that twelve inches make one foot; arbitrary in the sense that there is no reason why it could not be ten inches or fourteen, or any other number. The reason may be that we fail to understand the purpose of the law; or we may not be sufficiently familiar with all sides of the problem to recognize that the rule is just in the sense that it is the best rule that could be devised under the circumstances.

Sec. 1-B. Specific Objectives of the Law. The objectives of the Constitution of the United States are included in the preamble, and important statutes frequently include a statement of their objectives. In many instances, however, the objective of the law is not stated or it is expressed in very general terms. Whether stated or not, each law has an objective; and it is helpful in understanding the nature and purpose of the law to know what these objectives are.

In the following enumeration the more important specific objectives of the law are discussed against the background of our understanding of the general objective of creating, maintaining, and restoring order, stability, and justice.

(1) Protection of the State. A number of laws are designed to protect the existing governments, both state and national. Laws condemning treason, sedition, and subversive practices are examples of society taking measures to preserve governmental systems. Less dramatic are the laws that impose taxes to provide for the support of those governments and that provide for compulsory military service to protect them from enemy aliens.

(2) Protection of Public Health, Safety, and Morals. The law seeks to protect the public health, safety, and morals in many ways. Laws relating to quarantine, food inspection, and compulsory vaccination are designed to protect the public health. Laws regulating the speed on the highway and those requiring fire escapes or guard devices around moving parts of factory machinery protect safety. Laws prohibiting the sale of liquor to minors and those prohibiting obscenity protect the morals of the public.

(3) Personal Protection. At an early date laws developed to protect the individual from being injured or killed. The field of criminal law is devoted to a large extent to the protection of the person. In addition, under civil law a suit can be brought to recover damages for the harm done by such acts. For example, a negligent driver of an automobile who injures a pedestrian is subject to a penalty imposed by the state in the form of imprisonment or a fine, or both.

He is also liable to the injured person for the payment of damages, which may include not only medical and hospital cost but also loss of time from work and mental anguish. In time, the protection of personal rights has broadened to protect reputation and privacy and to protect contracts from malicious interference by outsiders. (See p. 12, Nature and Purpose of Cases, and p. 14, Korn v. Rennison)

(4) Property Protection. Just as both criminal and civil laws have developed to protect the individual's physical well-being, such laws also have developed to protect one's property from damage, destruction, and other harmful acts. If the negligent driver runs into a parked car, he must account to the state for his negligence and to the owner of the damaged automobile for the cost of the necessary repairs even if that loss is covered by insurance.

(5) Title Protection. Because of the importance of ownership of property, one of the objectives of the law has been to protect the title of an owner to his property so that he remains the owner until it is clearly proved that he has transferred the title to someone else. Thus, if property is stolen, the true owner may recover it from the thief. He may even recover his property from a person who purchased it in good faith from the thief without any knowledge that the goods had been stolen.

(6) Freedom of Personal Action. In the course of the passing centuries, man became concerned with what he himself could do as well as with protection against what others might do to him or his property. At one time he was increasingly concerned with the restrictions that the monarchs were placing upon his freedom to act. This became particularly pronounced in the era before the American Revolution when the rulers of Europe, acting under the mercantilist theory, regulated the economy to benefit themselves. In the Anglo-American stream of history, man's desires for freedom from political domination gave rise to the American Revolution, and the desire for freedom from economic domination gave rise to the free enterprise philosophy. Today we find freedom as the dominant element in the constitutional provisions for the protection of freedom of religion, press, and speech and also in such laws as those against trusts or business combinations in restraint of trade by others.

This right of freedom of personal action, however, cannot be exercised by one person in such a way that it interferes to an unreasonable extent with the rights of others. Freedom of speech, for example, does not mean freedom to speak or write a malicious, false statement about another person's character. In effect, this means that one person's freedom of speech must be balanced with another person's right to be free from defamation of character or reputation.

(7) Freedom of Use of Property. Closely related to the objective of protection of freedom of action is that of protecting the freedom of the use of property. This freedom is achieved by prohibiting, restraining, or penalizing acts of others that would hamper the reasonable use of property by its owner.

Absolute freedom of this kind would permit its owner to make any use he chose of his property—even in a way that would harm others, to sell it at any price he desired, or to make any disposition of it that he wished. Such freedom is not recognized today, for everywhere we find some limitation of the right of the owner of property to do as he pleases with it.

The law prohibits an owner from using his property in such a way as to injure another or another's property. Further, zoning laws may limit the use of his land. Building restrictions in a deed may restrict the type of building that the owner may construct on his land. Fire laws and building codes may specify details of construction of his building. Labor laws may require that he equip a business building with safety devices.

(8) Enforcement of Intent. The law usually seeks to enforce the expressed intention of a party to a contract. This objective is closely related to the concept that the law seeks to protect the individual's freedom of action. For example, if a person provides by his will for the distribution of his property when he dies, the law will generally allow the property to pass to the persons intended by the deceased owner. The law will likewise seek to carry out the intention of the parties to a business transaction. To illustrate, if you and an electrician agree that he shall rewire your house for $200, the law will ordinarily enforce that contract because that is what was intended by both parties.

The extent to which the intent of one person or of several persons will be carried out has certain limitations. Sometimes the intent is not effective unless it is manifested by a particular formality. For example, a deceased person may have intended that his friend should receive his house, but in most states that intent must be shown by a written will signed by the deceased owner. Likewise, in some cases the intent of the parties may not be carried out because the law regards the purpose of the intent as illegal or otherwise improper.

(9) Protection from Exploitation, Fraud, and Oppression. Many rules of law have developed in the courts and many statutes have been enacted to protect certain groups or individuals from exploitation by others. Thus, the law developed that a minor (a person under legal age) could set aside his contract, subject to certain exceptions, in order to give the minor an opportunity to avoid a bad bargain.

Persons who buy food that is packed in tin cans are given certain rights against the seller and the manufacturer. Since they cannot see the contents, buyers of such products need special protection against unscrupulous canners who would pack improper foods. The consumer is also protected by laws against adulteration and poisons in foods, drugs, and household products because he would ordinarily be unable to take care of himself. Laws prohibiting unfair competition and discrimination, both economic and social, are also designed to protect from oppression.

For the purpose of brevity "oppression" is here used to include not only conscious wrongdoing by another but also cases of hardship or misfortune where the consequences to the victim may be regarded as extreme or oppressive. (See p. 15, Falcone v. Middlesex County Medical Society)

(10) Furtherance of Trade. Society may seek to further trade in a variety of ways, as by establishing a currency as a medium of payment; by recognizing and giving legal effect to installment sales; by adopting special rules for checks, notes, and similar instruments so that they can be widely used as credit devices and substitutes for money; or by enacting laws to mitigate the harmful effects of alternating periods of depression and inflation.

Laws that have been considered in connection with other objectives may also serve to further trade. For example, laws protecting against unfair competition have this objective, as well as the objective of protecting certain classes from exploitation by others.

(11) Creditor Protection. Society seeks to protect the rights of creditors and to protect them from dishonest or fraudulent acts of debtors. Initially creditors are protected by the law which declares that contracts are binding and which provides the machinery for the enforcement of contracts, and by the provision of the federal constitution that prohibits states from impairing the obligation of contracts. Further, creditors may compel a debtor to come into bankruptcy in order to settle his debts as far as his property permits. If the debtor has concealed his property or transferred it to a friend in order to hide it from his creditors, the law permits the creditors to claim the property for the payment of the debts due them.

(12) Debtor Rehabilitation. Society has come to regard it as unsound that debtors should be ruined forever by the burden of their debts. The passing centuries have seen the debtor's prison abolished. Bankruptcy laws have been adopted to provide the debtor with a means of settling his debts as best he can and then starting upon a new economic life. In times of widespread depression the same objective has been served by special laws that prohibit the foreclosure of

mortgages and regulate the amount of the judgments that can be entered against mortgage debtors.

(13) Stability. Stability is particularly important in business transactions. When you buy a house, for example, you not only want to know the exact meaning of the transaction under today's law but you also hope that the transaction will have the same meaning in the future. When the businessman invests money, he desires that the law will remain the same as it was when he acted.

Because of the objective of stability, the courts will ordinarily follow former decisions unless there is some valid reason to depart from them. When no former case directly bears on the point involved, the desire for stability will influence the courts to reach a decision that is a logical extension of some former decision or which follows a former decision by analogy rather than to strike off on a fresh path and to reach a decision unrelated to the past. Thus stability is achieved through continuity based on the assumption that many problems of today and tomorrow will be basically the same as those that were settled yesterday.

If stability were an absolute objective of the law, the cause of justice would often be thwarted. The reason that originally gave rise to a rule of law may have ceased to exist. The rule then appears unjust because it reflects a concept of justice that is outmoded or obsolete. For example, a rule of law, such as capital punishment, which one age believes just may be condemned by another age as unjust. We must not lose sight of the fact that the rule of law under question was created to further the sense of social justice existing at that time, but since our concepts of justice may change, the law may not always coincide with current concepts.

The law itself may be flexible in that it makes provision for changes in rules to meet situations that cannot be anticipated or for which an explicit set of rules cannot be developed satisfactorily in advance. Our constitutions state the procedures for their amendment. Such changes in constitutional law are purposely made difficult in order to serve the objective of stability, but they are possible when the need for change is generally recognized by the people of the state or nation.

Changes by legislative action in federal and state statutes and local ordinances are relatively easier to make. Furthermore, some statutes recognize the impossibility of laying down in advance a hard and fast rule that will do justice in all cases. The typical modern statute, particularly in the field of regulation of business and enterprise, will therefore contain "escape clauses" by which a person can escape from the operation of the statute under certain circumstances. Thus a rent control law may impose a rent ceiling, that is, a maximum above which landlords cannot charge, but it may also authorize a greater charge when special circumstances make it just to allow such exception, as when the landlord has made expensive repairs to the property or when his taxes have increased materially.

The rule of law may be stated in terms of what a reasonable or prudent man would do. Thus, whether you are negligent in driving your automobile is determined in court by whether you exercised the same degree of care that a prudent man would have exercised had he been driving your car under the circumstances in question. This is a vague and variable standard as to how you must drive your car, but it is the only standard that is practical. The alternative would be a detailed motor code specifying how you should drive your car under every possible situation that might arise: a code that obviously could not foresee every possible situation and which obviously would be too long for any driver to know by heart.

(14) Practical Expediency. Frequently the law is influenced by what is practical and expedient in the situation. In some of these situations, the law will strive to make its rules fit the business practices of society. For example, a signature is frequently regarded by the law as including a stamping, printing, or typewriting of a name, in recognition of the business practice of "signing" letters and other instruments by mechanical means. A requirement of a handwritten signature would impose a burden on business that would not be practically expedient.

The concept of practical expediency may also apply when the courts are influenced by the effect upon the courts themselves of the adoption of a particular rule of law. For example, courts will not ordinarily render advisory opinions, that is, give legal advice to people when there is no real lawsuit. It would not be practical for courts to perform that function, for, if they did, the courts would be overburdened with "advice" work.

Sec. 1-C. Conflicting Objectives. As we have seen, the specific objectives of the law sometimes conflict with each other. When this is true, the problem is one of social policy, which in turn means a weighing of social, economic, and moral forces to determine which objective should be furthered. Thus we find a conflict at times between the objectives of the state seeking protection from the conduct of individuals or groups and the objective of freedom of action by those individuals and groups. (See p. 18, United States v. Bonanno)

Considering more in detail the interplay and conflict of objectives, let us turn to rent control. If we wish to protect the freedom of the use of property, we will then allow the landlord to rent his property in any condition he chooses and at any price he chooses. Underlying this decision will be our belief that if his property is not in good condition, the competition of other landlords will force him to improve his property or to reduce his rent. An examination of the facts, however, may show such a serious housing shortage that property in poor condition can be rented at a high price. Under such circumstances we cannot depend upon the forces of supply and demand to make the landlord improve his property or reduce his rent. Society therefore adopts a law regulating the condition of leased property or specifying the maximum rents which landlords may charge. That is, society seeks to protect the tenant from exploitation by the landlord. By adopting such a control law, society is sacrificing the objective of protecting the freedom of the use of property by the landlord to the objective of protecting the tenant from the landlord's exploitation.

As another example, the objective of protecting title may conflict with the objective of furthering trade. Consider again the example of the stolen property that was sold by the thief to one who purchased it for value and in good faith, without reason to know that the goods had been stolen. If we are to further the objective of protecting the title to the property, we will conclude that the owner can recover the property from the innocent purchaser. This rule, however, will discourage trade, for people will be less willing to buy goods if they run the risk that the goods were stolen and may have to be surrendered. If we instead think only of taking steps to encourage buying and selling, we will hold that the buyer takes a good title because he acted in good faith and paid value. If we do this, we then destroy the title of the original owner and obviously abandon our objective of protecting title to property. As a general rule, society has followed the objective of protecting title. In some instances, however, the objective of furthering trade is adopted by statute, and the buyer is given good title as in certain cases of the purchaser of negotiable instruments (notes, drafts, and checks) or of the purchaser from a regular dealer in other people's goods.

Sec. 1-D. Law as an Evolutionary Process. As of any one minute, or even over a number of years, law appears to be static and, in fact, a number of legal principles have remained the same over the centuries. But many rules of law have changed and are changing. (See p. 20, New Jersey v. Culver)

In the first place, the law changes as society seeks to improve its existing rules in order to attain more closely the standards of justice and morality. This change in the law, in turn, may be a reflection of a social and economic change. For example, the law governing relations between landlord and tenant originated in the era of feudalism in which the owner of the land was economically, socially, and politically dominant. The law at that time, therefore, reflected his desires and was designed primarily to protect his interests. In modern society the owner of the land no longer holds that position of dominance; and the law has changed to conform to new concepts of justice and fairness, and greater recognition and protection are given to the rights and interests of the tenant.

Let us consider another example of this type of change. When the economy was patterned on a local community unit in which everyone knew each other and each other's product, the concept of "let the buyer beware" expressed a proper basis on which to conduct business. Much of the early law of the sales of goods was predicated on this philosophy. In today's economy, however, with its emphasis on interstate, national, and even international activities, the buyer has little or no direct contact with the manufacturer or seller, and the packaging of articles makes their presale examination impossible. Under the circumstances the consumer must rely on the integrity of others to an increasing degree. Gradually practices that were tolerated and even approved in an earlier era have been condemned, and the law has changed to protect the buyer by warranties when his own caution can no longer protect him.

Moreover, new principles of law are being developed to meet the new situations that have arisen. Every new invention and every new business practice introduces a number of situations for which there is no satisfactory rule of law. For example, how could there have been a law governing the liability of a food canner to the consumer before canning was invented? How could there have been a law relating to stocks and bonds before those instruments came into existence? How could there have been law with respect to the liability of radio and television broadcasters before such methods of communication were developed? This pattern of change will continue as long as man strives for better ways to achieve his desires.

Sec. 1-E. Law as a Synthesis. Law as a synthesis may be illustrated by the law relating to contracts for the sale of a house. Originally such a contract could be oral, that is, merely spoken words with nothing in writing to prove that there was such a contract. Of course, there was the practical question of proof, that is, whether the jury would believe that there was such a contract, but no rule said that the contract must be in writing. This situation made it possible for a witness in court to swear falsely that Jones had agreed to sell his house for a specified sum. Even though Jones had not made such an agreement, the jury might believe the false witness, and Jones would be required to give up his house on terms to which he had not agreed. To help prevent such a miscarriage of justice, a statute was passed in England in 1677 which declared that contracts for the sale of houses had to be in writing.

This law ended the evil of persons lying that there was an oral agreement for the sale of a house, but was justice finally achieved? Not always, for cases arose in which Jones did in fact make an oral agreement to sell his land to Smith. Smith would take possession of the land and would make valuable improvements at great expense and effort, and then Jones would have Smith thrown off the land. Smith would defend on the ground that Jones had orally agreed to sell the land to him. Jones would then say, "Where is the writing that the statute requires?" To this Smith could only reply that there was no writing. No writing meant no legal agreement and therefore Smith lost the land, leaving Jones with the land and all the improvements that Smith had made, without Smith getting one penny for his trouble. That certainly was not just. What then?

Gradually the law courts developed the rule that in spite of the fact that the statute required a writing, the court would enforce an oral contract for the sale of land when the buyer had gone into possession and made valuable improvements of such a nature that it would be difficult to determine what amount of money would be required to make up the loss if he were to be put off the land.

Thus, the law passed through three stages: (1) The original concept that all land contracts could be oral. Because the perjury evil arose under this rule of law, society swung to (2) the opposite rule that no such contract could be oral. This rule gave rise to the hardship case of the honest buyer under an oral contract who made extensive improvements. The law then swung, not back to the original rule, but to (3) a middle position, combining both (1) and (2), that is, combining the element of the written requirement as to the ordinary transaction but allowing oral contracts in the special cases to prevent hardship.

This example is also interesting because it shows the way in which the courts "amend" the law by decision. The flat requirement of the statute was "eroded" by decisions and by exceptions created by the court in the interest of furthering justice.

Sec. 1-F. A Final Word. As you study the rules of business law in the chapters that follow, consider each rule in relationship to its social economic, and moral background. Try to determine the particular objective of each important rule. To the extent that you are able to analyze law as the product of man striving for justice in society, you will have a greater insight into the law itself, the world in which you live, the field of business, and the mind of man.

*   *   *   *   *   *   *

Nature and Purpose of Cases. Following the text in each chapter, cases are included for analysis and study. They illustrate how certain principles of law are applied in lawsuits by our courts. The information for each case is presented in three parts: (1) the heading, (2) the facts of the case, and (3) the opinion. In this explanation, the first case, Korn v. Rennison, page 14, will be used as an example. In some cases a Code Comment is added to indicate what the decision would be if the case were governed by the Uniform Commercial Code.[1]

(1) Heading. The heading of the case consists of the title and the source.

(a) TITLE. The title of the case usually consists of the names of the parties to the action. In the illustrative case, Korn, as plaintiff, sued Rennison (and others) as defendants.

The title of an appealed case may not reveal who was the plaintiff in the original or lower court and who was the defendant. When the action is started in the lower court, the first party named is the plaintiff and the second is the defendant. When the case is appealed, the name of the party who takes the appeal generally appears first on the records of the higher court. If the defendant takes the appeal, the original order of the names of the parties is then reversed.

(b) SOURCE. The second part of the heading gives the source of the opinion. The opinion is found in "21 Conn.Sup. 400, 156 A.2d 476." This means that the opinion is found in the 21st volume of the Connecticut Supplement (Conn.Sup.) reporter beginning at page 400; and that it is also found in the Atlantic (A.) sectional reporter[2] in volume 156 of the second series beginning at page 476.

(2) Facts. The paragraph in smaller type following the heading is a summary of the facts of the case, which provides a background for an understanding and analysis of the opinion. Read the statement of facts for Korn v. Rennison. Keep in mind the principles of law that

---

[1] See p. 51.
[2] The sectional reports are: Atlantic—A. (Connecticut, Delaware, District of Columbia, Maine, Maryland, New Hampshire, New Jersey, Pennsylvania, Rhode Island, Vermont); Northeastern—N.E. (Illinois, Indiana, Massachusetts, New York, Ohio); Northwestern—N.W. (Iowa, Michigan, Minnesota, Nebraska, North Dakota, South Dakota, Wisconsin); Pacific—P. (Alaska, Arizona, California, Colorado, Hawaii, Idaho, Kansas, Montana, Nevada, New Mexico, Oklahoma, Oregon, Utah, Washington, Wyoming); Southeastern—S.E. (Georgia, North Carolina, South Carolina, Virginia, West Virginia); Southwestern—S.W. (Arkansas, Kentucky, Missouri, Tennessee, Texas); and Southern—So. (Alabama, Florida, Louisiana, Mississippi). There is also a special New York State reporter known as the New York Supplement and a special California State reporter known as the California Reporter. In addition to these state reporters, a Federal Supplement reports the opinions of the Federal District Courts and the United States Court of Claims; the Federal Reporter, which formerly reported the lower federal court decisions, now reports the decisions of the courts of appeals; and the Supreme Court Reporter and the Lawyers' Edition each reports the decisions of the United States Supreme Court.

you studied in the chapter. Then read the opinion carefully to see how the court made its decision, what it decided, and whether it agrees with what you thought would be decided.

(3) Opinion. The opinion of the court includes the name of the judge, excerpts from the reasoning of the court, and the judgment.

(a) JUDGE. At the beginning of the opinion is the name of the judge who wrote it. The opinion in the first case was written by Judge Alcorn. If the case has been appealed, the judge in writing the opinion is speaking for the entire court, unless otherwise indicated. In cases that have not been appealed, one judge is disposing of the case himself, as in the Korn case.

The letter or letters following the name of the judge indicates his rank or title. J. stands for Judge or Justice. (JJ. is the plural form). Other abbreviations include C.J. for Chief Justice or Circuit Judge, D.J. for District Judge, P.J. for Presiding Judge or President Judge, and C. for Chancellor or Commissioner.

(b) BODY OF THE OPINION. The material following the judge's name is quoted from the opinion of the court. Words enclosed in brackets [ ] did not appear in the original opinion but have been added to explain a legal term, to identify a party, or to clarify a statement. Ellipses (three or four periods) are used to indicate that something has been omitted that is not pertinent to the point of law in which we are concerned at this time.

Decisions vary in length from less than a page to more than a hundred pages, and opinions frequently involve several points of law. Each case in this book has been carefully edited so that the excerpts reprinted here will be convenient for student use.

The edited opinion in Korn v. Rennison consists of five paragraphs. In the first paragraph the Judge indicates that more than a half-century ago the existence of a right of privacy was recognized by some as a matter of common or nonstatutory law. In the second paragraph he brings the subject down to date, pointing out the present state of the law and the social and scientific factors which influenced the growth of the law. The third paragraph points out the conflict of interests that are involved, and a further recognition of the growth of the law is made. The fourth paragraph is a formal statement of the present-day rule as made by the Restatement of the Law of Torts. The final paragraph states the conclusion of the Judge that there is a common-law right of privacy and that whether it has been violated in a given case depends upon the facts of the case.

Opinions do not follow a standard pattern of organization; but usually the well-written opinion will carefully examine the arguments presented by all parties and then explain why the court accepts or rejects those arguments. In this process the opinion may discuss the opinion of the lower court, the decisions in similar cases in other courts, the opinions of legal writers, and material from other sources.

(c) JUDGMENT. The case is concluded with a statement of the court's decision. If the case has been appealed and the court agrees with the lower court, the decision may simply be "Judgment affirmed," or a similar expression. If the appellate court disagrees, the decision may be expressed as "Judgment reversed." "Case remanded" means that the case is returned to the lower court to proceed further in harmony with the appellate court's decision. In lower court cases when the judgment is on a narrow issue, the judgment of the court is limited to "Objection sustained" or "Objection dismissed."

A judge of the court who disagrees with the majority may simply declare as part of the record that he dissents; or he may file a dissenting opinion, as occurred in the case on page 31.

Cases for Chapter 1

Checklist for Case Study: *Suggested questions for use in the analysis of each case are listed on page 54.*

Korn v. Rennison

21 Conn.Sup. 400, 156 A.2d 476 (1959)

The substance of this complaint was that, through an arrangement and agreement between Rennison and other defendants, a photograph of Korn, the plaintiff, was published for advertising purposes in the defendant newspaper without the knowledge, consent, or permission of the plaintiff and in violation of her personal liberties and private rights. As a result, the defendants received monetary benefits and advantages while the plaintiff received none and was subjected to ridicule, embarrassment, vexation, and humiliation. The plaintiff, a minor, brought this action by her mother to recover damages.

ALCORN, J. . . . The defendants argue that . . . a right [of privacy] was not recognized at common law [3] and therefore, in the absence of statute, it cannot exist in Connecticut today. When Samuel D. Warren and Louis D. Brandeis first gave form and substance to the right of privacy in 1890, it was one objective of their discussion in 4 Harvard Law Review 193 to demonstrate that the right found support in common-law principles. Underlying their reasoning is the premise that the common law is not static and its protecting arm does not become immobilized from lack of precedent.

---

[3] See p. 50.

In the years intervening since the right was thus defined, a constantly increasing number of jurisdictions have recognized its independent existence. Press, photography, radio, and television represent elements in constantly changing conditions which impinge upon individual privacy. With the environmental changes of modern living has grown the need that man's inner nature and feelings as well as his body and possessions receive the protection of the law. Hence, the right of privacy has become established in nearly half the states. . . .

The line to be drawn between reasonable demands of individual privacy and public interest in legitimate news is not always easy to define, but the boundary is more readily perceived in the case of commercial advertising. . . . No case decided within the last fifteen years has been found in which the existence of a right of privacy has been denied. Decisions which originally denied the right have, with apparently a single exception, since been overruled, modified, or altered by statute. Rhode Island appears to stand alone as an unqualified precedent for denying a recovery in damages for an invasion of the right of privacy. . . .

The right of privacy, as developed, finds expression in the Restatement, 4 Torts § 867, as follows: "A person who unreasonably and seriously interferes with another's interest in not having his affairs known to others or his likeness exhibited to the public is liable to the other."

The statement of the rule emphasizes the importance of the facts of the individual case presented. The recognition of the right as a basis for . . . [an] action in jurisdictions faced with the question unaided by statute, and the practical unanimity of recent opinion, place the right within the purview of the common law. . . .

[Objection of defendants dismissed.]

Falcone v. Middlesex County Medical Society

34 N.J. 582, 170 A.2d 791 (1961)

Dr. Falcone was admittedly a licensed and qualified physician and surgeon, holding degrees from a Philadelphia school and from the College of Medicine of the University of Milan, who practiced surgery and obstetrics. He met all the requirements of the bylaws of the Middlesex County Medical Society. The Society, however, refused him membership on the ground that it had an unwritten rule requiring that every applicant have four years of study in a medical school recognized by the American Medical Association. Dr. Falcone did not meet this requirement since the Philadelphia school was not AMA-approved and, although the University of Milan was so approved, the course was not four years. Dr. Falcone brought suit against the Society for refusing to admit him to membership.

JACOBS, J. . . . The Society's declaration of his ineligibility and its refusal to admit him to membership have had seriously adverse economic and professional effects on Dr. Falcone. He was a member of the medical staffs of the Middlesex General Hospital and St. Peter's General Hospital in New Brunswick but was dropped because they, like other hospitals in the area, require that their staff physicians be members of the County Medical Society. It seems entirely evident that Dr. Falcone cannot successfully continue his practice of surgery and obstetrics or properly serve his surgical and obstetric patients without the use of local hospital facilities; he testified that in order to earn a livelihood it is necessary "to belong to the local society" for "otherwise, you cannot use the hospitals." The virtual monopoly which the Society possesses in fact over the use of local hospital facilities results from the well-known interrelationship between the County Society, the State Medical Society, the American Medical Association, and the Joint Commission on Accreditation of Hospitals. . . .

Over thirty years ago Professor Chafee, in his discussion of non-profit associations, pointed to the distinction between the customary social and fraternal organizations on the one hand and trade unions and professional societies on the other hand; he noted that whereas exclusion or expulsion from a social or fraternal organization may result in little more than hurt feelings, exclusion or expulsion from a trade union or a professional society may result, as here, in deprivation of the invaluable opportunity "to earn a livelihood." . . . In a more recent discussion addressed specially to medical societies, the editors of the Yale Law Journal, after pointing out that exclusion or expulsion from a local medical society results, as a practical matter, in the deprivation of hospital facilities, descriptively noted that "nonmembership amounts to a partial revocation of licensure to practice medicine." 63 Yale L.J. at p. 953. . . .

Throughout his formative writings, Holmes repeatedly stressed the vital part played by public policy considerations in the never ending growth and development of the common law. Over eighty years have passed since he expressed his now well known thought that "every important principle which is developed by litigation is in fact and at bottom the result of more or less definitely understood views of public policy." See Holmes, "Common Carriers and the Common Law," 13 Am.L.Rev. 609, 631 (1879); Holmes, The Common Law 35 (1881). And while earlier day judges displayed hesitancy in its acknowledgment, modern day judges display no comparable hesitancy; in recent decisions our courts have repeatedly acknowledged that public policy is the dominant factor in the molding and remolding of common-law principles to the high end that they may soundly serve the public welfare and the true interests of justice. . . .

We are here concerned with . . . an organization, membership in which may . . . be viewed as "an economic necessity"; in dealing with such an organization, the court must be particularly alert to the need for truly protecting the public welfare and advancing the interests of justice by reasonably safeguarding the individual's opportunity for earning a livelihood while not impairing the proper standards and objectives of the organization. . . .

When courts originally declined to scrutinize admission practices of membership associations, they were dealing with social clubs, religious organizations, and fraternal associations. Here the policies against judicial intervention were strong, and there were no significant countervailing policies. When the courts were later called upon to deal with trade and professional associations exercising virtually monopolistic control, different factors were involved. The intimate personal relationships which pervaded the social, religious, and fraternal organizations were hardly in evidence and the individual's opportunity of earning a livelihood and serving society in his chosen trade or profession appeared as the controlling policy consideration. . . .

It must be borne in mind that the County Medical Society is not a private voluntary membership association with which the public has little or no concern. It is an association with which the public is highly concerned and which engages in activities vitally affecting the health and welfare of the people. . . . Through its interrelationships, the County Medical Society possesses, in fact, a virtual monopoly over the use of local hospital facilities. As a result it has power, by excluding Dr. Falcone from membership, to preclude him from successfully continuing in his practice of obstetrics and surgery and to restrict patients who wish to engage him as an obstetrician or surgeon in their freedom of choice of physicians. Public policy strongly dictates that this power should not be unbridled but should be viewed judicially as a fiduciary power to be exercised in reasonable and lawful manner for the advancement of the interests of the medical profession and the public generally. . . .

In the light of all of the foregoing, the effort of the County Society to apply its unwritten requirement of four years' attendance at an AMA approved medical college so as to exclude Dr. Falcone from membership, must be viewed as patently arbitrary and unreasonable and beyond the pale of the law. When the County Society engages in action which is designed to advance medical science or elevate professional standards, it should and will be sympathetically supported. When, however, as here, its action . . . runs strongly counter to the public policy of our State and the true interests of justice, it should and will be stricken down. . . .

[Admission ordered.]

United States v. Bonanno

180 F.Supp. 71 (D.C. S.D. N.Y., 1960)

When the local police noticed that a large number of persons were gathering in Apalachin, New York, at the country estate of a person they had been investigating, they set up a road check on all persons leaving the estate. Those who were not already known to them were taken to a local police station, without any objection, and questioned as to name, age, address, occupation, criminal record, the reason for being at the estate, and other relevant matters. No examination lasted for more than a half hour, after which the person was allowed to leave. Bonanno and others who were so stopped and questioned claimed that the stopping was an illegal arrest and seizure and that the statements obtained by the police should therefore be suppressed and not allowed to be used as evidence.

KAUFMAN, D.J. . . . It is axiomatic that before a finding can be made that there has been an *illegal* arrest, a showing must be made that there has been an arrest. Thus, an immediate problem of definition arises. Joined to that problem is the danger that the defining process will cast an air of deceptive simplicity over the broader task actually faced by the Court. One must never forget that this is a decision on the rights of individuals and the duties of government, and not an abstract exercise in definition. In dealing with words, there is always a temptation to allow them to become separated from their objective correlatives in the everyday world, and to treat them as if they have, or ought to have, one single simple meaning, unaffected by the contexts in which they occur and divorced from the world of things and events which give them their content and justification.

"Arrest" is just such a word, not only because it is necessarily unspecific and descriptive of complex, often extended processes, but because in different contexts it describes different processes, each of which has built up, in both legal and common parlance, sharply divergent emotional connotations. . . . [The court held that there had not been an "arrest."]

But, to rely solely upon the fact that there was no technical arrest, or no arrest as that term is commonly understood, would be to fall into the very semantic trap alluded to above. The problem, as I see it, is not whether the challenged police procedures constituted an "arrest," but whether these procedures were of such a character that all evidence stemming from them must be suppressed. . . .

While the Fourth Amendment may be construed as [prohibiting unlawful] "seizure" of an individual, it cannot be contended that every detention of an individual is such a "seizure." If that were the case, police investigation would be dealt a crippling blow, by imposing a radical sanction unnecessary for the protection of a free citizenry.

Under such a theory, a policeman could not stop and question a person standing next to a bloody corpse. . . .

All would agree that the officer in the situation referred to would be justified in detaining the suspect and questioning him with a view toward establishing his identity and his reasons for being on the scene. This is so even though the policeman could not know at the time of the stoppage that a crime had been committed, since the corpse could quite likely have been the product of accident or suicide. Furthermore, could it be seriously questioned that it would be good police activity for the officer to question each member of the limited group gathered at the scene. In such a situation it would be almost certain that not everyone present was a participant in the crime and likely that no one present had participated. . . .

I can see no difference in principle between the detention of an individual on the street and the stoppage of a car, so long as there is no violence or highhandedness involved. . . . Police activity without a warrant may be more reasonable in the case of an automobile, which if not stopped is not likely to be seen again, than in the case of a fixed abode. This has been recognized in the line of cases dealing with the transportation of contraband. . . .

The administration of justice is not an exact science. Its subject matter encompasses very nearly the totality of human experience, and is concentrated upon that area of life least subject to mathematical precision: relationships among persons. Furthermore, the administration of justice is a personal venture; no machine has yet been designed that can do justice, and none seems likely in the near future.

When mere human beings are confronted with such a complexity of subject matter, errors must occur. In order to compensate for inevitable mistakes the persons charged with the administration of justice indulge in certain techniques developed over the years in order to assure, as adequately as possible, that the expected errors should balance the scales toward an end thought most conducive to our concept of justice.

One of the most common, but most important, of these corrective efforts is the philosophy that justice is better served if a guilty person is allowed to go free, rather than condemning an innocent person as a criminal. Like most judicial philosophies, this one is expressed in legal rules. Thus a defendant is presumed innocent until proven guilty. He may not be compelled to be a witness against himself. A coerced confession or admission is not admissible against the defendant who gave it. . . . These are vital and necessary rules of law for they tend to assure that innocent men will not be convicted of crime and that overzealous police officers will be restrained.

But, the fact that a certain rule tends toward a desired end does not mean that an expansion of that rule will tend toward the same end. The opposite might well be the result. If the right of police to investigate a crime before formally arresting and charging a person is restricted too severely, not only will guilty persons go free, but innocent persons will suffer unnecessarily. Police officers tend, by and large, to uphold and be ruled by the law. There are overzealous policemen, just as there are bad members of other occupations and professions, but they are the exceptions in generally creditable callings. If the police are told that they may not question a person until he has been formally arrested and arraigned, they will carry out that precept to the letter, especially if to do otherwise would be likely to result in an escape from punishment by guilty men. Instead of giving a person an opportunity to exculpate himself from any suspicion of wrongdoing, they will arrest him first and ask questions afterwards. . . .

There are many occasions where a man appears guilty enough to be arrested and arraigned, when in fact he is entirely innocent of wrongdoing. This innocence may be easy to establish, once the suspect is allowed to give his story to the police [without the harm to his reputation of being "arrested. . . .]"

Thus, if in an effort to protect innocent persons, we restrict too much the right of the police to investigate before a formal arrest, the circle of the unprotected will be widened. The true end must be kept in sight. There is no value in the limitation of police power merely for the sake of limitation. The true and ultimate end is to protect innocent persons from false charges. If allowing law enforcement officers to question persons as part of the investigation of a crime, will further this end, forbidding that procedure would divert us from the objective. Sweeping generalities ought not be indulged in, and the focus should be on the facts of the particular case. General propositions no more decide concrete cases in criminal law than they do in the area of economic regulation. Here the police moved with restraint after they had reasonable grounds to believe that a crime might have been committed. . . .

[Objections of defendants dismissed.]

New Jersey v. Culver

23 N.J. 495, 129 A.2d 715 (1957)

Culver was given a life sentence under a habitual criminal statute on the basis that he was a fourth offender. After he had been in prison seven years, it was determined that there were only two prior offenses and that the life sentence was therefore illegal. The court then entered the correct sentence. Culver appealed on the ground that the court had no authority to correct the illegal sentence and therefore he must be allowed to go free.

VANDERBILT, C.J. . . . . No one can question that the release of the defendant, a properly convicted criminal offender, . . . is an undesirable result. . . . Nor can it be said, apart from any statutory considerations, that our courts, according to present-day concepts and standards, are without power to correct an illegal or improper sentence. One of the great virtues of the common law is its dynamic nature that makes it adaptable to the requirements of society at the time of its application in court. There is not a rule of the common law in force today that has not evolved from some earlier rule of common law, gradually in some instances, more suddenly in others, leaving the common law of today when compared with the common law of centuries ago as different as day is from night. The nature of the common law requires that each time a rule of law is applied it be carefully scrutinized to make sure that the conditions and needs of the times have not so changed as to make further application of it the instrument of injustice. Dean Pound posed the problem admirably in his Interpretations of Legal History (1922) when he stated, "Law must be stable, and yet it cannot stand still." And what has been done in the past is but one of the factors determinative of the present course of our law—a truism which has not gone unrecognized among the great thinkers of the legal profession. Thus, Mr. Justice Holmes recognized that: "To rest upon a formula is a slumber that, prolonged, means death"; Collected Legal Papers 306 (1920) . . . .

The factors to be weighed in the balance in determining the present course of the law include the reasons for the rule, the present requirements of the environment in which the rule is to be applied, the dangers incident to any change, and the evils resulting from its continuance. The power of growth is inherent in the common law. . . .

In State v. Gray, 37 N.J.L. 368 (Sup.Ct., 1875), the court set aside the defendant's sentence to a term in prison at hard labor as illegal because the specific offense for which he had been convicted was not punishable at hard labor. In discharging him from custody, the court held that at common law it had no power to impose the proper sentence or to remand for that purpose; and in the absence of statute granting such power, the only course open to it was to set the prisoner free. The court relied for its authority on an ancient rule dating back to the time of Lord Coke and on decisions in other states which in turn had relied on the English precedents. . . .

The majority of the courts in this country have seen fit to distinguish the English rule. The greater number of American cases have adopted the rule that . . . an invalid or illegal sentence, which is beyond the power of the trial court to impose, may be corrected after the execution of the sentence has begun and without regard to the term of court at which it is done. . . .

It is easy to see from our own cases the sound basis for the ancient English rule. In Patterson v. State, 48 N.J.L. 381, 383, 4 A. 449, 450 (Sup.Ct., 1886), we are told that:

"In the early days of English criminal jurisprudence, when even a trifling larceny was punishable with death, there was reason why the judicial mind should exhaust its ingenuity in aid of the defense, and seize upon every technicality to avert from the prisoner a punishment so disproportionate to his crime. In our time a more humane system of criminal law has been adopted, which graduates the punishment according to the magnitude of the offense, and in which there is nothing to shock our sense of justice. The reason for resorting to mere technicality to enable the criminal to evade the sanctions of the law no longer exists, and the practice to which that reason led should therefore cease. Men who make their lives a scourge to society must answer its violated laws, and can justly demand in a judicial tribunal nothing except a fair trial according to the laws of the land, in which no substantial right is denied them. . . . It is of the utmost importance to society that its criminal classes shall understand that the penalty surely follows the crime."

By the time of the decision in State v. Gray, 37 N.J.L. 368 (Sup. Ct., 1875), however, our criminal jurisprudence had advanced to the stage reflected in the Patterson case and the reason for construing the law in favor of a dangerous criminal had long since disappeared.

Certainly, time itself has indicated that the tide has run against the view taken in State v. Gray, supra. As long ago as 1609, in Milborn's case, 7 Coke 7a (K.B., 1609), Lord Coke stated that the reason for the law is the soul of the law, and if the reason for a law has changed, the law is changed. More recently, Mr. Justice Holmes said:

"It is revolting to have no better reason for a rule of law than that so it was laid down in the time of Henry IV. It is still more revolting if the grounds upon which it was laid down have vanished long since, and the rule simply persists from blind imitation of the past." Collected Legal Papers 187 (1920).

Blind imitation of the past is what we find as the basis for holding in State v. Gray, supra. . . .

We believe that the sentences originally imposed on this defendant were in fact improper and that the court's jurisdiction to impose a correct sentence had not expired until a valid sentence was imposed. "To hold otherwise would allow the guilty to escape punishment through a legal accident." . . .

[Judgment affirmed.]

CHAPTER 2

Legal Rights and Wrongs

In order to preserve our freedom and to protect the rights that give meaning to that freedom, society, through rules of law and government, imposes certain limitations that apply to everyone. Three areas of the law that determine whether conduct is wrongful are contract law, the law of torts, and criminal law.

A claim based upon contract law arises, for example, when an employee sues his employer for failing to pay him his proper wages, or when a homeowner sues the contractor for failing to complete his house in time, or when a beneficiary brings suit on a life insurance policy. Contract law in general is discussed in Part II. Special types of contracts, such as those for sales and insurance, constitute the subject matter of several other parts that follow.

The law of torts and criminal law are subjects for discussion in this chapter.

Torts

Sec. 2-A. Definition. A *tort* is a private injury or wrong arising from a breach of a duty created by law. It is often defined as a wrong independent of contract. Most torts, although not all, involve moral wrongs, but not all moral wrongs are torts.

The area of tort law includes harm to the person, as well as to property caused negligently or intentionally. In some instances, liability is imposed merely because the activity of the wrongdoer is so dangerous that it is deemed proper that he should pay for any harm that has been caused. Torts that affect business security [1] include defamation of reputation (slander and libel); infringement of patents, copyrights, and trademarks; and unfair competition.

---

[1] See Chapter 65.

(1) Tort and Breach of Contract. The wrongs or injuries caused by a breach of contract arise from the violation of an obligation or duty created by consent of the parties. A tort arises from the violation of an obligation or duty created by law. The same act may be both a breach of contract and a tort. To illustrate, when an agent exchanges property instead of selling it as directed by the principal, he is liable for breach of contract and for the tort of conversion.

(2) Tort and Crime. A crime is a wrong arising from a violation of a public duty, whereas a tort is a wrong arising from a violation of a private duty. An act may be both a crime and a tort as in the case of the theft of an automobile.

Although the state recognizes both crimes and torts as wrongs, it attaches different effects to the acts or omissions. In the case of a crime, the state brings the action to enforce a prescribed penalty or punishment. On the other hand, when an act or omission is a tort, the state allows an action for redress by the injured party.

Sec. 2-B. Wrongdoers. In general, all persons are responsible for their torts. In a few instances when a public officer acts for the state, there is no liability on the part of the officer. Ordinarily the state cannot be sued by an individual except with its consent.

A tort may be caused by several wrongdoers. If they are joint wrongdoers, each is liable for the entire injury regardless of the extent of his participation; that is, each is ordinarily both jointly and severally liable for all the harm caused. A *joint wrong* exists when there is concert of action or agreement between the parties although the injury is done by one; a joint wrong is also committed when the parties act independently but produce a single injury. Courts differ as to the extent of the liability of each tort-feasor or wrongdoer in such cases. (See p. 31, Maddux v. Donaldson)

Some states allow contribution between joint tort-feasors when they have acted independently without any concert or agreement, or when the conduct of each amounts only to negligence. The trend of decisions has been to widen the exceptions so as to permit contribution in more types of cases. In a number of states this result has been achieved by the adoption of a statute expressly authorizing contribution.

Sec. 2-C. Basis of Tort Liability.

(1) Voluntary Act. The defendant must be guilty of a voluntary act or omission. Acts that are committed or omitted by one who is confronted with sudden peril or pressing danger, not of his own making, are considered as having been committed or omitted involuntarily.

(2) Intent. Whether intent to do an unlawful act or intent to cause harm is required as a basis for tort liability depends upon the nature of the act involved. Liability is imposed for some torts even though the person committing the tort acted in complete ignorance of the nature of his act and without any intent to cause harm. Thus a person entering land or a person cutting trees in a forest is liable for the tort of trespass if the land or trees do not belong to him, unless he has permission from the owner.

In the case of other torts, such as assault, slander, malicious prosecution, or interference with contracts, it is necessary for the plaintiff to show that there was an intent on the part of the defendant to cause harm or at least the intent to do an act which a reasonable man would anticipate as likely to cause harm.

(3) Motive. As a general rule motive is immaterial except as it may be evidence to show the existence of intent. In most instances any legal right may be exercised even with bad motives, and an act that is unlawful is not made legal by good motives.

(4) Negligence. One is entitled to be free from injuries to his person or to his property that are caused by the failure on the part of another to exercise a proper degree of care. The party who violates his legal duty to exercise the degree of care required by the circumstances and causes another to suffer damages is guilty of a tort known as *negligence.*

The elements of this tort are a duty on the part of the defendant to exercise care in respect to the plaintiff; a failure to perform that duty; and a resulting injury to the plaintiff that is proximately related to the defendant's act.

(a) DUTY OF CARE. A person is under a duty to act carefully with respect to those persons or things which are likely to be within the area in which they might be affected by his conduct.

At one time the zone of duty to exercise care was narrower when the question involved the negligence of a seller or a manufacturer. For a time it was held that the only person to whom a manufacturer or vendor owed any duty was his own purchaser. If the purchaser was injured because of the negligence of the manufacturer or vendor in making the product, the purchaser could sue the vendor; but if someone else was injured, there was no liability. This rule has gradually been abandoned so that the seller or manufacturer is liable to third persons whom he should have foreseen would be injured by his negligence.

A person is under a duty of care to other persons whose presence he should reasonably anticipate, but he is not under a duty to anticipate the presence of persons unlawfully on his property. With respect to those persons whom he invites on his property, the landowner must take reasonable measures to insure that the property is safe and must warn the persons of any dangers present. In the case of the trespasser, the owner may ignore him until he knows that he is present. Once he knows that a trespasser is on his property, he cannot take any action which a reasonable man would recognize as exposing the trespasser to unreasonable risk. The owner of the land cannot make his land unsafe for trespassers for the purpose of injuring them, as by setting spring guns.

(b) DEGREE OF CARE. The degree of care required of a person is that which an ordinarily prudent man would exercise under similar circumstances. It does not mean such a degree of care as would have prevented the harm from occurring, nor is it enough that it is just as much care as everyone else exercises. Nor is it sufficient that one has exercised the degree of care which is customary for persons in the same kind of work or business, or that one has employed the methods customarily used. If one is engaged in services requiring skill, the care, of course, measures up to a higher standard. The degree of care exercised must be commensurate with the danger that would probably result if such care were lacking. In all cases it is the diligence, care, and skill that can be reasonably expected under the circumstances. Whether one has exercised that degree of care is a question which is determined by the jury.

(c) PROOF OF NEGLIGENCE. The plaintiff ordinarily has the burden of proving that the defendant did not exercise reasonable care. In some instances, however, it is sufficient for the plaintiff to prove that the injury was caused by an inanimate thing within the control of the defendant. If injury only results from such objects when there is negligence, the proof of these facts is prima facie proof that the defendant was negligent. This is expressed by the maxim *res ipsa loquitur,* the occurrence or thing speaks for itself. (See p. 34, Thompson v. Burke Engineering Sales Co.)

(d) CONTRIBUTORY NEGLIGENCE. Generally, one cannot recover for injuries caused by another's negligence if his own negligence has contributed to the injury. The plaintiff's negligence, however, must be a proximate cause of the injury, that is, it must contribute to the injury in order to defeat recovery.

In this connection there has developed a doctrine variously called the *doctrine of last clear chance,* the *humanitarian doctrine,* or the *doctrine of discovered peril.* Under this doctrine, although the plaintiff is negligent, the defendant is held liable if he had the last clear chance to avoid the injury. In such a case the theory is that the plaintiff's negligence is not the proximate cause and therefore does not contribute to the injury.

When the plaintiff is guilty of contributory negligence, he is ordinarily denied recovery without regard to whether the defendant was more negligent than he. The common law does not recognize comparative degrees of negligence, nor does it try to apportion the injury to the two parties in terms of the degree of their respective fault. As an exception to these principles, a number of states provide by statute that the negligence does not bar his recovery but merely reduces the amount which he recovers in proportion to the degree or extent of his own negligence.

The burden of proving that the plaintiff was contributorily negligent is upon the defendant.

(5) Proximate Cause. In order to fix legal responsibility upon one as a wrongdoer, it is necessary to show that the injury was the proximate result of his voluntary act. Whether an act is the proximate cause of an injury is usually a question of fact for the jury to determine.

(6) Liability Without Fault. Ordinarily there must be some fault on the defendant's part to impose tort liability for his acts. He must either be negligent or intend harm to result, or he must volitionally do the act which causes the harm, as in a trespass to land, even though he did not intend that result. As an exception to these principles, liability is imposed in some cases, not because of the fault or intent of the defendant, but because the activity in which he has engaged, though lawful, has such a high potential of danger to others that society will make him pay for any harm which results. This is known as the *rule of absolute liability* or *rule of liability without fault.*

This doctrine has been applied to impose liability upon a person keeping vicious, wild animals; a person storing inflammable gases and liquids, and explosives; and persons engaged in blasting or drilling for oil wells. In some states that reject the doctrine, the courts achieve the same result by terming the defendant guilty of a nuisance of such a character that he must pay for the harm done without regard to fault or by applying the rule of res ipsa loquitur. In some states liability without fault is imposed upon railroads for fires caused by locomotives emitting sparks. The basic principle of workmen's compensation statutes is liability without fault. In a number of states statutes have been adopted making the owner or operator of aircraft absolutely liable for any damage caused by the aircraft in the course of its ascent, descent, or flight. (See p. 36, Adler's Quality Bakery v. Gaseteria, Inc.)

Crimes

Sec. 2-D. Definition and Classification. A *crime* is a violation of the law that is punished as an offense against the state or government. The field of criminal law as it affects business security [2] includes obtaining property by false pretenses; using false weights, measures, or labels; using the mails for the purpose of defrauding another; and forgery.

Crimes may be classified (1) in terms of the source of the law prohibiting them, (2) in terms of their seriousness, or (3) in terms of their nature.

(1) Source of Criminal Law. Crimes are classified in terms of their origin as common-law and statutory crimes. Some offenses that are defined by statute are merely declaratory of the common law. Each state has its own criminal law, although a general pattern among the states may be observed.

(2) Seriousness of Offense. Crimes are classified in terms of their seriousness as treason, felonies, and misdemeanors. *Treason* is defined by the Constitution of the United States, which states that "treason against the United States shall consist only in levying war against them, or in adhering to their enemies, giving them aid and comfort." [3]

Felonies include the other more serious crimes, such as arson, homicide, and robbery, which are punishable by confinement in prison or by death. In some instances a statute may convert an act, previously a minor offense, into a felony.

Crimes not classified as treason or felonies are *misdemeanors*. Illegal parking, weighing and measuring goods with scales and measuring devices that have not been inspected, and disturbing the peace by illegal picketing are generally classified as misdemeanors. An act may be a felony in one state and a misdemeanor in another.

(3) Nature of Misconduct. Crimes are also classified in terms of the nature of the misconduct. *Crimes mala in se* include acts that are inherently vicious or, in other words, that are naturally evil as measured by the standards of a civilized community. *Crimes mala prohibita* include those acts that are wrong merely because they are declared wrong by some statute, such as a law prohibiting parking.

Sec. 2-E. Responsibility for Acts.

(1) Minors. Some states have legislation fixing the age of criminal responsibility of minors. At common law,[4] when a child is under the

---

[2] See Chapter 65.
[3] Art. III, Sec. 3.
[4] See p. 50.

age of seven years, the law presumes him to be incapable of committing a crime; after the age of fourteen he is presumed to have capacity as though he were over twenty-one; and between the ages of seven and fourteen, no presumption of law arises and it must be shown that the minor has such capacity. The existence of capacity cannot be presumed from the mere commission of the act.

(2) Insane Persons. An insane person is not criminally responsible for his acts because he cannot form a criminal intent. There is a conflict of opinion as to what constitutes such insanity as to excuse a person from the normal consequence of his acts. All courts, however, agree that intellectual weakness alone is not such insanity.

A test commonly applied is the right-and-wrong test. The responsibility of the defendant is determined in terms of his ability to understand the nature of his act and to distinguish right from wrong in relation to it. (See p. 38, Minnesota v. Finn)

Some courts also use the irresistible-impulse test. The essence of this theory is that, although the defendant may know right from wrong, if he acts under an uncontrollable impulse because of an unsound state of mind caused by disease of any nature, he has not committed a voluntary act and is not criminally responsible. If the mental instability is not caused by disease, the irresistible-impulse test is not applied.

When insanity takes the form of delusions or hallucinations, the defendant is not legally responsible when the imagined facts, if they were true, would justify the act.

(3) Intoxicated Persons. Involuntary intoxication relieves a person from criminal responsibility; voluntary intoxication generally does not. An exception to this rule is made in the case of a crime requiring specific intent when the accused was so intoxicated that he was incapable of forming such intent.

(4) Corporations. The modern tendency is to hold corporations criminally responsible for their acts. A corporation may also be held liable for crimes based upon the failure to act.

Certain crimes, such as perjury, cannot be committed by corporations. It is also usually held that crimes punishable only by imprisonment or corporal punishment cannot be committed by corporate bodies. If the statute imposes a fine in addition to or in lieu of corporal punishment, a corporation may be convicted for the crime. Thus a corporation may be fined for violating the federal antitrust law by conspiring or combining to restrain interstate commerce. A corporation may be fined for committing criminal manslaughter when death has been caused by the corporation's failure to install statutory safety equipment.

Sec. 2-F. Parties to a Crime. Two or more parties may directly or indirectly contribute to the commission of a crime. At common law participants in the commission of a felony are sometimes known as *principals* and *accessories*. By statute, the distinction has frequently been abolished and all participants are principals. In the case of a misdemeanor all the parties, as a general rule, are responsible as principals.

(1). Principals. Principals are divided into two classes: (a) *principals in the first degree* who actually engage in the perpetration of the crime, and (b) *principals in the second degree* who are actually or constructively present and aid and abet in the commission of the act. For example, a person is a principal in the second degree if he assists by words of encouragement, stands ready to assist or to give information, or keeps watch to prevent surprise or capture.

The distinction as to degree is frequently abolished by statute so that all persons participating in a crime are principals.

(2) Accessories. Accessories to a crime are also divided into two classes, accessories before the fact and accessories after the fact. An *accessory before the fact* differs from a principal in the second degree only by reason of his absence from the scene of the act. An *accessory after the fact* is a person who knowingly assists one who has committed a felony. Thus a person is an accessory after the fact if, after the commission of the crime and with intent to assist a felon, he gives warning to prevent arrest or shelters or aids in an escape from imprisonment.

Sec. 2-G. Basis of Criminal Liability. A crime generally consists of two elements: (1) an act or omission, and (2) a mental state. In the case of some crimes, such as the illegal operation of a businesss without a license, it is immaterial whether the act causes harm to others. In other cases, the defendant's act must be the sufficiently direct cause of harm to another in order to impose criminal liability, as in the case of unlawful homicide. (See p. 40, Pennsylvania v. Root)

Mental state does not require an awareness or knowledge of guilt. In most crimes it is sufficient that the defendant voluntarily did the act that is criminal, regardless of motive or evil intent. In some instances, a particular mental state is required, such as the necessity that a homicide be with malice aforethought to constitute murder. In some cases, it is the existence of a specific intent that differentiates the crime committed from other offenses, as an assault with intent to kill is distinguished by that intent from an ordinary assault or an assault with intent to rob.

Sec. 2-H. Prevention of Crimes. The usual method employed to prevent crime is punishment. (See p. 43, Carnley v. Cochran) This may take the form of fines, imprisonment, or other penalties. In some states the punishment for a crime is increased if the criminal is a repeating or habitual offender. The legislatures may prescribe any punishment for crime, subject to federal constitutional provisions that prohibit "excessive fines" and "cruel and unusual punishments."

Statutes sometimes require a restitution of property that has been stolen or the payment of damages to the owner upon conviction of larceny. At common law, courts may require a bond to secure the future good behavior of a person who has been convicted of a serious misdemeanor. Statutes sometimes authorize the requirement of a bond for this purpose when a person has been convicted two or more times of violating a specific law.

Cases for Chapter 2

Maddux v. Donaldson

362 Mich. 425, 108 N.W.2d 33 (1961)

Maddux was injured when the car in which she was riding was hit by a skidding truck, which was driven by Donaldson, and then by the car following the truck. Maddux sued Donaldson for injuries caused by both collisions. Donaldson claimed that he could only be sued for those injuries which Maddux could show were caused by him and not for the total amount of damages. Because Maddux could not show what part of her injuries were caused by Donaldson, the trial court dismissed the action. Maddux appealed.

SMITH, J. . . . This is one of the most baffling of our current legal problems, critical because of the extensive use of expressways upon which large numbers of cars travel at high speeds in close proximity to one another. . . . The difficulty arises from the fact that we do not have a "joint" tort in the ordinary sense of the word, and thus it is argued that there cannot be joint and several liability. . . . Actually what we have is injury to plaintiffs resulting from the independent and tortious acts of two tort-feasors.

There is authority, in this situation, that plaintiff must separate the injuries, ascribing some to one tort-feasor and the balance to the other, much as a housewife separates the colored and the white goods before laundering. Such authority concludes that if plaintiff cannot make such differentiation he cannot recover from either. This type of decision is well illustrated by the case of Adams v. Hall, 1829, 2 Vt. 9. In this case an owner of sheep suffered loss to his flock through the depredations of two dogs. The owners he sued jointly. It was shown at the trial, however, that they were not joint owners. In addition, there was no testimony as to which dog killed which sheep. In approving a [dismissal of the action] it was held that neither owner was liable for the actions of the other's dog, merely because they "did the mischief in company."

However defensible such a result may have been in this and cases similar in principle in an agrarian economy shortly after the American Revolution (and even this is open to question) we do not regard it as precedent governing the liability of automobile owners in what are known as "chain collisions" on today's highways. It should be unnecessary to spell out the differences between the social problems presented or the judicial policies involved in their solution. When we impose upon an injured plaintiff the necessity of proving which impact did which harm in a chain collision situation, what we are actually expressing is a judicial policy that it is better that a plaintiff, injured through no fault of his own, take nothing, than that a tortfeasor pay more than his theoretical share of the damages accruing out of a confused situation which his wrong has helped to create. . . . It is . . . utterly inconsistent with the [basis] of precedents going back at least to the year 1613 when the rule of joint and several liability dispensed with the necessity of plaintiff's proof of just which ruffian inflicted which injury when he was set upon by three. The reason behind the rule was impossibility, the impossibility of plaintiff's proving the origin of each of his injuries. Where the same impossibility exists today, our sensitivity to plaintiff's injury should be no less than that of the King's Bench to its plaintiff, whose "wounding . . . in a cruel and barbarous manner" was held to impose joint and several liability upon the defendants. It is clear that there is a manifest unfairness in "putting on the injured party the impossible burden of proving the specific shares of harm done by each. . . . Such results are simply the law's callous dullness to innocent sufferers. One would think that the obvious meanness of letting wrongdoers go scot free in such cases would cause the courts to think twice and to suspect some fallacy in their rule of law." . . .

It is our conclusion that if there is competent testimony, adduced either by plaintiff or defendant, the injuries are factually and medically separable, and that the liability for all such injuries and damages, or parts thereof, may be allocated with reasonable certainty to the impacts in turn, the jury will be instructed accordingly and mere difficulty in so doing will not relieve the triers of the facts of this responsibility. This merely follows the general rule that "where the independent concurring acts have caused distinct and separate injuries to the plaintiff, or where some reasonable means of apportioning the damages is evident, the courts generally will not hold the tort-feasors jointly and severally liable."

But if, on the other hand, the triers of the facts conclude that they cannot reasonably make the division of liability between the tort-feasors, this is the point where the road of authority divides. Much ancient authority, not in truth precedent, would say that the case is now over, and that plaintiff shall take nothing. Some modern courts, as well, hold that this is merely the case of the marauding dogs and the helpless sheep relitigated in the setting of a modern highway. The conclusion is erroneous. Such precedents are not apt. When the triers of the facts decide that they cannot make a division of injuries, we have, by their own finding, nothing more or less than an indivisible injury, and the precedents as to indivisible injuries will control. They were well summarized in Cooley on Torts in these words: "Where the negligence of two or more persons concur in producing a single, indivisible injury, then such persons are jointly and severally liable, although there was no common duty, common design, or concert action." . . .

Is it better, as we asked heretofore, that a plaintiff, injured through no fault of his own, take nothing, rather than that a tort-feasor pay no more than his theoretical share of the damages accruing out of a confused situation which his wrong has helped to create? . . .

Here, then, is the essence of the problem—Where is the likelihood of injustice? We think it is in denying the blameless victim of traffic chain collision any recovery whatever. We perceive no reason why his tort-feasors should escape liability because of the very complexity of the injury created by their wrong. . . .

[Judgment reversed and new trial ordered.]

BLACK, EDWARDS, KAVANAGH and SOURIS, JJ., concurred with SMITH, J.

CARR, J. (dissenting). . . . The rule has been consistently recognized in Michigan, as well as in other states, that a tort-feasor may not be held liable for damages for an injury not caused by such defendant's wrongful conduct. In 15 Am. Jur., p. 404, it is said:

"A defendant is liable only to the extent to which his acts have caused the injury complained of, and it follows that separate wrongs done by independent agents cannot be joined together to increase the responsibility of one of the wrongdoers, notwithstanding any difficulty there may be in determining what part of the injury or loss was the result of the acts or omissions of the defendant, and what part was the result of other causes."

In Rodgers v. Canfield, 272 Mich. 562, 262 N.W. 409, an action for damages for malpractice was brought against two physicians. The testimony indicated that one of said physicians had not participated in all of the alleged acts of malpractice charged against the other. The trial court, however, directed the jury to return a verdict against both defendants for the full amount of the damages shown. This Court reversed on the ground that the defendant whose participation was partial only could not be held liable for the acts of the other defendant in which he did not take part. . . .

There is another aspect of the situation before us that merits consideration. The 14th amendment to the Federal Constitution forbids any State to "deprive any person of life, liberty, or property, without due process of law." The Constitution of Michigan, Article II, § 16, contains a like inhibition. . . . If a defendant in a case of the nature under consideration is adjudged to pay damages for injuries not shown to have been caused by wrongful conduct attributable to him, does such result comport with the basic requirement pertaining to due process of law? . . .

To compel one to respond in damages because of injuries not shown by proof to be attributable to him involves a denial of due process. . . .

DETHMERS, C.J., and KELLY, J., concurred with CARR, J.

BLACK, J. (concurring in reversal). Until now the Michigan rule has been settled. Where two or more wrongdoers separately cause the plaintiff to suffer an unknown or uncertain part or portion of the damages he has shown, each—hitherto—stood responsible to the plaintiff only for the harm caused by his tort, however, difficult it may have been to establish the same. . . .

Now we affirm that, where the trier or triers of fact find they cannot ascertain the amount of damages each wrongdoer has inflicted, then such trier or triers are authorized to assess the plaintiff's damages against any one or all of such wrongdoers on ground that the latter have—in law—participated in the infliction of "a single, indivisible injury." . . .

These sentiments are recorded solely that lawyers may know that the former rule is now definitely modified to the extent, and only to the extent, we now attest by majority vote. Otherwise such former rule remains in full force.

Thompson v. Burke Engineering Sales Co.

252 Iowa 146, 106 N.W.2d 351 (1960)

Burke Engineering Sales Co. installed a ceiling in the Normandy Restaurant. Fifteen months later part of the ceiling fell and injured Thompson, an employee of the restaurant. She sued Burke and proved the above facts but could not prove why the ceiling fell. The lower court dismissed the plaintiff's case on the ground that there was no proof of negligence on the part of Burke. The plaintiff appealed.

GARFIELD, J. . . . Defendant installed the ceiling and had exclusive control thereof until it was turned over to plaintiff's employer as completed for its use and that of its employees and the public; neither plaintiff nor her employer nor any other person did anything to cause the occurrence which arose solely from the condition of the ceiling as installed by defendant; neither plaintiff nor her employer knew what caused the ceiling to fall nor had access to the evidence thereof and such evidence is exclusively within defendant's knowledge; no one had access to the ceiling from above or disturbed it from below after its installation by defendant; it was fully protected from all the elements of nature; there was no [evidence of any] intervening cause of the occurrence. . . .

Under the doctrine of res ipsa loquitur, where (1) injury is caused by an instrumentality under the exclusive control of defendants and (2) the occurrence is such as in the ordinary course of things would not happen if reasonable care had been used, the happening of the injury permits but does not compel an inference that defendant was negligent. . . .

In considering the applicability of res ipsa loquitur, the question whether the occurrence is such as would not happen if reasonable care had been used rests on common experience and not on evidence in the particular case that tends to show the occurrence was or was not the result of negligence. . . .

Traditionally the rule of res ipsa loquitur has frequently been applied in cases of injuries from falling objects. A number of decisions throughout the country apply the doctrine to the fall of plaster from a ceiling. . . .

As stated in Windas v. Galston & Sutton Theatres, supra [35 Cal. App.2d 533, 96 P.2d 171], "Plaster does not ordinarily fall from a ceiling if proper care has been used to see that the ceiling is safe." It would seem the fall of "a large piece of metal ceiling" might be found to be more unusual than the fall of plaster. . . .

In most of the many cases that apply the res ipsa doctrine, the instrumentality which causes the injury is under defendant's exclusive control at the time the injury occurs. However, there is a growing number of decisions which apply the rule where defendant was in exclusive control of the instrumentality at the time of the alleged negligent act, although not at the time of the injury, *provided* plaintiff first proves there was no change in the condition of the instrumentality after it left defendant's control which could reasonably have caused the injury. . . . Of course this assumes existence of the second foundation fact . . . that the occurrence is one which would not ordinarily happen if reasonable care had been used.

Perhaps most numerous of the precedents last referred to are those where a bottler of beverages has been held liable for injuries from the explosion of a bottle after it left defendant's control provided intervening causes are eliminated. . . .

"The real test is whether defendants were in control at the time of the negligent act or omission which either at that time or later produced the accident." . . .

There are also many precedents which apply the res ipsa rule, under the same proviso, to injuries from the presence of broken glass or other foreign substance in a bottle of beverage. . . .

Other decisions apply the res ipsa doctrine under varying facts where defendant was not in control of the instrumentality causing the injury at the time, provided plaintiff proves [that] no change in condition of the instrumentality after it left defendant's control caused the injury. Hercules Powder Co. v. Automatic Sprinkler Corp., 151 Cal.App.2d 387, 311 P.2d 907 (explosion allegedly caused by malfunctioning of sprinkler system installed by defendant at least 19 months previously and checked by it about every six months, the last time 30 days before the fire) ; Plunkett v. United Electric Service, 214 La. 145, 36 So.2d 704, 3 A.L.R.2d 1437, 1444 (plaintiff's house burned by failure of furnace installed by defendant to function properly) ; Saunders v. Walker, 229 La. 426, 86 So.2d 89, 93 (plaintiff's residence damaged by water caused by slipping of a rubber hose in an air conditioning system installed by defendant in the attic) ; Peterson v. Minnesota Power & Light Co., 207 Minn. 387, 291 N.W. 705, 707 (plaintiff burned by flash of electricity from electric stove installed by defendant); Rafferty v. Northern Utilities Co., 73 Wyo. 287, 278 P.2d 605 (fire allegedly caused by defendant's negligently cleaning and reinstalling a gas heater) . . . .

[Judgment reversed.]

Adler's Quality Bakery v. Gaseteria, Inc.

32 N.J. 55, 159 A.2d 97 (1960)

Gaseteria, Inc., owned an airplane which crashed into a television tower. The falling debris damaged the property of Adler's Quality Bakery and other persons. They brought suit against Gaseteria for this damage and claimed that because of a statute in New Jersey the defendant was absolutely liable without proof of negligence. Gaseteria claimed that the statute was unconstitutional. From a judgment for the plaintiffs, the defendant appealed.

BURLING, J. . . . The statute . . . provides:

"The owner of every aircraft which is operated over the land or waters of this State is absolutely liable for injuries to persons or property on the land or water beneath, caused by ascent, descent, or flight of the aircraft, or the dropping or falling of any object therefrom, whether such owner was negligent or not, unless the injury is caused in whole or in part by the negligence of the person injured, or of the owner or bailee of the property injured. If the aircraft is leased at the time of the injury to person or property, both owner and lessee shall be liable, and they may be sued jointly, or either or both of them may be sued separately." . . .

The Legislature has not improperly exercised [its] . . . power . . . merely because it imposes absolute liability on a person causing injuries. . . . Rather, when such action has been taken, the question is whether the law is reasonable, not arbitrary or capricious, and whether it bears a real and substantial relation to the end sought to be attained.

The essential reasonableness of the statutory imposition of absolute liability in question stems, at least arguably, from the problems of proof of fault encountered by a person damaged by falling aircraft (or falling debris from aircraft) who seeks recovery for those damages. Proof of negligence, for many different reasons, is difficult to obtain in a large number of such cases. . . . Even if such proof is obtainable, the expense involved is frequently very high, and often prohibitive. . . . Application of the doctrine of res ipsa loquitur is an uncertain means of overcoming these problems. . . . A practical alternative, therefore, is to place the risk of ground damages caused by aircraft, or at least the risk of recovering from the person responsible for the fault causing such damages, on a person other than the damaged party—such as the owner of the aircraft as was done in the statute in question. . . . These considerations, some scholars argue, indicate that the aircraft industry should bear common-law absolute liability. Restatement Torts § 20, comment (d) (1938). Both France and Italy, by statute, impose absolute liability on some segment of the aviation industry in favor of the victim of a falling aircraft. . . . England has enacted several statutes with the same effect. . . . Concerning the latter, the British Aerial Transport Committee Report of 1918, recommending the passage of the [British] act, stated:

> Admittedly persons on land are practically powerless to ensure their own safety by precautionary measures against damage caused by the fall of aircraft or of objects carried therein. . . . [A]s far as damages done by aircraft is concerned, the deprivation of the land-owner of what is almost certainly an existing right of property should be compensated by what will be in effect insurance of himself and his property against such damage. Nor do we think that in practice the expense of insuring himself against third party risks will prove very burdensome to the owner of aircraft. . . .

The statute to which the Committee referred bears striking resemblance to Section 5 of the Uniform Aeronautics Act (which was enacted in this State . . .) and the comments of the Committee are as cogent now as then. Manifestly, to shift the risk of ground damages caused by aircraft from the victim thereof to the better risk bearer is within the legislative power to act in behalf of the general welfare.

The above discussion reveals that the statute in question is a reasonable measure, not arbitrary or capricious, and bears a real and substantial relation to the end sought to be achieved. The statute therefore does not violate Gaseteria's rights under Art. I, Par. 1 or 20 of N.J.Const. 1947, or under the due process clause of the Fourteenth Amendment of the Federal Constitution. . . .

[Judgment affirmed.]

Minnesota v. Finn

257 Minn. 138, 100 N.W.2d 508 (1960)

Finn, when prosecuted for murder, raised the defense that he was of unsound mind and was not criminally responsible for his acts. The trial judge instructed the jury that Finn was sufficiently sane to be punished if he knew the difference between right and wrong with respect to his act. The trial judge also refused to instruct the jury that Finn was not responsible if he acted under an irresistible impulse. From a conviction, Finn appealed.

DELL, C.J. . . . The jury was charged in accordance with the [statute] which provides:

". . . [A] person . . . shall not be excused from criminal liability except upon proof that at the time of committing the alleged criminal act he was laboring under such a defect of reason, from one of these causes [idiocy, imbecility, lunacy, or insanity], as not to know the nature of his act, or that it was wrong."

This statute, originally enacted in 1885, had its origin in the rules promulgated in M'Naghten's Case, 10 Clark & Finnelly 200, 8 Eng.Rep. 718, commonly referred to as the "right-and-wrong" test of criminal insanity. Under this test every man is accountable for offenses committed by him unless, by reason of a diseased mind, (1) he did not know the nature of the act or (2) that it was wrong. For many years the right-and-wrong test has been subjected to severe attack on the ground that it is archaic and inadequate. Those who oppose the rule argue, among other things, that under modern psychiatric concepts man's reason is not the sole determinant of his conduct and that emotional drives and pressures must be recognized in attempting to formulate a guide of an accused's responsibility. In short, it is urged that the M'Naghten test is unrealistic and deals in concepts of no real psychological significance.

Several jurisdictions have modified the M'Naghten rule by using, in conjunction therewith, the so-called "irresistible impulse" test. Under this test the defendant is relieved of responsibility if he acted upon an impulse made irresistible by mental disease regardless of whether he knew the act was wrong. However, in the leading case of Durham v. United States, 94 U.S.App.D.C. 228, 214 F.2d 862, 45 A.L.R.2d 1430, even the modified M'Naghten test was found inadequate. The court reasoned that the irresistible-impulse test failed to recognize mental illness characterized by brooding and reflection. It adopted the broad test that a defendant should be found not guilty by reason of insanity if his unlawful act was the product of mental disease or mental defect. The defendant argues that the trial court erroneously denied his requested instructions couched in the language of the Durham and irresistible-impulse tests.

Both the irresistible-impulse test and the Durham test have been challenged for a variety of reasons as being unworkable and of questionable merit. Still other guides have been suggested as being substantial improvements over any test heretofore devised. But whatever the merit of these various concepts may be, if any change is to be made in this jurisdiction in the accepted standard of criminal responsibility, it must be done by the legislature. [The statute] defines clearly and unequivocally, in the language of the M'Naghten case, the only grounds upon which the defense of insanity is allowed. (See also . . . § 610.09, which provides in part: "A morbid propensity to commit prohibited acts existing in the mind of a person who is not shown to have been incapable of knowing that such acts were wrong shall constitute no defense.") . . .

Similarly, in other states where the M'Naghten rules have been reenacted by statute, the courts have declined to effect any change in the tests. . . . Even in the absence of controlling statutes, at least one jurisdiction has insisted that the formulation of any new test is a legislative function. . . .

Nor can it be said that we are authorized to make a change in the law by virtue of § 610.03, which, it is urged, gives the court wide discretion in interpreting statutes in accordance with advances in science. It provides: "The rule that a penal statute is to be strictly construed shall not apply to any provision of Part V of the Minnesota Statutes, but every such provision shall be construed according to the fair import of its terms to promote justice and effect the purpose of the law."

This section, which was intended to abolish the common-law rule that penal statutes must be strictly construed in favor of an accused, has no application in the instant case. While changing conditions can and often do affect the construction of statutes, the courts cannot go beyond the plain and clear meaning of the statute to spell out some different meaning. . . . If more adequate standards of determining criminal responsibility can be devised, it is the function of the legislature and not this court.

[Conviction affirmed.]

Pennsylvania v. Root

403 Pa. 571, 170 A.2d 310 (1961)

Root was challenged to an illegal auto race at night on a public highway. While the challenger was doing 70 to 90 miles an hour in a 50-mile-an-hour no-passing zone, he crossed the dividing line in attempting to pass Root, struck an oncoming truck, and was killed. Root was prosecuted for involuntary manslaughter. From a conviction, Root appealed.

JONES, C.J. . . . While precedent is to be found for application of the tort law concept of "proximate cause" in fixing responsibility for criminal homicide, the want of any rational basis for its use in determining criminal liability can no longer be properly disregarded. When proximate cause was first borrowed from the field of tort law and applied to homicide prosecutions in Pennsylvania, the concept connoted a much more direct causal relation in producing the alleged culpable result than it does today. Proximate cause, as an essential element of a tort founded in negligence, has undergone in recent times, and is still undergoing, a marked extension. More specifically, this area of civil law has been progressively liberalized in favor of claims for damages for personal injuries to which careless conduct of others can in some way be associated. To persist in applying the tort liability concept of proximate cause to prosecutions for criminal homicide after the marked expansion of *civil* liability of defendants in tort actions for negligence would be to extend possible *criminal* liability to persons chargeable with unlawful or reckless conduct in circumstances not generally considered to present the likelihood of a resultant death. . . .

Legal theory which makes guilt or innocence of criminal homicide depend upon such accidental and fortuitous circumstances as are now embraced by modern tort law's encompassing concept of proximate cause is too harsh to be just. A few illustrations should suffice to so demonstrate.

In Mautino v. Piercedale Supply Co., 1940, 338 Pa. 435, 12 A.2d 51—a civil action for damages—we held that where a man sold a cartridge to a person under 16 years of age in violation of a State statute and the recipient subsequently procured a gun from which he fired the cartridge injuring someone, the injury was proximately caused by the act of the man who sold the cartridge to the underage person. If proximate cause were the test for criminal liability and the injury to the plaintiff in the Mautino case had been fatal, the man who sold the bullet to the underage person (even though the boy had the appearance of an adult) would have been guilty of involuntary manslaughter, for his unlawful act would, according to the tort law standard, have been the proximate cause of the death. . . .

In Marchl v. Dowling & Company, 1945, 157 Pa.Super. 91, 41 A.2d 427, . . . where a truck driver had double parked his truck and the minor plaintiff was struck by a passing car when she walked around the double parked truck, the truck driver's employer was held liable in tort for the plaintiff's injuries on the ground that the truck driver's act of double parking, which violated both a State statute and a city ordinance, was the proximate cause of the plaintiff's injuries. Here, also, if proximate cause were the test for criminal liability and the plaintiff's injuries had been fatal, the truck driver would have been guilty of involuntary manslaughter since his unlawful act would have been the proximate cause of the death for which his employer was held liable in damages. . . . To be guilty of involuntary manslaughter for double parking would, of course, be unthinkable, yet if proximate cause were to determine criminal liability, such a result would indeed be a possibility. . . .

If the tort liability concept of proximate cause were to be applied in a criminal homicide prosecution, then the conduct of the person whose death is the basis of the indictment would have to be considered, not to prove that it was merely an *additional* proximate cause of the death, but to determine, under fundamental and long recognized law applicable to proximate cause, whether the subsequent wrongful act *superseded* the original conduct chargeable to the defendant. If it did in fact supervene, then the original act is so insulated from the ensuing death as not to be its proximate cause. . . .

In this case, the conduct of the defendant was not the proximate cause of the decedent's death as a matter of law. . . .

The deceased was aware of the dangerous condition created by the defendant's reckless conduct in driving his automobile at an excessive rate of speed along the highway but, despite such knowledge, he recklessly chose to swerve his car to the left and into the path of an oncoming truck, thereby bringing about the head-on collision which caused his own death.

To summarize, the tort liability concept of proximate cause has no proper place in prosecutions for criminal homicide and more direct causal connection is required for conviction. . . . In the instant case, the defendant's reckless conduct was not a sufficiently direct cause of the competing driver's death to make him criminally liable therefor. . . .

[Conviction reversed.]

EAGEN, J. (dissenting). . . . If the defendant did not engage in the unlawful race and so operate his automobile in such a reckless manner,

this accident would never have occurred. He helped create the dangerous event. He was a vital part of it. The victim's acts were a natural
reaction to the stimulus of the situation. The race, the attempt to pass
the other car and forge ahead, the reckless speed, all of these factors
the defendant himself helped create. He was part and parcel of them.
That the victim's response was normal under the circumstances, that
his reaction should have been expected and was clearly foreseeable, is
to me beyond argument. That the defendant's recklessness was a substantial factor is obvious. All of this, in my opinion, makes his unlawful conduct a direct cause of the resulting collision. . . .

Acts should be judged by their tendency under the known circumstances, not by the actual intent which accompanies their performance.
Every day of the year, we read that some teen-agers, or young adults,
somewhere in this country, have been killed or have killed others,
while racing their automobiles. Hair-raising, death-defying, law-
breaking rides, which encompass "racing," are the rule rather than
the exception, and endanger not only the participants, but also every
motorist and passenger on the road. To call such . . . [conduct] unlikely to result in death, is to ignore the cold and harsh reality of everyday occurrences. . . .

1 Wharton, Criminal Law and Procedure § 68 [Anderson Edition]
(1957), speaking of causal connections, says: "A person is only
criminally liable for what he has caused, that is, there must be a
causal relationship between his act and harm sustained for which he
is prosecuted. It is not essential to the existence of a causal relationship
that the ultimate harm which has resulted was foreseen or intended
by the actor. It is sufficient that the ultimate harm is one which a
reasonable man would foresee as being reasonably related to the acts
of the defendant." Section 295, in speaking about manslaughter, says:
"When homicide is predicated upon the negligence of the defendant,
it must be shown that his negligence was the proximate cause or a
contributing cause of the victim's death. It must appear that the death
was not the result of misadventure, but the natural and probable result
of a reckless or culpably negligent act. To render a person criminally
liable for negligent homicide, the duty omitted or improperly performed must have been his personal duty, and the negligent act from
which death resulted must have been his personal act, and not the act
of another. But he is not excused because the negligence of someone
else contributed to the result, when his act was the primary or proximate cause of the negligence of the other did not intervene between
his act and the result."

Professor Joseph Beale, late renowned member of the Harvard Law
School faculty, in an article entitled, The Proximate Consequence of
an Act, 33 Harv.L.Rev. 633, 646, said, "Though there is an active

force intervening after defendant's act, the result will nevertheless be proximate if the defendant's act actually caused the intervening force. In such a case the defendant's force is really continuing in active operation *by means of the force it stimulated into activity.*" ... 2 Bishop, New Criminal Law § 424 (1913), says: "He whose act causes in any way, directly or indirectly, the death of another, kills him, within the meaning of felonious homicide. It is a rule of both reason and the law that whenever one's will contributes to impel a physical force, whether another's, his own, or a combined force, proceeding from whatever different sources, he is responsible for the result, the same as though his hand, unaided, had produced it."

But, says the majority opinion, these are principles of tort law and should not in these days be applied to the criminal law. But such has been the case since the time of Blackstone. These same principles have always been germane to both crimes and tort. ... They have been repeatedly so applied throughout the years and were employed in a criminal case in Pennsylvania as long as one hundred and seventeen years ago. See Commonwealth v. Hare, 1844, 2 Clark 467. In that case, two separate bands of men were fighting each other with firearms in a public street and, as a result, an innocent citizen was shot and killed. The person firing the fatal shot could not be ascertained. Hare, one of the rioters, was convicted of homicide and the judgment was affirmed. Can anyone question the logic or correctness of this decision? Under the rationale of the majority opinion, what would be the result in the Hare case? Certainly, under its reasoning, if the truck driver met death under the circumstances the case at hand presents, the defendant would not be legally responsible. Again with this conclusion, I cannot agree.

While the victim's foolhardiness in this case contributed to his own death, he was not the only one responsible and it is not he alone with whom we are concerned. It is the people of the Commonwealth who are harmed by the kind of conduct the defendant pursued. Their interests must be kept in mind. . . .

Carnley v. Cochran

118 So.2d 629 (Fla., 1960)

Carnley was convicted of forgery and was sentenced to a term of 6 months to 10 years under a Florida statute authorizing an indeterminate sentence within specified minimum and maximum limitations. He brought a suit against Cochran, the Director of the Corrections Division, seeking release on the ground that the statute was unconstitutional and violated the prohibition of the Florida constitution against "indefinite imprisonment."

THORNAL, J. . . . In . . . ancient . . . centuries . . . a basic concept of punishment for the commission of crime was retribution. It was thought that if an individual violated the laws prescribed for the governance of the community he should compensate in kind, whether physical or material, as a retributive punishment for the offense which he had committed. So it was that . . . God instructed Moses:

"And if any mischief follow, then thou shalt give life for life,
"Eye for eye, tooth for tooth, hand for hand, foot for foot,
"Burning for burning, wound for wound, stripe for stripe."
See Exodus 21:23-25.

This concept of retributive justice . . . continues to influence the thinking of many.

With the passage of time, and especially during the current century, penologists and sociologists have arrived at the conclusion that retribution, in and of itself, is unjustifiable as the sole and only objective of punishment for crime.

An enlightened society is rapidly coming to the view that the results to be accomplished by a sentence in a criminal matter are two-fold, to wit: (1) deterrence, and (2) rehabilitation. . . .

The currently accepted guide to a sentence in a criminal matter is that it should be sufficiently severe to deter the particular offender and others similarly conditioned from committing other breaches of the criminal law. Nevertheless, it should be sufficiently flexible to permit opportunity to consider the individual involved in order to take advantage of every possibility for rehabilitation. . . .

The sentencing judge must evaluate the qualities and potentials of the individual before him in the light of his judicial responsibility to the community. . . .

The so-called indeterminate sentence . . . makes possible a more flexible opportunity for rehabilitation. It constantly holds out to the individual law violator the incentive to minimize his term of imprisonment. It offers him every chance to re-establish himself as a useful member of society, provided he has the courage and ambition to accomplish this desirable result. . . .

[Relief denied.]

CHAPTER 3

Enforcement of Legal Rights

Legal rights are meaningless unless they can be enforced. The purpose of this chapter is to present the means and methods of such enforcement. The discussion will conclude with a prologue to the study of business law.

Enforcement by Court Action

Government provides a system by which the rights of the parties under the law can be determined and enforced. Generally the instrumentality of government by which this is accomplished is a court; the process involved is an action or a lawsuit.

Sec. 3-A. The Courts. In every state there is a system of state courts, and throughout the United States there are the federal courts.[1] Some of these courts are created by constitution, others by statute. Some courts are trial courts, which hear the witnesses, determine the facts of the case, and make a decision; while other courts are appellate courts, which make decisions only as to cases that are appealed or brought to them for review. The latter courts do not hear witnesses but base their decision on the record of the proceedings in the trial court.

In addition to the distinction in terms of function, each court has its own particular class of claims which it may consider, such as civil cases, criminal cases, adoption cases, and so on. This power to hear and decide a particular class of claims is termed the *jurisdiction* of the court.

(1) Determination of Facts. The facts of a case are determined in the trial court. When the case is tried with a jury, the jury determines the facts. In some instances there is no jury because (a) the parties have agreed to try the case without a jury; or (b) the case is

---

[1] For a discussion of the court system generally, see the Appendix.

of such a nature that there is no right to a jury trial; or (c) the action
is brought in a magistrate's court or before a justice of the peace, in
which court there is ordinarily no trial by jury. In such instances, the
facts of the case are determined by the primary officer of the court—
the judge, magistrate, or justice of the peace.

The determination of the facts is made on the basis of evidence
that is brought into court. Generally this evidence will be the testimony of witnesses who saw or were present when the important facts
occurred. They testify under oath what they saw and heard. Sometimes the witness is not one who observed but is an expert who
expresses his opinion on the basis of information presented at the
trial or who states in court the result of a particular test made by
him. For example, the fingerprint expert may state his opinion as to
the identity of fingerprints, a handwriting expert as to the authenticity
of a signature, a ballistics expert may state that a given bullet was fired
from a particular gun, or a person familiar with the market value of
property may testify as to its value.

(2) Rules of Evidence. The evidence that is offered at the trial
must be competent, relevant, and material before it can be accepted
or admitted. To be *relevant evidence,* it must have some relationship
to the matter involved. To be *material evidence,* it must be sufficiently
related to the facts in dispute that it tends to prove the existence of
some important fact. To be *competent evidence,* it must be in such
form or of such nature that the law will allow it to be introduced.

The fact that the evidence is hearsay is one of the most common
grounds of exclusion on the ground of incompetence. *Hearsay* means
that the witness is testifying in court to what he has heard someone
else say or what someone else has written. Practical necessity, however,
has resulted in the making of a number of exceptions to the hearsay
evidence rule. For example, the records kept by a businessman or
enterprise are generally admissible in evidence to establish the facts
set forth in those records even though the person in court is only
testifying on the basis of what the records show and although he has
no personal knowledge of the facts which so appear.

(3) Determination of Law. In any court the law is determined
by the judge. When there is a trial by jury, the judge determines the
law and instructs the jury as to the rules of law that will be applied,
depending upon the facts which the jury finds to exist. For example,
when the plaintiff brings suit for breach of contract and the defendant
denies that there was a contract, the judge could instruct the jury:
"If you find that there was a contract and that the defendant without
cause violated the contract, you will return a verdict for the plaintiff
in the amount of the damages which the plaintiff sustained by the

breach of the contract. If, however, you find that there was no contract, you will return a verdict in favor of the defendant. Likewise, if you find that there was a contract but also find that the defendant was justified in not performing the contract, you shall return a verdict in favor of the defendant."

When an appeal is taken, the higher or appellate court is concerned only with the legal correctness of the action or decision from which the appeal was taken. Thus there is no question of fact to be determined on appeal but merely the question of whether the lower court acted correctly.

(4) Finality. The judgment of a court of jurisdiction determines or ends the dispute. The question may be examined a number of times, however, before such a final judgment is reached. The verdict of the jury, except in the case of an acquittal in a criminal prosecution, may be set aside by the court when manifestly wrong; and the final action of the trial court may be reviewed on appeal to a higher court.

In many instances an appeal cannot be taken beyond a particular court because there is no other court with jurisdiction to hear the appeal. The right to take an appeal is also subject to the limitation that it must be taken within a specified period of time. Furthermore, the verdict of a jury cannot be set aside either by the trial judge or by an appellate court merely because the reviewing judge or court would not have reached the same decision as the jury. Otherwise stated, the verdict must be allowed to stand unless it can be said that no reasonable man could have arrived at the same verdict as the jury.

Sec. 3-B. The Lawsuit. In most instances, legal rights are enforced by a lawsuit in a court, as contrasted with a proceeding before an administrative agency or an arbitration board. Reduced to simplest terms, the lawsuit is brought by a plaintiff against a defendant, and papers called *pleadings* are filed by each to set forth his version of the facts and to raise any questions of law.[2] If only questions of law are raised, the court will decide them on the basis of the pleadings and a trial is not required. If, however, there is a disagreement as to one or more important facts, the case goes on trial so that the facts can be determined. In order to assist the parties both in the preparation of the pleadings and in preparing for trial, it is commonly provided that prior to trial the parties can question witnesses outside of court under oath and compel the production of documents and records for examination.

At the trial, if there is one, both parties present evidence. When any of the evidence is not relevant, material, or competent, the court

---

[2] For a discussion of the lawsuit in greater detail, see the Appendix.

will refuse to admit it if the adverse party objects to it. After all of the evidence is presented to the jury, the judge will analyze or explain to the jury the substance of the evidence that has been presented and will instruct them as to the law which is to guide them in making their decision. This summarization is subject to certain exceptions. For example, the case can be taken away from the jury and disposed of by the judge alone when there is no evidence which justifies the case going to the jury or if the evidence is so much in favor of one side that the jury would not be allowed to return a verdict in favor of the other.

Following the return of the verdict by the jury, any party dissatisfied with it may attack the verdict. According to the circumstances of the case, the trial judge will then sustain the verdict or set it aside. From this action any objecting party can obtain a review of the case by the trial judge, and ultimately any dissatisfied party may appeal.

After the decision in the case is final, because no further appeal is possible or because the time for taking any appeal has expired, the judgment may be enforced by the sheriff when it is a money judgment or when it provides for the surrender or delivery of property to any person.

A lawsuit may be a long proceeding. Because the winning party does not recover all of his expenses, even he may have less than he would have had if there had been no lawsuit. The losing party has his own expenses and costs to bear, in addition to any judgment for damages that he must pay to the other party. Knowledge of the law before you enter into business transactions, or guidance by one who has the knowledge, therefore, may save you much difficulty and expense.

Other Agencies and Procedures for Settling Disputes

In addition to courts, administrative agencies have been created to enforce law and to determine rights within certain areas; arbitration has developed as an out-of-court method of dispute determination; and the declaratory judgment has been added as an alternative to the traditional type of lawsuit.

Sec. 3-C. Administrative Agencies. During the last half century, governments, both state and national, have adopted extensive regulations of business. The traditional courts of law are not well suited to determining matters arising in connection with such regulations because the judges and the juries lack an expert knowledge of the particular business that is being regulated. For this and other reasons, a special agency has been created to handle each particular field of government regulation.

Violation of government regulations of business are heard in some manner before the administrative agency in charge of such regulations. In general, the procedure is similar to that before a court except that the government administrator acts as the judge, there is no jury, and under most statutes the administrator is not limited by the courtroom rules as to what is admissible as evidence. Thus we find the Interstate Commerce Commission regulating interstate commerce and passing upon whether conduct of a carrier is a violation of its regulations. The commission is thus a lawmaker, an executive that enforces the law, and a court which interprets and applies the law. This is also true of the Civil Aeronautics Administration, the Federal Trade Commission, the Securities and Exchange Commission, the National Labor Relations Board, and many other federal and state administrative agencies.

Any person aggrieved with the action of the administrative agency can generally appeal to a court. In such a case, the appellate court generally disposes of the case in the same manner as though an appeal were taken from a trial court; that is, it accepts the findings of fact by the agency when supported by substantial evidence, even though the appellate court may disagree with such conclusions, but the court reverses the agency if it disagrees with it as to a question of law.

Sec. 3-D. Arbitration. The need for a speedier determination of technical matters by specialists has led to the rise of arbitration. By this procedure a dispute is brought before one or more arbitrators who make a decision which the parties have agreed to accept as final.

When a case is tried in court, the members of the jury and the judge frequently are not familiar with the business practices involved. The attorneys find it necessary, therefore, to explain these business practices before presenting the facts of the case. Arbitration enables the parties to present the facts before trained experts because the arbitrators are familiar with the practices that form the background of the dispute.

Parties to a contract which is to be in effect for some time may specify in the contract that any dispute shall be submitted to arbitrators to be selected by the parties. In some instances the contract will name the arbitrators in advance, who will then be a standing board of arbitrators for the duration of the contract. Frequently the parties provide their own remedy against failure to abide by the award of the arbitrators. The parties may execute a mutual indemnity bond by which each agrees to indemnify the other for any loss caused by his failure to carry out the arbitration award.

Sec. 3-E. Declaratory Judgment. In recent years a new procedure for settling disputes, authorized by statute, has made its appearance.

This is the *declaratory judgment* procedure. Under it a person, when confronted with the early prospect of an actual controversy, may petition the court to decide the question before loss is actually sustained. A copy of the petition is served on all parties. They may file answers. After all the pleadings have been filed, the court then decides the questions involved just as though a lawsuit had been brought.

The advantage of this procedure is that it enables the court to decide the dispute before any loss is sustained or an act done which causes harm. Since the decision is made in advance of any loss, it is a decision of law and does not involve questions of disputed fact in most cases.

Although the declaratory judgment procedure has these advantages, it cannot always be invoked. Courts have traditionally, with few exceptions, refused to render *advisory opinions*, that is, to give advice in advance of an actual law case. The declaratory judgment tends to become an advisory opinion unless it is clear that there is an actual dispute. Many courts accordingly refuse to allow a petition for a declaratory judgment unless convinced that there are present "the ripening seeds of a controversy."

Prologue to Business Law

The preceding discussion in Part I has been concerned with the social forces that determine the law (Chapter 1), the nature of legal rights and wrongs (Chapter 2), and the enforcement of legal rights (Chapter 3). In the parts that follow, an intensive study of the law of business transactions will be undertaken. The following prologue dealing with the sources of the law and the nature and branches of business law will provide a helpful background for that study.

Sec. 3-F. The Sources of the Law. The "law" is a composite of rules from many sources. In the United States the basic stock from which the law springs is in most instances the common law of England. In Louisiana the Code Napoléon and in parts of the Southwest the Spanish law form either the basis for the law or exercise a profound influence.

In England, common or community law developed in the centuries following the Norman Conquest in 1066. This *common law* was a body of unwritten principles that were based on customs and usages of the community. These principles were recognized and enforced by the courts. By the time the colonies were founded in America, the English common law had become a definite, established body of principles and was brought over to the New World to become the basis for the law of the colonies and of virtually all of the states of the United States.

To the basis of English common law have been added the decisions of the courts (*case law*); ordinances of cities and towns, and statutes of state legislatures and the United States Congress (*statutory law*); regulations of administrative agencies; executive orders and proclamations; international treaties; and state and national constitutions (*constitutional law*).

Through the general body of law run certain basic principles which have come to be known as equitable principles or rules. During the early centuries following the Norman Conquest, it was common for subjects of the English Crown to present to the King petitions requesting that particular favors or relief that could not be obtained in the ordinary courts of law be granted. The extraordinary or special relief granted by the chancellor, to whom the King referred such matters, was of such a nature as was dictated by principles of justice and equity. This body of principles was called *equity*.

Within the twentieth century there has been a marked trend toward the adoption of special statutes as general statements or codifications of particular areas of the law. The Commission on Uniform Laws, including representatives from all the states, has drafted recommended statutes on various business subjects and submitted them to the states for adoption. To the extent that these statutes have been adopted without modification, the law is the same in those states.

With the passage of the years and the accumulation of experience, the need for revision of some of these statutes became apparent. The Commission on Uniform Laws and the American Law Institute have accordingly prepared a Uniform Commercial Code for adoption to replace some of the former uniform laws.

Sec. 3-G. Uniform Commercial Code. The most important code to the businessman and to the business community in general is the Uniform Commercial Code.[3] Its importance lies in the fact that it regulates such a broad segment of the business world. Specifically, it

---

[3] As of August 1, 1963, the Code had been adopted in the following states, effective as noted:

Alaska (December 31, 1962)	Nebraska (Sept. 1, 1965)
Arkansas (January 1, 1962)	New Hampshire (July 1, 1961)
California (January 1, 1965)	New Jersey (January 1, 1963)
Connecticut (October 1, 1961)	New Mexico (January 1, 1962)
Georgia (January 1, 1964)	New York (September 27, 1964)
Illinois (July 1, 1962)	Ohio (July 1, 1962)
Indiana (July 1, 1964)	Oklahoma (January 1, 1963)
Kentucky (July 2, 1960)	Oregon (September 1, 1963)
Maine (December 31, 1964)	Pennsylvania (July 1, 1954)
Maryland (February 1, 1964)	Rhode Island (January 2, 1962)
Massachusetts (October 1, 1958)	Tennessee (June 30, 1964)
Michigan (January 1, 1964)	West Virginia (July 1, 1964)
Missouri (July 1, 1965)	Wisconsin (July 1, 1965)
Montana (January 1, 1965)	Wyoming (January 2, 1962)

regulates the fields of sales of goods; commercial paper, such as checks; bank collections and letters of credit; warehouse receipts; bills of lading; investment securities; and secured transactions in personal property.

This book is written on the basis of the Uniform Commercial Code; that is, it sets forth the law of business as it is in force in those states which have adopted the Code. In many instances this law is also the same in states that have not adopted the Code and, unless otherwise indicated, the principles stated are the same in both Code and non-Code states. Where this is not the case, it is specifically pointed out that the statement of law is based exclusively on the Code.

Sec. 3-H. Branches of Business Law. Some two centuries ago, Blackstone set forth the principles of the law of England in four small volumes. Today even 400 volumes would be inadequate to make an accurate statement of the law in the United States. The rise of new ways of social and business life, the development of an industrial society, and the increased daily use of mechanical devices have led not merely to an increase in the quantity of laws but also in the number of the fields of laws.

This book is devoted to a consideration of the basic or fundamental principles in those fields of law which are of the greatest importance to the citizen and the businessman in his personal and business life. *Business law*, then, includes the various laws that determine the rights and liabilities of persons taking part in business transactions, whether as individuals or as businessmen.

(1) Contract Law. A contract is a binding agreement. The general principles governing contracts are discussed in Part II. Certain types of contracts have developed special principles which govern them, in addition to the general principles applicable to all kinds of contracts. Thus it is necessary to give particular attention to contracts for the sale of goods (Part IV); the contracts or obligations that arise in connection with commercial paper, such as checks (Part V) ; secured credit sales and other security devices, such as those used in installment selling (Part VI); contracts of agency and employment (Part VII) ; contracts of insurance (Part X) , and suretyship and guaranty (Chapter 36) .

(2) Property Law. The law governing property is classified in terms of the particular kind of property involved, and particular transactions relating to it. Some of these principles relate to personal property, the transfer of title to personal property, and bailments of personal property which arise when it is given to another person to store, repair, or transport (Part III) . The law of real property, which

is ordinarily land and buildings, is discussed both generally, and with respect to the transfer of title, and the renting and mortgaging of real property (Part IX).

In a general sense, the chapter relating to business security (Chapter 65) may also be regarded as relating to property law for the security considered is the security of various property rights against harm from various types of misconduct.

(3) Business Organizations. Business today is to a very large degree conducted by groups or associations. The law governing the two most common forms of business organizations is set forth in the chapters devoted to partnerships and corporations (Part VIII).

(4) Estates. Property that belongs to one person often is administered or is nominally owned by another. This situation arises most commonly when property is held by one person in trust for another, when the owner has died and his property is being collected and distributed by his executor or administrator, or when the owner has become bankrupt and his property is being distributed through the bankruptcy court in order to pay his debts (Part XI). Although these situations are not of everyday occurrence, they are of sufficient importance to require an understanding of the basic applicable principles.

(5) Government Regulation of Business. The law of government regulation of business is considered with respect to the regulation of business enterprises, and the regulation of labor-management relations (Part XII). Although briefly treated because of limitations of space, the importance of the power of government to regulate business and the scope of such regulations must not be minimized. Both as a member of society and as a person whose welfare is affected by the business world, each individual must recognize the importance of the laws that regulate business. The importance of his right to vote and of his duty to exercise that right in an intelligent manner will be appreciated when it is understood that there is little or no protection against unwise regulatory legislation except the vote of the people. The courts will not protect the individual or the economy from unsound business laws. As stated by the United States Supreme Court:

It is not for this Court to reweigh the relevant factors and, perchance, substitute its notion of expediency and fairness for that of Congress. This is so even though the [Act of Congress] may demonstrably be disadvantageous to certain areas or persons. This Court is not a tribunal for relief from the crudities and inequities of complicated experimental economic legislation.[4]

---

[4] Secretary of Agriculture v. Central Roig Refining Company, 338 U.S. 604.

Checklist for Case Study

The questions in the following checklist will serve as a guide for the analysis of each case. It should be understood, however, that not every case will provide answers to all of these questions.

(1) Court. In what court was the action brought, and which court filed the opinion being studied?

(2) Purpose of the Action. What was the relief or remedy sought in the action?

(3) Parties. Who were the parties to the action? Were they the parties to the original transaction, or were there strangers such as creditors?

(4) Action Appealed from. What was done in the lower court which the appellant deemed wrong and from which he appealed?

(5) Arguments of the Parties. What were the arguments made by the respective parties?

(6) Decision of the Court. What did the court decide?

(7) Basis for Decision. What authority did the court give to support its opinion? Was it common law, statute, other cases, Restatements of the Law and texts, logic, or the personal belief of the court?

(8) Appraisal of the Opinion. Is the opinion in accord with the general body of law? What social objectives are advanced by the decision? What social objectives are hindered or defeated by the decision? Is the decision socially desirable? Is it practical in application? Does it give rise to any dangers?

CHAPTER 4

Nature and Classes

An essential part of free enterprise in our economic system is that the rights created by contracts are protected. Each party must observe the terms of the contract, and generally government cannot impair the obligations of a contract. Economic life would be most uncertain and it would be impossible to plan ahead if we did not have the assurance that agreements once made would be binding.

Sec. 4-A. Definition of a Contract. By one definition, "a *contract* is a promise or set of promises for the breach of which the law gives a remedy or the performance of which the law in some way recognizes as a duty." [1] Contracts arise out of agreements; hence a contract is often defined as "an agreement creating an obligation." [2]

Generally a contract is an exchange of promises or assents by two or more persons, resulting in an obligation to do or to refrain from doing a particular act, which obligation is recognized or enforced by law. A contract may also be formed when a promise is made by one person in exchange for the act or the refraining from the doing of an act by another. The substance of the definition of a contract is that by mutual agreement or assent the parties create legally enforceable duties or obligations that did not exist before.

In order to be an enforceable contract, there must be (1) an agreement, (2) based upon the genuine assent of the parties, (3) supported

---

[1] Restatement, Contracts, Sec. 1. See the Appendix for a discussion of the nature and purpose of the Restatements.

[2] *H. Liebes & Co.* v. *Klengenberg*, (C.C.A. 9th) 23 F.2d 611.

by consideration, (4) made for a lawful object, (5) between competent parties, and (6) in the form required by law, if any. These requirements will be considered in the following seven chapters.

Sec. 4-B. The Nature of Contracts. Contracts arise under a wide variety of circumstances. They may arise from face-to-face conversations or from conversations by telephone, from the exchange of letters or telegrams, or by any other means of communication.

When the contract is part of a common business transaction, a printed form is often used. In such a case, all that is usually necessary to complete the contract is to add the date, the names of the parties, the price, the particular performance or commodity which is the subject matter of the contract, and the signatures of the parties. Familiar types of standard contract forms are leases and the various forms used for the installment purchase of automobiles, refrigerators, and television sets. One of the most detailed of the common types of contract forms is the life insurance policy.

Sometimes the contract must comply with certain standards. One law may declare that a particular type of contract shall be in writing. Another law may prescribe that certain provisions must be included in the contract. Thus state laws commonly provide that an insurance policy must contain a clause giving the policyholder a 30-day or 31-day period in which to pay overdue premiums before he may be declared in default. The law may state that when a contract calls for the payment of money and interest on that money, the interest cannot be greater than a specified per cent of the amount owed. Certain provisions of contracts may be prohibited entirely by law or may be declared contrary to public policy by the courts.

The subject matter may relate to the performance of personal services, such as contracts of employment to work on an assembly line in a factory, to work as a secretary in an office, to sing in an opera, or to build a house. The contract may provide for the transfer of the ownership of property, such as a house, an automobile, or an account receivable, from one person to another. A contract may also call for a combination of these things. For example, a builder may contract to supply materials and do the work involved in installing the materials, or a person may contract to build a house and then transfer the house and the land to the buyer.

Sec. 4-C. The Parties to a Contract. A person who makes a promise is the *promisor*, and the person to whom the promise is made is the *promisee*. If the promise is binding, it imposes upon the promisor a duty or obligation and he may be called the *obligor*. The promisee who can claim the benefit of the obligation is also called the *obligee*.

The parties to a contract are said to stand in privity with each other, and the relationship between them is termed *privity of contract.*

A party to a contract may be an individual, a partnership, a corporation, a government. A person may act for himself, or he may act on behalf of another. There may be just one person on each side of the contract, or there may be two or more persons on either side.

Sec. 4-D. Formal and Simple Contracts. Contracts are classified in terms of their form as (1) contracts under seal, (2) contracts of record, and (3) simple contracts. The first two classes are known as *formal contracts;* they are binding even though not supported by consideration.[3]

(1) Contracts Under Seal. When the terms of an obligation are written or printed on paper that is signed, sealed, and delivered, the obligation constitutes a *contract under seal.* It is also known as a deed, a bond, and a common-law speciality. The distinguishing feature of this form of contract is the seal.

A contract is sealed when it is executed by affixing a seal or, in other words, by making an impression upon the paper or upon some tenacious substance, such as wax, attached to the instrument. Although at common law an impression was necessary, the courts now treat various signs or marks to be the equivalent of a seal. To illustrate, some states hold that there is a seal if a person's signature or a corporation's name is followed by a scroll or scrawl, the word "Seal," or the letters "L.S." [4] When such devices are used as substitutes for the common-law seal, however, some states require that the document recite that it is intended to be a contract under seal. For example, the signature "H. C. Walker (Seal)" with such a recital was held to be a promise under seal; whereas the signature "Church Lumber Co. (Seal)" without such a recital was held not to be a promise under seal.

Two or more persons may use the same seal. When one signer affixes a seal, the subsequent signers, if they deliver the instrument, are presumed to have adopted the seal "unless extrinsic circumstances show a contrary intention."[5]

In some states the common law relating to seals has been changed by statute. The Uniform Commercial Code abolishes the law of seals with respect to contracts for the sale of goods.[6]

---

[3] R., Sec. 7. The Restatement includes in the class of formal contracts commercial paper or negotiable instruments (see Part V) that are commercial specialties as distinguished from sealed contracts that are common-law specialties.

[4] "L.S." stands for "locus sigilli," the Latin for "the place for the seal."

[5] R., Secs. 98, 99.

[6] Uniform Commercial Code (UCC), Sec. 2-203.

(2) Contracts of Record. An obligation imposed by the judgment of a court and entered upon its records is often called a *contract of record.* It cannot accurately be described as a contract, however, because it is really not based upon an agreement of the parties.

One form of contract of record is in fact a contract. This type exists when one acknowledges before a proper court that he is obligated to pay a certain sum unless a specified thing is done or not done. For example, a party who has been arrested may be released on his promise to appear in court and may bind himself to pay a certain sum in the event that he fails to do so. An obligation of this kind is known as a *recognizance.*

(3) Simple Contracts. All contracts other than contracts of record and contracts under seal are called *simple contracts* or informal contracts, without regard to whether they are oral or written.

Sec. 4-E.   Express and Implied Contracts.   Simple contracts may be classified in terms of the way in which they are created as express contracts and implied contracts.

(1) Express Contracts. An *express contract* is one in which the parties have made oral or written declarations of their intentions and of the terms of the transaction.

(2) Implied Contracts. An *implied contract* (or, as sometimes stated, a contract implied in fact) is one in which the evidence of the agreement is not shown by words, written or spoken, but by the acts and conduct of the parties. Such a contract arises, for example, when one person, without being requested to do so, renders services under circumstances indicating that he expects to be paid for them, and the other person, knowing such circumstances, accepts the benefit of those services. The benefited person is then required by law to pay a reasonable value for the service rendered. An implied contract cannot arise when there is an existing express contract on the same subject.

It is more accurate to describe contracts of this nature as contracts "expressed by conduct," as distinguished from contracts expressed in words, for an agreement by conduct differs from an express agreement only in the manner by which its existence is established. It is more common, however, to refer to these contracts as implied. (See p. 60, Victor's Executor v. Monson.)

Sec. 4-F.   Quasi-Contracts.   Under certain circumstances the law creates and enforces legal rights and obligations when no real contract, express or implied, exists. These obligations are known as *quasi-contracts.* "It is an obligation which the law creates, in the absence of any agreement, when and because the acts of the parties or others have placed in the possession of one person money, or its equivalent, under such circumstances that in equity and good conscience he ought not to retain it, and which *ex aequo et bono* (in justice and fairness) belongs to another. Duty, and not a promise or agreement or intention of the person sought to be charged, defines it." [7]

Conversely, no quasi-contractual obligation arises when the plaintiff merely confers upon the defendant a benefit to which he was already entitled.

Sec. 4-G. Valid Contracts, Voidable Contracts, and Void Agreements. Contracts may be classified in terms of their enforceability or validity as (1) valid contracts, (2) voidable contracts, and (3) void agreements. (See p. 61, Griffin v. Smith)

(1) Valid Contracts. A *valid contract* is an agreement that is binding and enforceable. It has all the essential requirements mentioned on page 55.

(2) Voidable Contracts. A *voidable contract* is an agreement that is binding and enforceable but, because of the circumstances surrounding its execution or the capacity of one of the parties, it may be rejected at the option of one of the parties. For example, one who has been forced to sign an agreement against his will may in some instances avoid liability on the contract. The right to avoid a contract must be exercised within a reasonable time, however, or the right to do so is lost.

(3) Void Agreements. A *void agreement* is without legal effect. Thus, an agreement that contemplates the performance of an act prohibited by law is usually incapable of enforcement; hence it is void. Although the distinction between a void agreement and a voidable contract is clear in principle, there is frequently confusion because some courts describe a given transaction as void while others regard it as merely voidable.

Sec. 4-H. Executed and Executory Contracts. Contracts may be classified in terms of the extent to which they have been performed as executed contracts and executory contracts.

(1) Executed Contracts. An *executed contract* is one that has been completely performed. In other words, an executed contract is one under the terms of which nothing remains to be done by either party. A contract may be executed at once, as in the case of a cash sale; or it may be executed in the future.

(2) Executory Contracts. In an *executory contract* something remains to be done. For example, if a utility company agrees to

---

[7] *Miller* v. *Schloss*, 218 N.Y. 400, 113 N.E. 337.

furnish electricity to another party for a specified period of time
at a stipulated price, the contract is executory. If the entire price is
paid in advance, the contract is still deemed executory; although,
strictly speaking, it is executed on one side and executory on the other.

Cases for Chapters 4

Victor's Executor v. Monson [8]

283 S.W.2d 175 (Ky.App., 1955)

Monson requested payment from Kate Victor's estate for services rendered and money advanced on behalf of Victor under an express contract.
The estate refused to pay, and Monson sued. His evidence showed that he
had managed Victor's house, took constant care of her, and attended to all
her business affairs during the last two years of her life. There was, however, no proof that Victor expressly agreed to compensate Monson for
such services. Judgment was entered for Monson, and the estate appealed.

STEWART, C.J. . . . If the proven facts and circumstances are
such as to fairly show that both the party rendering the services or
furnishing the necessities and the one receiving them expected, understood, and intended compensation should be paid, the court or the
jury trying the case will be authorized to find an express contract for
payment was entered into. . . . This particular type of agreement is
denominated a "contract implied in fact"; it differs from an "express
contract" only in the mode of proof required; and it is implied only
in that it is to be inferred from the circumstances, the conduct, and
the acts or relations of the parties, rather than from their spoken
words. In short, from the evidence disclosed the court may conclude
the parties entered into an agreement, although there is no proof of
an express offer and a definite acceptance. . . .

It is insisted that since appellee [Monson] occupied a position of
family relationship to Mrs. Victor, he had to prove an express contract and . . . he cannot recover on an implied contract.

Where all the parties live together in a close family relationship,
each contributing work or money to the common cause and each receiving mutual benefits from the joint efforts, there will be no implied
contract raised in favor of any of them against any of the others for
recompense for mutual services rendered. . . . It is recognized, however, despite such a presumption of gratuity arising from a family
relationship, recovery can still be had on an express contract for
the services claimed. . . .

Assuming . . . appellee sustained toward Mrs. Victor a family
relationship, which necessitated his proving an express contract to

---

[8] The structure or anatomy of a judicial opinion is considered on page 13. See also
p. 54, Checklist for Case Study.

sustain his action, he may recover on a contract implied in fact for the reasons already written. We have shown he did in fact come forward with the essentials of a contract implied in fact. . . .

[Judgment reversed because certain instructions to the jury not relevant to the subject here considered were erroneous. Case remanded.]

Griffin v. Smith

101 F.2d 348 (C.A. 7th, 1938)

The directors of a corporation paid Griffin, one of the directors, a bonus. He paid the federal income tax on the bonus in addition to his regular income. Later a suit was brought by the shareholders of the corporation to recover the bonus on the ground that it was excessive and therefore illegal. To settle the suit, Griffin returned the greater portion of the bonus and then sued the government for a refund of the tax that he had paid on that part of the bonus he returned. From a judgment allowing a tax refund, the federal tax collector appealed.

LINDLEY, D.J. [The court stated that as a question of income tax law the returned bonus money was not subject to tax if the contract for its payment was void, but that it was subject to tax if the contract was voidable.]

. . . The expression "void contract" is often used to denote that the parties to the transaction have gone through the form of making a contract, but that none has been made in law by reason of lack of some essential element of a contract. . . . Such a contract creates no legal right of any kind, and either party thereto may ignore it at his pleasure, in so far as it is executory; and being void, an absolute nullity, it is incapable of ratification. . . . A voidable contract, on the other hand, is one wherein one party has the privilege of electing it to be either valid or void at his pleasure. . . . The party in whom the law lodges such option is thus clothed with a right in the nature of an equitable election. A void contract, one made in the face of absolute inhibition by statute, is ineffective for all purposes, . . . whereas a voidable contract may be rescinded at the option of the party who has the right to complain. The use of the terms "void" and "voidable" as indicative of the transaction is unsatisfactory and often misleading. . . . The two words are frequently misused. . . .

Where contracts of directors in violation of their duties to stockholders involve unreasonableness of an exercise of power, it is quite universally the rule that they are voidable. . . . The contract [for the payment of the bonus] was voidable at the option of the stockholders as to all sums in excess of a reasonable allowance, and the court was in error in concluding that it was wholly void. . . .

[Judgment for plaintiff taxpayer reversed.]

Questions and Case Problems

1. What objective of the law (from the list in Chapter 1, pages 3-8) is illustrated by each of the following quotations?

(a) "Economic life would be most uncertain . . . if we did not have the assurance that contracts once made would be binding."

(b) "A person shall not be allowed to enrich himself unjustly at the expense of another."

2. McNulty signed a contract with the Medical Service of District of Columbia, Inc. The contract which was on a printed form prepared by the corporation, concluded with the clause: "In witness whereof, the party of the first part has caused its corporate seal to be hereunto affixed and these presents to be signed by its duly authorized officers and the party of the second part has hereunto set his hand and seal the day and year first above written." The contract had been sent to McNulty who signed and sealed it, and then returned it to the corporation. The latter signed but did not seal it, and then sent an executed copy of the contract to the plaintiff without referring to the lack of a seal. When McNutly sued on the contract, the corporation claimed that it was an unsealed contract because it had not been sealed by both parties. Was it correct? (McNulty v. Medical Service of the District of Columbia [M.C. App.Dist. Colo.] 176 A.2d 783)

3. Tetrauld made a written agreement to sell his land to Bauer. Tetrauld died. Bauer claimed that after the agreement for the sale of the land had been made, they had orally agreed that Tetrauld would give the land to Bauer for his past services instead of selling it to him. Monroe, who was administering the estate of Tetrauld, objected to changing the written contract. A Montana statute provided that a "contract in writing may be altered by a contract in writing or by an executed oral agreement, and not otherwise." Was the oral agreement barred by this statute? (Bauer v. Monroe, 117 Mont. 306, 158 P.2d 485)

4. Mrs. Herbert, the owner of an orchard, and Cantor, to whom she had leased the orchard, desired to borrow money so that a crop could be grown by the tenant. Part of the money required by them was loaned by the Pinnacle Packing Co. and the Medford National Bank. The loan agreement stated that the lenders would "furnish" the money and that when the crops were sold, there would be deducted a sufficient amount "to repay the advances made by [the lenders] before any payments would be made to the borrowers." There was no express provision in the agreement that the borrowers would repay the money. No oral agreement to repay was made by either borrower. Pinnacle Packing Co. then sued Herbert to recover the amount of the money advanced. She defended on the ground that she had not expressly agreed to repay the money borrowed. Decide. (Pinnacle Packing Co. v. Herbert, 157 Ore. 96, 70 P.2d 31)

CHAPTER 5

The Agreement — Offer

A contract is a legally binding agreement. This agreement results from an exchange of promises or assents by the parties involved. These assents may be expressed by words or by conduct.

The Agreement

Sec. 5-A. How an Agreement Arises. An agreement arises when one person, the *offeror*, makes an offer and the person to whom the offer is made, the *offeree*, accepts. In every case there must be both an offer and an acceptance. If either is lacking, there is no contract.

An offeror may make an offer to a particular person because he wants only that person to do what he has in mind. On the other hand, he may make the offer to the public at large because he does not care by whom something is done so long as it is done. The latter case arises, for example, when a reward is offered to the public for the return of lost property.

It is frequently said that a meeting of the minds is essential to an agreement or a contract. Generally this is a satisfactory statement. Modern cases do not stress the meeting of the minds, however, because in some situations the law finds an agreement even though the minds of the parties have not in fact met. (See p. 70, Industrial Products Case) The real test is not whether the minds of the parties met, but whether under the circumstances one party was reasonably entitled to believe that there was an offer and the other to believe that there was an acceptance.

Sec. 5-B. Bilateral and Unilateral Contracts. In making an offer, the offeror is in effect extending a promise to do something, such as to pay a sum of money, if the offeree will do what the offeror requests. If the offeror extends a promise and asks for a promise in return and if the offeree accepts the offer by making the promise, the contract is called a *bilateral contract* because one promise is given in exchange for another.

In contrast, the offeror may agree to obligate himself only when something is done by the offeree. Since only one party is obligated to perform after the contract has been made, this kind of contract is called a *unilateral contract*. This is illustrated by the reward case because the offeror does not care for a mere promise by members of the public that they will try to return the lost property. The offeror wants the property, and he promises to pay anyone who returns the property. When this is done, his offer is accepted, a contract arises, and the offeror is bound by his agreement. The offeree has nothing more to do because he returned the property called for by the offer.

The Offer

An *offer* expresses (or, in the case of an apparent offer, appears to express) the willingness of the offeror to enter into a contractual agreement regarding a particular subject. It is a promise which is in its terms conditional upon an act, a forbearance, or a return promise that is given in exchange for the promise or its performance.

Sec. 5-C. Requirements of an Offer. A valid offer must meet the tests of (1) contractual intention, (2) definiteness, and (3) communication to the offeree.

(1) Contractual Intention. To constitute an offer, the offeror must intend to create a legal obligation or it must appear that he intends to do so. When there is a lack of such intention on his part, it makes no difference whether the offeree takes any action concerning the offer. The following are examples of a lack of contractual intention on the part of the offeror:

(a) SOCIAL INVITATIONS. Ordinary invitations to social affairs are not "offers" in the eyes of the law. The acceptance of a social invitation, such as an invitation to go to dinner, does not give rise to a legally binding agreement or contract.

(b) OFFERS MADE IN JEST OR EXCITEMENT. If an offer is made in obvious jest, the offeree cannot accept it and then sue the offeror for breach of the agreement. Here the offeree, as a reasonable man, should realize that no contract is intended and therefore no contract arises even though the offeror speaks words which, if seriously spoken, could be accepted and result in a contract. Under the same theory an extravagant offer of a reward made in the heat of excitement cannot be acted upon as a valid offer.

It is not always obvious or apparent to the offeree when the offer is made in jest or under excitement. If it is reasonable under the circumstances for the offeree to believe that the offer was made seriously, a contract is formed by the offeree's acceptance. (See p. 72, Lucy v. Zehmer)

(c) INVITATIONS TO NEGOTIATE. The first statement made by one of two persons is not necessarily an offer. In many instances there may be preliminary discussion or an *invitation* by one party to the other *to negotiate* to talk business. (See p. 74, Lonergan v. Scolnick)

Ordinarily, when a seller sends out circulars or catalogs listing prices, he is not regarded as having made an offer to sell at those prices but as merely indicating that he is willing to consider an offer made by a buyer on those terms. The reason for this rule is in part the practical consideration that since a seller does not have an unlimited supply of any commodity, he cannot possibly intend to make a binding contract with everyone who sees his circular. The same principle is applied to merchandise that is displayed with price tags in stores or store windows and to most advertisements.

The circumstances may be such, however, that even newspaper advertising constitutes an offer. Thus it has been held that the seller made an offer when he advertised specific items which would be sold at a clearance sale at the prices listed and added the words: "First come, first served."

Quotations of prices, even when sent on request, are likewise not deemed offers in the absence of previous dealings between the parties or the existence of a trade custom which would give the recipient of the quotation reason to believe that an offer was being made to him. Although the businessman is not bound by his quotations and price tags, he will as a matter of goodwill make every effort to deliver the merchandise at those prices.

In some instances, it is apparent that an invitation to negotiate and not an offer has been made. When construction work is done for the national government, for a state government, or for a political subdivision, statutes require that a printed statement of the work to be done be published and circulated. Contractors are invited to submit bids on the work, and the statute generally requires that the bid of the lowest responsible bidder be accepted. Such an invitation for bids is clearly an invitation to negotiate, both from its nature and from the fact that it does not specify the price to be paid for the work. The bid of each contractor is an offer, and there is no contract until the government accepts one of these bids. This procedure of advertising for bids is also commonly employed by private persons when a large construction project is involved. (See p. 75, Olson v. Beacham)

(d) AGREEMENTS TO MAKE A CONTRACT AT A FUTURE DATE.
No contract arises when the parties merely agree that at a future date
they shall consider making a contract or shall make a contract on
terms to be agreed upon at that time. In such case, the agreement is
merely to enter into future negotiations since, until the future contract
is made, neither party is under any obligation.

If part of a contract provides for the execution of a future agreement pertaining to certain matters and that part is by itself too vague
to be binding, such a provision does not affect the enforceability of
other parts of the same contract that are otherwise binding. (See p.
76, Fincher v. Belk-Sawyer Co.)

(2) Definite Offer. An offer must be definite and certain. If it is
indefinite or vague or if an essential provision is lacking, it cannot be
accepted. The reason is that the courts cannot tell what the parties
are to do. (See p. 77, Bonnevier v. Dairy Cooperative Association)
Thus an offer to conduct a business for such time as should be prof-
itable is too vague to be considered a valid offer.

Although an offer must be definite and certain, not all of its terms
need be expressed. Some of the terms may be implied. For example,
an offer "to pay fifty dollars for a watch" does not state the terms of
payment. A court would consider that these terms were implied,
specifically, that cash payment was to be made upon delivery of the
watch.

The offer and contract may also be made definite by reference to
another writing, as when the parties agreed that the written lease
which was to be executed by them should be the standard form of lease
with which both were familiar.

(3) Communication of Offer to the Offeree. The offer must be
communicated directly to the offeree by the offeror or by another
person acting as agent or employee of the offeror or with his consent.
Until the offer is made known to the offeree, he does not know that
there is something which he can accept. Sometimes, particularly in
the field of unilateral contracts, the offeree performs the act called
for by the offeror without knowing of the offer's existence. Thus,
without knowing that a reward is offered for the arrest of a particular
criminal, a person may arrest the criminal. If he learns thereafter
that a reward was offered for the arrest, he cannot recover the reward
in most states. (See p. 79, Fidelity & Deposit Co. Case)

Termination of the Offer

An offer gives the offeree power to bind the offeror by contract.
This power does not last forever, and the law specifies that under
certain circumstances the power shall be terminated.

Once the offer is terminated, the offeree cannot revive it. If he attempts to accept the offer after it has been terminated, his act is meaningless, unless the original offeror is willing to regard the "late acceptance" as a new offer which he then accepts.

Sec. 5-D. Methods of Termination of Offer. Offers may be terminated in any one of the following ways: (1) revocation of the offer by the offeror, (2) lapse of time, (3) rejection of offer by offeree, (4) counteroffer by offeree, (5) death or disability of either party, and (6) subsequent illegality.

(1) Revocation of the Offer by the Offeror. Ordinarily the offeror can revoke his offer before it is accepted. If he does so, the offeree cannot create a contract by accepting the revoked offer. Thus the bidder at an auction sale may withdraw (revoke) his bid (offer) before it is accepted. The auctioneer cannot thereafter accept the withdrawn bid.

An ordinary offer may be revoked at any time before it is accepted, even though the offeror had originally stated that the offer would be good for a stated period which has not yet expired, or he had expressly promised the offeree that he would not revoke the offer before a specified later date.

(a) WHAT CONSTITUTES A REVOCATION. No particular form of words is required to constitute a revocation. Any expression or act indicating that the offer is revoked or the communication of information inconsistent with a continuation of the offer is sufficient. A notice sent to the offeree that the property which is the subject of the offer has been sold to a third person is a revocation of the offer. An order for goods by a customer, which is an offer by him to purchase at certain prices, is revoked by a notice to the seller of the cancellation of the order, provided such notice is communicated before the order is accepted.

(b) COMMUNICATION OF REVOCATION. A revocation of an offer is ordinarily effective only when it is made known to the offeree or his agent or employee. Until it is so communicated to him, he has reason to believe that there is still an offer which he may accept; and he may rely on this belief.

Except in a few states, a letter or telegram revoking an offer made to a particular offeree is not effective until received by the offeree. It is not a revocation when it is written and signed by the offeror nor even when it is mailed or dispatched. A written revocation is effective, however, when it is delivered to the offeree's agent, or to the offeree's residence or place of business under such circumstances that the offeree would be reasonably expected to be aware of its receipt.

It is ordinarily held that there is a sufficient "communication" of the revocation when the offeree learns indirectly of the offeror's intent to revoke. This is particularly true when the seller-offeror, after making a written offer to sell land to the offeree, sells the land to a third person, and the offeree, who indirectly learns of such sale, necessarily realizes that the seller cannot perform his offer and therefore must be deemed to have revoked it.

If the offeree accepts an offer before its effective revocation, a valid contract is created. This may occur when the offeree mails or telegraphs his acceptance without knowing that a letter of revocation has been mailed to him.

When an offer is made to the public, it may usually be revoked in the same manner in which it was made. For example, an offer of a reward that is made to the general public by an advertisement in a newspaper may be revoked in the same manner. A member of the public cannot recover the amount of the reward by thereafter performing the act for which the reward was originally offered. This exception is made to the rule requiring communication of revocation because of the necessities of the situation. The offeror does not know which members of the general public know of his offer so that it would be impossible for him to communicate to every person the fact that he revokes his offer. The public revocation of the public offer is effective even though it is not seen by the person attempting to accept the original offer.

(c) OPTION CONTRACTS. An *option contract* is a binding promise to keep an offer open for a stated period of time or until a specified date. The offeror cannot revoke his offer if he has received consideration, that is, has been paid, for his promise to keep the offer open. If the owner of a house gives a prospective purchaser a sixty-day written option to purchase the property at $15,000 and the customer pays the owner a sum of money, such as $500, the agreement is valid and the owner cannot revoke the offer within the sixty-day period. Even though he expressly tells the purchaser within that time that the option contract is revoked, the purchaser may exercise the option, that is, he may accept the offer. If the option is exercised, the money paid to obtain the option is ordinarily applied as a down payment on the purchase price. If the option is not exercised, the offeror keeps the $500.

In those jurisdictions in which the seal retains its common-law force, the option contract is binding on the offeror if it is set forth in a sealed writing, even though he does not receive any payment for his agreement.

Frequently an option contract is combined with a lease of real estate or personal property. Thus, the parties may enter into a transaction by which one of them rents a building for a period of years, at the end of which time he has the option of purchasing the building for a specified amount.

(d) FIRM OFFERS. As another exception to the rule that an offer may be revoked at any time before acceptance, it is provided by statute in some states that an offeror cannot revoke an offer prior to its expiration when he has made a *firm offer*, that is, an offer in writing which states that it is to be irrevocable for a stated period.

The Uniform Commercial Code adopts this doctrine with respect to a merchant's offer to buy or sell goods, but sets a maximum of three months on its duration.[1]

(e) REVOCATION OF OFFER OF UNILATERAL CONTRACT. Since the offer of a unilateral contract can be accepted only by performing the act called for, it theoretically follows that there is no acceptance until that act is fully performed by the offeree and that the offeror is free to revoke his offer even though the offeree has partly performed and has expended time and money. To avoid this hardship, a number of courts hold that after the offeree has done some substantial act toward acceptance, the offeror cannot revoke the offer until after the lapse of a reasonable time in which the offeree could have completed performance.

(2) Lapse of Time. When the offer specifies that it is good for a specified time only, the offer terminates with the expiration of that period of time. It cannot be accepted thereafter.

If the offer does not specify a time, it will terminate after the lapse of a reasonable time. What constitutes a reasonable time depends upon the circumstances of each case, that is, upon the nature of the subject matter, the nature of the market in which it is sold, the time of the year, and other factors of supply and demand. If the commodity is perishable in nature or fluctuates greatly in value, the reasonable time will be much shorter than if the commodity or subject matter is a staple article. An offer to sell a harvested crop of tomatoes would expire within a very short time.

(3) Rejection of Offer by Offeree. If the offeree rejects the offer and communicates this rejection to the offeror, his agent, or employee, the offer is terminated, even though the period for which the offeror agreed to keep the offer open has not expired. The offeree thereafter cannot revive the offer by attempting to accept it. It may be that the offeror is willing to renew the offer; but unless he does so, there is no offer for the offeree to accept.

The fact that the offeree replies to the offeror without accepting the offer does not constitute a revocation when it is apparent that

---

[1] Uniform Commercial Code, Sec. 2-205.

the failure to accept at that time was not intended as a revocation. For example, when the seller on receiving an order from a customer sent a reply that he would send a "formal confirmation" of the order as soon as the seller received confirmation from his source of supply that the goods were available, the reply of the seller was not a rejection of the offer made by the customer.

(4) Counteroffer by Offeree. Usually if *A* makes an offer to *B*, such as to sell a used automobile for $1,000, and *B* makes an offer to buy at $750, the original offer is terminated. *B* is in effect saying, "I refuse your original offer, but in its place I make a different offer." Such an offer by the offeree is known as a *counteroffer.* In substance, the counteroffer presupposes a rejection of the original offer. (See p. 80, Garrett v. International Milling Co.)

In some instances, however, it is held that the circumstances showed that both parties knew and intended that the counteroffer was not to be regarded as a definite rejection of the original offer but merely as further discussion on the subject or as a request for further information.

Counteroffers are not limited to offers that directly contradict the original offers. Any departure from, or addition to, the original offer is a counteroffer even though the original offer was silent as to the point added by the counteroffer. For example, when the offeree stated that he accepted and added that time was of the essence, the "acceptance" was a counteroffer when the original offer had been silent on that point.

A counteroffer is by definition an offer and, if the original offeror (who is now the offeree) accepts it, a binding contract results.

(5) Death or Disability of Either Party. If either the offeror or the offeree dies or becomes insane before the offer is accepted, it is automatically terminated.

(6) Subsequent Illegality. If the performance of the contract becomes illegal after the offer is made, the offer is terminated. Thus, if an offer is made to sell alcoholic liquors but a law prohibiting such sales is enacted before the offer is accepted, the offer is terminated.

Cases for Chapter 5

Industrial Products Mfg. Co. v. Jewett Lumber Co.

185 F.2d 866 (C.A. 8th, 1950)

On February 22, the Jewett Lumber Company placed an order with the Elaterite Company, which order in turn was to be filled by Industrial Products Mfg. Co. The latter refused to deal with the Elaterite Company because of its poor credit standing. Jewett then suggested that Industrial ship to and bill Jewett directly. This offer as to the order of February 22 was made by Jewett by a telegram of March 7, and a letter of March 10. When the goods were shipped by Industrial to Jewett, the latter returned them on the ground that on March 3, it had made a new agreement with the Elaterite Company which modified the order of February 22, by expressly giving Jewett the right to return goods for credit. Industrial contended that since it did not know of such amendment, it was not bound and sued Jewett. From a judgment for Jewett, Industrial appealed.

WOODROUGH, C.J. . . . At the conclusion of all the evidence on the jury trial, the defendant moved for directed verdict in its favor on the . . . ground . . . that the telegram of March 7 and the letter of March 10 from defendant to plaintiff were not sufficient to effect a new contract because there was no meeting of the minds—each party having meant a different thing when referring to "the order of February 22," the lumber company meaning the order as amended on March 3, and the Industrial company meaning the order as it stood, not amended.

The motion for directed verdict for the defendant was sustained, and judgment of dismissal followed. . . .

The phrase adopted by the defendant—"meeting of the minds"—is an ancient and venerable term, and it is widely accepted that there must be a "meeting of the minds" if there is to be a contract. The difficulty arises, however, in trying to determine when the minds of the parties have met. Defendant's position, in effect, is that only the terms in the minds of each of the parties to a contract constitute the terms of the contract, and that the mental processes of each party must concur before a contract can result. But courts are not so limited in their enforcement of contracts. On the contrary, it is what is expressed by the parties that constitutes the contract which courts enforce. . . . "Though there must be a meeting of the minds of the parties to constitute a contract, such meeting of the minds is to be determined by the expressed, and not by the secret, intention of the parties."

In Canister Co. v. National Can Corp., D.C. 63 F.Supp. 361, 365, it is well stated: "It is true that mutual assent is an essential prerequisite of the formation of a contract. But the test as to whether there is mutual assent is objective and does not depend upon the undisclosed intentions of the parties. Since the test is objective, the formation of a contract does not require 'the meeting of the minds' of the parties. Despite early dicta to the contrary, this view is now almost universally accepted." Holmes, in "The Path of the Law," (10 Harv.L.R. 457, 464) says: "In my opinion no one will understand the true theory of contract or be able to discuss some fundamental questions intelligently until he has understood that . . . the making of a contract depends not on the agreement of two minds in

one intention, but on the agreement of two sets of external signs—
not on the parties having meant the same thing but on their having
said the same thing."

. . . It follows that in some cases the minds of the parties never
did meet and that in interpreting and applying offers and their
acceptance 'what the other party is justified as regarding as assent,
is essential.' . . ."

In this case there was no lack of agreement on the part of the
offeree, the plaintiff. The telegram of March 7 and the letter of
March 10, coupled with a reference to the merchandise order of
February 22, the original copy of which plaintiff had in its hands
led to one definite, unambiguous contract. . . . The defendant's . . .
telegram and letter did not refer to the order of February 22, as
amended by the agreement of March 3. Instead, the defendant made
only a definite reference to the contract of February 22, when it was
well known to it that that contract had been amended by Elaterite and
the lumber company on the duplicate copy retained by the defendant,
and when it was also known to it that somewhere the original of that
contract was in existence without the supplemental agreement endorsed upon it.

The plaintiff was fully justified in acting as it did. The only fair
inference the plaintiff could draw from defendant's communications
was that the lumber company offered to make a new contract. The
terms of this new contract were clearly set out—plaintiff was to ship
directly to the defendant and was also to bill it directly. The materials
to be shipped and the prices were to be determined by reference to
the prior contract between the lumber company and Elaterite. . . .
Knowledge that the contract referred to had been amended could not
be imputed to the plaintiff. The defendant therefore is bound by the
plain words it chose to employ in its offer made to and accepted by
plaintiff.

[Judgment reversed and case remanded for new trial.]

Lucy v. Zehmer

196 Va.App. 493, 84 S.E.2d 516 (1954)

Zehmer discussed selling a farm to Lucy. After some discussion of a
first draft of a contract, Zehmer and his wife signed a paper stating:
"We hereby agree to sell to W. O. Lucy the Ferguson Farm complete for
$50,000.00, title satisfactory to buyer." Lucy agreed to purchase the farm
on these terms. Thereafter the Zehmers refused to transfer title to Lucy
and claimed that they had made the contract for sale as a joke. Lucy
brought an action for specific performance of the contract. From a judgment for the Zehmers, Lucy appealed.

BUCHANAN, J. . . . The defendants insist that the evidence was ample to support their contention that the writing sought to be enforced was prepared as a bluff or dare to force Lucy to admit that he did not have $50,000; that the whole matter was a joke; . . . and no binding contract was ever made between the parties. . . .

The appearance of the contract, the fact that it was under discussion for forty minutes or more before it was signed; Lucy's objection to the first draft because it was written in the singular, and he wanted Mrs. Zehmer to sign it also; the rewriting to meet that objection and the signing by Mrs. Zehmer; the discussion of what was to be included in the sale, the provision for the examination of the title, the completeness of the instrument that was executed, the taking possession of it by Lucy with no request or suggestion by either of the defendants that he give it back, are facts which furnish persuasive evidence that the execution of the contract was a serious business transaction rather than a casual, jesting matter as defendants now contend. . . .

If it be assumed, contrary to what we think the evidence shows, that Zehmer was jesting about selling his farm to Lucy and that the transaction was intended by him to be a joke, nevertheless the evidence shows that Lucy did not so understand it but considered it to be a serious business transaction and the contract to be binding on the Zehmers as well as on himself. The very next day he arranged with his brother to put up half the money and take a half interest in the land. The day after that he employed an attorney to examine the title. The next night, Tuesday, he was back at Zehmer's place and there Zehmer told him for the first time, Lucy said, that he wasn't going to sell and he told Zehmer, "You know you sold that place fair and square." After receiving the report from his attorney that the title was good, he wrote to Zehmer that he was ready to close the deal.

Not only did Lucy actually believe, but the evidence shows he was warranted in believing, that the contract represented a serious business transaction and a good faith sale and purchase of the farm.

In the field of contracts, as generally elsewhere, "We must look to the outward expression of a person as manifesting his intention rather than to his secret and unexpressed intention. 'The law imputes to a person an intention corresponding to the reasonable meaning of his words and acts.' " . . .

The mental assent of the parties is not requisite for the formation of a contract. If the words or other acts of one of the parties have but one reasonable meaning, his undisclosed intention is immaterial except when an unreasonable meaning which he attaches to his manifestations is known to the other party. . . .

[Judgment reversed and case remanded.]

Lonergan v. Scolnick
129 Cal.App.2d 179, 276 P.2d 8 (1954)

Scolnick, who owned real estate, desired to sell it and placed an ad for that purpose in a newspaper. He and Lonergan then corresponded about the land, and Lonergan claimed that he had a binding contract with Scolnick for the purchase of the land. Scolnick denied there was a contract and sold the land to a third person. Lonergan then sued Scolnick for damages. From a judgment in favor of Scolnick, Lonergan appealed.

BANARD, P.J. . . . During March, 1952, the defendant placed an ad in a Los Angeles paper reading, so far as material here, "Joshua Tree vic. 40 acres, . . . need cash, will sacrifice." In response to an inquiry resulting from this ad the defendant, who lived in New York, wrote a letter to the plaintiff dated March 26, briefly describing the property, giving directions as to how to get there, stating that his rock bottom price was $2,500 cash, and further stating that "This is a form letter." On April 7, the plaintiff wrote a letter to the defendant saying that he was not sure he had found the property, asking for its legal description, asking whether the land was all level or whether it included certain jutting rock hills. On April 8, the defendant wrote to the plaintiff saying "From your description you have found the property"; giving the legal description; and then saying, "If you are really interested, you will have to decide fast, as I expect to have a buyer in the next week or so." On April 12, the defendant sold the property to a third party for $2,500. The plaintiff received defendant's letter of April 8 on April 14. On April 15 he wrote to the defendant thanking him for his letter "confirming that I was on the right land," stating that he would . . . deposit $2,500 . . . "in conformity with your offer." . . .

There can be no contract unless . . . the parties have . . . mutually agreed upon some specific thing. This is usually evidenced by one party making an offer which is accepted by the other party.

The language used in Niles v. Hancock, 140 Cal. 157, 73 P. 840, 842, "It is also clear from the correspondence that it was the intention of the defendant that the negotiations between him and the plaintiff were to be purely preliminary," is applicable here. The correspondence here indicates an intention on the part of the defendant to find out whether the plaintiff was interested, rather than an intention to make a definite offer to the plaintiff. The language used by the defendant in his letters of March 26 and April 8 rather clearly discloses that they were not intended as an expression of fixed purpose to make a definite offer. . . .

The advertisement in the paper was a mere request for an offer. The letter of March 26 contains no definite offer, and clearly states that it is a form letter. It merely gives further particulars, in clarification of the advertisement, and tells the plaintiff how to locate the property if he was interested in looking into the matter. The letter of April 8 added nothing in the way of a definite offer. It merely answered some questions asked by the plaintiff, and stated that if the plaintiff was really interested, he would have to act fast. The statement that he expected to have a buyer in the next week or so indicated that the defendant intended to sell to the first-comer, and was reserving the right to do so. From this statement, alone, the plaintiff knew or should have known that he was not being given time in which to accept an offer that was being made, but that some further assent on the part of the defendant was required. Under the language used the plaintiff was not being given a right to act within a reasonable time after receiving the letter; he was plainly told that the defendant intended to sell to another, if possible, and warned that he would have to act fast if he was interested in buying the land.

[Judgment affirmed.]

Olson v. Beacham

102 N.W.2d 125 (N.D., 1960)

Beacham and McElroy advertised for bids for the installation of a cooling system in a building they owned. Olson submitted the lowest bid, but the owners accepted the slightly higher bid of another contractor. Olson sued the owners for breach of contract. From a judgment in favor of the owners, Olson appealed.

SATHRE, C.J. . . . It is the contention of the plaintiff that having submitted the lowest bid . . . a contract resulted between the parties, and that failure on the part of the defendants to accept plaintiff's bid constituted a breach of contract resulting in damages to the plaintiff. . . .

The defendants in advertising for bids stated. . . : "The owner reserves the right to reject any or all bids when such rejection is in the interest of the owner. . . ."

The plaintiff in his bid stipulated: "The undersigned, as bidder, hereby proposes, and if this proposal is accepted, agrees to enter into a contract." . . .

The defendants did not accept the bid of the plaintiff. . . . They clearly had the right under the terms of their advertisement for bids and instruction to bidders to accept or reject any of the bids that might be submitted. The plaintiff recognized the right of the owners and stated . . . he would enter into a contract . . . *if the defendants accepted his bid.* The defendants having rejected the bid of the plaintiff were under no obligation to him and they had the right to determine for themselves which bid submitted would be to their best interest. The plaintiff was aware of this fact when he submitted his bid. The advertisement of the defendants for bids was merely an invitation for offers and was not an offer to accept any particular bid. The advertisement could result in a contract only upon acceptance of a bid submitted by a bidder. . . .

[Judgment affirmed.]

Fincher v. Belk-Sawyer Co.

127 So.2d 130 (Fla., 1961)

Fincher was employed by Belk-Sawyer Co. as fashion coordinator for the latter's retail stores. The contract of employment also provided for additional services of Fincher to be thereafter agreed upon in connection with beauty consultation and shopping services to be established at the stores. After Fincher had been employed as fashion coordinator for several months, Belk-Sawyer Co. refused to be bound by the contract on the ground that it was too indefinite. From a judgment in favor of Belk-Sawyer Co., the plaintiff Fincher appealed.

HORTON, C.J. . . . The basis of the defendant's motion . . . was that the so-called contract was not a contract, but an agreement to agree; that it was so vague and indefinite as to not be susceptible of enforcement. . . .

The agreement . . . provided for the employment of the plaintiff to supervise and direct defendant's respective fashion departments, shopping services, and beauty salon, and specified her duties as fashion coordinator of the defendant's stores; she was to schedule and supervise fashion shows in connection therewith. Plaintiff granted to defendant the exclusive right within the State of Florida to distribute the Gloria De Haven line of cosmetics and women's wear, the plaintiff having complete authority as to all fashions pertaining to these lines. Plaintiff was to act as a consultant in an advisory capacity in conjunction with the fashion purchasing department in regard to all defendant's other line of women's wear and accessories. The defendant was to establish a beauty consulting service in conjunction with its beauty salon and establish a shopping service at a time mutually agreed.

Plaintiff further agreed to make various personal appearances in connection with the promotion of the above described departments. The agreement further provided for the use by the defendant of plaintiff's name in connection with merchandise and merchandising activities. . . .

It is apparent that if a purported agreement is so vague and so uncertain in the specifications of the subject matter that the court cannot identify that subject matter or determine its quality, quantity, or price, it will be unenforceable. This is true because the courts cannot make a contract for the parties. . . . This . . . principle is expressed in Williston on Contracts, Third Edition, Section 45, where the following language is used:

". . . If an essential element is reserved for the future agreement of both parties, the promise can give rise to no legal obligation until such future agreement. Since either party by the very terms of the promise may refuse to agree to anything to which the other party will agree, it is impossible for the law to affix any obligation to such a promise."

However, in 1 Corbin, Contracts, § 29, that authority points out that "two persons may fully agree upon the terms of a contract, knowing that there are other matters on which they have not agreed and on which they expect further negotiation. Such an expectation does not prevent the agreement already made from being an enforceable contract. This may be true even though they expressly provide in their agreement that the new matters, when agreed upon, shall be incorporated into a written lease or other formal document along with the contract already made." . . .

Clearly where the matters left for future agreement are unessential, the remainder of the contract may be enforced. . . .

Accordingly we must determine whether the indefinite promises were so essential to the contract that the inability to enforce them would make unfair the enforcement of the remainder of the contract.

The contract leaves to the future agreement of the parties the establishment by the defendant of a beauty consulting service, shopping service, and the amount of additional compensation based upon the gross sales of the defendant's fashion department, beauty consulting service and shopping service. In addition, personal appearances by the plaintiff were to be mutually agreed upon and were not to interfere with any of her outside commitments.

We conclude that these provisions left for future agreement do not render the remaining promises, which are definite and certain, unenforceable. . . .

[Judgment for defendant reversed and remanded.]

Bonnevier v. Dairy Cooperative Association
227 Ore. 123, 361 P.2d 262 (1961)

Bonnevier, an employee of the Dairy Cooperative Association, lived in his own home near the employer's plant. The employer wished to expand the plant and decided to purchase Bonnevier's house. Bonnevier was not then working because of an injury. He claimed that an agreement was made to sell the house to the Association in return for which he would be paid $12,000 and would be given employment. The Association did not thereafter employ Bonnevier, and he and his wife sued for breach of contract. Neither party was satisfied with the action of the lower court, and both appealed.

ROSSMAN, J. . . . A purported [agreement] . . . in order to effect a contract must render reasonably certain all of the terms of the would-be undertaking so that a court, in the event of litigation, may know what each of the . . . parties bound himself to do. If a court is to enforce an alleged agreement . . ., it must be able to ascertain from the agreement itself . . . the duties of those who, it is claimed, bound themselves to the alleged future course of action.

However reluctant the courts may be to reject the suit of parties who thought that they had effected a contract, yet if the parties, in negotiating, spoke only in terms of generalities and left uncertain what each was expected to do, the court could not enforce the purported agreement unless it itself wrote the contract. The court will not write contracts for parties. . . .

Corbin on Contracts § 95 declares:

"A court cannot enforce a contract unless it can determine what it is. It is not enough that the parties think that they have made a contract; they must have expressed their intentions in a manner that is capable of understanding. It is not even enough that they have actually agreed, if their expressions are not such that the court can determine what the terms of that agreement are. Vagueness of expression, indefiniteness and uncertainty as to any of the essential terms of an agreement, may prevent the creation of an enforceable contract."

Seiss v. McClintic-Marshall Corporation, 324 Pa. 201, 188 A. 109, was an action for breach of an alleged contract [to employ an injured employee] . . . for life. He testified, "The meaning of it was that they were supposed to take care of me in regard to suitable employment I was to do, and they were to take care of all medical attention afterwards. It said in the agreement they would take care of me for life in employment that I would be able to do." We now quote from the opinion:

"The contract here set up is so lacking in precision, so indefinite and vague, that nothing certain about it can be formulated. . . . What is 'suitable employment'? Who is to determine what it is? What is implied by 'any employment that I was able to do'? Without more these words are too indefinite to predicate anything upon with certainty. . . . No rate of pay is specified; no arbiter is provided to determine what work plaintiff will be able to perform. . . ."

In the case at bar the purported agreement which the plaintiffs seek to enforce mentions no specific job, nor do the plaintiffs claim that . . . the subject of wages was even once broached. . . .

Significant is the fact that the plaintiffs do not claim that any term was mentioned for the employment which they say the defendant promised. If the employment was without term the plaintiff could be discharged the following day, and that would, of course, indicate that no contract had been effected. But, if it was to run permanently, then the parties surely would have approached its formation with more attention to details than was indicated by the accounts which they gave. . . . They would have discussed wages, type of work, and similar partinent facts. . . .

In their agreement concerning the sale of their real property the plaintiffs agreed upon precise details, but discussed nothing of that character concerning the employment. We do not believe that they effected any agreement [as to employment]. . . .

[Judgment for defendant.]

Fidelity & Deposit Co. of Maryland v. Messer

112 Miss. 267, 72 So. 1004 (1916)

The Fidelity & Deposit Company offered "one hundred dollars reward for the apprehension and conviction of each person burglarizing, robbing, or holding up" any banks that it insured against burglary. One of these banks, located at New Hebron, was burglarized by two persons. Messer and others met an incoming train at Hattiesburg and apprehended the burglars, who were subsequently convicted and sentenced. Messer and the others did not, however, know of the reward at the time of the capture. They brought an action against the company to recover the reward. The company appealed from a judgment in favor of Messer and the others.

SMITH, C. J. The contract here sought to be enforced is one alleged to have been created by the acceptance by appellees of appellant's offer of a reward for the capture of the persons who burglarized the New Hebron Bank. It appears, however, from the agreed statement of facts that when appellees arrested the burglars, they did not know that appellant had offered a reward therefor; consequently they cannot be said to have accepted the offer.

"The publication of an advertisement offering a reward is a general offer to make a contract with any person who is able to perform the required services and to meet the conditions of the proposal. The performance of the service or the performance of the condition on which the promise is made, with knowledge, is an acceptance of the offer and, when done, concludes the contract. The matter rests exclusively in the domain of contracts involving an offer and its acceptance. This being true, it logically follows that a reward cannot be earned by one who did not know it had been offered; for there can be no acceptance of an uncommunicated offer."

[Judgment for plaintiffs reversed.]

Garrett v. International Milling Co.

223 S.W.2d 67 (Tex.Civ.App., 1949)

The International Milling Company sued Garrett for breach of a contract to purchase flour. A written contract, made with Garrett by the company's salesman, expressly stated that the salesman had no authority to bind the company and that the contract was not binding unless confirmed by the company. The company sent Garrett a letter which stated that it confirmed his offer, but the confirmation added new terms. The company sued Garrett for breach of the contract. From a judgment for the company, Garrett appealed.

LINCOLN, J. . . . The general rules of contract apply to agreements between seller and buyer of personal property. . . . Such contracts, like all others, must arise upon an offer and acceptance. The acceptance must be unqualified and unconditional, and in the exact terms of the offer. . . .

"It does not matter that the difference of terms between the parties may not seem to be very material. If a diversity exists, that fact is enough. To make a contract, there must be a mutual assent. 'The assent must comprehend the whole of the proposition; it must be exactly equal to its extent and provisions, and it must not qualify them by any new matter.' If the answer, 'either in words or effect, departs from the proposition, or varies the terms of the offer, or substitutes for the contract tendered one more satisfactory to the respondent,' there is no assent and no contract. . . . 'If a proposition be accompanied with certain conditions or limitations, the acceptance must correspond to it exactly, for if any alteration be suggested, or any exception be made to its exact terms, the provisional acceptance becomes merely a new proposition, which also requires an acceptance.' ". . .

Applying the principles above stated to the facts of this case, we think that the instrument . . . which was signed by [Garrett] and by the salesman for appellee [company] was not a contract but constituted an offer by buy 1200 cwt. of Robin Hood Flour at $7.50 per cwt. The order required acceptance or confirmation by the appellee before it became effective. . . . The confirmation given was not unconditional, did not "comprehend the whole proposition," and it was not "exactly equal to its (the order's) extent and provisions." The offer embraced within the order was qualified in the confirmation. . . .

The confirmation, therefore, resulted in no acceptance of the order. The most that can be said for [the confirmation] is that it constituted a new offer from the seller to the buyer, and did not put the order . . . into effect as a binding contract. It was necessary for [Garrett] to accept or confirm in some manner the order with its change or modification as embraced within the writing . . . purporting to be a confirmation. We find no instrument of writing in the record constituting a confirmation by [Garrett] of the counteroffer made by the [company] in its purported confirmation. Neither is there anything in the record constituting a rejection. We do not think that a rejection was necessary, but an acceptance or confirmation of the counteroffer was necessary.

[Judgment for the company reversed.]

Questions and Case Problems

1. What is the objective (from the list in Chapter 1, pages 3-8) of each of the following rules of law?

　(a) Certain statements, as well as certain listings or quotations of prices, are invitations to negotiate and are not binding as offers.

　(b) An offer is terminated by the lapse of a reasonable time when no time has been stated.

2. Sandeman was employed by Sayres and others. The written contract of employment specified a salary of $750 a month and added that a commission or bonus would be paid "and will be decided upon, after the first three (3) months of our marketing operations. . . . This period of time is specified to enable us to properly evaluate the market and acceptability of our product. . . ." Sandeman was paid his regular salary but never received any bonus. He then sued Sayres, claiming that a reasonable bonus would be 2½ per cent of the gross national sales of the defendant. Was Sandeman entitled to recover? (Sandeman v. Sayres, 50 Wash. 2d 539, 314 P.2d 428)

3. The Brewster Fruit Growers Association did business in Seattle under the name of M. L. Davies Co. On May 23, it sent Coleman a written offer to purchase a carload of 30 pound-tins of frozen raspberries at "packer's opening price." This price would be determined for the industry on or about July 15. On August 2, Coleman accepted the contract offered, signed it, and mailed it to Brewster. Brewster refused to purchase the raspberries under the contract. Coleman sued for breach of contract. Was there a contract? (Coleman v. Davies, 39 Wash. 2d 312, 235 P.2d 199)

4. Malcolm, as salesman of the National Refining Co., received an order for 60 barrels of oil from Miller. The order expressly stated that it was "positive and not subject to change or countermand." Nevertheless, Miller countermanded the offer. The National Refining Co. sent the oil, but Miller refused to accept it and to pay for it. The refining company brought an action to recover damages for breach of contract. Was it entitled to judgment? (National Refining Co. v. Miller, 1 S.D. 548, 47 N.W. 962)

5. Whitney wrote to Park on May 16 offering to purchase certain shares of stock in a given corporation at any time after the following January 1. About 14 months later Park wrote to Whitney, accepting the offer. Whitney refused to purchase and pay for the stock. Thereupon Park brought an action against Whitney to recover damages for breach of contract. Was he entitled to judgment? (Park v. Whitney, 148 Mass. 278, 19 N.E. 169)

6. Hedden, a general contractor, planned to bid on the construction of a state government building. Lupinsky telephoned him and offered to do the tile work at a specified price. Hedden determined its bid to the state on the basis of Lupinsky's bid. Hedden was awarded the contract by the state. He then sent Lupinsky a written contract form to be executed by him for the tile work. This written contract contained a number of provisions which were different than, or added matters not included in, the government's general specifications for the work to be done. Lupinsky refused to sign the contract. Hedden then sued him for breach of contract. Decide. (Hedden v. Lupinsky, 405 Pa. 609, 176 A.2d 406)

7. Wilson and the Southern Oil Co. made an agreement that called for the payment of the "current market price" for the property leased to the oil company. The parties later disagreed as to the meaning of the quoted phrase. It was claimed that there was no contract because there was no "meeting of the minds." Decide. (Southern Oil Co. v. Wilson, 22 Tex.Civ.App. 534, 56 S.W. 429)

8. Owen wrote to Tunison asking if Tunison would sell his store for $6,000. Tunison replied, "It would not be possible for me to sell unless I received $16,000 cash." Owen replied, "Accept your offer." Tunison denied that there was a contract. Decide. (Owen v. Tunison, 131 Maine 69, 158 A. 926)

9. Boro-Heat Sealed Plastics manufactured plastic telephone directory covers, which it distributed to physicians in the county. On October 30, 1960, it entered into an agreement with Bartlett to run an ad for him on such covers. The agreement specified that Boro-Heat had the right to cancel at any time before publication. Shortly thereafter Boro-Heat mailed Bartlett a proof copy of his ad for his approval. Another request for approval of a proof copy was mailed to Bartlett on January 3, 1961. On January 9, Bartlett requested Boro-Heat to cancel the contract. On January 14, Boro-Heat replied that it was too late in the publication to cancel the contract. On February 8, Boro-Heat mailed out the covers. It then transferred the contract to Eaton Factors Co., which sued Bartlett for the amount due. Bartlett raised the defense that there was no binding contract because Boro-Heat could have canceled at any time before publication. Was this a defense? (Eaton Factors Company v. Bartlett, 24 Conn. Sup. 40, 186 A.2d 166)

10. Certain property was leased to Cohen for a period of time ending December 31, 1922. On or about April 11, 1919, the landlord offered Cohen the right to renew the lease and gave him six months before the end of the lease to accept. In January, 1920, the landlord sold the property to a third person. Cohen knew of the sale but thereafter gave written notice that he renewed the lease. The purchaser claimed that the lease was not renewed. Decide. (William Weisman Realty Co. v. Cohen, 157 Minn. 161, 195 N.W. 898)

CHAPTER 6

The Agreement — Acceptance

Once the offeror expresses or appears to express his willingness to enter into contractual agreement with the offeree, the latter is in a position to accept the offer.

Sec. 6-A. Nature of the Acceptance. An *acceptance* is the assent of the offeree to the terms of the offer. The acceptance must be absolute and unconditional. It must accept just what is offered. If the offeree changes any term of the offer or adds any new term, he does not accept the offer because he does not agree with what was offered. (See p. 87 Southern Real Estate Case) An acceptance that states what is implied by law, however, does not add a new term within this rule. Thus a provision in an acceptance that payment must be made in cash will usually not introduce a new term since a cash payment is implied by law in the absence of a contrary provision. Similarly, a provision in an acceptance relating to routine or mechanical details of the execution of a written contract will usually not impair the effect of the acceptance. (See p. 88, Carver v. Britt) Likewise, an acceptance otherwise unconditional is not impaired by the fact that an additional matter is requested as a favor rather than being made a condition or term of the acceptance. Accordingly, there is an effective acceptance when the buyer, upon accepting, simply requests additional time in which to complete the transaction.

No particular form of words or mode of expression is required for an acceptance. Any expression of an intention to agree is sufficient. An acceptance may be indicated, for example, by an informal "O. K.," by a mere affirmative nod of the head, or, in the case of an offer of a unilateral contract, by performing the act called for.

(1) Who May Accept. An offer may be accepted only by the person to whom it is directed. If anyone else attempts to accept it, no agreement or contract with that person arises. (See p. 89, Grieve v. Mullaly)

If the offer is directed not to a specified individual but to a particular class, it may be accepted by anyone within that class. If the offer is made to the public at large, it may be accepted by any member of the public at large who has knowledge of the existence of the offer.

(2) Manner of Acceptance. The acceptance must conform to any conditions expressed in the offer concerning the manner of acceptance. If the offeror specifies that the acceptance must be written, an oral acceptance is ineffective. If the offeror calls for an acceptance by a specified date, a late acceptance has no effect. When an acceptance is required by return mail, it is usually held that the letter of acceptance must be mailed the same day that the offer was received by the offeree. If the offer specifies that the acceptance be made by the performance of an act by the offeree, he cannot accept by making a promise to do the act but must actually perform it.

Under the Uniform Commercial Code an order or offer to buy goods for prompt or current shipment may be accepted by the seller either by making the shipment or by promptly promising to do so.[1]

(3) Silence as Acceptance. In most cases the silence of the offeree and his failure to act cannot be regarded as an acceptance. (See p. 90, Phelan v. Everlith) Ordinarily the offeror is not permitted to frame his offer in such a way as to make the silence and inaction of the offeree operate as an acceptance. When a seller writes to another with whom he has not had any prior dealing that "unless notified to the contrary" he will send that person specified merchandise to be paid for at specified prices, there is no acceptance if the offeree ignores the offer and does nothing. The silence of the person receiving the letter was not intended by him as an acceptance, and the seller as a reasonable man should not have believed that it was so intended. This rule applies to magazines and tickets sent to a person through the mail when he has not ordered them and does not use them. The fact that he does not return them does not mean that he accepts them.

In the case of prior dealings between the parties, the offeree may have a duty to reject an offer expressly, and his silence may be regarded as an acceptance.

Under the Uniform Commercial Code provisions relating to the sale of goods, silence is in some instances treated as an acceptance when the parties are both merchants.[2]

(4) Insurer's Delay in Acting on Application. The great weight of authority holds that the fact that an insurance company delays in acting upon the application for insurance does not constitute an

---

[1] Uniform Commercial Code, Sec. 2-206(1)(b).
[2] See p. 51.

acceptance. A few cases hold that an acceptance may be implied from the failure of the company to reject the application promptly and that there is accordingly a binding contract and the application cannot be rejected, particularly when the applicant has paid the first premium and the insurer fails to return it.

Some decisions hold the insurer liable for tort if, through its unjustified delay in rejecting the application, the applicant remains unprotected by insurance and then, in the interval, suffers loss that would have been covered by the insurance if it had been issued. For practical purposes, the result of this doctrine may be the same as though the application were deemed accepted.

Sec. 6-B. Communication of Acceptance. If the offeree accepts the offer, must he notify the offeror that he accepts? The answer depends upon the nature of the offer. When communication is required, the acceptance must be communicated directly to the offeror or his agent. A statement made to a third person is not effective as an acceptance of the offer.

(1) Communication of Acceptance in a Bilateral Contract. If the offer pertains to a bilateral contract, an acceptance is not effective unless communicated to the offeror. Until the offeree makes known that he agrees to perform in the future, there is no way for the offeror to know whether the offeree accepts the offer or not.

(2) Communication of Acceptance in a Unilateral Contract. If the offeror makes an offer of a unilateral contract, communication of acceptance is ordinarily not required. (See p. 91, Ross v. Leberman) In such a case, the offeror calls for a completed or accomplished act. If that act is performed by the offerer with knowledge of the offer, the offer is accepted without any further action by way of notifying the offeror. As a practical matter there will eventually be some notice to the offeror because the offeree who has performed the act will ask the offeror to carry out his promise.

Under the Uniform Commercial Code, when the shipment of goods is relied upon to constitute an acceptance of the buyer's order, the seller must notify the buyer of such acceptance within a reasonable time.[3]

(3) Communication of Acceptance in a Guaranty Contract. The general rule that notification of acceptance is not necessary in cases of an offer requesting the performance of an act is not applied in many states when the offer calls for the extension of credit to a buyer

---

[3] UCC Sec. 2-206(2).

in return for which the offeror promises to pay the debt if it is not paid. In such a guaranty case, the merchant must notify the promisor within a reasonable time after extending credit. Some courts take the view that this type of case is an exception and that notice is essential to complete the contract itself. Others take the view that the failure to give notice is a condition subsequent that discharges the contract which was created when credit was given.

Sec. 6-C. Acceptance by Mail or Telegraph. When the offeree conveys his acceptance by mail or telegraph, questions may arise as to the right to use such means of communication and as to the time when the acceptance is effective.

(1) Right to Use Mail or Telegraph. Express directions of the offeror, prior dealings between the parties, or custom of the trade may make it clear that only one method of acceptance is proper. For example, in negotiations with respect to property of rapidly fluctuating value, such as wheat or corporation stocks, an acceptance sent by mail may be too slow. When there is no indication that mail or telegraph is not a proper method, an acceptance may be made by either of those instrumentalities without regard to the manner in which the offer was made.

In former years there was authority for the proposition that an offer could only be accepted by the same means by which the offer was communicated. This view is being gradually abandoned. The trend of the modern decisions supports the following provision of the Uniform Commercial Code relating to sales of personal property: "Unless otherwise unambiguously indicated by the language or circumstances, an offer to make a [sales] contract shall be construed as inviting acceptance in any manner and by any medium reasonable in the circumstances." [4]

(2) When Acceptance by Mail or Telegraph Is Effective. If the offeror specifies that an acceptance shall not be effective until received by him, the law will respect the offeror's wish. If there is no such provision and if acceptance by letter is proper, a mailed acceptance takes effect when the acceptance is properly mailed. The letter must be properly addressed to the offeror, and any other precaution that is ordinarily observed to insure safe transmission must be taken. If it is not mailed in this manner, the acceptance does not take effect when mailed, but only when received by the offeror.

The rule that a properly mailed acceptance takes effect at the time it is mailed is applied strictly. The rule applies even though the acceptance letter never reaches the offeror.

---

[4] Sec. 2-206(1).

An acceptance sent by telegraph takes effect at the time that the message is handed to the clerk at the telegraph office, unless the offeror specifies otherwise or unless custom or prior dealings indicate that acceptance by telegraph is improper.

Sec. 6-D. Acceptance by Telephone. Ordinarily acceptance of an offer may be made by telephone unless the circumstances are such that by the intent of the parties or by the law of the state no acceptance can be made or contract arise in the absence of a writing. If acceptance by telephone is otherwise proper, the acceptance takes effect at the place where the acceptance is spoken into the phone. (See p. 92, Linn v. Employer's Reinsurance Corp.)

Sec. 6-E. Auction Sales. At an auction sale the statements made by the auctioneer to draw forth bids are merely invitations to negotiate. Each bid is an offer, which is not accepted until the auctioneer indicates that a particular offer or bid is accepted. Usually this is done by the fall of the auctioneer's hammer, indicating that the highest bid made has been accepted. As a bid is merely an offer, the bidder may withdraw his bid at any time before it is accepted by the auctioneer.

The Uniform Commercial Code also provides that at an auction sale of goods when a bid is made while the auctioneer's hammer is falling in acceptance of a prior bid, the auctioneer may in his discretion reopen the bidding or declare the goods sold under the bid on which the hammer is falling.[5]

Ordinarily the auctioneer may withdraw any article or all of the property from the sale if he is not satisfied with the amounts of the bids that are being made. Once he has accepted a bid, however, he cannot cancel the sale. In addition, if it had been announced that the sales was to be made "without reserve," the goods must be sold to the person making the highest bid regardless of how low that may be.

Cases for Chapter 6

Southern Real Estate & Finance Co. v. Park Drug Co.
344 Mo. 397, 126 S.W.2d 1169 (1939)

The Park Drug Co. negotiated with the Southern Real Estate & Finance Co. for a lease of office space. The drug company wrote a letter dated May 6, 1932, in which it stated the terms on which it wished to lease the property. On May 10, 1932, the finance company sent the drug company unsigned forms of leases that contained terms beyond those in the letter of the drug company. The drug company refused to sign the leases. The finance company sued to recover damages for breach of contract. From a judgment for the defendant, the plaintiff appealed.

---

[5] Sec. 2-328(2).

BRADLEY, C. . . . "In order to make a bargain, it is necessary that the acceptor shall give in return for the offeror's promise exactly the consideration which the offeror requests. If an act is requested, that very act and no other must be made absolutely and unqualifiedly. This does not mean necessarily that the precise words of the requested promise must be repeated, but by a positive and unqualified assent to the proposal the acceptor must in effect agree to make precisely the promise requested; and if any provision is added to which the offeror did not assent, the consequence is not merely that this provision is not binding and that no contract is formed but that the offer is rejected.

"The new condition is as fatal when its inconsistency with the offer appears by implication only, as when it is explicitly stated. . . ."

Section 58, Restatement of the Law of Contracts, says: "Acceptance (of an offer) must be unequivocal in order to create a contract," and comment (a) says: "An offeror is entitled to know in clear terms whether the offeree accepts his proposal. It is not enough that the words of a reply justified a probable inference of assent."

". . . The contract is not complete or consummated until the proposition of the one is presented to the other and by him accepted as presented without conditions or qualifications. In other words, the acceptance of the proposition presented by the one must be accepted by the other in the form tendered; and if the acceptance omits, adds to, or alters the terms of the proposition made, then neither party to the negotiations is bound. So long as any element of the proposition is left open, the contract is not complete and, of course, not binding on any one."

[Judgment for defendant affirmed.]

Carver v. Britt

241 N.C. 538, 85 S.E.2d 888 (1955)

Carver owned real estate which he listed for sale with Britt, a broker. Britt obtained a buyer and notified Carver of the buyer's offer. Carver sent Britt the following telegram: "Your telegram relative sale my property is accepted subject to details to be worked out by you and my attorney. . . ." Thereafter Carver sold and deeded the property to Vallejo, another buyer, for a greater price. Britt sued Carver for his commissions on the theory that he had obtained a buyer and that Carver by his telegram had entered into a binding contract to sell to that buyer. From a judgment for Carver, Britt appealed.

PARKER, J. . . . The defendant contends that his telegram of acceptance was conditional upon the working out of the details, and as these were never worked out, he never accepted the offer and therefore is not liable to plaintiff for commissions.

It seems that the contention of the defendant arises out of his failure to distinguish between a condition which goes to the making of a contract and a statement relating only to its ultimate performance or execution.

Where an offer is squarely accepted in positive terms, the addition of a statement relating to the ultimate performance of the contract does not make the acceptance conditional and prevent the formation of the contract. . . .

It is elementary learning that an acceptance to be enforceable must be identical with the offer and unconditional. . . . In order for the words "subject to details to be worked out by you and [my attorney]" to invalidate the contract, these words must amount to a qualification or condition imposed as a part of the acceptance itself, and defendant's telegram must be construed as a qualified acceptance to the effect that "I will accept your offer, provided the details are worked out."

The looking up of a title, the drafting and execution of a deed, the time and place of payment of the purchase price are customary details in working out a real estate conveyance. . . .

We are satisfied that the words as to the working out of the details relate to the performance of the contract, and that the telegrams contain all of the essential elements of a valid contract. . . .

[Judgment reversed and case remanded.]

Grieve v. Mullaly
211 Cal. 77, 293 P. 619 (1930)

The Mullaly brothers sent Grieve a signed written statement that "we . . . agree to lease for a period of three years with privilege of one more year (certain specified land) to J. D. Grieve of Davis, Cal." Grieve sold his rights under this writing to Adams. Adams tendered to the Mullaly brothers a formal lease for them to sign. The lease named Adams as the tenant. The Mullaly brothers refused to sign the lease. Adams sued the brothers. From a judgment in their favor, Adams appealed.

WASTE, C.J. . . . In legal effect, the writing [sent to Grieve by the Mullaly brothers] was no more than an offer. . . .

. . . The writing . . . in no way bound Grieve, and it in no way bound defendants until accepted. It amounted to an offer to Grieve to enter into a lease. It is elementary that . . . an offer to contract is not assignable; it being purely personal to the offeree. In this case the offer was made to Grieve. The evidence does not disclose any acceptance by him. Adams attempted to accept the offer, not as the agent or representative of Grieve, but in his own right. This is conclusively shown by the fact that Adams tendered to the Mullalys a lease for their signatures, naming him, Adams, as lessee. . . .

[Judgment affirmed.]

Phelan v. Everlith
22 Conn.Sup. 377, 173 A.2d 601 (1961)

Everlith obtained a one-year liability policy of insurance from the insurance company's agent, Phelan. Prior to the expiration of the year, Phelan sent Everlith a renewal policy covering the next year, together with a bill for the renewal premium. The bill stated that the policy should be returned promptly if the renewal was not desired. Everlith did not return the policy or take any other action relating to the insurance. Phelan sued for the renewal premium.

WISE, J. . . . The only dealings the parties had with each other was the issuance of the original policy in January, 1959, and the alleged renewal policy. There had been no prior dealings between them. The defendant never made an application for the renewal of the policy; never ordered it or asked that it be renewed; never indicated that he wanted it renewed; nor indicated an acceptance of the renewal; nor was any part of the premium paid by the defendant.

The fundamental and basic requisites that there must be an offer and an acceptance to make a valid contract have been applied to insurance contracts. "It is a thoroughly established principle of the law of contracts, within the field of which insurance largely lies, that ordinarily a bare offer imposes no liability upon the person to whom it is made until it is accepted; he need make no reply to it at all, and if he fails to do so for any reason, because he does not propose to accept it, or because he has forgotten it, or under other circumstances, the only result the law recognizes is that no contract comes into existence." . . . A renewal policy is a separate contract, independent of the original policy, requiring its own elements of offer and acceptance. . . . The unsolicited issuance of a renewal policy prior to the expiration of the original policy is but a proposal or an offer to insure. . . .

An express acceptance of an offer of renewal is not always necessary but may be implied under some circumstances. A familiar illustration of this is where, in accordance with prior dealings between the parties, the agent writes and delivers a policy to his customer prior to the expiration date and bills him for the premium upon the assumption that in the absence of notice to the contrary the policy will be accepted and the premium paid as in the past. Here, failure of the customer to notify the agent to the contrary will signify the customer's implied acceptance of the policy and his promise to pay the premium within a reasonable time. However, the doctrine that in view of a general custom among insurance agents to renew the insurance of their policyholders without request, a failure by the insured to reject the renewal is tantamount to its acceptance may not be availed of unless the custom is established and it is shown that the party relying thereon knew of it and there had been a course of dealings between the parties from which it could be implied that the policyholder's silence or failure to reject the offer would be regarded as an acceptance. . . . Applying these principles to the instant case, it is clear that there was no acceptance by the defendant of the renewal policy.

Only in a single instance, which occurred in January, 1959, had the plaintiff issued a policy to the defendant. Never had he previously renewed a policy for the defendant. A single transaction does not establish a course of conduct or course of dealing. There had been no course of dealing between the parties which would lead the plaintiff to think that defendant's silence would result in the renewal of the policy, nor was there anything in the conduct on the part of the defendant to lead the plaintiff to believe that the policy would be renewed.

In the absence of circumstances from which an acceptance may be implied, an acceptance will not be presumed from a mere failure to decline a proposal. . . .

[Judgment for defendant.]

Ross v. Leberman

298 Pa. 574, 148 A. 858 (1930)

Ross, N. Leberman, S. Leberman, and another person each owned one fourth of the stock of a corporation. Ross moved to England but offered to pay one third of the expenses of the corporation in order to keep the business going. These expenses soon totaled over $100,000. Ross then refused to pay his share. When Ross was sued by the Lebermans for his share of the expenses, judgment was entered in favor of Ross. The Lebermans appealed.

SADLER, J. . . . [The defense was raised that no] notice was given by the Lebermans of the acceptance of the offer of Ross made in 1923, and the contract was therefore unenforceable. The promise in this case was not to pay third parties sums which might be borrowed by the Lebermans, as in the ordinary case of guaranty, nor was there a contingent liability to pay, but an understanding to underwrite one third of the advances made for the corporation in which Ross was interested. The necessary amounts were directed to be taken from the balance then due by the Lebermans, provided the defendants should supply the remaining two thirds, which they claim to have expended between 1923 and 1926. No notice of the outlays made was furnished directly to Ross, nor did he ask to be advised as to the amount. As one-fourth owner of the stock of the corporation it would seem he was in position to secure the information if desired. No revocation of his undertaking appeared. . . .

"It is often said that notice of acceptance is necessary for the completion of a contract; but it is not true and never has been true, as a general proposition, that where an offeror requests an act in return for his promise and the act is performed, notice to the offeror of the performance is necessary to create a contract." . . . [The court notes that in some cases notice of acceptance is required (1 Williston on Contracts 118), although according to Williston:] "The contract is complete on the performance of the act but is subject to a condition subsequent that if notice of the performance of the act is not given within a reasonable time by the promisee, the promisor is freed from obligation." But, as the writer observes, the rule which he suggests is most frequently applied to strict guaranties. . . .

An attempt has been made to formulate a rule by the American Law Institute in Section 56 . . . when it states: "But if the offeror has no adequate means of ascertaining with reasonable promptness and certainty that the act or forbearance has been given and the offeree should know this, the contract is discharged unless, within a reasonable time after performance of the act or forbearance, the offeree exercises reasonable diligence to notify the offeror thereof." But, as there said by the authors: "It is only in the exceptional case where the offeror has no convenient means of ascertaining whether the requested act has been done that notice is requisite. Even then, it is not the notice which creates the contract, but lack of notice which ends the duty." . . .

[Judgment reversed and new proceeding ordered.]

Linn v. Employers' Reinsurance Corporation

392 Pa. 58, 139 A.2d 638 (1958)

Linn, an insurance broker, sued the Employers' Reinsurance Corporation for breach of a contract based upon the acceptance of Linn's offer to the Corporation by its agent, Ehmann. In order to determine whether the contract was properly executed, it was necessary to know in which state the contract was made. From a nonsuit [6] of the plaintiff, an appeal was taken.

COHEN, J. . . . In the case of acceptance by mail or telegraph, the act of acceptance is held to be effective where the acceptance was posted . . . or received by the telegraph company for transmission. . . .

Professor Williston and the Restatement of Contracts take the position that a contract made over the telephone is no different from a contract made where the parties orally address one another in each other's presence. In the latter case the offeror does not have the risk of hearing an acceptance addressed to him, and a contract is formed only if the acceptance is heard. Consequently, the place of contracting is where the acceptance is heard and not where the acceptance is spoken. 1 Williston, [Contracts] supra, § 82A; Restatement, Contracts

---

[6] See Appendix.

§ 65 (1934). While we agree that this analysis represents a sound theoretical view, the reported cases which consider this issue are uniform in holding that by analogy to the situations in which acceptance is mailed or telegraphed, an acceptance by telephone is effective and a contract is created at the place where the acceptor speaks. . . .

We believe that in this day of multistate commercial transactions it is particularly desirable that the determination of the place of contracting be the same regardless of the state in which suit is brought. The absence of uniformity makes the rights and liabilities of parties to a contract dependent upon the choice of the state in which suit is instituted. . . . For this reason we chose to follow the established pattern of decisions and hold that acceptance by telephone of an offer takes place where the words are spoken.

Applying this principle to the facts before us, we conclude that the state where the contract was made is the state from which Ehmann telephoned the defendant's acceptance to Linn. However, . . . there is no evidence in the record to indicate from which state Ehmann spoke. It is likely that he telephoned from his New York office, but it is also possible that he called from Kansas City [home office] or even Philadelphia; we cannot substitute speculation for evidence. The record of this case, therefore, must be remitted to the court below for determination of the question. . . .

[Judgment reversed and new trial ordered.]

Questions and Case Problems

1. What is the objective of each of the following rules of law?

   (a) No particular form of words or mode of expression is required for an acceptance.
   (b) An acceptance takes effect when it is properly mailed, in the absence of any contrary specification by the offeror.

2. Sierota signed a paper calling for the printing of advertising material by Union Interchange. The paper contained the clause: "This agreement shall become effective only when accepted by your office [the printer's office] in Los Angeles, California. You shall notify me of such acceptance." Sierota heard nothing more about the transaction until he was sued for payment. Did he have any defense? (Union Interchange v. Sierota, 144 Colo. 293, 355 P.2d 1089)

3. Sass sent to Lucas an offer by mail for the exchange of land. Lucas received the offer two days later and on the following day wired his acceptance to Sass. The latter disposed of his land before receiving the telegram. Lucas claimed this was a breach of contract. Decide. (Lucas v. Western Union Telegraph Co., 131 Iowa 669, 109 N.W. 191)

4. Shuford offered to sell a specified machine to the State Machinery Co. The Nutmeg State Machinery Corp. heard of the offer and notified Shuford that it accepted. When Shuford did not deliver the machine, the

Nutmeg corporation sued him for breach of contract. Could it recover? (Nutmeg State Machinery Corp. v. Shuford, 129 Conn. 659, 30 A.2d 911)

5. Bennett made an offer through an agent, Treadaway, to purchase certain real estate. Unknown to Bennett, the owner had died and therefore court approval was necessary for such a sale. While Bennett was at sea, the executor of the owner's estate gave Treadaway a written acceptance of Bennett's offer which stated that is was "subject to court approval." When Bennett returned, he claimed that his offer had never been accepted because he had never made an offer subject to court approval. The defendant answered that an executor was by law required to sell by court approval and therefore adding the clause "subject to court approval" was not the introduction of a new term but only the statement of one implied by law. Was a contract formed when the executor "accepted" the offer "subject to court approval"? (Bennett v. Treadaway, [La.App.] 134 So.2d 668)

6. The Great A. & P. Tea Co. rented a store from Geary. On February 25, the company wrote Geary offering to execute a lease for an additional year, commencing on May 1. At 10:30 a.m. on March 7, Geary wrote a letter containing a lease for the additional year and accepting the offer. On the same day at 1:30 p.m. the company mailed Geary a letter stating that it withdrew the offer to execute the new lease. Each party received the other's letter the following day. Was there an effective acceptance of the offer to make a lease? (Geary v. Great A. & P. Tea Co., 366 Ill. 625, 10 N.E.2d 350)

7. Hill offered $350 cash for a deed to certain lands that would guarantee the title to that property. The offeree accepted the offer as to the cash sum but stated that the title would not be guaranteed. Was there a contract? (Hill v. Bell, 111 Vt. 131, 11 A.2d 211)

8. Raysor made an offer to Mallance, Superintendent of the Berkeley County Railway & Lumber Co. Mallance made no reply during the next several months. Raysor brought an action against the Berkeley County Railroad & Lumber Co. in which he claimed that there had been an acceptance because of the failure of Mallance to reject his offer. Do you agree? (Raysor v. Berkeley County Railway & Lumber Co., 26 S.C. 610, 2 S.E. 119)

9. Calo, Inc. decided to open a bowling alley. It sent a purchase order dated November 26, 1958 to AMF Pinspotters, Inc., setting forth what equipment it wished to purchase and to rent, and the terms of payment that it would make. The purchase order contained the condition that "acceptance of this order by seller at seller's office in New York or Chicago shall be necessary to constitute a contract." Thereafter Calo paid and AMF accepted a deposit of $5,000 according to the terms of the order, AMF prepared plans for remodeling the premises of Calo and assured it that the work would be completed in ample time for 1959 summer business, and the remodeling was done under the supervision of AMF. The contract was not fully performed by AMF, however. Calo sued it for breach of contract. AMF raised the defense that there was no contract because Calo's offer had never been accepted since there was no writing to show acceptance of the purchase order. Was this a valid defense? (Calo, Inc. v. AMF Pinspotters, Inc., 31 Ill.App.2d 2, 176 N.E.2d 1)

CHAPTER 7

Genuineness of Assent

An agreement is the result of an offer and an acceptance. The enforceability of a contract based upon an agreement may be affected, however, because a mistake was made by either or both of the parties or because the assent of one of the parties was obtained through fraud, undue influence, or duress.

Sec. 7-A. Mistakes. The law does not treat all mistakes the same. Some have no effect whatever; others make the agreement voidable or unenforceable.

(1) Unilateral and Mutual Mistakes. Mistakes may be unilateral or mutual (bilateral).

(a) UNILATERAL MISTAKE. Ordinarily a unilateral mistake regarding a fact does not affect the contract unless the contract states that it shall be void if the fact is not as believed, or unless the mistake is known to or should be recognized by the other party.

A unilateral mistake of law or as to expectations does not have any effect upon the contract. (See p. 104, Harrod v. Kelly Adjustment Co.) The courts refuse to recognize ignorance of law as an excuse. If they did, the unscrupulous could avoid their contracts at will by saying that they did not understand the law.

(b) MUTUAL MISTAKE. When both parties make the same mistake of fact, the contract is void. When the mutual or bilateral mistake is one of law, the contract generally is binding. A few courts have refused to follow this rule, and in several states statutes provide that a mutual mistake of law shall have the same vitiating effect as a mutual mistake of fact. A bilateral mistake with respect to expectations ordinarily has no effect on the contract unless the realization of those expectations is made a condition of the contract.

(2) Mistake as to Possibility of Performance. A contract is void
if there is a mutual mistake as to the possibility of performing the
contract. Assume that *A* meets *B* downtown and makes a contract
to sell to *B* his automobile, which both believe to be in *A's* garage.
Actually the automobile was destroyed by fire an hour before the
agreement was made. Since this fact was unknown to both parties,
there is a mutual mistake as to the possibility of performing the contract, and the contract is void.[1]

It is possible to make the contract absolute so that it obligates
the seller to perform or to pay damages regardless of whether the
goods or the subject matter of the contract existed at the time. The
law will not reach such a result, however, unless the contract expressly
imposes such absolute liability.

(3) Mistake as to Identity of Subject Matter. A contract is void
if there is a mutual mistake as to the identity of the subject matter
of the contract. For example, if a buyer and seller discuss the sale of
an electrical transformer, but one is thinking of a one-phase transformer and the other is thinking of a three-phase transformer, there is
no contract.

The same result could be obtained by applying the rule that a
contract must be certain in all of its material terms. If the contract
does not specify which type of transformer is purchased, an essential
term is lacking and there is no contract.

(4) Mistake as to Identity of Parties. When the parties deal face
to face, a contract is not affected by the fact that one party may be
mistaken as to the identity of the other. When the mistake as to the
identity of a party is induced by trick or deception of that party, however, the contract is voidable and may be set aside by the deceived
party.

(a) OBJECTIVE VERSUS SUBJECTIVE TEST. A different question
arises when the parties do not deal face to face. The courts differ as
to the effect of such a mistake, influenced by whether they follow the
modern objective test of "appearances to a reasonable man" or the old
subjective test of "meeting of the minds." The objective test is a better
one because the seller, for example, is always in a position to make a
credit examination and, if he makes a mistake, it is his own fault.
Furthermore, it is illogical to require a buyer to send an inquiring
letter to the seller to check whether the seller really knows who the
buyer is and intends to make the contract with him. Thus there is
the possibility of a binding contract between an impostor and the
person with whom he deals.

---

[1] Uniform Commercial Code, Sec. 2-613; Uniform Sales Act, Sec. 7.

(b) CREDIT CARDS. The impostor's conduct may impose a liability on the person he is thought to be and on other persons. For example, when an impostor steals or finds a credit card and then represents himself to be the lawful owner of the card, the credit-extending agency is liable to the person dealing with the impostor for credit extended to him. Furthermore, the lawful owner of the credit card is, in turn, liable to the credit-extending agency after it has paid the bills incurred by the impostor if the owner failed to report the loss or theft of the card to the agency promptly.

Sec. 7-B. Misrepresentation. Suppose that one party to a contract makes a statement of fact which is false but that he does so innocently without intending to deceive the other party. Can the other party set aside the contract on the ground that he was misled by the statement? It is often held he cannot. In certain instances, however, the law protects the deceived person by permitting him to avoid the contract.

Equity will permit the rescission of the contract when the innocent misstatement of a material fact induces another to make the contract. (See p. 104, In re New Jersey Refrigerating Co.) If the deceived person is a defendant in an action at law, it is generally held that he cannot use as a defense the fact of innocent deception by the plaintiff. There is a tendency, however, for the law courts to adopt the rule of equity. For example, it may be possible for an insurance company to avoid its policy because of an innocent misstatement of a material fact by the applicant.

Contracts between persons standing in confidential relationships, such as guardian and ward or parent and child, can be set aside for the same reason.

Sec. 7-C. Concealment. Generally, one party cannot set aside a contract because the other party failed to volunteer information which the complaining party would desire to know. Ordinarily if *A* does not ask *B* any questions, *B* is not under any duty to make a full statement of material facts.

If *A* and *B* stand in a confidential relationship, such as that of attorney and client, however, *B* has a duty to reveal anything that is material to *A's* interests, and his silence is given the same effect as though he had knowingly made a false statement that there was no material fact to be told *A*. In such a case *A* can avoid the contract.

Concealment may be more than the passive failure to volunteer information. It may consist of a positive act of hiding information from the other party by physical concealment, or it may consist of furnishing the wrong information. Conduct of such nature is generally classified and treated as fraud.

Sec. 7-D. Fraud. *Fraud* exists when a person makes a misrepresentation of a material fact, known to him to be untrue or made with reckless indifference as to whether it is true, with the intention of causing the other party to enter into a contract, and the other party is entitled to rely thereon and enters into the contract. When one party to the contract is guilty of fraud, the contract is voidable and may be set aside by the injured party.

Some elements of fraud are given a liberal interpretation by the courts, and further consideration of them is necessary. For convenience, the following illustrations refer to fraudulent statements, but any kind of communication may be used. The misrepresentation may also be made by conduct as well as by words.

Fraud is not easy to define because the law tries to balance its desire to protect the injured person from the act of the wrongdoer and its unwillingness to protect the careless person from the consequences of his own neglect.

(1) Mental State. The speaker must intend to deceive. This means that he must either know or believe that what he is saying is false and must intend to mislead, or that he is recklessly indifferent as to whether what he says is true or not. The deceiver must intend that the injured party rely upon the statement and be deceived. Since it is practically impossible to show this directly, it is sufficient if the surrounding circumstances make it so appear.

(2) Misstatement of Past or Present Fact. A misstatement of a past or present fact may constitute fraud. A statement that a painting is the work of Rembrandt, when the speaker knows that it is the work of an art student in a neighboring school, is such a misstatement.

An intentional misrepresentation of the nature of the transaction between the parties is fraudulent. A person is guilty of fraud when he falsely makes another believe that the contract about to be signed is not a contract but is a receipt or a release.

(3) Misstatement of Intention. A misstatement of intention can constitute fraud when a promise is made by a person who does not intend to keep it. To illustrate, a customer purchases goods from a merchant on credit and agrees to pay for them in sixty days. The merchant sells the goods to the customer because he believes the customer's statement that he will pay in sixty days. Actually, the customer does not intend to pay for the goods, and he does not do so. He is guilty of fraud in misstating his intention. Suppose that the customer had purchased the goods, intending to pay for them, but that he discovered later that he was unable to do so or decided later not to pay for them. In that event, he would not be guilty of fraud. He would be liable, however, for a breach of his contract to pay as promised.

(4) Misstatement of Opinion or Value. Ordinarily a misstatement of opinion or value is not regarded as fraudulent, on the theory that the person hearing the statement recognizes or should recognize that it is merely the speaker's personal view and not a statement of fact. When the speaker has expert knowledge or information not available to the other and he should realize that his listener relies upon his expert opinion, however, a misstatement by him of his opinion or of value, if intentionally made, amounts to fraud.

(5) Misstatement of Law. A misstatement of law is treated in the same manner as a misstatement of opinion or value. Ordinarily the listener is regarded as having an opportunity of knowing what the law is, an opportunity equal to that of his speaker, so that he is not entitled to rely on what the speaker tells him. When the speaker has expert knowledge of the law or represents that he has such knowledge, however, his misstatement can be the basis of fraud.

(6) Materiality of Misstatement. Does it make any difference if the misstatement concerns a trivial matter, or must it be something that a reasonable man would regard as material? Generally the misstatement must pertain to a material matter. The Restatement of the Law of Contracts, however, adopts the view that any statement, whether material or not, constitutes fraud if all the other elements are present.

(7) Investigation Before Relying on Statement. If the injured person has available the ready means of determining the truth, as by looking at something in front of him, he cannot rely on the false statement. The fact that he relies on the other person, that he is too busy to read the paper, or that he is in a hurry does not protect him. He takes the risk that the paper will read as he thinks it does when he signs it without reading it. When an illiterate person or one physically unable to read signs a paper without having it explained or read to him, he is ordinarily bound by its contents.

If an examination by the injured person does not reveal the defect, or if the injured person cannot be expected to understand what he sees because of its technical nature, or if a simple examination is not available, the injured person may rely on the statements of the other party and raise the issue of fraud when he learns that they are false. A misrepresentation made to prevent further inquiry also constitutes fraud. (See p. 105, Bob Wilson, Inc. v. Swann)

(8) Reliance and Damage. A person can complain of the misrepresentation of another only if he was misled by it and acted in reliance on it. (See p. 106, Trustees of Columbia University v. Jacobsen) If *A* says that his house is in good condition when it is

infested with termites but *B* does not buy the house, *B* cannot complain that *A's* statement was false since *B* cannot show that he was harmed in any way. Even if *B* purchased the house, he cannot recover from *A* when it can be shown that *B* knew there were termites and purchased the property anyway or that he did not care because he intended to tear down the building and erect a new building on the land.

When a person seeks to avoid a contract for fraud, it is theoretically immaterial whether the defrauded person is damaged in the sense that he can show a definite financial loss as the result of the fraud. As a practical matter, however, the defrauded person would probably not raise the question if he did not suffer some damage. If the injured person wishes to sue the wrongdoer for damages, as distinguished from avoiding the contract, then he must show that he has sustained some loss or injury.

(9) Who May Complain. The wrongdoer is liable only to the person he intended to deceive. Ordinarily a fraudulent statement is made directly by the wrongdoer to his intended victim. Suppose, however, that unknown to the speaker a third person overhears him or looks at a letter containing his false statement. Can that third person complain of the speaker's fraud when he thereafter relies upon it? Since the wrongdoer did not intend to harm the third person, no liability results.

This rule does not require that the speaker make the misrepresentation directly to the intended victim. If the speaker makes a public announcement, any member of the public defrauded can bring an action against him. As an illustration, if *A*, in organizing a corporation, issues a prospectus that falsely describes the corporation and its financial status, any person who purchases the stock in reliance on that false prospectus may sue *A*.

When the speaker gives false information to one person intending that it will be communicated to another whom he hopes to deceive, the latter person may sue for fraud.

(10) Use of Assumed Name. The use of an assumed name is not necessarily fraudulent or unlawful. (See p. 107, Fidelity & Deposit Co. v. Bodenstedt) It is such only when the impostor assumes the name of another person or makes up a name for the purpose of concealing his identity from persons to whom he owes money or a duty, or to avoid arrest, or for the purpose of deceiving the person with whom he is dealing, or of imitating the name of a competitor.

In the absence of any intent to evade or deceive by the use of the assumed name, it is lawful for a person to go by any name he chooses, although other persons may refuse to deal with him unless he uses his actual name. If a person makes a contract in an assumed or fictitious name or in a trade name, he will be bound by his contract because that name was in fact intended to identify him.

(a) CHANGE OF NAME. In most states, a person may obtain a decree of court officially changing his name upon filing a petition with the court, setting forth the reason for the desired change and satisfactory proof that there is no fraudulent or criminal purpose in effecting the change. In addition, a person's name may be changed as an incident to being adopted or divorced.

(b) FICTITIOUS NAME REGISTRATION. If a person or a group of persons, other than a corporation do business under a fictitious name, a statement must generally be filed in a specified government office setting forth the names and addresses of the persons actually owning or operating the business, together with the name, address, and nature of the business. Violation of such a statute is made a crime and, if the statute expressly so declares, prevents the enterprise from bringing suit on a business contract so long as the name is not registered. No violation generally exists, however, when the other contracting party knows the identity of the persons doing business under the unregistered fictitious name.

(11) Fraud as a Tort. Apart from its effect upon the validity of the contract, the fraud of one party is a tort or civil wrong upon the injured party. The injured party may bring a tort action, called trespass in common-law jurisdictions, in which he may recover the money damages that he has sustained as the result of the fraudulent statement.

Sec. 7-E. Undue Influence. An aged parent may entrust all his business affairs to his son; an invalid may rely on his nurse; a client may follow implicitly whatever his attorney recommends. The relationship may be such that for practical purposes the one person is helpless in the hands of the other. In such cases, it is apparent that the parent, the invalid, or the client is not in fact exercising his free will in making a contract suggested by the son, nurse, or attorney, but is merely following the will of the other person. Such relationships are called *confidential relationships.* Because of the great possibility that the person dominating the other may take advantage of him, the law presumes that the dominating person exerts *undue influence* upon the other person whenever the dominating person obtains any benefit from a contract made by the dominated person. The contract is then voidable and may be set aside by the other person unless the dominating person can prove that no advantage was taken by him.

The class of confidential relationships is not well-defined. It includes the relationships of parent and child, guardian and ward, physician and patient, attorney and client, and any other relationship of trust and confidence in which one party exercises a control or influence over another.

Whether undue influence exists is a difficult question for the court (ordinarily the jury) to determine. The law does not regard every "influence" as undue. Thus a nagging wife may drive a man to make a particular contract, but that is not regarded as being undue influence. Persuasion and argument are not in themselves undue influence.

An essential element of undue influence is that the person making the contract does not exercise his own free will in so doing. (See p. 108, Trigg v. Trigg) In the absence of a recognized type of confidential relationship, such as that between parent and child, the courts are likely to take the attitude that the person who claims to have been dominated was merely persuaded and wanted to make the contract.

Sec. 7-F. Duress. A person can claim *duress* if a threat of violence or other harm would restrain the free choice of any person of similar mentality, physical health, experience, education, and intelligence. It is sufficient that the victim is in fact deprived of his free will (See p. 109, Rubenstein v. Rubenstein), although whether other persons would have been similarly affected may influence the jury in determining whether the victim had in fact been deprived of his free will.

The threats may be directed against third persons who are near relatives of the intimidated person making the contract. Thus a threat to injure one's parent, child, husband, wife, brother, aunt, grandchild, or son-in-law may be duress. The threat may be directed at the property of the intimidated person, such as a threat to burn down his house if he does not sign the contract. When the effect is to prevent the intimidated person from exercising his own free will, duress exists.

Generally a threat of economic loss, such as a threat to prevent a contractor from securing further credit necessary to obtain building materials, is not regarded as duress. Some courts have held it to be duress when so serious a loss threatened the victim, if he did not agree, that he in fact was not exercising a free choice when he made the contract. In any case, in order to prove duress by business or economic compulsion, it is necessary to show that the victim would suffer irreparable loss for which he could not adequately recover, if at all, by suing the wrongdoer.

A threat to prosecute a person or a member of his family for a crime is usually held to constitute duress without regard to whether the person is guilty of the crime or not. However, a threat to resort to civil litigation made in the belief that there is a right to sue is not duress even though the belief is unfounded.

Sec. 7-G. Remedies. Mistake, fraud, undue influence, and duress may make the contract voidable or, in some instances, void. If the contract is voidable, it can be rescinded or set aside by the party who has been injured or of whom advantage has been taken. If he does not elect to avoid it, however, the contract is valid and binding. In no case can the other party, the wrongdoer, set aside the contract and thus profit by his own wrong. If the contract is void, neither party can enforce it and no act of avoidance is required by either party to set the contract aside.

If the injured party elects to rescind the contract, he is entitled to recover anything that he had paid or given the other in performance of the contract. If the injured party has received any money or property from the wrongdoer, he must return it as a condition to rescission. If restoration is not possible, as when the injured party has spent the money or consumed the property that he has received, or has sold the property to a third person, or had received personal services under the contract, the injured party is generally barred from rescinding the contract.

When a contract is voidable, the right to rescind the contract is lost by any conduct that is inconsistent with an intention to avoid it. The right to rescind the contract is lost if the injured party, with full knowledge of the facts, affirms the transaction, or when, with such knowledge, he fails to object to the guilty party within a reasonable time. (See p. 110, Frailey v. McGarry) In determining whether a reasonable time has expired, the court considers whether the delay benefited the injured party, whether a late avoidance of the contract would cause unreasonable harm to the guilty person, and whether avoidance would harm intervening rights of third persons acquired after the original transaction.

If the other party was guilty of a wrong, such as fraud, as distinguished from making an innocent mistake, the injured party may sue him for damages caused by such wrong.

When the contract has resulted in the transfer of property from the guilty person to the victim, the latter also loses the right to rescind if, with knowledge of the true situation, he retains and uses the property, sells it to another, or uses it after the guilty person refuses to take it back.

When the result of a mutual mistake is merely that a writing does not correctly state the agreement made by the parties, either party can have the court reform or correct the contract to express the intended meaning.

Cases for Chapter 7

Harrod v. Kelly Adjustment Co.

179 A.2d 431 (M.C.App.D.C., 1962)

When Harrod was seventeen years of age, he purchased a watch on credit. He signed a contract which recited that it was sealed, and the printed word "Seal" appeared after his signature on the contract. Ten years later, Kelly Adjustment Co. sued him for the balance due on the contract. Harrod claimed that the suit was brought too late because it was an ordinary contract. Kelly claimed that the statutory twelve-year limitation applied because it was a sealed contract. From a judgment for Kelly, Harrod appealed.

QUINN, A.J. . . . Appellant [Harrod] first contends that it was error for the trial court to allow the action under the twelve-year limitation for sealed instruments, instead of dismissing it on the three-year . . . [limitation] for simple contracts. Not having known the meaning and effect of a sealed instrument, he maintains that he could not have intended to execute one, with the result that the sales contract should have been treated as a simple contract. In this way he seeks to avoid the effect of the language "witness my hand and seal," which appears prominently in the contract, and the word "seal," in parenthesis, which appears opposite his signature. This he may not do. Appellant's ignorance of the seal's significance and his avowed lack of actual intent to execute an agreement of such dignity do not determine the character of the instrument; whatever reservations he may have had then are unavailing now. In deciding the issue, the court is concerned not with a maker's undisclosed intent but with that expressed or manifested on the paper under examination. "And, as the word 'seal' in parenthesis is in common use as a seal, its presence upon an instrument in the usual place of a seal, opposite the signature, undoubtedly evinces an intention to make the instrument a sealed instrument, which should be held conclusive by the court, in the absence of other indications to the contrary appearing on the face of the instrument itself." Far from any such contrary indication being demonstrated here, the words "witness my hand and seal" lend added and conclusive force of an intention to make a sealed contract, and the trial court was correct in so holding. . . .

[Judgment reversed on other grounds.]

In re New Jersey Refrigerating Co.

100 N.J.Eq. 537, 136 A. 179 (1927)

Jasinski purchased a building owned by the New Jersey Refrigerating Co. at an auction sale held by receivers appointed for the company. The auctioneer's notice stated that the estimated annual rentals of the property were $3,648. Actually the rentals were $2,388. Jasinski petitioned to set aside the purchase because of this misstatement. From a decree confirming the sale, Jasinski appealed.

BLACK, J. . . . Rentals are an important factor for bidders to know. There is no reason for inaccuracies or misrepresentations as to rentals. The slightest care on the part of the receivers could have stated this item with substantial accuracy. . . . The petitioner became the purchaser under misapprehension, relying upon the truth of the statements in the auctioneer's notice of sale, issued in the name of the receivers.

. . . The reason advanced for confirming the sale is that the auctioneer's notice of sale . . . contained the following paragraph: "All statements are subject to errors and omissions, and all dimensions of lands are more or less." The further statement was that the yearly rentals were estimated. The petitioner bought at her own risk, and she was bound to satisfy herself, in advance of sale, the condition of the property. With this conclusion . . . we cannot agree.

. . . A court of equity will rescind a transaction entered into upon the faith of a material representation, false in fact, if the person to whom it was made relied upon it, and in consequence suffered injury. In equity the complainant may succeed although the misrepresentation was innocent.

The description of the property offered for sale should be in language so clear and unambiguous that persons of ordinary understanding will not be deceived as to either its character or identity. A misdescription in a material matter, upon which the purchaser might reasonably rely and did rely to his damage, is ground for avoidance of the contract. This is so even though the conditions of sale provide that errors and misdescriptions shall not avoid the contract. . . .

[Judgment against Jasinski reversed.]

Bob Wilson, Inc. v. Swann

168 A.2d 198 (App.D.C., 1960)

Swann traded in his old car and purchased a used car from Bob Wilson, Inc. The latter's President, Lenoff, wrote down the terms of the sale on a top sheet and then requested Swann to sign the top sheet and the sheets underneath, stating that they were duplicates. Lenoff thereafter had Swann acknowledge each of the sheets before a notary public and write in the margin of each sheet, "We have read this contract; it is correct and complete." Swann did not read the contract and did not see that the copies had additional interest and charges totaling $613.20 which he was required to pay. He sued the company for overcharging him. From a judgment in his favor, the company appealed.

QUINN, A.J. . . . It is settled that one who refrains from reading a contract and in conscious ignorance of its terms voluntarily assents thereto will not be relieved from his bad bargain. The question whether the same risk falls upon a person who has been disarmed by fraud has not received uniform treatment. The approach taken by some jurisdictions denies redress where the party victimized neglected available means to discover the duplicity. Other courts, adopting what commentators regard as the better view, afford relief where misrepresentation has induced a party to forego the ordinary precaution of investigation. The fact that by so doing the party exercised less vigilance than most people would have employed under the circumstances does not protect the wrongdoer.

We need not consider here whether appellee Swann was unreasonable in trusting Lenoff's representations and in failing to insist on an examination of the papers before signing. In Stern v. Moneyweight Scale Co., (1914), 42 App.D.C. 162, the United States Court of Appeals for the District of Columbia ruled that fraud constituted a good defense to a contract which appellee's salesman had misrepresented despite appellant's apparent lack of good judgment in accepting the former's word without question. Such misconduct has also served as a basis for setting aside a contract, and, we believe, warrants a recovery at law. The record shows that Lenoff deliberately sought to mislead Swann and was successful in the attempt. Appellant may not shield itself from the consequences of its agent's deception by saying that Swann should not have been fooled.

[Judgment affirmed.]

Trustees of Columbia University v. Jacobsen
53 N.J.S. 574, 148 A.2d 63 (1959)

Columbia University sued Jacobsen for the balance of his tuition. He made a counterclaim against the University that it had made false representations as to what it would teach him. From a judgment in favor of the University, Jacobsen appealed.

GOLDMANN, S.J.A.D. . . . At the heart of defendant's counterclaim is a single complaint. He concedes that "I have really only one charge against Columbia: that it does not teach Wisdom as it claims to do. . . ."

We agree with the trial judge that wisdom is not a subject which can be taught and that no rational person would accept such a claim made by any man or institution. We find nothing in the record to establish that Columbia represented, expressly or even by way of impression, that it could or would teach wisdom or the several qualities which defendant insists are "synonyms for or aspects of the same Quality." The matter is perhaps best summed up in the supporting affidavit of the Dean of Columbia College, where he said that "All that any college can do through its teachers, libraries, laboratories, and other facilities is to endeavor to teach the student the known facts, acquaint him with the nature of those matters which are unknown, and thereby assist him in developing mentally, morally, and physically. Wisdom is a hoped-for end product of education, experience, and ability which many seek and many fail to attain."

Defendant's extended argument lacks the element of fraudulent representation indispensable to any action of deceit. We note, in passing, that he has cited no legal authority whatsoever for his position. Instead, he has submitted a dictionary definition of "wisdom" and quotations from such works as the *Bhagavad-Gita*, the *Mundaka Upanishad*, the *Analects of Confucius* and the *Koran;* excerpts from Euripides, Plato and Menander; and references to the Bible. Interesting though these may be, they do not support defendant's indictment of Columbia. If his pleadings, affidavit, and exhibits demonstrate anything, it is indeed the validity of what Pope said in his Moral Essays: "A little learning is a dangerous thing; Drink deep, or taste not the Pierian spring: . . ."

The papers make clear that through the years defendant's interest has shifted from civil engineering to social work, then to physics, and finally to English and creative writing. In college he became increasingly critical of his professors and his courses; in his last year he attended classes only when he chose and rejected the regimen of examinations and term papers. When his nonattendance at classes and his poor work in the senior year were called to his attention by the Columbia Dean of Students, he replied in a lengthy letter that "I want to learn, but I must do it my own way. I realize my behavior is nonconforming, but in these times when there are so many forces that demand conformity I hope I will find Columbia willing to grant some freedom to a student who wants to be a literary artist." In short, he chose to judge Columbia's educational system by the shifting standards of his own fancy, and now seeks to place his failure at Columbia's door on the theory that it had deliberately misrepresented that it taught wisdom. . . .

[Judgment affirmed.]

Fidelity & Deposit Co. v. Bodenstedt
170 Neb. 799, 104 N.W.2d 292 (1960)

Fred Clair Clay, the grandson of Fred Jarvis, purchased an automobile and signed the papers "Fred C. Jarvis." The Fidelity & Deposit Co., in suing a party on the note given for the purchase price, claimed that Fred had made a forged signature on the papers. Fred had been reared by his grandfather and had always gone under the name of Fred C. Jarvis, although that was not his actual name. When he signed the papers for the automobile, he acted in good faith, intending to designate himself as the person who was buying the auto. From a judgment that the signature was forged, an appeal was taken by Bodenstedt who would be liable if the signature in question were a forgery.

YEAGER, J. . . . "In general, in the absence of statutory prohibition, a person, without abandoning his real name, may adopt or assume any name, wholly or partly different from his name, by which he may become known, and by which he may transact business, execute contracts, and carry on his affairs, unless he does so in order to defraud others, or he is inhibited by judicial adjudication, since it is the identity of the individual that is regarded, and not the name which he may bear or assume." . . .

The signing of the note and mortgage was not, under the undisputed facts in this case and the law, a forgery. Generally defined, forgery is the false making or materially altering, with intent to defraud, of any writing which, if genuine, might apparently be of legal efficacy, or the foundation of a legal liability. . . . In the record here, there is an absence of anything indicating the existence of a fraudulent intent.

In the light of the record, therefore, the court erred in [holding that the signature "Fred C. Jarvis" was a forgery]. . . .

[Judgment reversed.]

Trigg v. Trigg

37 N.M. 296, 22 P.2d 119 (1933)

Trigg conveyed a large ranch to his wife. Shortly thereafter she deserted him. He then brought an action to cancel the deed, claiming that the transfer had been made because of constant importunities by his wife and threats of desertion and divorce. From a judgment for the plaintiff, the defendant appealed.

ZINN, J. . . . In an Indiana case, the court said: "The threat of a husband to abandon his wife if she does not execute a mortgage on her separate real estate to secure his debt is an improper pressure; and a mortgage executed by a wife, under such a threat, may be avoided by her, if the threat induced the execution of the mortgage."

The books abound with cases . . . where the husband obtained the property from the wife, where the guardian obtained property from the ward, where children obtained the property from the aged father or mother, the attorney from the client; generally the weaker or subservient having conveyed to the stronger or dominant, and equity had granted relief because of undue influence, duress, or fraud.

Here, however, we have the reverse, the clinging vine inducing the oak to convey to her all his interest in fourteen thousand broad acres on the Pablo Montoya grant, the weaker sex importuning, "nagging," and obtaining from the stronger and dominating member of the life partnership a conveyance of community real estate. She adopted the device, as alleged by the appellee, of threatening abandonment of his bed and board, and dissolving the marriage by securing a divorce unless he gave her a deed to the ranch.

Domestic tranquillity, the companionship and affection of a companionable mate and peaceful household, are more priceless than jewels and cannot be measured in dollars and cents; and a social or domestic force exercised in such a manner as might put fear into the mind of a husband that unless a conveyance is made of property so as to vest the same in the wife, a divorce would follow, with the consequences attendant thereto upon the domestic and social affairs of the threatened husband, might be considered as undue influence and force preventing the true and free action of his will and consent; and where a deed of conveyance has been made after persistent "nagging," followed by threats of divorce and abandonment unless the deed is executed, it is a legitimate inference that such a deed was made under the exercise of a domestic or social force which prevented the free action of the will of the donor and that such gift was made as the result of undue influence. . . .

[Judgment for plaintiff affirmed.]

Rubenstein v. Rubenstein

20 N.J. 359, 120 A.2d 11 (1956)

Rubenstein and his wife owned real estate. He transferred the real estate to a corporation owned solely by his wife. He later sued to set aside the transaction on the ground that he had made the conveyance because he had been threatened with personal violence and death by arsenic poison if he did not do so. At the time, his wife's father was serving a life sentence for murder committed as a member of an "arsenic ring" engaged in killing to defraud insurance companies. From a judgment against him, the husband appealed.

HEHER, J. . . . Conveyances . . . procured by means of duress . . . are inoperative and voidable. Actual violence is not an essential element of duress of the person, even at common law, because consent is the very essence of a contract and, if there be compulsion, there is no actual consent. And moral compulsion, such as that produced by threats to take life or to inflict great bodily harm, as well as that produced by imprisonment, came to be regarded everywhere as sufficient in law to destroy free agency, indispensable to the consent without which there can be no contract.

It would seem to be basic to the legal concept of duress, proceeding as it does from the unreality of the apparent consent, that the controlling factor be the condition at the time of the mind of the person subjected to the coercive measures, rather than the means by which the given state of mind was induced, and thus the test is essentially subjective. . . .

In the modern view, moral compulsion or psychological pressure may constitute duress if, thereby, the subject of the pressure is overborne and he is deprived of the exercise of his free will. The question is whether consent was coerced; that is, was the person complaining "induced by the duress or undue influence to give his consent, and would not have done so otherwise." . . . It was said in the early books that there could not be duress by threats unless the threats were such as "to put a brave man in fear"; but the tendency of the more recent cases, and the rule comporting with reason and principle, is that any "unlawful threats" which do "in fact overcome the will of the person threatened, and induce him to do an act which he would not otherwise have done, and which he was not bound to do, constitute duress. The age, sex, capacity, relation of the parties and all the attendant circumstances must be considered. . . ."

But the pressure must be wrongful. And means in themselves lawful must not be so oppressively used as to constitute, e.g., an abuse of legal remedies. . . . The act or conduct complained of need not be "unlawful" in the technical sense of the term; it suffices if it is "wrongful in the sense that it is so oppressive under given circumstances as to constrain one to do what his free will would refuse." . . . It was said in a recent case that duress is tested, not by the nature of the threats, but rather by the state of mind induced thereby in the victim.

. . . Wherever motive, belief, or intent of a party is material to the issue, it may be proved by his own direct testimony. . . .

[Judgment reversed and new trial ordered.]

Frailey v. McGarry

116 Utah 504, 211 P.2d 840 (1949)

McGarry sold land to Frailey. The purchaser sued to rescind the contract on the ground that the seller had defrauded him by making false statements as to the availability of water for irrigation. From a judgment for the defendant, the plaintiff appealed.

LATIMER, J. . . . After reviewing the record of events as they transpired, we find it unnecessary to determine whether defendant, by fraud, induced the plaintiff to enter into the contract. There are facts present in the instant case which preclude plaintiff from rescinding the contract for the reasons he alleges. It is well settled by decisions from this court that a person claiming the right to rescind a contract because of misrepresentations or fraud must, after discovery of the fraud, announce his purpose and adhere to it. . . . We have also held that the purchaser must evidence his intent to rescind by some unequivocal act either by notice or some act amounting to notice of intent to rescind. . . . Moreover, a defrauded party, after learning the truth, will not be permitted to go on deriving benefits from the transaction and later elect to rescind. . . .

Nor will he be permitted to go on with the contract for the purpose of securing benefits which, although not directly conferred by the contract, are nevertheless made possible as a result of the contract, only to later claim a right to rescind when he discovers the benefits to be acquired will not be great enough to compensate him for the loss he will sustain by reason of the fraud.

The fraud alleged by plaintiff as grounds for rescission consisted of the alleged statements made by defendant that there was ample water available to irrigate the 960 acres covered in the contract and that it was a mere formality to secure the right to drill wells in order to obtain that water. The falsity of such statements, if made, was made known to the defendant many months before he decided to rescind the contract. He became aware . . . that there was a supposed shortage of water . . . on March 2, 1946. Yet he did not notify defendant of his intention to rescind until some ten months later.

Black in his work on Rescission and Cancellation, Sec. 536, states the law to be: ". . . It must be remembered that a contract induced by fraud, false representations, mistake, etc., is not void but only voidable, and it is entirely within the right of the injured party to affirm it or treat it as valid and subsisting. In this respect he has a choice or election, and he should not be required to make his decision instantly. The true doctrine is that, after discovering the facts justifying rescission, the party is entitled to a reasonable time in which to decide upon the course he will take. But this does not mean that he will be indulged in a vacillating or hesitating course of conduct, but that he must act with such a measure of promptness as can fairly be called 'reasonable' with reference to all the circumstances of the particular case. Particularly, he must, if possible, avoid such a delay as will make the ensuing rescission injurious to the other party or to the intervening interests of third persons. He must use reasonable diligence in ascertaining the facts which may entitle him to rescind, and must act so soon after the discovery of them as that the opposite party will not be unnecessarily prejudiced by the delay. 'The rule is that he who would rescind the contract must offer to do so promptly on discovering the facts that will justify a rescission, and while he is able of himself, or by the judgment of the court, to place the opposite party substantially in statu quo.' "

Plaintiff had little or no cause for an extended delay in rescinding as he does not claim he was subsequently led to believe that he would be able to secure water sufficient to irrigate 960 acres or any substantial part thereof. Even when he received permission to drill two wells at his own risk, he could not possibly have thought they would be sufficient to irrigate the entire tract. As a matter of fact, he attempted to induce defendant to reduce the number of acres he would be required to purchase under the contract when it became apparent to him that it would be difficult if not impossible to secure enough water for his purposes. For almost a year plaintiff vacillated between reliance on the contract, obtaining a modified contract, abandonment of the contract, and finally rescission. When he finally concluded to adopt the latter course, he still maintained his right to retain the benefits he received under the contract.

In attempting to justify his delay in electing to rescind the contract, plaintiff argues this is not a case which permits a party to readily ascertain whether there is sufficient water available to supply the needs of the land which plaintiff sought to purchase. While we agree that the situation in which plaintiff found himself prevented him from being able to tell how much, if any, water he would eventually be given, we think the record is clear that he was informed early in 1946 that in all probability he would not get any water for at least one year and that he never would secure enough water to irrigate 960 acres or any acreage approximating that amount. No good reason appears to justify a delay of some ten months' time.

Plaintiff further contends that his acts and conduct after he learned he would not be able to secure the water he needed, made it clear to defendant that he, the plaintiff, did not intend to be bound by the contract. We do not so interpret them. There is a difference between an expression of dissatisfaction and one of intent to rescind. While the record contains evidence of the fact that plaintiff was dissatisfied with the contract, we are convinced that plaintiff's conduct was insufficient to convey to the defendant the impression that plaintiff was electing to rescind the contract. . . .

[Judgment for defendant affirmed.]

Questions and Case Problems

1. What is the objective of each of the following rules of law?

  (a) One party generally cannot set aside a contract because the other party failed to volunteer information which the complaining party would desire to know.

  (b) In certain close relationships that are regarded as confidential, it is presumed that a contract which benefits the dominating person was obtained by undue influence, and he has the burden of proving the contrary.

2. The Adjustment Bureau held for collection a claim against Rogers. Rogers executed an agreement to pay the money to Adjustment Bureau. When the bureau sued him on the agreement, he claimed that it had been obtained from him by duress because Adjustment Bureau had threatened to attach his wages if he did not execute the agreement. Was the agreement binding? (Adjustment Bureau, Inc. v. Rogers, 143 Colo. 480, 354 P.2d 605)

3. Auerbach was the president of the Emancipator Boat Co. and owner of 98 per cent of the stock. Forbes sold lumber to the company on credit. Forbes was about to stop extending credit when Auerbach referred him to a financial statement that he had prepared for Dun & Bradstreet, a credit rating agency. The report showed that the company was successful, and Forbes extended further credit on the basis of the statement. The statement was false as the company had been insolvent at all times. The company was unable to pay Forbes, who then sued Auerbach for the loss caused by the fraudulent financial statement. Auerbach raised the defense that the false credit statement had not been furnished to Forbes but had been furnished to the credit rating agency and therefore Forbes had no right to rely on it. Was he correct? (Forbes v. Auerbach, [Fla.] 56 So.2d 895)

4. The Manning Lumber Co. made a written contract to sell 602,000 board feet of logs to Voget. The seller represented that there were that many logs although the buyer knew that it was not possible to measure the lumber accurately and that the seller was trying to sell all of its lumber for a lump sum. After executing the contract, the buyer suggested the inclusion of a provision for credit to the buyer in the event of a shortage. The seller refused to agree to this. When the seller later sued the buyer for the purchase price, the buyer claimed that there was a shortage and that the contract should be reformed or modified to give him credit for the amount of the shortage. Was the buyer entitled to this relief? (Manning Lumber Co. v. Voget, 188 Ore. 486, 216 P.2d 674)

5. Platt made a contract with Locke to construct a swimming pool. Platt was not incorporated but did business under the assumed name of Crystal Pools, Inc. The name was not registered as required by a statute making it a crime to engage in business under a fictitious name that was not registered. The statute made no further provision. When Platt sued Locke on the contract, the latter claimed that Platt could not recover because he had not registered his name. Platt proved that Locke knew

that he was actually contracting with Platt in spite of the assumed corporate name. Decide. (Platt v. Locke, 11 Utah 2d 273, 358 P.2d 95)

6. Tucker purchased an automobile from Central Motors, relying on the representation that it was the latest model available. The sale was completed on February 9. On February 10, Tucker learned that the representation that the automobile was the latest model was false. He continued to drive the car and after having driven it in excess of one thousand miles, he demanded on April 7 that the purchase be set aside for fraud. Decide. (Tucker v. Central Motors, 220 La. 510, 57 So.2d 40)

7. Murphy was a man 86 years of age and of impaired faculties. A friend falsely told him that he was giving his time to religious and educational work without compensation. The friend aroused a prejudice in Murphy against leaving his property to others. By appealing to Murphy's religious and charitable instincts, the friend persuaded Murphy to make a promissory note for $2,300 payable to him personally at Murphy's death. After Murphy's death, payment of the note was refused. Could the note be enforced? (Geddes v. McElroy, 171 Iowa 633, 154 N.W. 320)

8. An agent of Thor Food Service Corp. was seeking to sell Makofske a combination refrigerator-freezer and food purchase plan. Makofske was married and had three children. After being informed of the eating habits of Makofske and his family, the agent stated that the cost of the freezer and food would be about $95 to $100 a month. Makofske carefully examined the agent's itemized estimate and made some changes to it. Makofske then signed the contract and purchased the refrigerator-freezer. The cost proved to be greater than the estimated $95 to $100 a month, and Makofske claimed that the contract had been obtained by fraud. Decide. (Thor Food Service Corp. v. Makofske, 218 N.Y.S.2d 93)

9. Dunham ran a department store in which the fur coat department was operated as a concession by Hurwitz, although to the general public it appeared that Dunham was running that department. Hurwitz would send the fur coats of Dunham's customers to be cleaned and stored with Kudra. Hurwitz went bankrupt and Dunham canceled the concession. Kudra, however, had 412 coats of Dunham's customers which it refused to surrender until he was paid $622.50 for charges relating to those coats and an additional $3,232.55 owed for back bills. It was the end of November, the temperature was dropping to 15 degrees above zero, and Dunham's customers were demanding the return of their coats from storage. Kudra insisted that he be paid both amounts. Dunham paid all the money demanded, received the coats, and then sued Kudra for the return of the $3,232.55. Decide. (S. P. Dunham Co. v. Kudra, 44 N.J.S. 565, 131 A.2d 306)

10. Roberts, an educated person, purchased real estate from Morrison. Roberts merely "half-read" the contract which she signed. As a result, she did not notice the provision in the contract with respect to interest on the unpaid portion of the purchase price. She refused to pay the interest specified in the contract. Morrison sued her. Could he recover? (Morrison v. Roberts, 195 Ga. 45, 23 S.E.2d 164)

CHAPTER 8

Consideration

To constitute a valid contract, the agreement must meet requirements other than genuine mutual assent. Ordinarily one of these requirements is consideration.

Sec. 8-A. Definition of Consideration. In simplest terms *consideration* is what a promisor demands and receives as the price for his promise. A promise usually is binding upon a person only when he has received consideration. It must be something to which the promisor is not otherwise entitled, and it must be the very thing that the promisor specifies as the price for his promise.

Although some cases define consideration in terms of benefit to the promisor or detriment to the promisee, it is immaterial whether benefit or detriment is present. The essential element is that the act or thing which is done or promised has been specified by the promisor as the price to be paid in order to obtain his promise. (See p. 123, Baehr v. Penn-O-Tex Oil Corporation)

A promise to make a gift or a promise to do or not to do something without receiving consideration is unenforceable, but an executed gift or a performance without consideration cannot be rescinded for lack of consideration.

If the contract is bilateral, each party to the contract is a promisor and must receive consideration to make his promise binding. A unilateral contract has only one promisor, and the performance of the act which he called for is the consideration for his promise.

Consideration is sometimes qualified or described as "valuable consideration." This is done to distinguish it from the so-called "good consideration," that is, the love and affection existing between near relatives. In most states good consideration is not consideration at all but is merely a matter of inducement in the making of the promise. (See p. 124, Wright v. Polk General Hospital) Moral obligation is likewise not consideration.

115

Sec. 8-B. Forbearance as Consideration. In most cases consideration consists of the performance of an act or the making of a promise to act. But consideration may also consist of *forbearance*, which is refraining from doing an act, or a promise of forbearance. In other words, the promisor may desire to buy the inaction of the other party or his promise not to act. (See p. 125, Hofmann v. DeFelice)

The waiving or giving up of any right, legal or equitable, can be consideration for the promise of another. Thus the relinquishment of a right in property, of a right to sue for damages, or of a homestead right will support a promise given in return for it.

The right that is surrendered in return for a promise may be a right against a third person or his property, as well as one against the promisor or his property. There is no consideration when the right is known to be worthless by the person surrendering it.

Sec. 8-C. Present Versus Past Consideration. Since consideration is what the promisor states must be received for his promise, it must be given after the promisor states what he demands. Past consideration is not valid. (See p. 126, Warner & Co. v. Brua) When one person performs some service for another without the latter's knowledge or without an understanding that compensation is to be paid, a promise made later to pay for such services is not supported by consideration and is unenforceable.

Some courts hold that when benefits are derived by fraud or under circumstances that create a moral obligation, a promise to compensate is supported by consideration. When one promises to pay a debt that was unenforceable because of his infancy, or that is barred by the Statute of Limitations, or that has been discharged in bankruptcy, the promise is binding. There must be clear proof, however, that a subsequent promise was in fact made. The better theory is that the new promise is a waiver of the bar or defense to the action and that no consideration is necessary. Some courts regard the new promise as supported by moral consideration to pay the old debt. This is not a satisfactory explanation since ordinarily neither a moral obligation nor a past performance is deemed consideration.

Sec. 8-D. Binding Character of Promise. To constitute consideration, the promise must be binding, that is, it must impose a liability or create a duty. (See p. 127, Mandel v. Liebman) Suppose that a coal company promises to sell to a factory all the coal which it orders at a specified price, and that the factory agrees to pay that price for any coal which it orders from the coal company. The promise of the factory is not regarded as consideration because it does not obligate the factory to buy any coal from the coal company.

If, however, the factory promises to purchase all the coal it requires for a specified period and the coal dealer agrees to supply it at a specified price per ton, there is a valid contract according to most courts. It is true that it cannot be known beforehand how much coal will be ordered. The factory may have a strike or a fire and not operate at all during the year, and therefore require no coal. Moreover, the factory might convert to oil. In spite of these possibilities such a contract is usually regarded as valid.

Although a contract must impose a binding obligation, it **may** authorize one or either party to terminate or cancel the agreement under certain circumstances or upon giving notice to the other party. The fact that the contract may be terminated in this manner does not make the contract any the less binding prior to such termination.

In some instances where it is manifest that a particular act is impossible to perform, a promise to do that act is not regarded as valid consideration. If there is a possibility that the performance can be made, the consideration is valid.

Sec. 8-E. Promise to Perform Existing Obligations. Ordinarily, a promise to do, or the performance of, what one is already under legal obligation to do is not consideration. (See p. 128, Marion Production Credit Assn. v. Smith) It is immaterial whether the legal obligation is based upon contract, upon the duties pertaining to an office held by the promisor, or upon statute or general principles of law. This rule is based on the theory that in such instances the promisor receives nothing for his promise since he was entitled to the conduct called for without paying anything extra.

For example, a promise to pay a stated sum of money to a police officer for making an arrest in the line of duty is unenforceable since the promisor receives only that which he has a right to demand without making any promise. If the act requested is over and beyond the call of duty, however, the performance of that act will make the promise binding.

Similarly, a promise to refrain from doing what one has no legal right to do is not consideration.

(1) Completion of Contract. When a contractor refuses to complete a building unless the owner promises him a payment or bonus in addition to the sum specified in the original contract, and the owner promises to make that payment, the question arises whether the owner's promise is binding. A few courts hold that the promise is binding on the theory that the first contract was mutually rescinded and that a second contract including the promise to pay the bonus was executed. Some courts hold the promise enforceable on the theory that the contractor has given up his right of election (a) to perform or (b) to

abandon the contract and pay damages. Most courts, however, hold that the second promise of the owner is without consideration. (See p. 129, Leggett v. Vinson)

The courts holding that there is no consideration for the second promise make an exception when there are extraordinary circumstances caused by unforeseeable difficulties or mistakes and when the additional amount demanded by the contractor is reasonable for the extra work done by him. They do so usually upon the theory that the first contract was discharged because of an implied condition that the facts would be or would continue to be as supposed by the parties and that the completion of the contract was the consideration for the new promise. Generally, however, unanticipated difficulty or expense, such as a strike or price increase, does not affect the liabilities of the parties. Such risks one takes in making a contract in the same sense that when you buy a coat or a house, you take the risk that you may not like it as much as you thought you would.

If the promise of the contractor is to do something that is neither expressly nor impliedly a part of the first contract, then the promise of the other party is binding. For example, if a bonus of $1,000 is promised in return for the promise of a contractor to complete the building at a date earlier than that specified in the original agreement, the promise would be binding.

(2) Compromise and Release of Claims. The rule that doing or promising to do what one is bound to do is not consideration applies to a part payment made in satisfaction of an admitted debt. For example, if one person owes another $100, the promise of the latter to take $50 in full payment is not binding upon him and will not prevent him from demanding the remainder later because the partial payment by the debtor is not consideration.

This rule has been severely criticized because it seems unfair to permit the creditor to go back on his promise even though the debtor does owe him the money. In some instances it has been changed by statute or by court decision. Some courts treat the transaction as a binding gift of the remainder on the part of the creditor. Other courts seize the slightest opportunity to find some new consideration.

If the debtor pays before the debt is due, there is, of course, consideration since on the day when payment was made the creditor was not entitled to demand any payment. Likewise, if the creditor accepts some article, even of slight value, in addition to the part payment, the agreement is held to be binding.

If there is a bona fide dispute as to the amount owed or whether any amount is owed, a payment by the debtor of less than the amount claimed by the creditor is consideration for the latter's agreement to release or settle the claim. Under this rule it is generally regarded as sufficient if the claimant believes in his claim. Conversely, if the claimant knows that his claim does not have any merit and he is merely pressing it in order to force the other party to make some payment to buy peace from the annoyance of a lawsuit, the settlement agreement based on the part payment is not binding. A minority of states qualify the "actual-belief" rule by holding that the claimant must also have a reasonable ground for believing that his claim is valid.

Under the Code, the acceptance of a check for part of a debt releases the entire debt, without regard to the existence of a dispute, if the check bears a notation that it is intended as final or full payment of the debt.

(3) Composition of Creditors. A problem also arises when there is a *composition of creditors.* Here the different creditors of the one debtor mutually agree to accept a fractional part of their claims in full satisfaction thereof. Such agreements are binding and are deemed supported by consideration, but there is disagreement as to the theory for so holding.

Sec. 8-F. Adequacy of Consideration. Ordinarily the courts do not consider the adequacy of the consideration given for a promise. In the absence of fraud or other misconduct, the courts usually will not interfere to make sure that each side is getting a fair return. (See p. 130, Smith v. Smith) The courts leave each person to his contract and do not seek to reappraise the value that he has placed upon the consideration which he has received. The fact that the consideration given may seem small to other persons or to a reasonable man does not, in the absence of fraud, affect the validity of the contract.

If forbearance is called for by the promisor as the price of his promise, it is not material whether the parties agree that the forbearance shall be for a long or a short time. The promisee must forbear for the period called for by the promisor, but the law will not attempt to say whether the period of forbearance is adequate consideration for the promise.

When no specific period of forbearance is stated, the promisee is under a duty to forbear for a reasonable time. If, however, there is no duty to forbear for any period at all, as when the promisee merely agrees to forbear as long as he wishes, there is no consideration since the promisor has not bought anything with his promise.

There are some exceptions to the rule that the courts will not weigh the consideration, as follows:

(1) Statutory Exceptions. In a few states statutes require that the consideration be adequate, or fair or reasonable, in order to make a contract binding.

(2) Evidence of Fraud. The smallness of the consideration may be evidence of fraud. It does not mean that the transaction is necessarily made in bad faith or for a fraudulent purpose but, if there is some other evidence indicating the presence of fraud, the smallness of the consideration corroborates that evidence.

(3) Exchange of Different Quantities of Identical Units. A promise to pay a particular amount of money or to deliver a particular quantity of goods in exchange for a promise to pay or deliver a greater amount or quantity of the same kind of money or goods at the same time and place is not adequate consideration.

If there is a difference between the nature of the units promised by the different parties, the law will find that there is consideration and will not ask whether the consideration is adequate. A promise to pay $60 in return for a promise to pay one penny would not be supported by consideration if both amounts of money are current legal tender. On the other hand, a promise to pay $60 of current money for a coin collector's penny would be supported by consideration since the units are not equivalent.

Sec. 8-G. Exceptions to Requirement of Consideration. Ordinarily, a promise is not binding unless supported by consideration. There are certain exceptions to this rule.

(1) Voluntary Subscriptions. When charitable enterprises are financed by voluntary subscriptions of a number of persons, the promise of each one is generally enforceable. For example, when a number of people make pledges or subscriptions for the construction of a church, for a charitable institution, or for a college, the subscriptions are binding.

The theories for sustaining such promises vary. One view is that the promise of each subscriber is consideration for the promises of the others. This view is not sound because the promises are not given in exchange for each other. Another view is that the liability of the promisor rests upon a promissory estoppel [1] because obligations have been incurred in reliance upon the promise. Still another view treats a subscription as an offer for an act which is accepted by creating liabilities or making expenditures. Under this theory the promise would be revocable until the act is performed. It is also held by some courts that the acceptance of a subscription carries an implied promise creating an obligation to perform in accordance with the offer.

The real answer is that in these cases consideration is lacking according to the technical standards applied in ordinary contract cases. Nevertheless, the courts enforce such promises as a matter of public policy.

---

[1] See p. 122.

(2) Commercial Paper. When a negotiable instrument, such as a check or promissory note, has been executed and delivered, there is a prima facie presumption of consideration, which, however, may be rebutted as between the immediate parties. In some states, by statute, the same rule applies to all simple agreements that have been reduced to writing. In the case of commercial paper, however, lack or failure of consideration is no defense as against certain other persons to whom the instruments are thereafter transferred.[2] The result is that the negotiable instrument may be enforceable even though no consideration was given.

(3) Sealed Instruments. At common law consideration was not necessary to support a promise under seal. In a state which gives the seal its original common-law effect, a gratuitous promise or a promise to make a gift is enforceable when it is set forth in a sealed instrument.

The common-law rule that a promise under seal does not need consideration has been abolished or modified in most states. In some states a promise under seal must be supported by consideration, just as though it did not have a seal. Other states take a middle position and hold that the presence of a seal is prima facie proof that there is consideration to support the promise. This means that if nothing more than the existence of the sealed promise is shown, it is deemed supported by consideration. The party making the promise, however, may prove that there was no consideration. If he does, the promise is not binding upon him.

Even in those states in which the contract under seal is binding, the courts of equity will refuse to grant special relief, such as specifically enforcing the contract, if there is not a fair or reasonable consideration for the promise.

(4) Debts of Record. No consideration is necessary to support an obligation of record, such as a judgment or recognizance. These obligations are enforceable because of their form since it would be contrary to public policy to permit obligations formally entered in a court record by court order to be questioned on the ground that there was no consideration.

(5) Model Written Obligations Act. Under statutes in some states no consideration is necessary in order to make certain written promises binding. The Model Written Obligations Act provides that "no release (or promise) hereafter made and signed by the person releasing (or promising) shall be invalid or unenforceable for lack

---

[2] See p. 501.

of consideration, if the writing also contains an express statement, in any form of language, that the signer intends to be legally bound" [3] by his promise.

(6) Uniform Commercial Code. Under the Code, consideration is not required (a) for a merchant's written firm offer as to goods, stated as irrevocable for a fixed time not over three months; [4] (b) to discharge in writing a claim for breach of a commercial contract; [5] or (c) to modify a contract for the sale of goods.[6]

(7) Promissory Estoppel. Some courts enforce promises that are not supported by consideration upon the *doctrine of promissory estoppel.* By this doctrine, if a person makes a promise to another and that other person acts upon that promise, the promisor is barred from setting up the absence of consideration in order to avoid his promise. The enforcement of the promise, even though there is no consideration, is deemed proper when the promisor should reasonably expect to induce and does induce action or forfearance of a definite and substantial character on the part of the promisee and when "injustice can only be avoided by enforcement of the promise." [7] In some instances, the doctrine of promissory estoppel is applied to keep open an offer that would otherwise be revocable because no consideration was given to create a binding option. (See p. 131, Drennan v. Star Paving Co.) The doctrine of promissory estoppel, however, is not given very wide recognition and is rejected in most states as conflicting with the basic requirement of consideration.

Sec. 8-H. Failure of Consideration. When a promise is given as consideration, the question arises as to whether the promisor will perform his promise. If he does not perform his promise, the law describes the default as a "failure of consideration." This is a misnomer since the failure of the promisor is one of performance, not of consideration.

Sec. 8-I. Legality of Consideration. The law will not permit persons to make contracts that violate the law. Accordingly, a promise to do something which the law prohibits or a promise to refrain from doing something which the law requires is not valid consideration and the contract is illegal. This subject is further discussed in Chapter 9.

---

[3] Model Written Obligations Act (MWOA), Sec. 1. The Act has been adopted in Pennsylvania.
[4] See p. 69.
[5] UCC Sec. 1-107.
[6] Sec. 2-209(1).
[7] Restatement, Contracts, Sec. 90.

Cases for Chapter 8

Baehr v. Penn-O-Tex Oil Corporation

258 Minn. 533, 104 N.W.2d 661 (1960)

Kemp leased a gas filling station from Baehr. Kemp, who was heavily indebted to the Penn-O-Tex Oil Corporation, transferred to it his right to receive payments on all claims. When Baehr complained that the rent was not paid, he was finally assured by the corporation that the rent would be paid to him. Baehr did not sue Kemp for the overdue rent but later sued the corporation. From a judgment for the defendant, the plaintiff appealed.

LOEVINGER, J. . . . Unfortunately, contract, like most of the basic terms constituting the intellectual tools of law, is conventionally defined in a circular fashion. By the most common definition, a contract is a promise or set of promises for the breach of which the law gives a remedy or the performance of which the law recognizes as a duty. This amounts to saying that a contract is a legally enforceable promise. But a promise is legally enforceable only if it is a contract. . . .

Although the definition of contract does not help much in determining what expressions shall be held to impose legal obligations, it does direct attention to a promise as the starting point of inquiry. Both in popular and legal usage, a promise is an assurance, in whatever form of expression given, that a thing will or will not be done. . . .

There was an unequivocal assurance given that the rents would be paid. This cannot be anything but a promise.

However, the fact that a promise was given does not necessarily mean that a contract was made. It is clear that not every promise is legally enforceable. Much of the vast body of law in the field of contracts is concerned with determining which promises should be legally enforced. On the one hand, in a civilized community men must be able to assume that those with whom they deal will carry out their undertakings according to reasonable expectations. On the other hand, it is neither practical nor reasonable to expect full performance of every assurance given, whether it be thoughtless, casual, and gratuitous, or deliberately and seriously made.

The test that has been developed by the common law for determining the enforceability of promises is the doctrine of consideration. This is a crude and not altogether successful attempt to generalize the conditions under which promises will be legally enforced. Consideration requires that a contractual promise be the product of a bargain. However, in this usage, "bargain" does not mean an exchange of things of equivalent, or any, value. It means a negotiation resulting in the voluntary assumption of an obligation by one party upon condition of an act or forbearance by the other. Consideration thus insures that the promise enforced as a contract is not accidental, casual, or gratuitous, but has been uttered intentionally as the result of some deliberation, manifested by reciprocal bargaining or negotiation. In this view, the requirement of consideration is no mere technicality, historical anachronism, or arbitrary formality. It is an attempt to be as reasonable as we can in deciding which promises constitute contracts. . . .

Consideration, as essential evidence of the parties' intent to create a legal obligation, must be something adopted and regarded by the parties as such. Thus, the same thing may be consideration or not, as it is dealt with by the parties. In substance, a contractual promise must be of the logical form: "If . . . [consideration is given] . . . then I promise that. . . ." Of course, the substance may be expressed in any form of words, but essentially this is the logical structure of those promises enforced by the law as contracts.

Applying these principles to the present case, it appears that although defendant's agent made a promise to plaintiff, it was not in such circumstances that a contract was created. Plaintiff correctly states that an agreement of forbearance to sue may be sufficient consideration for a contract. Plaintiff further contends that his failure to institute suit immediately . . . permits an inference of an agreement to forbear from suit in consideration for defendant's assurance of payment of rents to plaintiff. . . . However, such an inference must rest upon something more than the mere failure to institute immediate suit. The difficulty with plaintiff's case is that there is no more than this. . . .

There is nothing in the evidence to suggest that plaintiff deferred initiating legal action any longer than suited his own personal convenience. There is nothing in the evidence to suggest that defendant sought any forbearance by plaintiff or thought that it was securing such action; nor is there any evidence that plaintiff's delay from the middle of February until April or May in undertaking legal action was related to defendant's promises. There is no evidence that either of the parties took defendant's assurances seriously or acted upon them in any way. There was, therefore, no consideration, and the promises did not amount to a contract. . . .

[Judgment affirmed.]

Wright v. Polk General Hospital

95 Ga.App. 821, 99 S.E.2d 162 (1957)

Wright's brother had been a patient in the Polk General Hospital. When the brother was discharged, the hospital sued Wright on the ground that he had agreed to pay for the medical services furnished his brother. From a judgment for the hospital, Wright appealed.

FELTON, C.J. . . . This action was brought to recover for medical services rendered to the defendant's brother and for which the defendant allegedly agreed to pay. It is contended that after the medical services had been rendered and at the time the brother was discharged from the hospital, the defendant signed a paper whereby he assumed the debt of the brother. This paper contained the brother's personal data and at the bottom contained the following: "Signature of person responsible for this bill. /s/ James O. Wright." Nowhere is there contained in this paper any recited consideration or other agreement by the defendant except his signature following the above quoted phrase. The evidence showed no consideration other than possibly love and affection. A promise to answer for the debt of another must not only be in writing [8] and contain a clear statement of the agreement . . . , but must also be supported by a good and sufficient consideration. Assuming for the sake of argument only that the paper showed a clear agreement on the part of the defendant to answer for the debt of his brother, neither the agreement nor the evidence showed any consideration for such an agreement. No benefit accrued to the defendant, and there was no detriment to the plaintiff. The plaintiff was under the duty to release and discharge the brother whether or not the defendant promised to pay for the medical services rendered to his brother. Love and affection only is not sufficient consideration for a promise to answer for the debt of another. . . .

[Judgment reversed.]

Hofmann v. DeFelice

136 Conn. 187, 70 A.2d 129 (1949)

While Raye DeFelice was a minor, her parents purchased furniture from Hofmann. Some of the furniture was paid for, but a balance was still due when Raye became twenty-one. Hofmann's attorney told her that unless she would agree to pay the balance due of $175, suit would be brought against her parents. She signed an agreement to pay the money. When she failed to do so, suit was brought by Hofmann against her on the agreement. From a judgment in her favor, Hofmann appealed.

DICKENSON, J. . . . The agreement reads as follows: "Agreement. New Haven July 21, 1947. The undersigned, Raye N. DeFelice of 107 Franklin St. in consideration of forbearance of further prosecution of suit against Dominick DeFelice & Mrs. Pauline DeFelice and an extension of time within which to pay, hereby acknowledge owing Hofmann Furniture Store of the sum of $175.00; and hereby agree to pay said sum at the office of Nelson Harris, Attorney, with a payment of 50 cents on the 21 day of July, 1947, and the balance at the

---

[8] See p. 177.

rate of 50 cents weekly until said sum is paid in full. Provided, however, if any of said installment payments shall remain unpaid for a
period of three days after same become payable, the balance shall be
and become due and payable, at once, in the option of said Attorney.
[signed] Raye N. DeFelice."

. . . The trial court's . . . finding that the real consideration was
forbearance to sue the defendant herself is refuted by the contract,
which recites that the consideration was the forbearance of further
prosecution of an action against the defendant's parents and an extension of time in which to pay, and this the defendant is estopped
to deny.

An agreement to forbear to sue in consideration of a written promise by a third person to pay the debt of another constitutes a valid
contract. . . . From the finding now before us, with the necessary
corrections, it appears that the defendant's parents owed the plaintiff
the sum in suit; that is was an existing debt; that the plaintiff demanded
payment of it; and that as a result the defendant signed the forbearance
contract. On these facts, the trial court was in error in ruling that the
contract was invalid. . . .

[Judgment reversed and new trial ordered.]

Warner & Co. v. Brua

33 Ohio App. 84, 168 N.E. 571 (1929)

Warner & Co. procured a purchaser for the property of Brua and submitted to Brua sales papers to be signed. The papers contained a promise
to pay Warner & Co. commissions for finding a purchaser. Brua signed the
paper but later refused to pay Warner & Co. Thereafter Warner & Co.
brought a suit to recover the commissions from Brua who contended that
there was no consideration for his promise. From a judgment for the defendant, the plaintiff appealed.

HAMILTON, J. . . . The law of Ohio requires a promise to pay
commissions for the sale of real estate to be in writing before an action can be maintained therefor. The situation, then, here is that the
parties had performed all the services without any promise in writing,
and then sought at the time of the presentation of the contracts signed
by the purchasers to bring themselves within the law by adding the
promises in writing. The general rule is that past consideration will
not support a promise. After the signing of the promises, plaintiffs
did nothing toward procuring buyers or toward the sale of the property.
All this work had been done prior thereto. The facts bring the case
within the rule laid down in the case of Shields v. Sterrat, 77 N.J. Law,
414, 71 A. 1129, wherein it was held:

"As no service was rendered by the agent after the written agreement was executed, the written contract was nothing more than a

subsequent promise to pay for services already rendered, and [has] no consideration to support it. . . ."

There being no supporting consideration for the written promise to pay commissions, the judgment [for the defendant] will be affirmed.

Mandel v. Liebman
303 N.Y. 88, 100 N.E.2d 149 (1951)

Liebman was an author and entertainment director. He and Mandel executed a contract by which Mandel agreed to act as Liebman's agent and manager. The contract specified that Mandel "shall only devote as much time and attention to the activities and affairs" of Liebman "as the opinion and judgment" of Mandel "deems necessary." Mandel was to receive 10 per cent of the earnings of Liebman during the period of the contract and on contracts made with third persons that continued beyond that five-year period. Mandel sued Liebman for his compensation. From a judgment for Liebman, Mandel appealed first to the Appellate Division and later to the Court of Appeals.

CONWAY, J. . . . The majority in the Appellate Division . . . held that the original contract of May 8, 1946 . . . "was void and unconscionable and against public policy." . . . In reaching that conclusion, the court pointed out that . . . the plaintiff [Mandel] was not required to render any services to defendant [Liebman]. . . .

There might be some force to the claim of unconscionability in the case at bar if the contract could properly be construed as was done by the majority in the Appellate Division. That court held that under the express terms of the contract of May 8, 1946, plaintiff was not required to render any services to defendant. We do not think that that is a permissible construction under our decisions. . . . Here, the contract provided that it is "Mutually agreed by the parties," among other things, that the defendant "hereby employs" the plaintiff "as his personal representative and manager to use his ability and experience as such manager and personal representative in the guidance and furtherance" of defendant's career and "to advise him in connection with all offers of employment and contracts for services, and conclude for him such contracts." Thus, there is a clear implication that plaintiff was required to do that for which he was employed. Even if the contract had merely provided that plaintiff was employed "as personal representative and manager," with no further description of his duties, that would have been sufficient, for it could be shown that to these parties, in a specialized field with its own peculiar customs and usages, that phrase was enough to measure the entire extent of plaintiff's required services. . . .

The further provision in the contract—that plaintiff "shall only devote as much time and attention to the activities and affairs" as plaintiff "deems necessary"—must be given a reasonable interpretation consonant with the purpose of the contract. It would be an unnatural and bizarre construction of the document to hold that that provision was intended to excuse plaintiff from any obligation to render service under the contract, while continuing to reap benefits thereunder. The provision seems merely to constitute an attempt on the part of plaintiff to protect himself from excessive and unreasonable demands upon his time. See Meyers v. Nolan, 18 Cal.App.2d at page 323, 63 P.2d at page 1217, where it was said: "The fact that the contract provided that the managers could devote as much time to defendant's affairs as they deemed necessary does not destroy its mutuality. The very nature of the business of the parties was such that representation of other actors was to be expected. The clause was evidently inserted to avoid any misunderstanding on the subject and to more clearly define the rights and obligations of the managers." Of course, as defendant urges, it is theoretically possible that plaintiff, under this provision, could deem it necessary to devote no time to the activities and affairs of defendant, but in that event, it is clear that plaintiff would not be performing the contract but would be breaching it and foregoing his right to compensation.

Since plaintiff, as we hold, was required to render some service to defendant under the contract, it cannot be said that the contract was unconscionable. Defendant was the best judge of the necessity and worth of plaintiff's services, and of the price he wished to pay to obtain them. In return for plaintiff's contractual obligation to render such services, defendant agreed to pay as compensation an amount based upon a percentage of his earnings. It is not for the court to decide whether defendant made a good or bad bargain. We fail to see how the contract can be described as one "such as no man in his senses . . . would make" . . . or one which would "shock the conscience and confound the judgment of any man of common sense" . . . or even one which is "so extreme as to appear unconscionable according to the mores and business practices of the time and place" . . . particularly since, as we are told, without denial, the contract of May 8, 1946, is similar in most respects to contracts in current and general use in the entertainment industry. . . .

[Judgment reversed and case remanded.]

Marion Production Credit Assn. v. Smith

221 S.C. 172, 69 S.E.2d 705 (1952)

Smith gave the Marion Production Credit Association a promissory note on May 29, 1950, for $9,329.43 due on October 1, 1950, with interest at 5½ per cent. On April 9, 1951, the Association sued Smith on the note claiming a balance of $8,675 and interest from April 2, 1951. Smith raised the defense that on April 2, 1951, he had paid an installment on the note and the interest then due in consideration of the agreement of the Association to extend the note for a number of years. From a judgment for the Association, Smith appealed.

PER CURIAM. . . . The only issue before the Court is whether the allegation in the answer of the appellant that, after the note had become due, he had made payments on the note and had paid the interest to April 2, 1951, and that for this valuable consideration respondent entered into an agreement to extend the date for the payment of the note as hereinabove set out, was any defense to the action.

". . . All jurisdictions are unanimous in holding that an agreement to do that which one is already legally bound to do is not sufficient to support a new contract. The defendant is alleging a new agreement and bases his defense . . . thereon, but it is quite obvious the new agreement he attempts to allege embodies terms and conditions to do that which he is already legally bound to do. . . ."

[Judgment affirmed.]

Leggett v. Vinson

155 Miss. 411, 124 So. 472 (1929)

Vinson entered into a contract with Leggett to construct a building. Vinson found that he could not complete the work at the price fixed in the contract. He claimed that when he informed Leggett to that effect, Leggett agreed to pay him whatever loss he would sustain in completing the building. After completing the building, Vinson sued Leggett for the amount of the loss. From a judgment for the plaintiff, the defendant appealed.

COOK, J. . . . While there is some authority to the contrary, notably from the courts of Massachusetts, Indiana, and Illinois, the great weight of authority seems to establish as the general rule the proposition that a promise to do that which a party is already legally bound to do is not a sufficient consideration to support a promise by the other party to the contract to give the former an additional compensation or benefit, and such promise cannot be legally enforced although the other party had completed his contract in reliance upon it; and with this general rule, prior decisions of this court are in accord. . . .

From the appellee's [contractor's] own testimony, it appears merely that after having spent several weeks in the prosecution of the work which he had contracted to do, he discovered that the completion of the contract would require more money than he had calculated upon and that he had made a losing contract. He admits that at the time the promise of additional compensation was made by the appellant [owner], he was under obligation to complete the building for the contract price of $3,950, and as to the payment in full of this contract, there is no real conflict in the testimony. By this oral contract the appellee assumed no obligations or burdens other than those already imposed by the written contract. . . .

It is undoubtedly true that the parties to a contract may modify it, or waive their rights under it, and ingraft new terms upon it; and in such case the promise of one party will be sufficient consideration for the promise of the other. But where the promise of one is merely a repetition of a subsisting legal promise, and the duties, obligations, and burdens imposed upon such party by the contract are in no way varied, altered, or changed, there is no consideration for the promise of the other. Such is the case made by the appellee's proof, and therefore the alleged promise of appellant was without consideration.

[Judgment for plaintiff reversed.]

Smith v. Smith

340 Ill. 34, 172 N.E. 32 (1930)

Upon the death of their mother, the children of James Smith **gave their** interest in the mother's estate to their father in consideration of his payment of $1.00 to each and of his promise to leave them property on his death. The father died without leaving them the property. The children sued their father's second wife to obtain the property in accordance with the agreement. From a judgment for the plaintiffs, the defendant appealed.

EDMUND, C. . . . Appellant [second wife] attacks the contract on the ground that the consideration was inadequate. It is the general rule that inadequacy of consideration, exorbitance of price, or improvidence in a contract will not, in the absence of fraud, constitute a defense. . . . The present record contains no evidence of fraud. Appellant insists, however, that there was such gross inadequacy of consideration as to show that the contract was unconscionable, and that such a degree of inadequacy calls for setting it aside. . . .

In considering the argument based upon alleged inadequacy of consideration, it is essential to bear in mind the sound suggestion of Story that the value of a thing must depend upon its nature, fluctuating, admitting of no precise standard, "and will depend upon 10,000 different circumstances," and that "if courts of equity were to unravel all these transactions, they would throw everything into confusion and set afloat the contracts of mankind." . . . While there may sometimes be such gross inadequacy of consideration as to vitiate an agreement, such inadequacy must be such as shocks the conscience and amounts, in itself, to conclusive and decisive evidence of fraud in the transaction. . . . The mere fact that one party may have "gotten . . . the best of" a transaction is not conclusive. . . . Making due allowance for the principle that in this class of cases the ordinary rules, . . .

which furnish reasonable safeguards against fraud, should be rigidly applied . . . , it must be said that there is here no such degree of inadequacy of consideration as to warrant us in saying that the agreement was unconscionable. . . .

[Judgment for plaintiffs affirmed.]

Drennan v. Star Paving Co.

51 Cal.2d 409, 333 P.2d 757 (1958)

Drennan was a general contractor preparing a bid for the construction of a school building. He obtained bids by telephone from subcontractors for various phases of the work. Star Paving gave the low bid for the paving work, the Drennan used it in computing his bid. Drennan's bid for the school construction was the lowest, and he was awarded the contract. The next morning Drennan went to Star's office to notify it that its paving bid was accepted. Before Drennan could make any statement, Star declared that its bid was a mistake and that it required more than double the amount quoted to do the work. Drennan insisted that Star live up to the terms of the bid and sued it for breach of contract when it failed to do so. From a judgment for Drennan, Star appealed.

TRAYNOR, J. . . . Defendant contends that there was no enforceable contract between the parties on the ground that it made a revocable offer and revoked it before plaintiff communicated his acceptance to defendant. . . .

Plaintiff contends, however, that he relied to his detriment on defendant's offer and that defendant must therefore answer in damages for its refusal to perform. Thus the question is squarely presented: Did plaintiff's reliance make defendant's offer irrevocable?

Section 90 of the Restatement of Contracts states: "A promise which the promisor should reasonably expect to induce action or forbearance of a definite and substantial character on the part of the promisee and which does induce such action or forbearance is binding if injustice can be avoided only by enforcement of the promise."

The very purpose of section 90 is to make a promise binding even though there was no consideration "in the sense of something that is bargained for and given in exchange." . . . Reasonable reliance serves to hold the offeror in lieu of the consideration ordinarily required to make the offer binding. In a case involving similar facts the Supreme Court of South Dakota stated that "we believe that reason and justice demand that the doctrine [of section 90] be applied to the present facts. We cannot believe that by accepting this doctrine as controlling in the state of facts before us we will abolish the requirement of a consideration in contract cases, in any different sense than an ordinary estoppel abolishes some legal requirement in its application. We are of the opinion, therefore, that the defendants in executing the agreement [which was not supported by consideration] made a promise which they should have reasonably expected would induce the plaintiff to submit a bid based thereon to the Government, that such promise did induce this action, and that injustice can be avoided only by enforcement of the promise." . . .

When plaintiff used defendant's offer in computing his own bid, he bound himself to perform in reliance on defendant's terms. Though defendant did not bargain for this use of its bid neither did defendant make it idly, indifferent to whether it would be used or not. On the contrary it is reasonable to suppose that defendant submitted its bid to obtain the subcontract. It was bound to realize the substantial possibility that its bid would be the lowest, and that it would be included by plaintiff in his bid. It was to its own interest that the contractor be awarded the general contract; the lower the subcontract bid, the lower the general contractor's bid was likely to be and the greater its chance of acceptance and hence the greater defendant's chance of getting the paving subcontract. Defendant had reason not only to expect plaintiff to rely on its bid but to want him to. Clearly defendant had a stake in plaintiff's reliance on its bid. Given this interest and the fact that plaintiff is bound by his own bid, it is only fair that plaintiff should have at least an opportunity to accept defendant's bid after the general contract has been awarded to him. . . .

In the present case plaintiff promptly informed defendant that plaintiff was being awarded the job and that the subcontract was being awarded to defendant.

Defendant contends, however, that its bid was the result of mistake and that it was therefore entitled to revoke it. . . . Of course, if plaintiff had reason to believe that defendant's bid was in error, he could not justifiably rely on it, and section 90 would afford no basis for enforcing it. . . . Plaintiff, however, had no reason to know that defendant had made a mistake in submitting its bid, since there was usually a variance of 160 per cent between the highest and lowest bids for paving. . . . He committed himself to performing the main contract in reliance on defendant's figures. Under these circumstances defendant's mistake, far from relieving it of its obligation, constitutes an additional reason for enforcing it, for it misled plaintiff as to the cost of doing the paving. . . . It presented its bid with knowledge of the substantial possibility that it would be used by plaintiff; it could foresee the harm that would ensue from an erroneous underestimate of the cost. Moreover, it was motivated by its own business interest. . . . These considerations . . . are persuasive that defendant's mistake should not defeat recovery under the rule of section 90 of the Restatement of Contracts. As between the subcontractor who made the bid and the general contractor who reasonably relied on it, the loss resulting from the mistake should fall on the party who caused it.

Leo F. Piazza Paving Co. v. Bebek & Brkich, 141 Cal.App.2d 226, 296 P.2d 368, 371, [is] . . . not to the contrary. In the Piazza case the court sustained a finding that defendants intended, not to make a firm bid, but only to give the plaintiff "some kind of an idea to use" in making its bid; there was evidence that the defendants had told plaintiff they were unsure of the significance of the specifications. There was thus no offer, promise, or representation on which the defendants should reasonably have expected the plaintiff to rely. . . .

[Judgment affirmed.]

Questions and Case Problems

1. What is the objective of each of the following rules of law?
   (a) An executed gift or a performance that has been rendered without consideration cannot be rescinded for lack of consideration.
   (b) In the absence of fraud, the adequacy of consideration is usually immaterial.

2. Mangus and Present were both real estate brokers. Mangus was trying to sell certain houses for his customers who had listed the properties with him for sale. Mangus made a contract with Present that if Present produced a purchaser for any of these properties, Mangus and Present would divide the commissions on the sale. Present produced a purchaser and received commissions from his customer but refused to divide them with Mangus. Mangus then sued Present for breach of contract. The latter raised the defense that there was no consideration for the promise to divide the commissions since Mangus did not have the exclusive agency to sell the real estate in question, which therefore could have been sold by the owner or any other agent, in which case Mangus would not have been entitled to any commissions. Decide. (Mangus v. Present, [Fla.] 135 So.2d 417)

3. The Association of Army and Navy Stores gave a price discount to customer members of the association. The association agreed to list Young's Store as a member store, and Young agreed to pay the association a percentage of the sales made at its store to association customer members plus a fixed monthly charge of $2.50. No new customers purchased at Young's Store. He refused to pay the association the monthly charge on the grounds that the consideration for the contract had failed. Decide. (Association of Army and Navy Stores v. Young, 296 Ky. 61, 176 S.W.2d 136)

4. Irene Dewein studied nursing. She did not entre that profession, however, but went to live with and take care of her parents. This she did for 27 years, during which time the father was invalided until his death in 1948. In 1957 the mother died after being frequently bedridden for a period of 2 years. In October, 1956, Irene's brother Edward had said to her, "Sis, I am so grateful you are taking care of mother, and I am certainly going to see you are taken care of for life. You deserve it. Don't worry about the future. I am going to see you are taken care of." The brother died in 1959 without having made any provision in his will for Irene. She

sued his estate for the value of her services for 27 years. Decide. (Dewein v. Dewein's Executors, 30 Ill.App.2d 446, 174 N.E.2d 875)

5. Cobb was appointed a deputy prosecuting attorney under an agreement with the prosecuting attorney, Scoggins, that Cobb would be paid more compensation than was provided by law. Cobb served as a deputy for some time. He was later discharged and then sued Scoggins to enforce the agreement. Was Cobb entitled to judgment? (Cobb v. Scoggins, 85 Ark. 106, 107 S.W.2d 188)

6. When Helen Suske sued John Straka on a promissory note that he had given her, he raised the defense that his note was a gift and that he had not received any consideration for it. She claimed that at the time John was obligated to her in several ways and that such obligations constituted consideration. It was claimed that he had promised to marry the plaintiff, that he owed the plaintiff for room rent and money loaned to him, and that he had caused her some inconvenience. Was the note binding? (Suske v. Straka, 229 Minn. 408, 39 N.W.2d 745)

7. Waters was induced by fraud to enter into an agreement with White. Upon learning of the false representations, Waters determined to repudiate the transaction. When White's wife learned of the intention of Waters, she signed a note in consideration that Waters would forbear exercising his right to rescind the agreement with her husband. Was the forbearance on the part of Waters a valid consideration for the promise of the wife? (Waters v. White, 75 Conn. 88, 52 A. 401)

8. Tappan gave Friedman a writing which stated that Tappan offered to sell Friedman "certain lots" in the borough at the rate of $400 an acre. The writing provided that Friedman was to pay the cost of preparing the description of any real estate to be conveyed. After receiving this writing, Friedman requested a title company to examine the records to determine what land Tappan owned in the borough. A few days later Tappan notified Friedman that he would not go through with the agreement. Friedman did not tell the title company to stop its examination and later sued Tappan for specific performance. He claimed that since he had gone to the expense of having the title company make its search, Tappan was estopped to deny that there was a binding contract. Decide. (Friedman v. Tappan Development Corp., 22 N.J. 523, 126 A.2d 646)

9. Schwerdt promised in writing to pay $1.50 a week as his share in the support of his father. Schwerdt then broke his promise, and the father brought an action against him to recover damages. Decide. (Schwerdt v. Schwerdt, 235 Ill. 386, 85 N.E. 613)

10. Saxon executed a written contract by which he promised to teach all pupils that Goff of the Arts Club assigned to him for instruction. By the same contract, Goff agreed to assign to Saxon for instruction such students as Goff desired. Thereafter Goff brought an action against Saxon to enforce the promise that he had made. Was she entitled to judgment? (Goff v. Saxon, 174 Ky. 331, 92 S.W. 24)

CHAPTER 9

Legality of Contract

A contract is illegal when, under the common law or statute, either the formation or the performance of the agreement is deemed a crime or a tort, or is opposed to public policy or interest. Ordinarily an illegal contract is void.

Sec. 9-A. Effect of Illegal Contracts. When a contract is illegal, the parties are usually regarded as being beyond the pale of the courts and not entitled to their aid. If the illegal contract has not been performed, neither party can sue the other to obtain performance or damages. If the contract has been performed, neither party can sue the other for damages or to set the contract aside.

There are the following exceptions to the rule that the court will not aid the parties to an unlawful contract:

(1) When the law which the agreement violates is intended for the protection of one of the parties, that party may seek relief. For example, when in order to protect the public the law forbids the issuance of securities or notes by certain classes of corporations, a person who has purchased them may recover his money.

(2) When the parties are not equally guilty or, as it is said, are not *in pari delicto*, the one less guilty is granted relief when public interest is advanced by so doing. This rule is applied to illegal agreements that are induced by undue influence, duress, or fraud.

(3) Another exception exists in most states when a consideration has been paid for an illegal act that has not been performed. Thus, a person who had placed money with a stakeholder for the purpose of swindling another by a pretended race was allowed to recover when he repudiated the agreement and requested his money before the race was scheduled to be run.

(4) An exception may also exist when the illegality is collateral or incidental, as when one of the parties has not obtained a government

135

permit or license to perform the contract. (See p. 144, Meissner v. Caravello)

Sec. 9-B. Partial Illegality. An agreement may involve the performance of several promises, some of which are illegal and some legal. The legal parts of the agreement may be enforced, provided that they can be separated from the parts which are illegal. The same rule applies when the consideration is illegal in part. The rule is not applied, however, to situations in which the illegal act or consideration is said to taint and strike down the entire agreement.

When there is an indivisible promise to perform several acts, some of which are illegal, the agreement is void. Also when there is a single promise to do a legal act, supported by several considerations, some of which are illegal, the agreement cannot be enforced.

If a contract is susceptible of two interpretations, one legal and the other illegal, the court will assume that the legal meaning was intended unless the contrary is clearly indicated.

Sec. 9-C. Crimes and Civil Wrongs. A contract or agreement is illegal and therefore void when it calls for the commission of any act that constitutes a crime. To illustrate, one cannot enforce a contract by which the other party agrees to commit an assault, to steal property, to burn a house, to print a libelous article, or to kill a person.

An agreement that calls for the commission of a civil wrong is also illegal and void. Examples are agreements to damage the goods of another, to slander a third person, to defraud another, or to infringe another's patent, trade-mark, or copyright. Thus, an agreement for *A's* orchestra to use the name of *B*, a skilled musician, is illegal as a fraud upon the public when *B* is not actually to appear with the orchestra. The use of his name would give the impression that the orchestra was conducted by him.

Sec. 9-D. Contracts Injuring Public Service. Any contract that tends to interfere with the proper performance of the duties of a public officer, whether legislative, administrative, or judicial, is contrary to public policy and void. Thus an agreement to procure the award of a public contract by corrupt means is not enforceable. Other examples are agreements to sell public offices, to procure pardons by corrupt means, or to pay a public officer more or less than his legal fees or salary. (See p. 146, Goodrich Case)

One of the most common contracts within this class is the *illegal lobbying contract*. This term is used to describe a contract by which one party agrees to use bribery, threats of a loss of votes, or any other improper means to procure or prevent the adoption of particular legislation by a lawmaking body, such as Congress or a state legislature. Such agreements are clearly contrary to the public interest since they interfere with the workings of the democratic process. They are accordingly illegal and void.

Some courts hold illegal all agreements to influence legislation, regardless of the means contemplated or employed. Other courts adopt the better rule that such agreements are valid in the absence of the use of improper influence or the contemplation of using such influence. According to the latter courts, since an individual has the right to state his cause to the lawmaker in the hope of influencing his action, it is perfectly proper for the individual to retain and pay an agent or attorney to present his case to the lawmaker. So long as no improper inducement or threat is to be made to the lawmaker and the agent is to confine himself to stating the facts of the case, leaving it to the free will of the lawmaker to decide for himself, no illegality is present.

Sec. 9-E. Contracts Obstructing Legal Processes. Any agreement intended to obstruct or pervert legal processes is contrary to public interest and therefore void. Contracts that promise to pay money in return for the abandonment of the prosecution of a criminal case, for the suppression of evidence in any legal proceeding, for the stirring up of litigation, or for the perpetration of any fraud upon the court are therefore void.

An agreement to pay an ordinary witness more than the regular witness fee allowed by law or a promise to pay him a greater amount if the promisor wins the lawsuit is void. The danger here it that the witness will lie in order to help his party win the case, resulting in perjury and the miscarriage of justice.

Contracts providing for the arbitration of disputes are generally recognized as valid by modern decisions and statutes. Earlier cases held them void as interfering with the jurisdiction of the courts.

Sec. 9-F. Usury. A person is guilty of *usury* when he makes a loan of money that is to be paid unconditionally and he specifies a rate of interest which is greater than allowed by statute. In determining whether a transaction is usurious, the court will look through the form of the transaction to determine whether there is in fact a loan on which excessive interest is charged.

Most states prohibit by statute the taking of more than a stated annual rate of interest. These statutes provide a *maximum contract rate* of interest—usually 6, 8, or 10 per cent, which is the highest annual rate that can be exacted or demanded under the law of a given state. It is usually recoverable only when there is an agreement in writing to pay that amount.

All states provide for a legal rate of interest. When there is an agreement for interest to be paid but no rate is specified or when the law implies a duty to pay interest, as on judgments, the *legal rate* is applied. In all but ten states the legal rate of interest is 6 per cent

Contract and Legal Rates of Interest

STATES AND TERRITORIES	MAXIMUM CONTRACT RATE PER CENT	LEGAL RATE PER CENT	STATES AND TERRITORIES	MAXIMUM CONTRACT RATE PER CENT	LEGAL RATE PER CENT
Alabama	8	6	Montana	10	6
Alaska	8	6	Nebraska	9	6
Arizona	8	6	Nevada	12	7
Arkansas	10	6	New Hampshire	Any rate	6
California	10	7	New Jersey	6	6
Colorado	Any rate ᵃ	6	New Mexico	10 ᵇ	6
Connecticut	12	6	New York	6	6
Delaware	6	6	North Carolina	6	6
D. of Columbia	8	6	North Dakota	7	4
Florida	10	6	Ohio	8	6
Georgia	8	7	Oklahoma	10	6
Hawaii	12	6	Oregon	10	6
Idaho	8	6	Pennsylvania	6	6
Illinois	7	5	Puerto Rico	9 ᶜ	6
Indiana	8	6	Rhode Island	30	6
Iowa	7	5	South Carolina	7	6
Kansas	10	6	South Dakota	8	6
Kentucky	6	6	Tennessee	6	6
Louisiana	8	5	Texas	10	6
Maine	Any rate	6	Utah	10	6
Maryland	6	6	Vermont	6	6
Massachusetts	Any rate	6	Virginia	6	6
Michigan	7	5	Washington	12	6
Minnesota	8	6	West Virginia	6	6
Mississippi	8	6	Wisconsin	10	5
Missouri	8	6	Wyoming	10	7

ᵃ When any rate is permitted for contracts, there usually is a limit for a small loan of approximately $300 or less, although this limit may be as high as 3 per cent a month.
ᵇ When a loan is not secured by collateral, the contract rate may be 12 per cent.
ᶜ When the amount is more than $3,000, the maximum contract rate is 8 per cent.

per year. In some states the maximum contract rate is the same as the legal rate of interest.

If the maximum contract rate of interest is specified for a short-term loan (not exceeding a year), the collection of the interest in advance as a discount from the nominal amount of the loan does not constitute usury even though the amount of interest collected represents a rate of interest in excess of that permitted by law. The usury statutes do not apply, either, to contracts that provide for the payment of the annual interest charge at the maximum rate in several installments, such as quarterly or monthly, even though collection of the interest in this manner benefits the creditor more than the collection of the total interest in one amount at the end of the year.

Usually state statutes permit small loan associations, pawnbrokers, and similar licensed money lenders to charge a higher rate of interest than is permissible in ordinary business transactions on the theory that a much greater risk is involved.[1]

The effect of an agreement that violates the usury laws differs in the various states. In some states the entire amount of interest is forfeited. In other states, the recovery of the excess only is denied. In still others, the agreement is held to be void. If the interest has been paid, the states differ as to whether the borrower recovers merely the amount of the interest paid or whether he recovers two or three times that amount as a penalty.

Usury statutes generally do not apply to sales made on credit, such as installment sales. In some states corporations are prohibited from raising the defense of usury. If a loan is nominally made to a corporation, however, in order to bar the defense of usury, it may be shown that the loan was actually made to an individual who may then raise the defense of usury.

Sec. 9-G. Wagers and Lotteries. Largely as a result of the adoption of antigambling statutes, wagers or bets are generally illegal. Lotteries containing the three main elements of prize, chance, and consideration, or similar affairs of chance, also are generally held illegal. Raffles are usually regarded as lotteries. Sales promotion schemes calling for the distribution of property according to chance among the purchasers of goods are held illegal as lotteries, without regard to whether the scheme is given the name of a guessing contest, raffle, or gift. (See p. 147, Jasper v. Rossman)

Sec. 9-H. Transactions in Futures. A person may contract to deliver in the future goods which he does not own at the time he makes the agreement. The fact that the seller does not have the goods at the time the contract is made, or that he intends to obtain securities by buying them on margin rather than paying cash in full, does not affect the legality of the transaction. If, however, the parties to the sale and purchase intend that delivery shall not be made but merely that one party shall pay the other the difference between the contract price and market price on the date set for delivery, the transaction is a gambling contract or a wager upon the future market price and the

---

[1] Small loan statutes have been adopted in Alabama, Alaska, Arizona, California, Colorado, Connecticut, Florida, District of Columbia, Georgia, Illinois, Indiana, Iowa, Kansas, Kentucky, Louisiana, Maine, Maryland, Massachusetts, Michigan, Minnesota, Missouri, Nebraska, New Hampshire, New Jersey, New Mexico, New York, Ohio, Oklahoma, Oregon, Pennsylvania, Rhode Island, South Dakota, Tennessee, Utah, Vermont, Virginia, Washington, West Virginia, Wisconsin.

contract is void and illegal. Generally, an undisclosed intention of either party or both parties that actual delivery should not be made does not affect the validity of the transaction. Furthermore, it is the intent at the time of the making of the contract which governs. Accordingly, a contract is not rendered illegal because after its formation the parties agree that instead of making actual delivery a payment representing the market price differential shall be made.

Transactions calling for the future purchase or delivery of commodities such as wheat, corn, and soybeans, through organized commodity exchanges, provide a valuable means by which a dealer or manufacturer can protect himself from future price fluctuations. This is *hedging*. By means of this device the manufacturer or dealer who buys one of these commodities (wheat, for example) for the purpose of processing it and selling the product (flour) makes a simultaneous speculative contract to sell the same quantity of the commodity (wheat) at a future date when the processed product (flour) will be ready for sale. Any change in price that will cause a loss on one transaction is offset by a gain on the other transaction.

Sec. 9-I. Sunday Laws. Under the English common law, an agreement or contract could be executed on any day of the week. Today, however, most states have statutes that prohibit to some extent the making or performance of contracts on Sunday. The terms of the statutes vary greatly from state to state. The statutes may expressly declare agreements void if they are made on Sunday or if they call for performance on Sunday. They may prohibit only "servile" or manual labor, prohibit "worldly employment," or prohibit labor or business of one's "ordinary calling." Under a provision of the last type, one could legally enter into an agreement to do work outside of his regular calling.

Sunday laws expressly provide that they do not apply to works of charity or necessity. *Works of charity* include those acts that are involved in religious worship or in aiding persons in distress. In general a *work of necessity* is an act which must be done at that time in order to be effective in saving life, health, or property.

When an offer is made on Sunday but the acceptance is not made until the next day, the agreement is valid because in law it is made on the weekday when it is accepted. If a contract is made on Sunday, some courts hold that it can be ratified on another day. Other courts, however, hold the contrary on the ground that the contract was illegal when made, and an illegal contract or transaction cannot be ratified.

Sec. 9-J. Licensed Callings or Dealings. Statutes frequently require that a person obtain a license, certificate, or diploma before he can practice certain professions, such as law or medicine, or carry on a particular business or trade, such as that of a real-estate broker, peddler, stockbroker, hotelkeeper, or pawnbroker. If the requirement is imposed to protect the public from unqualified persons, a contract to engage in such a profession or business without having obtained the necessary license or certificate is void. Thus a contract with an unlicensed physician for services cannot be enforced by him.

On the other hand, a license may be imposed solely as a revenue measure by requiring the payment of a fee for the license. In that event an agreement made by one not licensed in violation of the statute is generally held valid. The contract may also sometimes be held valid when it is shown that no harm has resulted from the failure to obtain a permit to do the work contemplated by the particular contract.

It is likewise frequently held that the absence of a license cannot be raised as to transactions between persons who should all be licensed, such as dealers, when the purpose of the license requirement is not to protect such persons as against each other but to protect the public generally against such persons. (See p. 148, Fomco, Inc. v. Joe Maggio, Inc.)

Sec. 9-K. Regulation of Business. Local, state, and national laws regulate a wide variety of business activities and practices. A businessman violating such regulations may under some statutes be subject to a fine or criminal prosecution, or under others to an order to cease and desist entered by the administrative agency or commission.

Whether a contract made in connection with business conducted in violation of the law is binding or void depends upon how strongly opposed the public policy is to the prohibited act. Some courts take the view that the contract is not void unless the statute expressly so specifies. In some instances, as in the case of the failure to register a fictitious name under which the business is done, the statute expressly preserves the validity of the contract by permitting the violator to sue on a contract made while illegally conducting business after his name is registered as required by the statute.

Sec. 9-L. Fraudulent Sales. Statutes commonly regulate the sale of certain commodities. Scales and measures of grocers and other vendors must be checked periodically, and they must be approved and sealed by the proper official. Certain articles must be inspected before they are sold. Others must be labeled in a particular way to show their contents and to warn the public of the presence of any dangerous or poisonous substance. Since the laws are generally designed for the protection of the public, transactions in violation of such laws are void.

When the aim of the law is to raise revenue by requiring the payment of a fee, the violation merely makes the wrongdoer liable for the penalty imposed by the law but does not make the transaction void. The fact that a fee must be paid under the statute does not by itself determine that the statute is a revenue measure. The fee may be imposed to defray the expenses of administration, in which case the character of the law as designed to protect the public is not affected.

Sec. 9-M. Contracts in Restraint of Trade. A contract that unreasonably restrains trade is illegal and void on the ground that it is contrary to public policy. Such agreements take many forms, such as a combination to create a monopoly or to obtain a corner on the market, or an association of merchants to increase prices. In addition to the illegality of the contract based on general principles of law, statutes frequently declare monopolies illegal and subject the parties to such agreements to various civil and criminal penalties.[2] In some instances, however, the law expressly authorizes combined action.

(1) Agreements Not to Compete. When a going business is sold, it is commonly stated in the contract that the seller shall not go into the same or a similar business again within a certain geographical area, or for a certain period of time, or both. In early times, such agreements were held void since they deprived the public of the service of the person who agreed not to compete, impaired the latter's means of earning a livelihood, reduced competition, and exposed the public to monopoly. Gradually the law began to recognize the validity of some restrictive provisions. At first the courts held valid an agreement not to compete when there was a limitation on the time the restriction was to remain in effect or the area in which it was to operate. To the modern courts, the question is whether under the circumstances the restriction imposed upon one party is reasonable or whether the restriction is more severe than is required to protect the other party. If the restriction is reasonable, it is valid.

A similar problem arises when an employee agrees with his employer that he will not compete with the employer should he leave his employment. The courts recognize that business and professional men would be reluctant to employ and instruct assistants unless they could require such employees to refrain from competing with them after learning the details and secrets of their business. Restrictions to prevent such competition are held valid when reasonable and necessary to protect the interest of the employer. (See p. 149, Mutual Loan Co. v. Pierce)

---

2 *Sherman Antitrust Act*, 15 USC, Secs. 1-7; *Clayton Act*, 15 USC, Secs. 12-27; *Federal Trade Commission Act*, 15 USC, Secs. 41 to 58.

(2) Resale Price Maintenance Agreements. Under antitrust legislation, an agreement between a manufacturer and distributor or between distributor and dealer that the latter should not resell below a specified minimum price was void. Congress and virtually all of the states have adopted statutes, called *fair trade acts,* which change this rule and sustain the validity of such agreements when they relate to trade-mark or brand-name articles.[3]

The theory of such laws is that it is reasonable and desirable to prevent a party from reselling in the course of regular business an established article at too low a price because such sales may harm the reputation or market established by the manufacturer or distributor of the article. If the article is not a trade-mark or brand-name article, an agreement against price cutting on resale is illegal as a restraint on trade in violation of the antitrust laws.

The federal statute and most state laws apply not only to the parties to the price maintenance agreement but also to anyone having knowledge of the agreement who thereafter in the course of regular business resells the article under its trade name or mark.[4]

Sec. 9-N. Illegality in Performing Contract. When a contract is otherwise legal, the fact that one of the parties in performing his part of the contract commits illegal acts not contemplated by the other party does not ordinarily prevent the wrongdoer from recovering on the contract. In some instances the wrong may be regarded as so serious that the wrongdoer is punished by denying him the right to recover on the contract which he has performed. (See p. 151, McConnell v. Commonwealth Pictures Corp.)

Sec. 9-O. Statutory Regulation of Contracts. In order to establish uniformity or to protect one of the parties to a contract, statutes frequently provide that contracts of a given class must follow a statutory model or must contain specified provisions. For example, statutes commonly specify that particular clauses must be included in insurance policies in order to protect the persons insured and their beneficiaries.

---

[3] Such laws have been adopted in substantially all of the states and the District of Columbia. The state acts apply only to intrastate sales. The federal statute applies to interstate sales and permits resale price maintenance agreements when such agreements are lawful in the state in which the goods are to be resold or into which they are to be sent.

[4] *Miller-Tydings Act,* 50 Stat. 693, 15 USC Sec. 1; *McGuire Act,* 66 Stat. 632, 15 USC, Sec. 45. It is commonly provided that the parties to such a contract may recover damages from third persons who sell the article below the agreement price or may obtain an injunction to compel the observance of that price. About one third of the state courts have held unconstitutional the provisions of the state laws binding nonsigners. *Olin Mathieson Chemical Corp.* v. *Francis,* 134 Colo. 160, 301 P.2d 139; *Shakespeare Co.* v. *Lippman's Tool Shop Sporting Goods Co.,* 334 Mich. 109, 54 N.W.2d 268.

In a majority of states the problem of price cutting is also regulated by statutes prohibiting resale below cost when the purpose is to injure competitors.

Others require that contracts executed in connection with credit buying
and loans contain particular provisions designed to protect the debtor,
as by specifying that he may pay off his debt at an earlier date or buy
back the property that has been used as security within a specified
period. Motor-vehicle-financing statutes commonly specify that an
installment sale contract must contain the cash price, the down payment, the trade-in value if any, the cash balance, the insurance costs,
the finance charges, the amount and time of installments, and similar
details of the transaction.

Noncompliance with the statutory requirements may in some instances make the entire contract void; while in others the contract
will be enforced as though it did not contain the improper or illegal
clauses but did contain the provisions required by the statute.

Cases for Chapter 9

Meissner v. Caravello

4 Ill.App.2d 428, 124 N.E.2d 615 (1955)

The Ilice Construction Company made masonry alterations to a building occupied by Caravello as tenant and owned by Rose. A city ordinance
required that anyone making such alterations must first obtain a building
license. Ilice had not obtained a license. Caravello and Rose refused to
pay Ilice for the work. Ilice joined in an action brought by Meissner,
another contractor, to enforce a mechanic's lien against the property. No
claim was made that the work as done by Ilice did not satisfy the requirements of the building code, and Ilice obtained a permit for the past work
after the action had been brought on the mechanic's lien. From a judgment against it, Ilice appealed.

FRIEND, J. . . . In their motion . . . defendants contended that plaintiff's failure to obtain a building permit before commencement of the
improvement made illegal the contract under which the work was
performed, and consequently barred plaintiff from enforcing its claim
for mechanic's lien. It may be conceded that a valid contract is one
of the prerequisites for the mechanic's lien, but it does not follow
that plaintiff's contract in the instant proceeding was illegal because
a building permit had not been issued before the work was commenced.
The contract itself contained no trace or suggestion of illegality. . . .

"In general, unless a bargain necessarily contemplates an illegal
act, it is not unenforceable; and if it is later performed in a way that
involves some slight violation of law, not seriously injurious to the
public order, the person performing may recover on his bargain. This
principle may be stated more broadly: 'Where a bargain does not in
terms necessarily involve a violation of law, the fact the plaintiff performs it in a way not allowed by law, does not preclude recovery, if
not seriously injurious to the public order.' " . . . ". . . Where a con-

tract could have been performed in a legal manner as well as in an illegal manner, it will not be declared void because it may have been performed in an illegal manner, since bad motives are never to be imputed to any man where fair and honest intentions are sufficient to account for his conduct. The rule has been stated to be that if an agreement can by its terms be performed lawfully, it will be treated as legal, even if performed in an illegal manner. . . ." "The laws and the public policy of the state permit and require the utmost freedom of contracting between competent parties, and it is only when a contract expressly contravenes the law or the known public policy of the state that courts will hold it void." In the instant case the contract did not provide for or require the violation of any law and was therefore not an illegal contract.

The provisions of the City of Chicago ordinances . . . do not prevent recovery in the event a permit is not first obtained, but exact penalties for their violation. We construe the ordinances to mean that penalties may be exacted in case of violation, but there are no prohibitory words indicating that a party is precluded from recovering on the contract. The ordinances were presumably enacted in order to give the building department an opportunity to deny a permit for valid reasons, but if the work has been done safely and lawfully, no harm has been done. . . .

. . . [In] Bairstow v. Northwestern University, 287 Ill.App. 424, 5 N.E.2d 269, . . . a mechanic's lien was denied for excavation work and removal of trees done without having obtained a building permit, as required by the ordinances of the City of Evanston. It appears from the opinion that the building which was to be constructed violated the zoning provisions of the municipality. Two parcels of land were involved in that case. The building to be erected on one of the parcels complied with the zoning law, the building to be erected on the other did not. A building permit was obtained for the former but not for the latter, and it was for the latter that the mechanic's lien was denied. It thus appears that a building permit could not have been obtained because the contemplated structure failed to meet the zoning requirements, but this is not true in the case at bar. There is nothing to suggest that a building permit could not have been obtained, or that the work was in violation of the building code; and in fact, after the improvements had been completed, and when plaintiff first obtained knowledge that a building permit had not been obtained, it made application for, and was given, one. Hence, in the present case the work done was not in violation of any law, whereas in the Bairstow case the failure to obtain a building permit was integrally connected with the illegality of the construction which was in violation of the zoning ordinance. . . .

[Judgment reversed and case remanded.]

Goodrich v. Northwestern Telephone Exchange Co.

161 Minn. 106, 201 N.W. 290 (1924)

Goodrich and seventeen other persons, including the mayor of Anoka, Minnesota, and three members of the city council, which was composed of six members and the mayor, entered into an agreement with the Northwestern Telephone Exchange Company by which, in return for the charging of certain rates by Northwestern, Goodrich and the others promised to use their influence to prevent the Tri-State Telephone Company from obtaining any concessions in the city. Goodrich brought a suit for an injunction to restrain the Northwestern Telephone Company from raising the agreed rates. From a judgment for the plaintiff, the defendant appealed.

WILSON, C.J. . . . The restrictions upon the council under consideration, placed there by a majority of its members, and the agreement by private citizens to use their influence upon the existing and future councils introduce elements into the transaction that do not have the approval of public policy. . . .

Persons with these secret agreements in mind, and relying upon them for their gain, do not act toward the public and third persons as they would without them. Whatever tends to divert the attention of the councilmen from their judgment, or to substitute other motives for their conduct, or subject them to follow sinister and secretive motives, must necessarily tend to impair the integrity of official conduct. But such agreements are so contrary to the principles of American government and our jurisprudence, and so fraught with temptation, that they should be condemned at every appearance. The law closes the door to temptation by refusing recognition to any such contracts, regardless of purity of motive. Private citizens, much less public officials, cannot sell their personal influence over a city council; and public officials cannot bargain away their future judgment and discretion upon matters of public concern. Such contracts are contrary to sound public policy and void. Obviously they lead to inefficiency in the public service. In the instant case, not only was competition completely stifled, but it was in fact put to death. These men, in their zeal to give service to their community, doubtless acted in the best motives; but if a rule is established that will permit an act of such character to stand, it will also let others stand which are inspired by a different motive. . . .

In fact, the prevailing rule is that such agreements are illegal, and the conclusions have not been reached upon the theory that improper influences were to be used, but upon the corrupting tendency of such agreements. "The law meets the suggestion of evil, and strikes down the contract from its inception." Such agreements are not consistent with good morals. Straw should be kept away from fire. In other words, the best punishment is to prevent the wrong. The law guards against the incidental temptation that must necessarily accompany such agreements. . . .

Of course, the individual has the right to approach legislative bodies, and by petition, by legitimate argument, and by a fair showing of the circumstances [to] appeal to the judgment and reason of the legislative officials for or against any proposed measure. But this is not that case. We hold the contract void as contrary to public policy.

[Judgment for plaintiff reversed.] *preventing competition or restrain trade*

Jasper v. Rossman
73 S.D. 222, 41 N.W.2d 310 (1950)

Jasper sued to recover the purchase price of punch boards that he had sold to Rossman. The defendant claimed that the contract could not be enforced because the punch boards were gambling devices and that the contract was therefore void as against public policy. Judgment was entered for the defendant. The plaintiff appealed.

ROBERT, J. . . . Section 25, Article III of the State Constitution, provides: "The legislature shall not authorize any game of chance, lottery, or gift enterprise, under any pretense, or for any purpose whatever.". . .

As defined by the [legislature], a lottery is "any scheme for the disposal or distribution of property by chance, directly or indirectly, among persons who have paid or promised to pay any valuable consideration for the chance of obtaining such property, or a portion of it, or for any share of, or interest in such property, upon any agreement, understanding, or expectation that it is to be distributed or disposed of by lot or chance, whether called a lottery, a raffle, a gift enterprise, or by whatever name the same may be known."

. . . "Every lottery is unlawful and a public nuisance.". . . It is an offense to maintain and carry on lotteries and . . . "all property offered for sale or distribution in violation of the statutes relating to lotteries is forfeited to the people of this state as well as before as after the determination of the chance on which the same are dependent."

It is asserted that defendant did not purchase the articles in question for the purpose of using them but for resale, and that it follows that without participation or interest in an illegal act, the validity of the sale and the right to recover the price of the punch boards were not affected.

There have been many decisions to the effect that, where the sale is of an article that may or may not be used for an illegal purpose, it is no defense to an action to recover the price that the seller knew of the purpose of the buyer to devote it to the commission of a minor offense, without some further evidence implicating the seller.

The case before us rests upon different facts. . . . Hatton v. Casey, 93 Ind.App. 336, 178 N.E. 303, is an analogous case. The seller of punch boards brought the action to recover their price. The court held that the only practical use to which these articles could be put was to conduct a game of chance and that the seller could not recover. . . . True, the sale of punch boards in this state is not expressly prohibited, but their use for selling of chances to win money or prizes is unlawful. The ordinary use, if not the only use of the punch boards sold by plaintiff, was for gaming or lottery purposes; and for these reasons plaintiff cannot maintain this action.

[Judgment for defendant affirmed.]

Fomco, Inc. v. Joe Maggio, Inc.
8 Cal.Rep. 459, 356 P.2d 203 (1960)

Fomco, Inc. and Joe Maggio, Inc. were both in the business of growing, harvesting, and marketing carrots. Fomco made a contract with Maggio to harvest carrots on Maggio's land, to market them, and to divide the net profits with Maggio. The market price of carrots rose greatly above the contract rate, and Maggio refused to allow Fomco to harvest the full quantity of carrots specified in the contract. Maggio thereby obtained a $30,000 profit for itself by reselling the carrots. When Fomco sued for breach of contract, Maggio raised the defense that Fomco had failed to obtain a license as a "dealer" or "cash buyer" under the state Agricultural Code, and was thus guilty of misdemeanor. From a judgment for Fomco, Maggio appealed.

McComb, J. . . . "In some cases . . . the statute making the conduct illegal, in providing for a fine or administrative discipline, excludes by implication the additional penalty involved in holding the illegal contract unenforceable; or effective deterrence is best realized by enforcing the plaintiff's claim rather than leaving the defendant in possession of the benefit; or the forfeiture resulting from unenforceability is disproportionately harsh considering the nature of the illegality. In each such case, how the aims of policy can best be achieved depends on the kind of illegality and the particular facts involved. . . ."

Volume 6, Corbin on Contracts, section 1512, page 966: "The statute may be clearly for protection against fraud and incompetence; but in very many cases the statute breaker is neither fraudulent nor incompetent. He may have rendered excellent service or delivered goods of the highest quality, his noncompliance with the statute seems nearly harmless, and the real defrauder seems to be the defendant who is enriching himself at the plaintiff's expense. Although many courts yearn for a mechanically applicable rule, they have not made one in the present instance. Justice requires that the penalty should fit the crime; and justice and sound policy do not always require the enforcement of licensing statutes by large forfeitures going not to the state but to repudiating defendants.

"It must be remembered that in most cases the statute itself does not require these forfeitures. It fixes its own penalties, usually fine or imprisonment of minor character with a degree of discretion in the court. The added penalty of nonenforceability of bargains is a judicial creation. In most cases, it is wise to apply it; but when it causes great and disproportionate hardship, its application may be avoided."

The case of John E. Rosasco Creameries v. Cohen, 276 N.Y. 274 [11 N.E.2d 908, 909, 118 A.L.R. 641] . . . , is illuminating: . . .

"We have here a statute which provides that milk dealers shall not sell milk unless duly licensed. The statute imposes penalties for its violation by way of fine and imprisonment, but it does not expressly provide that contracts made by milk dealers shall be unenforceable. Nothing in this statute reveals an implied intent to deprive unlicensed dealers of the right to recover the reasonable value of the milk sold by them, and where the wrong committed by the violation of the statute is merely malum prohibitum,[5] and does not endanger health or morals, such additional punishment should not be imposed unless the legislative intent is expressed or appears by clear implication." . . .

To permit defendant to retain this profit [of approximately $30,000], merely because plaintiff did not have a license to do business would impose upon plaintiff a hardship out of all proportion to the technical violation of law committed by it. . . .

If plaintiff was required to have a license, defendant Joe Maggio, Inc., was equally obligated to have one. Hence, neither corporation was within the class for whose protection the statute was passed.

The applicable rule is stated in Kennoy v. Graves (Ky.), 300 S.W. 2d 568, an action brought by an unlicensed consulting engineer against another member of his own profession. In upholding plaintiff's right to recover for services rendered the court said . . . : "The statute involved, and similar ones, are designed to protect the public from being imposed upon by persons not qualified to render a professional service. The reason for the rule denying enforceability does not exist when persons engaged in the same business or profession are dealing at arms length with each other. . . ."

[Judgment affirmed.]

---

[5] See the Glossary.

Mutual Loan Co. v. Pierce

245 Iowa 1051, 65 N.W.2d 405 (1954)

Pierce worked for the Mutual Loan Company in Sioux City, Iowa. By the written contract of employment he agreed not to enter the employ of any competing small loan business in the same town while employed or for one year thereafter. Upon the termination of his employment with Mutual, he went to work for a competing personal loan company. Mutual sought an injunction to prevent him from continuing in such employment. From a judgment for Pierce, Mutual appealed.

MULRONEY, J. . . . Not all restrictive covenants in hiring contracts will be enforced. The agreement not to engage in a competing business on leaving employment is an agreement in restraint of trade, and it is unenforceable unless reasonably necessary to protect the employer.

The courts will not enjoin the taking of the new employment merely because it is within the negative restriction. Every man has a right to earn his livelihood in any legitimate employment or business, and his covenant not to follow a certain calling cannot be enforced by the covenantor as any sort of penalty. The covenantor who seeks the enforcing injunction in equity has the burden of showing the restrictive covenant is fair and reasonably necessary for the protection of his business.

It is to be expected, when courts are applying a rule of reason, that the limits of enforceability of negative covenants in employment contracts are not sharply outlined. Plaintiff argues in effect that such covenants are enforceable when limited as to time and area; such as here where it was limited to one year and a certain city. That is not quite true though it is generally held that one that is unlimited as to time or area is unreasonable and unenforceable. . . . The length of time and extent of area contained in the covenant will be taken into consideration in appraising the reasonableness of the restriction. . . . The covenantor's first burden is to show the reasonable necessity for the enforcement of the covenant at all in order to protect its business. . . . He cannot have the covenant enforced to preclude his former employee from exercising general skill and knowledge in the personal loan business, acquired by his employee while in his service, even if this skill and knowledge will be used in competition to plaintiff's business. . . . There is nothing unique about the personal loan business. Plaintiff's witness said there were some 10 or 12 of them doing "similar business in Sioux City and South Sioux City" and if you add banks and credit unions, there are about 18 in the small loan field. . . .

Plaintiff would not be entitled to the injunction without some showing that defendant, when he left plaintiff's employment, pirated or had the chance to pirate part of plaintiff's business; took or had the opportunity of taking some part of the good will of plaintiff's business; or it can reasonably be expected some of the patrons or customers he served while in plaintiff's employment will follow him to the new employment. Practically the only contact defendant had with plaintiff's customers was calling or telephoning the delinquent customers to try to get them to pay up. We can think of nothing less conducive to the building up of a personal following among plaintiff's patrons. The record shows he would occasionally close a loan when he was in South Sioux City, when he was alone in the office during the noon hour or the manager was out of town. Plaintiff and his present employer both testified there is no personal solicitation for loans in their business, the manager saying: "It is not an accepted ethical method of getting loans. We advertise by newspaper and radio." Their record shows that neither defendant nor his present employer ever advertised the fact that defendant was a former employee of Mutual in order to get customers.

The record shows this case is readily distinguishable from . . . [the case] where a physician, employed by a medical clinic, contracts on termination of his employment he will not practice his profession for a period of years in that locality. And it is distinguishable from Sioux City Night Patrol v. Mathwig, 224 Iowa 748, 277 N.W. 457, where the employee of a company engaged in guarding business houses covenanted not to engage in a similar business for a period of two years after the termination of his employment. The latter case might be called a "route case" for there are many decisions upholding restrictive covenants in employment contracts of employees serving milk routes, or laundry routes, or restrictive covenants in employment contracts of salesmen serving definite routes. In such cases the employee has had a close contact with his employer's customers and it is only fair, on termination of his employment, there be an interval when the new employee will be able to get acquainted with the customer. In such cases it is reasonable to expect some of the employer's customers will follow the employee to the new business. . . .

Under the whole record in this case we are convinced the trial court was right in denying the injunction. Plaintiff failed to make out a case where it can reasonably be said it will be harmed by its competitor because of defendant's new employment. The harm, if any, that plaintiff would suffer by defendant's new employment would be no greater than if Western had hired any other person with 20 months general experience in the small loan business. The benefit which plaintiff could possibly gain by the enforcement would be trivial and far out of proportion to the hardship to the defendant.

[Judgment affirmed.]

McConnell v. Commonwealth Pictures Corp.

7 N.Y.2d 465, 199 N.Y.S.2d 483 (1960)

Commonwealth Pictures Corp. agreed to pay McConnell $10,000 and a specified commission if he could persuade Universal Pictures Company to give Commonwealth the distribution rights on its pictures. Without the knowledge of either Universal or Commonwealth, McConnell obtained the distribution rights by bribing an agent of Universal with the $10,000 Commonwealth paid McConnell. McConnell thereafter sued Commonwealth for the agreed commission. From a judgment in favor of McConnell, Commonwealth appealed.

DESMOND, C.J. . . . [The lower court] said that, since the agreement sued upon—between plaintiff and defendant—was not in itself illegal, plaintiff's right to be paid for performing it could not be defeated by a showing that he had misconducted himself in carrying it out. The court found a substantial difference between this and the performance of an illegal contract. We take a different view. Proper and consistent application of a prime and long-settled public policy closes the doors of our courts to those who sue to collect the rewards of corruption.

New York's policy has been frequently and emphatically announced in the decisions. "It is the settled law of this State (and probably of every other State) that a party to an illegal contract cannot ask a court of law to help him carry out his illegal object, nor can such a person plead or prove in any court a case in which he, as a basis for his claim, must show forth his illegal purpose. . . . The money plaintiff sues for was the fruit of an admitted crime and 'no court should be required to serve as paymaster of the wages of crime.' "

. . . It is true that some of the leading decisions . . . were in suits on intrinsically illegal contracts, but the rule fails of its purpose unless it covers a case like the one at bar. . . .

We are not working here with narrow questions of technical law. We are applying fundamental concepts of morality and fair dealing not to be weakened by exceptions. So far as precedent is necessary, we can rely on Sirkin v. Fourteenth Street Store, 124 App.Div. 384, 108 N.Y.S. 830 . . . and Reiner v. North American Newspaper Alliance, 259 N.Y. 250, 191 N.E. 564, 83 A.L.R. 23. . . . Sirkin is the case closest to ours and shows that, whatever be the law in other jurisdictions, we in New York deny awards for the corrupt performance of contracts even though in essence the contracts are not illegal. Sirkin had sued for the price of goods sold and delivered to defendant. Held to be good was a defense which charged that plaintiff seller had paid a secret commission to an agent of defendant purchaser. There cannot be any difference in principle between that situation and the present one where plaintiff (it is alleged) contracted to buy motion-picture rights for defendant but performed his covenant only by bribing the seller's agent. In the Reiner case (supra), likewise, the plaintiff had fully performed the services required by his agreement with the defendant but was denied a recovery because his performance had involved and included "fraud and deception" practiced not on defendant but on a third party. It is beside the point that the present plaintiff on the trial might be able to prove a prima facie case without the bribery being exposed. On the whole case (again assuming that the defenses speak the truth) the disclosed situation would be within the rule of our precedents forbidding court assistance to bribers.

It is argued that a reversal here means that the doing of any small illegality in the performance of an otherwise lawful contract will deprive the doer of all rights, with the result that the other party will get a windfall and there will be great injustice. Our ruling does not go as far as that. It is not every minor wrongdoing in the course of contract performance that will insulate the other party from liability for work done or goods furnished. There must at least be a direct connection between the illegal transaction and the obligation sued upon. Connection is a matter of degree. Some illegalities are merely incidental to the contract sued on. . . . We cannot now, any more than in our past decisions, announce what will be the results of all the kinds of corruption, minor and major, essential and peripheral. All we are doing here is labeling the conduct described in these defenses as gross corruption depriving plaintiff of all right of access to the courts of New York State. Consistent with public morality and settled public policy, we hold that a party will be denied recovery even on a contract valid on its face, if it appears that he has resorted to gravely immoral and illegal conduct in accomplishing its performance.

Perhaps this application of the principle represents a distinct step beyond Sirkin and Reiner . . . in the sense that we are here barring recovery under a contract which in itself is entirely legal. But if this be an extension, public policy supports it. We point out that our holding is limited to cases in which the illegal performance of a contract originally valid takes the form of commercial bribery or similar conduct and in which the illegality is central to or a dominant part of the plaintiff's whole course of conduct in performance of the contract. . . .

[Judgment reversed.]

FROESSEL, J., dissenting. . . . This is not a case where the contract *sued upon* is intrinsically illegal . . . or was *procured* by the commission of a crime. . . .

In the instant case, the contract which plaintiff is seeking to enforce is perfectly valid, and it was not intended or even contemplated that plaintiff would perform the contract by illegal or corrupt means.

Having received and retained the full benefits of plaintiff's performance, defendant now seeks to "inject into" its contract with plaintiff,
"which was fair and legal in itself, the illegal feature of the other
independent transaction" . . . This court is now adopting a rule that
a party may retain the benefits of, but escape his obligations under, a
wholly lawful contract if the other party commits some illegal act
not contemplated nor necessary under the contract. By way of a
single illustration, an owner may thus avoid paying his contractor
for the cost of erecting a building because the contractor gave an
inspector a sum of money to expedite an inspection.

The majority opinion seeks to distinguish between "major" and
"minor" illegality and "direct" and "peripheral" corruption. It decides this case on the ground that the manner in which plaintiff performed his admittedly valid contract with defendant was "gravely immoral and illegal." Such distinctions are neither workable nor sanc-
tioned by authority. If a contract was lawfully made, and did not
contemplate wrongdoing, it is enforcible; if, on the other hand, it was
procured by the commission of a crime, or was in fact for the performance of illegal services, it is not enforcible. These are the criteria
distinguishing enforcible from unenforcible contracts—not "nice" distinctions between degrees of illegality and immorality in the performance of lawful contracts, or whether the illegal act of performance
was "directly" or "peripherally" related to the main contract. . . .

Here, the contract between plaintiff and defendant was perfectly
legal, and defendant is seeking to avoid its obligations under the contract—of which it has reaped the benefits for some 12 years—by asserting
the illegality of a *different* and subsequent agreement between plaintiff
and a third party. This it should not be permitted to do. . . .

VAN VOORHIS, J., dissenting. Public morals and fair dealing are
likely to be advanced by limiting rather than by enlarging the rule
that is being extended to the facts of this case. This rule is grounded
on considerations of public policy. Courts will not intervene between
thieves to compel them to divide the spoils. But in a situation like
the present, it seems to me that the effect of this decision will not be
to restrain the corrupt influencing of agents, employees or servants
but to encourage misappropriation of funds and breaches of faith
between persons who do not stand in corrupt relationships with one
another. The public interest is not served best by decisions which
put a premium on taking unconscionable advantage of such situations,
or which drive the enforcement of obligations of this kind under-
ground. . . .

Questions and Case Problems

1. (a) What is the objective of the law that usury statutes generally do not apply to prices charged for sales made on credit, such as installment sales.

(b) What rule of law in this chapter illustrates the evolutionary nature of the law?

2. Las Vegas Hacienda, Inc., advertised that it would pay $5,000 to anyone shooting a hole in one on its golf course. Gibson, who paid the fee of 50 cents, made a hole in one. The golf course corporation refused to pay the $5,000. When Gibson sued for breach of contract, it raised the defense that the contract was an illegal gambling contract and could not be enforced even though gambling as such was legalized in the state. Decide. (Las Vegas Hacienda, Inc. v. Gibson, 77 Nev. 25, 359 P.2d 85)

3. Griffith sued Dr. Bennett for malpractice. In the preparation of the case, Dr. Harris agreed to appear in the trial against Dr. Bennett and to testify favorably to Griffith. He later notified Griffith that he would not voluntarily appear as a witness and that if called as a witness, he would not testify in Griffith's favor. Griffith lost the suit against Bennett. He then sued Harris for breach of contract to appear and testify in his favor. Decide. (Griffith v. Harris, 17 Wis.2d 255, 116 N.W.2d 133)

4. Womack ran an unlawful gambling business. From time to time he paid Mainer, a local judge, $1,675 to obtain protection from prosecution. Womack sued Mainer for the return of the money. Decide. (Womack v. Mainer, 227 Ark. 786, 301 S.W.2d 438)

5. Burgess, a salesman for Bowyer, failed to turn over to Bowyer an indefinite amount of money collected by him. In order to avoid a criminal prosecution of Burgess by Bowyer, Burgess and his brother-in-law entered into a contract with the employer by which they agreed to pay Bowyer $5,000 if full restitution was not made. No restitution was made, and Bowyer sued Burgess and his brother-in-law on the contract for $5,000. Was he entitled to recover? (Bowyer v. Burgess, 54 Cal.2d 97, 4 Cal.Reptr. 521, 351 P.2d 793)

6. Ellis borrowed money from Small and executed a series of six promissory notes payable with the maximum rate of interest. The notes contained an acceleration clause by virtue of which, upon the borrower's default, the lender could declare the entire balance of the debt to be due, together with the contract rate of interest. By virtue of such acceleration, the creditor would be receiving more than the maximum rate since the borrower would have had the money for the shorter period only and not for the original period for which he bargained. Were the notes usurious? (Small v. Ellis, 90 Ariz. 194, 367 P.2d 234)

7. The Rhode Island Grocers' Association held an annual exhibition. As an added feature to attract public interest, arrangements were made with the Transocean Air Lines for a drawing of a door prize for a free round trip to Hawaii for two. Any spectator attending the exhibition could participate in the drawing by filling out a card with his name and address.

Was this a lottery? (Finch v. Rhode Island Grocers' Association, [R.I.] 175 A.2d 177)

8. A Virginia statute required builders and persons doing construction work to obtain a license and imposed a fine for failing to do so. F. S. Bowen Electric Co. installed equipment in a building being constructed by Foley. Bowen had not obtained a license. When Foley did not pay Bowen, the latter sued Foley for the money due. Could he recover? (F. S. Bowen Electric Co. v. Foley, 194 Va. 92, 72 S.E.2d 388)

9. McQuown was the night supervisor of the Lakeland Window Cleaning Co. His contract of employment with the company specified that he would not enter into a competing business in the same county within five years of the termination of his employment with the company. He thereafter left the employment and established his own cleaning and janitor service in the same county and competed with his former employer. The latter sued to enjoin the competition for five years. The court enjoined competition for one year. The former employer appealed on the ground that a one-year limitation was improper. The former employer appealed on the ground that any injunction was improper. What should the court have decided? (McQuown v. Lakeland Window Cleaning Co., [Fla.] 136 So.2d 370)

10. Jones sold to Groves cattle which, unknown to Groves, were infected with a contagious disease. A statute prohibited the sale of any domestic animals infected with a contagious, infectious, or communicable disease. Jones knew of the condition of the animals at the time of the sale. Groves brought an action to recover the purchase price. Could he recover? (Groves v. Jones, 252 Mich. 446, 233 N.W. 375)

11. Haines obtained a loan from the Commercial Mortgage Co. The company charged not only the maximum rate of interest but also a "service charge," which was computed as 3 per cent of the amount of the loan. Haines later sued the company to recover under a California statute that permitted the recovery of three times the amount of any usurious interest paid. Was the service charge usurious interest? (Haines v. Commercial Mortgage Co., 200 Cal. 609, 254 P. 956)

12. Rigney was selling houses. He and McDonnell agreed that for a specified sum of money McDonnell would appear at meetings of persons solicited to buy the houses and would pretend to buy some of the lots and talk to others with a view of inducing them to purchase also. Thereafter McDonnell brought an action against Rigney to recover the promised compensation. Was he entitled to judgment? (McDonnell v. Rigney, 108 Mich. 276, 66 N.W. 52)

13. R. A. Lazenby was the chief beneficiary of a will executed by R. H. Lazenby. After the latter's death, his heirs sought to have the will set aside. R. A. Lazenby entered into an agreement by which he promised to pay money to A. Lazenby if the latter would not present evidence in connection with the contest of the will. Thereafter A. Lazenby brought an action to enforce the promise made by R. A. Lazenby. Was he entitled to judgment? (Lazenby v. Lazenby, 132 Ga. 836, 65 S.E. 120)

CHAPTER 10

Capacity of Parties

All persons do not have the same legal capacity to make a contract. In some cases the legal capacity has no relation to the actual ability or capacity of the party. A person who is twenty years old, for example, may be just as capable or may have just as much ability to make a contract as an older person. Nevertheless, he may be under a legal incapacity. In other cases, such as those involving insane persons, the legal incapacity is based upon the inability to understand the consequences of the particular transaction.

Persons whose legal capacity is or may be restricted include minors, insane persons, intoxicated persons, convicts, and aliens. Such a limitation on married women is now largely historical. The restrictions on the contractual powers of corporations are discussed in Chapter 49.

Sec. 10-A. Minors. At common law any person, male or female, under twenty-one years of age is an infant or a *minor*. This period of minority usually ends the day before the minor's twenty-first birthday.[1]

In some states the common-law definition of minority has been modified. Some states provide by statute that a girl ceases to be a minor upon attaining the age of eighteen or upon being married. At least one state provides that a person of either sex attains majority upon marriage. In a few states minority does not end until the twenty-first anniversary of the minor's birth date.

(1) Minor's Right to Avoid Contracts. With exceptions that will be noted later, a contract made by a minor is voidable at his election. If the minor desires, however, he may perform his voidable contracts. The adult party to the contract cannot avoid the contract on the

---

[1] It is interesting to note that, in determining eligibility for old-age benefits under the Social Security Act and according to the regulations of the Internal Revenue Service, a person is considered as having reached the required age on the day before that birthday.

ground that the minor could do so if he wished. Until the minor avoids the contract, the other party is bound by it. If the minor dies, the personal representative of his estate may avoid a contract which the minor could have avoided.

Age of Majority and Effect of Marriage

STATE	AGE OF MAJORITY		STATE	AGE OF MAJORITY	
	MALE	FEMALE		MALE	FEMALE
Alabama a	21	21	Montana	21	18
Alaska	21	19	Nebraska g	21	21
Arizona b	19	21	Nevada	21	18
Arkansas	21	18	New Hampshire	21	21
California a	21	21	New Jersey	21	21
Colorado	21	21	New Mexico	21	21
Connecticut	21	21	New York	21	21
Delaware	21	21	North Carolina	21	21
District of Columbia	21	21	North Dakota	21	18
Florida c	21	21	Ohio	21	21
Georgia	21	21	Oklahoma h	21	18
Hawaii	20	20	Oregon	21	21
Idaho	21	18	Pennsylvania i	21	21
Illinois	21	18	Rhode Island	21	21
Indiana	21	21	South Carolina	21	21
Iowa c	21	21	South Dakota	21	18
Kansas d	21	21	Tennessee	21	21
Kentucky	21	21	Texas	21	21
Louisiana d	21	21	Utah c	21	18
Maine e	21	21	Vermont	21	21
Maryland	21	21	Virginia	21	21
Massachusetts	21	21	Washington j	21	21
Michigan	21	21	West Virginia	21	21
Minnesota f	21	21	Wisconsin	21	21
Mississippi	21	21	Wyoming	21	21
Missouri	21	21			

a Minority terminates when 18 or over and married.
b Minority as to community property only terminates upon marriage, if 18.
c Minority terminates upon marriage.
d Minority terminates upon marriage, if 18.
e Minority as to real or personal property transfers terminates upon marriage.
f Minority as to real property transfers terminates for women upon marriage.
g Minority terminates for women upon marriage.
h If married, may not avoid as to real property acquired after marriage.
i If married, may not avoid deed if joined with adult spouse.
j Married women may not avoid if husband is an adult.

In some jurisdictions the appointment of an agent or an attorney by a minor is void rather than voidable. There is no reason why this exception should be made, and there is a tendency to eliminate it.

(2) Minor's Misrepresentation of Age. Statutes in some states prevent a minor from avoiding his contract if he has fraudulently misrepresented his age. In the absence of such a statute, however, his fraud generally does not affect his right to avoid the contract when sued for its breach, although there is some authority that in such case

he must pay for any damage to, or deterioration of, the property he received under the contract. If the minor is not sued for the breach of the contract but is himself suing to recover what he has paid or given the other party, his fraud in misrepresenting his age generally will bar him from obtaining any relief.

In any case, the other party to the contract may avoid it because of the minor's fraud. There is a conflict of authority, however, as to whether the other party may sue the minor for damages because of the minor's fraud. Recovery is denied in some jurisdictions on the ground that to allow the other party damages for the minor's misrepresentation of his age would in effect deny the minor the right to avoid the contract. Elsewhere recovery is allowed because a minor, although he may avoid his contracts, is liable for his misconduct.

(3) Time for Avoidance. A minor's contract, whether executed or not, ordinarily can be disaffirmed or avoided by the minor at any time during minority or for a reasonable time after becoming of age. What is a reasonable time is a question of fact to be determined in the light of all the surrounding circumstances. After the expiration of a reasonable time following the attainment of majority, it is held that the minor has ratified the contract by his failure to avoid the contract within that time; but in some states an express affirmance is necessary to make a wholly executory contract binding.

As an exception to the right to disaffirm a contract during minority, a minor cannot fully avoid a conveyance or transfer of land made by him until he reaches his majority. Prior to that time, he may partially avoid the conveyance to the extent that he may retake possession of the land and enjoy its use or rent it to the others, but he cannot set aside the transfer of title until he is twenty-one.

(4) What Constitutes Avoidance. Avoidance or disaffirmance of a contract by a minor may be made by any expression of an intention to repudiate the contract. If the minor performs an act inconsistent with the continuing validity of the contract, that is deemed a disaffirmance. Thus, when a minor conveyed property to *A* and later, on reaching majority, made a conveyance of the same property to *B*, the second conveyance was deemed an avoidance of the first.

There is authority for the rule that if the contract is executory and the minor has not received any benefits, the contract is not binding upon him unless he affirmatively ratifies it after attaining the age of twenty-one. Under this rule the minor's silence or inaction is the equivalent of a disaffirmance. In certain states the silence of the minor may be considered in the light of all the other circumstances of the case to determine whether an affirmance may be implied. In some states no distinction is made between executory and executed contracts, and the minor is required to disaffirm both kinds.

When a minor avoids his contract, he must avoid it in all its parts. He cannot keep part of the contract and reject the balance.

(5) Restitution by Minor upon Avoidance. When a minor avoids his contract, must he return what he has received? What happens if what he received has been spent, used up, damaged, or destroyed? When the minor has in his possession or control the consideration received by him, or any part of it, he must return it or offer to do so before he can require the other party to undo the contract and set things back to their original position, or as it is called, to restore the *status quo ante*. Although the minor must make this restitution if he can, the right to disaffirm his contract is not affected by the fact that he no longer has the money or property to return, or that the property has been damaged. In those states which follow the general rule, the minor can thus refuse to pay for what he has received or he can get back what he has paid or given, even though he himself does not have anything to return or returns the property in a damaged condition.

This absolute right to disaffirm is modified in some states where, except as to transactions involving the conveyance of land, a minor must restore what he received or its money equivalent before he can disaffirm the contract. If he cannot make such restoration, he is denied the right to disaffirm. In a few states this limitation is imposed by statute on minors over a certain age. Most states require the minor to pay for any damage to the returned property if the minor had falsely represented his age when he obtained the property.

When a minor wishes to avoid an insurance contract, he can recover everything that he has paid without regard to whether the insurance company had made any payments to him. The unfairness of this rule has led some jurisdictions to limit the recovery of the minor to the amount of the premiums paid by him in excess of the actual cost of the protection he has enjoyed during the time the policy was in force. In some states the minor is by statute denied the right to avoid a life insurance policy on his own life.

(6) Recovery of Property by Minor upon Avoidance. When the minor avoids his contract, the other contracting party must return all the money or property of the minor that he had received, or the money equivalent of property which he cannot return. (See p. 166, O'Brien v. Small)

Can a minor who avoids a transaction involving personal property recover that property from a third person to whom the other party to the contract has transferred it? The Uniform Sales Act and the Uniform Commercial Code [2] make no provision for protecting the title of

---

[2] Uniform Commercial Code, Sec. 2-403 (1).

the minor under such circumstances. At common law there is authority
for the rule that when a minor avoids a transaction as to either real
or personal property, he may recover it from the third person, even
though that person did not know of the minority and purchased the
property for value. In a number of states the common-law rule has
been repudiated on the basis of equitable principles apart from statute.

(7) *Ratification.* A minor's voidable contract becomes binding
upon him when he ratifies or approves it. Of necessity, the minor can
only ratify a contract when he is no longer a minor. He must have
attained his majority or his "ratification" would itself be regarded
as voidable in order to protect the minor. In contrast, a minor can
usually avoid a contract at any time during minority.

Ratification may consist of any expression that indicates an intention to be bound by the contract. In some states a written ratification
or declaration of intention is required. An acknowledgment by the
minor that a contract had been made during his minority, without
any indication of an intention to be bound thereby, is not a ratification.

In addition to ratification based on statements or promises, ratification may be found in the conduct of the minor. If after attaining
majority the minor fails to disaffirm an executed contract within a
reasonable time, the contract is deemed ratified.[3] If the minor acquired
property under his contract and after reaching majority makes a use
or disposition of the property inconsistent with disaffirmance, he will
also be deemed to have ratified the contract. (See p. 167, Haydon v.
Hillhouse)

(8) *Contracts for Necessaries.* A minor is liable for the reasonable
value of necessaries that are supplied to him by another person at the
minor's request. This exception differs from the others that follow in
that the minor is ordinarily not bound by the terms of his contract.
In the case of necessaries he is usually required to pay only the reasonable value of what the seller actually delivers and which the minor
receives. This duty of the minor is called a quasi-contractual liability.[4]
It is a duty which the law imposes upon the minor rather than one
which he has created by the contract.

Originally necessaries were limited to those things absolutely
necessary for the sustenance and shelter of the minor. Thus limited,
the term would extend only to the most simple foods, clothing, and
lodging. In the course of time, the rule was relaxed to extend generally
to things relating to the health, education, and comfort of the minor.
Thus, the rental of a house used by a married minor, his wife, and

---

[3] See p. 159.
[4] See p. 58.

child, is a necessary. The rule has also been relaxed to hold that whether an item is a necessary in a particular case depends upon the financial and social status, or station in life, of the minor. The rule thus does not treat all minors equally. To illustrate, college education may be regarded as necessary for one minor but not for another, depending upon their respective stations in life.

Property other than food or clothing acquired by a minor is generally not regarded as a necessary. Although this rule is obviously sound in the case of ornaments and property used for pleasure, the same view is held even though the minor is self-supporting and uses the property in connection with his work, as tools of his trade, or an automobile which he must have to go to and from work. The more recent decisions, however, hold that property used by the minor for his support is a necessary. (See p. 168, Bancredit, Inc. v. Bethea) Thus it has been held that a tractor and farm equipment were necessaries for a married minor who supported his family by farming.

Money loaned to a minor is ordinarily not classified as a necessary, even though the minor thereafter purchases necessaries with the borrowed money. An exception is made to the rule when the lender advances money for that express purpose and makes certain that the minor purchases necessaries with the money. In such a case the minor must pay the lender the amount of the loan.

If the minor is adequately supplied with necessaries or if those purchased by him are excessive in quantity or too expensive, the courts hold that such purchases are not necessary and that the contracts are voidable by the minor.

(9) Contracts That Minors Cannot Avoid.

(a) MINOR IN BUSINESS. In order to prevent the minor from using the shield of his minority as a sword to injure others, some states, either by decision or statute, have the rule that when a minor engages in a business and operates in the same manner as a person having legal capacity, he will not be permitted to set aside contracts arising from that business.

(b) COURT-APPROVED CONTRACT. In some states permission of the court may be obtained for a minor to execute a contract. When this permission is obtained and the contract is made, it is fully binding upon the minor. In this manner, a minor may execute a binding contract for professional performances on the stage, in the movies, or on television.

(c) CONTRACTS IN PERFORMANCE OF LEGAL DUTY. A minor cannot avoid a contract which the law specifically requires or that provides for the performance of an act which he is legally bound to do. If the law authorizes a minor to make an enlistment contract with a branch of the armed forces, he cannot avoid it on the ground of minority. Many states require that a person file a bond when he brings certain kinds of lawsuits or takes an appeal. If a minor brings such an action or takes an appeal and executes the necessary bond, he cannot avoid liability on the bond by claiming that he was a minor.

If property of a father is held in the name of his minor child under an agreement that it is to be conveyed or sold in a particular manner, a conveyance by the son cannot be avoided by him. Here the transaction by the minor is in performance of the duty imposed upon him by his agreement with his father, and the law will not permit the minor to set the contract aside. In this type of case, the minor has no direct interest in the transaction but in a sense is acting as the agent for the father.

(d) VETERANS. In most states statutes permit veterans who are minors to execute binding contracts of certain types, particularly those concerning real property.

(e) BANK ACCOUNTS. By statute in some states a minor may open a bank account in his own name, and all acts of the minor with respect to the account are binding upon him as though he were of full age.

(f) STOCK TRANSFERS. By statute it is sometimes provided that when a minor transfers shares of stock, the transfer shall be as binding as though he were an adult with respect to anyone not knowing that he is a minor.

(10) Liability of Parent for Minor's Contract. Ordinarily a parent is not liable on a contract executed by a minor child. The parent may be liable, however, if the child is acting as the agent of the parent in executing the contract.[5] If the parent has neglected the child, the parent is liable to a third person for the reasonable value of necessaries supplied by that person to the child.[6] If a parent joins in a contract with a minor, as when the parent acts as a cosigner, the parent is liable on his own undertaking. He then remains bound by his contract even though the minor avoids the contract as to himself.

Sec. 10-B. Insane Persons. If a party to a contract is insane, he lacks capacity and his contract is either void or voidable. In order to constitute insanity within the meaning of this rule, the party must be so deranged mentally that he does not know that he is making a contract or that he does not understand the consequences of what he is

---

[5] See p. 569.
[6] See p. 573.

doing. If he lacks understanding, the cause of his mental condition is immaterial. It may be idiocy, senile dementia, lunacy, imbecility, or such excessive use of alcoholic beverages or narcotics as to cause mental impairment.

If at the time the party makes the contract he understands the nature of his action and its consequences, it is immaterial that he has certain delusions or insane intervals, or that he is eccentric. As long as the contract is made in a lucid interval and is not affected by any delusions, it is valid.

(1) Effect of Insanity. If a party to a contract is insane, he may generally avoid his contracts in the same manner as a minor. (See p. 170, Sjulin Case) Upon the removal of the disability, that is, upon his becoming sane, he may either ratify or disaffirm the contract. If a proper court has appointed a guardian for the insane person, the contract may be ratified or disaffirmed by the guardian. If the insane person dies, his personal representative or heirs may also affirm or disaffirm the contract made by him.

As in the case of minors, the other party to the contract has no right to disaffirm the contract merely because the incompetent has the right to do so.

(2) Exceptions. There are several exceptions to the rule that the contracts of an insane person are voidable:

(a) EXISTENCE OF GUARDIAN. It is commonly provided that when a court has appointed a guardian for the insane person, the latter cannot make any contract whatever and one made by him is therefore void.

(b) NECESSARIES. An insane person has a quasi-contractual liability to pay the reasonable value of necessaries furnished to him, his wife, or his children.

(c) BENEFICIAL CONTRACT. If the contract was fair and reasonable and was advantageous to the incompetent, a substantial number of states hold that he may not avoid the contract when the other party acted without knowledge of the incompetence and in good faith, and it would be impossible to restore the status quo ante.

Sec. 10-C. Intoxicated Persons. The capacity of a party to contract and the validity of his contract are not affected by the fact that he was drunk at the time of making the contract so long as he knew that he was making a contract. The fact that the contract was foolish and that he would not have made it had he been sober does not invalidate the contract unless it can be shown that the other party purposely caused the person to become drunk in order to induce him to execute the contract.

If the degree of intoxication is such that the person does not know at the time that he is executing a contract, there is no valid contract. (See p. 172, Coody v. Coody) The situation is the same as though he were so insane at the time that he did not know what he was doing. Upon becoming sober, the person may ratify the contract if he so desires. An unreasonable delay in taking steps to set aside a transaction entered into while intoxicated, however, may bar the intoxicated person from asserting this right.

As in the case of a minor, a drunkard is bound by a contract that carries out an obligation or duty imposed by law. He is also required to pay for the reasonable value of all necessaries furnished him.

If a person has been adjudicated a habitual drunkard or if a guardian has been appointed for him because of his inability to care for his property, the drunkard is placed under a continuing legal disability to make a contract. The statutes which provide for the appointment of a guardian or the adjudication of the status of the drunkard generally specify that after the court has acted, the drunkard has no power to make a contract even when he is sober.

Sec. 10-D. Convicts. The capacity to contract of a person convicted of a major criminal offense, a felony, or treason varies from state to state. In some he may make a valid transfer of his property. In other states such a person has either partial or total disability. When there is a disability, it exists only during the period of imprisonment.

Sec. 10-E. Aliens. An *alien* is a national or subject of a foreign country. Originally aliens were subject to many disabilities. These have been removed in many instances by treaty between the United States and the foreign country, under which each nation agrees to give certain rights to the subjects or citizens of the other. Generally the right of the alien to make a contract has been recognized.[7]

If this country is at war with a nation of which an alien is a subject, he is termed an *enemy alien*, without regard to whether he assists his country in the prosecution of the war. An enemy alien is denied the right to make new contracts or to sue on existing ones; but if he is sued, he may defend the action. Contracts made by him, even though made before the war began, will at least be suspended during the war. In some instances, if the contract calls for continuing services or performance, the war terminates the contract.

---

[7] In some states laws prohibit aliens from owning land. These have been held unconstitutional by the Supreme Courts of California, Montana, and Oregon as violating the Fourteenth Amendment of the Constitution of the United States. *Sei Fujii* v. *State*, 38 Cal.2d 718, 242 P.2d 617; *Montana* v. *Oakland*, 129 Mont. 347, 287 P.2d 39; *Kenji Namba* v. *McCourt*, 185 Ore. 579, 204 P.2d 569. Earlier decisions of the Supreme Court of the United States had sustained the California and Washington statutes. *Porterfield* v. *Webb*, 263 U.S. 225; *Terrace* v. *Thompson*, 263 U.S. 197.

Sec. 10-F. Married Women. At common law a married woman could not make a binding contract. Her contracts were void, rather than voidable, even when she lived apart from her husband. Consequently, she could not ratify a contract after the removal of the disability by the death of her husband.

The common-law disability of a married woman has almost been abolished by statute in practically all the states. There are still a few restrictions in some jurisdictions, mainly in instances where the wife might be unduly influenced by the husband, as in acting as surety for him, contracting with him, or joining with him in a conveyance of their property to a third person, for in such instances there is the danger that the transaction may be harmful to the wife's best interests.

Cases for Chapter 10

O'Brien v. Small

101 Ohio App. 408, 122 N.E.2d 701 (1954)

Peggy O'Brien purchased a 1952 Hudson automobile from Small when she was nineteen. Part of the purchase price was a trade-in of a 1941 Oldsmobile, and part was furnished by a note and a chattel mortgage. Several months later the finance company repossessed the automobile when installment payments were not made. O'Brien then sued Small to set aside the contract and to obtain the refund of what money had been paid on the contract. Small raised the defense that the purchase of the 1952 Hudson had in fact been made by Peggy's adult husband with his money and that the title to the automobile had been placed in Peggy's name. From a judgment for the minor, Small appealed.

SKEEL, J. . . . [The court first held that the lower court should have submitted to the jury the question whether the minor or her husband had been the other party to the contract with the automobile dealer.]

. . . There is evidence in the record tending to show that the money paid in cash on the purchase of the Hudson automobile, or at least part of it, was the property of Charles O'Brien. This issue should have been submitted to the jury under proper instructions from the court. A minor in disaffirming an executed sale is entitled to recover back only such property as was that of the minor, and which the minor parted with in the transaction. Whether or not the Oldsmobile which was turned in was the property of the plaintiff, or her husband, was also an issue in the case. . . .

. . . It is a well recognized principle of law that an infant is bound by and cannot disaffirm an obligation imposed by law. . . . Funds expended for sales tax . . . , fees expended to secure from the county clerk a certificate of title to a motor vehicle, and for the transfer of automobile license plates, are obligations of the purchaser and are imposed by law. The court was therefore in error in instructing the jury that money paid to the defendant to defray such obligations could be recouped by an infant in disaffirming the purchase of an automobile. . . .

The right of an infant upon the disaffirmance of the purchase of personal property is to receive back that which the infant parted with as consideration for the contract. If the plaintiff was the owner of the property in the Oldsmobile, then upon disaffirmance she would be entitled to have the Oldsmobile returned to her, or, if the other party to the contract has put it beyond his power to return the automobile, then the value thereof would be the basis of recovery. . . .

[Judgment reversed and case remanded.]

Haydon v. Hillhouse

223 Ark. 957, 270 S.W.2d 910 (1954)

Hillhouse, while a minor, purchased an automobile from Haydon. After becoming of age, Hillhouse made ten additional monthly payments, was in three collisions with the automobile and collected insurance for the damage, purchased a new top from Haydon at wholesale price as authorized by the purchase contract, and drove the automobile 35,000 miles. He then brought an action to rescind the contract on the ground that he was a minor when he made the contract. Judgment of rescission was granted, from which Haydon appealed.

Holt, J. . . . In the circumstances, we hold that appellee [Hillhouse], by his conduct and actions, ratified the contract in question, which he executed during his minority and is therefore bound by it.

. . . "One who has entered into a contract which he might avoid because of personal incapacity, such as an infant, an insane person, a drunkard, and the like, has the election to affirm such contract, or to disaffirm it, and when he has exercised his election, with full knowledge of the facts, such election is final. Accordingly, if such person elects to affirm the transaction, his election is final and conclusive without any new consideration."

Section 38-103, Ark.Stats. 1947, argued by appellee as supporting his contention, is not controlling here. This section provides: "No action shall be maintained whereby to charge any person upon any promise made after full age, to pay any debt contracted during infancy, unless such promise or . . . ratification shall be made by some writing signed by the party to be charged therewith." . . .

Appellants are not basing their claim of ratification by appellee, Hillhouse, on any promises in writing and signed by him, *after he became twenty-one,* but on a promise and contract made by him during his minority and ratified by him after reaching his majority.

Kentucky and South Carolina have statutes, in effect, the same as above, § 38-103, and the construction placed thereon by those cases, while not controlling, is persuasive on us. . . .

In the present case, we are dealing with a man who knew he could not legally buy a car until he became twenty-one, and was equally positive that he could legally buy a car after he had passed his twenty-first birthday. With this knowledge, after reaching his majority, he proceeded to sign and purchase money orders to apply on payments (10 of them), which he made. He also executed proofs of loss to recover for car damages growing out of three collisions, bought the new top, which was part of the original contract in question, and drove this used car in his own use approximately 35,000 miles within less than a year.

In the circumstances, we think the preponderance of the testimony shows that he affirmed the contract after his majority, became bound by it, is estopped from rescinding, and accordingly the decree is reversed and the cause is remanded for further proceedings consistent with this opinion.

Bancredit, Inc. v. Bethea

65 N.J.S. 538, 168 A.2d 250 (1961)

Bethea, aged 20, purchased an automobile on credit. When sued by Bancredit, Inc. for the purchase price, he raised the defense in his answer filed in court that he was not liable because he was a minor when he made the contract. He was still a minor when he filed the answer. The lower court held that the automobile was a necessary because the minor used it for transportation to and from his place of employment. From a judgment in favor of Bancredit, the minor appealed.

FREUND, J.A.D. . . . While an automobile has not generally been classed as a necessary, in accordance with the principle that articles used for pleasure or for business advantage are not bodily or mental essentials. . . , recent decisions have espoused the more realistic view that an occupational accessory may well be a link in the chain of physical survival. . . . For example, in Ehrsam v. Borgen, 185 Kan. 776, 347 P.2d 260 (Sup.Ct., 1959), the infant, at the time of contracting, was over 20 years of age and apparently supported himself. He owned his own automobile, driving approximately 20 miles to and from work each day. It was found . . . that "in order for defendant to hold his job and earn a livelihood, he had to get to and from work and, under such conditions, the arrangement made between the parties was necessary insofar as defendant was concerned." The Kansas court discussed the evolution of the automobile as a concomitant to modern living:

"It might be said that earlier in the history of our country, when industry was centralized in cities or industrial communities where housing was adequate and public transportation, by way of the street car, the bus or the community train was available to all, private transportation was not necessary for one getting to and from his work. However, since World War II there has been a tremendous growth in our country's population, and in this highly industrial age, where industry has the tendency to decentralize and move to less populated or rural communities within which there is a shortage of housing and very little, if any, public transportation available, the worker is, as a result, required to commute long distances to and from his place of employment. We are, therefore, of the opinion that private transportation for the worker is now a necessity, and an agreement made by a minor for such transportation is binding and not subject to disaffirmance for the reasons of minority alone." . . .

We are in accord with the recognition, implicit in these holdings, that modern transportation habits and the definitional flexibility of "necessary," dependent as the term is upon the social position and situation in life of the minor, . . . may well combine to dictate that, under certain circumstances, an automobile is sufficiently indispensable to bind an infant who contracts for one. Whether, therefore, the automobile in the case at hand—allegedly used by young Bethea in driving to and from work—is a necessary should have been determined by the jury, taking into account such considerations as the defendant's station in life, his personal need of the vehicle, the type of work in which he is engaged, the traveling distance involved in going to and from his job, convenient alternative means of transportation, and the terms of his contract of employment. . . . Also to be resolved by the jury is the question of whether, considering young Bethea's possession of another automobile (the one traded in) and the apparent willingness of his father to help him, the infant was in "actual need" of the car purchased. Finally, even if the automobile is found to be a necessary, the infant's liability must be limited to the reasonable value thereof; defendants have claimed all along that the worth of the vehicle is considerably less than the sales price.

We recognize that, in general, the burden of proving infancy is on the one who asserts it in defense. . . . However, once the defendant effectively demonstrates his infancy at the time of contracting, the party seeking to recover for materials furnished has the burden of proving both that the articles supplied in fact constituted necessaries, and that the infant was in "actual need" of them. . . . It is also the duty of the creditor to establish the reasonable value of the alleged necessaries. . . .

Should the automobile be found not to be a necessary, Lynn Bethea's release from liability on the note is not open to question.

It cannot be claimed that he ratified his obligation upon attaining majority, as he in fact disaffirmed before coming of age. Ratification cannot be effectually made until the coming of age. . . . Disaffirmance, however, at least with respect to contracts relating to personal property, may occur either during infancy or within a reasonable time after the attainder of full age. . . . The record indicates that Lynn Bethea reached his twenty-first birthday on September 26, 1959. Inspection of the docket shows that defendant's answer, in which Lynn raised the defense of infancy, was filed with the Union County District Court on July 27, 1959. Disavowal by an infant need not take any prescribed form or ceremony; the filing of the answer prior to the attainment of majority instituted disaffirmance as a matter of law. . . .

[Reversed and new trial ordered.]

Sjulin v. Clifton Furniture Co.

241 Iowa 761, 41 N.W.2d 721 (1950)

Sjulin purchased furniture from the Clifton Furniture Company. The company knew at the time that Sjulin was mentally incompetent. Two days later he was judicially declared incompetent, and a guardian was appointed for him. The guardian sought to return the furniture and avoid the contract. From a judgment for the guardian, the company appealed.

GARFIELD, J. . . . Sterling Sjulin, . . . age 24, purchased furniture from defendant Clifton . . . for which he paid $1,121.29. Two days later, Sterling was adjudged insane by the County Commission of Insanity and committed to the Veterans Administration Hospital for the Insane at Knoxville where he was still confined when this case was tried. . . . Sterling's father was appointed guardian of his property by the Fremont County District Court . . . , and brought this equity suit . . . to avoid the contract and recover the purchase price. . . .

To avoid the contract, it must appear not only that Sterling was of unsound mind when it was made, but that this unsoundness was such that he had no reasonable perception of the nature and terms of the contract. Mere mental weakness or unsoundness to some degree is not sufficient, in the absence of fraud or undue influence, to invalidate a contract.

[The court discussed in detail the evidence which showed that Sterling was insane.]

An executed contract may be avoided upon the ground one party was mentally incapable of making it when the other party may be placed in statu quo, even though the other did not know of the incapacity and the contract was fair and upon full consideration. . . .

However, where the executed contract of an incompetent has been entered into in good faith, for a fair consideration, without notice of the insanity and before an adjudication thereof, it will not be set aside unless the other party can be put in statu quo. . . .

Where the other contracting party has knowledge or notice of the insanity, restoration to him of the status quo is unnecessary; but the incompetent or his representative is required only to return what is left of what was received under the contract. . . .

Thus, if defendant is placed in statu quo, it is not important whether he had knowledge or notice of Sterling's incapacity. If defendant had such knowledge or notice, he would not be entitled to be put in statu quo but only to the return of such furniture as plaintiff was able to return.

The trial court found defendant had notice of Sterling's incapacity. Also that the furniture was in substantially the same condition as when delivered by defendant and its return to him, which was decreed at plaintiff's expense, would restore the status quo. Either finding, if warranted by the proof, would entitle plaintiff to recover provided, of course, Sterling was mentally incapable of making the contract. We feel the evidence supports each finding. . . .

Defendant's contention that return of the furniture will not restore the status quo is based on evidence that it declined in value 30 per cent between time of delivery and plaintiff's appointment as guardian, a little over three months, on the theory it became used furniture by the sale and delivery. Defendant also offered to prove the cost of the furniture to him was two thirds the retail price while his net profit was only 10 per cent of such price and that the difference between the wholesale cost and the net profit was cost of selling. Defendant argues he will not be put in statu quo unless plaintiff pays him the difference between his wholesale cost and net profit in addition to return of the furniture. Defendant cites no authority that supports his argument and none has come to our attention.

The basic principle upon which restoration of the status quo is required in order to avoid a contract is that he who seeks equity must do equity.

The rule requiring restoration of what was received is not to be applied strictly but in accordance with equitable principles; and the rescinding party is required to do only what he should equitably do. . . . We think return of the furniture is all the equities of the case require. . . .

Defendant is entitled to be put in the position he occupied before the transaction complained of. . . . Plaintiff should also be placed in the position his ward then occupied. We have said that the rescinding party is entitled to no profit from his bargain. . . . We know of no reason why the other party should have any part of his gross profit. If plaintiff were compelled to pay defendant money in addition to the return of the furniture, he would not be left in the position his ward occupied before the transaction, while defendant would occupy a better position.

[Judgment for guardian affirmed.]

Coody v. Coody

39 Okla. 719, 136 P. 754 (1913)

Edward Coody executed a number of deeds to D. R. Coody. Later Edward brought a suit to cancel these deeds on the ground that at the time he executed them, he was intoxicated and unable to understand what he was doing. From a judgment for the defendant, the plaintiff appealed.

SHARP, C. . . . If, at the time the deed . . . was executed, plaintiff was so under the influence of intoxicants as to be wholly unable to transact business and to understand the nature of the deed which he signed, he may plead his disability from such drunkenness in an action to cancel the deed. Intoxication which is absolute and complete, so that the party is for the time entirely deprived of the use of his reason and is wholly unable to comprehend the nature of the transaction and of his acts, is a sufficient ground for setting aside or granting other appropriate relief against a conveyance or contract made while in that condition, even in the absence of fraud, procurement, or undue advantage by the other party.

[The Court quoted early common-law writers who had stated that intoxication could not be raised as a defense because it was voluntarily caused.] But Blackstone observes that this doctrine sprung from loose authorities and . . . rejects the maxim as being contrary to reason. . . . So far as legal incapacity is concerned, it can make no difference from what cause it proceeded, whether from the party's own imprudence or misconduct, or otherwise. It is the state and condition of the mind itself that the law regards and not the causes that produced it. It from any cause his reason has been dethroned, his disability to contract is complete. . . .

The rule formerly was that intoxication was no excuse and created no privilege or plea in avoidance of a contract; but it is now settled according to the dictates of good sense and common justice that a contract made by a person so destitute of reason as not to know the consequences of his contract, though his incompetence be produced by intoxication, is voidable and may be avoided by himself, though the intoxication was voluntary and not produced by . . . the other party.

[Judgment for defendant reversed.]

Questions and Case Problems

1. (a) What is the objective of the rule of law that when a minor avoids a contract, he usually cannot recover his property if the other party has transferred it to a third person who did not know of the minority and purchased the property for value?

   (b) How is the evolutionary nature of the law illustrated by the changes in the definition of a minor's necessaries?

2. Saccavino made a contract with Carl Gambardella, then 15 years of age, and Carl's parents, that he would train Carl to be a horse rider and the he would receive in return a share of Carl's earnings from exhibitions and racing. When Saccavino sued on the contract years later, Carl claimed that it was void. Was he correct? (Saccavino v. Gambardella, 22 Conn. Sup. 168, 164 A.2d 304)

3. On February 28, 1958, Alice Sosik signed a note promising to make certain payments to Conlon. She later sued to have the note set aside on the ground that she lacked mental capacity. A letter from a physician was presented which stated that he had examined her on July 3, 1959 and that she "is suffering from a chronic mental illness and is totally incapable of managing her affairs." Was she entitled to set the note aside? (Sosik v. Conlon, [R.I.] 164 A.2d 696)

4. Martinson executed a note payable to Matz. At the time Martinson was drunk. The next day he was told that he had signed the note. Five years later, Martinson's wife told Matz's attorney that Martinson would not pay the note as he was drunk at the time he executed the note. Matz brought suit on the note two years after that. Could he recover? (Matz v. Martinson, 127 Minn. 262, 149 N.W. 370)

5. Byers was convicted of a felony and sentenced to the penitentiary. While in prison he hired Sheffler, an attorney, to obtain a parole for him. In order to pay the attorney, Byers gave him a promissory note for $1,000. Sheffler transferred the note to the Sun Savings Bank. He obtained the parole. When the bank sought to collect the amount of the note, Byers claimed that he was not bound by the note on the theory that a convict confined in jail had no capacity to make a contract. Decide. (Byers v. Sun Savings Bank, 41 Okla. 728, 139 P. 948)

6. Dobbins, who was engaged in the nursery business in Montgomery County, Iowa, sold and delivered shrubbery to Childs. Childs paid Dobbins $500. Thereafter, but before reaching majority, Childs disaffirmed the sale and brought an action to recover the money paid to Dobbins. Was he entitled to do so? (Childs v. Dobbins, 55 Iowa 205, 7 N.W. 496)

7. Squilache, an Italian subject, was injured in an explosion while working for the Tidewater Coal and Coke Co. He sued his employer claiming that the latter had violated his duties under the employment contract. Tidewater defended on the ground that Squilache was an alien and therefore could not enforce any rights under the contract. Decide. (Squilache v. Tidewater Coal and Coke Co., 64 W.Va. 337, 62 S.E. 446)

8. Wilkinson, when eighty years of age, executed a deed conveying 320 acres of land of an alleged value of $14,000 to the Physio-Medical College of Indiana, in consideration of "love and affection for the college." A few years later she died without having made a will. Her heirs brought an action to cancel the deed upon the ground of her unsoundness of mind. Assuming that incompetency, as alleged, existed, are they entitled to have the deed set aside? (Physio-Medical College v. Wilkinson, 108 Ind. 314, 9 N.E. 167)

9. Rich, a minor, borrowed money from Kilgore by having him pay a board bill that Rich had incurred while attending school. Thereafter Kilgore brought an action to recover the money. Decide. (Kilgore v. Rich, 83 Me. 305, 22 A. 176)

10. Baltzer, forty-two years of age, was a shrewd merchant in Bruneau Valley, Idaho. A reservoir and canal were being constructed nearby. This project had created the impression that agricultural lands would increase greatly in value. With a view of making a profit thereon, Baltzer in May purchased a ranch from Ratliff, to whom he gave a note for the unpaid purchase price and a mortgage on the ranch as security. During April and May, Baltzer occasionally acted peculiarly, such as dancing for a school teacher with whom he became enamored, singing and playing musical instruments when he could neither sing nor play such instruments, buying two peacocks that pleased his fancy and a mare which he took pleasure in riding. In June he was adjudged insane and was confined in an insane asylum. When an action was brought to enforce the mortgage, insanity was claimed as a defense. Decide. (Ratliff v. Baltzer's Administrator, 13 Idaho 152, 89 P. 71)

11. Mary McCoy, a married woman, sold land that she owned to Niblick. Her husband did not sign the contract. Niblick moved onto the property before a deed was delivered and made improvements. Later Mary sought to set the contract aside. A Pennsylvania statute provided that a married woman had the same right as an unmarried woman to sell or dispose of her property but that she could not execute a deed to the property without having her husband sign the deed. Who was entitled to the property? (McCoy v. Niblick, 221 Pa. 123, 70 A. 577)

12. Dostal sued Magee who was then a minor. Magee retained Petersen as his attorney. After becoming twenty-one years of age, Magee disaffirmed the acts of Petersen as his agent. Dostal claimed that Magee could not set aside the contract of employment of his attorney because (1) the contract had been ratified, as Magee's father had consulted with Petersen after Magee became of age; and (2) Magee was barred from avoiding the contract because of fraud, as he had not informed anyone that he was under twenty-one years of age. Could Magee set aside the contract? (Dostal v. Magee, 272 Wis. 509, 76 N.W.2d 349)

CHAPTER 11

Formality and Interpretation

As a practical matter, it is always desirable to put important contracts in writing. In the first place, each party knows just what he is agreeing to when the agreement is written. Second, the writing assures both parties that at a future date there will be less chance of disagreement as to what has been agreed upon. Third, it eliminates the possibility that either party to the contract can effectively deny having made the contract.

Sec. 11-A. General Rule. Generally a contract is valid whether it is written or not. As important exceptions to the general rule that a writing is not required, statutes provide that conveyances of land and negotiable instruments must be written. In some states, a promise affirming a contract made during minority must be in writing. The most common provisions concerning the form of contracts are to be found in the Statute of Frauds.

Apart from statute, the parties may agree that their oral agreement is not to be binding until a formal written contract is executed. (See p. 184, Breaux Bros. Construction Co. v. Associated Contractors) Conversely, they may agree that their oral contract is binding even though a written contract is to be executed. If one of the parties, with the knowledge or approval of the other contracting party, undertakes performance of the contract before it is reduced to writing, it is generally held that the parties intended to be bound from the moment of the making of the oral contract.

Sec. 11-B. Statute of Frauds. In 1677, a statute adopted in England aimed at reducing the evil of perjured testimony by providing that certain contracts could not be enforced if they depended upon the testimony of witnesses alone and were not evidenced by a writing. As stated in the preamble of the statute, its purpose was the "prevention of many fraudulent practices, which are commonly endeavored to be upheld by perjury and subornation of perjury." From this recital, the common name of the statute, *Statute of Frauds* or *Statute of Frauds and Perjuries*, is derived. Its provisions have been closely followed by statutes adopted in the various states of this country.

The statute is designed to prevent the use of the courts for the purpose of enforcing certain oral agreements or alleged oral agreements. It does not apply when an oral agreement has been performed by both sides or when the parties voluntarily perform the agreement. Sometimes special statutes apply to particular contracts and take the place of the general Statute of Frauds.

Sec. 11-C. Fourth Section of the Statute of Frauds. The fourth section of the Statute of Frauds provides that "no action shall be brought [on certain agreements] unless the agreement upon which such action shall be brought, or some memorandum or note thereof, shall be in writing, and signed by the party to be charged therewith, or some person thereunto by him lawfully authorized." The section does not apply to quasi-contracts.

The contracts governed by this section of the Statute of Frauds are of two general types: those that will not be performed within a relatively short time and those that deal with specified subjects.

(1) An Agreement That Cannot Be Performed Within One Year After the Contract Is Made. A writing is required by the Statute of Frauds when the contract by its terms cannot be performed within one year after the date of the agreement. (See p. 185, Longcope Case) In computing the year for the purpose of the Statute of Frauds, the day on which the contract was made is excluded. The year begins with the following day and ends at the close of the first anniversary of the day on which the agreement was made.

The fourth section of the Statute of Frauds does not apply if it is possible under the terms of the agreement to perform the contract within one year. Thus under the statute a writing is not required when no time for performance is specified and the performance will not necessarily take more than a year. In this case it would be possible to perform the contract within a year, and the statute is deemed inapplicable without regard to the time when performance is actually begun or completed.

A promise to do an act at or upon or until the death of a person does not require a writing, even though that event may not occur until more than a year from the time the agreement is made. In contrast, a contract to pay an agent a commission for new customers procured by the agent for as long as such customers continue to purchase contemplates acts that may be performed beyond the statutory year and a writing is therefore required.

In most states, this provision of the Statute of Frauds is not applicable if the contract may or must be fully performed within a year by one of the contracting parties. By this view, a loan made today to be repaid in three years does not come within the statute because the performance of the lender necessarily takes place within the year. In a minority of states, the statute is applicable as long as performance by one of the parties may be made after the period of a year.

(2) An Agreement to Sell or a Sale of Any Interest in Real Property. The Statute of Frauds requires that all contracts to sell and sales of land, buildings, or interests in land, such as mortgages, which are treated as such an interest, shall be in writing. The statute applies only to the agreement between the owner and the purchaser, or between their agents. It does not apply to other or collateral agreements, such as those which the purchaser may make in order to raise the money to pay for the property, or to agreements to pay for an examination or search of the title of the property. Similarly, a partnership agreement to deal in real estate is generally not required to be in writing. The statute generally does not apply to contracts between a real estate agent and one of the parties to the sales contract employing him. Special statutes may require a writing in such a case, however.

(3) A Promise to Answer for the Debt or Default of Another. When *A* promises *C* to pay *B's* debt to *C* if *B* does not do so, *A* is promising to answer for the debt of another. Such a promise must usually be in writing to be enforceable.[1]

The requirement of a writing does not apply when the promisor makes the promise primarily for his own benefit. (See p. 186, R. H. Freitag Mfg. Co. Case) No writing is required when the debt incurred is the debt of the person promising to pay, even though a third person designated by the promisor benefits thereby. Thus, if *A* buys on his own credit from *C* and directs that *C* deliver the goods to *B, A* is incurring his own debt.

(4) A Promise by the Executor or Administrator of a Decedent's Estate to Pay a Claim Against the Estate from His Personal Funds. The executor or administrator has the duty of winding up the affairs of a deceased person, paying the debts from the proceeds of the estate and distributing any balance remaining. The executor or administrator is not personally liable for the claims against the estate of the decedent. If the personal representative promises to pay the decedent's debts, however, the promise cannot be enforced unless it is in a writing that complies with the terms of the statute.

---

[1] See Ch. 36.

If the personal representative makes a contract in the course of administering the estate, this section of the Statute of Frauds does not require that the contract be in writing as the representative is then contracting on behalf of the estate and not on his own behalf. Thus, if he employs an attorney to settle the estate or makes a burial contract with an undertaker, no writing is required since he is not undertaking to make a payment from his personal funds.

(5) A Promise Made in Consideration of Marriage. If a person makes a promise to pay a sum of money or to give property to another in consideration of marriage or a promise to marry, the agreement must be in writing. This provision of the Statute of Frauds is not applicable to ordinary mutual promises to marry, and it is not affected by the statutes in some states that prohibit the bringing of any action for breach of promise of marriage.

Sec. 11-D. Seventeenth Section of the Statute of Frauds. With respect to the sale of personal property, a special provision was made by the English Statute of Frauds. Section seventeen provided that "No contract for the sale of any goods, wares or merchandise, for the price of ten pounds sterling, or upwards, shall be allowed to be good, except: (1) when the buyer shall accept part of the goods so sold and actually received the same, (2) or give something in earnest to bind the bargain, or in part payment, (3) or that some note or memorandum in writing of the said bargain be made and signed by the parties to be charged by such contract or their agents thereunto lawfully authorized."

The provisions of the seventeenth section have been copied in most states. The statutes commonly provide a sales price, usually ranging from $30 to $500, below which the statute does not apply.

The expression "goods, wares, and merchandise" includes practically all forms of personal property—tangible or intangible. Choses in action (documents representing intangible personal property, such as stock certificates and bonds) are expressly included by the Uniform Sales Act [2] and by separate provisions of the Uniform Commercial Code. [3]

Sec. 11-E. Note or Memorandum. The Statute of Frauds requires a writing for those contracts which come within its scope. This writing may be a note or memorandum, as distinguished from a formal contract. It may be in any form because its only purpose and effect is to act as evidence of the contract.

---

[2] Uniform Sales Act (USA) Sec. 4(1).

[3] Uniform Commercial Code, Sec. 8-319 as to securities, and Sec. 1-206 as to other choses in action.

The note or memorandum must contain all the material terms of the contract, however, so that the court can determine just what was agreed. The writing must name or identify the parties to the contract. The subject matter must be identified either within the writing itself or in other writings to which it refers.

The note or memorandum may consist of one writing or instrument or of separate papers, such as letters or telegrams, or of a combination of such papers. The memorandum may be made at the time of the original transaction or at a later date. It must, however, ordinarily exist at the time an action is brought upon the agreement.

The note or memorandum must be signed by the party sought to be charged or his agent. Many states require that the authorization of an agent to execute a contract coming within the Statute of Frauds must itself be in writing.[4] In the case of an auction, it is the usual practice for the auctioneer to be the agent of both parties for the purpose of signing the memorandum. If the seller himself acts as auctioneer, however, he cannot sign as agent for the buyer.

The signature may be made at any place on the writing, although in some states it is expressly required that the signature appear at the end of the writing. The signature may be an ordinary one or any symbol that is adopted by the party as his signature. It may consist of initials, figures, or a mark. When a signature consists of a mark made by a person who is illiterate or physically incapacitated, it is commonly required that the name of the person be placed upon the writing by someone else, who may be required to sign the instrument as a witness. A person signing a trade or an assumed name is liable to the same extent as though he signed in his own name. In the absence of a local statute that provides otherwise, the signature may be made by pencil, as well as by pen, or by typewriter, by print, or by stamp.

Sec. 11-F. Effect of Noncompliance. The majority of states hold that an agreement which does not comply with the Statute of Frauds is voidable. A small minority of states hold that it is void. In those jurisdictions where it is voidable, the Statute of Frauds is a defense personal to the defendant. This means that an action can be brought to enforce the contract, but the defendant can raise the objection that it is not written. It also means that no one other than the defendant can make the objection.

In some cases when a writing is not made as required by the statute, the courts will nevertheless enforce the agreement if there has been a sufficient part performance to make it clear that a contract existed. In other instances the court will not enforce the con-

---

4 See p. 570.

tract but will permit a party to recover the fair value of work and improvements that he has made in reliance upon the contract. This situation commonly arises when a vendee or purchaser of land under an oral agreement enters into possession of the land. If the purchaser has made valuable improvements to the land, the courts will commonly enforce the oral agreement. On the other hand, the fact that a purchaser has paid the purchase price or that he has gone into possession does not take the case out of the Statute of Frauds if he has not made improvements. Ordinarily the performance of personal services does not constitute such part performance as will take the case out of the Statute of Frauds, except in extraordinary cases when the value of the services cannot be measured by money.

Before the court dispenses with the need for a writing, it must find that there has been such reliance upon the existence of the oral contract that it would be grossly unfair to one of the parties to refuse to enforce the contract in his favor.

In most instances, a person who is prevented from enforcing a contract because of the Statute of Frauds is nevertheless entitled to recover from the other party the value of any services or property furnished or money given under the contract. Recovery is based not upon the terms of the contract but upon the quasi-contractual obligation of the other party to restore to the plaintiff what he has received in order to prevent his unjust enrichment at the plaintiff's expense.

Sec. 11-G. Parol Evidence Rule. Can a written contract be contradicted by the testimony of witnesses? The general rule is that spoken words, that is, *parol evidence*, will not be allowed to modify or contradict the terms of a written contract which is complete on its face unless there is clear proof that because of fraud, accident, or mistake the writing is not in fact a contract or the complete contract. This is called the *parol evidence rule*. It refers to words spoken before or at the time the contract was made.

If a written contract appears to be complete, the parol evidence rule prohibits its alteration not only by oral testimony but also by proof or other writings or memoranda made before or at the time the written contract was executed. An exception is made when the written contract refers to and identifies other writings or memoranda and states that they are to be regarded as part of the written contract. In such a case, it is said that the other writings are incorporated by reference.

(1) Reason for the Parol Evidence Rule. The parol evidence rule is based on the theory that either (a) there never was an oral agreement (see p. 187, Evans v. Borkowski) or (b) if there was, the parties **purposely abandoned it when they executed their written contract.**

(2) *When the Parol Evidence Rule Does Not Apply.*

(a) INCOMPLETE CONTRACT. The parol evidence rule is based on the theory that the written contract sums up or integrates the entire contract. Accordingly, if the written contract is on its face or is admittedly not a complete summation, the parties naturally did not intend to abandon the points upon which they had agreed but which were not noted in the memorandum.

(b) FRAUD, ACCIDENT, OR MISTAKE. A contract may appear on its face to be complete and yet not include everything the parties agreed upon. It must be remembered that there is no absolute standard by which to determine when a contract is complete. All that the court can consider is whether all essential terms of the contract are present, that is, whether the contract is sufficiently definite to be enforceable, and whether it contains all provisions which would ordinarily be included in a contract of that nature.

It may be, however, that a contract apparently complete on its face may have omitted a provision which should have been included. If the final copy is not a true copy in that it omits a provision because of fraud, accident, or mistake, and this fact is proved to the satisfaction of the court, it is proper to show by oral testimony what the terms of the omitted provision were.

(c) AMBIGUITY. If a written contract is not clear in all its provisions, parol evidence may generally be admitted to clarify the meaning. This is particularly true when the contract contains contradictory measurements or descriptions, or when it employs symbols or abbreviations that have no general meaning known to the court. Parol evidence may also be admitted to show that a word used in a contract has a special trade meaning or a meaning in the particular locality that differs from the common meaning of that word.

(d) CONDUCT OF PARTIES. The parol evidence rule does not prevent either party from showing by parol evidence that he was fraudulently induced to execute the contract or that the other party to the contract has not performed his obligations.

(3) *Existence or Modification of Contract.* The parol evidence rule prohibits only the contradiction of a complete written contract. It does not prohibit proof that an obligation under the contract never existed because a condition precedent was not satisfied or that the contract was thereafter modified or terminated.

When it is claimed that a contract is modified by a later agreement, whether written or not, consideration must support the modifying agreement.

Sec. 11-H. Interpretation of Contracts. The terms of a contract should be clearly stated, and all important terms should be included. If they are not, the parties may interpret the terms differently. When such differences cannot be resolved satisfactorily by the parties and the issue is brought into court, certain principles of construction and interpretation are applied. An understanding of these rules should help contracting parties to avoid many of the difficulties that may arise when a contract is not drafted carefully.

(1) Intention. A contract is to be enforced according to its terms. The court must examine the contract to determine and give effect to what the parties intended, provided that their objective is lawful. It is the intention of the parties as expressed in the contract that must prevail. (See p. 188, Liberty Storage Case) A secret intention of one party that is not expressed in the contract has no effect, and a court cannot remake a contract for the parties under the guise of interpreting it. Of course, if the contract is so vague or indefinite that the intended performance cannot be determined, the contract cannot be enforced.

In arriving at the meaning of a contract, a court must endeavor to give meaning to every word. In the absence of proof that a word has a peculiar meaning or that it was employed by the parties with a particular meaning, a common word is given its ordinary meaning and a technical word is given its ordinary technical meaning.

Clerical errors and omissions are ignored and the contract is read as the parties intended, provided that the errors or omissions are not so material or do not raise such a conflict as to make it impossible to determine the intention of the parties.[5]

(2) Whole Contract. The provisions of a contract must be construed as a whole. This rule is followed even when the contract is partly written and partly oral, but this principle does not apply when an oral agreement must be excluded according to the parol evidence rule.[6]

When several writings, letters, telegrams, and/or memorandums are executed as part of one transaction, either at the same time or at different times, they are all to be construed as a single writing when it can be determined that that was the intent of the parties.

Terms in a printed letterhead or billhead or on the reverse side of a printed contract form are not part of a contract written thereon unless a reasonable man would regard such terms as part of the contract.

---

[5] As to the extent to which parol evidence may be employed to explain the meaning of terms and to show the intent of the parties, see page 181.

[6] See p. 180.

(3) Contradictory Terms. When a contract is partly printed or typewritten and partly written and the written part conflicts with the printed or typewritten part, the written part prevails. When there is a conflict between a printed part and a typewritten part, the latter prevails. When there is a conflict between an amount or quantity expressed both in words and figures, the amount or quantity expressed in words prevails.

When it is possible to give a contract two interpretations and one is lawful and the other unlawful, it is assumed that the lawful interpretation was intended by the parties. Similarly, an interpretation that is fair is preferred over one that will work an unjust hardship or cause one of the parties to forfeit valuable rights.

A contract is interpreted more strictly against the party who drafted it. Thus printed forms of a contract supplied by one party to the transaction are interpreted against him and in favor of the other party when two interpretations are reasonably possible.

(4) Implied Terms. Although a contract should be explicit and provide for all reasonably foreseeable events, it is not necessary that every provision be set forth. In some cases, a term may be implied in the absence of an express statement to the contrary. To illustrate, an obligation to pay a certain sum of money is implied to mean payment in legal tender. Likewise, in a contract to perform work there is an implied promise to use such skill as is necessary for the proper performance of the work. In a "cost plus" contract there is an undertaking that the costs will be reasonable and proper. (See p. 190, Wendel v. Maybury)

A local custom or trade practice, such as that of allowing 30 days credit to buyers, may form part of the contract when it is clear that the parties intended to be governed by this custom or trade practice or when a reasonable man would believe that they had so intended.

Sec. 11-I. Conflict of Laws. Since we have 50 state court systems and the federal court system, questions sometimes arise as to what law will be applied by a court. *Conflict of laws* is that branch of law which determines which body of law shall apply in these situations.

(1) State Courts. It is important to distinguish between the state or states in which the parties are domiciled or have their permanent home, the state in which the contract is made, and the state in which the contract is to be performed. The state in which the contract is made is determined by finding the state in which the last act essential to the formation of the contract was performed. Thus, when an acceptance is mailed in one state to an offeror in another state, the state of formation of the contract is the state in which the acceptance is mailed if the acceptance becomes effective at that time.

If an action on a contract made in one state is brought in a court of another state, an initial question is whether that court will lend its aid to the enforcement of a foreign contract. Ordinarily suit may be brought on a foreign cause of action. But if there is a strong contrary local policy, recovery may be denied even though the contract was valid in the state where it was made. (See p. 190, Metropolitan Life Insurance Co. v. Kendall.)

The capacity of a natural person to make a contract is governed by the place of contracting; a corporation's capacity to do so is determined by the law of the state of incorporation. The law of the state where the contract is made determines whether it is valid in substance [7] and satisfies requirements as to form. Matters relating to the performance of the contract, excuse or liability for nonperformance, and the measure of damages for nonperformance are generally governed by the law of the state where the contract is to be performed. When a lawsuit is brought on the contract, the *law of the forum*, that is, of the court in which the action is brought, determines the procedure and the rules of evidence.

Whether there is any right that can be assigned is determined by the law of the state which determines whether the contract is substantively valid. The formal validity of the assignment is determined by the law of the state in which it is made.

(2) Federal Courts. When the parties to the contract are domiciled in different states and an action is brought on the contract in a federal court because of this diversity of citizenship, the federal court must apply the same rules of conflict of laws that would be applied by the courts of the state in which the federal court is sitting. Thus a federal court is Chicago deciding a case involving parties from Indiana and Wisconsin must apply the same rules of conflict of laws as would be applied by the courts of Illinois. The state law must be followed by the federal court in such a case whether or not the federal court agrees with the state law.

Cases for Chapter 11

Breaux Bros. Construction Co. v. Associated Contractors
226 La. 720, 77 So.2d 17 (1954)

Breaux Brothers Construction Co. negotiated with Associated Contractors for the excavation by Breaux of dirt from drainage ditches. It was contemplated by both parties that when the terms of a contract were

---

[7] The right of the parties to select their own law is recognized by the Uniform Commercial Code, which provides that whenever a transaction is governed by the Code, the parties may agree that their rights and duties shall be governed by the law of any state or nation which "bears a reasonable relation" to the transaction. UCC Sec. 1-105(1).

decided upon, the contract would be reduced to writing and signed by all parties. Agreement as to the terms was reached, but no written contract was ever executed. Breaux sued Associated, claiming that an oral contract had been entered into and that the oral contract had been broken by Associated. From a judgment for Associated, Breaux appealed.

HAWTHORNE, J. . . . It is elementary in our law that where the negotiations contemplated and provide that there shall be a contract in writing, neither party is bound until the writing is perfected and signed. The distinction is manifest between those cases in which there is a complete [oral] contract, which the law does not require to be reduced to writing, and a subsequent agreement that it shall be reduced to writing, and those in which, as in this case, it is a part of the bargain that the contract shall be reduced to writing. In the first class of cases the original oral contract is in no manner impaired by the failure to carry out the subsequent agreement to put it in writing. In the second class of cases, the final consent is suspended; the contract is inchoate, incomplete, and it can not be enforced until it is signed by all the parties. . . .

Since the parties in the instant case intended from the beginning to reduce their negotiations to a written contract, neither the plaintiff nor the defendant was bound until the contract was reduced to writing and signed by them. Therefore, even if all of the terms of the alleged contract between plaintiff and defendant had been [orally] agreed upon, no valid contract would have existed between the parties because this case falls within the second class of cases discussed . . . , and therefore in this case the final consent of the parties was suspended until such time as the contract should be reduced to writing and signed by all the parties.

[Judgment affirmed.]

Longcope v. Lucerne-in-Maine Community Assn.

127 Maine 282, 143 A. 64 (1928)

In December, 1925, Saddlemire, President of the Lucerne-in-Maine Community Association, by oral agreement employed Longcope at a specified weekly salary as a "co-ordinator" in the development of the state of Maine as a playground, as well as agriculturally and industrially. Longcope was told that the enterprise would "take a great many years to develop, and I want you with me, to act as my right-hand man during that time." After being discharged on May 1, 1926, he brought an action against the company to recover damages for breach of contract. From a verdict for the plaintiff, the defendant moved for a new trial.

DEASY, J. . . . The defendant's main reliance is upon the Statute of Frauds, which bars actions upon contracts not to be performed within a year, unless such contracts are evidenced by writing.

Contracts of employment for a specified period of more than a year or for the performance of undertakings which necessarily require more than that time are obviously within the statute.

Also within the statute are contracts wherein the manifest intent and purpose of the parties, affirmatively proved, is that more than one year shall be taken for their performance. . . .

Some authorities hold that mere possibility of literal performance within a year removes the bar of the statute. Such is not the law in this jurisdiction. The intent of the parties that the contract is not to be performed within a year, whether such intent is expressed in words or otherwise plainly manifested, is controlling.

Mr. Longcope's contract, as appears from his own testimony, required him to act with Mr. Saddlemire during the time that the latter is engaged in carrying into execution vast plans of state-wide vacational, agricultural, and industrial development. These ambitious projects certainly require more than a year for completion. The parties so understood and intended. It was, indeed, stated in the contract, as testified to by the plaintiff, that the work undertaken would take "a great many years," and that "during that time" the plaintiff was to act as Mr. Saddlemire's right-hand man.

This case is clearly within the legal principle as enunciated by the above authorities. . . .

[New trial granted on motion of defendant.]

R. H. Freitag Mfg. Co. v. Boeing Airplane Co.

55 Wash. 2d 334, 347 P.2d 1074 (1959)

Boeing Airplane Co. contracted with Pittsburgh-Des Moines Steel Co. for the latter to construct a supersonic wind tunnel. R. H. Freitag Mfg. Co. sold material to York-Gillespie Co., which subcontracted to do part of the work. In order to persuade Freitag to keep supplying materials on credit, Boeing and the principal contractor both assured Freitag that he would be paid. Freitag was not paid by the subcontractor and then sued Boeing and the contractor. They defended on the ground that the assurances given Freitag were not written. From a judgment in favor of the defendants, the plaintiff appealed.

Rossellini, J. . . . It is conceded that the Statute of Frauds . . . renders unenforceable any special promise to answer for the debt, default, or misdoings of another. However, this court has recognized and followed the very widely accepted doctrine that, where the leading purpose of the promisor is not to aid the third person in getting credit but to secure a benefit for himself, he will be considered a debtor himself, rather than a surety, and the statute will not apply. . . .

"The purpose of [the statute] was not to effectuate, but to prevent, wrong. It does not apply to promises in respect to debts created at the instance and for the benefit of the promisor, but only to those by which the debt of one party is sought to be charged upon and collected from another. . . .

It is so obviously just that a promisor receiving no benefits should be bound only by the exact terms of his promise, that this statute requiring a memorandum in writing was enacted. Therefore, whenever the alleged promisor is an absolute stranger to the transaction, and without interest in it, courts strictly uphold the obligations of this statute. But cases sometimes arise in which, though a third party is the original obligor, the primary debtor, the promisor has a personal, immediate and pecuniary interest in the transaction, and is therefore himself a party to be benefited by the performance of the promisee. In such cases the reason which underlies and which prompted this statutory provision fails, and the courts will give effect to the promise." . . .

The allegations of the complaint in this instance are ample to support a finding that the assurances of Pittsburgh and Boeing were given to secure a benefit to themselves, a technically satisfactory and expeditious construction of the needed parts, and there is no allegation to show that they had any motive or purpose to benefit York-Gillespie. . . .

[Judgment reversed.]

Evans v. Borkowski

139 So.2d 472 (Fla., 1962)

Evans made a written contract to buy property from Borkowski. Under the sales contract the buyer was to make payment in certain installments prior to the delivery of the deed. When the buyer could not make payments on time, the parties entered into a new written agreement, the buyer persuading the seller to do so by orally promising him that he would pay interest on late payments. He was late in making the payments and paid the interest under protest. The buyer later sued the seller to recover the interest payments. From a judgment in the seller's favor, the buyer appealed.

STURGIS, J. . . . Parol testimony is inadmissible to vary, contradict, or add to the terms of a written instrument. . . . "The [parol evidence rule] . . . obviously enables the judge to head off the difficulty at its source, not by professing to decide any question as to the credibility of the asserted oral variation, but by professing to exclude the evidence from the jury altogether. . . ." It . . . rests upon a rational foundation of experience and policy and is essential to the certainty and stability of written obligations. . . .

The seller insists that the buyer made the alleged parol agreement as an inducement to him to accept [the new agreement]. . . . By the same token, it is evident that the parol agreement, if any, was part and parcel of the [new agreement] and as such is inadmissible in evidence.

We deem it in order to note that our holding is based upon what we deem to be well-settled principles of law which have been established as the result of the dictates of experience and wisdom which takes into account the fact that when in conflict, written transactions must prevail over parol transactions; that stability and order compel that course. In so holding, we recognize that under this rule it is inevitable that there will be instances where, as appears to be the case here, an unsuspecting person will accept in good faith the promise of a dissembler and reap the consequences of ill-placed trust. It is regretful that the advantages of maintaining the rule outweigh the disadvantages occasionally suffered by such circumstances. . . .

[Judgment reversed.]

Liberty Storage Co. v. Kansas City Terminal Warehouse Co.

340 S.W.2d 189 (Mo.App., 1960)

Afton Realty Co. leased a warehouse to Liberty Storage Co. for a term of five years beginning January 21, 1949, and ending January 20, 1954, with an option to renew the lease for an additional five years. Liberty assigned the lease to Kansas City Terminal Warehouse Co. By the assignment Kansas City agreed to pay the rent to the "termination date of the present lease." Liberty thereafter had the lease extended for an additional five years to January 20, 1959. Kansas City paid the rent to the end of the original five-year term but refused to pay any rent for the additional five-year term. Liberty sued Kansas City for the rent for the additional term. From a judgment for the defendant, the plaintiff appealed.

Cross, J. . . . Fundamentally, the disputed question will be resolved by determining the intention of the parties as expressed in the language of the contract. "For the purpose of determining the intention of the parties and reaching a construction that is fair and reasonable under all the facts and circumstances, the court may consider the relationship of the parties, the subject matter of the contract, the usages of the business, the surrounding facts and circumstances attending the execution of the contract and its interpretation by the parties." . . .

The rules for interpreting contracts are not subtle, but are made for persons of common understanding. . . . The contract in dispute will be considered according to the plain, ordinary and usual meaning of the words and phrases contained in it, as there is nothing in the record to indicate that any word contained in the text of the contract was used in a legal or technical sense. Both parties were warehouse operators—not real estate brokers. No inference arises that any of their officers and employees were familiar with the usages and terminology of the real estate trade or were learned in any branch of the law. "All mercantile contracts ought to be interpreted according to their plain meaning, to men of sense and understanding, and not according to forced and refined interpretations which are intelligible only to lawyers, and scarcely to them." . . .

Under the foregoing prescription, we examine the following words of the contract, which alone define the period of defendant's obligation: "2. Second Party shall pay direct to the First Party an additional rent of One Hundred Dollars ($100.00) per month from November 1, 1950 to the termination date of the present lease."

Our first duty is to determine and apply to the contract the meaning and effect of the word "present," as used by the parties. We are not at liberty to ignore the presence of the word, but must attach meaning and significance to it, because every part of the contract must be given effect, if fairly and reasonably possible. . . .

Webster's New International Dictionary, Second Edition, defines the word "present," as "now existing, or in process; begun but not ended, now in view, being dealt with, or under consideration; being at this time; actual; contemporary; not past or future."

We believe that the foregoing lexicon definitions are in accordance with and express the ordinary use and understanding of the word "present," and that the parties understood and used that word in a sense equivalent to the quoted definitions.

The phrase "the present lease" was written into the contract for the useful purpose of identifying a certain lease or lease term as distinguished from some other or different one. By "the present lease" the parties meant the one then existing, within their view and being dealt with—not a lease which might (or might not) come into future being. We conclude that "the present lease" contemplated by the parties was the lease "for a term of five years beginning January 21, 1949 and ending on the 20th day of January, 1954." . . .

Another circumstance of import is the contract provision that the additional rentals were to be paid "to the termination *date* of the present lease"—not to its *termination*. At the time of the agreement there was only one termination date before the contracting parties. That date was January 20, 1954, as set out in the lease. Although it was evident, from the lease itself, that it might later be renewed as an additional term, yet the parties chose to limit defendant's obligation to the term then in duration. The use of the words "termination date" instead of the broader word "termination" points to their intent to contract with specific reference to the existing five year lease terminating on January 20, 1954. . . .

If the parties had intended that defendant pay rentals after January 21, 1949, and during an extension or renewal term, they could have so provided by using appropriate words. They could have used the words "for and during the term of said lease and any extensions or renewals thereof." . . . They could even have expressed such intention by refraining from using the word "present" in the contract. . . .

[Judgment affirmed.]

Wendel v. Maybury

75 So.2d 379 (La.App., 1954)

Maybury, who owned a piece of real estate, contracted with Wendel to construct a building thereon under a "cost plus" contract by which Maybury agreed to pay all costs of labor and material plus a commission on that cost. When the building was finished, the contractor presented a bill for $614.80 for "mill work, lumber, carpenter labor, hardware, nails, screws, and paving labor." Maybury refused to pay this lump sum and disputed what amounts had been used for labor and materials. From a judgment for Maybury, the contractor appealed.

McBride, J. . . . Under a cost-plus contract, the contractor is obligated to use his utmost endeavors to see that the owner gets value received. . . . Where there is such a contract to do a job for whatever it might cost, it is implicit that the price charged will not be whatever the contractor sees fit to charge, but will be whatever may be shown to be the reasonable and proper cost. . . .

The law being thus, we are of the opinion that plaintiff was under the duty of submitting an itemization of each and every expenditure made by him on the cost-plus contract, and that a bill in a lump sum for numerous items will not meet the requirements which are exacted from a contractor working on such basis. The defendants denied they were indebted to plaintiff, so plaintiff carried the burden of proving each and every item of expense in connection with the erection of defendants' building, . . . We do not believe he has successfully done so. . . .

[Judgment modified for other reasons.]

Metropolitan Life Insurance Co. v. Kendall

225 Ark. 731, 284 S.W.2d 863 (1955)

Blakely Kendall applied for and was issued a policy of life insurance in Missouri by the Metropolitan Life Insurance Co. After his death, his beneficiary, Amos Kendall, sued the insurance company in Arkansas. The insurance company sought to offer in evidence statements made by the insured to his doctors. Amos claimed that by the law of Arkansas such statements could not be admitted in evidence. The statements were excluded. From a judgment for Amos, the insurer appealed.

HOLT, J. . . . "The broad, uncontroverted rule is that the lex loci [8] will govern as to all matters going to the basis of the right of action itself, while the lex fori [9] controls all that is connected merely with the remedy. . . . It is well settled in this state that, when a party comes into court to enforce his remedy upon a contract, that remedy will be enforced in accordance with the laws of this state regulating the remedy and not according to the remedy of the state where the contract was made." . . .

For reversal appellant [insurer] relied on but one point, that: "The trial court erred in excluding from evidence the appellant's offered depositions of . . . [various doctors] as being privileged communications." . . .

[The court held that the evidence was properly excluded under the provisions of the Arkansas statute.]

[Judgment affirmed.]

Questions and Case Problems

1. What is the objective of each of the following rules of law?
   (a) A contract is generally valid whether it is written or not.
   (b) Parol evidence is not admissible for the purpose of modifying a written contract when that evidence relates to an agreement made before or at the time that the written contract was executed.

2. Claremont Management Company sold a house to McNeely. The contract was a blank form prepared by Claremont and filled in with the details of the sale. The form made certain warranties but stated that any complaint must be delivered to the seller not later than a date to be specified, and then indicated that the date should be one year from initial occupancy. Claremont, in preparing the contract for the sale to McNeely inserted "January 6, 1957" as the deadline for the notice. This was actually more than a year after the beginning of occupancy since McNeely had moved into the property on May 16, 1955. On October 4, 1956, McNeely gave notice of certain deficiencies to Claremont. Claremont refused to recognize the notice on the ground that the warranty period of one year from occupancy had expired. Was Claremont bound by the notice? (McNeely v. Claremont Management Co., 27 Cal.Reptr. 87)

3. Keith sued Heffernan on a contract for the sale of land. Heffernan raised the defense that there was no writing which satisfied the Statute of Frauds. Keith introduced into evidence: (1) a series of letters from the defendant to the defendant's real estate broker describing the property in question and putting it up for sale with the broker at $10,000; (2) the testimony of the broker that he telephoned to the defendant the offer

---

[8] The law of the place where the cause of action arose.
[9] The law of the court in which the action is brought.

received by the broker from the plaintiff as to the purchase of the property in question; and (3) a telegram received by the broker in response to his request to the seller for a confirming telegram, which telegram read: "Accept $10,000 net for 5 acres 125th Avenue deal to close by March 9th." Was Keith entitled to enforce the contract? (Heffernan v. Keith, [Fla.] 127 So.2d 903)

4. Talbott, a petroleum engineer, claimed that Gatty hired him to drill twenty oil wells on certain land. When Gatty hired another engineer to drill the wells, Talbott sued Gatty. The latter defended on the ground that there was no written contract. Could Talbott recover? (Talbott v. Gatty, 171 Kan. 141, 231 P.2d 205)

5. Milbrand and Castorri, both of Michigan, made an oral contract by which Milbrand was to employ Castorri for five years to do certain work in Florida. Later, Castorri sued Milbrand in Florida for breach of the contract. Milbrand raised the defense that the contract was void because there was no writing as was required by the law of Michigan. Castorri replied that under the law of Florida, where he was to perform the contract and where the suit was being brought, the contract with the defendant was binding even though it was oral. Could Castorri recover? (Castorri v. Milbrand, [Fla.] 118 So.2d 563)

6. Mary Kearney made an oral contract with Paul Lytle, an investment broker, by which Kearney was to obtain a loan by placing a new mortgage on certain property and Lytle was to receive the proceeds of the loan and thereafter make all payments on the mortgage as they became due. Lytle died and Kearney brought suit against his executor, the Mechanics National Bank, to enforce the oral contract. The executor claimed that the contract was not binding because it was a contract to pay the debt of another and was not in writing. Decide. (Kearney v. Mechanics National Bank of Worcester, [Mass.] 180 N.E.2d 667)

7. Lillie Lightner executed a note promising to pay to the order of M. S. Lightner approximately $11,000. Thomas Lightner later became the owner of the note and sued Lillie. She raised the defense that it was agreed between M. S. Lightner and herself that suit would not be brought against her on the note. Was this a defense? (Lightner v. Lightner, [W.Va.] 124 S.E.2d 355)

8. An employment agency advertised in the New York Times of October 30 for work in Venezuela for a period of not less than two years. The ad stated that "Client will interview in our office Monday and Tuesday, October 31 and November 1." The ad gave only the name of the agency and ended with "Please phone for appointment." The client, the Blaw-Knox Co., made employment contracts with Bachmann and 24 others. Seven of these contracts were made either before October 30 or in other states. Blaw-Knox discharged the 25 employees before the expiration of the two years. When the 25 employees sued Blaw-Knox, it defended on the ground of the Statute of Frauds. The plaintiffs relied on the New York Times advertisement of October 30 as a writing to satisfy the Statute. Decide. (Bachmann v. Blaw-Knox Company [W.D. Pa.] 198 F.Supp. 617)

CHAPTER 12

Nature and Transfer of Contract Rights

Ordinarily one person makes a contract with another person and no question arises as to the nature of the rights created. Rather frequently, however, two or more persons make a contract with one or more other persons. Furthermore, a person who was not a party to the original agreement may acquire rights under that contract. Under these circumstances questions concerning the nature of the rights created may arise.

Sec. 12-A. Joint, Several, and Joint and Several Contracts. When two or more persons make a contract with one or more other persons, the contract may be (1) joint, (2) several, or (3) joint and several.

(1) Joint Contracts. A *joint contract* is one in which two or more persons jointly promise to perform an obligation or in which two or more persons are jointly entitled to the benefit of the performance by the other party or parties. If *A, B,* and *C* sign a contract stating "we jointly promise" to do a particular act, the obligation is the joint obligation of *A, B,* and *C.* In the absence of an express intent to the contrary, a promise by two or more persons is generally presumed to be joint and not several. (See p. 201, Mintz v. Tri-County Natural Gas Co.)

Each of two or more joint promisors is liable for the entire obligation, but an action must be brought against all who are living and within the jurisdiction of the court. When a judgment is obtained against two joint promisors, execution on the judgment may be levied wholly on the property of one promisor or partially on the property of each one. However, if only one (or less than all) is sued and if he does not object to the fact that all are not sued, he cannot object after he has lost the action because the defect is regarded as cured by the entry of a judgment. At common law the entry of the judgment in such a case also barred the plaintiff from subsequently suing the joint obligors whom he had not sued in the first action. This rule has been changed by statute in many states so that the plaintiff can bring a later action against those whom he had not sued originally.

If one of the joint promisors dies, the surviving promisors remain bound to perform the contract unless it was personal in character and required the joint action of all the obligors for its performance. If the deceased obligor had received a benefit from the contract, a court of equity will also hold his estate liable for the performance of the contract.

Generally the release by the promisee of one or more of the joint obligors releases all.

These rules apply equally to joint promisees.

(2) Several Contracts. Several contracts arise when two or more persons separately agree to perform the same obligation even though the separate agreements are set forth in the same instrument. At common law these persons were liable individually and could not be sued jointly in one action. This rule has been changed in many jurisdictions by the adoption of statutes, or by rules of courts making procedural reforms, that permit persons liable on related causes of action to be sued at one time.

If *A, B,* and *C* sign a contract stating "we severally promise" or "each of us promises" to do a particular act or to pay a specified sum of money, the three signers are severally bound to perform or to pay, that is, each signer is individually bound.

Upon the death of a several obligor, his liability descends to his estate and not to the surviving parties to the contract. Thus, upon the death of a person making a several contract, the promisee may maintain an action against the personal representative of the deceased obligor.

Since the liability of each obligor to a several contract is by definition separate or distinct, the release of one or more of the joint obligors by the promisee does not release the others.

The same principles apply when the rights of two or more obligees are several.

(3) Joint and Several Contracts. As the name implies, a *joint and several contract* is one in which two or more persons are bound both jointly and severally. If *A, B,* and *C* sign a contract stating "we, and each of us, promise" or "I promise" to pay a specified sum of money, they are jointly and severally bound. In such a contract, the obligee may treat the claim either as a joint claim or as a group of separate claims. He may bring a suit against all or against one at a time. Under modern procedural rules and statutes, the plaintiff may sue any number of the severally liable parties instead of suing them either singly or all at one time.

In some states it is declared by statute that a joint contract is to be interpreted as a joint and several contract.

Sec. 12-B. Third Party Beneficiary Contracts. A third person who is expressly benefited by the performance of a contract may enforce it against the promisor when such was the intention of the parties to the contract. The third person may be either a creditor beneficiary or a donee beneficiary. A *creditor beneficiary* is a creditor of the promisee whose obligation to the creditor will be discharged to the extent that the promisor performs his promise A *donee beneficiary* is a person to whom no legal duty was owed by the promisee, and as to whom the performance by the promisor is a gift. Employees are ordinarily allowed to sue their employer for benefits conferred by a collective bargaining contract made by the employer and the union, on the theory that the employees are third party beneficiaries of such a contract. (See p. 202, Springer v. Powder Power Tool Corp.)

It is generally held that the rights of a third party beneficiary cannot be revoked even though the original parties to the contract change their minds. The creation of the contract gave the beneficiary definite rights, and in the absence of an express reservation those rights cannot be destroyed without his consent.[1]

Sec. 12-C. Incidental Beneficiaries. Although the right of a third party beneficiary to sue is now generally recognized, not everyone who benefits from the performance of a contract between others is deemed such a beneficiary. If a city makes a contract with a contractor to pave certain streets, property owners living along those streets will naturally receive a benefit from the performance. This fact, however, does not confer upon them the status of third party beneficiaries. Accordingly, the property owners cannot sue the contractor if he fails to perform. The courts reason that such beneficiaries are merely incidentally benefited. The city contracted for the building of the streets to further the general public interest, not primarily to benefit individual property owners.

Sec. 12-D. Assignments. Generally an *assignment* is a transfer by a party to a contract of some or all of his rights under the contract to a person not a party to the contract. The party making the assignment is the *assignor,* and the person to whom the assignment is made is the *assignee.* An assignee may generally sue in his own name as though he were a party to the original contract. (See p. 203, Compton v. Atwell) A *delegation of duties* is a transfer of duties by a party to a contract to another person who is to perform them in his stead.

---

[1] The Restatement of Contracts to some extent authorizes a contrary conclusion. Secs. 142, 143.

(1) Form of Assignment. Generally any form of an assignment is sufficient. Any words, whether written or spoken, that show an intention to transfer or assign will be given the effect of an assignment. Statutes may require that certain kinds of assignments be in writing or be executed in a particular form. This requirement is common in respect to statutes that limit the assignment of claims to wages.

An assignment is a transfer, not a contract. It is therefore immaterial whether there is any consideration for the assignment. An assignment may be made as a gift, although more commonly it is part of a business transaction.

In a contract to make an assignment, which is executory as far as the assignor is concerned (as contrasted with an assignment, which is executed), there must be consideration as in any other contract.

(2) Assignment of Rights to Money. A person entitled to receive money, such as payment of the purchase price or payment for work done under a contract, may generally assign that right to another person. A contractor entitled to receive payment from the owner can assign that right to the bank as security for a loan, or he can assign it to anyone else. The fact that the assigned right represents money not yet due does not prevent the application of this rule so long as the contract itself exists at the time of the assignment. Thus a contractor on January 15 may assign an installment payment that will be due on February 1 by the terms of the contract which was signed on January 10. Similarly a person entitled to receive payment of money under a contract of employment may ordinarily assign his right to future wages.

(a) NONEXISTING CONTRACTS. If the contract is not in existence at the time the assignment is made, the attempt to assign money due on the contract in the future does not have the effect of a legal assignment. If the assignment has been supported by consideration, however, a court of equity will treat the assignment as a promise to assign and compel the assignor to make a transfer when the money is due.

(b) RESTRICTIONS UPON ASSIGNMENT. There is a division of authority as to the effect of a prohibition in a contract against its assignment. In some jurisdictions, if a right to money is otherwise assignable, the right to transfer cannot be restricted by the parties to the contract. Such a restriction is regarded in those states as contrary to public policy because it places a limitation on the assignor's right of property. In other states such a prohibition is recognized as valid on the theory that the parties to the original contract may include such a provision if they choose to do so. (See p. 204, Allhusen v. Caristo Construction Corp.)

The Uniform Commercial Code recognizes the validity of a prohibition against assignment by declaring that rights under contracts for the sale of goods may be assigned, "unless otherwise agreed," except when the assignment would materially change the performance of the other party. It is also declared that unless the circumstances indicate the contrary, a prohibition of the assignment of "the contract" is to be construed only as prohibiting a delegation of performance.[2]

Statutes may validly prohibit the assignment of rights to money. Contractors who build public works are frequently prohibited from assigning money due or money that will become due under the contract. If some states wage earners are prohibited from assigning their futures wages, or the law limits the percentage of their wages that can be assigned. In some instances an assignment of wages is lawful, but the assignment must be a separate instrument complete in itself and not included in the body of any other instrument. The purpose of such a provision is to protect employees from signing printed forms containing "hidden" wage assignment clauses.

(3) Assignment of Right to a Performance. When the right of the obligee under the contract is a right to receive a performance by the other party, he may assign his right, provided the performance required of the other party to the contract will not be materially altered or varied by such assignment. If the assignor has the right to buy a certain quantity of a stated article and to take such property from the seller's warehouse, this right to purchase can be assigned. If, however, the sales contract stipulated that the seller should deliver to the buyer's premises and the assignee lived or had his place of business a substantial distance from the assignor's place of business, the assignment would not be given effect. In this case, the seller would be required to give a performance different from that which he contracted to make. Similarly a right to purchase goods on credit cannot be assigned since the seller would be required to accept a new purchaser whom he had not approved as a credit risk.

In the cases in which an attempted assignment is held void because the performance would be changed if the assignment were given effect, the law ignores whether the change in the performance would be to the disadvantage of the obligor.

(a) PERSONAL SATISFACTION. A similar problem arises when the goods to be furnished must be satisfactory to the personal judgment of the buyer. Since the seller only contracted that his performance would stand or fall according to the buyer's judgment, the law will not permit the buyer to substitute the judgment of his assignee.

---

[2] Uniform Commercial Code, Sec. 2-210 (2), (3).

(b) PERSONAL SERVICES. The foregoing principle also prohibits the assignment of a right to receive or obtain personal services. An employer cannot assign to another the employer's right to have an employee work for him. The relationship of employer and employee is so personal that the right cannot be assigned. The performance contracted for by the employee was to work for a particular employer at a particular place and at a particular job. To permit an assignee to claim the employee's services would be to change the contract that the employee made.

(4) Delegation of Duties. Under certain circumstances a contracting party may obtain someone else to do the work for him. When the performance is standardized and nonpersonal so that it is not material who performs, the law will permit the delegation of the performance of the contract. In such cases, however, the contracting party remains liable for the default of the person doing the work just as though the contracting party himself had performed or attempted to perform the job. If the contract expressly prohibits delegation, this cannot be done.

If the performance by the promisor requires his personal skill or is a performance in which his credit standing or the other party's confidence in his ability was material in selecting him, delegation of performance is prohibited. A doctor or an artist hired to render a particular service cannot delegate the performance of that duty to another as it is obvious that the other party to the contract relied upon his personal skill in selecting him. The law will not permit him by means of delegation to remake the other party's contract without that party's consent.

Whether a contract calls for a performance of such a nature that it cannot be delegated is a matter which may be difficult to determine. There are necessarily many borderline cases where reasonable persons might disagree as to whether a performance is such a routine matter that it can be done by anyone or is a matter which rests upon the skill, judgment, credit, or reliability of the contracting party.

(a) INTENTION TO DELEGATE DUTIES. A question of interpretation arises as to whether an assignment of "the contract" is an assignment only of the rights of the assignor or is both an assignment of those rights and a delegation of his duties. The trend of authority is to regard such a general assignment as both a transfer of rights and a delegation of duties. (See p. 205, Radley v. Smith)

The Uniform Commercial Code provides with respect to contracts for the sale of goods that "an assignment of 'the contract' or of 'all my rights under the contract' or an assignment in similar general terms is an assignment of rights and unless the language or the circumstances (as in an assignment for security) indicate the contrary, it is a delegation of performance of the duties of the assignor and its acceptance by the assignee constitutes a promise by him to perform those duties. This promise is enforceable by either the assignor or the other party to the original contract." [3]

(b) NOVATION. One who is entitled to receive performance under a contract may agree to release the person who is bound to perform and to permit another person to take his place. When this occurs, it is not a question of merely assigning the liability under the contract but is really one of abandoning the old contract and substituting in its place a new contract. This change of contract and parties is called a *novation*. For example, if *A* and *B* have a contract, they, together with *C*, may agree that *C* shall take *B's* place. If this is done, there is a novation. *B* is then discharged from his contract, and *A* and *C* are bound. It must be shown that a novation was intended.

(5) Partial Assignment. The common law refused to recognize a partial assignment unless the obligor had consented to it. Here again, however, courts of equity have come to the aid of a person left remediless by the courts of law. In equity and under modern procedural reforms in many states, a partial assignee may sue provided that he makes the holders of the remaining fractional parts of the obligation coparties to the action.

(6) Defenses and Setoffs. The assignee's rights rise no higher than those of the assignor. If the other party to the contract could sucessfully defend against a suit brought by the assignor, then he will also prevail against the assignee. The obligor may also assert against the assignee a defense based on a setoff or counterclaim for damages against the assignor or for defective workmanship of the assignor.

If the obligor does not know of the assignment, it is immaterial whether these defenses, or setoffs and counterclaims, arise before or after the assignment is made. Those defenses, setoffs, and counterclaims which are based on acts of the assignor after the obligor has been informed or has learned of the assignment cannot be asserted by the obligor against the assignee. In such case the obligor did not regard the assignor as the holder of a claim when the defense, setoff, or counterclaim against him arose. It would therefore be unfair to permit the obligor to assert such claim or defense against the assignee.

The fact that the assignee takes the assignment in good faith and pays value and does not know or have any reason to know that the obligor has a defense or counterclaim available against the assignor

---

[3] UCC Sec. 2-210(4).

does not affect the applicability of these rules. The only way in which the assignee can protect himself is to ask the obligor whether he has any defense or setoff or counterclaim against the assignor. If the obligor states that he has none or makes a declaration of no setoff, he is estopped (barred) from contradicting his statement and in most cases is not permitted to prove a defense, setoff, or counterclaim based on facts arising prior to the time of his statement to the assignee.

(7) Notice of Assignment. An assignment, if otherwise valid, takes effect the moment it is made. It is not necessary that the assignee or the assignor give notice to the other party to the contract that the assignment has been made. It is highly desirable, however, that the other party be notified as soon as possible after the making of the assignment because, if notice is not given, the assigned right may be impaired or possibly destroyed.

(a) SETOFFS. The setoffs and counterclaims that may be asserted by the obligor against the assignee not only include those acquired by the obligor before the assignment is made but also include those based on acts committed up to the time that the obligor receives notice of the assignment. The giving of prompt notice to the obligor therefore reduces the period during which such setoffs or counterclaims can be acquired by the obligor.

(b) DISCHARGE. Until the obligor knows that there has been an assignment, he is legally entitled to pay to or perform for the assignor just as though there were no assignment. Such payment or performance is a complete discharge of his obligation under the contract; but in such a case the assignee could proceed against the assignor to require him to account for what he had received. If the assignee has given the obligor notice of the assignment, however, the obligor cannot discharge his obligation to the assignee by making a payment to or a performance for the assignor.

(c) PRIORITY. It sometimes happens that a person assigns the same right to two different assignees. A number of states hold that the assignee taking the first assignment prevails over the subsequent assignees. Other states adopt the English view by which the assignee first giving notice to the obligor is entitled to the payment. Under this rule, however, the first assignee may recover the payment made to the subsequent assignee if the latter knew of the prior assignment when he received the payment. This right of the prior assignee is restricted to suit against the subsequent assignee and does not give him the right to sue the obligor.

(8) Warranties of Assignor. When the assignment is made for a consideration, the assignor is regarded as impliedly warranting that

the right he assigns is valid, that he is the owner of the claim which he assigns, and that he will not interfere with the assignee's enforcement of the obligation. He does not warrant that the other party will pay or perform as required by the contract.

Cases for Chapter 12

Mintz v. Tri-County Natural Gas Co.
259 Pa. 477, 103 A. 285 (1918)

Mintz sold gas from a tract of land to the Tri-County Natural Gas Co. When the company failed to pay him for the gas, he sued. The company raised as a defense the fact that Mintz and five other persons had failed to perform another contract to sell gas to the company from a different tract of land. From a judgment for Mintz, the gas company appealed.

MOSCHZISKER, J. . . . The question whether a contractual promise, made by two or more persons, is joint, several, or joint and several depends upon the intention of the parties as evidenced by the language employed in the agreement under consideration; the general rule being that, in the absence of an apparent intent to the contrary, such promises are presumed to be joint and not several. . . .

"It is a general presumption of law, when two or more persons undertake an obligation, that they undertake jointly. Words of severance are necessary to overcome this primary presumption."

In the present instance, no such words appear; hence we say that the plaintiff and his fellow lessors are all jointly liable for a failure to deliver the gas sold to defendant, and the latter cannot maintain a suit against the plaintiff alone for such a breach of contract. At common law, there are three distinct forms of obligations ex contractu, i.e., (1) joint, (2) several, and (3) joint and several. In an action on the first, it was necessary to sue all the obligors together, or the survivors of them; on the second, the obligors had to be sued separately; but, on the third, the plaintiff could elect either to sue separately or jointly. . . . Except where changed by statute, these principles are still applicable. . . .

Since the defendant cannot maintain a suit against the present plaintiff alone for the breach of contract which it contends it has a right to take advantage of in this action, it follows that the defendant is not in a position to use this alleged breach in defense as a setoff; for the rule requiring mutuality of debts, where setoff is pleaded, forbids the setting off of a joint debt against a separate one. . . .

The cases which hold that two or more persons sued jointly may set off a debt due by the plaintiff to any one of them . . . have no application here since they rest upon the theory that defendants have the right to agree among themselves as to the adjustment of the proceeds of the setoff, and hence no harm is done to any one. This rule also permits one of two joint obligees, with the consent of the other, to use the obligation as an equitable defense in an action by the obligor against one of them alone . . . for again no harm is done; but a claim due from the plaintiff and others jointly cannot be set off in an action by plaintiff alone because to allow such a setoff would compel the latter to pay, individually, a debt for which he is liable only when called upon jointly with others. . . .

[Judgment for plaintiff affirmed.]

Springer v. Powder Power Tool Corp.
220 Ore. 102, 348 P.2d 1112 (1960)

The local labor union made a collective bargaining agreement with the Powder Power Tool Corp. governing the rates of pay for the latter's employees. Springer brought a suit on behalf of certain employees of the corporation who had not received the full pay under the agreement. From a judgment for the defendant, the plaintiff appealed.

McALLISTER, C.J. . . . There are several theories on which the right is granted . . . an employee [to] sue his employer to collect benefits accruing to the employee under a collective labor agreement made between his employer and the union. . . . "First, a collective agreement, while not thought to be itself enforceable by anyone, was considered to be a 'custom or usage' which could be incorporated by the individual into his personal employment contract. Second, the agreement was treated by a few courts as a 'mutual general offer to be closed by specific acceptance.' Third, some courts thought the collective agreement itself was enforceable by the individual on the ground that the employees were parties to the agreement, the union merely negotiating it on their behalf as a duly authorized agent. Fourth, a majority of courts allowed the individual to sue on the agreement itself on the theory that it was a third party beneficiary contract between the union and the employer for the benefit of the individual members of the union."

The great weight of modern authority adopts the legal theory that the employee is a third-party beneficiary of the labor agreement. . . .

There are also many cases holding that individual employees may sue under a collective bargaining agreement without mentioning the theory under which the right is recognized. . . . In at least a few instances there has been a conscious recognition that these cases do not fit precisely into the traditional concept of third-party beneficiary actions and that the rule applied may be [a new distinct rule]. . . .

Defendant relies heavily on Shelley v. Portland Tug & Barge Co., 158 Ore. 377, 76 P.2d 477, but we think the case is clearly distinguishable. In that case, decided in 1938, an employee sued to recover benefits which he claimed were due him under a contract made between his employer and a union. In holding that the employees could not sue on the contract, this court relied almost entirely on the admitted fact that no employee of the company was a member of the union. However, if the case is inconsistent with what is said here, it must yield to modern developments in the law of labor relations. . . .

[Judgment reversed.]

Compton v. Atwell

86 A.2d 623 (M.C.App.D.C., 1952)

Compton owed money to Atwell and three other persons. To save the expenses of litigation, the other three persons assigned their claims to Atwell, who then brought one lawsuit in his own name against Compton to recover on all four claims. The local rule of court required that actions be brought in the name of the real party in interest. Compton claimed that Atwell was not the real party in interest on the assigned claims because it was intended that Atwell should turn over any money recovered to the three assignors. From a judgment for Atwell, Compton appealed.

CLAYTON, C.J. . . . "Is an assignment valid when made only for the purpose of permitting the assignee to manage the litigation and to act as plaintiff for the real parties in interest?"

[Compton] argues that Atwell had no right to maintain the suit on the claims assigned to him because under Municipal Court Rule 17 he was not the real party in interest. But we note that the same rule provides that ". . . a party with whom or in whose name a contract has been made for the benefit of another, or a party authorized by statute may sue in his own name without joining with him the party for whose benefit the action is brought." This plaintiff was "authorized by statute" to sue in his own name. Code, 1940, 28-2503 provides, "All nonnegotiable written agreements for the payment of money . . . all open accounts, debts, and demands of a liquidated character . . . may be assigned in writing, so as to vest in the assignee a right to sue for the same in his own name." Long ago it was recognized that under the Code an assignee has the right to sue in his own name. . . .

Appellant [Compton] says the assignment transferred to Atwell only a naked legal title. This contention is seemingly based on the testimony that the assignment was made for the purpose of permitting him to act as plaintiff for the assignors, "in order to save Court costs and the additional expense to plaintiff and defendant which would be necessary for each person to sue the defendant in a separate suit. . . ." But assuming that Atwell was merely an assignee for collection, he would still not be prevented from maintaining the suit in his own name. In Overbury v. Platten, 2 Cir., 108 F.2d 155, 126 A.L.R. 185, certiorari denied, 311 U.S. 664, 61 S.Ct. 21, 85 L.Ed. 426, where a similar statute was involved, Judge Learned Hand wrote that an assignee of the title to a chose in action may sue in his own name though he had no interest in it, citing Titus v. Wallick, 306 U.S. 282, 59 S.Ct. 557, 561, 83 L.Ed. 653. There the Supreme Court, speaking through Justice Stone, held that where an assignment under a New York statute had operated to vest the assignee with title to the claim ". . . the fact that it was given for the purpose of enabling petitioner to bring the suit, and that he was bound to account to a stranger to the suit for its proceeds, are immaterial, since neither the court nor respondent was prejudiced by petitioner's failure to disclose them." The decision went on to say that such an assignee is qualified as "the real party in interest" even though the assignment is for the purpose of suit only and the assignee is obligated to account for the proceeds of the suit to his assignor. . . .

[Judgment affirmed.]

Allhusen v. Caristo Construction Corp.

303 N.Y. 446, 103 N.E.2d 891 (1952)

The Caristo Construction Corp. executed a contract with New York City for the construction of school buildings. It then made a subcontract with the Kroo Painting Co. to do the painting work. The contract with Kroo specified that any assignment of any money due or to become due under the contract was void unless made with the written consent of Caristo. Without obtaining any consent, Kroo assigned his claim to money due under the contract to Allhusen, who then sued Caristo to collect the money. From a judgment in Caristo's favor, Allhusen appealed.

FROESSEL, J. . . . Whether an antiassignment clause is effective is a question that has troubled the courts not only of this State but in other jurisdictions as well. . . .

Our courts have not construed a contractual provision against assignments framed in the language of the clause now before us. Such kindred clauses as have been subject to interpretation usually have been held to be either (1) personal covenants limiting the covenantee to a claim for damages in the event of a breach . . . or (2) ineffectual because of the use of uncertain language. . . . But these decisions are not to be read as meaning that there can be no enforcible prohibition against the assignment of a claim; indeed, they are authority only for the proposition that, in the absence of language clearly indicating that a contractual right thereunder shall be nonassignable, a prohibitory clause will be interpreted as a personal covenant not to assign.

In the Manchester case, [Manchester v. Kendall,] it was held, 103 N.Y. at page 463, that the words, " 'This contract not to be assigned, or any part thereof, or any installments to grow due under the same,' " must be construed as an agreement not to assign, the breach of which would give rise to a claim for damages by the covenantee. The court stated, 103 N.Y. at page 463, that the quoted words "would not make the assignment void." In the clause now before us, however, it is expressly provided that the "assignment . . . shall be void.". . .

In Devlin v. Mayor of City of N. Y., 63 N.Y. 8 at pages 17, 20, we said: "Parties may, in terms, prohibit the assignment of any contract [and the interest of the contractor under it] and declare that neither personal representatives nor assignees shall succeed to any rights in virtue of it, or be bound by its obligations." In Fortunato v. Patten, 147 N.Y. 277, 41 N.E. 572, where the contract with the city provided in substance that the contractor shall not assign the contract, or any moneys payable thereunder, without the consent of the city, we noted, 147 N.Y. at page 281, 41 N.E. at page 573: "It was inserted in the contract solely for the benefit of the city, and prevents any claim being asserted against it in the absence of consent.". . .

This is in harmony with Restatement of the Law of Contracts (§ 151): "A right may be the subject of effective assignment unless . . . (c) the assignment is prohibited by the contract creating the right.". . .

In the light of the foregoing, we think it is reasonably clear that, while the courts have striven to uphold freedom of assignability, they have not failed to recognize the concept of freedom to contract. In large measure they agree that, where appropriate language is used, assignments of money due under contracts may be prohibited. When "clear language" is used, and the "plainest words . . . have been chosen," parties may "limit the freedom of alienation of rights and prohibit the assignment.". . . We have now before us a clause embodying clear, definite, and appropriate language, which may be construed in no other way but that any attempted assignment of either the contract or any rights created thereunder shall be "void" as against the obligor. One would have to do violence to the language here employed to hold that it is merely an agreement by the subcontractor not to assign. The objectivity of the language precludes such a construction. We are therefore compelled to conclude that this prohibitory clause is a valid and effective restriction of the right to assign. . . .

[Judgment affirmed.]

Radley v. Smith
6 Utah 2d 314, 313 P.2d 465 (1957)

Smith, who owned the Avalon Apartments, sold individual apartments under contracts that required each purchaser to pay $15 a month extra for hot and cold water, heat, refrigeration, taxes, and fire insurance. Smith assigned his interest in the apartment house and under the various contracts to Roberts. She failed to pay the taxes on the building. Radley and other tenants sued Smith and Roberts to compel them to pay the taxes. The action was dropped as to Smith. From a judgment against Roberts, she appealed.

CROCKETT, J. . . . The first of defendant's contentions is that the trial court erred in finding she had assumed any of the duties and obligations arising under the contracts between Smith and the plaintiffs. She maintains that in purchasing Smith's interest she was acquiring only the right to collect payments from the plaintiffs and that she had no intention of assuming the burdens of the contracts. While it is no doubt possible for a party to become the assignee of the rights under a contract without becoming responsible for the duties, the question whether a purported assignment of an entire contract includes such assumption depends upon its terms and the intent of the parties. Whenever uncertainty or ambiguity exists with respect thereto, it is proper for the court to consider all the facts and circumstances, including the words and actions of the parties forming the background of the transaction.

It appears that the defendant had available Smith's contracts which set forth the corresponding rights and duties of the parties, and expressly stated that the provisions would bind the "successors and assigns." She, therefore, knew of the services required of the seller and in fact initially accepted and performed those responsibilities, and further, accepted the $15 per month which the contract recited was to pay for them, and for the payment of taxes. Applicable to this situation is the rule of construction stated in § 164 (1) of the Restatement of Contracts:

> "Where a party to a bilateral contract, which is at the time wholly or partially executory on both sides, purports to assign the whole contract, his action is interpreted, in the absence of circumstances showing a contrary intention, as an assignment of the assignor's rights under the contract and a delegation of the performance of assignor's duties."

There is nothing in this case to affirmatively indicate anything other than that defendant was to assume the responsibilities of the seller under the contracts and the trial court's finding with respect to that issue must therefore be affirmed. . . .

[Judgment affirmed.]

Questions and Case Problems

1. What is the objective of each of the following rules of law?
   (a) An incidental beneficiary cannot recover damages for breach of the contract by which he is benefited.
   (b) Contractors who build public works are frequently prohibited by statute from assigning money due or money that will become due under their contracts.

2. The Rhode Island Grocers' Association made an agreement with *donee* Transocean Air Lines to supply the airline with a booth at its annual *beneficiary* exhibit and to give the airline certain publicity, in return for which the airline would provide a ⌐door prize⌐ for the exhibition of a round trip to Hawaii for two. Finch won the door prize and received the winning tickets but by the time she was able to make the trip, the airline had suspended operations. She sued the Rhode Island Grocers' Association as a third party beneficiary. Was she entitled to recover? (Finch v. Rhode Island Grocers' Association, [R.I.] 175 A.2d 177)

3. Hudgens purchased a used car from Mack, a dealer. Mack falsely *fraud* informed Hudgens that the car was in good condition when, in fact, it *void* needed extensive repairs. Mack also refused to live up to his 30-day *Contract* guarantee when the car was brought back within a few days after the sale. The day following the sale Mack had assigned the contract to Universal C.I.T. Credit Corp. When Hudgens refused to pay on the contract, he was sued by Universal. Hudgens claimed the right to set aside the contract for fraud. Was he entitled to do so? (Universal C.I.T. Credit Corp. v. Hudgens, [Ark.] 356 S.W.2d 658) *yes*

4. Enos had a policy of insurance with the Franklin Casualty Insurance *3rd* Company providing for the payment of all reasonable hospitalization ex- *party* penses up to $500 for each person injured while a passenger in or upon *beneficiary* entering or leaving the insured's automobile. Wagner, a guest in the automobile, was injured in a highway accident. She was treated by Dr. Jones, who then sued the insurer to obtain payment. Decide. (Franklin Casualty Insurance Company v. Jones, [Okla.] 362 P.2d 964)

5. Consumers Mart, which sold on credit, assigned its contracts to Federal Finance Co. Under the agreement between them, Federal would not pay Consumers Mart the full amount due it but held back a specified percentage as a reserve against possible loss in connection with such assigned contracts. Consumers Mart owed money to Mid-America Appliance Corporation and assigned to it the rights of Consumers Mart in the reserve fund. Mid-America gave Federal Finance notice of the assignment. Federal continued to purchase contracts from Consumers Mart and took out of the reserve fund amounts covering losses sustained by it on contracts assigned to it both before and after notice of the assignment. Mid-America claimed that the notice of the assignment prevented Federal from charging the reserve fund with any losses from contracts purchased by it after notice of the assignment. Was it correct? (Mid-America Appliance Corp. v. Federal Finance Co., 172 Neb. 270, 109 N.W.2d 381)

6. Deaton made a contract with Dr. Lawson by which he was to receive certain medical treatment in return for the payment of a specified fee. A physician employed by Lawson was assigned to give the treatments to Deaton. Deaton insisted on performance by Lawson. Decide. (Deaton v. Lawson, 40 Wash. 486, 82 P. 879) *OK special talent subject contract the assigned*

7. Summerwill, who owned 40 acres near Iowa City, sold part of the tract to the Independent School District of Iowa City and part to Hutt. The contract with these purchasers required them to make a street between their two lots, each to pay one half of the cost of construction. Hutt made his portion of the road as a dirt road. He then sold certain lots to Birchwood Builders, and they sold a lot to Olney. This area was later annexed by Iowa City and paved by it. Olney then sued Hutt for the assessment made by the city for the paving work. Was Hutt liable? (Olney v. Hutt, 251 Iowa 1379, 105 N.W.2d 515)

8. A Michigan statute bars a minor from avoiding a contract because of infancy if he makes an intentionally false statement of his age "in writing in a separate instrument containing only the statement of age, date of signing, and the signature, or by admission in open court." Funston Chevrolet sold a car to Poli who was then 17 years of age and later assigned the contract to the National Bank of Detroit which made the purchase without knowledge that Poli was a minor. When Poli did not pay the balance due, the bank sued him. Assuming that the automobile was not a necessary, did Poli have any defense? (Poli v. National Bank of Detroit, 355 Mich. 17, 93 N.W.2d 925)

9. Blackard and Mills were partners doing business under the name of Monarch's Manufacturers and Distributors. The partnership was terminated by an agreement providing for the sale of Blackard's interest to Mills and the formation of a corporation under the name of Monarch's Manufacturers and Distributors, Inc., which was to continue the former partnership business. This agreement further provided that shares of stock of the corporation would be issued to Blackard, that he would be employed as its vice-president, and that he would not compete with the corporation in any other business in Indiana or adjacent states for a period of four years. Seven months later an agreement was executed between Blackard and the corporation by which he released it from the employment contract, and a separate agreement was executed between Blackard and Mills by which Blackard was released from his covenant not to compete. Three months later Blackard began to compete with Monarch as the principal stockholder and major officer of another corporation. Monarch then sued Blackard on his covenant not to compete. Blackard proved that Mills had released him from his agreement not to compete. Decide. (Blackard v. Monarch's Manufacturers and Distributors, Inc., [Ind.] 169 N.E.2d 735)

10. Page was a contractor who was financed by Bailey. They agreed that Page should bid to obtain a government contract for construction at Matagorda. Among other things, the contract specified that Page would pay Bailey from the payments received under the new contract for a prior debt which had resulted from construction work at Port Lavaca. Was this an assignment of the contractor's rights under the contract? Decide. (Page v. Bailey, [C.A. 5] 290 F.2d 483)

CHAPTER 13

Discharge of Contracts

Ordinarily a contract is terminated by the performance of the terms of the agreement, but termination may also occur by agreement, impossibility of performance, operation of law, or acceptance of breach. The first four methods of discharge are discussed in this chapter. Discharge by acceptance of breach is treated in Chapter 14.

Sec. 13-A. Discharge by Performance. In the great majority of cases the parties carry out their promises; that is, the contract is discharged by performance according to its terms. If a dispute arises as to whether there has been performance, the party claiming that he has performed has the burden of proving that fact.

(1) Payment. When payment is required by the contract, performance consists of the payment of money or, if accepted by the other party, the delivery of property or the rendering of services in lieu of the payment of money.

Payment by executing a negotiable instrument, such as a check, is deemed a conditional payment, unless it is expressly specified that it is accepted as absolute payment without regard to whether the parties bound by the instrument pay the amount due on it. When a negotiable instrument is taken as conditional payment, the payment is not effective if the instrument is not paid and the original debt may be sued upon. Under the Uniform Commercial Code [1] the instrument merely suspends the debt until it is presented for payment. If payment is made, the debt is discharged; if not paid, suit may be brought on either the debt or the instrument.

(2) Application of Payments. If the debtor owes more than one debt to the creditor and pays him money, a question may arise as to

---

[1] Uniform Commercial Code, Sec. 3-802(1)(b).

which of the debts has been paid. If the debtor specifies the debt to which the payment is to be applied and the creditor accepts the money, the creditor is bound to make the application specified by the debtor.

If the debtor does not specify the application to be made, the creditor may apply the payment to any one or more of the debts in such manner as he chooses. As between secured and unsecured claims, the creditor is free to apply the payment to the unsecured claim. The creditor, however, must apply the payment to a debt that is due as contrasted with one which is not yet due. He cannot apply payment to a claim that is illegal or invalid, but he may apply the payment to a claim which cannot be enforced because it is barred by the Statute of Limitations [2] and, according to some authority, to a claim which cannot be enforced for want of a writing required by the Statute of Frauds.

If neither the debtor nor the creditor has made any application of the payment, application will be made by the court. There is a division of authority, however, whether the court is to make such application as will be more favorable to the creditor or debtor.

(3) Time of Performance. When the date or period of time for performance is stipulated, performance should be made on that date or in that time period. It may usually occur later than the date, however, unless the nature or terms of the contract indicate clearly that time of performance is vital, as in the case of contracts for the purchase or sale of property of a fluctuating value. When time is vital, it is said to be "of the essence."

In the absence of an express stipulation as to the time of performance, it is generally held that performance must be made within a reasonable time.

In some contracts the time of performance is conditional, that is, it depends upon the happening of a particular event, the failure of such an event to happen, or the existence of a certain fact. If the condition is not fulfilled, the promisor has no obligation to perform. To illustrate, a fire insurance policy does not impose any duty for performance on the insurance company until there is a loss within the coverage of the contract.

(4) Tender of Performance. An offer to perform is known as a *tender.* If performance requires the doing of an act, a tender that is refused will discharge the party offering to perform. If performance requires the payment of a debt, however, a tender that is refused does not discharge the obligation. But it stops the running of interest charges and prevents the collection of court costs if the party is sued, providing the tender is kept open and the money is produced in court.

---

[2] See p. 216.

A *valid tender of payment* consists of an unconditional offer of the exact amount due on the date when due or an amount from which the creditor may take what is due without the necessity of making change. It is unnecessary for the debtor to produce the money, however, if the creditor informs him in advance that he will not accept it. The debtor must offer *legal tender* or, in other words, such form of money as the law recognizes as lawful money and declares to be legal tender for the payment of debts. The offer of a check is not a valid tender since a check is not legal tender.

(5) Substantial Performance. If the plaintiff in good faith substantially performed the contract, he can sue the other party for payment. He then recovers the contract price subject to a counterclaim for the damages caused the other party by the plaintiff's failure to perform to the letter of the contract. (See p. 217, Cassinelli v. Stacy)

This rule is most frequently applied in actions upon building contracts. Thus, if a contractor undertakes to erect a building for $10,000 but the work that he does is not exactly according to specifications in certain minor respects, he may still sue for the amount due on the contract. Assume that it would cost the owner $500 to correct the defects in the contractor's work. The contractor could recover $10,000 minus $500. The owner would then have $500 with which to have the defects corrected so that he would have his building at the original contract price of $10,000.

If, however, the defect is of such a nature that it cannot be remedied without rebuilding or materially injuring a substantial part of the building, the measure of damages is the difference between the value of the building as constructed and the value it would have had if it had been built according to the contract.

This rule of substantial performance applies only when the departure from the contract or the defects are not made willfully, and provided that the contract is substantially performed. If the contractor intentionally departs from the contract or if the amount of work he has completed is not substantial, he is in default and cannot recover anything from the other party.

(6) Satisfaction of Promisee or Third Person. When the agreement requires that the promisor perform an act to the satisfaction, taste, or judgment of the other party to the contract, the courts are divided as to whether the promisor must so perform as to satisfy the promisee or whether it is sufficient that he perform in a way that would satisfy a reasonable man under the circumstances. When personal taste is an important element, the courts generally hold that the performance is not sufficient unless the promisee is actually satisfied, although in some instances it is insisted that dissatisfaction be shown in good faith and not merely to avoid paying for the work that has been done. The personal satisfaction of the promisee is generally required under this rule when one promises to make clothes, to write a novel, or to paint a portrait to the satisfaction of the other party.

There is a similar division of authority when the subject matter involves the fitness or mechanical utility of the property. With respect to things mechanical, however, the courts are more likely to hold that the promisor has satifactorily performed if a reasonable man should be satisfied with what was done. (See p. 218, Johnson v. School District #12)

When performance is to be approved by a third person, the tendency is to apply the "reasonable man" test of satisfaction, especially when the third person has become incapacitated or has wrongfully withheld his approval.

Sec. 13-B. Discharge by Agreement. A contract may be terminated by the operation of one of its provisions or by a subsequent agreement.

(1) Provision of Original Contract. The contract may provide that it shall terminate upon the happening of a certain event, such as the destruction of a particular building, or upon the existence of a certain fact, even though the intended performance by one party or both parties has not been completed.

A contract may also provide that either party or both parties can terminate it upon giving a particular notice, such as a 30-day notice, as in the case of an employment contract or a sale with an option to return,[3] or that one party may terminate the contract if he is not satisfied with the performance of the other. Notice to terminate must be clear and definite.

(2) Rescission by Agreement. The parties to a contract may agree to undo the contract and place each one in his original position by returning any property or money that had been delivered or paid. It is said that they agree to rescind the contract or that there is a *mutual rescission.* Ordinarily no formality is required for rescission, and an oral rescission or conduct evidencing such an intent may terminate a written contract. (See p. 219, Jensen v. Chandler) An oral rescission is ineffective, however, in the case of a sealed instrument or a sale of an interest in land. In the latter case the purpose of a rescission is to retransfer the interest in land. Accordingly, the retransfer or rescission must satisfy the same formality of writing that the Statute of Frauds applies to the original transfer.

(3) Waiver. A contractual obligation is discharged by *waiver* when one party fails to demand performance by the other party or to object

---

[3] See p. 68.

when the other party fails to perform according to the terms of the contract. Unlike rescission, a waiver does not return the parties to their original positions; it leaves the parties where they are at the time.

(4) Substitution. The parties may decide that their contract is not the one they want. They may then replace it with another contract. If they do so, the original contract is discharged by *substitution*.

It is not necessary that the parties expressly state that they are making a substitution. Whenever they make a new contract which is clearly inconsistent with a former contract, the court will assume that the former contract has been superseded by the latter. Since the new contract must in itself be a binding agreement, it must be supported by consideration.

(5) Novation. In a novation, as explained in Chapter 12, the original contract is discharged by the new contract.

(6) Accord and Satisfaction. In lieu of the performance of an obligation specified by a contract, the parties may agree to a different performance. Such an agreement is called an *accord*. When the accord is performed or executed, there is an *accord and satisfaction*, which by its terms discharges the original obligation. (See p. 220, Puett v. Walker) Ordinarily an accord and satisfaction will not take effect until it is executed, that is, until the performance which is agreed to by the accord is actually rendered.

When the performance of one party under the accord and satisfaction consists of paying a sum of money smaller than that claimed by the other party, it is frequently required that there be a bona fide dispute as to the amount due or that the accord and satisfaction be supported by independent consideration. Under the Uniform Commercial Code, however, no dispute is required when a check is accepted which states that it is in full settlement of a claim.

Sec. 13-C. Discharge by Impossibility. Except in the four instances that are discussed in the following paragraphs, impossibility that arises subsequent to the making of the contract has no effect; but some courts have attempted to qualify this rule. Acts of God, such as tornadoes, lightning, and sudden floods, usually do not terminate a contract even though they make performance difficult or impossible. Likewise, strikes, riots, shortages of materials, and similar factors do not excuse the promisor from performing his contract. The fact that it will prove more costly to perform the contract than originally contemplated, or that the obligor has voluntarily gone out of business, does not constitute impossibility which excuses performance. (See p. 222, Safe Harbor Fishing Club Case)

Frequently this problem is met by a provision of the contract which expressly excuses a contractor or provides for extra compensation in the event of certain unforseen or changed conditions. A party seeking to excuse himself by such a clause has the burden of establishing the facts that justify its application. (See p. 224, Morrison v. Oregon)

(1) Destruction of Particular Subject Matter. When the parties contract expressly for or with reference to a particular subject matter, the contract is discharged if the subject matter is destroyed through no fault of either party. When a contract calls for the sale of the wheat crop growing on a specific parcel of land, the contract is discharged if that crop is destroyed by blight.

On the other hand, if there is a contract merely to sell a given quantity of wheat, the seller is not discharged because his wheat crop is destroyed by blight. In this case, the seller makes an absolute undertaking, not limited or restricted in any way to any particular property. His obligation is to deliver a certain quantity of wheat regardless of where it is obtained.

(2) Change of Law. A contract is discharged when its performance is made illegal by a subsequent change in the law of the state or country in which the contract is to be performed. Thus, a contract to construct a nonfireproof building at a particular place is discharged by the adoption of a zoning law prohibiting such construction within that area. Mere inconvenience or temporary delay caused by the law, however, does not excuse performance. The entry of a court order that makes performance impossible is a defense to a party to a contract, provided such order is not the result of his own conduct.

(3) Death or Disability. When the contract obligates a party to perform an act that requires personal skill or which contemplates a personal relationship with the obligee or some other person, the death or disability of obligor, obligee, or other person (as the case may be) discharges the contract. If the act called for by the contract can be performed by others or by the promisor's personal representative, however, this rule does not apply.

(4) Act of Other Party. When the promisee prevents performance or otherwise makes performance impossible, the promisor is discharged from his contract. Thus, a subcontractor is discharged from his obligation when the principal contractor refuses to deliver to him the material, equipment, or money as required by the subcontract.

Sec. 13-D. Discharge by Operation of Law. Under certain circumstances either a contract is discharged or the right to enforce it is destroyed by operation of law.

(1) Alteration. A written contract, whether under seal or not, may be discharged by alteration. To have this effect (a) it must be a *material alteration,* that is, it must change the nature of the obligation; (b) it must be made by a party to the contract, as alterations made by a stranger have no effect; (c) it must be made intentionally, and not through accident or mistake; and (d) it must be made without the consent of the other party to the contract. For example, when one party to an advertising contract, without the consent of the other party, added "on a monthly payment basis" thus making the rate of payment higher, the advertiser was discharged from any duty under the contract.

(2) Merger. In some instances contract rights are merged into or absorbed by a greater right. If an action is brought upon a contract and a judgment is obtained by the plaintiff against the defendant, the contract claim is merged into the judgment.

(3) Bankruptcy. Subject to many specific regulations and some exceptions discussed in Chapter 62, any individual or corporate debtor may voluntarily enter into a federal court of bankruptcy or be compelled to do so by creditors. The trustee in bankruptcy then takes possession of the debtor's property and distributes it as far as it will go among his creditors. After this is done, the court grants the debtor a discharge in bankruptcy if it concludes that he had acted honestly and had not attempted to defraud his creditors.

Even though all creditors have not been paid in full, the discharge in bankruptcy is a bar to the subsequent enforcement of their ordinary contract claims against the debtor. The cause of action or contract claim is not destroyed, but the bankruptcy discharge bars a proceeding to enforce it. Since the obligation is not extinguished, the debtor may waive the defense of discharge in bankruptcy by promising to pay the debt.[4] Such a waiver is governed by state law. In a few states such a waiver must be in writing.

(4) Statute of Limitations. It is provided by statute that after a certain number of years have passed, a contract claim is barred. Technically, this is merely a bar of the remedy and does not destroy the right or cause of action. A few states hold that the statute bars the right as well as the remedy and that there is accordingly no contract after the lapse of the statutory period.

The Statute of Limitations begins to run the moment that the cause of action of the plaintiff arises, that is, when he is first entitled to bring suit. When the party entitled to sue is under a disability, such as insanity, at the time the cause of action arises, the period of the statute does not begin to run until the disability is removed.

---

4 See p. 116.

Statutes of Limitations

STATE	OPEN AC-COUNTS	WRITTEN CON-TRACTS	JUDG-MENTS OF RECORD	STATE	OPEN AC-COUNTS	WRITTEN CON-TRACTS	JUDG-MENTS OF RECORD
	YEARS	YEARS	YEARS		YEARS	YEARS	YEARS
Alabama	3	6	20	Missouri	5	10	10
Alaska	6	6	10	Montana	5	8	10
Arizona	3	6	5	Nebraska	4	5	5
Arkansas	3	5	10	Nevada	4	6	6
California	4	4	5	New Hampshire	6	6	20
Colorado	6	6	20	New Jersey	6	6	20
Connecticut	6	6	No limit	New Mexico	4	6	7
Delaware	3	3*	10	New York	6	6	20
District of				North Carolina	3	3	10
Columbia	3	3	12	North Dakota	6	6	10
Florida	3	5	20	Ohio	6	15	21
Georgia	4	6	10	Oklahoma	3	5	5
Hawaii	6	6	10	Oregon	6	6	10
Idaho	4	5	6	Pennsylvania	6	6	20
Illinois	5	10	20	Rhode Island	6	6	20
Indiana	6	20	20	South Carolina	6	6	10
Iowa	5	10	20	South Dakota	6	6	20
Kansas	3	5	5	Tennessee	6	6	10
Kentucky	5	15	15	Texas	2	4	10
Louisiana	3	10	10	Utah	4	6	8
Maine	6	6	20	Vermont	6	6	8
Maryland	3	3	12	Virginia	3	5	20
Massachusetts	6	6	20	Washington	3	6	6
Michigan	6	6	10	West Virginia	5	10	10
Minnesota	6	6	10	Wisconsin	6	6	20
Mississippi	3	6	7	Wyoming	8	10	5

* Promissory notes, 6 years.

The Uniform Commercial Code (Sec. 2-725) specifies a four-year period for actions on contracts for sales of goods.

When a condition or act prevents the period of the Statute of Limitations from running, it is said to *toll the running of the statute.*

Statutes of limitations do not run against governments as it is contrary to the public policy that the rights of society generally, as represented by the government, should be prejudiced by the failure of the proper governmental officials to take the necessary action to enforce the claims of the government.

The defense of the Statute of Limitations may be waived by the debtor. The waiver must be in the form of an express promise to pay or such an acknowledgment of the existence of the debt that the law can imply a promise to pay the debt from the acknowledgment. In some states the promise or acknowledgment must be in writing. Part payment of the principal or interest is also regarded as a waiver of the bar of the statute and revives the debt.

Cases for Chapter 13

Cassinelli v. Stacy
238 Ky. 827, 38 S.W.2d 980 (1931)

Stacy contracted to construct a building for Cassinelli according to plans and specifications. When the work was finished, Stacy sued Cassinelli for the contract price. Cassinelli counterclaimed against Stacy on the ground that the construction had not been in accordance with the terms of the contract. From a judgment for the plaintiff, the defendant appealed.

RICHARDSON, J. . . . Originally at common law, it was the rule that a literal performance with respect to building contracts was applied in such cases. This rule has been changed to the extent of allowing the equitable doctrine relating to substantial performance to be applied.

Two reasons are given by the courts for the rule that a substantial performance for a building contract will support a recovery. One is that it is next to impossible for a builder literally to comply with all the minute specifications in a building contract. The other is that for the erection of a building on the lot of the owner, such owner must receive the benefit of the contractor's labor and materials, and it is therefore deemed equitable to require him to pay for what he gets. . . . The rule of substantial performance cannot be invoked where the defects in the construction or the omissions from the requirements set forth in the building contract are intentional, and not the result of an attempt in good faith to perform the contract. . . . But an intentional omission to do certain things called for by the contract, if the contractor believes they are not required of him and intends in good faith to do all that he has agreed to do, does not prevent the application of the doctrine of substantial performance from controlling his rights and remedies. . . . The doctrine of substantial performance permits the builder to recover on the entire building contract if the work has been done under a building contract, but is defectively done, allowing damages for incompleteness. The measure of recovery for a breach of the contract by the builder in such event is the difference between the contract price of the building constructed according to the contract and its reasonable value as it is at the date of completion. . . . But, if any work or material required by the contract has been omitted, and . . . may be done or furnished at reasonable cost, . . . the measure of recovery is the cost of doing the work or furnishing the material so omitted.

It is shown by the evidence that the defects and omitted parts of the building can be corrected or installed at a reasonable cost. . . .

There is no evidence controverting the items as given by him, or his estimated cost of repairing or installing them in the building.

[Judgment for plaintiff reversed.]

Johnson v. School District #12
210 Ore. 585, 312 P.2d 591 (1957)

Johnson was operating a school bus for School District #12 under a two-year written contract which specified that Johnson "is to have option for next 3 years if a bus is run and his service has been satisfactory." At the end of the two-year period Johnson notified the School District that he had selected to exercise the option, but the School District refused to renew the contract. Johnson sued the School District for breach of the option provision. From a nonsuit entered against him, Johnson appealed.

KESTER, J. . . . In granting the nonsuit, the trial court held that the contractual provision that plaintiff's service be "satisfactory" was akin to those contracts where fancy, taste, or personal judgment are involved, and where lack of satisfaction on the part of the promisor is not reviewable. In effect, he held that the option was unenforceable against the school district. . . .

Plaintiff's option to renew the contract if his service has been satisfactory presents a question similar to those arising under contracts giving one party a right to terminate or be relieved from obligation if performance is unsatisfactory. Such contracts are generally grouped into two categories:

(1) Those which involve taste, fancy or personal judgment, the classical example being a commission to paint a portrait. In such cases the promisor is the sole judge of the quality of the work, and his right to reject, if in good faith, is absolute and may not be reviewed by court or jury.

(2) Those which involve utility, fitness, or value, which can be measured against a more or less objective standard. In these cases, although there is some conflict, we think the better view is that performance need only be "reasonably satisfactory," and if the promisor refuses the proffered performance, the correctness of his decision and the adequacy of his grounds are subject to review.

[Employment] cases, where the contract provides that the employment shall continue as long as the employee's services are satisfactory, are usually classed with the first group; and it is generally held that the employer has an absolute right to discharge the employee if he, in good faith, is actually dissatisfied, without regard to the sufficiency of his reasons. . . .

Where, in a given contract, it is doubtful whether the promise is intended to be conditional on the promisor's personal satisfaction or on the sufficiency of the performance to satisfy a reasonable man, the latter interpretation is adopted. Restatement of Contracts § 265.

Even in cases where the right to terminate is absolute, the dissatisfaction must be actual and honest, and not merely feigned in order to escape liability. . . .

After study of the contract in question here, we are of the opinion that the standard of performance involved is not the mere personal satisfaction of the school board, unsupported by reason, but it is such performance as would satisfy a reasonable man under the circumstances.

Plaintiff was not an employee, but an independent contractor; and while his services involved some intangible factors, we think they were not of the character to come within the rule of taste, fancy, or personal judgment. . . . Such construction does not, as argued by defendant, render meaningless the requirement of satisfaction, as reasonable satisfaction is still required.

In our opinion, therefore, plaintiff would establish a prima facie case for renewal of the contract by proving that his performance was of a quality that should have satisfied a reasonable man under the circumstances.

[Judgment of nonsuit affirmed for other reasons.]

Jensen v. Chandler

77 Idaho 303, 291 P.2d 1116 (1955)

Chandler purchased an Austin automobile from the Jensen Motor Sales Co. by trading in a Chevrolet and making a payment by check. He returned the Austin on the next business day, demanded the return of the Chevrolet, and stopped payment of his check. Jensen sued him for the price due. Chandler sued Jensen for the return of the Chevrolet, claiming that the sales contract had been rescinded. From a judgment in favor of Chandler, Jensen appealed.

PORTER, J. . . . Respondent [Chandler] in the late afternoon of July 3, delivered the Chevrolet trade-in with its certificate of title to appellant's [Jensen'] place of business and took the Austin automobile to his home.

Appellant's place of business was closed on Saturday, July 4, and Sunday, July 5. On Monday, July 6, respondent returned the Austin automobile to appellant's garage where it was received by one of appellant's employees and placed on the floor in approximately the same position that it had occupied at the time of its being shown to respondent. Respondent demanded the return of his Chevrolet car which was refused. He stopped payment on his check at the bank; advised the bank not to purchase the conditional sales contract and secured a cancellation of the registration certificate and received back his $5.00.

On July 9, appellant wrote a letter to respondent demanding that he rescind his actions in order that the sale might be consummated; and advised respondent that the Austin was being held to respondent's account.

Appellant did not at any time either actually or by his pleadings tender the Austin automobile and its certificate of title to respondent. Respondent's witness, James H. Moore, testified that on July 22, appellant showed such Austin automobile to the witness and offered to sell the same to him at the price of a new car. . . .

The [Trial] Court concluded: "That the acts and conduct of the plaintiff as set forth in the foregoing findings of fact, coupled with the acts and conduct of the defendant as set forth in the foregoing findings of fact resulted in a mutual rescission of the sale."

A contract may be discharged by conduct as well as by words. . . . An abandonment of a contract by consent may be implied from acts of the parties. . . .

A contract will be treated as abandoned where the acts of one party inconsistent with its existence are acquiesced in by the other party. . . .

In the instant case the trial court found a refusal to comply with the contract by respondent and acts on the part of appellant thereafter inconsistent with the continued existence of the contract and concluded therefrom as an ultimate fact that there had been a mutual rescission of the conditional sales contract covering the Austin automobile. . . .

[Judgment affirmed.]

Puett v. Walker

332 Mich. 117, 50 N.W.2d 740 (1952)

Puett, who claimed that he and Walker had been in a common business or enterprise, sued Walker for what Puett claimed was his share. Walker claimed that he had paid Puett in full, as he had sent him a check for $296.61 which Puett had accepted and cashed, and that he was released from further liability. From a judgment in favor of Puett, Walker appealed.

NORSE, C.J. . . . In a letter from appellant [Walker] to appellee [Puett] dated November 16, . . . appellant embodied an itemization of what he claimed were the respective debit and credit items of the account between the parties. The result as asserted by appellant was that he was indebted to appellee for $296.61. It was appellant's check for that amount which was endorsed by appellee and the proceeds retained by him. This letter of November 16 . . . began with the following words: "The enclosed is our final accounting"; and immediately following the numerous items of debit and credit, which as contained in the letter resulted in an apparent indebtedness of defendant to plaintiff of $296.61, appellant wrote: "I am enclosing my check for $296.61 which completes the business. . . ."

Appellant relies upon the two quoted statements in his letter of November 16 in asserting that appellee's receipt of the statement embodied therein, accompanied by the check for $296.61, which appellee endorsed and retained the proceeds, constituted the accord and satisfaction, in consequence of which appellee's suit should be barred. And in any event, it is appellant's contention that since appellee accepted and retained the proceeds of the check, and has not at any time tendered return of the same to appellant, appellee's present action should be held to be barred.

Appellee in denying there was an accord and satisfaction and in asserting his right to maintain this suit urges various reasons, among which are the following: "(1) Doing only what the defendant was legally bound to do affords no consideration for accord and satisfaction; (2) Part performance of an accord is not accord and satisfaction; (3) There cannot be an accord and satisfaction without a meeting of the minds of the parties."

As to (1), it is apparent that in forwarding his check for $296.61 appellant did no more than what he admitted he was legally bound to do. In fact, he did only a portion of that which he was legally bound to do, as we are about to note herein.

"An accord and satisfaction, being a contract, must be supported by a good or valuable consideration in order to be given effect.". . .

"It is too well settled to require the citation of authorities that doing what one is legally bound to do is not a consideration for a new promise."

As to (2) above, the record discloses that appellant in his letter of November 16, wrote: "I will forward you the wax credit of 1,500 lbs. as soon as two things you agreed to do this past summer are done." It appears from the record that while appellant admits his obligation to do so, he has never accounted to appellee relative to the 1,500 pounds of wax. So, it quite conclusively appears that appellant tendered only a partial settlement of matters in controversy. The situation in its legal aspect is quite the same as though appellant had admitted an indebtedness of $500, but offered to pay presently only $250. . . .

"The retention and use of a check accompanied by a letter stating that it is in full of a certain account does not preclude action for a balance in fact due.". . .

As to (3), . . . it is apparent from this record that there never has been [an agreement] between these litigants which resulted in an accord and satisfaction.

"To work an accord and satisfaction the tender of payment as being *in full* should be made in unequivocal terms, so that the creditor in accepting the conditional payment will surely do so understandingly.". . .

When the assent of the creditor is sought to be inferred from the acceptance of a less sum than that claimed to be due, that fact that such amount is offered in full discharge of the whole claim must have been communicated to the creditor in some unmistakable manner. Consequently, where a check is tendered, even though it accompanies an account, if there is no expression of the condition that it must be accepted in full payment, the acceptance of the check does not constitute an accord and satisfaction, as no agreement to that effect can be implied from the transaction. . . .

While appellant at the beginning of his letter to appellee said: "The enclosed is our final accounting," it was not until practically at the close of his long letter, with the intervening itemization of the account which occupies more than four pages of the printed record, that he said: "I am enclosing my check for $296.61 which completes the business. . . ." Nowhere in his communication, or by notation on his check, did appellant state or clearly indicate that appellee's keeping the check or its proceeds would be on condition of its being accepted as a final settlement between the parties rather than in payment of what appellant was willing to admit he owed appellee. Under the circumstances appellee's endorsement of the check and his retention of the amount for which it was drawn cannot be construed as a binding acceptance by appellee of appellant's claim as to the status of this account. As held by the trial judge, it did not constitute accord and satisfaction between these parties. . . .

[Judgment affirmed.]

Code Comment: The same decision would be made under the Uniform Commercial Code since it was not clear that the check was to be accepted as payment in full. See UCC Sec. 3-408.

Safe Harbor Fishing Club v. Safe Harbor Realty Co.
34 Del.Ch. 28, 107 A.2d 635 (1953)

The Safe Harbor Realty Co. made a written contract to sell certain land to the Safe Harbor Fishing Club. As part of the consideration, the fishing club agreed to construct a club house on the land and to make other improvments that would have the effect of benefiting other real estate in the development. The realty company failed to convey the land. The fishing club sued for specific performance of the contract.[5] The realty company defended on the ground that the fishing club had failed to construct the club house. The fishing club replied that it was impossible to do so for the amount of money originally contemplated.

BRAMHALL, V.C. . . . The members of the fishing club contended that it was unreasonable for defendants to require plaintiff to erect a club house on this site since, because of the marshy condition of the land, piling would have to be driven six or eight feet before solid

---
[5] See p. 230.

ground could be reached. Objection was also made on the ground that it would be impossible to erect a club house at the club house site because there was no road leading to it. . . .

Plaintiff contends that it was relieved from its duty to erect a club house on the club house site by reason of the excessive cost which would be entailed in the erection of a club house on that site and by reason of the serious difficulty, if not impossibility, of moving materials to the club house site in the absence of the construction of the road. Plaintiff entered into a binding contract. At the time of the execution of the agreement there was no road leading to the club house site. From the testimony of the various witnesses it was obvious that a road leading to the site of the proposed club house would have to be constructed. Nevertheless, plaintiff executed an agreement which contained nothing relative to the construction of the road or as to whose responsibility its construction would be. . . .

Mere inconvenience or substantial increase in the cost of compliance with a contract, though they might make compliance a hardship, cannot excuse a party from the performance of an absolute and unqualified undertaking to do a thing that is possible and lawful. Courts cannot alter contracts merely because they work a hardship. A contract is not invalid, nor is the obligor therein in any manner discharged from its binding effect, because it turns out to be difficult or burdensome to perform. . . . Mere inability to perform a contract will not alone relieve the defaulting party. . . . Accepting the testimony offered by plaintiff, it amounts, at most, to a substantial increase in cost of the erection of the club house by reason of necessity of using piling and by reason of the necessity of constructing a road to the club house site. As far as the club house site is concerned, it was a marshy foundation. It was therefore obvious to plaintiff at the time of the execution of the contract that there might be considerable difficulty in erecting a club house on that site. . . . Admittedly, there is hardship, serious inconvenience, and a substantial increase in cost involved, but nothing more. I conclude that the erection of the club house on the club house site is not impossible of performance.

Plaintiff has asked this court to decree specific performance of the contract. Specific performance is a matter of grace and not of right and rests in the sound discretion of the court. That power will not be exercised in favor of a complainant who fails to show either substantial performance on his part or that he offered to discharge the duty imposed upon him by his contract. . . . Plaintiff has failed to comply with the terms of the contract between the parties providing for the construction of the club house at the club house site. This is a default in a substantial obligation of the plaintiff as set forth in the contract. Since plaintiff is in default in this material respect, specific performance will not be decreed. . . .

Morrison v. Oregon

225 Ore. 178, 357 P.2d 389 (1960)

Morrison and Lamping made a contract with the State of Oregon to construct a highway across an irrigated field. They knew that it was the irrigation season and that the owner Estes would turn water into the field. More water was turned into the field than they had expected with the result that their construction work was slowed down more than they had contemplated. They then sued the state for extra compensation under the provision of the contract which entitled them to extra compensation if they were delayed by "changed conditions." From a judgment for the contractors, the state appealed.

HOWELL, J. . . . The "Changed Conditions" clause of the contract [covered]: . . . *unknown conditions of an unusual nature differing materially from those ordinarily encountered and generally recognized as inhering in work of the character provided for in the plans and specifications.* . . .

The contract between the parties also included . . . as part of the "Special Provisions" [provisions relating to construction in irrigated areas]. . . .

Basically, the plaintiffs' position is: they expected irrigation water in the ditches, not in the fields; they expected the irrigation water to cause work delay and interruption and allowed for it in their bid, but did not expect the volume of water or the extent of the delay. . . .

Whether the circumstances constitute a "Changed Condition" depends upon the facts in each case. . . .

"The term 'unusual' does not refer to a condition which would be deemed a geological freak but rather a condition which would not be anticipated by the parties to the contract in entering into their initial agreement.". . .

The . . . following . . . were held to constitute a changed condition within the meaning of the clause: . . . unexpected rock ledge; . . . ancient roots encountered in excavation for levee; . . . handling excessively wet materials consisting of decayed vegetation and water; . . . disintegration of the road caused by spring thaw.

The following . . . [were] held . . . not [to] constitute a changed condition: . . . flooding of work areas; . . . flooding of site—Act of God; . . . scouring effect of a hurricane; . . . waves from storm damaged levee construction; . . . more ledge rock and nearer to surface than contractor anticipated; . . . seasonal flood destroying portion of flood control dam project; . . . unexpected ground water causing wet fill material. . . .

In the instant case plaintiffs contracted to build a highway across an irrigated field, knowing it was irrigation season and that Estes planned to turn the water into his field at the time. Plaintiffs' contention that they expected water in the ditches but not in the field is hardly plausible, because they should have anticipated that the area between the ditches would also be irrigated. The plaintiffs admit they anticipated the water might slow down their operations and allowed an additional amount in their bid for this contingency. The latter fact alone would indicate not that the condition was unexpected but that the plaintiffs misjudged the extent thereof. Plaintiffs' complaint that the amount of water was unexpected applies only to the proportion and not to the character of the condition. . . . The difficulties from the irrigation were within the contemplation of the plaintiffs when they entered into the contract.

[Judgment reversed.]

Questions and Case Problems

1. What is the objective of each of the following rules of law?

   (a) When a construction contract is substantially performed in good faith, the contractor may recover the contract price less damages caused by other party for shortcomings in his performance.

   (b) Impossibility of performance that arises subsequent to the making of the contract ordinarily does not excuse the promisor from his obligations.

2. Greif obtained credit cards from Socony Mobil Oil Co. for himself and his wife. The card specified, "This card is valid unless expired or revoked. Named holder's approval of all purchases is presumed unless written notice of loss or theft is received." Later Greif returned his card to the company, stating that he was canceling it, but that he could not return the card in his wife's possession because they had separated. Subsequently Socony sued Greif for purchases made by the wife on the credit card in her possession. He defended on the ground that he had canceled the contract. The company claimed that the contract was not revoked until both cards were surrendered since otherwise purchases could still be made on the outstanding card. Decide. (Socony Mobil Oil Co. v. Greif, 10 App.Div.2d 119, 197 N.Y.S.2d 522)

3. J. Siler gave land to his son, L. Siler, in consideration for which the son agreed to support the father as long as the father should live. The son died before the father. The son's estate was sued for failing to continue to support the father after the death of the son. Decide. (Siler v. Gray, Administrator of Siler's Estate, 86 N.C. 566)

4. Ferric Industries made a contract to purchase scrap copper from Bay State Smelting Co. The contracts called for shipment date of "Jan./Feb." on one lot and "Feb./first half March" on the other. In order to make delivery, it was necessary for the buyer to procure export licenses. Bay State notified the buyer that it was ready to make delivery and would do so on production of necessary licenses. The buyer did not have the licenses. The market price in scrap copper was fluctuating. Bay State notified Ferric that it was canceling the contracts because of the failure

to procure the necessary export licenses, notifying the buyer on February 28 as to lot No. 1 and March 11 as to lot No. 2. Ferric obtained the export licenses about March 23 and demanded that Bay State perform its contract. Ferric sued Bay State for breach of contract. Decide. (Bay State Smelting Co. v. Ferric Industries, Inc., [C.A. 1] 292 F.2d 96)

5. The Tri-City Concrete Co. sent a letter to the A.L.A. Construction Co. proposing to supply the contractor with concrete required in connection with certain construction at the Otis Air Force Base, Falmouth, Massachusetts. The letter stated that the supplier must be notified every day of the contractor's need for the next day and that such orders could be made by telephone. The letter also stated that the telephone orders "will be supplemented with a sales memo to accompany the first delivery which will confirm your order as we understand it and which will be acknowledged by your representative on the job." Each sales memo contained certain general printed provisions, including a promise by the contractor to pay for any damage to the concrete company's truck while on private property. On October 4, 1956, one of the plaintiff's trucks fell into an excavation. The sales memo for that day's delivery was signed by a laborer of the defendant. The concrete company sued the contractor for the damage to the truck on the basis of the sales memo provision. Decide. (Tri-City Concrete Co. v. A.L.A. Construction Co., [Mass.] 179 N.E.2d 319)

6. Maze purchased 50 shares of stock in the Union Savings Bank, but he did not pay the full purchase price. Maze was later discharged in bankruptcy. Thereafter he was sued for the balance of the purchase price due. Decide. (Burke v. Maze, 10 Cal.App. 206, 101 P. 438)

7. Claterbaugh was the owner and president of the Madison Park Appliance and Furniture, Inc. Acting in his individual capacity and without naming Madison Park or indicating that he was acting as its agent, Claterbaugh borrowed money from Hays. A few days later Claterbaugh made another loan from Hayes in the same manner and gave Hays a promissory note of the corporation for the total of both loans. Later a payment was made on the loans by a money order in the name of Madison Park. Later, when Hays sued Claterbaugh for the loans, he claimed that there had been a novation by which the corporation was substituted in his place. Was he correct? (Hays v. Claterbaugh, [La.] 140 So.2d 737)

8. Hayden did roofing work for Coddington. There was no dispute as to the amount due, but Coddington did not want to pay the full amount. He sent a check to Hayden on the back of which was written "Cashing this check is acknowledgement of payment in full for gutter job at 6949 Blenheim St. Pgh. Pa." When Hayden received this check, he crossed out these words, indorsed the check, cashed it, and then sued for the balance due on the contract. Decide. (Hayden v. Coddington, 169 Pa.Super. 174, 82 A.2d 285)

CHAPTER 14

Breach of Contract and Remedies

When termination is the result of a breach of contract by one party, the other party may have a choice of several remedies.

Sec. 14-A. Discharge by Acceptance of Breach. There is a *breach of contract* whenever one or both parties fail to perform the contract. A contract is discharged by breach if, when one party breaks the contract, the other party accepts the contract as ended. When a breach occurs, however, the injured party is not required to treat the contract as discharged. Since the contract bound the defaulting party to perform, the injured party may insist on the observance of the contract and he may resort to legal remedies.

A breach of a part of the contract is not deemed a breach of the entire contract if it is a *divisible contract*, that is, when the agreement consists of two or more parts and calls for corresponding performances of each part by the parties. Thus, in a promise to buy several separate articles at different prices at the same time, the agreement may sometimes be construed to be in effect separate or divisible promises for the articles. When a contract calls for performance in installments, there is a conflict of authority as to whether it is divisible.

A breach does not support a discharge of a contract when the term broken is not sufficiently important. A term of a contract that does not go to the root of the contract is a *subsidiary term*. When there is a failure to perform such a term, the agreement is not terminated, although the defaulting party may be liable for damages for its breach.

In addition to the effect of a breach as such, the occurrence of a breach also excuses the injured party from his performance if it is conditioned or dependent upon the performance of the defaulter's obligation. (See p. 231, K & G Construction Co. v. Harris and Brooks)

(1) Renunciation. When a party to a contract declares in advance of the time for performance that he will not perform, the other party

may (a) ignore this declaration and insist on performance in accordance with the terms of the contract, (b) accept this declaration as an *anticipatory breach* and sue the promisor for damages, or (c) accept this declaration as a breach of the contract and rescind the contract. It is for the injured party to determine what he wishes to do when the other party has made a renunciation.

The same rule applies when one party to the contract insists on a clearly unwarranted interpretation of the contract, since this indicates that he refuses to abide by the contract as it stands.

If the promisee does not elect to rescind the agreement, the contract continues in force; and his remedy is damages for breach either at once or at the time of performance specified by the contract. (See p. 233, Reliance Cooperage Corp. v. Treat) After renunciation, however, the promisee cannot continue to carry out his part of the agreement, thus increasing the damages which he sustains from the failure of the other party to perform.

(2) Incapacitating Self. Another form of anticipatory breach exists when the promisor makes it impossible for himself to perform his obligation. Under such circumstances, the promisee is entitled to treat the contract as discharged. For example, when one who is bound by the terms of the contract to turn over specific bonds, stocks, or notes to another transfers them to a third party instead, the promisee may elect to treat the contract as discharged or he may hold the promisor accountable for nonperformance when the time for performance arrives. The same is true when one agrees to sell specific goods to another person and then sells them to a third person in violation of his original contract.

Sec. 14-B. Remedies for Breach. There are three remedies for breach of contract, one or more of which may be available to the injured party: (1) the injured party is always entitled to bring an action for damages; (2) in some instances he may rescind the contract; (3) in some instances he may bring a suit in equity to obtain specific performance by the other party.

Local practice must be checked to determine the form of action and the court in which these actions are to be brought. In some states, the action will be an action in assumpsit or upon contract, or an equity action; while in many others it will be merely a civil action. Also the action in some states is classified as either an action at law or an action in equity; this distinction is not made in those states in which the courts of law and courts of equity have been merged. Regardless of the name of the action or of the court in which the remedy is prosecuted, the substance of the rights asserted will conform to the following general pattern.

(1) Damages. Whenever a breach of contract occurs, the injured party is entitled to bring an action for damages to recover such sum of money as will place him in the same position as he would have been in if the contract had been performed. (See p. 235, Numon v. Stevens) The injured party is under a duty, however, to *mitigate the damages* if reasonably possible. That is, he must not permit the damages to increase if he can prevent them from doing so by reasonable efforts. He may thus be required to stop performance of his part of the contract when he knows that the other party is in default. To illustrate, when an architect agreed to prepare preliminary drawings and to complete working drawings and specifications but the other party repudiated the contract upon the completion of the preliminary drawings, the architect could not recover for his services after the repudiation in preparing the working drawings and specifications. In the case of the breach of an employment contract, the employee is required to seek other similar employment and the wages earned or which could be earned from the other similar employment must be deducted from the amount of damages claimed.

(a) MEASURES OF DAMAGES. When the injured party does not sustain an actual loss from the breach of the contract, he is entitled to a judgment of a small sum, such as one dollar, known as *nominal damages.* If the plaintiff has sustained actual loss, he is entitled to a sum of money that will, so far as possible, compensate him for that loss; such damages are termed *compensatory damages.*

As a general rule, damages that are in excess of actual loss for the purpose of punishing or making an example of the defendant cannot be recovered for breach of contract; such damages are known as *punitive damages* or *exemplary damages.*

Damages may not be recovered for loss caused by remote injuries unless the plaintiff, at the time the contract was executed, had informed the defendant of the existence of facts which would give the defendant reason to foresee that his breach of the contract would cause such loss. What constitutes remote loss for which there can be no recovery depends largely upon the facts of each case.

(b) LIQUIDATED DAMAGES. The parties may stipulate in their contract that a certain amount shall be paid in case of default. This amount is known as *liquidated damages.* The provision will be enforced if the amount specified is not excessive and if the contract is of such a nature that it would be difficult to determine the actual damages.

It is very difficult, if not impossible, to determine what loss the owner of a building under construction suffers when the contractor is late in completing the building. It is therefore customary to include a liquidated damages clause in a building contract, specifying that the contractor is required to pay a stated sum for each day of delay. When a liquidated damage clause is held valid, the injured party cannot collect more than the amount specified by the clause and the defaulting party is bound to pay that much damages once the fact is established that he is in default and has no excuse for his default.

(c) LIMITATION OF LIABILITY. A party to a contract generally may include a provision that he shall not be liable for its breach generally, or for a breach that is due to a particular cause. When the provision is extended so as to free the contracting party from liability for his own negligence, the provision is sometimes held void as contrary to public policy. (See p. 236, Fedor v. Mauwehu Council). This is particularly likely to be the result when the party in question is a public utility, which is under the duty to render the performance or to provide the service in question in a nonnegligent way. (See p. 237, Southwestern Public Service Co. Case)

(2) Rescission upon Breach. The injured party may also have the right to treat the contract as discharged. When he elects to do so, his duty to perform is ended. For example, if a party fails to receive substantially the performance for which he bargained, he may rescind the contract and free himself from any further responsibility under the contract, provided that he returns to the other party whatever he has received or gives him credit for what he cannot return.

If the injured party exercises the right to rescind after he has performed or paid money due under the contract, he may recover the value of the performance rendered or the money paid. (See p. 238, Green v. Camlin) He sues, not on the express contract, but on a quasi-contract which the law implies in order to compel the wrongdoer to pay for what he has received and to keep him from profiting by his own wrong.

The rescinding party must restore the other party to his original position as far as circumstances will permit, and he must rescind the entire contract. If he cannot make restoration because of his own acts, he cannot rescind the contract. Thus a buyer who has placed a mortgage on property purchased by him cannot rescind the sales contract because he cannot return the property the way he received it.

The party who takes the initiative in repudiating the contract acts at his risk that he has proper cause to do so. If he does not have proper cause, he is guilty of a breach of the contract.

(3) Specific Performance. Under special circumstances, the injured party may seek the equitable remedy of *specific performance* to compel the other party to carry out the terms of his contract. The granting of this relief is discretionary with the court and will be refused (a) when the contract is not definite; (b) when there is an

adequate legal remedy; (c) when it works an undue hardship or an injustice on the defaulting party; (d) when the agreement is illegal, fraudulent, or immoral; or (e) when the court is unable to supervise the performance of such acts. The right to specific performance is also lost by unreasonable delay in bringing suit.

As a general rule, contracts for the purchase of land will be specifically enforced on the theory that each parcel of land is unique and the payment of money damages would only enable the injured person to purchase similar land but not the land specified in the contract.

Specific performance of a contract to sell personal property generally cannot be obtained. Money damages are deemed adequate on the basis that the plaintiff can purchase identical goods. Specific performance will be granted, however, when the personal property has a unique value to the plaintiff or when the circumstances are such that identical articles cannot be obtained in the market. Thus, specific performance is granted of a contract to sell articles of an unusual age, beauty, unique history, or other distinction, as in the case of heirlooms, original paintings, old editions of books, or relics. Specific performance is also allowed a buyer in the case of a contract to sell shares of stock essential for control of a close corporation,[1] having no fixed or market value, and not being quoted in the commercial reports or sold on any stock exchange.

Ordinarily contracts for the performance of personal services will not be specifically ordered, both because of the difficulty of supervision by the courts and because of the restriction of the Thirteenth Amendment of the Federal Constitution prohibiting involuntary servitude except as criminal punishment. In some instances, equity will issue a negative injunction which prohibits the defendant from rendering a similar service for anyone else. This may indirectly have the effect of compelling the defendant to work for the plaintiff.

Cases for Chapter 14

K & G Construction Co. v. Harris and Brooks
223 Md. 305, 164 A.2d 451 (1960)

K & G Construction Co., as contractor, made a subcontract with Harris and Brooks to perform part of the work. The subcontractor was obligated to perform all work "in a workmanlike manner, and in accordance with the best practices." The contractor was required to pay the subcontractor in monthly installments as the work progressed. The subcontractor did his work in such a negligent way that he damaged a wall being constructed by K & G. The latter refused to pay the subcontractor the next monthly pay-

---

[1] In a close corporation the stock is owned by a few individuals and there is no opportunity for the general public to purchase shares.

ment under the subcontract. The subcontractor then abandoned the work and sued the contractor for breach of the duty to make payments. From a judgment in favor of the subcontractor, the contractor appealed.

PRESCOTT, J. . . . Promises and counter-promises made by the respective parties to a contract have certain relations to one another, which determine many of the rights and liabilities of the parties. Broadly speaking, they are (1) independent of each other, or (2) mutually dependent, one upon the other. They are independent of each other if the parties intend that *performance* by each of them is in no way conditioned upon *performance* by the other. . . . A failure to perform an independent promise does not excuse nonperformance on the part of the adversary party, but each is required to perform his promise, and, if one does not perform, he is liable to the adversary party for such nonperformance. . . . Promises are mutually dependent if the parties intend *performance* by one to be conditioned upon *performance* by the other. . . .

The modern rule, which seems to be of almost universal application, is that there is a presumption that mutual promises in a contract are dependent and are to be so regarded, whenever possible. . . .

While the courts assume, in deciding the relation of one or more promises in a contract to one or more counter-promises, that the promises are dependent rather than independent, the intention of the parties, as shown by the entire contract as construed in the light of the circumstances of the case, the nature of the contract, the relation of the parties thereto, and the other evidence which is admissible to assist the court in determining the intention of the parties, is the controlling factor in deciding whether the promises and counter-promises are dependent or independent. . . .

Considering the presumption that promises and counter-promises are dependent and the statement of the case, we have no hesitation in holding that the promise and counter-promise under consideration here were mutually dependent, that is to say, the parties intended performance by one to be conditioned on performance by the other; and the subcontractor's promise was, by the explicit wording of the contract, precedent to the promise of payment, monthly, by the contractor. It would, indeed, present an unusual situation if we were to hold that a building contractor, who has obtained someone to do work for him and has agreed to pay each month for the work performed in the previous month, has to continue the monthly payments, irrespective of the degree of skill and care displayed in the performance of work, and his only recourse is by way of suit for illperformance. . . .

As the promises were mutually dependent and the subcontractor had made a material breach in his performance, this justified the contractor in refusing to make the August 10 payment; hence, as the contractor was not in default, the subcontractor again breached the contract when he, on September 12, discontinued work on the project, which rendered him liable (by the express terms of the contract) to the contractor for his increased cost in having the excavating done. . . .

[Judgment reversed.]

Reliance Cooperage Corp. v. Treat
195 F.2d 977 (C.A.8th, 1952)

Treat made a contract in July to deliver barrel staves to the Reliance Cooperage Corp. Delivery was to be completed by December 31. In the latter part of August, Treat notified Reliance that he would not make the delivery of any staves under the contract. The price of staves rose steadily during the rest of the year. Reliance sued Treat for breach of contract, claiming damages representing the difference between the contract price and the market price on December 31. The trial judge limited Reliance to damages representing the difference between the contract price and the market price in August. Reliance appealed.

SANBORN, C.J. . . . "The law is that, where the promisor before the time of performance expressly renounces his contract, the promisee is thereby entitled either to treat the contract as broken and sue at once for its breach without averring an offer or readiness to perform, or he may wait until the time of performance has expired, and then sue for the consequences of nonperformance.". . .

. . . While as a general rule an action upon an executory contract cannot be maintained until the time for performance has expired, the repudiation of the contract by one of the parties before that time gives to the other party the option to treat the contract as ended and to sue for the damages resulting from the anticipatory breach. In other words, unless the injured party chooses to treat the contract as breached by the anticipatory repudiation, his claim for damages does not accrue until the expiration of the time for performance.

There is no doubt that a party to an executory contract such as that in suit may refuse to accede to an anticipatory repudiation of it and insist upon performance and, if he does so, the contract remains in existence and is binding on both parties, and no actionable claim for damages arises until the time for performance expires. . . .

It is our opinion that, under the undisputed facts in this case, the unaccepted anticipatory renunciation by the defendant of his obligation to produce and deliver staves under the contract did not impair that obligation or affect his liability for damages for the nonperformance of the contract, and that the measure of those damages was no different than it would have been had no notice of renunciation been given by the defendant to the plaintiff. If there had been no anticipatory repudiation of the contract, the measure of damages for nonperformance by the seller would have been the difference between the contract price and the market price of the staves on the date when delivery was due, and that is the measure which should have been applied in assessing damages in this case.

Moreover, the measure of damages would have been the same had the plaintiff accepted the anticipatory repudiation as an actionable breach of the contract. The plaintiff would still have been entitled to recover what it had lost by reason of the defendant's failure to produce and deliver by December 31 . . . the staves contracted for, namely, the difference between the market price and the contract price of the staves on that date. The Comment in Restatement of the Law of Restatement of the Law of Contracts, § 338, Measure of Damages for Anticipatory Breach, contains the following statement (page 549): "The fact that an anticipatory repudiation is a breach of contract (see § 318) does not cause the repudiated promise to be treated as if it were a promise to render performance at the date of the repudiation. Repudiation does not accelerate the time fixed for performance; nor does it change the damages to be awarded as the equivalent of the promised performance.". . .

It seems safe to say that ordinarily no obligation to mitigate damages arises until there are damages to mitigate. No damages for the nonperformance of the contract in suit accrued before December 31. . . . Until that time the defendant, notwithstanding his anticipatory repudiation of the contract, was obligated and was at liberty to produce and deliver the staves, and had he done so the plaintiff would have been required to take and to pay for them. There is no justification for ruling that, after the plaintiff was advised that the defendant did not intend to perform, it must hold itself in readiness to accept performance from him and at the same time, at its own risk and expense, buy the staves contracted for upon the open market in the hope of reducing the defendant's liability for damages in case he persisted in his refusal to fulfill his obligations. The plaintiff did nothing to enhance its damages and seeks no special damages.

. . . The general rule in the United States is that a buyer who refuses to accept a seller's anticipatory refusal to deliver the commodities contracted for, and who insists upon performance by the latter, is not required to go upon the open market and purchase upon receipt of notice that the seller does not intend to perform. He has a right to treat the notice as inoperative, to wait until the time for performance has passed, and them buy on the open market, charging the seller with the difference between the contract price of the goods and the market price which prevailed at the time that performance should have been forthcoming. . . .

"There are two reasons for this rule. First, to require the innocent party to make an immediate purchase or sale upon receipt of notice of the other's repudiation would encourage such repudiation on the part of the seller or of the buyer as the market rose or fell. . . . Second, the immediate action of the innocent party might not have the effect of mitigating his damages, but might, on the other hand, enhance them. . . .

The doctrine of anticipatory breach by repudiation is intended to aid a party injured as a result of the other party's refusal to perform his contractual obligations, by giving to the injured party an election to accept or to reject the refusal of performance without impairing his rights or increasing his burdens. Any efforts to convert the doctrine into one for the benefit of the party who, without legal excuse, has renounced his agreement should be resisted.

The plaintiff is entitled to recover as damages the amount by which on December 31 . . . the market price of the staves contracted for exceeded their contract price. What the market price of such staves was on that date is a question of fact which has not as yet been determined.

The judgment is reversed and the case is remanded with directions to grant a new trial limited to the issue of the amount of damages.

Numon v. Stevens

162 Neb. 339, 76 N.W.2d 232 (1956)

Numon and his wife contracted with Davies to move their house. In the course of transit the house was damaged. The Numons sued Davies, Stevens, and others who had some part in the work for the damage sustained. The Numons claimed that they were entitled to recover damages representing the amounts spent to restore the house to its former condition. From a judgment in their favor, Davies appealed.

WENKE, J. . . . The evidence, establishes that appellees' [Numon and his wife] house suffered extensive damage while being moved and that such damage was caused by appellants [Davies and others] failing to perform the work in connection with moving the house in a workmanlike manner and in failing to exercise reasonable and necessary care for the prevention of damage thereto. In fact, the evidence establishes the work was performed in a careless manner.

"The measure of damages in the case of a breach of contract is the amount which will compensate the injured person for the loss which a fulfillment of the contract would have prevented or the breach of it has entailed. . . ."

"The measure of damages for injuring a building . . . is the cost of restoring it to its former condition."

The house had a dining room, living room, bathroom, three bedrooms, and a kitchen. It was an old house but before being moved was in good condition, both inside and out, and livable. After it was moved and set on the foundation at 2809 Avenue H, the opposite was true. Apparently the whole building was twisted and wrenched during the process of moving. This resulted in the plaster being cracked and loosened from the walls and ceiling, causing much of it to fall on the floors; the doors and frames were twisted and sprung so the doors would not open and close; the windows were twisted and some of the glass therein cracked; a floor joist was broken; the floors, which were mostly oak, were buckled and the finish badly scratched and marred; and the electric wiring was damaged.

In order to restore it to its former condition and make it livable, the appellees had to employ labor and purchase materials, the fair and reasonable value of which the evidence establishes was in excess of $1,705.99. Naturally the materials used, which were new, replaced materials that were old. Appellants suggest depreciation should be taken on the cost of the new material used to restore the building as it is more valuable than that replaced. In other words, appellants contend, "depreciation must be made from the cost of restoring the house with new material more valuable than that which was repaired and replaced," stating, "it stands to reason it (the house) was a more valuable property (after the repairs were made) than at the time it was purchased." This court has held to the contrary.

In Koyen v. Citizens' Nat. Bank [107 Neb. 274, 185 N.W. 414], we quoted, with approval, . . . "Where a bridge owned by a county was so injured by the wrongful act of defendant that a portion had to be rebuilt, the county is not to be denied recovery of damages in substantially the amount expended, because the rebuilt structure may be of greater value than the old and it is impossible to make a nice estimate of the difference in value."

We said of the old boiler involved in Koyen v. Citizens' Nat. Bank, supra: "And, what is more, it served the purpose as well as a new one." We think that is true of the old material here replaced by new through the fault of appellants. The house was livable and, except for damage caused thereto by appellants, would not have needed the repairs made.

[Judgment affirmed.]

Fedor v. Mauwehu Council

21 Conn.Sup. 38, 143 A.2d 466 (1958)

Charles Fedor, a minor, went to a summer camp. His father signed an agreement as a condition to his being admitted to the camp that the minor would not make any claim against the camp for any injury. When Charles was injured at the camp, he sued the camp claiming that the injury was caused by the camp's negligence. It raised the defense that the waiver agreement barred the suit. From a decision for the camp, Charles appealed.

MacDonald, J. . . . Generally speaking, agreements exempting parties from liability for their own negligence are not favored by the law and, if possible, are construed so as not to confer immunity from liability. . . . This general policy against construing agreements of the type involved here so as to confer immunity from liability for negligence is especially desirable in cases where a relationship once entered upon involves a status requiring of one party greater responsibility than that of the ordinary person and where the parties have not equal bargaining power and one party must either accept what is offered or be deprived of the relation. Certain language in defendant's [brief] . . . would appear to a certain extent to indicate the applicability of the foregoing language to the facts of this case—notably where defendant argues: "If this meritorious function [summer camp] is to be kept within the financial means of the greatest number of boys, some concession must be made. The concession in this case was the waiver of liability provision in the camp contract for which has been substituted a personal accident insurance policy to protect the boys and their parents from unfortunate casualties. These were the only terms available to the plaintiff and his parents and they accepted them readily."

In other words, low-income families desiring to take advantage of the opportunity to give their sons the advantages of a Boy Scout camp have no choice other than to sign a waiver absolving the camp from liability for acts of negligence of those responsible for the safety and lives of their sons. In this situation, the language of the court in Parillo v. Housing Authority . . . seems particularly in point, where it is stated (16 Conn.Sup. at page 107): "It can hardly be said to be in the public interest to countenance a policy which would deprive families of low income, otherwise eligible, of the opportunity to obtain dwelling accommodations expressly made available for them by the use of public funds unless they consented to assume the risks flowing from the negligence of the authority in carrying on its operations."

We must bear in mind this general public policy against agreements exempting parties from liability for their own negligence when we consider whether the alleged waiver is binding. . . .

It is doubtful that either the mother or father of this minor plaintiff had the power or authority to waive his rights against the defendant arising out of acts of negligence on the part of the defendant. . . .

[Judgment reversed.]

Southwestern Public Service Co. v. Artesia Alfalfa Growers' Ass'n
67 N.Mex. 108, 353 P.2d 62 (1960)

The Southwestern Public Service Co. negligently supplied excessively high voltage electricity over its power lines, thereby causing damage to the

electrical equipment of the Artesia Alfalfa Growers' Association. In a suit
for such damage, the service company denied liability on the ground that
its service contract provided that it was not liable for harm caused by
negligence. From a judgment in favor of the association, the service company appealed.

CHAVEZ, J. . . . The rule is well established that a provision in a
contract seeking to relieve a party to the contract from liability for his
own negligence is void and unenforceable, if the provision is violative
of law or contrary to some rule of public policy. Under this limitation
the courts are in complete accord in holding that a public service corporation, or a public utility such as an electric company, cannot contract against its negligence in the regular course of its business, or in
performing one of its duties of public service, or where a public duty
is owed, or where a public interest is involved. . . .

An electric company cannot contract against its negligence when
discharging its primary duty to the public, as any other holding would
put the individual or corporation using and paying for its power at
the mercy of the public service corporation, and [a contract so providing is] against public policy [and] null and void. . . .

We hold that . . . Southwestern Public Service Company cannot
validly contract against its liability for negligence in the performance
of a duty of public service, since such stipulation would be in con-
travention of public policy. . . .

[Judgment affirmed.]

Green v. Camlin

229 S.C. 129, 92 S.E.2d 125 (1956)

Camlin held a dealer's franchise to sell Tucker automobiles. The franchise agreement specified that it could not be assigned without the consent
of Tucker. Camlin sold his Tucker franchise to Green for $2,500 but failed
to obtain Tucker's consent to the assignment. Green sued Camlin for the
return of the purchase price. From a judgment for Green, Camlin appealed.

Moss, J. . . . [The Tucker franchise agreement stated:] . . . "This
Tucker Dealer Franchise Agreement constitutes a personal contract
between the Company and Dealer and is nonassignable; and, Dealer
covenants it will not transfer or assign same, or any part thereof,
or any rights thereunder without the written consent of the Company.
. . ."

The appellant [Camlin] alleges . . . as a defense that he had
complied with the contract but due to circumstances beyond his control, the actual written approval and transfer of the franchise by
Tucker Corporation to the respondents had not been made. . . .

It is apparent . . . that the parties contemplated the contract to be completed when the respondents received the right to sell Tucker automobiles in Conway, South Carolina. He [Camlin] was aware that no part of his agreement with Tucker Corporation could be assigned without the written consent of Tucker Corporation. This written consent was never obtained, and hence the respondents never received the right or franchise to sell automobiles in Conway, South Carolina. The failure to obtain the sales agency or franchise right to sell Tucker automobiles at Conway, South Carolina constituted a breach of the contract between the appellant and respondents and entitled the respondents to recover the consideration paid therefor.

Rights arising out of a contract cannot be transferred if they are coupled with liabilities, or if they involve a relationship of personal credit and confidence. It has been held that a sales agency agreement cannot be assigned without the consent of the principal. . . .

We therefore, must conclude that since the appellant had an exclusive sales agency for Tucker automobiles, he could not assign any rights thereunder to the respondents without the consent of the Tucker Corporation. This consent not having been obtained, the contract failed.

It follows that the respondents were entitled to recover the consideration paid. . . .

[Judgment affirmed.]

Questions and Case Problems

1. What is the objective of each of the following rules of law?
    (a) A party injured by a breach of contract is under a duty to mitigate the damages to the extent that is possible by a reasonable effort.
    (b) Specific performance of certain contracts is granted as an equitable remedy.

2. The Commodity Credit Corporation advertised the sale of lots of rice held by it. The Estherwood Rice Mill sent bids to the Commodity Credit Corporation by way of the Western Union Telegraph Company. Estherwood paid Western Union an additional fee for which the telegraph company sent Estherwood a "repeat message" so that Estherwood could verify that the correct message had been transmitted. The telegraph company transmitted Estherwood's bid on lot 315 as a bid on 316. Then the repeat message showed the original telegram as having referred to lot 315. Consequently Estherwood was not able to learn that a mistake had been made in the first message, prior to the deadline for receiving offers. When the mistake was discovered, Commodity Credit insisted that Estherwood go through with the terms of its contract. Estherwood adhered to the terms of the mistake and then sued Western Union for the loss. Was it entitled to recover? (Estherwood Rice Mill, Inc. v. Western Union Tel. Co., [La.] 127 So.2d 231)

3. John B. Robeson Associates was given a contract to direct sales for the lots in a new cemetery, the Gardens of Faith, Inc. Robeson guaranteed a minimum of $700,000 gross sales in excess of cancellations per year. The contract specified that quarterly in the second year and semiannually in the third year "the quota attained by Robeson will be reviewable by the cemetery, with the right in the cemetery to terminate this contract at its option if Robeson has substantially failed to attain guaranteed quota." In the first year Robeson exceeded the quota. In each of the first two quarters of the second year, Robeson fell under the quota. This was discussed with Gardens of Faith, but the contract was not terminated. Robeson adopted new selling methods and sales increased substantially in the last two quarters so that the annual sales for the second year were only slightly below the agreed quota. The cemetery then elected to terminate the contract. Was it entitled to do so? (John B. Robeson Associates, Inc. v. Gardens of Faith, 226 Md.App. 215, 172 A.2d 529)

4. Contrary to its subscription contract, the Southern Bell Telephone & Telegraph Co. failed to list the trade name of Scheinuk The Florist, Inc. in the white pages of the phone directory and only listed it in the yellow pages. In order to offset this omission, Scheinuk spent $508 in advertising. He sued the telephone company for damages of $25,147.53 which he asserted was the loss sustained in the 13-month period before the new directory was published. He showed that he was the second largest florist in New Orleans with a mailing list of 20,000 customers, doing approximately 95 per cent of its business over the phone. Scheinuk showed that his loss of gross profits during the 13-month period was $2,912.81. He claimed that since florists in the city had a general increase of business of 11.4 per cent, the amount of $16,726.72 was the gross profit on the income from sales he would have received if he had been properly listed and thus able to increase at the same rate. He also estimated that he would lose $5,000 in the future as the result of the past omission. The trial judge, hearing the case without a jury, allowed Scheinuk damages of $2,008. To what amount was he entitled? (Scheinuk The Florist, Inc. v. Southern Bell Tel. & Tel. Co., [La.App.] 128 So.2d 683)

5. Dankowski contracted with Cremona to perform construction work on a house for $5,060 and to make a down payment of $2,500. When the work was about 80 per cent completed, Dankowski refused to permit Cremona to do any further work because the work done was defective. Cremona brought suit for breach of contract. It was found that the defects in the work could be remedied at a cost of $500 and that Cremona had spent $4,167.26 in performance of the contract. He was awarded damages of $4,167.26 less the $500 necessary for repairs and less the down payment of $2,500, making damages of $1,167.25. The owner appealed from this decision. Decide. (Dankowski v. Cremona, [Tex.Civ.App.] 352 S.W.2d 334)

PERSONAL PROPERTY

CHAPTER 15

Nature and Classes

At one time trade and commerce were concerned only with movables, such as jewelry, fabrics, and furs. In the course of time immovables, such as land and houses, were freed of the restrictions of the feudal system and became articles of commerce.

Property in General

Property means the rights and interests which one has in anything subject to ownership, whether that thing be movable or immovable, tangible or intangible, visible or invisible. A right in a thing is property, without regard to whether such right is absolute or conditional, perfect or imperfect, legal or equitable.

Property includes the rights of any person to possess, use, enjoy, and dispose of a thing. It is not necessary that all of these rights be held by the same person at one time.

The term "ownership" is used synonymously with rights in property. Thus one is said to be the owner of a certain property, meaning that he has certain interests in the designated thing. Although the term "ownership" is often used to indicate that one has the highest rights possible to possess, it may be used when one does not have all of the rights in a thing. Thus we say that a person is the owner of a house even though he has rented it to a tenant who has exclusive use of the house during the term of the lease.

The term "property" is also commonly used to designate the thing itself in which one has rights or interests.

Sec. 15-A. Classifications of Property.

(1) Real and Personal Property. Real property means the rights and interests of a certain nature that one has in land and things closely pertaining to land. Technically *real property* is an interest of indeterminate or unfixed duration in things real. Personal property includes all property that is not real property. Technically *personal property* means any interest of determinate or fixed duration in things real and any interest in all other things that we know as things personal.

(2) Private and Public Property. The term *private property* designates things in which one or more persons have exclusive rights. The term *public property* designates things that are owned by a government, such as a state or municipality.

Sec. 15-B. Limitations on Ownership. When one has all possible existing rights in and over a thing, he is said to have *absolute ownership.* The term "absolute," however, is somewhat misleading, for one's rights in respect to the use, enjoyment, and disposal of a thing are subject to certain restrictions, such as the following:

(1) Rights of Government. All property is subject to the right of the government to compel the owner to give up a part for public purposes. This *power to tax* is an inherent right of sovereign states. By another power, called the *police power,* the government can pass reasonable rules and regulations in respect to the use and enjoyment of property for the protection of the safety, health, morals, and general welfare of the community. This police power is in substance the power to govern for the common good. Zoning laws that restrict the use of property within specified areas may be adopted under this power.

Private property is also subject to the right of the government to take it for public purposes. (See p. 247, Rabinoff v. District Court) This right of *eminent domain* may also be exercised by certain corporations, such as railroads and public utilities. Constitutional provisions require that fair compensation be paid the owner when property is taken by eminent domain.

(2) Rights of Creditors. Property is subject to the rights of one's creditors. It may be taken by judicial proceedings to satisfy just claims against the owner or his estate. A person cannot dispose of his property in any way so as to defeat the rights of his creditors.

(3) Rights of Others. The law restricts the use and enjoyment of property in that the owner is not allowed to use it unreasonably in a way that will injure other members of society.

Sec. 15-C. Forms of Ownership. All interests in a particular object of property may be held by one person alone. It may occur, however, that several persons have concurrent interests in the same object.

A further distinction may be made in terms of the relative interest of co-owners as between themselves. For example, when the owner of a bank account causes the bank to add the name of another person to the account so that either may draw checks on the account, both the original and the new owner are co-owners of the account as far as the bank is concerned. As between themselves, however, they may in fact be co-owners or the one whose name is added may merely be an agent for the other. In the latter case, while the agent "owner" has the right to withdraw money, he cannot keep the money for himself.

The forms of ownership include: (1) severalty, (2) tenancy in common, (3) joint tenancy, (4) tenancy by entirety, (5) community property, and (6) tenancy in partnership.

(1) Severalty. When property is owned by one person, it is said to be held in *severalty*.

(2) Tenancy in Common. A *tenancy in common* is a form of ownership by two or more persons. The interest of a tenant in common may be transferred or inherited, in which case the taker becomes a tenant in common with the others. This tenancy is terminated only when there is a partition, giving each a specific portion, or when one person acquires all of the interests of the co-owners.

(3) Joint Tenancy. A *joint tenancy* is another form of ownership by two or more persons. A joint tenant may transfer his interest to a third party, but this destroys the joint tenancy. In such a case the remaining joint tenant becomes a tenant in common with the third person who has acquired the interest of the other joint tenant.

Upon the death of a joint tenant, the remaining tenants take the share of the deceased, and finally the last surviving joint tenant takes the property as a holder in severalty. (See p. 252, Osterloh's Estate v. Carpenter)

Courts do not favor this form of ownership and will construe a transfer of property to several persons to be a tenancy in common whenever possible. Statutes in many states have abolished or modified joint tenancy, especially as to survivorship.

(4) Tenancy by Entirety. At common law a *tenancy by entirety* or tenancy by the entireties was created when property was transferred to husband and wife in such a manner that it would create a joint tenancy if transferred to other persons, not husband and wife. It differs from joint tenancy, however, in that the right of

survivorship cannot be extinguished and one tenant alone cannot convey his interest to a third person, although in some jurisdictions he may transfer his right to share the possession and the profits. This form of property holding is popular because creditors of one of the spouses cannot reach the property. Only a creditor of the husband and wife under the same obligation can obtain execution against the property. Moreover, the tenancy by entirety is in effect a substitute for a will since the surviving spouse acquires the complete property interest upon the death of the other.

Generally a tenancy by the entirety is created by the mere fact that property is transferred to two persons who are husband and wife, even though it is not expressly stated that such a tenancy is thereby created, unless, of course, it is expressly stated that a different tenancy is created. This type of tenancy may also be created by either husband or wife. Thus, when a husband opens a bank account in the name of himself and his wife, or the suvivor of them, and either the husband or wife may make withdrawals, a tenancy by the entirety is created as to any money that is deposited in the account, even though all deposits are made by the husband.

In some jurisdictions the statutes giving a married woman the capacity to contract and to own her own property are not regarded as affecting or abolishing tenancy by the entirety. In other jurisdictions it is held that by virtue of such statutes a creditor of either spouse may issue execution upon the chance of right of survivorship of the debtor spouse, with the result that if the debtor is the surviving spouse, who otherwise would acquire the property, the purchaser at the execution sale acquires the property.

(5) Community Property. In some states property acquired during the period of marriage is the *community property* of the husband and wife. Some statutes provide for the right of survivorship; others provide that half of the property of the deceased husband or wife shall go to the heirs, or permit such half to be disposed of by will. It is commonly provided that property acquired by either spouse during the marriage is prima facie community property, even though title is taken in the spouse's individual name, unless it can be shown that it was obtained with property possessed by that spouse prior to the marriage.

In states having community property statutes, it is generally held that husband and wife may each file a separate state income tax return covering only one half of the community income. The federal income tax law also permits husband and wife to pay a federal income tax of twice the tax due on one half of the aggregate income of both, without regard to whether it is community property or not.

(6) Tenancy in Partnership. In states that have adopted the Uniform Partnership Act, a special form of joint tenancy known as a "tenancy in partnership" exists as to property owned by the firm.[1]

Sec. 15-D. Ownership of Proceeds of Sale. When cotenants sell property, they hold the proceeds of the sale by the same type of tenancy as they held the original property.

Personal Property

Personal property rights are also known as chattel interests. The term "chattel" is more comprehensive than the word "goods," which is ordinarily confined to movable things.

Sec. 15-E. Classes of Personal Property.

(1) Chattels Real. Chattels real are interests in land or real estate which are limited as to their duration. The modern lease given by a landlord to his tenant is an illustration of a chattel real.

(2) Chattels Personal. Chattels personal consist of personal property, either tangible, such as furniture and books, or intangible, such as money claims and debts. Articles of tangible personal property are called *choses in possession,* or things in possession.

Rights in intangible personal property are called *choses in action.* Common forms of choses in action are insurance policies, stock certificates, bills of lading, and evidences of indebtedness, such as notes, bonds, and drafts. Choses in action ordinarily also include rights of action, whether arising *ex contractu,* that is, out of the breach of a contract, or *ex delicto,* based upon the infliction of a tort.

Sec. 15-F. Fixtures. Movable chattels may lose their nature as personal property by being annexed or affixed to the land or to a building. They are then known as *fixtures.* The parties may agree that chattels affixed to land are or are not to retain their character as personal property. The customs of the community may be significant in determining whether personal property is to be deemed a fixture.

The decision that certain property is a fixture has the effect of changing its classification from personal to real property. This is important for the purpose of tax laws because the fixture is subject to a real estate tax but not a personal property tax. If held to be real estate, it belongs to the land and whoever is entitled to the land or becomes its owner is entitled to the fixture. This is true even to the extent that the owner of personal property loses his ownership

---

[1] See p. 649.

when he attaches it in such a way as to become a fixture on the land of another person, the latter person thereby becoming the owner.

The distinction is also important with respect to a sale of the fixture, for as real estate it may be subject to or free from certain restrictions and taxes, whereas such would not be the case if it were still personal property. Likewise the seller of personal property makes certain guarantees or warranties by the mere act of selling, whereas the seller of real estate, including a fixture, makes only those warranties that are included in the deed to the land. (See p. 253, Voight v. Ott)

In the absence of an agreement, the courts apply three tests to determine whether the personal property has become a fixture:

(1) Annexation to the Realty. Generally the personal property becomes a fixture if it is so attached to the realty that it cannot be removed without materially damaging the realty or destroying the personal property itself. If the property is so affixed as to lose its specific identity, as bricks in a wall, it becomes part of the realty.

(2) Adaptation to or Usefulness of the Personal Property for the Purpose for Which the Realty Is Used. Personal property especially adapted or suited to the building may constitute a fixture. By the *industrial plant doctrine,* machinery reasonably necessary for the operation of an industrial plant usually becomes part of the realty when installed, without regard to whether it is physically attached or not.

(3) Intention of the Person Affixing the Property at the Time It Was Affixed. This is the true test; but in the absence of direct proof, it is necessary to resort to the nature of the property, the method of its attachment, and all the surrounding circumstances to determine what the intent was. Generally, when a tenant installs equipment for the operation of a store or business, the equipment is regarded as personal property or *trade fixtures* which the tenant may remove when he leaves the rented premises. As against third persons, the mere intention to make personal property a part of the realty may be insufficient when the property has not been attached or is not adapted in such a way as to indicate that it is part of the realty.

Sec. 15-G. Severed Realty. Property may be changed from real property to personal property by *severance.* If part of a house or building is removed or if material or stones are taken out of the earth, the property thus severed becomes personal property.

In some instances there may be a *constructive severance.* Thus, as soon as a contract for the sale and severance of standing timber is made, the timber is deemed personal property even though it has not been severed.[2]

---

[2] Uniform Commercial Code Sec. 2-107(1) is applicable when the seller is to sever.

Cases for Chapter 15

Rabinoff v. District Court

145 Colo. 225, 360 P.2d 114 (1961)

Rabinoff and others filed a petition to stop a proceeding in the district court under the Colorado Urban Renewal Act. This statute authorized a local agency or Authority to condemn large areas of land as slum or blighted, to demolish the buildings thereon, and then to resell the land to private persons, who could utilize the property as their own, subject to certain building and improvement restrictions. The petitioners, who owned homes and businesses in the area affected, claimed that the Act was unconstitutional on the ground that their property was being taken for a private and not a public purpose.

DOYLE, J. . . . The parties agree that the properties in question are not slums in the sense that the entire area is in disrepair or deterioration. On the other hand, it would appear . . . that the area poses a future hazard to the health and welfare of the community. Some allegedly do not comply with the Denver Health and Safety Ordinances, while others are conceded to be in full compliance with these ordinances. . . .

The petitioners argue that the act in question is devoid of public purpose and public use; that by authorizing the taking of private property, the demolishing of buildings thereon, the reselling to private persons with restrictions, it is not a public use as contemplated by the Colorado Constitution. It is said that this is a giant private real estate development designed to take private property from one group of individuals for the purpose only of vesting it in a different group. The present efforts are compared to the sequestration of property by Henry VIII. On this it is said:

"It is strange to find abhorred historic parallels reenacted in our own polity, without even being recognized. No difference obtains at all between the policy whereby in Medieval and Renaissance periods lands were redistributed or sequestered for the benefit of those who enjoyed state favor at the moment, and this procedure, whereby the lands of the many are taken deliberately to be redistributed to and agglomerated in the hands of the few, because the uses as so agglomerated concur more completely with the notions of the supra-governmental 'planners' as to what is good for the community." . . .

The narrow inquiry . . . is whether the power of eminent domain can be exercised in circumstances such as the present, wherein the public authority does not intend to permanently retain the property which it proposes to condemn. We do not consider the actual use by the public after the taking to be the appropriate test as to whether or not the use is a public one. The main object of this legislation is to eliminate slum and blighted areas. . . .

The acquisition and transfer to private parties is a mere incident of the chief purpose of the act which is rehabilitation of the area. . . .

The fact that when the redevelopment is achieved, the properties are sold to private individuals for the purpose of development does not rob the taking of its public purpose. . . .

The high courts of 26 states have upheld such statutes. On the other hand, a decision of unconstitutionality has been reached in only two states, Florida and South Carolina. . . .

Does the fact that the buildings here in question are not in an extremely dilapidated condition render the statute inapplicable or its application invalid?

The definitions of slum and blighted areas contained in . . . the act are sufficiently broad to include the Avondale area. A slum area is one which by reason of dilapidation, deterioration, age, obsolescence, insufficient light, air, sanitation, or overcrowding [creates] a fire hazard or [constitutes] a menace to the health, safety, morals or welfare of the community. A blighted area is somewhat more broadly defined as one which by reason of a substantial number of slum *deteriorated* or *deteriorating* structures or by reason of inadequate street layout endangers life or property, retards the growth of the community, constitutes a social or economic liability, etc.

In view of the scope of these definitions, it is not essential that the properties affected shall be in a state of disrepair calling for condemnation as nuisances. The cases which have considered the present issue point out that the approach to urban redevelopment cannot be on a structure to structure basis, inconsistent with its basic objectives. . . . There is a strict viewpoint in some of the cases that the area must be one which has deteriorated rather than one which is in the process of deteriorating. Most of the decisions, however, take a more liberal view and hold that the authority is not powerless to prevent deterioration. . . .

In the case at bar the City Council and the Urban Renewal Authority would appear to have carefully considered the pros and cons of undertaking renewal of the Avondale section prior to determining that it was properly subject to the act. There is no indication from the record before us that their action was arbitrary or capricious. There is an express finding in the authorizing ordinance that the area included within the Avondale Project is slum and blighted. . . .

The fact . . . that there are not widespread violations of building and health ordinances does not of itself establish arbitrariness on the part of the responsible authorities.

We must conclude therefore that the facts before us are not inconsistent with the statutory definitions and further that the condition of the properties does not render the particular plan an unconstitutional taking. We are not unmindful of the individual hardship nor are we unsympathetic toward it. On the other hand, it was within the power of the Assembly to determine that the public interest outweighs these considerations. . . .

[Petition dismissed.]

McWILLIAMS, J. . . . concurs in this opinion.

HALL, C.J. . . . and MOORE and FRANTZ, JJ. dissent.

MOORE, J. (dissenting). The opinion of the majority, as I view it, is so heavily weighted in the direction of unrestrained exercise of totalitarian and potentially tyrannical power by those in positions of governmental authority, and so repugnant to the limitations upon the exercise of governmental power, that I must dissent. . . .

I am primarily interested in the protection of constitutional limitations upon the power of any man, or group of men, to govern the people. This involves the preservation of individual freedom of action, and individual liberty, of which we talk so much and concerning which we do so little. With every passing year, by judicial opinions of the kind to which I now dissent, we nibble upon and whittle away the freedoms of the people; subjecting them more and more to unreasonable restraints, compelling compliance with governmental commands which are far in excess of any powers constitutionally authorized.

On March 4, 1939 . . . the then Chief Justice of the Supreme Court, Charles Evans Hughes, said, concerning the purpose of the constitution: "We protect the fundamental rights of minorities, in order to save democratic government from destroying itself by the excesses of its own power. The firmest ground for confidence in the future is that more than ever we realize that, while democracy must have its organization and controls, *its vital breath is individual liberty.*"

Under the act being considered the Urban Renewal Authority is given discretionary power of the most fantastic nature which could be exercised in a most arbitrary manner—to acquire *without the consent of the owner* the private property of untold thousands of citizens. And this may be accomplished notwithstanding that the "contemplated use" to be made of the property completely excludes the public, and on the contrary involves a private use and development of a kind to be bargained for, said *use* to be carried on for private profit! Vast amounts of public funds are to be expended in forcing unwilling owners of real estate to convey their property even though such property in no way whatever threatens to the public health, safety, or morals. The Urban Renewal Authority then conveys the property to private interests who undertake to create an atmosphere in the area purchased which is more to the liking of those who occupy the seats of power in the new dictator agency. These private interests, introducing new, or continuing the old private uses, anticipate a profit.

Thus the state plunges into the business of underwriting and financing private transactions in real estate and land development as a partner of those who speculate in real estate ventures, and in land development for profit.

If the . . . provisions of the constitution are impotent to prevent this socialistic plunge by the state into financial partnership with specially selected real estate promoters and developers of subdivisions who thereby acquire privately owned property without the consent of the owners, with the avowed purpose of putting to private uses for profit, then the constitution is dead in so far as it purports to assure the citizens that they have the "inalienable" right "of acquiring, possessing and protecting property." If countless thousands of property owners in practically any section of the city which happened to be conveniently "old" can thus be compelled to surrender their property to new purchasers for uses strictly private, we should discontinue the pretense that individual freedom of choice in matters pertaining to property has any constitutional protection against a tyrannical exercise of governmental power. If, as the majority opinion holds, the constitution is impotent in the instant situation then there is no point at which extreme encroachments upon rights guaranteed by the constitution can be stopped, since no grandiose multimillion dollar project can be conceived which would not carry with it some incidental or colorable public purpose.

It is usual and customary for those who seek to water down the effectiveness of the constitution as a bulwark of strength protecting individual freedom of action to claim some benefit to the public if the loss of individual liberty is sustained. It is true that no rights are absolute. However, I insist that "nothing is better settled than that the property of one individual cannot, *without his consent,* be devoted to the *private use* of another, even when there is an incidental or colorable benefit to the public." . . .

Under the holding of the majority there are few areas in the city of Denver which would not be subject to aggregate acquisition by the all-powerful Urban Renewal Authority, whether the owners of homes or business property located therein consented to being dispossessed or not. . . .

The Constitution of Colorado was created for the protection of minorities, for the protection of the individual against tyrannical rule. The fact that there may be a substantial clamor (largely contributed to by those who expect to profit from the scheme) for the sacrifice of individual liberty to advance private interests, does not mean that the constitution is ineffective to prevent the sacrifice.

Progress in this field should be and can be achieved within the framework of the constitution. The failure of local authorities to use the police power to eradicate "slums" adversely affecting the public health, safety, or morals does not warrant a judicial abandonment of the constitutional guaranties relating to property rights. As stated by Chief Justice Hughes, the "vital breath" of our way of life is the individual freedom of the citizen to act with a minimum of governmental compulsion. . . .

FRANTZ, J. concurs in the views hereinabove expressed.

HALL, C.J. . . . joins in the dissent of MOORE, J.

FRANTZ, J. (dissenting) . . . . Those in this court who deem the law consonant with the Constitution of this state and those who believe it sets the authority of this fundamental document at naught are equally in favor of progress and advancement. Our differences arise from considerations of the general good as opposed to those of the individual as they are expounded and made the subjects of rights and duties in the Constitution. The collision of doctrinal thought involves the primacy of the majority and the subordination of the individual, and, as in this case in some of its phases, a minority. . . .

Vindication for the Urban Renewal Law is expressly found in the police power. But police power cannot be exercised in respect to unoffending property. The measure of the right to exercise the police power is the right to regulate the use of property or to destroy it because either in the use or existence thereof it has a detrimental effect on the public health, safety, morals or general welfare. In this respect, properties must be considered individually. Individual properties which are not harmful to the public health, safety, morals, or general welfare are not, and cannot be, the proper subjects of regulation or destruction in the exercise of the police power.

Lawful, harmless properties may not be destroyed under a police power measure because located in an area containing properties which may be so treated, or nestled between such properties as are or may be proper subject for exerting the police power. What becomes of the natural, essential, and inalienable right to acquire, possess, and protect property if lawful, harmless buildings and improvements can be razed because so located? Lawful, harmless structures are the proper subjects of acquisition, possession, and protection. To hold otherwise would render empty and meaningless declarations of rights in the Constitution which have been considered precious to and inherent in man.

There are other disturbing elements in this case which provoke comment in view of the right of persons, regardless of their station in life, to acquire, possess, and protect property inoffensive from the standpoint of health, safety, morals, and welfare of the public. How are the great masses of the people to realize their aspirations of acquiring and possessing property, pursuing happiness, and enjoying life and liberty unless they are permitted to acquire and hold property, however humble in character? Are persons in extremely humble circumstances to be denied the opportunity to acquire and possess a home? . . .

And where do the persons of meager means in the area involved go if this project becomes reality? Probably they can do no better than seek the equivalent of that which they presently have. In all probability that means the removal to an area having the same characteristics as the one from which they are evicted. Continuing with probabilities, they would eventually face the same fate that will befall them in this case. An alternative would be to become renters, for it is not likely that they can afford homes of better quality. Thus, their constitutional right to acquire and possess property becomes a mirage —expressed in ghostly words with only a semblance of substance. . . .

"There is a proneness to regard constitutions as instruments of boundless accommodation, taking on so many shapes as in truth to be shapeless . . . That their generalities make for living documents covering changes in a developing society, no one will deny; but there are 'no trespass' signs in these constitutions effective against enroachment by the executive, legislative and judicial departments in certain areas, and among these areas are the natural rights of man enumerated in the Bill of Rights." . . .

History is monotonously repetitive. History in essence is little more than a chronicle of the struggle for the recognition and preservation or the abridgment of certain rights. In recent years the fortunes of the struggle have swung toward abridgment. The Urban Renewal Law is another effort to curtail individual rights in disregard of constitutional protections. At least the struggle should be in the forum of elections, to ascertain if the people desire to surrender these rights.

In addition to the foregoing, I join in the views expressed by MOORE, J.

Osterloh's Estate v. Carpenter
337 S.W.2d 942 (Mo., 1960)

Agnes Osterloh purchased securities within the two years prior to her death and had the certificates issued jointly in her name and the name of her sister. Upon her death, Carpenter, the inheritance tax collector, claimed that this transaction constituted a transfer of property by Agnes to her sister made within two years of her death and was therefore subject to inheritance tax. From a decision against the tax collector, he appealed.

STORCKMAN, J. . . . The most distinctive characteristic of an estate in joint tenancy is the right of survivorship. . . . When a joint tenancy is created, each of the cotenants acquires a right of survivorship which may or may not ripen into sole ownership of the property. . . .

Whether a cotenant will ever attain absolute ownership of the property and the accompanying right to exclusive possession is contingent and uncertain. The conveyance creating the joint tenancy does not determine this, and it cannot be ascertained until the death of one of the cotenants eliminates his right of survivorship.

A joint estate with right of survivorship is so distinctive that, unless specifically covered, it is not ordinarily held to be within the purview of a law taxing transfers by will or the intestacy laws, or transfers in contemplation of death. . . . "Joint tenancies with the right of survivorship are in a class by themselves. It is held that the entry into complete ownership and possession by one joint tenant of a piece of property, or a tenant by the entirety, upon the decease of the other, by virtue of the right of survivorship, is not subject to an inheritance tax under a statute which taxes the passing of property by will or by the laws regulating intestate succession. The same has been held under a statute taxing transfers."

Most jurisdictions by express provision have brought the entry of one of the joint tenants into sole ownership and possession under the inheritance and estate tax laws. These acts have separate provisions for taxing transfers in contemplation of death and for taxing the right of the surviving joint tenant to the immediate ownership or possession and enjoyment of the property. . . . On two occasions in recent years, attempts to bring Missouri in line with the federal act and those of other states have failed. . . .

The creation of a joint tenancy cannot be said to be a completed grant of the present or future possession or enjoyment of an ascertainable property interest. The interest of a cotenant in a joint tenancy may be entirely obliterated by his prior death and the alleged gift or grant may revert completely to the transferor free from any claim by the heirs or creditors of the deceased cotenant.

While the absolute title of the joint tenant who survives stems from the transaction which created the joint estate, the event which gives it completeness and permanence is the death of the cotenant. . . .

Our conclusion is that the transaction creating the joint tenancy was not a transfer of a property interest within the meaning of existing inheritance tax statutes. . . .

[Judgment affirmed.]

Voight v. Ott

86 Ariz. 128, 341 P.2d 923 (1959)

The Voights sold the sample house in a real estate development to the Otts. Mr. Ott, before buying, had inquired about the air conditioning and was given a folder which described the advantages of the air conditioning and heating system in the house. No mention was made about the system in the sales agreement or the deed to the house. Some time thereafter the Otts sued the Voights because the air conditioning did not work, on the theory that the system was personal property sold to them by the Voights who by the act of selling such property impliedly warranted that it would work. The Voights defended on the ground that the system was not personal property but was a fixture. From a judgment in favor of the Otts, the Voights appealed.

HENDERSON, J. . . . The question before us is whether such an item is a fixture or remains personalty and subject to the implications of warranty attributable thereto.

It is the general rule of law that implied warranties as to quality or condition do not apply to realty . . . If the item in question be realty, then there is no implied warranty applicable thereto. If the item be personalty, then the provisions of the statute as to implied warranties is made applicable. . . .

The parties may, as between themselves, by agreement determine that items of personal property shall be considered as a part of the realty. . . .

In the instant case, there was no mention made of the refrigeration or heating system of any portion thereof in any agreement or in any instrument whatsoever pertaining to the sale or conveyance of the residence property, and there was no separate agreement pertaining to such air conditioning system or any part thereof. In the absence of an agreement between the parties respecting fixtures, therefore, the answer to the question of whether an air conditioning system (heating and refrigeration) is a fixture or remains personalty depends upon the facts and circumstances attending each particular case, the relationship between the parties, and the application of the test . . . as to annexation, adaptability, and intention.

The modern tendency is to place less emphasis on the method or mode of annexation of the chattel and to give greater consideration to the intention of the parties as respects the use and adaptability thereof. . . .

It is common knowledge that the expanding economy of the valley areas of central and southern Arizona is due in large part to the widespread use of refrigeration systems, not only in business and commercial establishments but in residence properties. These plaintiffs, as practically all purchasers of residence properties in the Phoenix area, were materially concerned with the cooling system in the home. Many homes are purchased primarily because a refrigeration system exists therein. The plaintiff, James B. Ott, testified that the air conditioning system in this house was an integral part of the house and that it was very necessary for convenient living therein. He testified he wanted an air conditioned home and that the information about the system as contained in the brochure influenced him in regard to the purchase. Some purchasers will not purchase homes unless there is a refrigeration system, while others are content with an evaporative cooling system, but it is almost universal that no new residence property in the Phoenix area can be sold without one or the other of the two general methods of cooling. We can, therefore, say that the intent of the parties in practically all home purchases presupposes the existence and inclusion therein of some type of cooling system and, unless special mention be made to the contrary, it seems to us that whatever cooling system is included in the house passes with the house as a component part thereof and necessary for the comfortable and more convenient living of the occupants. . . .

We hold the test for a determination that the property in question is a part of the realty has been met. In view of this conclusion, it is not necessary to discuss the questions raised on the measure of damages. The remedy, if any, of the plaintiffs was not a suit for breach of warranty.

[The judgment is reversed.]

Questions and Case Problems

1. What is the objective of each of the following rules of law?
   (a) An owner is not allowed to use his property unreasonably in such a way as to injure other members of society.
   (b) Growing annual crops of grain and vegetables are regarded as personal property although still in or attached to the earth.

2. Cattie leased a building to Joseph P. Cattie & Brothers, Inc. In order to conduct its manufacturing business in the building, the corporation installed a crane track and a tram track that were embedded in a concrete foundation on the floor or supported by crossbeams embedded in walls of the building. When the lease was about to end, the corporation removed these tracks. This required cutting them with acetylene torches and removing them piece by piece. The equipment was thereby destroyed and, instead of having its original value of approximately $70,000, had a scrap metal value of approximately $10,000 for which it was sold by the corporation. Cattie then sued the corporation for $70,000 on the theory that the tenant had no right to remove the fixtures in question. Was the landlord entitled to the value of the fixtures. Decide. (Cattie v. Joseph P. Cattie & Brothers, Inc., [Pa.] 168 A.2d 313)

3. Adele Barret purchased corporate stock jointly in her name and the name of her niece, Mary Oliver, with the right of survivorship. When Adele died, the persons who received her estate claimed that the taxes on the estate should be paid proportionately by Mary since she was benefiting from the death of Adele. Decide. (Barret's Estate, [Fla.] 137 So.2d 587)

4. The Urban Redevelopment Law of Oregon authorized the condemning of blighted urban areas and the acquisition of the property by the Housing Authority by eminent domain. Such part of the land condemned as was not needed by the Authority could be resold to private persons. Foeller and others owned well-maintained buildings within the Vaughn

Street area that was condemned under this statute by the Portland Housing Authority as "physically substandard and economically deteriorated." The plaintiffs brought an action to have the statute declared unconstitutional. Decide. (Foeller v. Housing Authority of Portland, 198 Ore. 205, 256 P.2d 752)

5. Head, who owned a large tract of timber land, sold the timber to the Wood Mosaic Co. to be removed immediately. He then sold the land to Cheatham. The latter then sued Head claiming that Head had broken his contract in that he had already sold the timber to the Wood Mosaic Co. Decide. (Cheatham v. Head, 203 Ky. 489, 262 S.W. 622)

6. The Otis Elevator Corp. of Missouri made a contract to install elevators in the building owned by the Fifteenth Street Investment Corp. in Denver and to furnish both the labor and materials for such installation. A Denver ordinance imposed a tax on all sales of personal property. It was claimed that the materials that were to be installed were personal property and therefore that the transaction was subject to the tax. The Fifteenth Street Investment Corp. denied that the transaction was subject to tax on the ground that the materials were to be attached to realty. What was the nature of the materials? (Fifteenth Street Investment Corp. v. Colorado, 102 Col. 571, 81 P.2d 764)

7. The Aldrich Mining Co. mined coal from a strip of land in Alabama. Pearce claimed title to the land and brought an action for conversion of personal property against the company to recover the value of the coal. It was contended that the action was improper in that it should have been an action for injury to real property. Do you agree with this contention? (Aldrich Mining Co. v. Pearce, 169 Ala. 161, 52 So. 911)

8. Hughes and Kay were not married, but property was deeded to them as "husband and wife." Subsequently they brought an action to determine their rights in the property. What type of tenancy was created by the deed? (Hughes v. Kay, 194 Ore. 507, 242 P.2d 788)

9. A zoning ordinance of the city of Dallas, Texas, prohibited the use of property in a residential district for gasoline filling stations. Lombardo brought an action against the city to test the validity of the ordinance. He contended that the ordinance violated the rights of the owners of property in such districts. Do you agree with this contention? (Lombardo v. City of Dallas, 124 Tex. 1, 73 So.2d 475)

CHAPTER 16

Acquiring Title to Personal Property

Title to personal property may be acquired in several different ways. In this chapter the following ways will be discussed: copyrights and patents, accession, confusion, gifts, lost property, occupation, and judgments. Personal property may also be transferred by methods discussed in other chapters in this text, as follows: sales, adverse possession, marriage, bankruptcy, execution, and testate and intestate succession.

Sec. 16-A. Copyrights and Patents. Under its constitutional authority Congress has adopted copyright and patent right laws to further the arts and sciences by granting artists and inventors exclusive rights in the product of their mental labors.

(1) Copyrights. A *copyright* is a grant to authors giving them the exclusive right to possess, make, publish, and sell copies of their intellectual productions, or to authorize others to do so, for a period of 28 years, with the privilege of a renewal and an extension for an additional term of 28 years.

A copyright may be secured for lists of addresses, books, maps, musical compositions, motion pictures, and similar productions, provided the work is an original expression of an idea and not seditious, libelous, immoral, or blasphemous.

In 1955 the United States ratified the Universal Copyright Convention, and Congress amended our basic copyright statute. As a result, works of domestic origin exported to foreign countries that have ratified the Universal Copyright Convention may use the internationally accepted copyright symbol © in place of or in addition to the word "Copyright" or its abbreviation. Note the form of the copyright notice on the back of the title page of this book.

Independently of statute, the author or artist who creates a literary or artistic work has an absolute property right in his production as long as it remains unpublished.

(2) Patents. A *patent* is a grant to one who has given physical expression to an idea, giving him the exclusive right to make, use, and sell, and to authorize others to make, use, and sell the invention for a period of 17 years. A patent is not renewable. The invention must be a new and useful art, machine, or composition of matter not previously known and used.

Sec. 16-B. Accession. Property may be acquired by *accession,* that is, by means of an addition to or an increase of the thing that is owned, as in the case of produce of land or the young of animals. As a general rule repairs become a part of the article that is repaired. Likewise, when materials are furnished to another to be manufactured into an article, title to the finished article is in the owner of the materials. If the manufacturer, however, adds a large proportion of the materials, title will then usually vest in him.

A more difficult problem arises when a change in property is made against the wishes or at least without the consent of the owner. In such a case, the gaining of property by accession depends upon whether the act was done intentionally and willfully, or unintentionally and innocently.

In other instances the courts determine whether title has passed by accession on the basis of whether or not the labor and materials of the trespasser have changed the property into a different specie. Another rule frequently used is that title does not change by accession when the former value of the goods has been changed, so long as there is no loss of identity. Under this rule the owner of the original material may follow it and seize it in its new shape or form, regardless of the alteration which it has undergone, so long as he can prove the identity of the original material. The factor that influences the courts in applying one or the other rule is the desire to attain as fair a result as possible under the circumstances.

These rules merely relate to the right of the original owner to obtain the return of the property taken from him. They do not relate to his right to sue the person taking the property. Under other rules of property and tort law, the person taking the owner's property from him, however innocently, is liable for money damages representing the value of the property.

Sec. 16-C. Confusion. Personal property may be acquired when the property of two persons becomes intermingled under such circumstances that one owner forfeits his right in his goods. Under this *doctrine of confusion of goods,* if a person willfully and wrongfully mixes his own goods with those of another so as to render them indistinguishable, he loses his part of the property and the innocent party acquires title to the total mass.

The doctrine of confusion does not apply when (1) the mixture is by consent of the parties; (2) the mixture is made without fraudulent intent, as by accident or mistake; or (3) the goods that have been mixed are of equal kind and grade, therefore not capable of being distinguished, as in the case of oil, tea, and wheat. In these three cases each owner is entitled to his proportionate share of the mixture.

Sec. 16-D. Gift. Title to personal property may be transferred by the voluntary act of the owner without receiving anything in exchange, that is, by *gift.* The person making the gift, the *donor,* may do so because of things which the recipient of the gift, the *donee,* has done in the past or which he is expected to do in the future, but such matters of inducement are not deemed consideration so as to alter the "free" character of the gift.

Personal property may be given either absolutely or subject to a condition. The most common type of conditional gift is the *escrow delivery of a gift* by which the donor delivers the item of personal property to a third person who is not to give physical control to the donee until the latter has performed a specified condition.

(1) Inter Vivos Gifts. The ordinary gift that is made between two living persons is an *inter vivos gift.* For practical purposes the rule is that the gift takes effect upon the donor's expressing an intention to make a gift and making delivery, subject to the right of the donee to divest himself of title by disclaiming the gift within a reasonable time after learning that it has been made. Since there is no consideration for a gift, the donor cannot be sued for breach of contract, and the courts will not compel the donor to complete the gift.

The intent "to make" a gift requires an intent to transfer title at that time. In contrast, an intent to confer a benefit at a future date is not a sufficient intent to create any right in the intended donee. (See p. 262, Dudley v. Uptown National Bank)

The delivery of a gift may be a *symbolic delivery,* as by the delivery of means of control of the property, such as keys to a padlock or ignition keys to an engine, or by the delivery of papers that are essential to or closely associated with ownership of the property, such as documents of title or ship's papers. (See p. 264, Hardy v. St. Matthew's Community Center)

(2) Gifts Causa Mortis. A *gift causa mortis* is made when the donor, contemplating his imminent and impending death, delivers personal property to the donee with the intent that the donee shall own it if the donor dies. This is a conditional gift, and the donor is entitled to take the property back (a) if he survives the contemplated death; (b) if he revokes it before he dies; or (c) if the donee dies before the donor does. It can only be made when the donor contemplates death because of an existing illness or an impending peril.

(3) United States Government Savings Bonds. Government Savings Bonds, Series E, F, and G, are issued under a Treasury regulation which specifies that they are payable only to the registered owner and may be transferred only in the manner authorized by the regulation. Because of these limitations, some courts have held that neither an inter vivos gift nor a gift causa mortis may be made of such bonds. Some courts recognize a gift causa mortis but not a gift inter vivos of such bonds, while some recognize a gift when made by one of the original co-owners of a bond to the other.

(4) Uniform Gifts to Minors Act. Most states have adopted the Uniform Gifts to Minors Act,[1] which provides an additional method for making gifts to minors of money and of registered and unregistered securities. Under the act, a gift of money may be made to a minor by depositing it with a broker or a bank in an account in the name of the donor or another person or trust company "as custodian for [name of minor] under the [name of state] Uniform Gifts to Minors Act." If the gift is a registered security, the donor registers the security in a similar manner. If the gift is an unregistered security, it must be delivered by the donor to another person or trust company accompanied by a written statement signed by the donor and the custodian, in which the donor sets forth that he delivers the described property to the custodian as custodian for the minor under the uniform act and that the custodian acknowledges receipt of the security.[2]

Under the uniform act, the custodian is in effect a guardian of the property for the minor, but he may use it more freely and is not subject to the many restrictions applicable to a true guardianship. The gift is final and irrevocable for tax and all other purposes upon complying with the procedure of the act. The property can be transferred by the custodian to a third person free from the possibility that a minor donee might avoid the transfer.

----

[1] This Act has been adopted with varying minor modifications in the District of Columbia and all states except Alaska, Georgia, Louisiana, and New Jersey. This uniform act is based on a similar statute known as the Model Act Governing Gifts of Securities to Minors, which had been adopted in a number of states.

[2] Uniform Gifts to Minors Act (UGMA), Sec. 2.

Sec. 16-E. Lost Property. Personal property is *lost property* when the owner does not know where it is located but intends to retain title or ownership to it. The person finding lost property does not acquire title by his act of taking possession of it. Ordinarily the finder is entitled to possession as against everyone except the true owner.

In some states statutes have been adopted permitting the finder to sell the property if the owner does not appear within a stated period. In such a case, the finder is required to give notice, as by newspaper publication, in order to attempt to reach the owner.

The finder of lost property is not entitled to a reward or to compensation for his services in the absence of a statute so providing or a contract with the owner.

If property is found in a public place, such as the public part of a hotel, under such circumstances that to a reasonable man it would appear that the property had been intentionally placed there by the owner and that he is likely to recall where he left it and return for it, the finder is not entitled to possession of the property but must give it to the proprietor or manager of the public place to keep for the owner.

Sec. 16-F. Transfer by Nonowner. Ordinarily a sale or other transfer by one who does not own the property will pass no title. Accordingly, no title is acquired by theft. The thief acquires possession only, and if he makes a sale or gift of the property to a third person, the latter only acquires the possession of the property. The true owner may reclaim the property from the thief or from his transferee, or he may sue them for the conversion of his property and recover the value of the stolen property. (See p. 265, Farm Bureau Mutual Automobile Insurance Co. v. Moseley)

In some states this rule is fortified by statutes which declare that the title to an automobile cannot be transferred, even by the actual owner, without a delivery of a properly-endorsed title certificate. The states that follow the common law do not make the holding of a title certificate essential to the ownership of an automobile, although as a matter of police regulation the owner must obtain such a certificate.

As an exception to the rule that a nonowner cannot transfer title, an agent, who does not own the property but who is authorized to sell it, may transfer the title of his principal. Likewise certain relations create a power to sell and transfer title, such as a pledge or pawn of property. An owner of property may also be barred or estopped from claiming that he is still the owner when he had done such acts as deceive an innocent buyer in believing that someone else was the owner or had authority to sell the property.

Sec. 16-G. Occupation. Title to personal property may be acquired under certain circumstances by *occupation*, that is, by taking and holding possession of property of which no one has title. For example, in the absence of restrictions imposed by game laws, the person who acquires dominion or control over a wild animal becomes its owner.

Title to abandoned personal property may be acquired by the first person who reduces it to his possession and control. Personal property is deemed *abandoned property* when the owner relinquishes possession of it with the intention to disclaim title to it.

Sec. 16-H. Judgments. The entry of a judgment ordinarily has no effect upon the title to personal property owned by the judgment debtor. Exceptions arise when (1) the purpose is to determine title to the property as against the whole world, or (2) the action is brought to recover the value of converted personal property. In the latter case the payment of the judgment entered against the converter for the value of the goods transfers title to him as though there had been a voluntary sale. Some courts hold that title passes to the converter upon the mere entry of a judgment against him although it has not yet been paid.

Cases for Chapter 16

Dudley v. Uptown National Bank of Moline
25 Ill.App.2d 514, 167 N.E.2d 257 (1960)

Cecle Voss deposited money in the Uptown National Bank and received a certificate of deposit payable to her and P.O.D. (payable on death) to Pamela Dudley, a minor. Voss later had the deposited money withdrawn. After her death, Pamela, by her guardian, sued the bank for the amount of the deposit on the ground that she was the donee of a gift of the amount of the deposit. From a judgment in favor of the guardian, the bank appealed.

CROW, J. . . . A gift is a voluntary, gratuitous transfer of property by one to another. To constitute a legally effective gift inter vivos, there must be an intent by the claimed donor to make such a gift, an absolute and irrevocable delivery of the property to the claimed donee or the claimed donee's agent or trustee, with the intention of presently vesting the title and the immediate right of possession absolutely and irrevocably in the claimed donee, without restrictions, the claimed donor parting with all present and future dominion, power, and control over the property. . . . Intention, alone, by the claimed donor to make such a gift is not enough to make an effective gift. Delivery, alone, without an intent to pass title and possession, is not enough. . . .

The burden of proving all facts required for a valid gift inter vivos is on the claimed donee. To sustain the claimed gift, the proof must be clear, satisfactory, unequivocal, and convincing—there should be no uncertainty as to either the claimed intent or the claimed delivery. If a claimed gift does not take effect as an executed and completed transfer to the claimed donee during the life of the claimed donor, it is an attempted testamentary disposition not valid unless made by a proper will. . . .

In the present case we find the certificate of deposit was made payable by the decedent to herself "P.O.D. (payable on death to) Miss Pamela L. Dudley." This, alone, restricted Pamela L. Dudley in the collection of the money evidenced thereby until the death of Cecle Voss. Pamela, or her guardian, could not, under the terms of the certificate, have collected the money thereon during the life of Cecle Voss.

Cecle Voss was evidently familiar with the phraseology "P.O.D.," or "payable on death," having used it before in certain government bonds, having had it particularly explained here by a lawyer and Mr. Ely, of the bank, and having had the words " (payable on death to) " written out thereon in full after the abbreviated letters "P.O.D.," and presumably that phraseology expressed her intent, or is strong evidence of her intent. But she continued to keep the certificate in her possession from its issuance, July 11, 1957, to sometime in May, 1958. Then in May, 1958 just before she left home to go back to the hospital, she gave Brendon Dudley, Pamela's mother, a bundle of papers and other things which Cecle Voss described as important family things, family papers, and which Brendon Dudley referred to as the pile of things Mrs. Voss had asked her to care for, and which included various documents relating to some divorces, a Bible, some deceased parties' papers, etc., and she asked Brendon to keep them, or, as Brendon says, care for them. The certificate of deposit was in the bundle of papers, but Brendon Dudley did not know it was there. Cecle Voss either did not know it was there, or it is obscure and uncertain whether she knew it was there, and it was not endorsed or assigned by her.

Although indorsement or assignment may not have been essential if there otherwise was a perfected, executed gift inter vivos, the absence of indorsement or assignment by Cecle Voss is a significant and important evidence of no gift where the question of gift or no gift is in doubt; mere physical possession at one time by Brendon Dudley is not alone sufficient to prove a valid gift; an acquisition of physical possession without an intent by the owner to pass title and right to possession is not an effective delivery. . . . And the certificate at that time still remained in its original form—"P.O.D. (payable on death to) Miss Pamela L. Dudley"—which, alone, is inconsistent with a complete relinquishment in praesenti, inter vivos, by Cecle Voss of all dominion or control over the same. Later Brendon Dudley returned the certificate to Mr. Voss, who took it to Mrs. Voss at the hospital, and he, at Mrs. Voss' request, indorsed her name thereon, surrendered it to the bank, and the proceeds, with interest, were placed in their joint bank account. There is nothing to indicate Mrs. Voss was not aware that she was dealing with the certificate of deposit at that time and was asking Mr. Voss to do the mechanical job of indorsing and cashing it for her at the bank, which she was not physically able to do herself.

A general donative intent of the character here evidenced is quite different from, and opposed to, an intent to make a gift inter vivos, which is the type of intent required to sustain a claimed gift inter vivos. There was no absolute and irrevocable delivery of the property to Pamela or to Brendon Dudley, as Pamela's agent, with the intention of presently vesting the title and immediate right of possession absolutely and irrevocably in Pamela, without restrictions. . . .

[Judgment reversed.]

Hardy v. St. Matthew's Community Center
267 S.W.2d 725 (Ky.App., 1954)

Juanita Hardy bought ten tickets for a lottery on a Buick car run by St. Matthew's Community Center. On one of the ticket stubs she wrote the name of her niece, Dixie Lee Williams, a minor, and returned the stub to the Center. She later phoned the niece's mother and told her that she had bought a chance for Dixie. The chance with Dixie's name won. Juanita sued the Community Center, claiming that the Buick belonged to her. From a judgment against her, she appealed.

WADDILL, C. . . . The only question before us is whether or not the evidence was sufficient to support a finding that appellant made a gift to her niece, . . . of her chance to win the Buick automobile.

The elements necessary to constitute a gift inter vivos are a competent donor who intends to make an irrevocable gift; a donee capable of taking the gift; actual, constructive, or symbolic delivery to the donee; and acceptance of the gift by the donee. . . .

In the case of an advantageous gift to an infant, acceptance is presumed. . . .

Delivery may be symbolic, and we have held that the deposit of money in the name of infant donees, coupled with subsequent declarations of a purpose to vest ownership in the infants, is sufficient to constitute a gift, despite the fact the pass books were retained by the donor. . . .

We are of the opinion that appellant's act of writing Dixie Lee Williams' name on the ticket stub and returning the stub to the holder of the lottery, coupled with her declaration of intention to the infant's mother constitute a delivery of the subject matter of the gift to the infant. . . .

[Judgment affirmed.]

Farm Bureau Mutual Automobile Insurance Co. v. Moseley

47 Del. 256, 90 A.2d 485 (1952)

Grunwell's automobile, which he insured with the Farm Bureau Mutual Auto Insurance Co., was stolen. The insurance company paid Grunwell under the policy. The car was thereafter found in the possession of Moseley who had purchased it from a used car dealer. The identity of the thief was never established, but both Moseley and the used car dealer had acted in good faith. A new engine had apparently been placed in the car by the thief. Moseley had also made additions to the car. The insurance company sued Moseley to recover the automobile. From a judgment in favor of the insurance company, Moseley appealed.

RICHARDS, P.J. . . . The owner of goods or chattels which have been stolen is not divested of his ownership of the property by the larcenous taking. He may follow and reclaim the stolen property wherever he finds it.

A sale by the thief, or by any person claiming under the thief, does not vest title to the property in the purchaser as against the legal owner. The fact that the sale was made in the ordinary course of business and the purchaser acted in good faith makes no difference.

The subsequent possession by the thief is a continuing wrong; and if the wrongdoer increases the value of the property by his labor upon it, or by substituting parts for those which were on it when he acquired it, or by adding new parts to it, the property in its enhanced value or changed condition, still belongs to the original owner and he may retake it with the accessions thereto. . . .

The automobile in question having been identified as stolen property, the defendant Mosely has no title to it as against the claim of the plaintiff, who acquired title from Mr. Grunwell, the owner from whom it was stolen.

The property right to the automobile being in the plaintiff, I render judgment in its favor for the automobile.

The engine which was in the automobile at the time it was stolen from Mr. Grunwell, having been removed by the thief or someone who claimed under the thief and another engine put in its place, the new engine became a part of the automobile and the plaintiff is entitled to retain it as his property.

It does not appear that the defendant Moseley knew that the automobile had been stolen when he purchased it, consequently there was no willful wrongdoing by him. This being true, he is entitled to the sun visor, seat covers, and gasoline tank which he attached to the automobile while it was in his possession. The distinction between a willful and involuntary wrongdoer is recognized by the authorities.

[Judgment affirmed with modification.]

Questions and Case Problems

1. What is the objective of each of the following rules of law?

(a) A patent gives an inventor the exclusive right to make, use, and sell the invention for a period of 17 years.

(b) The owner of stolen property may sue not only the thief but also a transferee of the thief for conversion of the property.

2. Brogden acquired a biblical manuscript in 1945. In 1952 he told his sister Lucy that he wanted Texas A. & M. College to have this manuscript. He dictated a note so stating and placed it with the manuscript. He made some effort to have an officer of the college come for the manuscript. In 1956 he delivered the manuscript to his sister stating that he was afraid that someone would steal it. Later in the year he told a third person that he was going to give the manuscript to the college. In 1957 he was declared incompetent. In 1959 the sister delivered the manuscript to the college. In April, 1960, Borgden died and his heirs, Bailey and others, sued Harrington and other officers of the college to have the title to the manuscript determined. Decide. (Harrington v. Bailey, [Tex.Civ.App.] 351 S.W.2d 946)

3. Kenyon, an artist, had painted a picture entitled "Song of the Bluebird." The theme of the painting was taken from another picture entitled "Spring Song," but showed distinguishable variations. Kenyon sold and assigned all her rights in the picture to the Gerlack-Barklow Co. In an action in respect to the copyright brought by the buying company against Morris & Bendien, Inc., a question arose whether such a picture was the subject of copyright. What is your opinion? (Gerlack-Barklow Co. v. Morris & Bendien, Inc., [C.C.A. 2d] 23 F.2d 159)

4. Gates was engaged in lumber operations. By mistake he cut a quantity of white pine situated upon the adjoining land of Rust Bros. & Co. These logs were mixed with other logs of Gates and were banked on the west branch of the Rifle River. The next year the intermingled logs were driven down the stream and received in the boom of the Rifle Boom Co. Gates sued the Rifle Boom Co. for his logs. Decide. (Gates v. Rifle Boom Co., 70 Mich. 309, 38 N.W. 245)

5. Anne Nichols was the author of a play, "Abie's Irish Rose," which, was based upon the religious prejudices of the parents of a young man and a young woman who desired to marry. The ideas upon which the play was based were utilized in a photoplay, "The Cohens and The Kellys." In an action brought by Anne Nichols against the Universal Pictures Corp., a question arose whether the property of a playwright by virtue of copyright extends to ideas. What is your opinion? (Nichols v. Universal Pictures Corp., [C.C.A. 2d] 45 F.2d 119)

6. Gikas gave Nicholis an engagement ring and certain personal property when they became engaged. The engagement was later broken, and he demanded the return of the ring and the gifts. She refused to return them. Gikas brought suit for the conversion of the property. Decide. (Gikas v. Nicholis, 96 N.H. 177, 71 A.2d 785)

BAILMENTS

CHAPTER 17

Nature and Termination

Many instances arise in which the owner of personal property entrusts it to another. A person checks his coat at a restaurant or loans his car to a friend. He delivers a watch to a jeweler for repairs, takes furniture to a warehouse for storage, or delivers goods to a railroad for shipment. The delivery of property under such circumstances is a bailment.

Sec. 17-A. Definition. A *bailment* is the legal relation that arises whenever one person delivers possession of personal property to another person under an agreement or contract by which the latter is under a duty to return the identical property to the former or to deliver it or dispose of it as agreed. The person who turns over the possession of the property is the *bailor*. The person to whom he gives the possession is the *bailee*.

(1) Agreement. The bailment is based upon an agreement. Technically the bailment is the act of delivering the property to the bailee and the relationship existing thereafter. The agreement that precedes this delivery is an agreement to make a bailment rather than the actual bailment. Generally this agreement will contain all the elements of a contract so that the bailment transaction in fact consists of (a) a contract to bail and (b) the actual bailing of the property.

Ordinarily there is no requirement that the agreement of bailment be in writing. In some states, however, a writing or recording of the bailment agreement may be necessary to protect the interest of the bailor. Thus a statute may provide that if the bailor does not record his title to the bailed property, creditors of the bailee may treat it as the bailee's property when the bailment has lasted more than five years.

(2) Personal Property. The subject of a bailment may be any personal property of which possession may be given. Real property cannot be bailed.

(3) Bailor's Interest. The bailor is usually the owner of the property, but ownership by him is not required. It is sufficient that the bailor have physical possession. Thus an employee may be a bailor in leaving his employer's truck at a garage. Whether possession is lawful or not is immaterial. A thief, for example, may be a bailor.

(4) Delivery and Acceptance. The bailment does not arise until, pursuant to the agreement of the parties, the property is delivered to the bailee and accepted by him as subject to the bailment agreement. (See p. 271, Theobald v. Satterthwaite) This may be an actual delivery, as when the bailor physically hands a book to the bailee. Or it may be a *constructive delivery*, as when the bailor points out a package to the bailee who then takes possession of it.

(5) Specific Property. A bailment places a duty upon the bailee to return the specific property that was bailed or to deliver or dispose of it in the manner directed by the bailor. If the bailee has an option of paying money or of returning property other than that which was delivered to him, there is generally no bailment. Thus, when a farmer delivers grain to a warehouse which gives him a receipt and promises to return either the grain or a certain amount of money upon presentation of the receipt, the relationship is not a bailment. The importance of this distinction lies in the fact that when the relationship is not a bailment but another relationship, such as a sale, the risk of loss if the property is damaged or destroyed will ordinarily be on the warehouse; whereas if it is a bailment, the bailor would ordinarily bear the loss.

In a number of states a rental of property coupled with an option to purchase is classified as a bailment.[1]

Sec. 17-B. Classifications of Bailments. Bailments are classified as ordinary and extraordinary. *Extraordinary bailments* are those in which the bailee is given unusual duties and liabilities by law, as in

---

[1] If the parties have agreed on a sale at the beginning and a bailment lease is executed merely for the protection of the seller, the transaction is governed by the Uniform Commercial Code, Article 9—Secured Transactions. See Chapter 35.

the case of bailments in which a hotel or a common carrier is the bailee. *Ordinary bailments* include all other bailments.

Bailments may or may not provide for compensation to the bailee. Upon that basis they are sometimes classified as *contract bailments* and *gratuitous bailments*.

Bailments may also be classified as for the (1) sole benefit of the bailor, as when a farmer gratuitously transports another's produce to the city; (2) sole benefit of the bailee, as when a person borrows the automobile of a friend; or (3) benefit of both parties, as when one rents an automobile.

Sec. 17-C. Constructive Bailments. When one person comes into possession of personal property of another without the owner's consent, the law treats the possessor as though he were a bailee. Sometimes this relationship is called a *constructive bailment*. It is thus held that the finder of lost property must treat the property as a bailee.

A police officer taking possession of stolen goods is deemed a bailee for the true owner. A seller who has not yet delivered the goods to his buyer is treated as the bailee of the goods if title has passed to the buyer. Similarly, a buyer who is in possession of goods, the title to which has not passed to him, is a bailee.

Sec. 17-D. Bailment of Contents of Container. It is a question of the intention of the parties as that appears to a reasonable man whether the bailing of a container also constitutes a bailment of articles contained in it; that is, whether a bailment of a truck is a bailment of articles in the truck, whether a bailment of a coat is a bailment of articles in the pockets of the coat, and so on. When the contained articles are of a nature that are reasonable or normal to be found within the container, they are regarded as bailed in the absence of an express disclaimer. If the articles are not of such a nature and their presence in the container is unknown to the bailee, there is no bailment of such articles.

Sec. 17-E. Bailee's Interest. Title to the property does not pass to the bailee, and he cannot sell the property to a third person. If he attempts to do so, his act only transfers possession and the owner may recover the property from the third person.

The bailor may cause third persons to believe that the bailee is the owner of the bailed property. If he does so, he may be estopped to deny that the bailee is the owner as against persons who have relied on the bailor's representations.

(1) Bailee's Right to Possession. The bailor may retake possession whenever he chooses if the bailment is at will. If the bailment is

for a set term, the bailor under ordinary circumstances is not entitled to take back the property before the expiration of the term. If he should do so, the bailee may treat him as though he were a third person unlawfully trying to take the property. Moreover, if the bailee has a lien on the property for services performed by him, as a repairman, public warehouseman, or carrier, the bailor is not entitled to the return of the property until he has paid the amount due.

The bailee is usually entitled to retain possession as against third persons. If a thief takes the bailed property from the bailee or if a third person damages the bailed property, the possessory interest of the bailee is harmed and he may therefore sue the thief or third person for damages. Under modern law either the bailor or the bailee may sue the third person in such instances, although suit against the third person for the total damage to the property bought by either the bailor or the bailee bars a second action against the third person by the other. It has also been held that the bailee is entitled to the protection of a statute specifically designed for the protection of "owners."

As an exception to this right of possession as against third persons, the bailee must usually surrender the bailed property to one who establishes that he is the true owner and that he is entitled to immediate possession as against the bailor.

(2) Interpleader. Ordinarily a bailee is not permitted to question whether the bailor is the true owner, but must surrender the property to the bailor when the bailment ends. He cannot refuse to do so on the ground that a third person owns the property. A legal procedure called *interpleader* has been devised by which a bailee may require the bailor and a third person who claims to be the owner to litigate their rival claims so that the bailee will know to whom the property should be delivered. This procedural device is given to the bailee because, although he is under a duty to recognize the bailor, he also runs the danger that if the third person claiming ownership is in fact the owner, that third person may sue the bailee for damages as a converter of the property.

Sec. 17-F. Termination of Bailment. A bailment may be terminated by (1) agreement, (2) acceptance of breach, (3) destruction of subject matter, (4) act of the bailor, and (5) operation of law.

(1) Agreement. Since a bailment is based upon an agreement or contract, it may be terminated in accordance with its own terms (See p. 273, Adair v. Roberts) or by a subsequent agreement.

(2) Acceptance of Breach. If either party materially violates his obligations under the bailment, the other party has the option of

treating the bailment at an end. (See p. 274, Carstensen v. Gottesburen) Accordingly, the bailor may accept the bailee's breach of his
duties as a termination of the bailment. Thus, if the bailee unlawfully sells the property to a third person, the bailor may treat the
relationship as ended.

Even though the bailor does not terminate because the bailee
makes an improper or unauthorized use of the property, the bailee
remains liable for any harm caused thereby.[2]

(3) Destruction of Subject Matter. There is an implied condition
in a bailment that the bailed property be in existence and that it be
in either the same condition or form as when bailed or in a condition
or form which is suitable for the purpose of the bailment. Consequently the bailment ends if the property is destroyed by a third
person or by an act of God, or if it deteriorates so that it is unfit for
use for the purpose of the bailment.

If the property has been damaged through the bailee's fault the
bailment is not terminated automatically but there is a breach of the
agreement which the bailor may treat as terminating the bailment.

(4) Act of Bailor. If the bailment is terminable at the will of the
bailor, either because expressly made so or because no consideration
has been given to keep the bailment in existence for a specified fixed
period, the bailor may terminate the bailment at any time by demanding the return of the property, by retaking the property, or by
doing any other act which indicates that he has exercised his will to
terminate the bailment.

(5) Operation of Law. Death, insanity, or bankruptcy of a party
to the bailment will terminate the bailment when it is thereafter
impossible for the bailee to perform his duties, or when the bailment
is for the sole benefit of the bailee who has died, or when the bailment is terminable at will. If the bailment is for a fixed period and
is based upon a binding contract, however, the death or incapacity
of a party to the bailment does not terminate it.

Cases for Chapter 17

Theobald v. Satterthwaite

30 Wash.2d 92, 190 P.2d 714 (1948)

Theobald went to the beauty parlor operated by Satterthwaite. She left
her fur coat in the outer reception room. When she returned to the reception room, she found that the coat had been stolen. She then sued the
defendant for the value of the coat. From a judgment in her favor, the
defendant appealed.

---

[2] See p. 280.

MALLERY, C.J. . . . Theobald had patronized the shop on a number of occasions previous to the day in question and knew the arrangements of the rooms. On a previous occasion she had inquired of appellant, Satterthwaite, if the reception room was a safe place to leave her coat and had been assured that it was safe. Nothing had been stolen from the reception room in twenty years of operation, and the hooks in that room were the only places provided for customers on which to hang their wraps. There was no bell or warning device on the door that sounded when it was opened. A thief could see into the reception room and if a garment hung there, could open the door, take it off the hook, and leave without being seen from the operating room.

On December 24, 1946, . . . Theobald came into the beauty shop by appointment to get a permanent wave. She sat in the reception room with her fur coat on until the appellant . . . invited her into the operating room. Whereupon she removed her coat, which was natural and expected, for the period while receiving her permanent wave. She hung it on a hook provided for wraps in the reception room. [The appellant was not] aware that she had worn her fur coat on that day. When Satterthwaite had finished the work on respondent's hair, respondent went into the reception room to get her coat and found that it had been stolen. An alarm was given and the police were called, but to no avail. She valued the coat at $300 for which amount the lower court gave her judgment upon the theory that the [appellant was bailee] of the coat and had been negligent in caring for it because of having furnished an unsafe place to leave it.

The [appellant contends that she is] not liable because there was no bailment. Respondent contends that there was a bailment and relies upon the rule in Bunnell v. Stern, 122 N.Y. 539, 25 N.E. 910. . . . In that case a lady had gone to a clothing store to buy a coat. In order to try on a new garment, she took off her coat and laid it down in the presence of store attendants some distance away from the mirror she used in her fitting. Of this the store employees had knowledge. After her fitting she returned for her coat and found it gone. The court said: "Under these circumstances we think that it became their duty to exercise some care for the plaintiff's cloak because she had laid it aside with their invitation and with their knowledge and, without question or notice from them, had put it in the only place she could." . . .

While we are not inclined to view the element of delivery in any technical sense, still we think there can be no delivery unless there is change of possession of an article from one person to another. . . . One who takes off a garment and deposits it in his own presence as one would do in a restaurant retains the power of surveillance and control in himself, and the burden of care is not transferred with regard to such an article because the operators of the restaurant have not knowingly received the exclusive possession and dominion over it. In the instant case the respondent may not have had an adequate opportunity for surveillance; nevertheless she had not transferred control of it to the appellant by a delivery, and [she was] unaware that a valuable fur coat had been left in the reception room.

We therefore agree with the appellant's contention that there was no bailment in this case because there was no change of possession of the coat and hence no delivery. It follows that, in the absence of a bailment, the appellants owed the respondent no duty of care or were not negligent in failing to guard it effectively.

[Judgment for plaintiff reversed.]

Adair v. Roberts
276 S.W.2d 565 (Tex.Civ.App., 1955)

Adair contracted to haul certain pipe casings for the Ace Oil Co. from one well site to another. A month or more after he had unloaded all the pipe at the second site, it was taken unlawfully by Roberts. Adair sued Roberts for this conversion on the ground that he was the bailee of the Ace Oil Co. Roberts defended on the ground that Adair was not the bailee at the time when the pipe was taken and therefore had no authority to sue him. From a judgment in favor of Roberts, Adair appealed.

FANNING, J. . . . To constitute the relationship of bailor and bailee, there must be a contract expressly entered into or one arising by implication, growing out of the delivery of property to the party entrusted with its care. There must be a delivery of the property to the bailee and an actual acceptance of it by him. An acceptance by the alleged bailee must be shown because the relation is founded upon contract. The duties and liabilities springing from the relationship cannot be thrust upon one without his knowledge or consent. His acceptance of the property and of the responsibilities accompanying the relationship may be proved directly or by circumstances, but the proof must show that the person sought to be charged as bailee knew he was assuming such relationship and responsibilities concerning the property before he can be charged with the duties and responsibilities growing out of it. . . .

There was no . . . contract between plaintiff and Ace whereby plaintiff ever agreed to take exclusive possession of the casing and store and hold it until Ace called upon him for redelivery. . . . Plaintiff . . . testified that as far as he was concerned when his trucks took the pipe to the pumper's house and unloaded it there, he thought he was through with it and that he never expected Ace to pay him anything other than for hauling the pipe to the pumper's house. He never attempted to charge any "storage" and his bill . . . shows that it was solely for hauling. . . . Also it is clearly apparent from the record that plaintiff Adair only had possession of the casing on one day, December 24, 1952, the day he hauled the casing. . . . The alleged conversion of the pipe took place a month or more later, either in late January or early February, 1953, at a time when same had been out of the possession of plaintiff for a month or more.

It is our view that the only bailment contract that plaintiff Adair agreed to was one to move the casing . . . which was done on December 24, 1952, which bailment was completed insofar as plaintiff Adair was concerned on that date by delivery of the casing. . . . It is our further view that since Adair never agreed to store, safekeep, or return the property thereafter, no bailment therefor existed between Adair and Ace on the date of the alleged conversion. . . .

Since . . . there was no bailment between Adair and Ace on the date of the alleged conversion, it follows that Adair could not legally maintain the suit in question against Roberts. . . .

[Judgment affirmed.]

Carstensen v. Gottesburen
215 Cal. 258, 9 P.2d 831 (1932)

Carstensen and another leased a fishing barge to Gottesburen for a period of three years at a specified rental. The lease provided that it was not assignable and that the lessee should not sublet any part of the barge without the written consent of the lessors. Within three months Gottesburen assigned an undivided one-half interest in the lease to Shelton. Later the rent was not paid. The lease did not provide for forfeiture in case of default in rent. The lessors brought an action against Gottesburen and Shelton to recover the barge. From a judgment for the plaintiffs, the defendant Gottesburen appealed.

WASTE, C.J. . . . Appellant's principal contention . . . is that in the absence of a clause in the lease providing therefor, a breach of covenant (as distinguished from a condition) does not work a forfeiture. In support thereof he refers to Section 1931 of the Civil Code as specifying the only conditions and circumstances warranting the termination of a bailment by the lessor before the end of the term. That section reads as follows:

"The letter [bailor-lessor] of a thing may terminate the hiring and reclaim the thing before the end of the term agreed upon:

"1. When the hirer uses or permits a use of the thing hired in a manner contrary to the agreement of the parties; or,

"2. When the hirer does not, within a reasonable time after request, make such repairs as he is bound to make."

By the first subdivision of the foregoing section, the lessor may terminate the hiring when the lessee "permits a use of the thing hired in a manner contrary to the agreement of the parties." Under the terms and provisions of the lease here involved, the barge was placed in the appellant's possession for his sole and exclusive use and operation as a fishing barge. That the parties intended confining its use and operation exclusively to the appellant is established by the clause in the instrument which precludes and prohibits the appellant from assigning the lease or subletting any part of the barge without having first procured the written consent of the respondents. They did not consent to an assignment of the lease, and therefore to permit of the use and operation of the barge by one not a party to the hiring (and one not acting as agent or employee of the lessee) is to permit "a use of the thing hired in a manner contrary to the agreement of the parties" just as effectively and as completely as though the lessee had used the barge for illicit "rum-running" purposes when the provisions of the lease required that it be engaged only as a fishing boat. Therefore, for the appellant to transfer the lease or any interest therein to Shelton, a stranger to the hiring, or to a corporation, a partnership, or any other entity, having no connection therewith, when the lease by its terms forbade such a transfer and engaged only to permit the appellant's use of the barge, constituted, in our opinion, a positive violation of the terms of hiring and permitted "a use of the thing hired in a manner contrary to the agreement of the parties" within the meaning of Subdivision 1 of Section 1931. . . . This being so, the respondents, as lessors, were authorized by the cited section to terminate the hiring and reclaim the barge before the end of the term agreed upon. . . .

[Judgment for plaintiffs affirmed.]

Questions and Case Problems

1. What is the objective of each of the following rules of law?

(a) In a bailment, title to the property does not pass to the bailee and he cannot sell the property to a third person.

(b) A bailment is not terminated by the death of the bailor when it is based upon a contract providing for a bailment for a fixed period.

2. Mrs. Mushkatin placed her mink jacket in the unattended cloakroom of the Commodore Hotel. She did not inform the hotel or any employee that she was doing so. When she returned for the jacket, it could not be found. Her insurance company, the National Fire Insurance Co., paid the loss and then sued the hotel on the ground that it was a bailee. Was it a bailee? (National Fire Insurance Co. v. Commodore Hotel, Inc., [Minn.] 107 N.W.2d 708)

3. Rackliff rented road construction equipment to the Coronet Construction Co. on a monthly basis for the duration of a particular construction job. The agreement called for the payment by Coronet of $4,000 a month begining on June 13 and requiring Coronet to return the equipment to Rackliff's yard at the termination of the bailment. On July 27, Coronet notified Rackliff that it no longer desired the equipment and told Rackliff to come and get it. On August 1, Rackliff came and took the equipment back. Rackliff thereafter sued Coronet for the rental to August 1. Coronet claimed that no rental could be due after July 27, since the bailment had terminated on that date. Was Coronet correct? (Rackliff v. Coronet Construction Co., [Cal.App.2d] 321 P.2d 50)

4. The Vulcanite Portland Cement Co. delivered a quantity of cement to the Atlantic Building Supply Co. under a contract of bailment for one year. Thereafter the Atlantic Building Supply Co. took and used part of the cement for its own purposes. The Vulcanite Portland Cement Co. terminated the bailment relation. Was it entitled to do so? (Atlantic Building Supply Co. v. Vulcanite Portland Cement Co., 203 N.Y. 133, 96 N.E. 370)

5. Taylor parked his automobile in a garage operated by the Philadelphia Parking Authority and paid a regular monthly charge therefor. There was a written agreement between them which provided: "The Authority shall have the right to move the applicant's automobile to such location as it may deem necessary in order to facilitate the most effective use of the parking space on the roof. Ignition keys must be left in the automobile at all times." It was thereafter agreed between the parties that the plaintiff could retain the ignition key at all times and lock the auto in order to protect the valuable merchandise which Taylor carried in his car. Taylor brought the car into the garage, locked it, and left with the keys. The car was missing when he returned. He sued the parking Authority on the theory that it had breached a duty as bailee. The Authority claimed that it was not a bailee. Was the Authority correct? (Taylor v. Philadelphia Parking Authority, [Pa.] 156 A.2d 525)

6. Hubbard rented two trucks to Godde, one equipped with a drilling rig and the other with a water tank, by a written "lease" which gave Goode the option to purchase at a specified price and imposed upon Goode the obligation to pay taxes and to insure the property. Thereafter, without Hubbard's knowledge, Goode assigned his interest in the equipment to Hair and Russell who took possession and began drilling operations. When Hubbard learned that this assignment had been made, he sued Goode and the assignees to recover possession. Hubbard claimed that the assignment could not be made without his consent because "the equipment . . . was of a highly specialized nature and required special skill for its operation, [and he] relied upon the experience and ability of . . . Goode." Was the assignment valid? (Hubbard v. Goode, [N.Mex.] 335 P.2d 1063)

CHAPTER 18

Ordinary Bailments

A bailment creates certain rights and imposes certain duties and liabilities upon each party. These may generally be increased or modified by statute or custom, or by the express agreement or contract of the parties to the bailment.

Sec. 18-A. Rights of the Bailee.

(1) Right to Use the Property for the Bailment Purpose. It is a question of intention whether the bailee may use the property for his benefit. If none is expressed, the intention of the parties must be determined from the surrounding circumstances, including the nature of the property and the nature and purpose of the bailment.

In a bailment for the sole benefit of the bailee, the right of the bailee to use the property is strictly limited to the use contemplated by the bailor when he agreed to the relation. If a person borrows property to use in one city, for example, he cannot use it in another. When the bailment is for the sole benefit of the bailor, the bailee may not use or handle the property except to the extent necessary to protect it.

In a mutual-benefit bailment the bailee has the right to use the property in accordance with the terms of the contract. When this type of bailment is for storage only, the right to use the property does not exist unless some use is necessary to preserve and protect it.

(2) Right to Insure the Property. The bailee has an insurable interest in the property bailed and may take out insurance on the property. Generally he is not required to do so, although in some instances the bailee may be required by custom, agreement, or statute to insure the property. A commercial bailee, such as a warehouseman, may do so voluntarily in order to make his service more attractive to the public.

(3) Right to Compensation for Services. Whether the bailee is entitled to compensation for what he does depends upon the agreement. In the absence of an agreement to the contrary, courts assume that the bailor intended to pay the reasonable value of services rendered, unless the circumstances are such that reasonable men in the position of the parties would have realized that the services were rendered without the intention to charge or the expectation to pay.

In a mutual-benefit bailment the bailee is ordinarily entitled to compensation provided he has fully performed according to the terms of the contract. When the bailee is to perform services upon goods furnished by the bailor and the goods are lost, stolen, or destroyed without fault of the bailee, the latter is usually entitled to payment for the work done. Custom or the terms of the contract may, however, place the loss on the bailee. For example, if the bailee is to perform services on goods under an agreement which provides for payment "only after delivery in good order to our store," he assumes the risk that he will not be paid if he fails to make such delivery, whether or not he was at fault.

In a bailment for the sole benefit of the bailee, the bailee is not entitled to compensation for services rendered. If *A* borrows *B's* automobile for his own use, *A* cannot charge *B* a fee for the care he takes of the automobile during the period of the bailment.

(4) Bailee's Lien. A bailee who according to agreement performs services that enhance the value of the property has a specific common-law lien on the goods. Other bailees for hire are not entitled to a lien, but the parties can expressly provide for such a lien in their contract.

Statutes in many states have changed to a considerable extent the common law in regard to the liens of bailees. In some instances the bailee has the right of lien even though his services do not bestow value upon the subject matter of the bailment. (See p. 283, Braufman Case) Statutes commonly require a public sale of the property subject to the lien, and in some instances they provide for the recording of the lien.

In the absence of statute, the lien merely confers the right to retain possession and is lost if the lienholder voluntarily parts with possession.

Under common law and under statute, no lien arises when the work is done on credit.

(5) Action Against Third Persons. The bailee has a possessory right in the goods bailed. This qualified property right entitles him to bring an action against third persons for interfering with his possession or for injury to or destruction of the goods.

Sec. 18-B. Duties and Liabilities of the Bailee.

(1) Performance. If the bailment is based upon a contract, the bailee must perform his part of the contract and is liable to the bailor for any loss arising out of his failure to do so. For example, when the bailee was required to ship goods to one city but sent them to another, he was held liable for their loss en route. Similarly, if the bailment is for repair, the bailee is under the duty to make the repairs properly. The fact that the bailee uses due care does not excuse him for failing to perform according to his contract.

(2) Care of the Property. The bailee is under a duty to care for the property entrusted to him. If the property is damaged or destroyed, the bailee is liable for the loss (a) if the harm was caused in whole or in part by the bailee's failure to use reasonable care under the circumstances, or (b) if the harm was sustained during unauthorized use of the property by the bailee. Otherwise the bailor bears the loss. Thus, if the bailee was exercising due care and was making an authorized use of the property, the bailor must bear the loss of or damage to the property caused by an act of a third person, whether willful or negligent, by an accident or occurrence for which no one is at fault, or by an act of God. In this connection the term *act of God* means a natural phenomenon that it is not reasonably foreseeable, such as a sudden flood or lightning.

(a) STANDARD OF CARE. The standard for all ordinary bailments is reasonable care under the circumstances, that is, the degree of care which a reasonable man would exercise in the situation in order to prevent the realization of reasonably foreseeable harm. In some types of bailments the bailor may reasonably expect or demand that the bailee use greater care than in others. The significant factors in determining what constitutes reasonable care in a bailment are the time and place of making the bailment, the facilities for taking care of the bailed property, the nature of the bailed property, the bailee's knowledge of its nature, and the extent of the bailee's skill and experience in taking care of goods of that kind. Whether due care has been exercised under the circumstances is a question for the jury to decide.

The bailor has the burden of proving that the bailee was guilty of a breach of duty, but the bailee has the burden of presenting evidence to explain what happened. (See p. 284, Fox Chevrolet Sales Case) In any case, however, the jury must decide in favor of the bailee if it is not convinced by a preponderance of the evidence that he has violated his duties. If the jury believes the bailee's testimony that he took proper care of the goods, the bailee is not liable for the loss even though he cannot explain or show what happened.

(b) CONTRACT MODIFICATION OF LIABILITY. A bailee's liability may be expanded by contract. A provision that he assumes absolute liability for the property is binding, but there is a difference of opinion as to whether a stipulation to return the property "in good condition" or "in as good condition as received" has the effect of imposing such absolute liability. (See p. 285, St. Paul Insurance Case) An ordinary bailee may limit his liability, except for his willful conduct, by contract. Modern cases hold that a specialized commercial bailee, such as an auto parking garage, cannot limit liability for either its willful or negligent conduct.

(3) Unauthorized Use. The bailee is liable if he uses the property without authority or uses it in any manner to which the bailor had not agreed. The bailee is liable for conversion, just as though he stole the property. Ordinarily he will be required to pay compensatory damages, although punitive damages may be inflicted when the improper use was deliberate and the bailee was recklessly indifferent to the effect of his use upon the property.

(4) Return. The bailee is under a duty to return the identical property which is the subject of the bailment or to deliver it as directed. The redelivery to the bailor or delivery to a third person must be made in accordance with the terms of the contract as to time, place, and manner. When the agreement does not control these matters, the customs and usages of the community govern.

The bailee is excused from delivery when the goods are lost, stolen, or destroyed without his fault. If his fault or neglect has caused or contributed to the loss, however, he is liable. To illustrate, certain goods are destroyed by a flood while in the possession of the bailee. If the bailee could have protected the goods from the flood by taking reasonable precautions, the bailee is liable for the loss.

The bailee is excused from the duty to return the goods when they have been taken from him under process of law. To illustrate, if the police seize the property as stolen goods, the bailee is no longer under a duty to return the goods to the bailor.

If the bailee has a lien on the property, he is entitled to keep possession of the property until he has been paid the claim on which the lien is based.

Sec. 18-C. Rights of the Bailor. The exact scope of the rights of the bailor varies with the nature of the bailment.

(1) Compensation. The bailor is entitled to the compensation agreed upon in the bailment contract. If the agreement is silent as to compensation, the bailee must pay the reasonable rental value when

the circumstances are such that, as reasonable men, the parties would have expected that there would be compensation.

The bailor loses his right to compensation if the bailment is terminated through his fault. If the bailee loses possession or use of the goods through no fault of his own, the bailor is entitled to compensation only during the period of use, unless their agreement stipulates otherwise. For example, the bailee is not liable for compensation during a period when he cannot use the property because it is being repaired for a defect for which the bailor is liable. The same rule is applied when the goods are stolen or destroyed, or when they are retaken by the bailor through no fault of the bailee.

(2) Rights Against the Bailee. The bailor may sue the bailee for breach of contract if the goods are not redelivered to the bailor or delivered to a third person as specified by the bailment agreement. He may also maintain actions for negligence, destruction, and unlawful retention or conversion of the goods when the bailee is guilty of such conduct. Actions for unlawful retention or conversion can only be brought when the bailor is entitled to possession.

(3) Rights Against Third Persons. The bailor may sue third persons damaging or taking the bailed property from the bailee's possession, even though the bailment is for a fixed period that has not expired. In such a case the bailor is said to recover damages for injury to his *reversionary interest,* that is, the right which he has to regain the property upon the expiration of the period of the bailment.

Sec. 18-D. Duties and Liabilities of Bailor. Duties and liabilities of the bailor arise from the bailment relationship, although they may be modified by statute or by the contract of the parties.

(1) Condition of the Property. In a mutual-benefit bailment for hire, the bailor is under a duty to furnish goods reasonably fit for the purpose contemplated by the parties. If the bailee is injured or if his property is damaged because of the defective condition of the bailed property, the bailor may be liable. If the bailment is for the sole benefit of the bailee, the bailor is under a duty to inform the bailee of those defects of which he is actually aware, but he is not under any duty to look for defects. If the bailee is harmed by a defect that was known to the bailor, the bailor is liable for damages. If the bailor receives a benefit from the bailment, he must not only inform the bailee of known defects, but he must also make a reasonable investigation to discover defects. The bailor is liable for the harm resulting from defects which would have been disclosed had he made such an examination, in addition to those which were known to him.

If the defect would not have been revealed by a reasonable examination, the bailor, regardless of the classification of the bailment, is not liable for harm which results.

In many cases the duty of the bailor is described as an implied warranty that the goods will be reasonably fit for their intended use. (See p. 286, McNeal v. Greenberg) Apart from an implied warranty, the bailor may expressly warrant the condition of the property, in which event he will be liable for the breach of the warranty to the same extent as though he had made a sale rather than a bailment of the property.[1]

In any case the bailee, if he knows of the defective condition of the bailed property, is barred by his contributory negligence or assumption of risk if, in spite of that knowledge, he makes use of the property and sustains injury because of its condition.

(2) Repair of the Property. Under a rental contract the bailor has no duty to make repairs that are ordinary and incidental to the use of the goods bailed. The bailee must bear the expense of such repairs, in the absence of a contrary contract provision. If, however, the repairs required are of an unusual nature or if the bailment is for a short period of time, the bailor is required to make the repairs unless they were caused by the negligence or fault of the bailee.

(3) Reimbursement for Payments by Bailee. The bailor must reimburse the bailee for any payments made by the bailee that should have been made by the bailor. If the bailee makes repairs that should have been made by the bailor, the bailee may recover the amount so paid. If the bailee is sued by a third person who demands the bailed property on the ground that the bailor did not own it, the bailee is entitled to reimbursement for expenses incurred in the litigation. If the expense is incurred by reason of the bailee's negligence, misconduct, or misuse of the property, however, the bailor is not required to reimburse him.

(4) Performance of Contract by Bailor. The bailor is, of course, under a duty to perform his part of the contract of bailment. If he violates its provisions, he is answerable to the bailee for damages.

Sec. 18-E. Liability to Third Persons. When the bailee injures a third person with the bailed property, as when a bailee runs into a third person while he is driving a rented automobile, the bailee is liable to the third person to the same extent as though the bailee were the owner of the property. When the bailee repairs bailed property, he is liable to third persons who are injured in consequence

---

[1] See Ch. 24 as to sales warranties.

of the negligent way in which he has made the repair. Conversely, the bailee is not liable to a third person who is injured by a thief who steals the bailed property from the bailee even though the theft was possible because the bailee was negligent.

The bailor is ordinarily not liable to a third person. Unless the bailee is acting as the employee or agent of the bailor, a fault or negligence of the bailee is not imputed to the bailor.

The bailor is liable, however, to the injured third person: (1) if the bailor has entrusted a dangerous instrumentality to one whom he knew was ignorant of its dangerous character; (2) if the bailor has entrusted an instrumentality such as an automobile to one whom he knows to be so incompetent or reckless that injury of third persons is a foreseeable consequence; or (3) if the bailor has entrusted property with a defect that causes harm to the third person when the circumstances are such that bailor would be liable to the bailee if the latter were injured because of the defect.

Cases for Chapter 18

Braufman v. Hart Publication
234 Minn. 343, 48 N.W.2d 546 (1951)

Park Square Corporation delivered a carload of paper to Hart Publication to be held by the latter and printed into special forms as requested. Hart printed a portion of the forms but did not deliver them because Park refused to pay for them. Hart then claimed a lien for the printing on both the printed and unprinted portions of the paper. The rights of Park Square Corporation were assigned to Braufman, who sued Hart for conversion for asserting a lien on the unprinted paper. From a judgment for the defendant, the plaintiff appealed.

LORING, C.J. . . . Where goods are delivered to a lien claimant under a single contract for services relating to all of the goods, the goods retained in the lien claimant's possession may be charged not only with the value of services performed upon them, but also with the value of services performed upon other goods delivered under the same contract, the entire mass of goods being treated as a unit. In strict logic, if a lien claimant may charge goods in possession not only with the value of services which have enhanced their value, but also with the value of services performed upon other goods no longer in his possession but which were delivered under the same contract, it follows that he may do likewise with retained goods on which no services have been performed; for, in each case, the retained goods are being charged for services which have not been performed upon them. In both cases, the value of the retained goods is not enhanced to the extent of the lien claim. . . .

The absence of express language in our lien statute altering the common-law single-contract rule obliges us to hold that it is a subsisting rule of law. The application of that rule dictates that several articles of personal property, delivered under the same contract, be treated as a unit under our lien statute. We concur with the trial court's determination that defendant's lien attaches to both the printed and unprinted paper in its possession as security for the entire amount due for printing any portion of the paper delivered to defendant under the single contract.

[Judgment for defendant affirmed.]

Fox Chevrolet Sales v. Middleton
203 Md. 158, 99 A.2d 731 (1953)

Middleton took her auto to Fox Chevrolet Sales for repairs. The shop was located in the industrial section of the city and was bounded on two sides by extensive railroad yards. At night the rear of the shop building was out of the sight and hearing of persons passing by the shop. The two rear doors were locked by padlocks on hasps nailed to the wood. Because there had been breaking of windows of the shop by vandals and the stealing of equipment, a night watchman was employed but he often failed to report for duty. On one of the nights when the watchman failed to report, a thief broke the locks on the two rear doors of the shop and stole Middleton's car. It was later found in a damaged condition. Middleton sued Fox for the damages. From a judgment in favor of Middleton, Fox appealed.

HAMMOND, J. . . . When an automobile is delivered to one who, for a consideration, undertakes to repair it, the contract is one of bailment for hire, or for mutual benefit, so that where, in such case, a demand and an unexplained refusal to deliver is proven, a prima facie case of negligence is made out; yet, when the loss or injury is accounted for as having been occasioned by a cause which would excuse the bailee, such as a burglary of his premises, then the defense is complete, unless the bailor follows by showing that the bailee, by the exercise of ordinary care and diligence might have avoided the loss or injury. The burden of proving negligence never shifts from the plaintiff. He must prove the delivery, the bailment, and the failure to return; thereupon, it is incumbent upon the bailee to explain that failure. If he does so, the bailor must prove that the bailee failed to use ordinary care and diligence to safeguard such property and that his failure to perform that duty caused the loss. . . .

We think that the evidence in this case clearly meets the tests which have been set up by the cases which on similar facts have held that the question of negligence is for the jury. Reasonable men could well find, as the jury did in this case, that the appellant had failed to live up to its duty to use ordinary care and diligence in safeguarding the property entrusted to it. . . . This is not to say . . . that the failure to employ a watchman in every mercantile establishment, as, for example, a jewelry store, would be evidence of negligence if a theft occurred. . . . The test to be applied is whether, in the particular situation, there was failure to use such care as persons of common prudence in their own situation and business usually use in the custody and keeping of similar property belonging to themselves. . . . There was no evidence offered in the instant case as to custom or usage in the trade. Each case must be decided on its own facts. What we hold here is that the building's environment, its physical arrangement, the evidence of prior thefts, the customary employment of the watchman and his absence when the theft took place, and the locks used, considered together, are sufficient to present a jury question. . . .

[Judgment affirmed.]

St. Paul Fire & Marine Insurance Co. v. Chas. H. Lilly Co.
48 Wash.2d 528, 295 P.2d 299 (1956)

Chas. H. Lilly Co. rented a Scoopmobile from Air-Mac, Inc. on a month-to-month basis. The agreement required Lilly to return the machine in good mechanical condition, except for usual wear and depreciation such as might be caused by reasonable use and wear. Four months later the machine was destroyed by fire. Air-Mac collected the amount of its loss from its insurance company, the St. Paul Fire & Marine Insurance Co., and then assigned to it the claim against Lilly. The insurance company then sued Lilly. From a judgment in favor of the company, Lilly appealed.

FINLEY, J. . . . In a simple bailment . . . where the parties do not contract explicitly or by inference respecting damages, loss, or destruction of the bailed property, the rule is that a bailee who is without fault is not liable for damages to the bailed property or for its loss or destruction. The risk or loss in such cases falls on the bailor. . . . As a corollary to the foregoing, it should be pointed out that a bailee may become an insurer when he explicitly contracts that he will be absolutely liable, irrespective of fault, if the bailed property is damaged or destroyed. . . . In cases where the bailee has contracted to "return the property in the condition received, except for normal wear and tear," or words to the effect, there is a split of authority as to the interpretation and the effect to be given to the indicated language. A so-called minority view is that the indicated language implies an assumption of absolute, or an insurer's, liability by the bailee. On the contrary, the so-called majority view refuses to supply an implied or an inferred meaning to the above indicated language, and the result is that absolute liability is not imposed . . . upon the bailee.

. . . We explicitly hold that the so-called majority rule is controlling in this jurisdiction. It is more realistic as to the probable intentions of the parties to a bailment contract, and as to what was contemplated and understood by them. We are convinced that it is the more just and equitable rule. This conclusion on our part seems more reasonable and more convincing if the problem of interpretation relative to the phrase, *to return in the condition received, except for normal wear and tear,* is approached initially in terms of the implied obligations or liabilities of an ordinary common-law bailee. In other words, if *A* rents his automobile to *B* so that the latter can make a trip, and nothing more is agreed to by the parties, *B* is under an implied legal obligation (1) to return the car, and (2) to observe ordinary care in the use of it, and (3) to make good any damages, loss, or destruction caused by his negligence. But *B* is not liable for damages or loss occurring without his fault. Now what, if anything, is added to the obligation of such a common-law bailee by a covenant to return in the condition received, except for normal wear and tear? . . .

If the parties intended that a bailee, irrespective of fault, was to be an absolute insurer, they could have so provided with little difficulty, merely by using clear and explicit language to that effect.

[Judgment reversed.]

McNeal v. Greenburg
30 Cal.2d 740, 255 P.2d 810 (1953)

Greenberg and two others who operated Sam's U-Drive, rented a tractor to McNeal. The brakes failed to hold on a hillside when used by McNeal, as the result of which he was injured. He sued Greenberg and his associates. From a judgment in their favor, McNeal appealed.

EDMONS, J. [It is claimed] that the lessors [Greenberg and associates] negligently . . . failed to make a proper test or inspection of the tractor before renting it to McNeal. As a result of such failure, it is alleged, he received the vehicle in a dangerous and defective condition. Section 408 of the Restatement of the Law of Torts . . . declares that a bailor for hire of a chattel must use reasonable care to make it safe for its intended use or disclose its actual condition to the bailee.

In comment "a" under that section it is said: "The fact that a chattel is leased for immediate use makes it unreasonable for the lessor to expect that the lessee will do more than give it the most cursory of inspections. The lessor must, therefore, realize that the safe use of the chattel can be secured only by precautions taken by him before turning it over to the lessee. . . . If the chattel is made by a third person, the lessor is required to exercise reasonable care to inspect it before turning it over to the lessee. . . . In addition to the inspection required when the chattel is acquired, the lessor is required to make from time to time such inspections of the articles, which he keeps for hire, as a reasonably careful man would make in view of the nature of the article and the use to which it is to be put."

The second count of the complaint is based upon the theory of a breach of an implied warranty of fitness. It is alleged that the lessors warranted the tractor to be fit for the purpose for which it was hired and that McNeal accepted it in reliance upon such warranty. McNeal asserts that the defective condition of the brakes made the machine unsafe and unfit for its contemplated use and caused the injuries for which he claims damages.

A bailor's implied warranty of fitness does not make him an insurer against all personal injuries suffered from the defective operation of the bailed chattel. He impliedly warrants only that he has exercised reasonable care to ascertain that the chattel is safe and suitable for the purpose for which it is hired. . . .

In this count, as in the one based upon the theory of negligence, the essential inquiry is whether the Greenbergs made such inspection of their equipment as was necessary to discharge their duty of reasonable care. . . .

Where a motor vehicle was obtained from an automobile dealer and shortly thereafter the brakes failed to operate, such failure . . . is sufficient basis for an inference that the brakes were defective at the time of the delivery of the vehicle and that a reasonable inspection would have disclosed the defect. . . .

[Judgment reversed.]

Questions and Case Problems

1. What is the objective of each of the following rules of law?
(a) By virtue of statute, a bailee may retain his lien for work done on the bailed article even though he has surrendered possession.
(b) The bailee is liable for any harm that befalls the bailed article when he makes an unauthorized use of the property, even though he was acting carefully.

2. Nutrodynamics delivered a quantity of loose pills that it manufactured to Ivers-Lee for the latter to place them in foil packages and then in shipping containers suitable for delivery to customers of Nutrodynamics. Approximately 193 cartons of packaged pills were finished and in Iver-Lee's possession when Beck brought a suit against Nutrodynamics and directed the sheriff to attach the pills in the possession of Ivers-Lee. Ivers-Lee had not been paid for its work in packaging. It claimed the right to keep the goods until paid but nevertheless surrendered them to the sheriff. Was it entitled to any claim on the goods in the hands of the sheriff? (Beck v. Nutrodynamics, Inc., 77 N.J.S. 448, 186 A.2d 715)

3. Goldfarb leased a taxicab to Niewinski. While driving Mason, a passenger, Niewinski collided with another automobile when his steering wheel "snapped" and he lost control of the car. Mason sued Niewinski and Goldfarb. The trial judge instructed the jury that "Goldfarb agreed to furnish Niewinski with a serviceably-operating cab [and that if] he failed in that [there could be recovery] for breach of warranty for the damages which proximately flowed from the breach of contract." The trial judge based this instruction on the provision of the lease agreement which stated that "the owner agrees and covenants with the lessee to make all necessary repairs and replacements, whether caused by collision, wear and tear or otherwise, at his, the owner's own cost and expense." Was the trial judge correct? (Mason v. Niewinski, [N.J.] 169 A.2d 195)

4. Miller took his auto to the Hand Ford Sales, Inc. to be repaired. Because there was a holiday and the repairs could not be done immediately, he decided to leave his auto at the repair garage. He then asked Hand Ford if he could be supplied with a temporarily loaned automobile. Hand Ford supplied him with an auto. Unknown to Hand Ford, a metal strip that was not noticeable to an occupant in the front seat projected from the underside of the car radio. In sliding across the front seat, Miller was cut by the strip. He sued Hand Ford on the theory that there was a mutual benefit bailment of the loaned automobile and that Hand Ford therefore had the duty to inspect the auto to determine that it was reasonably safe for use, and since it had not done so, it was liable for the harm caused by the strip which such investigation would have disclosed. Was he correct? (Miller v. Hand Ford Sales, Inc., [Ore.] 340 P.2d 181)

5. Morse, who owned a diamond ring valued at $2,000, took the ring to Homer's Inc., to sell for him. Homer placed the ring in the window display of his store. There was no guard or grating across the opening of the window inside his store. There was a partitioned door that was left unlocked. On two former occasions Homer's store had been robbed. Several weeks after Morse left his ring, armed men robbed the store and took several rings from the store window, including Morse's ring. He sued Homer, who defended on the ground that he was not liable for the criminal acts of others. Decide. (Morse v. Homer's, Inc., 295 Mass. 606, 4 N.E.2d 625)

6. Redmon rented a moving van from the U-Haul Company to move from Albany, Georgia, to Knoxville, Tennessee. The rental agreement stated that "lessee agrees to assume liability for any and all damage to personal property transported in said truck, including damage caused by fire, water, theft, or collision." Redmon drove the van through very heavy rain and, on arriving at the end of the trip, found several inches of water in the floor of the van and his household goods damaged. He sued the U-Haul company for breach of an implied warranty that the moving van was waterproof. Was he entitled to recover? (Redmon v. U-Haul Company, [Tenn.] 358 S.W.2d 300)

CHAPTER 19

Special Bailments

In addition to the ordinary bailment, a bailment relation arises when goods are stored in a warehouse or delivered to a merchant to sell for the owner. In some instances, a hotelkeeper may have a bailee's liability.

Hotelkeepers

A *hotelkeeper* is regularly engaged in the business of offering living accommodations to all transient persons. In the early law he was called an innkeeper or a tavernkeeper.

Sec. 19-A. Liability of Hotelkeeper. In the absence of a valid limitation, the hotelkeeper is generally an insurer of the safety of goods entrusted to his care. As exceptions to the general rule, the hotelkeeper is not liable for loss caused by an act of God, a public enemy, the inherent nature of the property, or the fault of the guest.

In many states statutes limit or provide a method for limiting the liability of a hotelkeeper. The statutes may limit the extent of liability, reduce the liability of the hotelkeeper to that of an ordinary bailee, or permit him to limit his liability by contract or by posting a notice of the limitation. Some statutes relieve the hotelkeeper from liability when directions for depositing valuables with the hotelkeeper are posted on the doors of the rooms occupied and the guest fails to comply with the directions. The hotelkeeper may adopt rules requiring the deposit of valuables in the hotel safe and other rules similar to the provisions of the statutes just noted. If a guest, knowing of such rules, fails to comply with them, the hotelkeeper is relieved from liability for losses that could have been avoided had the guest complied with the regulations.

It is held, in contrast, that the duty of a hotelkeeper is only to exercise due care when the goods of the guest, with his actual or implied consent, are placed by the hotelkeeper in the custody of a third person not employed by the hotelkeeper, such as a nearby garageman or dry cleaner.

With respect to the safety of persons, the hotelkeeper must use reasonable care to keep the premises and facilities of the hotel reasonably safe for the purposes for which they are to be used by guests and other invitees.

Sec. 19-B. Who Are Guests. A hotelkeeper owes a duty as such only when the patron of the hotel is a guest. The essential element in the modern definition of *guest* is that he is a transient. Under this definition a guest need not be a traveler nor come from a distance. A person living within a short distance of the hotel who engages a room at the hotel and remains there overnight is a guest.

The relationship of guest and hotelkeeper does not begin until a person is received as a guest by the hotelkeeper. Many persons enter a hotel without the expectation of receiving accommodations offered to transients and are not guests.

The relationship terminates when the guest leaves or when he ceases to be a transient, as when he arranges for a more or less permanent residence at the hotel and thereby becomes a boarder or lodger. In the former case all duties of the hotelkeeper end. In the latter case the extent of the duties is reduced. The transition from the status of guest to the status of boarder or lodger must be clearly indicated. It is not established by the mere fact that one remains at the hotel for a long period, even though it runs into months.

Sec. 19-C. Lien of Hotelkeeper. The hotelkeeper is given a lien on the baggage of his guests for the agreed charges or, if no express agreement was made, the reasonable value of the accommodations furnished. Statutes permit the hotelkeeper to enforce his lien by selling the goods at public sale.

(1) Persons Subject to Lien. The hotelkeeper's lien does not arise out of contract but is provided by law. It exists even when the guests are minors or other persons under a legal incapacity to make binding agreements.

(2) Property Subject to Lien. In general, all property brought by a guest to a hotel, except wearing apparel actually being worn, is subject to this lien. The lien extends to the property of another person brought by the guest if the hotelkeeper is ignorant of the true ownership. (See p. 296, Lines Music Co. v. Holt) This rule has been modified or abolished by statute in some jurisdictions. In many states the hotelkeeper's lien now applies to the goods of a third person that are in the guest's possession, even if the ownership is known to the hotelkeeper, when the goods were entrusted to the guest by the owner

with the understanding or realization that he would take them to the hotel.

(3) Termination of Lien. The lien of the hotelkeeper is terminated by (a) the guest's payment of the hotel's charges, (b) any conversion of the goods by the hotelkeeper, and (c) surrender of the goods to the guest, except when they are given to him for temporary use.

Sec. 19-D. Boarders or Lodgers. To those persons who are permanent boarders or lodgers, rather than transient guests, the hotelkeeper owes only the duty of an ordinary bailee of their personal property under a mutual benefit bailment.

A hotelkeeper has no common-law right of lien on property of his boarders or lodgers, as distinguished from his guests, in the absence of an express agreement between the parties. In a number of states, however, legislation giving a lien to a boardinghouse or a lodging-house keeper has been enacted.

Warehousemen

A person engaged in the business of storing the goods of others for compensation is a *warehouseman*. A *public warehouseman* holds himself out generally to serve the public without discrimination.

Sec. 19-E. Rights and Duties of Warehousemen. The common-law rights and duties of a warehouseman, in the absence of modification by statute, are in the main the same as those of a bailee in an ordinary mutual-benefit bailment.[1] (See p. 296, Brace v. Salem Cold Storage Co.) The public warehouseman has a lien against the goods for reasonable charges.[2] It is a specific lien in that it attaches only to the property with respect to which the charges arose and cannot be asserted against other property of the same owner in the possession of the warehouseman. The warehouseman, however, may make a lien carry over to other goods by noting on the receipt for one lot of goods that a lien is also claimed thereon for charges as to other goods.[3] The warehouseman's lien for storage charges may be enforced by sale after due notice has been given to all persons who claim any interest in the property stored.

---

[1] Uniform Commercial Code, Sec. 7-204; Uniform Warehouse Receipts Act, Sec. 21. As to states that have adopted the Code, see p. 51. The UWRA is in force in either its original form or with minor variations in all other states, and in the District of Columbia, Panama Canal Zone, Puerto Rico, and also in the Philippine Islands.

[2] UCC Sec. 7-209 (1); UWRA Sec. 27.

[3] UCC Sec. 7-209 (1).

Most states have passed warehouse acts defining the rights and duties of the warehouseman and prescribing regulations as to charges and liens, bonds for the protection of patrons, the maintenance of storage facilities in a suitable and safe condition, inspections, and general methods of transacting business.

Sec. 19-F. Warehouse Receipts. A *warehouse receipt* is a written acknowledgment by a warehouseman that the property of a named person has been received for storage. It also sets forth the terms of the contract of storage. The warehouse receipt is a document of title because the person lawfully holding the receipt is entitled to the goods or property represented by the receipt. The form and the effect of warehouse receipts are regulated by statute.[4]

The receipt can be issued only if goods have actually been received by the warehouseman. If a receipt is issued without the goods having been so received, the warehouseman is liable to a good-faith purchaser of the receipt for the loss he sustains thereby.[5] The issuance of a receipt when goods have not been received by the warehouseman is also a crime.

Sec. 19-G. Rights of Holders of Warehouse Receipts.

(1) At Common Law. At common law a warehouse receipt was nonnegotiable and could only be assigned by a written assignment or by a physical delivery of the receipt. The purchaser was in the position of an ordinary assignee, and took the instrument subject to any defenses which were valid against his transferor.

(2) Negotiability Under Statutes. The common-law rule of the nonnegotiability of warehouse receipts has been changed in part by statute. A receipt in which it is stated that the goods received will be delivered to the depositor, or to any other specified person, is still a *nonnegotiable warehouse receipt;* but a receipt in which it is stated that the goods received will be delivered to the bearer, or to the order of any person named in such receipt, is a *negotiable warehouse receipt.*[6]

The transfer of negotiable warehouse receipts is made by delivery or by indorsement and delivery, in a manner similar to the transfer of commercial paper, that is, negotiable instruments.[7] It is the duty of the warehouseman to deliver the goods to the holder of a negotiable receipt and to cancel such receipt before making delivery of the goods. The surrender of a nonnegotiable receipt is not required.

---

[4] UCC Sec. 7-202 et seq.; UWRA Sec. 2 et seq.
[5] UCC Sec. 7-203.
[6] UCC Sec. 7-104; UWRA Secs. 5, 6.
[7] See Chapter 28.

Negotiable warehouse receipts are negotiable to the extent that (a) the holder of the receipt may sue in his own name; (b) he is not required to give notice of a transfer to the warehouseman; and (c) the bona fide purchaser of the receipt has a right to the goods free from most claims of prior parties that are not shown on the face of the instrument, or which are not known by the purchaser from other sources. For example, when the owner gives a receipt for cotton in payment of a gambling debt, the transferee may give to a bona fide purchaser a valid title as against the original owner.

If the person who deposited the goods with the warehouse did not own the goods or did not have the power to transfer title to them, the holder of the warehouse receipt is subject to the title of the true owner. Accordingly, when goods are stolen or delivered without authority to a warehouse and a receipt is issued for them, the true owner prevails over the holder of the receipt.[8]

(3) Warranties Under Statutes. The transferee of a warehouse receipt is also given the protection of certain warranties from his immediate transferor; namely, that the instrument is genuine, that its transfer is rightful and effective, and that the transferor has no knowledge of any facts that impair the validity or worth of the receipt.[9]

Sec. 19-H. Field Warehousing. Ordinarily, stored goods are placed in a warehouse belonging to the warehouseman. The owner of goods, such as a manufacturer, may keep the goods in his own storage room or building, however, and have a warehouse company take control of the room or building. When the warehouseman takes exclusive control of the property, it may issue a warehouse receipt for the goods even though they are still on the premises of the owner. Such a transaction has the same legal effect with respect to other persons and purchasers of the warehouse receipt as though the property were in the warehouse of the warehouseman. This practice is called *field warehousing* since the goods are not taken to the warehouse but remain "in the field."

The purpose of this device is to create warehouse receipts which the owner of the goods is able to pledge as security for loans. The owner could, of course, have done this by actually placing the goods in a warehouse, but this would have involved the expense of transportation and storage.

As to the mechanics of field warehousing, the warehouseman may place a man on the premises of the owner to exercise control of the goods. Control may also be exercised by placing the goods under lock

---

[8] UCC Sec. 7-503 (1).

[9] UCC Sec. 7-507; UWRA Sec. 44. These warranties are in addition to any that may arise between the parties by virtue of the fact that the transferor is selling the goods represented by the receipt to the transferee. See Chapter 24 as to a seller's warranties.

and key on the owner's premises and giving the warehouseman the keys. In some jurisdictions it is required that in addition to the maintenance of an exclusive control by the warehouseman, the goods or premises must be marked or posted with signs so as to indicate that the warehouseman is in possession of the particular goods.

Factors

A *factor* is a special type of bailee who sells goods consigned to him as though he were the owner of the goods. In modern usage the device of entrusting a person with the possession of property for the purpose of sale is commonly called *selling on consignment.* The owner who sends or consigns the goods for sale is the *consignor.* The person or agent to whom they are consigned is the *consignee;* he may also be known as a commission merchant. His compensation is known as a *commission* or *factorage.* The property remains the property of the owner, and the consignee acts as his agent to pass title to the buyer.

Sec. 19-I. Factor as Agent. The relation of principal and factor is a form of agency [10] as well as a special bailment. The main difference between an agent and a factor is that the agent need not have possession of the principal's property, while the factor must have actual or constructive possession of it. The chief difference between a factor and an ordinary bailee is that the former receives goods to sell to purchasers, but the bailee receives them to be returned to the bailor or delivered in accordance with the bailment agreement.

Ordinarily an agent does not guarantee in any way that the third person with whom he makes a contract on behalf of his principal will perform the contract. If a sale is made by the agent on credit, the agent is under the duty to exercise due care in selecting the third person as a credit risk. If he exercises due care, the agent is not responsible when the third person does not pay or perform his part of the contract. In the case of some factors the custom has developed of guaranteeing that the purchaser is solvent and that he will perform the contract. A factor who makes such a guarantee is termed a *del credere factor.*

In some business areas the word "factor" is used to describe a sales broker or agent without regard to whether the possession of the goods is in fact entrusted to him. When possession is not given, the rights and liabilities of the parties are determined by principles of agency law because no element of bailment is present.

Sec. 19-J. Duties and Rights of Factors. The factor must exercise reasonable care in the protection of the goods. The care required is

---

10 See Part VII.

that of a bailee in an ordinary mutual-benefit bailment. Although the factor has power to insure the goods, he is ordinarily under no duty to do so. Such a duty can commonly be found, however, based either upon custom or trade, upon a course of dealings between the parties, or upon express instructions from the owner.

The factor must not mix the goods consigned to him with his own or another's property (1) unless he is authorized to do so by all parties in interest, or (2) unless the goods are fungible [11] in nature.

The factor must maintain accounts or records so that the proceeds to which the consignor is entitled can be accurately determined.

The factor, in making a sale of goods, must act in accordance with the instructions of the consignor. In the absence of express directions, the factor may sell in the manner usually and customarily employed by him. He cannot sell or pledge the goods for his own purposes unless expressly or impliedly authorized to do so by the principal. (See p. 298, Commercial Investment Trust v. Stewart) He has no power to exchange or barter the goods.

The factor has a lien on the goods of the principal in his possession and on the proceeds of sales of such goods for expenses, advances, and compensation. It is a general lien in that it may be exercised against any of the principal's goods coming into his possession at any time later. It is a possessory lien and is lost by relinquishment of possession of that property to the principal. The lien may also be lost by misconduct of the factor.

Sec. 19-K. Factor's Acts and the Code. At common law, if the factor unlawfully transfers the goods, the transferee acquires no title or right against the owner. This rule led to the defrauding of innocent third persons who purchased in good faith from the factor. To protect such persons, factor's acts have been adopted which provide that a sale by a factor in possession of goods or document of title may give a valid title as against the true owner.[12] The loss caused by an unauthorized sale then falls upon the owner who placed the factor in possession of the goods.

The Uniform Commercial Code expands this protection by providing that when any one entrusts property to a merchant who regularly deals in goods of that kind, the dealer has the power to pass a valid title to a purchaser in the ordinary course of business regardless of whether the goods were entrusted for sale, repair, storage, or any other purpose.[13] Likewise, creditors of the consignee may reach the goods as though they were owned by him.[14]

---

[11] See p. 338.
[12] Uniform Sales Act, Sec. 23 (2) (a).
[13] UCC Sec. 2-403(2).
[14] See Sec. 22-I (2), p. 340.

Cases for Chapter 19

L. E. Lines Music Co. v. Holt

332 Mo. 749, 60 S.W.2d 32 (1933)

Brown was a guest at Holt's Kentwood Hotel. He had the Lines Music Company deliver a radio to his room for demonstration purposes on the pretext of contemplating its purchase. Shortly thereafter Brown, upon leaving the hotel, informed the hotel that he was leaving the radio with the hotel until he returned to pay his bill. In reliance on the possession of the radio, the hotel permitted him to take his baggage. The music company brought an action against the hotel to recover the radio. The defendant contended that it had a lien on the property under a statute. From a judgment for the plaintiff, the defendant appealed.

WESHUES, C. . . . The agreed statement of facts discloses that plaintiff did not inform the defendant of the fact that Brown had not purchased the radio. Brown had legal possession thereof. The applicable rule to the facts at hand is . . . as follows: "Except in jurisdictions where the rule has been modified or abrogated by statute, the lien of an innkeeper may attach to goods which are not the property of the guest but which were brought by him to the inn and were received by the innkeeper in his capacity as such without knowledge of their true ownership or with knowledge that while the title is in another, yet that the guest as agent, servant, or otherwise, is in lawful possession thereof." . . . An innkeeper is obliged to receive guests and their goods and luggage. By virtue of this relationship, innkeepers become insurers of the property of the guest, the title to which the innkeepers cannot question. These obligations of innkeepers are stressed in the cases cited as reasons for the rule existing at common law, extending a lien to all property in the guest's possession for the payment of the hotel fare irrespective of the ownership of the property. [Plaintiff] in this case delivered the radio in question to the guest at the hotel and clothed him with lawful possession and control thereof. . . .

[Judgment for plaintiff reversed.]

Brace v. Salem Cold Storage, Inc.

118 S.E.2d 799 (W.Va., 1961)

Brace and his brother delivered cabbage to the Salem Cold Storage Company for refrigerated storage. The cabbage was later returned to them in a damaged condition. They sued Salem on the ground that through its negligence it had failed to keep the cabbage at a proper temperature. The jury returned a verdict in favor of the plaintiffs, but the trial judge set the verdict aside on the ground that the negligence of the warehouseman had not been established and that therefore the verdict in favor of the plaintiffs was not proper. The plaintiffs appealed from this action.

CALHOUN, J. . . . The liability of a warehouseman for negligence is stated in Code, 1931, 47-5-21, as follows: "A warehouseman shall be liable for any loss or injury to the goods caused by his failure to exercise such care in regard to them as a reasonably careful owner of similar goods would exercise; but he shall not be liable, in the absence of an agreement to the contrary, for any loss or injury to the goods which could not have been avoided by the exercise of such care." Statutes of this nature are merely declaratory of the common law.". . .

"It is well settled that when goods are stored in a warehouse, the relation of bailor and bailee, with its correlative rights and duties, is created between the depositor or owner of the goods and the warehouseman. The warehouseman is a bailee for hire. . . ."

"Where goods in cold storage are damaged, the burden of proof of negligence of the warehouseman rests on the depositor or owner of the goods. The depositor or owner is not necessarily required, however, to show specific acts of negligence causing the damage. It is generally held that where the owner shows that the goods were in good condition at the time they were delivered to the cold-storage warehouse, and that they were returned in a damaged condition from a cause not inherent in the goods themselves, the owner has made out a prima facie case, and it is incumbent on the warehouseman to account for the injury to the goods in some manner consistent with the exercise of due care on his part, unless the damage is of such nature as to result from natural causes, or deterioration, or internal defects without fault on the part of the warehouseman. If the evidence of the warehouseman gives an explanation of the injury which is consistent with reasonable care on his part, the bailor must show positive negligence on the part of the coldstorage operator. A statute requiring only the exercise of due care by a cold storer is not conclusive upon the question of burden of proof, where perishable goods have been injured while in cold storage." . . .

The defendant was not an insurer of the cabbage stored in its cold storage warehouse, but was required to exercise only ordinary care. It was, nevertheless, required to employ the skill and peculiar knowledge requisite to the operation of the business in which it was engaged. In order to recover in this action, it was incumbent upon the plaintiffs to establish negligence on the part of the defendant, and that such negligence caused the damage to the cabbage. In a case such as this, if the owner of the goods proves that the goods when placed in the cold storage warehouse were in good condition and that, when demanded within a reasonable time, they were in a damaged condition, there may be cast upon the defendant warehouseman thereby a burden of going forward with the evidence, in accordance with principles previously stated herein; but the ultimate burden of proof remains upon the plaintiff throughout the trial to establish his case by a preponderance of the evidence. . . .

"When the evidence is conflicting, or when the facts, though undisputed, are such that reasonable men may draw different conclusions from them, the question of negligence is for the jury.". . . "As in other cases, the question whether the damage to or loss of perishable property in a cold-storage warehouse is due to the negligence of the warehouseman is one for determination by the jury, where there is substantial evidence on which to submit such issue." . . . [The Court then considered the conflicting testimony as to the warehouseman's negligence.] On the whole case, we feel that the facts bearing both upon the right to recover and upon the amount of the verdict were peculiarly for jury determination; and that the trial court would not have been warranted in setting aside the verdict on the ground of insufficiency of evidence to support such verdict. . . .

The judgment . . . is reversed, the verdict of the jury is reinstated, and judgment for the plaintiffs . . . is rendered in this court.

Code Comment: The provision of the West Virginia Statute cited in the opinion is virtually identical with UCC Sec. 7-204 stating the duty of care of a warehouseman. The same result would be reached under the Code.

Commercial Investment Trust v. Stewart
235 Mich. 502, 209 N.W. 660 (1926)

Gaylord was engaged in selling Studebaker automobiles in Ann Arbor, Michigan. He received from the manufacturer in Detroit certain automobiles for sale at a specified price. Gaylord guaranteed payment of such sums to the Commercial Investment Trust, the holder of a time draft drawn on him by the manufacturer. He turned over two of the cars to Stewart to whom he was indebted. The Commercial Investment Trust brought an action against Stewart to recover the cars, contending that Gaylord, as a del credere factor, had no right to transfer the cars to satisfy such debt. From a judgment for the defendant, the plaintiff appealed.

CLARK, J. . . . Plaintiff . . . contends rightly, we think, that Gaylord was a del credere factor of plaintiff, his principal.

"A factor is one whose business it is to receive and sell goods for a commission. He differs from a broker in that he is intrusted with the possession of the goods to be sold, and usually sells in his own name."

"A del credere factor or a factor with a del credere commission or agency is one who, in consideration of a higher compensation, expressly engages to pay his principal the price of all goods sold by himself if the purchaser fails so to do."

The factor did not own the cars. He might sell them in due course for cash, or for cash and purchasers' notes indorsed and acceptable, which proceeds he was to keep distinct and separate from his own funds. He had no right to turn over the cars to satisfy a pre-existing debt of his own.

"In the absence of a statute protecting such pledges, the rule is well established that a factor has no implied authority to pledge the principal's goods for the factor's own debt or for advances made to himself. This doctrine results from the fact that the factor is but an agent, and as such can bind his principal only when his acts are within the scope of his authority. Authority to sell for the benefit of his principal can in no way be stretched into authority to pledge for his own benefit. Nor does it make any difference that the pledgee was ignorant of the extent of the factor's authority, or supposed him to be the real owner of the goods. As in the case of other agents, the person dealing with the factor must ascertain the extent of his authority and omits to do so at his peril. Mere local usages not known and assented to cannot change the rule." . . .

[Judgment for defendant reversed.]

Code Comment: The same decision would be made under the Code. While the factor may transfer title to a "buyer in ordinary course of business" under Sec. 2-403(2), a person taking property "as security for or in total or partial satisfaction of a money debt" is not such a protected "buyer." Sec. 1-201(9).

Questions and Case Problems

1. What is the objective of each of the following rules of law?

(a) The owner of stolen goods may recover them from the holder of a negotiable warehouse receipt representing such goods, even though the holder had purchased the receipt for value and in good faith.

(b) A factor has a general lien for expenses, advances, and compensation, which may be asserted against any property of the principal that comes into the factor's possession at a later time.

2. Sewell was a guest at the Mountain View Hotel. Three parking lots adjoining the hotel were marked for the use of guests. No hotel attendant was present at any of the lots, and the hotel did not know whose cars were on the lots. Without any direction from the hotel management, Sewell parked his car on one of these lots. Three days later the car, while so parked, was severely damaged when a car operated by an intoxicated driver in no way connected with the hotel careened off the highway and ran into the parking lot. Sewell sued the Mountain View Hotel on the ground that it was practically an insurer of the goods of a guest. Was the hotel liable? (Sewell v. Mountain View Hotel, Inc., [Tenn.] 325 S.W.2d 626)

3. Milford Packing Co. stored goods in Isaacs' warehouse. When Milford did not pay the storage charges, the warehouse sold the goods at public sale. The warehouse purchased the goods at the sale for $1. One and a half years later it resold the goods to a third person for an amount

greater than the storage charges and costs of making the sale. The ware-house then sued Milford for the storage charges. Was it entitled to recover? (Milford Packing Co. v. Isaacs, [Del.] 90 A.2d 796)

4. Francis owned and operated Uncle Bill's Dinner Bell Motel and Cafe. Armwood, who came to the cafe for a meal, complained of the service and thereafter brought suit against Francis on the ground that there had been a violation of a statute applicable to "innkeepers." Francis claimed that he was not subject to such statute. Decide. (Armwood v. Francis, [Utah] 340 P.2d 88)

5. Norvell took certain trunks containing samples to the St. George Hotel. The hotelkeepers knew that the sample trunks belonged to J. R. Torrey & Co. The trunks were retained to secure payment of Norvell's unpaid board bill under an alleged statutory right. The statute gave any hotelkeeper a "specific lien upon all property or baggage deposited with them for the amount of the charges against them or their owners if guests at such hotel." J. R. Torrey & Co. brought an action against the owners of the hotel to recover for a wrongful retention of the trunks. Was it entitled to judgment? (Torrey v. McClellan, 17 Tex.Civ.App. 371, 43 S.W. 64)

6. The Harbor View Marine Corp. operated a fish freezing plant and warehouse. During the course of several years the Pearl Fisheries, Inc., delivered fish for storing and freezing. The corporation issued a nonnego-tible warehouse receipt to the fishery for each lot so delivered. Subsequently the fishery was adjudged bankrupt. At that time there were eleven lots of fish stored with the corporation, which then asserted a lien against the fish for charges incurred with respect to those lots and also with respect to lots that had been frozen and stored before and had been removed from the corporation warehouse by the fishery before bankruptcy. Was it entitled to such a lien? (Harbor View Marine Corp. v. Braudy, 189 F.2d 481)

7. Hallman, stopping at the New Colonial Hotel as a guest, asked the desk clerk if the hotel had parking facilities for a car. He was told that the bellboy would take care of the car. The bellboy, following the usual procedure, drove the car to an open parking lot operated by the Federal Parking Services. The lot was owned and managed independently of the hotel. The bellboy gave Hallman a parking lot receipt on which appeared the name of the lot and the stamped name of the hotel. At the lot the auto was locked by the lot attendant who retained the keys. The next morning Hallman found that a window had been broken and valuable property in the car was missing. He sued the parking lot and the hotel. The hotel raised the defense that no negligence on its part had been shown, Hallman replied that the hotel was liable as an insurer for the property of its guests. Decide. (Hallman v. Federal Parking Services, [Mun.C.A. D.C.] 134 A.2d 382)

CHAPTER 20

Common Carriers

A *carrier* is one who undertakes the transportation of goods, regardless of the method of transportation or the distance covered. The *consignor* or shipper is the person who delivers goods to the carrier for shipment. The *consignee* is the person to whom the goods are shipped and to whom the carrier should deliver the goods.

Sec. 20-A. Classification of Carriers. A carrier may be classified as (1) a *common carrier*, which holds itself out as willing to furnish transportation for compensation without discrimination to all members of the public who apply, assuming that the goods to be carried are proper and that facilities of the carrier are available; (2) a *contract carrier*, which transports goods under individual contracts (see p. 309, Ace-High Dresses Case); or (3) a *private carrier*, such as a truck fleet owned and operated by an industrial firm. These three types of carriers are distinct in that the common carrier law applies to the first, bailment law to the second, and the law of employment to the third.

Sec. 20-B. Freight Forwarders. A *freight forwarder* accepts freight from shippers who send less-than-carload lots, combines such freight into carloads, delivers them as carloads to a carrier for shipment to a particular point where the carload lots are separated and the items carried to their respective destinations. A freight forwarder does not own or operate any of the transportation facilities. By court decision or statute, freight forwarders in some jurisdictions have been declared subject to the same government regulations as common carriers.

Sec. 20-C. Bills of Lading. When the carrier accepts goods for shipment or forwarding, it ordinarily issues to the shipper a *bill of lading* [1]

---

[1] In order to avoid the delay of waiting for a bill of lading mailed to the destination point from the point where the goods were received by the carrier, the Uniform Commercial Code Sec. 7-305 (1) authorizes the carrier at the request of the consignor to provide for the issuance of the bill at the destination rather than the receipt point.

in the case of rail or marine transportation or an *airbill* [2] for air transportation. This instrument is both a receipt for the goods and a contract stating the terms of carriage. (See p. 310, Schwalb v. Erie Railroad Co.) Title to the goods may be transferred by a transfer of the bill of lading made with that intention.

With respect to intrastate shipments, bills of lading in most states are governed by the Uniform Commercial Code [3] or the Uniform Bills of Lading Act.[4] Interstate transportation is regulated by the Federal Bills of Lading Act.[5]

A bill of lading is a negotiable or *order bill of lading* when by its terms the goods are to be delivered to bearer or to the order of a named person.[6] Any other bill of lading, such as one that consigns the goods to a specified person, is a nonnegotiable or *straight bill of lading*.[7]

(1) Contents of Bill of Lading. The form of the bill of lading is regulated in varying degrees by administrative agencies.[8]

As against a bona fide transferee of the bill of lading, a carrier is bound by the recitals in the bill as to the contents, quantity, or weight of goods.[9] This means that the carrier must produce the goods as described, even though they had not existed, or pay damages for failing to do so. This rule is not applied if facts appear on the face of the bill that should keep the transferee from relying on the recital.

As an illustration of the rule that the carrier is bound by the bill of lading, if an employee of a carrier issues a bill of lading for goods when none have been received, a bona fide transferee of the bill of lading for value may generally sue the carrier for failing to deliver the goods described in the false bill of lading. It is immaterial, whether the bill is negotiable or not.[10] In those states in which none of the bill of lading statutes is in force, some courts hold that the carrier is not liable on the theory that the agent who issued the false bill exceeded

---

[2] UCC Sec. 1-201 (6).

[3] UCC Article 7. As to the states adopting the Code, see p. 51.

[4] Alabama, Arizona, California, Delaware, Idaho, Iowa, Louisiana, Maine, Minnesota, Missouri, Nevada, North Carolina, North Dakota, South Carolina, Vermont, Washington, and Wisconsin as of April, 1963, although note subsequent Code adoptions, p. 51.

[5] United States Code Sec. 81 et seq.

[6] UCC Sec. 7-104 (1) (a). See also Uniform Bills of Lading Act Secs. 4, 51.

[7] UCC Sec. 7-104 (2). UBLA Sec. 8 also requires that bills be plainly marked "nonnegotiable" or "not negotiable" in such case. Interstate Commerce Commission regulations applicable to rail shipments require nonnegotiable bills to be printed on white paper and negotiable bills on yellow paper.

[8] The Code contains no provision regulating the form of the bill of lading as constrasted with UBLA Sec. 10, which imposes minimum requirements of stating the date of issue, the place where and the person from whom the goods are received, a description of the goods or the packages, the place and person to whom the goods are to be transported, and the signature of the carrier. Regardless of statutory or administrative regulation, this information would be expected in any bill as a matter of orderly business administration.

[9] UCC Sec. 7-301 (1); UBLA Sec. 23.

[10] UCC Sec. 7-301 (1); UBLA Sec. 23; Federal Bills of Lading Act, 49 USC Sec. 102.

his authority because he had no authority to issue a bill unless he received the goods described in the bill of lading. Other courts follow the rule declared by the statutes.

(2) Negotiability. By statute, varying degrees of negotiability have been conferred upon order bills of lading. A minority of the states give order bills of lading complete negotiablility. The large majority of states and the federal law do not go that far. The trend, however, is in the direction of increased negotiability in order to protect innocent purchasers.[11]

The Uniform Commercial Code provides that the person to whom a bill of lading has been negotiated acquires the direct obligation of the carrier to hold possession of the goods for him according to the terms of the bill of lading as fully as if the carrier had contracted with him, and ordinarily he acquires the title to the bill and the goods it represents. The rights of the holder of a negotiable bill are not affected by the fact (a) that the owner of the bill of lading had been deprived of it by fraud, accident, mistake, duress, undue influence, loss, theft, or conversion; or (b) that the goods had already been surrendered by the carrier or had been stopped in transit.[12] In the former case, the holder owns the document and the goods free of the claim of the former owner; in the case of the second category, the holder is entitled to damages from the carrier for failure to produce the goods described in the bill of lading.[13]

The rights of the holder of a bill of lading are subject to the title of a true owner who did not deliver or authorize the delivery of the goods to the shipper. For example, when a thief steals the goods, delivers them to the carrier, and then negotiates the bill of lading, the title of the owner prevails over the claim of the holder of the bill.[14]

(3) Warranties. The transferee for value of either a negotiable or nonnegotiable bill of lading acquires from his transferor, in the absence of any contrary provision, the benefit of implied warranties that (a) the bill of lading is genuine, (b) its transfer is rightful and is effective to transfer the goods represented thereby, and (c) the transferor has no knowledge of any facts that would impair the validity or worth of the bill of lading.[15]

---

[11] UCC Secs. 7-501 to 7-504; Uniform Sales Act Sec. 27-36.

[12] UCC Sec. 7-502(2). The Code expands the protection of the holder somewhat beyond that afforded by the UBLA Secs. 32, 38; and the FBLA, 49 USC Sec. 83, 107 et seq., 117.

[13] UCC Sec. 7-502(1) (d).

[14] Sec. 7-503 (1).

[15] UCC Sec. 7-507; UBLA Sec. 35; FBLA, 49 USC Secs. 114, 116. When the transfer of the bill of lading is part of a transaction by which the transferor sells the goods represented thereby to the transferee, there will also arise the warranties that are found in other sales of goods. See Chapter 24.

Sec. 20-D. Rights of Common Carriers.

(1) In General. A common carrier of goods has the right to make reasonable and necessary rules for the conduct of its business. It has the right to charge such rates for its services as yield it a fair return on the property devoted to the business of transportation, but the exact rates charged are now regulated by the Interstate Commerce Commission in the case of interstate carriers and by state commissions in the case of intrastate carriers. As an incident of the right to charge for its services, a carrier may charge *demurrage* for the detention of its cars or equipment for an unreasonable length of time by either the consignor or consignee. (See p. 312, Schumacher v. Chicago & Northwestern Railway Co.)

(2) Carrier's Lien. As security for unpaid transportation and service charges, a common carrier has a lien on goods that it transports. By statute, contract, or usage, the carrier's lien also secures demurrage charges, the costs of preservation of the goods, and the costs of sale to enforce the lien.[16]

The lien of a carrier is a specific, and not a general, lien. It attaches only to goods shipped under the particular contract, but includes all of the shipment even though it is sent in installments. Thus, when part of the shipment is delivered, the lien attaches to the portion remaining in possession of the carrier.

When the carrier extends credit for its charges for transportation, it waives its lien. The carrier also loses its lien if it voluntarily surrenders possession of the goods to the consignee, if it refuses a valid tender of charges, or if it demands excessive charges.[17]

As a general rule the lien of the carrier has priority over claims of other persons, such as general creditors or attaching creditors. In a few instances, however, the claim of a creditor is superior to the lien of the carrier. For example, a mortgagee has a prior claim if the carrier has proper notice of the mortgage.[18]

The carrier is also entitled to a lien on goods that are delivered to it for transportation without the owner's express or implied consent, with respect to goods which by law it must accept for shipment when tendered to it.[19]

Sec. 20-E. Duties of Common Carriers.

(1) Proper Goods. A common carrier is generally required to receive and carry the goods of all persons who offer them if the

---

[16] UCC Sec. 7-307 (1); UBLA Sec. 26; FBLA, 49 USC Sec. 105.
[17] UCC Sec. 7-307 (3).
[18] UCC Sec. 7-307 (2); UBLA Sec. 43; FBLA, 49 USC Sec. 120.
[19] UCC Sec. 7-307 (2). The lien could not be asserted against the owner in such case under the prior law, and the carrier was limited to asserting the lien against the shipper.

goods are proper and lawful. The shipper can recover damages from the carrier if it wrongfully refuses to accept and carry his goods, and he may in some instances obtain a court order to compel the carrier to receive and transport the goods offered to it.

(2) Facilities. The carrier is under a duty to furnish facilities that are adequate for the transportation of freight in the usual course of business, and to furnish proper storage facilities for goods awaiting shipment or awaiting delivery after shipment. If the carrier is a railroad, it must furnish on reasonable notice by the shipper sufficient cars to transport goods which are ready for shipment, except in cases of extraordinary and unusual emergencies that cannot be reasonably anticipated.

(3) Proper Shipment. The carrier is under a duty to follow shipping, handling, and routing directions given to it. It is liable to the shipper for any loss or damages caused him by its failure to do so.

(4) Loading and Unloading. Generally, it is the duty of the carrier to load and unload goods delivered to it for shipment in less-than-carload lots, but the shipper or consignee may by contract or custom assume this duty. It is customary for the shipper to load and the consignee to unload bulky freight, such as ore, grain, coal, and lumber, at private sidings when shipped in carload lots.

(5) Pick-Up and Delivery. There is generally no duty of a carrier to pick up or call for freight. The burden is upon the shipper to bring the freight to the carrier.

It is the duty of the carrier to deliver the goods to the consignee, except when custom or special arrangement relieves if of this duty. A wrongful refusal to make delivery renders the carrier liable for conversion, as well as for a breach of contract.[20] Likewise, when the carrier is instructed not to deliver the shipment unless the consignee produces the original bill of lading, the carrier is liable if it does not follow instructions, even though the bill is nonnegotiable.

(a) PLACE OF DELIVERY. Goods must be delivered at the usual place for delivery at the specified destination. In the case of railroads and certain other carriers, the station or the warehouse of the railroad is the usual place of delivery of inanimate goods, except when delivery is made from the car. When delivery is to be made of carload lots or under other circumstances requiring the consignee to unload, the car must be so placed as to be reasonably accessible to the consignee. Express companies are ordinarily required to deliver goods to the place of business or to the home of the consignee.

---

[20] UCC Sec. 7-403; UBLA Sec. 13.

(b) DELIVERY TO WHOM. The carrier is under a duty to deliver the goods to the person to whom they are consigned, or to his authorized agent. When goods are shipped under a negotiable bill of lading, the carrier must not deliver the goods without obtaining possession of the bill properly indorsed.[21]

When goods are shipped under a straight bill of lading, the carrier is justified in delivering to the consignee unless notified by the shipper to deliver to someone else. If a person other than the consignee does present the straight bill of lading, he is not entitled to the goods unless he holds an assignment or authorization from the person then entitled to receive the goods.

The carrier is liable for conversion and breach of contract if it delivers the goods to the wrong person. It is not liable, however, if in good faith and while observing reasonable commercial standards it delivers the goods to the holder of a bill of lading who acquired the bill by fraud or to the holder of an invalid bill.[22]

(c) NOTICE OF NONDELIVERY. Sometimes delivery of the goods is not possible, or the goods are not accepted by the third person to whom they are consigned or by the person who is to be notified of their arrival when the shipper consigns the goods to himself in order to retain title but directs the carrier to notify his customer of their arrival. In such cases there is a conflict of authority as to whether or not the carrier must give notice to the consignor. Some courts hold that there is no duty to notify the consignor, others hold that such a duty exists, and still others state that a duty to notify arises only if under the circumstances reasonable care requires the giving of notice.

Sec. 20-F. Liabilities of Common Carriers.

(1) Delivery of Goods to Carrier. The relationship of shipper and common carrier does not arise until the goods have been delivered by the shipper to the carrier. A carrier may make reasonable regulations as to the place and time freight will be received. A delivery at any other time or place does not as a general rule place any responsibility on the carrier in respect to the goods. Ordinarily the goods are delivered to a clerk or agent of the carrier. Notice is not required when, by agreement or custom, the carrier is willing to receive goods left at a particular place or platform even though no one is there to receive them.

(2) Liability of Carrier Before Transportation. When goods that are not for immediate transportation are delivered to the carrier, the

---

[21] UCC Sec. 7-403 (3); UBLA Sec. 14.
[22] UCC Sec. 7-404.

liability of the carrier for any loss or damage is that of an ordinary bailee in a mutual-benefit bailment. This situation arises when actual shipment is to be delayed until freight is paid or shipping directions given.

(3) Liability of Carrier During Transportation. When goods are delivered to a common carrier for immediate shipment and while they are in transit, the carrier is absolutely liable for any loss or damage to the goods unless it can prove that it was due solely to one or more of the following excepted causes: (a) act of God, or a natural phenomenon that is not reasonably foreseeable; (b) act of public enemy, such as pirates at sea or the military forces of an opposing government, as distinguished from ordinary robbers; (c) act of public authority, such as a health officer removing goods from the train; (d) act of the shipper, such as fraudulent labeling or defective packing; or (e) inherent nature of the goods, such as those naturally tending to spoil or deteriorate. (See p. 313, Anderson, Clayton & Co. Case)

(4) Liability of Carrier After Transportation. By the general rule, the period during which the carrier is subject to the rule of liability just stated continues after the goods have reached their destination until they have been removed from the carrier, and until the consignee has been notified of their arrival and a reasonable time thereafter has elapsed. After the expiration of that time, the carrier is held only to the duty of an ordinary bailee with respect to the goods.

(5) Carrier's Liability for Delay. A carrier is liable for losses caused by its failure to deliver goods within a reasonable time. Thus the carrier is liable for losses arising from a fall in price or a deterioration of the goods caused by their unreasonable delay. The carrier, however, is not liable for every delay. The law merely requires the carrier to transport and deliver the goods within a reasonable time. Risks of ordinary delays, incidental to the business of transporting goods, are assumed by the shipper.

In some cases the carrier is in fact under a duty to delay the shipment of goods, such as when there are known dangers to which the goods would be exposed if sent more quickly. When the cause excusing the delay ceases to operate, the carrier must deliver the goods within a reasonable time thereafter.

(6) Liability of Initial and Connecting Carriers. When goods are carried over the lines of several carriers, a question arises as to which carrier is liable for loss or damages sustained during transportation. Except as noted above, a common carrier on whose line the loss is sustained is liable to the shipper or the owner of the goods.

By statute [23] it is also provided that the first or initial carrier and the last or terminal carrier in the chain of rail or motor carriers are also liable for the loss sustained on any line (a) when the shipment is a through shipment sent to another state or to Canada or Mexico, (b) when the loss on the other carrier's line was sustained while a common carrier-shipper relationship existed, and (c) when the loss was such as would impose liability on a common carrier. In the event that an initial or terminal carrier is required to pay for loss for which another carrier is liable, the initial or terminal carrier may sue such other carrier to recover what it has paid. A similar liability is imposed with respect to intrastate shipments by the Uniform Commercial Code. [24]

(7) Limiting Liability. It is generally held that in the absence of a constitutional or statutory prohibition, a carrier has the right to limit its liability by contract. Generally a clause limiting the liability of the carrier is not enforceable unless consideration is given for it, usually in the form of a reduced rate, and provided further that the shipper is allowed to ship without limitation of liability if he chooses to pay the higher or ordinary rate. [25]

(a) RISKS. A carrier may by contract relieve itself from liability for losses not arising out of its own negligence. A carrier accepting freight for shipment outside the state cannot require the shipper to agree that the carrier will only be liable for losses occurring on its line or only for losses due to its neglect.

(b) AMOUNT. A common carrier may make an agreement with the shipper as to the value of the property. If the amount is reasonable, such an agreement will usually bind the shipper whether or not the loss was due to the carrier's fault. Some courts, however, hold such an agreement void if the loss was caused by the negligence of the carrier.

In the absence of a statute to the contrary, it is generally held that a carrier may limit its liability to the value of the property at the time and place of shipment, to the invoice price charged the consignee, or to the amount specified unless a greater value was declared by the shipper and a higher freight rate paid by him.

The carrier may limit the amount of its liability with respect to the period in which it is treated as a warehouseman.

(8) Making of Claim. When a shipper sustains loss, he will ordinarily inform the carrier of his loss and demand payment for his damages. In the absence of any contrary provision in the bill of

---

[23] 49 USC Sec. 20 (1).
[24] UCC Sec. 7-302.
[25] Sec. 7-309 (2).

lading or other binding contract between the shipper and the carrier, no special form of claim is required. It is commonly required, however, that the claim be submitted in writing.

It is likewise commonly specified in the bill of lading that the shipper must make his claim within a stated period after the loss or destruction occurs. Sometimes the provision requires the giving of a preliminary notice of the existence of the shipper's claim and then the filing of a formal written notice setting forth the details. If a claim is not presented within the time and in the manner prescribed by such provisions, the claim is barred. Such provisions in effect create special statutes of limitations.

With respect to interstate shipments, the Interstate Commerce Act prohibits the initial or terminal carrier from limiting the period for the filing of claims to less than nine months.[26]

Under the Uniform Commercial Code "reasonable provisions" as to the time and manner of presenting claims and instituting actions may be included in an intrastate bill of lading.[27]

(9) Liability for Baggage. A common carrier of passengers is required to receive a reasonable amount of baggage. Its liability in this respect is the same as the liability of a carrier of goods. If the passenger retains custody of his baggage, the carrier is liable only for lack of reasonable care or willful misconduct on the part of its agents and employees.

A passenger in a Pullman car cannot recover for loss of or damage to personal property which he has brought with him unless he can show that the railroad or the employees in the Pullman car failed to exercise reasonable care under the circumstances. A few cases hold the Pullman car employees and the railroad to the standard of care required of hotelkeepers. In the great majority of states this degree of liability applies only to property that is entrusted by the passenger to the Pullman employees for safekeeping.

Cases for Chapter 20

Ace-High Dresses v. J. C. Trucking Co.
122 Conn. 578, 191 A. 536 (1937)

The J. C. Trucking Co., Inc., was engaged under contracts to transport dress material from New York City to dressmaking establishments in New Haven, Hartford, and Bridgeport, Connecticut and then to transport the finished dresses back to New York City. Dresses that were being carried to Ace-High Dresses, Inc., were stolen from the trucking company.

---

[26] 49 USC Sec. 20 (11).
[27] UCC Sec. 7-309(3).

Ace-High Dresses sued the trucking company and claimed that the latter was liable for the loss as a common carrier. From a judgment for the defendant, the plaintiff appealed.

BANKS, J. . . . "A common carrier or public carrier is one who undertakes as a business, for hire or reward, to carry from one place to another the goods of all persons who may apply for such carriage, provided the goods be of the kind which he professes to carry, and the person so applying will agree to have them carried upon the lawful terms prescribed by the carrier. . . .

. . . The controlling factor is the public undertaking, either express or implied from a course of business, to carry for hire the goods of all persons who may apply for such carriage. . . . The fundamental distinction is the the [contract] carrier enters into a contract with each of his customers and assumes no obligation to carry for any other, while the common carrier undertakes to carry for all persons indifferently. The one is a contract carrier, the other carries without contract other than that implied from his public undertaking to carry for all.

The defendant had a limited number of customers, with each of whom it had a contract for the transportation of dresses to New York. During the year which elapsed between the time when it commenced business and the date of the loss of plaintiff's property, it had taken on no new customers and had solicited no new business. The only change in its business during this period was the loss of three customers. There is nothing in the record to indicate that it held itself out as willing to carry dresses for all who might apply, or that it would carry for anyone without first entering into a contract for such carriage. It called at the factories of its customers for the dresses which it had contracted to carry, and it does not appear that it undertook to carry others. It was distinctly a contract carrier as distinguished from a common carrier. That it was authorized to do a general trucking business for the public generally is not of importance since the test is, not what is was empowered to do, but what it was actually engaged in doing. . . .

[Judgment for defendant affirmed.]

Schwalb v. Erie Railroad Co.

161 Misc. 743, 293 N.Y.S. 842 (1937)

Hamilton delivered two carloads of grapes to the Atchison, Topeka & Sante Fe Railroad Co. for shipment to a consignee in New York City. The carrier issued a bill of lading which stated that it received "the property described below, in apparent good order, except as noted (contents and condition of contents of packages unknown.)" The goods arrived in a damaged condition. Schwalb brought an action against the Erie Railroad

Co., which also handled the shipment, to recover for the damage to the goods. The defendant claimed that there was no evidence as to their condition at the point of shipment and moved to set aside the verdict rendered in favor of the plaintiff.

GENUNG, J. . . . A bill of lading serves three distinct functions: First, as a receipt for the goods; second, as a contract for their carriage; and third, as documentary evidence of title to the goods. As a receipt, it recites the place and date of shipment, describes the goods as to quantity, weight, dimensions, identification marks, and condition, quality, and value. As a contract, it names the contracting parties which include the consignee, fixes the route, destination, and freight rate or charges, and stipulates the rights of and obligations assumed by the parties. As documentary evidence, it is proof of ownership if a "straight" bill of lading, and title to the goods themselves if an "order" bill of lading. . . .

The real issue . . . is whether or not these bills of lading function as a description of the goods as to condition when shipped so as to constitute prima facie evidence of good condition. One of the first functions of a bill of lading, as stated above, is to describe the quantity, condition, and quality of the goods shipped. The bills of lading in this case expressly state that the initial carrier: "Received at Reedley, California . . . the property described below, in apparent good order, except as noted." There was no exceptions noted thereon.

The defendant urges that the parenthetical clause in the bill of lading, "contents and condition of contents of packages unknown," destroys the effect of the bills of lading as prima facie evidence of contents and condition of contents. There was no dispute with respect to the identity of the contents in this case.

The shipments consisted of 1,008 lidded lugs of grapes in each car. . . . The testimony agreed that the grapes in these shipments were packed in standard containers, that they were loaded in the car in the usual and customary way for shipping this commodity, that it was possible and customary to inspect loaded cars, and that on such an inspection the lugs and the contents of the lugs in any part of the car could be observed.

The clause relied on by the defendant applies only where the contents of packages are actually unknown and cannot be ascertained by the carrier from a reasonable examination of the shipment. . . .

The defendant is sued for damage to the property in transit and not for a misdescription of the lading. The damage complained of in this case consisted of physical damage to the containers and their contents caused by external forces as distinguished from inherent forces. The nature of the damage was easily discernible at destination, and the absence of such damage at the point of origin was as

readily observable. The clause relied on by the defendant can coun-
teract the prima facie effect of the statements as to contents and
condition of contents in the bill of lading only where in fact the contents and condition thereof are actually concealed from the carrier
and are not observable or the carrier is deprived of an opportunity
to inspect the shipment. The bills of lading, therefore, were prima
facie evidence of the good condition of the property when shipped.
    [Judgment entered for the plaintiff.]

    Code Comment: The same decision would be made under the Code.
Sec. 7-301(1) declares that the carrier is not liable for a misdescription in a
bill of lading which "indicates" that the carrier did not know the nature
of the shipment, as by a notation "contents or condition of contents of
packages unknown" provided "such indication be true." In the Schwalb
case the facts were such that the "indication" was not true and therefore
the protection of Sec. 7-301(1) would not exist. Likewise, the same distinction would be made between liability for misdescription and liability for
physical damage.

Schumacher v. Chicago & Northwestern Railway Co.
207 Ill. 199, 69 N.E. 825 (1904)

    Schumacher of Highland Park, Illinois, was the consignee of two cars
of coke. He delayed unloading the goods for several days. The Chicago &
Northwestern Railway Co. included as part of its charges one dollar a
day or fraction thereof for the use of cars and tracks held for unloading
after the expiration of 48 hours. When Schumacher refused to pay this
charge, the railway company refused to allow him to remove about three
tons of coke which remained in one car. Schumacher brought an action
against the carrier to recover the goods. From a judgment for the defendant, the plaintiff appealed.

    RICKS, J. . . . "Section 5 of the act in relation to receiving, carrying,
and delivering grain in this state provides that a consignee of grain
transported in bulk shall have twenty-four hours, free of expense,
after actual notice of arrival, in which to remove the same from the
cars of such railroad corporation. . . . There would seem to be an
implied right, under the statute, to charge for a longer detention
than the twenty-four hours which the statute names. Indeed, no
reason is perceived, in law or justice, why any unreasonable and unnecessary detention of cars by consignees should not be paid for. . . .
The charges so made were . . . reasonable. . . . Demurrage . . . has
arisen in a practical way only within late years, and long after our
statutes for the regulation of railroads were passed. It does not, however, follow that because there is no statutory regulation of the question there is no law."

Mr. Elliott, in his work on railroads . . . says: . . . "After a carrier has completed its services as such, it has a right to charge extra compensation for storing the goods in a warehouse and keeping them, after the consignee has had a reasonable time in which to remove them. Why, then, when its duties as a carrier have been performed and a reasonable time has elapsed, is it not as much entitled to additional compensation for the use of its cars and tracks as for the use of its warehouse? Certainly a customer whose duty it is to unload, or who unreasonably delays the unloading of a car for his own benefit, ought not to complain if he is made to pay a reasonable sum for the unreasonable delay caused by his own act. But this is not all. The public interests also require that cars should not be unreasonably detained in this way." . . .

[Judgment for defendant affirmed.]

Code Comment: The same conclusion would be reached under the Code, which recognizes the right to demurrage and gives the carrier a right to a lien therefor. UCC Sec. 7-209(1).

Anderson, Clayton & Co. v. Yazoo & Mississippi Valley Railroad Co.

174 La. 762, 141 So. 453 (1932)

Anderson, Clayton & Company delivered 42 bales of cotton to the Yazoo & Mississippi Valley Railroad Co. for immediate shipment from Choudrant, Louisiana, to New Orleans. The cotton was loaded and inspected by the railroad company, and the car closed and sealed about noon. At three o'clock the next morning the cotton was destroyed by a fire inside the car while still at Choudrant. In an action brought by the shipper against the railroad company to recover the value of the cotton, the latter contended that the loss was caused by a fire concealed in the cotton at the time of the delivery. From a judgment for the plaintiff, the defendant appealed.

OVERTON, J. . . . In approaching the liability of defendant [railroad] for the loss of the cotton, it is advisable to ascertain whether the shipment was an interstate or an intrastate shipment to learn by what law it is governed—whether by the act of Congress, in connection with the common law, or by the civil law as established in this state. The shipment was from one point in this state to another point in the state, but the shipment, in order to reach its destination over defendant's railway, had to go from the point of its origin to Vicksburg, Mississippi, and thence some distance through the state of Mississippi until it re-entered the state of Louisiana to reach New Orleans, its point of destination. . . . It is therefore controlled by the act of Congress, interpreted in connection with the common law. . . .

There is nothing in the bill of lading, nor would there seem to be anything in the act of Congress, which either enlarges or contracts defendant's liability. Under the common law the rule governing the liability of a common carrier is as follows:

"The liability of the common carrier by law is, as has been seen, an unusual and extraordinary one, based upon considerations of public policy which have survived the wonderful change in the circumstances under which they first arose. By that law the common carrier is regarded as a practical insurer of the goods against all losses of whatever kind with the exception of (1) those arising from what is known as the act of God and (2) those caused by the public enemy; to which in modern times have been added (3) those arising from the act of public authority, (4) those arising from the act of the shippers, and (5) those arising from the inherent nature of the goods.". . .

Defendant does not contend that it is relieved from liability by virtue of any one of the first three exceptions, and obviously it is not. As to the fourth exception, which comprises those losses arising from the act of the shipper, defendant is not liable if the shippers delivered to it cotton with fire smouldering and concealed on the inside of any bale in the shipment, which caused the loss. While the evidence points rather strongly to the hypothesis that the cotton was destroyed by reason of the fact that the shippers delivered a bale with fire concealed in it, of which neither they nor defendants had knowledge, nevertheless this does not appear with legal certainty. The evidence, which is circumstantial, does not exclude every other reasonable hypothesis as to the cause of the loss except the hypothesis that it was occasioned in the manner advanced, namely, by the delivery of what is known as a fire bale, or that it was occasioned by any other act of the shippers. As [to] defendant's nonliability by virtue of the fifth exception to the general rule, which comprises losses from the inherent nature of the goods, it does not appear, and there is no reason to hold, that the nature of cotton in bales is such as to make is subject to spontaneous combustion. Hence, as the burden of proof was on defendant, defendant having received the cotton, to show that the loss was occasioned by one of the five causes named, and having failed to do so, defendant is liable for the loss. . . .

[Judgment for plaintiff affirmed.]

Code Comment: The same decision would be made under **the Code.** Although the Code does not go beyond declaring that a carrier must exercise reasonable care, it expressly declares that any rule of law creating an insurer's liability, as was applied in the Anderson case, shall remain in force in spite of the adoption of the Code. UCC Sec. 7-309(1).

Questions and Case Problems

1. What is the objective of each of the following rules of law?

(a) As against a bona fide transferee of the bill of lading, a carrier is bound by recitals in the bill as to the contents, quantity, or weight of goods.

(b) An interstate railroad can require that a shipper furnish proof of his claim to damages for loss within a specified time provided it is not less than nine months.

2. The Utah Public Service Commission granted a contract carrier permit to the Salt Lake Transportation Company to transport passengers between the Salt Lake airport for four principal airlines and the three leading hotels in the city. The Realty Purchasing Company and various hotels and taxicab companies objected to the granting of the permit on the ground that the company performed a taxicab service and was therefore a common carrier. Decide. (Realty Purchasing Co. v. Public Service Commission, [Utah] 345 P.2d 606)

3. The United States shipped four rectifiers by the Hoover Motor Express Co. Each rectifier weighed some 1,500 pounds and was mounted in a cabinet which in turn was crated. On arrival at their destination, the crates were undamaged but it was found that the rectifiers were damaged because a number of supporting bolts had worked themselves loose and had fallen inside the cabinets. The bill of lading stated that the goods had been received "in apparent good order . . . (contents and condition of packages unknown)." Was Hoover Motor Express liable for the damage? (Hoover Motor Express Co. v. United States, [C.A.6th] 262 F.2d 832)

4. Gardner delivered a number of stoves to the New Orleans & Northeastern Railroad Co. for transportation. The stoves were damaged while in transit as a result of water from a rainstorm leaking through the roof of the car in which they were being transported. Gardner sued the company to recover damages. Could he recover? (Gardner v. New Orleans & Northeastern Railroad Co., 8 Miss. 640, 29 So. 469)

5. Trees owned a carload of cattle. At Dolton, Illinois, he had the car connected to a freight train of the Pennsylvania Railroad Co. for shipment to Woodstock, Ohio. The car was attached to the first freight train that stopped at Dolton. This train was a through freight from Dolton to Columbus, Ohio. On its way, the freight train passed through Woodstock, Ohio, but in accordance with its schedule on file with the Interstate Commerce Commission it did not stop there. The cattle were carried by the railroad from Dolton to Columbus and then back to Woodstock. When they arrived, they showed signs of being worn by the travel. Trees claimed that if the railroad had stopped the through freight in Woodstock, the cattle would have been in a better condition. Was the carrier liable? (Trees v. Pennsylvania Railroad Co., Ohio App. 109 N.E.2d 29)

6. Nichols ordered cars of the Oregon Short Line Railway Co. to be furnished on a certain date for transportation of 3,370 head of sheep from Soda Springs, Idaho, to Omaha, Nebraska. Thereafter, other shippers placed orders for cars. These subsequent orders were filled by the railroad company before Nichols was furnished with cars for his shipment, causing him to keep his sheep near the corrals for ten days awaiting means of transportation. In an action brought by Nichols against the railroad company to recover damages, it was contended that there had been an unlawful discrimination. Do you agree? (Nichols v. Oregon Short Line Railway Co., 24 Utah 83, 66 P. 768)

7. The Brown & Haywood Co. delivered a carload of glass to the Pennsylvania Railroad Co. for shipment from Pennsylvania to Washington. The shipper directed that the goods be shipped via the Chicago, St. Paul & Kansas City and the Northern Pacific lines. The Pennsylvania Railroad Co. carried the car over its own line but, wrongfully or by mistake, sent the car over the Union Pacific. The Union Pacific company sent the goods by boat from Portland, Oregon, to Seattle, Washington, and employed Heath, a drayman, to transfer the glass to the station of the Northern Pacific company. While being transferred, part of the glass was broken. The shipper brought an action against the Pennsylvania railroad to recover damages arising out of the loss. Was it entitled to judgment? (Brown & Haywood Co. v. Pennsylvania Railroad Co., 63 Minn. 546, 65 N.W. 961)

8. Nuside Metal Products delivered two shipments to Eazor Express to be shipped C.O.D. Eazor Express delivered the shipments to a connecting carrier, Albrent Freight & Storage Corporation. The latter delivered the shipments to the consignee, collected the purchase price, and then remitted by its check directly to Nuside Metal Products. Albrent went bankrupt, and the bank on which its check was drawn refused to make payment because of insufficient funds. Nuside Metal Products then sued Eazor Express. Eazor defended on the ground that the claim against it was not made within nine months as required by its bill of lading which stated: "As a condition precedent to recovery, claims must be filed in writing with the receiving or delivering carrier, or carrier issuing this bill of lading, or carrier on whose line the loss, damage, injury, or delay occurred, within nine months after delivery of the property. . . ." Decide. (Nuside Metal Products, Inc. v. Eazor Express, Inc., [Pa.] 152 A.2d 275)

9. Keenan was engaged in the business of receiving for sale and commission, buying and selling, and shipping livestock at the Union Stockyards in Chicago, Illinois. Four carloads of cattle were shipped to him from Kansas City, Missouri, over the Atchison, Topeka & Santa Fe Railroad. The carrier with its own engines and switching crew removed the cars from a point on the Chicago end of its line, over the track of the Union Stockyards & Transit Co. to the Union Stockyards. For this transfer from its own line to the stockyards, the carrier charged a certain fee per car. Was it entitled to do so? (Walker v. Keenan, 19 C.C.A. 668, 73 F. 755)

PART IV
SALES

CHAPTER 21

Nature and Form

A *sale of goods* is a transfer of title to tangible personal property in consideration of a payment of money, an exchange of other property, or the performance of services. The consideration in a sale is known as the *price*. The parties to a sale are the person who owns the property and the person to whom the title is transferred. The transferor is the seller or vendor, and the transferee is the buyer or vendee. If the price is payable wholly or partly in goods, each party is a seller insofar as the goods he is to transfer are concerned.

The law of sales is a fusion of the law merchant and the common law of England, as modified and codified in most states by the Uniform Commercial Code [1] or the Uniform Sales Act. [2]

A sale of an interest in real property, such as a house, store, or farm, is governed by different principles discussed in Chapter 53.

Nature and Legality

Sec. 21-A. Sale Distinguished. A sale of goods must be carefully distinguished from several other closely related transactions.

(1) Bailment. A sale is an actual present transfer of title. If there is a transfer of a lesser interest than ownership or title, the transaction

---

[1] For the states that have adopted the Uniform Commercial Code, see p. 51.

[2] Alabama, Arizona, California, Colorado, Delaware, District of Columbia, Hawaii, Idaho, Iowa, Maine, Minnesota, Nebraska, Nevada, North Dakota, Panama Canal Zone, South Dakota, Utah, Vermont, Washington, and Wisconsin as of April, 1963, although note subsequent Code adoptions, p. 51.

is not a sale. Thus, a bailment is not a sale because only possession is transferred to the bailee. The bailor remains the owner.

(2) Gift. There can be no sale without consideration, or a price. A gift is a gratuitous transfer of the title of property.

(3) Contract to Sell. When the parties intend that title to goods will pass at a future time and they make a contract providing for that event, a *contract to sell* or a contract to make a sale in the future is created.[3]

(4) Option to Purchase. A sale, a present transfer of title, differs from an option to purchase. The latter is neither a transfer of title nor a contract to transfer title but a power to require a sale to be made at a future time.

(5) Conditional Sale. A conditional sale is technically any transfer of title on a condition. A conditional sale, however, customarily refers to a "condition precedent" transaction by which title does not vest in the purchaser until he has paid in full for the property purchased. This is the customary type of sale today when personal property is purchased on credit and payment is to be made in installments. Under this type of transaction the title to the property is retained by the seller until all payments have been made. In addition, the conditional sales agreement gives the seller the right to retake possession of the property upon the buyer's default.[4]

(6) Furnishing of Labor or Services. A contract for personal services is to be distinguished from a sale of goods even when some transfer of personal property is involved in the performing of the services. For example, the contract of a repairman is a contract for services even though in making the repairs he may supply parts necessary to perform his task. The supplying of such parts is not regarded as a sale because it is merely incidental to the primary contract of making repairs. The same principle is applied to a contract of a contractor to build a house, using materials which he supplies. (See p. 327, Dibblee Case)

Sec. 21-B. Subject Matter of Sales. The subject matter of a sale is anything that is movable when it is identified as the subject of the transaction.[5]

---

[3] UCC Sec. 2-106 (1), USA Sec. 1(1).

[4] This type of sale is known as a secured transaction under the Code, Article 9 (see Chapter 34), and in non-Code states is expressly called a conditional sale.

[5] UCC Sec. 2-105(1). It may also include things which are attached to the land, such as those consisting of (a) timber or minerals or buildings or materials forming part of buildings if they are to be removed or severed by the seller, and (b) other things attached to land to be removed by either party. UCC Sec. 2-107. Under the USA the subject matter of the sale is goods or tangible personal property.

The subject matter of a sale may not be investment securities, such as stocks and bonds, the sale of which is regulated by Article 8 of the Code; choses in action, since they are assigned, rather than sold, or because of their personal nature are not transferable in any case; [6] or real estate.

Sec. 21-C. Nonexistent and Future Goods. Generally a person cannot make a present sale of nonexistent or future goods or goods that he does not own. He can make a contract to sell such goods at a future date; but since he does not have the title, he technically cannot transfer that title now. For example, an agreement made today that all the fish caught on a fishing trip tomorrow shall belong to a particular person does not make him the owner of those fish. Where the parties purport to effect a present sale of future goods, the agreement therefore only operates as a contract to sell the goods.[7] Thus a farmer purporting to transfer the title today to the future crop would be held subject to a duty to transfer title to the crop when it came into existence. If he did not keep the promise, he could be sued for breach of contract; but the contract would not operate to vest the title in the buyer automatically.

Sec. 21-D. Law of Contracts Applicable. A sale is a voluntary transaction between two persons. Accordingly most of the principles that apply to a contractual agreement are equally applicable to a sale. Modern commercial practices, however, have modified the strict principles of contract law, and this approach to the problem is carried into the Code. Thus it is provided that the sales contract can be made in any manner and that it is sufficient that the parties by their conduct recognize the existence of a contract, even though it cannot be determined when the contract was made, and generally even though one or more terms are left open.[8] In some instances the Code treats all buyers and sellers alike. In others, it treats merchants separately, in contrast with the occasional or casual buyer or seller. Thus the Code recognizes that the merchant is experienced in his field and has a specialized knowledge of the relevant commercial practices.[9]

(1) Offer. The law as to offers is applicable except that an offer by a merchant cannot be revoked by him, even though there is no consideration to keep the offer open, if the offer expresses an intention

---

[6] As to rights that cannot be transferred because of their personal character, see p. 178.

[7] UCC Sec. 2-105(2), USA Sec. 5(3).

[8] UCC Sec. 2-204. This provision of the Code is limited by requiring that there be "a reasonably certain basis for giving an appropriate remedy."

[9] Sec. 2-104(1).

that it will not be revoked, is made in writing, and is signed by the merchant.[10] The expressed period of irrevocability, however, cannot exceed three months. If nothing is said as to the duration of the offer, this irrevocability continues only for a reasonable time.

(2) Acceptance. The Code redeclares the general principle of contract law that an offer may be accepted in any manner and by any medium which is reasonable under the circumstances, unless a specific manner or medium is clearly indicated by the terms of the offer or the circumstances of the case.

(a) ACCEPTANCE BY SHIPMENT. Unless otherwise clearly indicated, an order or other offer to buy goods that are to be sent out promptly or currently can be accepted either by actually shipping the goods, as though a unilateral contract offer were made; or by promptly promising to make shipment, as though a bilateral contract, that is, an exchange of promises, had been offered.[11] If acceptance is made by shipping the goods, the seller must notify the buyer within a reasonable time that the offer has been accepted in this manner.

(b) ADDITIONAL TERMS. Unless it is expressly specified that an offer must be accepted just as made, the offeree may accept a contract but at the same time propose additional terms. These new terms, however, do not become binding unless the offeror thereafter consents to them. If the transaction is between merchants, the additional terms become part of the contract if no objection is made to them and the additional terms do not materially alter the terms of the offer.[12]

(3) Determination of Price. The price for the goods may be expressly fixed by the contract, or the parties may merely indicate the manner of determining price at a later time.[13] Ordinarily, if nothing is said as to price, the buyer is required to pay the reasonable value of the goods. This is generally the market price, but not necessarily, as when the market price is under the control of the seller.

In recent years there has been an increase in use of the "cost plus" formula for determining price. Under this form of agreement the buyer pays the seller a sum equal to the cost to the seller of obtaining the goods plus a specified percentage of that cost.

The contract may expressly provide that one of the parties may determine the price, in which case he must act in good faith in so doing.[14] Again the contract may specify that the price shall be deter-

---

[10] Sec. 2-205.

[11] Sec. 2-206(1) (b).

[12] Sec. 2-207.

[13] UCC Sec. 2-305, USA Sec. 9(1).

[14] Good faith requires that the party in fact act honestly and, in the case of a merchant, also requires that he follow reasonable commercial standards of fair dealing which are recognized in the trade. UCC Secs. 1-201 (19), 2-103 (b).

mined by some standard or by a third person. If for any reason other than the fault of one of the parties the price cannot be fixed in the manner specified, the buyer is required to pay the reasonable value for the goods unless it is clear that the parties intended that if the price were not determined in the manner specified there would be no contract. In the latter case, the buyer must return the goods and the seller refund any payment made on account. If the buyer is unable to return such goods as he has received, he must pay their reasonable value at the time of delivery.

(4) Output and Requirement Contracts. Somewhat related to the open-term concept concerning price is that involved in the output and requirement contracts in which the quantity which is to be sold or purchased is not a specific quantity but is such amount as the seller should produce or the buyer should require. Although this introduces an element of uncertainty, such sales contracts are valid. To prevent oppression, they are subject to two limitations under the Code:

(a) The parties must act in good faith.

(b) The quantity offered or demanded must not be unreasonably disproportionate to prior output or requirements or to any estimate stated.[15]

When the sales contract is a continuing contract, as one calling for periodic delivery of fuel, but no time is set for the life of the contract, the contract runs for a reasonable time but may be terminated on notice by either party unless otherwise agreed.[16]

(5) Seals. The existence of a seal on a contract or an offer of sale has no effect. Thus in determining whether there is consideration or if the Statute of Limitations is applicable, the fact that there is a seal on the contract is ignored.[17]

(6) Implied Conditions. The field of implied conditions under contract law is broadened to permit the release of a party from his obligation under a sales contract when performance has been made commercially impracticable, as distinguished from impossible: (a) by the occurrence of a contingency, the nonoccurrence of which was a basic assumption on which the contract was made; or (b) by compliance in good faith with any applicable domestic or foreign governmental regulation or order, whether or not it is later held valid by the courts.[18]

---

[15] Sec. 2-306.

[16] Sec. 2-309(2).

[17] Sec. 2-203.

[18] Sec. 2-615. If under the circumstances indicated in the text the seller is totally disabled from performing, he is discharged from his contract. If he is able to produce some goods, he must allocate them among customers, but any customer may reject the contract and such fractional offer. Sec. 2-615(b), 2-616.

(7) Fraud and Other Defenses. The defenses that may be raised in a suit on a sales contract are in general the same as on any other contract. When one party is defrauded, he may rescind the transaction and recover what he has paid or the goods that he has delivered, together with damages for any loss which he has sustained. If title has passed to the buyer because of a fraud, the title is voidable while the goods are still owned by him and the sale may be set aside if the innocent seller so elects. If the fraudulent buyer has resold the goods to a buyer who acted in good faith, the right of the seller to obtain the goods is lost, although he may still sue the fraudulent buyer for his loss.

Sec. 21-E. Illegal Sales.

(1) Illegality at Common Law. At common law a sale is illegal if the subject matter is itself bad, as in the case of an indecent picture. The transaction may also be illegal even though the subject matter of the sale may be unobjectionable in itself, as when the agreement provides that the object of the sale shall be employed for some unlawful purpose or when the seller assists in the unlawful act. To illustrate, when the seller falsely brands goods, representing them to be imported, to assist the buyer in perpetrating a fraud, the sale is illegal. The mere fact, however, that the seller has knowledge of the buyer's unlawful purpose does not, under the general rule, make the sale illegal unless the purpose is the commission of a serious crime.

(2) Illegality Under Statutes. Statutes in many states prohibit business transactions, including sales, on Sunday. Practically every state has legislation prohibiting certain sales when they are not conducted according to the requirements of the statutes. Thus a statute may require that a particular class of goods, such as meat, be inspected before a legal sale can be made. In addition to statutes which invalidate the sale, a number of statutes make it criminal or impose a penalty for making a sale under certain circumstances. Statutes commonly regulate sales by establishing standards as to grading, size, weight, and measure, and by prohibiting adulteration.

In addition to the restrictive state statutes, federal legislation regulates the sale of goods in interstate commerce. The Federal Food, Drug, and Cosmetic Act, for example, prohibits the interstate shipment of misbranded or adulterated foods, drugs, cosmetics, and therapeutic devices. Other statutes considered in Sec. 63-B further protect the consumer from fraud and physical harm.

(3) Effect of Illegal Sale. An illegal sale or contract to sell cannot be enforced. This rule is based on public policy. As a general rule courts will not aid either party in recovering money or property trans-

ferred pursuant to an illegal agreement. Relief is sometimes given, however, to an innocent party to an unlawful agreement. For example, if one party is the victim of a fraudulent transaction, he may recover what he has transferred to the other party even though the agreement arose out of some illegal scheme.

Sec. 27-F. Bulk Transfers. *of inventory assets or HARDWARD* A common statutory regulation is designed to protect creditors of a merchant from the danger that he may sell all his inventory, pocket the money, and then disappear, leaving them unpaid. The Code provides that whenever a merchant is about to transfer a major part of his materials, supplies, merchandise, or other inventory, not in the ordinary course of business, advance notice of the transfer must be given to his creditors. If the statute is not followed, the creditors may still reach the sold property in the hands of the transferee if he knew of the breach of the Code or did not pay value.[19] (See p. 328, Berger v. Berger) The protection given to creditors by the bulk transfer legislation is in addition to the protection which they have against their debtor for fraudulent transfers or conveyances.[20]

Formality of the Sales Contract

In order to protect the parties to a sales contract from false claims, the English Statute of Frauds of 1677, Sec. 17, required, subject to certain exceptions, that all sales above a certain amount must be evidenced by writing. This requirement is followed in most states and is incorporated in the Uniform Commercial Code [21] and the Uniform Sales Act.[22]

Sec. 21-G. Amount. The Statute of Frauds provision of the Code applies whenever the sales price is $500 or more. In non-Code states that specify a minimum amount, it is most commonly $500. In two states all sales are subject to these requirements. In six states the statute does not apply to any sales.

If the total contract price equals or exceeds the statutory amount, the Statute of Frauds applies even though the contract covers several articles, the individual amounts of which are less than the statutory amount, provided the parties intended to make a single contract rather than a series of separate or divisible contracts. In the latter case, if each contract is for less than the statutory amount, no writing is required.

---

19 Sec. 6-101 et seq. Some states that have not adopted the Code have similar statutes called "bulk sales" acts.
20 See p. 322.
21 UCC Sec. 2-201.
22 USA Sec. 4.

Minimum Amounts for Sales of Goods to Make Statute of Frauds Applicable

Alabama	$ 500	Montana d	$ 500
Alaska	500	Nebraska	500
Arizona	500	Nevada	50
Arkansas	500	New Hampshire	500
California	500	New Jersey	500
Colorado	50	New Mexico	500
Connecticut	500	New York	500
Delaware	500	North Carolina	No requirement
District of Columbia	50	North Dakota	500
Florida	All sales	Ohio	500
Georgia	500	Oklahoma	500
Hawaii	100	Oregon	500
Idaho	500	Pennsylvania	500
Illinois	500	Rhode Island	500
Indiana	500	South Carolina	50
Iowa	All sales	South Dakota	500
Kansas	No requirement	Tennessee	500
Kentucky	500	Texas	No requirement
Louisiana	No requirement	Utah	500
Maine	500	Vermont	50
Maryland a	500	Virginia	No requirement
Massachusetts	500	Washington	50
Michigan b	500	West Virginia e	500
Minnesota	50	Wisconsin f	500
Mississippi	50	Wyoming	500
Missouri c	500		

a Prior requirement, $50.   b Effective January 1, 1964; $100 prior to that date.
c Effective July 1, 1965; $30 prior to that date.
d Effective January 2, 1965; $200 prior to that date.
e Effective July 1, 1964; no prior requirement.
f Effective July 1, 1965; $50 prior to that date.

Sec. 21-H. Nature of the Writing Required.

(1) Terms. The writing required by the Statute of Frauds provision of the Code need only give assurance that there was a sale.
Specifically it need only indicate that a sale or contract to sell has been
made and state the quantity of goods involved. Any other missing
terms, such as the price and time of delivery, may be shown by parol
evidence in the event of a dispute over the terms of the contract.[23]

(2) Signature. The writing must be signed by the person who is
being sued or his authorized agent. It may be signed by both parties,
but this is not required.

The signature must be placed on the writing with the intention
of authenticating the writing. It may be initials, printed, stamped,
or typewritten, as long as made with the necessary intent. In contrast,

---

[23] UCC Sec. 2-201(1). This contrasts with the interpretation given the Uniform Sales
Act under which the writing must state all material terms of the contract.

the mere fact that a writing contains an actual signature is not sufficient when the paper was merely signed for the purpose of identification or as an acknowledgment.

When the transaction is between merchants, the Code makes an exception to the requirement of signing. It provides that the failure of a merchant to repudiate a confirming letter sent him by another merchant binds him just as though he had signed the letter or other writing.[24] This ends the evil of a one-sided writing under which the sender of the letter was bound but the receiver could safely ignore the transaction or could hold the seller as he chose, depending upon which alternative gave him the better financial advantage.

(3) Time of Execution. A writing to satisfy the Statute of Frauds may be made at any time at or after the making of the sale. It may even be made after the contract has been broken or a suit brought on it, since the essential element is the existence of written proof of the transaction when the trial is held.

(4) Particular Writings. The writing which satisfies the Statute of Frauds may be a single writing or it may be several writings considered as a group. (See p. 329, Morris Furniture Co. v. Braverman) Formal contracts, bills of sale,[25] letters, and telegrams are common forms of writings that satisfy the Statute of Frauds. Purchase orders, cash register receipts, sales tickets, invoices, and similar papers generally do not satisfy the requirement as to a signature and sometimes they do not specify any quantity or commodity.

Sec. 21-I. Effect of Noncompliance. A sales agreement that does not comply with the statute is not enforceable by action nor can noncompliance be raised as a defense.[26] The defense that a sales contract does not satisfy the requirements of the Statute of Frauds may be waived and the contract then enforced as though the statute had been satisfied.

Sec. 21-J. When Proof of Oral Contract Permitted. In some instances the absence of a writing does not bar the proof of a sales contract.

(1) Receipt and Acceptance. An oral sales contract may be enforced if it can be shown that some of the goods were delivered by the seller and were received and accepted by the buyer.[27] Both a receipt and an acceptance by the buyer must be shown.

---

[24] Sec. 2-201(2). The confirming letter must be sent within a reasonable time after the transaction, and the receiving merchant must give written notice of his objection thereto within ten days after receiving the confirming letter.

[25] See p. 326.

[26] UCC Sec. 2-201(1), USA Sec. 4(1). Moreover, the contract itself is not unlawful and may be voluntarily performed by the parties.

[27] The contract may be enforced only in so far as it relates to the goods received and accepted. UCC Sec. 2-201(3)(c).

(2) Payment. An oral contract may be enforced if the buyer has made full or part payment on the contract.[28] There is some uncertainty in the law as to the effectiveness of a payment by check or a promissory note executed by the buyer. Under the law of commercial paper a check or note is conditional payment when delivered, and it does not become absolute until the instrument is paid. The earlier decisions held that the delivery of a negotiable instrument was not such a payment as would make the oral contract enforceable unless it was agreed at that time that the instrument was to be accepted as absolute and not conditional payment. A modern contrary view, which is influenced by the fact that businessmen ordinarily regard the delivery of a check or note as "payment," hold that the delivery of such an instrument is sufficient to make the oral contract enforceable.[29]

When the buyer has negotiated or assigned to the seller a negotiable instrument that was executed by a third person and the seller has accepted the instrument, a payment has been made within the meaning of the Statute of Frauds.

A check or promissory note that is tendered as payment but which is refused by the seller does not constitute a payment under the Statute of Frauds.

(3) Judicial Admission. No writing is required when the person alleged to have made the contract voluntarily admits in the course of legal proceedings that he has done so.

(4) Nonresellable Goods. No writing is required when the goods are specifically made for the buyer and are of such an unusual nature that they are not suitable for sale in the ordinary course of the seller's business. For this exception to apply, the seller must have made a substantial beginning in manufacturing the goods, or if he is a middleman, in procuring them, before receiving notice of an repudiation by the seller.[30]

Sec. 21-K. Bill of Sale. Regardless of the requirement of the Statute of Frauds, the parties may wish to execute a writing as evidence or proof of the sale. Through custom, this writing has become known as a *bill of sale.* It is not a bill or a contract. It is merely a receipt or writing signed by the seller in which he recites that he has transferred the title of the described property to the buyer.

---

[28] A contract may be enforced only with respect to goods for which payment has been made and accepted. UCC Sec. 2-201(3) (c).

[29] The Restatement of Contracts, Sec. 205, adopts this view. It would appear that the draftsmen of the Uniform Commercial Code are also in favor of this view, for the comment to Sec. 2-201 states that "part payment may be made by money or check, accepted by the seller."

[30] UCC Sec. 2-201(3) (a). The same exception is made by USA Sec. 4 (2) except that there is no requirement that the seller had begun the performance of the contract.

In many states provision is made for the public recording of bills of sale when goods are left in the seller's possession. In the case of the sale of certain types of property, a bill of sale may be required in order to show that the purchaser is the lawful owner. Thus some states require the production of a bill of sale before the title to an automobile will be registered in the name of the purchaser.

Cases for Chapter 21

Dibblee v. Dr. W. H. Groves Hospital

12 Utah 2d 241, 364 P.2d 1085 (1961)

Bowen, a patient in the Groves Hospital, was given a blood transfusion and died therefrom. It was admitted that there was no negligence, and independent tests made before and after the death established that the blood of the decedent and the blood given were compatible. Dibblee, the administrator of the estate of Bowen, sued the hospital on the theory that there was an implied sales warranty that the blood was fit for its intended purpose. The hospital defended on the ground that there had not been any "sale." From a judgment in its favor, Dibblee appealed.

HENRIOD, J. . . . Does a hospital, *free from negligence*, insure against negative results when it furnishes blood on proper order for transfusion into a patient.

Three cases and one statute have met this problem. All of them say no sale; . . . their upshot: That furnishing blood by a hospital at the specific request of a patient or his doctor, and for a charge, is a part of a *service*, not a *sale*. . . .

We find support in the California [statute]. There recently and in an obvious rejection of any idea that blood may be included in any expanded legislative inclusion of consumer goods as being subjects of insurism against negative consumer physical reaction, it was said, with no ambiguity, that "the procurement, processing, distribution, or use of whole blood, plasma, blood products, and blood derivatives for the purpose of injecting or transfusing the same, or any of them, into the human body" is *not a sale* but "*the rendition of a service*." To the . . . philosophy of this enactment we subscribe. . . .

We think of hospitals not as profit-seeking vendors in the market place as might be attributed to General Foods, General Motors, chain stores, super druggeries, national restaurants, or a cereal company that appeals to muscle-building qualities of its food. We do not say that hospitals should be immune from negligence. But we think they should not be strapped with an insurability of blood purity, absent negligence. . . .

The plaintiff, of necessity, must bottom his claim of recovery on some kind of kinship between a hospital furnishing blood and the commercial enterprise that beseeches the public to buy its products, in preference to its competitors. No hospital gives green trading stamps on the occasion of a blood transfusion as some commodity vendors do, or a car for one having the lucky blood purchase order number. We know of none that fills out forms under any Fair Trade or Unfair Competition Act, U.C.A. 1953, 13-4-1 et seq., 13-5-1 et seq. We are not aware of any that pays a sales tax on furnishing blood, or has a sales or advertising agent, telecasts with commercials, billboard bits of art, health suggestions, or muscle-building come-ons incident to a "sale." . . .

[Judgment affirmed.]

Code Comment: The same decision would be made under the Code. Although a literal application of the definition of "goods," see Sec. 2-105 (1), would result in a contrary conclusion, the same is true of a literal construction of "goods" as used in the Uniform Sales Act. The same social considerations that persuaded the court in the reported case would undoubtedly persuade a court to interpret the Code in the same way.

Berger v. Berger
271 Wis. 292, 73 N.W.2d 503 (1955)

Berger, who owned and operated a tavern, sold the property and the business to Drews. The sale included the fixtures in the tavern. Two weeks after the sale, Berger signed papers to comply with the Bulk Sales Act. Creditors of Berger claimed that the sale was void as to them because the Bulk Sales Act had not been satisfied. Drews claimed that the act did not apply to the sale of fixtures and that in any event the act had been satisfied. From a judgment in favor of the creditors, Drews appealed.

BROADFOOT, J. . . . The appellant [Drews] contends that . . . the bulk sales law . . . does not apply to the sale of [tavern] fixtures. . . . The appellant cites cases from other jurisdictions where the statutes do not seem to be identical in wording with our own. Our own statute is very comprehensive. It refers to the sale of any stock of goods, wares, and merchandise, or of the fixtures pertaining to the same, or of such goods, wares, and merchandise and fixtures. Thus it applies to the sale of merchandise alone, to the sale of fixtures pertaining to a stock of merchandise, or to a sale of both in combination. These fixtures had pertained to and were used for the sale of merchandise before the sale, and they were bought to pertain to and to be used in the sale of merchandise after the transfer. From the language of our particular statute we are compelled to say that the bulk sales law does apply to the sale of the tavern fixtures under the circumstances here presented.

The appellant's last contention is that there was a substantial compliance with the statute. . . . [The trial court] found as a fact not only that the appellant purchased the fixtures on July 1, 1953, but that he took possession thereof on the same date. Therefore the attempted compliance with the bulk sales law on July 13 did not meet the requirements of the law. . . .

[Judgment affirmed.]

Code Comment: The same decision would be made as to the first point, for the Code treats equipment as subject to the bulk transfer article when made in connection with a bulk transfer of inventory. Sec. 6-102 (2). The Code also requires compliance not less than ten days before the buyer takes possession or makes payment. Sec. 6-105.

Morris Furniture Co. v. Braverman
210 Iowa 946, 230 N.W. 356 (1930)

Braverman gave the Morris Furniture Co. an unsigned written order for furniture. A few days later he wrote a signed letter asking the seller to "hold out order of Sept. 17 until we give you further notice." When the goods were shipped, the buyer refused to accept and pay for them. In an action brought by the seller against the buyer to recover the agreed price, the defendant contended that the contract was unenforceable because of the Statute of Frauds. From a judgment for the plaintiff, the defendant appealed.

WAGNER, J. . . . In order to take the case without the Statute of Frauds it is not necessary that the contract be signed by the party to be charged but only that some note or memorandum in writing of the contract be signed by the party to be charged. The note or memorandum is required only as evidence of the contract and not to constitute it. Neither is it necessary that the note or memorandum should have been signed by the party to be charged with the intent to comply with the statute. . . . "The note or memorandum required by the Statute of Frauds need not be contained in a single document nor, when contained in two or more papers, need each paper be sufficient in contents and signature to satisfy the statute. Two or more writings properly connected may be considered together, matters missing or uncertain in one may be supplied or rendered certain by the other, and their sufficiency will depend upon whether, taken together, they meet the requirements of the statute as to contents and signature. The rule is frequently applied to two or more, or a series of, letters or telegrams, or letters and telegrams sufficiently connected to allow their consideration together. But the rule is not confined in its application to letters and telegrams; any other documents can be read together when one refers to the other. . . . The rule has been applied so as to allow the consideration together, when properly connected, of a letter . . . and an order for goods. . . . Matters not contained in one paper, or not stated therein with sufficient definiteness and certainty, . . . are frequently found to be adequately stated in another paper which is sufficiently connected with the former paper to justify their consideration together.". . .

In the instant case, the letter of September 25 in unmistakable language refers to "our order of September 17th." The order of September 17 was in writing and contained the prices and all the terms relative to the sale. There is in the subsequent letter of September 25 internal reference to the only order given by the appellant on September 17. Clearly, the letter of September 25, which is signed by the appellant, the party to be charged, and which unmistakably refers to the order of September 17, constitutes a memorandum sufficient within the meaning of the law to take the contract without the Statute of Frauds. . . .

[Judgment for plaintiff affirmed.]

Code Comment: The same decision would be made under the Code. Although there is no express provision on the subject in the Code, the same practical considerations which led to the conclusion that all writings should be combined for the purpose of satisfying the Uniform Sales Act will lead to the same conclusion under the Code.

Questions and Case Problems

1. What is the objective of each of the following rules of law?

(a) A "cost plus" contract is valid even though at the time it is made the exact price cannot be known.

(b) A writing that satisfies the requirements of a Statute of Frauds may ordinarily be executed at any time.

2. Stone agreed that he would aid Krylon, Inc. in developing a product, in return for which the corporation would grant him an exclusive agency to sell certain goods. Was this a sales contract? (Stone v. Krylon, Inc., [D.C. Pa.] 141 F.Supp. 785)

3. Knox ordered goods from the Elray Tool & Die Corp. The goods were received and accepted by Knox, but at no time was anything agreed as to the price for the goods. Was there a binding sales contract? (Elray Tool & Die Corp. v. Knox, [Pa.] 68 Dauphin Co. 7)

4. Williamson sold two milk vats for $1,600 to Martz who made a down payment of $100. There was no writing to show that the contract had been made. Martz later refused to take the vats. Was he liable for breach of contract? (Williamson v. Martz, [Pa.] 11 D.&C.2d 33, 19 Montg.Leg.Reg. 24, 29 Northum.Leg.J. 32)

5. The Rock Springs Commercial Co. sold and delivered grapes and barrels to Perko. Later it sued him for the purchase price. Perko defended on the ground that the sale was void because the seller knew at the time of the transaction that Perko intended to use the goods to make liquor in violation of the law. Was Rock Springs entitled to recover the purchase price? (Perko v. Rock Springs Commercial Co., 37 Wyo. 98, 259 P. 520)

6. Crocker printed and distributed Christmas cards. At certain intervals such cards which could not be sold would be destroyed. Crocker's employees took a large quantity of Christmas cards for that purpose to McFaddin who ran a dump and salvage operation. Persons bringing material to McFaddin would pay one fee for material that could be salvaged by him and a higher fee if instructions were given to destroy the material. When Crocker's employees took the Christmas cards to McFaddin, nothing was said as to the disposition to be made of them and only a salvage fee was paid. Later, Crocker learned that McFaddin had resold the cards. He sued McFaddin, claiming that McFaddin could not make such a sale because the transaction between Crocker and McFaddin was a bailment. McFaddin defended on the ground that the transaction was a sale, an abandonment, or a gift, and that in any instance McFaddin could sell the property and otherwise treat it as his own. Decide. (H. S. Crocker Co. v. McFaddin, [Cal.App.2d] 307 P.2d 429)

7. Suburban Gas Heat of Kennewick sold propane gas for domestic consumption. As the result of its negligence in supplying propane gas mixed with water, there was an explosion which caused damage to Kasey. When Kasey sued to enforce the liability of Suburban Gas Heat as a seller, Suburban raised the defense that it was engaged in furnishing a public service and not in the sale of personal property within the meaning of the Uniform Sales Act. Was Suburban correct? (Kasey v. Suburban Gas Heat of Kennewick, Inc., [Wash.] 374 P.2d 549)

8. Members of the Colonial Club purchased beer from outside the state and ordered it sent to the Colonial Club. The club then kept it in the club refrigerator and served the beer to its respective owners upon demand. The club received no compensation or profit from the transaction. The club was indicted for selling liquor unlawfully. Decide. (North Carolina v. Colonial Club, 154 N.C. 177, 69 S.E. 771)

9. Property of Harrison was sold at an auction to Wright. The auctioneer gave the purchaser a memorandum reciting the making of the sale. Harrison later claimed that the sale was void because he had not executed any memorandum of the sale. Decide. (Wright v. Harrison, 137 Tenn. 157, 192 S.W. 716)

10. Because of the fraudulent statements of the seller's agent, Wachtman was induced to subscribe in writing to a food distribution plan operated by Derran. Derran claimed that the parol evidence rule barred Wachtman from proving the agent's oral fraudulent statements. Was Derran correct? (Wachtman v. Derran Food Plan, [Pa.] 71 Dauphin Co. 121)

11. The Smith Co. made a contract to sell beet pulp in bags of 88 pounds each to the Southern Flour & Grain Co. A Georgia statute stated that "all concentrated commercial feeding stuff shall be in standard weight bags or packages of 50, 75, 100, 125, 150, or 200 pounds each." Violation of this statute was punishable by a fine or imprisonment, or both. The flour company refused to take the goods, and the seller brought an action to recover damages. Decide. (Southern Flour & Grain Co. v. Smith, 31 Ga.App. 52, 120 S.E. 36)

CHAPTER 22

Title and Risk in Sales Contracts

In the great majority of sales transactions the buyer receives the proper goods, makes payment, and the transaction is thus completed. The following problems, however, may arise:

(1) Creditors of the seller may seize the goods as belonging to the seller, or the buyer's creditors may seize them on the theory that they belong to the buyer. In such cases the question arises whether the creditors are correct as to who owns the goods. The question of ownership is also important in connection with the consequence of a resale by the buyer, of liability for or computation of certain kinds of taxes, and liability under certain registration and criminal statutes.[1]

(2) Until the buyer has received the goods and the seller has been paid, both the seller and buyer have an economic interest in the sales transaction.[2] The question arises as to whether either or both have enough interest to entitle them to insure the property involved, that is, whether they have an insurable interest.[3]

(3) If the goods are damaged or totally destroyed without any fault of either the buyer or the seller, must the seller bear the loss and supply new goods to the buyer; or is it the buyer's loss, so that he must pay the seller the purchase price even though he now has no goods or damaged goods?[4]

For the most part, these types of problems can be avoided if the parties by their sales contract or agreement make express provision. When the parties have not by their contract specified what results they desire, however, the following rules are applied by the law.

---

[1] Uniform Commercial Code, Sec. 2-401.
[2] UCC Sec. 2-501(1)(a).
[3] To insure property, a person must have such a right or interest in the property that its damage or destruction would cause him financial loss. When he would be so affected, he is said to have an insurable interest in the property. See Chapter 59.
[4] UCC Sec. 2-509.

Sec. 22-A. Nature of the Transaction. The answer to be given to each of the three preceding questions depends upon the nature of the transaction between the seller and the buyer. Sales transactions may be classified according to (1) the nature of the goods and (2) the terms of the transaction.

(1) Nature of Goods. The goods may be *existing goods,* which means that they are physically in existence and are owned by the seller. It is immaterial whether the existing goods are in the condition required by the contract or whether the seller must do some act or complete the manufacture of the goods before they satisfy the terms of the contract.[5]

In addition to existing goods, there are the classifications of identified goods and future goods. The seller and buyer may have agreed which goods are to be received by the buyer, or the seller may have picked out the goods. When such a selection has been made, the goods are described as *identified goods.*[6] If the goods are not both existing and identified at the time of the transaction, they are *future goods.*[7]

(2) Terms of the Transaction. The terms of the contract may obligate the seller to deliver the goods at a particular place, for example, to make delivery at destination. In contrast, the contract may only require that the goods be sent or shipped to the buyer, that is, that the seller make shipment. Under the latter contract, the seller's part is performed when he hands over the goods to a carrier for shipment to the buyer; as contrasted with the delivery at a destination provision, under which the seller's part of the contract is not completed until the goods are brought to the destination point and there tendered to the buyer. Ordinarily only delivery to the carrier is required in the absence of an express requirement of delivery at destination.

Instead of calling for the actual delivery of goods, the transaction may relate to a transfer of the document of title representing the goods. For example, the goods may be stored in a warehouse, the seller and the buyer having no intention of moving the goods, but intending that there should be a sale and a delivery of the warehouse receipt that stands for the goods. Here the obligation of the seller is to produce the proper paper as distinguished from the goods themselves. The same is true when the goods are represented by a bill of lading issued by a carrier or by any other document of title.

As a third type of situation, the goods may be stored with, or held by, a third person who has not issued any document of title for the goods, but the seller and buyer intend that the goods shall remain

---

[5] Under the USA, goods that could be delivered under the terms of a contract, in that they satisfied all its terms, were described as in a deliverable condition. Goods that did not meet the contract terms were described as in a nondeliverable condition.

[6] Such goods are comparable to specific goods under the Uniform Sales Act.

[7] Such goods are generally described as unascertained goods under the USA.

Transfer of Title, Special Property Interests, and Risk Under the Code

Fact Situation / Problem	Transfer of Title	Transfer of Special Property Interests	Transfer of Risk of Loss Without Breach
(1) Existing goods identified at time of contracting	Time and place of contracting. Sec. 2-401 (3) (b)	Time and place of contracting. Sec. 2-501 (1) (a)	Receipt of goods from merchant seller; tender of goods by nonmerchant seller. Sec. 2-509 (3)
(2) Delivery of documents of title only	Time and place of delivery of documents. Sec. 2-401 (3) (a)	Time and place of contracting. Sec. 2-501 (1) (a)	Receipt of negotiable document of title. Sec. 2-509 (2) (a)
(3) Acknowledgment by bailee	Time and place of contracting. Sec. 2-401 (3) (b)	Time and place of contracting. Sec. 2-501 (1) (a)	Time of bailee's acknowledgment of buyer's right. Sec. 2-509 (2) (b)
(4) Marking future goods for buyer	No transfer	At time of such act. Sec. 2-501 (1) (b)	No transfer
(5) Shipping contract for future goods	Time and place of shipment. Sec. 2-401 (2) (a)	Time and place of shipment. Sec. 2-501 (1) (b)	Delivery to carrier. Sec. 2-509 (1) (a)
(6) Delivery-at-destination contract for future goods	Tender at destination. Sec. 2-401 (2) (b)	Time and place of shipment. Sec. 2-501 (1) (b)	Tender at destination. Sec. 2-509 (1) (b)

in that bailee's hands, the transaction being completed without any delivery of the goods themselves or of any document.

Sec. 22-B. Title and Risk in Particular Transactions. The various kinds of goods and transaction terms may be combined in a number of ways. Only the more common types of transactions will be considered.[8] Keep in mind that the following rules of law apply only in the absence of an agreement by the parties concerning these matters.

(1) Existing Goods Identified at Time of Contracting, Without Documents. The title to such goods passes to the buyer at the time and place of contracting. (See p. 343, Moffitt v. Hieby) Since the buyer becomes the owner of the goods,[9] he has an insurable interest in them. Conversely, the seller no longer has an insurable interest unless he has reserved a security interest to protect his right to payment.[10]

If the seller is a merchant, the risk of loss passes to the buyer when he receives the goods from the merchant; if a nonmerchant seller, when the seller tenders or makes available the goods to the buyer. Thus the risk of loss remains longer on the merchant seller, a distinction which is made on the ground that the merchant seller, being in the business, can more readily protect himself against such continued risk.

(2) Negotiable Documents Representing Existing Goods Identified at Time of Contracting. Here the buyer has a property interest, but not title, and an insurable interest in the goods at the time and place of contracting; but he does not ordinarily acquire the title nor become subject to the risk of loss until he receives delivery of the documents.[11] Conversely, the seller has an insurable interest and title up to that time.

(3) Existing Goods, Identified at Time of Contracting, Held by Bailee, Without Documents. Here the goods owned by the seller are held by a warehouseman, garageman, repairman, or other bailee, but there is no document of title and the sales contract does not call for a physical delivery of the goods, the parties intending that the goods should remain where they are. In such a case the answers to the various problems are the same as case (1) above except that the risk

---

[8] This discussion and the balance of the text of this chapter are based upon the UCC. In many of the situations discussed, the same or nearly the same result would be reached under the USA. The changes introduced by the Code have in general been directed at affording the buyer greater protection, particularly when dealing with a merchant seller, or of stating the rules of law in terms of the actual commercial practices which exist today.

[9] This is the counterpart of specific goods in a deliverable condition under the USA.

[10] Secured transactions are discussed in Chapter 34.

[11] Express provision is made for the case of a nonnegotiable document and other factual variations. UCC Sec. 2-509 (2) (c), Sec. 2-503(4). When delivery of documents is to be made, the seller may send the documents through customary banking channels as well as make a tender in person or by an agent. Sec. 2-503(5)(b).

of loss does not pass to the buyer, but remains with the seller, until the bailee acknowledges that he is now holding the goods in question for the buyer.

(4) Seller's Marking Future Goods for Buyer. If the buyer sends an order for goods to be manufactured by the seller or to be filled by him from inventory or by purchases from third persons, one step in the process of filling the order is the seller's act of marking, tagging, labeling, or in some way doing an act for the benefit of his shipping department or for himself to indicate that certain goods are the ones to be sent or delivered to the buyer under the contract. This act of unilateral identification of the goods is enough to give the buyer a property interest in the goods and gives him the right to insure them.[12] However, neither title nor risk of loss passes to the buyer at that time but remains with the seller who, as the continuing owner, also has an insurable interest in the goods. Thus no title, interest, or liability passes to the buyer until some other event, such as a shipment or delivery, occurs.

(5) Shipping Contract for Future Goods. In this situation the buyer has placed an order for goods that will be shipped to him later, and the contract is performed by the seller when he delivers the goods to a carrier for shipment to the buyer. (See p. 344, Storz Brewing Co. v. Brown) Under such a contract the title and risk of loss pass to the buyer when the goods are delivered to the carrier, that is, at the time and place of shipment, at which time he also acquires an insurable interest in them. The seller then has no insurable interest unless he has reserved a security interest in the goods.[13]

The fact that a shipment of goods is represented by a bill of lading or an airbill issued by the carrier, and that in order to complete the transaction it will be necessary to transfer that bill to the buyer, does not affect these rules or bring the transaction within case (2).

(6) Destination Delivery of Future Goods. When the contract requires the seller to make delivery at a particular destination point, the buyer acquires a property right and an insurable interest in the goods at the time and place of delivery to the carrier; but the risk of loss and the title do not pass until the carrier tenders or makes the goods available at the destination point. The seller retains an insurable interest until that time; and if he has a security interest in the goods, he continues to retain that interest until the purchase price has been paid.

---

[12] Sec. 2-501(1)(b). Special provision is made as to crops and unborn young animals. Sec. 2-501(1)(c).

[13] The reservation of a security interest by the seller does not affect the transfer of the risk to the buyer.

Sec. 22-C. Damage or Destruction of Goods.

(1) Damage to Identified Goods Before Risk of Loss Passes. When goods that were identified at the time the contract was made suffer some damage without the fault of either party before the risk of loss has passed, the contract is avoided if the loss is total. If the loss is partial or if the goods have so deteriorated that they do not conform to the contract, the buyer has the option, after inspection of the goods, (a) to treat the contract as avoided, or (b) to accept the goods subject to an allowance or deduction from the contract price. In either case, the buyer cannot assert any claim against the seller for breach of contract.[14]

(2) Damage to Identified Goods After Risk of Loss Passes. If partial damage or total destruction occurs after the risk of loss has passed, it is the buyer's loss. It may be, however, that the buyer will be able to recover the amount of the damages from the person in possession of the goods or from a third person causing the loss. To illustrate, in many instances the risk of loss passes at the time of the transaction even though the seller is to deliver the goods later. During the period from the transfer of the risk of loss to the transfer of possession to the buyer, the seller has the status of a bailee of the goods and is liable to the buyer under the circumstances for which an ordinary bailee would be liable.

(3) Damage to Unidentified Goods. So long as the goods are unidentified, no risk of loss has passed to the buyer. If any goods are damaged or destroyed during this period, it is the loss of the seller. The buyer is still entitled to receive the goods for which he contracted. If the seller fails to deliver the goods, he is liable to the purchaser for the breach of his contract. The only exception arises when the parties have expressly provided in the contract that destruction of the seller's supply shall be deemed a release of the seller's liability or when it is clear that the parties contracted for the purchase and sale of part of the seller's supply to the exclusion of any other possible source of such goods.

(4) Reservation of Title or Possession. When the seller reserves title or possession solely as security to make certain that he will be paid, the risk of loss is borne by the buyer if the circumstances are such that he would bear the loss in the absence of such reservation.

In any of the preceding situations, the parties may by their agreement shift or divide the risk so as to change the result specified by the Code.[15]

---

[14] UCC Sec. 2-613.
[15] Sec. 2-303.

Sec. 22-D. Sales on Approval and with Right to Return. A sales transaction may give the buyer the privilege of returning the goods. In a *sale on approval*, the sale is not complete until the buyer approves. A *sale or return* is a completed sale with the right of the buyer to return the goods and thereby set aside the sale. The agreement of the parties determines whether the sale is on approval or with return; but if they have failed to indicate their intention, it is deemed a sale on approval if the goods are purchased for use, that is, by a consumer, and a sale or return, if purchased for resale, that is, by a merchant.[16]

(1) Consequence of Sale on Approval. In the absence of a contrary agreement, title and risk of loss remain with the seller under a sale on approval. Use of the goods by the buyer consistent with the purpose of trial is not an election or approval by him. There is an approval, however, if he acts in a manner that is not consistent with a reasonable trial, or if he fails to express his choice within the time specified or within a reasonable time if no time is specified. If the goods are returned, the seller bears the risk and the expense involved.[17] Since the buyer is not the "owner" of the goods while they are on approval, his creditors cannot reach them.[18]

(2) Consequence of Sale or Return. In a sale or return, title and risk of loss pass to the buyer as in the case of an ordinary or absolute sale. In the absence of a contrary agreement, the buyer under a sale or return may return all of the goods or any commercial unit thereof. A *commercial unit* is any article, group of articles, or quantity which commercially is regarded as a separate unit or item, as a particular machine, a suite of furniture, or a carload lot.[19] The goods must still be in substantially their original condition, and the option to return must be exercised within the time specified by the contract or within a reasonable time if none is specified. The return under such a contract is at the buyer's risk and expense.[20] As long as the goods are in the buyer's possession under a sale or return contract, his creditors may treat the goods as belonging to him.[21]

Sec. 22-E. Sale of Fungible Goods. *Fungible goods* are goods of a homogeneous nature that may be sold by weight or measure. They are goods of which any unit is from its nature or by commercial usage treated as the equivalent of any other unit.[22] Wheat, oil, coal, and

---

16 Sec. 2-326 (1). An "or return" provision is treated as a sales contract for the purpose of applying the Statute of Frauds, and cannot be established by parol evidence when it would contradict a sales contract indicating an absolute sale. Sec. 2-326(4).
17 Sec. 2-327(1).
18 Sec. 2-326(2).
19 Sec. 2-105 (6).
20 Sec. 2-327 (2).
21 Sec. 2-326(2).
22 UCC Sec. 1-201(17), USA Sec. 76.

similar bulk commodities are fungible goods since, given a mass of the same grade or uniformity, any one bushel or other unit of the mass will be exactly the same as any other bushel or similar unit.

Title to an undivided share or quantity of an identified mass of fungible goods may pass to the buyer at the time of the transaction making the buyer an owner in common with the seller.[23] For example, when a person sells to another 600 bushels of wheat from his bin which contains 1,000 bushels, title to 600 bushels may pass to the buyer at the time of the transaction, making him a 6/10ths co-owner of the mass. The courts in some states, however, hold that the title does not pass until a separation has been made.

Sec. 22-F. Sale of Undivided Shares. The problem of the passage of title to a part of a larger mass of fungible goods is distinct from the problem of the passage of title when the sale is made of a fractional interest without any intention to make a later separation. In the former case the buyer is to become the exclusive owner of a separated portion. In the latter case he is to become the co-owner of the entire mass. Thus there may be a sale of a part interest in a radio, an automobile, or a flock of sheep. The right to make a sale of a fractional interest is recognized by statute.[24]

Sec. 22-G. Auction Sales. When goods are sold at an auction in separate lots, each lot is a separate transaction, and title to each lot passes independently of the other lots.[25] Title to each lot passes when the auctioneer announces by the fall of the hammer or in any other customary manner that the auction is completed as to that lot.[26]

Sec. 22-H. Reservation of a Security Interest. The seller may fear that the buyer will not pay for the goods. The seller could protect himself by insisting that the buyer pay cash immediately. This may not be pratical for geographic or business reasons. The seller may then retain a security interest in the goods by entering into a secured transaction.[27]

(1) Form of Bill of Lading. The seller may retain varying degrees of control over the goods by the method of shipment. Thus he may send the goods to himself in the buyer's city, receiving from the carrier the bill of lading for the goods.[28] In such a case, the buyer cannot

---

[23] UCC Sec. 2-105(4).
[24] UCC Sec. 2-403(1), USA Sec. 6(1).
[25] UCC Sec. 2-328 (1), USA Sec. 21 (1).
[26] UCC Sec. 2-328(2), USA Sec. 21(2).
[27] As to the security transactions under the Code, see Chapter 34. As to other security devices, see Chapter 35.
[28] UCC Sec. 2-505.

obtain the goods from the carrier since the shipment is not directed to him, in the case of a straight bill of lading, or because he does not hold the bill of lading, if it is a negotiable or order bill. Conversely, the seller's agent in the buyer's city can arrange for or obtain payment from the buyer and then give him the documents necessary to obtain the goods from the carrier.

If the goods are sent by carrier under a negotiable bill of lading to the order of the buyer or his agent, the seller may also retain the right of possession of the goods by keeping possession of the bill of lading until he receives payment.[29]

(2) C.O.D. Shipment. In the absence of an extension of credit a seller has the right to keep the goods until paid, but he loses his right if he delivers possession of the goods to anyone for the buyer. However, where the goods are delivered to a carrier, the seller may preserve his right to possession by making the shipment C.O.D., or by the addition of any other terms indicating an intention that the carrier should not surrender the goods to the buyer until the buyer has made payment. Such a provision has no effect other than to keep the buyer from obtaining possession until he has made payment. The C.O.D. provision does not affect the problem of determining whether title has passed.

Sec. 22-I. Effect of Sale on Title. As a general rule, a person can sell only such interest or title in goods as he possesses. If the property is subject to a bailment, a sale by the bailor is subject to the bailment. Similarly, the bailee can only transfer his right under the bailment, assuming that the bailment agreement permits his right to be assigned or transferred. The fact that the bailee is in possession does not give him the right to transfer the bailor's title.

Moreover, a thief or finder generally cannot transfer the title to property since he can only pass that which he has, namely the possession but not the title. In fact, the purchaser from the thief not only fails to obtain title but also becomes liable to the owner as a converter of the property even though he made the purchase from the thief in good faith.

There are certain instances, however, when either because of the conduct of the owner or the desire of society to protect the bona fide purchaser for value, the law permits a greater title to be transferred than the seller possessed.

(1) Sale by Entrustee. If the owner entrusts his goods to a merchant who deals in goods of that kind, the latter has the power to transfer the entruster's title to anyone who buys from him in the ordinary

---

[29] UCC Sec. 2-505 (1) (a), USA Sec. 20(3).

course of business. (See p. 345, Al's Auto Sales Case) It is immaterial why the goods were entrusted to the merchant. Hence the leaving of a watch for repairs with a jeweler who sells new and secondhand watches would give the jeweler the power to pass the title to a buyer in the ordinary course of business.[30]

(2) Consignment Sales. A manufacturer or distributor may send goods to a dealer for sale to the public with the understanding that the manufacturer or distributor is to remain the owner and the dealer in effect is to act as his agent. When the dealer maintains a place of business at which he deals in goods of the kind in question under a name other than that of the consigning manufacturer or distributor, the creditors of the dealer may reach the goods as though they were owned by him.[31]

(3) Estoppel. The owner of property may estop himself from asserting that he is the owner and denying the right of another person to sell the property. A person may purchase a product and have the bill of sale made out in the name of a friend to whom he then gives possession of the product and the bill of sale. He might do so in order to deceive his own creditors or to keep other persons from knowing that he made the purchase. If the friend should sell the product to a bona fide purchaser who relies on the bill of sale as showing that the friend was the owner, the true owner is estopped or barred from denying the friend's apparent ownership or his authority to sell.

(4) Powers. In certain circumstances, by common law or statute, persons in possession of someone else's property may sell the property. This arises in the case of pledgees,[32] lienholders, and, in some instances, finders who are given authority to sell the property either to enforce their claim or when the true owner cannot be found.

(5) Documents of Title. By statute, certain documents of title, such as bills of lading and warehouse receipts, have been clothed with a quality of negotiability when executed in proper form.[33] By virtue of such provisions, whoever is in possession of a negotiable document of title may transfer title to the property to a purchaser for value acting in good faith. In such cases it is immaterial that the seller was not the lawful owner of the document of title.

(6) Recording and Filing Statutes. In order to protect subsequent purchasers and creditors, statutes may require that certain transactions

---

[30] UCC Sec. 2-403 (2), (3).

[31] Sec. 2-326(3). The manufacturer or dealer may protect himself from this result by entering into a secured transaction agreement or by complying with any local statute that protects him in such case. Sec. 2-326(3).

[32] See p. 549.

[33] UCC Sec. 7-502 (2), USA Secs. 27 to 40.

be recorded or filed and may provide that if that is not done, the transaction has no effect against a purchaser who thereafter buys the goods in good faith from the person who appears to be the owner or against the execution creditors of such an apparent owner. Thus if a seller retains a security interest in the goods sold to the buyer but fails to file a financing statement in the manner required by the Code, the purchaser appears to be the owner of the goods free of any security interest and subsequent bona fide purchasers or creditors of the buyer can acquire title from him free of the vendor's security interest.[34]

(7) Voidable Title. If the buyer has a voidable title, as when he obtained the goods by fraud, the seller can rescind the sale while the buyer is still the owner. If, however, the buyer resells the property to a bona fide purchaser before the seller has rescinded the transaction, the subsequent purchaser acquires valid title.[35] It is immaterial whether the buyer having the voidable title had obtained title by fraud as to his identity, or by larceny by trick, or that he had paid for the goods with a bad check, or that the transaction was a cash sale and the purchase price had not been paid.[36]

(8) Goods Retained by the Seller. When the seller after making the sale is permitted to retain possession of the goods, he has the power to transfer the title to a buyer in the ordinary course of business. Such permitted retention is an entrusting within the sale by entrustee rule described in (1) above. The purpose of this provision is to protect the second purchaser from the claim of the first purchaser, on the ground that the second had the right to rely on the apparent ownership of his seller.

(a) PROTECTION OF THE SELLER. As will be discussed in connection with the remedies of the parties, a seller who is lawfully in possession of property that he has sold may resell it to a second purchaser if the first purchaser is in default in the payment of the purchase price. Here the object of the statute is not to protect the second purchaser but to enable the seller to remedy the situation created by the first purchaser's default.

(b) PROTECTION OF CREDITORS OF THE SELLER. The continued possession of goods by the seller after their sale is generally deemed evidence that the sale was a fraud upon creditors, that is, that the sale was not a bona fide actual transfer of title but was merely a device to place the title out of the reach of the creditors of the seller. When the sale is fraudulent by local law, the Code provides that creditors of the seller may treat the sale as void and may have the

---

34 See p. 339.
35 UCC Sec. 2-403(1). See also USA Sec. 24.
36 UCC Sec. 2-403(1)(a) to (d).

property put up for sale on execution as though the property still belonged to the seller. However, the retention of possession by a merchant seller is declared not fraudulent when made in good faith in the current course of business and when it does not exceed a period of time which is commercially reasonable.[37] For example, the fact that the merchant retains possession until means for transporting the goods to the buyer can be arranged is not fraudulent as to the creditors of the seller.

Cases for Chapter 22

Moffitt v. Hieby

149 Tex. 161, 229 S.W.2d 1005 (1950)

Mrs. Hieby sold growing grapefruit to Moffitt. The written contract specified: "All terms of this agreement have been reduced to writing herein." The contract provided for the harvesting of the crop nine weeks later and stated: "Seller agrees that if harvesting is paid by buyer, it is to be charged to seller's account." The crop was damaged by the failure of Mrs. Hieby to care for and water the orchards after making the sale. Moffitt refused to take the grapefruit. Mrs. Hieby sued him for damages for the breach of the contract. From a judgment for the plaintiff, the defendant appealed.

HARVEY, J. . . . The agreement entered into by the parties appears on its face to be an executed contract. . . .

Inasmuch as title to the grapefruit on the trees passed to the buyer as of the date of the contract, with a consequent delivery thereof made in the orchards, and there was nothing on the part of the seller that remained to be done in the matter, there was no implied obligation on the part of the seller to water the orchards or perform any other act with reference thereto. Had the parties so desired and had so agreed, it would have been quite easy for them to have inserted a stipulation in the contract to the effect that the seller should do whatever might have been deemed advisable under the circumstances with reference to the care to be taken of the orchards, as well as in regard to any other matters. This they did not do, and there is no occasion for the courts to add to the contract as made by them. . . .

[Judgment for plaintiff affirmed.]

HART, J. (dissenting) . . . The defendants pleaded that the breach of the implied obligation of the plaintiff to care for the orchards, resulting in the failure of the fruit to reach normal or full size, was a material breach of the contract which released the defendants from the obligation to harvest and pay for the fruit. . . .

---

[37] Sec. 2-402 (2).

Assuming the facts to be as pleaded and testified to by the defendants and their witnesses, an obligation should be implied in fact that the seller would, after the date of the contract, with reasonable diligence and prudence continue to water and otherwise properly care for the orchards so that the fruit would attain the size and quality which would normally be expected. Otherwise, it seems apparent that the intention of the parties would not be accomplished but, on the other hand, would be defeated. The contract discloses on its face that the buyer would be permitted a period of more than two months in which to gather the fruit and that the seller would pay the expense of harvesting. Aside from their right to enter the orchards for the purpose of gathering the fruit, the buyers were given no control over the orchards; and it would follow that if the trees were to be watered and otherwise cared for, this would have to be done by the seller. Regardless of whether, as a matter of law, the title to the grapefruit had passed to the buyers, the seller, since she remained in charge of the orchards, should be under an obligation implied in fact (assuming the defendant's testimony to be true) to care for the orchards so that the fruit would normally develop and not be rendered unfit for the purposes for which the defendant's were buying it.

Code Comment: The same decision and the same dissent would be made under the Code since there is no direct provision in point.

Storz Brewing Co. v. Brown

154 Neb. 204, 47 N.W.2d 407 (1951)

Brown was a local distributor for the Storz Brewing Company. Under the distribution contract, sales were made at prices set by the company "all f.o.b. Storz Brewing Company's plant, from which shipment is made. . . . Distributor agrees . . . to pay all freight and transportation charges from Storz Brewing Company's place of business or to the delivery point designated by the distributor and all delivery expenses." Brown wrote the company to deliver a quantity of beer to a trucker by the name of Steinhaus as soon as the latter would accept the goods. The company delivered the goods to Steinhaus. Snow delayed the transportation and caused the beer to freeze. Brown rejected the beer and was sued by the company for the purchase price. From a judgment for the defendant, the plaintiff appealed.

WENKE, J. . . . This agreement, taken as a whole, provides that prices and shipments are f.o.b. the appellant's [company's] plant. Any order by the appellee [Brown] thereunder would be on that basis unless a contrary intent is shown as having been understood and agreed to by the parties at the time the order was given, accepted, and filled. . . .

"The letters 'f.o.b.' are an abbreviation of the words 'free on board' and, standing alone in a contract of sale, they simply mean that the subject of the sale is to be loaded for shipment without expense to the buyer. . . . However, if delivery is made by carrier, unless a contrary intent appears, the place of shipment is ordinarily considered the place of delivery. . . .

". . . The universal holding of the courts is that where the contract between the vendor and vendee is silent upon the subject of the place of delivery, the delivery of the property by the vendor to a carrier, for transportation to the vendee, of itself then and there divests the vendor's title to the property, and the vendee's title to such property, from the moment of such delivery to the carrier, attaches. . . . In such case the carrier is, in contemplation of law, the bailee of the person to whom and not by whom the goods are sent.". . .

"Where the goods are lost or destroyed after they have been delivered to the buyer with the intention of passing the title to the buyer, the loss must fall upon the buyer. . . . So, where delivery to a carrier is delivery to the buyer and passes title to him at the place of shipment, the risk of loss or injury after such delivery is on the buyer.". . .

From an examination of the record we find nothing upon which a jury could base its verdict that the parties, by what was done, intended any departure from the general rule that delivery to the carrier was to be considered as delivery to the buyer with the resulting effect that the title to the products passed to appellee immediately therewith. This being true, it was prejudicial error to submit such issue to the jury.

[Judgment for defendant reversed and new trial ordered.]

Code Comment: The same conclusion would be reached under the Code although the analysis would be based on transfer of risk of loss rather than transfer of title. In view of the fact that the contract was f.o.b. the seller's plant, the delivery point is the plant, and the risk of loss passes to the buyer when the goods are delivered to the carrier. UCC Secs. 2-319 (1) (a), 2-509 (1) (a).

Al's Auto Sales v. Moskowitz

203 Okla. 611, 224 P.2d 588 (1950)

Al's Auto Sales sold and delivered a used car to Cross Motor Co. on December 18, the title certificate to be delivered when payment was made. Cross gave Al a bank draft for the amount of the purchase price on the same day. On December 23, Cross resold the car to Moskowitz. Al attached the certificate of title of the car to Cross' draft and sent it through another bank for payment on January 4. The draft was dishonored and returned to Al together with the certificate of title. Al then learned that the car had been resold to Moskowitz and sued him to recover the car. From a judgment for Moskowitz, Al appealed.

JOHNSON, J. . . . No one can transfer or confer a better title than he has, unless some principle of estoppel operates to bar a claim under an otherwise better title. The mere possession of chattels, by whatever means acquired, if there is no evidence of property right therein, or of authority to sell, given by or for the true owner, will not enable the possessor to give a good title. . . .

A purchaser of personal property from one who has only the possession of the property under an incomplete conditioned sale cannot in general defeat a recovery by the true owner. . . .

But where an owner consigns personal property to a dealer in such goods, with express or implied authority to sell, . . . but with title reserved in the owner until the payment of the purchase price, a purchaser who pays value for such goods and gets possession thereof without notice of the terms or conditions of the original delivery, consignment or sale, obtains a good title as against the original owner. . . .

It is contended by plaintiffs [Al's] that the sale of the automobile in question was illegal and void for failure to comply with the provisions of the Motor Vehicle License and Registration Act . . . in that no certificate of title was delivered to defendant Cross Motor Company, or by said company to Moskowitz. This contention is untenable. The act does not expressly provide that sales made without complying with the requirements shall be void. . . .[38]

Where one of two innocent parties must suffer through the act or negligence of a third person, the loss should fall upon the one who by his conduct created the circumstances which enabled the third party to perpetrate the wrong or cause the loss.

The plaintiffs made it possible for . . . Cross Motor Company to make the sale to Moskowitz, defendant, without fault on the part of the latter. . . . There was nothing to indicate to defendant that such dealer had not paid for the car, or that the car was not delivered to the dealer for sale in the Cross Motor Company's well-known business as a dealer. The plaintiffs took no steps to acquaint purchasers from the dealer that such dealer had no right to sell, although they knew of the dealer's selling business, and . . . [plaintiffs are] estopped from claiming title as against a bona fide purchaser for value, from the dealer without actual or constructive notice of the condition on which the car was delivered to the dealer. . . .

[Judgment affirmed.]

Code Comment: The same decision would be made under the Code since there was an entrusting within the scope of UCC Sec. 2-403 (2), (3).

---

[38] In a number of jurisdictions no title to a motor vehicle can be transferred without the delivery of a properly indorsed or assigned certificate of title. In such a jurisdiction, no estoppel can arise when a certificate of title is not so delivered.

Questions and Case Problems

1. What is the objective of the following rules of law?

(a) In the absence of any statement to the contrary, title to existing goods identified at the time of contracting and not involving documents passes to the buyer at the time and place of contracting.

(b) Although a buyer is guilty of fraud in obtaining the sale to him, the seller cannot recover the property from the buyer's purchaser who has bought in good faith and for value.

2. Eastern Supply Co. sent to Metropolitan Distributors a purchase order that contained the provision, "Ship direct to [buyer's address]." Metropolitan later claimed that title to the goods did not pass until they reached the buyer's address. Was this correct? (Metropolitan Distributors v. Eastern Supply Co., [Pa.] 21 D.&C.2d 128, 107 Pittsburgh Leg.J. 451)

3. Coburn bought cattle from Regan and paid for them with a check at the time of sale. The parties agreed that Regan would hold the cattle for a few days. The day before Coburn was to take the cattle, Regan sold them to Drown who gave him a check at that time. After Regan took the check but before Drown had taken possession of the cattle, Regan told Drown that Coburn had purchased the cattle. Drown took the cattle. Coburn sued Drown for their value. Decide. (Coburn v. Drown, 114 Vt. 158, 40 A.2d 528)

4. Di Lorenzio had possession of certain goods that belonged to Wolf, a dealer in household furniture. The goods were destroyed by fire. Not knowing of this, the parties made an agreement for the sale of the goods. The dealer brought an action against Di Lorenzio. Decide. (Wolf v. Di Lorenzio, 22 Misc. 323, 49 N.Y.S. 191)

5. The Wisconsin Central Railway Co. advertised that it would sell goods at public auction. In bidding for certain property, one person bid $675; Anderson then bid $680. The auctioneer refused to accept his bid on the grounds that the increase was too small and sold the property to the next highest bidder. Anderson sued the railroad. Decide. (Anderson v. Wisconsin Central Railway Co., 107 Minn. 296, 120 N.W. 39)

6. The Saddler Machinery Co. of Michigan purchased a machine from Ohio National, Inc., a manufacturer at Upper Sandusky, Ohio. The purchase was made "f.o.b. Cars Upper Sandusky, Ohio." After the sale was made, Saddler wrote National on January 15 to hold the machine for "a week or two" as Saddler might resell the machine immediately. The machine was in National's plant and had not yet been loaded on cars when it was destroyed by fire on January 30. Saddler sued National to recover the purchase price, which had been paid in advance. National claimed that title had passed to Saddler. Upon which party would the risk of loss fall? (Saddler Machinery Co. v. Ohio National, Inc., [D.C.N.D. Ohio] 102 F.Supp. 652)

7. Logan made a written contract with Cross, the owner of a hay ranch, for the purchase of 200 tons of hay out of a certain stack at the agreed

price of $4,000. In an action brought by Logan against Cross, it was contended that title to the 200 tons of hay passed to the buyer without separation from the mass. Do you agree with this contention? (Logan v. Cross, 101 Ore. 85, 198 P. 1097)

8. Wolcov purchased goods from Russell. Later, the buyer claimed that he had the right to return the goods because the parties had orally agreed that he could do so at the time the written contract was signed. The written contract contained no provision for a return of the goods. Was the buyer entitled to return the goods? (Wolcov v. Russell, [Pa.] 46 Delaware County 202)

9. The Auburn Motor Co. sold five automobiles to Levasseur of Rhode Island to be shipped C.O.D. via the Adams Express Co. from Indiana to Providence, Rhode Island. While the goods were in transit, Levasseur borrowed money from the New England Auto Investment Co. to pay for the cars and executed a mortgage on the cars to secure payment of the loan. On the day the cars were received, Levasseur transferred one of them to the Whitten Motor Vehicle Co. The Whitten company sold the car to Andrews. In an action brought by the New England Auto Investment Co. against Andrews, the defendant alleged that the mortgage was invalid and contended that the Auburn Motor Co. had retained title and right of possession. Do you agree with this contention? (New England Auto Investment Co. v. Andrews, 47 R.I. 108, 132 A. 883)

10. The Atlantic Woolen Mills ordered from George Boiko & Co., a corporation engaged in the buying and selling of woolen rags, two bales of khaki overcoat clippings and one bale of khaki worsted clippings and agreed to send for them. The George Boiko & Co. set aside and tagged the three bales for the Atlantic Woolen Mills. The truckman who was sent for the bales called at the noon hour and left without them. In an action for the price, it was contended that title to the goods had passed when they had been set aside and tagged. Do you agree? (George Boiko & Co. v. Atlantic Woolen Mills, 195 App.Div. 207, 186 N.Y.S. 624)

11. The Brown & Lowe Co. delivered a secondhand road machine to Potolsky, who took the machine under an agreement to try it out and to pay an agreed sum if the machine proved satisfactory. The machine was used under two road contracts for a period of one year and four months, after which Potolsky claimed that it was unsatisfactory and refused to pay for it. The Brown & Lowe Co. brought an action to recover the agreed price. Was it entitled to judgment? (Brown & Lowe Co. v. Potolsky, 221 App.Div. 299, 223 N.Y.S. 71)

12. Perkins, an importer of dress goods, made an unconditional contract to sell Halpren goods which were in the warehouse of Murphy & Co. at the time the contract was made. Subsequently, Perkins brought an action against the buyer to recover the purchase price. The buyer claimed that title had not passed to him. Decide. (Perkins v. Halpren, 257 Pa. 402, 102 A. 741)

CHAPTER 23

Obligations of Parties and Performance

The parties to a sales contract are bound to perform according to its terms. Each is likewise under the duty to exercise good faith in its performance [1] and to do nothing that would impair the expectation of the other party that the contract will be duly performed.[2]

Sec. 23-A. Conditions Precedent to Performance. In most sales contracts the duties of the seller and buyer are concurrent. Each one has the right to demand that the other perform at the same time. That is, as the seller hands over the goods, the buyer theoretically must hand over the purchase money. If either party refuses to act, the other party has the right to withhold his performance.[3]

The duty of a party to a sales contract to perform his part of the contract may be subject to a *condition precedent,* that is, by the terms of the contract he is not required to perform until some event occurs or until some act is performed. Quite commonly the condition precedent is performance by the other party. Thus a contract may provide that the seller shall deliver merchandise but that the buyer must first pay for it in full. Under this contract the duty of the seller to deliver the merchandise is subject to the condition precedent of payment in full by the buyer. If the buyer never performs his part of the contract, the duty of the seller never arises.

In the event that a condition precedent to the obligation of one party is not fulfilled, he may either repudiate the transaction or waive

---

[1] Uniform Commercial Code, Sec. 1-203. In the case of a merchant, good faith means honesty in fact and the observance of reasonable commercial standards of fair dealing in the trade. UCC Sec. 2-103(1)(b).

[2] Sec. 2-609(1). As to demand for assurance of performance, see p. 355.

[3] UCC Sec. 2-511, USA Sec. 11(1), 42.

nonfulfillment of the condition and hold the other party to his promise. If there is a promise that the condition shall happen or be performed, the promisee may treat nonperformance as a breach of contract and claim damages of the other party for failing to bring about the fulfillment of the condition.

Sec. 24-B. Seller's Duty to Deliver. It is the seller's duty to transfer the possession of the goods to the buyer. The delivery must be made in accordance with the terms of the sale or contract to sell.[4]

(1) Place, Time, and Manner of Delivery. The terms of the contract determine whether the seller is to send the goods or the buyer is to call for them, or whether the transaction is to be completed by the delivery of documents without the movement of the goods. In the absence of a provision in the contract or usage of trade, the place of delivery is the seller's place of business, if he has one; otherwise, it is his residence. If, however, the subject matter of the contract consists of specific goods that are known by the parties to be in some other place, that place is the place of delivery. Documents of title may be delivered through customary banking channels.[5]

If the seller is required to send the goods but the agreement does not provide for the time of sending them, he must send the goods within a reasonable time. (See p. 356, Bound Brook Stove Works v. Ellis) An effectual tender or offer of delivery by the seller must be made at a reasonable hour.[6] The same rule applies to a demand for possession of the goods by the buyer. What constitutes a reasonable hour is a question of fact to be determined in view of the circumstances of each case.

(2) Quantity Delivered. The buyer has the right to insist that all the goods be delivered at one time. If the seller delivers a smaller quantity than that stipulated in the contract, the buyer may refuse to accept the goods. If the buyer accepts or retains part of the goods with knowledge of the seller's intention to deliver no more, he must pay the full contract price, unless the contract is divisible so that it is possible to apportion the contract price, in which case the buyer need only pay the proportionate price representing the items or units which he has received. If the goods are used or disposed of by the buyer before he learns of the seller's intention, the buyer is only required to pay the fair value of the goods he has received.

(3) Delivery in Installments. The buyer is under no obligation or duty to accept delivery of goods by installments unless the contract

---

[4] UCC Sec. 2-301, USA Sec. 41.
[5] UCC Sec. 2-308.
[6] UCC Sec. 2-503 (1)(a), USA Sec. 43.

contemplates such deliveries [7] or unless the circumstances are such as to give rise to the right to make delivery in lots.[8]

When the contract provides for delivery and payment by installments, a difficult problem is presented when the seller fails to make a proper delivery or when the buyer fails to pay for one or more installments. For example, *A* agrees to sell 6,000 tons of coal to *B* to be delivered in three equal monthly installments. During one month *A* delivers only 150 tons. The courts in some states hold that the buyer must accept the remaining installments, although he is entitled to damages for the deficiency in the short delivery. Other states take the view that time is of the essence of such contracts and that a failure to deliver or to pay a particular installment goes to the root of the contract, entitling the other party to rescind the entire transaction.

Under the Code there is a breach of the entire contract whenever the seller's default as to one or more installments substantially impairs the value of the whole contract.[9] This in effect continues the rule under the Uniform Sales Act by which the question as to whether the breach of contract is so material that it justifies the injured party in refusing to carry out the remaining terms of the contract and suing for damages for breach of the entire contract, or whether the breach applies only to the defective or missing installments so that the buyer is only entitled to damages as to them, depends on the terms of the contract and the circumstances of the case.[10] (See p. 357, Continental Grain Co. Case)

According to the Restatement of the Law of Contracts, if payment is to be made for each installment, the delivery of each installment and the payment for each installment are conditions precedent to the respective duties of the buyer to accept and of the seller to deliver subsequent installments.[11]

(4) Delivery to Carrier. When the seller is required to or may send the goods to the buyer but the contract does not require him to make a delivery at a particular destination, the seller, in the absence of a contrary agreement, must put the goods in the possession of a proper carrier and make such contract for their transportation as is reasonable in view of the nature of the goods and other circumstances of the case. The seller must also obtain and promptly deliver or tender in properly

---

[7] UCC Sec. 2-307, USA Sec. 45(1).

[8] UCC Sec. 2-307. This situation would arise whenever it is physically impossible because of the buyer's limited facilities or commercially impractical for any reason for the seller to make complete delivery.

[9] Sec. 2-612(3). The buyer, however, may waive the breach and he is deemed to reinstate the contract if he accepts a nonconforming installment without seasonably notifying the seller that he cancels the contract, or if he sues with respect only to past installments, or if he demands the delivery of future installments.

[10] USA Sec. 45(2).

[11] Restatement of Contracts, Sec. 272, Illus. 1.

indorsed form any document, such as a bill of lading, which is required by the buyer in order to obtain possession of the goods. The seller must likewise promptly notify the buyer of the shipment.[12] If the seller fails to notify the buyer or to make a proper contract of carriage, the buyer may reject the goods when material delay or loss is caused by such breach.[13]

(5) Delivery at Destination. If the contract requires the seller to make delivery at a destination point, the duty of the seller is the same as though he were dealing with the buyer face to face, rather than placing the goods in the possession of a carrier. In addition, however, if any documents are issued by the carrier that are necessary to obtain possession of the goods, the seller must also tender such documents.[14]

(6) Cure of Defective Tender. The Code gives the seller the right to make a second tender or delivery after the first is properly rejected by the buyer because it does not conform to the contract. If the time for making delivery under the contract has not expired, the seller need only give the buyer timely or seasonable notice of his intention to make a proper delivery within the time allowed by the contract, and he may then do so. If the time for making the delivery has expired, the seller is given an additional reasonable time in which to make a substitute conforming tender if he so notifies the buyer and if he had acted reasonably in making the original tender, believing that it would be acceptable.[15]

Sec. 23-C. Buyer's Duty to Accept Goods. It is the duty of the buyer to accept the delivery of proper goods.

(1) Right to Examine Goods. Unless otherwise agreed, the buyer, when tender of the goods is made, has the right before payment for or acceptance of the goods to inspect them at any reasonable place or time and in any reasonable manner to determine whether they meet the requirements of the contract.[16] A C.O.D. shipment, however, bars the right of inspection before payment is made unless there is an agreement to the contrary.[17]

(2) What Constitutes Acceptance. Acceptance ordinarily is an express statement by the buyer that he accepts or approves the goods. It may also consist of conduct which expresses such an intent, such as the failure to object within a reasonable period of time or the use

---

[12] UCC Sec. 2-504.
[13] Sec. 2-504.
[14] Sec. 2-503(3).
[15] Sec. 2-508.
[16] UCC Sec. 2-513 (1), USA Sec. 47(1)(2).
[17] UCC Sec. 2-513(3)(a), USA Sec. 47(3).

of the goods in such a way as would be inconsistent with a rejection of them by the buyer.[18] (See p. 359, Knobel v. J. Bartel Co.)

(3) Effect of Acceptance on Breach. Acceptance of the goods by the buyer does not discharge the seller from liability in damages or other legal remedy for breach of any promise or warranty in the contract to sell or the sale. But the seller is not liable if, after acceptance of the goods, the buyer fails to give notice to the seller of the breach of any promise or warranty within a reasonable time after the buyer knows or ought to know of the breach.[19]

Sec. 23-D. Buyer's Duty to Pay. The buyer is under a duty to pay for the goods at the contract rate for any goods accepted.[20] In the absence of a contrary provision, payment must be made in cash and must be made concurrently with receipt of the goods; and, conversely, payment cannot be required before that time.[21]

The seller may accept a negotiable instrument, such as a check, in payment of the purchase price. This form of payment, unless the parties expressly agree otherwise, is merely a conditional payment, that is, conditional upon the instrument's being honored and paid. If the instrument is not paid, it ceases to be payment of the purchase price and the seller is then an unpaid seller.[22]

The parties may agree to a sale on credit. This may be done for each sale individually or for sales generally, as in the case of a charge account in a department store. When a sale is made on credit, the parties may include special provisions to protect the seller should the buyer's credit standing become impaired. (See p. 361, Wessel v. Seminole Phosphate Co.)

Tender of the purchase price has the same effect as actual payment in imposing upon the seller the duty to make delivery. If the seller fails to make delivery when a proper tender or offer of payment is made, he is in default under the contract.

It must also be remembered that if the seller is in default, the buyer may rescind the contract; in which case, after making the rescission, he is no longer under a duty to maintain the tender.

Sec. 23-E. Duties Under Particular Terms. A sale may be as simple as a face-to-face exchange of money and goods, but it frequently involves a more complicated pattern, with some element of transporta-

---

[18] UCC Sec. 2-606.

[19] Sec. 2-607(2), (3). This section rejects the view followed in some states that acceptance of the goods is a waiver of any claim for damages.

[20] Sec. 2-301, 2-607(1).

[21] Sec. 2-310(a). If delivery under the contract is to be made by a delivery of document of title, payment is due at the time and place at which the buyer is to receive the document regardless of where the goods are to be received. Sec. 2-310(c).

[22] UCC Sec. 2-511, USA Sec. 52(b).

tion, generally by a common carrier. This, in turn, generally results in the addition of certain special terms to the sales transaction.

(1) F.O.B. The term "f.o.b.," or "free on board," may be used with reference to the seller's city, or the buyer's city, or an intermediate city, as in the case of a transshipment. It may also be used with reference to a named carrier, such as f.o.b. a specified vessel, car, or other vehicle. In general, an f.o.b. term is to be construed as requiring delivery to be made at the f.o.b. point, as contrasted with merely a shipment to that point,[23] and as imposing upon the seller the risk and expense involved in getting the goods to the designated place or on board the specified carrier.[24]

(2) C.I.F. The term "c.i.f." indicates that the payment by the buyer is a lump sum covering the selling price of the goods, insurance on them, and freight to the specified destination of the goods. The c.i.f. term imposes upon the seller the obligation of putting the goods in the possession of a proper carrier, of loading and paying for the freight, of procuring the proper insurance, and of preparing an invoice of the goods and any other document needed for shipment, and of forwarding all documents to the buyer with commercial promptness.[25]

Under a c.i.f. contract the buyer bears the risk of loss after the goods have been delivered to the carrier.[26] He must pay for the goods when proper documents representing them are tendered to him, which in turn means that he is not entitled to inspect the goods before paying for them, unless the contract expressly provides for payment on or after the arrival of the goods.[27]

(3) Ex-ship. If the contract provides for delivery ex-ship, the seller bears the risk of loss until the goods have left the ship's tackle or have otherwise been properly unloaded. He must discharge all liens arising from the transportation of the goods and must furnish the buyer with such documents or instructions as enables him to obtain the goods from the carrier.[28]

(4) No Arrival, No Sale. When goods are sent under such a term, the seller bears the risk of loss during transportation; but if the goods do not arrive, he is not subject to that liability for in such case there is no sale. The buyer is protected in that he is only required to pay for the goods if they arrive.

---

[23] See p. 352.
[24] UCC Sec. 2-319(1).
[25] Sec. 2-320(1), (2). The term "c. & f." or "c.f." imposes the same obligations and risks as a c.i.f. term with the exception of the obligation as to insurance.
[26] Sec. 2-320(2) (a). The c.i.f. and c. & f. contracts may be modified to place the risk of deterioration during shipment on the seller by specifying that the price shall be based on the arrival or "out turn" quality, or by having the seller warrant the condition or quality of the goods on their arrival. Sec. 2-321(2).
[27] Sec. 2-320 (4), 2-321(3).
[28] Sec. 2-322(2).

The "no arrival, no sale" contract requires the seller to ship proper conforming goods and to tender them on their arrival if they do arrive. He must, of course, refrain from interfering in any way with the arrival of the goods.[29]

Sec. 23-F. Adequate Assurance of Performance. Whenever a party to the sales transaction has reason to believe that the other party may not perform his part of the contract, he may make a written demand upon the other party for adequate assurance that he will in fact perform his contract. For example, when goods are to be delivered at a future date or in installments over a period of time, the buyer may become fearful that the seller will not be able to make the future deliveries required. The buyer may in such case require assurance from the seller that the contract will be performed.[30]

(1) Form of Assurance. The person upon whom demand for assurance is made must give "such assurance of due performance as is adequate under the circumstances of the particular case."[31] The Code does not specify the exact form of assurance. When the party upon whom demand is made has an established reputation, his reaffirmance of his contract obligation and a statement that he will perform may be sufficient to assure a reasonable man that it will be performed. In contrast, the person's reputation or economic position at the time may be such that there is no assurance that there will be a proper performance in the absence of a guarantee by a third person or the furnishing of security by way of a pledge or other device to protect the demanding party against default.[32]

(2) Failure to Give Assurance. In response to the demand for assurance, the party on whom demand is made may state he will not perform; that is, instead of giving assurance of performance, he repudiates the contract. In contrast with a flat repudiation of the contract, the party upon whom demand is made may fail to reply to the demand for assurance or may give only a feeble assurance that is not sufficient to assure a reasonable man that performance will be made. This problem is met by the Code by expressly declaring that the failure to provide adequate assurance within thirty days after receiving the demand, or a lesser time when thirty days would be unreasonable, constitutes a repudiation of the contract.[33]

---

[29] Sec. 2-324 (a).

[30] Sec. 2-609 (1). Between merchants the reasonableness of the grounds for insecurity is determined according to commercial standards. Sec. 2-609(2).

[31] Sec. 2-609(4).

[32] Between merchants the adequacy of any assurance is determined according to commercial standards. Sec. 2-609 (2).

[33] Sec. 2-609(4). This enables the adverse party to take steps at an earlier date to protect himself against the default of the other party, as by making substitute contracts to replace the repudiated contracts.

Cases for Chapter 23

Bound Brook Stove Works v. Ellis

98 N.J.L. 523, 122 A. 690 (1923)

The Bound Brook Stove Works entered into a contract to sell Ellis a certain quantity of pig iron. No time was specified for deliveries, which were to be made in installments. Thirteen hundred and fourteen tons of pig iron were delivered and accepted, the last 49 tons on October 28, 1917. A tender of 78 tons of pig iron on November 13, 1917, was refused on the ground of late delivery. The stove company brought an action against the buyer to recover damages. The defendant contended that delivery was not made within a reasonable time. From a judgment for the plaintiff, the defendant appealed.

BLACK, J. . . . The only . . . question involved is whether it was error for the trial court to find that the offer of deliveries of pig iron on November 13, 1917, was within a reasonable time. The contract, as stated, is dated April 4, 1917. No specific time for the deliveries is stated. The contract recites that the Bound Brook Stove Works, the plaintiff, had contracts for the purchase of pig iron, five in number, with various mills, upon the terms and conditions therein stated; that the buyer, Herman Ellis, the defendant, desires to purchase the pig iron to be delivered pursuant to the said contracts, subject to the terms thereof, as to quality and deliveries, and as and when the pig iron is delivered under the contracts. The deliveries are subject to the conditions in the contracts or any other causes not within the control of the seller.

The Uniform Sale of Goods Act . . . provides, where by contract "no time for sending them is fixed (i.e. the goods), the seller is bound to send them within a reasonable time."

This question under the circumstances of the case was clearly one of fact to be decided by the trial court. . . .

The finding of the trial court is supported by the evidence, and is therefore not reviewable on appeal. . . .

[Judgment for plaintiff affirmed.]

Code Comment: The same decision will be made under the Code. Sec. 2-309 (1) restates the substance of the provision of the USA quoted in the reported opinion. The principle relating to the scope of appellate review, namely, that lower court findings supported by evidence will not be reviewed or set aside on appeal, is not affected in any way by the Code.

Continental Grain Co. v. Simpson Feed Co.

102 F.Supp. 354 (E.D. Ark., 1951),
affirmed 199 F.2d 284 (C.A. 8th, 1952)

The Continental Grain Co., a grain dealer, made a contract with the Simpson Feed Co., a grain elevator company, to purchase approximately five carloads of soy beans, delivery to be made from October 1 to November 30 at seller's option, with the buyer to furnish the seller shipping instructions as each of the cars was loaded. On October 30, the first car was loaded and shipping instructions given by the buyer the same day. The next day a second car was loaded, but instructions were not given until after 48 hours. The seller refused to accept such delayed instructions and canceled the contract. The buyer then purchased four carloads of soy beans in the market and brought suit for the difference between the market and the contract price.

LEMLEY, D.F. . . . In determining whether or not a breach on the part of a buyer, with respect to one installment of a contract for the sale of goods to be delivered and paid for in installments, is so material as to justify the seller in refusing to perform further, numerous factors are to be considered. In [Helgar Corp. v. Warner Features, Inc., 222 N.Y. 449, 119 N.E. 114], the Court was concerned with whether or not a failure on the part of the buyer to pay for certain installments within the time fixed by the contract for such payments justified the seller in refusing to make further deliveries; and the Court said: "The vendor who fails to receive payment of an installment the very day that it is due may sue at once for the price. But it does not follow that he may be equally precipitate in his election to declare the contract at an end. . . . That depends upon the question whether the default is so substantial and important as in truth and in fairness to defeat the essential purpose of the parties. Whatever the rule may once have been, this is the test that is now prescribed by statute.

The failure to make punctual payment may be material or trivial according to the circumstances. We must know the cause of the default, the length of the delay, the needs of the vendor, and the expectations of the vendee. If the default is the result of accident or misfortune, if there is a reasonable assurance that it will be promptly repaired, and if immediate payment is not necessary to enable the vendor to proceed with performance, there may be one conclusion. If the breach is willful, if there is no just ground to look for prompt reparation, if the delay has been substantial, or if the needs of the vendor are urgent so that timely performance is imperiled, in these and in other circumstances, there may be another conclusion. Sometimes the conclusion will follow from all the circumstances as an inference of law to be drawn by the judge; sometimes, as an inference of fact to be drawn by the jury."

In the Restatement of the Law of Contracts, Section 275, it is said that the factors to be considered in measuring the materiality of a breach of such contract include the following: (1) the extent to which the injured party will obtain the substantial benefits which he could reasonably have anticipated; (2) the extent to which the injured party may be adequately compensated in damages for lack of complete performance; (3) the greater or less hardship on the party failing to perform in terminating the contract; (4) the willful, negligent, or innocent behavior of the party failing to perform, and (5) the greater or less uncertainty that the party failing to perform will perform the remainder of the contract. In the following section, 276, of the Restatement, it is stated that in mercantile contracts performance at the time agreed upon is important, and if the delay of one party is considerable, "having reference to the nature of the transaction and the seriousness of the consequences," and is not justified by the conduct of the other party, the latter need not perform further.

Assuming that the conduct of the plaintiff with respect to the second carload of soybeans amounted to a breach of its contract, nevertheless, when such breach is viewed in the light of the above-mentioned factors, we believe that, as a matter of law, it was insubstantial and did not have the effect of relieving the defendant of its obligation to perform its contract further, either with respect to the 2,000 bushels of soybeans loaded on October 31 or as to the remaining 6,000 bushels, which were never loaded.

While it appears that the parties contemplated that deliveries were to be made in installments and paid for separately, no particular number of installments or times for shipment were specified, and the defendant had the right, had it seen fit to do so, to tender all of the beans either on the first or the last day of the contract period. Plaintiff had no right to insist on delivery of any part of the beans prior to November 30. As a matter of fact, no beans were loaded until October 30, approximately six weeks after the contract was entered into and almost at the end of the first month of the contract period. The fact that the defendant was given approximately two and one-half months from the date of the contract to complete delivery, coupled with the fact that it did not undertake to perform until the month of October was practically gone, demonstrates to our mind that neither party was in a particular hurry with respect to these deliveries, and that time was not of the essence of the contract, except to the extent that the defendant was obligated to complete its deliveries by the end of Novmber. At the time of the assumed breach, twenty-eight days of the month remained.

There is no suggestion that the plaintiff's delay in furnishing shipping instructions manifested any inability on its part to perform its contractual obligations, or that it evidenced any intent on its part to repudiate the contract or to abandon further performance under it, and there is no evidence that the defendant so construed it. On the contrary, the undisputed evidence is that on and after November 2 plaintiff advised the defendant that it intended to perform fully and urged the defendant to do likewise, even going so far as to offer it an extension of time within which to complete deliveries.

Defendant sustained no substantial damages as a result of the plaintiff's delay, nor did it run the risk of future damage. The marked rise in the price of soybeans between September 14 and November 2 gave it a considerable margin of safety had the market begun to fall, which it did not do. Moreover, defendant was under contract to furnish beans to others at even lower prices than that at which it had contracted with the plaintiff. The only damages that the defendant could have suffered as a result of the plaintiff's delay, under the evidence in this case, would have been demurrage on the car, or the expense of unloading it, and interest for two days on the money which it had tied up in the second carload of beans. The plaintiff, on the other hand, as a result of the defendant's refusal to perform further has sustained damages to the extent of several thousand dollars.

There is no showing here that the plaintiff's delay was either willful or negligent. Its explanation that it spent the 48 hours in obtaining clearances from New Orleans, and that as soon as such clearances were obtained it furnished the defendant shipping instructions, is unchallenged.

Under such circumstances we do not feel that any reasonable man, in the exercise of fair and impartial judgment, could conclude that plaintiff's delay was such a material breach as to justify the defendant in canceling the contract either in whole or in part.

Code Comment: The same decision would be made under the Code since on the analysis of the facts as made by the court it would reach the conclusion that the breach of the buyer as to one installment did not "substantially impair the value of the whole contract," the latter being the test for determining whether breach as to an installment causes a breach of the whole contract. UCC Sec. 2-612(3). As a further element supporting this conclusion under the Code is the fact that the buyer volunteered an assurance of performance without waiting for the seller to demand it of him, as he could do under UCC Sec. 2-609.

Knobel v. J. Bartel Co.
176 Wis. 393, 187 N.W. 188 (1922)

The J. Bartel Company ordered coats from Knobel to be shipped from the seller's factory in New York to the buyer's store in Wisconsin. When the goods were received, some of the coats were damaged; but all were given the regular store tags by the buyer and hung up in the store. The buyer also attempted by a steaming process to remedy the defect. Later the buyer offered to pay the seller in full for those coats that were in good condition but not for the defective coats. The seller then sued for the total contract price. The buyer defended on the ground that it had not accepted the coats. From a judgment for the plaintiff, the defendant appealed.

JONES, J. . . . "The buyer is deemed to have accepted the goods when he intimates to the seller that he has accepted them, or when the goods have been delivered to him, and he does any act in relation to them which is inconsistent with the ownership of the seller, or when, after the lapse of a reasonable time, he retains the goods without intimating to the seller that he has rejected them."

The court based its ruling that there had been an acceptance on the grounds: First, that the action of defendant was inconsistent with the ownership of the goods by the plaintiffs; and, second, that it delayed for an unreasonable time in giving notice of the refusal to accept.

It was undisputed that the defects claimed were of such a nature that they could be easily discovered without very close inspection and that they were noticed when unpacked by persons having experience in handling such goods. Defendant not only made no objection to the quantity or quality of the goods for 25 days but did promptly object on other grounds which were not tenable. Under such circumstances the absence from the store of another person who may have had more experience in examining goods did not afford sufficient excuse for the retention of the goods for so long a period without objection. We also agree with the trial court that the manner of dealing with the goods was inconsistent with the ownership of the seller.

It is true that what a reasonable time for acceptance is, is usually a question for the jury; but the time may be so long that a court can and should say as a matter of law that the acceptance has been made. . . .

[Judgment for plaintiff affirmed.]

Code Comment: The same conclusion would be reached under the Code which redeclares the principle recognized by this case as to the effect of failure to object or the doing of an act inconsistent with the seller's ownership. UCC Sec. 2-606 (1).

To the extent that the decision relates to whether a question is one of fact for determination by the jury or one of law to be decided by the court, the decision is unaffected by the Code since it contains no provision with respect to the function of the jury or the review of its verdict.

Wessel v. Seminole Phosphate Co.

13 F.2d 999 (C.C.A. 4th, 1926)

Wessel and others contracted to sell 600 tons of nitrate of soda to the Seminole Phosphate Company. The agreement provided for payment 30 days from the average date of delivery, except that in case the sellers deemed the financial responsibility of the buyer to be impaired or unsatisfactory, the sellers had the right to require payment in advance or satisfactory security for the payment when due. It was also stipulated that the sellers could cancel the contract in case the goods were not paid for in accordance with the agreement. The buyer wired for a quick shipment of 25 tons of nitrate which the sellers refused to make unless the buyer paid in advance or gave satisfactory security. The sellers later brought an action for breach of contract against the buyer who contended that the sellers had canceled the contract. From a judgment for the defendant, the plaintiffs appealed.

PARKER, C.J. . . . We think that the learned District Judge erred in holding that the mere failure on the part of the plaintiffs to ship the nitrate on 30 days' terms amounted to a cancellation of the contract. . . .

In the absence of contrary provision in a contract of sale, it is the duty of the buyer to pay cash on delivery. . . . It was provided in the body of this contract that payment should be made 30 days from average date of delivery; but upon the margin was printed the condition that, if the financial responsibility of the buyer should become impaired or unsatisfactory to sellers, they should have the right to require payment in advance or satisfactory security. The effect of this provision was merely to preserve to the sellers the right to demand, as a condition of performance on their part, what they would have a right to demand at law in the absence of the 30-day provision. In other words, the effect of the condition in the margin was to confer upon the sellers the right to eliminate the provision as to the 30 days' terms if the credit of buyer should become impaired. Immediately after the sentence in the margin setting forth this condition, there followed another sentence providing that, if the buyer should fail to comply with the terms of payment or any other terms of sale, sellers should have the right to cancel unfilled portions of the contract, buyer remaining liable for unpaid accounts. It is argued in behalf of defendant that this sentence prescribes the exclusive remedy of the seller upon the buyer's failure to pay cash in advance or provide security, but we do not so interpret it. The right to cancel is given, not upon failure to pay cash in advance or furnish security, but upon failure "to comply with the terms of payment," which, in case payment in advance is not demanded on account of impaired credit, would mean failure to pay within 30 days of the average date of delivery of any lot of nitrate delivered under the contract. The right to cancel was also given by the provision in question upon failure of the buyer to comply with any other term of the contract, which clearly indicates that it was not the intention of the parties that the right of cancellation should be limited to the breach of conditions contained in the preceding sentence, and certainly not that it should furnish the sole remedy of the sellers. . . .

To give the language the interpretation contended for by defendant would lead to the absurd result that upon the buyer's credit being impaired coincident with a decline in the market, the sellers would be faced with the alternative of shipping the nitrate on 30 days' time and taking the risk of loss through failure of the buyer, or of cancelling the contract and taking the loss resulting from the decline in the market. Certainly no such result was contemplated by the parties. The obvious purpose of the sentences printed on the margin was to provide additional and independent safeguards for the sellers: First, the right to demand cash or security upon the buyer's credit becoming impaired; and, second, the right to cancel upon the buyer's failure to comply with payment or any other term of the contract. It was clearly not their purpose to diminish the safeguards of the seller or to provide that he must cancel and accept the loss due to a decline in the market, if unwilling to extend terms because of the impairment of buyer's credit. Such an interpretation would virtually give the buyer the option of canceling the contract upon the impairment of his own credit. . . .

[Judgment for defendant reversed and new trial ordered.]

Code Comment: The same decision would be made under the Code since it expressly declares that a remedy referred to in a sales contract is an additional or cumulative remedy unless it is "expressly agreed to be exclusive." UCC Sec. 2-719 (1) (b).

Note that under the Code the exercise of an "insecurity clause," that is, a clause giving a right when the party deems himself insecure, must be made in good faith. UCC Sec. 1-208.

Questions and Case Problems

1. What is the objective of each of the following rules of law?
(a) Ordinarily the place of delivery of goods is the seller's place of business.
(b) In the absence of a contrary provision, a seller cannot require payment before delivery of the goods.

2. The Clark Appliance Co. purchased stoves from the Dearborn Stove Co. It used them as demonstrators for seven and a half months and then notified Dearborn Stove Co. that the stoves did not work. Clark Appliance offered to return the stoves. Was Dearborn Stove Co. required to take back

the goods? (Dearborn Stove Co. v. Clark Appliance Co., [Pa.] 104 Pittsburgh Leg.J. 403)

3. Price agreed to purchase two barge-loads of coal from Brown. The
coal was delivered on barges of the buyer on the Green River at or near
Mining City, Kentucky, in accordance with the agreement. The buyer,
after being given an opportunity to inspect the coal, hooked onto the
barges and transported them up the river to Bowling Green, several miles
away. During subsequent litigation the buyer contended that he had not
accepted the coal. Do you agree? (Brown v. Price, 207 Ky. 8, 268 S.W. 598)

4. International Minerals and Metal Corporation contracted to sell
Weinstein scrap metal to be delivered within 30 days. Later the seller informed the buyer that it could not make delivery within that time. The
buyer agreed to an extension of time, but no limiting date was set. Within
what time must the seller perform? (International Minerals and Metal
Corp. v. Weinstein, 236 N.C. 558, 73 S.E.2d 472)

5. The Rock Glen Salt Co. agreed to sell to Segal of Massachusetts
some bags of salt. It obtained from the Watkins Salt Co., New York, the
bags of salt ordered by Segal and 15 barrels of salt ordered by another
customer. The bags and barrels of salt were placed in a car and shipped to
Boston. The bill of lading for the entire shipment was made out to the
seller, and indorsed and sent to Segal, who was notified by the carrier of the
arrival of the car. In an action brought by the salt company against Segal
to recover the purchase price, he contended that (a) he could accept the
salt in the bags and reject the salt in the barrels or (b) reject the entire
shipment. What is your opinion? (Rock Glen Salt Co. v. Segal, 229 Mass.
115, 118 N.E. 239)

6. George A. Ohl & Co. made a contract "to sell to A. J. Ellis a No. 5
press . . . for the sum of $680." The press was known by both parties to
be stored in the factory of another company. The agreement contained no
stipulation as to the place of delivery, and there was no usage of the trade
governing the question. In an action brought by Gruen, assignee of Ellis,
against the Ohl company, the place of delivery was a point of contention.
Decide. (Gruen v. George A. Ohl & Co., 81 N.J.L. 626, 80 A. 547)

7. The Tri-Bullion Smelting & Development Co. agreed to sell and
Jacobsen to buy the seller's output of zinc concentrates for a two-year
period. A year and a half later, the Tri-Bullion Co. closed its mine and
notified Jacobsen that it would make no further deliveries. Jacobsen refused
to pay for the last shipment. Jacobsen sued the Tri-Bullion Co. The defendant contended that the plaintiff had breached the contract by failure to
pay for the goods delivered. Do you agree? (Tri-Bullion Smelting &
Development Co. v. Jacobsen, 147 C.C.A. 454, 233 F. 646)

8. The Spaulding & Kimball Co. ordered from the Aetna Chemical Co.
75 cartons of window washers. The buyer received them and sold about
a third to its customers. The buyer later refused to pay for them, claiming
that the quality was poor. The seller sued for the price, claiming that the
goods had been accepted. Decide. (Aetna Chemical Co. v. Spaulding &
Kimball Co., 98 Vt. 51, 126 A. 582)

CHAPTER 24

Warranties and Product Liability

The seller may make a guarantee with respect to the goods. If they are not as guaranteed, he may be held liable for the breach of his guarantee. Even when he has not made a guarantee, the law will in some instances hold him responsible as though he had made a guarantee. This type of obligation is called a *warranty*.

Sec. 24-A. Kinds of Warranties.

(1) Express Warranties. An *express warranty* is a part of the basis for the sale; [1] that is, the buyer has purchased the goods on the reasonable assumption that they were as stated by the seller. Thus a statement by the seller with respect to the quality, capacity, or other characteristic of the goods is an express warranty. (See p. 372, Standard Stevedoring Co. v. Jaffe) To illustrate, the seller may say: "This cloth is all wool," "This paint is for household woodwork," or "This engine can produce 50 horsepower."

(a) FORM OF EXPRESS WARRANTY. No particular form of words is necessary to constitute an express warranty. A seller need not state that he makes a warranty nor even intend to make a warranty. [2] It is sufficient that the seller assert a fact which would naturally induce the buyer to rely and act on the seller's statement. It is not necessary that the seller make an express statement, for the express warranty may be found in his conduct. Accordingly, if the buyer asks for a can of outside house paint and the seller hands him a can of paint, the seller's conduct expresses a warranty that the can is outside house paint.

A statement as to the goods may also bind the seller even though it was actually made by the manufacturer, as in the case of a label placed

---

[1] Uniform Commercial Code, Sec. 2-313(1).
[2] UCC Sec. 2-313 (2).

by the latter on the can of household paint. Here the seller is bound by an express warranty even though the buyer selected the can of paint from a shelf and without comment paid for it. The seller, by exposing the can to sale with the manufacturer's label appearing on it, has in effect adopted that label as his own statement and it therefore constitutes an express warranty by the seller.

(b) TIME OF MAKING EXPRESS WARRANTY. It is immaterial whether the express warranty is made at the time of or after the sale. No separate consideration is required for the warranty when it is part of a sale. If a warranty is made after the sale, no consideration is required since it is regarded as a modification of the sales contract.[3]

(c) SELLER'S OPINION OR STATEMENT OF VALUE. The Code states without any exception that "an affirmation merely of the value of the goods or a statement purporting to be merely the seller's opinion or commendation of the goods does not create a warranty." [4] A purchaser, as a reasonable man, should not believe such statements implicitly, and therefore he cannot hold the seller to them should they prove false. Thus "sales talk" by a seller that "this is the best piece of cloth in the market" or that glassware "is as good as anyone else's" is merely an opinion which the buyer cannot ordinarily treat as a warranty.

It is probable, however, that the Code will permit an exception to be made, as under the prior law, where the circumstances are such that a reasonable man would rely on such a statement. If the buyer has reason to believe that the seller is possessed of expert knowledge of the conditions of the market and the buyer requests his opinion as an expert, the buyer would be entitled to rely on the seller's statement as to whether a given article was the best obtainable. The criterion is whether a reasonable man would rely on the statement. Thus a statement by a florist that bulbs are of first-grade quality may be relied upon as a warranty.

As another exception to the principle that there is no liability for an opinion, which will probably be recognized under the Code, the seller may be liable when he does not have the belief that he asserts. For example, when the seller knows that a dog is sick and refuses to warrant the animal but states that it is sound as far as he knows, his statement is a warranty as to the absence of his knowledge of any unsoundness.

(2) Implied Warranties. An *implied warranty* is one that was not made by the seller but which is implied by the law. In certain instances the law implies or reads a warranty into a sale although the seller did

---

[3] Sec. 2-313, Official Comment point 7. Under the Uniform Sales Act and prior law, separate consideration was required when the warranty was made after the sale.
[4] Sec. 2-313(2).

not make it. That is, the implied warranty arises automatically from the fact that a sale has been made; as compared with express warranties, which arise because they form part of the basis on which the sale has been made.

(3) Cumulative and Conflicting Warranties. The fact that express warranties are made does not exclude implied warranties, and both express and implied warranties should be deemed to coexist. In case of an unreasonable conflict, an express warranty prevails over an implied warranty as to the same subject matter except in the case of an implied warranty of fitness for a particular purpose.[5]

Sec. 24-B. Particular Warranties of All Sellers. The Code makes a distinction in some cases between a merchant seller and the casual seller, and provides for a greater range of warranties in the case of the merchant seller. The following warranties apply to all sellers:

(1) Warranty of Title. Every seller by the mere act of selling makes a warranty that his transfer is rightful and transfers good title.[6] It is immaterial whether he is the manufacturer or grower of the goods, or whether he had possession of the goods.

A warranty of title may be specifically excluded, or the circumstances may be such as to prevent the warranty from arising. The latter situation is found when the buyer has reason to know that the seller does not claim to hold the title or that he is claiming to sell only such right or title as he or a third person may have.[7] For example, no warranty of title arises when the seller makes the sale in a representative capacity, such as a sheriff, an auctioneer, or an administrator. Likewise no warranty arises when the seller makes the sale by virtue of a power of sale possessed by him as a pledgee or mortgagee.[8]

(2) Warranty Against Encumbrances. Every seller by the mere act of selling makes a warranty that the goods shall be delivered free from any security interest or any other lien or encumbrance of which the buyer at the time of the sales transaction had no knowledge.[9] The Code takes the practical position that this warranty refers to the goods only at the time they are delivered to the buyer and is not concerned with an encumbrance which existed before or at the time the sale was made.[10] For example, a seller may not have paid in full for the goods which he is reselling and the original supplier may have a lien on the

---

5 UCC Sec. 2-317, USA Sec. 15(16).
6 UCC Sec. 2-312(1)(a), USA Sec. 13(1).
7 UCC Sec. 2-312 (2).
8 See Chs. 35, 57.
9 UCC Sec. 2-312(1)(b).
10 USA Sec. 13(3) implied a warranty that the goods should be free of encumbrances at the time of the sale.

goods. Under the Code, the seller may resell the goods while that lien is still on them and his only duty is to pay off the lien before he delivers the goods to the buyer.

The warranty against encumbrances may be excluded expressly or by the circumstances of the case in the same manner as a warranty of title.[11] By definition, a warranty against encumbrances does not arise if the buyer knows of the existence of the encumbrance in question, although this must be an actual knowledge as contrasted with a constructive notice, which the law deems possessed by everyone by virtue of the fact that an encumbrance is filed or recorded on the public record.

(3) Warranty of Conformity to Seller's Statement or Promise. Whenever a statement or promise made by the seller constitutes an express warranty,[12] it is binding on the seller regardless of the type of seller involved.

(4) Warranty of Conformity to Description, Sample, or Model. When the contract is based in part on the understanding that the seller will supply goods according to a particular description or that the goods will be the same as the sample or a model, the seller is bound by an express warranty that the goods shall conform to the description, sample, or model.[13] Ordinarily a *sample* is a portion of a whole mass that is the subject of the transaction, while a *model* is a replica of the article in question.

(5) Warranty of Fitness for a Particular Purpose. If the buyer intends to use the goods for a particular or unusual purpose, as contrasted with the ordinary use for which they are customarily sold,[14] the seller makes an implied warranty that the goods will be fit for the purpose when the buyer relies on the seller's skill or judgment to select or furnish suitable goods, and when the seller at the time of contracting knows or has reason to know the buyer's particular purpose and his reliance on the seller's judgment.[15] By way of illustration, if the buyer asks the seller to ship a number of clay bottles that are suitable for heating and retaining molten glass, the buyer relies on the judgment of the seller and the seller impliedly warrants that the bottles which he then sells to the buyer are fit for that purpose.

---

[11] See p. 366.

[12] See p. 364.

[13] UCC Sec. 2-313(1)(b)(c). This in general follows USA Secs. 14, 16(a) as judicially construed, although the latter act classifies the warranties in question as implied.

[14] See p. 368.

[15] UCC Sec. 2-315. This warranty applies to every seller, but as a matter of fact it will probably always be a merchant seller who has such skill and judgment that the Code provision could be applicable. The Code in substance continues the implied warranty of USA Sec. 15(1).

Sec. 24-C. Additional Warranties of Merchant Seller. In addition to the warranties made by every seller, a merchant seller makes the following additional implied warranties.

(1) Warranty Against Infringement. Unless otherwise agreed, every seller who is a merchant regularly dealing in goods of the kind which he has sold warrants that the goods shall be delivered free of the rightful claim of any third person by way of patent or trademark infringement or the like.[16]

(2) Warranty of Merchantability or Fitness for Normal Use. A merchant seller who makes a sale of goods in which he customarily deals [17] makes an implied warranty of merchantability.[18] The warranty is in fact a group of warranties, the most important of which is that the goods are fit for the ordinary purposes for which they are sold. (See p. 374, Sams v. Ezy-Way Foodliner Company) It also includes implied warranties as to the general or average quality of the goods, and their packaging and labeling.[19]

The implied warranty of merchantability relates to the condition of the goods at the time the seller is to perform under the contract. Once the risk of loss has passed to the buyer,[20] there is no warranty as to the continuing merchantability of the goods unless such subsequent deterioration or condition is proof that the goods were in fact not merchantable when the seller made delivery.

Sec. 24-D. Warranties in Particular Sales. Particular types of sales may present considerations or give rise to warranties in addition to those already discussed.

(1) Sale of Food or Drink. The sale of food or drink, whether to be consumed on or off the seller's premises, is a sale and, when made by a merchant, carries the implied warranty that the food is fit for its ordinary purpose, that is, human consumption.[21] It is likely that the limitations of the prior law will continue under the Code so that there is no breach of warranty when a harmful object found in the food is of such a nature that it could be expected to be found in it or was natural to the particular kind of food, such as an oyster shell in oysters, a

---

[16] UCC Sec. 2-312(3).

[17] This includes the seller of food or drink to be consumed on the premises or to be taken out. UCC Sec. 2-314(1).

[18] UCC Sec. 2-314 (1). Under USA Sec. 15(2), it was also necessary that the sale be made by description, as when a buyer orders certain described articles which the seller agrees to sell.

[19] UCC Sec. 2-314 (2). Other implied warranties on the part of a merchant may also arise from a course of dealing or usage of trade. UCC Sec. 2-314(3).

[20] See Ch. 22.

[21] UCC Sec. 2-314(1), (2)(c).

chicken bone in chicken, and so on. (See p. 376, Bethia v. Cape Cod Corporation)

(2) Sale of Article with Patent or Trade Name. The sale of a patent or trade-name article is treated by the Code with respect to warranties in the came way as any other sale. The fact that the sale is made on the basis of the patent or trade name does not bar the existence of a warranty of fitness for a particular purpose when the circumstances giving rise to such a warranty otherwise exist.[22]

It is a question of fact, however, whether the buyer relied on the seller's skill and judgment when he made the purchase. That is, if the buyer asked for a patent or trade-name article and insisted on it, it is apparent that he did not rely upon the seller's skill and judgment and therefore the factual basis for an implied warranty of fitness for the particular purpose is lacking.[23] If the necessary reliance upon the seller's skill and judgment is shown, the warranty arises in that situation.[24]

(3) Sale on Buyer's Specifications. When the buyer furnishes the seller with exact specifications for the preparation or manufacture of goods, the same warranties arise as in the case of any other sale of such goods by the particular seller. No warranty of fitness for a particular purpose can arise, however, since it is clear that the buyer is purchasing on the basis of his own decision and is not relying on the seller's skill and judgment.

In sales made upon the buyer's specifications, no warranty against infringement is impliedly made by the merchant seller;[25] and conversely the buyer in substance makes a warranty to protect the seller from liability should the seller be held liable for patent violation by following the specifications of the buyer.[26]

(4) Sale of Secondhand or Used Goods. Under the Code no warranty arises as to fitness of used property for ordinary use when the sale is made by a casual seller. If made by a merchant seller, such a warranty appears to be implied. Prior to the Code a number of states followed the rule that no warranty arose in connection with used or secondhand goods, particularly automobiles and machinery; whereas some courts found a warranty of fitness for ordinary use in the sale of secondhand goods, particularly airplanes. It is likely that this division of authority will continue under the Code.

---

[22] See p. 367.
[23] UCC Sec. 2-315, Official Comment point 5.
[24] This changes the rule under USA Sec. 15(4), although many courts had by interpretation reached the same result under that section, which is now expressly authorized by the Code.
[25] See p. 368.
[26] UCC Sec. 2-312(3).

Sec. 24-E. Exclusion and Modification of Warranties. Warranties may be waived subject to the limitation that the waiver is not effective if the result be unreasonable or unconscionable.[27] If a warranty of fitness is waived, the provision effecting the waiver must be made in writing and be conspicuous to assure that the buyer will be aware of its presence. If the implied warranty of merchantability is excluded, the exclusion clause must be in writing and must expressly mention the word "merchantability."

(1) Particular Provisions. Such a statement as "there are no warranties which extend beyond the description on the face hereof" excludes all implied warranties of fitness.[28] Implied warranties are waived by the statement of "as is," "with all faults," or other language which in normal common speech calls attention to the exclusion of warranties and makes it clear that there is no implied warranty.[29]

(2) Examination. There is no implied warranty with respect to defects in goods that an examination should have revealed when the buyer before making the final contract has examined the goods, or a model or sample, or has refused to make such examination.[30]

(3) Dealings and Customs. An implied warranty may be excluded or modified by course of dealings, course of performance, or usage of trade.[31]

Sec. 24-F. Caveat Emptor. In the absence of fraud on the part of the seller or circumstances in which the law finds an express or an implied warranty, the relationship of the seller and buyer is aptly described by the maxim of *caveat emptor* (let the buyer beware). Courts at common law rigidly applied this rule, requiring the purchaser in the ordinary sale to act in reliance upon his own judgment except when the seller gave him an express warranty. The trend of the Uniform Sales Act, the Uniform Commercial Code, and decisions of modern courts has been to soften the harshness of this rule, primarily by implying warranties for the protection of the buyer. The rule of caveat emptor is still applied, however, when the buyer has full opportunity to make such examination of the goods as would disclose the existence of any defect and the seller is not guilty of fraud.

Sec. 24-G. Product Liability. When harm to person or property results from the use or condition of an article of personal property, the person

---

[27] Secs. 2-316 (1), 2-302(1).
[28] Sec. 2-316(2).
[29] Sec. 2-316(3)(a).
[30] Sec. 2-316(3)(b).
[31] Sec. 2-316(3)(c).

injured may be entitled to recover damages. This right may be based on the theory that there was a breach of warranty or that the person sued was negligent.

(1) Breach of Warranty. At common law the rule was that only the parties to a transaction had any rights relating to it. Accordingly, only the buyer could sue his immediate seller for breach of warranty. The rule was stated in the terms that there could be no suit for breach of warranty unless there was a privity of contract between the plaintiff and the defendant.

In most states an exception to the privity rule developed under which members of the buyer's family and various other remote persons not in privity of contract with the seller or manufacturer can sue for breach of warranty when injured by the harmful condition of food, beverages, or drugs. As a limiting factor, the right to sue the manufacturer of a bottled or packaged food might be denied when there is evidence that another person has or might have tampered with the food before it reached the buyer or consumer.

The Code expressly abolishes the requirement of privity to a limited extent by permitting a suit for breach of warranty to be brought against the seller by members of the buyer's family, his household, and his guests, with respect to personal injury sustained by them.[32] Apart from the express provision made by the Code, there is a conflict of authority as to whether privity of contract is required in other cases, with the trend being toward the abolition of that requirement. In many states, the doctrine is flatly rejected when suit is brought by a buyer against the manufacturer or a prior seller. In many instances, recovery by the buyer against the remote manufacturer or seller is based on the fact that the defendant had advertised directly to the public and therefore made a warranty to the purchasing consumer of the truth of his advertising. (See p. 378, Hamon v. Digliani) Recovery may also be allowed when the consumer mails to the manufacturer a warranty registration card which the manufacturer had packed with the purchased article.

(2) Negligence. Independently of the provisions of the Code, a person injured through the use or condition of personal property may be entitled to sue the manufacturer for the damages which he sustains on the theory that the defendant was negligent in the preparation or manufacture of the article. Historically, such suits were limited by the concept of privity of contract so that only the buyer could sue the seller for the latter's negligence but could not sue the manufacturer. This

---

[32] Sec. 2-318. Note that this does not cover property loss which the beneficiary might sustain, and that it does not extend to employees of the buyer nor such third persons as pedestrians. The Code expressly leaves open for local state law to determine whether the requirement of privity is abolished further than declared by the Code.

requirement of privity has generally been abolished, and the modern rule is that whenever the manufacturer as a reasonable man should foresee that if he is negligent a particular class of persons will be injured by his product, the manufacturer is liable to an injured member of that class without regard to whether such plaintiff purchased from him or from anyone.

(3) Comparison of Liability for Breach of Contract and for Negligence. In many states, an injured plaintiff has the choice of suing for breach of warranty or for damages for negligence. The importance of the distinction between the two remedies lies in the fact that to prove his case for breach of warranty the plaintiff is only required to prove facts of which he has direct knowledge or about which he can readily learn. That is, he need only show that there was a sale and a warranty, that the goods did not conform to the warranty, and that he was injured thereby. In the case of the action for negligence against the manufacturer, the plaintiff figuratively must go into the defendant's plant or factory and learn how the given article was made and prove in court that there was negligence. Unless the plaintiff is able to show that the design of the manufacturer's product or his general method of manufacture was faulty, it is likely that the plaintiff will be unable to prove that there was negligence. It has been the recognition of this difficulty which, to a large degree, has led the courts to expand the warranty liability under which proof of negligence is not required.

(4) Effect of Reprocessing by Distributor. Liability of the manufacturer or supplier to the ultimate customer, whether for warranty or in tort, does not arise when the manufacturer or supplier believes or has reason to believe that the immediate distributor or processor is to complete processing or is to take further steps that will remove an otherwise foreseeable danger. Accordingly, although the supplier of unfinished pork to a retailer should realize that it might contain trichinae and be dangerous to the ultimate consumers, he is not liable to an ultimate consumer who contracts trichinosis when the retailer in purchasing the unfinished pork told the supplier that he would finish processing it, which would destroy any trichinae, and the supplier did not know or have reason to know that the retailer failed to do so.

Cases for Chapter 24

Standard Stevedoring Co. v. Jaffe

42 Tenn.App. 378, 302 S.W.2d 829 (1956)

Standard Stevedoring Co. purchased a motor crane from Jaffe. Standard based its decision to purchase the crane on an advertisement in a trade publication. Part of the ad described it as a "15-20 ton P & H mechanical crane." Standard sent a representative to look at the crane and thereafter purchased it. Standard then learned that the capacity of the crane was substantially less than 15 tons. Standard sued to rescind the sale. From a decision in its favor, Jaffe appealed.

CARNEY, J. . . . There was an express warranty on the part of the defendant that the crane had a 15 to 20 ton capacity and . . . the crane which was sold had a capacity of substantially less tonnage and . . . therefore, the express warranty had been breached.

The defendant contended that since the complainant [Standard] sent employees to inspect the machine, the complainant did not rely on any warranty or statement of the defendant but relied upon the examination of his employees. The preponderance of the proof is that a person cannot tell the lifting capacity of one of these machines simply by looking at it. Also we think the preponderance of the proof is that no attempt was made by the employees of complainant who inspected the machine to ascertain its maximum lifting capacity by actual tests or demonstration. . . .

. . . The defendant was guilty of no fraud or intentional wrongdoing in warranting the . . . machine to have a 15 to 20 ton capacity. The defendant is not an engineer. That fact does not relieve the defendant of liability.

[The Sales Act declares] "Any affirmation of fact or any promise by the seller relating to the goods is an express warranty if the natural tendency of such affirmation or promise is to induce the buyer to purchase the goods, and if the buyer purchases the goods relying thereon. No affirmation of the value of the goods, nor any statement purporting to be a statement of the seller's opinion only shall be construed as a warranty."

. . . Where a seller of goods makes an affirmation of fact which has a tendency to induce and does induce a buyer to purchase, there is an express warranty; and if it is false, the seller is liable irrespective of any fraud or knowledge on his part that the affirmation was untrue and irrespective of whether he intended to warrant the goods or not.

Under the Uniform Sales Act a purchaser has an absolute right to rescind where there has been a breach of an express warranty. . . .

[Judgment affirmed.]

Code Comment: The same decision would be made under the Code because the description of the crane formed part of the basis of entering into the bargain and was therefore an express warranty. UCC Sec. 2-313-(1)(b). Since an examination of the crane would not reveal the defect, the buyer was not barred because he examined the crane. See Sec. 2-316(3)(b). Since there was a breach of warranty, the buyer, among other things, had the right to revoke his acceptance of the goods, and to cancel the contract. See p. 371.

Sams v. Ezy-Way Foodliner Company

157 Maine 10, 170 A.2d 160 (1961)

Sams purchased some frankfurts at Ezy-Way's Self Service Food super-market. They were contained in a sealed plastic bag labeled "Jordan's Hot Dogs." The manufacturer had a good reputation and there was no evidence of any negligence. In eating one of the hot dogs, Sams was cut by pieces of glass which it contained. He sued Ezy-Way for his damages. From a judg-ment in favor of the supermarket, Sams appealed.

WILLIAMSON, C.J. . . . The controlling issue in this action of a plaintiff purchaser-consumer against a defendant-retailer is whether there is a "sealed container exception" from the implied warranty of merchantability under our Sales Act. . . .

Liability of the defendant in this action rests solely upon an implied warranty of merchantability under Section 15 II of the Uniform Sales Act. R.S. c. 185, first enacted P.L. 1923, c. 191. It arises, if at all, by contract and is not dependent in the slightest degree upon fault of the defendant. The pertinent portions of Section 15 read:

"Sec. 15. Implied warranties of quality.—Subject to the provisions of this chapter and of any statute in that behalf, there is no implied warranty or condition as to the quality or fitness for any particular pur-pose of goods supplied under a contract to sell or a sale, except as follows: . . .

"II. Where the goods are bought by description from a seller who deals in goods of that description, whether he be the grower or manu-facturer or not, there is an implied warranty that the goods shall be of merchantable quality. . . .

"IV. In the case of a contract to sell or a sale of a specified article under its patent or other trade name, there is no implied warranty as to its fitness for any particular purpose.". . .

The plaintiff does not contend that he relied upon the defendant in selecting the particular brand of frankfurts purchased by him. He brings his case solely upon the warranty of merchantability.

A "hot dog" containing glass is, of course, not fit to eat and is there-fore not of merchantable quality. . . .

The frankfurts in the sealed plastic bag were sold by description within the meaning of Clause II. Assuming (we need not decide) that "Jordan's Hot Dogs" was a trade or brand name under Clause IV, the warranty of merchantability under Clause II was not thereby destroyed. Indeed, the trade name of "Jordan's Hot Dogs" was fairly intended to describe the goods to the prospective customer. . . .

The fact that the frankfurts were sold in a self-service market does not affect the result. The sign, or label, effectively described the goods in the market and in the package. The printed word was the silent salesman. The vitality of Clause II does not rest upon the presence of a clerk. Compare Mead v. Coca Cola Bottling Co., [329 Mass. 440, 108 N.E.2d 757] holding a warranty of merchantability under Clause II attached to the sale of coca cola in an automatic vending machine. . . .

We come to the issue of whether the retailer of food in a sealed container is insulated from an implied warranty of merchantability under the Sales Act. We make no distinction between [a] can of asparagus . . . , [a] package of macaroni . . . , bread wrapped in paper and sealed [referring to cases involving such containers], and the "hot dogs" in the sealed plastic bag. In each instance we have a sealed container or an original package effectively preventing inspection by the retailer at any time and by the purchaser until the container is opened. The basis of the "sealed container exception" is that the purchaser could not have placed reliance upon the retailer's skill or judgment in determining that the contents were fit to eat. . . .

The Uniform Sales Act codified, extended, and liberalized the common law. Rules inconsistent with the Act were thereby abolished. . . .

In Bigelow v. Maine Cent. R.R., [110 Maine 105; 85 A. 396] decided in 1912 before the adoption of the Uniform Sales Act in Maine, the Court held that a dining car operator was not liable for breach of an implied warranty of fitness to a diner for illness resulting from defective canned asparagus. The decision, although limited on its facts to the liability of a restaurant keeper to his guest, may fairly be said to state the common law of our state applicable, as here, in the case of the purchaser-consumer against the retailer. . . .

Under the Sales Act, by the great weight of authority there is no "sealed container exception.". . .

In the instant case for the first time since the Sales Act we have the problem of the sealed container presented to us. . . .

Vast changes have taken place in the manufacture and distribution of food products since the dining car case of 1912. The purchase of food in a can, jar, package, or sealed bag under brand or trade name is commonplace. The pantry shelf, the refrigerator, and the "deep freeze" evidence the fact. Sales are made over the counter, at self-service markets, and by vending machines. Inspection of such products which will uncover the defect within the container, as the defective asparagus, or the pin in the bread, is impossible as a practical matter until at least the container is opened, or in many instances, as here, until the product is eaten.

There is as well the problem of the latent defect in the product not sold in a container. The pin in the unwrapped loaf of bread may be, and probably is, hidden from the retailer and buyer no less than the pin in the wrapped loaf of "Ward's bread.". . .

If the frankfurts here had not been sold in a sealed bag, inspection would not have disclosed the glass within the edible casing. . . .

Without the sealed container exception, the retailer's exposure to liability is without question increased. Obviously liability based on fault alone is less burdensome than liability without fault based on an implied warranty of fitness or merchantability.

The burden is, however, rendered the less by the ability of the retailer to reach out on his warranty against his seller, and so in turn to the manufacturer. . . .

The Uniform Sales Act in establishing implied warranties under Section 15 ended our "sealed container" rule at common law. The rule of the Bigelow case is not, in our view, sound under the Sales Act.

[Judgment for defendant reversed and remanded.]

Code Comment: The same conclusion would be made under the Code. The considerations which persuaded the court in the Sams case would be equally persuasive under the Code. This is particularly true since, to introduce an exception that is not found in the Code, would tend to defeat the purposes and policies of the Code and to destroy uniformity throughout the country.

Bethia v. Cape Cod Corporation

10 Wis. 2d 323, 103 N.W.2d 64 (1960)

Bethia, while a patron of the Cape Cod Inn, in Milwaukee, Wisconsin, ordered, consumed on the premises, and paid for a chicken sandwich. The sandwich, which consisted of a layer of two or three pieces of sliced white chicken meat and a layer of lettuce between two slices of bread, was served cut diagonally and pinned with toothpicks. The plaintiff first ate the meat and then bit into the portion of the sandwich containing the bread and the lettuce. Embedded in the lettuce was a sharp fragment of chicken bone about one and one-half inches long and about one-eighth of an inch in diameter at its thickest point. As the plaintiff swallowed, he felt a sharp pain in the lower part of his throat. The bone eventually became lodged, causing severe laceration and infection, which required surgery. From a decision for the defendant, Bethia appealed.

HALLOWS, J. . . . Is the implied warranty of reasonable fitness of food for human consumption breached because of the presence of a chicken bone in a chicken sandwich? [Mix v. Ingersoll Candy Co., 6 Cal.2d 674, 59 P.2d 144 (1936)], which represents one view, held that as a matter of law a harmful substance present in food which is natural to it cannot be a legal defect or a breach of the implied warranty of reasonable fitness of such food. That case was brought both on the theory of implied warranty and of common-law negligence. The plaintiff was injured by a chicken bone in chicken-pot pie. On demurrer the court held the defendant was not liable under either theory because

what matter is proven

chicken bones were natural to the meat served and not a foreign substance, and it was common knowledge chicken pies occasionally contain chicken bones, and therefore their presence ought to be anticipated and guarded against by the consumer.

This reasoning is fallacious because it assumes that all substances which are natural to the food in one stage or another of preparation are, in fact, anticipated by the average consumer in the final product served. It does not logically follow that every product which contains some chicken must as a matter of law be expected to contain occasionally or frequently chicken bones or chicken-bone slivers because chicken bones are natural to chicken meat and both have a common origin. Categorizing a substance as foreign or natural may have some importance in determining the degree of negligence of the processor of food, but it is not determinative of what is unfit or harmful in fact for human consumption. A bone natural to the meat can cause as much harm as a foreign substance such as a pebble, piece of wire, or glass. All are indigestible and likely to cause injury. Naturalness of the substance to any ingredients in the food served is important only in determining whether the consumer may reasonably expect to find such substance in the particular type of dish or style of food served.

However, the reasoning of the Mix Case has been followed by four intermediate appellate courts: [Cal.] a turkey bone embedded in the dressing of a special plate of roast turkey; [Cal.] a fragment of chicken bone in chicken pie; [Ill.] a bone in creamed chicken made from turkey meat (query: Whether a turkey bone is natural to creamed chicken) ; [Ga.] a particle of bone in a barbecued pork sandwich; [Ga.] turkey bone in creamed turkey.

The naturalness doctrine was applied in [Iowa] to a sliver of bone in a pork chop swallowed by the deceased; in [N.C.] a partially crystallized grain of corn in corn flakes; and in [Cal.] a fish bone in Hot Barquette of Seafood Mornay, made of several kinds of fish. . . .

The "foreign-natural" test applied as a matter of law does not recommend itself to us as being logical or desirable. It is true one can expect a t-bone in T-bone steak, chicken bones in roast chicken, pork bone in a pork chop, pork bone in spare ribs, a rib bone in short ribs of beef, and fish bones in a whole baked or fried fish; but the expectation is based not on the naturalness of the particular bone to the meat, fowl, or fish, but on the type of dish served containing the meat, fowl, or fish. There is a distinction between what a consumer expects to find in a fish stick and in a baked or fried fish, or in a chicken sandwich made from sliced white meat and in roast chicken. The test should be what is reasonably expected by the consumer in the food as served, not what might be natural to the ingredients of that food prior to preparation. What is to be reasonably expected by the consumer is a jury question in most cases; at least, we cannot say as a matter of law that a patron of a restaurant must expect a bone in a chicken sandwich either because chicken bones are occasionally found there or are natural to chicken.

This test as applied to an action for breach of the implied warranty is keyed to what is "reasonably" fit. If it is found that the chicken bone of the size alleged ought to be anticipated in a chicken sandwich and guarded against by the consumer plaintiff, then the sandwich was reasonably fit under the implied warranty. As applied to the action for common-law negligence, the test is related to the foreseeability of harm on the part of the defendant. He is not an insurer but has the duty of ordinary care to eliminate or remove in the preparation of the food he serves such harmful bones as the consumer of the food, as served, would not ordinarily anticipate and guard against.

[Judgment reversed.]

Code Comment: While the Code provides for the warranty of fitness of food for human consumption as an aspect of fitness for normal use, the Code does not define "fitness." Accordingly the court in the Bethia case and other courts to which the opinion refers would reach the same conclusion as they did before the Code since the question here involved is the meaning of "fitness."

Hamon v. Digliani
148 Conn. 710, 174 A.2d 294 (1961)

Hamon purchased Lestoil, a household detergent, from Digliani. She was severely burned by it and sued the seller and its manufacturers, the Lestoil Corporation and the Adell Chemical Company. The manufacturers had extensively promoted the product by television, radio, and newspapers, stating that it could be used safely for household and cleaning tasks and that it was "the all-purpose detergent—for all household cleaning and laundering." The manufacturers defended on the ground that Hamon had not purchased the bottle of Lestoil from them. From a judgment in their favor, Hamon appealed.

MURPHY, A.J. . . . The plaintiff, by her appeal, is endeavoring to change the rule, which has existed in this state at least since Welshausen v. Charles Parker Co., 83 Conn. 231, 76 A. 271, that in order to sustain an action for breach of express or implied warranty there has to be evidence of a contract between the parties, for without a contract there could be no warranty. We held in that case (83 Conn. at page 233, 76 A. 271,) that the ultimate purchaser, or subvendee, of a gun manufactured by the defendant had no cause of action for breach of warranty against the manufacturer, with whom he had not dealt directly, but who had sold the gun to a dealer, who in turn sold it to a third party, from whom the plaintiff purchased it. The rule was reiterated in Borucki v. MacKenzie Bros. Co., 125 Conn. 92, 96, 3 A.2d 224, 225, wherein we quoted from Gearing v. Berkson, 223 Mass. 257,

260, 111 N.E. 785, L.R.A. 1961D, 1006, as follows: "The implied warranty, or to speak more accurately the implied condition of the contract, to supply an article fit for the purpose required, is in the nature of a contract of personal indemnity with the original purchaser. It does not 'run with the goods.' "

As we understand the argument advanced by the plaintiff, it is that, despite the lack of a sale directly from the manufacturer, the consumer should have a right of action against the manufacturer for breach of express or implied warranty where the consumer, in reliance on the representations made by the manufacturer, purchases a sealed container of the manufacturer's product from a retailer and sustains injury as the result of the use of the product in the manner intended.

Within recent years, numerous cases have arisen in other jurisdictions in which the courts have extended breach of warranty law to encompass a right of action against the manufacturer for breach of either an express or an implied warranty of his product and have eliminated privity of contract as an element essential to recovery. Dean Prosser, in an extensive review of the cases and trends in this regard, points out that the privity requirement was abolished by judicial fiat in cases involving the sale of food and that since 1934 thirteen jurisdictions have applied against the manufacturer a rule of strict liability for statements which prove to be false, if they were made to the public in labels on the goods or in the manufacturer's advertising or disseminated literature and it can be found that the plaintiff relied on the statements in making his purchase. . . . Since its publication, the Court of Appeals of New York, in Greenberg v. Lorenz, 9 N.Y.2d 195, 213 N.Y.S.2d 39, 173 N.E.2d 773, has ruled in a food case that lack of privity did not bar recovery by a child when the food had not been purchased by her but by her father. . . . Also, the opinion states . . . that about twenty states have abolished the requirement of privity, the latest being Virginia and New Jersey. . . .

The representation made by a manufacturer on the packages of its detergent was held to be a warranty to the ultimate consumer in Worley v. Proctor & Gamble Mfg. Co., 241 Mo.App. 1114, 1122, 253 S.W.2d 532, despite the absence of privity between the parties. Similarly, it was held in Rogers v. Toni Home Permanent Co., 167 Ohio St. 244, 249, 147 N.E.2d 612, 75 A.L.R.2d 103, that the representations made by the manufacturer of a home permanent lotion in its advertisements, on which the plaintiff relied, constituted an express warranty for breach of which the plaintiff could maintain her action, although there was no contractual relationship between her and the manufacturer. . . .

These cases, and others of similar import, rely on the original concept of an action for breach of warranty, that is, that it sounds in tort and is based on the plaintiff's reliance on deceitful appearances or representations rather than on a promise. . . . The recognition of such a right of action rested on the public policy of protecting an innocent buyer from harm rather than on the insuring of any contractual rights. . . . With the development of the merchandising concepts of the past quarter of a century, the ultimate consumer rarely has the opportunity to inspect the goods offered for sale. That was not the case when the Sales Act was adopted in Connecticut [in] 1907. Originally drafted to govern the relations between the immediate buyer and seller, two of the implied warranties of quality were expanded in 1939 and 1951 so that all members of the buyer's household were covered. . . . In the latter year, legislation was also enacted imposing an implied warranty of fitness of food and drink for consumption on or off the premises for the benefit of the buyer and all persons for whom the purchase was intended. [Both statutes are repealed but restated by UCC Secs. 2-314, 2-318].

The neighborhood storekeeper who called all of his customers by their first names and measured or weighed out the desired amount of the commodity ordered before packaging it has practically disappeared from the commercial world. Where one occasionally survives, his method of displaying and dispensing his wares has radically changed. The shelves and showcases in his store contain, for the most part, packages and containers which have been packed and sealed by the manufacturer or by a producer who puts out as his own the products made by another. Neither the retailer nor the consumer can sample or otherwise examine the product. The maxim "caveat emptor" has become a millstone around the necks of dealer and customer. While the customer may maintain an action under the Sales Act against the retailer for breach of implied warranty, the dealer in turn must sue his supplier to recoup his damages and costs where the customer prevails. Eventually, after several separate and distinct pieces of costly litigation by those in the chain of title, the manufacturer is finally obliged to shoulder the responsibility which should have been his in the first instance.

The supermarkets and other retail outlets of our day dispense with the need for clerks behind counters to wait on customers. The goods are displayed on shelves and counters lining the aisles, and the customer, as he searches for a product, is bewitched, bewildered, and bedeviled by the glittering packaging in riotous color and the alluring enticement of the products' qualities as depicted on labels. The item selected is apt to be the one which was so glowingly described by a glamorous television artist on the housewife's favorite program, just preceding the shopping trip Or the media of advertising might have been radio, magazine, billboard or newspaper. All are widely used in the appeal directed to the ultimate consumer. There appears to be no sound reason for depriving a plaintiff of the right to maintain an action against the manufacturer where the plaintiff alleges that he was

induced to purchase the product by the representations in the manufacturer's advertising and that he sustained harm when the product
failed to measure up to the express or implied representations. . . .

The manufacturer or producer who puts a commodity for personal
use or consumption on the market in a sealed package or other closed
container should be held to have impliedly warranted to the ultimate
consumer that the product is reasonably fit for the purpose intended
and that it does not contain any harmful and deleterious ingredient
of which due and ample warning has not been given. . . . Where the
manufacturer or producer makes representations in his advertisements
or by the labels on his products as an inducement to the ultimate purchaser, the manufacturer or producer should be held to strict account-
ability to any person who buys the product in reliance on the representations and later suffers injury because the product fails to conform
to them. . . . Lack of privity is not a bar to suit under these circumstances. . . .

[Judgment reversed and action remanded.]

Code Comment: The decision would be the same under the Code since
the Code does not establish any rule as to the privity of contract beyond
that allowing the members of the buyer's family or household, and his
guests, to sue for personal injuries resulting from breach of a warranty
made by the immediate seller. Sec. 2-318. This is not a statutory declaration
that privity should be retained in other cases, because point 3 of the official
Code comment to that section states "beyond this, the section is neutral and
is not intended to enlarge or restrict the developing case law on whether
the seller's warranties, given to his buyer who resells, extend to other
persons in the distributive chain."

Questions and Case Problems

1. What is the objective of each of the following rules of law?

(a) A statement by a seller may constitute a warranty even though he
does not state that he makes a warranty and generally even though
he does not intend to make a warranty.

(b) A manufacturer-seller may in some cases be liable for harm caused
by negligence in the manufacture of his product as well as for
breach of warranty as to its fitness.

2. Frank purchased a used automobile from the McCafferty Ford Co.
The person who sold the auto to McCafferty was not the owner, and the
true owner successfully reclaimed it from Frank. Frank then sued McCafferty although McCafferty had said nothing about the title to the automobile. Was McCafferty liable to Frank? (Frank v. McCafferty Ford Co.,
192 Pa.Super. 435, 161 A.2d 896)

3. Lowe was induced to buy a diamond ring from Lamb by the seller's
statement that the ring was worth twice the purchase price and that al-

though it was a yellow diamond, it was worth as much as a white diamond. When Lowe later learned that the diamond did not have the value as represented, he sued Lamb for breach of warranty. Was Lamb liable? (Lowe v. Lamb, [Pa.] 2 Crawford Co. 125)

4. Queen ordered goods by sample from Loomis Bros. Corp., a dealer in that kind of goods. The goods that were delivered conformed to the sample but were not fit for the normal intended use. Loomis claimed that it had fully performed its contract since it was only required to deliver goods that conformed to the sample. Was it correct? Loomis Bros. Corp. v. Queen, [Pa.] 17 D.&C.2d 482, 46 Del.Co. 79)

5. Sensabaugh purchased from Morgan Brothers Farm Supply construction equipment that was manufactured by J. I. Case Co. No warranty was stated in the sales contract. Several days after the transaction was completed, Morgan gave Sensabaugh a manual of instructions on the back of which was a printed warranty of the J. I. Case Co. When the equipment proved defective, Sensabaugh sued Morgan Bros., which raised the defense that Sensabaugh was bound by the warranty as stated on the back of the manual. Decide. (Sensabaugh v. Morgan Brothers Farm Supply, Inc., [Md.] 165 A.2d 914)

6. Hodge Chile Company negotiated for the purchase of food cartons from Interstate Folding Box Co. Interstate sent samples of its boxes to Hodge without making any statement as to their qualifications. Hodge subjected the samples to various tests and then placed an order for the boxes with Interstate. Hodge did not pay for the boxes and, when sued for their purchase price, claimed that there was a breach of an implied warranty of fitness of the boxes for use for their intended purpose. It was shown that the defects of which Hodge complained had not been revealed in the tests because the cartons had been filled by hand instead of by machine and the chile that had been put in the boxes was poured at a lower temperature than when poured by machine. Did Hodge have a valid defense? (Interstate Folding Box Co. v. Hodge Chile Co., [Mo.App.] 334 S.W.2d 408)

7. Kaspirowitz asked his druggist to recommend something for a skin condition. The druggist recommended a bottle of Sebizon manufactured by Schering Corporation. The bottle bore a warning on the front label of "Caution: Federal law prohibits dispensing without prescription." On the reverse side of the bottle were four numbered instructions entitled: "Directions to the Patient." The last direction stated: "Repeat applications as directed by physician." The druggist sold the Sebizon to Kaspirowitz without prescription. Its use caused an extreme rash and swelling. Kaspirowitz sued Schering Corporation on the ground that by putting the product on the market for sale without warning of possible dangerous consequences from use, Schering Corporation had made a warranty that Sebizon was safe to use. Was Kaspirowitz entitled to recover from Schering? (Kaspirowitz v. Schering Corporation, [N.J.] 175 A.2d 658)

CHAPTER 25

Remedies for
Breach of Sales Contracts

In the event that one of the parties to a sales contract fails to discharge his responsibilities, the other party has several remedies available to him by provision of the law. In addition, the parties may have agreed upon certain provisions pertaining to remedies in their contract.

Sec. 25-A. Remedies of the Seller.

(1) Seller's Lien. In the absence of a provision for the extension of credit to the purchaser, the seller has a lien on the goods or the right to retain possession of the goods until he is paid for them. Even when the goods are sold on credit, the seller has a lien on the goods if the buyer becomes insolvent or the period of credit expires while the goods are in the seller's possession.

The seller's lien is a specific lien, which attaches to the particular goods and only for the purchase price due on them. It cannot be exercised by the seller for the purpose of collecting any other debt or charge owed him by the purchaser.

Delivery of part of the goods to the buyer does not bar a lien on the remainder of the goods unless the parties intended that it should have that effect. Moreover, if the buyer is insolvent, the seller may refuse to deliver any further goods unless paid for in cash, not only for those goods but also for any previously supplied under the contract.[1]

(2) Completion or Salvage of Repudiated Contract. It may be that the buyer repudiates or otherwise breaches the contract while the seller has some or all of the goods in his possession in either a finished and ready-to-deliver stage or in a partially manufactured stage. If the seller has in his possession goods that satisfy or conform to the contract with the buyer, he may identify those goods to the contract which the buyer has broken.[2] This will enable the seller to sue the buyer for the

---

[1] Uniform Commercial Code, Sec. 2-702(1).
[2] UCC Sec. 2-704(1)(a).

purchase price and to make a resale of the goods, holding the buyer responsible for any loss thereon.

If the goods intended for the buyer are in an unfinished state, the seller must exercise reasonable commercial judgment to determine whether (a) to sell them for scrap or salvage or (b) to complete their manufacture, then identify them to the buyer's contract, and resell them.[3] In any case the buyer is liable for the loss sustained by the seller if the latter has acted properly.

(3) Stopping Delivery by Carrier or Bailee. The goods may be in transit on their way to the buyer. They also may be in the hands of a bailee who is to surrender them to the buyer. Under the Code the seller may stop delivery of the goods to the buyer, without regard to the quantity involved, if the buyer is insolvent.[4] In addition, the seller may stop delivery if the quantity involved is a carload, truckload, or planeload, or more, whenever the buyer has repudiated the contract or failed to make a payment due before delivery or if for any reason the seller would have the right to retain or reclaim the goods.[5]

Except for a carrier's lien for transportation or a bailee's lien for storage charges, the right to stop delivery is superior to other claims. Thus, when the creditors of the buyer attach the goods en route, their claims are subject to the right of the seller.

After the seller regains possession of the goods by stopping delivery, he is in the same legal position as though he had not placed them on the carrier or delivered them to the bailee and may assert against them a seller's lien. When the seller reserves title or the right to possession, the seller need not invoke the right to stop delivery since he can withhold the property from the buyer by virtue of such reservation.

(a) EXERCISE OF THE RIGHT. The seller exercises the right to stop delivery by notifying the carrier or bailee that the goods are to be returned to or held for him. If the seller gives the carrier or bailee proper notice in sufficient time so that through the exercise of due diligence it can stop delivery, the carrier or bailee must obey the seller's order. Any additional cost involved must be borne by the seller. If the carrier or bailee fails to act, it is liable to the seller for any loss he sustains.

After proper notice has been given, the carrier or other bailee must follow the instructions of the seller as to the disposal of the goods. When a negotiable document of title for the goods is in circulation,

---

[3] Sec. 2-704(1)(b),(2).

[4] A person is "insolvent" when he has ceased to pay his debts in the ordinary course of business, or cannot pay his debts as they become due, or is insolvent within the meaning of the Federal Bankruptcy Law. Sec. 1-201 (23).

[5] Sec. 2-705(1). This expands the right of stopping in transit under the Uniform Sales Act, Secs. 57 to 59, which existed only in case of insolvency and when the goods were in possession of a carrier.

however, the carrier or bailee is not obliged to deliver the goods until the document is surrendered. The holder of such a document may defeat the seller's right of stopping delivery.[6]

(b) TERMINATION OF RIGHT TO STOP DELIVERY. The seller's right to stop delivery is terminated or lost, even though a proper notification is given, when (1) the goods have been delivered to the buyer, (2) the carrier acknowledges the right of the buyer by reshipping at his direction or by agreeing to hold for him as a warehouseman; (3) the bailee in possession acknowledges that he holds the goods for the buyer, or (4) the seller has negotiated to the buyer a negotiable document of title covering the goods.[7]

(4) Reclamation of Goods Received by Insolvent Buyer. The buyer may have obtained goods from the seller on credit when unknown to the seller, the buyer was insolvent. If the buyer made a false written statement to the seller that he was solvent and received the goods within three months after that time, the seller may at any time demand and reclaim the goods sold to the buyer on credit.[8] If the buyer never made a false written statement of solvency, or if he made it more than three months before he received the goods, the seller, in order to reclaim the goods, must demand the return of the goods within ten days after they are received by the buyer.[9]

(5) Resale. When the buyer has broken the contract by wrongfully rejecting the goods, wrongfully revoking his acceptance, failing to pay, or repudiating the contract, the seller may resell the goods or the balance of them remaining in his possession, or the goods over which he has reacquired possession as by stopping delivery. After the resale, the seller is not liable to the original buyer upon the contract or for any profit obtained by him on the resale. On the other hand, if the proceeds are less than the contract price, the seller may recover the loss from the original buyer.[10]

Unless otherwise agreed, the resale may be made either as a public or auction sale or as a private sale, as long as the method followed is commercially reasonable. The Code prescribes certain formalities for the resale but provides that a person who purchases in good faith acquires the goods free of all claims of the original buyer, even though the resale was irregular because the seller did not follow the procedure prescribed for such a sale.[11]

---

[6] Sec. 2-705(3)(c).
[7] Sec. 2-705(2).
[8] Sec. 2-702(2).
[9] Sec. 2-702(2).
[10] Sec. 2-706(1),(6).
[11] Sec. 2-706(5).

Reasonable notice must be given to the original buyer of the intention to make a private sale. Such notice must be given him of a public sale unless the goods are perishable in character or threaten to decline speedily in value. Notice of a public sale must also be given to the general public in such manner as is commercially reasonable under the circumstances.

(6) Cancellation. When the buyer wrongfully rejects the goods, wrongfully revokes an acceptance of the goods, repudiates the contract, or fails to make a payment due on or before delivery, the seller may cancel the contract.[12] Such action puts an end to the contract, discharging all obligations on both sides that are still unperformed, but the seller retains any remedy with respect to the breach by the buyer.[13] Cancellation necessarily revests the seller with title to the goods.

(7) Action for Damages. If the buyer wrongfully refuses to accept the goods or if he repudiates the contract, the seller may sue him for the damages that the seller sustains. In the ordinary case the amount of damages is to be measured by the difference between the market price at the time and place of the tender of the goods and the contract price.[14] (See p. 392, Hugo Lowei Case)

If this measure of damages does not place the seller in the position in which he would have been placed by the buyer's performance, recovery may be permitted of lost profits, together with an allowance for overhead.[15] The seller may in any case recover as incidental damages any commercially reasonable charges, expenses, or commissions incurred in enforcing his remedy, such as those sustained in stopping delivery; in the transportation, care, and custody of the goods after the buyer's breach; and in the return or resale of the goods.[16]

(8) Action for the Purchase Price. The seller may bring an action to recover the purchase price, together with incidental damages as described in connection with the action for damages, if (a) the goods have been accepted and there has not been any rightful revocation of acceptance; (b) conforming goods were damaged or destroyed after the risk of loss passed to the buyer; or (c) the seller has identified proper goods to the contract but after the buyer's breach has been or will be unable to resell them at a reasonable price.[17] In consequence of these limitations, the right to sue for the contract price, as distinguished from a suit for damages for breach of the sales contract, is a relatively unusual remedy.

----

12 Sec. 2-703 (f).
13 Sec. 2-106 (4).
14 Sec. 2-708(1).
15 Sec. 2-708(2).
16 Sec. 2-710.
17 Sec. 2-709(1).

Sec. 25-B. Remedies of the Buyer.

(1) Rejection of Improper Delivery. If the goods or the tender made by the seller do not conform to the contract, the buyer has the choice (a) of rejecting the entire quantity tendered, (b) of accepting the entire tender, or (c) of accepting any one or more commercial units thereof and rejecting the rest.[18] The rejection must be made within a reasonable time after the delivery or tender, and the buyer must notify the seller of his action.[19]

After rejecting the goods, the buyer may not exercise any right of ownership as to the goods but must hold them awaiting instructions from the seller. When the goods are perishable or threaten to decline in value rapidly, the buyer is required to make reasonable efforts to sell the goods if he is a merchant and the seller does not have any agent or place of business in the market of rejection.[20] In any case, if the seller does not furnish the buyer any instructions, the buyer has the option of reshipping the goods to the seller at the seller's expense, or of storing or reselling them for the seller's account.[21]

(2) Revocation of Acceptance. The buyer may revoke his acceptance of the goods when they do not conform to the contract to such an extent that the defect substantially impairs their value to him, provided (a) he accepted the goods without knowledge of the nonconformity, because it could not be reasonably discovered or because the seller has assured him that the goods were conforming; or (b) he accepted the goods with knowledge of the nonconformity but reasonably believed that the defect would be cured by the seller.[22] Revocation of acceptance may be made not only with respect to the entire quantity of goods but also with respect to any lot or commercial unit that is nonconforming. A buyer who revokes his acceptance stands in the same position as though he had rejected the goods when they had been originally tendered.

The acceptance of goods cannot be revoked unless the buyer gives the seller a notice of revocation. This notice must be given within a reasonable time after the buyer discovers that the goods do not conform or after he should have discovered it. The notice must also be given before there has been any substantial change in the condition of the goods, apart from the change resulting from their own defective condition.[23]

---

[18] Sec. 2-601.
[19] Sec. 2-602. The failure to specify the particular ground for rejection may bar the buyer from proving it in a subsequent action. Sec. 2-605. As to the right of the seller to cure the default, see Sec. 2-508.
[20] Sec. 2-603(1).
[21] Sec. 2-604.
[22] Sec. 2-608(1).
[23] Sec. 2-608(2).

(3) Possession of Goods on Seller's Insolvency. The buyer may have paid in advance for the goods that are still in the seller's possession. Assuming that the seller then becomes insolvent, can the buyer claim the goods from the possession of the seller or is he limited to making a general claim for the refund of the amount paid for them? Under the Code, if the goods have been identified to the contract by either or both the buyer and seller, and the seller becomes insolvent within ten days after receipt of the first installment of the price, the buyer is entitled to recover the goods. The buyer who makes a partial payment has a similar right of reclamation if the seller becomes insolvent within ten days after the first payment is made, but he must pay the balance due.[24]

(4) Action for Damages for Breach of Contract. If the seller fails to deliver as required by the contract or repudiates the contract, or if the buyer properly rejects tendered goods or revokes his acceptance as to such goods, the buyer is entitled to sue the seller for damages for breach of contract. The buyer is entitled to recover the difference between the market price at the time the buyer learned of the breach and the contract price.[25]

Within a reasonable time after the seller's breach, the buyer may *cover*, that is, procure the same or similar goods elsewhere. If the buyer acts in good faith, the measure of damages for the seller's nondelivery or repudiation is then the difference between the cost of cover and the contract price.[26] The buyer is not under duty to cover and his right to damages is not affected by his failure to cover.[27]

In any case the buyer is entitled to recover incidental and consequential damages, but he must give the seller credit for expenses saved as a result of the seller's breach.

(a) DAMAGES FOR BREACH OF CONTRACT AS TO ACCEPTED GOODS. If the buyer has accepted goods that do not conform to the contract or as to which there is a breach of warranty, he must notify the seller of the breach within a reasonable time after he discovers or should have discovered the breach. Otherwise he is not entitled to complain. If the buyer has given the necessary notice of breach, he may recover damages measured by the loss resulting in the normal course of events from the breach.

If suit is brought for breach of warranty, the measure of damages is the difference between the value of the goods as they were when accepted and the value that they would have had if they had been as warranted. In all cases the buyer may recover any incidental or conse-

---

[24] Sec. 2-502.
[25] Sec. 2-713(1).
[26] Sec. 2-712 (2).
[27] Sec. 2-712(3).

quential damages sustained.[28] For example, if the merchant seller sells a preservative that he knows will be used by the buyer in the process of preserving other goods, the merchant seller is liable for the destruction of the other goods if the preservative he supplies is not fit for that purpose.

Whenever the buyer would be entitled to recover damages from the seller, he may deduct the amount of them from any balance remaining due on the purchase price provided he notifies the seller that he intends to do so.[29]

(b) NOTICE OF THIRD-PARTY ACTION AGAINST BUYER. The buyer may be sued in consequence of the seller's breach of warranty, as when the buyer's customers sue him because of the condition of the goods which he has resold to them. In such a case it is optional with the buyer whether or not he gives the seller notice of the action against him and requests the seller to defend the action.[30] The buyer may also be sued by a third person because of patent infringement. In this case he must give notice of the action to the seller. Moreover, the seller can demand that the buyer turn over the defense of that action to him.[31]

When the seller is given notice of a suit against the buyer but fails to defend the buyer, the seller cannot dispute the facts shown in that action when he in turn is sued by the buyer.

In any case a buyer has the burden of proving that the goods were not as represented or warranted when he so alleges, whether as a claim in a suit against the seller or as a defense when sued by the seller. (See p. 393, Vanadium Corporation Case)

(5) *Cancellation.* The buyer may cancel the contract if the seller fails to deliver the goods or if he repudiates the contract, or if the buyer has rightfully rejected tendered goods or revoked his acceptance of the goods. The fact that the buyer cancels the contract does not destroy his cause of action against the seller for breach of the contract. (See p. 395, Lester v. Percy) The buyer may therefore recover from the seller not only any payment made on the purchase price but, in addition, damages for the breach of the contract. The damages represent the difference between the contract price and the market price, or the price of cover if the buyer has purchased other goods.[32]

The fact that the goods are returned by the buyer does not in itself establish that there has been a cancellation, since a return of the goods

---

28 Sec. 2-714.
29 Sec. 2-717.
30 Sec. 2-607(5) (a).
31 Sec. 2-607 (3), (5)(b).
32 Sec. 2-711(1). Note that the Code abolishes the prior rule that the rescinding buyer could not also recover damages, the former theory being that it was inconsistent to rescind the contract and still sue for its breach.

is consistent with an intent to preserve the contract and receive other goods in exchange. That is, the buyer may be doing nothing more than revoking his acceptance of the goods.

(6) Resale of Goods. When the buyer has possession of the goods that he has rightfully rejected or as to which he has properly revoked his acceptance, he is treated the same as a seller in possession of goods after the default of a buyer. That is, he has a security interest in the goods for his claim against the other party and may resell the goods as though he were a seller.[33] From the proceeds of the sale he is entitled to deduct for himself any payments made on the price and any expenses reasonably incurred in the inspection, receipt, transportation, care and custody, and resale of the goods.[34] (See p. 398, Walter E. Heller Case)

(7) Action for Conversion or Recovery of Goods. When, as a result of the sales agreement, ownership passes to the buyer and the seller wrongfully refuses or neglects to deliver the goods, the buyer may maintain any action allowed by law to the owner of goods wrongfully converted or withheld. Hence, a buyer having the right to immediate possession may bring an action of replevin to recover possession of the goods wrongfully withheld, or he may bring an action to recover the value of the goods on the ground of conversion. Likewise, by virtue of the Code, the buyer may replevy the goods when he satisfies the security interest of the seller in the goods shipped under a security reservation but delivery to the buyer is refused.

The buyer is also given the right of replevin when the seller has identified the goods to the contract and the circumstances are such that similar goods cannot be reasonably procured by the buyer in the open market.[35] Here it is immaterial whether the title has passed to the buyer, and the action of replevin is in effect an action of specific performance granted to protect the buyer from a harm which would follow from the fact that he is not able to obtain similar goods in the market if he does not obtain them from the seller.

The obligation of the seller to deliver proper goods may be enforced by an order for specific performance when the goods are "unique or in other proper circumstances." [36] This permits the buyer to obtain specific performance, not only when the goods have a peculiar or special quality that makes them unique, but also when it would be a hardship on the buyer to deny him that right. Accordingly, a contract calling for the sale of the seller's output or the supplying of the buyer's requirements may present circumstances where specific performance will be required to permit the buyer to obtain the benefit of his contract.

---

[33] See p. 385.
[34] UCC Sec. 2-715.
[35] Sec. 2-716(3).
[36] Sec. 2-716(1).

(8) Remedies for Fraud of Seller. Independently of the preceding remedies the buyer has the right to sue the seller for damages for the latter's fraud or to rescind the transaction on that ground.[37] As these remedies for fraud exist independently of the provisions of the Code, the buyer may assert such remedies even though he is barred by the Code from exercising any remedy for a breach of warranty.

Sec. 25-C. Contract Provisions on Remedies.

(1) Limitation of Damages. The parties may in their sales contract specify that in the event of breach by either party the damages are to be limited to a certain amount. If this amount is unreasonably large, it is void as a penalty. If the amount is reasonable, the injured party is limited to recovering that amount. Whether the limitation is reasonable is determined in the light of the actual harm that would be caused by breach, the difficulty of proving the amount of such loss, and the inconvenience and impracticality of suing for damages or enforcing other remedies for breach.[38]

(2) Down Payments and Deposits. The buyer may have made a deposit with the seller or an initial or down payment at the time of making the contract. If the buyer breaches the contract, the seller is permitted only to retain as much of the down payment or deposit as will compensate him for his actual damages.

If the contract contains a valid liquidation-of-damages provision, the seller must return any part of the down payment or deposit in excess of the amount specified by the liquidated damages clause. In the absence of such a clause, the seller's damages are computed as 20 per cent of the purchase price or $500, whichever is the smaller. The extent to which the down payment exceeds such amount must be returned to the buyer.[39]

The rule just stated applies to payments made by the buyer in goods as well as in cash as, for example, by making a trade-in. Such goods given in payment are assigned a dollar value for the purpose of determining the payment made by the buyer. If the goods have been resold, their value is the proceeds of the resale; if not, it is the reasonable value of such goods.[40]

(3) Limitation on Remedies. The parties may validly limit the remedies. Thus a seller may specify that the only remedy of the buyer

---

[37] Sec. 1-103. As to what constitutes fraud, see Chapter 7. As to the expansion of the damages recoverable, see Sec. 2-721.
[38] Sec. 2-718(1).
[39] Sec. 2-718 (2).
[40] Sec. 2-718 (4). If the seller has notice of the buyer's breach before resale is made, the seller must observe the same standards that apply to the ordinary seller who resells upon breach by the buyer. See p. 353.

for breach of warranty shall be the repair or replacement of the goods, or that the buyer shall be limited to returning the goods and obtaining a refund of the purchase price. How much further the restrictions may go is not clear, but the limitation is not binding if it is unreasonable or unconscionable. The exclusion of damages for personal injuries caused by defective goods is prima facie unconscionable, and therefore not binding, when the goods are sold for consumption by the buyer.[41] Moreover, when the seller would be liable to his buyer for a breach of warranty, the seller cannot exclude liability for personal injuries to members of the buyer's family, his household, or his guests.[42]

Cases for Chapter 25

Hugo Loewi, Inc. v. Geschwill

186 F.2d 849 (C.A. 9th, 1951)

Hugo contracted to purchase growing hops from Geschwill. The contract stipulated that the measure of damages for the breach of the contract by either party would be the difference between the contract price and the market value at the time and place of delivery, and that such damages were fixed as liquidated damages. Hugo refused to accept the hops, which were then sold by Geschwill to another buyer. Geschwill sued Hugo for the difference between the contract price and the resale price. Damages were awarded on this basis because there was no evidence of an established market value. From a judgment for the plaintiff, the defendant appealed.

Bone, C.J. . . . Appellant [Hugo] contends that the trial court erred in finding that title to the hops passed to the appellant and therefore an action for the price may not be maintained. In the text of our opinion we assume, without deciding, that title did not pass. . . .

We are of the opinion that the Oregon Uniform Sales Act does not preclude the method of recovery adopted by the trial court. . . [It] provides:

"(1) Where the buyer wrongfully neglects or refuses to accept and pay for the goods, the seller may maintain an action against him for damages for nonacceptance.

"(2) The measure of damages is the estimated loss directly and naturally resulting, in the ordinary course of events, from the buyer's breach of contract.

"(3) Where there is an available market for the goods in question, the measure of damages is, in the absence of special circumstances showing proximate damage of a greater amount, the difference between the contract price and the market or current price at the time or times

---

[41] Sec. 2-719 (3).
[42] Sec. 2-318.

when the goods ought to have been accepted or, if no time was fixed for acceptance, then at the time of the refusal to accept."

Subdivision (3) of the above law is applicable only when there is an available market for the goods in question while subdivision (2) is applicable where there is no available market. . . . Under the facts of the instant case as found by the trial court we hold that subsection (2) is the proper measure of damages and that the difference between the contract price and the amount realized by appellee from the resale of the hops represented appellee's loss directly and naturally due to and resulting from the buyer's breach of contract.

Appellant contends that in any event the recovery is limited by the terms of the contract as to the measure of damages. . . .

The so-called "liquidated damages" clause provides only one method of recovery regardless of how or when the contract is breached. This carries the implication that the parties contemplated that there would be an available market for the hops.

. . . Where as here, there was no available market for the goods in question and such a market was obviously contemplated by the parties by the terms of the damage clause, the clause did not stand as a bar to the measure and theory of damages here adopted by the trial court which worked out substantial justice between the parties. . . .

[Judgment for plaintiff affirmed.]

Code Comment: The same decision would be made under the Code. Sec. 2-706 of the Code, which is in effect in Oregon, in substance restates the provision of the former Uniform Sales Act quoted in the opinion. Under the Code, the absence of an available market would also nullify the damage clause of the parties by virtue of the provision that "where circumstances cause an exclusive or limited remedy to fail of its essential purpose," the case is determined as though there were no such limitation. UCC Sec. 2-719(2).

Vanadium Corporation v. Wesco Stores Co.

135 Colo. 77, 308 P.2d 1011 (1957)

About December 1, Vanadium contracted with Voytilla to purchase 400 dressed, unfrozen turkeys for Christmas gifts to Vanadium's employees. Voytilla in turn purchased the turkeys from Wesco Stores. The turkeys were then delivered at Vanadium's direction to the Durango Ice and Produce Co. The turkeys were delivered in vacuum bags and, when opened four and a half days later, were in spoiled condition. Payment for the turkeys was refused. Wesco sued for the purchase price. Voytilla brought Vanadium into the action, and the latter raised the defense of breach of warranty of fitness of the turkeys for food. From a judgment for Wesco, Vanadium appealed.

HALL, J. . . . [There was evidence that the persons cleaning the freshly killed turkeys had failed to clean them properly, that Wesco had not kept the unfrozen turkeys at a sufficiently low temperature, and that Durango had only partially frozen the turkeys.]. . .

All parties were aware of the fact that Vanadium expected to receive turkeys that would be edible on Christmas day, and it is conceded that on such sale there was an implied warranty that the turkeys would be suitable for human consumption. . . .

By Vanadium's direction the turkeys were delivered to Durango Ice and Produce Co., and it is claimed that this amounted to an acceptance. Our statute . . . provides: "The buyer is deemed to have accepted the goods when he intimates to the seller that he has accepted them, or when the goods have been delivered to him, and he does any act in relation to them which is inconsistent with the ownership of the seller, or when, after the lapse of a reasonable time, he retains the goods without intimating to the seller that he has rejected them."

Vanadium, having taken physical possession and control of the turkeys, partially froze them and retained them for five days, is presumed to have accepted them.

Having accepted the turkeys and now seeking to avoid payment therefore because of breach of the implied warranty of suitability for human consumption, Vanadium is charged with the burden of proving unsuitability at the time of delivery and acceptance.

"The burden is on the buyer seeking to recover damages for defects in quality, or setting up such defects as an affirmative defense in an action for the price, to prove that the defects existed at the time of sale and did not result from deterioration after shipment, or from the buyer's negligence after he came into possession of the property, since there is no presumption that the defects discovered after delivery existed at the time of sale.". . .

Counsel for Vanadium contend that proof of the spoiled condition of the turkeys four and one-half days after delivery and acceptance was sufficient to prove the turkeys were in a defective condition when delivered, and in support thereof refer to several cases in which it has been held that the fact that canned or bottled goods on opening, by a buyer, are defective is some evidence that they were defective when delivered to buyer. These cases are not persuasive in the circumstances before us. Here there was evidence of questionable handling of the turkeys by Vanadium or its agent for a period of four and one-half days before opening of the bags. The trial judge determined the facts and concluded from all of the evidence that Vanadium had not met the burden of proving the turkeys were defective at the time of delivery. This finding is sufficiently supported by the evidence and will not be disturbed.

[Judgment affirmed.]

Code Comment: The same decision would be made under the Code. The Vanadium case involves two issues: (1) burden of proof, and (2) extent of appellate review. As to the first, the Code declares that "the burden is on the buyer to establish any breach with respect to the goods accepted." Sec. 2-607(4). The Code does not in any way regulate appellate review; accordingly, the principle applied in the Vanadium case, that a finding of fact supported by the evidence will not be set aside when appealed, would still be followed.

Lester v. Percy

58 Wash.2d 501, 364 P.2d 423 (1961)

Gloria Lester purchased from Stenger, acting as agent for Percy, a washer and drying machine for use in the nursing home which she and her husband ran. The equipment proved defective and, after several attempts at its repair by Stenger, Lester sued for rescission of the contract. Percy claimed that she had waived the right to rescind by her conduct subsequent to learning of the defective condition of the equipment. From a decision in Percy's favor, Lester appealed.

OTT, J. . . . [The appellant buyer established] that during the conversation leading to the sale, she informed Mr. Stenger of the nature and extent of the nursing home washing requirements, consisting of approximately eleven or twelve separate washings in a twenty-four hour period. Mr. Stenger assured her that the equipment was adequate for her extensive washing needs, in that it was "heavy-duty commercial type" equipment. The washing machine motor was guaranteed for five years, and other parts and service for one year. The dryer was similarly guaranteed for one year. She relied upon Mr. Stenger's representations and judgment, and purchased the equipment on contract. The washer was installed in July, 1957. The dryer was installed in October, 1957.

Mrs. Lester encountered mechanical difficulty with the equipment shortly after it was installed. The respondent replaced the washer in August, 1957. The dryer was also defective and was replaced in February, 1958. It was necessary for respondent to repair and service the newly installed equipment on numerous occasions. There was no charge to appellant for the calls, which were covered by respondent's warranty of service. Appellant did pay respondent $10.33 and $15.50 for service calls, and $4.65 to the Peninsula Propane Company for repairs to the dryer, which respondent contended were not within the service contract. She also paid the installments on the contract of purchase in full.

March 28, 1958, the washing machine motor burned out, and appellant called the respondent for service. Mrs. Lester testified that: "He [Mr. Percy] came up and we had a verbal argument. He said he had done all he could do, and he was going to wash his hands of me and the equipment, and he left, and he was very angry with me."

April 9, 1958, Mrs. Lester gave notice of her intention to rescind the contract because of the breach of various warranties, and thereafter commenced this action. . . .

Respondent [seller] contends that the rule in this state is that one who seeks to rescind a contract upon the ground of breach of warranty must do so promptly upon discovery of the breach, otherwise the right to rescind is waived. We agree with respondent's statement of the general rule, but it is subject to certain exceptions, two of which are (1) the waiver must be voluntary and intentional, and (2) the right to rescind is not waived when the delay in claiming it is induced by the vendor. . . .

The equipment which the appellant purchased carried two warranties: First, a warranty of fitness to meet appellant's requirements, and, second, a warranty to furnish necessary parts and service for a specified period of time. The difficulty experienced by the appellant immediately after the machines were installed would have supported an action for rescission, but to hold that she was required to rescind at that time would render the warranty on parts and service a nullity, and deny to the vendor an opportunity to repair and service the equipment to meet the requirements of the vendee. The appellant's failure to rescind immediately upon acquiring knowledge that the equipment was defective is justified by her election to afford the respondent an opportunity to service and repair the equipment to meet the standard of the warranty of fitness. Appellant's tolerant conduct in this regard does not warrant an inference that she relinquished the right to rescind, or that she intended to waive her right to do so.

Applying the general rule, together with the exceptions here applicable, appellant's conduct in paying the miscellaneous repair costs, under the circumstances here present, did not in and of itself establish an intentional or voluntary waiver of the right to rescind. On March 28, 1958, the vendor, for the first time, made known its intent to disavow its contractual obligations. Until that date, the vendor's conduct led the appellant to believe that the vendor would fully honor its contract; thus, the appellant was induced to postpone the exercise of her right to rescind. Appellant's notice of rescission on April 9, 1958, was timely under these circumstances. . . .

[Judgment is reversed.]

HUNTER, J., dissenting.

I disagree with the holding of the majority that rescission was timely made. The washer and the one replaced were continuously used for washing sheets in the appellants' nursing home for approximately nine months, and the dryer and the one replaced were used there for about six months. The record discloses the use of the equipment was to the extent of ten to twelve washings a day of at least seven sheets per washing, for the above periods, during which time the appellants knew the equipment was not as represented.

The rule stated by the majority in Eliason v. Walker, 1953, 42 Wash.2d 473, 477, 256 P.2d 298, 300 is that ". . . Diligence in rescission is a relative question, and whether or not there has been an unreasonable delay in a given case depends upon the particular circumstances of that case. . . ."

The circumstances of the instant case, in my opinion, support the finding of the trial court that the rescission was waived by reason of the long and extensive use of this equipment. It is inherent in the relief afforded by rescission that circumstances must be such to permit the parties being placed within at least reasonable reach of status quo, . . . unless it be due to the fault of the seller. This is, of course, the basic reason that diligence must be exercised by the person seeking rescission; otherwise a restoration to status quo will be denied the party against whom the rescission is sought. Where the status quo is so unapproachable by reason of the delay of the person seeking rescission, as in the instant case, the person seeking rescission stands in a position to gain an unconscionable advantage, for which no compensation by that person has been paid, to the total loss of the other.

The appellants should not be permitted in a court of equity to have free use of this equipment to their substantial benefit. Under the majority holding, they will have obtained a benefit incident to their relief requested which a court of equity should not countenance. . . .

I am in agreement with the rule . . . that a buyer who continues in possession and uses the property may still elect to rescind the contract for a breach of warranty when the delay was induced by the promise of the seller to make the equipment comply with the warranty. However, under these conditions, delay in rescinding may not be extended beyond a reasonable time. When the use has been as extensive as in the instant case and where, as here, the equipment cannot be returned to the seller in substantially as good condition as it was when delivered to the purchaser, a reasonable time for rescinding the contract has elapsed. . . .

Code Comment: The same decision would be made under the Code. Sec. 2-711(1) gives the buyer the right to "cancel" the contract; but it does not specify the scope or limitations of cancellation beyond declaring that it puts an end to the contract, although any existing claim or cause of action for breach is not extinguished by such cancellation. Sec. 2-106(4), 2-720. In view of the preservation of principles of equity and estoppel, Sec. 1-103, it would undoubtedly be held that a waiver of any right is subject to the same limitations as imposed in the Lester case.

Walter E. Heller & Co. v. Hammond Appliance Co.

29 N.J. 589, 151 A.2d 537 (1959)

The Peerless Corporation sold 50 appliances to a dealer, the Hammond Appliance Co. The seller then assigned its contract to Walter E. Heller & Co. When Heller sued Hammond for the purchase price, the latter showed that following the purchase the seller and it had agreed that the goods were defective and had mutually rescinded the contract. In spite of this, the seller never came to pick up the goods although Hammond repeatedly requested it to do so. After about a year Hammond began repairing the appliances and finally sold 27 of the 50, still having possession of the remaining 23 at the time of the trial. At the trial, in addition to denying liability, Hammond made a counterclaim for the cost of repairing the appliances, the cost of their storage while waiting for the seller to retake them, and the cost of moving the appliances from one store to another in the effort to sell them. From a judgment against the assignee, Heller appealed. The Appellate Division held that the defendant buyer had waived the rescission by making repairs and sales and was therefore liable for the total purchase price. He appealed to the state supreme court.

PER CURIAM. . . . Upon the happening of the rescission, defendant became a bailee of the goods . . . and the title reverted to the seller. However, the seller, having undertaken to reassume possession, was under a duty to do so within a reasonable time. Not only did failure to perform that duty create a liability for reasonable storage charges, but defendant was not obliged to retain possession indefinitely. . . . He was entitled to undertake a good faith sale without further notice and to hold the proceeds for the benefit of the seller subject to certain rightful credits. . . . 3 Black, Rescission and Cancellation (2d ed. 1929), § 629; 3 Williston, Sales (rev. ed. 1948), § 498. And see Uniform Commercial Code, section 2-711(3), and comment 2.

The statement of principle in Black, supra, is clearly applicable by analogy . . . : "When the seller of goods persistently refuses to take them back, after being notified of the rescission of the sale by the purchaser for sufficient cause, it is proper, if not obligatory, for the purchaser to take such measures as are expedient to save unnecessary loss to the seller, and if the best method of accomplishing this end is to sell the property (as, in the case of perishable goods), he may sell it 'for account' of the vendor for the best price obtainable, and retain out of the proceeds enough to reimburse him for necessary expenses, and hold the balance subject to the vendor's demand. . . . But one selling property for account of another in this manner must act with reasonable promptness. He will be entitled to storage charges and other expenses only for a reasonable length of time, and whether he has waited an unreasonable time or incurred unreasonable expense, before selling the property, is a question of fact for the jury."

Accordingly, we are of the view that because of the unreasonable delay of the seller and the plaintiff assignee in retaking the goods, defendant was legally justified in selling them. And out of the proceeds he is entitled to retain such sum as represents reasonable storage charges, the reasonable cost of moving and transporting the goods from one store to another (as the proof indicates was done), and the reasonable cost of putting the appliances in a fit condition for sale in the market. . . .

The unsold appliances which have remained in defendant's possession during the pendency of this litigation are still the property of the plaintiff. They may be reclaimed, subject to reasonable storage charges. But if this is not done within a reasonable time after judgment in this court, defendant may dispose of them by bona fide sale in accordance with the views expressed herein.

The judgment of the Appellate Division is modified and the matter is remanded for trial of the issues outlined. . . .

Code Comment: The same decision would be made under the Code. Since the right of the parties to rescind the sales contract and the effect of such rescission is not affected by the Code, the prior law continues. Sec. 1-103. Even without the mutual agreement of the parties, the buyer under the Code would have been entitled to revoke his acceptance of the goods because of their defective condition, cancel the contract, resell the goods, and recover the damages sustained. Sec. 2-711.

Questions and Case Problems

1. What is the objective of each of the following rules of law?
(a) When the seller stops goods in transit, the carrier's lien for transportation is superior to the seller's rights.
(b) A provision in a sales contract that limits the damages for breach by either party to a certain amount is void if the amount is unreasonably large.

2. Braginetz purchased an automobile from the Foreign Motor Sales, Inc. The automobile proved defective, and notice thereof was given promptly by the buyer. The seller made four successive attempts to remedy the defect, each time assuring the buyer that the defect had been remedied. After these unsuccessful attempts, the buyer notified the seller that he revoked the acceptance of the goods. The seller claimed that the buyer had lost the right to revoke acceptance because of his unreasonable delay. Decide. (Braginetz v. Foreign Motor Sales, Inc., [Pa.] 73 Dau. Co. 1)

3. Koscove sold Brunger a quantity of furniture, fixtures, and equipment located in a storeroom for $3,000. It was later learned that Koscove did not own the goods, and Brunger brought an action to rescind the sale. Koscove defended on the ground that Brunger was unable to return all of the property since he had disposed of two coolers. The evidence showed that the two coolers were given by Brunger to a fixture dealer on his

agreeing to remove them from the building and there was no evidence that they had any cash value. Was Brunger entitled to rescind the contract? (Koscove v. Brunger, [Colo.] 352 P.2d 961)

4. Marks contracted with Lehigh Brickface, Inc. to put brickfacing on his house. The brickfacing was not as durable as it was claimed and deteriorated rapidly. Marks notified Lehigh Brickface that it rescinded the contract. Lehigh Brickface defended on the ground that the rescission was not effective because the buyer had not made an offer to return the goods. Was the seller correct? (Marks v. Lehigh Brickface, Inc., [Pa.] 19 D.&C.2d 666, 73 Dau. Co. 244)

5. Skopes Rubber Corp. purchased skin-diving suits from the United States Rubber Co. The sale was made on the basis of a sample on which the vinyl coating on the suits had been hand applied and was smooth. The suits that were delivered were wrinkled because the vinyl had been machine applied. In use, the suits split at the wrinkle lines. Skopes returned the first installment of the suits because of this defect. He then sued United States Rubber Co. for breach of warranty. It raised the defense that by returning the first installment, Skopes had rescinded the contract and could not thereafter sue for damages. Was this correct? (Skopes Rubber Corp. v. United States Rubber Co., [C.A. 1st] 299 F.2d 584)

6. Grucella purchased an automobile from General Motors Corp. There were a number of defects, but they disappeared after the car was broken in or repaired by General Motors. Grucella notified General Motors that he revoked his acceptance of the automobile because of these defects. General Motors contended that Grucella could not revoke his acceptance. Decide. (Grucella v. General Motors Corp., [Pa.] 10 D.&C.2d 651)

7. Walters purchased goods from Garson. The goods did not conform to a warranty. Walters nevertheless retained and used the goods, but he then sued Garson for breach of warranty. Was Walters entitled to recover and, if so, how much? (Walters v. Garson, [Pa.] 24 Fayette County 99)

8. Chaplin purchased a walk-in hardening box from Bessire & Co. for approximately $7,000. In effect, it was an insulated room for the storage of ice cream and similar products. It was especially manufactured for Chaplin and installed in the fall of 1957. It developed leaks at once, and Bessire made repairs and guaranteed that it would work properly, which it did during that winter, but in the summer of 1958 it developed other defects which required a modification of the corrective repairs that had been made the fall before. The box worked through the cold months of 1958 and 1959, but in the spring it developed leaks again. In May, 1959, a fuse blew, and within a few hours the temperature of the box rose 30 degrees causing the contents to spoil. Bessire refused to take the box back. Chaplin sued Bessire for breach of warranty, claiming the right to rescind the contract, to recover payments paid on the contract, and to recover special damages for lost merchandise. During the course of the lawsuit, Chaplin made unsuccessful attempts to sell the box. Bessire defended on the ground that Chaplin had delayed too long before seeking to rescind and that, by attempting to sell the box, he lost any right of rescission. Decide. (Chaplin v. Bessire & Co., [Ky.App.] 361 S.W.2d 293)

PART V
COMMERCIAL PAPER

CHAPTER 26

Nature, Kinds, and Parties

Under the law of contracts a promise, when supported by consideration, creates certain legal rights that may be assigned to another person. Even before these common-law rules relating to contracts were developing, another body of law, the law merchant, was creating principles relating to a different type of obligation and the transfer of rights arising therefrom. In the course of time this obligation became the bill of exchange, which today we also know as a draft, a trade acceptance, or, with certain modifications, a check. In time another type of instrument, the promissory note, appeared. Both drafts and promissory notes may have the quality of negotiability that distinguishes them from ordinary contracts. As a group, they are known today as commercial paper or negotiable instruments.

Sec. 26-A. Nature and Functions. Much of the importance of negotiable instruments lies in the fact that they are more readily transferred than ordinary claims or contract rights and that the transferee of a commercial paper may acquire greater rights than would an ordinary assignee. A person who acquires a commercial paper may therefore be subject to less risk.

Negotiable instruments often serve as substitutes for money. When a person pays a debt by check, he is using a negotiable instrument. He might have paid in cash, but for convenience and possibly for safety, he used a negotiable instrument. Of course, such payment is usually conditional upon the instrument being paid.

Negotiable instruments may create credit. If a debtor gives his creditor a promissory note by which he agrees to pay him in sixty days, that is the same as an agreement that the creditor will not collect the claim until sixty days later.

Sec. 26-B. Development of the Law of Commercial Paper. The use of negotiable instruments developed as a result of the efforts of early merchants to avoid the dangers of transporting money to pay for purchases in distant lands. In England the principles relating to these instruments first became a part of the law merchant, which was enforced by special merchants' courts. Later these principles were incorporated in the common law.

In the United States, first the common law and later various state statutes governed the use of negotiable instruments. The subject was then codified by the Uniform Negotiable Instruments Act, which was drafted in 1896.[1] The Uniform Commercial Code was drafted in the middle of the present century.[2] Article 3 of the Code governs negotiable instruments, or as called by the Code, commercial paper.[3] In many instances the law under the Code and under the NIL is the same for the obvious reason that the former statute has built upon the principles of, and the experience acquired under, the latter statute. At the same time, significant changes have been made by the Code with the objective of making the law conform to modern commercial practices and to provide a better resolution of current commercial problems. The law of commercial paper as set forth in Chapters 26 to 33 is the law under the Uniform Commercial Code, although from time to time reference is made to the NIL for comparative or historical purposes.

Sec. 26-C. Kinds of Commercial Paper. Negotiable instruments fall into four categories: (1) promissory notes, (2) drafts or bills of exchange, (3) checks, and (4) certificates of deposit.

(1) Promissory Notes. A negotiable promissory note is an unconditional promise in writing made by one person to another, signed by the maker, engaging to pay on demand, or at a particular time, a sum certain in money to order or to bearer.[4] It may be described simply as a written promise by one person to pay money to another.

---

[1] The Uniform Negotiable Instruments Act is cited in this book by the initials, NIL (Negotiable Instruments Law). It is in effect in all states that have not adopted the Uniform Commercial Code.

[2] The Uniform Commercial Code is cited in this book by its initials, UCC.

[3] As to the states that have adopted the Code, see p. 51.

[4] UCC Sec. 3-104 (1).

The person who makes the promise is called the *maker* of the note. The person to whom payment is to be made is called the *payee*.

$ 600.⁰⁰   HARRISBURG, PA.   May 14   19 64

Six months   AFTER DATE I   PROMISE TO PAY TO

THE ORDER OF David L. Snyder

Six hundred and ⁰⁰⁄₁₀₀ —————————————DOLLARS

PAYABLE AT First National Bank

VALUE RECEIVED WITH INTEREST AT 5 %

No. 31   DUE Nov 14, 1964   Charles Burnet

Promissory Note

Parties: maker—Charles Burnet; payee—David L. Snyder.

If the promissory note is payable "on demand," that is, immediately, it may be used as a substitute for money. If it is not payable until a future time, the payee in effect extends credit to the maker of the note for the period of time until payment is due.

Special types of promissory notes may or may not be negotiable, depending upon their form. The following are commonly used:

A *mortgage note* is a note secured by a mortgage, which can be foreclosed if the note is not paid when due.

A *collateral note* is a note accompanied by collateral security given to the payee by the borrower. Thus a person borrowing money might give the lender certain property, such as stocks or bonds, to hold as security for the payment of the note.

A *judgment note* contains a clause which gives the holder the right to enter a judgment against the maker if the note is not paid when due. This power to confess judgment for the maker means that the delay and expense of a lawsuit are avoided should the promisor default on his note. A minority of the states recognize judgment notes, which are also known as *cognovit notes*. Other states either do not recognize them or prohibit their use.

A *conditional sales note* is a promissory note given by the purchaser of personal property under a conditional sales agreement. This note is ordinarily a part of the contract signed by the buyer of goods on the installment plan.

(2) Drafts. A *draft* or *bill of exchange* is an unconditional order in writing addressed by one person to another, signed by the person giving it, requiring the person to whom it is addressed to pay on demand or at a particular time a sum certain in money to order or to bearer.[5] In effect, then, it is an order by one person upon a second

---

[5] Sec. 3-104(1).

person to pay a sum of money to a third person. The person who makes
the order is called the *drawer* and is said to draw the bill. The person

Draft (Bill of Exchange)

Drawer—Van Horn; drawee—Benton; payee—Central Trust Bank.

on whom the order to pay is drawn is the *drawee*. The person to whom
payment is to be made is called the *payee*. The drawer may designate
himself as the payee.

The drawee who is ordered to pay the money is not bound to do
so unless he accepts the order. After he accepts, he may be identified
as the *acceptor*. From the practice of "accepting" a bill of exchange,
the term "acceptance" is sometimes applied to these instruments.

(a) SIGHT AND TIME DRAFTS. A *sight draft* is one that is payable on sight or when the holder presents it to the drawee for payment.
A *time draft* is payable at a stated time after sight, such as "30 days
after sight" or "30 days after acceptance," or at a stated time after a
certain date, such as "30 days after date" (after date of instrument).

(b) DOMESTIC AND INTERNATIONAL BILLS. If a draft is drawn
and payable in the same state, or is drawn in one state and payable in
another, it is a *domestic bill*. If it appears on the face of the instrument that it was made in one nation and payable in another, it is an
international bill of exchange or a foreign draft.[6]

(c) TRADE ACCEPTANCES. A draft may be sent by a seller of
goods to a purchaser, as the drawee, with the understanding that if
he approves of the goods sent him, the drawee will accept the instrument immediately. This type of draft is a *trade acceptance*.

(3) Checks. A *check* is a bill of exchange drawn on a bank payable
on demand.[7] It is an order by a depositor, the *drawer*, upon his bank,
the *drawee*, to pay a sum of money to the order of another person, the

---

[6] Under the NIL, Sec. 129, a draft both drawn and payable within the same state
is classified as an inland bill of exchange, and any other bill is a foreign bill of
exchange. In other words, a draft drawn in one state and payable in another is
classified as a foreign bill.

[7] UCC Sec. 3-104(2)(b).

payee. A check is always drawn upon a bank as drawee and is always payable upon demand.

| PAUL HARRIS | | No. *126* |
| 3610 Iris Lane | | |

DES MOINES, IOWA *April 17* 19 *64*   33–1 / 713

PAY TO THE ORDER OF *Mefford Electric Company* $*200.00*

Two hundred and 00/00 ———————— DOLLARS

FIRST NATIONAL BANK
DES MOINES, IOWA   *Paul Harris*

⑈0713⑈0001⑈ 136 323 8⑈

Check

Drawer—Harris; drawee—bank; payee—Mefford Electric Company.

A *cashier's check* is drawn by a bank on itself, ordering itself to pay the stated sum of money to the depositor or to the person designated by him. The latter requests his bank to issue a cashier's check for a given amount, which amount either the depositor pays the bank or the bank charges against the depositor's account. The depositor then forwards the cashier's check, instead of his own, to the seller or creditor.

A *bank draft* is in effect a check drawn by one bank upon another bank in which the first bank has money on deposit, in the same way that a depositor draws a check upon his own bank. It is commonly used for the same purpose as a cashier's check.

(4) Certificates of Deposit. A *certificate of deposit* is an instrument issued by a bank that acknowledges the deposit of a specific sum of money and promises to pay the holder of the certificate that amount, usually with interest, when the certificate is surrendered.[8]

Sec. 26-D. Parties to Commercial Paper. A note has two original parties—the maker and the payee; and a draft or a check has three original parties—the drawer, the drawee, and the payee. In addition to these original parties, a negotiable instrument may have one or more of the following parties:

(1) Indorser.[9] A person who owns a negotiable instrument may transfer it to another person by signing his name on the back of the instrument and delivering it to the other person. When he does so,

---

[8] A certificate of deposit "is an acknowledgement by a bank of receipt of money with an engagement to repay it," as distinguished from a note which "is a promise other than a certificate of deposit." UCC Sec. 3-104(2)(c), (d).

[9] The form *endorse* is commonly used in business. The form *indorse* is used in the UCC and NIL.

he is an *indorser*. Thus, if a check is made payable to the order of
A to pay a bill owed to him, *A* may indorse it to *B* to pay a debt which
A owes *B*. In such a case *A*, who was the payee of the check since it
was originally made payable to him, is now also an indorser.

(2) Indorsee. The person to whom an indorsement is made is
called an *indorsee*. He in turn may indorse the instrument; in that
case he is also an indorser.

(3) Bearer. The person in physical possession of a negotiable
instrument which is payable to bearer is called a *bearer*.

(4) Holder. A *holder* is a person in possession of a negotiable
instrument which is payable at that time either to him, as payee or
indorsee, or to bearer.

(a) HOLDER FOR VALUE. Ordinarily negotiable instruments are
given to persons in the course of business in return for or in payment
for something. If the holder gives consideration for the instrument
or takes it in payment of a debt, he is a *holder for value*. Thus, if an
employee is paid wages by check, he is a holder for value of the check
since he received it in payment of wages earned and due. If he indorses
the check to his landlord to pay the rent, the landlord becomes the
holder for value.

A person may receive a negotiable instrument without giving anything for it. Thus, when an aunt gives her niece a check for $100 as
a Christmas present, the niece becomes the owner or holder, but she
has not given anything for the check and she does not become a holder
for value.

(b) HOLDER IN DUE COURSE. A person who becomes a holder
of the paper under certain circumstances is given a favored standing
and is immune from certain defenses. He is termed a *holder in due
course*.[10]

(c) HOLDER THROUGH A HOLDER IN DUE COURSE. A person
who holds an instrument at any time after it was once held by a
holder in due course is called a *holder through a holder in due course*
and ordinarily is given the same special rights as a holder in due
course.[11]

(5) Accommodation Party. A person who becomes a party to a
negotiable instrument in order to add the strength of his name to the
paper is called an *accommodation party*. If he is a maker, he is called
an accommodation maker; if an indorser, an accommodation indorser.
For example, *A* applies to a bank for a loan and is willing to give the
bank a promissory note naming it as payee. The bank may be un-

----

10 See p. 496.
11 See p. 499.

willing to lend money to *A* on the strength of his own promise. It may be that *B,* who has a satisfactory credit standing, will sign the note as a comaker with *A.* If *B* does this without receiving any value from the payee but only for the purpose of bolstering *A's* credit, it is said that he signs for accommodation and is an accommodation maker.

It is immaterial whether the accommodation party signs the paper merely as a friend or because he is paid for doing so.[12]

An accommodation party is liable on the instrument to a holder for value even though the latter knows that he is merely an accommodation party.[13] (See p. 408, Union Bank Case) If the accommodation party is required to pay the instrument, he may recover the amount of the payment from the person accommodated. If the holder did not become a holder for value, the accommodation party is not liable to that holder unless there has been consideration for his undertaking.

(6) Guarantor. A *guarantor* is a person who signs commercial paper and adds a statement that he will pay the instrument under certain circumstances. Ordinarily this is done by merely adding "payment guaranteed" or "collection guaranteed" to the signature of the guarantor on the paper.

The addition of "payment guaranteed" or similar words means that the guarantor will pay the instrument when due even though the holder of the paper has not sought payment from any other party. "Collection guaranteed" or similar words means that the guarantor will not pay the paper until after the holder has sought to collect payment from the maker or acceptor and has been unable to do so. In such a case the holder must first obtain a judgment against the maker or acceptor, which judgment remains unpaid because the sheriff cannot find sufficient property of the debtor in question to pay it, or the debtor must be insolvent.[14]

Sec. 26-E. Liability of Parties. A person who by the terms of the instrument is absolutely required to pay is primarily liable. For a note, the maker is primarily liable; for a draft, the acceptor, or drawee who has accepted, is primarily liable. A guarantor of payment is primarily liable in any case. Other parties are either secondarily liable or not liable in any capacity.

Sec. 26-F. Interest and Discount. When a commercial paper is used as a credit device, it may provide for the payment of interest. For

---

[12] UCC Sec. 3-415(1).
[13] Sec. 3-415(2).
[14] Sec. 3-416(1)(2). If the meaning of the guaranty is not clear, it is construed as a guaranty of payment. Sec. 3-416(3). The guaranty written on the commercial paper is binding without regard to whether it may not satisfy the requirements of a local Statute of Frauds. Sec. 3-416 (6).

example, a six-month note dated March 1 for a loan of $1,000 may specify interest at 5 per cent. Payment on September 1 would be $1,025.

A note or time draft may be discounted. Interest that is paid in advance in this way is known as *discount*. For example, if the note in the preceding illustration were non-interest-bearing, it could be discounted by the lender by substracting the amount of interest from the face of the note at the time that the loan was made. In that case, the amount received by the borrower on March 1 would be $975 and the payment at the date of maturity would be $1,000. Interest-bearing negotiable instruments may also be discounted.

Case for Chapter 26

Union Bank & Trust Co. v. Pine Ridge Coal Co.

255 Mich. 295, 238 N.W. 261 (1931)

The Pine Ridge Coal Company became the exclusive sales agent of the Buffalo Thacker Coal Company. Cronin, the president of the Pine Ridge company, signed two trade acceptances for the accommodation of the Buffalo company at the request of Reese, the president of the latter company, so that the company could obtain an order for 100 cars of coal from the West Virginia Coal Company. The acceptances were discounted by Archer, the president of the Union Bank & Trust Company, a state bank located in West Virginia; and they were subsequently turned in to the bank. In an action by the bank against the Pine Ridge company to recover the amount of the acceptances, the defendant contended that no recovery could be had because the bank knew that the defendant was merely an accommodation acceptor. From a judgment for the defendant, the plaintiff appealed.

SHARPE, J. . . . Section 62 [of the Negotiable Instruments Law] provides: "The acceptor by accepting the instrument engages that he will pay it according to the tenor of his acceptance. . . ."

Under this provision the acceptor of a bill of exchange is no longer to be considered as secondarily liable thereon. By his acceptance he becomes the principal debtor precisely like the maker of a note. . . .

That Archer knew that defendant's acceptance was in the nature of an accommodation to the Buffalo company in no way affects defendant's liability. Section 29 of the act . . . reads: "An accommodation party is one who has signed the instrument as maker, drawer, acceptor, or indorser, without receiving value therefor, and for the purpose of lending his name to some other person. Such a person is liable on the instrument to a holder for value, notwithstanding such holder at the time of taking the instrument knew him to be only an accommodation party."

It clearly appears, as before stated, that plaintiff gave value for the acceptances. In Irwin v. Wolcott, 183 Mich. 92, 98, 149 N.W. 1035,

1037, wherein a somewhat similar question was presented, it was said: "The agreement authorized the discount of the note, and the fact that it was known to the cashier of the bank that the paper had been drawn for accommodation would not prevent the bank which discounted it for value, by giving credit to the company for the amount of the discount upon its account, from recovering thereon."

The defense must rest upon the claim of Mr. Cronin that it was agreed between him and Mr. Archer that the defendant should not be liable thereon.

It is difficult to understand how such an agreement could have been made when that coal company was in no way a party to the arrangement then being made. Mr. Archer, as a witness, denied that he had any conversation with Mr. Cronin relative to the payment of the acceptances. . . .

[Judgment for defendant reversed.]

Code Comment: The same decision would be made under the Code. NIL Sec. 62 relating to the acceptor's liability is continued under UCC Sec. 3-413 (1). NIL Sec. 29 relating to an accommodation party is continued under UCC Sec. 3-415, although under the Code the accommodation party may be compensated. This variation does not affect the decision in this case.

Questions and Case Problems

1. What is the objective of each of the following rules of law?
(a) The transferee of a commercial paper may acquire greater rights than would an ordinary assignee.
(b) A holder for value may recover from an accommodation party even though he knew of his character as such.

2. Cortner and Wood, in payment for certain sheep, executed and delivered an instrument whereby they promised to pay $2,000 to the order of W. C. Thomas. Thomas signed his name on the back and delivered the note to Fox, at the latter's bank in Lewisburg, Tennessee. Who of the foregoing parties, if any, are properly described as (a) payee, (b) maker, (c) drawer, (d) indorser, (e) acceptor, (f) drawee, and (g) indorsee? (Fox v. Cortner, 145 Tenn. 482, 239 S.W. 1069)

3. McCormick & Co. brought suit against the Gem State Oil Co. on an instrument that bore the following notation in the margin:

> The obligation of the acceptor of this bill arises out of the purchase of goods from the drawer. Upon the acceptor hereof suspending payment, giving a chattel mortgage, suffering a fire loss, [or] disposing of his business, . . . this [instrument], at the option of the holder, shall immediately become due and payable.

What kind of an instrument was this? (McCormick & Co. v. Gem State Oil & Products Co., 38 Idaho 470, 222 P. 286)

4. Montgomery Ward & Co. brought suit against Newman upon the following writing:

Rutland, Vt., Feb. 17, 1930

A. Newman
Dear Sir:

Please pay Montgomery Ward & Co. ($800.00) Eight Hundred Dollars and charge to my account.

This is the second payment on plumbing and heating for three houses, 82-84 Killington Avenue, 15 Vernon Street.

C. W. YOUNG

Does this writing meet the tests of a commercial paper as stated in the definitions of a promissory note, a draft, or a check? (Montgomery Ward & Co. v. Newman, 104 Vt. 115, 157 A. 824)

5. Bonds were to be issued by the Belgian Government. In selling these bonds in the United States, J. P. Morgan & Co. issued to purchasers certificates stating that the bearer was entitled to a specified number of bonds "when, as, and if delivered" by the Belgian Government to J. P. Morgan & Co. Were these certificates negotiable instruments as stated in the definitions of a promissory note, a draft, or a check? (Manhattan Co. v. Morgan, 242 N.Y. 38, 150 N.E. 594)

6. Inman of Masonville, Michigan, executed and delivered to Dousay a bill of exchange for $128.05, drawn on Mason, who resided and had his place of business in Chicago, Illinois. The draft was not paid at maturity. In an action brought by Dousay against Mason, it was contended that the instrument was a foreign bill of exchange. What determines whether a negotiable instrument or commercial paper is a foreign or an inland bill of exchange? (Mason v. Dousay, 35 Ill. 424, 85 Am.Dec. 368)

7. Fowler, Allen, and Flanagan signed a promissory note as makers When Majors sued them on the note, Flanagan claimed that he had signed for the accommodation of the other parties and therefore was only liable as a surety (undertaking to become primary liability for the obligation), and that his liability was therefore not determined under the law governing negotiable instruments. Was he correct? (Flanagan v. Majors, [Ga.] 67 S.E.2d 786)

CHAPTER 27

Negotiability

In order to be negotiable, an instrument must (1) be in writing (2) signed by the maker or drawer; it must contain (3) a promise or order (4) of an unconditional character (5) to pay in money (6) a sum certain; (7) it must be payable on demand or at a particular future time; and (8) it must be payable to order or to bearer.[1] (9) If one of the parties is a drawee, he must be identified with reasonable certainty.

In addition to these formal requirements, the instrument must be delivered or issued by the maker or drawer to the payee or the latter's agent with the intent that it be effective and create a legal obligation.

Sec. 27-A. Requirements of Negotiability.

(1) Writing. A commercial paper must be in writing. Writing includes handwriting, typing, printing, engraving, and any other method of setting words down.

The instrument may be written in ink or pencil, but the use of pencil is not wise because such writing is not as durable as ink and the instrument may be more easily altered. A negotiable instrument may be written partly in ink and partly in pencil, or it may be partly printed and partly typewritten with a handwritten signature.

Since a negotiable instrument is in writing, the parol evidence rule applies. This rule prohibits modifying the instrument by proving the existence of a conflicting oral agreement alleged to have been made before or at the time of the execution of the commercial paper. Thus an instrument payable on a certain date cannot be shown by parol evidence to be payable at a later date, nor can parol evidence be used to prove the existence of an option to renew the instrument.

A carbon copy of an instrument is not admissible as evidence until the loss or destruction of the original has been shown. (See p. 420, Chrismer v. Chrismer, Executor)

---

[1] Uniform Commercial Code, Sec. 3-104(1).

(2) Signature. The instrument must be signed by the maker or drawer. His signature usually appears at the lower right-hand corner of the face of the instrument. It is immaterial, however, where the signature is placed. If the signature is placed on the instrument in such a manner that it does not in itself clearly indicate that the signer was the maker, drawer, or acceptor, however, he is held to be only an indorser.

The signature itself may consist of the full name or of any symbol adopted for that purpose. It may consist of initials, figures, or a mark.[2] A person signing a trade or an assumed name is liable to the same extent as though he signed in his own name.[3]

In the absence of a local statute that provides otherwise, the signature may be made by pencil, by typewriter, by print, or by stamp, as well as by pen.

(a) AGENT. A signature may be made for a person by his authorized agent.[4] No particular form of authorization to an agent to execute or sign a commercial paper is required, and the existence of his authority is established as in other cases.

An agent signing should indicate that he does so in a representative capacity, and he should disclose his principal. When he does both, the agent is not liable if he has acted within the scope of his authority.[5] (See p. 421, Betz Case)

(b) NONDISCLOSURE OF AGENCY. If a person who signs a negotiable instrument in a representative capacity, such as an agent or officer of a corporation, executes the instrument in such a way as to make it appear that it is his own act, he is personally bound regardless of whether he intended it to be his own act or his act in representative capacity. In such a case, parol evidence is not admissible to show that it was not intended that the agent or representative be bound or to show that it was intended to bind the undisclosed principal.

(c) PARTIAL DISCLOSURE OF AGENCY. The instrument may read or the agent may sign in such a way that his principal is identified or his representative capacity is disclosed, but not both. In such a case, the agent is personally liable on the instrument to third persons acquiring the instrument; but if sued by the person with whom he dealt, he may prove that it was intended that the principal should be bound.[6] The representative capacity of an officer of an organization is

---

[2] When a signature consists of a mark made by a person who is illiterate or physically incapacitated, it is commonly required that the name of the person be placed upon the instrument by someone else, who may be required to sign the instrument as a witness. Any form of signature is sufficient in consequence of the definition of "signed" as including any symbol executed or adopted by a party with the present intention to authenticate a writing. UCC Sec. 1-201(39).

[3] Sec. 3-401(2).

[4] Sec. 3-403(1).

[5] Sec. 3-403.

[6] Sec. 3-403(2)(b).

sufficiently shown under the Code when he signs his name and the title of his office either before or after the organization name.[7]

(3) Promise or Order to Pay. If the instrument is a promissory note, it must contain a promise to pay money.[8] No particular form of promise is required; the intention as gathered from the face of the instrument controls. If the maker uses such phrases as "I certify to pay" or "the maker obliges himself to pay," a promise is implied even though the word "promise" is not used.

A mere acknowledgment of a debt, such as a writing stating "I.O.U.," is not a negotiable instrument. It is not a promise to pay, and a promise is not implied from the fact that the existence of the debt is admitted.

If the instrument is a draft or a check, it must contain an order or command to pay money.[9] As in the case of a promise in a note, no particular words are required.

(4) Unconditional Character. The promise or order to pay must be unconditional. For example, when an instrument makes the duty to pay dependent upon the completion of the construction of a building or upon its placement in a particular location, the promise is conditional and the instrument is nonnegotiable. A promise to pay "when able" is generally interpreted as being conditional, but a minority of states regard it as requiring payment within a reasonable time and as therefore being an absolute promise.

The use of a term of politeness, such as "please," before an otherwise unconditional order to pay does not destroy the effect of the order within the meaning of the requirements for negotiability. But if the effect of the provision is no more than to seek the payment of money or to request it if certain facts are true, the order to pay is conditional and the instrument is nonnegotiable.

Whether a promise or an order to pay is conditional or unconditional is determined from an examination of the instrument itself. An unconditional or absolute promise in an instrument cannot be shown to be conditional by a provision found in a separate written agreement or based upon an oral agreement.

An order for the payment of money out of a particular fund, such as ten dollars from next week's salary, is conditional.[10] If, however, the instrument is based upon the general credit of the drawer and the reference to a particular fund is merely to indicate a source of reimbursement for the drawee, such as "you may take the payment out of the money due me" or "charge my expense account," the order

---

[7] Sec. 3-403(3).
[8] Sec. 3-104(1)(b).
[9] Sec. 3-104(1)(b).
[10] Sec. 3-105(2)(b).

is considered to be absolute.[11] (See p. 424, Brown v. Cow Creek Sheep Co.)

A promise or order that is otherwise unconditional is not made conditional by the fact that it "is limited to payment out of a particular fund or the proceeds of a particular source, if the instrument is issued by a government or governmental agency or unit; or is limited to payment out of the entire assets of a partnership, unincorporated association, trust, or estate by or on behalf of which the instrument is issued." [12]

(5) Payment in Money. A negotiable instrument must call for payment in *money*, that is, in any circulating medium of exchange which is legal tender at the place of payment. It is immaterial, as far as negotiability is concerned, whether it calls for payment in a particular kind of current money. If the order or promise is not for money, the instrument is not negotiable. For example, an instrument which requires the holder to take stock or goods in lieu of money is nonnegotiable.

An instrument is also nonnegotiable when the promise or order to pay money is coupled with an agreement to do something else unless that agreement will make it easier for the holder of the instrument to collect the money due on the instrument. A provision of the latter type is deemed not to impair negotiability because the effect of its inclusion is to make the paper more attractive to a purchaser and thus it encourages the exchange or transfer of the commercial paper.

(6) Sum Certain. The instrument must not only call for payment in money but also for a sum that is certain. Unless the instrument is definite on its face as to how much is to be paid, there is no way of determining how much the instrument is worth.

When there is a discrepancy between the amount of money as written in words and the amount as set forth in figures on the face of the instrument, the former is the sum to be paid. If the words that indicate the amount are ambiguous or uncertain, reference may be made to the amount in figures to determine the amount intended.[13] When there is an uncertainty of this type in connection with a check, it is common practice for a bank officer or teller to telephone the drawer in order to learn just what amount was intended before payment is made on the instrument.

The fact that the instrument may require certain payments in addition to the amount due as specified does not make the instrument nonnegotiable when such additional amounts come within any of the following categories:

----

[11] Sec. 3-105(1)(f).
[12] Sec. 3-105(1)(g),(h).
[13] UCC Sec. 3-118(c), NIL Sec. 17(1) and (4).

(a) INTEREST. A provision for the payment of interest does not affect the certainty of the sum, even though the interest rate changes upon default.[14]

(b) INSTALLMENTS. A provision for payment in installments does not affect certainty. Nor is certainty affected when the installment provision is coupled with a provision for acceleration of the date of payment for the total amount upon default in any payment.

(c) EXCHANGE. A provision for the addition of exchange charges does not affect the certainty of the sum payable since its object is in effect to preserve the constancy of the value involved. In this connection, the fact that the money due on the instrument is stated in a foreign currency does not make the instrument nonnegotiable.[15]

(d) COLLECTION COSTS AND ATTORNEY'S FEES. The certainty of the sum is not affected by a provision adding collection costs and attorney's fees to the amount due, although general principles of law may place a limit upon the amount that can be recovered for such items.

(e) DISCOUNT AND ADDITION. The certainty of the sum and the negotiability of the instrument are not affected by a provision that allows a discount if earlier payment is made or which increases the amount due if late payment is made.[16] (See p. 425, Waterhouse v. Chouinard)

(7) Time of Payment. A negotiable instrument must be payable on demand or at a particular time. If it is payable "when convenient," the instrument is nonnegotiable because the day of payment may never arrive. An instrument payable only upon the happening of a particular event that may never happen is not negotiable. For example, a provision to pay when a person marries is not payable at a particular future time since that event may never occur. It is immaterial whether the contingency in fact did happen because from an examination of the instrument alone it still appears to be subject to a condition that may never happen.

(a) DEMAND. An instrument is payable on demand when it is expressly specified to be payable "on demand;" or at sight; or on presentation, that is, whenever the holder tenders the instrument to the party required to pay and demands payment; or when no time for payment is specified.[17]

---

[14] Sec. 3-106(1)(b).
[15] Sec. 3-107(2). The Code follows banking practice in stating that an instrument payable in a foreign currency calls for the payment of a sum certain of money which, in the absence of contrary provision, is the number of dollars that the foreign currency will purchase at the buying sight rate on the due date or demand date of the instrument.
[16] Sec. 3-106(1)(c).
[17] Sec. 3-108.

(b) DEFINITE TIME. The time of payment is definite if it can be determined from the face of the instrument.

An instrument satisfies the requirement of providing for payment at a definite time when it is payable (1) on or before a stated date, (2) at a fixed period after a stated date, (3) at a fixed period after sight, (4) at a definite time subject to any acceleration, (5) at a definite time subject to extension at the option of the holder, (6) at a definite time subject to extension to a further definite date at the option of the maker or acceptor, or (7) at a definite time subject to an extension to a further definite date automatically upon or after the occurrence of a specified date or event.[18]

An instrument payable in relation to an event which though certain to happen will happen on an uncertain date, such as a specified time after death, is not negotiable.[19]

(8) Order or Bearer. A negotiable instrument must be payable to order or bearer.[20] This requirement is met by such expressions as "Pay to the order of John Jones," "Pay to John Jones or order," "Pay to bearer," and "Pay to John Jones or bearer." The use of the phrase "to the order of John Jones" or "to John Jones or order" is important in showing that the person executing the instrument is indicating that he does not intend to restrict payment of the instrument to John Jones and that he does not object to paying anyone to whom John Jones orders that paper to be paid. Similarly, if the person executing the instrument originally states that it will be paid "to bearer" or "to John Jones or bearer," he is not restricting the payment of the instrument to the original payee. If the instrument is payable "to John Jones" or "to bearer, John Jones," however, payment is restricted to John Jones and the instrument is not negotiable.

It is not necessary that the instrument actually use the words "order" or "bearer." Any other words indicating the same intention are sufficient. It has been held that the words "pay to holder" could be used in place of "order" or "bearer" without affecting the negotiability of the instrument.

(a) ORDER PAPER. An instrument is payable to order when by its terms it is payable to the order or assignees of any person specified therein with reasonable certainty (Pay to the order of E. A. Stacey), or to such a person or his order (Pay to E. A. Stacey or his order).[21]

---

18 Sec. 3-109(1). Although an acceleration provision may be added without affecting negotiability, a power to accelerate "at will" or when the holder "deems himself insecure" must be exercised in good faith. Sec. 1-208.

19 Sec. 3-109(2).

20 Under the Code, while an instrument not payable to order or bearer is not negotiable, it is nevertheless governed by Article 3 of the Code governing negotiable instruments except that there cannot be a holder in due course. Sec. 3-805.

21 An instrument is also payable to order when it is conspicuously designated on its face as "exchange" or the like, and names a payee. Sec. 3-110(1).

(b) BEARER PAPER. An instrument is payable to bearer when by its terms it is payable (1) to bearer or the order of bearer, (2) to a specified person or bearer, or (3) to "cash," or "the order of cash," or any other indication that does not purport to designate a specified person.[22]

An instrument payable to order and indorsed in blank becomes payable to bearer and may be negotiated by delivery alone until specially indorsed.[23]

(c) IMPOSTORS. The Code does not contain any provision for a fictitious, as contrasted with an impersonal, payee but deals with the problem more broadly by declaring that in certain instances an indorsement is valid although it has been made by a person who is an impostor or who was not intended to have any beneficial interest in the instrument. It is provided that an indorsement in the name of a named payee is effective if (1) an impostor has induced the maker or drawer to issue the instrument to him or a confederate in the name of the payee; (2) the person signing as, or on behalf of, the drawer intends that the named payee shall have no interest in the paper; or (3) an agent or employee of the drawer has given the drawer the name used as the payee intending that the latter should not have any interest in the paper. The last situation is illustrated by the case of the employee who fraudently causes his employer to sign a check made to a customer or other existing person, but the employee does not intend to send the check to that person but rather intends to forge the latter's indorsement to cash the check, and to keep the money for himself.

These impostor case provisions are based upon the social desire to place the loss upon the employer who could have prevented it through the exercise of greater care to protect subsequent holders of an instrument who have no reason to know of any wrongdoing. (See p. 427, Prugh Case)

Although the impostor's indorsement is effective, his civil or criminal liability for making such an indorsement continues under the Code.[24]

(9) Drawee. In the case of a draft or check, the drawee must be named or described in the instrument with reasonable certainty.[25] This requirement, which is based upon practical expediency, is designed to enable the holder of the instrument to know to whom he must go for payment.

---

22 Sec. 3-111.
23 Sec. 3-204(2). The Code does not classify as bearer paper an instrument on which the last indorsement is blank, as did the NIL, but the same result is obtained by virtue of the provision stated in the text.
24 Sec. 3-405.
25 Sec. 3-102 (1)(b).

When there are two or more drawees, they may be either joint drawees or alternative drawees.[26]

Sec. 27-B. Provisions for Additional Powers or Benefits to Holder of Instrument.

The Code expressly authorizes certain provisions in an instrument that give the holder certain additional powers and benefits.[27]

(1) Collateral. The inclusion of a power to sell collateral security upon default does not impair negotiability. An instrument secured by collateral contains as absolute a promise or order as an unsecured instrument. The Code also provides that negotiability is not affected by a promise or power to maintain or protect collateral or to give additional collateral,[28] or to make the entire debt due, if the additional collateral is not supplied.

(2) Acceleration. A power to accelerate the due date of an instrument upon a default in the payment of interest or of any installment, or upon the failure to maintain or provide collateral does not affect the negotiability of an instrument. (See p. 428, Cassiani v. Bellino) However, a power to accelerate "at will" or when a person "deems himself insecure" must be exercised in good faith.[29]

(3) Confession of Judgment. Negotiability is not affected by a provision authorizing the entry of a judgment by confession upon a default. In a judgment note the confession of judgment saves the holder the expense and delay of a lawsuit. If the holder of the instrument is authorized to confess judgment at any time, whether before maturity or not, however, it is generally held that the instrument is nonnegotiable. Local law may, however, invalidate a power to confess judgment.

(4) Waiver of Statutory Benefit. State statutes commonly provide that when a person is sued for a debt, a certain amount or kind of his property is exempt from the claim. If the party who executes a commercial paper promises to waive his rights under such a statute in order that it will be a little easier to collect the amount due, negotiability is not affected. A waiver of this kind is void in some states, however.

(5) Requirement of Another Act. The inclusion of a provision authorizing the holder to require an act other than the payment of

---

[26] Sec. 3-102(1)(b). The instrument is nonnegotiable if there are successive drawees. Successive drawees exist when, if one drawee fails to pay, the holder is required to go to the next drawee for payment rather than proceed at once against secondary parties.

[27] Sec. 3-112.

[28] Sec. 3-112(1)(c).

[29] Sec. 1-208.

money, such as the delivery of goods, makes the instrument non-negotiable.[30]

Sec. 27-C. Additional Documents. The fact that a separate document is executed that gives the creditor additional protection, as by a lien on goods or the right to repossess property sold to the maker of the instrument, does not impair its negotiability. (See p. 430, Mann v. Leasko)

Sec. 27-D. Immaterial Provisions. The addition or omission of certain provisions has no effect upon the negotiability of an otherwise commercial paper.

A negotiable instrument is not affected by the omission of the date. In such case it is regarded as carrying the date of the day on which it was executed and delivered to the payee. If the date is essential to the operation of the instrument, such as when the instrument is payable a stated number of days or months "after date," any holder who knows the true date may insert that date.

When a negotiable instrument is dated, the date is deemed prima facie to be the true date, whether the date was originally inserted or was thereafter added.[31] If the wrong date is inserted, the true date can be proved unless the holder is a holder in due course or a holder through a holder in due course, in which case the date, even though wrong, cannot be contradicted.

A negotiable instrument may be antedated or postdated, provided that is not done to defraud anyone. The holder acquires title as of the date of delivery without regard to whether this is the date stated in the instrument.

It is immaterial, so far as negotiability is concerned (1) whether an instrument bears a seal;[32] (2) whether it calls for payment in a particular kind of current money; (3) whether it fails to state that value has been given; or (4) whether it recites the giving of value without stating its nature or amount.

Some forms for checks provide a special space in which the drawer can note the purpose for which the check is given or set forth the items discharged by the check. Some statutes require that instruments state the purpose for which they are given in order to help avoid certain types of fraud. The Negotiable Instruments Law provided that it did not "repeal any statute requiring . . . the nature of the consideration to be stated in the instrument." The same conclusion would be reached under the Code.[33]

---

[30] Sec. 3-112, Official Comment.
[31] Sec. 3-114 (3).
[32] At common law the addition of a seal destroyed the negotiable character of the instrument.
[33] Compare UCC Sec. 3-112(1)(a),(2).

Negotiability is not affected by a provision that by indorsing or cashing the instrument the person receiving it takes it in full settlement of a specified claim or of all claims against the drawer.[34]

Cases for Chapter 27

Chrismer v. Chrismer, Executor

103 Ohio App. 23, 144 N.E.2d 494 (1956)

Francis M. Chrismer executed and delivered a promissory note and a carbon copy duplicate of the note payable to his son, Vern, and his daughter-in-law, Marie. After the death of Francis, suit was brought by the payees against his estate on the carbon copy duplicate. The estate contended that the carbon copy was not a negotiable instrument and that it could not be sued upon without proof of the loss or destruction of the original copy. From a judgment in favor of the estate, the plaintiffs appealed.

WISEMAN, J. . . . First, is the instrument a negotiable instrument within the meaning of the Negotiable Instruments Act? We think it is not. Without question, the instrument is but a carbon copy of an original. The signature is made by imprint of the carbon paper. In our opinion the signature of the maker must be an original signature to be genuine and legal within the meaning of the Act.

. . . In our opinion, the execution of a duplicate original negotiable promissory note is not contemplated by the Act, and, further, to do so would not be a sound trade practice or usage. We are cognizant of the fact that in modern trade practice carbon copies of negotiable promissory notes are made and retained for limited record purposes. However, in no sense can a carbon copy meet the statutory requirements of negotiability.

Since the instrument in question does not meet the test of a negotiable promissory note, we must consider its admissibility from the view point of a nonnegotiable promissory note. Promissory notes are divided into two classes: Negotiable and nonnegotiable; the former must comply with the Negotiable Instruments Act; the latter need not comply. . . .

In resolving this issue we leave the field of statutory law and enter the field of general contract law. Under the rules of evidence controlling the admission of written contracts, was this instrument admissible without first laying the foundation for its introduction under the best evidence rule? . . .

"Copies of written documents and instruments are merely secondary evidence, and except in the case of public documents or records which the public has the right to inspect and which cannot without

---

[34] Sec. 3-112(1)(f).

inconvenience be removed from their place of custody, copies are as a general rule inadmissible if the originals are available, unless proper foundation has been laid for their admission, or unless the admission thereof is provided for by statute."

"While a few cases have admitted carbon copies of other written instruments without requiring a foundation to be laid explaining the absence of the originals, the weight of authority is to the effect that some foundation must be laid to account for the absence of written instruments other than letters, before carbon copies thereof will be receivable."

[Case remanded for new trial to allow plaintiff opportunity to lay foundation for absence of original note.]

Code Comment: The same arguments sustain the same conclusion under the Code. Note also that the conclusion of the court would be strengthened by UCC Sec. 1-201 (39), which requires that a signature be placed with "present intention to authenticate a writing." The intent of the signer to authenticate is ordinarily limited to authenticating the original document that he signs, and it is unlikely that by a carbon paper duplicate of his signature he thereby means to authenticate the copy.

Betz v. Bank of Miami Beach

95 So.2d 891 (Fla., 1957)

The bank held two promissory notes. The notes were on printed forms which read ". . . the undersigned jointly and severally promise to pay to the bank. . . ." Each was executed as follows:

Corvette of Miami, Inc.

Hal Kaye	(Seal)
Howard Betz	(Seal)

The name of the corporation was typewritten. The names of the individuals were signed by them. The bank sued Betz on the notes. From a judgment for the bank, Betz appealed.

O'CONNELL, J. . . . Betz raises two questions on appeal. They are:

(1) Does the form of the note impose the liability thereof upon any person other than the corporation, as a matter of law?

(2) May parol evidence be introduced to prove the intent of the parties as to whether liability extends to the signer of the notes as individuals?

We are of the opinion that the notes as a matter of law impose liability as a maker on Betz. This makes it unnecessary for us to answer the second question posed by appellant, Betz, for his second question presupposes that the notes are ambiguous as to the liability of Betz. We do not find such to be the case. . . .

It is not disputed that Betz signed and intended to sign the notes as maker. The dispute is that Betz contends that he intended to sign as maker only in his representative capacity as secretary-treasurer of the corporation. The Bank contends that he signed and that it was intended that he sign as maker, individually. . . .

At first glance [Section 17 (6) of the NIL] might appear to control and answer appellant's first question. Appellee Bank argues that it does. That section reads:

(6) Where a signature is so placed upon the instrument that it is not clear in what capacity the person making the same intended to sign, he is deemed to be an indorser.

However, the apparent weight of authority and what seems to us to be the better rule is that the above quoted section is not applicable to a situation such as now before us where the question is not whether one intended to sign as endorser or maker, but whether one intended to sign as maker for himself, or maker for another, by acting in a representative capacity.

. . . This section was intended to settle doubt fairly arising from location of the name of a person, as where the signature is placed at the side, on the end or across the face of the instrument thus creating a doubt as to whether the signer intended to be bound as maker or as endorser. . . .

We next must consider [Section 20 which] provides that:

Where the instrument contains or a person adds to his signature words indicating that he signs for or on behalf of a principal, or in a representative capacity, he is not liable on the instrument if he was duly authorized; but the mere addition of words describing him as an agent, or as filling a representative character, without disclosing his principal does not exempt him from personal liability.

"It is well settled that whether a principal, or his agent, is the party liable upon a promissory note or bill of exchange, must be ascertained from the instrument itself. All evidence [outside of] the instrument is to be excluded. . . . 'If it is left ambiguous on the face of the instrument whether they have so signed it, the construction most against the person signing should prevail.' "

Appellee, the Bank, contends that this last statement . . . is controlling. . . .

In the case of Lazarov v. Klyce, 1953, 195 Tenn. 27, 255 S.W. 2d 11, a note had thereon the signature of B without indication that he had signed in a representative capacity. B contended that the note was ambiguous as to him and that he had intended to sign only in his representative capacity as an officer of the corporation. The court held that he had signed as maker and was bound as such. The court held there was no ambiguity. . . .

In Toon v. McCaw, 1913, 74 Wash. 335, 133 P. 469, L.R.A. 1915A, 590, a note was signed with the name of Aberdeen Tug Boat Co. followed by the names of three individuals, which names were not preceded by prepositions or followed by titles. The three contended they had signed only in their representative capacity. The court held the note not to be ambiguous as to them, refused to allow parol evidence to show that they signed only in a representative capacity, and held them liable as makers.

In Murphy v. Reimann Furniture Mfg. Co., 1948, 183 Ore. 474, 193 P.2d 1000, 1002 we find an identical factual situation. The note provided "we promise to pay." Two individuals signed below the name of a corporation without indicating that they did so in a representative capacity. There was no such indication in the body of the note. The court held there was no ambiguity in the note as to the liability of the two individuals, refused to allow them to introduce parol evidence to show they intended to sign only in their representative capacity, and held them personally liable as makers.

In Coal River Collieries v. Eureka Coal and Wood Company, 1926, 144 Va. 263, 132 S.E. 337, 338, 46 A.L.R. 485, a note was signed

"Eureka Coal & Wood Co., Inc.
"J. Liebman, Treasurer., N. Orleans."

It appears that N. Orleans was president of the corporation under which name he signed and that he had intended to sign only in such capacity. The court held there was no ambiguity, allowed no parol evidence, and held Orleans personally liable as a maker. It remarked that Orleans had signed exactly as he would have signed had he intended to bind himself individually, and that the parol evidence was offered first to create an ambiguity where none existed, and then to remove it.

We construe Sec. [20] supra, to provide a means by which one who signs a negotiable instrument for or on behalf of a principal, as maker, may escape personal liability thereon by following the provisions of the section. It seems clear to us therefore that where the body of the instrument or the person signing does not indicate that the maker is signing in a representative capacity, it is the intention of the statute that he be bound individually.

In the notes before us, there is nothing other than the name of the corporation typed above the signatures of Kaye and Betz to indicate that the payee and makers of the notes considered the instrument not to be binding on Betz as an individual maker. Betz signed exactly as he would have if it had been his intention to bind himself individually. His signature as written makes him personally liable as maker.

Not having availed himself of the opportunity, expressed in Sec. [20] supra, to escape a personal liability, we feel it clear that he is bound individually as a maker, that there is no ambiguity in the notes as to Betz, and therefore it is unnecessary to consider whether parol evidence should be admitted to allow him to show his liability to be contrary to what it appears to be from the face of the notes as they were actually signed, as they were delivered to the Bank and as they were sued on.

The result of this decision may be considered to be harsh. Yet in view of the importance of negotiable instruments in business, banking, and finance, the need for certainty and stability in the meaning of what appears on the face of such instruments and, in view of what we believe the intention and meaning of the pertinent sections of the Negotiable Instruments Law to be, we believe the rule we have adopted to be the better view. We believe this rule will cause less harm to commerce and result in less litigation than if we adopted the opposite view. . . .

[Judgment affirmed.]

Code Comment: The same result would be reached under the Code. Betz did not sign in a representative capacity because he did not add the title of his office as specified by UCC Sec. 3-403 (3). Betz is therefore liable under Sec. 3-403 (2) (b), which provides that "except as otherwise established between the immediate parties, [an authorized representative] is personally obligated if the instrument names the person represented but does not show that the representative signed in a representative capacity."

Brown v. Cow Creek Sheep Co.

21 Wyo. 1, 126 P. 886 (1912)

Wilkes, the agent of the Cow Creek Sheep Co., drew a company check on the First National Bank payable to Brown. On the check was the notation "For Wilkes." Before Brown cashed the check, the company told the bank not to pay the check. When the bank refused to make payment, Brown sued the company. The company defended on the ground that there was no consideration for the promise and that consideration was necessary because the check was nonnegotiable since it did not contain an unconditional order to pay. From a judgment for the defendant, the plaintiff appealed.

POTTER, J. . . . . The objections urged . . . present the question whether the check upon which the action is founded is . . . either a negotiable instrument, or one for the unconditional payment of money; it being contended . . . that the check is not such an instrument, and that the petition is therefore insufficient for the failure to aver consideration; and, further, that the check was drawn upon and payable out of a particular fund. . . . It is argued by counsel for defendant that the words "For Wilkes" constitute the instrument an order payable out of a particular fund, and therefore not negotiable or unconditional. . . .

The contention that the check is payable out of a particular fund cannot be sustained. The words "For Wilkes" do not, in our opinion, import that the check is drawn otherwise than upon the general personal credit of the drawer; but they appear, on the contrary, to be merely a statement of the object for which the check is drawn, or the person or account to which the amount was to be charged. Nor do they impress upon the check any element of contingency. . . .

. . . We perceive no reason for holding that the words "For Wilkes" indicate anything more than the purpose or consideration for which the check was drawn. . . .

It has not generally been held that a statement in or upon a bill, note, or check, indicating the consideration therefor, or the account to be charged with the amount, and the like, renders the payment, promise, or order conditional or affects the negotiability of the instrument. There is a clear distinction between such a statement and an order or promise to pay out of a particular fund; and this distinction is usually recognized in statutes defining negotiable instruments as it is in our statute by the provision that an order or promise to pay out of a particular fund is not unconditional, but that an unqualified order or promise to pay is unconditional though coupled with an indication of a particular fund out of which reimbursement is to be made, or a particular account to be debited with the amount, or a statement of the transaction which gives rise to the instrument. We hold, then, that the direction contained in this instrument is not to pay out a particular fund, as distinguished from an order upon the general credit of the drawer. . . .

[Judgment for defendant reversed.]

Code Comment: The same decision would be made under the Code. Such a notation would not impose any condition upon the instrument. UCC Sec. 3-105 (1) (a), (b), (f).

Waterhouse v. Chouinard

128 Me. 505, 149 A. 21 (1930)

Chouinard executed and delivered a promissory note to Currier. The instrument called for payment of $400 with the privilege of discharging the note by payment of the principal, less a discount of 5 per cent, within 30 days from date. Currier indorsed the note to Waterhouse for value, who thereafter brought suit upon the note against Chouinard. The latter claimed that the note was nonnegotiable and raised the defense of failure of consideration. From a judgment for the plaintiff, the defendant appealed.

FARRINGTON, J. . . . The first question, therefore, to be determined is whether the note in the case is a negotiable note under the Uniform Negotiable Instruments Act. . . . Does it contain "an unconditional promise or order to pay a *sum certain* in money"? . . . It becomes pertinent, as bearing on the question of whether the note was given for "a sum certain," to consider the effect on the promise to pay of the provision that it was "with the privilege of discharging this note by payment of principal less a discount of 5 per centum within thirty days from the date hereof."

As to whether or not such a provision in a note renders it nonnegotiable, the cases are in conflict. The Uniform Negotiable Instruments Act is silent as to the effect of such a provision. . . .

In the two lines of cases there is a slight preponderance numerically in favor of those holding such an instrument negotiable, but this court is unable to escape the conclusion that the maker of the note in the case under consideration, in promising to pay $400 one year after date in six-months' installments of $200 each, "with the privilege of discharging this note by payment of principal *less* a discount of 5 per centum within thirty days from the date hereof," did not promise to pay a "sum certain," and we so find. There should be such a degree of certainty that the exact amount to become due should be clearly ascertainable at the date of the note, uninfluenced by any conditions not certain of fulfillment. . . .

The Uniform Negotiable Instruments Act is the product of careful and deliberate thought. If it had been the intention that a note like the one in the instant case should be regarded as containing a promise to pay "a sum certain," a provision to that effect could have been included in the section defining what constitutes "a sum certain" as has been done, for example, in the provision for costs of collections or attorneys' fees, with reference to which there was a conflict of decisions before the Negotiable Instruments Law was generally adopted.

Assume a note made payable in one year after date with a discount of 15 per cent if paid within 30 days from date, and if not paid within 30 days, with the privilege of paying in full within 60 days with a discount of 10 per cent, and, if not then paid, with a 5 per cent discount if paid in full within 90 days. The element of uncertanity is brought out and emphasized more clearly as the differing sums contained in such a promise are made manifest.

. . . We therefore hold that the note is nonnegotiable. . . .

[Judgment for plaintiff reversed.]

Code Comment: Contrary to the decision, the instrument is negotiable under the Code. UCC Sec. 3-106 (1) (c) provides that "the sum payable is certain even though it is to be paid . . . with a stated discount . . . if paid before . . . the date fixed for payment." The note in the Waterhouse case did not literally contain a provision for discount upon payment before a fixed date, but its provision for discount if paid within a specified time after issuance would be interpreted as coming within the scope of the Code provision.

Prugh, Combest & Land, Inc. v. Linwood State Bank

241 S.W.2d 83 (Mo.App., 1951)

Prugh, Combest & Land, Inc., was a brokerage company. Ryan, a salesman of the company, falsely represented to the company that two of their customers, Harvey and Young, each desired to make a loan from the company. Ryan drew two checks on the company's bank, the Linwood State Bank, to the order of the customers. After having the checks signed by the president and cashier of the company, Ryan forged indorsements of the names of the payees on the checks, cashed them at the South Side Bank, which then forwarded them to the Linwood Bank for collection. The Linwood Bank paid the amounts of the checks and charged the account of the company therewith. The company then sued the bank for having so charged its account. From a judgment in favor of the bank, the company appealed.

Bour, C. . . . Linwood Bank and the . . . South Side Bank denied liability and defended mainly on two grounds. The banks asserted, first, that the two checks described in plaintiff's petition were, under the facts, payable to bearer. . . . If the checks were "bearer" instruments within the meaning of the [NIL, as amended] and therefore transferable by delivery, then it becomes immaterial whether the indorsements were forged or genuine, and plaintiff cannot recover. In such case the indorsements of the names of the designated payees, by whomever made, may be treated as superfluous and disregarded. . . .

Prior to the amendment of 1945, the Negotiable Instrument Law provided, Sec. [9 (3)]: "The instrument is payable to bearer: . . . (3) when it is payable to the order of a fictitious or nonexisting person and such fact was known to the person making it so payable." . . . As stated in 118 ALR, 15, 17, "that provision has been a prolific source of litigation on the questions as to when the paper is 'payable to a fictitious or nonexisting person' and when 'such fact is known to the person making it so payable.' " . . .

The Statute, as amended, Laws 1945, p. 594, Mo.R.S.A. § 3025 (3) R.S. 1949, § 401.009 (3), reads as follows: "The instrument is payable to bearer . . . (3) When it is payable to the order of a fictitious or nonexisting person *or to a living person not intended or entitled to have any interest in it* and such fact was known to the person making it so payable or was known to his employee or other agent who supplies or causes to be inserted the name of such payee. . . ." (Italicized words added by the amendment.)

... Ten other states have adopted similar amendments. . . . Thus, the Illinois negotiable instrument act was amended in 1931 so as to make an instrument payable to bearer "When it is payable to the order of a fictitious or nonexistent or living person not intended to have any interest in it, and such fact was known to the person making it so payable, *or known to his employee or other agent who supplies the name of such payee*.". . . (Italicized words . . . added by the amendment. . . .)

In the case at bar, Ryan represented to Land, plaintiff's secretary-treasurer, that Harvey and Young wished to borrow money on their securities, which representations were wholly false. . . . When Ryan made the false representations to Land, "the said Ryan did not intend that the said Harvey or the said Young should receive said checks or any beneficial interest therein . . . ," and "that when said checks were delivered to Ryan for delivery to the payees named therein, he, in fact, had no intention of delivering the said checks to the named payees but instead intended to convert said checks and their proceeds to his own use and benefit.". . . In view of these facts, it is clear that each check was payable to the order of "a living person not intended . . . to have any interest in it." The conduct of the employee, Ryan, as disclosed by the evidence, amounted to supplying the names of the payees within the meaning of the 1945 amendment. The plaintiff corporation was the "person" who in the statutory sense made the checks payable to the named payees; but it is bound by the guilty knowledge and intent of Ryan. This is so notwithstanding the fact that Ryan had no authority to prepare, execute, or issue the checks in question. . . .

[Judgment affirmed.]

Code Comment: The same result is obtained under the Code, which redeclares the "employee" amendment to the NIL on which the case is based. UCC Sec. 3-405 (1) (c).

Cassiani v. Bellino

338 Mass. 765, 157 N.E.2d 409 (1959)

Bellino was a maker of a promissory note payable in installments which contained the provision that upon default in the payment of any installment the holder had the option of declaring the entire balance "due and payable on demand." The note was negotiated to Cassiani who sued Bellino for the full debt when there was a default on an installment. Bellino raised the defense that no notice of acceleration had been given to her prior to the suit. From a judgment in favor of Cassiani, Bellino appealed.

WILKINS, C.J. . . . Because of the words "on demand," it is insisted that the note in suit is conditional. . . . We cannot accept this contention. The defendants do not argue that they were ready and able to make payment of the installment of interest but did not know where to make it. . . . Nor is this a case where the defendants were not given a fair opportunity to pay. . . .

The acceleration clause is valid. . . . The note was negotiable notwithstanding that clause. . . . To enforce a note payable on demand, the bringing of suit is in itself a sufficient demand. . . . As we said as to the institution of another type of suit, "A more definite and insistent form of 'written demand' could hardly be imagined." . . .

The defendants also argue that after default the principal was not due without a demand for payment of the accelerated amount. . . . This point is of first impression [35] in this Commonwealth. The views of other courts are divided [citing Texas and Connecticut cases]. . ., holding that demand upon the maker is necessary to accelerate the payment of the entire debt. . . .

To the contrary and to the effect that a demand for the full amount, or notice of an intention to exercise the option to collect it, is not a condition precedent to bringing suit, are cases in many jurisdictions. Some are of long standing. . . .

The interpretation of the acceleration clause is governed by the law of contracts and was not covered by the negotiable instruments law. . . . In the existing state of the authorities, we have a free choice of the rule which, to our thinking, is better suited to negotiable instruments and commercial practice. Ours is now the decision whether the signer of a note containing an acceleration clause upon default optional with the holder is, after default, entitled to a special notice, as a condition precedent to suit, that the holder has elected to avail himself of the benefits of that clause. A maker must be held to know what he signed. We do not favor placing this unnecessary burden upon the recovery of the loan. We are aware of no policy in this Commonwealth which would handicap the enforcement of a contract, freely made, for the repayment of cash borrowed. We are not informed of any reason why the defendants should be given the advantage of the defense asserted. It cannot be denied that before suit presentment for payment and demand for the full amount of the note would have precluded this defense. Such presentment and demand could have preceded service of the writ by the briefest period of time. . . .

[Judgment for plaintiff affirmed.]

---

[35] A case of first impression is one which raises a point that has never been decided in the jurisdiction in question.

Code Comment: The same decision would be made under the Code because the Code recognizes the validity of an acceleration clause, UCC Secs. 1-208, 3-109 (1) (c). The decision in the Cassiani case did not rest on any particular provision of the NIL but rather on general principles of construction of contracts, which principles would be applicable as well to cases arising under the Code. See UCC Sec. 1-103, declaring the continuing operation of general principles of law.

Mann v. Leasko

179 Cal.App.2d 692, 4 Cal.Rep. 124 (1960)

Leasko purchased a water softener from Mission Supply Co. In payment, he executed a negotiable promissory note and also signed a nonnegotiable contract in which he created a lien on his house to secure the note. Mission sold the note to a finance company operated by Mann. Later Mann sued Leasko on the note and brought an action to foreclose the lien. Leasko claimed that the note was nonnegotiable because it was secured by a nonnegotiable contract creating a lien. From a judgment for Leasko, Mann appealed.

HERNDON, J. . . . . The promissory note in the case at bar clearly meets all the formal requirements for a negotiable instrument. . . .

Under the Negotiable Instruments Law, adopted in California in 1917, authorities in many jurisdictions, including California, have taken the view that concurrent execution of a note and a contract under which the payee has certain executory obligations will not, in and of itself, impair the negotiability and resulting commercial value of the note. . . . This view has obtained where the note is secured by a conditional sales contract. . . , even where the note refers to the contract or is physically attached to the contract when executed. . . . Similarly, except where a statute provides to the contrary, it is generally conceded that the mere fact that a promissory note is secured by a chattel mortgage does not impair the negotiability of the note. . . . This view obtains in California where a note is secured by a mortgage on real or personal property, by virtue of section 3265 of the Civil Code, providing in relevant part that ". . . the negotiability of a promissory note otherwise negotiable in form, secured by a mortgage or deed of trust upon real or personal property shall not be affected or abridged by reason of a statement therein that it is so secured, nor by reason of the fact that said instrument is so secured nor by any conditions contained in the mortgage or deed of trust securing the same.". . .

Pursuant to these rules and in keeping with the purpose of furthering the integrity of commercial paper underlying the Negotiable Instruments Law, we hold that contemporaneous execution and transfer of a promissory note and a nonnegotiable contract securing performance by a lien on real property does not, in and of itself, impair the negotiability of the note. And, since the transfer of the note constitutes a transfer of the lien which is an incident thereof . . . if appellant is entitled . . . to bring suit on the note, he is similarly entitled to foreclose the lien. . . .

[Judgment reversed.]

Code Comment: The same conclusion is reached under the Code, which recognizes that the negotiability of an instrument is not impaired by the fact that there is collateral security for it, even though the instrument expressly states that it is secured by such collateral. UCC Secs. 3-105 (1) (e), 3-112 (1) (b).

Questions and Case Problems

1. What is the objective of each of the following rules of law?

(a) A signature on a commercial paper may be made by pencil, by typewriter, by print, or by rubber stamp, as well as by pen.

(b) An instrument is nonnegotiable if it contains a clause authorizing acceleration when the holder deems himself insecure.

2. Cortis made a contract for storm windows and gave the seller a promissory note in payment. The note promised to pay $3,400 in installments as set forth in the schedule of payments stated in the note. The schedule of payments, however, was left blank. Was the note void? (Liberty Aluminum Products Co. v. Cortis, [Pa.] 14 D.&C.2d 624, 38 Wash.Co. 223)

3. Conville, as an officer of the Hughesville Mfg. Co., signed a note but did not name the corporation in the note nor indicate that he was acting as an officer for it. Later, he was sued by the Grange National Bank, the holder of the note. He raised the defenses that: (1) the corporation, and not he, was liable on the note; (2) the note could be reformed to show that he had been acting as an officer for the corporation. Decide. (Grange National Bank v. Conville, [Pa.] 8 D.&C.2d 616, 5 Lyc.Rep. 170)

4. Hunter executed a note payable "to Beeson & Foley." Aamoth, who purchased the note in good faith before maturity, sued Hunter on the note. Hunter claimed that the note was nonnegotiable. Was he correct? (Aamoth v. Hunter, 33 N.D. 582, 157 N.W. 299)

5. Mr. and Mrs. Gulas took care of Dulak. When the latter desired to draw checks, Mr. Gulas would prepare the checks and Dulak would sign them. Six days before Dulak died, he told Mr. and Mrs. Gulas that he was obligated to their two sons for $3,000 each, requested his checkbook, and directed Gulas to prepare a check for each son for $3,000. Dulak then signed each check, and the two checks were torn from the checkbook but were not separated from each other. The checks were replaced in the checkbook, which was then put in the dresser drawer in Dulak's room where it was usually kept. After his death, Mrs. Gulas showed the checkbook and the checks to the executors under Dulak's will, and they kept possession of the checks. The two sons then sued to enforce the payment of the checks. Decide. (Dulak's Will, 209 N.Y.S.2d 928)

6. After the death of Cecelia Donohoe, her son, Richard, presented for payment a note that she had executed. Mrs. Donohoe had signed her name in the body of the note rather than at the end, and then acknowledged the note before a notary public, as follows:

$13,070.86.   August 30th, 1910.

I, Cecelia W. Donohoe, after date, *August 30th*, promise to pay to the order of *Richard Donohoe, thirteen thousand and seventy dollars and 86/100*, with interest at *6%*. . . .
Witness *my* hand and seal.

   (Seal.)   Hester Johnson,
                   Notary Public.

The note was on a printed form, and the words italicized were in the handwriting of Mrs. Donohoe. Her estate claimed that it was not liable on this writing because it had not been signed by Mrs. Donohoe. Was it correct? (Donohoe's Estate, 271 Pa. 554, 115 A. 878)

7. Leonard executed a promissory note which authorized the holder to confess judgment at any time. Was the note negotiable? (Atlas Credit Corp. v. Leonard, [Pa.] 15 D.&C.2d 292, 56 Lanc.L.Rev. 57)

8. Keel executed a promissory note payable to Day four months after date. The blank for the date was left unfilled. A subsequent holder of the note, the Bank of Houston, brought suit on the note against Day. It was shown that the cashier of the bank who knew the true date of issue had inserted a date a month later than the day the note was executed by Keel. Day claimed that the wrongful dating released him from liability. Decide. (Bank of Houston v. Day, 145 Mo.App. 410, 122 S.W. 756)

9. Von Dolcke gave Gross a promissory note payable on or before a fixed date. Gross wrote and signed a notation on the instrument that if the amount could not be paid in full when due, "a partial payment will be acceptable of any amount available and the note extended from time to time until it can be paid in full." Was this a negotiable instrument? (Gross v. Von Dolcke, 313 Mich. 132, 20 N.W.2d 838)

10. Koch executed an instrument by which he promised to pay to Schultz money and wheat amounting to the sum of $3,400 on or before six years from date. Was this instrument negotiable? (Thomson v. Koch, 62 Wash. 438, 113 P. 1110)

11. Granger and Cottrell were partners engaged in business under the name of "The Oregon Locators." Granger, for partnership purposes, gave to Masten a promissory note for the sum of $100 that was signed "The Oregon Locators." In an action brought by the holder of the note against Granger and Cottrell to recover on the note, the defendants claimed that the note was not validly signed. Was this contention sound? (Frazer v. Cottrell, 82 Ore. 614, 162 P. 834)

12. Wade executed a promissory note for $3,100 payable to Keister or order. When Keister brought an action to recover on the note, Wade contended that it was nonnegotiable because it specified no time of payment. Decide. (Keister v. Wade, 191 App.Div. 870, 182 N.Y.S. 119)

CHAPTER 28

Transfer of Commercial Paper

Commercial paper may be transferred by negotiation or assignment. When a negotiable instrument is transferred by a negotiation, the rights of the transferee may rise higher than those of the transferor, depending upon the circumstances attending the negotiation. When the transfer is made by assignment, the assignee has only those rights which the assignor possessed and the assignee is subject to all defenses existing against the assignor prior to notice of the assignment.

Indorsements

The person to whom an instrument is payable or the person in possession of bearer paper may indorse it for the purpose of negotiating it by merely signing his name on it or he may add certain words or statements as part of his indorsement. By definition, an indorsement is properly written on the back of the instrument.

Sec. 28-A. Kinds of Indorsements. The four principal kinds of indorsements are (1) blank, (2) special, (3) qualified, and (4) restrictive.

(1) Blank Indorsement. When the indorser signs only his name, the indorsement is called a *blank indorsement* since it does not indicate the person to whom the instrument is to be paid, that is, the indorsee. This is the most common form of indorsement because it is the simplest and the easiest to write. It may be a dangerous form of indorsement since it has the effect of making the instrument payable to bearer and it can be negotiated by delivery by anyone, even a finder or a thief. Such an indorsement usually may be made with safety on a check when the holder is in a bank where he intends to deposit or cash the check. The holder of an instrument on which the last indorsement is blank may protect himself by writing above the signature of the blank indorser a statement that the instrument is made payable to him.[1] This is called "completing" the indorsement

---

[1] Uniform Commercial Code, Sec. 3-204(3); Negotiable Instruments Law, Sec. 35.

433

or "converting" the blank indorsement to a special indorsement by specifying the identity of the indorsee. This has the same effect as though the indorser had named the holder as indorsee.

Negotiation by a blank indorsement does three things: (a) it passes the ownership of the instrument; (b) it makes certain warranties;[2] and (c) it imposes upon the indorser a liability to pay the amount of the instrument if the maker or drawee fails to do so and certain conditions are then satisfied by the holder.

(2) Special Indorsement. An indorsement that consists of the signature of the indorser and words specifying the person to whom the indorser makes the instrument payable, that is, the indorsee, is a *special indorsement.* Common forms for this type of indorsement are "Pay to the order of Harold Newman, F. J. Baker" and "Pay to Harold Newman or order, F. J. Baker." It is not necessary that the indorsement contain the words "order" or "bearer." Thus a negotiable instrument indorsed in the form "Pay to Harold Newman, F. J. Baker" continues to be negotiable and may be negotiated further. In contrast, an instrument which on its face reads "Pay to Harold Newman" is not negotiable.

When the last indorsement on the instrument is special, an indorsement and delivery by or on behalf of the last indorsee is required for further negotiation.[3]

As in the case of the blank indorsement, a special indorsement transfers title to the instrument and results in the making of certain warranties[4] and in imposing a liability upon the indorser to pay the amount of the instrument under certain conditions.

(3) Qualified Indorsement. A *qualified indorsement* is one that qualifies the effect of a blank or a special indorsement by disclaiming or destroying the liability of the indorser to answer for the default of the maker or drawee. This may be done by including the words "without recourse" in the body of the indorsement, or by using any other words that indicate an intention to destroy the indorser's secondary liability for the default of the maker or drawee.[5]

The qualifying of an indorsement does not affect the passage of title or the negotiable character of the instrument. It merely limits the indorser's liability to the extent of the qualification. (See p. 442 Cressler v. Brown)

---

[2] See p. 440.
[3] UCC Sec. 3-204(1), NIL Sec. 34.
[4] See p. 440.
[5] UCC Sec. 3-414(1), NIL Sec. 38.

This form of indorsement is most commonly used when the qualified indorser is admittedly a person who has no personal interest in the transaction, as in the case of an attorney or an agent who is merely indorsing to his principal or client a check made payable to him by a third person. Here the transferee recognizes that the transferor is not a party to the transaction and therefore is not in a position where he should be asked to guarantee the paper.

(4) Restrictive Indorsements. A *restrictive indorsement* specifies the purpose of the indorsement or the use to be made of the paper. Restrictive indorsements may be of the following types:

(a) INDORSEMENT FOR DEPOSIT. This indorsement indicates an intent that the instrument be deposited, such as "For deposit only," "For deposit only to the account of Paul A. Ogden," and "Pay to the First National Bank for deposit only." [6]

(b) INDORSEMENT FOR COLLECTION. This indorsement indicates an intention that the instrument be received by the indorsee for the purpose of effecting the collection of the instrument, such as "For collection only," or "Pay to any bank or banker." [7]

(c) INDORSEMENT PROHIBITING FURTHER NEGOTIATION. The indorsement, "Pay to Alex White only," indicates an intent that no further negotiation should occur and is therefore restrictive. [8]

(d) AGENCY OR TRUST INDORSEMENT. An indorsement that makes the indorsee the agent of the indorser, such as "Pay to (indorsee, agent) on account of (indorser, principal)," or which makes the indorsee the owner subject to a trust for another person, such as "Pay to (indorsee, mother) to hold for use of (third person, son)," are restrictive indorsements [9] in that they state that the indorsement is for the benefit or use of the indorser or another person. [10]

(e) CONDITION AS A PART OF THE INDORSEMENT. An indorsement which indicates that it is to become effective only upon the satisfaction of a particular condition, such as "Pay to Jones upon completion of Contract #251," is a restrictive indorsement. [11]

---

6 UCC Sec. 3-205 (c).

7 Sec. 3-205(c). The same view was declared by the Bank Collection Code, Sec. 4, adopted in Idaho, South Carolina, and Washington. The Bank Collection Code had also been adopted in Indiana, Illinois, Kentucky, Maryland, Michigan, Missouri, Nebraska, New Jersey, New Mexico, New York, Oregon, Pennsylvania, West Virginia, Wisconsin and Wyoming but was repealed upon the adoption of the Uniform Commercial Code in those states.

8 UCC Sec. 3-205(b), NIL Sec. 36.

9 NIL Sec. 36.

10 UCC Sec. 3-205(d).

11 Sec. 3-205(a).

Sec. 28-B. Effect of Restrictive Indorsement. A restrictive indorsement does not have the effect of prohibiting further negotiation even though it expressly attempts to do so.[12] In all cases the transferee may therefore be a holder, just as is true under a nonrestrictive indorsement. A bank may ignore and is not affected by the restrictive indorsement of any person except the holder transferring the instrument to the bank or the person presenting it to the bank for payment. However, a depositary bank, that is, the one in which the customer deposits the item, and persons not in the bank collection process must recognize the restrictive indorsement to the extent of applying any value [13] given in a manner consistent with the indorsement.[14]

Sec. 28-C. Irregular Form of Indorsement. The indorser may make an indorsement that does not fall into any of the standard categories of indorsements. For example, he may write "I hereby assign all my right, title, and interest in the within note," and then sign his name. The signature in such a case is effective as an indorsement in spite of the added words, on the theory that the indorser actually intended to indorse and was merely attempting to make certain that he transferred his interest. "Words of assignment, condition, waiver, guaranty, limitation or disclaimer of liability, and the like accompanying an indorsement do not affect its character as an indorsement." [15]

Sec. 28-D. Irregular Indorser. Sometimes the capacity in which a particular party has signed a negotiable instrument cannot be determined by looking at the instrument. For example, a note may be indorsed by A to the order of B, and then by B to the order of C, and by C to the order of D. Assume that on the back of the note there also appears the signature of M. How does M enter into the history of the instrument? It may be that when A was about to indorse the note to B, B would not accept the note unless M signed it also as an accommodation party. This fact, however, cannot be determined just by looking at the back of the note. An *irregular indorser*,[16] then, is a person who signs his name as an indorser before delivery but who is otherwise not a party to the instrument.

An indorsement which is not in the chain of title, that is, which is irregular or anamalous, thereby gives notice of its accommodation character.[17] In any case, the accommodation party is liable to the holder for value according to the capacity in which he has signed.[18]

---

[12] Sec. 3-206(1).
[13] See p. 496.
[14] UCC Sec. 3-206(2). Additional limitations are imposed in the case of collection and conditional indorsements, Sec. 3-206 (3), and trust indorsements, Sec. 3-206(4).
[15] Sec. 3-202(4).
[16] The irregular indorser is also called an *anomalous indorser*. NIL Sec. 64.
[17] UCC Sec. 3-415(4).
[18] Sec. 3-415(1),(2).

Sec. 28-E. Correction of Name by Indorsement. Sometimes the name of the payee or indorsee to a negotiable instrument is improperly spelled. Thus John H. Jones may receive a pay check which improperly is payable to the order of "John A. Jones." If this was a clerical error and the check was intended for John H. Jones, the employee may ask his employer to write a new check payable to him in his proper name. This may cause a great deal of inconvenience as well as delay the employee in receiving his pay.

The payee or indorsee whose name is misspelled may indorse the wrong name, his correct name, or both. A person giving or paying value for the instrument may require both.[19]

This correction of name by indorsement may only be used when it was intended that the instrument should be payable to the person making the corrective indorsement. If there were in fact two employees, one named John H. Jones and the other John A. Jones, it would be illegal as a forgery for one to take the check intended for the other and by indorsing it obtain for himself the benefit or proceeds of the check.

Sec. 28-F. Bank Indorsements. In order to simplify the transfer of commercial paper from one bank to another in the process of collecting items, the Code provides that "any agreed method which identifies the transferor bank is sufficient for the item's further transfer to another bank." [20]

Likewise, when a customer has deposited an instrument with a bank but has failed to indorse it, the bank may make an indorsement for him unless the instrument expressly requires the payee's personal indorsement. Furthermore the mere stamping or marking on the item of any notation showing that it was deposited by the customer or credited to his account is as effective as an indorsement by the customer would have been.[21] In this way the annoyance and loss of time of returning the instrument to the customer for his indorsement are eliminated. The exception as to "personal indorsement" is commonly applicable in the case of pay checks issued by governments and some corporations.

Negotiation

The method of negotiating an instrument depends upon the terms of the instrument or its indorsement. If it is order paper, it can be negotiated only by indorsement and delivery. If it is bearer paper, it may be negotiated by delivery alone.

---

[19] UCC Sec. 3-203. See NIL Sec. 43.
[20] UCC Sec. 4-206.
[21] Sec. 4-205(1).

Sec. 28-G. Methods of Negotiation.

(1) Negotiation of Order Paper. An instrument payable to order may be negotiated only by the indorsement of the person to whom it is payable at the time (see p. 443, American Motors Acceptance Corp. Case) and delivery by him or with his authorization. (See p. 444, Cartwright v. Coppersmith) The indorsement must be written on the instrument itself.[22] (See p. 445, Bailey v. Mills) The indorsement must be placed on the instrument by the person to whom it is then payable, unless the indorsement is made for accommodation. The indorsement ordinarily must be genuine or authorized in order to make negotiation of the instrument effective.

(a) MULTIPLE PAYEES AND INDORSERS. Ordinarily one person is named as payee by the instrument, but two or more payees may be named. In that case, the instrument may specify that it is payable to any one or more of them or that it is payable to all jointly. If nothing is specified, the instrument is payable to all of the payees [23] and they are *joint payees.* For example, if the instrument is made payable "to the order of *A* and *B*," the two persons named are joint payees. The importance of this kind of designation is that it requires the indorsement of both *A* and *B* to negotiate the instrument further. This protects *A* against the action of *B*, and vice versa. Each knows that the other cannot secretly negotiate the instrument and pocket the proceeds. This rule does not apply, however, when the payees are partners or when one person is authorized to act for all and he indorses for all.

Joint payees or joint indorsees who indorse are deemed to indorse jointly and severally.[24] If the instrument is payable to alternate payees or if it has been negotiated to alternate indorsees, as *A* or *B,* it may be indorsed and delivered by either of them.

(b) AGENT OR OFFICER AS PAYEE. The instrument may be made payable to the order of an officeholder. For example, a check may read, "Pay to the order of the Receiver of Taxes." Such a check may be received and negotiated by the person who at the time is the Receiver of Taxes. This is a matter of convenience since the person writing the instrument is not required to find out the name of the Receiver of Taxes at that time.

If the instrument is drawn in favor of a person as "Cashier" or some other fiscal officer of a bank or corporation, it is payable to the

---

[22] Sec. 3-202(2). If there is no more space on the instrument itself, the indorsement may be written on another piece of paper provided it is so firmly attached to the instrument that it becomes part of it. This additional paper is called an *allonge.* See NIL Sec. 31.

[23] UCC Sec. 3-116, NIL Sec. 41.

[24] UCC Sec. 3-118(e), NIL Sec. 68.

bank or corporation of which he is such an officer, and may be negotiated by the indorsement of either the bank or corporation, or of the named officer.[25]

(c) PARTIAL NEGOTIATION. A negotiation of part of the amount cannot be made.[26] The entire instrument must be negotiated to one person or to the same persons. If the instrument has been partly paid, however, the unpaid balance may be transferred by indorsement. This is proper since the amount then due, although it is only a portion of the original amount due, is being transferred.

(d) MISSING INDORSEMENT. Although order paper cannot be negotiated without indorsement, it can be assigned to another without indorsement. In such a case, if the transferee has given value for the paper, he has the same rights as the transferor. In addition, he has the right to require that the transferor indorse the instrument to him and thereby effect a negotiation of the instrument.

(2) Negotiation of Bearer Paper. Any negotiable instrument payable to bearer may be negotiated by merely delivering it, that is, by physically handing it over to another person.[27] This is true not only when the instrument expressly states that it is payable to bearer, but also when the law interprets it as being payable to bearer, as in the case of a check payable to the order of "Cash."

Although bearer paper may be negotiated by delivery, the person to whom it is delivered may insist that the bearer indorse the paper so as to impose upon the transferor the liability of an indorser. This situation most commonly arises when a check payable to "Cash" is presented to a bank for payment.

Because bearer paper can be negotiated by delivery alone, a thief, a finder, or an unauthorized agent can pass title as though he owned or had the right to negotiate the instrument. This means that the use of bearer paper should be avoided whenever possible.

(3) Time for Determining Character of Paper. The character of the paper is determined as of the time when the negotiation is about to take place, without regard to what it was originally or at any intermediate time. Accordingly, when the last indorsement is special, the paper is order paper without regard to whether it was bearer paper originally or at any intermediate time, and the holder cannot ignore or strike out intervening indorsements, or otherwise treat it as bearer paper because it had once been bearer paper.

---

[25] UCC Sec. 3-117(a), NIL Sec. 42.

[26] UCC Sec. 3-202(3), NIL Sec. 32. Under the Code, the partial negotiation is not a nullity but is given the effect of a partial assignment.

[27] UCC Sec. 3-202 (1), NIL Sec. 39.

Sec. 28-H. Effect of Incapacity or Misconduct on Negotiation. A negotiation is effective even though (a) it is made by a minor or a person lacking capacity; (b) it is an act beyond the powers of a corporation; (c) it is obtained by fraud, duress, or mistake of any kind; (d) or the negotiation is part of an illegal transaction or was made in breach of duty. Under general principles of law apart from the Code, the transferor in such cases may be able to set aside the negotiation or to obtain some other form of legal relief. If, however, the instrument has in the meantime been acquired by a holder in due course, the negotiation can no longer be set aside.[28]

Sec. 28-I. Assignment of Commercial Paper. In addition to transfer by negotiation, a negotiable instrument may be transferred by assignment. Such an assignment of a negotiable instrument may be made (1) by act of the parties or (2) by operation of law.

(1) Assignment by Act of the Parties. A negotiable instrument is regarded as assigned when a person whose indorsement is required on the instrument transfers it without indorsing it. In such a case the transferee has only the rights of an assignee, and he is subject to all defenses existing against the assignor prior to notice of the assignment. He is entitled, however, to require that the transferor indorse the instrument.[29] If the indorsement is obtained, then the transferee is deemed a holder but only as of the time when the indorsement is made.

(2) Assignment by Operation of Law. An assignment by operation of law occurs when by virtue of the law the title of one person is vested in another. If the holder of a negotiable instrument becomes a bankrupt or dies, the title to the instrument vests automatically in the trustee in bankruptcy or in the personal representative of the estate.

Warranties of Transferor

The transferor, by the act of making the transfer, warrants the existence of certain facts. The warranties of the transferor are not always the same but vary according to the nature of the indorsement he makes or whether he transfers the instrument without indorsement. The Code also distinguishes between warranties arising in connection with acceptance or payment[30] and those arising in connection with transfer. In connection with the latter, it also provides that in the case of transfer by indorsement the warranty may run to a subsequent holder but in the case of transfer by delivery only to the immediate transferee.

---

[28] UCC Sec. 3-207.
[29] UCC Sec. 3-201(3), NIL Sec. 49.
[30] See p. 463.

Sec. 28-J. Warranties of Unqualified Indorser. When the holder of a negotiable instrument negotiates it by an unqualified indorsement, and receives consideration, several warranties are implied by the Code. The transferor warrants that:

(1) He has a good title, which includes the genuineness of all indorsements necessary to his title to the instrument, or that he is authorized to act for one who has such good title.[31]

(2) His act of transferring the instrument is rightful, independent of the question of his title or authority to act.[32]

(3) The signatures on the instrument are genuine or executed by authorized agents.[33]

(4) The instrument has not been materially altered.[34]

(5) He has no knowledge of the existence or commencement of any insolvency proceeding against the maker or acceptor of the instrument, or against the drawer of an unaccepted bill of exchange.[35]

(6) No defense of any party is good as against him.[36]

These warranties made by the unqualified indorser pass to his transferee and to any subsequent holder who acquires the instrument in good faith.[37]

Sec. 28-K. Warranties of Other Parties.

(1) Warranties of Qualified Indorser. The qualified indorser makes the same warranties as an unqualified indorser except that the warranty as to "no defenses" is limited to a warranty that the indorser does not have knowledge of any defense, rather than that no such defense exists.[38] The warranties of a qualified indorser run to the same persons as those of an unqualified indorser.

(2) Warranties of Transferor by Delivery. The warranties made by one who transfers a negotiable instrument by delivery are the same as those made by a qualified indorser except that they run only to the immediate transferee and then only if he had given consideration for the transfer.[39] Subsequent holders cannot enforce such warranties regardless of the status or character of such holders.

(3) Warranties of Selling Agent or Broker. A selling agent or broker who discloses the fact that he is acting as such only warrants

---

[31] UCC Sec. 3-417(2)(a).
[32] Sec. 3-417 (2)(a).
[33] Sec. 3-417(2)(b).
[34] Sec. 3-417(2)(c).
[35] Sec. 3-417(2)(e).
[36] Sec. 3-417(2)(d).
[37] Sec. 3-417(2).
[38] Sec. 3-417(3). The qualified indorsement does not exclude other warranties unless it is specified to be "without warranties."
[39] Sec. 3-417(2).

his good faith and authority to act. If he does not disclose such capacity, he is subject to the warranties of an ordinary transferor who transfers in the manner employed by him.[40]

Cases for Chapter 28

Cressler v. Brown

79 Okla. 170, 192 P. 417 (1920)

Brown executed and delivered a promissory note to E. E. Cressler, who negotiated the note to C. W. Cressler by indorsement without recourse. When C. W. Cressler sued to enforce the note, Brown claimed that there was a lack of consideration. From a judgment for the defendant, the plaintiff appealed.

RAMSEY, J. . . . Under the Negotiable Instruments Law . . . the indorsement of the note by E. E. Cressler to C. W. Cressler without recourse is a qualified indorsement, and made C. W. Cressler a mere assignee of the title.

Such qualified indorsement . . . made E. E. Cressler a warrantor (1) that said note is genuine and in all respects what it purports to be; (2) that he had a good title to it; (3) that the makers had capacity to contract; and (4) that he (E. E. Cressler) had no knowledge of any fact which would impair the validity of the instrument or render it valueless. . . . [The Court found] that the alleged invalidity of the note and its alleged want of consideration were personally known to E. E. Cressler. If E. E. Cressler obtained the note without consideration, and then assigned it, as alleged, to C. W. Cressler for a valuable consideration, indorsing it "without recourse," when as a fact said note was without consideration, E. E. Cressler is responsible to C. W. Cressler for breach of warranty.

An indorsement "without recourse" by the payee of a negotiable promissory note contains as a term thereof, with the same force and effect as if expressly written therein, the statutory warranty on the part of the indorser "that he has no knowledge of any fact which would impair the validity of the instrument or render it valueless.". . .

[Judgment for defendant reversed on other grounds and case remanded.]

Code Comment: The decision would be the same under the Code since the qualified indorser makes the same warranty of absence of knowledge of any defense under UCC Sec. 3-417 (3), as he does under the NIL.

---

[40] Sec. 3-417 (4).

American Motors Acceptance Corp. v. Heckerman

332 S.W.2d 345 (Tex.Civ.App., 1960)

Whitten, who did business under the assumed name of Fashion Plate, also was an officer of a Texas corporation by the name of Fashion Plate Wares, Inc. Heckerman executed a promissory note payable to the order of Fashion Plate in payment of uniforms supplied by that business. Whitten then indorsed the note to the American Motors Acceptance Corp. by an indorsement reading: "The Fashion Plate, Inc. By William Edward Whitten." There was a Missouri corporation named Fashion Plate, Inc., but this was another business that had no connection with the persons or business involved. When American Motors sued Heckerman, he claimed that it was not the holder of the note. From a judgment in his favor, American Motors appealed.

LANGDON, C.J. . . . . [The NIL] provides, in substance, that title to a note payable to the order of a named person may be transferred without indorsement, but such a transfer passes only an equitable title; it is not a transfer within the law of negotiable instruments. Negotiation of the instrument . . . takes effect only as of the time, and at the date, when the indorsement is actually made. In the absence of such an indorsement, the transferee's title is subject to whatever equities exist against his transferor. . . .

Here we have two separate and distinct legal entities: the named payee, "Fashion Plate," the assumed name of William Edward Whitten, under which he conducted a business as an individual, constituting the first legal entity; and, the corporation, Fashion Plate Wares, Inc., the second legal entity. Whitten was the sole owner of "Fashion Plate," an unincorporated business, and was one of the incorporators of "Fashion Plate Wares, Inc.," a Texas corporation. We do not believe that this case falls within that line of cases wherein the name of the payee is wrongly designated, misspelled, or abbreviated. The defendant, maker of the note in question, is shown, without dispute, to have dealt with Whitten in his individual capacity, under his assumed name of "Fashion Plate," and the payee in said note was so designated. Also, it was established without equivocation that plaintiff dealt with Whitten only in his corporate capacity, as a representative of Fashion Plate, Inc., or Fashion Plate Wares, Inc. Since the indorsement was not that of the payee, the plaintiff transferee was not a holder. . . .

[Judgment for defendant affirmed.]

Code Comment: The same decision would be made under the Code, which continues the substance of the requirement of the NIL in that an instrument payable to order "is negotiated by delivery with any necessary indorsement." UCC Sec. 3-202 (1). This is, of course, the indorsement of the payee of the instrument.

Cartwright v. Coppersmith

222 N.C. 573, 24 S.E.2d 246 (1943)

Coppersmith executed and delivered negotiable notes to Elliott. The payee indorsed the notes to Whitehurst but kept the notes in her possession because she wanted to collect the interest during her life and wanted the indorsee to have the notes upon her death. After Elliott's death, her executor, Cartwright, found the notes. Both Cartwright and Whitehurst sought to enforce the notes against Coppersmith. From a judgment in favor of Cartwright, an appeal was taken by Whitehurst.

DEVIN, J. . . . We think the testimony . . . was insufficient to show a valid transfer of the title to the notes . . . from Elliott to . . . Whitehurst since there was no evidence of delivery of the notes, actual or constructive. . . .

"If a negotiable instrument is made payable to order (as were these notes), the transfer from one person to another is 'by the indorsement of the holder, and completed by delivery.' To constitute delivery, there must be a parting with the possession and with power and control over it by the maker or indorser for the benefit of the payee or indorsee. To constitute delivery, it must be put out of possession of the indorser. . . . An actual delivery, however, is not essential, and a constructive delivery will be held sufficient if made with the intention of transferring the title; but there must be some unequivocal act, more than the mere expression of an intention or desire. . . .

"While it is not indispensable that there should be an actual manual transfer of the instrument from the maker to the payee, yet, to constitute a delivery, it must appear that the maker in some way evinced an intention to make it an enforceable obligation against himself, according to its terms, by surrendering control over it and intentionally placing it under the power of the payee or of some third person for his use. . . .

"It is true the fact of retention of possession by the indorser is not always fatal to a claim of constructive delivery; . . . there may be a delivery, notwithstanding the maker keeps the note in his possession, where it is apparent that he intended to hold it for the benefit and as the agent of the payee.". . .

But here the . . . testimony falls short of coming within that principle. . . .

[Judgment for Cartwright affirmed.]

Code Comment: The same decision would be made under the Code since UCC Sec. 3-202 (1) requires delivery by the payee as well as indorsement. Continuing principles of prior general law, UCC Sec. 1-103, would require that the delivery be made by the payee or under the payee's authority during the lifetime of the payee.

Bailey v. Mills

257 Ala. 239, 58 So.2d 446 (1952)

Mills and another executed and delivered a note and a mortgage. Before maturity the payee transferred the note and mortgage by a separate written assignment to the Bailey Company, a partnership. The assignment, note, and mortgage, held together by a paper clip, were delivered to the partnership. Mills later sued Bailey to cancel the note and mortgage because of fraud by the payee. Bailey and his partners claimed that this could not be done as they were holders of a negotiable instrument by indorsement. From a judgment in favor of the makers of the note, the partners appealed.

SIMPSON, J. . . . The real question is whether the appellants [Bailey and his partners], as transferees of the holder, acquired the note (and the mortgage securing) by proper indorsement so as to constitute them holders in due course, with the defense unavailing against the validity of the instruments.

The trial court decided the issue against appellants and granted appellees [the makers] relief. We think the authorities in this jurisdiction, as well as generally, sustain that conclusion. The note was "payable to order" and the indorsement of the payee nowhere appeared on it (or for that matter on the mortgage either), although there was ample space for such, [with the result] that the transfer was a common-law assignment merely and the transferees took no better title than the original holder.

For one to be a holder . . . "the indorsement must be written on the instrument itself or upon a paper attached thereto.". . . A written indorsement upon another and entirely distinct instrument is not permissible and will not have the effect of passing the legal title of such a negotiable instrument so as to make the transferee a holder. . . . "It is indispensably necessary, if such instruments are to fulfill the object for which they were designed, that they should carry with them the indicia by which their ownership is to be determined; otherwise, their value as a circulation medium would be largely curtailed, if not entirely destroyed. Adding an allonge when necessary or convenient is permissible only because furthering the object of their creation, viz. free and unrestrained negotiability. . . ."

Here there was no such requisite indorsement. The instruments purported to have been transferred to appellants by a separate instrument of assignment given by payee to appellants, all three documents (according to appellants' testimony) being fastened together with a [paper clip.] This was not sufficient to meet the rule of the instruments so as to make appellants holders. . . .

The negotiable instruments law with respect to the indorsement of a negotiable instrument by "a paper attached thereto" . . . is but a statutory affirmation of the rule of the old law merchant, which allowed indorsements to be made upon an "allonge"; that is, upon a slip of paper tacked or pasted on to the instrument so as to become a part of it. . . . But the use of the allonge was allowable only when the back of the instrument itself was so covered with previous indorsements that convenience or necessity required additional space for further indorsements. . . . [The N.I.L.] sanctions the use of the allonge, but certainly it was not intended to establish the loose and undesirable practice of making regular indorsements of commercial paper by a writing on the back of any other paper or document to which it might be temporarily attached, as by pinning, and, more especially, when there is ample space for indorsement on the back of the instrument itself.

[Judgment affirmed as to point discussed above.]

Code Comment: The same decision would be reached under the Code, for UCC Sec. 3-202 (2) requires that the paper on which the indorsement is written, when not written on the instrument itself, be "so firmly affixed thereto as to become a part thereof." This language is more explicit than the general language of the NIL Sec. 31 that the indorsement be "on the instrument itself or upon a paper attached thereto."

Questions and Case Problems

1. What is the objective of each of the following rules of law?

    (a) Bearer paper may be negotiated by a physical delivery without an indorsement.

    (b) The holder of an instrument under a blank indorsement may protect himself from theft or loss of the instrument by writing above the signature of the blank indorser a statement that the instrument is made payable to him.

2. Benton, as agent for Savidge, received an insurance settlement check from the Metropolitan Life Insurance Co. He indorsed it "For deposit" and deposited it in the Bryn Mawr Trust Company in the account of Savidge. What was the nature and effect of this indorsement? (Savidge v. Metropolitan Life Insurance Co., 380 Pa. 205, 110 A.2d 730)

3. The Carolina Petroleum Co. executed and delivered its promissory note for $1,200 payable to the order of the Beaufort Bank. Thereafter, the Federal Intermediate Credit Bank brought an action against the Carolina Petroleum Co. The note, when received by the Federal Intermediate Credit Bank, did not bear the indorsement of the Beaufort Bank. It was contended that the plaintiff was not a holder of the instrument. Do you agree with this contention? (Federal Intermediate Credit Bank v. Carolina Petroleum Co., 154 S.C. 435, 151 S.E. 738)

4. Humphrey drew a check for $100. It was stolen and the payee's name forged as an indorser. The check was then negotiated to Miller who had no knowledge of these facts. Miller indorsed the check to the Citizens' Bank.

Payment of the check was voided on the ground of the forgery. The Citizens' Bank then sued Miller as indorser. Decide. (Citizens' Bank of Hattiesburg v. Miller, 194 Miss. 557, 11 So.2d 457)

5. Kavlich hired Rothman to do construction work and paid him by a note. Rothman indorsed the note "without recourse" to the Eastern Acceptance Corp. The corporation sued Kavlich on the note. He defended on the ground that the consideration for the note had failed and that this defense was available against the corporation because it could not be a holder in due course on account of the form of the indorsement. Decide. (Eastern Acceptance Corp. v. Kavlich, 10 N.J.S. 253, 77 A.2d 49)

6. Mobilla indorsed a negotiable instrument "without recourse." He was later sued by the Union Bank as holder of the instrument for breach of his warranty as a transferor of the instrument. He claimed that he was not liable. Decide. (Union Bank v. Mobilla, [Pa.] 43 Erie Co.L.F. 45)

7. Searcy executed and delivered a promissory note payable to the order of the Bank of Ensley. A later holder, the First National Bank of Birmingham, sued Searcy on the note. A dispute arose as to whether the First National Bank was the holder of the instrument on January 10, before the closing of the Ensley Bank on January 11. The First National Bank proved that on January 10 the note was indorsed to it by the Ensley Bank. Did this prove that the First National Bank was the holder on January 10? (First National Bank of Birmingham v. Searcy, 31 Ala.App. 553, 19 So. 2d 559)

8. Filter Laboratories, Inc. installed a water conditioner in the property of Richir in June, 1959. Richir signed an installment contract and executed a negotiable promissory note payable to the order of Filter Laboratories, Inc. The sale was made on a six month's trial approval, but this fact was not stated on the note. In July, 1959, Filter Laboratories, Inc. sold the note to the Marine Trust Co., which notified Richir that it had purchased the note. Richir told the bank that it was not satisfied with the unit and was not going to pay for it. The bank then sued Richir, who claimed that the bank was subject to any defense on the theory that the note was not negotiable because the indorsement made the note nonnegotiable. The indorsement read as follows:

WITHOUT RECOURSE

The undersigned represent(s) and warrant(s) in addition to the warranties implied by law, that the transaction which gave rise to this note was the furnishing of goods or services for repairs, alterations, or improvements upon or in connection with real property at the request of the maker(s) of this note and that the furnishing of such goods and services has been completed to the satisfaction of such maker(s).

Was Richir correct? (Marine Trust Co. of Western New York v. Richir, 228 N.Y.S.2d 694)

CHAPTER 29

Notes and Presentment for Payment

A promissory note is a two-party commercial paper, which means that originally only the maker and payee are involved. The maker is liable for payment on the maturity date of the note; but if the maker dishonors the note when it is presented to him for payment, the payee and indorsers, if any, may become secondarily liable for payment.

The procedures for presenting a negotiable instrument for payment and for giving notice of dishonor, which are explained in this chapter in terms of a promissory note, apply to all commercial paper.

Sec. 29-A. Liability of Maker. The liability of a maker of a promissory note is primary. This means that payment may be demanded of him and that he may be sued by the holder as soon as the debt is due. The maker is under the duty to pay the note at the time and at the place named, if any place is specified by the note, unless he can set up a defense that is valid against the holder.

By the very act of signing the promissory note, the maker deprives himself of two possible defenses. He admits (1) the existence of the payee named in the instrument and (2) the payee's capacity at that time to indorse the paper.[1] When the payee of a note is a minor or a bankrupt, the maker cannot deny the validity of the title of a subsequent holder of the instrument on the ground that the payee lacked capacity to transfer title.

When a note is issued in payment of a debt, the original obligation is suspended until the instrument is due or until presentment for payment in the case of demand paper. If the note is dishonored for non-payment, the holder may sue either on the note or on the underlying obligation.[2] (See p. 455, In re Eton Furniture Company)

---

[1] Uniform Commercial Code, Sec. 3-413(3); Uniform Negotiable Instruments Law, Sec. 60.

[2] UCC Sec. 3-802 (1)(b).

Sec. 29-B. Need for Presentment for Payment. The holder of a promissory note need not present the instrument to the maker for payment in order to hold the latter liable on the note.[3] If the note has a specified maturity date, the maker is under a duty to pay the holder the amount due on the instrument as soon as that date is reached. The liability of the maker continues until barred by the Statute of Limitations. If the note is demand paper, the holder may even begin a lawsuit against the maker without first making a demand for payment since the act of bringing suit is regarded as the making of a demand.

An unqualified indorser is secondarily liable for the payment of the instrument, which means that he must pay the amount of the instrument to the holder under certain circumstances. Generally this duty arises only if (1) the instrument was presented for payment to the primary party on the due date or at maturity, (2) the primary party defaulted by failing to pay the amount of the instrument to the holder, and (3) the secondary party in question was given proper notice of the primary party's default.

A qualified indorser or a former holder of bearer paper who negotiated the instrument without indorsing it is not liable for payment. However, such parties, as well as an unqualified indorser who does have a secondary liability, may be liable to the holder for a breach of warranty.

Sec. 29-C. Presentment for Payment.

(1) Person Making Presentment. Presentment for payment, when made, must be made by the holder of the paper or by one authorized to act and receive payment for him.

(2) Manner of Presentment. Any demand for payment is sufficient as a presentment. The party to whom the demand is made may require, however, that greater formality be observed, such as by requiring (a) reasonable identification of the person making presentment and evidence of his authority if he acts for another; (b) production of the instrument for payment at a place specified in it or, if there be none, at any place reasonable in the circumstances; and (c) a signed receipt on the instrument for any partial or full payment and its surrender upon full payment. If the party presenting the instrument does not comply with such a request at the time of making presentment, he is allowed a reasonable time within which to do so; but if he does not so comply, the presentment has no effect.[4]

---

[3] UCC Sec. 3-501(1), NIL Sec. 70. Under the Code, if timely presentment of a note payable at a bank is not made, the maker is discharged to the extent that he has lost money on deposit in the bank because the bank has failed during the delay. See p. 483. Paper payable at a bank is described as "domiciled" paper.

[4] UCC Sec. 3-505.

In addition to a presentment for payment made directly between the parties, presentment may be made by sending the paper through the mail to the debtor, or by sending it through a clearing house.[5] A collecting bank may also make presentment for payment by sending merely a notice to the nonbank party that it holds the note on which payment is due.[6] If the party so notified fails to act within a specified time, his inaction is treated as a dishonor of the note.[7]

(3) On Whom Presentment Is Made. Presentment for payment must be made to the party primarily liable, that is, the maker of the promissory note, or to a person who has authority to make or refuse payment on his behalf.[8] In the case of two or more makers, presentment may be made upon any one.[9] If the instrument is payable at a bank, it must be presented to a proper person in the bank who is authorized to pay the note.[10]

(4) Place of Making Presentment. Presentment for payment is properly made at the place specified in the instrument. When a place of payment is not specified, presentment is to be made at the place of business or the residence of the person from whom payment is to be demanded.[11]

(5) Time of Making Presentment. A note payable at a stated date must be presented for payment on that date.[12] If the balance due on the note has been accelerated, payment must be made within a reasonable time after acceleration.[13] When the question is the secondary liability of any party, presentment for payment must be made within a reasonable time after such person became liable on the instrument.[14]

With respect to the hour of the day, presentment must be made at a reasonable hour and, if made at a bank, must be made during its banking day.[15]

(a) COMPUTATION OF TIME. In determining the date of maturity of an instrument, the starting day is excluded and the day of payment is included. Thus an instrument dated July 3 and payable 30 days from date is due on August 2.[16]

---

5 Sec. 3-504(b).
6 Sec. 4-210(1). This provision is not applicable if the paper is payable by, through, or at a bank.
7 Sec. 4-210(2).
8 Sec. 3-504(3).
9 Sec. 3-504(3)(a).
10 Sec. 3-504(4).
11 Sec. 3-504(2)(c).
12 UCC Sec. 3-503(1)(c), NIL Sec. 71.
13 UCC Sec. 3-503(1)(d).
14 Sec. 3-503(1)(e).
15 Sec. 3-503(4).
16 In business practice, when the time is expressed in terms of months rather than days, such as 1 month after date, the date of maturity is the same date in the month of maturity.

(b) INSTRUMENT DUE ON LEGAL OR BUSINESS HOLIDAY. When the presentment of the paper is due on a day that is not a full business day, presentment is due on the next following full business day. This rule is applied whether the due day is not a full business day because it is a legal holiday or merely because the person required to make payment or the bank, as a matter of its business practice, is closed all day or for a half day.[17]

This rule is also applied when the due date is a business holiday for either party, that is, if either the person required to present the instrument or the person who is required to pay upon presentment is not open for a full business day on the due date. The date for presentment is extended to the first day that is a full business day for both of them.[18]

(c) EXCUSE FOR DELAY IN MAKING PRESENTMENT. Failure to present an instrument for payment at the proper time will be excused when the delay is caused by circumstances beyond the control of the holder. It must not, however, be caused by his conduct, negligence, or fault. Mere inconvenience, such as that arising from inclement weather, is not a valid excuse for delay. When the circumstances that excuse the delay are removed, presentment must be made within a reasonable time.[19]

(d) EFFECT OF DELAY. An unexcused delay in presentment for payment discharges an indorser. If the note is *domiciled*, that is, payable at a bank, the delay may also operate to discharge the maker. The Code provides as to such paper that "any . . . maker of a note payable at a bank who because the . . . payor bank becomes insolvent during the delay is deprived of funds maintained with the . . . payor bank to cover the instrument may discharge his liability by written assignment to the holder of his rights against the . . . payor bank in respect of such funds, but such . . . maker is not otherwise discharged." [20]

Sec. 29-D. When Presentment for Payment Is Excused or Unnecessary. Presentment of a note for payment is not required in order to charge secondary parties under certain circumstances.

(1) Waiver. Presentment is not required if it has been waived by the express or implied agreement of the secondary party in question.[21] A waiver of presentment is binding upon all parties if it appears on

---

[17] UCC Sec. 3-503(3).
[18] Sec. 3-503(3).
[19] UCC Sec. 3-511(1), NIL Sec. 81. Delay is also excused when the holder does not know that the instrument is due, UCC Sec. 3-511(1), as could occur if the date had been accelerated by a prior holder.
[20] UCC Sec. 3-502(1)(b).
[21] UCC Sec. 3-511(2)(a), NIL Sec. 82.

the face of the original note. If the waiver is part of an indorsement, however, it binds only that indorser.[22]

(2) Inability. Presentment is not required if it cannot be made in spite of the exercise of due diligence (see p. 457, Cuddy v. Sarandrea), as when presentment is attempted at the place where payment is to be made but neither the person who is to make payment nor anyone authorized to act for him can be found at that place.[23]

(3) Death or Insolvency. Presentment for payment is not required if the maker of the note has died or if he has gone into insolvency proceedings after he had issued the note.[24]

(4) Refusal to Pay. The holder is not required to make presentment upon the maker if he has already refused to pay the note for no reason, or for any reason other than an objection that proper presentment was not made.[25]

(5) Belief or Conduct of Secondary Party. The secondary party cannot demand that presentment be made if he has no reason to expect that the instrument would be paid and no right to require that payment be made.[26] This situation could arise when the maker executed the note for the benefit of the secondary party but the latter has breached the agreement with the maker and therefore has no right to expect or require that the maker perform his part of the agreement by paying the note.[27]

Sec. 29-E. Dishonor of Note. If the maker fails or refuses to pay the note when it is properly presented to him, he has dishonored the instrument by nonpayment. The fact that the maker does not make immediate payment of the note when it is presented to him does not dishonor the note. He has the right to withhold making payment until he has made a reasonable examination to determine that the note is properly payable to the holder. He cannot, however, delay payment beyond the close of business on the day presentment is made.[28]

(1) Notice of Dishonor. If commercial paper is dishonored by nonpayment, any secondary party who is not given proper notice thereof is released from liability, unless the giving of notice is excused.[29]

---

[22] UCC Sec. 3-511(6).
[23] Secs. 3-504(2), 3-511(2)(c).
[24] Sec. 3-511(3)(a). Insolvency proceedings are defined by Sec. 1-201(22).
[25] Sec. 3-511(3)(b).
[26] UCC Sec. 3-511(2)(b), NIL Sec. 80.
[27] Sec. 3-511, Official Comment, point 4.
[28] Sec. 3-505(2). See also Sec. 3-506(2).
[29] UCC Sec. 3-501(2)(a), NIL Secs. 89, 109. In the case of a "domiciled" note payable at a bank, the maker must be given notice that the note was not paid when presented at the bank and, if notice is not so given, the maker is released to the same extent already noted in connection with the effect of failure to present at the bank. UCC Sec. 3-501(2)(b). See p. 450.

It is only necessary that a party be given notice once, because a notice operates for the benefit of all parties who have rights on the instrument against the party notified.[30]

(a) WHO MAY GIVE NOTICE. The notice of dishonor is ordinarily given by the holder who has been refused payment or by his agent. If the agent made the presentment for payment, he of course may give notice of the dishonor to his principal who in turn may give it to the secondary party in question. When any person who is liable on the paper receives notice of its dishonor, he may in turn give notice to other secondary parties.[31]

(b) PERSON NOTIFIED. The notice of dishonor may be given to any party who is liable on the instrument. Notice to one partner is notice to each, even though the firm has been dissolved. When the party to be notified is dead or incompetent, notice may be sent to his last-known address or be given to his personal representative. If insolvency proceedings were begun against a party after the note was issued, the notice may be given to him or to the representative of his estate.[32]

(c) FORM OF NOTICE. Notice may be given in any reasonable manner. It may be oral or written, and it may be sent by mail. It may have any terms as long as it identifies the instrument and states that it has been dishonored. A misdescription that does not mislead the party notified does not nullify or vitiate the notice. Notice may be effected by sending the instrument itself, with a stamp, ticket, or writing attached thereto, stating that payment has been refused or by sending a notice of debit with respect to the paper.[33] Although not required by the Code, it is a sound precaution to give a signed, dated, written notice, and to keep a copy.

(d) PLACE OF NOTICE. The Code does not specify a place to which notice is to be given, but it provides that notice generally shall be deemed given whenever such steps have been taken as may be reasonably required to inform the other person in ordinary course, whether or not he actually comes to know of it. Furthermore, a person is deemed to receive notice or notification whenever the matter comes to his attention, or when the notice is delivered at the place of business through which the contract was made or at any other place held out by him as the place for the receipt of such communications.[34]

(e) TIME OF NOTICE. Notice must be given before midnight of the third business day after dishonor. If the notice is given following

---

[30] Sec. 3-508(8).
[31] Sec. 3-508(1).
[32] Sec. 3-508(1),(5),(6),(7).
[33] Sec. 3-508(3).
[34] Sec. 1-201(26).

the receipt of notice of dishonor from another party, it must be given before the midnight of the third business day after receiving such notice. When required of a bank, notice of dishonor must be given before midnight of the banking day following the banking day on which the note is dishonored or the bank receives notice of such dishonor.[35] A written notice of dishonor is effective when sent even though it is not received. Hence a notice sent by mail is sufficient even though it was never received, provided it was properly addressed, bore the necessary postage, and was properly mailed.[36] (See p. 458, Durkin v. Siegel)

(2) Excuse for Delay or Absence of Notice of Dishonor. Delay in giving notice of dishonor is excused under the same circumstances as delay in making presentment.[37]

The absence of any notice of dishonor is excused for three of the reasons considered as excusing the absence of presentment; namely (a) waiver, (b) inability to give notice in spite of due diligence, and (c) the fact that the party not notified did not have any reason to believe that the instrument would be paid nor any right to require payment.[38]

The requirements as to notice of dishonor are not applicable in determining the rights of co-obligors as between themselves. For example, when two indorsers are jointly liable and one pays the full amount of the instrument, he is entitled to recover one half of such payment by way of contribution from his co-indorser without regard to whether the holder had given the co-indorser proper notice of dishonor. (See p. 460, Greenwald v. Weinberg)

Sec. 29-F. Proof of Dishonor. Since the liability of the secondary party depends upon whether certain steps were taken within the proper time, it is important for the holder to be able to prove that he has complied with the requirements of the law. In order to aid him in proving such essential facts, the Code declares that certain documents and records are admissible as evidence of dishonor and of any notice recited therein. The trier of fact must accept such evidence in the absence of proof to the contrary.[39] The Code makes this provision with respect to (1) protests, (2) bank stamps and memorandums, and (3) bank records.

(1) Protests. A *protest* is a memorandum or certificate executed by a notary public, or certain other public officers, upon information satisfactory to him, which sets forth that the particular indentified

---

[35] Secs 3-508(2), 4-104(1)(h).
[36] UCC Sec. 3-508(4), NIL Sec. 105.
[37] Sec. 3-511.
[38] Sec. 3-511(2). See p. 451.
[39] Secs. 3-510, 1-201(31).

instrument has been dishonored. It may also recite that notice of dishonor was given to all parties or to specified parties.[40]

(2) Bank Stamps and Memorandums. If the stamp put on the paper by a bank or the memorandum attached to the note by the bank is consistent with a dishonor, it is evidence of that fact. For example, a notation "Not sufficient funds" or "Payment stopped" indicates a dishonor or nonpayment of the instrument and therefore comes within this rule. On the other hand, a notation of "Indorsement missing" is not consistent with dishonor and is therefore not admissible as evidence of a dishonor.[41]

(3) Bank Records. Bank records kept in the usual course of business are admissible as evidence of dishonor even though it cannot be shown who made the entry in the books.[42]

Cases for Chapter 29

In re Eton Furniture Company

286 F.2d 93 (C.A. 3d, 1961)

Huntington was the general manager of the Eton Furniture Co. From time to time he borrowed money from the bank on behalf of Eton but would give his individual note to the bank and sometimes would pledge his own automobile as security. When Eton's checking account in the bank would have on deposit an amount greater than the loan to Eton, the bank would deduct the amount of the loan with interest from Eton's account. Eton was declared a bankrupt, and the trustee in bankruptcy demanded that the bank return the amounts which it had deducted from Eton's account. From a decision in favor of the bank, the trustee in bankruptcy appealed.

BIGGS, C.J. . . . The trustee asserted that the loans negotiated by Huntington from the Bank, and for which he gave his personal notes to the Bank were loans to him and not to Eton. It was argued that Eton received the proceeds of the loans from Huntington and not from the Bank, and that therefore the satisfaction of the obligations from Eton's account with the Bank constituted an unjustified appropriation of Eton's funds by the Bank to pay the debts of another.

. . . Huntington testified that when Eton was short of funds and not in a position to borrow from the Bank, he would procure a loan for Eton on the strength of his personal note, sometimes putting up his car as additional collateral. He stated that these loans were negotiated by him on behalf of Eton and that his notes which he gave to the Bank

40 Secs. 3-509, 3-510(a).
41 Sec. 3-510(b), Official Comment, point 2.
42 Sec. 3-510(c).

were collateral security for primary obligations of Eton. . . . "The course of dealing between Huntington and the Bank renders it clear that each understood that when Huntington borrowed money and credited the proceeds to Eton's account, Huntington was acting for the account of and in the interest of Eton, his principal.". . .

The single issue which this court must determine is whether Eton was indebted to the Bank in the amounts of the loans negotiated by Huntington, its general manager. The trustee makes two arguments which we must consider. First, relying on Section 3-401(1) of the Uniform Commercial Code, applicable in Pennsylvania, 12A P.S. § 3-401 (1), he contends that since Huntington's signature alone appears on the notes given by him to the Bank, Huntington alone can be held liable by the Bank for repayment of the loans. Second, he argues that Huntington was not authorized to borrow money for Eton and that, therefore, regardless of any understanding that may have existed between Huntington and the Bank, Eton, not being bound, could not be liable for repayment of the loans.

. . . We . . . start with the premise that Huntington's notes were intended to be collateral security, that all of the parties so understood the transaction, and that the money was in fact used by Eton for its own benefit.

Section 3-401(1) provides that "No person is liable on an instrument unless his signature appears thereon." On the basis of this provision the trustee contends that Eton, not having signed the notes given to the Bank, cannot be held liable for repayment of the loans. This argument finds no support in the words of the statute which provides merely that one who does not sign a note cannot be liable on the note. Contrary to the trustee's argument, the provision quoted cannot be read to mean that no person is liable on a debt whose signature does not appear on a note given as collateral security for that debt. Indeed, it has long been settled in Pennsylvania and elsewhere that the one to whom money is loaned or property advanced is liable for the debt regardless of the fact that his name may not appear on the security taken if that security was regarded by the parties purely as collateral. That Section 3-401 (1) was not intended to change this rule is demonstrated clearly by the comment to that section which states in pertinent part: "Nothing in this section is intended to prevent any liability arising apart from the instrument itself. The party who does not sign may still be liable on the original obligation for which the instrument was given. . . ."

The rule that a note given in a transaction as collateral security is not a bar to a suit on the primary obligation even though the primary obligor did not sign the note was enunciated clearly in In re Estate of Van Haagen Soap Mfg. Co., 1891, 141 Pa. 214, 21 A. 598, 599, 12

L.R.A. 223. . . . Other courts are in accord on substantially similar facts. . . .

In the present case, the evidence of Huntington, adopted "as verity" by the referee, similarly shows that the loans were for Eton's use, that the Bank, Eton, and Huntington understood this to be so, and that the money was in fact used by the Company for its own benefit. We hold that the finding of the referee and that of the court below that the debts were incurred by Eton is supported by the evidence and that their rulings are in accordance with the applicable law.

The trustee's contention that Huntington had no authority to incur debts on behalf of the corporation also is without merit. Even if it be assumed that Huntington did not have the authority to borrow money on behalf of Eton the actual receipt and use of the money, by Eton constituted ratification of Huntington's acts. . . .

[Judgment affirmed.]

Cuddy v. Sarandrea

52 R.I. 465, 161 A. 297 (1932)

Samuel and Annie Jacobson executed a promissory note payable to Frank and Angelo Sarandrea. The payees indorsed the note to Cuddy. The note was delivered for collection to Potter, a notary public. The makers of the note had moved, leaving no address, and presentment for payment was therefore not made. Notice of dishonor, however, was given to the indorsers. Cuddy then sued the indorsers for payment. From a judgment for the plaintiff, the defendants appealed.

STEARNS, C.J. . . . Defendants received notice of dishonor either the day the note was due or the following day.

A city directory for the year 1929 was admitted in evidence, over defendant's objection, showing the following address of the Jacobsons: "Jacobson, Samuel (Annie) Mgr., h. 55B Goddard." The notary went to two houses, the occupants of which were named Jacobson. He went to Somerset Street where he learned that the Jacobsons living there were the wrong parties. He went to the address at which the Jacobsons lived, according to the directory, found it had been their residence, but was told by the occupant that they had moved and their present address was unknown. The notary made the return on his record books and gave notice of dishonor by mail to the Sarandreas.

Cuddy had no information as to the whereabouts of either Jacobson or Sarandrea. He had last been in communication with the maker of the note in July, 1927, and with the payee in February, 1926. . . .

The provisions [of the NIL] for actual presentment or presentment at the usual place . . . of business or residence are not unconditional.

When presentment for payment cannot be made . . . , such presentment is dispensed with after the exercise of reasonable diligence. [NIL] Section 82.

The usual residence referred to in the statute is the regular ordinary and habitual residence. In the instant case Jacobson and his family had occupied several different tenements in the two years preceding the maturity of the note. When the presentment for payment was made, Jacobson was listed in the directory as residing where the presentment was made. He had recently moved and his residence was unknown to the occupants of his former tenement, . . . to plaintiffs, and the notary of the bank. It was the duty of the notary to exercise reasonably diligence to ascertain the usual place of residence of Jacobson. . . .

Defendants question the exercise of proper diligence because of the absence of evidence of any inquiry made of the payee. Such an inquiry, if practicable, should be made when neither the maker nor his residence can be found; it is always prudent and often essential. But such an inquiry is not required in all cases as a matter of law. Whether or not it is essential in any particular case depends on the circumstances. . . .

In view of all the evidence we do not think the failure to interrogate the payee can properly be regarded as sufficient cause to warrant the finding of a lack of diligence, particularly as there is only one day allowed for the presentment.

We are of the opinion that . . . the notary was not lacking in due diligence in failing to discover the actual residence of Jacobson. . . .

[Judgment for plaintiff affirmed.]

Code Comment: The court would reach the same decision under the Code since the absence of presentment is excused when it cannot be made in the exercise of "reasonable diligence." UCC Sec. 3-511 (2) (c). The NIL contained the same excuse of "reasonable diligence" and accordingly the problem, whether decided under the NIL or under the Code, is one of determining whether the holder had exercised "reasonable diligence." On the same facts, the same court should reach the same decision.

Durkin v. Siegel
340 Mass. 445, 165 N.E.2d 81 (1961)

Browne made a promissory note which was indorsed by Siegel. On the default of Browne, the holder of the note, Durkin, gave notice to Siegel by certified mail, return receipt requested. The notice was returned unopened and undelivered, marked refused, and with the blank form of post office receipt unsigned. From a judgment in favor of Durkin, Siegel appealed on the ground that he had not been given proper notice, that ordinary first class mail could have been forwarded, and that he had been in Canada at the time the notice was sent.

CUTTER, J. . . . The Negotiable Instruments Law . . . applies to this case, because these events occurred prior to October 1, 1958, the effective date of the Uniform Commercial Code. . . . The holder of a dishonored negotiable instrument must give prompt notice of dishonor to those secondarily liable. . . . [NIL § 105] . . . reads, "Where notice of dishonor is duly addressed and deposited in the post office, the sender is deemed to have given due notice, notwithstanding any miscarriage in the mails." Registered and certified mail, return receipt requested, are usually regarded by careful people as preferred methods of ensuring delivery. No exception is made in § [105] with respect to these or other types of first-class mail. The section has been carried over into the Uniform Commercial Code in somewhat different language but without attempt to change its meaning. See . . . § 3-508, which in par. (3) provides that "notice may be given in any reasonable manner" and that "it may be oral or written," and in par. (4) states, "Written notice is given when sent although it is not received." The comments of the draftsmen show that no changes in §§ 96 and 105 of the Negotiable Instruments Law . . . were intended. . . .

The most carefully supervised available methods of mail delivery, registered and certified first-class mail, are certainly a "reasonable manner" of giving notice of dishonor, for the propriety of the use of registered or certified mail for important notices has frequently been recognized in our statutes. Although some statutes permit notices by ordinary mail, in the absence of explicit language in a particular statute, a court would be slow to say that service by registered or certified mail was not a compliance with such a statutory requirement for notice by mail. . . . In the light of the foregoing considerations, we hold that § [105] makes reasonable use of any form of first-class mail (not excluding registered or certified mail) for a properly addressed notice of dishonor the equivalent of actual notice. Section [105] is not merely an application of the principle that the "mailing, postage prepaid . . . of a properly addressed letter is prima facie evidence of its receipt by the addressee". . . but, instead, is a legislative declaration that the mailing is itself notice. Under [§ 105], once proper mailing of the notice has been shown, the fact of notice is established. . . .

Persons who become secondarily liable upon negotiable instruments are not unfairly burdened if they are held bound by notices sent to them by any generally used form of first-class mail at a usual address. They can protect themselves by stipulating . . . that a particular address be used and by arranging at that address during any absence to have their mail received, opened, forwarded, and collected (in the event of the receipt of a notification from the postal authorities that it has not been possible to deliver to them a piece of registered or certified mail). That use of ordinary mail might have ensured delivery . . . is completely irrelevant in view of [§ 105]. Refusal of a registered or certified letter, of course, would not protect an indorser from the effect of notice. . . .

No . . . public policy allows an indorser to escape secondary liability on a negotiable instrument signed by him because its holder has reasonably used a better and a more expensive method of notifying him by mail of the dishonor of the instrument than ordinary first-class mail which the holder could have used quite properly and safely. . . . [Under § 105] mailing is made "due notice, notwithstanding any miscarriage in the mails.". . . The quoted words are broad enough to include nondelivery of certified or registered mail. . . .

[Judgment for plaintiff affirmed.]

Code Comment: As indicated in the opinion, the Code provision does not make any change in the substance of the NIL as to the point involved. This court would accordingly interpret the Code provision in the same manner as the NIL and reach the same conclusion.

Greenwald v. Weinberg

102 Pa.Super. 485, 157 A. 351 (1931)

Brown executed a promissory note payable to the order of Greenwald and Weinberg at the Peoples City Bank, McKeesport, Pennsylvania. The note was not paid at maturity. The holder mailed notices of dishonor to the payees, as indorsers, in separate enclosures but sent both notices to the address of Greenwald, who paid the amount of the note to the holder. In a suit for contribution brought by Greenwald against Weinberg, the latter disclaimed liability because of lack of notice of dishonor. From a judgment for the plaintiff, the defendant appealed.

LINN, J. . . . Defendant denied receiving notice of dishonor; he contended that without such notice he was discharged from all liability, not only of his liability to the holder of the note imposed by the Negotiable Instruments Act . . . but also the liability growing out of his contractual relations with his copayee. . . .

[The] plaintiff's right to recover from his copayee one half of what he paid to the bank does not depend on notice of dishonor. . . .

Appellant's [Weinberg's] liability to plaintiff depends, not on the note or the indorsements under the Negotiable Instruments Law, but on his relation with plaintiff as joint payee; they did not intend that liability [as between themselves] should depend on the Negotiable Instruments Law. Their joint relation imposed equality of burden; either, compelled by a holder to bear it all, may require contribution of the other. The note is evidence in the suit, but it is not the foundation of the right to recover. "Contribution," in the often quoted phrase of Lord Chief Baron Eyre, "is bottomed and fixed on general principles of justice and does not spring from contract, though contract may qualify it." . . . The obligation, it is said, arises from "the equitable principle that . . . 'the law requires equality. . . .'" That doctrine has so long been part of the law that persons engaged as co-obligors, in the absence of express understanding otherwise, are held to have dealt with it as an implied term in their relations. . . .

[Judgment for plaintiff affirmed.]

Code Comment: The same decision would be made under the Code. The right of contribution involved is based on the general principles of equity which the Code continues in force in the absence of an express provision of the Code to the contrary. UCC Sec. 1-103.

Questions and Case Problems

1. What is the objective of each of the following rules of law?
   (a) If a waiver of presentment for payment appears on the face of the instrument, it binds the party making it and all subsequent parties to the instrument.
   (b) If a commercial paper is dishonored by nonpayment, due notice of the dishonor, unless waived, must be given to a secondary party in order to hold him liable for the default.

2. Four promissory notes were executed by Continental Diamond Mines, Inc., payable to the order of M. Kopp. The notes were thereafter indorsed to M. Kopp, Inc. and then to Rafkin. Rafkin was the holder on the due date. Was it necessary for him to make a presentment of the notes to Continental Diamond Mines in order to hold it liable on the notes? (Rafkin v. Continental Diamond Mines, Inc., 228 N.Y.S.2d 317)

3. De Lise was secondarily liable on a note held by the First Pennsylvania Banking & Trust Co. When sued on the note, De Lise claimed that he was not liable because notice of the maker's default had been given by telephone. Was this a valid defense? (First Pennsylvania Banking & Trust Co. v. De Lise, 186 Pa.Super. 398, 142 A.2d 401)

4. The American Tool & Machine Co. executed a promissory note payable to the order of the Lancaster Foundry Co. After the note was indorsed by Robinson for the accommodation of the maker, the instrument was delivered to the payee. A demand for payment of the note was made by telephone. The stenographer that answered said that no one was in the office. The foundry company treated this as a refusal to pay, gave notice of dishonor, and then brought an action to recover from Robinson as indorser. Was it entitled to judgment? (Robinson v. Lancaster Foundry Co., 152 Md. 81, 136 A. 58)

5. Chaffee, the holder of a note payable four years from date, transferred the instrument by blank indorsement to Bardshar. Without presenting the instrument to the maker for payment or giving notice of dishonor to Chaffee, Bardshar brought an action to recover from Chaffee as an indorser. Was he entitled to judgment? (Bardshar v. Chaffee, 43 Wash. 698, 156 P. 388)

6. McCrow negotiated with Bedwell & Keyt for the purchase of stock. He delivered to them a promissory note payable to W. E. Davidson & Co., whom he believed to be the owner of the stock. Davidson, who did business under the name of W. E. Davidson & Co., indorsed the note to Hill. In an action brought by Hill against McCrow to recover on the note, McCrow denied the capacity of the payee to indorse the note. Could this defense be raised? (Hill v. McCrow, 88 Ore. 299, 170 P. 306)

7. Dubinsky borrowed money from the Columbian National Life Insurance Co. He sold his house to Cohen who promised to pay this debt to the insurance company and gave it a promissory note. Later Dubinsky gave the company a renewal note. In a suit upon the renewal note Dubinsky claimed that he was an accommodation maker. Decide. (Columbian National Life Insurance Co. v. Dubinsky, 349 Mo. 299, 160 S.W.2d 727)

8. In an action brought by Hughes against a corporation that had indorsed a promissory note, the latter claimed that notice of protest had not been properly given. It was shown that the notice had been left at the company's office during business hours after the holder was unable to find any of the officers of the corporation. Was sufficient notice given? (Hughes v. Rankin Realty Co., 108 N.J.L. 485, 158 A. 487)

9. Mellen-Wright Lumber Co., the holder of a note, sued McNett, as maker, and Kendall, as indorser. The latter claimed that he had not received notice of the dishonor of the note by the maker. The holder proved that he had sent the following letter, dated June 10, to Kendall:

Dear Sir: We hold note for $2,000 with interest at 7 per cent signed by Earl P. McNett and Anna J. McNett, his wife, on which you indorsed guaranteeing payment.

This note will be due June 12 and we are going to ask that you arrange to pay same promptly. We would appreciate this being paid by not later than Friday, June 18.

Kindly advise if you wish to make payment at our office or at one of our local banks.

We are enclosing stamped envelope for reply.

Was Kendall liable? (Mellen-Wright Lumber Co. v. McNett, 242 Mich. 369, 218 N.W. 709)

CHAPTER 30

Drafts and Presentment for Acceptance

A draft differs from a promissory note in that it is an order upon a third person to pay instead of a promise to pay. It is made by a drawer who orders the drawee to pay the payee or his order, or to pay the bearer.

A note and a draft differ in another respect. A note must be presented for payment in order to hold secondary parties liable; under certain circumstances a draft must be presented for acceptance as well as for payment.

If the drawer names himself as drawee, the paper is effective as a promissory note.[1] In such a case, the drawer is the primary party and procedures peculiar to drafts, such as presentment for acceptance, are eliminated.

Sec. 30-A. Liability of Drawee.

(1) Before Acceptance. An *acceptance* is the assent of the drawee to the order of the drawer. Before a drawee accepts a draft, he is not liable for its payment. In the absence of a prior contract to accept the draft, the drawee is not under any duty to do so. His act of refusing to accept the draft does not give the holder any right to sue him on the instrument, even though he may thereby break a contract with the drawer or some other party that he would accept the bill. Neither does the draft operate as an assignment of any money, even though the drawee has in his possession funds of the drawer.[2]

(2) After Acceptance. When the drawee accepts a draft, he is an acceptor and becomes primarily liable for its payment. By the accept-

---

[1] Uniform Commercial Code, Sec. 3-118(a).
[2] UCC Sec. 3-409(1), NIL Sec. 127.

ance he also admits (a) the existence of the payee and (b) the payee's capacity at the time to indorse the draft.[3]

If the drawee pays the instrument to a person who claims it through a forged indorsement, the drawee must bear the loss of such payment.

Sec. 30-B. Liability of Drawer. The drawer has a secondary liability. By executing the draft, he undertakes to pay the amount of the draft to the holder if, when the instrument is presented to the drawee for acceptance or payment, it is dishonored and proper proceedings are taken by the holder. (See p. 468, Gill v. Yoes) The drawer, however, may insert in the draft a provision to exclude or limit his own liability to the holder.[4]

The drawer, as in the case of the maker of a promissory note, admits two things by the act of drawing the draft. He admits (1) the existence of the payee and (2) the payee's capacity at the time to transfer the instrument. The effect of these statutory admissions is the same as in the case of the maker of a promissory note.[5]

When the drawer executes and delivers to the payee a draft in payment of a debt, the original obligation is suspended until the instrument is due, or until presentment for payment if it is demand paper. If the paper is dishonored, the holder may sue either on the paper or on the underlying obligation.[6]

Sec. 30-C. Liability of Indorser. The liability of an unqualified indorser of a draft is broader than that of unqualified indorser of a promissory note. In both cases, the unqualified indorser is under a secondary liability for the nonpayment of the instrument when due. In addition the unqualified indorser of a draft is under a secondary liability for the refusal of the drawee to accept the instrument when it is thereafter presented to him for acceptance.

In order to charge the unqualified indorser of the draft for either nonacceptance or nonpayment, it is necessary to prove that a presentment to the drawee had been properly made and due notice given to the indorser of the drawee's failure to accept or pay.

Sec. 30-D. Presentment for Acceptance. The best way for the payee to find out whether the drawee will pay the draft is to present it to the drawee for acceptance. If the drawee is not willing to pay the instrument according to its terms, he will reject it, that is, dishonor it by nonacceptance. If he is willing to pay the draft, he will do so

---

3 UCC Sec. 3-413(3), NIL Sec. 62.
4 UCC Sec. 3-413(2), NIL Sec. 61.
5 See p. 448.
6 UCC Sec. 3-802(1)(b). Special provisions apply when a bank is the drawer. Sec. 3-802(1)(a).

immediately in the case of demand paper or paper that has become due by that time. If the paper is not due but he is willing to pay it when it becomes due, he will accept it.[7]

(1) Necessity of Presentment for Acceptance. A draft may always be presented to the drawee for acceptance so that the holder can determine the intentions of the drawee. On the other hand, a presentment for acceptance must be made when (a) it is necessary in order to fix the date of maturity of the draft, such as when the instrument is payable a specified number of days after sight; (b) the draft expressly states that it must be presented for acceptance; or (c) the draft is made payable elsewhere than at the residence or place of business of the drawee.[8]

(2) Manner of Presenting for Acceptance. Presentment of a draft for acceptance is made in the same manner as the presentment of a note for payment,[9] with the obvious difference that the presentment is made upon the drawee rather than upon the maker.

(3) Time for Presentment for Acceptance. Unless a different time is specified in the draft, presentment for acceptance must be made on or before the date on which the instrument is payable by its express provisions. If it is payable after sight, it must be presented for acceptance within a reasonable time after its date or issue, whichever is later, or after it is negotiated to another person. With respect to the liability of any secondary party on any other form of instrument, presentment for acceptance must be made within a reasonable time after that party became liable on it.[10] (See p. 469, N.Y., N.H. & H. Railroad Co. Case)

The time for presentment of a draft for acceptance with respect to the hour and day or the effect of holidays is the same as in the case of presentment of a note for payment.[11]

(4) Delay or Absence of Presentment for Acceptance. Delay in a necessary presentment of a draft for acceptance and the failure to make any presentment are excused under the same circumstances as in the case of the presentment of a note for payment.[12]

An unexcused delay in making presentment for acceptance discharges all indorsers.[13] If the draft is domiciled, that is, payable at a bank, the drawer or acceptor is discharged under the same circum-

---

[7] UCC Sec. 3-410(1), NIL Sec. 132.
[8] UCC Sec. 3-501(1)(a), NIL Sec. 143.
[9] UCC Sec. 3-504.
[10] Sec. 3-503(1)(a),(b),(e).
[11] See p. 451.
[12] Sec. 3-511(1),(2),(3),(6). A minor qualification must be made in that in the case of a draft, it is the death or insolvency proceedings relating to the acceptor or drawee which is material, rather than the death or insolvency of a maker. See also Sec. 3-511(3)(a).
[13] UCC Sec. 3-502(1).

stances that apply to discharging the maker of a note for dishonor by nonpayment.[14]

(5) Time Allowed for Acceptance. It is not necessary that the drawee accept or dishonor the draft immediately upon its presentment to him. In order to afford him an opportunity of determining from his records whether he should accept, he may postpone making a decision, without thereby dishonoring the draft, until the close of the next business day following the presentment of the draft. Likewise the holder may allow the postponement of acceptance for an additional business day when he acts in good faith in the hope that he will be able to obtain an acceptance. When the holder agrees to such additional postponement, the liability of the secondary parties is not affected and the draft is not thereby dishonored.[15]

Sec. 30-E. Kinds of Acceptances.

(1) General Acceptance. A *general acceptance* (or simply an "acceptance") is one in which the acceptor agrees without qualification to pay according to the order of the drawer.

(2) Draft-varying Acceptance. A *draft-varying acceptance* is one in which the acceptor agrees to pay but not exactly in conformity with the order of the draft.[16] An acceptance varies the draft when it changes the time or place of payment, when it agrees to pay only a part of the amount of the draft, or when it sets up a condition that must be satisfied before the acceptance is effective.

An acceptance to pay at a particular bank or place in the United States is a general acceptance, unless it expressly states that the draft is to be paid there only and not elsewhere. In the latter case the acceptance varies the draft.[17]

If the holder does not wish to take the varying acceptance, he may reject it and treat the draft as dishonored by nonacceptance. After giving due notice, he can then proceed at once against the secondary parties.

If the holder assents to the draft-varying acceptance, however, he in effect consents to the execution of a new instrument; and each drawer and indorser is released from liability unless he affirmatively assents to such acceptance. The fact that a secondary party fails to object is not sufficient to prevent his release from liability.

Sec. 30-F. Form of Acceptance. An acceptance is the drawee's notation on the draft itself that he will make payment as directed thereby.

---

[14] Sec. 3-502(1)(b). See p. 449.
[15] Sec. 3-506.
[16] UCC Sec. 3-412(1), NIL Sec. 139.
[17] UCC Sec. 3-412(2), NIL Sec. 140.

It may be merely his signature, but customarily it will be the word "Accepted," and his signature, and generally the date. In any case, however, the acceptance must be written on the draft itself.[18] Usually it is written across the face of the instrument.

An acceptance cannot be oral, nor can it be contained in some other writing. The fact that the drawee is not liable on the draft because he has not accepted it does not necessarily prevent his being liable apart from the draft because of other obligations or principles of law. (See p. 471, Home Savings Bank Case)

Under the Code there can be no acceptance by misconduct. If the drawee retains the draft and refuses to return it on demand, he is guilty of conversion.[19] The measure of damages prescribed by the Code is the face amount of the instrument.[20]

Sec. 30-G. Dishonor by Nonacceptance. When a draft that is presented for acceptance is not accepted within the allowed time, the person presenting it must treat the draft as dishonored by nonacceptance.[21] If he fails to do so, the secondary parties are released from liability.

When a draft is dishonored by nonacceptance, the holder must give the same notice of dishonor as in the case of dishonor of a note by nonpayment. If the draft on its face appears to be drawn or payable outside of the United States, its territories, and the District of Columbia, it is also necessary to make protest of the dishonor in order to charge the drawer and the indorsers of the draft.[22]

Sec. 30-H. Presentment for Payment. The requirements and limitations upon the necessity of presentment of a draft for payment are the same as in the case of a promissory note, with the circumstances excusing delays in or failure to make presentment of a note likewise excusing delay or failure to make presentment of a draft for payment. The failure to present for payment is likewise excused with respect to a party who has countermanded payment of the draft.[23]

Furthermore, when a draft has been dishonored by nonacceptance, a later presentment for payment is excused unless the instrument has been since accepted.[24]

(1) Notice of Dishonor. The provisions governing notice of dishonor of a draft by nonpayment are the same as those for a note.[25]

---

[18] UCC Sec. 3-410(1).
[19] Sec. 3-419(1)(a).
[20] Sec. 3-419(2).
[21] UCC Sec. 3-507 (1) (a), NIL Sec. 149 (1).
[22] UCC Sec. 3-501(3). As to protest of dishonor and the effect thereof, see p. 454.
[23] Sec. 3-511(1),(2),(3).
[24] Sec. 3-511(4).
[25] Sec. 3-501(2). See p. 452.

(2) Protest of Dishonor. A protest of dishonor of a draft is not necessary unless the draft appears on its face to be drawn or payable outside of the United States, its territories, and the District of Columbia. The holder, however, may protest the dishonor of any instrument.[26] Delay in protesting dishonor or the absence of a protest are excused under the same circumstances that apply in the case of a note dishonored by nonpayment.[27]

A waiver of protest is effective to excuse the absence of an otherwise required protest. Protest is commonly waived, particularly in the case of out-of-town instruments, because protesting does involve an additional cost and some inconvenience. Frequently, therefore, the instrument will contain a clause stating that protest is waived, or it may be stamped with the words, "Protest waived" or "No Protest." A waiver of protest is a waiver of the requirement of presentment and notice of dishonor as well as of the protest itself even though protest is not required.[28]

When words of guaranty, such as "payment guaranteed" or "collection guaranteed," are used, presentment, notice of dishonor, and protest are not necessary to charge the person using such language.[29]

Cases for Chapter 30

Gill v. Yoes

360 P.2d 506 (Okla., 1961)

Gill sold his airplane to Hobson for $8,000. The purchase price was paid by delivering to Gill a draft drawn by Yoes on the Phoenix Savings & Loan Company to the order of Gill. Yoes had no money in the savings and loan association but had applied to it for a loan. The loan application was rejected and when the draft was presented on the association, it refused to pay it. Gill then sued Yoes on the draft. From a judgment for Yoes, Gill appealed.

PER CURIAM . . . The defendant claimed that she had nothing to do with the purchase of the plane except that she did sign the draft for $8,000 to pay for it; that she knew nothing about the dealings between Hobson and plaintiff; that she had no need for a plane and that she did not buy it. . . .

. . . [NIL Sec. 61] specifically deals with the liability of a drawer of the instrument. It provides in part, "The drawer by drawing the

---

26 UCC Sec. 3-501(3), NIL Sec. 118.
27 UCC Sec. 3-511(1),(2).
28 UCC Sec. 3-511 (5), NIL Sec. 111.
29 UCC Sec. 3-416 (5).

instrument . . . engages that on due presentment the instrument will be accepted and paid, or both, according to its tenor. . . ."

The defendant by her answer injected into this case the proposition that the draft given for the plane was for the benefit of a third party, one Hobson. It is really immaterial whether the draft was given for the purchase of the plane by either Hobson or the defendant just so long as it was given. We think that Haffner v. First National Bank of Seiling, 152 Okla. 169, 5 P.2d 351, 354, is controlling here and the following language is pertinent: "Where a benefit is conferred on a third party and a detriment is suffered by the payee of a note at the instance of the maker thereof, it will be sufficient 'consideration' to support the note, even though the maker thereof received no personal benefit by reason of the execution and delivery thereof."

The case was followed in Lacy v. Edwards, 170 Okla. 458, 41 P.2d 64, where a defendant gave his personal note in order to obtain funds to make a down payment on an automobile which a third person was buying. . . .

Defendant represented that she was putting the $8,000 into the transaction and she cannot avoid liability simply because the draft was not honored. . . .

[Judgment reversed.]

Code Comment: The same decision would be made under the Code. The substance of NIL Sec. 61 on which the decision is based is restated in UCC Sec. 3-413 (2) .

N. Y., N. H. & H. Railroad Co. v. First National Bank
105 Conn. 33, 134 A. 223 (1926)

The Goodhue Mill Company shipped a carload of flour, consigned to the National Grain Corporation, located in Bridgeport, Connecticut, and drew a draft on the grain corporation for the amount of the purchase price, payable "30 days after arrival of the car." The draft and bill of lading were sent to the First National Bank of Minneapolis, which forwarded it to the First National Bank of Bridgeport with instructions to deliver the bill of lading when the drawee accepted the draft. The grain corporation accepted the draft and received the bill of lading from the Bridgeport bank on November 12, and on the same day it assigned the bill of lading to the Bridgeport bank as security for a loan. On November 22, bankruptcy proceedings were begun against the National Grain Corporation. On November 27, the car of flour arrived. The mill company and the Bridgeport bank both claimed the flour. The N. Y., N. H. & H. Railroad Co. brought an action to determine title to the flour that was in its possession. From a judgment for the mill, the bank appealed.

HINMAN, J. . . . The . . . instruction accompanying the draft in question was unmistakably a direction to present the draft for acceptance; it contained no express direction [to] . . . the bank to delay presentment for acceptance until it had ascertained that the car had arrived, instead of presenting it, as it did, within a reasonable time after receiving it. . . .

The trial court has found a custom in the banking business in Bridgeport, as to drafts payable a specified time after arrival of car, to treat the acceptance of the draft as proof of the arrival of the car, without ascertainment by the bank as to whether the car had actually arrived, and that such acceptance established the due date of the draft as the specified time from the date of acceptance. This custom was followed as to the draft in question. . . . The court . . . found that neither the Goodhue Company nor the Minneapolis bank were aware that the Bridgeport bank permitted acceptance before actual arrival of cars, until after the bankruptcy of the grain corporation; and the mill company claims that, for this reason, the custom is not binding upon it and will not avail to justify the bank in acting in accordance therewith.

A bank is governed, in all matters concerning the presentment, acceptance, and collection of paper, by the laws and customs which prevail in the place of its own location. If the paper has been transmitted from a distant place, where the laws and customs are different, the transmitting party, if he wishes these to be conformed to, must send special instructions to that effect; and in the absence of express directions the collecting bank is not bound to inquire into the laws or usages of any place other than its own. The understanding which is assumed to be mutual and to enter into the contract of the parties is that the bank shall perform the various acts embraced in the business in accordance with the local laws, rules, and habitual course of dealing, providing that such usage is not illegal. The assent of all concerned to the pursuance of this course then becomes an implication of law by which all the parties are equally bound. . . .

Neither can we agree . . . that the custom was inconsistent with the specific instructions given or that it changed the intrinsic character of the transaction. The instructions were to "surrender documents upon drawee's acceptance of draft payable 30 days after arrival of car." The acceptance of the draft is indicated as the condition precedent to surrender of the bill of lading, and this direction was literally complied with. To make the custom inconsistent with the instructions and the act of the bank a violation of them, the language must be construed as if it directed surrender of the bill of lading "only after arrival of the car and acceptance of draft"; the direction given does not express, nor do we think fairly import, such a meaning. . . .

[Judgment for mill reversed, and judgment entered for bank.]

Code Comment: The same decision would be made under the Code. Except in the case of checks, the Code declares that "a reasonable time for presentment is determined by the nature of the instrument, any usage of banking or trade, and the facts of the particular case." UCC Sec. 3-503(2). A usage of trade is defined as "any practice or method of dealing having such regularity of observance in a place, location, or trade as to justify an expectation that it will be observed with respect to the transaction in question. . . . An applicable usage of trade in the place where any part of performance is to occur shall be used in interpreting the agreement as to that part of the performance." UCC Sec. 1-205(2), (5).

Home Savings Bank v. General Finance Corp.

10 Wis. 2d 417, 103 N.W.2d 117 (1960)

Schenk's Motor Sales had a checking account in the Home Savings Bank. The bank certified a check drawn by Schenk in reliance on the oral promise of the General Finance Corp. to accept a draft drawn on General by Schenk that had just been deposited in Schenk's account. The certified check was paid by the bank, but General refused to pay the draft on the ground that its oral acceptance was not binding. The bank sued General for the amount of the certified check. From a judgment in favor of General, the Bank appealed.

FAIRCHILD, J. . . . Plaintiff bank points out that it is not attempting to recover from General Finance upon an accepted bill of exchange. . . . "The acceptance must be in writing and signed by the drawee." [NIL § 132] Plaintiff bank does claim, however, that General Finance orally promised to accept the draft if the bank would certify the $9,700 check payable to General Finance; that the bank did so, and thereby accepted the offer and furnished consideration for the promise; that no statute requires such contract to be in writing to be enforceable. Secondly, plaintiff bank claims a cause of action for restitution of unjust enrichment. . . .

Separate contract theory. "If an acceptance or promise to accept is unenforceable under the Statute because it is not in writing, it is well settled that the drawee is liable neither on the bill nor on the promise, though if other consideration is given for the promise, as distinguished from the consideration supporting the bill, it should be binding as a simple contract." 4 Williston, Contracts (rev. ed.), p. 3435, sec. 1195. This theory appears to have been followed in several cases. . . . The difficulty we have with it is that if fully and logically followed, it would erode or evade the statutory requirement that an acceptance be written. A drawee's promise to accept or pay an outstanding bill is scarcely distinguishable from "signification by the drawee of his assent to the order of the drawer," the definition of acceptance in [NIL § 132], requiring an acceptance to be put in writing. . . .

Unjust enrichment. The essential elements of quasi contract are a benefit conferred upon the defendant by the plaintiff, appreciation by the defendant of such benefit, and acceptance and retention by the defendant of such benefit under circumstances such that it would be inequitable to retain the benefit without payment of the value thereof. . . . The conferring of the benefit and appreciation by defendant are clear.

It also seems clear that at least as to a part of the money, retention by General Finance is inequitable. It is beyond belief that General Finance could have obtained cash for the $9,700 check in any way except by persuading the bank president that the draft would be honored. No matter how gullible or careless it may have been for the president to rely upon an oral acceptance, the retention of the bank's money after refusal to honor the draft as promised cannot be considered equitable.

$3,080.56 was the balance in Schenk's account when the check was certified. The record does not disclose the payment of any checks by the bank after that except the one for $9,700. We think the amount which General Finance cannot equitably retain is the difference between $9,700 and $3,080.56, or $6,619.44. . . .

It has been suggested that since an acceptance of a bill must be in writing in order to be enforceable, it is against public policy to grant restitution in the situation here present. This question is considered in Restatement, Contracts, sec. 355. In comment *a* of subsec. 1, it is said: "The parties to a contract that is rendered unenforceable by the Statute of Frauds or some similar statute very frequently act in reliance on it by rendering the agreed performance, in part or in whole, or by making improvements on land that is the subject matter of the contract. In such cases, the refusal of all judicial remedy would result in harm to one party and unjust enrichment of the other. Therefore, restitution is enforced even though the Statute makes other remedies unavailable." . . .

In a recent case, we said: "Under the theory of unjust enrichment it is immaterial whether the defendant and the plaintiff entered into a void contract. The plaintiff is not seeking to have the defendant perform the alleged contract. It is seeking the return of its money. Money paid under an oral contract void because of the Statute of Frauds may be recovered on the theory that it was paid without consideration because the law implies a promise of repayment when no rule of public policy or good morals has been violated." . . .

. . . The purpose of requiring an acceptance to be in writing seems to us to fall within the latter class, and not to prevent the remedy of restitution where one party has paid money to another in reliance upon an oral and therefore unenforceable contract. . . .

[Judgment for defendant reversed.]

Code Comment: The same decision would be made under the Code because the principles on which the case was decided are general principles that are not displaced by the Code. UCC Sec. 1-103.

Questions and Case Problems

1. What is the objective of each of the following rules of law?
    (a) The failure of a drawee to act by the close of the business day following the presentment of a draft constitutes a dishonor of the instrument.
    (b) In states that have adopted the Uniform Commercial Code, there can only be an acceptance by a writing on the instrument itself.

2. J. J. and L. L. Morton executed and delivered to Lewis Hubbard & Co. a draft drawn on the West Virginia Timber Co. The timber company accepted the instrument by promising to pay it whenever certain timber was inspected. When the draft was not paid, the Hubbard corporation brought an action against the drawers. The drawers denied liability on the ground that the payee, without the drawers' consent, took a qualified acceptance. Were they liable? (Lewis Hubbard & Co. v. Morton, 80 W.Va. 137, 92 S.E. 252)

3. The Perfection Curing Co. gave the First National Bank of Winnfield a sight draft drawn by it on the Citizens' Bank of Campti. The First National Bank sent the sight draft to the Citizens' Bank for acceptance and payment. The Citizens' Bank received the draft on September 28. On October 11 the Citizens' Bank returned the draft to the First National Bank without either accepting or rejecting the draft. The First National Bank sued the Citizens' Bank on the draft. Can it recover? (First National Bank of Winnfield v. Citizens' Bank of Campti, 163 La. 919, 113 So. 147)

4. Lowe & Myers were contractors doing construction work for the Druid Realty Co. In order to pay for their materials they drew a draft on the realty company directing it to pay $2,000 to the order of the Crane Co. The realty company, through its president, wrote on the instrument that it accepted the instrument and agreed to pay it within 30 days after the completion of the work, provided the crane company continued to furnish materials to Lowe & Myers. What was the effect of the action by the realty company? (Crane v. Druid Realty Co., 137 Md. 324, 112 A. 621)

5. Rogers, Brown & Co., of New York City and other cities in the United States, sold iron to Soehne, iron merchants doing business in Vienna, Austria. They shipped the iron from Birmingham, Alabama, to the buyers in Austria, and drew in New York City a demand on the buyers for the amount of the purchase price of the iron. The bill, payable to the order of the drawers, was indorsed to G. Amsinck & Co. On February 21, payment was demanded and refused. When suit was brought upon the bill, the defendant claimed that the holder had failed to protest the bill for non-payment. Decide. (Amsinck v. Rogers, 103 App.Div. 428, 93 N.Y.S. 87)

6. Cobb purchased from the Woods National Bank of San Antonio, Texas, a draft drawn on the Milmo National Bank. Thereafter the instrument was presented for acceptance by Thaison, an agent of Cobb. An action was brought later by Cobb against the Milmo National Bank and Morris, the receiver of the Woods National Bank. It was claimed that the presentment to the drawee was not valid because it was not made by the holder in person. Decide. (Milmo National Bank v. Cobb, 54 Tex.Civ.App. 1, 115 S.W. 345)

7. Slack drew a draft on the Clayton Drug Co. payable to the Clayton Town Site Co. The draft was accepted orally by the drawee. The Clayton Town Site Co. sued the Clayton Drug Co. when the former refused payment. Could it recover? (Clayton Town Site Co. v. Clayton Drug Co., 20 N.M. 185, 147 P. 460)

8. Rello, Inc., drew a bill of exchange on the Philadelphia Wholesale Drug Co. The drug company accepted the instrument by writing on the bill: "Accepted for payment as per Rello contract for amount and date shown hereon." When the International Finance Corp. brought an action against the drug company for payment, it was contended that the acceptance was a qualified acceptance. Was this contention sound? (International Finance Corp. v. Philadelphia Wholesale Co., 312 Pa. 280, 167 A. 790)

9. Crozer purchased from the American Express Co. four drafts drawn by the company on itself. One of the drafts was payable to the Western Evergreen, another to the Western Evergreen Co., and two of them to the West Coast Co. Unknown to the drawer, these payees were fictitious payees. Crozer indorsed the names of the payees and cashed the draft with the People's Savings Bank. In an action by the express company against the bank, it was claimed that the drawer admitted the authority of the purchaser to indorse the names of the payees. What is your opinion? (American Express Co. v. People's Savings Bank, 192 Iowa 366, 181 N.W. 701)

10. Whetmore was the general agent and manager of the New York Iron Mine, a corporation carrying on mining operations near Marquette, Michigan. He executed a draft drawn on Tildon, president and treasurer of the corporation, at New York City. The draft was postdated, being drawn on June 16 and dated July 5, but purported to be payable at sight. The draft was discounted at the Citizens' Bank in Marquette. Was it necessary for the bank to present the draft to the drawee for acceptance? (New York Iron Mine v. Citizens' Bank, 44 Mich. 344, 6 N.W. 823)

11. Fuller Brothers, as the holder, brought an action against Bovay, as indorser. It was shown that the notice of default of the primary party was given to Bovay by a letter addressed "Jonesboro Rice Mill Co., Jonesboro, Ark., Attention Mr. Bovay." Was this a proper notice? (Bovay v. Fuller, 63 F.2d 1143)

12. Drummond executed a draft on the Webb Packing Co. to pay for cattle purchased from Hales. The Webb Packing Co. refused to accept or to pay the draft. Hales gave proper notice to Drummond and then sued him on the draft. Drummond raised the defense that he had been acting merely as the agent of the Webb Packing Co. and that it was understood with Hales that Drummond should not be personally liable on the instrument. Was this a defense? (Drummond v. Hales, [C.A. 10th] 191 F.2d 972)

CHAPTER 31

Checks and Bank Collections

Of the various types of commercial paper in use today, by far the most common is the check. By means of checks it is possible to make payment safely and conveniently without the need of safeguarding a shipment of money. A book of blank checks can be kept without fear of financial loss if it is stolen. The checkbook stub and the canceled check make a written record which may be used at a later date to show that a payment was made. The more common aspects of checks and of their payment and collection are considered in this chapter.

Sec. 31-A. Nature of a Check. A check is a particular kind of bill of exchange. The following features of a check distinguish it from other drafts or bills of exchange: [1]

(1) The drawee of a check is always a bank.

(2) As a practical matter, the check is drawn on the assumption that the bank has on deposit in the drawer's account an amount sufficient to pay the check. In the case of a draft there is no assumption that the drawee has any of the drawer's money with which to pay the bill. Actually, the rights of the parties are not affected by the fact that the depositor does not have funds on deposit with the bank sufficient to pay the check.

If a draft is dishonored, the drawer is civilly liable; but if a check is drawn with intent to defraud the person to whom it is delivered, the drawer is also subject to criminal prosecution in most states under what are known as "bad check" laws. Most states provide that if the check is not made good within a stated period, such as ten days, it will be presumed that the check was originally issued with the intent to defraud.

(3) A check is demand paper A draft may be payable either on demand or at a future time. The standard form of check does not

---

[1] Checks are governed by both Article 3 of the Code relating to commercial paper and Article 4 governing bank deposits and collections.

specify when it is payable, and it is therefore automatically payable on demand. This eliminates the need for an acceptance since the holder of the check will merely present it for payment.

One exception arises when a check is postdated, that is, when the check shows a date later than the actual date of execution and delivery. Here the check is not payable until that date arrives. This in effect changes the check to time paper without expressly stating so. (See p. 483, Commonwealth v. Kelinson)

The delivery of the check is not regarded as an assignment of the money on deposit. It therefore does not automatically transfer the rights of the depositor against his bank to the holder of the check, and there is no duty on the part of the drawee bank to pay the holder the amount of the check.[2]

Sec. 31-B. Indication of Purpose. Although not required by law, a notation on a check of the purpose for which it is delivered is desirable. It serves to identify the payment in case the purpose is questioned later. Customary notations are "Payment of invoice No. 548," "Painting house, 1963," or "Fees, drafting of will." If a person cashes a check bearing such a notation, he is estopped from denying that the payment was made and received for the purpose stated.

A common form of notation is the statement "In full payment (or settlement) of the claim of. . . ." When a check with such a notation is accepted by the payee, the claim referred to is discharged without regard to whether the amount of the check was the full amount of the claim or only a part, and without regard to whether there was any dispute as to the actual amount due.[3]

A special form of check, known as a *voucher check,* is used by some businesses. This form is larger than an ordinary check. The additional space is used for stating the purpose of the check or for listing the items of an invoice for which the check is issued in payment. When the payee receives a voucher check, he detaches the voucher portion of the form and keeps it in his files as a record of the payment that he has received.

Sec. 31-C. Liability of Drawer. If the check is presented for payment and paid, no liability of the drawer arises. If the bank refuses to make payment, the drawer is then subject to a liability similar to that in the case of the nonpayment of an ordinary draft. If proper notice of dishonor is not given the drawer of the check, he may be discharged from liability to the same extent as a drawer of an ordinary bill of exchange.

---

[2] Uniform Commercial Code, Sec. 3-409(1); Negotiable Instruments Law, Sec. 189.
[3] UCC Sec. 3-408.

Sec. 31-D. Rights of Drawer.

(1) Refusal of Bank to Pay. The bank is under a general contractual duty to its depositor to pay on demand all of his checks to the extent of the funds deposited to his credit. When the bank breaches this contract, it is liable to the drawer for damages. In the case of a draft, there is ordinarily no duty on the drawee to accept it or to make payment if he has not accepted it, and there is therefore no liability on his part to the drawer when he does not do so.

A bank is obligated to pay a proper order by a depositor even though he does not use a regular printed form supplied by the bank. Any writing that contains the substance of a regular printed check must be honored by the bank.

Although the drawee bank is liable for improperly refusing to pay a check, this liability runs in favor of the drawer alone. Even though the holder of the check or the payee may be harmed when the bank refuses to pay the check, the holder or payee has no right to sue the bank. The holder or payee is limited to proceeding against the secondary parties on the instrument. He may also proceed, however, against the person from whom he received the check on the original obligation, which has not been discharged because the check was not paid.[4]

A bank acting in good faith may pay a check presented more than six months after its date but, unless the check is certified, it is not required to do so.[5]

(2) Stopping Payment. The drawer has the power of stopping payment of a check. After the check is issued, he can notify the drawee bank not to pay it when it is presented for payment. This is a useful device when a check is lost or mislaid. A duplicate check can be written and, to make sure that the payee does not receive payment twice or that an improper person does not receive payment on the first check, payment on the first check can be stopped. Likewise, if payment is made by check and then the payee defaults on his contract so that the drawer would have a claim against him, payment on the check can be stopped, assuming that the payee has not cashed it.

The stop order may be either oral or written. If oral, however, it is only binding on the bank for 14 calendar days unless confirmed in writing within that time. A written order is not effective after 6 months unless renewed in writing.[6]

If the bank makes payment of a check after it has been properly notified to stop payment, it is liable to the depositor for the loss he

---

[4] Sec. 3-802(1)(b).
[5] Sec. 4-404.
[6] Sec. 4-403(2).

sustains, in the absence of a valid limitation of the bank's liability. (see p. 485, Haman Case) The burden of establishing the loss resulting in such case rests upon the depositor.[7]

The act of stopping payment may in some cases make the depositor liable to the holder of the instrument. If the depositor has no proper ground for stopping payment, he is liable to the payee to whom he has delivered the check. In any case, he is liable for stopping payment with respect to any holder in due course or other party having the rights of a holder in due course, unless he stops payment for a reason that may be asserted against such a holder as a defense.[8] The fact that the bank refuses to make payment because of the drawer's instruction does not make the case any different from any other instance in which the drawee refuses to pay, and the legal consequences of imposing liability upon the drawer are the same.

Generally payment is stopped only when the drawer has good cause with respect to the payee. For example, the purchaser of goods may give the seller a check in advance payment for the goods. The seller may then declare that he is not going to deliver the goods. The purchaser is within his lawful rights if he stops payment on the check since the seller has no right to the check if he does not perform his part of the sales contract. Thus the payee could not sue the drawer-purchaser for stopping payment on the check. If the check has been negotiated to a subsequent holder who is a holder in due course or a holder through a holder in due course, the purchaser cannot assert this defense against such a holder. Accordingly, such a favored holder may hold the drawer liable on the dishonored check.

When the depositor does not give the bank the stop-payment notice in person but makes use of a means of communication such as the telegraph, he cannot hold the bank liable if the notice is delayed in reaching the bank which makes payment before receiving the notice. If negligence on the part of the telegraph company can be established, however, the depositor can sue that company.

Sec. 31-E. Presentment of Check for Payment. In the case of demand paper generally, presentment for payment must be made on any secondary party to the instrument within a reasonable time after such party becomes liable on it. Reasonable time is determined by the nature of the instrument, by any existing commercial usage, and by the facts of the particular case.[9]

Failure to make such timely presentment discharges all indorsers of the instrument. It also discharges the drawer, if the draft is payable

---

[7] Sec. 4-103(3).
[8] See p. 504.
[9] UCC Sec. 3-503(1)(e),(2). See NIL Sec. 193.

at a bank, to the extent that he has lost, through the bank's failure, money which he had on deposit at that bank to meet the payment of the instrument.[10]

As a modification to the foregoing principles, the Code establishes two presumptions as to what is a reasonable time in which to present a check for payment.[11] If the check is not certified and is both drawn and payable within the United States, it is presumed as to the drawer that 30 days after the date of the check or the date of its issuance, whichever is later, is the reasonable period in which to make presentment for payment. In the case of an indorser it is presumed to be 7 days after his indorsement.[12]

Sec. 31-F. Dishonor of Check. When a check is dishonored by nonpayment, the holder must follow the same procedure of notice to each of the secondary parties as in the case of a draft or bill of exchange if he wishes to hold them liable for payment. As in the case of any drawer of a draft or bill of exchange who countermands payment, notice of dishonor need not be given to the drawer who has stopped payment on a check. Notice is also excused under any circumstances that would excuse notice in the case of a promissory note. For example, no notice need be given a drawer or an indorser who knows that sufficient funds to cover the check are not on deposit, since such party has no reason to expect that the check will be paid by the bank.[13] (See p. 489, Plitt v. Grim)

A check that is dishonored by nonpayment may be presented to the drawee bank at a later time in the hope that by the later date there will be sufficient funds in the account of the drawer so that the drawee bank will be able to make payment. Although there is this right to make a subsequent presentation for payment, it is essential that notice be given secondary parties after the dishonor of the instrument upon the first presentation. If they are not duly notified at that time, they are discharged and no new rights can be acquired against them by making a subsequent presentment and then notifying the secondary parties of the second dishonor.

Sec. 31-G. Liability of Bank for Improper Payment of Check. As pointed out earlier, a bank that honors a check after the depositor

---

[10] UCC Sec. 3-502(1).

[11] A presumption means that the trier of fact is bound by the presumption in the absence of evidence that supports a contrary conclusion. Sec. 1-201 (31).

[12] Sec. 3-503(2). This abolishes the "1-day" rule recognized in many jurisdictions which required presentment not later than the next business day if the bank and all parties resided in the same city. This requirement had become very burdensome in the case of businesses which received a large volume of checks at one time, as at the end of the month, and persons, such as farmers, who would not want to interrupt their work to go to the bank every time a check was received.

[13] Sec. 3-511(2)(b).

has stopped payment is liable to the depositor for the loss he sustains. In addition, the bank is generally liable if it makes an improper payment under the following circumstances:

(1) Payment on Forged Signature of Drawer. The bank is liable to the depositor if it pays a check on which his signature has been forged since a forgery ordinarily has no effect as a signature.[14] The burden of knowing the signatures of all its depositors is thus placed on the bank. Accordingly, upon opening an account in a bank, the depositor is required to sign a card in the way in which he will sign his checks. This signature card remains on file in the bank and is used to make a comparison to determine whether checks presented to the bank for payment have been signed by the depositor.

Although the bank has no right to pay a check on which the drawer's signature is forged, the drawer may be barred from objecting that his signature was a forgery. If the drawer's negligence contributed substantially to the forging of his signature, he cannot assert that is was forged when the drawee bank makes payment of the check while acting in good faith and conforming to reasonable commercial standards.[15] For example, if the drawer signs his checks with a mechanical writer, he must exercise reasonable care to prevent unauthorized persons from making use of it to forge or "sign" his name with such a device. If the depositor's negligence enables a third person to make such improper use of it, the depositor is barred from objecting to the payment of the check by the bank.

When the depositor fails to examine his bank statement and canceled checks with reasonable care and promptness and to notify the bank promptly of any forgery, the depositor cannot hold the bank responsible if in making payment on the forged instrument it had used ordinary care. (See p. 491, Worthen Bank & Trust Co. Case) Even when the bank failed to exercise care, the depositor cannot object to the forgery of his signature unless he acts within one year.[16]

(2) Payment on Forged Indorsement. A bank that pays a check on a forged indorsement is liable for conversion.[17] However, a bank that has dealt with an instrument or the proceeds of it on behalf of one who was not the true owner is not liable to the true owner when the bank acted in good faith and in accordance with the reasonable commercial standards applicable to a bank. In the latter case, the liability of the bank is limited to surrendering the instrument or the proceeds of it to the true owner if the bank still has either in its possession.[18]

---

[14] Sec. 3-404(1).
[15] Sec. 4-406.
[16] Sec. 4-406.
[17] Sec. 3-419(1)(c).
[18] Sec. 3-419(3).

(3) Payment on Missing Indorsement. A drawee bank is liable for the loss when it pays a check that lacks an essential indorsement. In such a case, the instrument has not been properly presented and by definition the person presenting the check for payment is not the holder of the instrument and is not entitled to demand or receive payment. It is a defense to the bank, however, that although the person to whom payment was made was not the holder of the instrument, he was in fact the person whom the drawer or the last holder of the check intended should be paid.

When a person deposits a check in his bank but neglects to indorse it, the bank may make an indorsement for him unless the check contains a statement that it must be signed personally by that person. Even without the bank so doing, there is an effective negotiation from the customer to his bank when the check is stamped by the bank to indicate that it was deposited by the customer or was credited to his account.[19]

(4) Payment on Nonfiduciary Indorsement. The bank is not liable when it makes payment on a nonfiduciary indorsement to a person to whom the instrument had been made payable in a fiduciary capacity. Thus the bank is protected when it pays on an indorsement of "D. A. Jones" although the check was drawn to the order of "D. A. Jones, Trustee."

(5) Alteration of Check. If the face of the check has been altered so that the amount to be paid has been increased, the bank is liable to the drawer for the amount of the increase when it makes payment for the greater amount. The bank has the opportunity of examining the check when it is presented for payment and, if it fails to detect the alteration, it is responsible for the loss.

The drawer may be barred from claiming that there was an alteration by virtue of his conduct with respect to writing the check and his conduct after receiving the canceled check from the bank. As to the former, he is barred if in writing the check he was negligent and that negligence substantially contributed to the making of the material alteration and the bank honored the check in good faith and observed reasonable commercial standards in so doing.[20] For example, the drawer is barred when he leaves blank spaces on his check so that it is readily possible to change "four" to "four hundred," and the drawee bank pays out the latter sum without any cause to know of the alteration.

The drawer of the check may also be barred from objecting to the alteration by his failure to inform the bank after receiving his canceled

[19] Sec. 4-205 (1).
[20] Sec. 3-406.

checks and bank statement. In such a case he is barred under the same conditions as determine when he is barred from objecting to the drawee bank that his signature on the check is forgery.[21]

(6) Payment After Depositor's Death. The effectiveness of a check ordinarily ceases with the death of a drawer. Accordingly, when the drawer of a check dies, the bank cannot make payment of the check. If it does, the bank is liable to the estate of the depositor. Under the Uniform Commercial Code, however, the death of the drawer does not revoke the agency of the bank until it has knowledge of the death and has had reasonable opportunity to act. Even with such knowledge, the bank may continue for ten days to pay or certify checks drawn by the drawer unless ordered to stop payment by a person claiming an interest in the account.[22]

Sec. 31-H. Certified Checks. Checks are not accepted in the sense that drafts or bills of exchange are accepted by the drawee; but the bank may certify a check, which has the same legal consequence.[23] The effect of the certification is to set aside in a special account maintained by the bank as much of the depositor's account as is needed to pay the amount of the certified check. With respect to the holder of the check, the certification is an undertaking by the bank that when the check is presented for payment, it will make payment according to the terms of the check without regard to the standing of the depositor's account at that time.

By statute, the use of a certified check is frequently required for payments made at sheriff's sales and as filing fees sent to government agencies for various purposes. They are also commonly used when property is sold to a buyer who is not well known or who is deemed an unsatisfactory credit risk.

As in the case of an acceptance, any writing showing an intention to certify a check is sufficient. Ordinarily a certification is made by stamping or printing on the check the word "Certified," the name of the bank, the signature and title of the officer making the certification, and the date.

A check may be certified by a bank upon the request of the drawer or the holder. In the latter case all indorsers and the drawer are automatically released from liability.[24] Since the holder could have received payment, as the bank was willing to certify the check, and since the holder did not take the payment but chose to take the promise of the certification, the secondary parties are released from liability.

---

[21] See (1) supra this section.
[22] UCC Sec. 4-405.
[23] UCC Sec. 3-411(1), NIL Sec. 187.
[24] UCC Sec. 3-411(1). See NIL Sec. 188.

When the certification is obtained by the drawer, there is no release of the secondary parties.

Sec. 31-I. Agency Status of Collecting Bank. When a person deposits a negotiable instrument at a bank, he is ordinarily making it his agent to collect or obtain the payment of the instrument. Unless the contrary intent clearly appears, a bank receiving an item is deemed to take it as agent for the depositor rather than as becoming the purchaser of the paper from him. This presumption is not affected by the form of the indorsement nor by the absence of any indorsement. The bank is also regarded as being merely an agent although the depositor has the right to make immediate withdrawals against the deposited item. In consequence of the agency status, the depositor remains the owner of the item and is therefore subject to the risks of ownership involved in its collection, in the absence of fault on the part of any collecting bank.[25]

Cases for Chapter 31

Commonwealth v. Kelinson

199 Pa.Super. 135, 184 A.2d 374 (1962)

Kelinson was president of the Barkel Meat Packing Co., a wholesale meat packer. On February 2, a shipment of meat was delivered to the company. He gave the driver a check in payment for the full amount but dated it February 4. Approximately thirty checks given in payment of prior shipments had also been postdated. All prior checks had been paid, but the check of February 2 was not paid. Kelinson was prosecuted for the offenses of passing a worthless check and of obtaining money by false pretenses. From a conviction for both crimes, he appealed.

WATKINS, J. . . . The Commonwealth bases its case upon the issuance of the check in the amount of $8,453.44, which was returned for want of sufficient funds and has never been paid. Because of the nature of its business every check drawn by Barkel to this supplier was postdated. The instant check was the only one not paid.

The Act of 1939, June 24, P.L. 872, § 854, 18 P.S. § 4854, known as the "Worthless Check Act," provides inter alia: "Whoever, with intent to defraud, makes, draws, utters, or delivers any check, draft, or order for the payment of money, upon any bank, banking institution, trust company, or other depository, knowing, at the time of such making, drawing, uttering, or delivering, that the maker or drawer has not sufficient funds in, or credit with, such bank, banking institution, trust company, or other depository, for the payment of such check, although no express representation is made in reference thereto, is guilty of a

---

[25] UCC Sec. 4-201(1).

misdemeanor, and upon conviction thereof, shall be imprisoned not exceeding two (2) years, or fined not exceeding one thousand dollars ($1,000), or both."

The defendant contends that postdated checks do not come within the purview of the "worthless check act." . . .

The courts generally, in the more recent cases, have taken the view that such a check is not within the contemplation of "bad check" statutes, such as ours. . . . "By the terms of the act intent to defraud at the time of making or delivering the check is an essential element of the crime. This was a postdated check. As such, it differed from an ordinary check in that it carried on its face implied notice that there was no money presently on deposit available to meet it, with the implied assurance that there would be such funds on the day it became due. At most is amounted to a promise that on the day it became due the drawer would have in the bank a sufficient deposit to meet it.". . .

Postdated checks are today a form of negotiable paper, a credit instrument, containing a promise to pay on the date appearing on the face of the instrument, that are in everyday commercial use. Post-dating the check, in itself, is a manner in which commercial usage permits the drawer to put a payee on notice that he does not have sufficient funds on deposit, at the time of making, to pay the check. . . . "What the drawer undertakes is that on a day named he will have the amount of the check to his credit in the bank. In the meantime he wants the full and free use of his entire deposit."

A postdated check is one that is made and delivered at some time prior to the day of its date. It is generally held to be payable at sight or upon presentation at the bank at any time on or after the day of its date. It differs from an ordinary check in that it has on its face implied notice that there is no money presently on deposit available to meet it, with the implied assurance that there will be such funds on the day it becomes due. It is a familiar and useful form of negotiable paper and plays an important part in the role of commerce. Ordinarily its purpose is to obtain an extension of credit. . . .

The law in Pennsylvania is clear that the acceptance of a postdated check amounts to a delivery on credit and the remedies for the non-payment of such checks are set forth in the Uniform Commercial Code. "Where the instrument offered by the buyer is not a payment but a credit instrument such as a note or a check postdated by even one day, the seller's acceptance of the instrument insofar as third parties are concerned, amounts to a delivery on credit and his remedies are set forth in the section on buyer's insolvency. As between the buyer and the seller, however, the matter turns on the present subsection and the section on conditional delivery, and subsequent dishonor of the instrument gives the seller rights on it as well as for breach of the contract for sale." 1953, P.L. 3, § 2-511, 12A P.S. § 2-511, U.C.C. Comment No. 6. . . .

The appellant also contends that his conviction of obtaining money under false pretenses cannot stand because the evidence does not support it. To bring this case within the provisions of the law defining cheating by false pretenses, Act of 1939, P.L. 872, § 836, as amended, 18 P.S. § 4836, "there must be found to co-exist three separate elements: (1) a false pretense, as a false assertion of existing fact; (2) obtaining property or something of value thereby; (3) an intent to defraud." . . . A mere promise for future conduct does not suffice to constitute a false pretense even though the promisor never intended to perform. . . .

A postdated check is not a present promise; is not a false representation of a present existing fact that there are funds on deposit to pay the check. A postdated check declares boldly on its face that it is nothing more than a promise to pay in the future on or after the date appearing on the face of the instrument.

The Commonwealth has failed to establish by the evidence, as a matter of law, the offenses for which this defendant stands convicted. . . .

[Judgment arrested and the defendant discharged.]

Code Comment: Since the Code regulates only civil rights and liabilities, reference must be made to the criminal law of the state in which a person has acted in order to determine whether he has committed a crime. It is therefore possible that in some Code states the delivery of a postdated check will be held to be a violation of the bad check law or the obtaining of money by false pretenses. This likelihood is increased when the drawer draws the postdated check with no intention of ever depositing sufficient funds to meet the check.

Haman v. First National Bank

115 N.W.2d 883 (S.D., 1962)

Note: In this case the court is faced with two problems: (1) What did the parties mean by their words? (2) What was the legal effect of what they meant? The dissenting opinion disagrees with the majority of the court in the answer to both questions. As to the legal effect of the words, the Uniform Commercial Code adopts the view of the dissenting judge. In reading this case, bear in mind this conflict and observe the growth of the law.

Haman had a checking account in the First National Bank. On November 14, 1956, he issued a check to Calhoun for $1,000. The same day he telephoned the bank to stop payment on the check and, when so instructed by the bank officer, mailed a written stop-payment order to the bank on the same day. Three days later the bank paid the check and charged his account for $1,000. Haman's canceled checks, including the $1,000 Calhoun check, were returned to him on December 18, 1956. Haman reported the payment of the stopped check to the bank in the latter part of

January, 1957. The bank denied that it was liable because the deposit contract that appeared on the signature card which Haman had signed when he opened the account stated, "This bank will not be liable for any amount paid on any forged . . . check, nor for any difference of account, unless written notice thereof is delivered to this bank within 10 days after date of mailing or delivering the depositor's statement," and "Any request for stop payment must be in writing on a form prescribed by this bank, and this bank will not be liable . . . for paying the item through accident or oversight." From a judgment in favor of the bank, the depositor appealed.

ROBERTS, J. . . . Plaintiff urges that a notice was not necessary for the reason that the bank had actual knowledge of the claimed difference and that the law does not require a useless act. It can be said that the bank had knowledge of its own act, but the purpose of the notice is not only to inform the bank of the fact of improper payment but of plaintiff's claims and intentions. . . . Perhaps . . . defendant was at fault; but the point is if the notice had been given, it might have been able to have shown the contrary. At any rate, it appears to be a reasonable construction of the contract to conclude that notice should be given in such cases so that a bank with multiple transactions is forewarned in sufficient time so that it may ascertain the facts and protect itself against unjust claims. . . .

It is conceded that defendant bank owed plaintiff depositor the absolute duty to pay out his money only according to plaintiff's order. If there is a breach of a depositor's instruction to stop payment, a bank under accepted common-law principles becomes obligated to pay the depositor the amount charged against his account. It is contended that the stipulations referred to limit liability on paying a check in disregard of a stop-payment order and are valid and enforceable.

There can be no mistake in regard to the meaning of the words any "difference of account" in the deposit contract. . . . The relation of a bank and depositor is simply that of debtor and creditor. The bank agrees with the depositor to receive and credit his deposits and to honor his checks to the amount of his credit when checks are presented. The term "account" as used in such agreement is an account in the ordinary acceptation of that term, that is, a statement of debits and credits entered on the books of the bank during a stated period of time. . . . "The later decisions support the general rule that it is the duty of a depositor in a bank to examine the balanced pass book, statement of account, or canceled checks returned to him by the bank, within a reasonable time after receiving them, and to report to the bank any forgeries, or other discrepancies in the amounts, which he may discover." Under the general law and the terms of the deposit contract, plaintiff was required to examine the statement and to report any discrepancy resulting from debiting the check in controversy.

The deposit contract limits the time within which to examine and give notice of "difference of account" to ten days after date of mailing or delivery of bank statement to the depositor. A bank undoubtedly has the right to determine for itself whether or not it will accept a deposit, and it may agree upon the terms and conditions on which the deposit will be accepted so long as they are not in conflict with a controlling statute or other rule of law. . . .

. . . The deposit contract whereby the depositor agreed to examine monthly statements and to report forgeries or other discrepancies in the amounts which he may discover became a part of the contract between the bank and the depositor and in the absence of waiver or other special circumstance are binding.

The deposit contract, as we have indicated, also includes the limitation that the bank shall not be liable for paying a stop-payment item through "accident or oversight." Such stipulations relieving banks from liability for payment of checks in disregard of stop-payment orders are usually contained in stop-payment orders. The weight of authority supports the view that such a stipulation in a stop-payment order constitutes a valid and enforceable contract. . . .

Other authorities are to the effect that such a stipulation in a stop-payment order is invalid on the ground of want of consideration and as against public policy. These courts reason that a bank having money to the credit of a depositor is not at liberty to demand a waiver of liability before undertaking performance of the legal duty to honor a stop payment order. . . . The provisions of the deposit contract releasing the bank from liability from paying a stop-payment item as the result of accident or oversight absolves the bank except, of course, for willful disregard of a stop-payment order. . . .

. . . The provisions requiring notice to the bank of "difference of account" and those relieving the bank from liability for payment of a stop-payment item through "accident or oversight" except, of course, for willful disregard of such an order, constituted binding contractual obligations upon the plaintiff barring recovery. . . .

[Judgment affirmed.]

HANSON, J., dissenting. . . . The ultimate issue here is whether the defendant bank or the plaintiff depositor should sustain loss of a check negligently paid by the bank in disregard of the depositor's timely and valid order to stop payment. The failure of the bank to honor the stop-payment order is unexplained. Likewise, there is no evidence to show the bank exercised, or attempted to exercise, ordinary or reasonable care in the matter. Instead, the bank seeks to exonerate itself from all liability for its negligent conduct by reason of the following two provisions written in fine print on the reverse side of the depositor's signature card·

I. "This bank will not be liable for any amount paid on any forged or altered item including forged indorsements, nor for any missing canceled check, nor for any difference of account, unless written notice thereof is delivered to this bank within 10 days after date of mailing or delivering the depositor's statement; and if the depositor fails to give such notice, or if any statement or canceled checks are lost in transit, the bank's record of the account shall be accepted as correct," and

II. "Any request for stop payment must be made in writing on a form prescribed by this bank, and this bank will not be liable in any way for refusing payment of the item nor for paying the item through accident or oversight."

The Depositor's Contract was written and prepared by the bank. Its provisions serve to limit, restrict, or entirely exonerate the bank from its common-law duties and responsibilities to its depositors. As such, it should be construed most strongly against the bank and most liberally in favor of its depositors. . . .

The two contractual provisions are patently incompatible and cannot reasonably be conjointly construed together in favor of the bank. The second provision deals expressly and exclusively with stop payment requests. It purports to relieve the bank from all liability "in any way . . . for paying the item through accident or oversight." This absolute exemption from liability is inconsistent with the 10-day notice of any difference of account clause. In other words, the difference-of-account clause allows a depositor ten days of grace. If he gives the bank notice of any difference of account within that period the bank is liable. Thus, the "difference of account" clause obviously was never intended to apply to checks paid by the bank in disregard of a stop payment request. The express provision which purports to relieve the bank from all liability for failure to honor a request to stop payment precludes application of the general inconsistent "difference of account" clause in accord with the elementary rule of construction that the express mention of one thing implies the exclusion of another. . . .

In my opinion the remaining stipulation which purports to release the bank of all liability for negligently paying a check after receiving a request to stop payment is contrary to public policy and void.

There is little freedom of contract between a depositor and a bank. Their bargaining positions are not equal. A depositor must accept the services of a bank on its terms or not at all. We have said that commercial banking is affected with public interest. . . . Banks are franchised and statutorily protected against open competition. Most communities of this state have only one bank. Charters are sparingly granted only after a showing of public convenience and necessity. . . . It would logically follow that banks, like . . . other franchised businesses affected with a public interest, should not be allowed to relieve themselves from all liability for negligent conduct by contract. . . .

Other courts have considered the validity of similar stipulations. Some courts have upheld validity . . .: [citing Indiana, Massachusetts, and New York cases].

Early annotators have referred to these cases as the "weight of authority" . . . and, more recently, as the "slight preponderance of authority." . . . However, numerous recent cases have swung the pendulum in the opposite direction. Today the decided weight of authority holds such stipulations invalid either as against public policy or for lack of consideration: [citing Alabama, California, Connecticut, New Jersey, Ohio, Pennsylvania, and South Carolina cases]. . . .

Since 1926, Indiana has been the only court to uphold the validity of a contract stipulation relieving a bank from liability for payment order. Seven courts have declared them invalid. Sound reasoning dictates we should do likewise.

It is interesting to note the Uniform Commercial Code reflects the prevailing view on this question. According to Section 4-103 Subsection 1 thereof ". . . no agreement can disclaim a bank's responsibility for its own lack of good faith or failure to exercise ordinary care or can limit the measure of damages for such lack or failure. . . ."

I would accordingly reverse the judgment appealed from.

Code Comment: As noted by the dissenting opinion, the exoneration or no-liability clause would be held invalid under the Code. The defense of the bank would then rest solely on the depositor's failure to have given notice within the 10-day period. As a matter of construction, the dissenting view is preferable as to the point that this 10-day clause had no application to the stopping of payments since that was governed by the other clause. Even if the 10-day clause is applicable to stop-payment cases, it would appear to be void under the Code section noted by the dissent. This conclusion is strengthened by the policy of the Code to make loss from the disregard of stop-payment orders an incident of the operating expense of running a bank. See Official Code Comment to UCC Sec. 4-403 point 2.

Plitt v. Grim

220 Md. 632, 155 A.2d 672 (1959)

Grim, who operated a bookkeeping and tax service, acted as bookkeeper and financial advisor to the Wal-Tay Nursing Home. The latter was in great financial difficulty, which was temporarily met by Grim's obtaining a loan for the home from Plitt. The loan was represented by five postdated checks payable a month apart, drawn by the owners of the home, naming Grim as the payee, and indorsed by him to Plitt on receiving the money. At the time this was done, all the parties knew that the bank account of the drawers of the checks had been closed, that the first check would be paid from the current income of the home, and that the remaining checks could not be cashed. When those later checks were not paid on time,

Grim took part in obtaining extensions of time. Later when the checks were not paid, Plitt sued Grim as indorser. He defended on the ground that no presentment had been made nor notice of dishonor given. From a judgment in Grim's favor, Plitt appealed.

HAMMOND, J. . . . [The NIL] sec. 130 provides that "notice of dishonor may be waived, either before the time of giving notice has arrived, or after the omission to give due notice, and the waiver may be express or implied." Sec. 103 has similar provisions as to presentment. Section 130 is declaratory of the common law. . . . "A waiver of notice of dishonor may be implied by any conduct or words of the indorser by which the holder of the note is reasonably induced to believe that such waiver was intended," and . . . usage, words or acts which by fair and reasonable construction are of such a character as will satisfy the mind that a waiver was intended, or which will justify the holder in assuming, that the indorser intended to dispense with notice, will permit a finding of waiver. . . .

Waiver of presentment and of notice of dishonor by an indorser often have been inferred by the Courts, from acquiescence, or implied, in extension of the time for payment of the note. . . . "It is a well-supported view that consent by an indorser of a note to extension of the time of payment is of itself sufficient to indicate that presentment and notice of dishonor have been waived.". . .

We find the record almost to compel the inference that Grim waived presentment and notice of dishonor. Although it has been held that, standing alone, the indorser's knowledge of the maker's insolvency will not excuse the giving of notice of dishonor, there is more here. Plitt and Grim knew of Wal-Tay's almost desperate financial straits at the time of the making of the [loan]. A month later, they knew that the bank account had been closed, that the four remaining checks would never be presented for payment, and that Wal-Tay was using almost all of its income . . . to pay the first installment due April 12. . . . Grim participated in . . . extension arrangement[s as to the later checks]. Grim himself says that at the time of the arranging for the extension of payment of the second installment, "we" had made arrangements to keep on extending the times of payments of the checks until "we" got on our feet. . . .

. . . The record shows that Grim did not expect that [later] installments would be paid when due. . . . Grim's conduct was such as to fairly and reasonably have justified Plitt in assuming that he did not expect nor desire presentment or notice of dishonor.

Presentment and notice of dishonor were not required, under the circumstances, as a condition precedent to Grim's liability on his indorsement.

[Judgment reversed.]

Code Comment: The same decision would be made by this court under the Code, for the absence of presentment, notice, or protest is excused as to a party who "has waived it expressly or by implication either before or after it is due." UCC Sec. 3-511(2)(a). The same conclusion is also reached on the theory that because of Grim's knowledge of the financial condition of Wal-Tay Nursing Home, he did not have any reason to believe nor any right to require that the checks be paid. UCC Sec. 3-511(2)(b).

Worthen Bank & Trust Co. v. Kelley-Nelson Const. Co.

219 Ark. 882, 245 S.W.2d 405 (1952)

Kelley-Nelson Construction Co. had a bank account with the Worthen Bank & Trust Co. Over a period of 11 months Eldridge, a part-time employee of the construction company, forged 24 checks in the name of Nelson as drawer and cashed them at the bank. The bank charged the account of Kelley-Nelson with the amount of such checks. The construction company then sued the bank for the amount so charged. The bank defended on the ground that the construction company had failed to examine its monthly canceled checks and statements to determine whether there were forgeries. The trial court submitted to a jury the question whether the construction company was negligent in failing to make such an examination. From a judgment for the construction company, the bank appealed.

S. M. GOODWIN, S.J. . . . Notice should first be taken of certain evidence offered by the bank. Three of its officers and employees explained in great detail how meticulous the bank was in sight-posting and machine-posting these checks, always with the signatures of Kelley and Nelson before them. This evidence establishes beyond any question that the bank exercised a high degree of care in examining Nelson's signature to the checks before it cashed them and charged them to the company's account. And yet we are met by the stubborn fact that, entirely apart from the bank's good faith in the premises, it honored the forged checks sued on. . . .

Even if a bank has employed every known means, device, and test in an effort to avoid the payment of a forged check and has thereby exercised the highest degree of care in protecting its depositor, it will, if the check is forged, be liable to him unless the depositor "is precluded from setting up the forgery or want of authority"; and "no degree of care on the part of the bank will excuse it from liability." In other words, although the forgery is a "perfect" one, the bank is liable unless the depositor is precluded.

. . . The one material issue in this case is: Was it proper for the trial court to submit to the jury the question whether the depositor . . . exercised ordinary care in its monthly examination of the canceled checks and bank statements which the bank mailed to it?

In cases involving facts similar to those in the case at bar on the question whether a depositor has exercised the degree of care which the law imposes on him in detecting a forgery, there are three lines of authorities: (1) Those courts which hold the bank liable for forgery, even though the depositor never examined the monthly bank statement or his canceled checks; (2) those courts which hold that the depositor is liable as a matter of law for failure to examine the monthly bank statement and canceled checks with sufficient particularity to discover the forgery; and (3) those courts which hold that it is a question for the jury to determine whether the depositor exercised ordinary care in examining the monthly bank statement and canceled checks, even though the examination was not made with sufficient particularity to discover the forgery. . . .

We reject [the first] view, since we are of the opinion that the depositor does owe a duty to the bank where, as there and here, the bank returns to him monthly his canceled checks and a statement of his account. The extent of that duty will be considered later in this opinion. . . .

. . . We reject the [second view since it goes] too far in the other direction in holding, as a matter of law, that the depositor did not exercise ordinary care. . . .

The third line of authorities adheres to the rule which we have adopted in the Bank of Black Rock case [148 Ark. 11, 229 S.W. 1]. There the depositor kept a forged check seven days without complaining that it had been forged, and permitted the bank to charge the check to its account. The question was whether the depositor was "precluded from setting up the forgery." The trial court directed a verdict in favor of the depositor. This court reversed that judgment, holding that "it became its (the depositor's) duty to examine the checks when returned to it and exercise reasonable care to see whether any of them had been forged and, if so, to notify the bank of that fact," adding, 148 Ark. 17, 229 S.W. at page 3: "Under the circumstances, . . . the [trial] court erred in directing a verdict for appellee, and that it should have submitted to the jury the question of whether or not appellee had exercised ordinary care in examining the checks and discovering the forgery and reporting it to the bank.". . .

We come now to consider the evidence as to the nature of the examination of the bank statements and canceled checks made by the company in the case at bar, together with the related question whether this court can say, as a matter of law, that the examination so made fell short of ordinary care. If reasonable minds might conclude that the company exercised ordinary care in the premises, then the court below properly refused the peremptory instruction and submitted the case to the jury.

[The court then examined the evidence and concluded that the partners had no reason to suspect forgery by the bookkeeper since she had been highly recommended to them and her books balanced when audited. There was also evidence that one or both partners would go over the canceled checks each month having in mind the accounts to which they applied. The court concluded that this was sufficient evidence to make it proper to submit to a jury the question whether the firm had exercised due care to detect the forgeries.]

[Judgment affirmed.]

Code Comment: The same decision would be reached by this court under the Code. The Code requires that the depositor "exercise reasonable care and promptness to examine the statement and items to discover his unauthorized signature . . . and . . . notify the bank promptly after discovery thereof." UCC Sec. 4-406(1). With respect to whether it is the jury or the judge who determines whether such care has been exercised, a Code state would follow its general principles of jury trial practice (see Sec. 1-103), and hold that the court could make such determination when the facts were so clear that only one possible verdict could be allowed to stand. Conversely, if there could be two different views taken of the evidence so that a verdict either in favor or against the depositor would be allowed to stand as supported by substantial or reasonable evidence, then the question is to be determined by the jury.

Questions and Case Problems

1. What is the objective of each of the following rules of law?
    (a) A bad check that is not made good within a stated period will be presumed to have been issued originally with the intent to defraud.
    (b) The drawer has the power to stop payment of his check.

2. Pflaum mailed a check for $5,000 to the Laura Baker School and stated in the accompanying letter that it was a gift to the school which it could use for any purpose. Before the check was presented to the bank for payment, Pflaum stopped payment on it. The school then sued on the check. Decide. (Laura Baker School v. Pflaum, 225 Minn. 181, 30 N.W. 2d 290)

3. Bogash drew a check on the National Safety Bank and Trust Co. payable to the order of the Fiss Corp. At the request of the corporation, the bank certified the check. The bank later refused to make payment on the check because there was a dispute between Bogash and the corporation as to the amount due the corporation. The corporation sued the bank on the check. Decide. (Fiss Corp. v. National Safety Bank and Trust Co., 191 Misc. 397, 77 N.Y.S.2d 293)

4. Berg, who had a checking account in the Central National Bank, drew a check on that bank payable to the order of Anschutz. Colucci obtained the check from Berg by fraudulent misrepresentation and forged

the name of Anschutz as an indorsement. The check was subsequently negotiated several times and then presented by a subsequent holder to the Central National Bank for payment. The bank, without knowing that the payee's indorsement was a forgery, paid the amount of the check to the apparent holder. Thereafter Anschutz sued the bank for the amount of the check. Was the bank liable? (Anschutz v. Central National Bank, [Neb.] 112 N.W.2d 545)

5. Steinbaum executed and delivered a check payable to the order of the White Way Motors, which was the name under which DiFranco was doing business. Before the check was paid, Steinbaum stopped payment on the check. DiFranco sued Steinbaum on the check. Decide. (DiFranco v. Steinbaum, [Mo.App.] 177 S.W.2d 697)

6. Goldsmith told his employee to draw a check on the Atlantic National Bank to the employee's order for $10.10. The employee wrote the check in his own hand, leaving space to the left of the amount. After Goldsmith signed the check, the employee filled in the spaces to the left of the amount, thus raising the check to $2,110.10. The employee presented the check to the bank, which made payment of the raised amount. Goldsmith sued the bank for the raised amount. Decide. (Goldsmith v. Atlantic National Bank, [Fla.] 55 So.2d 804)

7. Silver, an attorney, had an account labeled "special account" in the Commonwealth Trust Co. Part of the fund on deposit was money belonging to his client, Goldstein. Silver drew a check on this account for his own use. Goldstein sued the bank claiming that it had no right to honor the check because the bank should have known that the account included the money of third persons and that the attorney was making improper use of the money. Decide. (Goldstein v. Commonwealth Trust Co., 19 N.J.S. 39, 87 A.2d 555)

8. Doodan, who owed money to Szawlinsky, delivered a check for the amount due Szawlinsky, but the latter never cashed the check. Doodan claimed that the continued retention of the check discharged the debt. Decide. (Doodan v. Szawlinsky, 197 Pa.Super 623, 179 A.2d 661)

9. Stone & Webster drew a check on the First National Bank of Boston payable to the order of Westinghouse in payment of a debt. Before the check could be mailed to Westinghouse, an employee of Stone & Webster forged the indorsement of Westinghouse and cashed the check at the First National Bank & Trust Company of Greenfield. The Greenfield bank then presented the check for payment to the drawee bank, the First National Bank of Boston. The latter paid the Greenfield bank the amount of the check and then debited the account of Stone & Webster with the amount of the check. Stone & Webster then sued the Greenfield bank for the amount of the check. Was the plaintiff entitled to recover? (Stone & Webster Eng. Co. v. First National Bank of Greenfield, [Mass.] 184 N.E.2d 358)

CHAPTER 32

Rights of Holders and Defenses

When a contract right is assigned, the assignee's right is subject to any defenses existing between the original parties prior to the notice of the assignment. For example, when the seller assigns his right to collect the purchase price, the buyer may assert against the seller's assignee the defense that the buyer never received the goods. It is immaterial through how many successive assignees the right has been transferred and whether or not the assignees acted in good faith, in ignorance of the original defenses, and gave value for their assignments. Such a principle of law should make a prospective assignee of a contract right extremely cautious. He should make inquiry as to the existence of defenses, particularly by the original obligor.

If the holder of a negotiable instrument were required to conduct such an investigation in every instance in order to protect himself, the utility of commercial paper would be greatly impaired. First the law merchant, then the Negotiable Instrument Law, and now the Uniform Commercial Code have met this problem by giving certain holders of commercial paper a preferred standing by protecting them from the operation of certain defenses. Such a favored holder may be either a holder in due course or a holder through a holder in due course. If the holder is not one of these favored holders, he has only the same standing as an ordinary assignee and is subject to all defenses to which an ordinary assignee would be subject.[1]

Holders—Rights and Special Classes

Sec. 32-A. Rights of Holders. A holder, whether favored or not, has the right to demand payment or to sue on the instrument.[2] Whether he recovers depends upon whether the person sued is liable to him and whether there is any defense that may be asserted against him.

---

[1] See p. 199.
[2] Uniform Commercial Code, Sec. 3-301; Negotiable Instruments Law, Sec. 51.

In accord with general principles of court procedure, the defendant in such a case has the burden of proof as to a defense. (See p. 506, Taylor v. Hamden Hall School)

The holder of the instrument is the only person who is entitled to demand payment or to sue on it. If a person is a holder, it is immaterial that he is merely a holder for collection, such as an agent holding the instrument under a restrictive indorsement in order to collect the amount due, or a trustee holding for the benefit of other persons.

Ordinarily a holder may sue any prior indorser without regard to the order of liability as between the indorsers themselves.

The holder is the only one who may grant a discharge of, or cancel liability on, the instrument.

Sec. 32-B. Holder in Due Course. In order to be a holder in due course, the person must first be a holder. This means that he must be either in possession of order paper properly indorsed or of bearer paper.

(1) Necessary Elements. In addition to being a holder, the holder in due course must meet certain conditions that pertain to (a) value, (b) good faith, (c) ignorance of paper overdue or dishonored, (d) ignorance of defenses and adverse claims.[3]

(a) VALUE. Since the law of commercial paper is fundamentally a merchant's or businessman's law, it favors only the holders who have given value for the paper. Accordingly, a person receiving a negotiable instrument as a gift, such as a check for a birthday present, cannot be a holder in due course.

A person has taken an instrument for value (1) when he has performed the act for which the instrument was given, such as delivering the goods for which the check is sent in payment; (2) when he has acquired a security interest in the paper, such as when it has been pledged with him as security for another obligation; or (3) when he has taken the instrument in payment or as security for a debt.[4]

When an instrument is deposited with a bank, the latter does not become a holder for value by the mere fact that it credits the customer's account with the amount of the deposit when the customer has not yet drawn upon the credit. It is at the latter time that the bank becomes a holder for value.[5]

(b) GOOD FAITH. The element of good faith requires that the taker of commercial paper has acted honestly in the acquisition of the

---

[3] UCC Sec. 3-302(1). See NIL Sec. 52.

[4] UCC Sec. 3-303. It is also provided that there is a taking for value when another negotiable instrument is given in exchange or when the taker makes an irrecoverable commitment to a third person as by providing a letter of credit. Sec. 3-303(c).

[5] See p. 483.

instrument. Bad faith may sometimes be indicated by the small value given. This does not mean that the transferee must give full value, but that a gross inadequacy of consideration may be evidence of bad faith. Bad faith is established by proof that the transferee had knowledge of such facts as rendered it improper for him to acquire the instrument under the circumstances.

If the transferee takes the instrument in good faith, it is immaterial whether his transferor acted in good faith.

(c) IGNORANCE OF PAPER OVERDUE OR DISHONORED. Commercial paper may be negotiated even though (1) it has been dishonored, whether by nonacceptance or nonpayment; or (2) the paper is overdue, whether because of lapse of time or the acceleration of the due date; or (3) demand paper has been outstanding more than a reasonable time. In other words, ownership may still be transferred. Nevertheless the fact that the paper is circulating at a late date or after it has been dishonored is a suspicious circumstance that is deemed to put the person acquiring the paper on notice that there is some adverse claim or defense. A person who acquires title to the paper under such circumstances therefore cannot be a holder in due course.

If the fact that the paper is overdue or has been dishonored is not apparent from the paper itself, it is immaterial whether it was in fact overdue or dishonored. The new holder is not affected thereby unless he had knowledge or notice that it was overdue or dishonored.[6]

The purchaser of a commercial paper has notice that the instrument is overdue if he has reasonable grounds to believe " (a) that any part of the principal amount is overdue or that there is an uncured default in payment of another instrument of the same series; or (b) that acceleration of the instrument has been made; or (c) that he is taking a demand instrument after demand has been made or more than a reasonable length of time after its issue. A reasonable time for a check drawn and payable within the states and territories of the United States and the District of Columbia is presumed to be thirty days." [7]

(d) IGNORANCE OF DEFENSES AND ADVERSE CLAIMS. Prior parties on the paper may have defenses which they could raise if sued by the person with whom they had dealt. For example, the drawer of a check, if sued by the payee of the check, might have the defense that the merchandise delivered by the payee was defective. In addition to defenses, third persons, whether prior parties or not, may be able to assert that the instrument belongs to them and not to the holder or to his transferor. A person cannot be a holder in due course if he acquires the

---

[6] Notice, as here used, means that the new holder "from all the facts and circumstances known to him at the time in question . . . has reason to know" that the instrument was overdue or dishonored. UCC Sec. 1-201(25)(c).

[7] Sec. 3-304(3).

commercial paper with notice or knowledge that any party might have a defense or that there is any adverse claim to the ownership of the instrument. Thus he cannot be a holder in due course when he has knowledge of a failure of consideration in an earlier transaction involving the instrument.

When the transferee makes payment for the transfer of the paper in installments and learns of a defense after he has paid in part, he can be a holder in due course as to the payments made before, but not as to payments made after, learning of the existence of the defense.

Knowledge of certain facts constitutes notice to the person acquiring a negotiable instrument that there is a defense or an adverse claim. The holder or purchaser of the paper is deemed to have notice of a claim or defense (1) if the instrument is so incomplete, bears such visible evidence of forgery or alteration, or is otherwise so irregular as to call into question its validity, terms, or ownership, or to create an ambiguity as to the party who is required to pay; or (2) if the purchaser has notice that the obligation of any party is voidable in whole or in part, or that all parties to the paper have been discharged. The purchaser has notice of a claim of ownership of another person to the instrument if he has knowledge that a fiduciary has negotiated the paper in breach of his trust.[8]

A holder does not have notice or knowledge of a defense or adverse claim merely because he knows (1) that the instrument is antedated or postdated; (2) that it was issued or negotiated in return for an executory promise or accompanied by a separate agreement, unless the purchaser has notice that a defense or claim has arisen from the terms thereof; (3) that any party has signed for accommodation; (4) that an incomplete instrument has been completed, unless the purchaser has notice of any improper completion; (5) that any person negotiating the instrument is or was a fiduciary; or (6) that there has been a default in payment of interest on the instrument or in payment of any other instrument, except one of the same series. The fact that a document having some relation to the instrument has been filed or recorded does not constitute notice which will prevent a person from being a holder in due course.[9]

(2) Who May Be a Holder in Due Course. Any person may be a holder in due course. This includes the payee of the instrument provided he satisfies the necessary elements. Ordinarily the payee deals directly with the drawer and therefore would have knowledge of any defense that the latter might raise. The factual situation in which the payee becomes a holder in due course is therefore generally one

---

8 Sec. 3-304(1),(2)
9 Sec. 3-304(4),(5).

in which the payee acted through an intermediary so that in fact he did not deal with the drawer but acquired the paper from the intermediary, even though the paper was made payable to his order. The net result is the same as though the drawer had made the check payable to the intermediary who in turn indorsed it to the payee.

Certain types of purchases of commercial paper do not make the purchaser a holder in due course although he otherwise satisfies all the elements here considered; on the theory that the sales are not of an ordinary, everyday commercial nature and therefore the buyer need not be given the higher degree of protection afforded a holder in due course. Thus a person is not a holder in due course when he acquires the paper by means of a judicial sale or legal process, the sale of the assets of an estate, or a bulk sale not in the course of the business of the transferor.[10]

(3) Proof of Status as Holder in Due Course. The status of the holder does not become important until a person sued by the holder raises a defense that can be asserted against an ordinary holder but not against a holder in due course or a holder through a holder in due course. Initially the plaintiff in the action is entitled to recover as soon as the commercial paper is put in evidence and the signatures on it are admitted to be genuine. If the genuine character of any signature is specifically denied, the burden is then on the plaintiff to prove that the signature is genuine.[11] Once the signatures are admitted or established, the plaintiff-holder is entitled to recover unless the defendant establishes a defense. The plaintiff then has the burden of establishing that he is a holder in due course (see p. 507, Altex Aluminum Supply Co. v. Asay), or a holder through a holder in due course, in order to avoid such defense.[12]

Sec. 32-C. Holder Through a Holder in Due Course. Those persons who become holders of the instrument after a holder in due course are given the same protection as the holder in due course provided they are not parties to any fraud or illegality that would affect the instrument.[13]

This means that if an instrument is indorsed from *A* to *B* to *C* to *D* and that if *B* is a holder in due course, both *C* and *D* will enjoy the same rights as *B*. If *C* received the instrument as a gift or with knowledge of failure of consideration or other defense, or if *D* took

---

[10] Sec. 3-302(3).

[11] Sec. 3-307(1). The plaintiff is aided by a presumption that the signature is genuine or authorized except where the action is to enforce the obligation of a signer who has died or become incompetent. Sec. 3-307(1)(b).

[12] Sec. 3-307(3). If the defense is one that may be asserted against any holder, it is immaterial whether the plaintiff is a holder in due course.

[13] UCC Sec. 3-201(1), NIL Sec. 58.

the instrument after maturity, they could not themselves be holders in due course. Nevertheless, they are given the same protection as a holder in due course because they took the instrument through such a holder, namely, *B*. It is not only *C*, the person taking directly from *B*, but also *D*, who takes indirectly through *B*, who is given this extra protection.

These rights have been conferred by the law upon the holders through a holder in due course not to favor them but to protect the holder in due course. If such a person has a commercial paper which he can enforce but a prospective transferee from him will not be able to enforce it, he obviously would have difficulty in selling the instrument at a fair value. Thus in order to facilitate the sale of the instrument by the holder in due course, the transferee is given the protection that the instrument will be just as valid in his hands as it was in the hands of the holder in due course.

Defenses

The importance of being a holder in due course or a holder through a holder in due course is that those holders are not subject to certain defenses when they demand payment or bring suit upon a negotiable instrument. Another class of defenses may be asserted against any holder without regard to whether he is an ordinary holder, a holder in due course, on a holder through a holder in due course. A holder who is neither a holder in due course nor a holder through a holder in due course is subject to every defense just as though the instrument were not negotiable.[14]

Sec. 32-D. Defenses Available Against an Ordinary Holder. When suit is brought by the original payee, he is subject to every defense that the defendant may possess, unless he qualifies as a holder in due course.[15]

There is a growing tendency to hold that a finance company which takes an active part in arranging the details of a sale is not to be regarded as a holder in due course of a note given by the buyer to the seller and negotiated by the seller to the finance company. In such a case the finance company is regarded as a party to the original transaction and therefore an ordinary holder.

The fact that a person cannot recover on a negotiable instrument does not necessarily mean that he is not entitled to recover in another action or against another party. He may be able to recover on a

---

[14] The UCC eliminates the terminology of the former law of real and personal defenses and treats defenses as merely those that can and those that cannot be asserted against a holder in due course. For convenience the defenses that can only be asserted against an ordinary holder may be described as *limited* defenses and those that can be asserted against all holders may be described as *universal*.

[15] See p. 498.

contract that was part of the transaction in which the instrument was given. It is also possible that he may be able to hold a party to the instrument liable for breach of an implied warranty or to recover from a person expressly guaranteeing payment of the instrument.

Sec. 32-E. Limited Defenses—Not Available Against a Holder in Due Course. Neither a holder in due course nor one having the rights of such a holder is subject to any of the following defenses: [16]

(1) Simple Contract Defenses. In general terms, the defenses that could be raised against a suit on a simple contract cannot be raised against the holder in due course. Accordingly the defendant cannot assert against the holder in due course the defense of lack, failure, or illegality of consideration with respect to the transaction between the defendant and the person with whom he dealt. In contrast, in an action upon an ordinary contract, the promisor may defend on the ground that there was no consideration for his promise; or that if there was consideration in the form of a counterpromise, that promise was never performed; or that the consideration was illegal.[17] Thus, if contractor *C* promises to paint the roof of owner *O's* house but fails to perform properly, *O* would be entitled to sue *C* for breach of his contract or to refuse to pay him the contract price. If *C* should assign his right to payment to an assignee, *O* could raise the same defenses when sued by the assignee as though sued by *C*.

Assume, however, that *O* gives *C* a check in payment of the contract price before *O* learns that the work is improper. If the check is negotiated to a holder in due course, *O* cannot refuse to pay the check on the ground of failure of consideration. He must pay the check according to its tenor. His only remedy is to sue the contractor *C* for the loss which he has caused.

The fact that an instrument is not enforceable by a foreign corporation that has not registered to do business in the state does not affect the right of a holder in due course to sue thereon unless a statute expressly declares that the instrument is void. (See p. 509, Salitan Case)

(2) Incapacity of Defendant. The incapacity of the defendant, with the exception of minority,[18] may not be raised against a holder in due course unless by general principles of law that incapacity makes the instrument a nullity.[19]

(3) Fraud in the Inducement. When a person knows that he is executing a commercial paper and knows its essential terms but is

---

[16] UCC Sec. 3-305.
[17] See p. 122.
[18] See p. 157.
[19] UCC Sec. 3-305(2)(b).

persuaded or induced to execute it because of false statements or representations, he cannot defend against a holder in due course or a holder through a holder in due course on the ground of such fraud. As an illustration, *A* is persuaded to purchase an automobile because of *B's* statement concerning its condition. *A* gives *B* a note, which is negotiated until it reaches *E*, who is a holder in due course. *A* meanwhile learns that the car is not as represented and that *B's* statements were fraudulent. When *E* demands payment of the note, *A* cannot refuse to pay him because of the fraud of *B*. He must pay the instrument and then recover his loss from *B*, assuming that he can find *B* and that *B* can be made to pay the judgment.

(4) Prior Payment or Cancellation. When a commercial paper is paid before maturity, the person making the payment should demand the surrender of the instrument. If he fails to obtain the instrument, it is possible for the holder to continue to negotiate it. Another person may thus become the holder of the instrument. When the new holder demands payment of the instrument, the defense cannot be raised that payment had been made if the new holder is a holder in due course or a holder through a holder in due course. The fact that the person making the payment obtained a receipt from the holder does not affect the application of this principle.

When the holder and the party primarily liable have agreed to cancel the instrument but the face of the instrument does not show any sign of cancellation, the defense of cancellation cannot be asserted against a holder in due course. Similarly, an order to stop payment of a check cannot be raised as a defense by the drawer of a check against a holder in due course.[20]

(5) Nondelivery. A person may make out a commercial paper or indorse an existing instrument and then leave it on his desk for future delivery. At that moment the instrument or the indorsement is not effective because there has been no delivery.

Assume that through the negligence of an employee or through the theft of the instrument, it comes into the hands of another person. If the instrument is in such form that it can be negotiated, as when it is payable to bearer, a subsequent receiver of the instrument may be a holder in due course or a holder through a holder in due course. As against him, the person who made out the instrument or indorsed it cannot defend on the ground that he did not deliver it.

No distinction is made under the Code between a nondelivered instrument that was complete and one which had not been completed by the person executing it. In either case, the defense of nondelivery cannot be raised against the holder in due course.

---

[20] See p. 478.

(6) Conditional or Specified Purpose Delivery. As against a favored holder, a person who would be liable on the instrument cannot show that the instrument which is absolute on its face was in fact delivered subject to a condition that had not been performed, or that it was delivered for a particular purpose but was not so used. Assume that *A* makes out a check to the order of *B* and hands it to *C* with the understanding that *C* shall not deliver the check to *B* until *B* delivers certain merchandise. If *C* should deliver the check to *B* before the condition is satisfied and *B* then negotiates the check, a holder in due course or a holder through a holder in due course may enforce the instrument.

Similarly, if the instrument is itself restrictively indorsed to subject it to a condition, the defendant may not raise against the holder in due course the defense that payment to him would be inconsistent with the restriction.

Somewhat similar to the defense of a conditional delivery is the defense that delivery was made subject to a particular oral agreement or understanding. As against a holder in due course, a defendant-indorser cannot assert that he has negotiated the instrument to his indorsee under an oral agreement that the negotiation should be without recourse as to him.

(7) Duress. The defense that a person signed or executed a commercial paper under threats of harm or violence may not be raised as a defense against a holder in due course when the effect of such duress is merely to make the contract voidable at the election of the victim of the duress.

(8) Unauthorized Completion. If a maker or drawer signs a commercial paper and leaves blank the name of the payee, or the amount, or any other term, and then hands the instrument to another to be completed, the defense of an improper completion cannot be raised when payment is demanded or suit brought by a subsequent holder in due course or a holder through a holder in due course. That is, he may enforce the instrument as completed.[21]

This situation arises when an employer gives a signed blank check to an employee with instructions to make certain purchases and to fill in the name of the seller and the amount when these are determined. If the employee fills in the name of a friend and a large amount and then the employee and the friend negotiate the instrument, the employer cannot defend against a subsequent holder in due course or a holder through a holder in due course on the ground that the completion had been without the authority of the employer.

(9) Theft. As a matter of definition, a holder in due course will not have acquired the paper through theft and any defense of theft

---

[21] UCC Sec. 3-407 (3).

therefore must relate to the conduct of a prior party. Assuming that the theft of the paper does not result in a defect in the chain of necessary indorsements, the defense that the instrument had been stolen cannot be asserted against a holder in due course.[22]

Sec. 32-F. Universal Defenses—Available Against All Holders. Certain defenses are regarded as so basic that the social interest in preserving them outweighs the social interest of giving commercial paper the free-passing qualities of money. Accordingly, such defenses are given universal effect and may be raised against all holders, whether ordinary holders, holders in due course, or holders through a holder in due course.

(1) Fraud as to the Nature and Essential Terms of the Instrument. If a person signs a commercial paper because he has been fraudulently deceived as to its nature and essential terms, and if he was not negligent in allowing himself to be deceived, he has a defense available against all holders. This is the situation when an experienced businessman induces an illiterate person to sign a note by falsely representing that it is a contract for repairs.[23] (See p. 511, Bancredit, Inc. v. Bethea)

(2) Forgery or Lack of Authority. The defense that a signature was forged or signed without authority may be raised against any holder unless the defendant is estopped by his conduct or negligence from raising that defense.[24]

(3) Duress. When a person executes or indorses a commercial paper in response to a threat of such a nature that under general principles of law there is duress which makes the transaction a nullity, rather than merely voidable, such duress may be raised as a defense against any holder.[25]

(4) Incapacity. The fact that the defendant is a minor who under general principles of contract law may avoid his obligation is a matter that may be raised against any kind of holder. Other kinds of incapacity may only be raised as a defense if the effect of the incapacity is to make the instrument a nullity.[26]

(5) Illegality. If the law declares that an instrument is void when executed in connection with certain conduct, such as gambling or usury, or when issued by foreign corporations not authorized to do

---

[22] Sec. 3-305 (1).
[23] Sec. 3-305(2)(c).
[24] Sec. 3-404(1).
[25] Sec. 3-305(2)(b).
[26] Sec. 3-305(2)(b).

business within the state, that defense may be raised against any holder. If the law merely makes the transaction illegal but does not make the instrument void, the defense cannot be asserted against a holder in due course or a holder through a holder in due course.[27]

(6) Alteration. The fact that an instrument has been altered may be raised against any holder. Unlike other defenses, however, it is only a partial defense as against a holder in due course. That is, the latter holder may enforce the instrument according to its original terms prior to its alteration.[28] Moreover, if the person sued by the holder in due course has substantially contributed by his negligence to making the alteration possible, that defendant is precluded from asserting the defense of alteration.[29]

An alteration does not have any effect unless it is both material and is fraudulently made. An alteration is material when it changes the contract of any party in any way, as by changing the date, place of payment, rate of interest, or any other term. It also includes any modification that changes the number or the relationship of the parties to the paper, by adding new terms, or by cutting off a part of the paper itself.[30] Conversely, the adding or crossing out of words on the instrument which do not affect the contract of any party is not material.

An alteration must be made to the instrument itself. An oral or a collateral written agreement between the holder and one of the parties that modifies the obligation of the party is not an "alteration" within the sense just discussed, even though the obligation of the party is changed or altered thereby.

By definition an alteration is a change made by a party to the instrument. A change of the instrument made by a stranger has no effect, and recovery on the instrument is the same as though the change had not been made provided it can be proved what the instrument had been in its original form.

Sec. 32-G. Adverse Claims to the Instrument. Distinct from a defense which a defendant may raise against a plaintiff as a reason why he should not be required to pay the instrument is a claim of a third person that he and not the plaintiff is the holder or owner of the commercial paper. Assume that a check was made to the order of *A*, that thereafter blank indorsements are made by *B*, *C*, and *D*, and that *E* in possession of the check appears to be the holder. *B* might then claim and show, if such be the case, that he indorsed the check because

---

27 Sec. 3-305(2) (b).
28 Sec. 3-407 (3).
29 Sec. 3-406. This estoppel may also arise in favor of a drawee or other payor who pays the instrument as altered in good faith, when acting in accord with the reasonable commercial standards of his business. Sec. 3-406.
30 Sec. 3-407(1).

he was fraudulently deceived by *C*; that he avoids his indorsement because of such fraud; and that accordingly the check still belongs to him. *B* in such case is making an adverse claim to the instrument.

A holder in due course holds commercial paper free and clear from all adverse claims of any other person to the paper, including both equitable and legal interests of third persons, and the right of a former holder to rescind his negotiation.[31] In contrast, such adverse claims may be asserted against a holder who is not a holder in due course,[32] which means that the adverse claimant may bring such action against the holder since the law allows generally for the recovery of property by the owner from anyone else.

Ordinarily a defendant when sued by a holder cannot raise against the holder the defense that the holder's ownership is subject to an adverse claim. This may be done only when the adverse claimant has also become a party to the action or is defending the action on behalf of the defendant.[33] Otherwise it would be unfair to the adverse claimant to pass upon the merits of his claim in his absence, as well as being undesirable in opening the door to perjury by giving any defendant the opportunity of beclouding the issues by raising a false claim that a third person has an adverse interest.

Cases for Chapter 32

Taylor v. Hamden Hall School

182 A.2d 615 (Conn., 1962)

Taylor loaned money to Hamden Hall School. The school, on December 21, 1950, executed a promissory note and mortgage for $65,000 in favor of Taylor and his wife. Subsequently Taylor died. When the school was sued on the note by Taylor's widow, it claimed that there had not been any loan and therefore there was no consideration for the note. Judgment was entered in favor of the widow for $39,000, and interest was allowed from the date of Taylor's death on July 3, 1956. All parties appealed.

ALCORN, A.J. . . . . [The defendant's] argument is that the . . . facts fail to support the conclusion of a valid mortgage loan in any amount. The court has found, however, that the note and the mortgage are in proper form, duly executed and acknowledged by the proper officers of the defendant, and prima facie valid. The note was negotiable in form. . . . Therefore, it is deemed prima facie to have been issued for a valuable consideration, and the burden of proving absence or failure of consideration rested on the defendant. . . . The defendant [did not sustain] this burden.

---

31 Sec. 3-305(1), 3-207.
32 Sec. 3-306 (d).
33 Sec. 3-306(d).

The basic contention of the plaintiff on her cross appeal is that the court erred in concluding that the amount actually loaned by Taylor in connection with the gymnasium mortgage was only $39,000 and in fixing the mortgage debt, in its judgment, at that figure instead of at $65,000. . . . The court fixed the mortgage debt at $39,000 on the theory that the amount actually loaned must control the determination of the amount of the mortgage debt, that the burden of proving the amount loaned was on the plaintiff, and, therefore, that the inability of the [plaintiff] to demonstrate that the amount loaned exceeded $39,000 must redound to the plaintiff's disadvantage. We do not discuss the court's proposition that the amount loaned necessarily controls the determination of the debt. . . . The court, by shifting to the plaintiff the burden of proof on the issue of the amount loaned, placed its determination of the amount of the debt on an unsupportable basis.

The court found that interest was due on the note at the rate of 5 percent per annum from May 17, 1951. The judgment, however, allowed the recovery of interest only from July 3, 1956, the date of Taylor's death. The note does not specify the date from which interest was to run. Therefore, interest ran from the date of the instrument. . . . The plaintiff, however, claims interest only from May 17, 1951. The judgment should also be corrected, therefore, to award interest from that date.

[Action remanded for further proceedings.]

Code Comment: The same decision would be made under the Code. UCC Sec. 3-408, with an exception not here relevant, makes consideration a defense as against an ordinary holder. The burden of proving the absence of consideration is therefore on the defendant. The lower court was in error according to the Code in requiring the plaintiff to prove how much was loaned in return for the note. Under the Code, as soon as the signatures of an instrument are admitted or established, the holder is entitled to recover unless the defendant establishes a defense. UCC Sec. 3-307 (2). That is, even if it could be shown as between the immediate parties that the debt was actually less than the note, the burden of so doing was on the defendant. The same decision would be made as to interest on the note, for the Code provides that unless otherwise specified a provision for interest means interest at the judgment rate at the place of payment from the date of the instrument, or if undated, from the date of issue. UCC Sec. 3-118 (d).

Altex Aluminum Supply Co. v. Asay

72 N.J.S. 582, 178 A.2d 636 (1962)

Asay made a note payable to the order of Home Specialists, Inc. This note in turn was indorsed on behalf of the payee by its president to Altex Aluminum, which indorsee later sued Asay on the note. The latter raised a defense that the note had been delivered subject to a condition. The lower court held that Altex was a holder in due course and was entitled to recover without regard to any condition. The defendant appealed.

SULLIVAN, J.A.D. . . . Defendant . . . claims that his mere denial of the corporate payee's indorsement puts plaintiff to its proof not only that the indorsing signature . . . is genuine but also that such officer was actually authorized to execute such indorsement. . . .

. . . The authority of the president to execute an indorsement of a promissory note on behalf of the corporation in the normal course of business must be presumed; otherwise the negotiability of commercial paper would be seriously impaired. To become a holder in due course, one is not required to satisfy himself of the actual authority of such officer. . . .

It is to be noted that the Uniform Commercial Code, adopted in New Jersey (L. 1961, c. 120), effective January 1, 1963, in Article 3, revises and clarifies the Negotiable Instruments Law, R.S. 7:1 et seq., N.J.S.A. Section 3-307 thereof provides as follows: "(1) Unless specifically denied in the pleadings each signature on an instrument is admitted. When the effectiveness of a signature is put in issue, (a) the burden of establishing it is on the party claiming under the signature; but (b) the signature is presumed to be genuine or authorized except where the action is to enforce the obligation of a purported signer who has died or become incompetent before proof is required."

The comment on this section . . . includes the following: "The question of the burden of establishing the signature arises only when it has been put in issue by specific denial. . . . The burden is on the party claiming under the signature, but he is aided by the presumption that it is genuine or authorized stated in paragraph (b) . 'Presumption' . . . means that until some evidence is introduced which would support a finding that the signature is forged or unauthorized the plaintiff is not required to prove that it is authentic. The presumption rests upon the fact that in ordinary experience forged or unauthorized signatures are very uncommon, and normally any evidence is within the control of the defendant or more accessible to him. He is therefore required to make some sufficient showing of the grounds for his denial before the plaintiff is put to his proof. . . . Until he introduces such evidence, the presumption requires a finding for the plaintiff. Once such evidence is introduced the burden of establishing the signature by a preponderance of the total evidence is on the plaintiff."

Here, plaintiff is the holder of the note and produced testimony . . . that the president of the payee-corporation executed the indorsement. . . . Plaintiff has established that it is a holder in due course and is entitled to judgment. . . .

[Judgment affirmed.]

Salitan v. Carter, Ealey and Dinwiddie

332 S.W.2d 11 (Mo.App., 1960)

Carter, Ealey and Dinwiddie purchased materials in Missouri from the Sterling Materials Co., which was a New York corporation not legally qualified to do business in Missouri. By Missouri law, Sterling's activity of selling without having qualified to do business was unlawful and it could not bring suit on any contract until it had qualified to do business. In payment of the goods, Carter accepted a trade acceptance naming Sterling as the payee. Sterling sold the trade acceptance to Salitan and Jacobs who operated a finance company. The latter was a holder in due course. When suit was brought on the trade acceptance, the defense of illegality was raised. An appeal was made from a decision for the defendant.

HUNTER, J. . . . In 1943 our legislature adopted a new corporation code. . . . We quote therefrom: ". . . No foreign corporation, failing to comply with this act, can maintain any suit or action, either legal or equitable, in any of the courts of this state, upon any demand, whether arising out of the contract of tort, *while the requirements of this Act have not been complied with.*" . . .

It is the contention of defendant that an instrument, such as those before us, where given to a foreign corporation doing business in Missouri without qualifying is, under [section 351.635] a void instrument, and thus, is not enforceable even by a bona fide purchaser for value.

Thus, our first question is whether under new Section 351.635 a contract or trade acceptance is void or whether it is merely unenforceable in Missouri courts until the foreign corporation complies with the requirements of the mentioned chapter. . . .

It is our opinion that the quoted language . . . changed the prior law of Missouri to the end that contracts of nonlicensed foreign corporations are no longer "absolutely void" but rather under Section 351.635 are merely unenforceable until such time as the foreign corporation complies with the requirement of the mentioned chapter and that thereafter such contracts may be enforced just as may any other contract of a foreign corporation made at a time when such corporation was in full compliance with the requirements of the chapter. . . .

We are further strengthened in our views by the support of decisions in other jurisdictions where similar statutes are involved. . . .

There is an additional factor that must be considered; namely, the effect of our Negotiable Instrument Law on such a situation as is presented on this appeal. . . .

It is one thing to deny access to our courts to the unlicensed foreign corporation until it becomes qualified to do business in the state, and quite another thing to deny access to the courts to an innocent holder in due course of a negotiable instrument who seeks to enforce it against its maker. A penalty might be imposed on the unlicensed corporation for wrongfully doing business, and we note there is provision for such penalty in the Missouri Act. An injunction might issue against doing such unlicensed business. Access to the courts by the unlicensed corporation may be denied until there is compliance with the act. But to provide by judicial interpretation further penalties not provided in the statute against an innocent purchaser for value of an apparently negotiable instrument would seem unreasonable. . . .

The generally accepted rule is that where the statute does not declare the instrument to be void, a holder in due course can recover against the maker on a promissory note made to the order of a foreign corporation although it has not complied with the statutory conditions to the right to do business in the state. . . .

In 2 Daniel, Negotiable Instruments, Section 939 (Seventh Edition), it is stated: "A bona fide holder for value who has received the paper in the usual course of business is unaffected by the fact that it originated in an illegal consideration. . . . The law extends this peculiar protection to negotiable instruments, because it would seriously embarrass mercantile transactions to expose the trade to the consequences of having the bill or note passed to him impeached for some [hidden] defect. . . . Thus, where a note given to a nonresident corporation is not enforceable in the hands of the corporation because of doing business in the state in violation of the law of the state, yet it may be enforced in the hands of a purchaser without notice, the statute not declaring such a note void . . . ."

. . . Any other view would place the burden on Missouri business and banking institutions to investigate each and every payee and indorser on each and every instrument in order to determine whether a foreign corporation is unlicensed, and if so, whether it is or is not doing business in Missouri. Such a burden does not seem to be in accord with the basic purpose of the Negotiable Instruments Law. . . .

[Judgment for defendant reversed.]

Code Comment: The same decision is made under the Code once it is determined that as a matter of state corporation law the note given is not void but merely not enforceable by the corporation while it remains not qualified to do business. By UCC Sec. 3-305(2)(b) a holder in due course is not subject to a defense based upon the illegality of the transaction unless it "renders the obligation of the party a nullity."

Bancredit, Inc. v. Bethea

68 N.J.S. 62, 172 A.2d 10 (1961)

When Bethea executed a promissory note, he knew that it was a promissory note and that it required him to make money payments. The note was payable to the order of Bancredit. When it sued Bethea, he claimed that he was not bound by the note because he had understood that the note was payable to the order of the Beneficial Finance Company and that it was for a smaller amount. From a decision in favor of Bancredit, Bethea appealed. The court held that Bancredit was a holder in due course, 65 N.J.S. 538, 168 A.2d 250 (1960), but then allowed a rehearing on the question of the validity of Bethea's defense.

FREUND, J.A.D. . . . At the heart of the [defense of fraud as to the nature of the instrument] is the absence of that degree of mutual assent prerequisite to formation of a binding contract; absent the proverbial "meeting of the minds," one cannot be said to have obligated himself in law and the purported transaction is regarded as void. This is basic contract doctrine. . . .

Nevertheless, where the circumstances demonstrate the basic ingredient of voluntary, physical inscription, there has been at least an outward manifestation of assent on the part of the signer, thereby bringing into play—as against a holder in due course—additional considerations grounded in equity but phrased in terms of negligence. The signer must in such a situation exercise the caution of a reasonably prudent man to determine the character of the paper upon which he has purposefully placed his signature. The rationale of such a requirement may be found in the desirability of preserving general confidence in commercial paper, as well as in the equitable principle that where one of two innocent persons must suffer by the wrongful act of a third party, he who enabled the third party to perpetrate the wrong must sustain the loss. . . .

The cases on this subject . . . speak in terms of the basic knowledge of the signer and the reasonableness of his failure to obtain additional information as to the nature and terms of the paper obligation. . . . See Uniform Commercial Code (1958), § 3-305, providing that: "To the extent that a holder is a holder in due course he takes the instrument free from . . . (2) all defenses of any party to the instrument with whom the holder has not dealt except . . . (c) such misrepresentation as has induced the party to sign the instrument with neither knowledge nor reasonable opportunity to obtain knowledge of its character or its essential terms. . . ."

. . . With respect to the question of negligence, it is clear that the standard of care imposed on the signer may vary in degree according to the extent of his actual awareness of the nature of the instrument he is in fact signing. . . . Thus, where the signer does not intend to evidence a legal obligation, he is under a lesser duty of care than where he does mean to undertake a legal duty of some kind; and where he fully intends to bind himself on a commercial promissory instrument, he is under a duty to exercise the highest degree of care. . . .

. . . The identity of the contractee, as well as the [amount] of the obligation, is an essential component of the settled agreement. We would blind ourselves to commercial reality by denying that fraudulent identification of the obligee of an instrument, especially when considered in conjunction with alleged misrepresentations as to the amount of the obligation, could reasonably be interpreted as misstatement of an "essential term" of the document. See Uniform Commercial Code, supra, § 3-305 (2) (c), and especially comment 7, explaining the Code provision as an extension of the defense of fraud [as to the nature of the instrument] "to an instrument signed with knowledge that it is a negotiable instrument, but without knowledge of its essential terms." . . . Therefore, were we, solely for purposes of analysis, to separate the questions of knowledge and negligence, there would be some merit in the view that Tony Bethea's intent to sign a $500 note to Beneficial Loan did not, standing alone, sufficiently approximate the obligation, as actually written, as to preclude him as a matter of law from claiming fraud [as to the nature of the instrument.] . . .

The fact of the matter is, however, that the elements of knowledge and negligence cannot feasibly be [separated]. . . . The fact that the signer knew he was inscribing a negotiable document places upon him an unusually high degree of care in ascertaining its operative details. It is the failure of the instant defendant to demonstrate proper exercise of that duty, under the circumstances of his signing and his own particular status, that compels us to reaffirm his liability on the note as a matter of law.

The imposition upon the maker of the burden of establishing freedom from negligence, as an essential ingredient of his defense . . . is an explicit direction to the signer of the instrument to come forward either with evidence that the physical circumstances of the signing and the representations made to him were so far removed from the realm of negotiable paper that he could not reasonably have foreseen or otherwise observed the subsequent effect of his signature, or to produce proof of legally mitigating circumstances in the form of his own physical or mental inability to comprehend the essence of the deception. Factors to be considered in mitigation may include physical disability (e.g., blindness), illiteracy, unfamiliarity with the English language, low general intelligence, unfamiliarity with commercial transactions, unavailability of interpretative aid, and misrepresentation by means of physical deception. . . .

We have already mentioned the depth of defendant's understanding of the instrument in relation to its final character as negotiable paper. And while this may not, in itself, under the instant facts, defeat his right to have the jury consider his defense, when taken in conjunction with his failure to shoulder his burden of establishing freedom from negligence, he is clearly bound on the note to plaintiff. The record is devoid of proof of any mitigating circumstances. On the contrary, we are faced with a situation in which the evidence is indisputable that Bethea was aware he was signing a negotiable instrument, and uncontradicted as to both his literacy and his knowing signature of the printed documents which, when later filled in as to payee and amount, constituted the note and conditional sales contract. These are all factors weighing so heavily against defendant's freedom from negligence, which it was his burden in the first instance to establish, that we are compelled to conclude, as a matter of law, that defendant has failed to sustain his defense. . . .

[Judgment affirmed.]

Code Comment: The same decision would be made under the Code. By UCC Sec. 3-305(2) (c), all holders are made subject to the defense of "such misrepresentation as has induced the parties to sign the instrument with neither knowledge nor reasonable opportunity to obtain knowledge of its character or its essential terms." In the reported case, Bethea did not show that his claimed ignorance of the terms of the note was the result of misrepresentation and that he had not had reasonable opportunity to ascertain the truth. The plaintiff, as a holder in due course under the Code, would therefore take the paper free of Bethea's defense.

Questions and Case Problems

1. What is the objective of each of the following rules of law?
   (a) A person cannot be a holder in due course of a check that he has received as a gift.
   (b) Although certain defenses cannot be raised against a holder in due course, other defenses may be raised against him.

2. Ten negotiable notes were negotiated to the First National Bank which paid for them with a draft on another bank. The First National Bank then learned that the notes had been procured by fraud. Thereafter the bank on which the draft of the First National Bank had been drawn made payment. When First National Bank sued Motors Acceptance Corp., the latter claimed that the bank was not a holder in due course because it had not "paid" for the notes before it learned of the defense. Decide. (First National Bank of Waukesha v. Motors Acceptance Corp., [Wis.] 112 N.W.2d 381)

3. Insdorf, as holder of a check, sued the Wil-Avon Merchandise Mart, as drawer. The latter raised the defense that Insdorf did not plead that

consideration had been given for the check. Was Insdorf's claim defective? (Insdorf v. Wil-Avon Merchandise Mart, Inc., [Pa.] 8 Chester Co. 341)

4. Henry executed and delivered a check to Jesse Farley in payment of an automobile. On the face of the check was written "Car to be free and clear of liens." The check was indorsed and delivered by Farley to the Zachry company. When the latter sued Henry, he raised the defense of fraud in the inducement and failure of consideration, and claimed that Zachry was not a holder in due course because the words "Car to be free and clear of liens" written on the instrument gave notice of defenses. Was Henry correct? (C. C. Henry v. A. L. Zachry Co., 93 Ga.App. 536, 92 S.E.2d 225)

5. Rocchio executed and delivered a note payable to the order of Berta. When Berta sued Rocchio on the note, the latter offered parol evidence to show that the note had been given as payment for a business and its inventory and that less inventory had been delivered than had been agreed upon. Berta claimed that the obligation of the instrument could not be modified by parol evidence. Was he correct? (Berta v. Rocchio, [Colo.] 369 P.2d 51)

6. Lillie Lightner executed a promissory note for $10,900 to M. S. Lightner. After his death, suit was brought by the administratrix of his estate against Lillie. The administratrix took a nonsuit in the action. Nearly ten years after the note was issued, the administratrix sold the note and indorsed it to Thomas H. Lightner, who knew of the prior nonsuit. The transfer to him was made "without recourse" for $100. Thomas Lightner then sued Lillie. She raised the defense of absence of consideration. Could that defense be raised against Thomas? (Lightner v. Lightner, [W.Va.] 124 S.E.2d 355)

7. Panac and his wife were illiterate. Hart gained their confidence and persuaded them to sign a promissory note in the belief that it was a contract for the repair of their house. Panac and his wife did not know the true nature of the note and did not seek other advice because they relied on Hart's statements. The note was negotiated to the C.I.T. Corporation, which was a holder in due course. The corporation sued Panac and his wife, who defended on the ground of fraud. Was this a valid defense? (C.I.T. Corp. v. Panac, 25 Cal.2d 547, 154 P.2d 710)

8. Wolsky executed a promissory note payable to the order of Green. Green indorsed it "Pay to the order of M. E. Grasswick, (signed) Albert E. Green" and delivered it to Grasswick. Grasswick then indorsed and delivered it to McGuckin, a holder in due course. When the note was not paid, McGuckin sued Wolsky and the indorsers. Green claimed that the negotiation by him to Grasswick was agreed between them to be without recourse. Was this a valid defense? (McGuckin v. Wolsky, 78 N.D. 921, 53 N.W.2d 852)

9. Hawkins sold his real estate through Wood, a broker, to Morgan Brothers. The latter gave Wood a promissory note in payment of part of his commissions. When Wood sued Morgan Brothers on the note, they raised the defense that Hawkins had removed certain equipment from the property in violation of the sales contract. Was this a defense available against Wood? (Wood v. Morgan Brothers, [La.App.] 135 So.2d 692)

10. Parsons executed and delivered a note for $800 payable to the order of Burton & Co. The note was indorsed to Manchester, who was a holder in due course. He brought an action against Parsons to recover on the note. The defendant contended that the note was discharged by an agreement he had made with Burton & Co. in connection with the purchase and sale of some Percheron colts. From a judgment for the plaintiffs, the defendant appealed. Was this a valid defense? (Manchester v. Parsons, 75 W.Va. 793, 84 S.E. 885)

11. The Arizona Savings & Loan Association permitted Varner to withdraw $2,000 without complying with the statute and bylaws of the association governing notice of withdrawals. The Association gave Varner a check for $2,000 drawn on the First National Bank of Arizona. Varner indorsed the check and delivered it to the Bank of Douglas in return for its draft upon the Hanover Bank. The Bank of Douglas presented the Association check to the First National Bank of Arizona the drawee. It refused to make payment as the Superintendent of Banks who had taken possession of the Arizona Savings & Loan Association had stopped payment thereon. The Bank of Douglas then sued Colby, the receiver who had been placed in charge of the savings and loan association. Colby claimed that the check could not be paid to the Bank of Douglas because it had been illegally issued. Was this a valid contention? (Colby v. Bank of Douglas, [Ariz.] 370 P.2d 56)

12. In response to a radio ad, Green contacted Alderman Building Materials to arrange for the building of an additional room on his house. In the course of the preliminary negotiations, Green learned that the improvement would be financed by a loan from Home Credit Co. to which the papers to be executed by Green would be assigned and that all payments would be made directly to Home Credit. He also learned that it would be necessary for Home Credit to approve him as a credit risk and, further, that he would be required, before he could obtain a loan from Home Credit, to pay off a prior encumbrance on his house, in order that the debt to Home Credit would be a first lien on the house. Home Credit would also loan him the amount necessary for this purpose. Alderman and Home Credit were independent organizations but had worked together on 50 to 60 similar transactions in the past. When the contract was finally signed, Green executed two negotiable promissory notes, one for $4,999.20, representing $2,500 for the cost of the addition plus $2,499.20 as an "add on" price for permitting payment over a 10-year period; and $3,750 representing $2,500 for the discharge of encumbrances plus $1,250 as a "discount" for permitting payment over the 10-year period. The notes stated on their face that they were noninterest-bearing and provided for acceleration to maturity of the entire unpaid amount upon default as to any installment, without any reduction in the event of such maturity. The notes were negotiated by Alderman to Home Credit Co. "without recourse." Green made one payment and then died, whereupon Home Credit sued his administrator, Brown. Does Brown have any defense? (Brown v. Home Credit Co., [Fla.] 137 So.2d 887)

CHAPTER 33

Discharge of Commercial Paper

A party to commercial paper who would otherwise be liable on it may be discharged either individually or by some act that has discharged all parties to the paper at one time. The nature of the transaction or occurrence determines which occurs.

Discharge of Individual Parties

A party to a commercial paper, like a party to an ordinary contract, is usually discharged from liability by making payment to the proper person; but the discharge from liability may be effected in a number of other ways.

Sec. 33-A. Simple Contract Discharge. A party is discharged from liability to any other party (1) with whom he enters into an agreement for his discharge, or (2) with whom he enters into a transaction which under the law of contracts is effective to discharge liability for a simple contract for the payment of money.[1] Accordingly, there may be a discharge by accord and satisfaction, a novation, a covenant not to sue, rescission, or the substitution of another instrument. The liability may also be barred by operation of law as in the case of a discharge in bankruptcy, the operation of the Statute of Limitations, or by the merger of liability into a judgment in favor of the holder when an action has been brought on the instrument.

Sec. 33-B. Discharge by Payment. The obligation of a particular party on commercial paper is discharged when he pays the amount of the instrument to the holder.[2] A payment is not effective unless it is

---

[1] Uniform Commercial Code, Secs. 3-601(2), 3-305(2)(d); see Negotiable Instruments Law, Sec. 119(4).
[2] UCC Sec. 3-603(1), NIL Sec. 119(1),(2).

516

made to the holder of the instrument or his authorized agent; and payment to anyone else, even though in physical possession of the instrument, is not effective. (See p. 522, First National Bank v. Gorman) If the holder consents, however, payment may also be made by a third person, even a total stranger to the paper; and surrender of the paper to such a person gives him the rights of a transferee of the instrument.[3]

By definition, a negotiable instrument provides for the payment of a sum of money. Any party and the holder may, however, agree that the transfer or delivery of other kinds of property shall operate as payment. Sometimes a new instrument may be executed or delivered to the holder of the original instrument. In the absence of proof of an agreement to the contrary, a delivery of a subsequent instrument, without the destruction or other act to discharge the first, is merely the giving of additional security for the payment of the original instrument but is not in itself a payment or discharge of the first.

(1) Knowledge of Adverse Claim to the Paper. When the payment of the amount of the paper is made to the holder, the party making payment may know that some other person claims an interest in or ownership of the paper. The knowledge that there is such an adverse claimant does not prevent making a payment to the holder, and such payment is still a discharge of the obligation of the party making payment. Specifically, the existence of the adverse claim to the paper may thus be disregarded unless the adverse claimant furnishes the payor with a bond or other indemnity to protect him in the event that he does not pay and the adverse claim proves to be worthless or unless the adverse claimant obtains a court injunction against making payment to the holder.[4]

The purpose of this provision is to give commercial paper greater acceptance in the business world since the person writing such paper knows that he will be able to discharge the instrument by making payment in the ordinary case to the holder without the risk of deciding whether an adverse claim is valid.

(2) Satisfaction. The principles governing payment just described likewise apply to a satisfaction entered into with the holder of the instrument;[5] the difference being merely the factual one that instead of paying the holder in full in money, a payment of less than all is accepted as full, or some service is rendered or property is given by the party discharged.

---

[3] UCC Sec. 3-603(2).

[4] Sec. 3-603(1). Certain exceptions are made to this rule when payment is made in bad faith on a stolen instrument or when the instrument is restrictively indorsed. Sec. 3-603(1)(a),(b).

[5] Sec. 3-601(1).

(3) Tender of Payment. A party who is liable may offer to the holder the full amount when or after the instrument is due. If the holder refuses such payment, the party making the tender of payment is not discharged from his liability for the amount then due; but the holder cannot hold him liable for any interest that accrues after that date. Likewise, in the event that the holder sues the person making the tender, the holder cannot recover legal costs from him nor attorney's fees, as is commonly authorized by commercial paper.[6]

If the holder refuses a proper tender, his refusal may discharge third persons even though it does not affect the liability of the person making the tender. Specifically, any party to the paper who would have a right, if he made payment, to recover that amount from the person making the tender is discharged if the tender is not accepted.[7] For example, if the paper is negotiated through the unqualified indorsers *A, B,* and *C,* to the holder *D,* and if *B* or *C* is required to pay *D,* they each would have the right to sue *A,* the prior indorser, to recover from him the amount paid the holder *D.* In such a case, if *A* makes a proper tender of payment which *D* refuses, *B* and *C* are discharged from any liability to *D.*

Sec. 33-C. Cancellation. The holder of an instrument, with or without consideration, may discharge the liability of a particular party by cancellation, by a notation on the paper which makes that intent apparent, or by destroying, mutilating, or striking out the party's signature on the paper. (See p. 523, Broad & Market National Bank Case) The fact that by effecting such cancellation an indorsement necessary to the chain of title of the holder is destroyed does not affect his title to the paper,[8] since the fact remains that the paper had been properly negotiated to the holder.

A cancellation does not exist or take effect as such if it is made by a person who is not the holder or who is not acting by his authority, or when the physical destruction of the instrument is made by accident or mistake. The party who claims that an apparent cancellation should not take effect has the burden of proof.

Sec. 33-D. Renunciation. The holder of an instrument, with or without consideration, may discharge the liability of a particular party by renunciation. This is effected either (1) by surrendering the instrument to the party to be discharged, or (2) by executing a signed written renunciation which is then delivered to the party. If the holder surrenders the instrument in effecting the renunciation, he ceases to be the holder and thereafter cannot hold any party liable on the paper

---

[6] Sec. 3-604 (1).
[7] Sec. 3-604(2).
[8] UCC Sec. 3-605. See NIL Sec. 119(3).

although such other parties are not themselves discharged with respect to the person to whom the paper was surrendered or any other subsequent holder thereof.[9] (See p. 524, White System v. Lehmann)

Sec. 33-E. Impairment of Recourse. In most instances there is at least one party to commercial paper who, if required to pay, will have a right of recourse, or a right to obtain indemnity, from some other party. For example, in the least complicated situation, the payee of a note has indorsed it without qualification to the present holder. If the holder obtains payment from the indorsing payee, the latter has a right of recourse against the maker of the note. In order to protect that right of recourse, the Code provides that if the holder, without the indorser's consent, discharges the liability of the maker, extends the time for payment, or agrees not to sue him, the indorser is also discharged unless he consented thereto, on the theory that his right of recourse has been impaired.[10]

This same principle applies to other parties, as when the holder releases or agrees not to sue one indorser subsequent to him, since the other parties would each have a right of recourse against the prior indorser so released.

Sec. 33-F. Impairment of Collateral. When the commercial paper was executed, the maker or drawer may have given the holder property, such as stocks or bonds, to hold as security for the payment of the instrument. Likewise, any other party liable on the instrument may have given collateral security to the holder for the same purpose. The existence of this collateral security benefits all parties who would be liable on the paper because to the extent that payment is obtained from the security, they will not be required to make payment. Conversely, if the collateral security is impaired or harmed in any way that reduces its value, the parties liable are harmed since the possibility that they will be required to pay increases. The Code accordingly provides that a particular party is discharged if the holder unjustifiably impairs collateral security provided by that party or by any person against whom such party has a right of recourse.[11]

Sec. 33-G. Reacquisition of Paper by Intermediate Party. Commercial paper is sometimes reacquired by a party who had been an earlier

---

[9] UCC Sec. 3-605. See NIL Sec. 122.

[10] UCC Sec. 3-606(1)(a), NIL Sec. 120. Note that this is similar to the situation when a holder refuses to accept a proper tender of payment from the maker in which case the indorser is discharged. See p. 518. The operation of this section is avoided, and the other party not released, if the holder executes a reservation of his right against the other party at the time when he discharges the party subject to the latter's right of recourse. UCC Sec. 3-606(2).

[11] UCC Sec. 3-606(1).

holder. This occurs most commonly when that earlier party pays the then existing holder the amount due, thereby in effect purchasing the paper from that holder. When this occurs, the prior party may cancel all indorsements subsequent to his and then reissue or further negotiate the paper. When he does this, the intervening indorsers subsequent to him whose indorsements have been canceled are discharged as to the reacquirer and all subsequent holders.[12]

Sec. 33-H. Alteration. When an instrument is materially and fraudulently altered by the holder,[13] any party whose obligation on the paper is changed thereby is discharged, unless he had assented to the alteration or is barred by his conduct from asserting that he is discharged.[14] If the alteration does not meet all the conditions of being (1) fraudulent, (2) material, and (3) made by the holder, no party to the instrument is affected.[15]

The effect of the discharge by alteration is limited; for if the altered instrument is held by a holder in due course, he may enforce it according to its original terms.[16]

Sec. 33-I. Discharge for Miscellaneous Causes. In addition to the discharge of a party as discussed in the preceding sections, the conduct of certain parties with respect to the commercial paper or the enforcement of rights thereunder may release some of the parties to the paper. This occurs (1) when a check has been certified on the application of the holder; [17] (2) when the holder accepts an acceptance that varies the terms of the draft; [18] and (3) when a presentment, notice of dishonor, or protest, when required, is delayed beyond the time permitted or is absent and such delay or absence is not excused.[19]

In addition, federal or local statutes may provide for the discharge of a party by bankruptcy proceedings or by local laws declaring certain obligations not enforceable because they violate particular statutes.[20]

Discharge of All Parties

Sec. 33-J. Discharge of Party Primarily Liable. The primary party on an instrument, that is, the maker of a note or the acceptor of a

---

[12] Sec. 3-208.
[13] See p. 505.
[14] UCC Sec. 3-407(2)(a).
[15] Sec. 3-407(2) (b).
[16] UCC Sec. 3-407 (3), NIL Sec. 124.
[17] See p. 482.
[18] See p. 466.
[19] See p. 467.
[20] UCC Sec. 3-601, Official Comment, point 1.

draft,[21] has no right of recourse against any party on the paper. Conversely, every other party who may be held liable on the paper has a right of recourse against persons primarily liable. If the holder discharges a party who is primarily liable in any way, all parties to the instrument are discharged, since the discharge of the primary party discharges the persons who had a right of recourse against him.[22]

Sec. 33-K. Reacquisition of Paper by Primary Party. When a party primarily liable on the paper reacquires it in his own right at any time, whether before or after it is due, the paper is then held by one who has no right to sue any other party on the paper. Such reacquisition therefore discharges the liability of all intervening parties to the instrument.[23] Moreover, since the reacquisition by that party, if lawful, necessarily involves the negotiation or surrender by the person who was then the holder of the right against that party, no party remains liable on the paper. The Code therefore declares that the reacquisition by the party who has no right of action or recourse against anyone else on the paper discharges the liability of all parties on it.[24]

Effect of Discharge on Holder in Due Course

Sec. 33-L. Discharge of Individual Party. The fact that a party has been discharged of liability, and even that a new holder of the paper knows of it, does not prevent the new holder from being a holder in due course as to any party remaining liable on the paper.[25] If the holder in due course does not have notice or knowledge of a discharge of a party obtained before he acquired the paper, he is not bound by the discharge and may enforce the obligation of the discharged party as though he had never been discharged.[26] In order to protect himself, a party securing his own discharge should have a notation of it made on the paper so that any subsequent party would necessarily have notice of that fact.

Sec. 33-M. Discharge of All Parties. The fact that the liabilities of all parties to a negotiable instrument have been discharged does not destroy the negotiable character nor the existence of the commercial paper. If it should thereafter be negotiated to a person who qualifies

---

21 An accommodated payee is in effect also a primary party since the accommodating party, if required to pay, has a right of recourse against such payee.
22 UCC Sec. 3-601(3). In some instances this rule is modified by UCC Sec. 3-606.
23 Sec. 3-208.
24 UCC Sec. 3-601(3)(a). See NIL Sec. 119(5).
25 UCC Sec. 3-304(1)(b).
26 Sec. 3-602. As an exception to this rule, the holder in due course is bound by a prior discharge in insolvency proceedings, such as bankruptcy, whether he had notice thereof or not. Sec. 3-305(2)(d).

as a holder in due course, the latter may enforce the liability of any party on the paper, although otherwise discharged, of whose discharge the holder in due course had no notice or knowledge.[27]

Cases for Chapter 33

First National Bank v. Gorman

45 Wyo. 519, 21 P.2d 549 (1933)

Gorman executed and delivered a promissory note to the First National Bank. After several payments, the note was stolen from the bank. Subsequently, Gorman paid the remainder to one representing himself to be Richardson, who previously had been connected with the payee bank. In an action brought by the bank to collect the remainder of the note from Gorman, the latter pleaded payment and produced the note marked paid by the impostor. From a judgment for the plaintiff, the defendant appealed.

BLUME, J. . . . Counsel for the appellant [defendant] claims that defendant's possession of the note raises a presumption that it has been paid; that this presumption has not been overcome; that the plaintiff should have been more careful in not letting the note in question get out of its possession; that that carelessness made it possible for some one to hold himself out as the agent of the defendant; and that it is now estopped to claim that payment was made to one not authorized. Counsel relies partially upon cases which hold that where two innocent parties must suffer, that one should suffer who has made the loss possible. . . . There is some slight authority to sustain the position that mere possession of a note, though not indorsed, entitles the holder to collect the money due thereon. . . . Daniel on Negotiable Instruments . . . in commenting on the point under consideration . . . says:

"If the instrument be payable to a particular party or order, and unindorsed by him, it has been held that a payment to any person in actual possession will still be valid because, although he may have no legal title, he may be the agent of the actual owner. But this doctrine, it seems to us, goes too far. Such person in actual possession may perhaps be presumed to be agent of the holder prima facie. But even this is doubtful, and to us seems wrong, for nothing is more common than to indorse negotiable instruments to agents for collection; and if the bill or note be unindorsed . . . it might be that the owner had withheld his indorsement for the very purpose of preventing collection by a person not entitled to receive the money; and if this were so, the presumption of agency (if, indeed, it be at all admitted) would be rebutted. The contrary doctrine destroys a great and salutary safeguard to the rights of proprietors of negotiable instruments and to a large degree breaks down the distinction between those

---
[27] Sec. 3-601, Official Comment, point 3.

payable to order and those payable to bearer." The authorities generally are in full accord with this statement. . . .

In the case of Anderson v. Wm. H. Moore Dry Goods Company, . . . payment was made of an unindorsed note to one without authority to collect. Instead of contending in that case that the person who received payment was the apparent agent of the owner, counsel claimed that he was the holder of the note within the meaning of the Negotiable Instruments Law . . . , reading that "payment is made in due course when it is made at or after the maturity of the instrument to the holder thereof in good faith and without notice that his title is defective." The court, however, held that the term "holder" means the person who is legally in possession of the instrument, either by indorsement or delivery or both, and who is entitled to receive payment from the drawer or acceptor or maker of the note, and does not include a person in actual possession who has no right to such possession. . . . Thus we have arrived at the same conclusion by two different methods of reasoning. When the note was presented for payment by a stranger without a legal transfer, the presumption was that it was lost or purloined or otherwise improperly got into circulation. . . . The defendant took the risk of making payment to him, without being able to show that he had authority to collect. Moreover, he had other ample means by which he could have fully protected himself, namely, by obtaining a draft or check payable to the plaintiff bank. . . .

[Judgment for plaintiff affirmed.]

Code Comment: The same decision would be made under the Code since the requirements of the NIL as to who is the holder of an instrument and the necessity for proper indorsements are continued under the Code.

Broad & Market National Bank v. New York & E. Realty Co.

102 Misc. 82, 168 N.Y.S. 149 (1917)

Sicklick, who was president of the New York & Eastern Realty Company, with its authority, made its promissory note to his order for $750 due in four months from date. He indorsed and discounted the instrument with the Broad & Market National Bank. The note was reduced to $700 and paid by another note for that amount. When this note was due, Sicklick gave his check on the holder bank in payment and received the note stamped or punched "Paid." His check, although charged to his account, was not paid in part because a check for $550 drawn on a bank in Bangor, Pa., was uncollected. In an action brought by the Broad & Market National Bank against the New York & Eastern Realty Company to collect the amount of the note, the maker contended that the note had been discharged. From a judgment for the plaintiff, the defendant appealed.

BENEDICT, J. . . . The mere stamping of a negotiable instrument with the word "Paid," or the cancellation of it in any other way, is not conclusive evidence of its discharge, for the reason that such cancellation may have been done through error or mistake. . . .

Section 204 of the Negotiable Instruments Law provides that:

"A cancellation made unintentionally, or under a mistake, or without the authority of the holder, is inoperative; but where an instrument or any signature thereon appears to have been cancelled, the burden of proof lies on the party who alleges that the cancellation was made unintentionally, or under a mistake or without authority."

In the present case, however, the cancellation of the note was not unintentional nor the result of a mistake. It is not claimed nor shown that there was any fraud or deceit on the part of Sicklick practiced upon the bank in obtaining the cancellation and surrender of the notes . . . , and it was entirely competent for the bank to accept the check of its depositor in payment of the last note made by the appellant. If payment in such manner was accepted by it, the maker of the note was discharged. The evidence clearly establishes that fact. . . .

. . . The plaintiff is not entitled to recover upon the note, nor upon either of the two renewal notes . . . and . . . its remedy is solely against its depositor upon his unpaid check. . . .

[Judgment for plaintiff reversed.]

Code Comment: The same decision would be made under the Code, the act of stamping the instrument "paid" coming within the provision for discharging a party "in any manner apparent on the face of the instrument . . . as by intentionally canceling the instrument. . . ." UCC Sec. 3-605 (1) (a).

White System v. Lehmann

144 So.2d 122 (La.App., 1962)

White System sued Lehmann on a promissory note which he had executed as maker. Lehmann defended on the ground that the holder had renounced or canceled the obligation when, after Lehmann's default, it carried the note in its profit and loss account. From a judgment in favor of White System, Lehmann appealed.

MILLER, J. pro tem. . . . The primary defense is that the plaintiff, by transferring the obligation to the Profit & Loss Account in his bookkeeping records, has in effect renounced or canceled the debt and therefore the obligation is fully discharged. This defense is untenable. In order to renounce his rights, the holder must so expressly state in writing or must surrender or deliver the instrument to the person primarily liable thereon. . . . There is no evidence whatever to establish that the plaintiff executed such a written renouncement, and the fact that the note was attached to his petition clearly refutes that he surrendered or delivered it to the defendant. Obviously there was no renouncement of the debt.

Counsel for defendant in support of his contention that the transfer of the defendant's obligation to the Profit & Loss Account by the plaintiff constituted a discharge of the instrument, cites (LSA-) R.S. 7:119 (Pars. 3, 4) which respectively provide that a negotiable instrument is discharged by the intentional cancellation by the holder or by any other act which will discharge a simple contract for the payment of money.

The sections of the Statutes cited . . . are not applicable to the facts of this case. The action of the plaintiff in placing the obligation in the Profit & Loss Account, after its default, is merely an internal bookkeeping entry, utilized by the holder, who was apparently motivated by either recognized accounting principles or for income tax purposes. Unquestionably he could have transferred the defendant's indebtedness to any other account it he so desired, no approval of, nor communication to, the debtor being required. The fact that he carried the account on his books, even though in a substandard classification, clearly negatived any intentional cancellation of the obligation; otherwise his action would have been useless and in vain. The modes of discharging a negotiable instrument, as set forth above, could only be interpreted as meaning that the action of the holder is of such a definite or certain nature that there could be no question of his intention to discharge the obligation arising out of the negotiable instrument. Such were not the facts in this matter. . . .

[Judgment affirmed.]

Code Comment: The same decision would be made under the Code. There was no act done to the face or back of the paper itself, it was not surrendered to the party claiming that he was discharged, nor was any written renunciation delivered to him. In the absence of any of these, there could be no cancellation or renunciation. UCC Sec. 3-605.

Questions and Case Problems

1. What is the objective of each of the following rules of law?
   (a) Payment does not discharge an order instrument when it is not made to the holder of the instrument or to his authorized agent, even though payment is made to a person, not the holder, who was in possession of the instrument.
   (b) It is generally immaterial whether an alteration to a commercial paper was made innocently or with intent to defraud.

2. The Citizens State Bank issued a cashier's check payable to the order of Donovan. He indorsed it to Denny, who did business as the Houston Aircraft Co., and included in the indorsement a recital that it was "in full [payment of] any and all claims of any character whatever." Denny crossed

out this quoted phrase and wrote Donovan and the bank that he had done so. The Houston Aircraft Co. sued the Citizens National Bank on the check. Was the bank liable? (Houston Aircraft Co. v. Citizens State Bank, [Tex. Civ.App.] 184 S.W.2d 335)

3. Henry and Herbert Mordecai were partners doing business under the name of the Southern Cigar Co. They indorsed a promissory note executed by the firm to Henry Mordecai and delivered it to the District National Bank. They also delivered as security a certificate for certain stock in the Monumental Cigar Co. After maturity of the note, the indorsers made an assignment of a claim against the United States to the bank, which accepted it in satisfaction of its rights on the note. Was the note discharged? (District National Bank v. Mordecai, 133 Md. 419, 105 A. 586)

4. Burg executed and delivered a promissory note for $1,060 payable to Liesemer. When the note was due, Burg paid $893 and demanded credit for the remainder of the amount due because of the boarding expense incurred by Liesemer's daughter. Liesemer gave Burg the note so that he could compute the amount due. Burg refused to give credit for Liesemer's claim and kept the note. When Liesemer brought an action to recover the remainder of the note, it appeared that Burg had written across the face of the note, "Paid February 9th." It was contended that the note had been discharged by cancellation. Do you agree? (Liesemer v. Burg, 106 Mich. 124, 63 N.W. 999)

5. C. Neal executed and delivered a promissory note payable to the order of A. Neal who indorsed the instrument to his wife, Mary Neal, a holder in due course. Before maturity, the maker paid the amount of the note to the payee. After maturity, Mary, who had divorced A. Neal and resumed her maiden name of Fogarty, brought an action against C. Neal to recover on the note. Neal contended that the note had been discharged by payment. Do you agree with this contention? (Fogarty v. Neal, 201 Ky. 85, 255 S.W. 1049)

6. As part of a business plan Schwald executed and delivered a note to Montgomery. The parties then made a new business arrangement, and Montgomery intentionally tore up the note and threw it into the wastebasket. It was subsequently contended that this note had been canceled. Do you agree? (Montgomery v. Schwald, 117 Mo.App. 75, 166 S.W. 831)

7. Satek authorized his agent to execute a mortgage with Fortuna as mortgagor. Fortuna executed a note secured by the mortgage. Later Fortuna made a part payment on the note to the agent. This payment was made before maturity, and the agent at the time did not have possession of the note. Satek later sued to foreclose the mortgage. The court refused to allow Fortuna credit for the payment made to the agent. Why? (Satek v. Fortuna, 324 Ill.App. 523, 58 N.E.2d 464)

PART VI
SECURITY
DEVICES

CHAPTER 34

Secured Consumer Credit Sales

A characteristic of the modern American economy is the large volume of purchases of goods made on credit. Various devices have been developed to provide the seller with some protection beyond his general right to sue the buyer for the purchase price. Today such a device is known as a *secured transaction* and is governed by Article 9 of the Uniform Commercial Code.[1]

In this chapter, secured credit sales relating to consumer goods are considered. In Chapter 35, attention will be given to secured credit sales of inventory and equipment, and to secured loan transactions.

Sec. 34-A. Nature of a Secured Credit Sale. Under the Uniform Commercial Code, a *secured credit sale* is an ordinary sale in which the title, possession, and risk of loss pass to the buyer but the seller retains a security interest in the goods until he has been paid in full. This security interest entitles him to repossess the goods when the buyer fails to make payments as required or when in any other way he commits a breach of the purchase contract. This right of repossession is in addition to the right to sue on the purchase contract for the amount of the purchase price.

Forerunners of this credit device include: (a) a *conditional sale,* where the seller retained title until the condition of payment in full had been satisfied; (2) a *bailment lease,* under which transaction the

---

[1] For states that have adopted the Uniform Commercial Code, see p. 51.

buyer rented the property and, after the payment of sufficient rentals to equal the purchase price, could elect to take title to the property; and (3) a *chattel mortgage*, by which the buyer, upon taking title from the seller, in turn gave the seller a mortgage on the property for the amount of the purchase price. In these transactions the possession and risk of loss passed to the buyer, but the seller had the right of repossession to protect his interest as well as to sue for breach of contract. These three types of transactions have been replaced by the secured transaction under the Code.[2]

The Uniform Commercial Code is not designed solely to aid the sellers. The provisions of Article 9 increase the protection given to buyers over that available to them under the former law. Special statutes designed to protect buyers, in addition to the Code, may also be in force within a given state. For example, many states have adopted some form of a retail installment sales act to protect the buyer from improper practices, such as the charging of excessive interest through fictitious charges and the concealment from the buyer of the amount actually due on his purchase.[3]

Sec. 34-B. Creation of Security Interest. A security interest for the protection of the seller of goods to a consumer arises as soon as the seller and buyer agree that the buyer shall have property rights in particular goods and that the seller shall have a security interest in them.[4] It is immaterial whether or not the sales agreement provides for the passage of title to the buyer prior to his payment of the goods in full, for the location of title to the property involved, called *collateral*, is immaterial under the Code.[5]

(1) Consumer Goods. Consumer goods are those which are used or bought for use primarily for personal, family, or household purposes.[6] It is the intended use rather than the nature of the article which determines its character. For example, goods purchased by a buyer for resale to ultimate consumers are not consumer goods in the hands of such middleman.

(2) Security Agreement. The agreement of the seller and buyer that the seller shall have a security interest in the goods must be evidenced by a written *security agreement* which is signed by the buyer

---

[2] The Code, however, has not abolished these transactions nor made them illegal. The parties may still enter into a conditional sale, bailment lease, or chattel mortgage; but if they do, the transaction must satisfy the requirements of the secured transaction under the Code. Thus the Uniform Commercial Code establishes certain minimum requirements applicable to all types of security devices employed by the credit seller.

[3] Such laws continue in effect under the Code, UCC Secs. 9-201, 9-203(2), and supplement its provisions.

[4] Sec. 9-204 (1).

[5] Sec. 9-202.

[6] Sec. 9-109(1).

and which describes the collateral.[7] This description need only reasonably identify the collateral. It is not necessary that the goods be described specifically, as by serial number or by manufacturer's model.[8] A description is sufficient when it would enable a third person aided by inquiries made to others to determine what goods were involved. (See p. 534, In re Drane)

(3) Future Transactions. The security agreement may contemplate future action by extending to goods not in existence and which are to be acquired and delivered to the buyer at a future date. In general the security interest does not attach to future goods until the buyer has rights in such goods.[9]

Rights of Parties Independent of Default

In a secured credit sale of consumer goods, both the seller who has a security interest and the buyer have rights independent of default by either party.

Sec. 34-C. Rights of Seller Independent of Default. The seller stands in a dual position of being both a seller, having rights under Article 2 of the Code governing sales, and a secured creditor, having rights under Article 9 of the Code regulating secured transactions.[10]

The seller may transfer or assign his interest under the sales contract and under the security agreement to a third person, and the assignee acquires all the rights and interest of the seller. The rights of the assignee may rise higher than those of the seller to the extent that there is a defense or claim valid against the seller which is not effective against the assignee because the buyer has waived such a right as against an assignee.[11]

The secured credit seller of consumer goods has rights that are effective not only against the buyer but also against purchasers of the property of the buyer as soon as the security agreement is executed with respect to goods in which the buyer has acquired an interest. From that moment on, the seller's interest is fully effective against all third persons and is described as a *perfected security interest.*[12]

(1) Filing Not Required. In an ordinary sale of consumer goods under a secured transaction, no filing is required in order to perfect

---

[7] Sec. 9-203(1)(b).
[8] Sec. 9-110.
[9] Sec. 9-204(1),(2).
[10] Sec. 9-113. No civil liability rests upon the seller for harm sustained by third persons as a result of acts or omissions of the debtor or in consequence of the existence of the secured transaction. Sec. 9-317.
[11] See p. 195.
[12] UCC Sec. 9-201.

the secured seller's interest. Thus the seller is protected against purchasers from and creditors of the buyer who may acquire the property
thereafter.[13]

As an exception to the rule that the seller of consumer goods has a
perfected interest as soon as the agreement is executed and the buyer
has an interest in the property, the seller's security interest is not perfected, and filing is required to perfect it, if the goods purchased are
to be attached to buildings or land as a fixture or if they consist of
farm equipment sold for a purchase price of over $2,500. A security
interest in a motor vehicle required to be licensed is not perfected
unless the vehicle is licensed with a notation of the security interest
made in the title certificate, if such is required by law, or if not so
required, unless there is a filing under the Code.[14]

(2) Interstate Security Interests. The Code regulates not only
transactions within the state but also the effect to be given security
interests in property brought into the state from another state, whether
or not such other state is also a Code state. If the interest of the secured
party arising under the law of another state is perfected by the law of
that state, his interest will be regarded as perfected by the Code state
into which the property is brought, without regard to whether any
filing or recording was required in the foreign state. Within the Code
state, however, it is necessary to file within four months in order to
keep the security interest continuously protected. (See p. 536, Church-
hill Motors Case) If the secured party's interest in the goods was unperfected when they were brought into the state, that interest may be
perfected in the Code state, in which case the perfection of the secured
interest dates from such perfection in the Code state.[15]

If title to the property, such as an automobile, is represented by a
title certificate, the law of the state which issued the certificate determines whether an interest is perfected. Accordingly, if the law of the
certificate-issuing state requires that a security interest be noted on the
title certificate in order to be binding, that requirement is the exclusive means of perfecting the interest of the secured creditor.[16]

Sec. 34-D. Rights of the Buyer Independent of Default. The buyer
under a secured transaction has a double status under the Uniform
Commercial Code. By virtue of Article 2 he has certain rights because
he is a buyer, and by virtue of Article 9 he has certain rights because
he is a debtor under a secured transaction.

---

13 Sec. 9-312(4). The Code makes detailed provisions as to the priority of conflicting
security interests with respect to fixtures, accessions, and comingled and processed goods.
Sec. 9-313 and following.

14 Sec. 9-302(1)(c),(d),(3). As to the requirements of filing generally, see p. 546.

15 Sec. 9-103(3).

16 Sec. 9-103(4).

(1) Rights as a Buyer. The secured credit sale of consumer goods remains fundamentally a sale that is governed by Article 2 and therefore the debtor-buyer has the same rights as an ordinary buyer under that article.[17] (See p. 540, L. & N. Sales Co. v. Stutski)

The buyer has certain rights of ownership in the collateral. Under the Code it is not material whether technically he is the owner of the title. In any case, whatever interest he owns he may transfer voluntarily and his creditors may reach it by the process of the law as fully as though there were no security agreement.[18] Such third persons, however, cannot acquire any greater rights than the buyer, and therefore they hold the property subject to the security interest of the seller.

It is common practice for credit sellers to seek to protect themselves by prohibiting the buyer from reselling the property. Such a provision has no effect and does not prevent an effective resale, even though the security agreement in addition to prohibiting such resale also expressly makes it a default or breach of the contract to make a resale.[19]

(2) Rights as a Debtor. The secured transaction buyer is a debtor to the extent that there is a balance due on the purchase price. In order for the buyer to know just how much he owes and to check with his own records what the seller claims to be due, the Code gives the buyer the right to compel the seller to state what balance is owed and also to specify in what collateral the seller claims a security interest. This is done by the buyer's sending the seller a statement of the amount which he believes to be due, or a statement of the collateral which he believes to be subject to the security agreement, with the request that the seller approve or correct the statement. The seller must so indicate and if he has assigned the contract and the security interest to a third person, he must furnish the buyer with the name and address of such successor in interest.[20]

(3) Waiver of Defenses. It is common practice for finance companies that have a standing agreement to purchase sales contracts from a credit seller to provide him with forms to be signed by the buyer. These forms generally specify that the buyer waives, as against the assignee of the sales contract and security agreement, any right that he would have against the seller. In addition to an express agreement waiving his defenses, a buyer who, as part of the purchase transaction, signs both a commercial paper and a security agreement is deemed as a matter of law to waive such defenses, even though nothing is said as to any waiver.

---

[17] Sec. 9-206(2).
[18] Sec. 9-311.
[19] Sec. 9-311. The second buyer is of course subject to the security interest as was the first buyer if that interest was perfected.
[20] Sec. 9-208.

The validity of waiver clauses was uncertain under the prior law, but by the Code both the express and the implied waiver are valid and bind the buyer if the assignee takes his assignment for value, in good faith, and without notice or knowledge of any claim or defense of the buyer.[21] The validity of any waiver of defense is subject to two limitations: (a) those defenses which could be raised against the holder in due course of commercial paper cannot be waived; [22] (b) the waiver is not effective if a statute or decision establishes a different rule for buyers of consumer goods.[23]

Rights of Parties After Default

When the buyer under the secured credit sale defaults by failing to pay an installment due or commits any other breach of the contract, the secured creditor is given additional rights for his protection. The buyer is likewise given certain additional rights in order to protect his interest.

Sec. 34-E. Secured Seller's Repossession and Resale of Collateral. Upon the buyer's default, the secured party is entitled to take the collateral or purchased property, from the buyer. If he can do so without causing a breach of the peace, the seller may repossess the property without legal proceedings. In any case he may use legal proceedings if he desires.[24]

The seller who has repossessed the goods may resell them at a private or public sale at any time and place and on any terms. He must, however, act in good faith and in a manner that is commercially reasonable.[25] The seller must give the buyer reasonable advance notice of a resale, unless the goods are perishable, or threaten to decline speedily in value, or are of a type customarily sold on a recognized market.[26] The seller's resale destroys all interest of the buyer in the goods.

(1) Compulsory Resale. If the buyer has paid 60 per cent or more of the cash price of the consumer goods, the seller must resell them within 90 days after repossession, unless the buyer, after default, has signed a written statement surrendering the right to require the resale. If the seller does not resell within the time specified, the buyer may sue him for conversion of the collateral or proceed under the Code provision applicable to failure to comply with the Code.[27]

---

21 Sec. 9-206(1),(2).
22 Sec. 9-206(1). See p. 504.
23 Sec. 9-206(1).
24 Sec. 9-503.
25 Sec. 9-504(1),(3).
26 Sec. 9-504(3).
27 See p. 533.

(2) Redemption of Collateral. If the buyer acts in time, he may redeem or obtain the return to him of the goods by tendering to the secured party the amount that is owed him, including expenses and any legal costs that have been incurred. The right to redeem is destroyed if the seller has made a resale or entered into a binding contract for resale.[28]

(3) Accounting After Resale. When the secured party makes a resale of the goods, the proceeds of the sale are applied in the following order to pay (a) reasonable costs of repossession, storage, and resale of the goods; (b) the balance due, including interest and any proper additions such as attorney's fees; and (c) subsequent security interests on the property that are discharged by the sale.[29]

If any balance remains after the payment of these claims, the buyer is entitled to the surplus. Conversely, if the net proceeds of sale are insufficient to pay the costs and the debt due the seller, the buyer is liable to him for such deficiency unless it has been otherwise agreed.[30]

Sec. 34-F. Secured Seller's Retention of Collateral to Discharge Obligation. If a compulsory disposition of the collateral is not required, the secured party may propose in writing that he keep the collateral in payment of the debt. If the buyer does not object to this proposal, the secured party may do so and the secured obligation is automatically discharged.[31] If written objection to the retention of the collateral by the secured party is made within 30 days, he must then proceed to dispose of it by resale or other reasonable manner.

Sec. 34-G. Buyer's Remedies for Violation of Code by Secured Party. The Code authorizes both injunctive and money-damage relief against the secured party who violates the provisions of the Code applicable upon default. The remedies provided by the Code are not exclusive, and the buyer may also invoke any remedies authorized by any other statute applicable to the particular transaction. (See p. 542, Alliance Discount Corp. v. Shaw)

The buyer is entitled to recover the damages caused him by the secured party's failure to comply with the Code. In the absence of proof of a greater amount of damages, the buyer is entitled to recover not less than the credit service charge together with 10 per cent of the principal amount of the debt or the time price differential plus 10 per cent of the cash price.[32]

---

28 UCC Sec. 9-506.
29 Sec. 9-504(1).
30 Sec. 9-504(2).
31 Sec. 9-505.
32 Sec. 9-507(1).

If a resale has not yet been made nor a binding contract therefor entered into, the buyer may obtain a court order or injunction requiring the seller to comply with the Code provisions.

Cases for Chapter 34

In re Drane

202 F.Supp. 221 (D.C. Ky., 1962)

Note: In this case, the secured transaction or chattel mortgage was used to borrow money on the security of furniture already owned by the borrower. The same type of transaction may also be used to secure the seller; the buyer taking title and possession of the property and then giving back to his seller a chattel mortgage for the amount of the sales price, rather than for the amount of the loan. For most purposes it is immaterial whether the transaction is a borrowing or a selling device.

Willard Drane executed in favor of Popular Finance Corporation a mortgage on household furniture, and he also executed a "note and security agreement" which was properly recorded in the office of the county clerk. Later Drane was declared a bankrupt. The finance corporation claimed that it held a lien on the property which was superior to the trustee in bankruptcy. The latter claimed that the finance corporation did not have any lien because the property had not been sufficiently described in the recorded agreement. From a decision in favor of the trustee, the finance corporation appealed.

SHELBOURNE, D.J. . . . [The note and security agreement described the property as] . . .

    1—2 pc. living room suite, wine
    1—5 pc. chrome dinette set, yellow
    1—3 pc. panel bedroom suite, lime oak, matt. & spgs.

The referee [in bankruptcy] overruled the [finance company's claim] on the ground that the description of the chattels was insufficient to put a member of the general public, other than one engaged in the furniture business, on notice of the existence of the lien. . . .

[He] was of opinion that a member of the general public would not be able to determine what particular pieces of furniture composed the sets mentioned and held the description insufficient, stating: "A three-piece bedroom suite could be twin beds and a dresser, or chest, or a bed, dresser or mirror, and a chest. A two-piece living room suite could be a couch to be used only as such or a couch converted into a bed and a chair or overstuffed stool, or some item commonly used in a living room; and a five piece dinette, in addition to being a table and four chairs, could be a table, cabinet for dishes, or some other dining or breakfast room piece and three chairs." . . .

. . . The referee held that a description must be sufficiently definite to enable a member of the general public to identify the mortgaged property as contrasted with other similar property.

The sole question on review is whether the description of this property in the "Note and Security Agreement" is a sufficient description under the law of Kentucky.

The creditor relies on the Uniform Commercial Code, particularly Section 9-110 (KRS 335.9-110) which provides: "For the purposes of this article any description of personal property or real estate is sufficient whether or not it is specific if it reasonably identifies what is described."

The creditor insists that the description in the mortgage meets the test of the Uniform Commercial Code and also meets the test required by the Kentucky Court of Appeals before the adoption of the Code, as set forth in Liberty National Bank & Trust Co. v. Miles, Ky., 259 S.W.2d 474, and the cases relied on by the referee. . . . The creditor contends that a correct interpretation of these cases is that a general description of property is adequate if sufficiently intelligible to fix the lien; property need not be described with utmost particularity. A description is sufficient if the facts shown will enable a third party, assisted by external evidence, to identify the property.

Fifty-nine years ago, in Sparks v. Deposit Bank of Paris, 115 Ky. 461, 74 S.W. 185, 78 S.W. 171, the Kentucky Court of Appeals set forth the rule concerning the sufficiency of the description of mortgaged chattels: "The description need not be such as would enable a stranger to select the property. A description which will aid third persons, aided by inquiries which the instrument itself suggests, to identify the property, is sufficient. . . . It is enough if it puts the purchaser on inquiry which, if reasonably pursued, will result in his obtaining the exact information as to what property the mortgage incumbers."

The cases . . . relied upon by the referee in this case, both involved mortgages in which the address of the mortgagor was not stated. The general rule as to the importance of this information is stated in 10 Am Jur. 756, 7, Chattel Mortgages § 63: "A statement as to the location of the chattels is one of the most important elements in the description. Other details without this element often amount to little or nothing, whereas its presence with other slight details often makes easy the ascertainment of the property meant to be designated and may make sufficient a description which otherwise would be insufficient. There should be a designation of the property conveyed and of the place where it may be found."

In the "Note and Security Agreement" here, the address of the mortgagor is stated and the mortgage provides that the chattels "will be kept at the debtor's address above and not moved without the written consent of the secured party." . . .

... A third party would have had little difficulty in identifying the two-piece wine living room suite, whether comprised of a divan or davenport and a chair or two chairs. It would have been equally easy to identify the yellow dinette set, whether it consisted of a table and four chairs or a table, a sideboard, and fewer chairs. The same "external evidence" would have identified the lime oak panel bedroom suite, mattress, and springs. The location of the property at the address of the mortgagors and in their possession furnished reference to "external evidence" of identification.

While this Court is not in accord with the modern usage of highly abbreviated descriptions of property in mortgages of this type, the description of the property in the mortgage here involved is considered sufficient. It would hardly be doubted that one interested in or affected by the identity of the property would have little concern deciding whether the bankrupt owned more than one wine-colored living room suite, one yellow dinette set, or one lime oak bedroom suite. As stated in 14 C.J.S. Chattel Mortgages § 59, p. 668: "The scarcity or plentitude of chattels similar to those mortgaged is an element to be considered in determining the sufficiency of the descriptions of the chattels covered by the mortgage, and the nonexistence of other property to which the terms of the mortgage could apply frequently renders valid a description in a mortgage which otherwise would be indefinite."

The rule governing the problem posed here is perhaps a bit variable and each case may have certain convincing language of description and "external evidence." ...

[Judgment reversed and mortgage lien sustained.]

Churchill Motors, Inc. v. A. C. Lohman, Inc.

229 N.Y.S.2d 570 (App.Div., 1962)

On July 7, Mulry sold a Ford Thunderbird to Greene in Rhode Island by a conditional sales contract. The contract was never recorded or filed since this was not required in Rhode Island to perfect the interest of Mulry. Unknown to him, Greene took the automobile to Pennsylvania and sold it to Miracle Mile Motors on July 11. The latter obtained a Pennsylvania title certificate to the automobile which stated that it was the owner but bore a notation indicating that the automobile had been brought in from outside of the state. On July 25, Miracle Mile resold the automobile in Pennsylvania to A. C. Lohman, Inc., a New York automobile dealer, who brought the automobile back to New York and sold it on the following May to Churchill Motors, expressly warranting the title. On October 10, Mulry took the automobile from the parking lot of Churchill because he had never been paid by Greene. Churchill then sued Lohman for breach of the warranty of title. From a decision in favor of Churchill, Lohman appealed.

HALPERN, J. . . . This case presents the question of the right of the conditional vendor of an automobile, whose security interest therein had been perfected in accordance with the law of the state in which the automobile had been sold, to enforce the contract and retake the automobile upon default, where the vendee, without the vendor's knowledge or consent, had taken the automobile to another state and sold it to a purchaser for value who was unaware of the outstanding conditional sales contract.

The resale by the vendee in this case took place in Pennsylvania. Therefore the answer to the question turns upon the construction of the Uniform Commercial Code, which was promulgated in 1952 and which was adopted by the Commonwealth of Pennsylvania as of July 1, 1954 (Purdon's Pennsylvania Statutes, Title 12A).

At the time of the promulgation of the Uniform Commercial Code, the generally prevailing rule was that the interest of the conditional vendor would be protected in the circumstances stated. The conditional sales agreement usually prohibited the vendee from taking the automobile out of the state without the vendor's consent. The conditional vendor in such a case would have no reason to anticipate that the vendee would take the automobile out of the state and, in the absence of notice of removal, he would have no opportunity to file the contract in the state to which the automobile had been taken, prior to its resale. Therefore, the risk of loss was thrown upon the person who purchased the automobile from the wrongdoing vendee. . . . However, there were a few jurisdictions, of which Pennsylvania was one, which threw the risk of loss upon the conditional vendor. In those states, the purchaser from the conditional vendee was held to have acquired a title superior to the interest of the conditional vendor, because the vendor had not filed the contract in accordance with the law of the state to which the automobile had been taken. The interests of the local purchaser (and local creditors) were thus preferred over those of the out-of-state vendor. . . .

The Uniform Commercial Code chose a middle course between the majority and minority views in an effort to arrive at a fair compromise between the conflicting interests of the conditional vendor and the purchaser from the vendee.

Subsection (3) of Section 9-103 of the Uniform Commercial Code, 1952 Official Edition, as adopted by Pennsylvania . . . , reads as follows:

"(3) If personal property is already subject to a security interest when it is brought into this state, the validity of the security interest is to be determined by the law of the jurisdiction where the property was when the security interest attached, unless the parties understood at that time that the property would be kept in this state and it was brought here within thirty days thereafter for purposes other than transportation through this state. If the security interest was already perfected under the law of the jurisdiction where the property was kept before being brought into this state, the security interest continues perfected here for four months and also thereafter if within the four month period it is perfected here. The security interest may also be perfected here after the expiration of the four-month period; in such case perfection dates from the time of perfection in this state. If the security interest was not perfected under the law of the jurisdiction where the property was kept before being brought into this state, it may be perfected here; in such case perfection dates from the time of perfection in this state."

This subsection was amended in 1959, effective January 1, 1960, to conform to the 1958 Official Edition of the Uniform Commercial Code, but the amendments are not material in this case. . . .

As will be seen upon a reading of the quoted subsection, the draftsmen of the Code decided that the conditional vendor ought to try to keep track of the property covered by the conditional sales agreement and, when he discovers that the property has been taken to another state, he ought to take reasonably prompt steps to give notice to the public of his interest in accordance with the law of that state. On the other hand, subsequent purchasers and lienors in the state to which the property had been taken would have to take the risk of there being an outstanding security interest in the state from which the property had come, if they purchased the property or acquired a lien upon it shortly after it had been brought into the state and before the vendor had had an opportunity to discover the facts and to perfect his security interest in accordance with the law of the state. A four-month period was chosen as a reasonable period within which the vendor ought to be able to locate the property and to perfect his security interest in the state to which the property had been taken. . . .

. . . All the transactions in the state of Pennsylvania, with respect to the automobile, took place within four months from the time when it was brought into Pennsylvania. Therefore, under the provisions of subsection (3) of Section 9-103 of the Uniform Commercial Code, quoted above, the security interest of the conditional vendor was entitled to full protection in Pennsylvania. The interest had been perfected in Rhode Island, the state in which the automobile had been kept "before being brought into this state" and therefore the security interest continued "perfected here for four months." Therefore, Miracle Mile Motors and the Lohman Company both took subject to the outstanding interest of the conditional vendor (Casterline v. General Motors Acceptance Corp., 195 Pa.Super. 344, 171 A.2d 813 [1961]) . . . .

The defendant-appellant stresses the fact that the conditional vendor did not file the contract in Pennsylvania within four months after the automobile had been brought into the state or at any time thereafter. But the subsequent failure to file is not material in the situation before us. Under the provisions of the Uniform Commercial Code, the conditional vendor's interest continued to be a perfected interest for four months. At the end of that period, it ceased to be a perfected interest and became an unperfected one but there is no provision which forfeits the four-month period of protection because of the failure to file prior to its expiration. The four-month period under the Uniform Commercial Code is thus different from the ten-day grace period allowed under the New York conditional sales law for the original filing of a conditional sales contract (Personal Property Law, § 65). Under the New York statute, if the contract is filed within ten days, the interest of the vendor is deemed perfected from the beginning but if he fails to file within ten days, then the security interest of the vendor remains unperfected from the time of the original sale. (See the provision for a similar 10-day grace period for filing with respect to a purchase money security interest in Section 9-301, subsection (2), of the Uniform Commercial Code.) In contrast with this, the four-month period provided in Section 9-103 (3) of the Uniform Commercial Code is not a grace period for filing; it is an absolute period of protection of the vendor's security interest designed to give him adequate time to make an investigation and to locate the property. If the vendor fails to file within the four-month period, the protection of his security interest ceases upon the expiration of that period and his unperfected security interest is thereafter subject to being defeated in the same way in which any unperfected security interest may be defeated under the Code. A subsequent purchaser for value without notice of the unperfected security interest would take a title superior to it (Uniform Commercial Code, §§ 9-301, 9-307, 1-201 [subsection (9)]). But a prior purchaser who had purchased during the four-month period of statutory protection is not retroactively given a superior title. He is not in the same position as a subsequent purchaser who acquired his interest after the expiration of the four-month period. If the resale to the plaintiff Churchill Motors after the four-month period had taken place in Pennsylvania and had been governed by the provisions of the Uniform Commercial Code, the plaintiff would have acquired a superior title but, as we have seen, that transaction took place in New York and it was not subject to the provisions of the Uniform Code. . . .

Mention should be made of subsection (4), which was added to Section 9-103 by an amendment in 1959 . . ., reading as follows: "(4) Notwithstanding subsections (2) and (3), if personal property is covered by a certificate of title issued under a statute of this state or any other jurisdiction which requires indication on a certificate of title of any security interest in the property as a condition of perfection, then the perfection is governed by the law of the jurisdiction which issued the certificate."

This amendment was part of a general revision of the Uniform Commercial Code to take effect on January 1, 1960, to bring the Pennsylvania statute into conformity with a revision of the Uniform Commercial Code in 1958. The purpose of the amendment was stated by the Editorial Board as follows: "Subsection (4) is new to avoid the possible necessity of duplicating perfection in the case of vehicles subject to a certificate of title law requiring compliance therewith to perfect security interests. The certificate of title law requirements are adopted as the test for perfection." . . .

As the note by the draftsmen makes clear, subsection (4) does not have any application to an automobile which was sold under a conditional sale contract in a state which did not require "indication on a certificate of title of any security interest in the property as a condition of perfection," and which was subsequently brought into a state which had such a requirement. . . .

[Judgment affirmed.]

L. & N. Sales Co. v. Stutski

188 Pa.Super. 117, 146 A.2d 154 (1958)

Stutski purchased 123 beverage pourers from L. & N. Sales Co., which was the sales outlet for the manufacturer. Four writings were signed: (1) a purchase contract on September 28, 1955, which did not release or limit any warranties of the seller; (2) an express written warranty of marketability given on September 28, 1955, which stated that it was in place of any other warranty express or implied and all other liabilities or obligations of the seller; (3) a purchase money security agreement, in the nature of a conditional sales contract executed on October 5, 1955, to secure the purchase price due the seller, the latter reciting that no warranties, guarantees, or representations of any kind were made; and (4) a judgment note authorizing the seller to confess judgment against the buyer on default. The buyer thereafter refused to make payments because the pourers did not work. The sales company then entered a judgment on the note against Stutski. He filed a petition to open the judgment to permit him to make a defense and to rescind the purchase. From the refusal of the court to open the judgment, Stutski appealed.

WATKINS, J. . . . The defendant [buyer], according to the uncontradicted testimony, experienced difficulty with the pourers shortly after their installation in that the meters did not register accurately, the drinks poured were not consistent in that one would be large, another small, and that it was impossible to have any control over the business or inventory under these circumstances. The seller's serviceman attempted to correct the defects and prevent the mechanism from sticking by use of lubricating oil and other means, but was apparently unsuccessful. The defendant after making one monthly payment defaulted and judgment was confessed for the unpaid balance, plus collection fees. . . .

The conditional sales contract, although being a purchase money security interest . . . the sale being controlled by the [Code] article on sales, is still a security agreement and its force and effect controlled by Art. 9, Sec. 206 (3) which expressly prohibits such an agreement from limiting or modifying warranties made in the original contract of sale, as follows: " (3) When a seller retains a purchase money security interest in goods the sale is governed by the Article on Sales (Article 2) and a security agreement cannot limit or modify warranties made in the original contract of sale." Therefore, the conditional sales contract, regardless of language contained therein, under the present circumstances cannot be considered as limiting or releasing plaintiff from liability on any warranty made by the seller at the time the sales contract was executed, since the security agreement was executed subsequent thereto for the purpose of securing the credit extended to the defendant.

The express written warranty of merchantability also could not exclude or modify the warranty of fitness for a particular purpose because these warranties are not inconsistent, and the warranty of fitness is expressly saved from such exclusion by Art. 2, § 317 (c) of the Code, as follows: " (c) Express warranties displace inconsistent implied warranties other than an implied warranty of fitness for a particular purpose." And, although it ostensibly superseded all other warranties, the clear and specific language required by Art. 2, § 316(2)(a) of the Code was not used. This section reads as follows: " (a) All implied warranties are excluded by expressions like 'as is,' 'as they stand,' 'with all faults' or other language which in common understanding calls the buyer's attention to the exclusion of warranties and makes plain that there is no implied warranty."

The time within which a contract of sale must be rescinded must be within a reasonable time under the existing circumstances. In the present case rescission was attempted a month and a half after the pourers were first used. The defendant, according to his uncontradicted testimony, was very desirous that the pourers should work properly, and gave the manufacturer every opportunity to make them work, which appears reasonable. That the manufacturer guaranteed the quality of material and offered to service or replace all the pourers, did not deprive the defendant of his right to rescind as soon as he was satisfied that the pourers could not be made to work satisfactorily.

[Judgment reversed.]

Code Comment: This decision was made under the 1952 text of the Code as adopted in Pennsylvania. The same decision would be made under the 1958 text of the Code, which has since been adopted in Pennsylvania.

Alliance Discount Corp. v. Shaw

195 Pa.Super. 601, 171 A.2d 548 (1961)

Shaw purchased an automobile from Countrywide Motors. The seller financed the purchase, with Shaw executing a contract and a judgment note. Countrywide then sold the contract and note to Alliance Discount Corp. When the installments were not paid on the purchase price, Alliance entered judgment on the note, repossessed the automobile, and sold it at a private sale for a very nominal amount. No notice was given to Shaw of any of the proceedings. He petitioned to open the judgment to permit the true value of the automobile to be shown so that the balance owed on the purchase price could be reduced by the fair value of the automobile. The court opened the judgment on the note, whereupon Alliance appealed.

WATKINS, J. . . . The defendant . . . filed her petition to open the judgment, . . . averring as her defense . . . that the plaintiff failed to give notice of the intention to resell the automobile and failed to give the petitioner any notice of the time and place of sale, as required by the Uniform Commercial Code . . . , which failure was admitted by the plaintiff.

The provision of the Uniform Commercial Code . . . reads as follows: " (3) Disposition of the collateral may be by public or private proceedings and may be made by way of one or more contracts. Sale or other disposition may be as a unit or in parcels and at any time and place and on any terms; but every aspect of the disposition including the method, manner, time, place and terms must be commercially reasonable. Unless collateral is perishable or threatens to decline speedily in value or is of a type customarily sold on a recognized market, reasonable notification of the time and place of any public sale or reasonable notification of the time after which any private sale or other intended disposition is to be made shall be sent by the secured party to the debtor. . . ."

The observation by the court below, in its opinion, is well put. "It is indeed questionable whether there is a 'recognized market' for used automobiles. No other article of commerce is subject to more erratic vacillation in pricing procedures. The so-called 'red book' purporting to fix prices of various makes and models of automobiles in accordance with their year of manufacture is adopted for the convenience and benefit of dealers and is not based on market prices which are arrived at in the open, based on asking prices of sellers and bids of prospective buyers." Notice, as required by the Act, should have been given.

The defendant alleged in her petition that the sale price was grossly inadequate and this was admitted by the plaintiff company. . . .

Further, this debtor was given no opportunity to have the reasonable value of the automobile determined upon resale as required by the Motor Vehicle Sales Finance Act. . . . This Act provided: ". . . That the buyer may have the reasonable value of the motor vehicle at the time of resale, determined in any action or proceeding brought by the seller or holder to recover the deficiency, the resale price being prima facie, but not conclusive evidence, of such reasonable value and the said reasonable value, as determined, or the resale price, whichever shall be higher, shall be credited to the buyer. . . ."

Plaintiff agrees that both the Uniform Commercial Code, supra, and the Motor Vehicle Sales Finance Act, supra, apply to this transaction; however, it is argued that defendant is limited in her rights of action to those set forth in Art. 9 § 504 of the Uniform Commercial Code, upon the failure of the secured party to comply with the Act. While these rights are available to the defendant, she is in no way limited in her means of exercising them. . . .

[Order affirmed.]

Questions and Case Problems

1. What is the objective of each of the following rules of law?
    (a) The seller's right of repossession in a secured credit sale is in addition to his right to sue on the contract for the amount of the purchase price.
    (b) A perfected security interest gives the seller of consumer goods rights that are effective against purchasers of the property from the buyer.

2. The United Gas Improvement Co. sold gas-burning equipment to McFalls for use in his home, the transaction being a lease under which title was retained by the seller until all the installments were paid. U.G.I. did not file the lease or make any other filing. McFalls claimed that it did not have a valid security interest. Decide. (U.G.I. v. McFalls, [Pa.] 18 D.&C.2d 713, 56 Lanc.L.Rev. 431)

3. Hileman purchased a washer from the Maytag Rice Co. on credit and executed a chattel mortgage. The mortgage gave the seller authority "to make use of such force as may be necessary to enter upon, with or without breaking into any premises, where the [goods] may be found." Maytag assigned the contract and mortgage to the Harter Bank & Trust Company. When Hileman failed to pay the installment due, Harter Bank had its employees remove a screen in Hileman's house and enter through a window for the purpose of removing the mortgaged washer. Hileman sued the Harter Bank for unlawfully trespassing upon his property. Was he entitled to damages? (Hileman v. Harter Bank & Trust Co., [Ohio] 186 N.E.2d 853)

4. Bailey purchased a freezer-and-food plan from Pen Del Farms on the installment plan. The latter sold its rights under the contract to the Associated Acceptance Corp. and gave it a copy of the original contract. When Associated sued Bailey, he claimed that the transaction was void under the Maryland Retail Installment Sales Act because the copy of the contract that had been given him had not been fully signed on behalf of the seller. Associated replied that the copy which it had received had been fully executed and that it contained the statement of Bailey that "purchaser acknowledges receipt of true, executed copy of this contract at time of execution hereof." Was Bailey's defense valid? (Associated Acceptance Corp. v. Bailey, [Md.] 174 A.2d 440)

5. Allen, who operated a trailer park, rented a trailer, which at all times remained in the park, to Cady under a lease which gave Cady the option to purchase the trailer. The lease stated that the cash price of the trailer plus various charges was $5,800, of which the down payment was $1,934, and specified that $17 of each weekly payment of $32 was to be applied to the down payment. The lease was for 24 months so that the total payments, if the trailer was not purchased, would be $3,578, or 62 per cent of the price of the trailer. Cady became bankrupt and Cohen, his trustee in bankruptcy, claimed that the interest of Allen in the trailer was void because the transaction was a conditional sale and there had not been any recording of the sales contract. Was Allen's claim to the trailer binding? (Allen v. Cohen, [C.A.2d] 310 F.2d 312)

6. Little Brown Jug, Inc., purchased goods from L. & N. Sales Co. Little Brown Jug later claimed that it was not bound by the conditional sales contract because its representative had been too busy to read it and thought that he was merely signing an order form. Is that a valid defense? (L. & N. Sales Co. v. Little Brown Jug, Inc., [Pa.] 12 D.&C.2d 469)

7. Cook sold to Martin a new tractor truck for approximately $13,000 with a down payment of approximately $3,000 and the balance to be paid in 30 monthly installments. The sales agreement provided that upon default in any payment Cook could take "immediate possession of the property . . . without notice or demand. For this purpose vendor may enter upon any premises the property may be." Martin failed to pay the installments when due, and Cook notified him that the truck would be repossessed. Martin had the tractor truck, attached to a loaded trailer, locked on the premises of a company in Memphis. Martin intended to drive to the West Coast as soon as the trailer was loaded. When Cook located the tractor truck, no one was around. In order to disconnect the trailer from the truck, as Cook had no right to the trailer, Cook removed the wire screen over a ventilator hole by unscrewing it from the outside with his penknife. He next reached through the ventilator hole with a stick and unlocked the door of the tractor truck. He then disconnected the trailer and had the truck towed away. Martin sued Cook for unlawfully repossessing the truck by committing a breach of the peace. Decide. (Martin v. Cook, [Miss.] 114 So.2d 669)

CHAPTER 35

Other Secured Transactions

Subject to certain exceptions, Article 9 of the Uniform Commercial Code regulates all secured transactions dealing with personal property. The secured transaction relating to consumer goods sold on credit has been discussed in Chapter 34. In this chapter other common forms of secured transactions under the Code are considered.

Secured Credit Sales of Inventory

In contrast with one who buys personal property for his own use, the buyer may be a merchant or dealer who intends to resell the goods. Under the Code the goods which such a merchant or dealer buys are classified as *inventory*. The financing of the purchase of inventory may involve a third person as creditor rather than the seller. For example, a third person, such as a bank or finance company, may loan the dealer the money with which to make the purchase and to pay the seller in full. In such a case the security interest given by the buyer in the goods he purchases is given to the third person and not to the seller.[1] Accordingly, the terms "creditor" and "secured party" as used in this chapter may refer to both a seller who sells on credit and a third person who finances the purchase of inventory.

In general, the provisions regulating a secured transaction in inventory follow the same pattern as those applicable to the secured credit sale of consumer goods. Variations are introduced by the Code in recognition of the differences in the commercial settings of the two transactions.

---

[1] Prior to the adoption of the Code, security was frequently provided the person financing the purchase of inventory by the device of a trust receipt, under which the purchaser-merchant would declare that he held the inventory in trust for the creditor. This device was regulated by the Uniform Trust Receipts Act (UTRA) which is in force in Alabama, Arizona, California, Delaware, Florida, Hawaii, Idaho, Maine, Minnesota, Mississippi, Nebraska, Nevada, North Carolina, North Dakota, Puerto Rico, South Dakota, Texas, Utah, Virginia, Washington, and Wisconsin. It had also been adopted in most of the states that have adopted the Code but has been replaced thereby. As to the states that have adopted the Code, see p. 51.

Sec. 35-A. Use of Property and Extent of Security Interest. A secured transaction relating to inventory will generally give the buyer full freedom to deal with the collateral goods as though he were the absolute owner and the goods were not subject to a security interest. Thus the parties may agree that the buyer-dealer may mingle the goods with his own existing inventory, resell the goods, take goods back and make exchanges, and so on, without being required to keep any records of just what became of the goods covered by the security agreement, or to replace the goods sold with other goods, or to account for what is done with the particular goods.[2]

The security agreement may expressly provide that the security interest of the creditor shall bind after-acquired property, that is, other inventory thereafter acquired by the buyer. The combination of the buyer's freedom to use and dispose of the collateral and the subjecting of after-acquired goods to the interest of the secured creditor permits the latter to have a floating lien on a changing or shifting stock of goods of the buyer. Conversely stated, the Code rejects the common-law concept that the security interest was lost if the collateral was not maintained and accounted for separately and that a floating lien upon the buyer's property was void as a fraud against the latter's creditors.

The security agreement also may expressly cover proceeds resulting from the resale of the goods.[3] If the financing statement covers the proceeds, the secured party's security interest continues in the proceeds obtained by the buyer on the resale of the goods. If the original financing statement does not cover such proceeds, the security interest in the proceeds continues for only 10 days unless within that time the secured party perfects his interest therein by filing or by taking possession of the proceeds.[4]

Sec. 35-B. Filing of Financing Statement. Filing is required to perfect the creditor's interest in inventory. An exception is made when a statute, such as a motor vehicle statute, requires the security interest to be noted on the title certificate issued for the property.[5]

(1) Financing Statement. The paper that is filed is a financing statement and is distinct from the security agreement which was executed by the parties to give rise to the secured transaction.[6] The

---

[2] Uniform Commercial Code, Sec. 9-205.

[3] UCC Sec. 9-203(1)(b).

[4] Sec. 9-306(3). Proceeds includes not only money but also checks and other commercial paper, and the account or debt owed by the subpurchaser. Sec. 9-306(1).

[5] Sec. 9-302(1),(3),(4). Reference must be made to the Code as adopted in a particular state as to the place of filing, for the Code as submitted to the states for adoption gave the states the option of providing for a system of state-wide-effective filing with the Secretary of State or of requiring in addition thereto a local county filing in order to perfect the secured interest. See Sec. 9-401.

[6] Sec. 9-402. However, the security agreement may be filed as a financing statement if it contains the required information and is signed by both parties.

financing statement must be signed by both the debtor and the secured party, and it must give an address of the secured party from which information concerning the security interest may be obtained and a mailing address of the debtor; and it must contain a statement indicating the types, or describing the items, of collateral.[7]

(2) Duration and Continuation of Filing. If the debt is due within less than 5 years, the filing is effective for the entire period until the debt matures and for 60 days thereafter. If the debt is not due within 5 years, a filing is effective only for 5 years. At the expiration of the designated period, the perfection of the security interest terminates unless a continuation statement has been filed prior thereto.[8] The *continuation statement* is merely a written declaration by the secured party which indentifies the original filing statement by its file number and declares that it is still effective. The filing of the continuation statement continues the perfection of the security interest for a period of 5 years after the last date on which the original filing was effective. The filing of subsequent continuation statements will continue the perfection indefinitely.[9]

(3) Termination Statement. When the buyer has paid the debt in full, he may make a written demand on the secured party, or the latter's assignee if the security interest has been assigned, to send the buyer a *termination statement* that a security interest is no longer claimed under the specified financing statement. The buyer may then present this statement to the filing officer who marks the record "terminated" and returns to the secured party the various papers which had been filed by him.[10]

(4) Assignments. The secured party may have assigned his interest either before the filing of the financing statement or thereafter. If the assignment was made prior to its filing, the financing statement may include a recital of the assignment and state the name and address of the assignee, or a copy of the assignment may be attached thereto. If the assignment is made subsequent to the filing of the financing statement, a separate written statement of assignment may be filed in the same office.[11]

Sec. 35-C. Protection of Customer of the Buyer. The customer of the buyer takes the goods free from the secured interest of the secured

---

[7] Sec. 9-402(1). The financing statement is effective if it substantially complies with the Code even though it contains minor errors which are not seriously misleading. Sec. 9-402(5).

[8] Sec. 9-403(2). If the obligation is payable on demand, the filing is effective for five years from filing. Code Text 1962.

[9] Sec. 9-403(3).

[10] Sec. 9-404.

[11] Sec. 9-405.

party. That is, one who buys in the ordinary course of business items of property taken from the original buyer's inventory is free of the secured party's interest, even though that interest was perfected and even though such ultimate customer knew of the secured party's interest.[12] (See p. 551, Taylor Motor Rental Case) As an exception to this rule, the buyer of consumer goods or of farm equipment not having an original purchase price in excess of $2,500 is subject to the security interest if it had been perfected by filing prior to the ultimate sale. If it had been perfected without filing, the ultimate buyer is also subject to that security interest unless he buys without knowledge of its existence, for value, and for his own personal, family, or household purposes, or his own farming operations.[13]

Sec. 35-D. Rights and Remedies After Default. The rights and remedies of the secured party and the buyer of inventory after a default on the part of the latter are the same as in the case of a secured credit sale of consumer goods.[14] As a modification of that pattern, however, the creditor taking possession of inventory on the buyer's default is not required to make a sale of the goods but may retain them in full discharge of the debt due, unless an objection is made by the buyer to such retention. In the latter case, the creditor must then make a sale.[15]

Secured Credit Sales of Equipment

The Code makes a distinction, for the purpose of secured transactions, as to the purpose for which a consumer purchases goods. If the ultimate consumer purchases primarily for his personal, family, or household use, the goods are described as consumer goods.[16] The consumer's purchase, however, is described as *equipment* if used or purchased for use primarily in a business, in farming, or in a profession; or if the goods do not constitute consumer goods, inventory, or farm products.[17]

In general, the equipment secured sale is treated the same as a secured transaction as to inventory, except that the various provisions relating to resale by the buyer and the creditor's rights in proceeds have no practical application because the buyer does not resell the property but makes the purchase with the intention to keep and use or operate it.

---

[12] Sec. 9-307(1).
[13] Sec. 9-307(2).
[14] See p. 532.
[15] UCC Sec. 9-505(2). In this situation, the secured creditor must give notice not only to his debtor but also to any other party who has a security interest in the goods and who has properly filed a financing statement, or any person known by the secured party to have a security interest in the goods.
[16] As to the secured credit sale of consumer goods, see Chapter 34.
[17] UCC Sec. 9-109(2).

Filing is required to perfect a purchase money security interest in equipment, with the exception of farm equipment having a purchase price not in excess of $2,500, and motor vehicles which must be licensed under a specific licensing statute.[18]

Secured Loan Transactions

In Chapter 34 and the first part of this chapter, consideration has been given to secured transactions as a means of protecting sellers or third persons financing the purchase of goods. The secured transaction may also be employed to protect one who lends on credit apart from the making of any sale. In the latter case the secured transaction may be one in which the collateral is delivered to or pledged with the creditor, or it may be one in which the borrower retains possession of the collateral.

Sec. 35-E. Pledge. A *pledge* is a secured transaction in which the lender is given possession of the property or collateral in which he has the security interest. More specifically, a pledge is a bailment created as security for the payment of a debt. Under a pledge, specific property is delivered into the possession of a bailee-creditor with the authority, express or implied, that in the event that the debt is not paid, the property may be sold and the proceeds of the sale applied to discharge the debt secured by the pledge. For example, a person borrowing $1,000 may give his creditor property worth $1,000 or more to hold as security. If the borrower repays the loan, the property is returned to him. If he does not repay the debt, the creditor may sell the property and reduce the debt by the amount of the net proceeds of such sale. (See p. 552, Elrae Corporation v. Bankers' Trust Co.)

In general terms, the rights of the debtor (the *pledgor*) and the creditor (the *pledgee*) under a pledge relationship are the same as the rights of a buyer and seller under a secured credit sale of consumer goods.[19] A distinction arises from the fact that the pledgee is given possession from the commencement of the secured transaction, whereas under a secured credit sale the secured party obtains possession only upon default. After a default occurs, the two transactions may be regarded as the same.

(1) Creation and Perfection. The pledge relation arises as soon as it is agreed that the pledgee shall have a security interest in the property which is delivered to him and on the basis thereof he gives value, such as lending money.[20] Filing is not required.[21]

---

[18] Sec. 9-302(1)(c),(3).
[19] See Chapter 34.
[20] UCC Sec. 9-204(1).
[21] Secs. 9-302(1)(a), 9-305.

(2) Duties of Pledgee. Because the secured party or pledgee is in possession of the property or collateral, he must use reasonable care in preserving the property and is liable for damage which results from his failure to do so.[22] The pledgee must keep the collateral separate and identified, although fungible goods [23] of the same kind and quality may be comingled.[24] If money, such as dividends, is received by the pledgee by virtue of his holding the collateral, he must apply such money to the reduction of the debt or send it to the debtor.[25]

Sec. 35-F. Pawn. The term *pawn* is often used to indicate a pledge of tangible personal property, rather than documents representing property rights. In such a case the pledgor is called the *pawner*, and the pledgee is called the *pawnee.*

A person engaged in the business of lending money at interest, in which he requires a pawn or tangible personal property as security, is known as a *pawnbroker.* In order to avoid usurious loan practices and trafficking in stolen goods, the business of professional pawnbroking is generally regulated by statute. State and municipal regulations commonly require the licensing of pawnbrokers, and regulate the general conduct of the business and the charges that may be made for loans. In many states pawnbrokers are permitted to charge a higher rate of interest on small loans than would otherwise be legal.

Sec. 35-G. Securing of Debt Without Change of Possession. This situation is illustrated by the owner of a television set who borrows money from the bank and, to protect the latter, gives the bank a security interest in his property. In general terms, the relation between the lender and the borrower is regulated in the same manner as in the case of a secured credit sale of inventory goods. Filing is required whether or not the collateral constitutes consumer goods.[26] When there is a default in the payment of the debt, the lender has the same choice of remedies under such a secured transaction as the secured credit seller of inventory. (See p. 553, In re Adrian Research and Chemical Co.)

Sec. 35-H. Secured Interest in Goods Being Manufactured. In certain industries, such as the textile industry, the practice developed of advancing money to manufacturers on the security of goods being manufactured or to be sold thereafter. In over half of the states this practice

---

[22] Sec. 9-207(1),(3). The reasonable expenses of caring for the collateral, including insurance and taxes, are charged to the debtor and are secured by the collateral. Sec. 9-207(2)(a).
[23] See p. 338.
[24] UCC Sec. 9-207(2)(d).
[25] Sec. 9-207(2)(c).
[26] Sec. 9-302(1).

was recognized by statutes providing for a *factor's lien* on the manufacturer's goods when a written agreement therefor was properly filed as a public record. These statutes have been replaced by Article 9 of the Code under which the financing party and the manufacturer execute a security agreement giving the lender a security interest in existing goods and, if desired, in goods to be manufactured thereafter, and the proceeds of all such goods. In general this security transaction follows the same pattern as a secured credit sale of inventory.[27]

Cases for Chapter 35

Taylor Motor Rental, Inc. v. Associates Discount Corp.

196 Pa.Super. 182, 173 A.2d 688 (1961)

Associates Discount Corp. held a perfected security interest in an automobile owned by McCurry Motors, Inc. The latter corporation sold the automobile to Taylor Motor Rental, Inc. When payments were not made of the installments due Associates, it repossessed the automobile. Taylor then sued it to recover the automobile. Associates showed that McCurry Motors and Taylor were two corporations that were both managed by Fred McCurry, that the two corporations had common officers, shareholders, and employees, and that Fred McCurry had applied for the state certificate of title in the name of Taylor. From a judgment in favor of Associates, Taylor appealed.

WOODSIDE, J. . . . [Quoting from the opinion of the lower court:] "The precise question in this case is which of the parties was entitled to possession of the automobile. Plaintiff claimed its right to possession by virtue of its purported purchase from McCurry, and the defendant claimed its right to possession of the automobile by virtue of its secured interest.

"There can be no question that the defendant had a valid and perfected security interest in the automobile under the provisions of the Uniform Commercial Code, 12A P.S. § 1-101, et seq. It gave value for the automobile by its payment of the purchase price to the Studebaker factory, it obtained a security agreement which described the automobile by serial number and it had on file in appropriate offices a properly executed financing statement which described the type of property it was financing for McCurry Motors. . . .

"Defendant's security interest in the automobile was enforceable against everyone, except as otherwise provided in the Commercial Code. . . . Plaintiff claims to be a buyer in the ordinary course of business and relies on (§ 9-307) . . . .

"It is clear that plaintiff was not a buyer in the ordinary course of business as defined by the Commercial Code. Both the relationship of

---

[27] See p. 545.

plaintiff and McCurry, with their interlocking officers, shareholders, and employees and the fact that both plaintiff corporation and McCurry Motors, Inc., were managed by Fred McCurry negates this. Moreover, Fred McCurry acted for both plaintiff and McCurry Motors, Inc., in applying for the certificate of title in the name of the plaintiff. . . . The purported sale by McCurry Motors, Inc., to the plaintiff was merely a paper transaction for the benefit of Fred McCurry [to obtain] the automobile for which defendant has never been paid.". . .

Only if the appellant were "a buyer in ordinary course of business" would it take free of the appellee's security interest. The facts set forth above clearly support the trial court's finding that the transaction was not in the ordinary course of business. . . .

[Judgment affirmed.]

Code Comment: UCC Sec. 9-307 (1) provides "a buyer in ordinary course of business . . . other than a person buying farm products from a person engaged in farming operations, takes free of a security interest created by his seller even though the security interest is perfected and even though the buyer knows of its existence." A buyer in ordinary course of business is defined as "a person who in good faith and without knowledge that the sale to him is in violation of the ownership rights or security interest of a third party in the goods buys in ordinary course from a person in the business of selling goods of that kind. . . ." Sec. 1-201(9).

Elrae Corporation v. Bankers' Trust Co.

105 N.J.Eq. 501, 148 A. 652 (1930)

The Elrae Corporation purchased land subject to a mortgage held by Proffett. Proffett pledged the mortgage to Schmeidler as security for debts owed the Second National Bank and Hanstein. Schmeidler, without giving proper notice to the pledgor, sold the mortgage to the Second National Bank, which claimed to be entitled to the interest due. The Bankers' Trust Company also claimed the interest as assignee of the mortgage under an assignment made by Proffett. The Elrae Corporation brought a bill of interpleader to determine to whom the interest should be paid.

INGERSOLL, V.C. . . . It is a well-settled rule of the common law that the pledgee, upon default, may sell at public auction the chattel pledged . . . upon giving the debtor reasonable notice to redeem. . . . The notice of his intention to sell and of the time and place of sale is always necessary for the making of a binding sale of the property pledged, unless by agreement of the parties such notice has been expressly or impliedly waived.

Again, if the debt secured is not one which becomes due at a fixed time, there can be no default upon the occurrence of which a sale of the pledge can be made until the pledgee makes demand of payment or gives notice of the occurrence of the event which constitutes a default; or it may be that the event upon which a default occurs is one peculiarly within the knowledge of the pledgee; or it may be that such event is one which it is his option to declare. In such cases, of course, there is no default until the pledgee makes demand of payment or gives notice of the default.

. . . Where the debt secured is not payable at a fixed time, a demand of payment, or that the pledge securing the debt be redeemed, should be made before the creditor can properly dispose of the pledged property; and . . . if the debtor be absent or cannot be found, judicial proceedings should be had to bar his right of redemption. . . . Also, . . . where provision is that the pledgee may sell in case the securities depreciate in their market value, the pledgor is entitled to notice to redeem. A sale without notice in such case will not pass the pledgor's right of redemption. . . .

There was no notice given by the pledgee to the pledgor. . . . The sale of the mortgage . . . must be set aside. . . .

Code Comment: The same decision would be made under the Code which requires notice of sale by the secured party. UCC Sec. 9-504(3),(4).

In re Adrian Research and Chemical Co.

269 F.2d 734 (C.A.3rd, 1959)

Adrian Research and Chemical Co. owed over $7,000 back rent to Kirkpatrick. To protect Kirkpatrick, Adrian gave him a judgment note for the amount of the overdue rent and entered into a security agreement that gave Kirkpatrick a security interest in the office, laboratory, and plant equipment of Adrian. Kirkpatrick entered judgment on the note. About six months later Kirkpatrick issued execution, the sheriff served the execution process, and the date of the sale of Adrian's property was advertised. Before the sale could take place, Adrian went into bankruptcy and Kirkpatrick filed a petition claiming the property covered by the security agreement. The referee in bankruptcy and the District Court refused to recognize Kirkpatrick's claim to the property and decided that he was merely a general creditor. From that decision, Kirkpatrick appealed.

KALODNER, C.J. . . . The single issue presented is whether the petitioner Kirkpatrick is deprived of the lien of his perfected secured claim because he took judgment against the debtor, issued execution, and caused a levy to be made. . . .

. . . The security arrangement was made pursuant to and perfected by compliance with the Pennsylvania Uniform Commercial Code. . . .

Also, on September 10, 1957, as evidence of his obligation, the debtor executed and delivered to the petitioner a judgment note in the sum of $7,600, and judgment was entered thereon on September 12, 1957.

On March 12, 1958, because of the debtor's default, the petitioner issued execution on the judgment and caused a levy to be made on all of the debtor's personal property, which included the personal property covered by the security agreement. Bills were posted advertising the sheriff's sale. . . .

The District Court held, as did the Referee, that since the petitioner elected to issue execution and to levy on the assets of the debtor, he was barred from asserting a security interest to "retake" the personal property on the ground that the execution was inconsistent with the right to take possession. . . .

The validity of petitioner's asserted lien is a question to be decided under Pennsylvania law, for it is not disputed that if petitioner has such a lien, he is in a protected position under the Bankruptcy Act. . . .

The Pennsylvania courts have emphasized that distinct remedies may be used concurrently or alternately if they are consistent in purpose and kind; they must be inconsistent and not merely cumulative in order for the selection of one to operate as a bar to the pursuit of the other. . . .

. . . The relationship of the petitioner to the bankrupt debtor was that of creditor and debtor, the debt being evidenced by the note. The chattels covered by the security agreement were collateral for the debt. The assertion by the petitioner of the note of obligation against the debtor in legal proceedings and his attempt to collect it by execution and levy can hardly be said to be inconsistent with the assertion of his claim upon the collateral.

The remedies are consistent both in kind and purpose, for each results in the application to the debt of the chattels covered by the security agreement and each has as its objective the reduction of the debt. The absence of inconsistency is highlighted by respondent's concession that petitioner could have proceeded first against the collateral, and if a deficiency remained, proceeded by execution and levy against any other property of the debtor.

What respondent suggests is a requirement that the collateral must first have been exhausted, and unless this occurred, the petitioner would lose his security by proceeding against the debtor to collect the debt. In the analogous case of a pledge, such is not the law of Pennsylvania. The holder of a note may maintain his action without realizing or attempting to realize upon the collateral. . . . Absent an agreement to the contrary, the creditor is entitled to hold the collateral security until the debt is paid and is not under obligation to sell; it is only upon payment of the debt that the debtor is entitled to the collateral. . . .

We can observe no essential factor in the case now before this Court which would place the petitioner in a different position, there being nothing in the security agreement to restrict the rights of the petitioner. The obligation of the debtor was to pay the debt, and neither he nor his successor, the trustee in bankruptcy, became entitled to the collateral security until the debt was discharged. It follows that the petitioner did not waive his right to rely on the collateral when he proceeded by execution and levy to enforce the judgment. . . .

[Order reversed and cause remanded.]

Questions and Case Problems

1. What is the object of each of the following rules of law?
   (a) In a secured credit sale of inventory, the buyer generally can deal with the collateral goods as if he were the absolute owner.
   (b) When the buyer in a secured credit sale of inventory has paid the debt in full, he is entitled to a termination statement from the secured party.

2. Warren Lepley Ford, Inc., a dealer, purchased new automobiles from the manufacturer and gave the Girard Trust Corn Exchange Bank a security interest. Were the automobiles consumer goods? (Girard Trust Corn Exchange Bank v. Warren Lepley Ford, Inc., No. 1, [Pa.] D.&C.2d 351)

3. Is any of the following statements sufficient for a description of the collateral subject to a security interest:
   (a) "Passenger and commercial automobiles financed by Girard Trust Corn Exchange Bank?" (Girard Trust Corn Exchange Bank v. Warren Lepley Ford, Inc., No. 2, [Pa.] 13 D.&C.2d 119)
   (b) "Future accounts receivable?" (Industrial Packaging Products Co. v. Fort Pitt Packaging International, Inc., 399 Pa. 643, 161 A.2d 19)
   (c) A description of an automobile that does not contain a serial number? (Girard Trust Corn Exchange Bank v. Warren Lepley Ford, Inc., No. 2, [Pa.] 13 D.&C.2d 119)

4. Gordetsky took his wife's jewelry without her consent and pledged it with Cohen, a pawnbroker, as security for a loan. When his wife learned of this, she sued Cohen to recover the jewelry. He defended on the ground that a New Jersey statute provides that a pawnbroker cannot be required to surrender the pledged property unless the pawn ticket is surrendered or unless a court has ordered the ticket impounded or has enjoined its negotiation. The wife did not have the pawn ticket, which was held by the husband. Was she entitled to the jewelry without the ticket? (Gordetsky v. Cohen, [N.J.S.] 89 A.2d 84)

5. The Girard Trust Corn Exchange Bank financed the purchase of new cars by Warren Lepley Ford, Inc., an automobile dealer. A security agreement was executed between the bank and the dealer, and proper filing was made. Thereafter, the dealer sold the cars that had been purchased as the result of this transaction with the bank and then purchased other cars with the proceeds of the money. Warren Lepley later became insolvent. Girard Trust claimed that it was entitled to a security interest in the subsequently-purchased cars in the hands of the receiver. The receiver contended that the right of the bank did not go beyond the cash

proceeds and was lost once the cash proceeds were spent in any way. Decide. (Girard Trust Corn Exchange Bank v. Warren Lepley Ford, Inc., No. 3, [Pa.] 25 D.&C.2d 395)

6. U.G.I. sold "one-houshold laundry dryer" to Henry by a sales agreement in the form of a lease under which title was retained by U.G.I. until all installments were paid. Later, Henry sold the dryer to McFalls, a dealer in used appliances, who purchased for a resale. No filing of any nature had been made, and McFalls purchased in ignorance of any claim of U.G.I. Later, U.G.I. demanded the return of the dryer because Henry had stopped making payments. When McFalls refused to return it, U.G.I. sued McFalls. Was U.G.I. entitled to recover? (U.G.I. v. McFalls, [Pa.] 18 D.&C.2d 707)

7. Maulding was in the business of selling trailers. In order to finance his transactions, he entered into a "floor plan agreement" with the Bank of Fairbanks. Thereafter, Manhattan Trailer Sales sold a trailer to the bank. The bank "floored" the trailer with Maulding after he executed a document which acknowledged receipt of the property, designated it as trust property, declared that the bank had a security interest in the trailer until Maulding paid a note which he gave for the purchase price. Maulding, described in the document as "trustee," likewise agreed to return the trailer "on demand and in good order and unused"; to sell it as "trustee" for the bank and, in the event of sale to notify the bank promptly, to hold the proceeds in trust for it, and to deliver such proceeds promptly to the bank. Maulding sold the trailer but kept all of the purchase price for himself. He was then prosecuted for the crime of "embezzlement by bailee." Was he guilty? (Maulding v. United States, [C.A. 9th] 257 F.2d 56)

8. McDivitt purchased two trucks from Harris Ford, Inc., under "bailment leases" which provided for the obtaining of title by McDivitt after the "rentals" paid under the leases reached a specified amount. Harris Ford sold its rights under the sales contract and bailment leases to the Universal C.I.T. Credit Corporation. Thereafter, McDivitt failed to pay the installments when due and was notified that if he did not pay up the back installments by a specified date, action would be taken by the finance company to enforce its rights. Subsequent thereto, but before any such action was taken, McDivitt was fined for having the two trucks driven with excess loads in violation of the Motor Vehicle Code. As the fine was not paid for this offense, the two trucks were put up for sale under the provisions of the local statute. This was proper if McDivitt was the owner of the trucks. The finance company objected that it was the owner and therefore the enforcement proceeding was illegal. Decide. (Commonwealth v. Two Ford Trucks, 185 Pa.Super. 292, 137 A.2d 847)

9. Leonard owned an automobile subject to a chattel mortgage held by Harvard Trust Co. His automobile struck the automobile of Racheotes as a result of the negligence of both parties. At the time of the accident the balance due on the chattel mortgage was $318. The damage to the automobile was $506. Harvard sued Racheotes for $506. Decide. (Harvard Trust Co. v. Racheotes, [Mass.] 147 N.E.2d 817)

CHAPTER 36

Suretyship and Guaranty

The relationship by which one person becomes responsible for the debt or undertaking of another person is used most commonly to insure that a debt will be paid or that a contractor will perform the work called for by his contract.

Nature and Creation

Sec. 36-A. Nature of the Relationship. A distinction may be made between two kinds of agreements by which a third person agrees to pay another's debt if the debtor does not. One kind is called a contract or undertaking of *suretyship,* and the third person is called a *surety.* The other kind is called a contract or undertaking of *guaranty,* and the third person is called the *guarantor.* In both cases, the person who owes the money or is under the original obligation to pay is called the *principal,*[1] the principal debtor, or debtor, and the person to whom the debt is owed is known as the *creditor.*

Both suretyship and guaranty undertakings have the common feature of a promise to answer for the debt or default of another; but they have a basic difference. The surety is primarily liable for the debt or obligation of the principal; ordinarily the guarantor is only secondarily liable. This means that the moment the principal is in default, the creditor may demand performance or payment of the surety. He generally cannot do so in the case of the guarantor; he must first attempt to collect from the principal. An exception is an "absolute guaranty" which creates the same obligation as a suretyship contract. A guaranty of the payment of a note creates an absolute guaranty.

---

[1] The word "principal" is also used by the law to identify the person who employs the agent. The "principal" in suretyship must be distinguished from the agent's "principal."

There is frequently confusion in the use of the terms suretyship and guaranty, and it becomes a question of construction to determine what the parties really intended by their contract. In some states it is provided by statute that an undertaking to answer for the debt of another is to be interpreted as a suretyship agreement in the absence of an express statement that only a guaranty agreement was intended.

Sec. 36-B. Indemnity Contract. Both suretyship and guaranty differ from an *indemnity contract* which is an undertaking by one person for a consideration to pay another person a sum of money to indemnify him when he incurs a certain loss. A fire insurance policy is a typical example of an indemnity contract.

Sec. 36-C. Creation of the Relation. Suretyship and guaranty are ordinarily based upon contract, express or implied. All of the principles applicable to the formation, validity, and interpretation of contracts are therefore generally applicable to the law of suretyship. The liability of a surety is measured by the terms of his contract or bond, and his obligation is not necessarily as broad as that of his principal. (See p. 561, Bevard v. New Amsterdam Casualty Co.)

(1) Offer and Acceptance. Generally the ordinary rules of offer and acceptance apply. Notice of the acceptance, however, must sometimes be given by the creditor or the guarantor.

(2) Consideration. A suretyship relation may be created by the contract of the parties either before, after, or at the same time as the principal obligation. Ordinarily there must be consideration for the promise of the surety.

If the suretyship undertaking is entered into before or at the time the principal obligation arises, a separate consideration is not required. (See p. 563, McMillan v. Dozier). If the suretyship promise is made afterwards, it must be supported by a separate consideration since the prior transaction would be "past" consideration.

When the surety or guarantor is a party to a commercial paper, he cannot raise the defense of lack of consideration if the instrument is in the hands of a holder in due course or a holder through a holder in due course.

(3) Capacity. Anyone with capacity to contract can be a surety for the obligation of another. In many instances the surety is a corporation organized for the purpose of acting as surety in return for a payment of a premium.

(4) Form. In most states the Statute of Frauds requires that contracts of guaranty be in writing in order to be enforceable, sub-

ject to the exception that no writing is required when the promisor makes the promise primarily for his own benefit.[2]

In the absence of a special statute, no writing is required for contracts of suretyship or indemnity, because they impose primary liability, and not a secondary liability to answer for the debt or default of another. Special statutes or sound business practices, however, commonly require the use of written contracts of suretyship and indemnity.

Sec. 36-D. Special Classes of Surety Contracts. Suretyship or guaranty undertakings are sometimes classified as general or special. If the offer is made to the general public or to anyone who becomes the owner of the debt, it is a *general guaranty*. If the offer is made to a particular person and cannot be accepted by another, it is called a *special guaranty*. This is an application of the principle of contract law that an offer can be accepted only by the person to whom it is made.

The undertaking may be classified in terms of its scope. It is a *continuing guaranty*, for example, when the promisor engages to answer for the payment of as many automobiles as another person desires to purchase or of as many loans as he might make in the future. A *limited guaranty* is restricted to transactions made during a stated period of time or to transactions not exceeding a stated amount. If no restrictions are imposed, an *unlimited guaranty* exists.

Rights of the Parties

Sec. 36-E. Rights and Duties of the Creditor.

(1) Right to Demand Payment or to Sue. In a suretyship and an absolute guaranty the creditor may proceed against the surety immediately upon the default of the principal, without proceeding against the principal. This explains why the surety is regarded as subject to a primary liability, or one in the same degree as the debtor.

In a conditional guaranty the creditor must first exercise due diligence to obtain payment from the debtor before he can make demand upon or sue the guarantor, unless the debtor is insolvent or bankrupt so that it is obvious that a suit against him would be worthless. This in turn explains why the guarantor is regarded as subject to a secondary liability.

A delay on the part of the creditor in bringing his action against the debtor will not ordinarily affect his right against the guarantor. If the delay has prejudiced the guarantor, as when the debtor went bankrupt in the interval, however, the latter is released from liability.

(2) Duty to Give Notice of Default. In the case of strict suretyship or absolute guaranty, the creditor is not required to give the

---

[2] See p. 177.

surety or guarantor notice of the default of the principal, unless he is expressly required to do so by the contract.

In a conditional guaranty, notice must be given by the creditor within a reasonable time so that the guarantor can take steps to protect himself. If notice is not given, the guarantor is released from liability to the extent that he can show that he was prejudiced by the creditor's failure to give notice.

(3) Security Held by the Surety. The surety may be unwilling to act as such unless the debtor transfers property to him as security. If the debtor gives property to the surety as security, the creditor is entitled to satisfy his claim out of such property.

When the right exists for the surety to reach the debtor's property given to the surety as security, the right of the creditor to obtain satisfaction from the security is not lost by virtue of the fact that the creditor has lost his right to sue the surety for any reason, such as the running of the Statute of Limitations.

Sec. 36-F. Rights of the Surety. The surety has a number of rights to protect him from sustaining loss, to obtain his discharge because of the conduct of others that would be harmful to him, or to recover the money that he has been required to pay because of his contract.

(1) Exoneration. If the surety finds his position threatened with danger, as when the debtor is about to leave the state and take his property with him, the surety may call upon the creditor to take steps to enforce his claim against the debtor while he can still do so. If at that time the creditor could proceed against the debtor and fails to do so, the surety is released or exonerated from liability to the extent that he can show that he has been harmed.

(2) Subrogation. When a surety pays a debt that he is obligated to pay, he is subrogated to the claim and the right of the creditor. That is, once the creditor is paid in full, the surety stands in the same position as the creditor and may sue the debtor, or enforce any security that was available to the creditor, in order to recover the amount that he has paid. The effect is the same as if the creditor, on being paid, made an express assignment of all his rights to the surety.

(3) Indemnity. A surety who has made payment of a claim for which he was liable as surety is entitled to indemnity from the principal, that is, he is entitled to demand from the principal reimbursement of the amount which he has paid.

(4) Contribution. If there are two or more sureties, each is liable to the creditor for the full amount of the debt, until the creditor has

been paid in full. As between themselves, however, each is only liable for a proportionate share of the debt. Accordingly, if the surety has paid more than his share of the debt, he is entitled to demand that his cosureties contribute to him in order to share the burden. The right to contribution does not arise until the debt due the creditor has been paid in full.

Sec. 36-G. Defenses of the Surety.

(1) Ordinary Defenses. Since the relationship of suretyship is based upon a contract, the surety may raise any defense that a party to an ordinary contract may raise, such as lack of capacity of parties, absence of consideration, fraud, mistake, or absence of a required writing.

Fraud and concealment are common defenses. Since the risk of the principal's default is thrown upon the surety, it is unfair for the creditor to conceal from the surety facts that are material to the surety's risk. (See p. 564, W. I. Carpenter Lumber Co. v. Hugill) Fraud on the part of the principal that is unknown to the creditor and in which he has not taken part does not ordinarily release the surety.

The creditor is not required to volunteer information to the surety and need not disclose that the principal was insolvent.

(2) Suretyship Defenses. In addition to the ordinary defenses that can be raised against any contract, the following defenses are peculiar to the suretyship relation:

(a) Invalidity of original obligation.

(b) Discharge of principal by release, payment, performance, or any other means.

(c) Material modification of the original contract to which the surety does not consent (see p. 565, Watkins Co. v. Eaker), particularly by a binding extension of time for performing the original contract.

(d) Loss of securities that had been given the creditor to hold as additional security for the performance of the original contract, to the extent of such loss.

Cases for Chapter 36

Bevard v. New Amsterdam Casualty Co.

132 A.2d 157 (M.C.App. D.C., 1957)

Bevard and other persons who had supplied labor and material used in the construction of a warehouse sued the New Amsterdam Casualty Co. on the bond which it had given to the owner of the warehouse to indemnify him from loss if the contractor failed to perform the contract.

The bond made no provision for the payment of labor and materialmen. From a judgment in favor of the surety, Bevard and others appealed.

HOOD, A.J. . . . The condition of the bond was: "That if the Principal (the contractor) shall indemnify the Obligee (the owners) against any loss or damage directly arising by reason of the failure of the Principal faithfully to perform said contract, then this obligation shall be void; otherwise it shall remain in full force and effect." . . .

Appellants argue that although the undertaking of the surety was in form an indemnity bond for the owners alone, it should be construed in connection with the contract to which it referred and that when so construed there is evidenced a clear intention that the bond was given for the protection not only of the owners but also for the laborers, materialmen, and subcontractors.

The contract provided for delivery by the contractor to the owners of "a performance and material and supplies and labor payment bond," securing the owners "the performance of this agreement and the payment of material and labor." Another part of the contract provided: "Wherever in this agreement the words 'performance bond and material and labor payments bonds' [are] mentioned, it is intended by the parties to mean a performance bond which will include requirement for the payment of labor and material."

It is perfectly plain that under the contract the owners could have demanded of the contractor a combined performance and labor and material payment bond; but it is just as plain that they did not, and instead accepted an indemnity bond. . . .

While many recent cases tend to find an intention to benefit materialmen and subcontractors in performance bonds and payment bonds, or a combination of the two, we have found no case holding that such parties may sue on a strict indemnity bond, as is the bond in this case. A surety's obligation must be measured by the condition stated in the bond, and when the condition is, as here, merely to indemnify the owner against loss or damage by reason of the failure of the contractor to perform, such condition cannot be construed to go further than its terms and give rights to others not mentioned either expressly or by intendment.

A recent case in our neighboring State of Maryland is very much in point. On facts very similar to those in our case, in denying recovery to a materialman and subcontractor, the court said:

"It is clear, under these provisions [of the contract], that the owner could have required the principal to furnish a payment bond, and not merely an indemnity bond, but the surety was not obliged to make its undertaking coextensive with that of the principal. The short answer is, that the bond furnished was not a payment, but merely an indemnity bond. The surety did not agree to be responsible for everything that the principal undertook to do, but only for such of his failures as caused loss to the owner." Board of Education of Montgomery County to Use of Breedon v. Victor N. Judson, Inc., 211 Md. 188, 126 A.2d 615, 616. . . .

[Judgment affirmed.]

McMillan v. Dozier

257 Ala. 435, 59 So.2d 563 (1952)

The president of the Dixie Provision Co. negotiated with Dozier for a loan. On August 29, they entered into a contract which the president did not have authority to make. The loan contract was submitted to the stockholders of the company and ratified by them by resolution adopted September 9. At the same meeting they adopted a resolution individually guaranteeing to pay the amount loaned to the corporation by Dozier. Thereafter when the loan was not repaid, Dozier sued McMillan and the other stockholders on their guaranty. They claimed that they had not received any consideration for the guaranty. From the judgment in favor of Dozier, the stockholders appealed.

LAWSON, J. . . . Appellants [stockholders], in support of their contention that the guaranty agreement . . . is invalid because without consideration, rely upon . . . the general rule . . . that the undertaking of one not a party to the original transaction who, in pursuance of some subsequent arrangement, signs an instrument as surety, grantor, or endorser, after the original contract has been fully executed and delivered and without agreement at the time of the execution of the original contract that additional security would be furnished, is a new and independent contract and to be binding must be supported by a new consideration, independent from that of the original contract.

We do not think the rule stated above has application to the instant case, for as we view the record, the . . . contract and guaranty agreement seem to us to have been parts of the same transaction, finally executed on the same day and, hence, there was no necessity for any independent consideration for the execution of the guaranty agreement. Where the contract of guaranty is made before or at the same time as the principal contract, and both contracts form parts of the same transaction, one consideration is sufficient. . . . The guaranty agreement which appellants claim was without consideration was signed on the same day as the resolution ratifying the financing agreement of August 29. . . .

It is our opinion that the contract of August 29, the resolution of September 9, ratifying that contract, as well as the resolution bearing the same date expressly guaranteeing the payment, were all parts of one continuing transaction and that the guaranty agreement was not a new and independent undertaking requiring a new consideration.

[Judgment affirmed.]

W. I. Carpenter Lumber Co. v. Hugill

149 Wash. 45, 270 P. 94 (1928)

Hugill agreed to deliver shingles to the W. I. Carpenter Lumber Co. He furnished a surety bond to secure the faithful performance of the contract on his part. After a breach of the contract by Hugill, the lumber company brought an action to recover its loss from the surety, the Fidelity & Deposit Co. of Maryland. The surety contended that the relation of suretyship had not been created because of the concealment of material facts on the part of the lumber company. From a judgment for the defendant, the plaintiff appealed.

FULLERTON, C.J. . . . It is the rule that parties to contracts of this sort, as in all other contracts, must exercise towards each other entire good faith and that any concealment of facts which materially affects the contract, or which induces a party to enter into a contract which he would not otherwise enter into, avoids it. . . .

"The contract of suretyship imports entire good faith and confidence between the parties in regard to the whole transaction. . . . So generally it has been said that, if a creditor induces a surety to enter into the contract of suretyship by any fraudulent concealment of material facts or by any express or implied misrepresentation of such facts, or by taking any undue advantage of the surety, either by surprise or by withholding proper information, there will be afforded a sufficient ground for the invalidation of the contract. . . .

In this instance, we are satisfied that the concealment was of material facts. There was a concealment, not only of the price to be paid for the shingles, but a concealment of the fact that a material advance payment was to be made to Hugill. The first, standing alone, would perhaps not operate to relieve the respondent [surety] from liability on the bond on the principle of noninjury, but the second clearly operates to the injury of the bondsman. The advancement represented, so the evidence disclosed, the profit Hugill could reasonably expect to make out of the transaction. The bondsman was thus deprived of the security the contract gave it, and the contractor was relieved of any incentive to perform the contract; [circumstances] sufficient . . . to render the bond nugatory.

[Judgment for defendant affirmed.]

Watkins Co. v. Eaker

56 N.Mex. 385, 244 P.2d 540 (1952)

The Watkins Co. contracted to supply Charles Eaker on credit with goods for resale for a period of forty months. Amanda Eaker and others gave the company a bond guaranteeing that Charles would pay for the goods. After six months the company refused to supply goods on credit and demanded cash from Charles. The company and Charles continued on a cash basis for almost two years when the company terminated the contract and then sued Charles and the sureties. The sureties raised the defense that they were released because of the company's refusal to continue to supply goods on credit. From an adverse judgment the company appealed.

McGHEE, J. . . . The finding . . . of the trial court that credit was wrongfully withdrawn from Eaker and his business so reduced that he could not continue it is sustained by the record.

The plaintiff still contends this would not discharge the sureties; that its action . . . was really of benefit to them in that Eaker's account was not increased, thereby relieving the sureties of an additional burden. . . .

The contract between the plaintiff and Eaker was made a part of the contract of suretyship. The plaintiff changed the contract from one of sales on credit to Eaker to one for cash. . . .

It is well settled . . . that a surety is liable only for the performance of the contract for which he becomes surety, and that any alteration thereof discharges such surety. . . .

To charge him beyond its terms, or to permit it to be altered without his consent, would be not to enforce the contract made by him, but to make another for him. . . . "And a discharge will be created by a departure from the terms of the contract respecting payments, though no injury is shown.". . .

"It will thus be seen that it is the deviation from the terms of the contract that operates to release the surety, and not the injury or damage done by such departure. . . ."

[Judgment affirmed.]

Questions and Case Problems

1. What is the objective of each of the following rules of law?
   (a) Even though the Statute of Limitations may prevent the creditor from suing the surety, he can obtain satisfaction from the debtor's property that has been given to the surety as security.
   (b) Fraud on the part of the principal that is unknown to the creditor and in which he has not taken part does not ordinarily release the surety from liability.

2. Cohen was a subcontractor under certain government contracts for work to be done at the Homestead Air Force Base in Florida. The Capital

Indemnity Insurance Co. was the surety on his bond to perform his contract and to pay labor and material claims. Cohen made a contract by which Maule Industries supplied him with materials. About a half year later, Cohen defaulted and told the plaintiff to look to Capital for payment of the balance then due of some $50,000. After negotiations, Maule Industries accepted a substantial partial payment from Capital and gave it a release from further liability. Maule then sued Cohen for the balance. He defended on the ground that he was released from liability when his surety, without his knowledge or consent, was given a release by Maule. Was Cohen liable for the unpaid balance? (Maule Industries, Inc. v. Cohen, [Fla.] 117 So.2d 37)

3. Lambert loaned Heaton $25,000 for six months. Heaton gave a promissory note, payable at the end of six months, in the face amount of $30,000, thereby concealing the fact that usurious interest was charged. Under the local statute, the loan contract was, in fact, void, because of the usury. Heaton obtained a bond from the United Bonding Insurance Co., which guaranteed to Lambert that the promissory note would be paid when due. When the note was not paid, Lambert sued Heaton and the bonding company. The latter raised the defense that its obligation was voided because the usurious character of the transaction had not been disclosed to it. Decide. (Lambert v. Heaton, [Fla.] 134 So.2d 536)

4. The State Highway Department entered into a contract with the Sloan Construction Co. for the construction of a section of highway. The Federal Insurance Co. furnished its bond to the Highway Department by which it guaranteed the faithful performance of the contract, including the payment of all lawful claims by reason of injuries received in and about the construction. Ward was injured through the alleged negligence of Miller, one of the highway employees. She sued Miller and obtained a judgment by default against him since he did not make any defense to the action. When the amount of the judgment was not paid, Ward sued Federal Insurance Co. It raised the defense that the judgment against Miller was improper because he had not been responsible for the accident and because the judgment had been entered against him without any defense having been made by him. Was Federal Insurance liable? (Ward v. Federal Insurance Co., [S.C.] 106 S.E.2d 169)

5. The Northwest Recapping Inc. negotiated with Industrial Credit Co. to obtain loans on the security of its accounts receivable. In order to persuade Industrial to enter into such an agreement, Dahmes executed a "guarantee" of the repayment of any such loans. The guarantee stated that the liability of Dahmes was "direct and unconditional" and "may be enforced without requiring lender first to resort to any other right, remedy, or security." Under the applicable local statute, the loans made by Industrial were usurious, but under the same law, Northwest Recapping could not raise the defense of usury because a statute prohibited corporations from raising such a defense. Later, when Industrial Credit sued Dahmes, he contended that his undertaking under the "guarantee" was his own personal contract so that he, as an individual, could assert the defense of usury. Decide. (Dahmes v. Industrial Credit Company, [Minn.] 110 N.W.2d 484)

CHAPTER 37

Creation and Termination

One of the most common legal relationships is that of agency. When it exists, one person can act for and can stand in place of another. The law might have held that each man must act for himself and that no one could act through another. This would have greatly handicapped the development of the modern economic world, for it would have limited each man to what he himself could do. Today, by virtue of the agency device, one man can make contracts at a hundred different places at the same time.

Nature of the Agency Relationship

Agency is a relation based upon an express or implied agreement whereby one person, the *agent,* is authorized to act under the control of and for another, his *principal,* in business transactions with third persons.[1] The acts of the agent obligate the principal to third persons and give the principal rights against the third persons.

Agency is based upon the consent of the parties and, for that reason, it is called a consensual relation. If consideration is present, the relationship is also contractual. The law sometimes imposes an agency relationship.[2]

The term "agency" is frequently used with other meanings. It is sometimes used to denote the fact that one has the right to sell certain products, such as when a dealer is said to possess an automobile

---

[1] Restatement of the Law of Agency, 2d, Sec. **1.**
[2] See p. 573.

agency. In other instances, the term is used to mean an exclusive right to sell certain articles within a given territory. In these cases, however, the dealer is not an agent in the sense of representing the manufacturer. The right of the dealer under such arrangements is frequently represented by a *franchise* which he purchases from the manufacturer or supplier.

Sec. 37-A. Agent Distinguished from Employee and Independent Contractor. An agent is distinguished from an employee in that the employee is not hired to represent the employer in dealings with third persons. It is possible, however, for the same person to be both an agent and an employee. For example, the driver of a milk delivery truck is an agent in making contracts between the milk company and its customers, but he is an employee with respect to the work of delivering the milk.

An agent or employee differs from an *independent contractor* in that the principal or employer has control over and can direct an agent or an employee, but the other party to the contract does not have control over the performance of the work by an independent contractor.

Sec. 37-B. Purpose of Agency. Usually an agency may be created to perform any act which the principal himself could lawfully do. The object of the agency may not be criminal, nor may it be contrary to public policy. Thus the courts will not enforce an agency contract by which one person is employed as a marriage broker. Such a transaction is considered contrary to the interests of society.

In addition, some acts must be performed by a person himself and cannot be entrusted or delegated to an agent. Voting, swearing to the truth of documents, filing tax returns, and making a will are instances where personal action is required. In the preparation of papers, however, it is perfectly proper to employ someone else to prepare the paper which is then signed or sworn to by the employing party.

Sec. 37-C. Who May Be a Principal. Any person, if he is competent to act for himself, may act through an agent. An appointment of an agent by a person lacking capacity is generally regarded as void or voidable to the same extent that a contract made by such person would be.

Groups of persons may also appoint agents to act for them. For example, three men, having formed a partnership, may employ an agent to act for them in the business transactions of the firm. Certain groups of persons, on account of the nature of the organization, must act through agents. Thus a group of persons organized as a corporation can only make a contract through an agent since the corporation is not a living person.

Sec. 37-D. Who May Be an Agent. Since a contract made by an agent is in law the contract of the principal, it is immaterial whether or not the agent has legal capacity to make a contract for himself. It is permissible to employ as agents aliens, minors, and others who are under a natural or legal disability. While ordinarily an agent is one person acting for another, an agent may be a group of persons.

In certain instances, the law imposes limitations upon the right to act as an agent. In order to protect the public from loss at the hands of dishonest or untrained "agents," it is common for statutes to provide that a person must obtain a license from an appropriate government agency or bureau before he can act as an auctioneer, a real-estate agent, or a broker.

Sec. 37-E. Classification of Agents. Agents are usually classified in terms of the extent of the business to be transacted by them as (1) special, (2) general, and (3) universal.

A *special agent* is authorized by the principal to transact a definite business transaction or to do a specific act. One who is authorized by another to purchase a particular house for him is a special agent.

A *general agent* is authorized by the principal to transact all of his affairs in connection with a particular kind of business or trade, or to transact all of his business at a certain place. To illustrate, a person who is appointed by the owner of a store as manager is a general agent.

A *universal agent* is authorized by the principal to do all acts that can be delegated lawfully to representatives. This form of agency arises when a person in the military service gives another person a "blanket" power of attorney to do anything that must be done while he is in the service.

Sec. 37-F. Agency Coupled with an Interest. An *agency coupled with an interest* exists when the agent has (1) an interest in the authority granted to him, or (2) an interest in the subject matter of the agency.

(1) Interest in the Authority. An agent has an *interest in the authority* when he has given consideration or has paid for the right to exercise the authority granted to him. To illustrate: when a lender, in return for making a loan of money, is given as security authority to collect rents due to the borrower and to apply those rents to the payment of the debt owed him, the lender becomes the borrower's agent with an interest in the authority given him to collect the rents.

(2) Interest in the Subject Matter. An agent has an *interest in the subject matter* when for a consideration he is given an interest in the property with which he is dealing. Hence, when the agent is authorized to sell certain property of the principal and is given a lien on such property as security for a debt owed to him by the principal, the agent has an interest in the subject matter.

Creating the Agency

An agency may be created in any one of the following four ways: authorization by appointment, authorization by principal's conduct, ratification, and operation of law.

Sec. 37-G. Authorization by Appointment. The usual method of creating an agency is by express authorization, that is, a person is appointed to act for and on behalf of another.

No particular form of language is necessary for the appointment of an agent. It is sufficient that the words used indicate that one person wishes another to represent him. In most instances the authorization of the agent may be oral. Some appointments, however, must be made in a particular way. Many states, by statute, require the appointment of an agent to be in writing when the agency is created to acquire or dispose of any interest in land. In a few states the appointment must be in writing when the agent is authorized to make any written contract for the principal. The fourth section of the Statute of Frauds [3] has the effect of requiring that a contract creating the authority of the agent be in writing when the relationship will necessarily exist for a period beyond one year from the date of the contract or is to start later than one year from that date. A written authorization of agency is commonly called a *power of attorney.*

At common law authority to execute an instrument under seal, such as a bond, could be conferred only by a writing of the same formality. This doctrine is still followed in a number of common-law states. The early common-law doctrine that required a sealed authorization for an agent of a corporation has been abandoned by most courts.

Sec. 37-H. Authorization by Principal's Conduct.

(1) Principal's Conduct as to Agent. Since agency is created by the consent of the parties, any conduct, including words, that gives the agent reason to believe that the principal consents to his acting as agent is sufficient to create an agency. If one person, knowingly and without objection, permits another to act as his agent, the law

---

[3] See p. 176.

will find in his conduct an expression of authorization to the agent, and the principal will not be permitted to deny that the agent was in fact authorized. Thus, if the owner of a hotel allows another person to assume the duties of hotel clerk, that person may infer from the owner's conduct that he has authority to act as the hotel clerk.

(2) Principal's Conduct as to Third Persons. In addition to conduct or dealings with the agent which cause him as a reasonable man to believe that he has authority, the principal may have such dealings with third persons as to cause them to believe that the "agent" has authority. When this occurs, it is said that the agent has *apparent authority* because he appears to be the agent, and the principal is estopped from contradicting the appearance that he has created. (See p. 577, M.F.A. Mutual Insurance Co. Case)

The term "apparent authority" is used only when there is merely the appearance of authority but it in fact does not exist, and it is essential that the appearance of authority of the agent be due to the acts of the principal. This apparent authority extends to all acts that a person of ordinary prudence, familiar with business usages and the particular business, would be justified in assuming that the agent has authority to perform.

It is also possible for a former agent who has acted in similar transactions to bind his former principal as to third persons who knew him as the agent of the principal if they have not been notified of the termination of the agency.[4]

Sec. 37-I. Agency by Ratification. An agent may attempt on behalf of the principal to do an act which he has not been authorized to do. Or a person who is not the agent of another may attempt to act as his agent. Ordinarily a person can ratify any unauthorized act done on his behalf which he could have authorized. The effect is the same as though he had authorized the act in the first place.

Initially, ratification is a question of intention. Just as in the case of authorization, where there is the question of whether or not the principal authorized the agent, so there is the question of whether or not the principal intended to approve or ratify the action of the agent. (See p. 579, Wilks v. Stone)

Although ratification may frequently be accompanied by reliance by the third party, it is not necessary that there be such reliance to constitute ratification.

(1) Form of Ratification. A ratification must generally meet the same requirements of form as a prior authorization. If a writing is not required, ratification may be by conduct indicating an intention to

---

[4] See p. 577.

ratify, as well as by words. If the other requirements of ratification are satisfied, a principal ratifies an agent's act when, with knowledge of the act, he accepts or retains the benefit of the act, or brings an action to enforce legal rights based upon the act or defends an action by asserting the existence of a right based on the unauthorized transaction, or fails to repudiate the agent's act within a reasonable time.

(2) Conditions for Ratification. In addition to the necessity of an intent to ratify, expressed in some instances with certain formality, the following conditions must be satisfied in order that the intention take effect as a binding ratification.

(a) The agent must have purported to act on behalf of the principal. If the person without authority informed the other person that he was acting as agent for the principal, this requirement is satisfied.

(b) The principal must have been capable of authorizing the act both at the time of the act and at the time when he ratified.

(c) A principal must ratify the entire act of the agent.

(d) The principal must ratify the act before the third person withdraws. If the third person brings an action against the agent because of lack of authority to make the contract, the bringing of the action is equivalent to a withdrawal that prevents the principal from thereafter ratifying the contract.

(e) The act to be ratified must generally be legal.

(f) The principal must have full knowledge of all material facts. If the agent conceals a material fact, such as that there is a lien upon the property or that the property is in a damaged condition, the ratification of the principal made in ignorance of such fact is not binding. Of course, there is no ratification when the principal had no knowledge of the making of the contract by his agent.

(3) Circumstances Not Affecting Ratification. Ratification is not affected by the fact (a) that the third person has not agreed again to the transaction after it has been ratified; (b) that the principal first repudiated but then changed his mind and ratified the transaction, provided the third party had not withdrawn prior to the ratification; (c) that the agent would be liable to the third person for breach of warranty of his authority or misrepresentation if the principal were not bound; (d) that the agent or the third person knew the agent was unauthorized; (e) that the agent died or lost capacity prior to the ratification; or (f) that the principal does not communicate his ratifying intent to anyone.

Although communication by the principal of his ratification is not essential, it may as a practical matter be necessary; for in the absence of some communication there may be no evidence from which it can be found that the principal did have the intent to ratify.

(4) Effect of Unratified Contract. If an unauthorized contract is not or cannot be ratified, there is no contract between the principal and the third party. In some instances the fact that a contract made by an unauthorized agent and a third person cannot be ratified will not prevent the principal from enforcing the contract. Thus, in some instances, the "agent" may assign his contract rights with the third person to the principal even though the principal might not be able to ratify the contract. Also, by definition, the existence of ratification is only of importance when the actions were initially unauthorized.

Sec. 37-J. Agency by Operation of Law. In certain instances the courts, influenced by necessity or social desirability, create or find an agency when there is none. For example: (1) A wife may purchase necessaries and charge them to her husband's account when he does not supply them. (2) A minor may purchase necessaries upon the credit of his father when the latter fails to supply them. A family relationship in and of itself, however, does not give rise to an agency by operation of law. (See p. 581, Barber v. Carolina Auto Sales Co.)

By the Restatement of Agency an emergency power of an agent to act under unusual circumstances not covered by this authority is recognized when the agent is unable to communicate with the principal and failure to act will cause the principal substantial loss.

Sec. 37-K. Proving the Agency Relationship. The burden of proving the existence of an agency relationship rests upon the person who seeks to benefit by such proof. In the absence of sufficient proof, the jury must find that there is no agency.

The existence of an agency cannot be established by the statements or admissions of the alleged agent alone. The fact that the latter told the third person that such relationship existed cannot be shown in evidence to establish that the person so stating was the agent of the principal. The person purporting to act as agent, however, may testify that on a certain day the principal gave him certain instructions and that in following those instructions he made a contract with a third person. This is testifying to the facts from which the court may conclude that there was an authorization.

Termination of the Agency

An agency may be terminated by the act of one or both of the parties to the agency agreement, or by operation of law. When the authority of an agent is terminated, the agent loses all right to act for the principal. The methods of termination will be discussed as they apply, first to the ordinary agencies, and then to agencies coupled with an interest.

Sec. 37-L. Termination of Ordinary Agency by Act of Parties. An ordinary agency may be terminated by act of the parties in the following ways: (1) expiration of contract, (2) agreement, (3) option of a party, (4) revocation by principal, and (5) renunciation by agent.

(1) Expiration of Agency Contract. The ordinary agency may expire by the terms of the contract. Thus the contract may provide that it shall last for a stated period, as five years, or until a particular date arrives, or until the happening of a particular event, such as the sale of certain property. In such a case, the agency is automatically terminated when the specified date arrives or the event on which it is to end occurs. When one appoints another to represent him in his business affairs while he is in Europe, the relation ends upon the return of the principal from abroad.

When it is provided that the agency shall last for a stated period of time, it terminates upon the expiration of that period without regard to whether the acts contemplated by the creation of the agency have been performed. If no period is stated, the agency continues for a reasonable time.

(2) Agreement. Since the agency relation is based upon consent, it can be terminated by the consent of the principal and agent.

(3) Option of a Party. An agency agreement may provide that upon the giving of notice or the payment of a specified sum of money, one party may terminate the relationship.

(4) Revocation by Principal. The relationship between principal and agent is terminated whenever the agent is discharged by the principal. If the agency was not created for a specified time but was to exist only at will, or if the agent has been guilty of misconduct, the principal may discharge the agent without further liability to him.

When the agency is based upon a contract to employ the agent for a specified period of time, the principal is liable to the agent for damages if the principal wrongfully discharges the agent. The fact that the principal is liable for damages does not, however, prevent the principal from terminating the agency by discharging the agent. In such a case it is said that the principal has the power to terminate the agency by discharging the agent but that he does not have the right to do so.

(5) Renunciation by Agent. The agency relationship is terminated if the agent refuses to continue to act as agent, or when he abandons the object of the agency and acts for himself in committing a fraud upon his principal. If the relationship is an agency at will, the agent has the right as well as the power to abandon the agency at

any time. In addition, he has the right of renunciation of the relationship in any case if the principal is guilty of making wrongful demands
upon him or of other misconduct. If, however, the agency is based
upon a contract calling for the continuation of the relationship for a
specified or determinable period, the agent has no right to abandon or
renounce the relationship when the principal is not guilty of wrong.

When the renunciation by the agent is wrongful, the agent is
liable to the principal for the damages that the principal sustains.
In some states the agent also forfeits his right to receive any compensation for the services rendered but not due prior to the renunciation. In other states he may recover the reasonable value of such
services, but not in excess of the contract price minus the damages
sustained by the principal. In all states the agent may recover any
salary or commission that had become due prior to the renunciation.
This remedy is subject, however, to the opposing claim of the principal for damages.

Sec. 37-M. Termination of Ordinary Agency by Operation of Law.
Under certain conditions it becomes impossible or socially undesirable
for the agency to continue. The law accordingly provides that the
agency shall be deemed terminated by the operation of law in the
following ways: (1) death, (2) insanity, (3) bankruptcy, (4) impossibility, (5) war, and (6) unusual events or change in circumstances.

(1) Death. The death of either the principal or agent ordinarily
terminates the authority of an agent automatically. Such termination
does not impose any liability for damages even though the contract
has not been completed. In an attorney-client relationship the death
of the client does not terminate the agency if the client had expressly
agreed that the attorney should conduct the proceeding to its conclusion.

(2) Insanity. The insanity of either the principal or agent ordinarily terminates the agent's authority. In spite of the termination
of the authority, the agent can still bind the principal with respect
to a third person who acts in good faith and without knowledge of
the insanity if it would work an injustice on the third party to hold
that the authority had terminated because of the insanity. If the
insanity of the principal or agent has been declared by a court, all
persons are deemed to know of the status of the incompetent and
accordingly they cannot come within this exception. If the incapacity
of the principal is only temporary, the agent's authority may be merely
suspended rather than terminated.

(3) Bankruptcy. Bankruptcy of the principal or agent usually
terminates the relationship. It is generally held, however, that the

bankruptcy of an agent does not terminate his power to deal with goods of the principal that are in his possession.

Insolvency usually does not terminate the agency. In some states it is accordingly held that the authority of an agent is not terminated by the appointment of a receiver to handle the principal's financial affairs.

(4) Impossibility. The authority of an agent is terminated when it is impossible to perform the agency for any reason, such as the destruction of the subject matter of the agency, the death or loss of capacity of the third person with whom the agent is to contract, or a change in law that makes it impossible to perform the agency lawfully.

(5) War. When the country of the principal and that of the agent are at war, the authority of the agent is usually terminated or at least suspended until peace is restored.

(6) Unusual Events or Change of Circumstances. The view is also held that the authority of an agent is terminated by the occurrence of an unusual event or a change in value or business conditions of such a nature that the agent should reasonably infer that the principal would not desire the agent to continue to act under the changed circumstances. For example, an agent employed to sell land at a specified price should regard his authority to sell at that price as terminated when the value of the land increases greatly because of the discovery of oil on the land.

Sec. 37-N. Termination of Agency Coupled with an Interest. The extent to which the agency may be terminated varies with the nature of the interest. If the agency is coupled with an interest in the authority, the agency cannot be terminated by the act of the principal, but in some states it is held to be terminated by his death. The Restatement of the Law of Agency, however, adopts the rule that the principal's death does not terminate such an agency.

An agency coupled with an interest in the authority is not revoked by the death of the agent. Thus, when the agent would have the right to receive periodic commissions under a continuing contract between the principal and the third person, the agent's estate, if the agency is coupled with an interest in the authority, may receive the commissions accruing after the agent's death. If not so coupled, the right to receive commissions terminates with the agent's death.

When the agency is coupled with an interest in the subject matter, the principal cannot terminate the agency nor is it terminated or affected by the death of either the principal or the agent.

Sec. 37-O. Effect of Termination of Authority. When the authority of an agent is terminated, the agent loses all right to act for the principal.

If the agency is revoked by the principal, the authority to act for the agent is not terminated until notice of revocation is given to or received by the agent. As between the principal and agent, the right of the agent to bind his principal to third persons generally ends immediately upon the termination of his authority. Such termination is effective without the giving of notice to third persons.

When the agency is terminated by the act of the principal, notice must be given to third persons. If such notice is not given, the agent may have the power to make contracts that will bind the principal and third persons. (See p. 582, Record v. Wagner) This rule is predicated on the theory that a known agent will have the appearance of still being the agent unless notice is given to the contrary.

When the law requires the giving of notice in order to end the power of the agent to bind the principal, individual notice must be given or mailed to all persons who had prior dealings with the agent or the principal. Notice to the general public can be given by publishing a statement that the agency has been terminated in a newspaper of general circulation in the affected area. If a notice is actually received, the power of the agent is terminated without regard to whether the method of giving notice had been proper. Conversely, if proper notice is given, it is immaterial that it did not actually come to the attention of the party notified. Thus a member of the general public cannot claim that the principal is bound to him on the ground that the third person did not see the newspaper notice stating that the agent's authority had been terminated.

Cases for Chapter 37

M.F.A. Mutual Insurance Co. v. Jackson

271 F.2d 180 (C.A. 8th, 1959)

Jackson and others owned and insured a poultry house with the M.F.A. Mutual Insurance Co. When Jackson paid the renewal premium, he told the soliciting agent of the company that he was going to use the building for manufacturing and asked whether that had any effect on the policy because of the change in the hazard. The agent said that it would not but that the agent would take care of any change that had to be made. Seventeen days later, Jackson and the other owners received a receipt for the payment on which was printed in large letters:

"M.F.A. Mutual Insurance Company is offering a free service of personal insurance analysis to all its policyholders. If you would like to know if your insurance program is in balance, ask your M.F.A. Mutual Agent.

He is an authorized insurance consultant and is qualified to advise you
on your insurance needs. See him today."

Eight months later the property was destroyed by fire. The insurer
denied liability on the ground that the change in the use of the property
avoided the policy and that its agent did not have authority to agree
thereto. Jackson and the others sued on the policy. From a judgment
in their favor, the insurer appealed.

GARDNER, C.J. . . . It is conceded that . . . a mere soliciting agent
for an insurance company is without authority to change or modify
the terms of an existing contract or to bind his principal by agreeing
to do so. . . . In the instant case the trial court found that the
soliciting agent had been given apparent authority to represent that
the change of the occupancy of the building insured would not in
fact increase the hazards and risks within the terms of the policy. The
company had in effect advised the plaintiffs that its agent was "an
authorized insurance consultant" and that the company was furnishing
"a free service of personal insurance analysis." . . . It is true that this
declaration of the agent's apparent authority was not received by
plaintiffs until some seventeen days after the agent had given assurance
that if there was any change in the character of the risk he would
take care of it, or words to that effect, but it was received some eight
months before the fire and the court was warranted in inferring that
this announcement warranted the insureds to rely upon what the
soliciting agent had already told them. . . .

In People's Fire Ins. Co. v. Goyne, 79 Ark. 315, 96 S.W. 365, 369,
16 L.R.A.,N.S., 1180, the soliciting agent knew that the application
stated that the building was a residence while in fact it was used as
a public hotel or tavern, yet he did not notify the company. The
court held that:

"When an agent does anything within the real or apparent scope
of his authority, it is (as) much the act of the principal as if done by
the principal himself. These are fundamental doctrines in the law
of principal and agent and have been applied in every court where the
common law prevails. When a person does an act or makes a representation which leads another person to a certain course of conduct
which he would not otherwise have pursued, the party causing this
action is estopped to take advantage of anything contrary in fact to
his misleading conduct or representation." . . .

In the instant case, the local agent was employed not only to solicit
business but to advise and counsel policyholders and the appellees
sought the advice of the local agent, told him of the pending proposed
change in the occupancy of the building, and in fact were advised
that this change would not increase the rate, but that if it did, he, the
agent, would take care of it. . . . As said by the trial court . . . "The
plaintiffs were entitled to believe, and the court has found that they

did believe, that the representation made by the agent was . . . within the competence and apparent authority of the agent to advise on insurance matters. . . . The agent's representation here was substantially a representation of fact made with apparent authority, and as such it estops the defendant from asserting a contrary proposition. In other words, the agent cannot with apparent authority represent that there is no increased hazard and, at the same time, leave available to the principal the contention that the hazard was in fact substantially increased." . . .

[Judgment affirmed.]

Wilks v. Stone

339 S.W.2d 590 (Mo.App., 1960)

Larry Wilks, aged 18, purchased a 1959 Chevrolet from Stone and paid in part by making a trade-in of his mother's 1957 Plymouth. She later sued Stone to recover that car. Stone offered evidence that after the purchase had been made, the mother knew what Larry had done but made no objection and that she thereafter consented to Larry's making a sale for his own benefit of the 1959 Chevrolet to a third person. This evidence was excluded. From a judgment against Stone, he appealed.

RUARK, J. . . . The principal issue and dispute is whether respondent Wilks was bound to the contract of exchange because she ratified the acts of her son, Larry, who purported to act as her agent . . . in making the purchase of the 1959 Chevrolet and in trading the 1957 Plymouth in as part of the purchasing price.

As relates to agency, "ratification" is an express or implied adoption or confirmation, with knowledge of all material matters, by one person of an act performed in his behalf by another who at that time assumed to act as his agent but lacked authority to do so. Ratification relates back and is the equivalent of authority at the commencement of the act. It is the affirmance of a contract already made. The existence of agency and the authority of the agent can be and often is implied by proof of facts, circumstances, words, acts, and conduct of the party to be charged. As applied to the agency or authority which is created or related back by means of ratification, it may be implied by any facts and circumstances from which it can be reasonably inferred that the party to be charged (with knowledge of the facts) acquiesced in and accepted the transaction as his own, or which are inconsistent with any other intention. The intent to ratify may be implied from the circumstances, and this implication may be made even though the person to be charged as principal may have had an intention *not* to ratify.

As to what facts, circumstances, and conduct will justify the inference of agency, no fixed rule can be stated. There is no particular mode by which it must be established. It depends upon the situation in each individual case. One of the circumstances to be considered is the relationship of the parties. Although the bare relationship of parent and child is not, in and of itself, sufficient to justify the inference, such relationship is a factor of "considerable weight" to be considered along with all other circumstances as tending to establish the fact. The prior conduct of the parties is also a factor to be taken into account if such conduct is a part of the "chain of circumstances" surrounding the transaction. Under some conditions the mere silence and inaction of the party to be charged, a failure to dissent or speak up when ordinary human conduct and fair play would normally call for some negative assertion within a reasonable time, tends to justify the inference that the principal acquiesced in the course of events and accepted the contract as his own.

Probably the most certain evidence of implied ratification is the acceptance and retention of the fruits of the contract with full knowledge of the material facts of the transaction. Although this ratification by acceptance of the fruits does not necessarily apply where the benefits went to the assumed agent or some third party, nevertheless we think the party to be charged as principal should not be permitted to escape if she, with full knowledge of the facts, knowingly channels the benefits into the hands of another, or assists, aids, and abets the benefited party in making away with the fruits of the transaction so that the *status quo* cannot be restored. Such conduct is inconsistent with a good faith claim of no authority at the outset.

Since ratification may be established by facts and circumstances, it is sufficient to make a question for the trier of the fact if the whole sum total of the facts and circumstances justifies *the reasonable inference* that the party charged as principal accepted the transaction as his own. . . . If there is any dispute as to the facts, or if different inferences can reasonably be drawn, ratification is a question of fact to be determined by the trier of the fact and not by the court.

In this case the defendant offered and attempted to prove . . . plaintiff knew her son had traded in the 1957 Plymouth on another car which he brought home and she did not object or express dissent at that time; . . . [and] she affirmatively consented to and approved of her minor son's sale of the 1959 Chevrolet received in the transaction to another dealer, for which sale the son received $2,200 in cash. By such conduct it could be found that she assisted in and made possible a transaction whereby the fruit of the transaction was appropriated and the return of the parties to *status quo* was made impossible.

We think these facts and circumstances [which the plaintiff sought to prove], had they been permitted in evidence, would have permitted a finding by the trier of such fact that Mrs. Wilks ratified the sale or exchange of her automobile, and that consequently the trial court was in error in excluding such evidence. We believe that, under the situation here involved, justice to all parties requires that the whole circumstances of the transaction be revealed. For such reason the judgment is reversed and the case is remanded for retrial.

Barber v. Carolina Auto Sales Co.

236 S.C. 594, 115 S.E.2d 291 (1960)

While Barber was in Germany in the United States Army, his wife used his 1950 automobile, which he had left at home for her use, as a trade-in on the purchase of a 1956 automobile from the Carolina Auto Sales Company. On his return to the United States he sued the sales company for the value of his 1950 automobile. The lower court held that he was not entitled to recover, on the theory that his wife was his agent and had authority to sell his automobile. He appealed.

OXNER, J. . . . It is well settled that the wife is not the agent of her husband by virtue of the marital relationship between them. . . . He may, however, make her his agent and be bound by her acts as such. "The agency relationship in such case ordinarily rests upon the same considerations as any other agency; she is his agent, and he is bound by her acts as his agent, only when her agency is express, implied, or ostensible." . . .

There may be circumstances where an agency may arise by implication of law, ex necessitate. But the scope of such an agency is very limited and is no broader than the exigencies which call it into being. The fact alone that the husband is away from home does not clothe his wife with implied authority to sell and dispose of his property as if it were her own. . . . "Where the wife is left in possession of the husband's property during his absence, as where he has absconded and his whereabouts are unknown, the law will imply or presume that she is acting as his agent and that she has authority to exercise the usual and ordinary control over the property. However, the mere fact that the husband is absent does not give rise to a presumption that the wife is his agent generally; her authority springs from and is limited to what can be reasonably presumed to be the intention of the husband, it does not extend beyond the authority which is usually and customarily conferred by husbands under the same or similar circumstances." . . .

It is equally clear that the fact that the owner of an automobile has left it in the possession of another does not give the latter implied authority to sell it. . . . This is true even though the relationship between the parties is that of husband and wife. . . . "The owner of an automobile, it has been held, by permitting his wife to use the vehicle, does not clothe her with such authority as to make binding upon him her sale of the automobile to a third person without the owner's knowledge or consent."

Under the foregoing principles, we conclude that [plaintiff's] wife was not empowered to sell his automobile while he was stationed in Germany. It is conceded that she had no express authority. The record discloses no circumstances from which an authority to sell may be implied from necessity. Nor is such authority usually and customarily given a wife during her husband's absence.

[Judgment reversed.]

Record v. Wagner
100 N.H. 419, 128 A.2d 921 (1957)

Record owned a farm that was operated by his agent, Berry, who lived on the farm. The latter hired Wagner to bale the hay in 1953 and told him to bill Record for this work. He did so and was paid by Record. By the summer of 1954, the agency had been terminated by Record but Berry remained in possession as tenant of the farm and nothing appeared changed. In 1954 Berry asked Wagner to bale the hay the same as in the prior year and bill Record for the work. He did so, but Record refused to pay on the ground that Berry was not then his agent. When Wagner sued him and recovered a judgment against him, Record appealed.

DUNCAN, J. . . . "It is a familiar principle of law that the authority of the agent to bind his principle continues, even after an actual revocation, until notice of the revocation is given." . . .

By paying the 1953 bill, the defendant recognized Berry's authority to hire the plaintiff on the former's credit. Berry then resided on the defendant's farm, and was properly found the defendant's agent at that time. In 1954, Berry continued to reside on the main farm, and to all appearances was operating it in the same manner and in the same capacity. If in fact he had ceased to occupy the farm as agent, but did so as a tenant, the defendant made no effort to notify the plaintiff of the change in Berry's status.

It could be found that in the exercise of reasonable diligence the plaintiff was justified as a result of the defendant's conduct in believing that Berry had authority to pledge the defendant's credit in 1954 for the same services which the defendant recognized as a proper charge against himself in 1953. . . . The important fact is that the defendant permitted the outward appearances of Berry's authority to remain unchanged in 1954 from what they were in 1953, and by not notifying the plaintiff of the termination of the agency permitted the plaintiff to be misled. Having done so, he rather than the plaintiff should bear the loss. . . . We do not consider the circumstance that Berry had previously pledged the defendant's credit upon only one occasion . . . to be of controlling importance. . . . The evidence that no question of the agent's authority was raised on that occasion, coupled with the evidence of the misleading circumstances of his continued occupancy and management of the farms and the cattle in the defendant's continued absence, was sufficient to warrant the verdict.

[Judgment for Wagner.]

Questions and Case Problems

1. What is the objective of each of the following rules of law?
    (a) The burden of proving the existence of an agency relationship rests upon the person who seeks to benefit by such proof.
    (b) If the principal fails to notify third persons when he terminates the agency, the agent may continue to make contracts that are binding to the principal.

2. In December, Shumaker authorized Hazen to act as agent to effect a sale of his shares of stock in the Utex Exploration Co. The power of attorney provided that it should be "irrevocable" for one year. In April of the next calendar year, Shumaker notified Hazen that the power of attorney was terminated. Could Shumaker terminate the agency? (Shumaker v. Hazen, [Okla.] 372 P.2d 873)

3. In 1946 the Ayrshire Corporation made a contract with a real estate agent, Wall, by which he was given the exclusive sales agency to sell the lots into which certain properties would be thereafter subdivided. No time was specified for the duration of the contract. After paying commissions on a number of transactions, Ayrshire canceled the contract in 1957. Wall claimed that the contract could not be terminated at will. Was he correct? (Wall v. Ayrshire Corporations, [Tex.Civ.App.] 352 S.W.2d 496)

4. Peters borrowed English's auto. Later that night, English phoned Peters to come to a designated place with the car and "pick him up." Peters started the trip to the designated point but on the way collided with a car driven by Dhane. Dhane sued English and Peters for the injuries he sustained. Dhane claimed that English was liable for the harm caused by Peters since the latter was his agent or employee in bringing the car to pick him up. Was Dhane correct? (English v. Dhane, [Tex.] 294 S.W.2d 709)

5. Through his agent, Davis, Fieschko executed a written agreement to sell his real estate to Herlich. The agreement had been negotiated by Dykstra as Herlich's agent. The contract for the purchase of the land was signed by Dykstra as the agent for Herlich. Thereafter Herlich sent a check for the down payment to Davis. The check did not contain any reference to the sale or the terms of the sale. Herlich did not go through with the sale and, when sued for breach of the contract, he argued that he was not bound by the contract since he had not signed it and Dykstra had not been authorized in writing to sign it. Fieschko claimed that Herlich had ratified the contract when he sent the check for the down payment. Decide. (Fieschko v. Herlich, [Ill.App.] 177 N.E.2d 376)

6. Greater Louisiana Corp. employed Jones as sales director to assist in the sale of corporate stock. As a term of the employment, Jones was to pay the cost of all printing involved in the stock promotion. In the presence of some of the directors of the corporation, Jones negotiated with Goldman and entered into printing contracts with him, placing the orders in the name of the corporation. When the printing work was finished, one of the directors called for part of it, took it, and gave a receipt in the name of the corporation. Goldman sued the corporation for the printing bill. It refused to pay on the ground that by the terms of the employment contract with Jones, such payments should have been made by him. Was this a valid defense? (Goldman v. Greater Louisiana Corp., [La.App.] 126 So.2d 771)

7. Coffin had a liability and property damage insurance policy on his automobile issued by the Farm Bureau Mutual Insurance Co. He purchased a new automobile and wanted to transfer the insurance. He phoned the home office of the insurance company, stated his request, and was transferred to two different girls who each stated that they did not have authority to make such a transfer and finally connected him with Pierson. Coffin stated to Pierson that he wanted to transfer his existing insurance and also to add comprehensive and collision coverage. Pierson told him that the new car was insured as requested from that moment on. Coffin had an accident in his car the next day before any change had been made to his policy. He sued the insurance company, which defended on the ground that no change had ever been made and that Pierson was merely a typing supervisor in the auto underwriters' department who had no authority to make any policy change. Was the new car covered by insurance? (Farm Bureau Mutual Insurance Company v. Coffin, [Ind.App.] 186 N.E.2d 180)

8. Meyer, a small contractor, learned that bids were being taken for the Glass Nursing Home. Since the job was too large for him, he contacted a number of larger contractors by finding their names in the telephone directory. He phoned Klensch and was told that he was out of town. He took the plans to Gilger and Klensch's brother, both of whom were in the latter's office. They informed Meyer that they were bosses for Klensch. Meyer and Gilger agreed that if Klensch was awarded the construction contract, Meyer would be paid 2 per cent of the contract price for furnishing the information. Later, Meyer phone Klensch who, when informed of this transaction, stated that he would not pay any commission as it was contrary to his principles. Klensch was awarded the contract and Meyer sued him for the 2 per cent commission, claiming that Gilger had made a binding contract which Klensch could not repudiate. Decide. (Meyer v. Klensch, [Ohio App.] 175 N.E.2d 870)

9. Barta executed a contract with the Manning-Winthrop Corp., a general contractor, for the construction of a house on a cost plus basis. The contractor sublet the installation of glass work to Goldberg. The contractor did not pay the subcontractor who then sued Barta, claiming that the contractor was Barta's agent. Decide. (Goldberg v. Barta, [Mun.Ct.App. D.C.] 109 A.2d 779)

CHAPTER 38

Principal and Agent

What authority does the agent have?

What are the duties and liabilities of the principal and agent to each other?

These are basic questions in the agency relationship.

Agent's Authority

Sec. 38-A. Scope of Agent's Authority. The authority of an agent includes that which is (1) expressly given by the principal; (2) incidental to the authority that is expressly given by the principal; and (3) customary for such an agent to exercise. In addition, an agent may have (4) apparent authority.

(1) Express Authority. If the principal tells the agent to perform a certain act, the agent has *express authority* to do so. Express authority can be indicated by conduct as well as by words.[1]

(2) Incidental Authority. In addition to his express authority, an agent has *incidental authority* to perform any act reasonably necessary to execute the express authority given to him. (See p. 591, Rock Wool Insulating Co. Case) To illustrate, if the principal authorizes the agent to purchase goods without furnishing funds to the agent to pay for them, the agent has implied incidental authority to purchase the goods on credit.

(3) Customary Authority. An agent has *customary authority* to do any act which, according to the custom of the community, usually accompanies the transaction for which he is authorized to act as agent. Thus one authorized to act as general manager has the power to make any contract necessary for the usual and ordinary conduct of business.

---

[1] See p. 570.

An agent with authority to receive checks in payment does not have implied authority to cash them. An agent does not have customary or incidental power to release or compromise debts owed his principal, even though he is designated as the "field representative" of the principal.

(4) Apparent Authority. As already noted, a person has apparent authority as an agent when the principal by his words or conduct reasonably leads a third party to believe that such a person has that authority.

Sec. 38-B. Duty to Ascertain Extent of Agent's Authority. A third person who deals with a person claiming to be an agent cannot rely on the statements made by the agent concerning the extent of his authority. If the agent is not authorized to perform the act involved or is not even the agent of the principal, the transaction between the alleged agent and the third person will have no legal effect between the principal and the third person.

The only certain way that the third person can protect himself is to inquire of the principal whether the agent is in fact the agent of the principal and has the necessary authority. If the principal states that the agent has the authority, the principal cannot later deny this authorization unless the subject matter is such that an authorization is not binding unless in writing.

If the authority of an agent is contingent upon the happening of some event, one may not ordinarily rely upon the statement of the agent as to the happening of that event. Thus, when an agent is authorized to sell for his principal a given quantity of oranges only in the event of the arrival of a specified ship, one dealing with the agent should ascertain for himself whether the ship has arrived and should not rely on the agent's statement that it has.

An exception to this rule is sometimes made in cases in which the happening of the event is peculiarly within the knowledge of the agent and cannot easily, if at all, be ascertained by the party dealing with the agent. As an illustration, if the agent of a railroad issues a bill of lading for goods without actually receiving the goods, the principal is held liable to one who accepts the bill in good faith and for value.[2]

The third party who deals with an agent is also required to take notice of any acts that are clearly adverse to the interest of the principal. Thus, if the agent is obviously making use of funds of the principal for his own benefit, the person dealing with the agent acts at his own peril.

---

[2] Uniform Commercial Code Sec. 7-301; Uniform Bills of Lading Act Sec. 23.

Sec. 38-C. Limitations on Agent's Authority. A person who has knowledge of a limitation on an agent's authority cannot disregard such limitation. If the authority of the agent is based on a writing or sealed instrument and the third person knows that there is such a writing, he is charged with knowledge of the limitations contained in it. The third person is likewise charged with such knowledge when the contract submitted to him indicates the existence of a limitation on the agent's authority. (See p. 592, Dixie Life & Accident Insurance Co. v. Hamm)

If the principal has clothed his agent with authority to perform certain acts but the principal has given him secret instructions which limit his authority, the third person is allowed to take the authority of the agent at its face value and is not bound by the secret limitations of which he has no knowledge.

Sec. 38-D. Delegation of Authority by Agent. As a general rule, an agent cannot delegate his authority to another. In other words, unless the principal expressly or impliedly consents, an agent cannot appoint *subagents* to carry out his duties. The reason for this rule is that since an agent is usually selected in reliance upon some personal qualifications, it would be unfair and possibly injurious to the principal if the authority to act could be shifted by the agent to another. This is particularly true when the agent was originally appointed for the performance of a task requiring discretion or judgment. For example, an agent who is appointed by his principal to adjust claims against an insurance company cannot delegate the performance of his duties to another.

An agent, however, may authorize another to perform his work for him in the following instances:

(1) When the acts to be done involve only mechanical or ministerial duties. Thus, an agent to make application for hail insurance on wheat may delegate to another the clerical act of writing the application.

(2) When a well-known custom justifies such appointment. To illustrate, if one is authorized to buy or sell a grain elevator, he may do so through a broker when that is the customary method.

(3) When the appointment is justified by necessity or sudden emergency. For instance, an agent to collect tolls, who is in charge of a bridge, may appoint another to collect tolls in his place when he is required to be on the bridge making repairs.

(4) When it was contemplated by the parties that subagents would be employed. For example, a bank in some states may use subagents to receive payment of notes that have been left for collection since the parties contemplated that this would be done.

Duties and Liabilities of Principal and Agent

Sec. 38-E. Duties and Liabilities of Agent to Principal. The agent owes to the principal the duties of (1) loyalty, (2) obedience and performance, (3) reasonable care, (4) accounting, and (5) information.

(1) Loyalty. An agent must be loyal or faithful to his principal. He must not obtain any secret profit or advantage from his relationship. To illustrate, if an agent knows that his employer is negotiating for a lease and secretly obtains the lease for himself, the court will compel the agent to surrender the lease to the principal. Likewise, an agent cannot purchase property of the principal which the agent was employed to sell, without the principal's express consent. Similarly, an agent's wife cannot purchase in her own name property of the principal which the agent was hired to sell.

If the agent owns property, he cannot purchase it from himself on behalf of his principal without disclosing to the principal his interest in the transaction. If he fails to disclose his interest, the principal may avoid the transaction even if he was not financially harmed by the agent's conduct. Or the principal can approve the transaction and sue the agent for any profit realized by the agent.

An agent cannot act as agent for both parties to a transaction unless both know of the dual capacity and agree to it. If he does so act without the consent of both parties, the transaction is voidable at the election of any principal who did not know of the agent's status.

An agent must not accept secret gifts or commissions from third persons in connection with his activities as agent. If he does, the principal may sue him for those gifts or commissions. It is immaterial whether the principal can show that he was harmed. Such practices are condemned because the judgment of the agent may be influenced by the receipt of gifts or commissions. A principal may also recover from his agent any secret profit that he has made in violation of his duty of loyalty to his principal. (See p. 593, Kribbs v. Jackson)

An agent is, of course, prohibited from aiding the competitors of his principal or disclosing to them information relating to the business of the principal. It is also a breach of duty for the agent to deceive the principal with false information.

(2) Obedience and Performance. An agent is under a duty to obey all lawful instructions given him. He is required to perform the services specified for the period and in the way specified. If he does not, he is liable to the principal for any harm caused him. For example, if an agent, without authority to do so, releases one who is in debt under circumstances that the release is binding upon the principal, the agent is liable to the principal for the loss.

If an agent is instructed to take cash payments only but accepts a check in payment, he is liable for any loss caused by his act, such as that which arises when the check accepted by him is not collectible because it is forged.

If the agent violates his instructions, it is immaterial that he acts in good faith or intends to benefit the principal. It is the fact that he violates the instructions and thereby causes his principal a loss which imposes a liability on him. In determining whether the agent has obeyed his instructions, they must be interpreted in the way that a reasonable man would interpret them.

(3) Reasonable Care. It is the duty of an agent to act with the care that a reasonable man would exercise under the circumstances. In addition, if the agent possesses a special skill, as in the case of a broker or an attorney, he must exercise that skill.

(4) Accounting. An agent must account to his principal for all property or money belonging to his principal that comes into the agent's possession. The agent should, within a reasonable time, give notice of collections made and render an accurate account of all receipts and expenditures. The agency agreement may state, of course, at what intervals or on what dates accountings are to be made.

An agent should keep his principal's property and money separate and distinct from his own. If an agent mingles his property with the property of his principal so that the two cannot be identified or separated, the principal may claim all of the commingled mass. Furthermore, when funds of the principal and of the agent are mixed, any loss that occurs must be borne by the agent. For example, when the agent deposits the funds of the principal in a bank in an account in his own name, he is liable for the amount if the bank should fail.

(5) Information. It is the duty of an agent to keep the principal informed of all facts pertinent to the agency that may enable the principal to protect his interests. In consequence, a principal's promise to pay a bonus to his agent for information secured by the agent in the performance of his duties is unenforceable on the ground that the principal was entitled to the information anyway. The promise was therefore not supported by consideration.

Sec. 38-F. Duties and Liabilities of Principal to Agent.

(1) Employment for Term of Contract. The principal is under the duty to permit the agent to continue to act as such for the period, if any, provided by the contract of agency. If the principal wrongfully discharges the agent, the latter has the choice of the following remedies:

(a) Treat the contract as nonexisting and sue the principal to recover the reasonable value of his services to the date of discharge, less any sums previously paid him.

(b) Treat the contract as existing and sue immediately to recover for the damages he has sustained. If he can show that, had he been allowed to complete the agency, he would have made a gain of $1,000, he can recover this sum as damages representing the injury caused him by the wrongful discharge. In some states, this recovery is denied on the theory that the amount of the gain which would have been derived is too speculative.

(c) Treat the contract as existing and, after the contract period of employment has expired, bring an action to recover actual damages. While waiting for this period to expire, the agent must attempt to mitigate his damages by securing similar employment. Thus, if an agent fails to use proper diligence in obtaining other employment, the amount he could have earned will be deducted from his claim against the principal. Some states require that the agent accept any position for which he is fitted; but, as a general rule, it is only necessary to accept work of the same general nature as that for which he had been employed by the principal.

(2) Compensation. The principal must pay the agent the compensation agreed upon. If the parties have not fixed the amount of the compensation by their agreement but intended that the agent should be paid, the agent may recover the customary compensation for such services. If there is no established compensation, he may recover the reasonable value of his services.

When one requests another to perform services under circumstances that reasonably justify the expectation of being paid, a duty to make payment arises. For example, when one requests an agent, as a broker or an attorney, to act in his professional capacity, it is implied that compensation is to be given.

When the agent is employed on the contingency that he is to be compensated only if he obtains or produces a specified result, the agent is not entitled to compensation or reimbursement if he does not achieve the desired result, regardless of how much time or money he has spent in the effort. Likewise an agent is not entitled to compensation with respect to transactions canceled by third persons as long as the principal was not at fault. (See p. 594, Eskin v. Acheson Mfg. Co.) In any case an agent may agree to work without compensation; for it is authorization to act, and not compensation for acting, that is the test of agency.

(3) Reimbursement. The principal is under a duty to reimburse the agent for all disbursements made at the request of the principal

and for all expenses necessarily incurred in the lawful discharge of the agency for the benefit of the principal. The agent cannot recover, however, for expenses caused by his own misconduct or negligence. By way of illustration, if the agent transfers title to the wrong person, he cannot recover from the principal the amount of expense incurred in correcting the error.

(4) Indemnity. It is the duty of the principal to indemnify the agent for any losses or damages suffered without his fault but occurring on account of the agency. For example, an agent compelled by law to pay damages because under the direction of his principal he, without knowledge, had unlawfully sold goods owned by a third person, was entitled to recover from his principal.

Cases for Chapter 38

Rock Wool Insulating Co. v. Huston
141 Colo. 13, 346 P.2d 576 (1959)   *read*

Reilly, who was president of the Rock Wool Insulating Co., borrowed money from Huston on behalf of the corporation and executed a promissory note for the amount of the loan. The minutes of the corporation showed that Reilly had general authority to make loans for the corporation but indicated nothing as to the execution of notes. When Huston sued on the note, the Rock Wool company claimed that Reilly had no authority to execute the note. From a judgment in favor of the corporation, Huston appealed.

DOYLE, J. . . . Reilly had actual authority to borrow money . . . on behalf of the company. . . . We recognize the principle of law . . . that "unless otherwise agreed an agent is not authorized to borrow unless such borrowing is usually incident to the performance of acts which he is authorized to perform for the principal." Restatement of the Law of Agency, Sec. 74. See also Montrose Land & Investment Co. v. Greeley National Bank, 78 Colo. 240, 241 P. 527, 529. In the Montrose case neither the bylaws nor the minutes of the corporation contained an express authorization to borrow money and the Court held that the authority to manage the company and control its affairs did not . . . carry with it the power to borrow money or make notes. . . .

In the case before us . . . actual authority existed [to make loans]. It is to be noted that authority to borrow money does include authority "to execute in the name of the principal such evidences of debt as are usually given." . . . Thus Reilly, having authority to borrow money on behalf of the company, was also empowered to execute evidence of the indebtedness, in this instance the note. . . .

[Judgment reversed as to this question.]

incidental authority

Dixie Life & Accident Insurance Co. v. Hamm

344 S.W. 2d 601 (Ark.,1961)

Hamm took out hospitalization insurance with the Dixie Life & Accident Insurance Co. and paid premiums to Mrs. Branscum, an agent of the company, who was authorized "to sell Hospitalization, forms D and R." When Hamm sued on the policy, the insurance company claimed that the policy had lapsed because the last premium due had not been paid. Hamm showed that he had paid the premium to Branscum. The company showed that Branscum had never paid the premium money to it. From a judgment for Hamm, the company appealed.

HARRIS, C.J. . . . The insurance company contends that Mrs. Branscum was only a soliciting agent and was without authority to accept the premium payment. . . . "A soliciting agent is merely a special agent, and, as a general rule, he has authority only to solicit insurance, submit applications therefor to the company, and perform such acts as are incident to that power."

. . . Certainly she was not a general agent. . . . "A general agent is taken to be one who has authority to transact all the business of the company of a particular kind, or in a particular place, and whose powers are prima facie coextensive with the business entrusted to his care. Stated differently, a person who has charge of the company's business in a state and who acts under general instructions, without special limitations upon his authority, is a general agent. Indeed, the view has been taken that whatever an insurance company may do can be done by its general agents. . . . We think it clear that under her contract with the company, Mrs. Branscum was no more than a soliciting agent, and as such, acted as a special agent with limited authority.

Appellee asserts that in the absence of notice to the contrary, one dealing with an admitted agent has the right to presume that he is a general agent, and acting within the scope of his authority. This assertion is erroneous. . . .

"A principal is not bound by the acts and declarations of an agent beyond the scope of his authority. A person dealing with an agent is bound to ascertain the nature and extent of his authority. No one has the right to trust to the mere presumption of authority, nor to the mere assumption of authority by the agent." . . .

Couch on Insurance, 2d Edition, Vol. 3, § 26:70, p. 547, states: "One who deals with soliciting and collecting agents of a life insurer must determine at his risk the extent of the agent's authority, as for example, whether the soliciting agent has authority to receive premiums other than the first, especially where the policy itself gives notice of the limitations of his authority."

The [plaintiff's] policy, paragraph 5, provides: "All premiums hereunder, except the initial premium herefor, shall be due and payable at the Home Office of the Company, but may be paid to any agent, cashier or collector duly authorized by the Company to accept premiums; provided, however, that if premiums be paid other than at the Home Office of the Company, they shall be paid only in exchange for the Company's Official Receipt signed by the President, Vice President or Secretary of the Company and countersigned by the Company's duly authorized agent, cashier or collector." . . .

Accordingly, . . . the insured had notice in the contract itself that the premiums were payable at the home office of the company, and he is precluded from recovery. . . .

"If it had been shown that the money was paid in fact to the insurance company, a different question would be presented; but there is no such question in this case of ratification, or estoppel of the company to deny the payment." . . .

[Judgment reversed.]

Kribbs v. Jackson

387 Pa. 611, 129 A.2d 490 (1957)

Kribbs owned real estate that had been rented through his agent, Jackson, at a monthly rental of $275. When this lease terminated, Jackson and a third person, Solomon, made an agreement that if the latter obtained a new tenant for a rental of $500 a month, Jackson would pay Solomon $100 a month. The latter obtained a new tenant who paid a monthly rental of $550. Jackson continued to send Kribbs $275 a month, less his commissions and janitor and utility costs, paid Solomon $100 a month, and kept the balance of the rental for himself. When Kribbs learned of these facts three years later, he sued Jackson for the money that he had kept for himself and which he had paid Solomon. From a judgment in his favor, an appeal was taken.

CHIDSEY, J. . . . There can be no doubt that Jackson was guilty of fraud and that he was personally liable to Kribbs for the entire amount fraudulently withheld from him. An agent owes a duty of loyalty to his principal. It is his duty in all dealings affecting the subject matter of his agency, to act with the utmost good faith and loyalty for the furtherance and advancement of the interests of his principal. . . . An agent who makes a profit in connection with transactions conducted by him on behalf of the principal is under a duty to give such profit to the principal. . . . All profits made and advantage gained by the agent in the execution of the agency belong to the principal. And it matters not whether such profit or advantage be the result of the performance or of the violation of the duty of the agent. If his duty be strictly performed, the resulting profit accrues to the principal as the legitimate consequence of the relation. If profit accrues from his violation of duty, that likewise belongs to the principal, not only because the principal has to assume the responsibility of the transaction but also because the agent cannot be permitted to derive advantage from his own default. . . ."

It is also the duty of the agent to give to his principal all information relating to the subject matter of his agency coming to the knowledge of the agent while acting as such. . . . Jackson, by deliberately concealing from his principal the amount of rent the [new tenant] agreed to pay under the lease, by intentionally failing to disclose to Kribbs his contract with Solomon, and by refusing to remit to Kribbs all receipts less proper deductions, was, . . . plainly guilty of actionable fraud and in violation of his duties as a fiduciary. Therefore he is liable to his principal, not only for the secret profit realized from the transaction, but he is also liable to account to Kribbs for the money which he fraudulently and without authority gave to Solomon. . . .

[Judgment affirmed.]

Eskin v. Acheson Manufacturing Co.
236 F.2d 135 (C.A. 3d, 1956)

Eskin was the sales agent of the Acheson Manufacturing Co. which produced brass products. During World War II, at a time when prices were subject to government control, Eskin obtained large orders. Because of the wartime conditions, these orders could not be filled at once. By the time they could be filled, government price controls were removed. Acheson then informed the customers that because of its increased costs it could not supply the purchases at the original price and would charge the prices existing when the goods were shipped. Acheson informed the customers that they could cancel their orders if they wished. Customers whose orders exceeded one million dollars canceled. Eskin then sued Acheson for the commissions he would have received on the orders if Acheson had not raised the price and caused their cancellation. From a judgment for Acheson, Eskin appealed.

HASTIE, C.J. . . . . A manufacturer's agent procured purchase orders which in all their terms, including the price offered, were satisfactory to the manufacturer when and as it received them from the agent. In our view, the arrangement between these parties was such that as each satisfactory order was received a unilateral contract was formed between the principal and the agent. The agent had completed the act which was his part of the bargain. The manufacturer then became bound by a conditional promise to pay the agent a 5 per cent commission if and when that order should be filled. This does not mean that any buyer's offer had ripened or would necessarily ripen into a contract of sale. The prospective seller had merely bound himself by a conditional promise to his agent. . . . [While] the condition must be fulfilled precisely as stipulated before the promise can be enforced, . . . [there is a] duty of the maker of the conditional promise not to prevent the fulfillment of the condition by unwarranted conduct. Such a breach of the promisor's implied obligation of reasonable cooperation in connection with the condition will entitle the promisee to the promised performance, despite the unfulfilled condition. . . . But there is no rule of thumb to indicate what frustrating conduct is "unwarranted," or "unreasonable" or "arbitrary" within this conception. . . . [The test] is to be found in the reasonable expectations of the makers of such a bargain in all the circumstances of the given case. . . .

Here we have parties doing business in an abnormal economy. Shortages of materials and resultant long delays in filling orders were the familiar experience of the industry. Prices were controlled, but controls were recognized as temporary. Any member of the business community must have recognized the likelihood that removal of controls in the not distant future would cause rather extreme price fluctuations.

In these circumstances, plaintiff solicited orders understanding that his right to a commission was conditioned upon the filling of the orders at a considerably later date in the uncertainties of an abnormal economy. It may well be that the parties reasonably anticipated that for the duration of stability imposed by the controlled price structure, the manufacturer would not subject orders to price increases after they were received. But it seems to us that reasonable persons contemplating the possibility of decontrol would not expect the manufacturer thereafter to produce and sell goods at the old controlled prices to meet accumulated orders received under basic conditions no longer existing. Indeed, the uncertainties of the abnormal economy and their impact on reasonable business behavior must be viewed as basic qualifying circumstances in this entire procedure of taking orders for filling in the indefinite future. It was not an unreasonable frustration of the agent's expectations for the manufacturer to subject outstanding orders to price increases which fairly reflected the influence of a basic change in our economy on production costs. . . .

[Judgment affirmed.]

Questions and Case Problems

1. What is the objective of each of the following rules of law?
   (a) A third person who deals with a person claiming to be an agent cannot reply on the statements made by the agent concerning the extent of his authority.

(b) If the parties have not fixed the amount of the compensation by their agreement but have intended that the agent should be paid, the agent may recover the customary compensation for his services.

2. Arcturus Mfg. Co., which operated a forging plant and machine shop, employed Rork as its general manager. In this capacity Rork designated the persons to do the metal inspection work for the corporation. In two years the persons he employed for that purpose paid back to him over $120,000 from the compensation received by them. The corporation, on learning of this, sued Rork for the amounts paid back to him. Decide. (Arcturus Mfg. Corp. v. Rork, [Cal.App.] 17 Cal.Reptr. 758)

3. Elger sued Lindsay and McConnell in connection with an auto collision. As one of the phases of the suit, McConnell asserted a claim against Allstate Insurance Co. and its agent, Snyder. McConnell showed that Snyder was known as the Allstate agent and that there was an official Allstate sign in Snyder's office, including a sign stating, "You are in good hands with Allstate," but that nothing indicated that Snyder was only a soliciting agent. McConnell also showed that he had paid the first premium to Snyder and that Snyder had told him that he was then covered by insurance. Allstate claimed that it was not liable since it had never issued a policy of insurance to McConnell and never received the premium which he had paid, and that Snyder with whom he had dealt had no authority to make contracts of insurance but was only authorized to receive applications and forward them to the home office for action. Decide. (Elger v. Lindsay, [N.J.S.] 176 A.2d 309)

4. Hockett employed Snearly as an agent in connection with the sales made at the Gilette Livestock Exchange operated by Hockett. Snearly was to perform various clerical operations in connection with the agent's work, and to write checks on the account of the principal for the payment of the persons selling their cattle and for the payment of his own salary. By the terms of compensation Snearly was to receive $25 on each sale made at the Exchange up to a certain date and $30 thereafter. According to this rate of compensation, Snearly was entitled to approximately $6,000 for the period in question, but he wrote checks to himself for approximately $27,000. Hockett sued Snearly to recover the excess compensation. Snearly defended on the ground that the additional compensation was taken for extra services rendered by him. The extra work was shown to have a value of approximately $2,000. Snearly also defended on the ground that the principal had waived any right to object to an overpayment by failing to take any action sooner. Decide. (Snearly v. Hockett, [Wyo.] 352 P.2d 230)

5. Adams was a sales agent employed by Shields, a real estate broker. The terms of her employment were set forth in a writing which also stated that Shields was not to be bound by any promise or representation of Adams as agent. Adams made a sale to Passarelli, stating to him that no commissions were to be charged. The purchaser knew that the house would be constructed thereon by Gottlieb under a general contract with Shields. When Gottlieb sent his bill for the construction work, he also sent a letter

stating that he determined the amount of the bill by adding to the cost of construction a claim for commissions for himself and also commissions for Shields. When Passarelli learned of this, he sued Shields for recovery of the commissions so paid, basing his claim on the agent's statements. Shields denied that the agent had power to make any agreement that no commissions would be charged. Decide. (Passarelli v. Shields, [Pa.Super.] 156 A.2d 343)

6. Bruch rented road construction equipment from Hatten Machinery Co. He made the rental arrangement over the phone with the president of Hatten and then sent an employee to Hatten to deliver the rental check and pick up the equipment. On getting the equipment, Bruch's employee signed the standard rental agreement used by Hatten. The agreement contained a provision that there were no express or implied warranties and that the landlord would not be responsible for any damages for breach of warranty. The equipment proved defective and broke down frequently. When Burch sued Hatten, the latter raised the defense that all warranties as to fitness had been waived. Decide. (Hatten Machinery Co. v. Bruch, [Wash.] 370 P.2d 600)

7. Harting owed money to Shinpaugh, who was an agent of the Midwest Life Insurance Co. In order to protect his interest, Shinpaugh obtained a policy of insurance on Harting in Midwest, which named him as beneficiary. At no time did he inform the insurance company of the reason for the policy or the fact that Harting suffered from advanced cancer which later caused his death. On Harting's death, Shinpaugh sued the insurance company. It defended on the ground that if it had been informed of the fact that the policy was securing the debt to its agent and that the insured had an advanced form of cancer, it would not have issued the policy. Decide. (Shinpaugh v. Midwest Life Insurance Co., [Ill.App.] 177 N.E.2d 426)

8. Hooks, a farmer, made an oral contract with Day, as plant manager of the Canyon State Canners, by which Hooks agreed to sell sweet potatoes to Canners. Day procured and furnished Hooks with potato plants and supplies. Canners refused to recognize the contract on the ground that Day did not have authority to make the contract. Hooks sued Canners for breach of contract. Decide. (Canyon State Canners v. Hooks, 74 Ariz. 70, 243 P.2d 1023)

9. Sexsmith was authorized by the California Development Co. to contract in behalf of the company for the use of a certain dipper dredge owned by the Yuma Valley Union Land & Water Co. He was instructed not to make the agreement unless the owner insured the machine. The Yuma company, without knowledge of the instructions, leased the machine without insuring it. In an action brought by the Yuma company to recover damages for breach of contract, the California Development Co. contended that it was not bound by the agreement made by Sexsmith. Do you agree? (California Development Co. v. Yuma Valley Union Land & Water Co., 9 Ariz. 366, 84 P. 88)

CHAPTER 39

Third Persons in Agencies

In agency transactions the third party has certain rights and liabilities as a result of the relationship with the agent with whom he deals directly and with the principal with whom he deals indirectly. The following discussion is organized in terms of the liabilities of the agent to the third party, the liabilities of the third party to the agent, the liabilities of the principal to the third party, and the liabilities of the third party to the principal. The liabilities of one party, of course, are the rights of the other.

Sec. 39-A. Liabilities of Agent to Third Party. If an agent makes a contract with a third person and has proper authority to do so, and if the contract is executed properly, the agent has no personal liability on the contract. (See p. 605, Petrando v. Barry) Whether the principal performs the contract or not, the agent cannot be held liable. If the agent lacks authority, however, or if certain other circumstances exist, he may be liable.

(1) Unauthorized Action. If a person purports to act as an agent for another but lacks authority to do so, the contract that he makes is not binding on the principal. His act may cause loss to the third person, however. The general rule is to hold the agent responsible for this loss on the theory that when he purported to act as agent for the principal, he made an implied warranty that he had authority to do so. Under this implied warranty it is immaterial that the agent acted in good faith or misunderstood the scope of his authority. The fact that he was not authorized imposes liability upon him, unless the third person knew that he exceeded his authority.

An agent with a written authorization may protect himself from liability on the implied warranty of authority by showing the written authorization to the third person and permitting the third person to determine for himself the scope of the agent's authority. When the third person wrongly decides that the agent has certain authority, the agent then has no liability if it is later held by the court that he did not have authority to make the contract.

The agent may also protect himself by having the third person agree that the agent shall not be liable in the event that he does not have authority, although ordinarily the third person would be reluctant to do business with the agent on those terms.

(2) No Principal with Capacity. When a person acts as an agent, he impliedly warrants that he has a principal and that the principal has legal capacity. If there is no principal or if the principal lacks legal authority, the agent is liable for any loss. As in the case of the implied warranty of authority, the agent can protect himself from liability on the implied warranty of the existence of a principal with capacity by making known to the third person all material, pertinent facts or by obtaining the agreement of the third person that the agent shall not be liable.

(3) Undisclosed and Partially Disclosed Principals. An agent becomes liable as a party to the contract, just as though he were acting for himself, when the third person is not told or does not know that the agent is acting for a specific principal, that is, when the principal is undisclosed. The agent is also liable on the contract when the third person is told or knows only that the agent is acting as an agent but the identity of the principal is not known or stated, that is, when the principal is partially disclosed.

(4) Wrongful Receipt of Money. If an agent obtains a payment of money from the third person by the use of illegal methods, the agent is liable to the third person.

If the third person makes an overpayment to the agent or a payment when none is due, the agent is also liable to the third person for the amount of such overpayment or payment. If the agent has acted in good faith and does not know that the payment is improperly made, however, he is liable to the third person only so long as he still has the payment in his possession or control. If in such a case he has remitted the payment to the principal before the time the third person makes a demand upon him for its return, the agent is not liable. In the latter case, the third person's right of action, if he has one, is only against the principal. But payment to the principal does not relieve the agent of liability when he knows that the payment was not proper.

(5) Assumption of Liability. An agent may intentionally make himself liable upon the contract with the third person. This situation frequently occurs when the agent is a well-established local brokerage

house or other agency and the principal is located out of town and is not known locally.

(6) Execution of Contract. If an agent executes a specialty (that is, a negotiable instrument or a sealed instrument in those states in which a seal retains its common-law force) and does so in such a way that he appears to be a party to the instrument rather than the agent for another person, he is bound by the specialty and he cannot show that the parties did not intend this result. Because of the formal character of the writing, the liability of the parties is determined from the face of the instrument alone and it cannot be modified or contradicted by proof of intention or other matters not set forth in the writing.

If the contract is not a specialty, the parties may prove by other evidence that a different result than that apparent on the face of the writing was intended. Thus a simple contract, which would appear to be the contract of the agent, can by oral testimony, if believed, be shown to have been intended as a contract between the principal and the third party. If the intention is established, it will be permitted to contradict the face of the written contract, and the contract as thus modified will be enforced.

To avoid any question of interpretation, an agent should execute an instrument by signing either *"J. B. Kyler, by A. O. Jackson,"* that is, "Principal, by Agent" or *"J. B. Kyler, per A. O. Jackson,"* that is, "Principal, per Agent." Such a signing is in law a signing by Kyler, and the agent is therefore not a party to the contract. The signing by an authorized agent of the principal's name without indicating the agent's name or identity is likewise in law the signature of the principal. (See p. 605, Treister v. Pacetty)

(7) Torts. An agent is liable for harm caused the third person by the agent's fraudulent, malicious, or negligent acts. The fact that he is acting as an agent at the time or that he is acting in good faith under the directions of his principal does not relieve him of liability if his conduct would impose liability upon him if he were acting for himself. The fact that he is following instructions does not shield him from liability any more than he would be excused from criminal liability if he committed a crime because the principal told him to do so.

Sec. 39-B. Liabilities of Third Party to Agent. Ordinarily the third party is not liable to the agent for a breach of a contract that the agent has made with the third person on behalf of his disclosed principal. In certain instances, however, the third party may be liable to the agent.

(1) Undisclosed and Partially Disclosed Principal. If the agent executed the contract without informing the third person or without the third party's knowing both of the existence of the agency and the identity of the principal, the agent may sue the third party for breach of contract. (See p. 606, Camp v. Barber)

In such instances, if the contract was a simple contract, the principal may also sue the third person even though the third person thought that he was contracting only with the agent. The right of the principal to sue the third person is, of course, superior to the right of the agent to do so. If the contract was a specialty, the undisclosed principal, not appearing on the instrument as a party, could not bring an action to enforce the contract.

(2) Agent Acting as Principal. If the third person knew that the agent was acting as an agent but nevertheless the parties intended that the agent should be personally bound by the contract, the agent may sue the third person for breach of the contract. This is true, also, when by custom it is recognized that the agent should have the right to sue the third person.

(3) Execution of Contract. The principles that determine when an agent is liable to the third person because of the way in which he has executed a written contract apply equally in determining when the third person is liable to the agent because of the way in which the contract is executed. If the agent could be sued by the third person, the third person can be sued by the agent. Thus, if the agent executes a sealed instrument in his own name, he alone can sue the third person on that instrument.

(4) Agent as Transferee. The agent may sue the third person for breach of the latter's obligation to the principal when the principal has assigned or otherwise transferred his claim or right to the agent, whether absolutely for the agent's own benefit or for the purpose of collecting the money and remitting it to the principal.

(5) Special Interest. If the agent has a special interest in the subject matter of the contract, he may bring an action against the third party. For example, a factor or a commission merchant has a lien on the principal's goods in his possession for his compensation and expenses. When the factor or merchant sells the goods, he therefore has an interest in the subject matter of the sale that entitles him to sue the buyer.

(6) Torts. The third party is liable in tort for fraudulent or other wrongful acts causing injury to the agent. If the third party by slander or other means wrongfully causes the principal to discharge

the agent, the latter may recover damages. The agent may also bring an action in tort against the third person for wrongful injuries to his person or property. If the agent has possession of the principal's property, he may sue any third person whose acts injure that property.

Sec. 39-C. Liabilities of Principal to Third Party. The principal is liable to the third person on the properly authorized and executed contracts of his agent and, in certain circumstances, for his agent's unauthorized contracts and torts as well.

(1) Agent's Contracts. When there is a principal with contractual capacity who had authorized or ratified the agent's action and when the agent properly executed the contract, a contract exists between the principal and the third person on which each can be sued by the other in the event of a breach. If the contract is a simple contract (that is, not under seal nor negotiable) the third person may sue the principal whether or not the principal has been disclosed. Since the agent acts for the principal, the law permits the third person to sue the principal directly even though his existence was not disclosed or was unknown and the third person therefore contracted with the agent alone.

The right to sue the undisclosed principal on a simple contract is subject to two limitations. First, a third person cannot sue the principal if the principal in good faith has settled his account with the agent with respect to the contract, although some states refuse to apply this limitation unless the third person reasonably had led the principal to believe that the account between the agent and the third person had been settled. (See p. 607, Poretta v. Superior Dowel Co.)

As a second limitation, the third person cannot sue the principal if he has elected to hold the agent and not the principal. To constitute such an election, the third person, with knowledge of the existence of the principal, must express an intention to hold the agent liable, or he must secure a judgment against the agent.

In those jurisdictions which permit the third person to join the principal and agent as codefendants, the third party, although he may sue both in one action, must make his election at the end of the trial. This rule of election does not apply when the principal is partially disclosed, for in that case the right of the third person is not to be regarded as alternatively against either the agent or the principal but as concurrent—that is, a right against both—and therefore the third person may recover a judgment against either without discharging the other.

It is also held that no election takes place when the agent is guilty of such misconduct as to constitute a bar to his suing the principal for indemnity.

(2) Agent's Statements. A principal is bound by any statement made by his agent while transacting business within the scope of his authority. This means that the principal cannot thereafter contradict the statement of his agent and show that it is not true. Statements or declarations of an agent, in order to bind the principal, must be made at the time of performing the act to which they relate or shortly thereafter.

(3) Agent's Knowledge. The principal is bound by knowledge or notice of any fact that is acquired by his agent while acting within the scope of his authority. This rule is extended in some cases to knowledge gained prior to the creation of the agency relationship. The notice and knowledge must appear to be reliable information. Thus, when the agent hears only rumors, the principal is not charged with notice.

The principal is not responsible for the knowledge of his agent, that is, he is not charged with having knowledge of what is known by his agent, under the following circumstances: (a) when the agent is under a duty to another principal to conceal his knowledge; (b) when the agent is acting adversely to his principal's interest; or (c) when the third party acts in collusion with the agent for the purpose of cheating the principal. In such cases it is not likely that the agent would communicate his knowledge to the principal. The latter is therefore not bound by the knowledge of the former.

(4) Agent's Torts. The principal is liable to third persons for the wrongful acts of his agent committed while acting within the scope of the agent's employment. These acts are usually acts of negligence, but the principal is sometimes liable for the willful acts of the agent. (See p. 609, Oddo v. Interstate Bakeries) He is always liable for the fraudulent acts or the misrepresentations of the agent made within the scope of his authority. In some states the principal is not liable when he did not authorize or know of the fraud of the agent at the time of the agent's fraudulent statement or misrepresentation.

In determining whether the principal is liable for the wrongful actions of his agent, it is immaterial that the principal did not personally benefit by those acts.

Ordinarily the principal is liable only for compensatory damages for the tort of the agent. If, however, the agent's act is of so offensive or extreme a character that the agent would be liable for punitive or exemplary damages, such damages may be recovered from the principal.

(5) Agent's Crimes. The principal is liable for the crimes of the agent committed at his direction. When not authorized, however, the principal is ordinarily not liable for the crime of his agent merely

because it was committed while otherwise acting within the scope of the latter's authority or employment.

Some states impose liability on the principal when the agent has in the course of his employment violated liquor sales laws, pure food laws, and laws regulating prices or prohibiting false weights. Thus, a principal may be held criminally responsible for the sale by his agent or employee of liquor to a minor in violation of the liquor law, even though the sale was not known to the principal and violated his instructions to his agent. Other courts follow the general rule that does not impose criminal responsibility on the principal.

When the principal is responsible for the agent's crime, he may be subjected through a criminal prosecution to imprisonment, a fine, or a penalty; or through a civil action, to the recovery of money improperly collected, depending upon the terms of the statute that is violated.

Sec. 39-D. Liabilities of Third Party to Principal. The third party may be liable to the principal either in contract or in tort, or he may be required to make restitution of property of the principal.

(1) Third Person's Contracts. If the principal is bound by a contract to the third person, the third person is usually bound to the principal. The third person is accordingly liable to the principal on a properly authorized contract that is properly executed as a principal-third party contract. The third person is likewise liable on an un-authorized contract that the principal has ratified. He is also liable to the principal even though the principal was not disclosed, except when the agent has made a sealed contract or negotiable instrument, in which case only the parties to the instrument can sue or be sued on it. In the case of a commercial paper or negotiable instrument, however, the undisclosed principal may sue on the contract out of which the instrument arose.

(2) Torts of Third Person. The third party is liable to the principal for injuries due to wrongful acts against the interests or property in the care of the agent. He is also responsible to the principal in some cases for causing the agent to fail in the performance of his agreement. Thus, when an agent is willfully persuaded and induced to leave an employment to which he is bound by contract for a fixed term, the principal may bring an action for damages against the party causing the contract to be violated. So, also, one who colludes with an agent to defraud his principal is liable for damages.

(3) Restitution of Property. When property of the principal has been transferred to a third person by an agent lacking authority to do so, the principal may ordinarily recover the property from the third person.

Cases for Chapter 39

Petrando v. Barry
4 Ill.App.2d 319, 124 N.E.2d 85 (1955)

Barry, an attorney, in taking an appeal for a client, contracted with Petrando to print the record and various other required papers in the case. Petrando knew that Barry was acting as attorney for the client. The printing bill was not paid, and Petrando sued Barry for the amount due. From a judgment for the plaintiff, Barry appealed.

FEINBERG, J. . . . The answer filed by defendant alleged that the order for the printing of said briefs and abstract was not on his own account but as agent for parties mentioned in said briefs and abstracts, which plaintiff at the time well knew; and that he never signed any memorandum in writing as required by the Statute of Frauds, to fix personal liability. He denies that he ever agreed to pay plaintiff the amount charged. . . .

"Where an agent in making a contract discloses his agency and the name of his principal, or where the party dealing with the agent knows that the agent is acting as an agent in making the contract, the agent is not liable on the contract, unless he agrees to become personally liable. . . .

". . . The relation of the attorney to his client, in some of its aspects, is a relation of agency, and is, in general, governed by the same rules which apply to other agencies. . . ."

In the instant case defendant's representative capacity is disclosed upon the printed briefs and abstract, and the name of his client, the principal, is disclosed. There is no evidence in the record that would take the instant case out of the rule of liability applicable to an agent . . . and fasten any liability upon defendant.

The mere fact that plaintiff billed defendant for the printing is not conclusive that the obligation is his rather than the client's. When the attorney orders printing of briefs and abstracts in a case on appeal, he will be deemed to have implied authority to order the printing and bind his client. . . .

[Judgment reversed.]

Treister v. Pacetty
85 So.2d. 605 (Fla., 1956)

Acting with the necessary authority, Brown, the agent for Pacetty, entered into a contract with Treister on behalf of his principal. Brown signed the contract with Pacetty's name without indicating in any way on the contract that it had been signed by an agent. Treister later sued Pacetty to enforce the contract. Pacetty denied that he was bound by the contract. From a judgment in his favor, Treister appealed.

O'CONNELL, J. . . . The simple issue presented . . . is whether or not a duly authorized attorney-in-fact can bind his principal by executing a contract in the name of the principal alone, without any indication of the fact of agency upon the face of the instrument. . . .

It is difficult in reason to perceive why . . . it may not be shown by evidence . . . that it was in fact executed by an agent. It cannot be said that this is to contradict, add to, or vary the deed by parol evidence, for its legal effect remains the same and it is nonetheless afterward what it purported to be before, the deed of the principal. Neither can it be said that in one case there is, while in the other there is not, evidence of the agency. In either event, the agency must be proved as a fact. It cannot be ₐestablished by mere recitals of authority or by any pretense of acting in that capacity." . . .

"As a matter of convenience in preserving testimony, it may be well that the names of all the parties who are in any way connected with a written instrument should appear upon the instruments themselves, but the fact that the name of the agent by whom the signature of the principal is affixed to an instrument appears upon the instrument itself neither proves nor has any tendency to prove the authority of such agent. That must be established . . . whether his name appears as agent or whether he simply places the name of his principal to the instrument to be executed."

It is the opinion of this Court that . . . a contract executed in the name of a principal by a duly authorized agent, acting within the scope of his authority, is binding upon the principal, although the fact that the agent acted for the principal is not apparent from the instrument itself.

[Judgment reversed.]

Camp v. Barber
87 Vt. 235, 88 A. 812 (1913)

Camp, acting as agent for an undisclosed principal, the Orange County Telephone Co., made a contract with Barber for running a telephone line over his land. Barber later violated his contract and was sued by Camp. Barber raised the defense that Camp could not sue in his own name. From a judgment for the defendant, the plaintiff appealed.

TAYLOR, J. . . . Can the plaintiff recover . . . in his own name? The defendant contends that he cannot because the plaintiff was acting for the Orange County Telephone Company in the making of the contract. . . . But this fact alone is not determinative. To escape liability to the plaintiff, the defendant attempts to show that the right of action, if any exists, is in the plaintiff's principal. While the general rule is that, where an agent makes a contract with a third person, *naming his principal,* the contract is made with the principal, and not with the agent, and no cause of action subsists in favor of the agent against the other party thereto, it has been held in some jurisdictions that, even where the principal is disclosed, a contract may be made by an agent with a third person in such terms that he, the agent, is personally liable for its fulfillment, and may therefore enforce the same in his own name. . . . Moreover, the authorities are practically uniform that, where the nominal promisee in a contract not under seal is an agent, and he has a beneficial interest in the performance of the contract or a special property in the subject-matter of the agreement, the legal interest is in him, and he may support an action upon the contract in his own name. . . .

. . . Where one beneficially interested in a contract, though made by him as agent, the contract containing apt words to bind the agent personally, seeks to enforce such contract in his own name, the other party to the contract, to defeat such action, must not only prove the fact of agency but must go further and show necessary facts to make the defense available, as, for example, that the principal was disclosed and that the agreement was in fact between himself and the principal. Defendant's failure to show more than the mere fact of agency leaves the agreement, as its terms import, a contract with an agent whose principal was undisclosed, and so subject to the rule governing such contracts.

It is a well-settled rule of law that, where an agent acts for an undisclosed principal, the agent becomes personally bound on the contract and is individually liable thereon to the other party. As a corollary to this rule, an action may be brought in the name of either the agent or the principal for the breach of such a contract by the other party, or . . . the agent may sue in his own name when he is beneficially interested in the contract. . . . This rule works no injustice to the other party to the contract since he may avail himself of all defenses that are good either against the agent or the principal. . . .

The contract by the defendant in terms imports to be an agreement with the plaintiff personally, though in fact acting for the Orange County Telephone Company. . . . In these circumstances he [the plaintiff] is entitled to support an action upon the contract in his own name. . . .

[Judgment for defendant reversed.]

Poretta v. Superior Dowel Co.

153 Maine 308, 137 A.2d 361 (1957)

Poretta sold wood to Young who was in fact acting for the Superior Dowel Co. an undisclosed principal. When Poretta learned of that fact, he sued Superior Dowel for the purchase price. The latter defended on the ground that it had paid Young the amount of the purchase price. From a judgment in favor of Poretta, Superior appealed.

DUBORD, J. . . . "Is an undisclosed principal absolved from liability to his agent's vendor who has sold goods to the agent upon the credit of the agent who has received payment or advances, or a settlement of accounts, from his undisclosed principal before discovery of the undisclosed principal by the agent's vendor?"

There are two different rules bearing upon the issue. The first one, which appears to be supported by the weight of authority is that an undisclosed principal is generally relieved of his ability for his agent's contracts to the extent that he has settled with his agent prior to the discovery of the agency. The other rule is, that an undisclosed principal is discharged only where he has been induced to settle with the agent by conduct on the part of the third person leading him to believe that such person has settled with the agent.

The decisions appear to be in a state of hopeless confusion. "The rule that an undisclosed principal, when discovered, may be held liable upon a contract made in his behalf will not be enforced for the advantage of a third party if it will work injustice to the principal. An undisclosed principal may be relieved from liability by reason of a changed state of accounts between him and the agent, the rule formerly laid down in England and now very generally followed in the United States being that, where the principal, acting in good faith, has settled with the agent so that he would be subjected to loss were he compelled to pay the third person, he is relieved from liability to the latter, and this doctrine is, in at least one jurisdiction, in effect prescribed by statute. This doctrine is now held in England, and in a few cases in the United States, to be too broad, and the better rule is stated to be that the principal is discharged only where he has been induced to settle with the agent by conduct on the part of the third person leading him to believe that such person has settled with the agent or has elected to hold the latter. . . .

The American Law Institute . . . adopted and promulgated the following rule:

"An undisclosed principal is discharged from liability to the other party to the contract if he has paid or settled accounts with an agent reasonably relying upon conduct of the other party, not induced by the agent's misrepresentations, which indicate that the agent has paid or otherwise settled the account." 1 Am.Law.Inst. Restatement of Agency, § 208. . . .

We cite § 292, 1 Williston on Contracts, Rev.Ed.:

"There is considerable confusion of authority in regard to the question whether settlement by the principal with his agent before the person with whom the agent dealt makes a claim upon the principal is a defense to the latter. The decision of the controversy depends upon whether the liability of an undisclosed principal is to be regarded as an absolute right of one who deals with the agent although confessedly the credit of the agent has been exclusively relied upon, or whether, on the other hand, a person who thus deals with an agent is to be given only such limited right against the undisclosed principal as is consistent with equity. If the first of these theories is sound, the person dealing with the agent cannot be deprived of his right against the principal unless in some way he has subjected himself to an estoppel by misleading the principal. If, however, the second theory is sound, the mere fact that the principal has innocently put himself in a situation where hardship will be caused by holding him liable on the agent's contract should be a defense. . . .

Mr. Mechem in his treatise on the Law of Agency, [in] . . . arriving at his conclusion that the law as now set forth in the Restatement was the correct law, . . . has this to say: . . .

"If the principal sends an agent to buy goods for him and on his account, it is not unreasonable that he should see that they are paid for. Although the seller may consider the agent to be the principal, the actual principal knows better. He can easily protect himself by insisting upon evidence that the goods have been paid for or that the seller with full knowledge of the facts has elected to reply upon the responsibility of the agent, and if he does not, but, except where misled by some action of the seller, voluntarily pays the agent without knowing that he has paid the seller, there is no hardship in requiring him to pay again. If the other party has the right, within a reasonable time, to charge the undisclosed principal upon his discovery,—and this right seems to be abundantly settled in the law of agency—it is difficult to see how this right of the other party can be defeated, while he is not himself in fault, by dealings between the principal and the agent, of which he had no knowledge, and to which he was not a party."

The Restatement may be regarded both as the product of expert opinion and as the expression of the law by the legal profession. . . .

We, therefore, adopt the rule as laid down in the Restatement of the Law of Agency. . . .

[Judgment affirmed.]

Oddo v. Interstate Bakeries, Inc.

271 F.2d 417 (C.A. 8th, 1959)

Oddo purchased baked goods from Interstate Bakeries for sale in his store. Cooley, the delivery man for Interstate, falsely altered the slips showing the daily deliveries to Oddo. In consequence, Interstate billed Oddo for more than was delivered. Each time after Oddo paid his current

bill, Cooley would embezzle the amount by which Oddo had been overcharged. When Oddo learned of the overcharges, he sued Interstate, which
claimed that it was not liable because Cooley had embezzled the money.
From a judgment in favor of Interstate, Oddo appealed.

WOODROUGH, C.J. . . . [The lower court held] that the fraud
which the agent Cooley practiced in falsely recording and reporting
the quantities of bakery products he delivered to plaintiff was the kind
of fraud from which he alone profited and from which his employer
did not benefit. It has been held as to such transactions . . . that the
money the agent himself thus obtains wrongfully from a customer
could not be recovered from the agent's principal. We do not express
opinion as to such cases because it seems clear that the fraud Cooley
practiced on plaintiff in this case was one from which defendant did
directly receive a benefit. Here Cooley did not obtain any money or
any goods from plaintiff by means of his fraud. It was the defendant
that adopted Cooley's false reports to it and defendant wrongfully
obtained plaintiff's money by the misrepresentations it made to the
plaintiff and by overcharging him. . . . The defendant suffered its
loss when its agent Cooley made off with the proceeds of its goods. But
that was a transaction with which the plaintiff had nothing to do.
There is no basis for connecting plaintiff with it and it affords no
justification for defendant to retain plaintiff's money. Defendant has
no right to say to plaintiff, "True, I overcharged you and obtained your
money without consideration upon false representations of what you
owed me, but I lost the same amount when my agent embezzled from
me and therefore I will keep your money." There is no basis on which
it can use that loss to offset what it owes the plaintiff for overcharging
him.

It appears from the court's summarizing of conclusions that the
decision to deny plaintiff any relief resulted largely from applying
to the case the principle that where one of two equally innocent
parties must suffer the consequences of the fraud of a third party, he
who made the fraud possible must bear the loss.

In respect to this principle, it appeared to the court that defendant was an "innocent" party as to the loss it suffered. That loss
occurred, as pointed out, when its agent Cooley failed to account to
it for the goods confided to him. But the evidence was that in the
course of the business through the years defendant never required
Cooley to present any record of what he did with any of the goods
turned over to him to sell except as to the part he sold on credit. As
to all the goods confided to him, he was charged in gross when he
went out in the morning and credited when he came back with the
charges and the cash he brought in. If defendant had required signed
delivery sheets and duplicate receipts in respect to all sales, the

particular fraud Cooley practiced would have been more difficult for him.

On the other hand, . . . when Cooley appeared at the store, his deliveries of bread sold to plaintiff were counted and found to accord with his delivery slip and that slip was duly signed by plaintiff's authority and the bills that came to plaintiff to be paid were computed on the figures over plaintiff's authorized signature. . . . There was no proof that it was an unusual and careless method on plaintiff's part. . . .

Plaintiff was deceived into believing the representation of the billings to be true by the willful fraud of the only agent of defendant that defendant sent to him to transact its business with him. That a principal is liable for the fraud of his agent committed in the very business in which the agent was appointed to act seems to be too elemental a proposition for serious discussion. . . .

[Judgment reversed.]

Questions and Case Problems

1. What is the objective of each of the following rules of law?
   (a) The principal is bound by knowledge or notice of any fact that is acquired by his agent while acting within the scope of his authority.
   (b) When property of the principal has been transferred to a third person by an agent lacking authority to do so, the principal may ordinarily recover the property from the third person.

2. Swilley organized the Central Finance Co. with J. J. Jones as president. In order to induce the Consumers Credit Corp. to deal with and extend credit to Central Finance Co., a letter was written by Jones and Swilley to Consumers Credit guaranteeing all notes sold to it by Central Finance "or which otherwise might come into (Consumer's) possession from Central Finance Co." Jones was personally indebted to Consumers and gave it a promissory note payable to its order. Jones stamped on the back of this note, "Payment of this note guaranteed. Central Finance Co., Inc., by," and then signed his name, "J. J. Jones." When the note was not paid, Consumers sued Swilley on the letter of guarantee. Was Swilley liable? (Consumers Credit Corp. of Mississippi v. Swilley, [Miss.] 138 So.2d 885)

3. Lee Steele owned a number of farms. His brother, John Steele, acted as Lee's agent in managing and renting the farms. One of the farms was leased to Skow. On that farm there was some unshelled corn that admittedly belonged to Lee. When John went to the Skow farm with men to shell the corn, Skow said that he did not want the corn shelled until certain other claims between Lee and Skow were settled. Skow left the farm to find his lawyer but was unable to do so. When he returned to the farm, the men were about to shell the corn. Skow asked John what he was going to do, whereupon John severely beat Skow. Skow sued both John and Lee. Decide. (Skow v. Steele, 74 S.D. 81, 49 N.W.2d 24)

4. Case owed money to Haddad. The latter retained Shepherd as his attorney to collect this debt. Case paid Shepherd $500 on the debt and received a receipt for the payment. Shepherd did not pay the money to Haddad but kept it as fees due him by Haddad for this and various other legal services. Haddad demanded that Case pay him $500. Case did so and then sued Shepherd to recover the $500 he had paid earlier. Decide. (Case v. Shepherd, 140 W.Va.App. 305, 84 S.E.2d 140)

5. Sawday, the local salesman and representative of the Sunset Milling and Grain Co., executed a contract with Anderson by the terms of which Sunset Milling Co. was to deliver certain goods. The contract was signed by Sawday as "C. Trevor Sawday, representative of the Sunset Milling and Grain Co." Anderson sued the Sunset Milling Co., which defended on the ground that it was not bound because of the form of execution of the contract. Decide. (Sunset Milling and Grain Co. v. Anderson, 39 Cal.2d 773, 249 P.2d 24)

6. Buge owned certain property. His agent, Lyon, leased the property to Mrs. Newman. The lease was signed and sealed by the tenant and by Lyon in his own name. Thereafter Buge sued Mrs. Newman to collect the rent. Was he entitled to do so? (Buge v. Newman, 61 Misc. 84, 113 N.Y.S. 198)

7. Blanche Trembley stated that she was agent for Trembley, Inc., and in the name of that corporation she made a contract with the Puro Filter Corp. of America. There was no corporation by the name of Trembley, Inc. The Puro Filter Corp. brought an action against Trembley to recover on the contract. Was it entitled to hold the agent liable? (Puro Filter Corp. v. Trembley, 266 App.Div. 750, 41 N.Y.S.2d 472)

8. Floyd, without authority, undertook to act as agent for the Wool Growers Exchange. Acting as agent, he made a contract for the exchange with the Farmers' Cooperative Trust Co. for the purchase of wool. After discovering the agent's lack of authority, the trust company brought an action against Floyd. Decide. (Farmers' Cooperative Trust Co. v. Floyd, 47 Ohio 525, 26 N.E. 110)

9. Waggoner was a salesman for the Providence Jewelry Co. As a result of a fraud perpetrated by him, he induced S. Fessler & Sons to sign a contract for the purchase of some cheap jewelry. Thereafter the Providence Jewelry Co. brought an action against S. Fessler & Sons to enforce the contract. Could it recover? (Providence Jewelry Co. v. S. Fessler & Sons, 145 Iowa 74, 123 N.W. 957)

10. Booth entered into a contract to purchase asphalt blocks from the Barber Asphalt Paving Co. In the transaction he was acting as the agent of an undisclosed principal, the Kelly Asphalt Block Co. The blocks that were delivered pursuant to the contract proved to be defective and unmerchantable. The Kelly Asphalt Block Co. brought an action against the Barber Asphalt Paving Co. to recover damages arising out of breach of the contract. Was the block company entitled to enforce the agreement? (Kelly Asphalt Block Co. v. Barber Asphalt Paving Co., 211 N.Y. 68, 105 N.E. 88)

CHAPTER 40

Creation and Termination

To a large extent, the law of employment is the same as that of agency. There are material differences, however, and the relationship has become subject to regulation by a large body of statutes generally described as labor legislation.

The relation of an employer and an employee exists when, pursuant to an express or implied agreement of the parties, one person, the *employee,* undertakes to perform services or to do work under the direction and control of another, the *employer.* In the older cases, this is described as the master-servant relationship. (See p. 619, Minneapolis Iron Store Co. v. Branum)

As already discussed,[1] an employee is hired to do work under the control of the employer, as contrasted with (1) an agent who is to make contracts with third persons on behalf of and under control of the principal, and (2) an independent contractor who is to perform a contract independent of, or free from, control by the other party.

Sec. 40-A. Creation of the Employment Relation. The contract upon which the relationship is based is subject to all the principles applicable to contracts generally. The relation of the employer and employee can be created only by consent of both parties. A person cannot be required to work against his will, nor can he become an employee without the consent of the employer.

The contract of employment may be implied, as when the employer accepts services which, as a reasonable man, he knows are

---

[1] See p. 568.

rendered with the expectation of receiving compensation. Thus it has been held that when a minor worked with his father under the supervision of the company's agent, the company impliedly assented to the relationship of employer and employee, even though the minor's name was not on the payroll.

As a result of the rise of labor unions, large segments of industrial life are now covered by *union contracts*. This means that the union and the employer agree upon a basic pattern or set of terms of employment. For example, a union contract will state that all workers performing a specified class of work shall receive a certain hourly wage.

Sec. 40-B. Terms of Employment. Basically the parties are free to make an employment contract on any terms they wish. The employment contemplated must, of course, be lawful; and by statute it is subject to certain limitations. Thus persons under a certain age and women cannot be employed at certain kinds of labor. Statutes commonly specify minimum wages and maximum hours which the employer must observe, and they require employers to provide many safety devices. A state may also require employers to pay employees' wages for the time that they are away from work while voting.[2]

Sec. 40-C. Reward of Labor. Historically, wages constituted the sole reward of labor. Today, in many fields of employment additional benefits are conferred upon the worker, either by virtue of the contract of employment or by statutory provision. In recent years the contract of employment, particularly in the case of union contracts, has increasingly included provisions relating to such matters as seniority in employment and promotion, promotion plans, sick leaves and vacations, pensions, and profit-sharing plans. In addition, both state and federal statutes provide a variety of benefits in the form of social security and unemployment insurance.[3]

Sec. 40-D. Methods of Termination. A contract of employment may, in general, be terminated in the same manner as contracts of any other kind. It may come to an end by the expiration of the term specified in the contract, by notice at the will of either party when the term is indefinite, or by mutual agreement at any time.

Death of the employee or his inability to perform his duties will terminate the relation. The same rule is applied upon the death of the employer except when the contract of employment is of such

---

[2] See Chapter 64 as to various statutory regulations of labor, such as those relating to fair labor standards, hours of service, fair employment practices, and labor-management relations.

[3] See Chapter 63.

nature that it can be carried out by the personal representative of the deceased employer.

A stipulation in the original agreement may give one or either of the parties the right to terminate the relation upon the happening of a certain contingency. For example, when the employee is hired as the manager of a branch store owned by the employer, the contract may stipulate that the employment is to terminate if the branch store is permanently closed by the employer for any reason. In such a case the closing of the branch is a *condition subsequent* which discharges the contract of employment.

The employment contract frequently stipulates that the employer may terminate the relation if he is not satisfied with the services of the employee. In such cases the employer is generally considered the sole judge of his reason provided that he acts in good faith.

When the right to terminate depends upon the giving of a stipulated notice, the parties must comply with such stipulation. The notice may be waived, however, by the one entitled to it.

Sec. 40-E. Justifiable Discharge by Employer. In the absence of a contract or statutory provision to the contrary, an employer may discharge an employee for any reason or for no reason if the employment is at will. If the employment may not be terminated at will, the employer will be liable for damages if he discharges the employee without justification.

(1) Nonperformance. The employer is justified in discharging an employee who refuses to carry out his part of the contract. Thus, if the employee refuses to work on the days specified in the contract, he may be rightfully discharged.

Employees who take part in a *"wildcat" strike* (one that is not approved or called by the union of which they are members) may be discharged by their employer.

(2) Fraud. The employer may rightfully discharge the employee when the relation has been established by means of fraud on the latter's part. To illustrate, when the employee falsely represents his experience in order to secure the contract of employment, he cannot complain of his discharge on that ground.

(3) Disobedience. In most states the employer is entitled to discharge the employee for willful disobedience of any proper order. Some courts add the qualification that such disobedience must relate to orders which are reasonably expected to be followed.

Disobedience as a ground for discharge involves a question of insubordination; hence there must be an act denoting a perverse disposition. A violation of an unknown rule, therefore, is not a valid ground for dismissal.

(4) Disloyalty. The discharge of the employee is justified when he engages in activities that are inconsistent with the interests of his employer. (See p. 620, Bernstein v. Lipper Mfg. Co.)

(5) Wrongful Misconduct. An employee may be dismissed when he is guilty of wrongful misconduct which harms the employer or his property, or interferes with the continued and peaceful operation of his business. In some instances the wrongful misconduct may also be an act of disobedience or of disloyalty.

(6) Incompetency. An employee may be dismissed when he is unable to perform in a reasonably skillful manner the duties for which he is employed. For example, the services of an accountant whose reports show errors may be dispensed with on this ground.

Sec. 40-F. Remedies of Employee Wrongfully Discharged. An employee who has been wrongfully discharged may bring against the employer an action for (1) wages, (2)) breach of contract, or (3) value of services already rendered. In certain instances, he may also bring (4) an action for specific performance of the employment contract, or (5) a proceeding under a federal or state labor relations statute.

(1) Action for Wages. The employee may bring an action for wages due at the time of his wrongful discharge. Most states hold that an action for wages can be brought only for services actually rendered and that the employee must resort to an action for breach of contract for claims in respect to the unexpired term.

(2) Action for Breach of Contract. The employee may bring an action for breach of a contract at the time of the wrongful discharge, at the expiration of the term, or at any intermediate time. When the contract expressly gives the employer the right to terminate the contract upon giving notice, recovery by the employee for a wrongful breach of the contract by the employer is limited to the wages the employee would receive during the notice period.

Whether the employee is suing for wages for the unexpired time or for damages, he is under a duty to seek similar employment in that community. The employer may reduce the amount recoverable by showing that the employee received or might have received wages for doing similar work.

(3) Action for Value of Services. When discharged wrongfully after having performed services under the contract, the employee

may treat the contract as rescinded and recover the reasonable value of his services. In such a case he cannot later bring an action for breach of contract because the remedies are inconsistent, the former denying and the latter relying upon the contract.

(4) Action for Specific Performance. Ordinarily, an employee is limited to bringing a suit for money whether as wages, damages for breach of contract, or the value of services rendered by him. When the employment is of such a peculiar character that merely receiving money would not be adequate compensation, the employee may obtain specific performance of the contract of employment to compel the employer to abide by its terms.

(5) Proceeding Under a Federal or State Labor Relations Act. In the case of a substantially large number of industrial workers, the provisions of either a state or national labor relations statute are applicable. These statutes commonly provide that if discharge of the employee by the employer is in itself an unfair labor practice, as a discharge because of union membership, the employee may bring proceedings before a labor relations board to compel the employer to reinstate the employee. This is in effect an action for specific performance brought before an administrative agency rather than a court of equity. In some instances the board, in addition to ordering reinstatement, may compel the employer to pay him "back wages" which the employee had lost since the date of his discharge.

Sec. 40-G. Justifiable Abandonment by Employee. The employee cannot, as a general rule, be compelled to perform his contract of employment. Hence he can at any time end the relation by a refusal to perform the services for which he was engaged. If the contract is not terminable at will, his refusal to carry out his part of the contract may or may not make him liable for damages, depending upon the ground for leaving his employment.

The employment relationship may be abandoned by the employee for (1) nonpayment of wages, (2) wrongful assault, (3) services not contemplated, (4) services not permitted, and (5) injurious conditions.

(1) Nonpayment of Wages. When the employer refuses or neglects to pay the wages fixed by the contract of employment, the employee is justified in abandoning the service. Anticipation of nonpayment of wages, however, is not sufficient.

(2) Wrongful Assault. The employee is justified in leaving his employment when he is wrongfully assaulted by his employer. Mere disagreement with the employer resulting in rude remarks or harsh

language is generally not sufficient, however. Whether the language used by the employer gives cause to quit depends largely upon the nature of service and the parties to the relation. To illustrate, it has been held that when the employee, with his wife and child, lived with the employer, harsh and profane language on the part of the employer justified an abandonment by the employee.

(3) Services Not Contemplated. When services that were not contemplated by the agreement are required of the employee, he is entitled to withdraw from the employment. So long, however, as the work is within the nature of the services for which the employee is engaged, he cannot complain of its severity or unpleasantness. It must also be clear that the employer requires the particular work. Thus, when the employer does not insist upon labor that has been requested, there is no cause for abandonment.

(4) Services Not Permitted. When the employer refuses to allow the employee to perform the work for which he was employed, the employee may abandon the employment.

(5) Injurious Conditions. Whenever the conditions of the employment, because of the negligence or acts of the employer, are such as are likely to result in harm to the employee's reputation, morals, health, or safety, the latter is justified in leaving the service.

Sec. 40-H. Remedies of the Employer for Wrongful Abandonment. When an employee has wrongfully abandoned his employment, the employer may bring (1) an action for breach of contract; and in certain circumstances he may also bring (2) an action against a third person maliciously inducing the breach of the contract, (3) an action for specific performance of the employment contract, or (4) a proceeding under a federal or state labor relations statute.

(1) Action for Breach of Contract. The employer may sue the employee for damages for breach of contract when the contract has not expired and the employee wrongfully abandons work. When the employee belongs to a labor union and the contract between the union and the employer contains a no-strike clause, the union may be liable in damages to the employer if it calls the men out on strike under circumstances that would not justify the employees quitting work individually.

(2) Action for Maliciously Inducing Breach of Contract. When a third person persuades an employee to quit work in violation of his employment contract, the conduct of the third person is sometimes deemed malicious. The employer is then permitted to sue the third

person for the tort of *maliciously inducing a breach of contract*. (See p. 621, Amatrudi v. Watson)

(3) Action for Specific Performance of the Contract. Ordinarily, equity will not grant a decree of specific performance to compel an employee to work. If the employee possesses peculiar abilities or talents so that it is clear that the employer could not obtain the same or similar services from another employee, however, equity can aid the employer by granting a negative decree of specific performance, particularly when the employee had expressly contracted that he would not work for anyone else. Instead of directing the employee to work for the employer, the decree prohibits the employee from working for anyone else during the life of the contract. If the identity of the prospective rival employer for whom the employee wants to work is known, the equity court may also enjoin that employer from hiring the employee. Since the employee cannot work for anyone else, it is probable that he will then work for the original employer and perform his contract.

(4) Proceeding Under Federal or State Labor Relations Act. Just as an employee may proceed before a labor relations board for wrongful discharge by the employer, the latter, in certain circumstances, may proceed against a union for making his employees stop work. When the circumstances amount to an unfair labor practice, the union will be ordered to refrain from interfering with the employment and to recall its strike command. Various penalties may be invoked to enforce such a decision.

For the most part the remedy before a labor relations board is directed only at the union of which the employee is a member. The labor relations statutes generally do not include unfair labor practices of individual employees.

Cases for Chapter 40

Minneapolis Iron Store Co. v. Branum
36 N.D. 355, 162 N.W. 543 (1917)

The Minneapolis Iron Store Company brought an action against Branum. A dispute arose as to the ownership of crops that had been raised by Branum. The rights of the parties depended upon whether Branum had raised the crops in the capacity of an employee of the owner of the farm land or as his tenant under a crop-sharing lease.

GRACE, J. . . . The distinguishing feature of the relation between master and servant is that the employer retains the control over the mode and manner of doing the work under the contract of hiring.

. . . It is impossible to make a relation which is one of landlord and tenant come under the relation known as master and servant. Those contracts in reference to leasing of lands by the owner thereof to a tenant, which reserves title and possession of the crops to the landlord until division, have been construed by this court . . . to be a contract of hiring; and under that theory the owner of the land would be master, and the tenant would be servant. . . .

We think that where one, the owner of land, leases the same to another for a certain period of time and puts the other in possession and control of the work, that in such case the relation of landlord and tenant exists. . . .

[The court concluded that the defendant was a tenant.]

Bernstein v. Lipper Mfg. Co.
307 Pa. 36, 160 A. 770 (1932)

The Lipper Manufacturing Company employed Bernstein as a salesman for a period of one year. Before the period of employment had expired, the company dismissed Bernstein on the ground that the employee did not devote himself during employment hours exclusively to the business of his employer. Bernstein brought an action against the company to recover under the contract of employment. From a judgment for the plaintiff, the defendant appealed.

KEPHART, J. . . . Plaintiff was engaged in Philadelphia . . . for one year as a salesman. . . . He was dismissed, and, as justification, it is asserted that he failed to devote himself exclusively to his employer's business during the hours of employment. Defendant charges that the plaintiff was interested in a rayon company in which his father had an interest, and that he tried to and did sell stock of this company during normal business hours. Plaintiff admits his father had an interest in such company; but explains that rayon was then a new and interesting subject of conversation to defendant's customers in the millinery trade, and that often, in discussing defendant's business, "rayon" would naturally come up. He claims he spoke of it to his friends and acquaintances as he might discuss any ordinary topic of the day. While naturally interested in his father's welfare, he denies working for the rayon company or for his father; and [he denies] that either he or his father [was] interested in the sale of stock, as another concern sold it. . . . The court below submitted the question to the jury in a clear and explicit charge, and instructed them that, if they believed plaintiff was not devoting his entire time exclusively to the interests of his employer, they should find for the defendant. The jury evidently believed plaintiff. . . .

The acts of an employee which will justify dismissal need not be such as injure the employer. . . . A master is not compelled to keep an employee for a given term in service . . .; if the employee is unfaithful, disobedient, disloyal, or does not properly perform his duties, he may be discharged.

Where an employee engages for a period of time to give exclusive services to his master, he cannot use such employment as a subterfuge to exploit other business; but whether he does so depends on the nature and character of his acts in connection with his employment and also on the character of the master's business.

In the present case the man was engaged as a salesman. To successfully pursue this occupation he must possess many qualities, none the least of which is ability to engage in what is commonly known as a line of "sales talk." Such an employee cannot rigidly adhere to "shop" or the subject-matter of his master's business but, to ingratiate himself with the buyer and to put himself on friendly terms, he must do many things of an incidental nature. The latitude to be permitted one acting in this capacity is uncertain, but his acts should certainly not detract from the furtherance of his master's business, nor should they, beyond the scope of such business, consume time otherwise than in the master's business.

The court below finds that rayon was an incident of defendant's business, and its customers would naturally be interested in the matter. Since the plaintiff's father was interested, this incident may have furnished the excuse to indulge in talk to aid his father; but the evidence does not disclose sufficient for us to say that he thereby violated the duties of his employment. It is a close case on this point, but we are not convinced the court below committed error in submitting the question to the jury. In all the cases wherein we have held there was sufficient justification, it was reasonably clear from undisputed evidence that the employee was guilty of misconduct. . . .

[Judgment for plaintiff affirmed.]

Amatrudi v. Watson

19 N.J.S. 67, 88 A.2d 7 (1952)

Amatrudi and another were engaged in the sandblast cleaning business. Communale was their foreman. One day Watson saw Communale and three laborers at work by themselves and thereupon hired Communale to sandblast the floor of his swimming pool. Communale and the laborers did the work for which Watson paid them $80, which was the amount that had been agreed upon. Amatrudi and his associate then sued Watson for $250, the reasonable value of the services of Communale and the laborers. From a judgment for the defendant, the plaintiffs appealed.

BIGELOW, J.A.D. . . . Communale testified that when defendant first approached him, he told defendant to call at plaintiffs' office where he would be given an estimate. But defendant countered with "Does the boss have to know about it?" After further parley, Communale agreed that he and the laborers (whom he consulted) would do the job on their own account and would split the money among themselves. Defendant denied the essence of the testimony. He testified that he assumed that Communale was his own boss and dealt with him in entire good faith and in ignorance that Communale was an employee of plaintiffs or of anyone else. . . .

The compressor, hose, and other equipment used for cleaning defendant's swimming pool belonged to plaintiffs as did the sand which was used and the greater part of which was lost in the operation. Plaintiffs could recover the value of the use, or reasonable rental value of their sand and equipment, even though defendant believed that Communale was the owner of it. . . . But plaintiffs did not prove what the use was worth. . . .

But restitution for the value of the services of Communale and the three laborers, or for the value of cleaning the pool—taking the operation as a unit—cannot be recovered if the defendant acted in good faith without notice that the men were employees of plaintiffs. A person who, knowing the [facts], entices an employee to break a subsisting contract of service, or to depart from his duty of loyal service to his employer, is guilty of a tort. . . . But unless the defendant has knowledge or notice of the relation of master and servant, he is guilty of no actionable wrong. . . .

Plaintiffs had the burden of proving defendant's [knowledge]. [The court concluded that the plaintiffs did not show that the defendant knew that Communale was the plaintiffs' employee.]

[Judgment for defendant affirmed.]

Questions and Case Problems

1. What is the objective of each of the following rules of law?
   (a) An employer is justified in discharging an employee for willful disobedience of a proper order.
   (b) An employer may recover damages from a third person who maliciously induces an employee to leave his employment.

2. Under a written agreement the Hippodrome Company of Baltimore employed Lewis for a period of two years at a specified salary. About six months after the agreement had been made, Lewis was wrongfully discharged. He thereafter brought an action against the company to recover damages arising out of breach of contract for the entire term of the contract. Decide. (Hippodrome v. Lewis, 130 Md. 154, 100 A. 78)

3. The Yazoo Yarn Mill employed Porter for a specified period. Before the expiration of that time, Porter went to work for Beale. The Yazoo Yarn Mill then sued Beale to recover damages. The defendant claimed that he was not liable because he did not know that Porter was employed by the

mill at the time he hired Porter. Decide. (Beale v. Yazoo Yarn Mill, 125 Miss. 807, 88 So. 411)

4. The Old Dominion Copper Mining and Smelting Co. employed Andrews at a salary of $200 a month, with provision for termination of employment upon three months' notice. Andrews was discharged without any notice. During the following three months he earned a total of $203.50 at other employment. What remedies, if any, did Andrews have against the company? (Old Dominion Copper Mining & Smelting Co. v. Andrews, 6 Ariz. 205, 56 P. 969)

5. Baugh was employed by the Lummus Cotton Gin Co. The contract of employment stated that his employment was "conditional on . . . conduct and service being satisfactory to us, we to be the sole judge. . . ." After some time, the company discharged Baugh solely because it could not afford to employ him longer. Baugh sued the company. Was it liable for breach of contract? (Lummus Cotton Gin Co. v. Baugh, 29 Ga.App. 498, 116 S.E. 51)

6. The Glen Rock Mineral Spring Co. employed Dore for one year. He was to receive a specified salary and a commission to be paid in twelve monthly installments. After several months Dore quit his employment because the company refused to pay him the compensation already due. Was Dore justified in the abandonment of the employment? (Dore v. Glenn Rock Mineral Spring Co., 147 Wis. 158, 132 N.W. 906)

7. Allen was employed by the firm of Aylesworth & Johnson for a period of two years and two months. One of the members of the firm told Allen that business was falling off and that Allen's brother-in-law, who was also employed by the firm, might be laid off. Allen then secretly and without knowledge of the firm examined the books to see the true condition of the business. When this fact was discovered, Allen was discharged. Was his discharge justified? (Allen v. Aylesworth, 58 N.J.Eq. 349, 44 A. 178)

8. Erickson sued Sorby, his employer, to recover compensation for his work. As a defense, Sorby claimed that Erickson had agreed to work for a specified period of time but had quit before the expiration of that period. Erickson admitted this claim but proved that he had quit because Sorby had struck him. Decide. (Erickson v. Sorby, 90 Minn. 327, 96 N.W. 791)

9. Lupher was employed as a brakeman by the Atchison, Topeka & Santa Fe Railway Co. He was only eighteen years of age at the time. In order to obtain the position, he stated that he was twenty-one years of age. Could the company discharge Lupher upon learning his true age? (Lupher v. Atchison, Topeka & Santa Fe Railway Co., 81 Kan. 585, 106 P. 284)

10. Craig was employed as a brakeman on the Missouri Pacific Railroad. By the company rules which formed part of the company's contract with the union, brakemen were required to live within the city and when leaving work were required to inform the employer where they could be located. Craig signed out one day, giving the employer a false address and took a trip out of the town, believing that he would not be called for duty for two days. He was called for duty the next day but could not be located at the false address. Craig was fired by the railroad. He then sued Thompson, the trustee of the railroad, for loss of wages. Decide. (Craig v. Thompson, [Mo.] 244 S.W.2d 37)

CHAPTER 41

Employer, Employee, and Third Persons

In the employment relation each of the parties, the employer and the employee, has certain duties, liabilities, and rights. Ordinarily third parties are not concerned; but when an injury to a third party results from the employment, the employer, the employee, or both, may be liable.

Duties and Defenses of the Employer

For most kinds of employment workmen's compensation statutes govern. They provide that the injured employee is entitled to compensation as long as the accident occurred in the course of his employment from a risk involved in that employment.

In some employment situations common law principles apply. Under them the employer is not an insurer of the employee's safety.[1] Accordingly, an employee injured in the course of his employment cannot recover damages from his employer unless he can prove that the employer had been negligent and that his negligence had been the cause of the employee's injury. In certain employment areas an injured employee must establish negligence on the part of the employer, but the employer is denied certain defenses which he could assert at common law.

Since the common-law principles still apply in certain types of employment, it is necessary to consider the duties and defenses of an employer apart from statute.

Sec. 41-A. Common-Law Duties of the Employer.

(1) Care. An employer is liable to his employees for injuries that result from a failure of the employer to exercise such ordinary and reasonable care as the nature and dangers of the business demand.

---

[1] Workmen's compensation statutes by their terms generally do not apply to agricultural, domestic, or casual employment. In addition, in some states it is possible for the employer or the employee to reject the plan of workmen's compensation.

(2) Place of Work. The employer is under a duty to furnish his employees with a reasonably safe place in which to work. The place of work includes not only the premises occupied while the employees are working, but also such other parts of the premises as may be used by the employees under express or implied permission or invitation of the employer. An employer is not liable, however, for the lack of a safe place in which to work when the employees are engaged in erecting or tearing down structures or in making repairs to a dangerous place and the nature of the work temporarily creates hazardous conditions.

(3) Tools and Appliances. The employer is under a duty to furnish his employees with reasonably safe tools and appliances necessary in the performance of the particular work. He is not obligated, however, to furnish the safest, best, or newest tools, machinery, or appliances.

(4) Competent Employees. The employer is under the duty to employ a sufficient number of competent employees for the task at hand. If special skill or experience is required, he must hire employees with such qualifications. He must exercise reasonable care in selecting and retaining competent employees, and he is liable for any injuries resulting from a failure to do so.

In determining whether the employer has exercised proper care, it must be remembered that incompetency extends to any kind of unfitness, including careless habits, which makes the employment of the worker dangerous to his fellow employees. On the other hand, infancy, physical incapacity, inexperience, lack of training, or inability to speak English does not necessarily establish incompetency.

(5) Warnings About Dangers. The employer must also give special warnings to his employees about unusual dangers peculiar to the business. The employer, however, need not give warning when the employee has knowledge of the dangers, or when such dangers are obvious or of common knowledge and the employee should know of them.

Sec. 41-B. Common-Law Defenses of the Employer.

(1) Assumption-of-Risk Doctrine. At common law the employer is not liable for injuries to his employees arising out of the ordinary risks or dangers of employment. This rule is known as the *doctrine of assumption of risk.*

Ordinary risks are the dangers of a particular business that cannot be prevented by the employer with the exercise of reasonable care. It is immaterial that the dangers are of a peculiarly hazardous nature if they are incidental to the service, for the employee is presumed to have contracted with reference to all the hazards and risks of such employment.

The employee does not assume unusual risks except in the following instances:

(a) The employee assumes such risks when he knows or should know that certain defects which the employer should remedy exist, but nevertheless continues voluntarily in the employment without complaint.

(b) When the employee complains of a dangerous condition but continues to work without any assurance that it will be removed or after a refusal on the part of the employer to remove it, the employee assumes the risk.

(c) The employee assumes the risk when the employer promises to repair equipment or to correct a dangerous condition and the employee continues to work, even though it is apparent that the employer will not keep his promise. When the promise is to repair by a certain time, the employee assumes the risk after the lapse of such time if the repair has not been made and the employee continues to work. If no time is stated, the employee does not assume the risk until after the lapse of a reasonable time.

(2) Fellow-Servant Doctrine. At common law the employer is not liable to his employee for injuries caused by another employee while at work. This *fellow-servant doctrine* is based on the theory that the negligence of one's fellow servant is an assumed risk.

It is frequently difficult in applying this doctrine to determine who are fellow servants. The definition of the term which is generally accepted is that *fellow servants* include all who are employed by a common employer to further the same general business when their work is so related by proximity or otherwise that there is a special risk of harm to one of them if the other is negligent. Thus it has been held that the brakeman of one train and the engineer of another of the same company are fellow servants.

Employees who are entrusted with carrying out the employer's duties are not fellow servants of the other employees. They are called *vice principals.* They perform duties for the employers that they cannot shift to another; and if they fail to carry out these duties, thus causing an injury, the employer cannot escape liability under the fellow-servant doctrine. Whether a subordinate is a vice principal depends upon the nature of the service performed, rather than the position or the name of the employee; hence one can change his relation to another employee from vice principal to fellow servant, or vice versa, during the day.

Some states have limited the fellow servant doctrine by the application of one of the following rules: (1) the *departmental rule,* under which those who do not work in the same department are not regarded as fellow servants, although employed by the same employer; (2) the *association rule,* which limits fellow servants to those whose work customarily requires their association with the injured employee; or (3) the *superior servant rule,* which excludes a fellow servant when he has been placed in a superior position over the injured employee.

(3) Contributory Negligence Doctrine. The employer is not generally liable to his employee for injuries that are caused by the employer's negligence when the employee has also been negligent.

The defense of contributory negligence is not available to the employer who intended to cause harm to the employee or who intentionally omitted precautions to protect the employee. Nor is the defense available to the employer when the employee's negligence does not concur with the employer's negligence, so as to be the proximate cause of the injury.

In some states the doctrine of last clear chance has been applied in order to avoid the defense by the employer of contributory negligence on the part of the employee.

Sec. 41-C. Statutory Changes. The rising incidence of industrial accidents, due to the increasing use of more powerful machinery and the growth of the industrial labor population, led to a demand for statutory modification of the common-law rules relating to the liability of employers for industrial accidents.

(1) Modification of Common-Law Defenses. One type of change was to modify by statute the defenses which an employer could assert when sued by an employee for damages. Under such statutes as the Federal Employers' Liability Act and the Federal Safety Appliance Act, which apply to common carriers engaged in interstate commerce, the plaintiff must still bring an action in a court and prove the negligence of the employer or of his employees but the burden of proving his case is made lighter by limitations on the employer's defenses.

In many states the common-law defenses of employers whose employees are engaged in hazardous types of work have also been modified by statute.

(2) Workmen's Compensation. A more sweeping development has been made by the adoption of workmen's compensation statutes in every state. With respect to certain industries or businesses, these statutes provide that an employee, or certain relatives of a deceased

employee, are entitled to recover damages for the injury or death of the employee whenever the injury arose within the course of the employee's work from a risk involved in that work. (See p. 632, Christian Case) In such a case compensation is paid without regard to whether the employer or the employee was negligent, although generally no compensation is allowed for a willfully self-inflicted injury or a harm sustained while intoxicated.

There has been a gradual widening of the workmen's compensation statutes, either by amendment or by the adoption of special statutes, so that compensation today is generally recoverable for accident-inflicted injuries and occupational diseases. In some states compensation for occupational diseases is limited to those specified in the statute by name, such as silicosis, lead poisoning, or injury to health from radioactivity. In other states any disease arising from the occupation is compensable.

Workmen's compensation proceedings differ from the common-law action for damages or an action for damages under an employer's liability statute in that the latter actions are brought in a court of law, whereas workmen's compensation proceedings are brought before a special administrative agency or workmen's compensation board.

Workmen's compensation statutes do not bar an employee from suing another employee for the injury caused him. (See p. 634, Ransom v. Haner)

Duties and Rights of the Employee

The duties and rights of an employee are determined primarily by the contract of employment. As to points not expressly covered by the contract of employment, the law implies certain provisions.

Sec. 41-D. Services. The employee is under a duty to perform or hold himself in readiness to perform such services as may be required by the contract of employment. If the employee holds himself in readiness to comply with his employer's directions, he has discharged his obligation and he will not forfeit his right to compensation because the employer has withheld directions and has thus kept him idle.

The employee impliedly agrees to serve his employer honestly and faithfully. He also impliedly agrees to serve him exclusively during his hours of employment. The employee may do other work, however, if the time and nature of the employment are not inconsistent with his duties to the first employer.

The employee impliedly purports that he will perform his duties in a workmanlike manner. This means that he will exercise due care and ordinary diligence in view of the nature of the work. When skill is required, the employee need exercise only ordinary skill.

Sec. 41-E. Trade Secrets. An employee is frequently given confidential trade secrets by his employer. He is under a duty not to disclose such knowledge. It is immaterial that the contract of employment did not stipulate against such disclosures. If he violates this obligation, the employer may enjoin the use of such information. (See p. 635, New England Overall Co. v. Woltmann)

The employee is under no duty to refrain from divulging general information of the particular business in which he is employed. Nor is he under a duty not to divulge the information of the particular business when the relation between employer and employee is not considered confidential. Mere knowledge and skill obtained through experience are not in themselves "trade secrets," and employees may make use of the fruits of their experience in later employment or in working for themselves.

Sec. 41-F. Inventions. In the absence of an express or implied agreement to the contrary, the inventions of an employee belong to him, even though he used the time and property of the employer in their discovery, provided that he was not employed for the express purpose of inventing the things or the processes which he has discovered.

If the invention is discovered during working hours and with the employer's material and equipment, the employer has the right to use the invention without charge in the operation of his business. If the employee has obtained a patent for the invention, he must grant the employer a nonexclusive license to use the invention without the payment of royalty. This *shop right* of the employer does not give him the right to make and sell machines that embody the employee's invention; it only entitles him to use the invention in the operation of his plant.

When the employee is employed in order to secure certain results from experiments to be conducted by him, the courts hold that the inventions equitably belong to the employer on the ground either that there is a trust relation or that there is an implied agreement to make an assignment.

In any case an employee may expressly agree that his inventions made during his employment will be the property of the employer. If such contracts are not clear and specific, the courts are inclined to rule against the employer. The employee may also agree to assign to the employer inventions made after the term of employment.

Sec. 41-G. Compensation. The rights of an employee with respect to compensation are governed in general by the same principles that apply to the compensation of an agent.

In the absence of an agreement to the contrary, when an employee is discharged, whether for cause or not, the employer must pay him his wages down to the expiration of the last pay period. The employee is generally not entitled to compensation for a fractional part of a pay period. The express terms of employment or union contracts, or custom, frequently provide for payment of wages for fractional terminal periods, however, and they may even require a severance pay equal to the compensation for a full period.

Sec. 41-H. Employee's Lien or Preference. At common law an employee was usually given no lien or claim against the employer's property for his wages. Most states today, however, protect an employee's claim for compensation either by a lien or a preference over other claimants of payment out of the proceeds from the sale of the employer's real property on which the employee has made improvements.

These statutes vary widely in their terms. They are usually called *laborers'* or *mechanics' lien laws.* Sometimes the statutes limit the privilege to the workmen of a particular class, such as plasterers, bricklayers, or stonemasons. Compensation for the use of materials or machinery is not protected.

Liability for Injuries of Third Persons

Sec. 41-I. Employee's Liability for Injuries of Third Person. Whenever the employee injures another person, whether another employee or an outsider, the liability of the employee for such injuries to the third person is determined by the same principles that would apply if the employee were not employed.

Sec. 41-J. Employer's Liability for Injuries to Third Persons. An employer is liable to third persons for the harm done them by the acts of his employee (1) when the employer expressly directed the act; (2) when the harm was due to the employer's fault in not having competent employees, or in failing to give them proper instructions, or a similar fault; (3) when the act by the employee was within the course of his employment; or (4) when the act was done by the employee without authority but the employer ratified or assented to it.

The third basis, by which the employer is made liable for the acts of his employee when committed within the scope of his employment,[2] is known as the *doctrine of respondeat superior.* (See p. 638, Kowaleski v. Kowaleski) If the act by the employee is not within the

---

[2] The Restatement, Agency, 2d, declares acts within the scope of the servant's employment to be acts of the kind that the employee was employed to perform; occurring substantially within the authorized time and space limits; and actuated, at least in part, by a purpose to serve the employer; and, if force is intentionally used against another, that its use was not unexpectable. Sec. 228 (1).

scope of his employment, the employer is not liable under this doctrine. An act does not cease to be within the course of employment merely because it was not expressly authorized nor even because it was committed in violation of instructions. Wanton and malicious injury is sometimes within the scope of employment when the employee inflicts such harm in the belief that he is furthering the employer's interest.[3]

There is a tendency toward widening the employer's liability for the tort of his employee, but there is great conflict among the decisions. There is a conflict of authority as to the liability of an employer for the use of force by an employee employed to guard property or in the protection of the employer's interest, with the weight of authority probably in favor of imposing liability. When the employee is employed to recapture or retake property of the principal, as the employee of a finance company employed to repossess automobiles on which installments have not been paid, the courts will generally impose liability on the employer for the unlawful force of the employee used in retaking the property or in committing an assault upon the buyer, but there is some authority to the contrary. In contrast, the majority of decisions do not impose liability on an employer for an assault committed by his bill collector upon the debtor. There is a conflict of authority as to whether the employer is liable for the assault of his employee committed during a dispute over a traffic accident in which the employee has been involved while driving the employer's truck or vehicle.

Sec. 41-K. Liability of Independent Contractor. If work is done by an independent contractor rather than by an employee, the employer or owner is not liable for harm caused by the contractor to third persons or their property. There is, however, a trend toward imposing liability on the employer or owner even in such case when the work undertaken is especially hazardous in nature.

Sec. 41-L. Enforcement of Claim by Third Person. When a third person is injured by an employee, he may have a cause of action or enforceable claim against both the employee and the employer. In most states, and in the federal courts, the injured person may now sue either or both in one action. If the injured person sues both, he may obtain judgment against both of them, although he can only collect the full amount of the judgment once.

If the employee was at fault, the employer may recover indemnity from the employee for the loss that the employer sustained when he was required to make payment to the third person. If the employer

---

[3] Some courts follow the older rule that the employer is never liable for a willful or malicious act by his employee regardless of its purpose.

was at fault and the employee was not, the employee then has a similar right of indemnity against the employer.

Sec. 41-M. Attachment and Garnishment of Wages. It is generally provided that a creditor may require a third person who owes money to his debtor to pay such amount to the creditor to satisfy the creditor's claim against the debtor. That is, if *A* has a valid claim for $100 against *B*, and *C* owes *B* $100, *A* can require *C* to pay him $100, which thereby satisfies both *C*'s debt to *B* and *B*'s debt to A. The necessary legal procedure, which is frequently regulated in great detail, generally requires the third person to pay the money into court or to the sheriff rather than directly to the original creditor. It is commonly provided that the original creditor may also by this process reach tangible property belonging to his debtor which is in the custody or possession of a third person. This procedure is commonly called *attachment* and the third person is called a *garnishee*.

In most states attachment or garnishment may be used when an employee owes money and his creditor then seeks to compel the employer to pay him the amount of the wages due the employee. It may generally be done after the entry of a judgment against the debtor. When the procedure is allowed, the employee may generally claim an exemption of part of his wages. In some states this is merely the minimum exemption which every judgment creditor is allowed regardless of the nature of the claim against him. In other states a special exemption is provided.

Cases for Chapter 41

Christian v. Chicago and Illinois Midland Railway Co.
412 Ill. 171, 105 N.E.2d 741 (1952)

John Christian was employed by the Peabody Coal Co. At the end of the working day, he drove away from the mine in his automobile and drove onto a public dirt road about 150 feet from the mine property. Tracks of the defendant railroad crossed the road. Christian was killed at the crossing by one of the defendant's trains. Eva Christian, his administratrix, sued the railroad in an action at law. The railroad claimed that the injury was compensable under workmen's compensation and that the plaintiff therefore could not bring an action at law. From a judgment for the defendant railroad, the plaintiff appealed.

BRISTON, J. . . . To be compensable, an accident resulting in death must "arise out of and in the course of employment." . . .

These phrases have been repeatedly defined by our courts. "In the course of" refers to the time covered by the employment, as well as reasonable conduct at a place where the workman might reasonably be while so employed. The test is triple, relating to time, conduct, and place. . . . . "Arising out of" refers to the requisite causal relation between the employment and the accident. Inasmuch as the phrases are used conjunctively, there must be a concurrence of both elements for the accident to be compensable. . . .

It has been held as a general guiding proposition that after an employee leaves the employer's premises at the close of his working hours, he is no longer in the course of his employment. . . .

Under certain circumstances, however, this rule that employment begins and ends at the employer's premises has been extended to include adjacent premises used by the employees as a means of ingress and egress with the express or implied consent of the employer. . . . Whether the rule can properly be extended so that an employee returning home from his place of employment may be deemed in the line of his employment depends ultimately upon the special circumstances in each case. . . . The inquiry of the court in each instance is whether the employee, when injured, was at a place where he was subject, by reason of his employment, to a hazard to which the public is not exposed, and to which he is exposed peculiarly and to a greater degree than the public. . . .

It is not sufficient, however, to establish that the employee would not have been at the place but for his job. Consequently, it has been held that if the employee's work for the day is ended and he is at a place off the employer's premises where the hazard to which he is exposed is the same, and of the same degree, as that to which the public is exposed, the injury is not compensable. General Steel Castings Corp. v. Industrial Com., 388 Ill. 66, 57 N.E.2d 454; Payne and Dolan v. Industrial Com., 382 Ill. 177, 46 N.E.2d 925.

The principles of compensation law have been applied by our courts in cases involving facts closely analogous to those in the case at bar and where the accidental injuries were held not to be compensable. . . .

The decedent in the case at bar had completed [his] day's work, had checked out, and had driven off the premises of [his] employer in the car of a fellow employee, and [was] enroute to [his home] and not engaged in any business of the coal company. As in the Steel Castings case, the approved road of egress involved crossing certain railroad tracks. At the moment of the collision [decedent was] on defendant's right of way located on a roadway which, though not a public highway, was open to all members of the public who wished to traverse thereon, and was sufficiently public to be within the jurisdiction of the highway commissioner of the township with respect to the portion extending north beyond defendant's right of way. Inasmuch as one end of the roadway ended at the property of the coal company, it is likely that the road would be traversed only by members of the public who had business with the coal company, or who wished to visit the families residing on the company premises; however, this fact did not convert it into a private road nor render it under the control of the coal company.

Moreover, all persons traveling on the roadway were subjected to the same hazard from defendant's trains, and the [decedent] at the time of the accident [was] not subjected to any greater risk than were other members of the public passing on the roadway. There was nothing in the nature of [his] employment as coal miner which enhanced the risks of this roadway. . . .

The foregoing analysis leads us to the conclusion that there is neither the requisite causal connection between the work of mining coal and the risk of crossing a railroad outside the mine property, nor the requisite finding that the accident occurred in the course of decedent's employment according to the threefold test of time, place, and conduct. . . . Therefore, the [death] of the [decedent was] not compensable within the terms of the Workmen's Compensation Act.

[Judgment for defendant reversed.]

Ransom v. Haner

362 P.2d 282 (Alaska, 1961)

Ransom was employed by the Ketchikan Pulp Co. Another employee of the company, Haner, negligently operated a crane, thereby causing injury to Ransom. The latter sued Haner who raised the defense that Ransom could not sue him because he was a fellow servant and therefore the only remedy available was a workmen's compensation proceeding against the employer. From a judgment in favor of the defendant, Ransom appealed.

AREND, J. . . . The Alaska Workmen's Compensation Act applicable to his case provides that "Where the injury for which compensation is payable hereunder was caused under circumstances creating a legal liability *in someone other than the employer* to pay damages in respect thereof, the employee may take proceedings against the one so liable to pay damages and against anyone liable to pay compensation under this Act, but shall not be entitled to receive both damages and compensation. . . ."

. . . Defendants contend that a fellow employee, . . . may not be regarded as a third party, i.e., "someone other than the employer," under the foregoing section of the act, and that therefore the plaintiff's exclusive remedy in this case is for compensation from the employer under the act and not by way of a common law action for damages against the fellow employees. The defendants have cited us to only four jurisdictions in which it is now squarely held that a fellow employee is not "someone other than the employer" within the meaning of the compensation law. There are other courts holding that the exclusive remedy of an employee injured by a fellow employee is under the Workmen's Compensation Act. The decisions of those courts, however, were usually based upon a more restrictive wording of the applicable state compensation act under consideration in respect to common-law liability of third persons to the injured employee.

Another line of authority holds that, under compensation acts containing a provision such as appears in [the Alaskan statute], immunity to common-law suit is extended only to the employer, and an injured employee can therefore *sue* his own coemployee for the latter's negligence. This is definitely the majority rule: . . . "There is no contract between coemployees, and they are subject to the provisions of the compensation act in their relationship with each other in no way. They pay nothing into the fund that entitles them to protection under its terms. We can perceive nothing in sound reasoning that would entitle a coemployee to gratuitous protection for his own misconduct. To hold that a coemployee is not liable for his own negligence would increase the hazard of employments and be contrary to public policy." . . .

The sizeable number of the majority alone would not persuade us, but sound reasoning, . . . does: "It is said that the defendant is not a 'third person,' within the meaning of the act. We see no reason for attributing to the words 'third person' any other meaning than the usual one. It must mean, as indeed the subsequent language of the section makes perfectly plain, a person other than the employer or employe."

We hold . . . that . . . a fellow employee is not immune to a suit by an injured employee. To declare otherwise would require us to assume the prerogative of the legislature.

[Judgment reversed.]

New England Overall Co. v. Woltmann

176 N.E.2d 193 (Mass., 1961)

Woltmann was employed by the New England Overall Co. as sales manager. Through the course of the years he acquired much information as to suppliers of material and the credit standing and requirements of the company's customers. The company was a small family corporation, and Woltmann was the first outsider to have a position that gave access to such information. Before he had been hired, he agreed that he would never use or divulge such information nor permit it to be used by anyone. After a number of years, Woltmann and one of the salesmen who had made a similar promise set up a rival business which competed with New England Overall. Later they left their jobs with New England, taking a customers' list with them, and then procured clothing articles from the company's suppliers that were almost identical to the company's stock which they sought to sell to the company's customers at lower prices. The company sued to compel Woltmann and the salesman to stop this competition within the area in which the company operated and to return the list of customers. From a judgment in favor of the company, the defendants appealed.

KIRK, J. . . . In situations where there has been no express contract of an employee not to use or disclose confidential information entrusted to him during his employment, this court has held that, although an employee may carry away and use general skill and knowledge acquired during the course of his employment, he may be enjoined from using or disclosing confidential information so acquired. . . . The theory [is] that "out of the 'relationship of employer and employee certain obligations arise, including that which precludes an employee from using, for his own advantage or that of a rival and to the harm of his employer, confidential information that he has gained in the course of his employment.' ". . .

The defendants contend that the granting of injunctive relief to protect an employer's confidential information in the absence of an express contract has been and should be limited to situations involving new or secret inventions and processes or knowledge of special circumstances.

We are unable to accept this contention. The defendants rely heavily upon Woolley's Laundry, Inc. v. Silva, 304 Mass. 383, 23 N.E.2d 899, 126 A.L.R. 752, where this court reversed a decree enjoining a laundry route solicitor and collector from doing business with customers whose names were on a list furnished by the employer with whom the employee had refused to sign a contract with post-employment restrictions. It was held that the list of customers in the circumstances was not confidential. . . . The conclusion was reached that "The questions to be determined in each case are whether the knowledge or information, the use of which the employer seeks to enjoin, is confidential, and whether, if it be confidential in whole or in part, its use ought to be prevented." . . .

We decide the case on its own facts. We do not rest our decision upon the existence or nonexistence of a restrictive covenant between the plaintiff and the defendants. The duties owed by the defendants to the plaintiff spring from the basic principles of equity as revealed in our own desicisons which are in accord with the Restatement 2d, Agency. Section 396 states the proposition as follows: "Unless otherwise agreed, after the termination of the agency, the agent: (a) has no duty not to compete with the principal; (b) has a duty to the principal not to use or to disclose to third persons, on his own account or on account of others, in competition with the principal or to his injury, trade secrets, written lists of names, or other similar confidential matters given to him only for the principal's use or acquired by the agent in violation of duty. The agent is entitled to use general information concerning the method of business of the principal and the names of the customers retained in his memory, if not acquired in violation of his duty as agent. . . ."

There is, of course, nothing secret or confidential about general business principles or methods, nor in general business information, nor in the data routinely gathered in a particular business. As a rule no effort is made to guard such information, and courts rarely would restrain its disclosure.

. . . [The facts of this case] present a different picture. The plaintiff is a corporation exclusively family controlled and managed for forty-nine years, engaged in a highly competitive business, dealing in a specialized type of wearing apparel the styles of which vary seasonally, buying from suppliers whose identity because of competition had to be kept secret and who would sell the particular style only to the plaintiff once it was determined, and selling to customers who would buy the commodity only from the plaintiff, and whose credit standing and foreseeable requirements were known to the plaintiff from years of business dealings. The exclusive family control for almost a half century coupled with the explicit understanding with Woltmann upon his admission to the inner councils of the plaintiff indicated not only a present intention and future purpose, but also a past policy on the part of the plaintiff, of keeping secret its internal business methods and practices, information, and schedules of marketing. The conclusion that factual data acquired over the years relating to styles, the customers' list and supporting material, and list of suppliers were confidential was right. The use of them by Woltmann in competition with the plaintiff after his employment terminated was a clear breach of duty under the principles earlier mentioned. . . .

We have considered the public interest aspect of the case and are aware of the public policy against unreasonably restraining freedom of employment and the growth of monopolistic businesses. . . . It is generally conceded that the clothing business is a highly competitive one. Within a very narrow segment of it the plaintiff as a family enterprise has prospered for many years, and through its internal business practices it has built a reservoir of good will which has insured, on the one hand, the certainty of an exclusive supply of styles created by it from its suppliers, and, on the other hand, the certainty of a market for its goods from its regular customers. The public interest will not be adversely affected by granting to the plaintiff whatever relief the injunction affords from the duplicity of the defendants. . . .

[Judgment affirmed.]

Kowaleski v. Kowaleski

227 Ore. 45, 361 P.2d 64 (1961)

Bernice and Andrew Kowaleski were husband and wife. Antone Kowaleski was the employer of the husband. Bernice was injured when the automobile she was driving was hit by Antone's truck driven by her husband, Andrew, as Antone's employee. Bernice sued Antone who defended on the ground that since Bernice was barred by general principles from suing Andrew, her husband, she could not sue her husband's employer. From a judgment in favor of the employer, Bernice appealed.

ROSSMAN, J. . . . This court has not ruled in the past upon the precise question which this case presents. The decisions of the other courts which were confronted with it are diametrically opposed to each other. The defendant . . . relies on . . . the theory . . . that . . . "the liability of the employer for the negligent acts of his servant is based upon the familiar doctrine of respondeat superior. Unless the servant is liable, there can be no liability on the part of the master. . . ."

The proposition that unless the servant is liable the master cannot be liable is an overgeneralization and inaccurate statement of the law. . . . It means merely that if the principal is sought to be held liable on the theory of respondeat superior, he is not answerable in damages unless the agent was negligent; the statement does not cover the situation when the agent is granted an immunity. . . .

Following the lead of Schubert v. August Schubert Wagon Co., 249 N.Y. 253, 164 N.E. 42, 64 A.L.R. 293, which was written by Cardoza, C. J., many courts have held that a wife may recover from her husband's employer for the husband's negligence. . . . In the Schubert case the wife was struck by the defendant's car which was being driven by her husband in the scope of his employment. In holding the employer responsible, the court reasoned that vicarious liability is not based on the servant's liability but upon his unlawful act and that the husband's individual immunity does not extend to his principal. . . .

Restatement of the Law, 2d, Agency, § 217 . . . reads:

"In an action against a principal based on the conduct of a servant in the course of employment: . . . (b) The principal has no defense because of the fact that. . . . (ii) the agent had an immunity from civil liability as to the act."

Comment b which accompanies § 217 states: ". . . On the other hand where the principal directs an agent to act, or the agent acts in the scope of employment, the fact that the agent has an immunity from liability does not bar a civil action against the principal. Thus, where a servant in the scope of employment negligently runs over his wife, an action against the master by the injured wife is not barred. This result is in accordance with the rule stated in this Section and is the rule adopted in most of the states." . . .

The English courts hold the employer liable for the husband's negligence toward his wife. In Broom v. Morgan, 1 QB 597 (1953), a wife sued her husband and his employer to recover damages for injuries sustained when the wife fell through a trap door which her husband left open and unprotected. Denning, L. J., said: . . .

"The reason for the master's liability is not the mere economic reason that the employer usually has money and the servant has not. It is the sound moral reason that the servant is doing the master's business, and it is the duty of the master to see that his business is properly and carefully done. Take the case of a master who sends a lorry out on to the road with his servant in charge. He is morally responsible for seeing that the lorry does not run down people on the pavement. The master cannot wash his hands of it by saying, 'I put a competent driver in charge of the lorry,' or by saying, 'It was only the driver's wife who was hurt.' It is his lorry, and it is his business that it is on. He takes the benefit of the work when it is carefully done, and he must take the liability of it when it is negligently done. He is himself under a duty to see that care is exercised in the driving of the lorry on his business. If the driver is negligent there is a breach of duty not only by the driver himself, but also by the master." . . .

Finally, respondent urges three policy reasons to prevent the wife's recovery. First, it is stated that there will be a disruption of the family unity and harmony. Historically, the husband and wife were considered a unit [but numerous] . . . statutes . . . changed this common law. . . . [In addition, another Oregon statute has] eliminated all civil disabilities from a wife which are not imposed on a husband and also confers on the wife all civil rights of the husband. . . . Thus, it is seen that the wife has gradually acquired a separate legal identity and there is not a complete unity in law between the spouses.

A harmonious family is still the basis of our society, but the law does not champion this ideal above all other objectives. Oregon allows recovery for a willful tort by one spouse against the other, . . . and a child against his parent, . . . A wife may also testify against her husband in certain criminal cases. . . . In these situations the harmony of the home is more likely to be disrupted than when a spouse sues her husband's employer. In the later case the employer is the real party defendant and not the husband. . . .

". . . Today there is a certain background of experience which was necessarily lacking when courts first denied personal tort actions between the spouses. There is nothing to show that in the states which permit such actions the peace and harmony of the home is disrupted to any greater extent, or that the courts are deluged with a greater flood of such litigation, than in the states which deny the action. . . ."

The second policy argument urged by the respondent is that there will be a diminution of the family wealth if a wife may sue her husband's employer for the husband's negligence. The theory is that a wife will recover from the employer and the recovery less costs goes into a common family fund. Then the employer is indemnified by the employee-husband; the net result is that the family has diminished the common fund by the cost of the two law suits. This hypothesis is not universally true because it does not cover the situation where there is no common fund, i.e., the husband and wife are separated or do not pool their individual resources. . . . Finally, whether the employer will sue the employee is collateral to this case and is not before the court. We cannot presume that the principal will sue his agent.

The third policy argument is the fear of collusion between the spouses. Why collusion is more dreadful in this case than when a child sues a parent . . . or one relative sues another is not apparent.

From the above analysis we conclude that a wife may sue her husband's employer for the husband's negligence. The husband's personal immunity should not extend to his employer. [The view] . . . denying recovery, is based on a rationale that the march of progress has rejected. Moreover, it would be a sad reflection upon the courts if a group of people were injured in one accident by an employee and everyone injured could recover from the employer but the wife of the negligent employee. The fact that the wife was injured by her husband when he was on the business of his employer should not relieve the defendant-employer of his legal responsibility.

[Judgment reversed.]

Questions and Case Problems

1. What is the objective of each of the following rules of law?
   (a) An employer is liable for injury to an employee sustained in the course of his employment from a risk involved in that employment.
   (b) An employee is entitled to compensation even though he has been idle when the idleness was caused by the employer's failure to give him directions as to what work to do.

2. Thouron did part-time housework in Acree's home in return for an hourly pay and free transportation to and from her home in Acree's automobile driven by Acree's full-time chauffeur. While she was being driven to Acree's house to work, there was a collision because of the chauffeur's negligence. Thouron sued Acree for damages caused by the negligence of the latter's chauffeur. The workmen's compensation law was not applicable since it excluded domestic employees. The liability of the

employer was thus governed by common law. Decide. (Thouron v. Acree, [Del.] 174 A.2d 702)

3. Wiltz was employed by the Esso Standard Oil Co. as a helper for a mechanic and pipe fitter. The area in which he worked was filled with various fumes and dust. The employer did not in any way ventilate the area or provide Wiltz with any protective equipment. After some time he developed tuberculosis from exposure to such conditions. Since tuberculosis was not an occupational disease within the general workmen's compensation act coverage, he sued Esso for its negligence in exposing him to the hazard when it knew of the danger involved. Esso defended on the ground that Wiltz had assumed the risk of developing tuberculosis. Was Esso liable? (Wiltz v. Esso Standard Oil Co., [La.App.] 126 So.2d 649)

4. Crutchfield, who had a contract to clear a right of way for a high voltage electric transmission line, employed Bogle to operate a bulldozer. After a sudden violent rain and electrical storm sprang up, Bogle was found dead from a bolt of lightning under a large tree that was on the strip being cleared. His bulldozer was found about 20 feet away with the engine running. His estate made a claim for workmen's compensation. This was opposed on the grounds that (a) death by lightning did not arise from and in course of Bogle's employment, and (b) he could have run under a smaller tree or into a wooden house nearby which would have been safer. Decide. (Crutchfield v. Bogle, [Okla.] 270 P.2d 640)

5. Complitano was an employee of Steel & Alloy Tank Co. The city in which the plant was located sponsored a softball league. Complitano and other employees of Steel & Alloy formed a team which represented the employer in the league. All games were played after hours and off the premises and were managed and controlled in all respects by the employees. Steel Alloy made a financial contribution to the support of the team but had no other interest in it. Complitano was injured while playing in one of the games and filed a claim for workmen's compensation on the theory that the activity was of mutual benefit to the employer and the claimant. Decide. (Complitano v. Steel & Alloy Tank Co., [N.J.S.] 164 A.2d 792)

6. Benson was employed as a switchman by the Chicago, Rock Island & Pacific Railway Company. While uncoupling a car from a train, Benson took hold of a grabiron on the preceding car. His glove was caught on the grabiron, and Benson was dragged some distance and severely injured. It was then discovered that his glove had caught on a piece of fence wire, with a hook on the end of it, which had been wrapped around the grabiron. He sued the railway for damages. Decide. (Chicago, Rock Island & Pacific Railway Co. v. Benson, 352 Ill. 195, 185 N.E. 244)

7. Deye, who was employed by the Quality Engraving and Electrotype Co., invented a new process for making molds and obtained a patent on it. He then made an assignment of the patent to the company but did not make any contract with the company for the payment to him of royalties. Although he had not been employed to discover the particular invention, he had done so on the employer's time and with the employer's materials. Was Deye entitled to the royalties? (Deye v. Quality Engraving and Electrotype Co., 90 Ohio App. 324, 106 N.E.2d 584)

8. Kirk made a contract with the Montana Transfer Co. to move her household furniture to another home. After the second load had been taken, Kirk notified the company that she did not want any more furniture moved. Van, an employee of the company, insisted on hauling the balance of the furniture. When Kirk refused his demand, Van took a refrigerator from Kirk as security for the amount of the unpaid charges. In so doing, he assaulted Kirk, who resisted the taking of the refrigerator. Then Kirk sued the moving company. The moving company meanwhile had been informed of what had happened, and at the time of the suit the company had the refrigerator in its warehouse. Decide. (Kirk v. Montana Transfer Co., 56 Mont. 292, 184 P.2d 987)

9. The Central Lumber Co. furnished material to Schroeder for the construction of certain buildings. It also loaned her $465 to enable her to pay the men working in the construction. A mechanics' lien law gave a lien to persons furnishing materials, machinery, or fixtures for the construction of buildings. Was the company entitled to a lien for the $465? (Central Lumber Co. v. Schroeder, 164 La. 759, 114 So. 644)

10. Nash, who owned a truck, contracted to haul Meguschar's timber. Nash was to do the hauling when he desired, and with his own equipment and assistants whom he would pay personally. Nash was killed in the hauling operations, and a workmen's compensation claim was presented for his death by his wife against Meguschar. Decide. (Nash v. Meguschar, 228 Ind. 216, 91 N.E.2d 361)

11. Buffo was employed by the Baltimore & Ohio Railroad Co. With a number of other workers he was removing old brakes from railroad cars and replacing them with new brakes. In the course of the work rivet heads and scraps from the brakes accumulated on the tracks under the cars, but these were only removed occasionally when the men had time. Buffo, while holding an air hammer in both arms, was crawling under a car when his foot slipped on scrap on the ground, which caused him to strike and injure his knee. He sued the railroad for damages under the Federal Employers' Liability Act. Decide. (Buffo v. Baltimore & Ohio Railroad Co., 364 Pa. 437, 72 A.2d 593)

12. Faunce was employed by the Boost Co., which manufactured a soft drink. After some years he left its employ and began manufacturing a different soft drink. The company claimed that he was using trade secrets learned while he was in its employ and sought to enjoin him. It was proved that the soft drink made by the defendant was not the same as that made by the plaintiff; that the difference between one soft drink and another was primarily due to the 1 per cent of the volume that represented flavoring; and that the drink made by the defendant could be made by anyone in the soft drink business on the basis of general knowledge of the trade. Was Boost entitled to an injunction? (Boost Co. v. Faunce, 17 N.J.S. 458, 86 A.2d 283)

PART VIII-A
PARTNERSHIPS

CHAPTER 42

Nature and Creation

The single proprietorship is the most common form of business organization, but many larger businesses have two or more owners. The partnership is a very common form of multiple ownership.

Modern partnership law shows traces of Roman law, the law merchant, and the common law of England. A Uniform Partnership Act, formulated by the National Commissioners on Uniform Laws for the purpose of bringing about uniformity in this branch of the law, has been adopted in most states.[1]

Sec. 42-A. Definitions. A *partnership* or copartnership is a legal relationship created by the voluntary "association of two or more persons to carry on as co-owners a business for profit." [2] The persons so associated are called *partners* or copartners.

A partnership can be described more realistically in terms of its characteristics:

(1) A partnership is a voluntary contractual relation; it is not imposed by law.

(2) The relation of partnership usually involves contributions by the members of capital, labor, or skill, or a combination of these.

(3) The parties are associated as co-owners and principals to transact the business of the firm.

---

[1] This Act has been adopted in Guam and all states except Alabama, Florida, Georgia, Hawaii, Iowa, Kansas, Louisiana, Maine, Mississippi, and New Hampshire.
[2] Uniform Partnership Act, Sec. 6 (1).

(4) A partnership is organized for the pecuniary profit of its members. If profit is not its object, the group will commonly be an unincorporated association.[3]

Sec. 42-B. Purposes of a Partnership. A partnership may be formed for any lawful purpose. It is immaterial whether it relates to the conduct of a business or a profession.

The partnership cannot be formed to carry out immoral or illegal acts, or acts that are contrary to public policy. The effect of an illegal purpose is a denial to the partners of a right to sue on the contracts that involve the illegality. Moreover, in such cases the partners cannot seek the aid of courts to settle their affairs among themselves. In addition, if the conduct of the partnership constitutes a crime, all persons involved in the commission of the crime are subject to punishment. (See p. 649, Vandegrift v. Vandegrift)

Sec. 42-C. Classification of Partnerships.

(1) General and Special Partnerships. A *general partnership* is created for the general conduct of a particular kind of business, such as a hardware business or a manufacturing business. A *special partnership* is formed for a single transaction, such as the purchase and resale of a certain building.

(2) Trading and Nontrading Partnerships. A *trading partnership* is organized for the purpose of buying and selling, such as a firm engaged in the retail grocery business. A *nontrading partnership* is one organized for a purpose other than engaging in commerce, such as the practice of law or medicine.

Sec. 42-D. Firm Name. In the absence of a statutory requirement it is not necessary that a partnership have a firm name, although it is customary to have one. The partners may, as a general rule, adopt any firm name they desire. They may use a fictitious name or even the name of a stranger. Moreover, a firm may have more than one name; as, for example, a firm that has branch houses or conducts business at two or more places.

There are, however, certain limitations upon the adoption of a firm name:

(1) The name cannot be the same as or deceptively similar to the name of another firm for the purpose of attracting its patrons.

(2) Some states prohibit the use of the words "and company" unless they indicate an additional partner.

---

[3] See p. 690.

(3) Many states require the registration of a fictitious partnership name. (See p. 650, Mason v. Martin)

Sec. 42-E. Classification of Partners.

(1) A *general partner* is one who publicly and actively engages in the transaction of firm business.

(2) A *nominal partner* holds himself out as a partner or permits others to hold him out as such. He is not in fact a partner since he neither shares in the management nor the profits; but in some instances he may be held liable as a partner.

(3) A *silent partner* is one who, although he may be known to the public as a partner, takes no active part in the business.

(4) A *secret partner* is one who takes an active part in the management of the firm but who is not known to the public as a partner.

(5) A *dormant partner* is one who takes no active part in transacting the business and who remains unknown to the public.

Sec. 42-F. Who May Be Partners.
In the absence of statutory provisions to the contrary, persons who are competent to contract may form a partnership. As has been indicated previously, however, certain persons have a legal or natural incapacity to contract. When the contracts of such a person are void, he cannot enter into partnership agreement. If his contracts are merely voidable, he may become a partner, assuming that the other partners will accept him under the circumstances; but he may thereafter avoid the relationship and withdraw from the firm. Thus a minor may become a partner, but he may avoid the contract of partnership and withdraw.[4]

In general, the capacity of an insane person to be a partner is similar to that of a minor, except that an adjudication of insanity usually makes subsequent agreements void rather than merely voidable. An enemy alien may not be a partner, but other aliens may enter into the relation. A corporation, unless expressly authorized by statute or its charter, may not act as a partner.

Sec. 42-G. Creation of Partnership.
A partnership is a voluntary association and exists because the parties agree to be in partnership. If there is no agreement, there is no partnership. If the parties agree that the legal relationship between them shall be such that they in fact operate a business for profit as co-owners, a partnership is created even though the parties may not have labeled their new relationship a "partnership." The law is concerned with the substance of what is done rather than the name.

---

4 See p. 157.

Conversely, a partnership does not arise if the parties do not agree to the elements of a partnership, even though they do name their enterprise a partnership.

Sec. 42-H. Articles of Partnership. As a general rule, partnership agreements need not be in writing. A partnership agreement must be in writing, however, if it is within the provision of the Statute of Frauds that a contract which cannot be performed within one year must be in writing. Thus an agreement to create a partnership two years hence or to create a partnership now that is to continue for more than one year must be written. If the duration of the partnership is not stipulated, a writing is not required under this section of the Statute of Frauds because such a partnership could terminate in less than a year.

In some situations, the agreement may come under the provision of the statute that requires a transfer of interest in land to be in writing. For example, if by the terms of the partnership agreement one partner is to gain an interest in real property owned by the other, the agreement must be in writing. Generally, however, the agreement need not be written solely because the partnership is formed to engage in the business of buying and selling real estate.

Even when unnecessary, it is always desirable to have the partnership agreement in writing to avoid subsequent controversies as to mutual rights and duties. The formal document that is prepared to evidence the contract of the parties is termed a *partnership agreement, articles of partnership,* or *articles of copartnership.*

Partnership articles, as in the case of any good contract, should cover all material points of the agreement. Generally, they will contain provisions relating to the following: (1) date of the agreement; (2) names of the partners; (3) recital of agreement to be partners; (4) nature of the enterprise; (5) duration of the relation; (6) name of the firm and location; (7) contributions to capital; (8) manner of sharing profits and losses; (9) withdrawals of money; (10) keeping of accounts; (11) duties of partners; (12) limitations upon partners; (13) special rights, duties, or compensation of any partner; (14) procedure upon the death of a partner as to the purchase of a deceased partner's share; and (15) final distribution of assets.

The partnership agreement may provide that certain matters, such as salaries to be paid the partners, may be determined from time to time. (See p. 651, Lentz v. Pearson)

Sec. 42-I. Determining Existence of Partnership. Whether a partnership exists is basically a matter of proving the intent of the parties. (See p. 652, Call v. Linn) As in the case of agency, the burden of proving the existence of a partnership is upon the person who claims that one exists.

When a written agreement recites that the parties have created a partnership and sets forth legal relationships characteristic of a partnership, the question is quickly settled unless the defendant claims that the agreement is forged or that it is invalid for some other reason or that the partnership created thereby had been terminated.

When the parties have not clearly indicated the nature of their relationship, the law has developed the following guides to aid in determining whether the parties have created a partnership:

(1) Sharing Profits and Losses. The fact that the parties share profits and losses is strong evidence of a partnership.

(2) Sharing Profits. An agreement that does not provide for sharing losses but does provide for sharing profits is evidence that the parties are united in partnership, as it is assumed that they will also share losses. The Uniform Partnership Act provides that sharing profits is prima facie evidence of a partnership, but that a partnership is not to be inferred when profits are received in payment (a) of a debt, (b) of wages, (c) of rent, (d) of an annuity to a deceased partner's widow or representative, (e) of interest, or (f) for the goodwill of the business. If there is no evidence of the reason for receiving the profits, it must be held that a partnership exists.

(3) Gross Returns. The sharing of gross returns is of itself very slight, if any, evidence of partnership. To illustrate, in a case in which one party owned a show that was exhibited upon land owned by another under an agreement to divide the gross proceeds, no partnership was proved because there was no co-ownership or community of interest in the business.

(4) Co-ownership. Neither the co-ownership of property nor the sharing of profits or rents from property which two or more persons own creates a partnership.

(5) Contribution of Property. The fact that all persons have not contributed property to the enterprise does not establish that the enterprise is not a partnership. A partnership may be formed even though some of its members furnish only skill or labor.

Sec. 42-J. Partners as to Third Persons. In some instances a person who is in fact not a partner or a member of a partnership may be held accountable to third persons as though he were a partner. This liability arises when a person conducts himself in such a manner that third persons are reasonably led to believe that he is a partner and to act in reliance on that belief to their injury. The person who incurs such a liability is termed a nominal partner, a partner by estoppel, or an ostensible partner.

Sec. 42-K. Partnership Property. In general, partnership property consists of all the property contributed by the partners or acquired for the firm or with its funds. There is usually no limitation upon the kind and amount of property that a partnership may acquire. The firm may own real as well as personal property, unless it is prohibited from doing so by statute or by the partnership agreement.

The title to firm property may be held in the name of all or one or less than all of the partners.

(1) Title to Personal Property in Firm Name. A partnership may hold and transfer the title to personal property in the firm name, whether the name is fictitious or consists of the names of living people. Thus a partnership may hold a mortgage on personal property in the firm name, such as "Keystone Cleaners."

(2) Title to Real Property in Firm Name. A majority of states now permit a partnership to hold or transfer the title to real property in the firm name alone, without regard to whether that name is fictitious or not.

In a minority of states the common-law rule still prevails that title to real property cannot be held in the firm name on the theory that such title must vest in either a natural or an artificial person and that the partnership has no legal existence as a separate person. Some of the minority states modify this view when the names of some or all of the individual partners are included in the firm name. In such instances it is held that the property is owned by those persons in trust for the use of the firm.

(3) Transferees of Firm's Real Property. In order for a transfer of a firm's real property to be technically correct, (a) it must have been made by a partner or agent with the authority to make the transfer and (b) it must have been made in the name of the holder of the title. When both conditions have been satisfied, the transferee has legal title as against the partnership.

If the transfer was authorized but was not made in the name of the title holder, the transferee acquires equitable title to the property and the right to have a proper deed or instrument of conveyance executed. If the transfer of the partnership property was not authorized, the firm may recover the property from the transferee if he knew that it was firm property or if he did not purchase it for value. When the title to the firm property is recorded but not in the name of the firm, a person who purchases from the record holder in

good faith, for value, and without notice or knowledge of the partnership title, may keep the property.

Sec. 42-L. Tenancy in Partnership. Partners hold firm property by
tenancy in partnership. The characteristics of such a tenancy are:

(1) In the absence of contrary agreement all partners have equal
right to use firm property for partnership purposes.

(2) A partner possesses no interest in any specific portion of the
partnership property that he can sell, assign, or mortgage. The
partner has no right in any specific property that he can transfer to
a third person, although he may transfer his interest in specific property to his sole surviving partner.

(3) In most states the creditors of a partner cannot levy on and
sell his interest in specific partnership property.

(4) The interest of a deceased partner in specific firm property
vests in the surviving partners, but only for partnership purposes.

(5) A partner's interest in specific property is not subject to dower
or curtesy.

This distinct form of tenure is sometimes confused with joint
tenancies and tenancies in common. The ordinary joint tenant has
full beneficial ownership upon the death of the cotenant, whereas a
surviving partner does not. A cotenant may alienate or transfer his
interest, putting another in his place, but a partner cannot do so.

Cases for Chapter 42

Vandegrift v. Vandegrift
226 Pa. 254, 75 A. 365 (1910)

John H. Vandegrift and his son, John M. Vandegrift, formed a partnership for manufacturing and selling spirituous liquors. Federal and Pennsylvania licenses to run the business were obtained under the son's name
without stating that the father had any interest. Both the federal and
Pennsylvania statutes required that the holder of such licenses disclose the
names of all persons interested in the firm and imposed criminal penalties
for failing to do so. Subsequently, the father sued the son for an accounting
of his profits of the partnership. From a decree for the defendant, the
plaintiff appealed.

POTTER, J. . . . The first question raised . . . is whether a partnership agreement to engage in the manufacture and sale of distilled
spirituous liquors, the business to be conducted under the name of one
of the partners only, is an illegal contract which a court of equity
will not enforce.

The fact is undisputed in this case that John M. Vandegrift each
year violated the laws of both Pennsylvania and of the United States
by making false statements that no one but himself was interested in

the business and thereby subjected himself to liability for the penalties prescribed in the acts. . . . These violations of law were expressly provided for in the agreement, which set forth that the business was "to be continued under the name of John M. Vandegrift as heretofore." So that at best the agreement contemplated the conduct of the business in an illegal manner. And the trial judge further finds as a fact that the concealment of plaintiff's interest in the business "was done with the knowledge of the said John H. Vandegrift, their purpose being to keep the creditors of John H. Vandegrift, who was insolvent, from learning that he had property that might be taken in execution by them." The fact that the partnership contemplated was to be formed in a manner forbidden by the statute would render it illegal, even though, aside from the statute, there would be no illegality. . . .

". . . To permit a recovery in this case is in substance to enforce an illegal contract, and one which is illegal because it is against public policy. . . . The court refuses to enforce such a contract. . . .

[Judgment for defendant affirmed.]

Mason v. Martin

57 S.D. 299, 232 N.W. 29 (1930)

T. Mason and his son, J. Mason, were partners engaged in business under the firm name of Mason's Funeral Home. They sued Martin for a bill due for the burial of her husband. She defended on the ground that the firm name of the partnership had not been registered, and that the plaintiff could therefore not bring suit. From a judgment for the plaintiffs, the defendant appealed.

BROWN, P.J. . . . As one defense appellant [Martin] pleaded failure of plaintiffs to comply with the statute requiring the filing of a certificate of the true names of the firm. . . . Rev. Code, 1919, Section 1334, provides that "every partnership transacting business in this state under a fictitious name, or a designation not showing the names of the persons interested as partners in such business, must file with the clerk of courts of the county in which its principal place of business is situated . . . a certificate stating the names in full of all the members of such partnership, and their places of residence, and publish the same once a week for four successive weeks in a newspaper published in the county"; and Section 1336 provides that, until such certificate has been filed and publication made, no action shall be maintained by such partners on any contract made or transaction had in the partnership name. It is conceded that the contract or transaction involved was had in the partnership name, and that Section 1334 has not been complied with by plaintiffs. The name "Mason's Funeral Home" in itself gives no indication that it designates a partnership. It would be equally applicable and appropriate to a corporation. Perhaps a reasonable inference might justify the belief that the name was meant to designate a single individual, but we think it clearly was not a designation showing the names of the persons interested as partners in the business, and that it was better adapted to give the impression that the business was that of an individual rather than that of a partnership. . . . In Andrews v. Glick, 205 Cal. 699, 272 P. 587, the Supreme Court . . . [holds] that the name Andrews-Cordano Plumbing Co., as the name of a partnership composed of Harry W. Andrews and Frank Cordano, does not designate the names of the persons interested as partners in the business, and that a partnership conducted under such name cannot maintain an action on a contract had in the partnership name. . . .

Plaintiffs were not entitled to maintain this action, not having filed a certificate as required by Section 1334. . . .

[Judgment for plaintiffs reversed.]

Lentz v. Pearson

246 Minn. 145, 74 N.W.2d 662 (1956)

Lentz and Pearson formed a partnership in 1948. Their partnership agreement provided that salaries should be paid the partners in such amounts as should be "determined by both persons from time to time, as the profits warrant." Later a dispute arose over the amount due Pearson as salary. He offered oral evidence to show that he was to receive $100 a week. From a judgment finding that Pearson was to receive $100 a week, Lentz appealed.

DELL, C.J. . . . There is testimony indicating that the parties had agreed, prior to and at the time of the execution of the articles of copartnership, that [Pearson's] salary should be $100 a week. However, [Lentz] contends that this testimony was inadmissible as being in violation of the parol evidence rule. He claims that such testimony contradicts or alters the articles of copartnership which provide that each partner shall draw a salary in an amount as determined by the parties from time to time. . . . Such testimony was admissible and not in violation of the parol evidence rule since the articles are silent as to the amount of salary allowance and specifically provide that that figure is to be set by agreement of the parties, which is what was done. . . .

Testimony of conversations, subsequent to the execution of the articles, fixing [Pearson's] salary was admissible and not in violation of the parol evidence rule. Such testimony does not contradict, alter, vary, or add to the terms of the written contract, in this instance the articles of copartnership. It merely shows the salary agreement of the parties reached from time to time during the course of the partnership which agreement was specifically provided for by the terms of the articles themselves. . . .

[Judgment affirmed.]

Call v. Linn

112 Ore. 1, 228 P. 127 (1924)

Call made a contract with Deverill to sell 5,100 head of lambs to Linn and Deverill, who were doing business under the name of Linn & Deverill. Subsequently in an action against Linn and Deverill to recover damages for breach of contract, Call contended that the defendants were partners. Linn objected that no partnership existed and that the transaction was simply a joint venture between him and Deverill. From a judgment for the plaintiff, the defendant appealed.

CoSHOW, J. . . . "Our law has always treated the partnership relation as founded upon voluntary contract. . . .

"This intention to form a partnership may be expressed in the contract, or it may be gathered from the acts of the parties and from the circumstances which may interpret the agreement between them. . . .

"In an action by a third person against alleged partners according to the rules elsewhere stated, it is sufficient to establish their liability to show admissions of such fact by the alleged partners, or that they have held themselves out to the public as such. The rule is that such proof may be made by parol. It is generally held that in actions by third persons against persons who are alleged to be partners, such partnership may be established by parol evidence even where it appears from the evidence on the trial of the case that there is a written agreement between the parties as to the partnership. . . . Partnerships may be established by proof of acts and conduct. No rule can be given as to what particular acts or conduct may be proved in order to establish the relation; nor can the nature and character of the acts be designated. It is only essential that the proof be sufficient to establish such acts and conduct from which the partnership may be reasonably inferred. . . . The fact of the existence of a partnership may be proved by the habit and course of dealing, and by the conduct and declarations of the partners.". . .

. . . A partnership may exist for one transaction only. It is not the quantity of business transacted, but the manner of transacting the business, the relation of the parties thereto and to each other, and their interest therein which constitute a partnership. . . .

[Judgment for plaintiff affirmed.]

Questions and Case Problems

1. What is the objective of each of the following rules of law?
   (a) The law does not conclude that a person is a partner from the fact that he shares in the partnership profits when he does so as payment of a debt, wages, or rent owed him.
   (b) A partnership may generally hold property in its own name.

2. Bates and Huffman formed a partnership to run a shoe business. In a lawsuit between the partners, Huffman claimed that the partnership agreement was void because Bates was a minor. Was he correct? (Huffman v. Bates, [Mo.] 348 S.W.2d 363)

3. The United States claimed that Coson was liable for taxes owed by a partnership, but Coson claimed that he was not a partner. The government showed that the income tax return filed by the firm listed Coson as a partner and also that one of the partners had assigned his interest in the firm to Coson. It was shown that Coson had no knowledge of the information contained in the income tax return. Was he liable as a partner? (United States v. Coson, [C.A.9th] 286 F.2d 453)

4. The H & R Construction Corporation entered into a contract for construction work, and the Seaboard Surety Co. executed a bond assuring that the contract would be performed. The Seaboard Surety Co. was required to pay damages for breach of the contract by the construction corporation, and then it brought suit against the contractor and the H. C. Nelson Investment Co. to recover the money it had paid. Its suit against the Nelson Investment Co. was based on the theory that the construction corporation and the investment company were partners. It was shown that the investment company financed the construction company to a large extent and also furnished machinery for the carrying out of its contracts under an agreement that it should in some cases receive a share of the profits of the contracts of the contractor. Was there a partnership? (Nelson v. Seaboard Surety Co., [C.A.8th] 262 F.2d 189)

5. A suit was brought by the heirs of members of a partnership to determine the right to the proceeds of sale of certain real estate. The real estate had been purchased by the partnership with partnership money and in the partnership name. The real estate was not used in the partnership business but was held only for investment purposes. It was claimed by the heirs that this real estate was not subject to the provisions of the Uniform Partnership Act governing tenancy by partnership because it was not used in the business. Were they correct? (Brown v. Brown, [Tenn.] 320 S.W.2d 721)

6. Only a licensed physician may practice medicine in Idaho. Abbot, Worlton, and Hulse formed a partnership called the Idaho Falls Clinic. The first two were licensed physicians, but Hulse was a layman who acted as business manager. Davis, a licensed physician, was employed by the clinic. In an action by Worlton and other parties against Davis, the defense was raised that the partnership was illegal. Decide. (Worlton v. Davis, 73 Idaho 217, 249 P.2d 810)

7. Edward and Robert Temm ran a business. An action was brought by Edward to declare the relationship a partnership. The defense was raised that because there was no agreement that losses should be borne equally, the relationship was not a partnership. Was this defense valid? (Temm v. Temm, 354 Mo. 814, 191 S.W.2d 629)

8. Brown and Pelkey entered into an agreement whereby Pelkey was to operate Brown's farm "to the halves." Each party received half of the proceeds and paid half of the expenses. Pelkey purchased from the Farmers' Exchange on credit a quantity of grain for use on the farm. He charged the purchase to Brown and himself. Brown paid half of the purchase price, and the creditor brought an action against him and Pelkey to recover the remainder. The Farmers' Exchange contended that the dedenfants were partners. Decide. (Farmers' Exchange v. Brown, 106 Vt. 65, 169 A. 906)

9. McMullen and Hoffman formed a partnership to do business under the name of Hoffman and Bater. The purpose of the partnership was to perform a contract for the manufacturing and laying of certain steel pipe from Mount Tabor to the lead works of the Bull Run Water System for the City of Portland. The partnership agreement stipulated that McMullen and Hoffman were to pretend to make competitive bids to obtain the contract but would secretly consult each other as to the amount of the bids. The former was to enter a bid under the name of the San Francisco Bridge Co.; and the latter, under the name of Hoffman and Bates. Subsequently McMullen brought a suit against Hoffman for an accounting. Was he entitled to an accounting? (McMullen v. Hoffman, 174 U.S. 639)

10. Farrell and Babbott entered into a partnership for the purpose of manufacturing refrigerating machines but did not agree upon a firm name. Later Babbott executed a promissory note payable to himself and signed with the name "Franklin Farrell & Co." The note was indorsed by Babbott to Gallaudet, who sold it to the Meriden National Bank. In an action brought by the bank against Gallaudet to recover the amount of the note, the plaintiff contended that there was no such firm as Franklin Farrell & Co. because there was no firm name. Decide. (Meriden National Bank v. Gallaudet, 120 N.Y. 298, 24 N.E. 944)

11. The Dempsey-Kearns Theatrical & Motion Picture Enterprises, Inc., agreed to include Jack Dempsey, then champion heavyweight fighter of the world, and Jack Kearns in a vaudeville show. In consideration therefor, Pantages, the theater manager, agreed to pay the Dempsey-Kearns Corporation $4,000 a week and one-half of the profits of each performance over and above a stipulated sum. The box-office receipts for a performance given in Kansas City, Missouri, were stolen from Pantages' safe in the office of the theater. Pantages refused to pay the agreed amount in connection with this performance, contending that the stolen funds were partnership funds. Do you agree? (Dempsey-Kearns Theatrical & Motion Picture Enterprises, Inc., v. Pantages, 91 Cal.App. 677, 267 P. 550)

CHAPTER 43

Authority of Partners

Decisions on business matters concerning the partnership are made by the partners, usually by a majority vote. In relationship to third persons, a partner's authority to act for the firm is similar to that of an agent to act for his principal.

Sec. 43-A. Authority of Majority of Partners. When there are more than two partners in a firm, the decision of the majority prevails on matters involving the manner in which the ordinary functions of the business will be conducted. (See p. 659, Cotton Plant Oil Co. Case) To illustrate, the majority of the partners of a firm decide to increase their advertising and enter into a contract for that purpose. The transaction is valid and binds the firm and all of the partners. The act of the majority is not binding, however, if it is contrary to the original agreement. For such matters unanimous action is required.

When there are two or any other even number of partners, there is the possibility of an even division on a matter that requires majority approval. In such a case no action can be taken, and the partnership is deadlocked. If the division is over a basic issue and the partners persist in the deadlock so that it is impossible to continue the business, any one of the partners may petition the court to order the dissolution of the firm.

Sec. 43-B. Authority of Individual Partners. An individual partner may have express authority to do certain acts, either because the partnership agreement so declares or because a sufficient number of partners have agreed thereto. In addition, he has authority to do those acts which are customary for a member of such a partnership. As in the case of an agent, the acts of a partner in excess of his authority do not ordinarily bind the partnership.

(1) Customary Authority. A partner, by virtue of the fact that he is a comanager of the business, customarily has certain powers necessary and proper to carry out that business. In the absence of express limitation, the law will therefore imply that he has such powers. The scope of such powers varies with the nature of the partnership and also with the business customs and usages of the area in which the partnership operates. The following are the more common of the implied powers:

(a) CONTRACTS. A partner may make any contract necessary to the transaction of firm business. He cannot make a contract of guaranty, however, merely because it will induce a third person to purchase from the partnership. (See p. 660, First National Bank v. Farson)

(b) SALES. A partner may sell in the regular course of business any part or all of the personal property of the firm and make the usual warranties incidental to such sales. This authority, however, is limited to the goods kept for sales.

(c) PURCHASES. A partner may purchase any kind of property within the scope of the business, and for this purpose he may pledge the credit of the firm. This authority is not affected by the fact that he subsequently misuses or keeps the goods.

(d) LOANS. A partner in a trading firm may borrow money for partnership purposes. In doing so, he may execute negotiable instruments in the firm name or give security, such as a mortgage or a pledge of the personal property of the firm. (See p. 661, Reid v. Linder) If the third person acts in good faith, the transaction is binding even though the partner misappropriates the money. A partner in a nontrading partnership does not ordinarily possess the power to borrow.

(e) INSURANCE. A partner may insure the firm property, cancel a policy of insurance, or make proof and accept settlement for the loss.

(f) EMPLOYMENT. A partner may engage such employees and agents as are necessary to carry out the purposes of the enterprise.

(g) CLAIMS AGAINST FIRM. A partner has the authority to compromise, adjust, and pay bona fide claims against the partnership. He may pay debts out of firm funds, or he may pay them by transferring firm property to creditors. Although he has no power to pay his own debts from firm assets, his creditors are protected if they receive such a payment in good faith and without knowledge that it comes from firm assets.

(h) CLAIMS OF FIRM. A partner may adjust, receive payment of, and release debts and other claims of the firm. He may take money or negotiable instruments but, as a rule, cannot accept goods in payment. One who makes a proper payment is protected even though the partner to whom payment is made fails to account to the firm.

(i) ADMISSIONS. A partner may bind the firm by admissions or statements that are adverse to the interests of the partnership if they are made in regard to firm affairs and in the pursuance of firm business.

(j) NOTICE. A partner may receive notice of matters affecting the partnership affairs, and such notice, in the absence of fraud, is binding on the others.

(2) Limitations on Authority. The partners may agree to limit the normal powers of each partner. When a partner, contrary to such an agreement, negotiates a contract for the firm with a third person, the firm is bound if the third person was unaware of the agreement. In such a case, the partner violating the agreement is liable to his partners for any loss caused by the breach of his contract.

A third person cannot assume that the partner has all the authority which he purports to have. (See p. 662, Samstag Case) The third person must be on the alert for the following situations in particular, as they serve to notify him that the partner with whom he deals either has restricted authority or no authority at all:

(a) NATURE OF BUSINESS. The third person must take notice of limitations arising out of the nature of the business. Thus an act of a partner that would ordinarily bind a commercial firm, such as the issuance of a note, would not bind a partnership engaged in a profession. A partner in a trading partnership has greater powers than one in a nontrading firm.

(b) SCOPE OF BUSINESS. A third person must recognize and act in accordance with limitations that arise from the scope of the business. A partner cannot bind the firm to a third person in a transaction not within the scope of the firm's business unless he has express authority to do so. Thus, when a partner in a dental firm speculates in land or when a partner in a firm dealing in automobiles buys television sets for resale, the third person, in the absence of estoppel or express authority, cannot hold the other partners on such a contract. The scope of the business is a question of fact to be determined by the jury from the circumstances of each case. In general, it means the activities commonly recognized as a part of a given business at a given place and time. The usual scope, however, may be enlarged by agreement or by conduct.

(c) TERMINATION OF PARTNERSHIP. A third person must watch for the termination of the partnership relation, either when the partnership is terminated under conditions requiring no notice or when notice of the termination has been properly given.

(d) ADVERSE INTEREST. A third person must take notice of an act of a partner that is obviously against the interest of the firm. To illustrate, if a partner issues a promissory note in the firm name and delivers it to his creditor in payment of a personal obligation, the latter acts at his peril because such an act may be a fraud upon the firm.

(3) Prohibited Transactions. There are certain transactions into which a partner cannot enter on behalf of the partnership unless he is expressly authorized to do so. A third person entering into such a transaction therefore acts at his peril when the partner has not been so authorized. In such a case, the third person should check with the other partners to determine whether the transaction is authorized.

The following are examples of prohibited transactions:

(a) CESSATION OF BUSINESS. A partner cannot bind the firm by a contract that would make it impossible for the firm to conduct its usual business.

(b) SURETYSHIP. A partner has no implied authority to bind the firm by contracts of surety, guaranty, or indemnity for the purposes other than the firm business.

(c) ARBITRATION. A partner in most states cannot submit controversies of his firm to arbitration. The Uniform Partnership Act expressly denies this power "unless authorized by the other partners or unless they have abandoned the business." [1]

(d) CONFESSION OF JUDGMENT. A partner cannot confess judgment against the firm upon one of its obligations because all partners should have an opportunity to defend in court. This power is expressly denied by the Uniform Partnership Act, except when the other partners consent or when "they have abandoned the business." [2]

(e) ASSIGNMENT FOR CREDITORS. A partner cannot ordinarily make a general assignment of firm property for the benefit of creditors. Exceptions are usually made in cases of bona fide acts in an emergency. The exceptions appear to be limited by the Uniform Partnership Act, which provides that "unless authorized by the other partners or unless they have abandoned the business, one or more but less than all the partners have no authority to assign the partnership property in trust for creditors or on the assignee's promise to pay the debts of the partnership." [3]

(f) PERSONAL OBLIGATIONS. A partner cannot discharge his personal obligations or claims of the firm by interchanging them in any way.

(g) SEALED INSTRUMENTS. In a minority of the states a partner cannot bind his copartners by an instrument under seal. A majority of

---

[1] Uniform Partnership Act, Sec. 9 (3) (e).
[2] Sec. 9 (3) (d).
[3] Sec. 9 (3) (a).

states, however, hold that instruments under seal are binding upon the firm when they are made in the usual course of business.

Cases for Chapter 43

Cotton Plant Oil Co. v. Buckeye Cotton Oil Co.

92 Ark. 271, 122 S.W. 658 (1909)

Pearce and others formed a partnership to operate a cotton gin. The partners agreed that Pearce was to buy and sell all of the cottonseed handled by the company. A few months later, after a controversy with the manager of the Cotton Plant Oil Co., Pearce began shipping the seed to the Buckeye Cotton Oil Co. As Pearce was preparing to ship a quantity of seed to the Buckeye Cotton Oil Co., four of the partners authorized two members to sell the seed then in freight cars to the Cotton Plant Oil Co., and this was done. Pearce, however, persuaded the agent of the railroad company to make the bill of lading in the name of the Buckeye Cotton Oil Co. Thereupon, the Cotton Plant Oil Co. brought an action against the partners to recover possession of the seed. The Buckeye Cotton Oil Co. intervened, claiming to own the two cars of seed and contending that only Pearce had authority to sell the seed. From a judgment for the Buckeye Cotton Oil Co., the plaintiff appealed.

HART, J. . . . It is earnestly insisted by counsel for appellee [Buckeye Cotton Oil Co.] that there was no complete contract by virtue of the bill of sale . . . because by the terms of the original agreement Pearce had exclusive authority to buy and sell seed, and this fact was known to appellant . . . , [But] a majority of the partners became dissatisfied with the way Pearce was conducting the selling of the seed, and . . . in good faith, for the interest of the partnership, they directed the bill of sale in question to be executed. This they had a right to do. Ordinarily, each partner is the general agent for the firm for the transaction of its business in the ordinary way. In this case the other partners delegated this power to Pearce. The power to grant the exclusive agency carries with it the right to revoke it. The rights of Pearce are not involved in this suit. . . . There was here a diversity of opinion between the partners as to the conduct of its affairs; and a majority of them, acting in the scope of the partnership business, directed a sale of the seed in controversy, and the partners to whom this authority was given executed a bill of sale to the two cars of seed in controversy. The act of the majority of the partners governs in such cases. . . .

[Judgment for Buckeye Cotton Oil Co. reversed.]

First National Bank v. Farson
226 N.Y. 218, 123 N.E. 490 (1919)

John Farson and his son, John Farson, Jr., were partners engaged in the business of buying and selling bonds and other securities under the name of Farson, Son & Co. A salesman of the firm sold to the First National Bank of Ann Arbor, Michigan, five bonds of the Eadon Irrigation and Land Co. As an inducement to buy the bonds, the bank was given a written guaranty of payment of the principal and interest executed in the firm name and delivered by the cashier of the partnership upon the authorization of John Farson, Sr. When the principal and interest were not paid, the bank brought an action on the guaranty against John Farson, Jr., the surviving partner, and another. The defendants contended that John Farson, Sr., had no power to bind the firm on a guaranty. From a judgment for the plaintiff, the defendants appealed.

COLLIN, J. . . . The partnership was a trading or commercial partnership. . . .

As to third persons, the authority [of] a partner must be found in the actual agreement of the partners or, through implication, in the nature of the business according to the usual and ordinary course in which it is carried on by those engaged in it in the locality which is its seat, or as reasonably necessary or fit for its successful prosecution. If it cannot be found in those, it may still be inferred from the actual, though exceptional, course and conduct of the business of the particular partnership itself, as personally carried on with the knowledge, actual or presumed, of the partner sought to be charged. The power or authority of a partner in a commercial partnership is to be tested and measured, when the actual agreements between the partners are unknown, by the ordinary usages of and the methods customarily used in partnerships conducting a business like unto, or by the usages and methods of his own partnership. Each partner is impliedly empowered to conduct the business in the way usual to that class of business or to his partnership. . . .

The instant case does not involve . . . a method or course of dealing peculiar to Farson, Son & Co., or a ratification of, or acquiescence in, the guaranty of John Farson, or an express or actual authorization to John Farson, Sr., to execute it. . . .

. . . [An agent's] implied authority, if he has it, springs from the usage of the business in which the principal or partnership is engaged. If in that business it is usual to give the guaranty in making the sale, the authority to sell carried with it the power to guarantee. . . .

There is not a finding that in the business in which Farson, Son & Co. were engaged the usage of guaranteeing the payment of the bonds or securities sold existed. . . .

[Judgment for plaintiff reversed.]

Reid v. Linder
77 Mont. 406, 251 P. 157 (1926)

Wilcomb, Linder, and Darnutzer were partners engaged in a farming and stock-raising business under the name of Trout Creek Land Co. One of the partners executed and delivered four promissory notes, each signed "Trout Creek Land Co., by A. J. Wilcomb." Reid, as receiver of the Bank of Twin Bridges, Montana, a corporation, brought an action against the members of the partnership to recover on the notes. Wilcomb's partners, as a defense, alleged that he had no authority to bind his partners on a firm note. From a judgment for the plaintiff, the defendants, other than Wilcomb, appealed.

MATTHEWS, J. . . . It is contended that the firm was a nontrading copartnership. The question is important, as in such a partnership a partner has no implied power to borrow money and give firm mercantile paper therefor. . . .

"The test of the character of the partnership is buying and selling. If it buys and sells, it is commercial and trading; if it does not buy or sell, it is one of employment or occupation.". . .

The firm engaged in buying and selling cattle, as well as farming and selling grain, and . . . it required capital and the use of credit; in fact, it operated from the beginning on credit alone, and established a custom within itself long prior to the issuance of the notes in question. . . . It appears that the issuance of negotiable paper was justified by custom and necessity of the firm as well as by the fact that the firm engaged in trading. . . .

As the firm was a trading partnership, each member of the firm was the agent for the partnership in the transaction of its business and had authority to do what was necessary to carry on such business in the ordinary manner, and for that purpose could bind the partnership by an agreement in writing . . . ; and notes executed by one of the partners for the benefit of the firm became partnership obligations, binding upon all the members of the firm, in the absence of bad faith on the part of the contracting parties and knowledge thereof on the part of the payee. . . .

But it is contended that Wilcomb used the firm credit for the purpose of playing the wheat market, without authority from the other members of the firm, and, in this, acted with bad faith toward his copartners. Even though this be admitted to be true, the borrowing was ostensibly authorized; and, if the bank was a bona fide lender, it was entitled to recover on the notes, even though the partner borrowing was actually obtaining the money for his own use. . . .

[Judgment for plaintiff affirmed.]

Samstag and Hilder Bros. v. Ottenheimer and Weil

90 Conn. 475, 97 A. 865 (1916)

A partnership, called Ottenheimer and Weil, was doing business in New Haven, Connecticut. Ottenheimer, who took no part in the firm's affairs, conducted a separate but similar business in New York City. He purchased in the firm name, Ottenheimer and Weil, certain goods from Samstag and Hilder Brothers. The goods were not used for the purpose of the firm of Ottenheimer and Weil but were purchased by Ottenheimer for the purpose of giving them away as Christmas presents to his customers in New York City. Later Samstag and Hilder Brothers brought an action against Ottenheimer and Weil to recover the purchase price of the goods, claiming that the firm was liable on the contract made by Ottenheimer. From a judgment for the plaintiff, the defendant appealed.

RORABACK, J. . . . One of the principal questions presented by reason of appeal is whether Ottenheimer, by virtue of his authority to represent the firm of Ottenheimer & Weil, could, in a transaction such as the record discloses in this case, make a contract binding upon the partnership in New Haven. It cannot be seriously claimed that this contract was within the scope of the partnership business of the defendant. It had nothing to do with the [business] in New Haven, in which the defendant company was engaged. It was not a company matter in regard to which each partner would, in his actions, represent himself and the defendant partnership. This co-partnership as it existed and its business transacted in New Haven could not, upon general principles, be made liable for goods which were sold and delivered to Ottenheimer and which were used by the Ottenheimer company for its business in New York City. In connection with this New York company the partnership of Ottenheimer & Weil had no interest. . . .

"Contracts made by one of several partners, in respect to matters not falling within the ordinary business, objects, and scope of the partnership, are not binding on the other partners and create no liability to third persons who have knowledge that the partner making the contract is acting in violation of his duties and obligations to the firm of which he is a member.". . .

It cannot be seriously claimed that the character of this transaction in New York City was such as to justify the plaintiff in assuming that the defendant could be made liable for these goods. The facts were such as to indicate the contrary. Under the circumstances surrounding this affair, it would have been reasonable for the plaintiff to have made an inquiry as to the liability of the defendant to pay a debt of this kind. There is nothing to show that the plaintiff was warranted in selling to Ottenheimer on the credit of the defendant on account of previous dealings between the parties. No business transaction had ever taken place between them. There was nothing in the general course of the defendant's business that would have warranted the plaintiff in treating Ottenheimer as the defendant's agent for buying goods on credit. It was not shown that Weil, or any one having authority to act for the defendant, assented to the purchase. Weil never heard of the matter until after the goods were bought. The record does not show any fact which indicates a ratification of the purchase by the defendant. It is not claimed that the defendant company had the goods purchased or any part of them. Neither does it appear that the defendant, as a company, was in any way benefited by the transaction. . . .

"Each member of a firm is the general agent of the firm in relation to all the business of the firm, and can bind the firm in what he says and does in such business. But when one partner has a transaction with a third person which is neither apparently nor really within the scope of the partnership business, the partnership is not bound by his declarations or acts in the transaction.". . .

[Judgment for plaintiff reversed and new trial ordered.]

Questions and Case Problems

1. What is the objective of each of the following rules of law?
    (a) A partner in a nontrading partnership does not have authority to borrow money in the firm name.
    (b) A partner cannot make an assignment of the firm's assets for the benefit of creditors.

2. Petrikis, Ellis, and others, who were partners, signed an agreement stating: "We, the undersigned, hereby agree to sell our interests in the partnership business. If and when the sale takes place and after all bills are accounted for, the remainder of the money is to be divided according to the share each partner now attains in the said business." Petrikis then began negotiations to sell the business to Hanges and finally made a contract selling the business to him for $17,500. Ellis, one of the partners, refused to accept the terms of the contract. Hanges then notified the partners that he called the deal off, whereupon the partners brought suit against him for breach of contract. Was Hanges liable for breach of contract? (Petrikis v. Hanges, 111 Cal.App.2d 734, 245 P.2d 39)

3. Milton Smith, Maude Smith, and Warren Ten Brook were partners doing business as "Greenwood Sales & Service." Pretending to act on behalf of the partnership, Ten Brook borrowed $6,000 from Holloway, giving her a note that was signed: "Greenwood Sales & Service, by Warren Ten Brook, Partner." In fact, Ten Brook borrowed the $6,000 so that he could make his capital contribution to the partnership. The check so obtained from Holloway was payable to the order of the partnership and was in fact deposited by Ten Brook in the partnership account. When the note was not paid, Holloway sued all of the partners. The other partners claimed that neither the partnership nor they were bound by

Ten Brook's unauthorized act committed for his personal gain. Was this defense valid? (Holloway v. Smith, 197 Va. 334, 88 S.E.2d 909)

4. Damsker and Carey, partners, entered into a contract with Goldberg for the construction of a building. The construction contract provided that disputes arising thereunder would be submitted to arbitration. A dispute arose relating to extra work, and Damsker gave notice that arbitration was requested on behalf of the partnership. Goldberg opposed the entry of an order to arbitrate on the ground that the application for arbitration was not made by both partners. Decide. (Application of Damsker, 283 App.Div. 719, 127 N.Y.S.2d 355)

5. Wilke, president of the Commercial Bank of Webster City, Iowa, and Wright entered into a farming and stock-raising partnership. The business was conducted under the name of Wilke and Wright Farm Co. The agreement stipulated that Wilke was "to have control and management of said business." Thereafter, Wright sold some partnership cattle to Gross and Gidley, cattle buyers, who resold the cattle to Simon. In an action brought against Simon to recover the cattle, Wilke alleged that Wright had no authority to sell them. Decide. (Wilke v. Simon, 46 S.D. 422, 193 N.W. 666)

6. O'Bryan, Sullivan, and Davis were partners engaged in operating freight steamers on the Yukon River. Sullivan purchased in the firm name and received from Merill certain lumber for the construction of firm warehouses at terminal points for the storage of freight. In an action on the contract of sale brought by Merrill against the members of the firm, it was contended that some of the partners had no power to bind the firm on this kind of contract. Do you agree with this contention? (Merrill v. O'Bryan, 48 Wash. 45, 93 P. 917)

7. Elrod and Hansford were partners under the name of Walter Elrod & Co. Hansford purchased on credit from the firm of Dawson Blakemore & Co. certain goods and merchandise for the firm. Before the sale, Elrod had notified Dawson Blakemore & Co. that he would not be bound to pay for any purchase for the firm made on credit or time by Hansford. Thereafter Dawson Blakemore & Co. brought an action against the members of Walter Elrod & Co. to recover the price of the goods. Elrod contended that he was not bound by the contract made by Hansford. Decide. (Dawson Blakemore & Co. v. Elrod, 105 Ky. 624, 49 S.W. 465)

8. Payson, Canda & Co. secured a contract to construct a portion of the railroad of the Northern Pacific Railroad Co. Sweet, Fleming, McCarthy, and Fenning entered into a partnership, under the name of Fleming, Kennedy and Co., for the purpose of executing a contract with Payson, Canda & Co. for building the South Dakota Division of the railroad. The terms of the agreement, in distributing the work to be done, assigned to Sweet, an engineer, the duty of "conducting" the final settlements and to his associates the work of grading. In the absence of Sweet, the other partners made a settlement with the firm of Payson, Canda & Co. Sweet contended that under the partnership agreement his partners had no authority to make a settlement. Do you agree with this contention? (Sweet v. Morrison, 103 N.Y. 235, 8 N.E. 396)

CHAPTER 44

Partners' Duties, Rights, and Remedies

"There is no stronger fiduciary relation known to the law than that of a copartnership, where one man's property and property rights are subject to a large extent to the control and administration of another." [1]

Sec. 44-A. Duties of Partners. In many respects the duties and responsibilities of a partner are the same as those of an agent.

(1) Loyalty and Good Faith. Each partner owes a duty of loyalty to the firm, which requires him to devote himself to the firm business. This duty bars him from making any secret profit at the expense of the firm or from using firm funds for his personal benefit. A partner must always act with strict fidelity to the interests of the firm. He must use his powers and the firm's property for the benefit of the partners and not for his individual gain. His duties to the firm must be observed above the furtherance of his own interests.

A partner, in the absence of an agreement to the contrary, is required to give his undivided time and energy to the development of the business of the partnership. Even when a partner is not required to give all of his time to the firm's business, he cannot promote a competing business. If he does so, he is liable for damages to the partnership.

(2) Obedience. Each partner is under an obligation to do all that is required of him by the partnership agreement, and to observe all restrictions and limitations imposed by the articles of the partnership or by a majority of the partners. If a majority of the partners have decided that no sales shall be made on credit, a partner who is placed in charge of the store must observe this limitation.

---

[1] *Salhinger* v. *Salhinger*, 56 Wash. 134, 105 P. 236.

(3) Reasonable Care. A partner must use reasonable care in the transaction of the business of the firm. He is liable for any loss resulting from his failure to do so. He is not liable, however, for honest mistakes or errors of judgment. Nor is he liable when the complaining partner likewise failed in his duty.

(4) Information. A partner has the duty to inform the partnership of matters relating to the partnership. He must "render on demand true and full information of all things affecting the partnership to any partner or the legal representative of any deceased partner or partner under legal disability." [2]

(5) Accounting. A partner must make and keep, or turn over to the proper person, correct records of all business that he has transacted for the firm. When the partners are equally at fault in not making and keeping proper records, however, none can complain.

One partner may be charged with maintaining the books and accounts of the firm. In such a case he has, of course, the duty to maintain proper records. (See p. 671, Hansen v. Hansen)

Sec. 44-B. Rights of the Partners as Owners. Each partner has the following rights in the absence of an agreement to the contrary:

(1) Management. All partners possess equal rights to participate in the conduct of the partnership business. It is immaterial that one partner contributed more than another to the firm.

(2) Inspection of Books. All partners are equally entitled to inspect the books of the firm. "The partnership books shall be kept, subject to any agreement between the partners, at the principal place of business of the partnership, and every partner shall at all times have access to and may inspect and copy any of them." [3]

(3) Share of Profits. Each partner is entitled to a share of the profits. The partners may provide, if they so wish, that profits shall be shared in unequal proportions. In the absence of such a provision in the partnership agreement, each partner is entitled to an equal share of the profits without regard to the extent of his capital contribution to the partnership or to the extent of services, if any, performed by him for the partnership.

The right to profits is regarded as personal property regardless of the nature of the partnership property. Upon the death of a partner, his right to sue for profits and an accounting pass to his executor or administrator. (See p. 673, Ewing v. Caldwell)

---

[2] Uniform Partnership Act, Sec. 20.
[3] Sec. 19.

(4) Compensation. Although one partner performs more duties or renders more valuable services than the other partner, he is not entitled to compensation for these extra services in the absence of an agreement to that effect. As an exception, "a surviving partner is entitled to reasonable compensation for his services in winding up the partnership affairs,"[4] although some states deny compensation even to the surviving partner.

(5) Repayment of Loans. A partner is entitled to have returned to him any money advanced to or for the firm. These amounts, however, must be separate and distinct from original or additional contributions to the capital of the firm.

(6) Payment of Interest. Contributions to capital do not automatically draw interest. The theory is that the profits constitute sufficient compensation. He may therefore only receive interest on the capital contributed by him from the date when repayment should be made. The partners, of course, may agree to pay interest on the capital contributions.

In earlier decisions courts were reluctant to allow interest on other advances until after an accounting was made, unless interest was provided for by agreement. A majority now treat advances in the form of loans as if they were made by a stranger. The Uniform Partnership Act provides that "a partner, who in aid of the partnership makes any payment or advance beyond the amount of capital which he agrees to contribute, shall be paid interest from the date of payment or advance."[5]

(7) Contribution and Indemnity. A partner who pays more than his share of the debts of the firm has a right to contribution from his copartners. Under this principle, if any employee of a firm negligently injures a third person while acting within the scope of his employment and the injured party collects damages from one partner, the latter may enforce contribution from the copartners. The partner has no right, however, to indemnity or reimbursement when he (a) acts in bad faith, (b) negligently causes the necessity for payment, or (c) has previously agreed to bear the expense alone.

(8) Distribution of Capital. Each partner is entitled to receive a share of the firm property upon dissolution after the payment of all creditors and the repayment of loans made to the firm by partners. Unless otherwise stated in the articles of partnership, each partner is entitled to the return of his capital contribution.

---

4 Sec. 18 (f).
5 Sec. 18 (c).

Sec. 44-C. Remedies of Partners. The remedies available to the members of a firm are, in some instances, limited because of the peculiar relation of the partners and because of the nature of their claims. In the following discussion the distinction between actions at law and actions in equity is preserved, although in many states and in the federal courts there is today only a civil action.

(1) Actions at Law. A partner cannot maintain an action at law against the firm upon a claim against the partnership. A partnership cannot bring an action at common law against one of its members on claims that the firm holds against him. In the absence of statute, a partnership cannot maintain an action against another firm when they have partners in common.

One partner cannot maintain an action at common law against another on claims involving partnership transactions. There are two exceptions to this general rule: (a) when the claim has been distinguished from the firm dealings by agreement; and (b) when the firm accounts have been balanced and show the amount to be due.

Partners may sue each other at common law in cases in which there is no necessity of investigating the partnership accounts. Situations of this kind exist when a partner dissolves the relation in violation of his agreement, when a partner fails to furnish capital or services agreed, or when a partner wrongfully causes injuries to his copartner, which in no way involve the partnership.

(2) Actions in Equity. The proper tribunal to settle all controversies growing out of partnership transactions is a court of equity. For example, an action by a partner to recover his share of profits should be brought in equity. The powers and the procedure of this court are such as to enable it to settle fully problems that arise in winding up the affairs of the firm.

In most instances the aid of the equity court is sought in connection with an accounting and a dissolution of the firm. It was at one time held that an accounting must be accompanied by a dissolution, but this view was later modified so as to permit a separate accounting. The Uniform Partnership Act states that a partner is entitled to an accounting (a) if he is wrongfully excluded from the partnership business or possession of its property by his copartners; (b) if the right exists under the terms of any agreement; (c) if he is a trustee; or, (d) if other circumstances render an accounting just and reasonable.

Sec. 44-D. Partner's Liability as to Particular Acts. Just as a principal is not liable for every act of his agent, so the partnership and the members of the partnership are not liable for every act of each partner. Just as an agent's act binds the principal only when it is within the agent's scope of authority, real or apparent, so a partner's act binds the firm and other partners only when it is within the scope of the partner's authority, real or apparent.

(1) Contracts. All members of the firm are liable on contracts made by a partner for the partnership and in its name if they were made within the scope of his actual or implied powers. This is true even though the partners may be unknown to the third persons. Thus a dormant partner, when discovered, is bound with the others.

When a partner makes a simple contract in his own name for the firm, the other members are nevertheless liable, but it must be clear that the third person did not deal with the partner as an individual rather than as a partner acting for the firm. To illustrate, a firm is not liable when a partner borrows money to make his contribution to the partnership capital.

If a partner signs a promissory note or any other commercial paper in his own name, the partnership, as undisclosed principal, cannot sue or be sued thereon.

(2) Torts. All partners are liable for torts, such as fraud, trespass, negligence, and deceit, committed by one partner while transacting firm business. The members of a firm are also liable for breach of trust by a partner in respect to goods or money of a third person held by the firm.

(3) Crimes. The partners of a firm and the partnership itself are liable for certain crimes committed by a partner in the course of the business, such as selling goods without obtaining a necessary vendor's license or selling in violation of a statute prohibiting sale. If carrying on the firm business does not necessarily involve the commission of the act constituting a crime, it is generally held that the firm and the partners not participating in the commission of a crime or authorizing its commission are not criminally liable. This exception is not recognized in some cases, such as the making of prohibited sales to minors or sales of adulterated products.

As a practical matter, the criminal liability of a partnership is limited to the imposition of a fine because it is not possible to imprison the partnership.

Sec. 44-E. Nature of Partner's Liability. By virtue of local statutes, partners are jointly liable on all firm contracts in some states; they are jointly and severally liable in other states. They are jointly and severally liable for all torts committed by an employee or one of the partners in the scope of the partnership business. (See p. 674, Johnson v. Gill) When one partner wrongfully injures a third person, the latter may sue all or any number of the members of the firm.

Sec. 44-F. Extent of Partner's Liability. Each member of the firm is individually and unlimitedly liable for the debts of the partnership regardless of his investment or his interest in its management. Moreover, the individual property of a partner, even before the firm property has been exhausted, may be sold in satisfaction of the judgment.

(1) Liability of New Partners. At common law a new partner entering an old firm is liable only for obligations arising thereafter. He may, however, expressly or impliedly assume the existing liabilities. Thus, when a new firm takes over the assets of an old firm, courts may infer an agreement to pay existing obligations.

The Uniform Partnership Act states that "a person admitted as a partner into an existing partnership is liable for all the obligations of the partnership arising before his admission as though he had been a partner when such obligations were incurred, except that his liability shall be satisfied only out of the partnership property." [6] Thus his liability does not extend to his individual property.

(2) Effect of Dissolution on Partner's Liability. A partner remains liable after dissolution unless the creditors expressly release him or unless the claims against the firm are satisfied. The Uniform Partnership Act states the following rules: "First, the dissolution of the partnership does not of itself discharge the existing liability of any partner. Second, a partner is discharged from any existing liability upon dissolution of the partnership by an agreement to that effect between himself, the partnership creditors, and the person or partnership continuing the business; and such agreement may be inferred from the course of dealing between the creditor having knowledge of the dissolution and the person or partnership continuing the business. Third, where a person agrees to assume the existing obligations of a dissolved partnership, the partners whose obligations have been assumed shall be discharged from any liability to any creditor of the partnership who, knowing of the agreement, consents to a material alteration in the nature or time of payment of such obligations." [7]

Sec. 44-G. Enforcement of Partner's Liability. The manner in which the civil liability of a partner may be enforced depends upon the form of the lawsuit brought by the creditor. The firm may have been sued in the name of all the individual partners doing business as the partnership, as "Plaintiff v. *A. B,* and *C,* doing business as the Ajax Warehouse." In such a case those partners named are bound by the judgment against the firm if they have been properly served in the suit. Partners either not named or not served are generally not bound by the judgment.

---

[6] Sec. 17; also see Secs. 41 (1) and (7).
[7] Sec. 36.

If the judgment binds an individual partner, the creditor may enforce the judgment against that partner before, at the same time, or after he seeks to enforce the judgment against the firm or other partners who are also bound by the judgment. If a partner is not bound by the judgment, the creditor must bring another lawsuit against the partner in which he establishes that the defendant is a partner in the particular partnership and that a judgment was entered against the partnership for a partnership liability. When this is established, a judgment is entered in favor of the creditor against the particular partner. The creditor may then have execution on this judgment against the property of the partner.

Sec. 44-H. Suit in the Firm Name. At common law a partnership could not sue or be sued in the firm name on the theory that there was no legal person by that name. If the partnership was composed of *A, B,* and *C,* it was necessary for them to sue or be sued as *A, B,* and *C.* If the firm name was "The X Bakery," some states required that they appear in the action as "*A, B,* and *C,* trading as The X Bakery." By statute or court rule this principle of the common law has been abolished in many states, and a partnership may sue or be sued either in the names of the partners or in the firm name. (See p. 674, Lewis Manufacturing Co. v. Superior Court)

The identity of the parties to an action is determined by the nature of the obligation on which the action is brought. If the action is brought on a negotiable instrument held by one partner, the action must be brought in his name, although he could readily change this situation by indorsing the instrument to the firm. If suit is brought on a sealed instrument executed by a partner in his own name, the action must be brought in his name in those states in which the seal has retained its common-law significance. Otherwise the firm may sue on the sealed instrument.

Cases for Chapter 44

Hansen v. Hansen
130 Mont. 175, 297 P.2d 879 (1956)

Dave and Ben Hansen formed a partnership to run a hotel, lunch counter, and bar. Ben, who was in full control of the conduct of the business, did not keep accurate books of the business. After several years Dave brought an action to have the partnership dissolved. Ben claimed that Dave was entitle only to a share of the profits shown on the partnership books. From a judgment in Dave's favor, Ben appealed.

BOTTOMLY, J. . . . The general rule is that where, as here, a partner assumes the responsibility of management and operation of a partnership business, and takes over the accounts, books, and bank accounts thereof, he acts as trustee for the partnership; and that his books and accounts of the partnership must be full, true, and exact; and that he cannot defeat the rights of his copartner to a true settlement and a proper distribution of the assets by failing to keep full and complete accounts. . . .

In regard to the books of the business the court found that such books of the business as were kept were kept by Dave, but that these books are utterly unreliable and furnish no basis whatever for a determination of the respective rights of the partners, and that Dave did make considerable money more out of the business than he accounted for. . . .

Dave, having assumed the trusteeship, is bound to perform the duties incident thereto. Dave used Ben's one-half interest in the partnership as well as his own. Under such circumstances Ben is entitled to one half the profits attributable to the partnership business. Dave may not profit from his own negligence in not keeping the partnership books and accounts so as to reflect the true status of the business. [The Uniform Partnership Act] provides: "Every partner must account to the partnership for any benefit, and hold as trustee for it any profits derived by him without the consent of the other partners from any transaction connected with the formation, conduct, or liquidation of the partnership or from any use by him of its property." . . .

In Wilson v. Moline, 229 Minn. 164, 38 N.W.2d 201, it is held that the burden of proving the accuracy of the accounts falls on the partner who has kept the records, once a breach of good faith is shown. Under such circumstances any doubt will of course be resolved against the partner who has charge of the books and accounts or the duty to keep them. . . . Compare Restatement, Trusts, § 172 in part as follows: "The trustee is under a duty to the beneficiary to keep and render clear and accurate accounts with respect to the administration of the trust." Comment (b) reads: "If the trustee fails to keep proper accounts, he is liable for any loss or expense resulting from his failure to keep proper accounts. The burden of proof is upon the trustee to show that he is entitled to the credits he claims, and his failure to keep proper accounts and vouchers may result in his failure to establish the credits he claims."

[The court then admitted oral testimony of third persons as to what the volume of business and profits of the business appeared to be and held that Ben was liable to Dave for one half of that amount. The judgment was affirmed with modifications relating to matters not discussed in this excerpt from the opinion.]

Ewing v. Caldwell

243 N.C. 18, 89 S.E.2d 774 (1955)

Armstrong and Caldwell formed a partnership and purchased land. Armstrong died, and the beneficiaries under her will brought an action against Caldwell for an accounting. Caldwell raised the defense that the action was not brought by the executor under the will of Armstrong. From a judgment in favor of the heirs, Armstrong appealed.

Bobbitt, J. . . . Prior to the adoption of the Uniform Partnership Act . . . the title to personal property owned by a partnership vested at once in the surviving partner; but . . . the interest of a deceased partner in real property owned by a partnership descended to his heir, subject to the right of the surviving partner to have such property applied, if necessary, to the payment of partnership debts and the settlement of accounts between the partners. . . .

But a radical change in this respect was made by the Uniform Partnership Act. Thereunder, "The property rights of a partner are (1) his rights in specific partnership property, (2) his interest in the partnership, and (3) his right to participate in the management." . . . As to specific partnership property, a partner is co-owner with his partners, "holding as a tenant in partnership." . . . Thus, a new kind of estate, "tenancy in partnership" was created.

The incidents of this tenancy are defined. . . . These include provisions that a partner's right in specific partnership property is not subject to attachment or execution, except on a claim against the partnership; that when partnership property is attached for a partnership debt, no partner or the representatives of a deceased partner can claim any right under the homestead or exemption laws; that a partner's right in specific partnership property is not subject to dower, curtesy, or allowances to widows, heirs, or next of kin; and, directly pertinent here, that "On the death of a partner his right in specific partnership property vests in the surviving partner or partners, . . ."— for partnership purposes. . . . "A partner's interest in the partnership is his share of the profits and surplus, *and the same is personal property.*" . . .

The deceased partner's interest being personal property, the statute requires the surviving partner to make settlement with *the personal representative* of the deceased partner; and there is placed upon the personal representative of the deceased partner the duty to require that a true accounting be made either by the surviving partner or by a receiver under court supervision. This is in accord with the statutory provision: "Upon the death of any person, all demands whatsoever, and rights to prosecute or defend any action or special proceeding, existing in favor of or against such person, except as hereinafter provided, shall survive to and against the executor, administrator, or collector of his estate."

The conclusion reached is that the right to sue for an accounting of the partnership assets and affairs vested exclusively in the personal representative of the deceased partner. . . .

[Judgment reversed.]

Johnson v. Gill
235 N.C. 40, 68 S.E.2d 788 (1952)

Johnson was injured by a truck driven by Gill and owned by Mattox. Johnson sued Gill and Mattox, claiming that they were liable as partners. From a judgment for Mattox, Johnson appealed.

WINBORNE, J. . . . At common law the liability of members of a partnership for a tort committed in the course of its business is joint and several. . . . And the common-law rule of joint and several liability of partners for a tort committed by one of the members of the partnership is incorporated in the Uniform Partnership Act. . . .

[That] Act declares that every partner is an agent of the partnership for the purposes of its business, and the act of every partner for apparently carrying on in the usual way the business of the partnership of which he is a mmber ordinarily binds the partnership . . . that where, by any wrongful act or omission of any partner acting in the ordinary course of the business of the partnership or with the authority of his copartners, loss or injury is caused to any person not being a partner in the partnership, or any penalty is incurred, the partnership is liable therefor to the same extent as the partner so acting or omitting to act . . . and that all partners are liable jointly and severally for everything chargeable to the partnership. . . .

Therefore, if defendants Gill and Mattox were partners, and plaintiff suffered injury by the wrongful act or omission of Gill acting in the ordinary course of the business of the partnership or with the authority of his copartners, Mattox would be liable jointly and severally therefor.

[It was found that there was not sufficient proof of the existence of a partnership between the defendants and judgment in favor of Mattox was affirmed.]

Lewis Manufacturing Co. v. Superior Court
140 Cal.App.2d 245, 295 P.2d 145 (1956)

The Lewis Manufacturing Co., a partnership consisting of persons living in Oklahoma, manufactured and sold safety belts. They sold such belts in California. One of the belts was used by a California workman who fell and was killed when it broke. His surviving widow and children sued the Lewis firm in California to recover damages for negligence in the manufacture of the belt. The Lewis firm claimed that it could not be sued in California in its firm name and applied to the Superior Court of California for an order to stop the action brought against it.

WOOD, J. . . . In Restatement of the Law of Judgments it is said at page 114, Section 24: "A court in a State in which a partnership or other unincorporated association is subject to be sued in the firm or common name acquires by proper service of process jurisdiction over it as to causes of action arising out of business done by the association in the State." It was also said therein at page 115: "Even though the partnership or association does business within the State, the courts of the State acquire jurisdiction over it only as to causes of action arising out of the business done in the State. . . . A court cannot exercise jurisdiction over a partnership or association unless there is such service of process as is reasonably calculated to give it notice of the action and an opportunity to be heard. . . . Service upon one of the partners or upon an agent in charge of the business is sufficient. . . . A judgment rendered against a partnership . . . in accordance with the rule stated in this Section is a binding adjudication as to the liability of the partnership or association with respect to its assets in other States as well as to its assets in the State in which it is rendered."

Section 388 of the Code of Civil Procedure provides: " When two or more persons, associated in any business, transact such business under a common name, . . . the associates may be sued by such common name, the summons in such cases being served on one or more of the associates; and the judgment in the action shall bind the joint property of all the associates, and the individual property of the party or parties served with process, in the same manner as if all had been named defendants and had been sued upon their joint liability." It thus appears that in California a partnership may be sued in the partnership or firm name and that judgment may be rendered against the partnership in the partnership name. . . .

[Application for order dismissed.]

Questions and Case Problems

1. What is the objective of each of the following rules of law?
   (a) Although each partner is an owner of the business, he must obey any limitations agreed to by a majority of the partners with respect to the ordinary details of the business.
   (b) A partner is unlimitedly liable for the obligations of the partnership.

2. Nelson, Kelly, and Bank were partners engaged in the hauling business. Nelson and Kelly excluded Bank from participating in managing the

business, paid themselves large salaries, and rented partnership property to themselves as individuals at a very low rental. Bank complained of their conduct. What was the legal basis for his complaint? (Bank v. Nelson, 199 Wash. 631, 92 P.2d 711)

3. Kittilsby and Velvelstad were partners doing work on a mining claim known as the Sea Level Claim. Kittilsby did the assessment work for one year and then went to Seattle, upon the promise of Velvelstad to do the work for the following year. Velvelstad did not do the work, and the claim became open to location. Velvelstad procured Singleton, who was to act for him, to locate and prove a claim covering the same district. After Singleton had conveyed the claim to him for a nominal consideration, Velvelstad sold the claim to the Juneau Sea Level Copper Mines. Thereafter Kittilsby brought an action against Velvelstad to recover half of the proceeds of the sale. Was he entitled to judgment? (Kittilsby v. Velvelstad, 103 Wash. 126, 173 P. 744)

4. Martinoff brought a suit against Triboro Roofing Co. and a partnership named Renray Realty Co. The plaintiff named the partnership in its firm name as a defendant and also each of the seven partners. Service of process was made on only one of the partners, namely David Raynes. What liabilities of the firm and the individual partners could be enforced in this action? (Martinoff v. Triboro Roofing Co., 228 N.Y.S.2d 139)

5. Delay and Foster entered into a partnership. Thereafter Foster wrongfully dissolved the partnership. Delay brought an action at law against Foster to recover damages arising out of the wrongful dissolution and breach of the partnership agreement. The defendant contended that the plaintiff was not entitled to bring an action at law but should have brought an action in equity. Do you agree? (Delay v. Foster, 34 Iowa 691, 203 P. 461)

6. The St. Johns Transportation Co., a corporation, made a contract with the firm of Bilyeu & Herstel, contractors, by which the latter was to construct a ferryboat. Herstel, a member of the firm of contractors, executed a contract in the firm name with Benbow for certain materials and labor in connection with the construction of the ferryboat. In an action brought by Benbow to enforce a lien against the ferryboat, called The James Johns, it was contended that all members of the firm were bound by the contract made by Herstel. Do you agree? (Benbow v. The James Johns, 56 Ore. 554, 108 P. 634)

7. Henslee and Boyd formed a partnership to operate a sawmill business. As part of the agreement, Henslee agreed to sell timber to the partnership at the prevailing market prices. Boyd later sued Henslee to set aside the agreement on the ground of fraud and breach of partnership duties. One of the objections made by Boyd was that Henslee had refused to sell timber to the partnership as required by the agreement. Henslee replied that he had refused to sell because the partnership could not pay in cash. Boyd then answered that Henslee should not have insisted on a cash sale since that would use up the partnership's ready cash. Was Henslee guilty of a breach of his partnership duty? (Henslee v. Boyd, [Ark.] 360 S.W.2d 505)

CHAPTER 45

Dissolution and Termination of Partnerships

Dissolution ends the right of the partnership to exist as a going concern. It is followed by a winding-up period, upon the conclusion of which the partnership's legal existence is terminated.

Sec. 45-A. Methods and Causes of Dissolution.

(1) Dissolution by Act of Parties.

(a) AGREEMENT. A partnership may be dissolved in accordance with the terms of the original agreement of the parties, as by the passing of the period for which the relation was to continue or by the performance of the object for which it was organized. The relation may also be dissolved by subsequent agreement.

(b) WITHDRAWAL. A partner has the power to withdraw at any time; but if his withdrawal violates his agreement, he becomes liable to his copartners for damages for breach of contract. When the relation is for no definite purpose or time, a partner may withdraw without liability at any time, unless a sudden withdrawal would do irreparable damage to the firm.

(c) EXPULSION. A partnership is dissolved by the expulsion of any partner from the business.

(d) ALIENATION OF INTEREST. Under the Uniform Partnership Act neither a voluntary sale [1] nor an involuntary sale for the benefit of creditors [2] works a dissolution of the partnership. A minority of states follow the contrary rule of the common law under which such sales dissolved the firm.

---

[1] Uniform Partnership Act, Sec. 27.
[2] Sec. 28.

(2) Dissolution by Operation of Law.

(a) DEATH. An ordinary partnership is dissolved immediately upon the death of any partner, even when the agreement provides for continuance of the business. Thus, when the executor of a deceased partner carries on the business with the remaining partner, there is legally a new firm.

(b) BANKRUPTCY. Bankruptcy of the firm or of one of the partners causes the dissolution of the firm; insolvency alone does not.

(c) WAR. A firm is ordinarily dissolved when there is war between the governments to which the different partners owe allegiance.

(d) ILLEGALITY. A partnership is dissolved "by any event which makes it unlawful for the business of the partnership to be carried on or for the members to carry it on in partnership." [3] To illustrate, when it is made unlawful by statute for judges to engage in the practice of law, a law firm is dissolved when one of its members becomes a judge.

(3) Dissolution by Decree of Court.

When a partnership is to continue for a certain time, there are several situations in which one partner is permitted to obtain its dissolution through a decree of court. A court will not order the dissolution for trifling causes or temporary grievances that do not involve a permanent harm or injury to the partnership. The causes that enable a partner to ask for a dissolution under the common law have been substantially codified by the Uniform Partnership Act. [4]

(a) INSANITY. A partner may obtain a decree of dissolution when his partner has been judicially declared a lunatic or when it is shown that he is of unsound mind.

(b) INCAPACITY. A decree of dissolution will be granted when one partner becomes in any way incapable of performing the terms of the partnership agreement. For example, a serious injury to one partner making it physically impossible for him to do his part is a cause for dissolution.

(c) MISCONDUCT. A partner may obtain a decree of dissolution when his partner has been guilty of conduct that tends substantially to affect the continuance of the business prejudicially. The habitual drunkenness of a partner is a sufficient cause for judicial dissolution.

(d) IMPRACTICABILITY. A partner may obtain a decree of dissolution when another partner habitually or purposely commits a breach of the partnership contract or so conducts himself in matters relating to the partnership business that it is not reasonably practicable to carry on the business in partnership with him.

---

[3] Sec. 31 (3).
[4] Sec. 32 (1).

(e) LACK OF SUCCESS. A decree of dissolution will be granted when the business of the partnership cannot be continued except at a loss.

(f) EQUITABLE CIRCUMSTANCES. A decree of dissolution will be granted under any other circumstances that equitably call for a dissolution. A situation of this kind, for example, is present when one partner has been induced by fraud to enter into partnership.

Sec. 45-B. Effect of Dissolution. Dissolution involves a change in the relation of the partners but does not end the partnership. "On dissolution the partnership is not terminated, but continues until the winding up of partnership affairs is completed." [5] The vested rights of the partners are not extinguished by dissolving the firm, and the existing liabilities remain. Thus, when the relation is dissolved by the death of a partner, the estate of the deceased member is liable for the existing debts of the firm.

The dissolution, however, does affect the authority of the partners. From the moment of dissolution the partners lose all authority to act in behalf of the firm, "except so far as may be necessary to wind up partnership affairs or to complete transactions begun but not finished." [6] (See p. 681, Bell v. Porter)

Sec. 45-C. Notice of Dissolution. The rule that dissolution terminates the authority of the partners to act for the firm requires some modification. Under some circumstances one partner may continue to possess the power to make a binding contract.

(1) Notice to Partners. When the firm is dissolved by an act of a partner, notice must be given to the other partners unless his act clearly shows an intent to withdraw or dissolve the firm. If he withdraws without notice to his partners, he is bound as between them upon contracts created for the firm. The Uniform Partnership Act declares that "where the dissolution is caused by the act, death, or bankruptcy of a partner, each partner is liable to his copartners for his share of any liability created by any partner acting for the partnership as if the partnership had not been dissolved, unless (a) the dissolution being by the act of any partner, the partner acting for the partnership had knowledge of the dissolution, or (b) the dissolution being by the death or bankruptcy of a partner, the partner acting for the partnership had knowledge or notice of the death or bankruptcy." [7]

(2) Notice to Third Persons. When dissolution is caused by the act of a partner or the agreement of the partners, notice must be

---

[5] Sec. 30.
[6] Sec. 33.
[7] Sec. 34.

given to third persons. Actual notice must be given to persons who have dealt with the firm. To persons who know of the relation but have had no dealings with the firm, a publication of the fact is sufficient. Such notice may be by newspaper publication, by posting a placard in a public place, or by any similar method. (See p. 682, Simmel v. Wilson) Failure to give proper notice continues the power of each partner to bind the others in respect to third persons on contracts within the scope of the business.

When dissolution has been caused by operation of law, notice to third persons is not required. This rule is modified to some extent by the Uniform Partnership Act, which requires knowledge or notice of dissolution by death and bankruptcy as between the partners.

Sec. 45-D. Winding Up Partnership Affairs. Although the partners after dissolution have no authority to create new obligations, they retain authority for acts necessary to wind up the business.

With a few exceptions, all partners have the right to participate in the winding up of the business. The Uniform Partnership Act provides that "unless otherwise agreed the partners who have not wrongfully dissolved the partnership or the legal representative of the last surviving partner, not bankrupt, has the right to wind up the partnership affairs; provided, however, that any partner, his legal representatives or his assignee, upon cause shown, may obtain winding up by court." [8]

When the firm is dissolved by the death of one partner, the partnership property vests in the surviving partners for the purpose of administration. They must collect and preserve the assets, pay the debts, and with reasonable promptness make an accounting to the representative of the deceased partner. In connection with these duties, the law requires the highest degree of integrity. A partner in performing these acts cannot sell to himself any of the partnership property. (See p. 683, Singleton v. Moore)

Sec. 45-E. Distribution of Assets. Creditors have first claim on the assets of the partnership. Difficulty arises when there is a contest between the creditors of the firm and the creditors of the individual partners. The general rule is that firm creditors have first claim on assets of the firm, and the individual creditors share in the remaining assets, if there are any. Conversely, individual creditors have priority in the distribution of individual assets; the claims of the firm creditors may be satisfied only after claims of individual creditors are settled.

After the firm liabilities to nonpartners have been paid, the assets of the partnership are distributed as follows:

---

8 Sec. 37.

(1) Each partner is entitled to a refund of advances made to or for the firm.

(2) Contributions to the capital of the firm are then returned.

(3) The remaining assets, if any, are divided equally as profits among the partners unless there is some other agreement. Likewise, if the partnership has sustained a loss, the partners share it equally in the absence of a contrary agreement.

If the distributable assets are withheld by a partner and wrongly used in the operation of another enterprise, he is liable to the injured partner for a share of the profits of the new enterprise. (See p. 685, Urzi v. Urzi)

Cases for Chapter 45

Bell v. Porter
261 Mich. 97, 246 N.W. 93 (1932)

Porter and Wyman were partners engaged in a general real-estate business. They employed Bell, chiefly as a salesman, at a salary of $100 a month and a percentage of the net profits of the business. After dissolution of the firm and an assignment of the firm property to the Muskegon Trust Co. for the purpose of winding up the affairs of the partnership, Bell brought an action against Porter, the surviving partner, to recover a sum of about $8,500 alleged to be due him. He introduced as evidence some writings in the books of the firm made by Wyman after dissolution of the partnership, indicating the alleged indebtedness. The defendant contended that the partnership was not bound by admissions made by a partner after dissolution of the firm. From a judgment for the plaintiff, the defendant appealed.

CLARK, C.J. . . . The partnership is not bound by any act of the partner after dissolution where the partner has no authority to wind up partnership affairs . . . , for plaintiff had knowledge of the dissolution and of the transfer to and appointment of the trust company for winding up partnership affairs.

[This suggests] that, because of the agreement of the partners, known to plaintiff, Wyman had no authority after dissolution to make a binding admission in respect to its affairs; but we cannot so hold.

Plaintiff as a creditor might proceed to judgment against the partners or the survivor [of them], irrespective of the transfer to and appointment of the trust company. Without his consent, the partners could not impair the obligation of his contract. As the partners may be sued in spite of the transfer to and appointment of the trust company, it follows, too, that, to avoid litigation, they must adjust and settle any claim against the partnership. It therefore appears that, in spite of the transfer to and appointment of the trust company, there remained in the partners full authority in respect to adjustment and compromise and settlement of claims against the partnership. To make a binding admission, an admission receivable in evidence, in respect of plaintiff's claim against the partnership, a past transaction, was therefore within the scope of Wyman's authority as a partner after dissolution and pending winding up the affairs. . . .

"While the dissolution of the partnership works a destruction of the power of any partner to bind another as a partner in any future business, it does not affect what is past, and that consequently the admissions of one partner made after the dissolution of the firm and relating to past transactions are admissible as against all the partners." . . .

The explanatory writing which Wyman caused to be made on the partnership books is no more than an admission respecting a past transaction. . . . Evidence of these admissions was properly received. This and other evidence, including the books and records of the partnership, as against evidence adduced by defendant, made the issue for the jury which was submitted without reversible error. . . .

[Judgment for plaintiff affirmed.]

Simmel v. Wilson

121 S.C. 358, 113 S.E. 487 (1922)

H. W. Wilson and H. G. Wilson were partners engaged in the brokerage business under the name of Wilson & Wilson in South Carolina. When war was declared in 1917, the former sold his interest to the latter and entered the military service of the United States. H. G. Wilson continued the business under the same name. In 1918, Simmel sold to "Wilson & Wilson, H. G. Wilson," a shipment of tomatoes. Simmel made the sale without any investigation, without knowledge whether he was dealing with an individual, partnership, or corporation, and without knowledge of the existence of such a person as H. W. Wilson. H. G. Wilson failed to pay the draft attached to the bill of lading that had been sent to the First National Bank. Simmel brought an action against the Wilsons, as partners, contending that insufficient notice of the dissolution of the firm had been given. From a judgment for the plaintiff, the defendant H. W. Wilson appealed.

MARION, J. . . . [The] rule [requiring notice of dissolution] is merely a branch of the doctrine of equitable estoppel, which precludes a person from denying a state of facts which he has permitted another to believe continues to exist when to do so would work a fraud upon the other party. . . . The object of giving notice is to remove the impression which has been created in the minds of those who have dealt with or had knowledge of the firm that certain persons continue to compose it. . . .

. . . With respect to [the right] to invoke the benefit of the doctrine of notice of dissolution, "men resolve themselves into two general classes, those who have had dealings with the firm and those who have not." Those who have had dealings with the partnership, who are presumed to know who compose it and to rely upon the credit of each and all of them, are entitled to act upon that knowledge until they have been informed that the partnership no longer exists. That they have received that information may be inferred from a notice in the public prints, and from any other pertinent facts and circumstances. . . . But advertisement of dissolution in a newspaper is not of itself notice to persons who have had dealings with the firm.

. . . A public advertisement in a newspaper [is not] a prerequisite to the discharge from liability of a retiring partner to creditors who have had no dealings with or knowledge of the firm prior to the dissolution. Unquestionably, strangers to the firm, who had not dealt with it but who had knowledge of it, would be entitled to . . . notice by advertisement in the public prints. . . .

There was evidence in this case tending to establish that the plaintiff not only had never dealt with the original partnership, but had never heard of it until more than a year after the dissolution, and that at the time of the transaction here involved he had no actual knowledge of the existence of the original partnership and of its membership. In that case and in the absence of evidence tending to show that he was in some way misled into his injury, the plaintiff was not entitled to any notice of the dissolution of the pre-existing firm. . . .

In addition . . . the testimony of the plaintiff himself was susceptible of the inference that he understood from the letters received from Wilson & Wilson that Harry G. Wilson was the owner of the firm and that there was not "any one else connected with the firm of Wilson & Wilson, other than H. G. Wilson." If the plaintiff had actual knowledge which was tantamount to a personal notice of the dissolution of any partnership which might formerly have existed . . . it could, of course, make no difference to him whether or not a general notice of dissolution of the former firm had been given. . . .

[Judgment for plaintiff reversed.]

Singleton v. Moore

262 F. 357 (C.C.A. 2d, 1919)

Upon the dissolution of the firm of E. B. Moore & Co., Moore, according to the terms of the partnership articles, became the liquidating partner. Singleton and other partners of the dissolved firm formed a new partnership under the name of Frankenberg, Morgan & Singleton. Moore continued business under the name of the old firm, as the partnership agreement provided he might do. Both Moore and the new firm actively purchased shares of stock of the Camden Woolen Co., seeking to gain control of the company so as to handle exclusively the output of the company. Moore did not sell 433 shares of stock in the Camden company, which formed part of the assets of the old firm, allegedly in order to control the annual meeting of the corporation. Singleton and the other partners brought a suit against Moore, asking for a receiver with orders to obtain and sell the stock owned by the firm. The defendant contended that the court was without authority to take the liquidation of the assets out of his hands. From a decree in favor of the plaintiffs, the defendant appealed.

ROGERS, C.J. . . . It is elementary that it is competent to provide in the partnership articles that, when the term fixed for the duration of the partnership business has expired, the power of liquidating the partnership business shall vest in some specified one of the partners. It then becomes the duty of the liquidating partner to collect the assets and adjust debts due to the firm. It is also his duty to turn the assets into money and then pay and discharge the outstanding liabilities. After these duties have been performed, he is to pay over to the other partners their proper share in the remaining surplus. . . . And the designation of a liquidating partner takes away from the other partners authority to act and confers it exclusively upon the liquidating partner. . . . He is the sole agent of the partnership for the purpose of winding up its affairs. And when the partnership articles intrust the charge of the property and the winding up of the partnership to one of the partners, the court will not interfere with his proceedings unless a palpable breach of the partnership articles is shown or misconduct appears which amounts to fraud or which endangers the property. . . .

. . . There is no question that under the partnership agreement, the appellant as the liquidating partner has the legal right to dispose of the stock in his own way, at his own time, and in his own discretion, unless in doing so he thereby would work a fraud upon his former partners. . . .

The activities of these parties in canvassing the shareholders to buy their stock created a market value for the stock which it had never had before, and which it is said it will not have again after the annual meeting is held. The 433 shares of Camden stock were carried on the books of E. B. Moore & Co. at about $20,000, or about $46 per share. The last previous sale . . . brought $55 per share, and the ordinary selling price was about $60 per share. Because of the active competition for purchase of the stock in order to control the annual meeting, the stock, if sold prior to the meeting, will bring $90 per share, and possibly $160 a share. After the annual meeting has been held, the evidence is that the stock will drop back to $80 per share. In other words, it appears that, if the 433 shares which belong to the partnership are sold at public auction prior to the annual meeting at even $90 per share, they will bring $38,970, and discharge the firm's "outstanding liability" of $32,657.57, and leave remaining a surplus of $6,312.43; whereas a sale after the annual meeting will, as defendant admits, bring the normal price of $60 a share, or a total of $25,980. This not only would fail to discharge "the outstanding liability" above referred to, but it would leave a deficit of $6,677.57, instead of a surplus of $6,312.43. There is, moreover, a possibility, as the evidence discloses, that the stock may bring as much as $43,300 in excess of its normal value. If this block of 433 shares is not sold, the liquidating partner can control the annual meeting; and for this reason he is opposed to a sale and asks that the court's order be reversed. The course he proposes is in his interest as an individual. It is not in the interest of the members of the firm.

. . . To withhold the stock from sale under the circumstances disclosed would operate as a fraud upon the rights of the other members of the firm . . . whose interests are intrusted to his keeping. His plain duty undoubtedly was to sell the stock at the high price obtainable under the peculiar conditions which existed. . . .

[Judgment for plaintiffs affirmed.]

Urzi v. Urzi
140 Cal.App.2d 589, 295 P.2d 539 (1956)

Louis and Sebastian Urzi ran a restaurant under an oral partnership agreement terminable at will. Sebastian, who owned the restaurant building, became dissatified, notified Louis that the partnership agreement was terminated, and retook possession of the restaurant building. He then formed a new partnership with a third person. This second partnership was dissolved, and another partnership formed with a fourth person. Louis sued Sebastian, claiming that he was entitled to one half of the profits made by the two subsequent partnerships. Sebastian claimed that Louis had taken from the original partnership more than his share of the profits and that the amount which he owed to the partnership at the time of its dissolution was in excess of the value of his interest in the partnership. From a judgment in favor of Sebastian, Louis appealed.

PETERS, P.J. . . . The main controversy is over whether plaintiff [Louis] is entitled to share in the profits of the two partnerships operated by defendant [Sebastian] after dissolution of the partnership with plaintiff. Plaintiff correctly points out that the dissolution . . . did not terminate the partnership. . . . He then relies on the well-settled general rule that "where the assets of a partnership are used by one partner in continuing the business after dissolution, he is accountable to the retiring partner for profits acquired after dissolution and before termination of the partnership. . . . This general rule has been codified in the Uniform Partnership Act and adopted in California in . . . the Corporations Code, which provides: "When any partner retires or dies, and the business is continued . . . without any settlement of accounts . . . , unless otherwise agreed, he or his legal representative . . . may have the value of his interest at the date of dissolution ascertained, and shall receive as an ordinary creditor an amount equal to the value of his interest in the dissolved partnership with interest or, at his option . . . in lieu of interest, the profits attributable to the use of his right in the property of the dissolved partnership."

. . . [The] general rule is predicated on the theory that a partner is entitled to share, after dissolution, in the profits derived in part from the use of assets in which he had an interest. But where, at the time of dissolution he has, in fact, no interest in such assets, he is not entitled to any division of profits earned by them. . . . If, by reason of . . . the excessive indebtedness of the partner to the firm, the partner has no interest, or at least only a nominal interest, remaining in the firm, he should not be entitled to a share of the subsequently earned profits. . . .

This . . . is clearly recognized by . . . the Corporations Code, because when [it] gives the partner the right to subsequently earned profits, it limits the amount to "the profits attributable to the use of his right in the property of the dissolved partnership." . . .

. . . Plaintiff, by his failure to report sales and retention of that money as well as of certain undistributed profits, on the date of dissolution, had in his possession $13,653.89. He thus was indebted to the partnership on the date of dissolution in that amount. On that date, far from having an interest in the partnership assets, he actually was indebted to defendant in the amount of $3,276.70. He had already received that much more than his interest in the assets were worth. Thus, he had no interest in such assets. . . .

[Judgment affirmed.]

Questions and Case Problems

1. What is the objective of each of the following rules of law?
    (a) Dissolution ends the right of the partnership to continue to exist as a partnership but does not terminate its existence.
    (b) When a partner upon dissolution wrongfully retains the share of another partner and invests it in a new business enterprise, the second partner is entitled to a share of the profits of the new enterprise.

2. The Consolidated Loan Co. was owned and operated by three partners. After the death of two of the partners, the surviving partner, Salabes, made an agreement with the estates of the other two to continue the partnership. Thereafter Salabes brought an action for a decree that she "is now the sole remaining partner in, or the sole proprietress of, Consolidated Loan Company" subject to the interests of the estates of the

decreased partners. Was she the sole owner of the enterprise? (Miller v. Salabes, [Md.] 169 A.2d 671)

3. The Weidlich Sterling Spoon Co., a partnership owned by three brothers, was dissolved. By agreement, one of the brothers was designated as liquidating partner. After he completed liquidation, he filed an account which related only to certain legal charges and expenses that had been incurred. Was this a proper accounting? (Weidlich v. Weidlich, [Conn.] 157 A.2d 910)

4. The Dahlin Bros. Coal Mining Co. was a partnership owned by two brothers. On the death of one, the survivor began, but did not complete, the liquidation of the business. Lee, who was appointed for the business, brought suit to compel the surviving partner to make an accounting. In addition to delay in liquidating, the liquidating partner used some of the partnership funds and took a partnership truck for his own use and never accounted for them. The liquidating partner claimed that he was entitled to compensation for his services under the Uniform Partnership Act which provides that the "surviving partner is entitled to reasonable compensation for his services in winding up the partnership affairs." Was he entitled to compensation? (Lee v. Dahlin, [Pa.] 159 A.2d 679)

5. Brown, Potter, and others were an insurance partnership. Potter and others brought an action against Brown to dissolve the partnership on the ground that he was exercising an exclusive control of the partnership and that there were constant disputes among the partners over many details. The written partnership agreement gave Brown exclusive control of the management of the firm. The firm had existed for many years and was prosperous. Should the partnership have been dissolved? (Potter v. Brown, 328 Pa. 554, 195 A. 901)

6. William Haff and his son, Harmon, were partners in the wholesale coal business. The partnership agreement provided that the firm was to continue for 60 days after either party gave notice of an intention to withdraw. In an action brought by Cahill, as executrix of the estate of William Haff, it was contended that the firm could have been dissolved by the withdrawal of one of the members at any time before the lapse of the 60 days after notice. Do you agree? (Cahill v. Haff, 248 N.Y. 377, 162 N.E. 288)

7. Edwards, who owned a store, formed a partnership with Arvin, who agreed to operate the store in return for half of the profits. Arvin made no capital investment. Later the partnership was dissolved. What proportion of the business assets should have been distributed to Arvin? (Edwards v. Arvin, 272 Ky. 528, 114 S.W.2d 778)

8. Ryan held by contract the exclusive right to sell Maxwell automobiles in certain townships of Madison County, Indiana. He formed a partnership for one year with Barnes for the purpose of selling the cars. About six months later, Ryan sold to other persons the exclusive right to sell the machines. Thereafter Barnes brought an action for an accounting against Ryan claiming that the firm had been dissolved by such sale. Do you agree with this contention? (Ryan v. Barnes, 72 Ind.App. 152, 125 N.E. 643)

CHAPTER 46

Special Partnerships and Associations

In addition to the general partnership and the ordinary business corporation, discussed in the next chapter, there are a number of hybrid organizations that are neither true partnerships nor corporations but which partake of the characteristics of one or both.

Sec. 46-A. Limited Partnership. A common form of modified partnership is the limited partnership. This form of partnership is solely a creature of statute; that is, it cannot be created in the absence of a statute authorizing it. Most of the states have adopted the Uniform Limited Partnership Act.[1]

In a *limited partnership* certain members can contribute capital without assuming personal liability for firm debts beyond the amount of their investment. These members are known as *special* or *limited partners*. The members who manage the business and assume full personal liability for firm debts are known as *general partners*. A limited partnership can be formed under the Uniform Limited Partnership Act by "one of more general partners and one or more limited partners." [2]

Unlike a general partnership, this special form can be created only by executing and swearing to a certificate stating the essential details of the partnership and the relative rights of the partners. The certificate, when executed, must be recorded in the office of the official in charge of public records, such as the Recorder of Deeds, of the county in which the principal place of business of the partnership is located.

The limited partner contributes cash or property, but not services. With certain exceptions, his name cannot appear in the firm name. His rights are limited to receiving his share of the profits or

---

[1] This Act has been adopted in all states except Alabama, Delaware, Kansas, Kentucky, Louisiana, Maine, Mississippi, Oregon, and Wyoming.
[2] Uniform Limited Partnership Act, Sec. 1.

a return of capital upon dissolution; he cannot exercise any control over the business. If improper use is made of his name, giving the public the impression that he is an active partner, or if he exercises a control over the business, he becomes liable as a general partner. In any case, a limited partner cannot withdraw his capital contribution when it is needed to pay creditors. (See p. 692, Neal v. United States)

In many respects the Uniform Limited Partnership Act follows the general pattern of the Uniform Partnership Act.

Sec. 46-B. Joint Venture. A *joint venture,* or joint adventure, is a relationship in which two or more persons combine their labor or property for a single undertaking and share profits equally, or as otherwise agreed. (See p. 693, Rehnberg v. Minnesota Homes) It is similar in many respects to a partnership, but it differs primarily in that the joint venture relates to the prosecution of a single venture or transaction, although its accomplishment may require several years, while a partnership is generally a continuing business or enterprise. This is not an exact definition because a partnership may be expressly created for a single transaction. Because this distinction is so insubstantial, many courts hold that a joint venture is subject to the same principles of law as partnerships.

An agreement for farming operations that provides for sharing expenses and profits, or an agreement to purchase real estate for development and resale, will often be regarded as a joint venture.

It is essential that there be a community of interest or purpose and that each co-adventurer have an equal right to control the operations or activities of the undertaking. The actual control of the operations may be entrusted to one of the joint adventurers. Thus the fact that one joint adventurer is placed in control of the farming and livestock operations and appears to be the owner of the land does not destroy the joint adventure relationship.

Sec. 46-C. Mining Partnership. A *mining partnership* is an association formed for the purpose of conducting mining operations. In some states it is declared by statute that a mining partnership exists when two or more persons engage in working a mine claim. Apart from statute, the formation of such a partnership is a matter of intention, as in the case of an ordinary partnership, evidenced by words or conduct of the parties. The intent to create a mining partnership must be shown.

In many respects the mining partnership is governed by the same principles as an ordinary partnership. It is primarily distinguished from an ordinary partnership in that the close, personal relationship of trust and confidence between partners is not present. In consequence of this, the authority of a partner to make contracts binding the mining partnership is more limited than in the case of a general partnership. That authority is limited to matters that are necessary and proper or usual for the purpose of working the mine. Moreover, the interest of a partner is transferable, and his transferee becomes a partner in the firm in his place without regard to the wishes of the other partners. Similarly, there is no dissolution when the interest of a partner passes to another person by operation of law, or when a partner becomes bankrupt or dies. Unlike a general partnership, profits and losses, unless otherwise stipulated, are shared proportionately according to the contributions made or shares held by each partner.

Sec. 46-D. Syndicate. A *syndicate* is generally defined as an association of individuals formed to conduct a particular business transaction, generally of a financial nature. Thus a syndicate may be formed by which its members agree to contribute sufficient money to purchase the control of a railroad. One of the common types of this form of business is the *underwriting syndicate*, which is an organization of investment banks for the purpose of marketing large issues of stocks or bonds.

A syndicate may be incorporated, in which case it has the attributes of an ordinary corporation. If it is not incorporated, it is treated in many respects the same as a general partnership, although it is held that, as in the case of the mining partnership, the personal factor or relationship between the partners is not important. When this is so held, it also follows that the interest of each member is freely transferable and that his transferee succeeds to his rights and membership in the syndicate.

Sec. 46-E. Unincorporated Association. An *unincorporated association* is a combination of two or more persons for the furtherance of a common nonprofit purpose. No particular form of organization is required, and any conduct or agreement indicating an attempt to associate or work together for a common purpose is sufficient. Social clubs, fraternal associations, and political parties are common examples of unincorporated associations.

Generally the members of an unincorporated association are not liable for the debts or liabilities of the association by the mere fact that they are members. It is generally required to show that they authorized or ratified the act in question. If either authorization or ratification by a particular member can be shown, he is unlimitedly liable as in the case of a general partner.

Except when otherwise provided by statute, an unincorporated association does not have any legal existence, such as has a corporation, apart from the members who compose it.

Sec. 46-F. Cooperative. A *cooperative* consists of a group of two or more independent persons or enterprises which cooperate with respect to a common objective or function. Thus farmers may pool their farm products and sell them as a group. Consumers may likewise pool their orders and purchase goods in bulk.

Initially the cooperative is itself an unincorporated association, and the rights and liabilities of all parties are determined in accordance with the principles governing an ordinary unincorporated association. In a majority of states, however, statutes subject cooperatives to regulation, particularly in the case of farm and dairy cooperatives. Incorporation by a special form of charter is commonly allowed and in some instances is required.

As the agreement by the members of seller's cooperatives that all products shall be sold at a common price is an agreement to fix prices, the seller's cooperative is basically an agreement in restraint of trade. By special legislation, such cooperatives have been exempted from the operation of antitrust laws. The Capper-Volstead Act of 1922 expressly exempts farmers' and dairymen's cooperatives from the operation of the federal Sherman Antitrust Act.

Sec. 46-G. Business Trust. A *business, common-law,* or *Massachusetts trust* arises when the owners of property transfer the ownership to one or more persons, called *trustees,* to be managed for business purposes by the trustees for the benefit of the original owners. Although the trustee or trustees, in a sense, are put in charge of the business for the benefit of the original owners, the relationship is more formal than an ordinary employer-employee relationship. In addition to the transfer of the legal title to the trustee or trustees, *trust certificates* or *shares* are issued to the former owners as evidence of their interest, and the profits from the enterprise are divided proportionately among the holders of the certificates.

Like shares in a corporation, shares in a business trust may be transferred. Unlike a corporation, the holders of the shares do not have control of the trustees running the business, as do stockholders over the board of directors of a corporation. Some courts hold that the business trust is merely a trust and the fact that it is designed for business operations, rather than to pay money for the support of certain persons or institutions, does not prevent the ordinary trust relationship law from applying.[3] (See p. 694, Hauser v. Catlett) Other

---

[3] See p. 865.

courts hold that for the purpose of taxation or the regulation of the business, the business trust is to be classified as a corporation.

One of the objectives of the business trust is to achieve a limited liability for the members or holders of trust certificates. In most jurisdictions it is held that the certificate holders are not liable for the debts of the business trust if they have relinquished all control over management to the trustees. The same conclusion is reached if there is a clause in the agreement establishing the trust by which it is stated that the certificate holders shall not be liable, at least with respect to persons dealing with the trust with knowledge or notice of such a limitation. In order to bring knowledge of such a limitation to third persons, it is common for the stationery of the business trust to state that such a limitation exists.

Sec. 46-H. Joint-Stock Company. Joint-stock companies are of common-law origin, although in a number of states they are now regulated by statute. This form of association has features resembling both a partnership and a corporation, or a business trust. Like a corporation, the shares of its members are transferable. The contract of the members provides that any member may transfer his share and that the person to whom the share is transferred shall be accepted as a partner. The management of the company is generally delegated to designated persons because as a general rule the membership is much larger than that of an ordinary partnership. The business is usually conducted under an impersonal name.

Cases for Chapter 46

Neal v. United States
195 F.2d 336 (C.A. 5th, 1952)

The War Assets Corporation sold a machine to Consolidated Machine Works, a limited partnership. The partnership was composed of Derrick, as a general partner, and Neal and Nauts, as limited partners. Subsequently the partnership was dissolved, and the capital contributions of the limited partners were returned to them. Such repayments made the partnership insolvent and unable to pay the War Assets Corp. for the machine. The United States then sued the limited partnership for the purchase price. From a judgment for the plaintiff, the defendant appealed.

STRUM, C.J. . . . At the time of its dissolution as a partnership, Consolidated was insolvent or "in contemplation of insolvency," within the provisions of . . . Texas Civil Statutes and . . . the purpose and effect of the entire transaction was to enable Neal and Nauts to withdraw their invested capital without first satisfying partnership creditors, further giving Neal an unlawful preference as a creditor on account of his loans to the partnership aggregating $25,000. The trial court held the transaction void under the Texas statutes. . . .

Accordingly, judgment was entered below against Neal and Nauts to the extent of their respective withdrawals of capital, with interest thereon to date of judgment, from which judgment they appeal.

We agree with the trial judge that the transaction, taken as a whole, was simply a device to enable the special partners to withdraw their capital without first satisfying their creditors. . . . and [was] therefore void as against creditors. . . . Texas Civil Statutes provide that any special partner who shall concur in or assent to such a transaction shall be liable as a general partner. . . .

[Judgment for plaintiff affirmed.]

Rehnberg v. Minnesota Homes
236 Minn. 230, 52 N.W.2d 454 (1952)

Rehnberg persuaded Hann and others to incorporate Minnesota Homes for the purpose of building houses. The corporation acquired title to certain land and employed Hann to construct houses for $500 per house, plus 25 per cent of the net profits from the sale of each house. The corporation employed Rehnberg to sell the houses at a fee of $150 per house, plus 25 per cent of the net profit to the corporation. Neither was entitled to his 25 per cent share until the net profits from all sales had been determined. An action was thereafter brought by Rehnberg to determine his rights. From a judgment for the defendant, the plaintiff appealed.

MATSON, J. . . . We come to the basic issue of whether we have a joint adventure. . . .

Although a joint adventure is not, in a strict legal sense, a copartnership, the rules and principles applicable to a partnership relation, with few if any material exceptions, govern and control the rights, duties, and obligations of the parties. No definite rule has been formulated for identifying the joint adventure relationship in all cases. Each case depends on its own peculiar facts. It is recognized, however, that an enterprise does not constitute a joint adventure unless each of the following four elements [is] present, namely:

(a) *Contribution*—the parties must combine their money, property, time, or skill in some common undertaking, but the contribution of each need not be equal or of the same nature.

(b) *Joint proprietorship and control*—there must be a proprietary interest and right of mutual control over the subject matter of the property engaged therein.

(c) *Sharing of profits but not necessarily of losses*—there must be an express or implied agreement for the sharing of profits (aside from profits received in payment of wages as an employee) but not necessarily of the losses.

(d) *Contract*—there must be a contract, whether express or implied, showing that a joint adventure was in fact entered into.

The first element of contribution is here present, in that plaintiff contributed his time, knowledge, and skill to the undertaking in discovering and promoting the enterprise, as well as in the subsequent sale of the house. The essential element of joint proprietorship and control is, however, lacking. There is no showing that plaintiff had any control over the manner in which the enterprise was carried on or that he even had any voice in the management of the corporation. In fact, the contract by its express terms identifies plaintiff's status as simply that of an employee.

Likewise, the third element of sharing in the profits in a manner consistent with a status of a joint adventure is absent. It is true plaintiff was to share in the profits, but only for the specific purpose of compensating him as an employee. In the analogous situation of a partnership, . . . the receipt by a person of a share in the profits is prima facie evidence that he is a partner, but . . . no inference shall be drawn if such profits are received in payment as wages of an employee. Furthermore, the indispensable element of a contract for the formation of a joint adventure is also absent.

We have a contract, but it is one that expressly creates an employment relation and thereby negatives any intent to create a joint adventure. . . .

[Judgment for defendant affirmed.]

Hauser v. Catlett

197 Okla. 668, 173 P.2d 728 (1946)

The Greer Investment Co. transferred money to F. H. Greer and others to hold as trustees under a business trust with the name of The Petroleum Royalties Co. The trust was to continue for 20 years. The trust agreement authorized the trustees to convey the property to new trustees when this was deemed judicious. Toward the end of the 20-year period, the trustees, then Hauser and others, decided to continue the business by conveying the assets to a new business trust, Petroleum Royalties, Limited, and to require the shareholders of the old trust to become shareholders of the new trust. To determine the validity of this plan, Hauser and the trustees brought an action against Catlett and the other shareholders in the original business trust. From a judgment in favor of the trustees, the shareholders appealed.

RILEY, J. . . . In the absence of prohibitive or controlling statutes, business trusts of the character of the one here involved, sometimes referred to as "Massachusetts Trust," which carry on a business for profit in the interest and for the benefit of the shareholders, are, generally speaking, legal and valid and not against public policy. . . .

Under a minority view, business trusts have been held to be generally invalid, at least to the extent of rendering invalid any attempted immunity from personal liability. But, in Oklahoma, [by statute] . . . business . . . trusts . . . are expressly authorized to conduct any lawful business . . . [although] such express trusts shall be limited in duration to a definite period not to exceed 21 years. . . . "The instrument creating the trust shall specify the period of duration thereof within the limitations herein provided."

The duration of trust creating the Petroleum Royalties Company conforms strictly to the statutory requirements. But by the provisions of the declaration, authority was vested in the trustees to transfer all the trust funds and other assets of the trust to a new trust or to a corporation. . . .

[Under the provision authorizing] transfer . . . to a new trust, . . . the trustees of the new trust could act with reference to the trust property for and only during that period of time fixed in the original declaration of trust. . . .

A business trust is a sort of hybrid form of organization, partaking in some respects the nature of a corporation and in other respects that of a partnership. Ordinarily a business trust differs from the corporation in that the trustees are given full power to conduct the business and affairs of the trust, free from interference from the individual shareholders. . . .

Any corporation chartered for a fixed term of years under the laws of this state may renew its charter and extend the time of its existence for a period not exceeding 20 years at any one time, by filing amended articles of incorporation. . . . Generally, the majority stockholders of a corporation have control of its management. They may determine whether its charter shall be renewed and whether the time of its existence shall be extended within statutory limitations.

There is no such provision with reference to business trusts. Shareholders have no such powers. The law does not specifically provide for the extension of its life. . . .

An organization such as Petroleum Royalties Company, "being a trust is subject to the same principles of law in determining the rights of trustees, cestuis que trust, creditors of the trust and others who deal with the trust as trusts which are older and historically traditional. . . ."

Generally, "If by the terms of the trust, the trust is to continue only until the expiration of a certain period or until the happening of a certain event, the trust will be terminated upon the expiration of the period or the happening of the event." Restatement of the Law of Trusts, § 334, p. 1011.

[Judgment reversed.]

Questions and Case Problems

1. What is the objective of each of the following rules of law?

 (a) Members of an unincorporated association are ordinarily not liable for debts of the group unless they had authorized, ratified, or in some way participated in creating the debt.

 (b) Farmers' and dairymen's cooperatives are exempt for the federal antitrust act.

2. In 1955 Booth, an experienced broker and trader in oil properties, and Wilson, who had been a jewelry merchant, made an oral agreement to work together in acquiring and trading in oil, gas, and mineral leases as a joint venture. As each lease was dealt in and disposed of, the two would take out whatever profit there was, divide it equally between themselves, and treat that operation as closed. In 1958 Booth and Wilson attempted to arrange a lease transaction with Gilbert but were unable to do so because of defects in the title. Booth then told Gilbert to revoke the contract, that he and Wilson did not have the money to go through with the deal, and that Gilbert should try to make the best deal with anyone else that he could. Thereafter, Wilson and Rector took a lease from Gilbert in their names. Booth then sued Wilson and Rector, claiming that he was entitled to share therein. Was he correct? (Booth v. Wilson, [Tex.] 339 S.W.2d 388)

3. Brenner was in the scrap iron business. Almost daily Plitt loaned Brenner money with which to purchase scrap iron. The agreement of the parties was that when the scrap was sold, Plitt would be repaid and would receive an additional sum as compensation for making the loan. The loans were to be repaid in any case, without regard to whether Brenner made a profit. A dispute arose as to the relationship between the two men. Plitt claimed that it was a joint venture. Decide. (Brenner v. Plitt, 182 Md. 348, 34 A.2d 853)

4. Merrilees, Hopkins, Mayer, and Adams formed a limited partnership but did not record their partnership agreement until 49 days after the partnership business began operations. Stowe, a creditor, claimed that a general partnership had been created because of the delay in filing the agreement. Decide. (Stowe v. Merrilees, 6 Cal.App. 2d 217, 44 P.2d 368)

5. Simpson and Saunders each had a used car dealer's license. They made an agreement to run their businesses independently but to share a lot, the building thereon, the furnishings, and the use of a telephone. Bates sued both Simpson and Saunders claiming that they were joint venturers and therefore both were liable for the fraudulent conduct of Simpson. Was Saunders liable? (Bates v. Simpson, 121 Utah 165, 239 P.2d 749)

6. Ettelsohn, Allen, and Levinson formed a limited partnership. The proceedings for the formation of the limited partnership complied with requirements of the statute except that Ettelsohn, the limited partner, contributed goods instead of cash as specified by the statute. In an action brought by Claflin, a creditor of the firm, it was claimed that Ettelsohn was a general partner. Decide. (Claflin v. Sattler, 41 Minn. 430, 43 N.W. 382)

CHAPTER 47

Nature and Classes

The corporation is one of the most important forms of business organization. To the large-scale enterprise it offers an easier way to finance itself by means of dividing its ownership into many small units that can be sold to a wide economic range of purchasers, including those with only small savings to invest. In addition to assisting financing operations, the corporate device offers a limited liability to the persons interested in the enterprise and a perpetual succession not affected by the death of any particular owner or by the transfer of his interest. Because of its limited liability, the corporation is also popular with many smaller businesses.

Sec. 47-A. Preliminary Survey. A corporation is formed by obtaining approval of articles of incorporation or a charter from the state or national government. The persons who develop the idea and induce others to join in the enterprise are called *promoters*. The persons who make the application to the government for the charter are called *incorporators*.

A corporation is controlled or managed by three groups of persons. The *board of directors* meets from time to time to determine the main policies of the corporation. This board selects the *officers* of the corporation, such as president, vice-president, treasurer, and secretary, who manage the corporation from day to day. In the ordinary business corporation *shareholders* or stockholders own shares of stock in the corporation and are the owners of the corporation.

The shares of some or all of the shareholders are voting shares, which give the holders the right to vote at the annual meeting. Through the election of the directors, the voting shareholders exercise an indirect control over the management of the corporation.

Shareholders have varying rights depending upon the nature of their stock. If the stock has no particular right or priority over any other stock, it is known as *common stock*. If the stock has a priority or preference over other stock, it is called *preferred stock*. There are several kinds of common and preferred stock.

Stock may also be distinguished in terms of whether the share of stock has a value specified in the stock certificate at the time it is issued, called a par value, or whether it is a share without any such specified value.

When a corporation is created, it is authorized to issue certain amounts and kinds of stock. If stock has been issued, it is said that the shares issued are outstanding. The outstanding stock of a corporation is also referred to as the capital stock of the corporation.

Since the shareholders are the owners of the corporation, they are entitled to share in the profits of the business. The profits are distributed to the shareholders in the form of *dividends* when the board of directors deems it advisable. Dividends are ordinarily paid in money, but they may also be paid in property.

Within the scope of its powers, the corporation may buy from and sell to other persons. A corporation may borrow money in the same way as an individual, that is, by making an unsecured loan, or one secured by a pledge or a mortgage on property. It is common practice for a corporation to issue bonds to raise money to finance its operations.

Like any other business enterprise, a corporation may go out of business. When this occurs, all creditors of the corporation are paid if possible; and if any balance remains, it is distributed among the shareholders. In addition, since the corporation exists by virtue of a charter obtained from a government, the government that granted the charter may revoke it because of corporate misconduct.

Sec. 47-B. Definition of a Corporation. A *corporation* is an entity, an artificial legal being, created by government grant and endowed with certain powers. (See p. 702, Perkins Case) That is, the corporation exists in the eyes of the law as though it were a person, separate and distinct from the people who own the corporation.

This concept means that property of the corporation is not owned by the persons who own shares in the corporation, but by the corporation. Debts of the corporation are debts of this artificial person and not of the people running the corporation or owning shares of stock in it. The corporation can sue and be sued in its own name with respect to corporate rights and liabilities, but the shareholders cannot sue or be sued as to those rights and liabilities. Furthermore, a corporation has independent life in the sense that it continues to exist without regard to the death of the individuals involved in its corporate affairs or the transfer by them of their interests in the corporation.

Sec. 47-C. Power to Create a Corporation. Since by definition a corporation is created by government grant, individuals cannot create a corporation merely by agreeing to do so. The right to be a corporation in the form of a *charter* or approval of *articles of incorporation* must be obtained from a government having authority to make that grant.

(1) Federal Power. The federal government is not expressly granted power to create corporations, but it may do so whenever appropriate to carry out the powers expressly granted to it. In addition, Congress has the right to authorize the creation of corporations in the District of Columbia and the territories of the United States.

(2) State Power. Generally a state by virtue of its police power may create any kind of corporation for any purpose. Some limitations on this power are found in state constitutions, and the power is, of course, subordinate to the federal powers. In many states the constitution provides that the legislature cannot create a corporation by a special act but only in accordance with a general law. (See p. 703, Sylvester Watts Smyth Realty Co. Case)

Most states have a *general corporation code* that lists certain requirements, and those groups which satisfy the requirements and which file the necessary papers with the government to prove compliance may automatically become corporations. Many states have several corporation codes, such as a code for the incorporation of business or profit corporations, another code for nonprofit or charitable corporations, and frequently special codes for such specialized corporate institutions as banks, savings and loan associations, insurance companies, and railroads. The American Bar Association has proposed a Model Business Corporation Act which has been adopted or is the basis for the business corporation code in Alaska, Colorado, Iowa, North Dakota, Oregon, Texas, Utah, Virginia, Wisconsin, Wyoming, and the District of Columbia. There is no uniform corporation act.[1]

---

[1] The Commissioners on Uniform State Laws had proposed a Uniform Business Corporation Act in 1928. This Act was adopted in Idaho, Kentucky, Louisiana, and Washington, and substantially influenced the corporation laws in a number of states. In 1943 the Commissioners designated it a model act, rather than a uniform act, to indicate that it was not believed that uniformity in the various states was essential. In 1957, as the result of the growth of the ABA model act, the Commissioners withdrew their model act.

Sec. 47-D. Classifications of Corporations.

(1) Public, Private, and Quasi-Public Corporations. A *public corporation* is one established for governmental purposes and for the administration of public affairs. A city is a public or municipal corporation acting under authority granted it by the state.

A *private corporation* is one established by private interests, whether for charitable and benevolent purposes or for purposes of finance, industry, and commerce. Private corporations are often called "public" in business circles when their stock is sold to the public.

A *quasi-public corporation,* which is also known as a public service corporation or a public utility, is a private corporation furnishing services upon which the public is particularly dependent. Examples of this class of corporations are those operating railroads, canals, and bridges or those supplying gas, electricity, and water. Such corporations are usually given special franchises and powers, such as the power of eminent domain.

(2) Stock and Nonstock Corporations. A *stock corporation* is one having its capital stock divided into shares, the rights and liabilities of the members being determined by ownership of such shares. A *nonstock corporation* is one in which the membership with attending rights and liabilities is acquired by agreement rather than by the acquisition of shares of stock, as in the case of incorporated lodges and fraternal organizations.

(3) Nonprofit and Profit Corporations. A *nonprofit corporation* (or an eleemosynary corporation) is one that is organized for charitable or benevolent purposes, such as certain hospitals, homes, and universities.

A *profit corporation* (or a business or civil corporation) is one organized for purposes other than charitable or benevolent purposes.

(4) Domestic and Foreign Corporations. If a corporation has been created under the law of a particular state or nation, it is called a *domestic corporation* with respect to that state or nation. Any other corporation going into that state or nation is called a *foreign corporation.* Thus a corporation holding an Illinois charter is a domestic corporation in Illinois but a foreign corporation in all other states and nations. This distinction becomes important in considering the extent of control that may be exercised by a government over corporations operating within its territorial boundaries. Whether a corporation is domestic is determined without regard to the residence of its shareholders or incorporators, or the state in which it conducts business. A corporation created under the law of one nation is also classified as an *alien corporation* in other nations.

Sec. 47-E. Regulation of Corporations.

(1) Domestic Corporations. Domestic corporations are regulated by the provisions of the code or general statutes under which they are organized and also by the tax laws and general laws of the state of their origin. The fact that a corporation goes outside its home state to conduct business does not remove it from all control by the incorporating state, although that control may in fact be very slight.

(2) Foreign Corporations. A foreign corporation is also subject to regulation and taxation, except as later noted, in every state in which it does business. Generally a foreign corporation must register to do business within the state, and it may be required to consent to be sued upon causes of action arising within the state. (See p. 705, Thomson v. Meridian Life Insurance Co.)

(3) Constitutional Limitations. In regulating a corporation, both state and national governments must observe certain limitations because corporations come within the protection of certain constitutional guarantees.

(a) THE CORPORATION AS A PERSON. The Constitution of the United States prohibits the national government and the state governments from depriving any "person" of life, liberty, or property without due process of law. Many state constitutions contain a similar limitation upon their respective state governments. A corporation is regarded as a "person" within the meaning of such provisions.

The federal Constitution prohibits states from denying to any "person" within its jurisdiction the equal protection of the laws. No such limitation is placed upon the federal government, although the due process clause binding the federal government has been liberally interpreted so that it would prohibit substantial inequality of treatment. Again it is held that a corporation enjoys the same equal protection of the laws as a natural person or individual.

(b) THE CORPORATION AS A CITIZEN. For certain purposes, such as determining the right to bring a lawsuit in a federal court, a corporation is today deemed a "citizen" of the state in which it was incorporated, without regard to the actual citizenship of the individual persons owning the stock of the corporation. Thus a corporation incorporated in New York is a New York corporation even though its shareholders are citizens of many other states.

The federal Constitution prohibits states from abridging "the privileges or immunities of citizens of the United States." A corporation, however, is not regarded as a "citizen" within this clause. Thus, with one exception, a foreign corporation has no constitutional right to do business in another state if that other state wishes to exclude it. For example, Pennsylvania can deny a New York corporation the right to come into Pennsylvania to do business. As a practical matter, most states do not exclude foreign corporations but seize upon this power as justifying special regulation or taxation. On this basis it is commonly provided that a foreign corporation must register or even take out a domestic charter, file copies of its charter, pay certain taxes, or appoint a resident agent before it can do business within the state. These regulations are sustained on the theory that since the foreign corporation could be excluded completely, it can be admitted on condition or at a price. Once the foreign corporation is admitted, however, the state cannot deny it due process or equal protection of the laws.

As an exception to the power of a state, it cannot exclude a foreign corporation when the latter engages solely in interstate commerce even though it is within the boundaries of the state. A state cannot require a license or registration of a foreign interstate commerce corporation or impose a tax on such a business.

Cases for Chapter 47

Perkins v. Benguet Consolidated Mining Co.
155 Ohio 116, 98 N.E.2d 33 (1951)

When Perkins sued the Benguet Consolidated Mining Co. service of process was made upon the president of the company. This service was proper if the company was a partnership. The company raised the objection that it was a corporation and that therefore the service was void. From a judgment for the defendant, the plaintiff appealed.

TAFT, J. . . . The decisions of this court have usually recognized that, in order to be a corporation, an organization must be a legal unit or be recognized as an entity by the law of the state or country in which it was organized. . . .

In determining whether an organization is a corporation, this court has never seemed very much concerned with what the organization is called. . . . Even if it is not called a corporation in the state from which it derives consent to be an entity or is called something else, an organization which has the essential attributes of a corporation is regarded in other states as a corporation. . . .

Section 116 of the Philippine Code of Commerce, under which defendant was organized, specifically provides that when a *sociedad anonima* is organized under its provisions, it becomes a legal entity.

The decisions of the highest court of the Philippine Islands have consistently and repeatedly treated *sociedad anonima* as legal units or entities having rights and obligations separate and distinct from the rights and obligations of their shareholders. . . .

That court has recognized that shares owned by shareholders of a *sociedad anonima* are transferrable without consent of the *sociedad anonima* or of its other shareholders and that changes in the ownership of shares do not in any way affect the rights and liabilities of a *sociedad anonima*. . . .

The death of a shareholder or other change in the identity of shareholders does not affect the continued existence of the *sociedad anonima*. . . .

Plaintiff further contends that a *sociedad anonima* is not a corporation because it receives no charter from the state. However, the statutes under which is was organized provide for the commencement of its existence on the filing of certain papers with a public official. . . . This is substantially the same procedure now followed in this state in incorporating a corporation under our General Corporation Act. . . .

[Judgment for defendant affirmed. This decision was reversed by the United States Supreme Court, 342 U.S. 437, which held that even though the association was a corporation, the service was valid.]

Sylvester Watts Smyth Realty Co. v. American Surety Co.
292 Mo. 423, 238 S.W. 494 (1921)

The Sylvester Watts Smyth Realty Co., a corporation, leased a tract of land to the Marsix Realty & Construction Co. Under the terms of the lease the tenant agreed to construct a modern office building on the tract. The American Surety Co. contracted as surety for the faithful performance of the tenant's obligation. When the tenant failed to construct the building, the lessor corporation sued the tenant and the surety company. The defendants claimed that the lease was void on the ground that the legislature could not create a corporation, such as the lessor corporation, for the purpose of dealing in real estate. From a judgment for the plaintiff, the defendants appealed.

RAGLAND, C. . . . Subject to the restrictions of constitutional provisions, the legislature of this state has plenary power to create corporations and prescribe the business in which they may engage. The only limitations on its power in this respect found in the Constitution are that corporations cannot be created by special law, . . . nor without the payment of certain incorporation fees, . . . and that no religious corporation can be established except for the purpose of holding the title to real estate for church edifices, parsonages, and cemeteries. . . . Clearly none of these prohibitions deprive the legislature of the power to create by general law corporations for the purpose of buying, selling, holding, and dealing in real estate as a business. The question then is whether the legislature has, in the exercise of its undoubted power, authorized by general laws the organization of corporations for such purposes.

At the times respectively when plaintiff and defendant were incorporated, the purposes for which manufacturing and business corporations might be created were prescribed by what is now Section 10151, R.S. 1919. The section, after specifically naming ten separate and distinct purposes for which such corporations may be formed, concludes as follows:

"Eleventh. For any other purpose intended for pecuniary profit or gain not otherwise especially provided for, and not inconsistent with the Constitution and laws of the state: Provided, that nothing in this section shall be construed to authorize the incorporation of a bond investment company. . . ."

This language is broad enough to authorize incorporation for all lawful business pursuits, for pecuniary profit or gain, which may engage capital and enterprise, and which are not specifically provided for by other provisions of the statutes relating to private corporations. . . . The buying, selling, and dealing in real estate and purchasing, owning, renting, selling, and exchanging of buildings for profit or gain are certainly lawful and usual business pursuits, and it seems entirely clear that they are comprehended within the broad and sweeping terms of the statute just quoted. . . .

But it is said that the statute in express terms excepts from its authorization the creation of corporations for purposes "inconsistent with the Constitution and laws of this state," and that the purposes for which plaintiff and defendant were organized are inconsistent with Section 7, Article 12, which provides:

"No corporation shall engage in business other than that expressly authorized in its charter or the law under which it may have been or hereafter may be organized, nor shall it hold any real estate for any period longer than six years, except such as may be necessary and proper for carrying on its legitimate business."

It is not apparent how this section of the Constitution can operate as a limitation on the power of the legislature to create corporations to buy and sell and deal in real estate, or to purchase, own, and rent buildings. It does not prescribe or limit the purposes for which corporations may be created; it does not even purport to deal with that subject. The portion of it pertinent to the question under consideration merely prohibits any corporation from holding any real estate for any period longer than six years except such as may be necessary and proper for carrying on its legitimate business; the converse of which is that, if the carrying on of its legitimate business makes it necessary and proper, a corporation can hold real estate indefinitely. . . .

[Judgment for plaintiff affirmed.]

Thomson v. Meridian Life Insurance Co.

38 S.D. 570, 162 N.W. 373 (1917)

The Meridian Life Insurance Co., an Indiana corporation, obtained permission to transact business in South Dakota. In order to obtain this permission, it agreed that in any action brought against it in South Dakota on an insurance policy, service of process could be made upon the insurance commissioner of South Dakota with the same effect as though the corporation were actually served. Thomson was the beneficiary of a policy issued by the company in Texas to a Texas resident. Thomson sued on the policy in South Dakota and made service on the insurance commissioner. The company objected that a state could not constitutionally compel a foreign corporation to appoint the insurance commissioner as its agent for service with respect to lawsuits brought on foreign causes of action. From a judgment for the plaintiff, the defendant appealed.

SMITH, J. . . . The precise question is whether the statutory consent of a corporation to be sued in this state extends to and includes causes of action upon a contract where the contract was entered into in, the cause of action arose in, and the plaintiff is a resident of, a foreign state. . . .

[By statute, South Dakota has required,] as a condition to transacting business in this state, . . . that every foreign insurance company shall stipulate and agree that all lawful process in any action or proceeding against the company in this state may be served upon the commissioner of insurance, "with the same effect as if the company existed in this state," and that such service "shall be of the same legal force and validity as if served on the company." . . . It seems to be the general policy of our law to place individuals and foreign corporations coming into this state upon the same basis, so far as the right to sue them is concerned, and it is our duty to give effect to that intent. . . .

We are also inclined to the view that the legislature intended . . . to cover transitory actions accruing in another jurisdiction in favor of nonresidents, and that service may be made upon foreign insurance corporations, under that section, with the same effect as if the company existed in this state, and that:

"The weight of modern authority . . . seems to support the proposition that a modern corporation may be sued on a transitory cause of action in any jurisdiction where it can be found in the sense that service may be perfected upon an agent or officer transacting business for the corporation within that jurisdiction, and that in the absence of statutory provisions to the contrary the residence of the plaintiff and the place at which the cause of action arose are not material questions to be determined to maintain jurisdiction if the corporation can be found and served." . . .

[Judgment for plaintiff reversed on other grounds.]

Questions and Case Problems

1. What is the objective of each of the following rules of law?
   (a) A corporation is created as an independent legal person by the act of the state in granting a charter or in approving articles of incorporation.
   (b) Incorporation is now generally obtained by complying with the requirements of a corporation code, rather than by obtaining a special grant or charter from the legislature.

2. Reisberg was the president and sole stockholder of the Carson Steel Co. His wife, driving an automobile owned by the corporation, collided at a grade crossing with a train of the Pittsburgh & Lake Erie Railroad. Reisberg sued the railroad for damage to the automobile. Was he entitled to recover? (Reisberg v. Pittsburgh & Erie R.R., 407 Pa. 434, 180 A.2d 575)

3. An action was brought by Alabama Tank Lines and other carriers against the Martin Truck Line, claiming that the truck line was operating without the necessary certificate of the state Public Service Commission. It was shown that Martin Truck Line had obtained a certificate at a time when all of its stock was owned by Thornbury, Cook, and Edwards. The stock was thereafter sold to Houghland and Page. No approval of the transfer of stock to them was obtained from the Public Service Commission. Was Martin Truck Line entitled to continue to do business under the certificate that had been originally issued? (Martin Truck Line v. Alabama Tank Lines, [Ala.] 73 So.2d 756)

4. The North River Bridge Co., which was incorporated by an act of Congress, brought proceedings against Luxton for the condemnation of the latter's land in Hoboken, New Jersey. The company needed this land for an approach to a bridge across the Hudson River between the states of New York and New Jersey. It was contended that Congress had no power to create a corporation for the construction of bridges. Do you agree with this contention? (Luxton v. North River Bridge Co., 153 U.S. 525)

5. A certificate of incorporation was filed with the Secretary of State, incorporating the Pittsburgh, Fort Wayne, and Chicago Railroad Co. Fifty years later, Lanier and others were running the affairs of the corporation. An action was brought by the state's attorney to question the right of Lanier and others to run the corporation. It was claimed that since they had not been original founders of the corporation, they had no right to run the corporation. Decide. (Illinois v. Wayman, 256 Ill. 151, 99 N.E. 941)

6. The Detroit Schuetzenbund borrowed $900 from the Detroit Agitations Verein. The debt was evidenced by a note signed on behalf of the Detroit Schuetzenbund by its president, secretary, treasurer, and two trustees. The Verein brought an action against the Schuetzenbund to recover the amount of the loan. It was claimed that the defendant was not a corporation because a charter had not been obtained from the state. Was this contention sound? (Detroit Schuetzenbund v. Detroit Agitations Verein 44 Mich. 312, 6 N.W. 675)

CHAPTER 48

Creation and Termination
of Corporations

A corporation receives its authority from government. Statutory law specifies the requirements that must be met for creating a corporation and the manner in which a corporation can be dissolved or terminated.

Creation of Corporations

Sec. 48-A. Requisites to Creation. Persons who wish to incorporate under general laws must substantially comply with the requirements of the statute, such as the following:

(1) Number and Qualifications of Incorporators. The statutes usually require a certain number of applicants who possess, in addition to the capacity to contract, the qualification of residence or citizenship. The ABA Model Business Corporation Act requires that the incorporators be "three or more natural persons of full age." [1]

In most states a minimum of three incorporators is required. About one fourth of the states require that the incorporators be shareholders, while the other states have abandoned this requirement.

Although many states exclude a corporation from acting as an incorporator, an exception is commonly made when corporations in existence are being consolidated to form a new corporation.

(2) Application for Incorporation. The organizers must make an application for a charter and file certain documents, such as the proposed articles of incorporation. The application must generally state the name, object, and capital stock structure of the proposed corporation.

---

[1] American Bar Association Model Business Corporation Act, Sec. 47.

(a) NAME OF THE PROPOSED CORPORATION. Subject to certain limitations, the incorporators may select any name for the corporation.[2]

(b) OBJECT OF THE PROPOSED CORPORATION. Sometimes the statute enumerates the purposes for which a corporation may be formed. The purpose or object must be lawful. A corporation may be forbidden to do acts that would be lawful if done by an individual. To illustrate, persons may be forbidden to incorporate for the purpose of practicing law, medicine, or related arts.[3] (See p. 714, State v. Zale Jewelry Co.) A corporation can neither practice one of the learned professions nor employ a licensed practitioner to practice for it. Some states also require a statement of the means to be used to attain the object of the corporation, particularly in the case of non-profit or charitable corporations.

(c) CAPITAL STOCK. The amount of capital stock to be authorized and the number and value of the shares into which it is divided must be specified. The Model Business Corporation Act also requires that the articles of incorporation state a description of the classes of stock, the number of shares in each class, the relative rights of each class, and that the corporation will not commence business until consideration of the value of at least $1,000 has been received for the issuance of shares.[4] Other statutes have similar requirements.

(d) PLACE OF BUSINESS. The location of the principal office or place of business of the proposed corporation must be stated.

(e) DURATION. The period during which the proposed corporation is to exist must be set forth. Most states permit the incorporators to select perpetual life for the corporation, but some states limit the number of years.

(f) DIRECTORS AND OFFICERS. The number of directors or the names and addresses of directors for the first year must be stated. Sometimes additional information regarding the directors is required. In some instances the names and addresses of the officers for the first year must also be stated.

The purpose of requiring the naming of the first board of directors is to provide the corporation with a body to govern or manage the corporation during the interval from the moment that the corporate life begins until the organization meeting of the shareholders is held. In some states that do not require the naming of the first board of

---

[2] See p. 721.

[3] In order to permit self-employed professional men to obtain the tax advantages of deferred retirement plans enjoyed by corporate employees, a number of states have adopted laws permitting the organization of professional corporations or associations. Such laws have been adopted in Alabama, Arkansas, Connecticut, Florida, Georgia, Illinois, Minnesota, Ohio, Oklahoma, Pennsylvania, South Dakota, Tennessee, and Washington. Note, however, that Opinion 303 of the American Bar Association Committee on Professional Ethics expresses "grave doubts" as to the propriety of lawyers forming organizations under such laws.

[4] ABA MBCA Sec. 48.

directors in this manner, the incorporators have the power of management during this period.

(g) INCORPORATORS. The names and addresses of the incorporators must be given, together with the number of shares subscribed by each. Sometimes the method of payment for those shares must also be stated.

(3) Advertisement. Statutes may require incorporators to give some form of public notice, such as by advertisement in a newspaper, of the intention to form the corporation. Provision is generally made that anyone objecting to the proposed corporation may file a written objection, ordinarily with the officer with whom incorporators are required to file their application. That officer may refuse to allow the incorporation when a sound objection is made; or he may require the incorporators to modify their plans, after which he will grant the charter.

Sec. 48-B. The Charter. After the application for a charter or the articles of incorporation are filed, the fee paid, and other conditions precedent fulfilled, usually an administrative official, such as the secretary of state, examines the papers. If the requirements of the law have been met, a certificate of incorporation, license, or charter is issued and recorded or filed, as specified by the terms of the local statute.

Under the Model Business Corporation Act corporate existence begins upon the issuance of the certificate of incorporation by the state official.[5] In some states corporate existence does not begin until an organization meeting is held under the charter to put the corporation in operation, and in others, not until a report on the organization is made. The statute may declare that the charter shall be void if the certificate of organization is not properly filed within a prescribed time. The organization meeting must be held within the state creating the corporation. If it is held elsewhere, the proceedings are not valid.

In theory it is required that the corporation accept the charter which is given to it; but unless expressly required by statute, it is not necessary for the corporation to inform any state officer that the charter is accepted. The acceptance of the charter can be inferred from conduct, such as the act of holding an organization meeting or doing business under the charter.

Since the charter is regarded as a contract, the corporation is protected from subsequent change or modification by the clause of the federal Constitution that prohibits states from impairing the obligation of contracts. This does not mean that in no case can the rights

---

[5] Sec. 50.

given by a charter be modified. Under many statutes it is expressly provided that the charter granted by the state is subject to the power reserved by the state to change the charter should it desire to do so. Independently of such a reservation, the rule has developed that permits the state, under the exercise of its police power, to modify existing contracts, including corporate charters, to further the public health, safety, morals, or general welfare.

Sec. 48-C. Proper and Defective Incorporations. If the legal procedure for incorporation has been followed, the incorporation has a perfect legal right to exist. It is called a *corporation de jure*, meaning that it is a corporation by virtue of law.

If there is a defect in the incorporation but it is not a material one, the law usually will overlook the defect and hold that the corporation is a corporation de jure.

(1) De Facto Corporation. The defect in the incorporation may be so substantial that the law cannot ignore it and will not accept the corporation as a de jure corporation. Yet there may be sufficient compliance so that the law will recognize that there is a corporation. When this occurs, the association is called a *de facto corporation.* It exists in fact but not by right, and the state may bring proceedings to have the corporate charter revoked because of the defects.[6] If, however, the state does not take proceedings against the defective corporation, the de facto corporation has all the rights and privileges of a regular lawful or de jure corporation, and third persons contracting with it cannot avoid their contracts on the ground that the corporation was merely a de facto corporation. The shareholders of a de facto corporation generally have limited liability. (See p. 715, Inter-Ocean Newspaper Co. v. Robertson)

Although there is conflict among the authorities, most courts hold that a de facto corporation must meet four tests: (a) there must be a valid law under which the corporation could have been properly incorporated; (b) the attempt to organize the corporation must have been made in good faith; (c) the attempt to organize must result in colorable compliance with the requirements of the statute; and (d) there must be a use of the corporate powers.

(2) Partnership v. Corporation by Estoppel. The defect in incorporation may be so great that the law will not accept the corporation even as a de facto corporation. In such a case, in the absence of a statute making the incorporation conclusive, there is no corporation. If the incorporators proceed to run the business in spite of such irregu-

---

[6] Sec. 50.

larity, they may be held liable as partners. In a minority of states the court will not hold the individuals liable as partners, but will hold liable the person who committed the act on behalf of the business on the theory that he was an agent who acted without authority and is therefore liable for breach of the implied warranties of the existence of a proper principal and of proper authorization.

The partnership liability rule is sometimes not applied when the third person dealt with the business as though it were actually a corporation. In such instances it is stated that the third person is estopped from denying that the "corporation" with which he did business has legal existence. The court in effect holds that there is a *corporation by estoppel* with respect to that creditor.

The doctrine of corporation by estoppel is not always applied, and it is difficult to bring one's case within the rule to show that the third person dealt with the defective corporation as a corporation. The doctrine is applied when one of the promoters or incorporators attempts to deny that there is a corporation. Having attempted or purported to create a corporation, the promoter or incorporator cannot deny that a corporation was created.

If the incorporators have failed to obtain a charter and have not done business together, neither the corporation by estoppel nor the partnership rule will be applied. (See p. 716, Southern Cotton Oil Co. v. Duskin)

Sec. 48-D. Promoters. The promoters are persons who plan the corporation and sell the idea to others. They may also file the necessary papers with the government to create the corporation. They are independent operators. They are not regarded as agents of the corporation since the corporation is not yet in existence.

A promoter, in the absence of statutory authority, cannot bind the corporation or give it rights by a preincorporation contract even though he purports to act for it. The corporation, upon coming into existence, may become a party to such a contract, however, by assignment or by novation. Moreover, when the corporation knowingly accepts the benefits of the promoter's contract, it becomes liable on that contract.

The promoter is personally liable for all contracts made in behalf of the corporation before its existence unless he is exempted by the terms of the agreement or by the circumstances surrounding it. (See p. 717, Quaker Hill v. Parr) He is also liable for all torts that he commits in connection with his activities as promoter. Although the corporation is not ordinarily liable for the torts of the promoter, it may become so by its conduct after incorporation. Thus, when a corporation, with actual or implied notice of the fraud of the promoter, assumes responsibility for the promoter's contract, it is liable for the fraud.

With respect to the other contracting party, the promoter's contract is binding even though it does not impose any duty upon him to form the corporation.

A promoter stands in a fiduciary relation to the corporation and to stock subscribers. He cannot make secret profits at their expense. Accordingly, if a promoter makes secret profits on a sale of land to a corporation, he must account to the corporation for those profits, that is, he must surrender the profits to it.

The corporation is not liable in most states for the expenses and services of the promoter unless it subsequently promises to pay for them or unless its charter or a statute imposes such liability upon it.

Dissolution and Termination

A corporation may be dissolved or terminated by agreement, insolvency, reorganization proceedings, consolidation, merger, and forfeiture of charter.

Sec. 48-E. Dissolution by Agreement.

(1) Expiration of Time. If the incorporators have selected a corporate life of a stated number of years, the corporate existence automatically terminates upon the expiration of that period. Some courts hold that the corporation may continue thereafter as a de facto corporation.

(2) Surrender of Charter. The shareholders may terminate the corporate existence by surrendering the charter to the state. The surrender is not effective until the state accepts the charter. The state will ordinarily not act, however, if any creditors have not been paid, since the state's acceptance of a surrender of the charter ends the corporate existence and generally extinguishes the liability of the corporation for debts.

(3) Repeal of Charter. The corporation may be formed with the provision that the legislature may terminate its existence at will or upon the happening of a certain contingency. This right may be contained in the provisions of the charter, or in the statute or constitution of the government. In exercising the right of repeal, however, the government cannot impair vested rights, as by taking the assets of the corporation from the shareholders or creditors.

Sec. 48-F. Insolvency. The insolvency of a corporation does not in itself terminate the corporate existence. Statutes in some states, however, provide that when the corporation is insolvent, creditors may commence proceedings to dissolve the corporation. Sometimes the statute merely dissolves the corporation as to creditors. This situation is sometimes called a *de facto* or *quasi dissolution.*

The appointment of a receiver for the corporation does not in itself dissolve the corporation, although the administration of the property by the receiver may result in the practical termination of the corporation. In some states the appointment of liquidators to wind up an insolvent corporation automatically dissolves the corporation. In the absence of statute, a court cannot appoint a receiver for a solvent corporation and order its dissolution.

Sec. 48-G. Reorganization. When a reorganization of a corporation occurs under the federal bankruptcy laws,[7] the corporate existence is not terminated. If the reorganization is successful, the result is the same as though the corporation merely exchanged obligations.

Under state law, however, reorganization proceedings are generally regarded as creating a new corporation.

Sec. 48-H. Consolidation. In a *consolidation* of two or more corporations, the separate corporate existences cease; a new corporation with the property and assets of the old corporations comes into being. When a consolidation is effected, the new corporation ordinarily succeeds to the rights, powers, and immunities of its component parts.[8] Limitations, however, may be prescribed by charter, constitution, or statute. As a general rule, the consolidated corporation is subject to all the liabilities of the constituent corporations.

Sec. 48-I. Merger. *Merger* differs from consolidation in that, when two corporations merge, one absorbs the other. One corporation preserves its original charter and identity and continues to exist, and the other disappears and its corporate existence terminates. (See p. 717, New Jersey v. National Power & Light Co.)

Sec. 48-J. Forfeiture of Charter. The government that granted the charter may forfeit or revoke the charter for good cause. Sometimes the legislature provides in a general statute that the charter of any corporation shall be automatically forfeited when certain acts are committed or omitted.

Common grounds for forfeiture are fraudulent incorporation; *willful nonuser,* that is, failure to exercise powers; or *misuser,* that is, abuse of corporate powers and franchises. When it is claimed that

---

[7] See p. 901.
[8] ABA MBCA Sec. 69.

a corporation has abused its privileges, such acts must be willful, serious, and injurious to the public. The action against the corporation to forfeit its charter must be brought by and in the name of the government, meaning ordinarily an action by the attorney general of the state. Forfeiture of a charter is an extreme penalty. Because of its severity, it is rarely used.

Cases for Chapter 48

State v. Zale Jewelry Company
179 Kan. 628, 298 P.2d 283 (1956)

The State of Kansas, on the complaint of the attorney general, brought an original action in the Supreme Court of Kansas against the Zale Jewelry Co., a corporation, to order it to stop the practice of optometry and to forfeit its charter for engaging therein. The State claimed that Dr. Marks, who practiced optometry in one part of the store, and the Douglas Optical Company, which also did business in part of the store, were in fact employees of the Zale Co., which, as their employer, was therefore engaging in optometry.

SMITH, C.J. . . . Defendant relies in the main on two leases . . . to establish that the relationship between it and Marks and it and Douglas was strictly that of lessor and lessee. . . . The two leases . . . each had the provision about defendant handling the business and financial affairs of both Marks and Douglas Optical. A reasonable inference is that such provision was in the lease so as to permit defendant to exercise control over both.

Rowe v. Standard Drug Co., 132 Ohio St. 629, 9 N.E.2d 609, 612, was a case where a drug company was charged with . . . practicing optometry. The arrangement between the drug company was somewhat analogous to what we have here. The drug company relied on leases between it and an optical company to establish the relationship of lessor and lessee. The court said:

"The court however, is not limited by the terms of the lease, but will consider the manner in which the optical business was conducted and the extent to which the corporation participated in transactions involving optometrists. . . .

. . . A lease, valid on its face, may be a mere sham or device to cover up the real transaction; but such a subterfuge will not be permitted to become a cloak for illegal practices. The courts will always pierce the veil to discover the real relationship. Where a corporation directly or indirectly engages in the practice of optometry, the lease will afford no protection on a proper challenge of the illegality." . . .

Besides the feature of the leases, . . . there is the fact that at first the neon sign near the stairway to the balcony read until this action was commenced "Optical Dept." [The] inference is that the business on the balcony was a part of the business of defendant. Even though it be held to refer to Douglas Optical and not Dr. Marks, still without Dr. Marks, the optical business would not have done well. . . . All Dr. Marks' prescriptions were filled by Douglas Optical. When glasses were charged, the account was carried in the name of defendant. . . .

The relationship between defendant and Dr. Marks is that of employer and employee. Dr. Marks is practicing optometry. He is employed to do so by defendant—hence defendant is practicing optometry, which it cannot do.

Judgment is in favor of plaintiff ousting defendant from the practice of optometry in the state. Plaintiff asks us to order the dissolution of defendant and the appointment of a receiver to wind it up. We find the record does not warrant such a drastic measure.

Inter-Ocean Newspaper Co. v. Robertson
296 Ill. 92, 129 N.E. 523 (1920)

Robertson and others incorporated as the Chicago Real Estate Show Co. Robertson made a contract for advertising with the Inter-Ocean Newspaper Co. The advertising was not paid for. The newspaper company brought suit against Robertson and the other incorporators, alleging that they had not filed the final certificate of incorporation and were therefore liable as partners. From a judgment for the plaintiff in the appellate court reversing the judgment of the trial court, the defendants appealed.

FARMER, J. . . . The Chicago Real Estate Show Co. was a corporation de facto, notwithstanding it neglected to file its final certificate of complete organization for record. . . .

Whether members and stockholders of a de facto corporation, as distinguished from a de jure corporation, are protected from liability to creditors as partners, the decisions are not in entire accord; but the great weight of the authorities hold they are not liable, in the absence of a statute making them so liable. That the stockholders of a de facto corporation, where the members in good faith supposed they were legally incorporated under a valid law authorizing such incorporation and honestly transacted business as a corporation, should not, in the absence of a positive statutory mandate, be treated and considered as partners as to persons dealing with it as a corporation seems to be absolutely sound.

A contrary rule would be far-reaching in its consequences, and often lead to great injustice and hardship to innocent stockholders. It is by no means always practicable for purchasers of stock to examine every step taken in the organization of the corporation; and to hold them individually liable for its debts seems contrary to reason and justice, where there had been no fraud, but an honest effort had been made to effect a legal organization, and both the incorporators and stockholders in good faith believed the corporation legal, but some mistake or omission had been made such as here—neglect to file the final certificate of its complete organization for record. . . .

[Judgment of the appellate court for plaintiff reversed.]

Southern Cotton Oil Co. v. Duskin

92 Ga.App. 288, 88 S.E.2d 421 (1955)

An application for a corporate charter for the Dawson Milling Co. was executed and filed by J. W. Duskin, Theodosia, his wife, and their son. After the filing of the articles and their advertisement, no further action was taken. The charter was not accepted, the corporation was not organized, no capital was paid in, and no stock was issued. Thereafter the husband executed and delivered two checks in payment of merchandise to the Southern Cotton Oil Co. The checks were signed "Dawson Milling Company" without indicating whether the drawer was an individual, partnership, or corporation. Southern sued the husband and the wife claiming that they were partners. From a judgment for the defendants, the plaintiff appealed.

QUILLIAN, J. . . . The plaintiff [Southern Cotton] contends that Mrs. Duskin was liable as a partner for the debts of Dawson Milling Company. This contention is based upon the rule that promoters of a corporation who are granted a charter, but make no effort to accept the charter by complying with its requirements, will be held liable as partners if they go forward with the business.

The plaintiff's position is that Mrs. Duskin was a promoter, and that she took part in the business of Dawson Milling Company and therefore is liable as a partner.

That Mrs. Duskin, her husband, and son jointly filed a petition and obtained a charter for a corporation which was never organized did not, without more, constitute them partners. Whether they became partners depended upon their engaging in business under the name of the proposed corporation.

If the promoters begin doing business before they organize the corporation and make no effort to accept the charter or [to comply] with its requirements, they are held liable as partners. . . .

"Merely participating in the signing and filing of articles of incorporation, however, will not render a person liable as a partner for obligations contracted by one of his associates who assumes to transact business under the proposed corporate name where the organization is never perfected and the one sought to be charged has not participated in the business or held himself out as a partner." . . .

[Judgment affirmed.]

Quaker Hill v. Parr

364 P.2d 1056 (Colo., 1961)

Quaker Hill made a contract for the sale of plants to the "Denver Memorial Nursery, Inc." The contract was signed by Parr as Denver's president. Quaker Hill knew that the corporation was not yet formed and the contract so stated, but Quaker Hill had insisted that the contract be executed in this manner rather than wait until the corporation was organized. The corporation was never formed, and Quaker Hill sued Parr and other promoters of the corporation. From a judgment in their favor, Quaker Hill appealed.

DOYLE, J. . . . The general principle which plaintiff urges as applicable here is that promoters are personally liable on their contracts, though made on behalf of a corporation to be formed. . . . A well recognized exception to this general rule, however, is that if the contract is made on behalf of the corporation and the other party agrees to look to the corporation and not to the promoters for payment, the promoters incur no personal liability.

In the present case, according to the trial court's findings, the plaintiff . . . was aware of that fact that the corporation was not formed and nevertheless urged that the contract be made in the name of the proposed corporation. . . . The entire transaction contemplated the corporation as the contracting party. Personal liability does not arise under such circumstances. . . .

The curious form of this transaction is undoubtedly explainable on the basis of the . . . great rush to complete it, the heavy emphasis on completion of the sale rather than on securing payment or a means of payment. No effort was made to expressly obligate the . . . defendants and this present effort must be regarded as pure afterthought.

[Judgment for defendants affirmed.]

New Jersey v. National Power & Light Co.

16 N.J. 486, 109 A.2d 607 (1954)

The attorney general of New Jersey brought an action against the National Power & Light Co., a New Jersey corporation. The defense was raised that the New Jersey corporation had merged with a Delaware corporation and that it had ceased to exist and could not be sued. From a judgment against the attorney general, he appealed.

OLIPHANT, J. . . . [The New Jersey statute provided that in case of a merger] "all rights of creditors and all liens upon the property of the former corporations shall be preserved unimpaired; and the respective former corporations may be deemed to continue in existence in order to preserve the same; and all debts, liabilities, restrictions, and duties of the former corporations shall thenceforth attach to such consolidated corporation, and may be enforced against it to the same extent as if they had been incurred or contracted by it."

. . . . There is no provision here, unlike the dissolution statute, that the corporation shall be continued a "body corporate" for the purposes of "prosecuting and defending suits by or against them" and "of disposing its property and closing its affairs but not to continue in business." Such provisions are found in the sections relating to voluntary and . . . involuntary dissolution. . . . These sections governing dissolutions are designed to protect creditors from the removal of assets. The continued existence of the dissolved corporation for purposes of suit is necessitated by the reason that the corporation retains ownership of the property out of which any obligation is to be satisfied. Under these sections the trustees in dissolution or the receiver hold the assets of the corporation as a trust fund which is a security for the performance of all liabilities direct or contingent.

The situation dealt with when two corporations merge is entirely different and hence the difference in the statutory provisions. Under this section, as pointed out, all the property of the former corporation vests in the successor corporation and all the liabilities of each become those of the successor corporation. Thus there is no necessity for the continuance of the existence of the merged corporation for purposes of suit. In a dissolution the assets are gathered together in a trust fund and then distributed to its creditors and stockholders. But when a merger or consolidation occurs, the assets are not distributed beyond the reach of creditors, but remain with the successor corporation subject to its liabilities and creditors, who may enforce their claims against such assets.

. . . It would seem to be indisputable that a corporation ceasing to exist by reason of the merger cannot be sued in the absence of an express provision for the continuance of life for the purposes of suit to enforce claims of creditors and to enforce its own claims against others. . . .

[Judgment affirmed.]

Questions and Case Problems

1. What is the objective of each of the following rules of law?
   (a) When a corporation knowingly accepts the benefits of a promoter's contract, it becomes bound by the contract.
   (b) A corporate charter is subject to revocation for misuse of power by the corporation.

2. The Maid of the Mist Steamboat Co. was organized for operating sight-seeing steamships on the Niagara River. It had a fifty-year charter which expired in 1942. No one realized that fact until 1947. In that year an application was made under the New York law to renew the charter of

the corporation. During the intervening period from 1942 to 1947 the corporation had continued to do business as usual. What kind of corporation was it during that period? (Garzo v. Maid of the Mist Steamboat Co., 303 N.Y. 516, 104 N.E.2d 882)

3. Woods executed and delivered a promissory note payable to the order of the Lowell-Woodward Hardware Co., which described itself as a Colorado corporation. The note was not paid at maturity, and an action was brought to recover thereon. As a defense, the maker alleged that the payee was not in truth a corporation. Was this a valid defense? (Lowell-Woodward Hardware Co. v. Woods, 104 Kans. 729, 180 P. 734)

4. Goodenow owned real estate which was listed for sale with White & Bollard, as real estate agents. The latter made a contract for the sale of the land to Lurie, a promoter for a corporation to be formed. From the contract it appeared that Lurie was the purchaser although, in signing, he added after his name, "as agent for a corporation to be formed." The contract stated that it was contingent upon the purchaser's obtaining satisfactory financing within 90 days and obligated the "purchaser to exercise reasonable speed and diligence in preparing plans and making all necessary applications for financing." Before the expiration of the 90-day period, Goodenow sold the land to another buyer. The real estate agents sued Goodenow and Lurie for the commissions that they would have made on the sale if the contract had been performed. Lurie raised the defense that there had been no intention that he should be bound by the contract. Was this a valid defense? (White & Bollard v. Goodenow, [Wash.2d] 361 P.2d 571)

5. The Burlington & Missouri Railroad Co. was organized under the general corporation laws of Iowa. Its rights were later transferred to the Chicago, Burlington & Quincy Railroad Co. The legislature of Iowa adopted a statute regulating the rates of fares and freight to be collected by railroads in that state. In a suit brought by the railroad against Cutts to enjoin the enforcement of the statute, it was contended that the charter of a corporation was within the meaning of the clause of the Constitution of the United States which prohibits a state from passing any law impairing the obligation of contracts. Do you agree? (Chicago, Burlington & Quincy Railroad Co. v. Cutts, 94 U.S. 155)

6. The Joint Stock Co. of Volgakama Oil & Chemical Factory, a Russian corporation, deposited money with the National City Bank of New York, making it appear that it was a corporation. Later it sued the bank for the money. The bank defended on the ground that the plaintiff was not a corporation. Assuming the Joint Stock Co. was not a corporation, could the bank raise that defense? (Joint Stock Co., etc. v. National City Bank, 210 App.Div. 665, 206 N.Y.S. 476)

7. A Wisconsin statute authorized the members of a church to organize as a corporation. Under the statute two churches attempted in good faith to organize as a single corporation. The organization thereafter admitted that it was not a corporation de jure but contended that it was a corporation de facto. Do you agree with this contention? (Evenson v. Ellingson, 67 Wis. 634, 31 N.W. 342)

8. Adams and two other persons were promoters for a new corporation, the Aldrelin Theaters Co. The promoters retained Kridelbaugh to perform legal services in connection with the incorporation of the new business and promised to pay him $1,500. The corporation was incorporated through Kridelbaugh's services, and the promoters became its only directors. Kridelbaugh attended a meeting of the board of directors at which he was told that he should obtain a permit for the corporation to sell stock because the directors wished to pay him for his prior services. The promoters failed to pay Kridelbaugh, and he sued the corporation. Was the corporation liable? (Kridelbaugh v. Aldrelin Theaters Co., 195 Iowa 147, 191 N.W. 803)

9. The Civil Code of California provided that "The articles of incorporation must be subscribed by five or more persons . . . and acknowledged before some officer authorized to take and certify acknowledgments of conveyances of real property." When incorporating the Montecite Water Co., five incorporators signed the articles of incorporation, but only four of them acknowledged the articles. In an action brought by the state against the water company, the latter contended that there had been a substantial compliance with the provisions of the statute and therefore the company was a corporation de jure. Decide. (California v. Montecite Water Co., 97 Cal. 276, 32 P. 236)

10. The American Malt Corporation was organized to hold the stock of the American Malting Co. At special meetings of the stockholders of both companies it was voted to merge the two companies. A provision of the New Jersey statutes authorized the merger of corporations engaged in business of a similar nature. The Board of Public Utility Commissioners refused to approve the merger, contending that the merger was not authorized by the statute. What is your opinion? (American Malt Corp. v. Board of Public Utility Commissioners, 86 N.J.L. 668, 92 A. 362)

11. The Shepard Broadcasting Service Co. broadcast a sponsored program on which lawyers stated the answers to legal questions submitted to the station by listeners. Rosenthal, an attorney, sued to cause the service company to stop this program on the ground that it violated a statute which prohibited any corporation from giving "legal advice in matters not relating to its lawful business, or to practice law." Should the program have been stopped? (Rosenthal v. Shepard Broadcasting Service, 299 Mass. 286, 12 N.E.2d 819)

CHAPTER 49

Corporate Powers

Either by common law or by virtue of the statute under which it is incorporated, a corporation has certain powers. Some of the powers possessed by a corporation are the same as those powers held by a natural person, such as the right to own property. Others are distinct powers not possessed by ordinary persons, such as the power to exist perpetually in those states where this is allowed.

Sec. 49-A. Nature of Corporate Powers. All corporations do not have the same powers. For example, those that operate banks, insurance companies, savings and loan associations, and railroads generally have special powers.

Except for limitations in the federal Constitution or the state's own constitution, a state may grant to a corporation any powers that it chooses. In addition, a corporation has certain powers that are incidental to corporate existence. These powers are implied because they are reasonably necessary to carry out and make effective the expressly granted powers.

(1) Perpetual Succession. One of the distinctive features of a corporation is its perpetual succession or continuous life—the power to continue as a unit forever or a stated period of time regardless of changes in stock ownership. When the period is limited, the corporation may in many states extend the period by meeting additional requirements of the statute.

(2) Corporate Name. A corporation must have a name to identify it. As a general rule it may select any name for this purpose. It may not, however, select for its exclusive use a name that all may lawfully use, such as a descriptive name, or one that another firm has the exclusive right to use.

The Model Business Corporation Act prohibits the use of the same or a deceptively similar name of any domestic corporation or any foreign corporation authorized to do business in the state.[1] Even though the practice of imitating another's name is not prohibited by the statutes of a particular state, the imitation may still be prohibited as unfair competition.

Statutes frequently require that the last word of the name be "Corporation" or that the word "Limited" or "Incorporated" be used in conjunction with the name selected. The Model Business Corporation Act requires that the name end with "Inc.," or include "Incorporated" or "Corporation," or include "Company" if not preceded by "and" or "&."

A corporation has the same right as an individual to assume a fictitous name under which it conducts business, provided that it complies with the statute relating to the registration of such names.

(3) Corporate Seal. A corporation has the right to have a seal. Under modern law, however, a corporation need not use a seal in a given transaction unless it is required by statute or unless a natural person in transacting the same business would be required to use a seal, as in a conveyance of land.

(4) Bylaws. The shareholders of a corporation have inherent power to make bylaws to supplement the charter of the corporation, but the right to do so is commonly expressed by statute or in the charter of the corporation.

The bylaws are subordinate to the general law of the state, including the statute under which the corporation is formed, as well as to the charter of the corporation. Bylaws that conflict with such superior authority or which are in themselves unreasonable are invalid. (See p. 725, Yager Case) Bylaws that are valid are binding upon all shareholders regardless of whether they know of the existence of those bylaws or were among the majority which consented to their adoption. Bylaws are not binding upon third persons, however, unless they have notice or knowledge of them.

(5) Borrowing Money. Corporations have the implied power to borrow money in carrying out their authorized business purposes. Statutes frequently prohibit corporations from raising the defense of usury.

(6) Execution of Commercial Paper. The power to issue or indorse negotiable instruments, or to accept drafts, is implied when the corporation has the power to borrow money and when such means

---

[1] American Bar Association Model Business Corporation Act, Sec. 7.

are appropriate and ordinarily used to further the authorized objectives of the corporation. (See p. 727, Burnett's Lumber Co. & Supply Co. Case)

(7) Bonds. A corporation, having the power to borrow money, has the implied power to issue various types of bonds.

(8) Transferring Property. The corporate property may be leased, assigned for the benefit of creditors, or sold. In many states, however, a solvent corporation may not transfer all of its property except with the consent of all or a substantial majority of its shareholders. In any case, the sale must be for a fair price. (See p. 728, Baron Case) A corporation, having power to incur debts, may mortgage or pledge its property as security for those debts. This rule does not apply to franchises of public service companies, such as street railways or gas and electric companies.

(9) Acquisition of Property. Although the power to acquire and hold property is usually given in the charter, a corporation always has the implied power to acquire and hold such property as is reasonably necessary for carrying out its express powers. In some states the power of a corporation to hold property is restricted as to the method of acquiring it or is limited as to the quantity or the value of the property or the period of time for which it may be held. Restrictions on holding real estate are also imposed upon corporations by the constitutions of some states. (See p. 729, Oklahoma v. International Paper Co.)

Under modern corporation codes a corporation may generally acquire the stock of other corporations. The stock-owning company may own such a percentage of the shares of another company that it controls the latter's operations. In such a case the first company is commonly called a *holding company.* Sometimes it is organized solely for the purpose of controlling other companies called *operating* or *subsidiary companies.*

If the holding company is merely a device to coordinate different phases of an economic activity, the holding company is a proper device. If its object is to eliminate competition between the operating companies whose stock is held, it may be illegal under state or federal antitrust laws. If a holding company that operates in interstate commerce holds stock of public utility companies, it may be ordered dissolved when it is found by the Securities and Exchange Commission to serve no economically useful purpose. It is no objection, however, that the subsidiary company engages in a business in which the holding company could not lawfully engage. (See p. 731, Connecticut General Life Insurance Co. Case)

(10) Acquisition of Own Stock. Generally a corporation may purchase its own stock, if it is solvent at the time and the purchase is made from surplus so that capital is not impaired. In a few states corporations are denied implied power to purchase their own stock, but are permitted to receive it as a gift, in payment of a debt, or for the security of a debt.

Stock that is reacquired by the corporation that issued it is commonly called *treasury stock.* Ordinarily, the treasury stock is regarded as still being issued or outstanding stock. As such, the shares are not subject to the rule that original shares cannot be issued for less than par.

Although treasury stock retains the character of outstanding stock, it has an inactive status while it is held by the corporation. Thus the treasury shares cannot be voted nor can dividends be declared on them.

(11) Business in Another State. A corporation has the inherent power and generally is expressly authorized to engage in business in other states. This grant of power by the incorporating state does not exempt the corporation, however, from satisfying the restrictions imposed by the foreign state in which it seeks to do business.

Sec. 49-B. Limitations on Corporate Powers. If a power is expressly prohibited to a corporation, the corporation cannot exercise that power. In addition, certain other powers cannot be implied and therefore cannot be exercised in the absence of express authorization. It is generally held that there is no implied power to lend credit, to enter a partnership, to consolidate, or to merge.

Sec. 49-C. Ultra Vires Acts. Any act that goes beyond the powers which the corporation can lawfully exercise is an *ultra vires act.* Such an act is improper because it is a violation of the obligation of the corporation to the state in that a power not granted has been exercised. It is also improper with respect to shareholders and creditors of the corporation because corporate funds have been diverted to unauthorized uses.

(1) Ultra Vires Acts and Illegality Distinguished. Although it is not lawful for a corporation to perform ultra vires acts, the objection to the commission of such acts is distinct from the objection of illegality. In the case of illegality the act would be wrong regardless of the nature of the person or the association committing it. The fact that an act is ultra vires merely means that this particular corporation does not have permission from the state to do the act. Thus it would ordinarily be beyond the powers of a business corporation, and therefore ultra vires, to engage in a charitable enterprise, such as the building of a church or college. But the activity would hardly be termed illegal.

(2) Effect of Ultra Vires Contracts. There is some conflict in the law as to the effect of an ultra vires act. Under the Model Business Corporation Act, ultra vires cannot be raised to attack the validity of any act, contract, or transfer of property,[2] except as noted under heading (3) below.

In the absence of statute, most courts recognize ultra vires as a defense but refuse to apply it in a particular case if it would be inequitable and work a hardship. The courts also refuse to recognize it as a defense against the holder of a commercial paper or negotiable instrument on which the corporation has, without authority, been an accomodation party. Likewise, a transfer or real or personal property cannot be set aside on the ground that it is ultra vires. Here the object of the law is to preserve the security of titles even though the result is to permit the wrongful act of the corporation to stand.

In most states, if the ultra vires contract has been completely performed, neither party can rescind the contract on the ground that it was originally ultra vires. Conversely, if neither party to the ultra vires contract has performed his part, the court will neither enforce the contract nor hold either party liable for a breach of the contract.

(3) Remedies for Ultra Vires Acts. In all states (a) a stockholder may obtain an injunction to stop the board of directors or other persons involved from entering into an ultra vires transaction; (b) the corporation or a stockholder acting on behalf of the corporation may sue the persons who made or approved the contract to recover damages for the loss caused the corporation by the ultra vires act; and (c) an action may be brought by the attorney general of the state to revoke the charter on the ground of its serious or repeated violation.

Cases for Chapter 49

Yager v. American Life Insurance Association
44 N.J.S. 575, 131 A.2d 312 (1957)

Yager was a member of the American Life Insurance Assn., an incorporated fraternal benefit society. In his application he agreed that he was bound by the existing bylaws and future bylaws of the corporation. At that time the bylaws permitted payment of weekly sick benefits only if the member "had need of at least two treatments weekly," but made "exceptions . . . in such cases, which, . . . do not require two treatments weekly." This bylaw was thereafter amended to exclude benefits "for any period . . . while the insured did not receive at least two treatments from the attending physician." Thereafter Yager became ill. During the first two weeks of his illness he was attended by a physician more than two times a week and the corporation paid him sick benefits. The doctor then decided that one

---

[2] ABA MBCA Sec. 6.

treatment a week was sufficient and continued to treat him once a week for ten weeks. The corporation refused to pay benefits for these ten weeks because of its bylaw. Yager sued the corporation. From a judgment in his favor, the corporation appealed.

JAYNE, J.A.D. . . . The fundamental question addressed to us by the present appeal is whether an [amendment] subsequent to the admission of the plaintiff to membership, imposing unqualifiedly the requirement of two medical treatments weekly to entitle the member to sick benefits, is valid. . . .

The certificate confers upon the member . . . a type of insurance.

A retrospective survey of the subject reveals historically that the so-called mutual benefit societies were originally organized principally to inculcate and promote the spirit of fraternity, benevolence, and charity amongst their members. Soon thereafter such societies additionally introduced to their membership sickness and burial benefits, and in many cases a form of life insurance, at an exceedingly moderate and inadequate premium cost. Experience forewarned them of the imprudence of that pursuit in defiance of sound actuarial principles, and financial losses gravely threatened them.

It was in such an exigency that the news spread, and quite universally the societies recognized the stern realities of economic forces and resorted to the use of the open contract clause in their certificates which provided that members would be bound by amendments to bylaws adopted subsequent to the date of their admission to membership.

Conflicting and complex considerations were immediately implicated. On the one side was the undeniable fact that the unbusinesslike practices of the societies in this field would inevitably guide them toward insolvency, while on the other hand to diminish or otherwise circumscribe the availability of existing benefit payments would visit an apparent injustice on the older members who, in numerous instances, had continuously paid their assessments over a long span of time. . . .

Our own courts . . . have adhered to the view that benefit certificates of this nature and import confer a vested interest upon the member which may not be impaired by a subsequent amendment, even though the power to amend be reserved in general terms, and that the subsequent alteration to have validity must be reasonable and be adopted in furtherance of the contractual right. . . .

In construing these conditional provisions, it is of material significance to recognize their basic object and purpose and rationalize from that point of view. Seemingly the paramount object is to guard the society against false or fraudulent claims, . . . to establish the good faith of the claim. . . . The attendance and treatment of a physician is

evidentiary of the sincerity and merit of the claim where those qualifying elements are in doubt. A practical and intelligent rather than a
strictly literal operative effect should be ascribed to a conditional
requirement of this signification according to the circumstances. . . .

A bylaw obliging the member of the society, in order to avoid a
forfeiture of his sick benefits in such circumstances, to have his physician needlessly administer to him . . . twice weekly is unreasonable,
if not fantastic and absurd. The courts are disinclined to enforce the
performance of futile acts, useless things, and idle formalities. . . .
It is the sickness in fact for which the benefits are accorded. Where
the intended reason for the application of such a conditional clause
disappears, its legal effectiveness vanishes with it. . . .

It has been said many times that our courts in the application of
the rules and principles of law cannot be insensible to the factual
surroundings of the particular case. The law must be recognized as
a living organism that moves in response to the dictates of reason
and justice.

[Judgment for plaintiff affirmed.]

Burnett's Lumber & Supply Co. v. Commercial Credit Corp.
211 Miss. 53, 51 So.2d 54 (1951)

Burnett's Lumber & Supply Co., which was incorporated to engage in
a wholesale and retail lumber business, owned three used trucks and a
trailer. The corporation sold the trucks on a conditional sales contract in
exchange for promissory notes, all of which the corporation assigned with
recourse to the Commercial Credit Corp. When the latter corporation sued
the lumber corporation, the defense was raised that the lumber corporation
had no authority to enter into such a transaction or to transfer the notes
and contracts with recourse. From a judgment for the plaintiff, the defendant appealed.

HALL, J. . . . It is here contended that the act of the corporation
in acquiring and selling this equipment and in assigning and indorsing the paper with recourse is [beyond its powers] and not binding
upon it. Appellant [lumber corporation] was engaged in a general
wholesale and retail lumber and supply business and under the . . .
provisions of its charter was fully authorized to transact any business which was incidental to its general corporate purposes. "A corporation may have implied power not only to acquire or purchase
personal chattels, but also to take choses in action which are transferable by assignment; and it may itself become the payee of commercial paper, bonds, etc., for indebtedness owing to it unless in
the pursuit of its authorized business there is no necessity for so
doing.". . . "A corporation has full power to alienate its property
both real and personal unless restricted by its charter, statute, or

considerations of public policy. The implied power of a corporation to alienate its property extends to commercial paper and other choses in action which are transferable by indorsement or assignment." . . . "An express grant is not necessary to confer upon a corporation the power, in the legitimate transaction of its business, to become a drawer, acceptor, or indorser of a bill of exchange or to become a party to any other negotiable paper. This power is generally implied in the case of a business corporation as a necessary incident of its express powers. Such power is, for example, incident to the power of a corporation to borrow money or incur indebtedness.". . . "It is well settled that where a corporation acquires commercial paper or bonds in the legitimate transaction of its business, it may sell them; and in furtherance of such a sale it may, in order to make them the more readily marketable, indorse or guarantee their payment.". . .

. . . We unhesitatingly hold that appellant [lumber] corporation's participation in the transaction was . . . within the implied powers granted under its corporate charter and that it is bound thereby.

[Judgment for plaintiff affirmed.]

Baron v. Pressed Metals of America
35 Del.Ch. 581, 123 A.2d 848 (1956)

The board of directors of Pressed Metals of America contracted to sell the assets of the company for approximately two and a half million dollars. The book value of the assets was approximately five million dollars. Baron, a minority stockholder of the corporation, brought an action to prevent the sale on the ground that the consideration was grossly inadequate. From a judgment against Baron, he appealed.

SOUTHERLAND, C.J. . . . If the book value be taken as indicating real value, the price is about one half of that amount. The disparity is substantial, but book value is not conclusive evidence of real value, as both sides agree. The "going concern value" is of much more importance in many cases of sales or of mergers. . . . "Going concern value" is based upon the demonstrated capacity of the corporation to earn money and pay dividends. . . . But at the time of the sale the earning capacity of the corporation was uncertain. . . .

In this case it is unnecessary to find a valuation wholly on the record of earnings. This is a case in which market value—the sum a willing purchaser would pay—is of especial importance. . . . In 1954 Pressed Metals was faced with a very serious loss of business and with serious labor troubles. The directors determined to sell the machinery, equipment, and plant. The best price they could hope to get was what someone would be willing to pay. The record shows that they made every effort to find a purchaser. . . . Three offers were made and rejected; and finally after eleven months the present offer was made. The directors negotiated a slightly better price and accepted it. "From the field of possible purchasers they took the best offer.". . . There is no suggestion that any director made any personal profit from the sale. The judgment of the directors is entitled to the presumption that it was exercised honestly and in good faith. . . .

When disparity is alleged between the value of the assets sold and the consideration received, plaintiff has the burden of showing such a gross disparity as will raise an inference of improper motives, or reckless indifference to or intentional disregard of stockholders' interests. . . .

Under the facts in this record we are of opinion that the disparity between the book value of the transferred assets and the consideration paid raises no inference of improper motives or reckless disregard of the stockholders' interests. . . .

[Judgment affirmed.]

Oklahoma v. International Paper Co.

342 P.2d 565 (Okla., 1959)

The State of Oklahoma sued the International Paper Company for the statutory penalty for unlawfully owning rural land in violation of the state constitutional provision that no corporation should own rural land "except such as shall be necessary and proper for carrying on the business for which it was chartered." The paper company claimed that the rural land it owned was being reforested by it. From a decision in the company's favor, the State appealed.

PER CURIAM. . . . [The defendant's charter authorized it, among other things to] acquire, own, occupy, use and develop and dispose of timber lands, timber, timber rights, cut-over lands, or other lands for the purpose of manufacture of lumber, timber, articles of lumber, and wood products. [The defendant claimed] that the lands in controversy were purchased and held and used for said purposes and that said lands were also owned and held for growing and producing timber under a reforesting program and that the timber therefrom has been and will be harvested and cut and converted into lumber and wood products. . . .

In Texas Company v. State ex rel. Coryell, 198 Okla. 565, 180 P.2d 631, 632, this court . . . said: "The words 'necessary and proper' used in the Constitution as expressive of the extent of the right of a corporation to acquire and hold land, do not import that which is indispensably necessary , but do import that which is proper, useful, and suitable and thus conducive to the accomplishment of the purposes of the corporation, which implies actual need therefor in contradistinction to mere preference.". . .

In the case now before us the evidence reflects the source of supply
of timber for lumber, poles, and pulp for paper has for some years
past been decreasing to the point where companies engaged in that
business have, in order to assure a constant supply of timber, been
compelled to engage in a program of reforesting on cut-over and other
suitable lands and for that purpose have acquired considerable tracts
of land; that an assured constant and sufficient supply of timber is
required before such concerns can justify expenditure of large sums
of money for the construction of processing plants for the carrying on
of the business for which such companies were formed and to supply
the demand for wood and paper products; that a period of time from
40 to 70 years is required to establish and bring to rotation a reforesting program complete with cutting and replacement and therefore requires the acquisition of [land] to assure a uniform and efficient
program and operation. . . .

The . . . acquisition of the [land] was . . . proper, useful, and suitable, and thus conducive to the proper carrying on of a lawful enterprise within the legitimate purposes provided for in the articles in
incorporation. . . .

[Judgment for defendant affirmed.]

BERRY, J., dissenting. . . . The ownership of land by corporations
tend[s] to create a perpetuity and thereby give corporations special
privileges not enjoyed by all; tend[s] to permit concentration of wealth
in the hands of a few and . . . to take real estate off the market and
thus prevent[s] individuals from acquiring [it] for use [as] homes. . . .

This Court, in Texas Co. v. State ex rel. Coryell, 198 Okla. 565,
570, 180 P.2d 631, 636, made this observation: "It is manifest from
the quoted debates that there was a determination to prevent corporate
ownership of farm lands because it was deemed to be inimical to home
ownership and to promote tenancy in the farming class. . . ."

The rationale of the majority opinion is such as to permit a corporation to own any given number of acres of land and minerals
underlying the land for any purpose irrespective of the character of
the land, provided ownership of the land and minerals is within the
framework of the corporation's charter. Therefore, that a corporation
can properly own and farm any given number of acres of agricultural
land. . . . The majority opinion is directly contrary to the proposition
heretofore recognized by this Court that the purpose of the cited
Constitutional provision and vitalizing legislation [is] "to prevent corporate ownership of farm lands (lands which could be used as homes)
because it was inimical to home ownership." . . .

If the people or the Legislature had intended to say that the
ownership of land by corporations was only prohibited where such
ownership was without the corporation's charter powers, then it would

have been a very easy task to have briefly so stated in the Constitutional provision and vitalizing legislation, and the considerable verbiage that was used in said Constitutional provision and vitalizing legislation would not have been used. . . . The purpose of said law was to preserve agricultural land for homes and deny it for vast commercial undertakings. . . . The pertinent language of the Constitution . . . that "except such as shall be necessary and proper for carrying on the business for which it was chartered or licensed" must be construed as excluding the ownership of rural land that can be used as homes except where the use is for office-building sites, warehouse sites, railroad right-of-ways, etc. . . .

This construction is in keeping with and not contrary to the construction that has been placed on the Constitutional provision and vitalizing statutes enacted pursuant thereto since the advent of Statehood. If the referred-to law is a remnant of the ox cart or horse-and-buggy age, it is the province of the people or the Legislature to change the law. . . .

[WILLIAMS, V.C.J., and BLACKBIRD and IRVIN, JJ., concurred in the dissent.]

Connecticut General Life Insurance Co. v. Superintendent of Insurance

10 N.Y.2d 42, 176 N.E.2d 63 (1961)

Connecticut General Life Insurance Co. is a Connecticut insurance company which obtained a license to write life insurance policies in New York. It thereafter proposed to acquire 80 per cent or more of the common stock of the National Fire Insurance Co. of Hartford, a fire and casualty insurance company licensed to write policies in New York. The New York State Superintendent of Insurance brought an action for a declaratory judgment to have the Connecticut company prohibited from writing life policies in New York if it acquired such stock because, through its subsidiary, it would then be writing fire and casualty insurance in New York. From a decision in favor of the Superintendent, the insurance company appealed.

FOSTER, J. . . . Undoubtedly [the New York statutes] forbid a foreign life insurance company licensed in this State from engaging in the business of writing fire or casualty insurance. . . . The real issue involved in this case is whether or not, by purchasing controlling interest in a fire or casualty company, the parent life insurance company actually is engaging in that business. . . . As appellant [insurance company] appropriately points out, the Legislature, in the Insurance Law, has used express language to prohibit certain activity through or by subsidiaries when that was its intention. [The Court then listed the specific sections of the statute expressly applying to holding companies and subsidiaries.]

The Insurance Law is replete with additional express references to subsidiaries and affiliates. . . . From these . . . and from the absence of express references to subsidiaries in [the sections here applicable], we may infer properly that the Legislature did not intend that the limitations [here applicable] be extended by implication to cover parent-subsidiary situations. This is a well-established canon of statutory construction. . . .

Such a construction, of course, is consistent with the general rule . . . that in no legal sense can the business of a corporation be said to be that of its stockholders . . . or the business of a subsidiary corporation be said to be that of a parent. . . . It is consistent also with the settled rule that a subsidiary corporation may engage in a business forbidden to its parent, unless the subsidiary entity is used as a cloak to cover for fraud or illegality. . . . On this issue we agree with the dissent below that the Superintendent may not presuppose, "without justification, that the plaintiff will utilize a fire or casualty subsidiary as a mere agent or tool to evade the provisions of said sections," and that "We are bound to assume that the mandate of the statute will be respected and that a subsidiary or plaintiff doing a fire or casualty business will carry on in the usual way, namely, as an independent corporate entity." Appellant, in seeking to purchase a controlling interest in a fire insurance company, admittedly desires to improve its competitive position, and to enable its agents to offer to the public both life insurance and casualty and fire insurance. This does not, as the Superintendent argues, mean that appellant desires to engage in the fire or casualty insurance business. If the time comes that appellant, through the guise of a subsidiary, actually engages in that business, that will be time enough to refuse to renew appellant's license.

No public policy would be offended by consummation of the proposed acquisition. Appellant's admitted assets, capital, and surplus apparently are sufficient to insure against insolvency and to protect policyholders in this State. . . .

[Judgment reversed.]

DESMOND, C.J., (dissenting) . . . . The majority opinion says: "No public policy would be offended by consummation of the proposed acquisition." We think this State's policy of protecting the trustheld funds of life insurers from any and all diversions is plain, compelling, and essential and that it positively forbids what petitioner is trying to do. . . .

A life insurance company holds its policyholders' funds in trust for the protection of their beneficiaries against want. Those trust funds, conservatively and prudently invested to serve the high trust purpose on the happening of the inevitable event insured against, should not be subjected even in the most remote way to the hazards of other kinds of insurance. Nor should the life insurer's trusteed funds be, by investment in other insurance stocks, indirectly subjected to the other company's less restrictive investment policies. If any further explanation of the public policy is sought, it can be found in the Armstrong Committee Reports of 1906 (see Vol. 10, p. 385 et seq.) which described the life insurance companies of that day as transacting through stock ownership "the business of banks and trust companies," reminded us of the life companies' duty of conservatism in investment, rejected the idea that life companies should be allowed to make more money by speculation, and warned that a life insurer which gets control of companies in other business will end up by managing those other companies and thus engaging in their separate businesses. . . .

[DYE and BURKE, JJ., concur in the dissent.]

Questions and Case Problems

1. What is the objective of each of the following rules of law?
    (a) In some states the defense of ultra vires cannot be raised in a suit between the corporation and the person with whom the ultra vires contract was made.
    (b) Corporations are persons within the constitutional protection of the life, liberty, and property of "persons."

2. The Columbia Chemical Co. was incorporated under the laws of New York for the purpose of manufacturing and selling chemicals. Thereafter a group of persons filed incorporation papers in the same state for an organization with the name of Columbian Chemical Co. It was contended that the second company had no right to adopt such a name. Do you agree? (New York v. O'Brien, 101 App.Div. 296, 91 N.Y.S. 649)

3. The Philadelphia Electric Co. was incorporated "for the purpose of supplying heating, lighting, and power by electricity to the public." The company supplied electricity but in addition began to sell electrical appliances. An action of quo warranto was brought by the attorney general against the corporation to forfeit its charter for engaging in ultra vires acts. Decide. (Commonwealth of Pennsylvania ex rel. Baldridge, Attorney General v. Philadelphia Electric Co., 300 Pa. 577, 151 A. 344)

4. The Plymouth Gold Mining Co., a corporation, agreed to purchase 4,000 shares of its own stock from Porter and Swan for $2,000. Thereafter it refused to accept and pay for the stock as agreed. In an action brought by Porter and Swan against the corporation, it was contended that a corporation has no implied power to purchase its own stock. Do you agree? (Porter v. Plymouth Gold Mining Co., 29 Mont. 347, 74 P. 938)

5. The H & R Construction Corporation entered into a contract for construction work, and the Seaboard Surety Co. executed a bond assuring that the contract would be performed. The Seaboard Surety Co. was required to pay damages when the contractor did not perform the contract.

It then sued the construction corporation and also the H. C. Nelson Investment Co. to recover the money it had so paid. Its suit against the Nelson Investment Co. was based on the theory that the construction corporation and the investment company were partners. Was there a partnership? (Nelson v. Seaboard Surety Co., [C.A. 8th] 262 F.2d 189)

6. An employee of the Archer Pancoast Co., a corporation, was killed as the result of falling through a hatchway in a building occupied by the company as a factory. Hoffman, superintendent of the factory, called Noll, an undertaker, and arranged for the funeral. Hoffman agreed to pay Noll $100 for his services. After performing the work, Noll brought an action against the Archer Pancoast Co. to recover the agreed sum. The defendant raised the defense of ultra vires. Decide. (Noll v. Archer Pancoast Co., 60 App.Div. 414, 69 N.Y.S. 1007)

7. The Louisville & Nashville Railroad Co. was incorporated in Kentucky as a common carrier. It entered into a contract with Lovejoy by which he was granted the exclusive right to display advertisements on the railroad's boxcars. Lovejoy assigned the contract to the National Car Advertising Co. Later when the railroad company refused to comply with the terms of the agreement, the advertising company brought an action for damages. Decide. (National Advertising Co. v. Louisville & Nashville Railroad Co., 110 Va. 413, 66 S.E. 88)

8. A bylaw of the Coleman Realty Co. provided that the corporation could not sell its stock to a person not a stockholder without first offering to sell it at its book value to the corporation or to the remaining stockholders in proportion to their interests. This bylaw was later repealed at a stockholders' meeting by the vote of Mrs. Ludgate who owned a majority of the stock. Bechtold, a minority stockholder, brought an action to declare that the repeal of the bylaw was invalid and had no effect. Was the repeal of the bylaw effective? (Bechtold v. Coleman Realty Co., 367 Pa. 208, 79 A.2d 661)

9. The Fountain-Head Railroad Co. made an agreement by which it subscribed to stock of the Knoxville and Fountain City Land Co. McCampbell, a stockholder of the Fountain-Head Railroad Co., brought an action against the railroad, contending that it had no implied power to make such a contract. Was this contention sound? (McCampbell v. Fountain-Head Railroad Co., 111 Tenn. 55, 77 S.W. 1070)

10. The Central Mutual Auto Insurance Co. was a Michigan corporation. A foreign corporation, the Central Mutual Insurance Co., was granted a license to do business in Michigan. Central Mutual Auto Insurance Co. brought an action to prevent the foreign corporation from doing business within Michigan under that name. Decide. (Central Mutual Auto Insurance Co. v. Central Mutual Insurance Co., 275 Mich. 554, 267 N.W. 733)

11. In an action by the Federal Savings State Bank as the holder of a note against Grimes, the maker of the note, the authority of the corporate payee, the Industrial Mutual Life Insurance Co., to accept the note from the maker was questioned. It was argued that the corporate payee possessed the power because there was no statute expressly prohibiting the exercise of that power. Was this argument valid? (Federal Savings State Bank v. Grimes, 156 Kan. 55, 131 P.2d 894)

CHAPTER 50

Corporate Stock

Membership in a corporation is usually based upon ownership of one or more shares of stock of the corporation. Each share represents a fractional interest in the total property possessed by the corporation. It confers the right to receive the dividends, when declared, and the right to participate in a distribution of capital upon the dissolution of the corporation. The shareholder does not own or have an interest in any specific property of the corporation; the corporation is the owner of all of its property.

Sec. 50-A. Certificate of Stock. The corporation ordinarily issues a *certificate of stock* as evidence of the shareholder's ownership of stock. Although the issuance of such certificates is not essential either to the existence of a corporation or to the ownership of its stock, it is an almost universal practice since it is a convenient method of proving ownership and since it makes transfer of ownership easier. Any form that identifies the interest owned by a person in a particular corporation is sufficient.

The Model Business Corporation Act requires that the certificate include (1) the state of incorporation; (2) the name of the person to whom issued; (3) the number and the class of shares represented and the designation of the series, if any; (4) the par value of each share or a statement that there is no par value; and (5) if there is more than one class of shares, a summary of the rights or restrictions of each class.[1] By virtue of statutes,[2] ownership of the certificate is essential

---

[1] American Bar Association Model Business Corporation Act, Sec. 21. The issuance of a certificate until the shares represented by it have been paid in full is prohibited.

[2] The statutes applicable to the transfer of share certificates are the Uniform Commercial Code (Article 8) and the Uniform Stock Transfer Act. The Stock Transfer Act is in force in all states that have not adopted the Code and in the District of Columbia in either its original form or with amendments. The Code Article is broader in scope than the Stock Transfer Act in that the Code also governs corporate bearer bonds, which were formerly governed by the Uniform Negotiable Instruments Law, and registered bonds and other types of investment paper, which were not covered by any uniform act. As to the states that have adopted the Code, see p. 51.

to owning an interest in the corporation, and the shareholder's interest cannot be fully transferred without transferring the certificate.

Sec. 50-B. Kinds of Stock. Certain definite varieties of stock have through usage acquired their particular names, such as common stock and preferred stock. Sometimes a corporation may issue two or more classes of the same kind of stock, such as "preferred stock A" and "preferred stock B," or "first preferred" and "second preferred."

(1) Common Stock. Common stock is ordinary stock. Each share of common stock entitles the holder to one vote and to a share of the profits in the form of dividends, when declared, and to participate in the distribution of capital upon dissolution of the corporation.

(2) Preferred Stock. Preferred stock has a priority over common stock with respect to dividends. Thus shares of "6% preferred stock of $100 par value" means that the holders of such shares are entitled to receive annual dividends of $6 for each share before any dividends are paid to the holders of the common stock. Preferred stock may also have a priority over common stock in the distribution of capital upon dissolution of the corporation. Preferred stock is ordinarily nonvoting.

(a) CUMULATIVE PREFERRED STOCK. Ordinarily the right to receive dividends is contingent upon the declaration of dividends by the board of directors for that particular period of time. If there is no fund from which the dividends may be declared or if the directors do not declare them from an available fund, the shareholder has no right to dividends.

In the absence of a statement that the right to dividends is noncumulative, it is frequently held that preferred stock has the right to cumulate dividends, particularly with respect to each year in which there was a surplus available for dividend declaration.

(b) PARTICIPATING PREFERRED STOCK. Sometimes the preferred stock is given the right of participation. For example, after the common shares receive dividends or a capital distribution equal to that first received by the preferred shares, thereafter both kinds share equally in the balance.

Sec. 50-C. Capital and Capital Stock.

(1) Capital. *Capital* refers to the net assets of the corporation. It signifies the actual worth, whether in money or property, of the corporation. It is the aggregate of the sums subscribed and paid in by the shareholders, together with all gains or profits arising from the business, less losses that have been incurred.

(2) Capital Stock. *Capital stock* refers to the declared money value of the outstanding shares of the corporation. Thus in a corporation

that has issued 1,000 shares of $100 par value, the capital stock of the corporation would be $100,000.

Sec. 50-D. Valuation of Stock.

(1) Par Value. Corporate stock commonly has a specified *par value*. This means that the person subscribing to the stock and acquiring it from the corporation must pay that amount. Shares are frequently issued with no par value. In such a case no amount is stated in the certificate, and the amount that the subscriber pays the corporation is determined by the board of directors.

(2) Book Value. The value found by dividing the value of the corporate assets by the number of shares outstanding is the *book value* of the shares.

(3) Market Value. The *market value* of a share of stock is the price at which it can be voluntarily bought or sold.

Sec. 50-E. Acquisition of Shares. Shares of stock may be acquired by (1) subscription, either before or after the corporation is organized, or (2) transfer of existing shares from a shareholder or from the corporation.

(1) Subscription. A *subscription* is a contract or agreement to purchase a specific number and kind of shares of stock when they are issued.

(a) FORMALITY. By the great weight of authority, a contract to subscribe for shares of a corporation not yet formed or for unissued shares of stock of an existing corporation is not within the Statute of Frauds and therefore need not be in writing. In contrast, a contract for the transfer of existing corporate shares comes within the Statute of Frauds.[3]

Apart from the Statute of Frauds, no particular formality is ordinarily required for a subscription to stock. Occasionally, however, a special statute requires a writing for a stock subscription, or stipulates that the subscription be accompanied by a cash payment or that the original subscribers sign the articles of incorporation.

(b) SUBSCRIPTION BEFORE ORGANIZATION. Many subscriptions are made prior to incorporation. In most states the corporation must expressly or impliedly accept the subscription before the subscriber is bound. Unless this is done, the subscription is regarded as an offer to the corporation to be formed; and the ordinary rules relating to

---

[3] Uniform Commercial Code, Sec. 8-319. In non-Code states the Statute of Frauds provisions applicable to the sales of personal property are applied to the sale of shares of stock.

offers apply. A few states hold that such subscriptions automatically become binding contracts when the organization has been completed.

The Model Business Corporation Act declares that, unless otherwise provided in the subscription agreement, or unless all the subscribers consent thereto, the preorganization subscription shall be irrevocable for the period of six months.[4] As in the case of any contract there may be a rescission upon proper grounds.

(c) SUBSCRIPTION AFTER ORGANIZATION. Subscriptions are also made after incorporation. In that event the transaction is like any other contract with the corporation. The offer of the subscription may come from the subscriber or from the corporation, but in either case there must be an acceptance. Upon acceptance the subscriber immediately becomes a shareholder with all the rights, privileges, and liabilities of a shareholder even though the subscriber has not paid any of the purchase price. The transaction, however, may only be a contract for the future transfer of shares rather than a present subscription. (See p. 742, Stern v. Mayer)

(d) CONDITIONS PRECEDENT. The subscription may provide that it shall be dependent upon the performance of some act or the happening of some contingency. Such a subscription, if made after incorporation, is valid, unless it is contrary to a charter or statutory provision, and the subscriber becomes a shareholder only upon the fulfillment of the condition. A conditional subscription made prior to incorporation is generally held void on the grounds that it is fraudulent as to unqualified subscribers and to creditors.

(2) Transfer of Shares. In the absence of restrictions imposed by statute, charter, bylaws, or agreement, a shareholder may transfer his shares to anyone he chooses. Restrictions on the transfer of stock are valid provided they are not unreasonable. It is valid to provide that a shareholder must give the corporation the option of purchasing his shares before he sells it to a third person. (See p. 743, Palmer v. Chamberlin)

There is a conflict of authority as to the validity of a provision that no transfer may be made of shares without the approval of the directors or the other shareholders. The trend is to sustain such a provision when the shareholders are the owner-tenants of an incorporated cooperative apartment house. In any case a restriction on transfer is interpreted in favor of transferability. For example, a restriction on the transfer by a retiring employee of the corporation was held not applicable to an employee who was discharged, and a restriction on the "sale" of shares was held not to bar a gift inter vivos or a bequest by will.

---

[4] ABA MBCA Sec. 16.

Under the Uniform Commercial Code a restriction upon the right to transfer is not valid as against a purchaser of the certificate unless the restriction is conspicuously noted on the certificate or the transferee has actual knowledge of the restriction.[5]

The transfer of shares may be absolute, that is, it may divest all ownership and make the transferee the full owner, or it may be merely for security, as when stock is pledged to secure the repayment of a loan. Since it is an essential element of a pledge transaction that the pledgee be able to sell the pledged property upon default, a pledge of stock requires the delivery to the pledgee of the stock certificate together with a separate assignment of or indorsement on the stock certificate in favor of the pledgee or bearer. When this is done, the pledgee will be able to transfer title to the shares in case of default.

Directors and officers of a corporation may purchase the stock held by shareholders of the corporation. It is generally held that in so doing, they purchase at arm's length and are not required to disclose to the shareholders facts known to them by virtue of their position which might affect the value of the shares. Exceptions to this rule are made when special facts are present, such as the concealment by the director of his identity.

(a) MECHANICS OF TRANSFER. The ownership of shares is transferred by the delivery of the certificate of stock indorsed by its owner in blank, or to a specified person, or by the delivery of the certificate by such person accompanied by a separate assignment or power of attorney executed by him.[6] A transfer made in this manner is effective as between the parties even though the corporate charter or bylaws specify that shares cannot be transferred until a transfer is made on the books of the corporation or the records of a corporate transfer agent.

Possession of the certificate is also essential to an involuntary transfer by execution of judicial process, and no attachment or levy upon shares of stock for which a certificate is outstanding is valid unless the certificate is actually seized by the officer making the attachment or levy.[7]

(b) NEGOTIABILITY. Under the common law the transferee of shares of stock had no greater right than the transferor because the certificate and the shares represented by the certificate were nonnegotiable. By statute, the common-law rule has been changed by imparting negotiability to the certificate and giving to the purchaser of the

---

[5] UCC Sec. 8-204. The USTA Sec. 15 requires the notation on the certificate, but the decisions thereunder are conflictifing as to the effect of actual knowledge of an unnoted restriction.

[6] UCC Sec. 8-309, USTA Sec. 1. The second alternative of a delivery of an unindorsed certificate is designed to keep the certificate "clean," as when the transfer is for a temporary or special purpose as in the case of a pledge of the certificate as security for a loan.

[7] UCC Sec. 8-317, USTA Secs. 13, 14.

certificate an absolute title to the shares if he pays value for the certificate and acts in good faith.[8]

In addition, just as various defenses cannot be asserted against the holder in due course of a commercial paper or negotiable instrument, it is provided that similar defenses cannot be raised against the person acquiring the certificate in good faith and for value. As against such a person, the defenses cannot be raised that his transferor did not own the shares, that he did not have authority to deliver the certificate, or that the transfer was made in violation of a restriction upon transfer not known to such person and not set forth in the certificate. A former owner cannot object as against a subsequent purchaser for value in good faith that his transferee obtained the certificate from him by fraud, duress, mistake, or did not give him any consideration.[9]

This concept of negotiability is also extended to liens of the corporation upon the stock. Although modern statutes commonly give the corporation a lien upon stock for a debt owed it by the shareholder, the corporation cannot assert a lien against a purchaser of the share unless the right of the corporation to the lien is noted conspicuously on the certificate.[10]

(c) TRANSFER AS AFFECTING CORPORATION. Until there is a transfer on the books in accordance with a lawful requirement, the corporation is entitled to treat as the owner the person whose name is on the books.[11] The corporation may properly refuse to recognize the transferee when the corporation is given notice or has knowledge that the transfer is void or in breach of trust. In such case the corporation properly refuses to effect a transfer until the rights of the parties have been determined.

The corporation may also refuse to register the transfer of shares when the outstanding certificate is not surrendered to it, in the absence of satisfactory proof that it had been lost, destroyed, or stolen. (See p. 744, Reynolds v. Reynolds)

Sec. 50-F. Protection for the Public.

(1) Blue-Sky Laws. In order to protect the public from the sale of securities of nonexistent or worthless corporations, many states have adopted regulations called *blue-sky laws.* The statutes vary greatly in detail. Some impose a criminal penalty for engaging in fraudulent practices, while others require the licensing of dealers in securities and approval by a government commission before a given security can be sold to the public. (See p. 746, Davis v. Walker)

---

[8] UCC Secs. 8-301, 8-315; USTA Sec. 7.
[9] UCC Secs. 8-301, 8-311, 8-315; USTA Secs. 4 to 8, 15.
[10] UCC Sec. 8-103. Similar provision is made by USTA Sec. 15.
[11] UCC Sec. 8-207, USTA Sec. 3.

(2) Federal Securities Act. The state blue-sky laws are subject to the very important limitation that they can apply only to intrastate transactions and cannot apply to sales made in interstate commerce. To meet this defect, the Federal Securities Act of 1933 was adopted. This act declares it unlawful for any issuer, underwriter, or dealer in securities to send either the securities or a prospectus for them through interstate commerce or in the mails without having first registered the issue with Securities and Exchange Commission. The effect of registration is to provide a full and adequate disclosure of information of which private investors may then avail themselves. The registration is not an approval of the security by the Commission or by the government, nor any guaranty of the safety of the investment. The act does not apply to the ordinary sale and purchase of stock by private individuals, nor does it apply to security issues under $100,000.

(3) Federal Securities Exchange Act. In addition to the evils connected with the issuing and floating of securities, a number of evils were due to practices at security exchanges. The Federal Securities Exchange Act of 1934 declares it unlawful for any broker, dealer, or exchange, directly or indirectly, to make use of the mails or any means of communication for the purpose of using the facilities of an exchange to effect any transaction in a security, unless such exchange is registered as a national securities exchange with the Securities and Exchange Commission or unless it is exempt from registration.

Various practices that were used in market manipulation are declared unlawful and prohibited by the act. Wash sales, matched orders, and circulation of false rumors and tips are made unlawful and prohibited. These devices attempt to create the impression of great trading activity in a particular stock, thus tending to increase the price that the public is willing to pay for it.

Other practices that can be used either for a lawful trading or an unlawful manipulating purpose are not prohibited by the act but are subject to the regulation of the Securities and Exchange Commission so that the Commission may see that they are used for a legitimate purpose. Speculative activity on exchanges is restricted by giving the Board of Governors of the Federal Reserve System power to fix the margin on which trading can be conducted and to restrict the extent to which money can be borrowed to finance stock transactions.

Control of corporations by insiders is checked to some extent by the act by requiring that solicitations for proxies state the identity and interest of the solicitor and what action is to be passed upon at the corporate meeting for which the proxy is solicited. Corporate insiders are also prohibited under certain circumstances from making a profit on the basis of information that they have but that the general public could not have.

(4) Later Federal Regulations. Later statutes provide for the registration of interstate utility holding companies with the Securities and Exchange Commission and authorize the Federal Power Commission to regulate the rates on interstate shipments of natural gas and electric power. In registering, the holding company must file detailed information concerning its corporate structure and financing.

Authority is given to the Securities and Exchange Commission to order the dissolution of holding companies that have been created merely for the purpose of corporate manipulation. If a holding company does not register as required by law, it is illegal for it to engage in any interstate business transactions. A holding company that has registered is subject to various restrictions as to financing and security issues, and the Commission is given supervisory powers over the company's financial records.

Cases for Chapter 50

Stern v. Mayer

166 Minn. 346, 207 N.W. 737 (1926)

Mayer made an agreement with the U. S. I. Realty Co. by which he was to receive five shares of stock upon payment of a specified sum. The agreement was set down in a printed "Application for Stock" in which Mayer stated "I hereby subscribe" and the corporation stated "The company accepts the subscription. . . ." The company became bankrupt; and Stern, its trustee in bankruptcy, sued Mayer for the unpaid balance on the stock. From a judgment for the defendant, the plaintiff appealed.

WILSON, C.J. . . . The important question is whether this writing is to be considered as a subscription to capital stock or a contract for the sale and purchase of shares of such stock. . . . Ordinarily, subscriptions to capital stock of a corporation are mutual agreements to take shares made upon the formation of a corporation. Yet the term is often applied to [agreements to] take stock entered into with the corporation itself after its formation. . . . If the instrument is a . . . subscription for stock, . . . the subscriber has the status of a stockholder. . . .

. . . The general rule is that the execution and delivery of the certificate are not conditions precedent to the liability of a subscriber to stock on his subscription or to calls or an action thereon by the corporation, unless the contract of subscription expressly requires a tender of certificate as a condition precedent to liability thereon. In this case the corporation has agreed to issue and deliver the stock when its purchase price is paid. It may, notwithstanding this reservation, be a subscription. The presence of such reservation is a circumstance indicative of a sale rather than a subscription. Whichever it may be, the complaint must plead that [the corporation] is able and willing to perform. In other words, where the contract in a stock subscription provides for delivery of stock when paid for, the acts must be regarded as contemporaneous. In such case the corporation's inability to perform should disable it from enforcement against the subscriber, although he may, by virtue of the terms of his contract, be a stockholder. . . .

. . . The wording of the contract that the corporation "agrees to issue and deliver the stock when the amount paid with interest" shall equal the price of the stock is explicit. The language of the instrument . . . leads to the inevitable conclusion that the contract is executory. . . . It would be executed upon the payment being made and the stock issued. . . . This agreement was not a subscription, but an executory contract for the sale and purchase of stock.

Is the plaintiff in a position to carry out this contract? . . . For all practical purposes the bankruptcy of a corporation is equivalent to its death. In fact, it must be held, as an implied term of every contract, that a party thereto will not permit himself, through bankruptcy, to become disabled from performance. . . .

[Judgment for defendant affirmed.]

Code Comment: The same decision would be made under the Code since it does not affect the principles of law here involved.

Palmer v. Chamberlin

191 F.2d 532 (C.A. 5th, 1951)

Palmer, Chamberlin, and others owned stock of the Graham Paper Co., a Missouri corporation. A bylaw of the corporation specified that in the event of death or severance of association with the corporation, the stock of any stockholder was to be offered to the members of the board of directors to purchase within 60 days at a valuation to be determined in the manner prescribed by the bylaws. The stock certificates contained a summary of the bylaw restriction. Palmer died and his executrix failed to offer his stock to the members of the board of directors. Chamberlin and others brought an action against Palmer's executrix to obtain specific performance of the obligation to offer the stock to the board of directors. From a judgment against the executrix, she appealed.

RIVES, C.J. . . . As is conceded, the validity of the bylaws as such would be governed by the law of Missouri, the state of incorporation. . . . Appellant [the executrix of Palmer] contends, however, that its validity when considered as a contract should be tested by the law of Louisiana where appellant claims that the decedent purchased his stock. . . . We think that the validity of the bylaw even as a contract is governed by the law of the State of Missouri. . . .

The things to be done under the contract centered in Missouri. The contract took the form of a bylaw of a Missouri corporation. That bylaw was unanimously agreed to or ratified by all of the stockholders, one hundred fifty-one in number. . . . The one-hundred fifty-one stockholders resided in various states. It was not intended that the validity and effect of the agreement should vary according to the laws of many different states, but rather that each stockholder should be alike bound. All these considerations clearly point to the intention of the stockholders that the validity and effect of the bylaw either as such or as a contract should be governed by the law of the State of Missouri. . . .

The validity of a restriction which precludes a shareholder from transferring his shares without first giving the company, or the other shareholders, an option to purchase within a limited time has often been sustained. . . .

The appellant further insists that the terms of the bylaws are against the best interests of the Company and unfair to its stockholders. Those are matters for the parties to decide for themselves. ". . . It is a matter of great public concern that freedom of contract be not lightly interfered with." . . .

What is best for their own business may safely be left to the stockholders. . . . In any event, that question is not for the Court, but for the parties to decide, unless there be such gross unfairness as to call for denial of the remedy of specific performance, and that we do not find. . . .

[Judgment affirmed.]

Code Comment: The same conclusion would be reached under the Code since it does not affect the question of when a transfer restriction is valid except to specify that it must be noted conspicuously on the certificate or the transferee must have actual knowledge of it in order for the restriction to be effective. UCC Sec. 8-204. In the Palmer case a summary of the restriction appeared on the certificate, and the executrix apparently had knowledge of the restriction since no objection was raised that the restriction was not binding because unknown to the executrix.

The same decision would be reached under the Code as to the point that the case was governed by Missouri law. UCC Secs. 1-105, 8-106.

Reynolds v. Reynolds
54 Cal.2d 669, 355 P.2d 481 (1960)

Charlotte Reynolds obtained a divorce from her husband Robert. The divorce court declared that shares of stock in certain companies held in the name of Robert were community property and decreed that Charlotte owned one half of the shares. Charlotte took the decree to the corporations and requested a new stock certificate in her name for these shares. The corporations refused to issue new certificates on the ground that the existing share certificates of Robert had not been surrendered. Charlotte then sued her husband and the corporations to compel the issuance of new certificates of stock. From judgments in her favor they appealed.

McComb, J. . . . In the early history of this state there was no requirement that certificates be issued evidencing shares of stock in a corporation. Where they were issued, their possession was not essential to the ownership of the shares, the . . . ownership of the shares being centered about the record on the corporate books. . . .

However, problems arose, particularly among assignees, pledgees, and attachment and execution creditors. As the problems multiplied, so did the demand for freer negotiability, commensurate with the developing importance of corporate investment in the national economy. . . .

In the years preceding 1931 recognition that the Corporation Law of California had become antiquated and a definite hindrance to the development of business in California as compared with other states led to a widespread demand for modernization. . . .

Consequently, the Legislature in 1931 enacted a new corporation law, with drastic changes from the old, incorporating the Uniform Stock Transfer Act with certain modifications. The key provision of the new law was that which defined, *exclusively,* the method of transferring title to corporate shares [by requiring a transfer of the certificate.] . . .

The immediate effect of the new law was that . . . ownership now centered in the stock certificates. As a result, for example, a bona fide purchaser of an endorsed stock certificate whose title was acquired even from a thief or a finder would acquire a good title to the shares. . . .

As the control of stock ownership moved away from the corporation's stock register and toward the free handling of stock certificates, business necessities demanded, and the Legislature granted, the necessary protection to the corporation. A major part of this protection, stated in section 2477 of the Corporations Code and adapted from section 13 of the Uniform Stock Transfer Act, is expressed in these simple, direct terms: "A corporation *shall not be compelled* to issue a new certificate for shares until the old certificate is surrendered to it, except when a certificate has been lost or destroyed, or the shares evidenced by a certificate have been sold for a delinquent assessment or nonpayment of the subscription price." (Italics added.) . . .

The judgments [appealed from] directing the issuance of new certificates without requiring a surrender of the old conflict with the statute as clearly as they possibly could; they order the corporations to do exactly what the statute says they shall *not* be compelled to do. . . .

The theme of the Uniform Stock Transfer Act . . . is negotiability of the certificates; and this cannot exist unless there is only one certificate for given shares, carrying with it the ownership of the shares themselves. . . .

[Judgments reversed.]

Code Comment: The same decision would be made under the Code under which there is no duty to recognize or register a transfer of shares until the properly indorsed outstanding certificate is surrendered (UCC Sec. 8-401(1)) unless it is shown that it was lost, destroyed, or stolen, and the special provisions then applicable are satisfied. UCC Sec. 8-405

Davis v. Walker

170 Neb. 891, 104 N.W.2d 479 (1960)

Davis purchased in Nebraska shares of stock and securities of the W & M Oil Company, a Nebraska corporation. No license had ever been obtained from the Department of Banking as was required by Nebraska law for making such sales. The shares of stock and securities purchased by Davis proved worthless. He then sued Walker and others, who were the directors and officers of W & M when he made the purchase, to recover the amount of his loss. From an adverse decision, Davis appealed.

CHAPPELL, J. . . . [The applicable sections of the Nebraska statute provide that an unlicensed vendor of securities] "shall be liable to the purchaser of the security for the value of the consideration paid by the purchaser less the amount of any income or recovery received thereon." . . .

[The sections] created a specific remedy which did not exist at common law, . . . [and] do not expressly purport by their language to make officers and directors of a corporation personally liable simply because they are officers and directors thereof. Be that as it may, such statutes did not change the preexisting responsibilities and duties of officers and directors of a corporation in handling its affairs and transacting its business. In that connection, as long ago as Ashby v. Peters, 128 Neb. 338, 258 N.W. 639, 99 A.L.R. 843, this court concluded that . . . where fraud is committed by a corporation, which is the situation in the case at bar, it is time to disregard the corporate fiction and hold the persons responsible therefor in their individual capacities. . . . "The general principle that a director or officer of a corporation does not incur personal liability for its torts merely by reason of his official character and is not liable for torts committed by or for the corporation unless he has participated in the wrong has been incorporated by express terms in some of the statutes providing for personal liability of directors and officers of a corporation which issues or sells securities in violation of statutory requirements. Most statutes of this type condition the personal liability of a corporate director or officer upon his personally participating, or aiding in any way, in making the illegal sale. The same principle is applied where personal liability of a corporate director or officer for an illegal sale of securities is predicated upon statutes which contain no express provisions as to the personal liability of such director or officer." . . .

In the case at bar, defendants . . . , while acting as officers and directors, . . . did know . . . that W & M Oil Company never had any license or permit to operate as a broker or salesman or to issue, sell, exchange, or transfer in Nebraska any security or interest in Wyoming, as here involved, and that no officer or salesman of said company had any license or permit to do so. . . . While officers and directors, [they] not only had the duty to be responsible for the transactions involved but also they participated both directly and indirectly in the illegal transactions for the use and benefit of the W & M Oil Company and themselves as shareholders and officers, and they received payment of their salaries as such officers at least in part from the proceeds of such transactions. . . .

[Judgment reversed with respect to the above phase of the case.]

Questions and Case Problems

1. What is the objective of each of the following rules of law?
   (a) A stockholder can be required to give the corporation the option of purchasing his stock before he may sell it to an outsider.
   (b) A transfer of stock is not possible under the Uniform Stock Transfer Act without a transfer of the certificate.

2. Smallwood made a contract to purchase stock of the Re-Mark Chemical Co. from Moretti. Moretti did not deliver the stock certificate to Smallwood but gave him a written assignment of 5,000 shares and directed the company to issue 5,000 shares to Smallwood. There was a delay in issuing the certificate because of certain stock registration problems. Meanwhile four dividends were declared on the stock. They were received by Moretti who paid them to Smallwood who accepted them without question. Shortly thereafter the Re-Mark Co. went into bankruptcy reorganization, and Smallwood then sought to set aside the purchase from Moretti. He claimed that the purchase was not effective because no stock certificate had been issued to him and therefore he had not been given the legal title to the stock. Was he entitled to set the sale aside? (Smallwood v. Moretti, [Fla.] 128 So.2d 628)

3. The Skinner Packing Co., which was incorporated under the laws of Maine, was authorized to do business in Nebraska where it had its principal place of business. The company sent an agent to Excelsior, Missouri, where he made a contract for the sale of 100 shares of stock in the company to Rhines. Within a year thereafter, Rhines concluded that he had been swindled and brought an action against the company to recover the purchase price of the stock. He based his claim upon a violation of the Missouri

Blue-Sky Law. The defendant asserted that the transaction was not governed by the Missouri statute. Do you agree? (Rhines v. Skinner Packing Co., 108 Neb. 105, 187 N.W. 874)

4. Tower subscribed for a certain number of shares of the Hudson Real Estate Co. Before incorporation, Tower gave notice that he withdrew from the enterprise. In an action brought by the company, Tower contended that a subscription before incorporation could be withdrawn up to the time of its acceptance. Do you agree? (Hudson Real Estate Co. v. Tower, 161 Mass. 10, 36 N.E. 680)

5. Flowers signed a written contract to subscribe to stock of the Positype Corporation on condition that his associates each pay a share of the purchase price. This was orally agreed to but was not put in writing. Later the corporation sued Flowers for the full purchase price. He defended on the ground that the condition had not been satisfied because his associates had not paid their share. Was this defense valid? (Positype Corp. v. Flowers, [C.C.A.9th] 36 F.2d 617)

6. Elizabeth Szabo, who owned stock of the American Telephone & Telegraph Co., was notified by the company that there had been a three-for-one split of the company's stock effective as of April 24, 1959, and that on May 29, 1959, the company would prepare and mail to her an additional stock certificate representing twice the number of shares already held by her. Upon receiving the notice from the company, Szabo indorsed on her certificate a transfer to herself and her son as joint tenants with the right of survivorship. She delivered the indorsed certificate to the stock transfer agent of the corporation but directed him to hold up the transfer of the stock until the new certificate for the split shares was available. The stock transfer agent was also notified to have the new certificate made out to Szabo and her son as joint tenants with the right of survivorship. Three days before the new certificate for the stock split was issued, Szabo died. Her son claimed the original shares of stock from her estate and the new shares issued on the stock split. Was he entitled to the share certificate? (Szabo's Estate, [N.Y.] 176 N.E.2d 395)

CHAPTER 51

Rights and Liabilities of Shareholders

The control of the shareholders over the corporation is indirect. Periodically, ordinarily once a year, the shareholders elect directors and through this means can control the corporation. At other times, however, the shareholders have no right or power to control the corporate activity so long as it is conducted within lawful channels. An exception to this rule is that frequently holders of a stated percentage of stock can call a special meeting of the shareholders and to that extent take affairs into their own hands.

Sec. 51-A. Rights of Shareholders.

(1) Certificate of Stock. A shareholder has the right to have issued to him a properly executed certificate as evidence of his ownership of shares.

(2) Transfer of Shares. Subject to certain valid restrictions, a shareholder has the right to transfer his shares as he chooses. He may sell the stock at any price or transfer it as a gift.

(3) Vote. The right to vote means the right to vote at shareholders' meetings for the election of directors and on such other special matters as must be passed upon by the shareholders.[1]

(a) WHO MAY VOTE. The articles of incorporation state which classes of shareholders can vote. Ordinarily only those common shareholders in whose names the stock appears on the books of the corporation are entiled to vote. Generally the directors may fix a date for determining the shareholders who may vote.[2]

---

[1] See p. 762.
[2] American Bar Association Model Business Corporation Act, Sec. 28.

(b) Number of Votes. Each shareholder is ordinarily entitled to one vote for each voting share. In some states, however, the number if votes allowed to each shareholder is limited by statute. A shareholder is not entitled to vote a fractional share.

In about half of the states cumulative voting in the election of directors may be provided for in the articles or automatically exists when the contrary is not stated in the articles. In nearly half of the states cumulative voting is mandatory, being imposed by either constitution or statute. A few states prohibit cumulative voting.

Under a *cumulative voting* plan each shareholder has as many votes as the number of shares he owns multiplied by the number of directors to be elected, and he can distribute them as he sees fit. To illustrate, if a person owns 30 shares and 10 directors are to be elected, he is entitled to cast 300 votes. He may cast 30 votes for each of 10 nominees, 50 for each of 6, 60 votes for each of 5, 75 for each of 4, 100 for each of 3, 150 for each of 2, or all of the 300 votes for 1.

There is a conflict of authority as to the validity of a provision for the election of the directors by classes, as when directors serve for three years and one third of the directors are elected each year. In some jurisdictions such a provision is held invalid as impairing the right of cumulative voting. In other jurisdictions such a system is valid and votes may be accumulated as to the directors within each class to be elected at each election. (See p. 755, Bohannan v. The Corporation Commission)

(c) Voting by Proxy. A shareholder has the right to authorize another to vote for him. This is known as *voting by proxy*. In the absence of restrictions to the contrary, any person, even one who is not a shareholder, may act as a proxy. Ordinarily authority to act as a proxy may be conferred by an informal written instrument.

(d) Voting Agreements and Trusts. Shareholders, as a general rule, are allowed to enter into an agreement by which they concentrate their voting strength for the purpose of controlling the management, unless their agreement is fraudulent or oppressive as to other members. A *voting trust* exists when by agreement a group of shareholders, or all of the shareholders, transfer their shares in trust to one or more persons, as trustees, who are authorized to vote the stock during the life of the trust agreement. In general, such agreements have been upheld if their object is lawful. In some jurisdictions such trusts cannot run beyond a specified number of years.

(4) Pre-emptive Offer of Shares. If the capital stock of a corporation is increased, each shareholder ordinarily has the pre-emptive right to subscribe to such a percentage of the new shares as his old shares bore to the former total of capital stock. This right is given in order to enable each shareholder to maintain his relative interest.

(5) Inspection of Books. A shareholder has the right to be informed about the business of the corporation. He has the right to inspect the books and property of his corporation so that he can keep himself informed about its condition. At common law the right to examine the corporate books and records is qualified. The shareholder must ask for examination in good faith, for proper motives, and at a reasonable time and place. This matter is frequently regulated by statutory and constitutional provisions. (See p. 756, Florida Telephone Corporation v. State) Inspection need not be made personally. A shareholder may employ an accountant or an attorney to examine the records for him.

(6) Dividends. A shareholder has the right to receive his proportion of dividends as they are declared, subject to the relative rights of other shareholders to preferences, accumulation of dividends, and participation. However, there is no absolute right to receive dividends.

(a) FUND AVAILABLE FOR DECLARATION OF DIVIDENDS. Statutes commonly provide that no dividends may be declared unless there is a "surplus" for their payment. This surplus is generally calculated as the amount of the corporate assets in excess of all outstanding liabilities and outstanding shares of the corporation. Thus, if a corporation owed $10,000 and had issued capital stock of $20,000, there could not be a fund for the declaration of dividends until the corporate assets were in excess of $30,000. The theory is that there must be preserved intact such a fund as will pay off all creditors of the corporation and return to each shareholder his capital investment before any dividends can be paid.

Cash dividends may be paid from paid-in surplus. This is the amount that is paid for stock in excess of its par value, if it is par-value stock, and of the amount designated by the board of directors as payment for shares having no par value.

A book surplus may be created by decreasing the capital stock or increasing the value of the corporate assets. Some states permit the declaration of a stock dividend,[3] but not of a cash dividend from a surplus based on such an unrealized appreciation of corporate assets. That is, a corporation cannot increase the valuation of its property on its books and then declare a cash dividend from the resulting paper surplus.

Conversely, for the purpose of dividend declaration, a corporation should write down its assets when because of their risk, nature, or depreciation they are in effect overvalued. The effect of these rules is to deny a corporation a right to declare dividends from current net profits if there is a deficit from prior years.

---

[3] See p. 752.

As an exception to these rules, a wasting assets corporation may pay dividends out of current net profits without regard to the preservation of the corporate assets. *Wasting assets corporations* include those enterprises that exhaust the assets of the corporation, as by extracting oil, coal, iron, and other ores, as compared with a manufacturing plant where the object is to preserve the plant as well as to continue to manufacture. A wasting assets corporation may also be formed for the purpose of purchasing and liquidating a bankrupt's stock of merchandise. If the stock of the wasting assets corporation provides for a preferred payment of principal on dissolution, the corporation must set aside or maintain a fund sufficient to meet those claims.

In about one fifth of the states, statutes provide that dividends may be declared from current net profits, without regard to the existence of a deficit from former years, or from surplus.

If dividends are about to be declared from an unlawful source, an injunction can be obtained to stop their declaration or payment. If the payment has already been made, the directors responsible for the action may be sued individually and be made to indemnify the corporation for the loss they have caused it by the improper payment; but generally it is necessary to show that the directors acted negligently or in bad faith in declaring the dividends.

(b) DISCRETION OF DIRECTORS. Assuming that a fund is available for the declaration of dividends, it is then a matter primarily within the discretion of the board of directors whether a dividend shall be declared.

In general, a court will refuse to substitute its judgment for the judgment of the directors and will interfere only when it is shown that their conduct is harmful to the welfare of the corporation or its shareholders. (See p. 758, Cron v. Tanner) The courts, however, will intervene and compel the declaration of a dividend when it is apparent that the directors have amassed a surplus beyond any practical business need.

Once dividends are declared, a debtor-creditor relation exists between the corporation and the shareholders as to those dividends. The shareholder may accordingly sue the corporation for the amount of his lawfully declared dividends if it fails to pay them.

(c) FORM OF DIVIDENDS. Customarily, a dividend is paid in the form of money, but it may be paid in property, such as a product manufactured by the corporation, in the shares of other corporations held by the corporation, or in the shares of the corporation itself. In the last case, referred to as a *stock dividend,* the result is the same as though the directors paid a cash dividend and all the shareholders then purchased additional stock in amounts proportionate to their original holdings. A stock dividend does not change the proportionate interest of each shareholder but only the evidence which represents that interest.

    (d) EFFECT OF TRANSFER OF STOCK. In determining who is entitled to dividends, it is immaterial when the surplus from which the distribution is made was earned. As between the transferor and the transferee, if the dividend is in cash or property other than the stock of the corporation declaring the dividend, the person who was the owner on the date the dividends were declared is entitled to the dividends. Thus, if a cash dividend is declared before the transfer is made, the transferor is entitled to it. If the transfer was made before the declaration date, the transferee is entitled to it. In applying this rule, it is immaterial when distribution of the dividend was made.

    The rule that the date of declaration determines which shareholder has the right to a cash dividend is subject to modification by the corporation. The board of directors in declaring the dividend may state that it will be payable to those who will be the holders of record on a later specified date.

    If the dividend consists of shares in the corporation declaring the dividend, ownership is determined by the date of distribution. Whichever party is the owner of the shares when the stock dividend is distributed is entitled to the stock dividend.

    The transferor and transferee may enter into any agreement they choose with respect to dividends.

    These rules determine the rights to dividends as between transferor and transferee. Regardless of what those rights may be, the corporation is generally entitled to continue to recognize the transferor as a shareholder until it has been notified that a transfer has been made and the corporate records are accordingly changed. If the corporation, believing that the transferor is still the owner of the stock, sends him a dividend to which the transferee is entitled, the transferee cannot sue the corporation. In that case, the remedy of the transferee is to sue the transferor for the money or property that the latter has received.

    (7) Shareholders' Actions. When the corporation has the right to sue its directors or officers or third persons for damages caused by them to the corporation or for breach of contract, one or more shareholders may bring such action if the corporation refuses to do so.[4]

    (8) Capital Distribution. Upon the dissolution of the corporation, the shareholders are entitled to receive any balance that remains after the payment of all creditors. Certain classes of stock may have a preference or priority in this distribution.[5]

---

[4] See p. 765.
[5] See p. 736.

Sec. 51-B. Liabilities of Shareholders.

(1) Limited Liability. The liability of a shareholder in an ordinary corporation is generally limited. This means that he is not personally responsible for the debts and liabilities of the corporation. The capital contributed by the shareholder may be exhausted by the claims of creditors, but he has no greater liability. The risk of the shareholder is thus limited to the original capital invested by him.

Ordinarily, the fact that a person owns all or substantially all of the stock of a corporation and that he has incorporated for the express purpose of insulating himself from liability does not constitute such fraud as justifies the court in ignoring the shielding effect of the corporation.

Similarly a parent company and its wholly owned subsidiary are regarded as separate entities. (See p. 759, Di Re Case)

Statutes sometimes provide that the shareholders shall be unlimitedly liable for the wage claims of corporation employees.

(2) Unpaid Subscriptions. Whenever shares issued by a corporation are not fully paid for, the original subscriber receiving the stock or any transferee who does not give value, or who knows that the shares were not fully paid, may be liable for the unpaid balance if the corporation is insolvent and the money is required to pay the debts of creditors.[6]

If the corporation has issued the shares as fully paid, or has given it as a bonus, or has agreed to release the subscriber for the unpaid balance, the corporation cannot recover that balance. The fact that the corporation is thus barred does not prevent the creditors of the corporation from bringing an action to compel payment of the balance. The same rules are applied when stock is issued as fully paid in return for property or services which are overvalued so that the stock is not actually paid for in full.

If a statute makes void the stock issued for less than par, it may be cancelled upon suit of the corporation.

(3) Unauthorized Dividends. If dividends are improperly paid out of capital, the shareholders are generally liable to creditors to the extent of such depletion of capital. In some states the liability of the shareholder depends on whether the corporation was insolvent at the time, whether the debts were existing at the time, and whether the shareholders had notice of the source of the dividend.

---

[6] Under ABA MBCA Sec. 23, the transferee is protected if he acts in good faith without knowledge or notice that the shares were not fully paid.

Cases for Chapter 51

Bohannan v. The Corporation Commission

82 Ariz. 299, 313 P.2d 379 (1957)

Bohannan and others presented the articles of a new corporation to the Arizona Corporation Commission for filing. The Commission refused to accept the charter for filing on the ground that the cumulative voting provision of the state constitution was violated by the articles in creating a nine-member elective board of directors, three of whom were to be elected each year. Bohannan brought an action to compel the commission to accept and file the charter. From a judgment in favor of the Commission, Bohannan appealed.

STRUCKMEYER, J. . . . Article 14, Section 10, of the Arizona Constitution provides:

"In all elections for directors or managers of any corporation, each shareholder shall have the right to cast as many votes in the aggregate as he shall be entitled to vote in same company under its charter multiplied by the number of directors or managers to be elected at such election; and each shareholder may cast the whole number of votes, either in person or by proxy, for one candidate, or distribute such votes among two or more such candidates; and such directors or managers shall not be elected otherwise." . . .

Any scheme, plan, or device which completely denies the effectiveness of cumulative voting must necessarily fall. . . .

It is urged by appellees that the general effect of staggering directors by term is to reduce the number of directors which can be elected by minority stockholders. . . . If this argument has any validity, it must be predicated on the proposition that the Constitution demands that minority stockholders be represented on corporate boards in proportion to or at least somewhat in the ratio to the number of shares owned or controlled by such minority. . . . If we are unable to find that the Constitution either by direct expression or fair implication requires proportionate representation, we will be compelled to render a construction which is consistent with the normal and ordinary meaning of the words. Such a construction merely guarantees that a means be provided whereby it is possible for some minority entitled to participate in the elections to secure representation on the board and would not guarantee to a minority stockholder or any particular percentage less than forty-nine per cent a director of his or their choosing.

In Wolfson v. Avery, [6 Ill.2d 78, 126 N.E.2d 710] the Illinois court [held invalid the election of directors by staggered terms and] found that the phrase . . . "to be elected" [a provision of the Illinois constitution similar to that of Arizona], expressed a recognition that the

number of directors varied as between corporations and did not
contemplate the possibility that less than the whole number of directors might be elected at any particular annual meeting. . . . In the
dissenting opinion it was pointed out that there was no express
prohibition in the Constitution against classification and the staggering
of directors when the words of the Constitution are taken in their
ordinary signification. We have examined both arguments advanced
. . . and can say that each has some element of logical plausibility. We
are more inclined to agree with the dissenting justice, but do not
expressly base our conclusions on this alone. Rather to the extent that
Article 14, Section 10, is susceptible of two possible interpretations in
that reasonable men may differ as to the import of its language, we
find it to be ambiguous.

We will, therefore, look beyond the article for assistance in determining its meaning. . . . And in so doing examine into, ascertain, and
give effect to the intent and purpose of the framers of the Constitution. . . . In this we are unable to conclude, as did the Illinois court,
that it was the intention of the framers of the Constitution to require
that minority shareholders be represented on corporate boards in proportion to the per cent of shares controlled by them, [as the statements
made at the Constitutional Convention referred only to *some* representation of minority stockholders.]

[Judgment reversed.]

Florida Telephone Corporation v. Florida ex rel. Peninsular Telephone Company [7]
111 So.2d 677 (Fla., 1959)

The Peninsular Telephone Company, which owned stock in the Florida
Telephone Corporation, requested permission to examine the latter's books
in order to learn the names and addresses of the shareholders so that it
could seek to buy their stock from them. When the corporation refused
to permit this inspection, Peninsular brought an action in the name of the
state to compel such inspection. From a decision in Peninsular's favor,
Florida Telephone Corporation appealed.

STURGIS, C.J. . . . [The Florida statute provides] "(1) . . . The
stock book or stock lists shall be open for at least three business hours
each business day for inspection by any judgment creditor of the
corporation or any person who shall have been for at least six months
immediately preceding his demand a record holder of not less than
one per cent of the outstanding shares of such corporation, or by any
officer, director, or any committee or person holding or authorized in

---

[7] This form of action is brought in the name of the state on the relation (ex rel.) or
complaint of the person actually wronged.

writing by the holders of at least five per cent of all its outstanding shares. Persons so entitled to inspect stock books or stock lists may make extracts therefrom.

" (2) If any officer or agent of any such corporation shall willfully neglect or refuse to make any proper entry in the stock book, or shall neglect or refuse to exhibit any stock book, or to allow it to be inspected and extracts taken therefrom as provided in this section, he and the corporation shall each forfeit and pay to the party injured a penalty of fifty dollars for every such neglect or refusal, and all damages resulting to him therefrom.

" (3) It shall be a defense to any action under this section that the person suing has used or purposes to use the information so obtained otherwise than to protect his interest in the corporation or has within two years sold or offered for sale any list of stockholders of such corporation or any other corporation, or has aided or abetted any person in procuring any stock list for any such purpose." . . .

At common law any shareholder had the right to examine all the books of a corporation at reasonable times and places and for proper purposes.

The statute in question differs from common-law principles in these respects: A distinction is made between the stock books and other books; it is limited in application to certain stockholders; creditors are given the right of inspection; it prescribes no motive to be asserted as a qualification for exercise of the right; and it provides a penalty of forfeiture to enforce the right. It is significant that by confining the broad statutory right to inspection of stock books and stock records, the legislature left the inspection of other corporate books and records to the more restrictive common-law provisions. Thus the lawmakers seem to have recognized the fundamental right of one owning as much as one per cent of the stock to know those with whom he is associated and the extent of their interests, and of making possible direct communication with them. This is readily seen to be an innocuous right as compared to the potential for abuse that might attend unrestricted examination of books of account, minutes, and other confidential papers. In restricting the right of inspection to shareholders who individually or collectively represent a substantial interest, the Florida statute avoids the pitfalls of earlier statutes of some states which are so framed as to permit professional litigants to buy one share and demand inspection of all the books of the corporation. . . .

Respondent [Florida Telephone Corp.] argues that it is unlawful to use such information for the purpose of seeking out the stockholders in an effort to purchase their shares, but this is untenable. It is unreasonable to suppose that the Legislature intended to further restrict such information to the corporate hierarchy or management, to those "in the know" by virtue of their position as corporate employees or officers, rather than to one who by virtue of the quantum of his stock ownership may indeed be the party most vitally interested and affected by improper management. . . .

The protection of interest by purchasing additional stock is a perfectly legitimate enterprise. . . . The desire to gain control is repugnant only to those seeking its retention for more of the same. . . .

[Judgment for plaintiff affirmed.]

Cron v. Tanner
171 Kan. 57, 229 P.2d 1008 (1951)

Cron owned a minority of the common stock of the Walnut Valley State Bank. He brought an action against Tanner and other directors of the bank to compel them to declare a dividend of not less than 15 per cent on the common stock. From a judgment for the plaintiff, the defendant appealed.

WERTZ, J. . . . The only allegation of wrongdoing alleged is that defendant Tanner and the other directors failed to vote in favor of plaintiff's motions at the directors' meetings to declare a dividend on the common stock, although sufficient funds were available in the undivided profits account, and passed a resolution increasing the salary of the defendant Tanner as president of the bank.

It is a well established rule of law that while courts have power to order payment of dividends out of undivided profits, they will not infringe upon the discretion vested in corporate officers, and in any instance are loath to act unless it clearly appears that the discretion is in bad faith abused. . . .

Declaration of a dividend on the stock of a corporation rests in the sound discretion of its board of directors. . . . The mere fact that a corporation has a large surplus or undivided profits account does not entitle the stockholders to a dividend as a matter of right. To what extent the net earnings should be distributed among the shareholders depends largely upon the bank's need for accumulated reserve to strengthen its credit, to increase its working capital, to carry out contemplated projects of expansion, and to provide contingencies against future hazards. These questions, in the absence of fraud, are to be determined by the governing board of the bank. . . .

. . . Plaintiff seeks to have a court of equity substitute its business judgment for that of the directors of the bank. It is not the function of the court to manage a corporation nor substitute its own judgment for that of the officers thereof. It is only when the officers are guilty of willful abuse of their discretionary power or of bad faith, neglect of duty, perversion of the corporate purpose, or when fraud or breach of trust are involved, that the courts will interfere. . . .

[Judgment for plaintiff reversed.]

Di Re v. Central Livestock Order Buying Company
246 Minn. 279, 74 N.W.2d 518 (1956)

Di Re was employed by the Central Livestock Order Buying Co., which was a subsidiary of the Central Livestock Association, Inc. The officers and directors of both corporations were identical. The subsidiary company had been formed because the Federal Packers and Stockyards Act had required the parent company to separate its buying and selling agencies. The subsidiary company notified Di Re that a reduction in staff was necessary and that he was discharged. The parent company then offered him another job. He refused to take the other job and applied for unemployment compensation. The Commissioner of the Department of Employment Security sustained Di Re's claim, from which the subsidiary company appealed.

DELL, C.J. . . . The subsidiary contends that the two companies must be deemed to be a single employer within the meaning of that Unemployment Compensation Act and that, therefore, the new position offered the employee was merely a "transfer" within the same employment. It argues that the termination of the employment was the voluntary act of the employee and, since it was not for "good cause attributable to the employer" . . . the employee is disqualified from receiving any benefits under the act. On the other hand, it concedes that, if the two companies were separate employers, then there was an involuntary termination of the employment which would not disqualify the employee from receiving unemployment benefits under the provisions of said section.

A corporation is an artificial person, created by law, or under authority of law, as a distinct legal entity, with rights and liabilities which are independent from those of the natural persons composing the corporation. Ordinarily two or more corporations are considered separate and distinct entities even though the same individuals are the incorporators of, or own stock in, the several corporations, and even though such corporations may have the same persons as officers.

In the instant case, due to the provisions of the Packers and Stockyards Act, the parent was faced with the choice of segregating its buying and selling activities or, in the alternative, of discontinuing one of these branches of its business altogether. It decided to separate the two functions and, as a result, the subsidiary was formed as a separate corporation in 1941. The two corporations were engaged in entirely different aspects of the livestock business. Their offices are on different floors of the Exchange Building and they maintain separate payroll records, as well as separate books of account. There is no question but that, if these corporations had been organized or used as an instrument to hinder, delay, or defraud creditors, or for any other wrongful purposes, then we should be justified in disregarding the separate and distinct corporate existence of the subsidiary. However, in the instant case the subsidiary's separate existence was required because of the provisions of the Packers and Stockyards Act, . . . and no claim is made that it was formed for fraudulent or wrongful purposes. In the absence of a claim and showing of fraud or other wrongful purposes, the subsidiary must be treated as a legal entity separate and apart from the parent.

[Judgment reversed and case remanded because other facts not relevant to the portion of the opinion above set forth had not been examined by the Department of Employment Security.]

Questions and Case Problems

1. What is the objective of each of the following rules of law?
   (a) Shareholders may generally vote cumulatively for directors of the corporation.
   (b) The directors have discretion whether dividends should be declared from a fund legally available for that purpose.

2. Mayer, who owned stock in the Cincinnati Economy Drug Co., requested permission from the company to make a list of its shareholders. The company refused to permit the inspection on the ground that Mayer also owned stock in competing drug companies. Was it justified in so doing? (Mayer v. Cincinnati Economy Drug Co., [Ohio] 103 N.E.2d 1)

3. Lehman was a stockholder of the National Benefit Insurance Co., which had been incorporated under the laws of Iowa. He brought an action to compel the corporation to permit him to inspect and copy records and documents of the corporation. It was admitted that he had the right to inspect the papers. Did he have a right to make copies of them? (Lehman v. National Benefit Insurance Co., [Iowa] 53 N.W.2d 872)

4. Carlson and others were in the business of buying up small telephone companies. The Ringgold County Mutual Telephone Co. had 365 shares outstanding. Carlson publicly advertised that his group was willing to purchase such shares at $200 per share, an amount slightly in excess of the book value. In this manner the Carlson group acquired 203 shares. The directors of the company, seeing that they no longer held control of the company, authorized the issuance of 644 shares at $40 a share upon the condition that such shares had to be offered to the company by shareholders before they could be resold. Acting under this resolution the directors sold 225 shares at $40 each, principally to their families, relatives, friends, and employees. On the making of each sale, the purchaser was also required to execute a proxy in favor of the defendant directors. When Carlson learned of the offering of these new shares, he brought suit to claim his pre-emptive right thereto. The company opposed the recognition of pre-emptive rights on the ground that Carlson's purpose was merely

to obtain control of the company and then to exploit it to the advantage of his group. Furthermore, a corporate bylaw provided that "transfers of stock shall be made only on approval of the board of directors," and Ringgold took the position that the board of directors refused to approve the transfer of additional shares to Carlson. Was Carlson entitled to shares by virtue of a pre-emptive right? (Carlson v. Ringgold County Mutual Telephone Co., [Iowa] 108 N.W.2d 478)

5. Siebrecht organized a corporation called the Siebrecht Realty Co. and then transferred his building to the corporation in exchange for its stock. The corporation rented different floors of the building to different tenants. Elenkrieg, an employee of one of the tenants, fell and was injured because of the defective condition of the hall stairway. She sued Siebrecht individually on the ground that the corporation had been formed by him for the purpose of securing limited liability. Decide. (Elenkrieg v. Siebrecht, 238 N.Y. 254, 144 N.E. 519)

6. Thomsen, a stockholder of the Yankee Mariner Corp., brought an action against it and a newly-elected board of directors to determine the validity of the election. It was shown that two of the stockholders, Langs and Napier, had given proxies to Donnelley on March 8 which were irrevocable for 90 days and gave him the right to vote their stock for the purpose of removing the then directors of the corporation and electing new directors. Although they had given their proxies, Langs and Napier appeared at the regular meeting and voted their stock. In the action by Thomsen it was claimed that their voting was illegal since their proxies were still outstanding. Decide. (Thomsen v. Yankee Mariner Corp. [Cal.] 235 P.2d 234)

7. Macomber owned stock in the Standard Oil Co. of California, which declared a stock dividend. Eisner, as Collector of Internal Revenue, claimed that the dividend was income received by Macomber and was subject to the federal income tax. Decide. (Eisner v. Macomber, 252 U.S. 189)

8. The Lewiston-Clarkston Co. owned and operated a hydroelectric plant. As part of the procedure for a reorganization of the company, the majority stockholders transferred their stock to trustees and authorized them to vote the stock. The trust agreement provided that the voting trust should automatically terminate when the preferred stock and outstanding bonds of the company were retired. The trustees decided to sell the plant. Clark, one of the parties to the agreement, sued Foster and the other trustees to restrain the sale on the ground that the "voting trust agreement" was illegal. Decide. (Clark v. Foster, 98 Wash. 241, 167 P. 908)

CHAPTER 52

Management of Corporations

A corporation is managed, directly or indirectly, by its shareholders, board of directors, and officers.

Sec. 52-A. Shareholders. Shareholders do not participate directly in the management of ordinary corporate affairs. Without express authorization by the corporation, a shareholder cannot bind it by contract. It is through the board of directors, the officers, and the employees hired by the corporation that a corporation conducts its business. Since the shareholders have the right to select the directors, they indirectly determine the policies to be followed in the management of the business.

When certain major matters are involved, as distinguished from the ordinary operations of the business, statutes commonly require action by the shareholders. Thus, when it is desired to change the character of the enterprise, the consent of all shareholders is required.[1]

Sec. 52-B. Meetings of Shareholders. Action by shareholders must be taken at a regular or special meeting; otherwise, it has no legal effect unless the consent of all shareholders is obtained.

(1) Place of Shareholders' Meeting. Generally shareholders' meetings, unless permitted by a statute,[2] cannot be held outside the state in which the corporation was created. Some courts hold that only the first meeting is required to be in the home state.

---

[1] The American Bar Association Model Business Corporation Act requires, in the absence of a provision in the articles of incorporation to the contrary, a majority of the voting power to change the name of the corporation and two thirds of the voting power to alter the articles of incorporation in any other respect. Sec. 38.

[2] The ABA MBCA provides that shareholders' meetings may be held in any state authorized by the bylaws, Sec. 26.

The place of holding stated meetings may be prescribed by the charter or bylaws, or it may be left in the hands of the directors. Unless otherwise prohibited by statute, a meeting improperly held as to place or time is binding on those who assent to it.

(2) Regular Meetings. The time and place of regular or stated meetings are usually prescribed by the charter or bylaws. Notice to shareholders of such meetings is ordinarily not required, but it is usually given as a matter of good business practice.

(3) Special Meetings. Unless otherwise prescribed by charter or bylaws, special meetings are called by the directors. It is sometimes provided that a special meeting may be called by a certain percentage of the shareholders. The purpose of this alternative of calling a special meeting is to prevent a board of directors from ruling the corporation with an iron hand.

Notice of the day, hour, and the place of a special meeting must be given to all shareholders. The notice must also include a statement of the nature of the business to be transacted. (See p. 767, In re William Faehndrich, Inc.) No other business may be lawfully transacted at such a meeting.

If proper notice is not given, the defect may be cured at a properly held meeting by ratification of the action taken by the earlier meeting.

(4) Quorum. A valid meeting requires the presence of a quorum of the voting shareholders. At common law any number of shareholders assembled at a proper meeting constituted a quorum, and action by the majority of such a quorum was binding. The purpose of this rule was to prevent a group of dissenters from blocking action by refusing to be present at a meeting. It is commonly provided by statute, charter, or bylaws, however, that in order to constitute a quorum, a specified number of shareholders or a number authorized to vote a stated proportion of the voting stock must attend.[3]

It is generally held that when a meeting opens with a quorum, the quorum is not thereafter broken if stockholders leave the meeting and those remaining would not have been sufficient to constitute a quorum originally. This principle is designed to prevent obstructionist tactics of groups of dissenting shareholders.

A charter or bylaw provision may lawfully require more than a simple majority vote of shareholders on any issue.

Sec. 52-C. Directors. The management of a corporation is usually entrusted to a board of directors who are elected by the shareholders.

---

[3] The ABA MBCA provides that a majority of shares entitled to vote constitute a quorum, Sec. 30.

(1) Qualifications. Eligibility for membership to a board of directors is determined by statute, charter, or bylaw. In the absence of controlling provisions, any person is eligible for membership, including a nonresident, a minor, or even a person who is not a shareholder.[4] Generally, however, it is required that all or some of the members on the board of directors meet certain requirements.

(2) Meetings of Directors. Corporate action by directors can only be taken at a proper meeting of the board. The statutes, charter, or bylaws sometimes require the meeting to be held at a particular place. In the absence of restrictions the meeting of the directors may be held outside the state.[5] Directors who participate without objection in a meeting held at a place or time other than as specified in the bylaws cannot object later.

A director is not allowed to vote by proxy. He must attend personally to the affairs of the corporation.

A quorum requires the presence of a majority of the directors, unless otherwise provided in the charter, statute, or bylaws. In the determination of whether the requisite number of directors to transact business is present, a director ordinarily cannot be counted if he has a personal interest in the matter before the board. The fact that he has such interest is deemed to disqualify him since, in the eyes of the law, he cannot act impartially. (See p. 767, Indurated Concrete Corp. v. Abbott) It is thus held that a director who also acts as general manager of the corporation cannot vote at a directors' meeting on a resolution to give him special compensation for his services as manager.

(3) Powers of Directors. The board of directors has authority to manage the corporation. The court will not interfere with its discretion in the absence of illegal conduct or fraud harming the rights of creditors, shareholders, or the corporation. (See p. 768, Noble v. Farmers' Union Trading Co.)

The board of directors may enter into any contract or transaction necessary to carry out the business for which the corporation was formed. The board may appoint officers and other agents to act for the company, or it may delegate authority to one or more of its members to do so.

Knowledge of a director of a corporation is knowledge of the corporation when the director acquires such knowledge while acting in the course of his employment and in the scope of his authority. Knowledge learned by a director while acting in his own interest, however, is not imputed to the corporation.

---

[4] Sec. 33.
[5] Sec. 39.

(4) Liability of Directors. Directors are fiduciaries entrusted with the management of the corporation. They are not liable for losses resulting from their management when they have acted in good faith and with due diligence, and have exercised reasonable care. For willful or negligent acts, however, they are held strictly accountable, and they are bound by all rules that the law imposes on those in a fiduciary position.

Actions against directors should be brought by the corporation. If the corporation fails to act, as is the case when the directors who are sued are in control of the corporation, one or more shareholders may bring the action in a representative capacity for the corporation. This is a secondary or derivative action in that the shareholder enforces only the cause of action of the corporation, and any money recovered is paid into the corporate treasury. Statutes commonly require that the plaintiffs own at least 5 per cent of the outstanding stock, in order to limit the danger of crank or nuisance suits.

Directors of a corporation are not personally liable for wrongs committed by the corporation merely by virtue of the fact that they are directors. It must be shown that they have authorized or ratified the improper conduct or have in some way participated therein.

When the director has dealt personally with his own corporation, as in the case when he has sold it his property, or when a transaction occurs between corporations with common directors, the burden is on the director or directors to show that the transaction was proper. (See p. 769, Shlensky v. South Parkway Building Corp.)

Sec. 52-D. Officers. Sometimes the officers are elected by the shareholders, but usually they are appointed by the board of directors. Ordinarily no particular formality need be observed in making such appointments. There are seldom particular qualifications required of officers. Unless prohibited, a director may hold an executive office.

(1) Powers of Officers. The officers of a corporation are its agents. Consequently their powers are controlled by the laws of agency, subject to limitations imposed by the charter and bylaws or by the instructions of the board of directors.

(a) PRESIDENT. It is sometimes held that in the absence of some limitation upon his authority, the president of a corporation has, by virtue of his office, authority to act as agent on behalf of the corporation within the scope of the business in which the corporation is empowered to engage. There is authority, however, that the president has such broad powers only when he is the general manager of the corporation and then such powers stem from the office of general manager and not from that of president. In any event, the president does not have authority by virtue of his office to make a contract which because of its unusual character would require action by the board of directors. The president, therefore, cannot make a contract to fix the compensation to be paid a director of the corporation, to make long term or unusual contracts of employment, to bind the corporation as a guarantor, to release a claim of the corporation, or to promise that the corporation will repurchase later shares which are issued to a subscriber.

(b) OTHER OFFICERS. The authority of other officers, such as secretary or treasurer, is generally limited to the duties of their offices. Their authority may, however, be extended by the conduct of the corporation, in accordance with the general principles governing apparent authority based on the conduct of the principal. An unauthorized act of an officer may, of course, be ratified.

When an officer is placed in the position of a general manager, irrespective of the name given to the office, he has implied power to do such acts as are necessary to carry out the particular business. This power includes authority to employ an attorney to represent the corporation. An officer, however, does not have authority to make contracts of an extraordinary nature, in the absence of proper authorization or ratification of his acts.

(2) Liability of Officers. The relation of the officers to the corporation, like that of the directors, is a fiduciary relationship. For this reason, the officers are liable for secret profits made in connection with the business of the corporation. They are also liable for willful or negligent acts that cause a loss to the corporation. On the other hand, they are not liable for mere errors in judgment committed while exercising their discretion, provided they have acted with reasonable prudence and skill.

Statutes commonly impose liability upon directors for commencing business before the statutory amount of capital has been paid in, making improper loans of corporate funds, declaring dividends from an improper source, purchasing shares of the corporation with improper funds, or distributing capital assets without making adequate provision for the payment of creditors. In addition, the directors may be liable for violating the Federal Securities Exchange Act or regulations adopted under the Securities and Exchange Commission, and a number of other federal statutes relating to securities.

Sec. 52-E. Agents. The authority, rights, and liabilities of an agent of a corporation are governed by the same rules applicable when the principal is a natural person.

Cases for Chapter 52

In re William Faehndrich, Inc.

2 N.Y.2d 468, 14 N.E.2d 597 (1957)

William Faehndrich founded a business which he later incorporated. His son grew up in the business and ultimately was its president with the father holding the offices of secretary and treasurer. The father and son held all the outstanding shares—the son, 161, and the father, 157. The son, as president, gave the father a notice that a special shareholders' meeting was called "for the purpose of electing directors of the corporation for the ensuing year, or for such action or further business, as may arise at said meeting." The father did not attend the meeting and the son, by voting his 161 shares, elected himself and his wife as directors. They then held a directors' meeting at which they voted to terminate the father's employment by the corporation. The father brought suit to declare the election of directors and the action of the directors' meeting void on the ground that the notice of the shareholders did not indicate that the object of the meeting was to terminate his employment. From a judgment in the father's favor, the son appealed.

FULD, J. . . . The notice of the stockholders' meeting, admittedly received, fairly and adequately apprised the petitioner of the purpose of the meeting; in so many words, it recited that the meeting was called "for the purpose of electing directors." It is quite likely that the father did not fully realize the significance of such an election or the consequences to himself that would flow therefrom, but it may not be said that the notice of the meeting was insufficient or misleading in any way. If the purpose of the meeting be clearly stated, there generally is no duty to specify the course of conduct contemplated by the directors after their election, and no requirement to explain the consequences that will follow from the action they plan to take. . . .

[Judgment reversed.]

Indurated Concrete Corp. v. Abbott

195 Md. 496, 74 A.2d 17 (1950)

Smith was a director and Abbott a director and president of the Indurated Concrete Corp. There were four directors in all. At a meeting at which one director was absent, Smith and Abbott presented claims that they held against the corporation for special services rendered by them. As directors, they voted in favor of paying their claims. The remaining director present voted against the claims. A new board of directors was elected the next year, and the corporation sued Smith and Abbott to recover the money that had been paid on those claims. From a judgment against Smith and Abbott, they appealed.

COLLINS, J. . . . There is an inherent obligation, . . . [on directors] that they will in no manner use their positions to advance their own individual interest as distinguished from that of the corporation, or acquire interests that may conflict with the fair and proper discharge of their duty. The corporation is entitled to the supervision of all the directors, in respect to all the transactions in which it may be concerned; and if one of the directors is allowed to place himself in the position of having his conduct and accounts made the subject of supervision and scrutiny, he, of course, cannot act, in regard to those matters, both for himself and the corporation; and the consequence is, that the corporation is deprived of the benefit of his judgment and supervision in regard to matters in which such judgment and supervision might be most essential to its interest and protection. Not only this, the remaining directors are placed in the embarrassing and invidious position of having to pass upon, scrutinize, and check the transactions and account of their own body, with whom they are associated on terms of equality in the general management of all the affairs of the corporation. The design of the rule, therefore, is to secure a faithful discharge of duty and, at the same time, to close the door, as far as possible, against all temptation to do wrong by subjecting the transactions between parties standing in such confidential relations to the most exact and rigid scrutiny whenever such transactions are brought in question before the courts. The transaction may not be ipso facto void, but it is not necessary to establish that there has been actual fraud or imposition practiced by the party holding the confidential or fiduciary relation—the onus of proof being upon him to establish the perfect fairness, adequacy, and equity of the transaction; and that too by proof entirely independent of the instrument under which he may claim." . . .

Looking at these claims with the "most exact and rigid scrutiny," it does not seem that the work done by them was more than that ordinarily done by directors in a small closely owned corporation in which it does not appear that salaries had been paid officers or directors during its existence. . . .

We must also note that the vote of . . . Abbott alone at the directors meeting . . . was the vote that decided whether his claim . . . should be paid. . . . Without his vote the claims would not have passed. For the reasons herein given, we are of opinion that the [board of directors] should not have paid . . . Abbott. . . .

[The court then disallowed the claim of Smith for the same reason.]

[Judgment entered for corporation.]

Noble v. Farmers' Union Trading Co.

123 Mont. 518, 216 P.2d 925 (1950)

Farmers' Union Trading Co., a corporation, was in possession of certain land, which the corporation believed it owned. Wiggins claimed title to a portion of this land. To avoid a lawsuit, the corporation agreed to pay Wiggins a monthly rental for the use of this portion of the land. Noble, who owned one share of the 785 or more shares of the outstanding corporate stock, brought an action against the corporation and Wiggins to establish that Wiggins had no title. From a judgment for the defendants, the plaintiff appealed.

ADAIR, C.J. . . . The functions of stockholders are exceedingly limited. Every stockholder impliedly agrees, on becoming a member of the corporation, to the execution of all the powers conferred by law on the corporation. . . .

"The minority stockholders . . . can only question the acts of directors or majority stockholders where such acts are ultra vires, illegal, or fraudulent. . . . There can be no interference by the minority stockholders with acts within the discretionary powers of the directors of majority stockholders, or pursuant to law. . . .

In the instant case the complaint does not allege that plaintiff requested the directors to call a special meeting of stockholders, . . . or that directors controlled a majority of the stock, or that plaintiff had procured a list of the stockholders, or that he had contacted or attempted to contact them, or that he had been denied the right to inspect the corporation's books to obtain the names and addresses of the stockholders; nor did plaintiff allege any ultra vires act, fraud, or bad faith on the part of the corporation's directors, or on the part of the defendant, Wiggins. Such complaint was and is clearly insufficient under the repeated decisions of this court. . . .

That a cause of action may exist in favor of the corporation and that the directors decline to commence the action does not empower a minority stockholder to institute and prosecute the suit in his own name. . . . "There may be a variety of things which a company may well be entitled to complain of, but which, as a matter of good sense, they do not think it right to make the subject of litigation" . . . ; and whether or not a corporation shall seek to enforce in the courts a cause of action existing in its favor is, like other business questions, a matter of internal management to be decided by the directors, as the executive representatives of the corporation. . . .

[Judgment for defendants affirmed.]

Shlensky v. South Parkway Building Corp.
19 Ill.2d 268, 166 N.E.2d 793 (1960)

Shlensky and others brought a suit on behalf of shareholders of the South Parkway Building Corp. against the directors of the corporation to recover from them damages for loss sustained by the corporation as the result of contracts made by the directors between the corporation and another corporation on the ground that some of the directors were also directors of

the other corporation and the effect of the contracts was to remove assets
from South Parkway for the benefit of the other corporation. The lower
court entered judgment in favor of Shlensky. The intermediate appellate
court reversed this judgment on the ground that Shlensky had not shown
that the contracts in question were unfair. Shlensky appealed.

BRISTOW, J. . . . In adjudicating this appeal, . . . we must strive . . .
to protect shareholders from exploitation by directors, and at the
same time to avoid undue restrictions of corporate activity. . . .

This court, in conformity with the practically universal judicial
opinion, has recognized that directors, or other officers of a corporation,
occupy a fiduciary relation toward it. . . .

"The directors of a corporation are trustees of its business and
property for the collective body of stockholders in respect to such
business. They are subject to the general rule, in regard to trusts and
trustees, that they cannot, in their dealings with the business or property of the trust, use their relation to it for their own personal gain.
It is their duty to administer the corporate affairs for the common
benefit of all the stockholders, and exercise their best care, skill, and
judgment in the management of the corporate business *solely in the
interest of the corporation.* . . . It is a breach of duty for the directors
to place themselves in a position where their personal interests would
prevent them from acting for the best interests of those they
represent." . . .

While a director is not disqualified from dealing with the corporation and buying its property, or selling property to it, the transaction
will be subject to the closest scrutiny, and if not conducted with the
utmost fairness, "to the end that the corporation shall have received
full value," it will be set aside. . . . Nevertheless, . . . transactions between corporations with common directors may be avoided only *if
unfair,* and that the directors who would sustain the challenged transaction have the burden of overcoming the presumption against the
validity of the transaction by showing its fairness. . . .

[This] rule, . . . is not only legally cogent, but is consistent with
the entire concept of the fiduciary relation in the fabric of our commercial law. The contrary rule, urged by defendants, whereby those
attacking the transactions of fiduciaries would have the burden of
establishing its unfairness or fraudulency is not only without substantial support in the case law, but would put a premium on sharp
practices by directors by putting the onus of proof on their victims,
and would also tend to further separate corporate management from
ownership.

In contrast, the [above] rule, . . . insofar as it provides that the
directors shall have the burden of establishing the fairness and propriety of the transactions, not only protects shareholders from exploitation, but permits flexibility in corporate dealings. While the concept

of "fairness" is incapable of precise definition, courts have stressed such factors as whether the corporation received in the transaction full value in all the commodities purchased; the corporation's need for the property; its ability to finance the purchase; whether the transaction was at the market price, or below, or constituted a better bargain than the corporation could have otherwise obtained in dealings with others; whether there was a detriment to the corporation as a result of the transaction; whether there was a possibility of corporate gain siphoned off by the directors directly or through corporations they controlled; and whether there was full disclosure—although neither disclosure nor shareholder assent can convert a dishonest transaction into a fair one. . . .

[The court then considered the evidence and concluded that the defendant directors] failed to establish the fairness of these five challenged transactions, and their conduct constituted a breach of fiduciary duty for which the chancellor properly ordered them to account. . . .

[Judgment for directors reversed.]

Questions and Case Problems

1. What is the objective of each of the following rules of law?
   (a) The action of shareholders at a meeting may ratify the action taken at an earlier meeting and cure the defect of an improper notice or lack of notice of the prior meeting.
   (b) If the corporation fails to sue a corporate officer for loss caused by him, shareholders may bring an action against the officer on behalf of the corporation.

2. The president of the Atlantic & North Carolina Railroad Co. published in one newspaper a notice of a special meeting of stockholders to be held in Newborn, North Carolina. After the stockholders assembled, they adjourned to meet in Morehead City on the same day. After reassembling, the stockholders voted to authorize a lease of the corporate property to the Howland Improvement Co. Twenty days later the regular annual meeting of the corporation was held. A resolution was then introduced by Foy, at the instance of Hill, instructing the proper officers to bring a suit to set the lease aside. The stockholders' meeting voted to take no action on this resolution and voted that it be tabled. On behalf of himself and other stockholders, Hill then brought a suit against the railroad company to have the lease annulled. He contended that the lease was not properly authorized because the notice of the meeting had not been given as required by the bylaws and because the meeting had not been held at the place of call. Was the special meeting properly held? (Hill v. Atlantic & North Carolina Railroad Co., 143 N.C. 539, 55 S.E. 854)

3. The directors of the American Founders Life Insurance Co. made a contract with the Colorado Management Corp. for certain services. American Founders later sued for the return of the money paid to Colorado on the ground that the contract could be set aside because it had been approved

by American Founders at a board of directors' meeting at which only six of the eight directors were present and three of these directors were also directors of Colorado and two of them were also officers of Colorado. The bylaws of American Founders required a majority, which was five, to constitute a quorum for a directors' meeting. Was American Founders entitled to recover? (Colorado Management Corp. v. American Founders Life Insurance Co., [Colo.] 359 P.2d 665)

4. Cholfin and his wife were two of the three directors of the Allied Freightways Corporation. Cholfin ran the business, and his wife and the other director took no active part in its management. Cholfin unlawfully used $16,857.25 of the corporate funds to pay his own debts and $3,086.39 of the corporate funds to pay those of his wife. Allied Freightways brought suit to recover from the Cholfin's the money improperly spent from the corporation. Allied Freightways claimed that each of the defendants was liable for the full amount of all improper expenditures. Was this correct? (Allied Freightways v. Cholfin, [Mass.] 91 N.E.2d 765)

5. The board of directors of the Haskell-Shaw Printing Co. consisted of five members. At one meeting, two members, Haskell and Wattles, attended and decided to make an assignment of certain corporate assets to Parker. In an action brought by the Calumet Paper Co. against the printing company, it was contended that the action of the directors was invalid. Do you agree? (Calumet Paper Co. v. Haskell-Shaw Printing Co., 144 Mo. 331, 45 S.W. 115)

6. Anthony Yee was the president of the Waipahu Auto Exchange, a corporation. As part of his corporate duties, he arranged financing for the company. The Federal Services Finance Corporation drew twelve checks payable to the order of the Waipahu Auto Exchange. These were then indorsed by its president: "Waipahu Auto Exchange, Limited, by Anthony Yee, President," and were cashed at two different banks. The Bishop National Bank of Hawaii, on which the checks were drawn, charged its depositor, Federal Services, with the amount of these checks. Federal Services then sued Bishop National Bank to restore to its account the amount of these twelve checks on the theory that Bishop National Bank had improperly made payment on the checks because Anthony Yee had no authority to cash them. Did Yee have authority to indorse and cash the checks? (Federal Services Finance Corp. v. Bishop National Bank of Hawaii, [C.A. 9th] 190 F.2d 442)

7. Sacks claimed that when he was a salesman for Helene Curtis Industries, its president, Stein, made an oral contract with him to the effect that Sacks was to act as the sales manager of the corporation at a compensation of a straight salary and a percentage of the increased volume of the corporation's sales. The corporation later refused to pay compensation on this basis and asserted that it had never been informed of any such agreement. The corporation denied that the contract had in fact been made and asserted that the president had no authority to make such an agreement. Was the agreement binding on the corporation? (Sacks v. Helene Curtis Industries, 340 Ill.App. 76, 91 N.E.2d 127)

CHAPTER 53

Nature and Transfer

The law of real property is technical and to a large extent uses a vocabulary drawn from the days of feudalism. Much of the earlier law of real property is no longer of practical importance in the modern business world. The following discussion is therefore a simplified, modern presentation of the subject.

Sec. 53-A. Definition. *Real property* includes (1) land, (2) buildings and fixtures, and (3) rights in the land of another. Real property, like personal property, may have one or more owners.

(1) Land. *Land* means more than the surface of the earth. It embraces the soil and all things of a permanent nature affixed to the ground, such as herbs, grass, or trees, and other growing, natural products. The term also includes the waters upon the ground and things that are embedded beneath the surface. For example, coal, oil, and marble embedded beneath the surface form part of the land.

Technically, land is considered as extending downward to the earth's center and upward indefinitely. Thus one cannot mine a tunnel at any depth beneath the surface of another's land, or build a structure which extends over it at any height, without violating the rights of the owner. How far an owner's right extends above the land is at present an unsettled question. The Uniform Aeronautics Act states that the owner of land owns the space above, subject to the right of flight in aircraft which does not interfere with the use of the land

and is not dangerous to persons or property lawfully on the land.[1]
(See p. 778, Johnson v. Airport Authority of Omaha)

(2) Buildings and Fixtures. A *building* includes any structure
placed on or beneath the surface of land, without regard to its purpose
or use. A *fixture* includes personal property that is attached to the
earth or placed in a building in such a way or under such circumstances
that it is deemed part of the real property.[2]

(3) Rights in the Land of Another. These rights include easements and profits.

Sec. 53-B. Easements. A person may have the right to cross his
neighbor's land in order to reach the nearest highway. This right is
an example of an easement. An *easement* is not only a right in the
land of another, but it is a right that belongs to the land which is
benefited. The benefited land is called the *dominant tenement,* and
the subject land is called the *servient tenement.*

An easement may be created by:

(1) An agreement under seal by the owner of the servient estate.

(2) An exception or reservation in a deed by one conveying a
parcel of land.

(3) Implication when one conveys part of his land that has been
used as a dominant estate in relation to the part retained. (See p. 779,
D'Amato v. Weiss) To illustrate, if water or drain pipes run from the
part alienated through the part retained, there is an implied right to
have such use continued. In order that an easement will be implied in
such a case, the use must be apparent, continuous, and necessary. The
last requirement is usually construed as meaning reasonably necessary.

(4) Implication when it is necessary to the use of the land alienated. This ordinarily arises when one sells land to which no entry
can be made, except over the land retained, or over the land of a
stranger. The right to use the land retained for the purpose of going
to and from the land is known as a *way of necessity.*

(5) Estoppel, as when the grantor states that the plot conveyed
is bounded by a street. If, in such a case, the grantor owns the adjoining plot, he cannot deny the public the right to use the area
which he has described as a street.

(6) Prescription by adverse use for a prescribed period.[3]

---

[1] The Uniform Aeronautics Act (UAA) has been adopted in Arizona, Delaware,
Georgia, Hawaii, Idaho, Indiana, Maryland, Minnesota, Missouri, Montana, Nevada, New
Jersey, North Carolina, North Dakota, Pennsylvania, South Carolina, South Dakota,
Tennessee, Utah, Vermont, and Wisconsin, but was withdrawn by the Commissioners on
Uniform Laws in 1943.

[2] See p. 245.

[3] See p. 778.

An easement may be terminated by release by deed to the owner of the servient land, by abandonment, by adverse possession, and in some states by the sale of the servient land for taxes.

Sec. 53-C. Profits. A person may have the right to cut and remove timber from his neighbor's woodland. This right in the neighbor's land is called a *profit à prendre* or a profit. A profit may extend to taking anything from the land of the other, such as minerals, coal, ice, or fish.

The profit may be attached to or be appurtenant to a dominant tenement, as in the case of an easement. In addition, it may be owned by a particular person without regard to his ownership of any land. In such a case it is termed a *profit in gross.*

Sec. 53-D. Duration and Extent of Ownership. The interest held by a person in real property may be defined in terms of the period of time for which he will remain the owner. He may have (1) a fee simple estate or (2) a life estate. These estates are termed *freehold estates.* In addition, either of these estates may be subject to a condition or may expire or terminate upon the happening of a specified contingency. Although a person may own property for a specified number of years, this interest is not regarded as a freehold estate, but is a *leasehold estate* and is subject to different rules of law.[4]

(1) Fee Simple Estate. An *estate in fee, fee simple,* or a *fee simple absolute,* is the largest estate known to our law. The owner of such fee has the absolute and entire property in the land. The important characteristics of this estate are as follows: (a) it is alienable during life; (b) it is alienable by will; (c) it descends to heirs generally if not devised (transferred by will) ; (d) it is subject to rights of the owner's surviving spouse; and (e) it is liable for debts of the owner before or after death.

(2) Life Estate. A *life estate,* as its name indicates, lasts only during the life of a person, ordinarily its owner. Upon his death no interest remains to pass to his heirs or by his will.

Sec. 53-E. Conditional Estates. An *estate on condition* is one in which the estate or interest will commence, be enlarged, or be defeated upon the performance or breach of a stated condition. This condition may be a (1) condition precedent or (2) a condition subsequent. When an estate does not arise until the happening of a contingency, it is on *condition precedent.* When the estate terminates upon the happening of a contingency, it is on *condition subsequent.*

---

[4] See p. 797.

Conditions, particularly conditions subsequent, are not favored in the law. When possible, courts will interpret conditions to be covenants. In that case a breach of a "condition" has no greater effect than a breach of a contract.

Sec. 53-F. Terminable Fees. A *terminable fee,* also called an estate upon limitation, is granted to exist while a specified use or condition continues but which terminates when that use or condition ceases. Thus a grant of land for "so long as the land should be used as a playground" gives ownership of the land for only so long as it is used for that purpose. If that use stops, the ownership ends and the land reverts to the prior owner. A terminable estate ends automatically when the contingency specified occurs; no re-entry by the former owner is required. This latter point is the most important distinction between a terminable estate and an estate on condition subsequent, for a re-entry is required to take advantage of the occurrence of a condition subsequent.

The fact that a deed merely recites the purpose for which land is granted does not make the estate terminable so that it would end if the land were not used for that purpose. (See p. 780, Ange v. Ange)

Sec. 53-G. Transferring Real Property.

(1) Public Grant or Patent. Real property may be acquired directly from the government. The method of transfer in such a case may be made by legislative grant or by patent. The latter method is commonly used by the federal government under the homestead laws.

(2) Deed. The most common form of transfer of title to real property is by the delivery of a deed by the owner.[5]

(3) Dedication. Any person possessing a legal or equitable interest in land may appropriate it to the use of the public. This is known as a *dedication.* There are two essentials to a valid common-law dedication:

(a) The real property must be set apart with the intention to surrender it to the use of the public. The intent may be express or implied.

(b) An acceptance is usually necessary on the part of the municipality or the state. An acceptance may be found in actual use by the public, (see p. 781, Lake Beulah Protective & Improvement Assn. v. Christenson) although in the latter case a duty of maintenance is generally not imposed on the local government.

---

[5] See p. 784.

(4) Eminent Domain.[6] Two important questions are involved in the transfer of property by this method; namely, whether there is a taking of property and whether the property is intended for public use. In respect to the first, it is not necessary that one be physically deprived of his land. It is sufficient if he is denied the normal use of his property. It is not necessary that the public actually use the land. It is sufficient that it is appropriated for a purpose that is intended for the public benefit.

(5) Accretion. The owner of land acquires or loses title to land that is added or taken away by the action of water upon his property. An increase of land caused by the action of water upon its borders is known as *accretion.* This gain or increase may result from alluvion or dereliction. *Alluvion* occurs when soil or sand is washed up by the water and becomes attached to the land. *Dereliction* occurs when the water recedes, leaving bare land which was formerly a part of its bed. Thus, when the boundary line between two farms is the middle of a stream, gradual changes in the course of the stream add to the land on one side and take away from the land on the other.

In order that the owner of land may acquire title to land by accretion, it is necessary that the accumulation result from a gradual and imperceptible growth. In case of sudden or perceptible changes, the ownership of the land remains unaltered. For example, if a river suddenly follows a different channel, the titles of the owners of the land formerly on each side are not affected.

(6) Adverse Possession. Title to land may be acquired by holding it adversely to the true owner for a certain period of time. In such a case one gains title by *adverse possession.* If such adverse possession is maintained, the possessor automatically becomes the owner of the property even though he admittedly had no lawful claim to the land before.

In order to acquire title in this manner, possession must be (a) actual, (b) visible and notorious, (c) exclusive, (d) hostile, and (e) continuous for a required period of years.

The period during which land must be held adversely in order to gain title varies in the different states. In many states the statute prescribes twenty or twenty-one years, whereas in others the period is less.

As a special exception to the requirement that adverse possession must be continued for a specific period, it is held that when the owners of neighboring lots have a bona fide dispute as to the location of the boundary line between them and in good faith agree upon and continue to recognize a boundary for a number of years, the boundary

---

6 See p. 242.

line will be deemed fixed where agreed although the time elapsed since the agreement is less than the adverse possession period.

(7) Prescription. The right to use another's land for some purpose, as in the case of an easement, may be acquired by adverse use. This is known as *prescription.* The elements requisite to the acquiring of rights by prescription are practically the same as in adverse possession, except that the use need not be exclusive of others. A modification is also made in that continuous use is not literally required.

(8) Marriage. At common law the husband and wife upon marriage each acquired specific, though differing, rights in the property of the other. Modern statutes have changed the common law by freeing the wife's property of the control of her husband. Property that she owned when she married remains her separate property; and her husband, during her lifetime, generally has no legal right to it by virtue of the marriage.

Under most statutes, if the deceased spouse did not leave a will, the surviving spouse is given absolute ownership of a fractional share of all property owned by the other spouse at the date of death. Provision is generally made for varying the share inversely to the number of children or other heirs, for rejecting the provisions of a will that deprive the surviving spouse of the statutory share,[7] and sometimes for permitting a spouse to claim an interest in property conveyed during the deceased spouse's lifetime without the consent of the surviving spouse.

(9) Abandonment. Unlike personal property,[8] title to real estate generally cannot be lost or transferred by abandonment. An easement may be lost by abandonment, however, if such intent is clearly shown.

Cases for Chapter 53

Johnson v. Airport Authority of Omaha
173 Neb. 801, 115 N.W.2d 426 (1962)

Johnson's land was located near the municipal airport of Omaha. The airport began proceedings to acquire by eminent domain the right to pass over Johnson's land in taking off and landing, and to remove two trees that obstructed the line of flight, which at its lowest point passed about 26 feet above the surface of his land. The airport contended that Johnson was entitled to damages only for the taking of the two trees, and was not entitled to damages for the effect upon the value of the land of the planes passing at low level. From a decision adverse to the airport, it appealed.

---

[7] See Ch. 61.
[8] See p. 261.

YEAGER, J. . . . . [The appellant airport's theory is] that since such
an easement [or right to fly across another's land] is authorized, empowered, and even commanded under the federal authority, and
authorized by Nebraska statutes, damage without physical taking is
not compensable. . . .

It is clear, of course, that land is the physical base of the easement,
and the base of the right within which navigation may be carried on is
a plane not less than 26 feet above the land. In order to arrive at
which is the topmost altitude of the easement, it becomes necessary to
refer to the Civil Air Regulations adopted under proper authority by
the Civil Aeronautics Board. Section 60.17 of the regulations, in the
description of minimum safe altitudes, provides that, except for takeoff
or landing, the minimum safe altitude in noncongested areas shall be,
for a situation such as is involved here, 500 feet above the surface.
Obviously this situation was treated for the purpose of the trial as a
noncongested area. This was the minimum safe distance. The area
above this was free for use. It is described as navigable airspace.
Navigable airspace is defined in 49 U. S. C. A. (1962 Supp.), § 1301,
p. 143, as follows: " 'Navigable airspace' means airspace above the
minimum altitudes of flight prescribed by regulations issued under
this chapter, and shall include airspace needed to insure safety in takeoff and landing of aircraft."

It may well be said therefore that the space between the lower limit
of 26 feet above the land of appellees and the minimum safe altitude
of 500 feet was the area of the avigation easement involved here. . . .

The legal authorities are in substantial accord in the view that a
taking of real property in the establishment of a navigation easement
which reduces the value of that to which the easement attaches entitles
the owner to damages in the amount of the difference in value before
and after the taking. . . . The damage contemplated is that which
flows from activity in the easement area up to the navigable airspace,
which in the instance here appears to be 500 feet. Clearly it could not
be less than that altitude above the ground. . . .

[Judgment affirmed.]

D'Amato v. Weiss

141 Conn. 713, 109 A.2d 586 (1954)

Villano owned a tract of land on which there was a hotel building and
a house. In back of the house ran a six-foot wide concrete alley that
extended to the lobby and kitchen doors of the hotel. Villano conveyed the
hotel building to a person who was the predecessor in title of Weiss and
others. No mention was made in the deed of any easement over the alley.
Thereafter, Villano conveyed the house to a person who was the predecessor
in title of D'Amato and others. D'Amato shut off the alley and sued for an

injunction to prevent Weiss and the others from using the alley. From a judgment in favor of the defendants, the plaintiffs appealed.

INGLIS, C.J. . . . "Where during the unity of title an apparently permanent and obvious servitude is imposed on one part of an estate in favor of another, which, at the time of the severance, is in use, and is reasonable necessary for the fair enjoyment of the other, then upon a severance of such ownership, whether by voluntary alienation or by judicial proceedings, there arises by implication of law a grant or reservation of the right to continue such use. In such case the law implies that with the grant of the one an easement is also granted or reserved, as the case may be, in the other, subjecting it to the burden of all such visible uses and incidents as are reasonably necessary to the enjoyment of the dominant heritage in substantially the same condition in which it appeared and was used when the grant was made." . . .

"There is ample authority that in so far as necessity is significant, it is sufficient, if the easement is 'highly convenient and beneficial' for the enjoyment of the portion granted. . . . The reason that absolute necessity is not essential is because fundamentally such a grant by implication 'depends on the intention of the parties as shown by the instrument and situation with reference to the instrument, and it is not strictly the necessity for a right of way that creates it.' . . ."

The conveyance from Mary E. Villano to the defendants' predecessor in title carried with it an implied right of way over the alley. . . .

[Judgment affirmed.]

Ange v. Ange
235 N.C. 506, 71 S.E.2d 19 (1952)

Eli Ange and others, as trustees of the Jamesville Christian Church, and L. W. Ange submitted to the court an agreed statement of facts in order to determine the effect of a provision in a deed to the Church that the Church was grantee to hold the property "for church purposes only." From a decision that the Church had an absolute fee, L. W. Ange appealed.

VALENTINE, J. . . . Do the words "for church purposes only" . . . have the effect of reducing the estate from an indefeasible title to some lesser estate? It will be noted that there is no language which provides for a reversion of the property to the grantors or any other person in case it ceases to be used as church property.

Ordinarily a clause in a deed will not be construed as a condition subsequent, unless it contains language sufficient to qualify the estate conveyed and provides that in case of a breach the estate will be defeated, and this must appear in appropriate language sufficiently clear to indicate that this was the intent of the parties. . . .

"A grantor can impose conditions and can make the title conveyed dependent upon their performance. But if he does not make any condition, but simply expresses the motive which induces him to execute the deed, the legal effect of the granting words cannot be controlled by the language indicating the grantor's motive."

It is clear from a fair interpretation of the entire deed under which the Church took title to the property that the grantors intended by the . . . clause only to express their motive in deeding the property to the Church. Upon the authorities herein cited, we reach the conclusion and so hold that the Christian Church of Jamesville acquired an indefeasible title to the property in question and has a right to convey the same in fee simple. . . .

[Judgment affirmed.]

Lake Beulah Protective & Improvement Assn. v. Christenson
272 Wis. 493, 76 N.W.2d 276 (1956)

Leach owned a large tract of land surrounding Lake Beulah, which he subdivided and sold. The individual owners formed a protective and improvement association. The association and the lot owners sought an injunction against Christenson to stop her from using an old road through the area on the theory that the road was not a public road open to her. From a judgment in favor of the association, Christenson appealed.

MARTIN, J. . . . Plaintiffs contend that the road was platted by Leach as a private road for the use of the lot owners in the subdivision and that it never became a public road, first, because the town never accepted it as a public highway, and, second, because any use of the road by others than the lot owners has been a permissive, not an adverse, user. . . .

" 'The essential requisites of a valid common-law dedication are that there must be an intent to dedicate on the part of the owner and an acceptance of the dedication by the proper public authorities, or by general user.'

"Dedications or offers thereof need not be in writing, nor in any particular form. The intention of the owner to dedicate and acceptance thereof by the public are the essential elements of a complete dedication." . . .

The evidence shows that there was an intention to dedicate on the part of the owner in this case. In the original plat offered for approval by the town board the road was not marked "private" as required by [statute], and it is a valid presumption that the platter intended a dedication. That the town board so understood it is indicated by the endorsement on the plat of its refusal to maintain any streets or alleys therein. There is no showing that the offer was thereafter withdrawn. We must hold there was a continuing offer to dedicate; there is no evidence to the contrary.

It is true that there has not been an acceptance by the town. . . . The record shows, however, that there has been an acceptance by public user. The road was never posted as a private road; no gates or barricades were ever erected to keep the public out. The evidence shows that it was freely used by the public without objection for 27 years before this action was brought. Plaintiffs argue that there was no duty on the lot owners to object to the use of the road by any traveler. It is significant that in 1953 a number of lot owners petitioned the town board to take over and maintain the road as a town road. This would indicate that they considered its use by the public sufficient to warrant its maintenance by the town as a public road. . . .

[Judgment reversed but case remanded because of other questions involved.]

Questions and Case Problems

1. What is the objective of each of the following rules of law?
    (a) An easement is created when entry to land sold can be made only over the land retained by the grantor.
    (b) Acceptance by government is usually necessary to make a dedication effective.

2. Smikahl sold to Hansen a tract of land on which there were two houses and four trailer lots equipped with concrete patios and necessary connections for utility lines. The tract purchased by Hansen was completely surrounded by the land owned by Smikahl and third persons. In order to get onto the highway, it was necessary to cross the Smikahl tract. Several years later, Smikahl put a barbed wire fence around his land. Hansen sued to prevent obstruction to travel between his land and the highway over the Smikhal land. Smikahl defended on the ground that no such right of travel had been given to Hansen. Was he correct? (Hansen v. Smikahl, [Neb.] 113 N.W.2d 210)

3. Wyatt owned Crow Island in the White river. By the government land surveys of 1826 and 1854, the river separated the island from land to the east owned by Wycough. The river abruptly changed its course and cut a new channel to the east, with the result that part of the Wycough land was no longer separated by water from Crow Island. Wyatt brought a suit against Wycough, claiming that he now owned that portion of land which had been joined to his as a result of the movement of the river channel. Was he correct? (Wyatt v. Wycough, [Ark.] 341 S.W.2d 18)

4. Whisnant sued Price for cutting and removing trees from certain land. Price defended on the ground that he owned the land by adverse possession. He proved that for a period of more than 21 years he had from time to time entered on the land and cut and removed logs. Was Price the owner of the land? (Price v. Whisnant, 236 N.C. 381, 72 S.E.2d 851)

5. McCormick and Miller owned land on the opposite sides of the Salt River, the middle of which was the boundary line. Over a period of 17 years the waters of the stream imperceptibly washed away soil on McCormick's side and deposited it on Miller's side until there was about 15 acres of land on Miller's side of the river that had previously belonged to McCormick. An action was brought by McCormick against Miller to gain possession of the 15 acres. Was McCormick entitled to judgment? (McCormick v. Miller, 239 Mo. 463, 144 S.W. 101)

6. Cole conveyed a tract of land to Jewell but reserved the right to remove gravel from that tract. Both parties sold their respective interests, which were finally owned by Rossi as successor to Cole, and by Beckwith as successor to Jewell. Rossi dug seven holes on Beckwith's land in search of gravel but, finding none, he covered the holes with a bulldozer. Beckwith then sued Rossi, claiming that Rossi had unlawfully damaged the topsoil. Decide. (Beckwith v. Rossi, [Maine] 175 A.2d 732)

7. Digirolamo owned a tract of land near the Philadelphia Gun Club. During shooting contests held by the club, buckshot from the contestants' guns fell on the plaintiff's land. He sued the club to compel it to stop. The club claimed that as it had held these contests for over 21 years, it had acquired an easement to do so. Decide. (Digirolamo v. Philadelphia Gun Club, 371 Pa. 40, 89 A.2d 357)

8. Tucker and Hankey were adjoining property owners. Tucker claimed that the fence which separated their properties was not located properly and that it should be moved back onto Hankey's land. Hankey claimed that he owned the strip between the fence and the alleged boundary line by adverse possession. He proved that for 40 years there had been on the strip in question a barn with a cement floor, which had been built by the person from whom he purchased his land, and that he had been told by the former owner that the fence was the boundary line. The fence consisted of a 5-foot high barbed wire set in cement. Did Hankey own the strip by adverse possession? (Tucker v. Hankey, 173 Kan. 593, 250 P.2d 784)

9. Maioriello and Arlotta owned neighboring tracts of land. Arlotta built a concrete wall 10 feet high on his own property, three inches from the party line and from the kitchen of Maioriello's house. Maioriello sought an injunction to remove the wall because it shut out the light and air from the kitchen, for the wall ran in front of the window of the kitchen. Arlotta defended on the ground that Maioriello could build a skylight in the kitchen. Decide. (Maioriello v. Arlotta, 364 Pa. 557, 73 A.2d 374)

CHAPTER 54

Deeds — Nature and Execution

Although many of the technical limitations of the feudal and old common-law days have disappeared, much of the law relating to the modern deed originated in those days. For this reason the drawing of a deed to transfer the title to land should be entrusted only to one who knows exactly what must be done.

Sec. 54-A. A Real-Estate Purchase. Ordinarily, the present owner and the future owner of real estate will make a contract by which one agrees to sell and the other to buy the property for a stated amount. This contract usually includes a down payment by the buyer. As this contract relates to the transfer of an interest in land, it must be in writing because of the Statute of Frauds.

The execution of the written contract to sell real property may itself be preceded by an option contract by which the seller agrees to keep his offer open for a specified period of time in exchange for a payment made by the buyer.

In these various transactions either the seller or the buyer, or both of them, may have made use of a real-estate salesman or broker. Such a broker or agent is entitled to a commission for his services, which is generally a percentage of the selling or buying price.

The day on which payment of the purchase price and delivery of the deed are to be made is called the *settlement day,* and the process of making payment and delivering the deed is called a *settlement.*

The actual mechanics of the settlement depend to a large degree on whether the parties have not acted without agents, attorneys, or a title company. If they have done so, the seller hands the deed to the buyer and the buyer hands over the money. If one or more real-estate men are involved, this transaction will probably take place at the real-estate office, and a real-estate man will act as intermediary.

784

An attorney or a title insurance clerk may also participate if their services have been employed. If the purchaser is borrowing money in order to finance the purchase, he will ordinarily give the lender a mortgage.[1] In that case the lender will usually be at the place of settlement and will bring with him a check for the money that he is lending, but which he will not hand over until the purchaser signs a mortgage on the newly acquired property.

After the deed is executed by the parties, it will be delivered to the grantee, and the buyer is then the new owner. Generally the deed will thereafter be recorded in order to protect the grantee (purchaser).

Sec. 54-B. Definition. A *deed* is an instrument or writing by which an owner or *grantor* transfers or conveys an interest in land to a new owner called a *grantee* or transferee. In some states that have retained the influence of the common law, the deed must be sealed.

Just as a sale was distinguished from a contract to sell in Chapter 21, so a deed must be distinguished from a contract to convey, that is, to execute and deliver a deed in the future. In a sale or a deed there is a present transfer of an interest. In the case of the *contract to convey* or to sell there is the creation of a binding contractual obligation to make a transfer in the future. At times it is difficult to determine whether a particular writing should be regarded as a present transfer or whether it is merely a contract to transfer thereafter. The problem is one of determining the intention of the parties from the face of the instrument.

Unlike a contract, no consideration is required to make a deed effective. Real property, as in the case of personal property, may either be sold or given as a gift. Although consideration is not required to make a valid deed or transfer of title by deed, the absence of consideration may be evidence to show that the transfer was made by the owner in fraud of his creditors who may then be able to set aside the transfer. A deed is necessary to transfer title to land, even though it is a gift.

Sec. 54-C. Classification of Deeds. Any writing executed with sufficient formality that clearly expresses an intention to transfer a specified interest of the grantor to an identified grantee is generally held sufficient as a conveyance. Through custom, however, deeds generally follow certain patterns. They may be classified in terms of the number of parties executing the deed as (1) a *deed poll*, which is executed by the grantor alone, or (2) a *deed of indenture,* which is executed by both the grantor and the grantee and is used when the grantee makes a promise of some nature to the grantor. They may be classified in

---

[1] See Ch. 57.

terms of the interest conveyed as (1) a *quitclaim deed,* which transfers merely whatever interest, if any, the grantor may have in the property, without specifying that interest in any way, and (2) a *warranty deed,* which purports to transfer a specified interest and which warrants or guarantees that such interest is transferred.

A deed may also be classified as (1) a statutory deed or (2) a common-law deed. The *common-law deed* is a long form that sets forth the details of the transaction, such as the names of the parties, the consideration paid, the words of grant which declare that an interest is conveyed, and a description of the property in question; a description of the estate or interest in the property that is conveyed; a description of any interests reserved by the grantor; a recital of any conditions imposed upon the grant and of any covenants made by the grantor or the grantee; and a recital of the execution of the deed by the grantor. The *statutory deed* eliminates much of the detail of the common-law form and in substance merely recites that a named person is making a certain conveyance to a named grantee. It is generally held that the existence of a statute authorizing a short form of deed does not preclude the use of the common-law form.

Sec. 54-D. Grantor's Warranties. In the common-law warranty deed the grantor expressly warrants or makes certain guarantees. The statutes authorizing a short form of deed provide that unless otherwise stated in the deed, the grantor shall be presumed to have made certain warranties.

The more important of the covenants or warranties of title which the grantor may make are: (1) *covenant of seizin,* or guarantee that the grantor owns the exact estate which he has purported to convey; (2) *covenant of right to convey,* or guarantee that the grantor, if he is not the owner, as in the case of an agent, has the right or authority to make the conveyance; (3) *covenant against encumbrances,* or guarantee that the land is not subject to any right or interest of a third person, such as a lien, easement, or dower right; (4) *covenant for quiet enjoyment,* or covenant by the grantor that the grantee's possession of the land shall not be disturbed either by (a) the grantor, in the case of a limited covenant, or (b) the grantor or any person claiming title under him, in the case of a general covenant; and (5) *covenant for further assurances,* or promise by the grantor that he will execute any additional document that may be required to perfect the title of the grantee.

In the absence of a warranty in the deed, no warranty arises. Unlike sales of personal property, there are no implied warranties in a sale or conveyance of land under the common law. (See p. 791, Steiber v. Palumbo)

Sec. 54-E. Execution of Deeds. Ordinarily a deed must be signed, by signature or mark, and sealed by the grantor. In order to have the deed recorded, statutes generally require that two or more witnesses sign the deed and that the grantor then acknowledge his deed before a notary public or other officer. In the interest of legibility, it is frequently required that the signatures of the parties be followed by their printed or typewritten names.

The deed remains binding as between the grantor and his grantee even though it has not been acknowledged or recorded.

Sec. 54-F. Delivery. A deed has no effect and title does not pass until the deed has been delivered. Delivery is a matter of intent as shown by both words and conduct; no particular form of ceremony is required. The essential intent in delivering a deed is not merely that the grantor intends to hand over physical control and possession of the paper on which the deed is written, but that he intends thereby to divest himself of ownership of the property described in the deed. That is, he must deliver the deed with the intent that it should take effect as a deed and convey an interest in the property.

A deed is ordinarily made effective by handing it to the grantee with the intention that he should thenceforth be the owner of the property described in the deed. (See p. 792, McCord v. Robinson) A delivery may also be made by placing the deed, addressed to the grantee, in the mail or by giving it to a third person with directions to hand it to the grantee.

When a deed is delivered to a third person for the purpose of delivery by him to the grantee upon the happening of some event or contingency, the transaction is called a *delivery in escrow*. No title passes until the fulfillment of the condition or the happening of the event or contingency.

Sec. 54-G. Acceptance. Generally there must be an acceptance by the grantee. In the absence of statute no particular mode of acceptance is necessary. Acceptance may be proved by words, formal or informal, or by conduct or acts, such as conveying or mortgaging of the land, retaining the deed instead of returning it to the grantor, or asserting rights with respect to the land, such as cultivating it, which are incidents of ownership and inconsistent with nonownership.

A more practical statement of the rule is that in all cases an acceptance is presumed but the grantee may disclaim the transfer if he acts within a reasonable time after learning that the transfer has been made.

Sec. 54-H. Cancellation of Deeds. A deed, although delivered, acknowledged, and recorded, may be set aside or canceled by the grantor

upon proof of such circumstances as would warrant the setting aside
of a contract. For example, when a conveyance is made in consideration of a promise to support the grantor, the failure of the grantee
to perform will ordinarily justify cancellation of the deed.

Sec. 54-I. Recording of Deeds. If the owner of the land desires to
do so, he may record his deed in the office of a public official sometimes called a recorder or commissioner of deeds. The recording is not
required to make the deed effective to pass title, but it is done so that
the public will know that the grantee is the present owner and thereby
prevent the former owner from making any other transaction relating
to the property. The recording statutes provide that a person purchasing land from the last holder of record will take title free of any
unrecorded claim to the land of which the purchaser does not have
notice or knowledge.

The fact that a deed is recorded charges everyone with knowledge
of its existence even though they in fact do not know of it because
they have neglected to examine the record. The recording of a deed,
however, is only such notice if the deed was properly executed. Likewise, the grantee of the land cannot claim any protection by virtue
of the recording of a deed when (1) an adverse claim is made by one
whose title is superior to that of the owner of record; (2) the grantee
had notice or knowledge of the adverse claim when he acquired title;
(3) a person acting under a hostile claim was then in possession of the
land; (4) the grantee received the land as a gift; or (5) the transfer
to the grantee was fraudulent.

Sec. 54-J. Additional Protection of Third Parties. Apart from the
protection given to buyers and third persons by the recorded title to
property, a buyer may generally also protect himself by procuring an
abstract of title or title insurance. An *abstract of title* is a summarized
report of the title to the property as shown by the records, together
with a report of all judgments, mortgages, and similar claims against
the property that have also been recorded. The buyer relies upon the
accuracy with which the abstract has been made and the correctness
of the interpretation given to it.

Under *title insurance,* a specialized type of insurance company
makes the same type of search of the records as is done in preparing an
abstract, but it then insures or guarantees the condition of the title
to the property. In other words, it stands in back of any errors or
mistakes made in its examination or interpretation of the record. In
some states the *Torrens System* has been adopted under which the
ownership of the land is officially registered and a certificate of title
is issued after a hearing, and from then on whoever is the lawful owner
of the certificate for the title is the lawful owner as to everyone.

Sec. 54-K. Donees and Purchasers with Notice. Donees or persons who do not give value and persons who have knowledge or notice of outstanding claims always take title to property subject to such claims, such as unrecorded deeds and equitable or statutory liens on the land.

Sec. 54-L. Creditors of Grantor. The transfer of title under a deed may be defeated in some instances by creditors of the grantor.

(1) Fraudulent Conveyances. Following an English statute,[2] it is held in most states that a conveyance for the purpose of hindering, delaying, or defrauding creditors is voidable as against such creditors. The rule is applicable in the case of subsequent creditors, as well as those existing at the time of the conveyance. For example, when one, just before entering into debt, makes a conveyance that he knows is likely to render him unable to pay his obligations, the subsequent creditor may avoid the conveyance. When the transfer is made to a bona fide purchaser without notice, the title passes under a deed free from the demands or claims of either existing or subsequent creditors. In any case the person who claims that a transfer of title has been made in fraud of creditors has the burden of proving that fact.

Under the Uniform Fraudulent Conveyance Act[3] conveyances in certain situations are classified as being in fraud of creditors. If the claim of a defrauded creditor of the grantor is due, he may have the fraudulent conveyance set aside or he may disregard the conveyance and attach or levy execution upon the property conveyed, subject to whatever consideration has been paid by the grantee. If his claim has not matured, he may have the conveyance set aside or a receiver appointed or obtain such relief as may be appropriate.

(2) Federal Bankruptcy Act. Another situation in which the claims of creditors may defeat the passing of title is that in which the conveyance violates a provision of the Federal Bankruptcy Act. Under the provisions of that statute a conveyance that operates to give a preference to one creditor as against another may be set aside if the conveyance was made within four months prior to the time when the grantor was adjudged a bankrupt. The trustee in bankruptcy is also authorized to avoid any conveyance that is a fraud upon creditors.[4]

Sec. 54-M. Grantee's Covenants. In a deed the grantee may undertake to do or to refrain from doing certain acts. Such an agreement

---

[2] *Statute 13, Elizabeth,* Ch. 5.
[3] This Act has been adopted in Arizona, California, Delaware, Maryland, Massachusetts, Michigan, Minnesota, Montana, Nevada, New Hampshire, New Jersey, New Mexico, New York, North Dakota, Ohio, Pennsylvania, South Dakota, Tennessee, Utah, Washington, Wisconsin, and Wyoming.
[4] See p. 897.

becomes a binding contract between the grantor and the grantee. The grantor may sue the grantee for their breach. When the covenant of the grantee relates directly to the property conveyed, such as an agreement to maintain fences on the property or that the property shall be used only for residential purposes, it is said not only that the covenant is binding between the grantor and the grantee but also that it *runs with the land*. This means that anyone acquiring the grantee's land from the grantee is also bound by the covenant of the grantee, even though this subsequent owner had not made any such agreement with anyone.

Similarly the right to enforce the covenant also runs with the land owned by the grantor to whom the promise was made.

A covenant which provides that the grantee shall refrain from certain conduct is termed a *restrictive* (or negative) *covenant*. It runs with the land in the same manner as a covenant that calls for the performance of an act, that is, an *affirmative covenant*. Negative covenants most commonly relate to the type of building that the purchaser will place on the land or the nature of the use to which he will put the land.

As a covenant is a contract, a grantee's covenant may be enforced in an action at law for damages. In the case of restrictive or negative covenants, the complaining person may also obtain the aid of the equity jurisdiction that will grant an injunction compelling the owner of the land to comply with the terms of the covenant. Equitable relief is generally denied, however, in the case of affirmative covenants.

Relief, whether at law or in equity, will not be afforded when enforcement of the restriction would amount to a discrimination prohibited by the Fourteenth Amendment of the Constitution of the United States, or when the circumstances and neighborhood have so changed that it would be absurd to continue to enforce the restriction. Thus restrictions in deeds delivered forty years ago stipulating that no private automobile garages could be erected or maintained have frequently been held invalid in recent years because the auto is now so commonplace that its exclusion would be ridiculous and would now make the ownership of the property less valuable. Restrictions requiring that premises be used only for residential purposes may often be ignored when stores and other commercial or industrial enterprises have entered the neighborhood in such a large number that the character of the neighborhood is no longer predominantly residential. However, every change in character does not warrant an abandonment of a restrictive covenant. (See p. 793, Cochran v. Long) Likewise the mere fact that the owner can make more money from the use of his property for commercial purposes is not in itself sufficient to justify ignoring the restriction that it be used only for residential purposes.

Cases for Chaper 54

Steiber v. Palumbo

219 Ore. 479, 347 P.2d 978 (1959)

Palumbo and his brothers, as builders and officers of the A and A Construction Co., built a house which they sold to the Steibers. Nothing was said at any time as to the condition of the ground or of the house. The ground was in fact a fill which gradually settled unevenly. The Steibers sued the Palumbos and the A and A Construction Co. on the ground that they had made an implied warranty that the house was of sturdy construction and that the land was capable of supporting it. For a judgment in favor of the defendants, the Steibers appealed.

ROSSMAN, J. . . . The complaint makes no charge of fraud, misrepresentation, overreaching, breach of express agreement, or lack of opportunity for adequate inspection before purchase. . . .

The deed contains the usual warranties of title but no others. It is apparent that if the plaintiff is entitled to prevail, she must do so on the basis of an implied warranty. [The Oregon statutes] provide: "No covenant shall be implied in any conveyance of real estate, . . ." [Also] Williston on Contracts, Revised Edition, Sec. 926, states: " . . . There can be no warranty of quality or condition implied in the sale of real estate." . . .

No decision has come to our attention which permitted recovery by the vendee of housing upon a theory of implied warranty although Allison Dunham, "Vendor's Obligation as to Fitness of Land for a Particular Purpose," 77 Minn. Law Rev. 108 (1953) argues that the law will move in this direction in the case of the supplier of new housing. Professor Dunham reasons that in this situation the vendee should have a right to rely on the contractor's skill and judgment that the house is fit for habitation. No such right would arise, as that author concedes, in the resale of used housing since the vendor normally has no greater skill than the buyer. As to the present state of the law Professor Dunham reports it as follows: "On the sale of completed new housing or second-hand housing there seems to be no obligation on the seller as to latent defects in the quality of the land and improvements unless the obligation is one sounding in fraud for concealment of defects known to the seller. . . ."

In Combow v. Kansas City Ground Investment Co., 1949, 358 Mo. 934, 218 S.W.2d 539, 541, 8 A.L.R.2d 213, the plaintiff and her husband purchased from the defendant an old house which the defendant had extensively remodeled. Six days after the completion of the transaction, the plaintiff was injured when the ceiling plaster of one of the rooms fell upon her. She thereupon sued in tort for her personal injuries. . . . In affirming the judgment [for the defendant], the

Supreme Court said: "It seems to be well settled in this state and other jurisdictions that, absent an express agreement to the contrary, a seller of real estate cannot be held liable for defective condition of the premises. . . .

"Whatever may be the reason, no case can be found in the books where the vendor has been held liable in damages to the vendee, or to third persons, for personal injuries arising from defects in the premises. Whether this be on grounds of public policy, or because the rule of caveat emptor governs, and no warranty will be implied . . . , or whether it be because the precedent negotiations are supplanted by the deed when the vendee receives it, . . . or whether such damages are not supposed to be within the reasonable contemplation of the parties—whatever be the reason, the fact remains.' "

The English courts also recognize that there is no warranty implied in the sale or lease of real estate. . . .

It will be noticed from the foregoing that even apart from legislation, such as [the Oregon statute], the law refuses to imply in favor of the purchaser of an existing house warranties as to quality. As to purchasers of that kind the rule of *caveat emptor* applies, and he must reduce his purported warranties to written contractual form if he expects to base an action upon them. . . .

[Judgment affirmed.]

McCord v. Robinson
226 Ark. 350, 289 S.W.2d 893 (1956)

Armstrong and his wife executed and delivered a deed to real estate to their daughter, Mildred, because they were afraid that they might lose the property to creditors. The conveyance to the daughter reserved a life estate to the grantor. At the time he handed the daughter the deed, Armstrong said, "This is for you and do not record it until my death, but upon my death, you get the deed on record . . . furthermore, you are going to have to take care of it." The daughter was living with her parents and kept the deed in a trunk that was accessible to them. She had the deed recorded when a brother-in-law threatened to destroy it. When Armstrong was informed that it had been recorded, he said, "Just let it be, just like it is." After Armstrong's death, his other heirs sued to have the deed to the daughter set aside on the ground that it had never been delivered to her. From a decision in her favor, they appealed.

MILLWEE, J. . . . Appellants argue there was no delivery of the deed, which remained at all times in the possession and under the dominion of the grantors. . . . We cannot agree. . . .

"A deed is defined to be 'a written instrument, signed, sealed, and delivered'; and it is essential to the validity of a deed that there should be a delivery of the instrument. But in order to constitute a sufficient delivery thereof, it is not necessary that there should be an actual manual transfer thereof to the grantee or a formal acceptance thereof by him. The question of a delivery of a deed is largely one of intent; and if it clearly appears from the words or acts of the grantor that it was his intention to treat the instrument as his deed, and to make a disposal thereof indicating that it should be effective, then the delivery is sufficient. . . . The registration of a deed raises a presumption of the delivery to and acceptance by the grantee thereof. It is evidence of a most cogent character tending to show delivery. It is a solemn proclamation to the world that there has been a transfer of the title to the property from the grantor to the grantee, of which our law makes every one take notice. . . . A deed signed, acknowledged, and recorded is complete and valid, although there is no evidence of a formal delivery thereof; and the presumption of delivery arising therefrom can only be overcome by clear and decisive proof that the grantor did not part, and did not intend to part, with the possession of the deed. The weight of authority is that a deed thus executed and recorded is valid and effective to pass title although retained by the grantor in his possession. . . ."

. . . The evidence clearly indicates that there was a manual transfer of the deed to appellee with the intention of the grantors that it pass out of their control and operate as a conveyance. . . . The fact that possession of the land was reserved to the grantors for life does not defeat the passing of the title to appellee upon delivery of the deed, which was shown by a preponderance of the evidence.

[Judgment affirmed.]

Cochran v. Long

294 S.W.2d 503 (Ky.App., 1956)

Long owned real estate in what was designated as Block #2 of Harrodsburg, Kentucky. All lots in this block were subject to a restrictive covenant that they could only be used for residential purposes. A state highway was relocated so that it ran through Block #2, and from 400 to 500 motor vehicles passed on the highway per hour. A number of commercial enterprises had been built outside of but near Block #2. Long and others brought an action against Cochran and others owning property in Block #2 to determine whether this change of conditions released their land from the covenant that it be used only for residential purposes. From a judgment that the covenant was not binding, Cochran appealed.

STEWARD, J. . . . The decisive issue in this case is whether there has been such a radical change in the status of lots 1, 2, 3, 4, 5, and 28 in Block 2, affected by the restrictive covenant, as to relieve them of the burden of this covenant. . . .

"A change of conditions which will . . . annul . . . a restrictive covenant is a change of such a character as to make it impossible longer to secure in a substantial degree the benefits sought to be realized through the performance of a promise respecting the use of the land. If it is still possible, despite a change in conditions, to secure the anticipated benefit in a substantial, though lessened, degree, the change of conditions will not alone be sufficient to warrant the refusal of injunctive relief against breach of the obligation arising from the promise." . . .

The problem before us is simply one of deciding whether the facts in this case disclose there has been such a basic change in the character of the restricted property as to cause the covenant in question to be inapplicable to what appellees claim is a new situation. . . .

The chancellor, in finding for appellees, [Long and others], held there had been such a complete change in the territory under scrutiny that the restriction as to residential use applicable to lots 1 through 5 and to lot 28 in Block 2 was no longer of any substantial value to these lots. This conclusion was reached primarily, because of the location of the new highway through this block, over which much traffic proceeds and from which considerable noise ensues. For this reason, it was believed the trend is toward a business district in this area, although in Block 2 only two commercial establishments have been built since the completion of the highway. It is true there was testimony to the effect that some distance to the north and outside of Block 2, particularly at a street intersection about a block distant, several business places have been located within the last year or so, but we do not believe this changes the basic picture at the present time.

It does not follow that the mere presence of a highway that has become one of the principal arteries of travel through the city of Harrodsburg automatically alters the character of property involved here to the extent that this property is released from the restrictions that adhere to it. . . .

Nor are we convinced that the evidence in this record shows there has been such a transition over to business in Block 2 and the surrounding area as to interfere in any material respect with the enjoyment by appellant lot owners of the benefit of the neighborhood as a place of residence. This is especially true where, as here, the restricted property, though it be small in extent, has not been invaded. Appellants do not claim that the approach of business on either side of the restricted lots along the highway has affected the restricted area's desirability for residential purposes or materially changed its character as a residential district. . . .

[Judgment reversed and case remanded.]

SIMS, J. dissenting. . . . This case is easily distinguished from Bickell v. Moraio, 117 Conn., 176, 167 A. 722. . . . There, the restricted property was already located on the Post Road which was merely widened, which resulted in an increase of traffic. While here, the trunk line highway was put through the restricted property which theretofore had not abutted any road and had suffered no annoyance or inconvenience from any traffic.

To my mind putting this highway through the property protected by the restricted covenant makes such a change in conditions of the property as to neutralize the benefits of the restriction and to defeat the purpose of the covenant. . . .

Questions and Case Problems

1. What is the objective of each of the following rules of law?

(a) No consideration is required to make a deed effective.

(b) A purchaser is charged with knowledge of a recorded deed even though he does not know that a deed has been recorded.

2. In 1959 the Chicago Land Clearance Commission brought proceedings to acquire by eminent domain real estate owned by George Loftus. In this proceedings, George's mother, Mary, filed a petition claiming that she was the owner and entitled to the compensation of $21,000 for the taking of the land. She admitted that in 1942 she had executed a deed to George and had delivered it to him and that the deed had been recorded. She contended, however, that she did not receive any consideration for the deed and had not intended to make a gift. Was she entitled to the condemnation money? (Chicago Land Clearance Commission v. Yablong, [Ill.] 170 N.E.2d 145)

3. Beaty, who owned 133 acres of land, conveyed a 3.67 acre tract to Dunlap by a deed which stated that Dunlap agreed that "no building on said premises shall ever be used as a store or for the conduct of mercantile business." From time to time Beaty sold other portions of land from the tract, and each deed contained similar restrictions. About 20 years later, Dunlap brought a declaratory judgment action against Beaty to have the restriction declared extinguished on the grounds (a) that it was not imposed as a part of a general scheme of improvement, and (b) that since the deed was executed, there had been such a radical change in the character of the neighborhood as to destroy the essential object and purpose of the restriction. Beaty defended on the ground that (a) the grantee could not bring an action against his grantor to extinguish the restriction, and (b) if the restriction were extinguished, it would lessen the commercial value of a part of the large tract still retained by the grantor on which there was a large shopping center. Decide. (Dunlap v. Beaty, [S.C.] 122 S.E.2d 9)

4. Whitaker dedicated to the city of Clear Lake a strip of land for public use as a street. The dedication was accepted by the city. The heirs of Whitaker gave Westfall a quitclaim deed to whatever property in the street had been owned by their ancestor. In a proceeding between a later owner, Kelroy, and the city, the question arose as to the effect of this quit-claim deed. Decide. (Kelroy v. City of Clear Lake, 232 Iowa 161, 5 N.W.2d 12)

5. Randall was about to sell his farm. He employed the Paine-Nichols Abstract Co. to make an abstract of the title. The abstract failed to list the existence of a water flow easement on the land, but Randall did not see the abstract since it was sent directly to the purchaser. Randall expressly told the purchaser that there was no easement and delivered to him a warranty deed to the property. When the easement was discovered, the purchaser recovered damages from Randall for the breach of the warranty. Randall sued the abstract company to recover the damages he paid the purchaser. Decide. (Randall v. Paine-Nichols Abstract Co., 205 Okla. 430, 238 P.2d 319)

6. Austin Combs conveyed the minerals underlying the tract of land owned by him to F. Combs. The minerals were next conveyed by F. Combs to Trigg, who in turn conveyed them to the Virginia Iron, Coal & Coke Co. After making the conveyance to F. Combs, the grantor had conveyed the tract of land to Jackson and Alonzo Combs, who had knowledge of the former deed that had not been properly certified and recorded. Jackson Combs brought an action against the coal company to determine title to the minerals in the land. Decide. (Virginia Iron, Coal & Coke Co. v. Combs, 186 Ky. 261, 216 S.W. 846)

7. Randall conveyed by deed certain land to his brother, O. Randall. The deed was not recorded, but the grantee took possession of the property and leased it to Gans. Thereafter J. Randall conveyed the land to Lingwall, who knew that Gans was in possession of the property but relied solely upon the record. Still later the deed to O. Randall was recorded. In an action brought by heirs of O. Randall against Lingwall, it was contended that the defendant was not a bona fide purchaser without notice. Do you agree? (Randall v. Lingwall, 43 Ore. 383, 73 P. 1)

8. Borstad agreed to sell certain lots to Grinne. Cone, who was employed to prepare the abstract of title, failed to include in the abstract a judgment that had been entered against Borstad and which was a lien on the land. In an action brought by Stephenson, administrator of the estate of Grinne, against Cone, it was contended that the abstract should have shown the existence of such judgment. Do you agree? (Stephenson v. Cone, 24 S.D. 460, 124 N.W. 439)

CHAPTER 55

Creation and Termination
of Leases

The relation of landlord and tenant exists whenever one person holds possession of the real property of another under an express or implied agreement.

Sec. 55-A. Nature. The person who owns the real property and permits the occupation of the premises is known as the *landlord* or *lessor*. The *tenant* or *lessee* is the one who occupies the property. A *lease* establishes the relationship of landlord and tenant. It is in effect a conveyance of a leasehold estate in land. The term "lease" is also used to designate the paper that is evidence of this transfer of interest.

The following elements are necessary in the establishment of the relation of landlord and tenant:

(1) The occupation must be with the express or implied consent of the landlord. (See p. 802, Williams v. Treece) For example, an occupancy by a trespasser does not create the relation.

(2) The tenant must occupy the premises in subordination to the rights of the landlord. To illustrate, the relation is not established if the person occupying the land claims ownership of the property.

(3) A reversionary interest in the land must remain in the landlord. That is, the landlord must be entitled to retake the possession of the land upon the expiration of the lease.

(4) The tenant must have an estate in the land of present possession. This means that he must have a right that entitles him to be in possession of the land now.

The requirement that a tenant have possession distinguishes the tenant's interest from the interests of others in the land. A person may receive permission from the owner of land to erect and maintain a billboard on the owner's land. This is merely a *license* and does not create a leasehold interest because a *licensee* has permission to do certain acts on the land but does not have any right to stay in possession of the land. Similarly, a person having a right of way, or a right to cross, over his neighbor's land is not in possession of that land. He has merely an easement and is not a tenant of the neighbor. A tenant also differs from a *sharecropper*, for the latter is in substance the servant of the landlord who is paid by a share of the crops he raises.

Sec. 55-B. Classifications of Tenancies. Tenancies are divided into four classes in terms of the duration of the estate created:

(1) Tenancy for Years. A *tenancy for years* is one under which the tenant has an estate of definite duration. Such a tenancy can run for any number of years, even beyond the life of the parties. The term "for years" is used to describe such a tenancy even though the duration of the tenancy is for only one year or for less than a year.

(2) Tenancy from Year to Year. A *tenancy from year to year* is one under which a tenant, holding an estate in land for an indefinite period of duration, pays an annual rent. A distinguishing feature of this tenancy is the fact that it does not terminate at the end of a year, except upon proper notice.

In almost all states a tenancy from year to year is implied if the tenant holds over after a tenancy for years with the consent of the landlord, as shown by his express statement or by conduct such as continuing to accept rent. The landlord may reject the holding over, however, and the tenant is then a trespasser. The lease will frequently state that a holding over shall give rise to a tenancy from year to year unless written notice to the contrary be given, or will expressly provide for an extension or renewal of the lease.

A lease may run from month to month or from week to week in the same manner as a lease from year to year.

(3) Tenancy at Will. When land is held for an indefinite period, which may be terminated at any time by the landlord, or by the landlord and the tenant acting together, a *tenancy at will* exists. A person who enters into possession of land for an indefinite period with the owner's permission but without any reservation of rent is a tenant

at will. An agreement that a person can move into an empty house and live there until he finds a home to buy creates a tenancy at will.

When the tenant may stay in the property for as long as he wishes, he literally has the right to stay in possession the rest of his life. Most courts accordingly hold that a life estate is created by such permission if there is a writing that satisfies the requirements of the Statute of Frauds. (See p. 803, Thompson v. Baxter) If there is no such writing, only a tenancy at will is created. Some courts hold that a tenancy at will is created even when there is a writing under the statute.

Statutes in some states and decisions in others require advance notice of the termination of this type of tenancy.

(4) Tenancy by Sufferance. When a tenant holds over without permission of the landlord, the latter may treat him as a trespasser or as a tenant. Until he elects to do one or the other, a *tenancy by sufferance* exists.

Sec. 55-C. Creation of the Relation. The relation of landlord and tenant is created by an express or implied contract. An oral lease is valid at common law, but statutes in most states require written leases for certain tenancies. Many statutes follow the English Statute of Frauds, which provides that a lease for a term exceeding three years must be in writing. Statutes in other states require written leases when the term exceeds one year. Some courts apply to leases the provision of the Statute of Frauds which states that an agreement not to be performed within the space of one year from its execution shall be in writing.

In the absence of an express statutory provision, the courts follow the rule that a tenancy from year to year is implied when the tenant goes into possession and pays rent under a lease which fails to comply with the Statute of Frauds. Statutes often provide that in such a case either a tenancy at will or a tenancy from year to year is created.

An option to renew a lease for more than one year must be in writing and, if it is not, the tenant becomes a tenant at will upon the expiration of the original term.

The fact that the tenant under an oral lease for which a writing is required by the Statute of Frauds has gone into possession and paid rent does not take the lease out of the Statute of Frauds when the tenant has not made any improvements to the property.

Sec. 55-D. Terms of Lease. Ordinarily a lease need not be in any particular form of language, provided it is clear and definite, showing an intention to transfer possession of the premises by lease. A written lease usually contains (1) the date of execution, (2) an identification of the parties, (3) a description of the premises, (4) a designation of the term for which the tenancy is to exist, (5) a statement as to the amount and the manner of payment of the rent, (6) a statement of any other obligations of the parties, and (7) the signatures of the parties.

The obligations of the parties that are referred to in point (6) in the preceding paragraph are frequently described as covenants. Thus a promise by the tenant to make repairs is called a *covenant to repair*. Sometimes it is provided that the lease shall be forfeited or terminated upon a breach of a promise, and the provision is then called a *condition* rather than a covenant.

If a statute prescribes certain requirements for a valid lease, as is sometimes the case, its provisions must, of course, be followed. In some states a lease for more than a specified period must be under seal, witnessed, acknowledged, and recorded.

Sec. 55-E. Termination of Lease. A lease is generally not terminated by the death, insanity, or bankruptcy of either party, except in the case of a tenancy at will.

(1) Expiration of Term in a Tenancy for Years. When a tenancy for years exists, the relation of landlord and tenant ceases upon the expiration of the agreed term, without any requirement that one party give the other any notice of termination. Express notice to end the term may be required of either or both parties by provisions in the lease, except when a statute prohibits imposing such a requirement.

(2) Notice in a Tenancy from Year to Year. A tenancy from year to year may be terminated at the end of a period by a prior notice to quit by the landlord or a notice of intention to quit by the tenant. In the absence of an agreement or a statute to the contrary, the landlord wishing to end the tenancy from year to year at the end of a period is required to give notice. The tenant is also usually required to give notice of his intention to quit. When either of them fails to give proper notice, the other party may elect to continue the relation for another period.

In the absence of an agreement of the parties notice is now usually governed by statutes. Thirty or sixty days' notice is generally required to end a tenancy from year to year. As to tenancies for periods of less than a year, the provisions of the statute may require only one week.

A notice to quit or the notice of intention to quit must be definite. Statute or lease provision may require that it be written.

(3) Release. The relation of landlord and tenant is terminated if the landlord makes a release or conveyance of his interest in the land to the tenant.

(4) Merger. If the tenant acquires the landlord's interest in any manner, as by inheritance or purchase, the leasehold interest is said to disappear by merger into the title to the land now held by the former tenant. The result is the same if the tenant has an estate for years and inherits a life estate in the same premises because a life estate is regarded as a greater interest.

(5) Surrender. A surrender or giving up by the tenant of his estate to the landlord terminates the tenancy if the surrender is accepted by the latter. A surrender may be made expressly or impliedly.

An express surrender must, under the Statute of Frauds, be in writing and signed by the person making the surrender or by his authorized agent.

A surrender by operation of law occurs only when the acts of the parties clearly show that both consider that the premises have been surrendered, as when the premises have been abandoned by the tenant and their return has been accepted by the landlord. (See p. 804, Duncan Development Co. Case) An acceptance may be inferred from the conduct of the landlord, but such conduct must clearly indicate an intention to accept. The mere taking of possession and re-entry by the landlord does not in itself prove an acceptance as he has the right to enter for the purpose of protecting or repairing the premises, and an entrance for that purpose or the performance of such work will not convert an abandonment by the tenant into a surrender and an acceptance. The same is true when the landlord leases the property to another tenant, or relets. Whether an acceptance of a surrender is implied in such a case depends on whether the landlord relets on his own or on the tenant's account in order to produce a rent to be applied in reduction of the landlord's claim against the tenant.

(6) Forfeiture. The landlord may terminate the tenancy by forfeiting the relation because of the tenant's misconduct or breach of a condition, if a term of the lease or a statute so provides. In the absence of such a provision the landlord may only make a claim for damages. This method of terminating the relation is not favored by courts, and the terms of a lease providing for a forfeiture are construed strictly against the landlord. Likewise the right to declare a forfeiture is generally waived by the landlord when, with knowledge of the breach of covenant giving rise to the right to forfeit the lease, he accepts rent that accrues thereafter.

(7) Destruction of Property. According to common law, when a lot and the building on it are leased, the destruction of the building does not terminate the lease or affect the duties of the tenant under the lease. He must continue to pay the full rental and is not entitled to a partial reduction proportionate to the building destroyed. This

rule of common law, however, is generally modified either by express provision in the lease or by a statute releasing the tenant from his liability under such circumstances, or reducing the amount of rent in proportion to the loss sustained. Such statutes do not impose upon the landlord any duty to repair or restore the property to its former condition.

When the lease covers rooms or an apartment in a building, a destruction of the leased premises terminates the lease.

Cases for Chapter 55

Williams v. Treece

184 Mo.App. 135, 168 S.W. 209 (1914)

Treece, a hunter and fisherman, went upon a tract of wild land partly adjacent to Cusion Lake in Missouri and built a tent in which he lived for several years. Thereafter he constructed a cheap house for the use of himself and his family. Williams, owner of the land, notified Treece to leave the property. He then brought an action against Treece, as a tenant, for unlawfully staying on the property after notice to leave had been given to him. For a judgment for the defendant, the plaintiff appealed.

NORTONI, J. . . . The real controversy in the instant case relates to the matter as to whether or not the relation of landlord and tenant existed between plaintiff and defendant. . . . Defendant insists no such arrangement was made whatever between the parties and he merely squatted upon the land, having told plaintiff he contemplated doing so. . . .

The instructions given by the judge to the jury seem to imply, at least, that in order to create that relation between the parties there should have been a renting of the place in the sense that a stipend of rent should be reserved. . . .

While a reversion of rent is usually incident to the relation of landlord and tenant, it is not absolutely essential. It is well settled that the relation of landlord and tenant may arise without a reservation of rent. . . . Indeed, the relation of landlord and tenant may be defined in general terms as that which arises from a contract by which one person occupies the property of another with his permission and in subordination to his right; the occupant in such case being known as the tenant, and the person in subordination to whom he occupies as the landlord. It is essential to the relation that the occupancy be both permissive and subordinate. When the two latter elements coexist, it is sufficient, though there be no actual reservation of rent. . . .

It is clear the instructions . . . misdirected the jury, and because of them the judgment should be reversed and the cause remanded.

Thompson v. Baxter
107 Minn. 122, 119 N.W. 797 (1909)

By a written lease, Thompson rented residential property in Albert Lea, Minnesota, to Baxter at an agreed monthly rental of $22 for "the full term of which he shall wish to live in Albert Lea." Later Thompson gave Baxter notice to leave. When he refused, Thompson brought an action to recover possession of the property. Baxter claimed that a life tenancy had been created which was not terminated by notice. From a judgment for the defendant, the plaintiff appealed.

BROWN, J. . . . . Tenancies at will may be created by express words, or they may arise by implication of law. . . .

A tenancy by sufferance arises where the tenant wrongfully holds over after the expiration of his term. . . .

A tenancy from month to month or year to year arises where no definite time is agreed upon and the rent is fixed at so much per year or month, as the case may be, and is terminable at the expiration of any period for which [rent] has been paid. . . . This form of tenancy can never exist where the lease or contract prescribes a fixed time. . . .

From these general principles of the law of tenancy it is quite clear that the lease under consideration does not come within any class mentioned. Its language does not expressly define it as a tenancy at will, and no such relation arises by implication for the reason that the term is not indefinite within the meaning of the law on this subject, nor is the right to terminate the lease reserved to the lessor. . . . In the lease under consideration the tenancy is limited by the time defendant [Baxter] shall continue to dwell in Albert Lea, and this limitation takes the case out of the class of tenancies at will. It is equally clear that a tenancy by sufferance was not created by the contract. There has been no wrongful or unlawful holding over the expiration of the term. Nor does the rule of tenancy from month to month apply. . . .

We therefore turn to the question . . . whether the instrument created a life estate in defendant. . . . It is thoroughly settled that a life estate may be created by deed, lease, or devise, either with or without a stipulation for the payment of rent. This class of tenancies differs in many essential respects from tenancies at will, or from year to year, or by sufference. . . . The lease under consideration embodies all the essentials of a life tenancy. It contains the usual words of inheritance, necessary at common law, running to defendant, "his heirs, executors, administrators, and assigns," and grants the right of occupancy for the term stated therein. . . .

[Judgment for defendant affirmed.]

Duncan Development Co. v. Duncan Hardware

34 N.J.S. 293, 112 A.2d 274 (1955)

Duncan Development Co. leased a store and basement to Duncan Hardware, Inc. When Development sued Hardware for rent, Hardware claimed that it was not liable because the lease had been surrenderd. Hardware showed that in May it had moved its store to another building across the street from the rented building. From July to September it moved its merchandise from the old to the new store although it continued to pay rent until December. In October, Development asked Hardware for a set of the keys to the old store so that a prospective tenant could be shown the premises. After Hardware's removal, Development used the garage of the old store on several occasions, dismantled and sold a heating blower which had been used to heat the old store, and removed signs from the window of the old store telling customers where the new store was located. In the following January, Development requested and was given the remaining keys to the premises. From a judgment for Development, Hardware appealed.

FRIEND, J.A.D. . . . Surrender by operation of law [requires] . . . acts . . . incompatible with the continued existence of the relationship of landlord and tenant under the lease.

. . . There must not only be an abandonment by the tenant, but an acceptance by the landlord. But the mere receipt of keys and the landlord's endeavor to relet the property may not, without more, constitute an acceptance of surrender. . . .

Whether there has been a surrender by operation of law depends on the intention of the parties to be deduced from their words and acts and is ordinarily a question of fact for the jury. The burden of proof is on the party alleging the surrender; and where it is to be inferred from circumstances or conduct inconsistent with an intention to perform, the proof must be clear. . . .

Surrender by operation of law "commonly occurs when the tenant abandons possession during the term in such manner as to indicate his intent to terminate the lease; and the landlord takes possession, in such manner as to show that he intends to reassume control for his own benefit, and not for the benefit of the outgoing tenant.". . . In the instant matter, any one of the acts of the parties might not as a matter of law constitute a surrender and an acceptance thereof, but in combination they were sufficient to raise a question of fact for the jury. . . . The case is reversed to the end that the question of termination of the lease by the tenant's voluntary surrender and the landlord's acceptance may be passed upon by a jury.

[Judgment reversed and case remanded.]

Questions and Case Problems

1. What is the objective of each of the following rules of law?
    (a) A notice to terminate a tenancy from year to year must be definite.
    (b) There is no acceptance of a surrender of a lease when the lessor retakes possession after abandonment of the premises by the tenant and then the lessor relets them in the name of the tenant.

2. Melson owned an oyster ground. Carruthers made an oral agreement to take care of the oyster beds, to harvest and sell the oysters, and to divide with Melson the net balance remaining after expenses were deducted. When Carruthers died, Hickman claimed that by virtue of Carruthers' will he acquired the latter's tenancy in the oyster grounds. Hickman sued Melson to prevent interference with his rights as a tenant of the oyster grounds. Decide. (Hickman v. Melson, [Va.] 107 S.E.2d 387)

3. Cropper "leased" to Timmons "appropriate space" for the operation of pinball machines on premises owned by Cropper on a "50-50 basis." The lease stated that no one else would be given a right to operate such machines on the premises. Contrary to the lease agreement, Cropper permitted other persons to install pinball machines in addition to those of Timmons. Timmons sued for an injunction on the ground that a landlord will be enjoined from violating his covenant as to his use of his property. Cropper claimed that this principle was not applicable. Decide. (Timmons v. Cropper, [Del.] 172 A.2d 757)

4. Clay, who owned a tract of land, permitted Hartney to occupy a cabin on the land. There was no agreement as to the length of time that it could be occupied, and either could terminate the relationship when he chose. There was no provision for rent. Hartney died. The next day Clay closed up the cabin and put Hartney's possessions outside the door. Paddock, who was appointed the executor under Hartney's will, claimed the right to occupy the cabin. Was he entitled to do so? (Paddock v. Clay [Mont.] 357 P.2d 1)

5. Williams leased a farm to Mershon for a period of one year, with an option of a further term of four years. During the year Mershon notified Williams that he would take the farm for one more year. Although notice to quit was not given to the tenant, Williams brought an action against Mershon to recover possession of the farm at the end of the first year. Was Williams entitled to judgment? (Williams v. Mershon, 57 N.J.L. 242, 30 A. 619)

6. Stockholm owned certain real estate. For a consideration he gave to the Borough Bill Posting Co. the exclusive privilege of erecting and using a signboard to be located on the land for bill posting purposes. He reserved the right, in case the property was sold or required for building purposes, to cancel all privileges upon returning to the company a pro rata amount of the consideration. In an action brought by Stockholm against the company, it was contended that a landlord-tenant relationship had been created. Do you agree? (Stockholm v. Borough Bill Posting Co., 144 App.Div. 642, 129 N.Y.S. 745)

7. Illinois Wesleyan University rented property in Mississippi to Brasher. The university was sued in Mississippi by Gillentine. Service in the action was made on Brasher on the theory that, as tenant, he was the agent of the university. If he was the agent, the service was valid. Was it valid? (Gillentine v. Illinois Wesleyan University, 194 F.2d 970 [C.C.A. 5th])

8. Hanson rented a dwelling to Pierce for seventeen and one-half months by an oral agreement. Pierce went into possession, varnished some of the floors, and altered his curtains to fit the windows. Hanson then notified him to leave. Pierce sued Hanson to restrain him from retaking possession of the property. The defendant contended that the lease was not binding because of the Statute of Frauds. Do you agree with this contention? (Pierce v. Hanson, 147 Minn. 219, 179 N.W. 893)

9. Louis De Marco rented a store from the Vineland Shopping Center, Inc. Since De Marco did not comply with all the provisions of the lease, Vineland desired to terminate the lease. The New Jersey statute required it to cause "a written notice of the termination of said tenancy to be served upon said tenant." The attorney of Vineland entered De Marco's store, inquired for Mr. De Marco, and then handed him a notice to terminate Sec., Vineland Shopping Center, Inc." Louis De Marco claimed that the father handed the notice to Louis who was present in the store. The notice did not state by whom it was given but was signed "by Sidney L. Brody, Sec., Vineland Shopping Center, Inc." Louis De Marco claimed that the notice was not effective because it had not been served upon him and was not given by and in the name of the landlord. Decide. (Vineland Shopping Center, Inc. v. Louis De Marco, [N.J.] 167 A.2d 414).

10. Boyar leased certain property to Wallenberg. The tenancy was from month to month at an agreed monthly rental, payable on the first of each month in advance. On the 27th of the following month, Wallenberg vacated the premises without giving any due notice of his intentions to move. Boyar brought an action against Wallenberg to recover one month's rent. Decide. (Boyar v. Wallenberg, 132 Misc. 116, 228 N.Y.S. 358)

11. Patcraft Mills leased a showroom from Gulbenkian. Patcraft Mills guaranteed a rent of $12,000 per year to be paid monthly with an additional amount of 1 per cent of total sales calculated at the end of the year. At the end of approximately 5 months Patcraft Mills left the premises. Gulbenkian sued for the defense that the lease was not for a year but only for a month at a time. Decide. (Gulbenkian v. Patcraft Mills, Inc., [Ga.App.] 121 S.E.2d 179)

CHAPTER 56

Tenant and Landlord

The rights and duties of the tenant and landlord relate to such matters as possession and use of the premises, rent, repairs and improvements, taxes and assessments, liability for injury on the premises, and assignment of the lease and subletting.

Sec. 56-A. Rights and Duties

(1) Possession. Possession involves both the right to acquire possession at the beginning of the lease and the right to retain possession until the lease is ended.

(a) TENANT'S RIGHT TO ACQUIRE POSSESSION. By making a lease, the landlord impliedly covenants that he will give possession of the premises to the tenant at the agreed time. If the landlord rents a building which is being constructed, there is an implied covenant that it will be ready for occupancy at the commencement of the term of the lease.

If the lease is obtained by fraud or if the tenant does not perform a condition precedent to the vesting of the estate, the landlord may rightfully withhold possession. The tenant's failure to perform any other agreement does not justify a refusal of possession. The landlord cannot withhold possession merely because the tenant has met financial reverses; although he may, with reason, be afraid that the tenant will not be able to make future payments of rent.

The tenant is entitled to damages for the landlord's refusal to give possession, and he is generally allowed to bring an action to obtain possession. He may, however, accept possession at a date later than that fixed by the terms of the agreement, or he may accept possession of a part of the premises. In either case he is entitled to any damages he has suffered, unless he waives his right to them.

The amount of damages that the tenant recovers is the difference between the actual rental value of the premises and the rent specified in the lease. The tenant cannot recover from the landlord profits that he expected to make by the use of the leased property because these are too speculative.

(b) TENANT'S RIGHT TO RETAIN POSSESSION. After the tenant has entered into possession, he has exclusive possession and control of the premises as long as the lease continues and so long as he is not in default under the lease, unless the lease otherwise provides. Thus the tenant can refuse to allow the landlord to enter the property for the purpose of showing it to prospective customers, although today many leases expressly give this right to the landlord.

If the landlord interferes with this possession by evicting the tenant, he commits a wrong for which the tenant is afforded legal redress. An *eviction* exists when the tenant is deprived of the possession, use, and enjoyment of the premises by the interference of the landlord or one acting under him. An eviction may be total or partial.

If the landlord wrongfully deprives the tenant of the use of one room when he is entitled to the use of the whole building, there is a *partial eviction.*

A tenant who has been evicted may in a proper action recover possession of the premises, or damages for the eviction, or both. The landlord, however, is not liable for the acts of others unless they are his agents. If the eviction is by one gaining possession through a title paramount to that of the landlord, the latter is usually liable for damages under an implied or express covenant for quiet enjoyment. Most written leases today contain an express covenant to protect the tenant in the quiet enjoyment of his possession.

(c) CONSTRUCTIVE EVICTION. An eviction may be actual or constructive. It is a *constructive eviction* when some act or omission of the landlord substantially deprives the tenant of the use and enjoyment of the premises. It is essential in a constructive eviction that the landlord intend to deprive the tenant of the use and enjoyment of the premises. This intent may, however, be inferred from the results of his conduct. The tenant must also abandon the premises in consequence of the landlord's conduct. If he continues to occupy the premises for more than a reasonable time after the acts claimed to constitute a constructive eviction, he is deemed to waive the eviction. He cannot thereafter abandon the premises and claim an eviction. (See p. 814, Bolding v. Clanton)

A landlord commits a constructive eviction when he intentionally drives the tenant out of the property by shutting off the heat, gas, or water supply, or keeps him from entering the property by refusing to operate the elevators.

(2) Use of Premises. In the absence of express or implied restrictions, a tenant is entitled to use the premises for any purpose for

which they are adapted or for which they are ordinarily employed, or in a manner contemplated by the parties in executing the lease. He is under an implied duty to use the premises properly even when the lease is silent as to the matter. What constitutes proper use of the premises depends, in the first place, upon the wording of the lease. The tenant is also under an implied duty to use the premises for lawful purposes.

The tenant is under an implied duty to refrain from willful or permissive waste. At common law the tenant of farm land is entitled to cut sufficient timber for fuel and for repairs to fences, buildings, and farm implements. This rule is extended in many jurisdictions to allow the tenant to clear timber to a reasonable degree so that he may put the land under cultivation. If this would involve any substantial area, it is likely that the lease would define the rights of the parties in this respect.

(3) Rent. The tenant is under a duty to pay rent as compensation to the landlord.[1] In times of emergency, war, and recovery from war, however, government may impose maximum limitations on rents that are charged.

It is generally held that a tenant is not excused from paying the rent because government restrictions prevent him from obtaining the goods which he expected to sell in the rented property.

The time of payment of rent is ordinarily fixed by the lease. When the lease does not control, rent generally is not due until the end of the term. Statutes or custom, however, may require rent to be paid in advance when the agreement of the parties does not regulate the point. Rent that is payable in crops is generally payable at the end of the term.

If the lease is assigned, the assignee is liable to the landlord for the rent. The assignment, however, does not in itself discharge the tenant from his obligations under the lease. The landlord may bring an action for the rent against either the tenant or the assignee, or both, but he is entitled to only one satisfaction. A sublessee ordinarily is not liable to the original lessor for rent, unless he assumes such liability or unless the liability is imposed by statute.

(4) Repairs. In the absence of an agreement to the contrary, the tenant has the duty to make those repairs that are necessary to prevent waste and decay of the premises, and he is liable for *permissive waste* if he fails to do so. When the landlord leases only a portion of the premises, or leases the premises to different tenants, he is under a duty to make repairs in connecting parts, such as halls, basements, elevators, and stairways, which are under his control. Some statutes require that

---

[1] For the effect of destruction of the premises on the duty to pay rent, see p. 801.

a landlord who leases a building for dwelling purposes must keep it in condition fit for habitation.

Most states deny the landlord the right to enter the leased premises to inspect them for waste and need of repairs except when the right is expressly reserved in the lease.

(5) Improvements. In the absence of special agreement, neither the tenant nor the landlord is under a duty to make improvements. Either may, however, make a covenant for improvements, in which case a failure to perform will render him liable in an action for damages for breach of contract brought by the other party. In the absence of an agreement to the contrary, improvements that are attached to the land become part of the realty and belong to the landlord.[2]

(6) Taxes and Assessments. In the absence of an agreement to the contrary, the landlord and not the tenant is usually under a duty to pay taxes or assessments. It the tax or assessment, however, is chargeable to improvements made by the tenant that do not become a part of the property, the tenant is liable.

If the tenant pays taxes or assessments to protect his interests, he may recover the amount, including damages, from the landlord, or withhold the amount from the rent.

When the premises are assigned by the tenant, the assignee is bound by any covenants of the tenant to pay taxes and assessments. Such covenants are said to "run with the land." The fact that the assignee is bound by the covenants does not, however, discharge the tenant from liability.

A sublessee is not bound by the covenants of the tenant, but he may expressly assume them. In the latter case, however, the tenant is not discharged from his covenants.

Sec. 56-B. Remedies of Landlord.

(1) Landlord's Lien. In the absence of an agreement or statute so providing, the landlord does not have a lien upon the personal property or crops of the tenants for money due him for rent. The parties may create by express or implied contract, however, a lien in favor of the landlord for rent, and also for advances, taxes, or damages for failure to make repairs.

(2) Suit for Rent. Whether or not the landlord has a lien for unpaid rent, he may sue the tenant on the latter's contract to pay rent as specified in the lease or, if payment of rent is not specified, he

---

2 As to the removal of improvements as trade fixtures, see pp. 245 and 774.

may enforce a quasi-contractual obligation to pay the reasonable value of the occupation and use of the property.

In order to avoid the expense of litigation, it is customary to provide in the lease that if the tenant fails to pay the rent, the landlord may enter or confess judgment in a proper court for the amount due. In some jurisdictions, the landlord is permitted to bring a combined action in which he recovers the possession of the land and the overdue rent at the same time.

(3) Distress. The common law has devised a speedy remedy to aid the landlord in collecting his rent. It permits him to seize personal property found on the premises and to hold it until the arrears are paid. This right is known as *distress.* It is not an action against the tenant for rent, but merely a right to retain the property as security until the rent is paid. Statutes have generally either abolished or greatly modified the right of distress, as by giving the landlord the right to sell the distrained property.

(4) Recovery of Possession. It is commonly provided in a lease that upon the breach of any of its provisions by the tenant, such as the failure to pay rent, the lease shall terminate or the landlord may, at his option, declare it terminated. When the lease is terminated for either reason, the landlord then has the right to evict the tenant and retake possession of the property.

At common law the landlord, when entitled to possession, may regain it without resorting to legal proceedings. This is known as the *right of re-entry.* The remedy is available in many states even when the employment of force is necessary. Other states deny the right to use force. The landlord is liable for damages in case of a re-entry made without right or in a wrongful manner.

The landlord may resort to legal process to evict the tenant in order to enforce his right to possession of the premises.

Sec. 56-C. Liabilities for Injuries on Premises.

(1) Landlord's Liability to Tenant. In the absence of a covenant to keep the premises in repair, the landlord is ordinarily not liable to the tenant for the latter's personal injuries caused by the defective condition of the premises that are by the lease placed under the control of the tenant. In other words, the landlord makes no implied warranty as to safeness. He is, however, liable to the tenant for injuries caused by nonapparent defects of which the landlord had knowledge. In some states the landlord also has a duty to notify the tenant of defects that the landlord could discover with due care and which are not known or obvious to the tenant.

When the landlord has agreed as a term of the lease, or by a subsequent contract, to make repairs, some courts hold that the tenant may recover in a tort action for injuries he receives. Other courts hold that he has only a right of action for breach of contract. Such a covenant, however, does not make the landlord an insurer of the tenant. (See p. 815, Glassman v. Martin)

When the landlord retains control of part of his building or land that is rented to others, he is liable to a tenant who is injured because of the defective condition of such retained portion if the condition was the result of his failure to exercise the proper degree of care.

(2) Landlord's Liability to Third Persons. If the landlord retains control over a portion of the premises, he is liable for injuries to third persons caused by his failure to exercise proper care in connection with that part of the premises. Thus a landlord who rents different parts of a building to various tenants and retains control of the stairways, passageways, hallways, or other methods of approach to the several portions of the building for the common use of the tenants, has resting upon him an implied duty to use reasonable care to keep such places in a reasonably safe condition, and he is liable for injuries which are sustained by persons lawfully in the building from a failure to perform such duty. The landlord of an apartment house who reserves control of and operates the elevators in the building is liable for neglect in the maintenance and operation of the elevators to persons lawfully in the building.

The owner may protect himself from such liability by obtaining insurance against public liability, including not only the general public but also the tenant and the latter's guests or friends.

(3) Tenant's Liability to Third Persons. Liability follows control. A tenant in complete possession has control of the property and is therefore liable when his failure to use due care under the circumstances causes harm to (a) licensees, or persons whom he permits on the premises, such as a person allowed to use his telephone, and (b) *invitees,* or persons whom he induces or desires to come on the premises, such as customers entering his store. With respect to both classes of third persons, the liability of the tenant is the same as any owner in possession of his property. It is likewise immaterial whether the property is used for residential, commercial, or manufacturing purposes, provided the tenant has control of the area where the injury occurs.

The liability of the tenant to third persons is not affected by the fact that the landlord may have contracted in the lease to make repairs, which if made would have avoided the injury. The tenant can protect himself, however, in the same manner that the landlord can, by procuring public liability insurance to indemnify him for loss by claims of third persons.

Both the landlord and the tenant may be liable to third persons for harm caused by the condition of the leased premises. For example, if the landlord maintains unhealthy or dangerous conditions amounting to a nuisance and then leases the property to a tenant who continues the nuisance, both parties may be liable, the one for creating and the other for maintaining the nuisance. In some states no liability is imposed upon a tenant in such circumstances unless the person injured by the nuisance first requests the tenant to stop or abate the nuisance and he refuses to do so.

Sec. 56-D. Transfer of Rights.

(1) Transfer of Reversionary Interest. The reversionary interest of the landlord may be transferred voluntarily by his act, or involuntarily by a judicial or execution sale. The tenant then becomes the tenant of the new owner of the reversionary interest, and the new owner is bound by the terms of the lease.

In the event of an assignment of the rent or of the reversion, notice must be given to the tenant. If the tenant in good faith and without notice of the assignment pays the rent to the assignor, he is discharged of his liability. After notice of the assignment, the tenant acts at his peril in making payments to any person other than the assignee or his agent.

The making of an assignment of the lease or a sale of the property does not affect the rights of a tenant. The assignee or new owner takes the property subject to the outstanding lease.

(2) Assignment of Lease and Sublease. An *assignment of a lease* is a transfer by the tenant of his entire interest in the premises to a third person. A tenancy for years may be assigned by the tenant unless he is restricted from doing so by the terms of the lease or by statute.

The lease may contain provisions denying the right to assign or sublet or imposing specified restrictions on the privilege of assigning or subletting. Such restrictions are enforceable in order to enable the landlord to preserve control of his property. (See p. 816, Segre v. Ring) Since the provision restricting the right of the tenant to assign the lease or requiring the landlord's written consent thereto is for the benefit of the landlord, it may be waived by him.

A *sublease* is a transfer of the premises by the tenant to a third person, the *sublessee*, for a period less than the term of the lease. The rules governing assignment are also applicable to subletting. In both cases restrictions in the lease are construed liberally in favor of the tenant. An ineffectual attempt to assign or sublet does not violate a provision prohibiting such acts. This is equally true when another is merely permitted to use the land. As a general rule a transfer of all or part of the premises by operation of law is not a breach of such a provision. The lease, however, may give the landlord the right to avoid the lease in such a case.

As neither the act of subletting nor the landlord's agreement to it releases the original tenant from liability under the terms of the original lease, it is customary and desirable for the tenant to require the sublessee to covenant or promise that he will perform all obligations under the original lease and that he will indemnify the tenant for any loss caused by default of the sublessee. An express covenant or promise by the sublessee is necessary to impose liability upon him. The fact that the sublease is made "subject" to the terms of the original lease merely recognizes the superiority of the original lease, but does not impose any duty upon the sublessee to perform the tenant's obligations under the original lease. If the sublessee promises the tenant that he will assume the obligation of the original lease, the landlord, as a third-party beneficiary, may sue the sublessee for breach of the provisions of the original lease. In contrast with a sublease, when the lease is assigned and the assignee takes possession of the property he becomes bound by the terms of the lease.

An assignment or a sublease must be in writing when the term transferred or sublet is of such duration that a writing would be required if any original lease were made for that period.

Cases for Chapter 56

Bolding v. Clanton

285 P.2d 213 (Okla., 1955)

Clanton and his wife owned a tract of land which they rented to Bolding and Pruett to use as a filling station. In April or May, the Clantons encroached on the leased property in connection with the use of the adjoining property which they occupied. Bolding and Pruett continued to use the rented property as a filling station until they left the property in December. They then sued the Clantons for having encroached on the property. The Clantons counterclaimed that rent was due them for the period from May to December. Bolding and Pruett replied that they had been constructively evicted from the property. From a judgment in favor of the Clantons, Bolding and Pruett appealed.

HALLEY, J. . . . "There can be no constructive eviction without a surrender of the possession by the tenant; a tenant who continues to occupy the premises for an unreasonable length of time after the acts or omissions that constitute a constructive eviction waives the

eviction, and cannot thereafter abandon the premises and assert it."
. . .

Lessees contend that the premises were restored to Lessors in such a reasonable time as to amount to an abandonment and that their claim of constructive eviction should stand. . . .

There are cases cited to the effect that constructive eviction may be established where the tenant abandons within a "reasonable time," but the facts before us show conclusively that the Lessees did not abandon the premises within a reasonable time before they claimed that the encroachment of Lessors amounted to a constructive eviction. They claim the wrongful action occurred mostly in April or May, . . . but they apparently made no effort to abandon until December, . . . and during all of these months they occupied the premises and continued to operate their filling station business.

We find no evidence in the record that the acts of the Lessors caused the Lessees the loss of a single customer or the sale of a single gallon of gas, or that the volume of their business decreased by reason of any of the alleged wrongful acts of the Lessors. . . .

[Judgment affirmed.]

Glassman v. Martin

196 Tenn. 595, 269 S.W.2d 908 (1954)

Glassman leased a house to Martin. Some time later Martin was injured from a fall when steps in the house that had been eaten by termites collapsed. Martin sued Glassman for his injury on the theory that Glassman had broken his covenant in the lease to make repairs. From a judgment in favor of the tenant, the landlord appealed.

NEAL, C.J. . . . The liability of the defendant for the wrongs and injuries turned upon whether or not he had breached his contract to keep the premises in repair during the plaintiff's tenancy. Conceding this to be true, we are constrained to hold that the contract did not make him an insurer of the safety of the premises. "Neither is the landlord 'liable for hidden defects from which injuries were received, without regard to the question of diligence and reasonable care.' " . . . The defendant could not be held to have breached his contract until after notice of the defect and a reasonable opportunity to repair.

The defect complained of, and which gave rise to this suit, was that the riser on the steps leading into the apartment had been eaten away by termite action. . . . While the steps, including the riser, were exposed to view, the effect of termite action was not so exposed. Both Mr. and Mrs. Martin testified they had noticed nothing wrong with the steps and they seemed solid.

. . . Termite damage occurs gradually. . . . The tenant had no reason to suspect that the steps were defective. The outward appearance gave no evidence whatever of the hidden defect.

The defendant and his carpenter inspected this duplex apartment periodically and testified they could see nothing wrong with the steps; that there was no evidence of any defect in the risers.

The contention seems to be that the defect could have been discovered by merely punching the steps and risers with a screw driver or ice pick, and it was his duty to do so under the circumstances. Our conclusion is that the law imposes no such legal duty. For us to announce such a rule would make the landlord an insurer of the leased premises. The cases . . . defining the duty of the landlord to discover latent defects hold: The law does not impose upon the landlord the duty of constant care and inspection of the premises. It imposes upon him the duty of reasonable care to inform himself of the condition of the property. . . .

[Judgment reversed.]

Segre v. Ring

103 N.H. 278, 170 A.2d 265 (1961)

Ring and other selectmen of the town of Hampton leased certain city property to Hall. The lease prohibited any assignment without the lessors' consent. Segre requested the town selectmen to permit Hall to make an assignment to him. When the selectmen refused, Segre brought an action to compel them to do so.

BLANDIN, J. . . . The instrument in question contains an unqualified provision "*that* the lessee will not assign this lease without the written consent of the lessor." It is undisputed that, were the transaction between private parties, the defendants would have the right to refuse assent to the assignment requested by the plaintiffs. . . .

However, the plaintiffs claim that since the defendants are selectmen and the contract is with the town, of which the selectmen are the agents, the lease should be construed in a different manner than if it were between private parties, and so as to compel consent to the assignment, or to force the selectmen to give reasonable excuse for not doing so, even though this be contrary to the clear intent of the parties to the lease. . . .

We have then a case where parties freely entered into a lease containing a plain and unqualified restriction against assignment without the consent of the lessor. They could easily have omitted this clause. . . . or qualified it in any number of ways. . . . They did not choose to do so.

Resort towns such as Hampton are faced with many and difficult problems in carrying on their affairs. The selectmen are entrusted with the management of such. . . . In this task a wide discretion should be given to them as to the methods they may employ. Many proper reasons may exist why the town should desire to keep a large measure of control over the renting of its property and why the selectmen should not be forced to delineate causes for their refusal to consent to an assignment in the face of an agreement which contains no requirement that they do so. . . .

In summary, we hold that an unequivocal and unqualified restriction against assignment in a lease, freely entered into between the parties, is valid. The Court will not rewrite the agreement to compel the selectmen to permit the assignment or to give their reasons for not doing so. . . .

[Judgment for defendants.]

Questions and Case Problems

1. What is the objective of each of the following rules of law?
   (a) A tenant is not ordinarily excused from paying the rent because government restrictions prevent him from selling goods on the premises as he planned to do.
   (b) The landlord is liable to third persons for injuries due to the condition of those parts of the rented building over which the landlord retains control.

2. The Awad's had rented a second floor from McColgan for some 7 years. By that time the porch steps obviously needed much repair. McColgan promised to repair the porch and steps, but he did not do so. The porch collapsed and Mrs. Awad was injured. She sued McColgan. Decide. (Awad v. McColgan, [Mich.] 98 N.W.2d 571)

3. Spears owned a building. On the first floor he rented space to a dry cleaner and a barber shop. The center door, which was at the top of an open stairway leading down into the basement, gave the appearance of a part of a double door leading into the dry cleaner's. There was no warning sign over the center door, and the door was unlocked. Trimble wanted to enter the dry cleaner's as a customer and by mistake opened the center door. Before she could realize her mistake, she fell down the stairs and was injured. When she sued Spears, he denied liability and further claimed that Trimble was guilty of contributory negligence. Decide. (Trimble v. Spears, [Kan.] 320 P.2d 1029)

4. Clawson, the owner of a summer resort hotel, leased the restaurant and kitchen to Cruse on a 100-day summer season lease. Next to the kitchen and cafe, but separated therefrom by a partition, was a lounge, barroom, and dance floor. A few days later, Clawson asked Cruse to agree to a removal of the partition. Cruse objected because if the partition were removed, he would be required to pay a 20 per cent cabaret federal tax and would have difficulty in maintaining separate operations so far as minors,

tourists, and guests were concerned. After closing hours a few days later, Clawson, unknown to Cruse, tore down the partition. Cruse then gave notice that he was quitting the premises because of Clawson's removal of the partition. He left and thereafter sued for damages from Clawson of $2,125 representing loss of profits and $500 as punitive damages. Was he entitled to any damages? (Cruse v. Clawson, [Mont.] 352 P.2d 989)

5. Carparking leased a store in its building to Harris. The lease contained a provision that it could not be assigned without the written consent of Carparking. Thereafter, Harris assigned the lease to Chappell's. No written approval of the assignment of the lease was obtained. Repairs to the store were required, and Chappell's had a number of discussions with Carparking as to when they could move in and were assured that the store would be ready on a specified date. Chappell's posted ads on the property while the repair work was going on announcing the opening of their store. After Chappell's moved into the property, it brought suit against Carparking, claiming that certain provisions of the lease had been violated. Carparking defended on the ground that Chappell's could not claim any breach of the lease because there had not been a written consent to the assignment of the lease to Chappell's. Was this a valid defense? (Carparking, Inc. v. Chappell's, Inc., [Ga.App.] 101 S.E.2d 894)

6. Martin leased a building for a 5-year period to a new tenant after making repairs to the building to fit it for the tenant and after having paid approximately $1,000 as commissions to a real estate agent to obtain the tenant. Under the lease the tenant was required to pay the last five months' rent in advance, or approximately $3,000. During the term of the lease the tenant defaulted in the payment of rent and Martin, acting within the terms of the lease, terminated it. Lochner, the receiver who was thereafter appointed for the tenant, sued for the return of the advance rent on the ground that there could be no "rent" due for an unexpired portion of a lease which had been terminated by the landlord and the landlord would be unjustly enriched if he were allowed to retain the advance payment. Decide. (Lochner v. Martin, [Md.App.] 147 A.2d 749)

7. Shelton leased certain property to Clinard for a specified period. Thereafter, she leased the same property to Stathos for a term of five years, beginning the day after the expiration of the lease to Clinard. In an action brought by Shelton against Clinard to recover possession of the premises, it was contended that it was the duty of the lessor to see that the first tenant vacated at the time the second tenant's right to possession arose. Do you agree with this contention? (Shelton v. Clinard, 187 N.C. 664, 122 S.E. 477)

8. The Steinway Building Co. leased a portion of a building to Paxinos for use as a restaurant. Another portion of the building was leased by the company to Brocum to be used "only for confectionery and ice cream business." Thereafter Brocum for the first time sold sandwiches, coffee, and cake. In an action brought by the Steinway Building Co. against Paxinos and Brocum to determine their rights under their leases, it was contended that Brocum was not using the premises rightfully in view of the terms of his lease. Do you agree? Steinway Building Co. v. Paxinos, 234 App.Div. 396, 255 N.Y.S. 202)

CHAPTER 57

Real Mortgages

A mortgage is a credit and a security device. By means of it, a person or business may borrow money by pledging property as security.

An agreement that creates an interest in property as security for an obligation and which is to cease upon the performance of the obligation is a *mortgage*. When the transaction relates to personal property, the agreement is a *chattel mortgage*.[1] When it relates to real property, the agreement is a *real mortgage*. The person whose interest in the property is given as security is the *mortgagor*. The person who receives the security is the *mortgagee*.

Nature and Creation

Sec. 57-A. Nature of Mortgage. A mortgage is based upon the agreement of the parties and arises only in connection with some debt or obligation to be secured. If there is no debt, there can be no mortgage. It is sometimes difficult to determine whether a given transaction creates a mortgage relationship or some other relationship. There are three outstanding characteristics of a mortgage: (1) the termination of the mortgagee's interest upon the performance of the obligation secured by the mortgage; (2) the right of the mortgagee to enforce the mortgage by foreclosure upon the mortgagor's failure to perform; and (3) the mortgagor's right to redeem or regain the property.

In any case, however, the intention of the parties determines whether there is a mortgage. If it appears from all circumstances that the parties intended to create a mortgage, the courts will treat the agreement as such. Thus, even when there is an apparent absolute conveyance or sale of property, the transaction will be given the effect of a mortgage if the court or jury is convinced that the

---

[1] The right to execute a chattel mortgage is generally based upon statute and is governed by the Uniform Commercial Code, Art. 9. See Chapter 34.

parties intended the conveyance to be for security only. (See p. 828, Mechtle v. Topp)

Sec. 57-B. Classification of Mortgages.

(1) Legal Mortgages. Under the common law a mortgage of land was an absolute conveyance of the title to the mortgaged property subject to a condition subsequent which divested the title of the mortgagee upon the satisfaction of the condition, namely payment of the debt. Most states have abandoned the title theory of the mortgage and treat it merely as a lien upon the property. Today there is not much practical difference between the two theories because many title theory states regard the mortgage as a lien with respect to third persons, that is, the mortgagor is still the owner of the land with respect to third persons.

The only practical difference today between the two theories is that under the lien theory the mortgagee is limited to foreclosing the lien of the mortgage, while under the title theory the mortgagee is entitled to go into possession upon default and collect the rents and profits as well as foreclose the mortgage. Under either theory the mortgagor may be sued on the mortgage debt.

(2) Equitable Mortgages. If the parties fail to comply with all of the requirements essential to the creation of a valid mortgage, equity may sometimes treat the transaction as giving rise to an equitable mortgage in spite of the fact that it would not be recognized at law. A court of equity will also enforce as an equitable lien or equitable mortgage an agreement of the parties to execute a mortgage.

Sec. 57-C. Property Subject to Mortgage.
In general, any form of property that may be sold or conveyed may be mortgaged. It is immaterial whether the right is a present right or a future interest, or merely a right in the land of another. It is not necessary that the mortgagor have complete or absolute ownership in the property. He may mortgage any interest, legal or equitable, divided or undivided, that he owns.

A mortgage binds after-acquired property that does not become part of the freehold only if the mortgage states in an *after-acquired property clause* that such property is bound. If the after-acquired property becomes part of the freehold, it is bound by the mortgage in any case.

Sec. 57-D. Obligations Secured.
A mortgage is by definition a right given to secure an obligation. The mortgage may be given to secure the performance of some act or the performance of a present or future,

contingent or absolute, liability. When given for a money claim, the amount may be liquidated or unliquidated, that is, for a fixed or for an uncertain amount. Generally the obligation secured includes all extensions or renewals of the original obligation. It does not, however, include any obligation not described in the mortgage. For example, if a mortgage recites that it is given as security for the purchase of goods, it cannot be enforced for other claims again the mortgagor held by the mortgagee.

The obligation itself may be evidenced by a bond, a note, or a series of notes. The mortgagee may sell or assign his rights under the mortgage transaction, in which case an assignment or a negotiation of the bond or note is made, together with the rights in the property subject to the mortgage.

A mortgage may be an *open-end mortgage,* that is, it may expressly declare that it is to cover not only a specified debt but also all advances which may be made at a later date, or all such advances up to a stated maximum. Most courts hold that a mortgage, given to secure future advances in whole or in part, has the same priority for such advances as if they were made at the time of the giving of the mortgage, when the mortgagee is required to make the later advances. If, however, the making of the future advances is optional with the mortgagee, such advances as are made after the mortgagee has actual knowledge of another encumbrance, rank subsequent to that encumbrance. (See p. 830, Batten v. Jurist) In some states, statutory restrictions have been placed on this kind of mortgage to prevent the incurring of excessive indebtedness.

Sec. 57-E. Form of Mortgage. A mortgage is almost universally required to be in writing. A mortgage upon real property, since it transfers an interest in the property, must be in writing by virtue of the Statute of Frauds. For the same reason, a contract to mortgage land to another must be in writing.

As a general rule, no particular form of language is required, provided the language used clearly expresses the intent of the parties. In title theory states, however, the mortgage must be in the form of a conveyance since it transfers a legal title. This form of mortgage is also usually employed in states following the lien theory. In many states the substance is practically identical to that of a deed with the exception that a mortgage contains a defeasance clause, a description of the obligation secured, and sometimes a covenant to pay or perform the obligation. The *defeasance clause* states that the mortgage shall cease to have any effect when the obligation is performed, as when the debt is paid. In many states statutes provide a form of mortgage that may be used.

Special forms of mortgages have been developed in the case of mortgages securing the payment of corporate bonds and mortgages given to finance real-estate developments.

Sec. 57-F. Parties to the Mortgage. The same rules governing the parties to a deed apply to the parties to a mortgage in those states that follow the title theory. In any case the mortgage must be executed by the persons who are the owners of the property. Thus, when two or more persons are co-owners of the property, all must join as mortgagors. When property is owned solely by the husband or wife, a mortgage executed by the owner should also be signed by the other spouse when necessary to release the marital right of that spouse in the land, except when it is a *purchase-money mortgage.* This is a mortgage that is given by the purchaser of property to the seller of property as settlement for all or part of the purchase price, as distinguished from a mortgage that the owner of property places upon it when he borrows money from another person.

Sec. 57-G. Recording or Filing of Mortgages. An unrecorded mortgage is valid and binding between the parties to it. The heirs, devisees, or donees of a mortgagor cannot defend against the mortgage on the ground that it had not been recorded. Recording statutes in most states, however, provide that purchasers or creditors who give value and act in good faith in ignorance of an unrecorded mortgage may enforce their respective rights against the property without regard to the existence of the unrecorded mortgage. Accordingly the purchaser of the land in good faith for value from the mortgagor holds the land free of the unrecorded mortgage, and the mortgagee's only remedy is against the mortgagor on the debt due to him. In such a case the mortgagee has the burden of proving that the transferee of the land did not purchase in good faith, for value, and in ignorance of the unrecorded mortgage.

Rights of Parties Before Default

The rights and duties of the parties before default pertain to the possession of the property, rents and profits, repairs and improvements, taxes, assessments, insurance, impairment of security, transfer of interests in the property, performance of the obligation, and evidence of discharge of the obligation.

Sec. 57-H. Possession of Property. In most title theory states the mortgagor is entitled to retain possession of the property until he is in default, whereupon the mortgagee is entitled to take possession, either actually or constructively by collecting rents and profits. Under the lien theory of mortgages, the mortgagor remains in possession until there has been a foreclosure sale, or a receiver is appointed by the court.

Even when the mortgagor is entitled to possession, he may agree with the mortgagee that the latter shall have possession. Moreover, those states that deny the mortgagee the right to possession upon default will permit him to remain in possession until the debt is paid or the obligation performed if he has already lawfully obtained possession. In some states "lawfully obtained" possession requires the consent of the mortgagor to the entry by the mortgagee, while in other states it is enough that the mortgagee has acquired possession without committing a breach of the peace.

Sec. 57-I. Rents and Profits.

(1) Mortgagor in Possession. As long as the mortgagor is in possession, he has sole rights to the rents and profits of the mortgaged property and may dispose of them without regard to the existence of the mortgage on the land unless the rents and profits, by express agreement, are also pledged to secure the obligation. This rule is followed even though the mortgagor is in default on the mortgage.

(2) Mortgagee in Possession. If the mortgagee is lawfully in possession, the mortgagor does not have the right to collect the rents and profits or to forfeit a tenant's deposit because of nonpayment of rent, but he does have the right to demand that they be properly expended by the mortgagee and that any surplus be paid to the mortgagor.

The duty of the mortgagee in possession is not merely to account for what he has received but also to use due diligence in keeping the property rented and in collecting the rents, and to use reasonable prudence in management and in the creation of profits. Failure to exercise such diligence or prudence renders him liable for losses that result from such a cause.

The fact that the mortgagee reduces rents or that the premises are vacant is not alone sufficient to establish liability for losses. For example, the vacancy may be caused by some act on the part of the mortgagor or to general economic conditions.

When the mortgagee is entitled to collect the rents, he is under a duty to pay the taxes on the property from them. If he fails to do so and the property is sold by the government for unpaid taxes, and he then buys the property at the tax sale, he cannot claim the property as his own. Since he would thereby be profiting from his own neglect, he must hold the property in trust for the mortgagor, who may then recover it from him after the mortgage is paid in full.

The mortgagee, receiving the rents and profits, is under a duty, after payment of necessary repairs and taxes, to apply them to the mortgage debt and to turn over any surplus to the mortgagor. When the property has been placed in the hands of a receiver, the mortgagee is also entitled to have the rents and profits applied to the payment of the mortgage debt.

Sec. 57-J. Repairs and Improvements. In the absence of an agreement to the contrary, a mortgagor is under no duty to make improvements or to restore or repair parts of the premises that are destroyed or damaged without negligence on his part.

The mortgagee, when in possession, must make reasonable and necessary repairs in order to preserve the estate. He is entitled to reimbursement for such repairs on the ground that they inure to the benefit of the mortgagor. Ordinarily, however, the mortgagee may not charge to the mortgagor expenditures for valuable or enduring improvements. A mortgagee will not be allowed to improve a mortgagor out of his estate by making it too costly for the mortgagor to redeem.

Sec. 57-K. Taxes, Assessments, and Insurance. The duty to pay taxes and assessments rests upon the mortgagor. However, if the mortgagee is in possession, he is under a duty to pay the taxes and assessments out of the rents and profits.

In the absence of an agreement neither party is under a duty to insure the mortgaged property. Both parties, however, may insure their respective interests. It is common practice for the mortgagor to obtain a single policy of insurance on the property payable to the mortgagee and the mortgagor as their interests may appear.

If the mortgagor fails to perform the duty of paying taxes, assessments, or insurance premiums, the mortgagee is entitled to make such payments and to receive reimbursement. Such payments, however, are treated as future advances and must be recorded to be valid against subsequent creditors and purchasers without notice. If the mortgagor fails to pay taxes that he is required to pay and then buys the property at the tax sale thereof, he continues to hold the land subject to the mortgage, as otherwise he would profit from his own wrong. (See p. 831, Dampier v. Polk)

Sec. 57-L. Impairment of Security. The mortgagor is liable to the mortgagee for any damage to the property, due to his fault, that impairs the security of the mortgage by materially reducing the value of the property. The impairment of security by fraudulent injury, concealment, sale, or removal on the part of the mortgagor is sometimes made a criminal act.

The mortgagee, whether or not he is in possession, is liable to the mortgagor for injuries to the property due to his fault. Both the mortgagor and the mortgagee have a right of action against a third person who wrongfully injuries the property. In some states the mortgagor loses this right after the mortgagee takes possession.

Sec. 57-M. Receivership Before Foreclosure. At the request of the mortgagee, the proper court may appoint a receiver for the mortgaged property prior to foreclosure in order to administer the property to prevent waste. In some states a receiver may be appointed only upon showing that the mortgagor is insolvent and is committing waste and that the mortgaged property is not by itself adequate security for the payment of the mortgage debt. In other states a receiver cannot be appointed for an individual, as distinguished from a corporate debtor.

Sec. 57-N. Transfer of Interest.

(1) Transfer by Mortgagor. In the case of a real mortgage, the mortgagor may ordinarily transfer his interest in the land without the consent of the mortgagee. A transfer by the mortgagor does not divest or impair the mortgage, and the grantee of the mortgagor holds the property subject to the mortgage, except the recording statutes may cut off the mortgage when it is not recorded and the mortgagor's grantee purchases in good faith for value, not knowing of the existence of the mortgage.

The transfer by the mortgagor of his interest does not affect the liability of the mortgagor to the mortgagee. Unless the latter has agreed to substitute the mortgagor's grantee for the mortgagor, the latter remains liable as though no transfer had been made. If, however, the mortgagor is required to pay the mortgage, he is subrogated to the rights of the mortgagee against his transferee.

(2) Liability of Mortgagor's Transferee. The purchaser of mortgaged property does not become personally liable for the debt secured unless he expressly assumes the debt. Even when he does so, the mortgagor continues to be liable unless released by the mortgagee. If the purchaser assumes liability for the debt, the mortgagee, after notice thereof, must treat the mortgagor as a surety to the extent that he must do nothing that will injure the mortgagor's interest.

(3) Transfer by Mortgagee. In most states a mortgage may be transferred or assigned by the mortgagee. A few states, following the title theory of a mortgage, hold that a mortgage is nonassignable at law and that the title of the mortgage can be transferred only by a formal conveyance. The assignability of mortgages, however, has

always been recognized by courts of equity. Although an equitable assignment only requires that the intent of the parties be shown, a written assignment is necessary as a general rule in order to pass a legal title. Formal assignment is sometimes required by statute, and it is usually necessary for recording purposes.

Sec. 57-O. Performance of Obligation. The mortgagee is entitled to the performance of the obligation secured by the mortgage according to its terms. When the obligation is a debt, its payment should be made to the mortgagee or to an agent authorized to receive payment when payment is due. A mortgagee need not accept payment from a stranger, but any person succeeding to the rights of the mortgagor or having an interest to protect, such as an executor, heir, or widow of the mortgagor, or a second mortgagee, may pay the debt.

The effect of a mortgagee's rejection of a valid tender or offer of the money due varies in the states. Some courts hold that a tender of the amount due on the due date does not discharge the lien. Most courts hold that the lien is discharged when the tender is arbitrarily or unreasonably refused. In any case, the debt is not discharged.

The courts are also in conflict as to whether a tender after default relieves the property of the lien. In order to be a valid tender, the total amount due, including interest, must be tendered. It is insufficient to tender merely the face amount of the mortgage.

If the debt is in any way discharged, the mortgage is also discharged. A discharge of the debtor from personal liability, however, does not release the lien of the mortgage. Thus the discharge of the mortgagor in bankruptcy does not affect the lien of the mortgage.

Sec. 57-P. Evidence of Discharge. The mortgagee, after receiving payment or satisfaction of the debt, is under a duty to give the mortgagor a receipt, certificate, or other evidence that the mortgage has been discharged. This duty may be enforced by various actions in the different states. Statutes usually require the filing of a discharge or an entry of satisfaction of the mortgage in the margin of the record book in which the mortgage has been recorded.

Rights of Parties After Default

Sec. 57-Q. Rights of Mortgagee After Default. Upon the mortgagor's default, the mortgagee in some states is entitled to obtain possession of the property and to collect the rents or to have a receiver appointed for that purpose.[2] In all states he may enforce the mortgage by foreclosure and sue to enforce the mortgage debt.

---

2 See p. 825.

(1) Foreclosure. In most states, *foreclosure* requires the mortgagee to sell the property under an order of the court or by a sale made by an officer of the court. If sufficient, the proceeds of the sale are used to pay the mortgage debt, interest, and costs of sale. There may also be taxes due on the real estate. If there is a surplus above these liabilities, the mortgagor is entitled to the surplus since it is his property that is being sold.

An exception to this disposition of the surplus arises when there are other liens upon the foreclosed property and those liens are discharged or destroyed by the foreclosure sale. It is generally held that the holders of such destroyed liens are entitled to receive payment from the surplus remaining after the taxes and the mortgagee's claims have been paid. Accordingly, it is only after all such claimants have been paid, as well as the mortgagee, that there is any surplus available for distribution to the mortgagor.

(2) Deficiency Judgment. A sale on the foreclosure of the mortgage destroys the mortgage, and the property passes at the sale free of the mortgage. But the extinction of the mortgage by foreclosure does not destroy the debt that was secured by the mortgage. The mortgagor remains liable for any unpaid balance or deficiency. This amount still due is determined by subtracting the net proceeds of the sale from the debt, interest, and costs due at the time of the sale. It is generally provided by statute that if the mortgagee purchases the property at foreclosure, the mortgagor may request that the appraised fair value of the property, rather than the net proceeds of the sale, be credited against the debt. (See p. 832, Gelfert v. National City Bank) Some states limit the period of time within which a deficiency judgment may be enforced against property that is used by the mortgagor as his home. Other states also provide that no deficiency judgment may be entered on a purchase money mortgage.

(3) Action on Mortgage Debt. In case of default a mortgagee, in the absence of statute or agreement, is not required to foreclose, but he may pursue any other remedy that he possesses. He may therefore bring an action on the debt, recover judgment, and obtain satisfaction of the debt by execution.

Sec. 57-R. Rights of Mortgagor After Default.

(1) Stay of Foreclosure. In certain cases, authorized by statute, a *stay* (or delay) *of foreclosure* may be obtained by the mortgagor to prevent undue hardship. The Federal Soldiers' and Sailors' Civil Relief Act prohibits the foreclosure of mortgaged property while the "owner" is in military service.

(2) Redemption. The *right of redemption* means the right of the mortgagor to free the property of the mortgage lien after default. By statute in many states the right may be exercised during a certain time following foreclosure and sale.

In general, redemption may be made only by a person whose interests will be affected by foreclosure. The right to redeem may be exercised by the executor or the heirs of the mortgagor, and in most states by a second mortgagee.

Cases for Chapter 57

Mechtle v. Topp
78 N.D. 789, 52 N.W.2d 842 (1952)

Topp agreed with Mechtle to pay to the sheriff, who was about to foreclose a mortgage on Mechtle's land, the sum needed to discharge the mortgage and pay the taxes. Topp did so, and Mechtle gave Topp a quit-claim deed to his land. The parties executed a written agreement under which Topp agreed to hold the land "in trust" for Mechtle for four months, during which time Mechtle could sell the land or any part of it in order to pay off the debt; if the land was not sold in two weeks, Topp was to be able to lease the land; if the land was not sold or the debt repaid in four months, the title to the land belonged to Topp absolutely. Mechtle brought an action to determine his rights under the above transaction.

MORRIS, C. J. . . . This is an action in equity to determine whether the transaction was one of sale or one of security. . . .

The defendant points out that there was no note or other evidence of debt given to the defendant by the plaintiff. The existence of an obligation is an essential element of a mortgage, but that obligation need not be reduced to writing as the defendant seems to infer. There can be no mortgage without a debt. . . . It is essential that there be an agreement, express or implied, on the part of the mortgagor or other person in whose behalf the mortgage is executed to discharge an obligation in some form owing to the mortgagee. . . . In this case, when Topp advanced the money to the sheriff to redeem Mechtle's land from foreclosure, there instantly arose an implied obligation on the part of Mechtle to repay the money so advanced. . . .

"The practical test is whether there is a liability, notwithstanding or independent of the conveyance and contract of reconveyance, which the grantee can enforce against the grantor. If a loan is made to the grantor at the time of executing the conveyance and the continued existence of his indebtedness therefor is evidenced by some collateral engagement given by the grantor, such as a note or bond, the case is simple and the transaction is clearly a mortgage. In the second place, if the conveyance is given in consideration of an antecedent debt due from the grantor and this debt yet remains, so that the grantee may enforce his claim at some time or another against the grantor, the transaction is also a mortgage. But if this antecedent debt is wholly satisfied and extinguished by the conveyance, so that no liability remains under any circumstances against the grantor, then there is no mortgage since there is no debt to be secured thereby. In such a case the surrender by the grantee of the written evidences of original indebtedness, or his cancellation thereof, would be very material circumstances. Thirdly, there may be neither a present loan nor an antecedent debt; but the grantee may undertake to assume some outstanding liability of the grantor or to pay off some claim against the grantor so that an obligation to reimburse him would rest upon the grantor, and the conveyance may be intended to indemnify the grantee and to secure the performance of the grantor's future continuing obligation, in which case it would clearly be a mortgage." . . .

In this case the defendant agreed to provide the plaintiff sufficient money to redeem from the mortgage foreclosure and to advance the further sum necessary to pay the 1947 and 1949 taxes. This agreement was carried out, the money was furnished to make the redemption and a debt created. That part of the transaction which was reduced to writing, namely, the giving of the deed and the execution of the agreement, did not pay that debt and did not pass absolute title to the defendant. The result is a security transaction. This conclusion is supported by the further fact that the property was worth considerably more than the amount of money which the defendant agreed to furnish at the beginning of the negotiations, which was about $4,000. Later it developed that there was something over $1,000 more due in taxes. The testimony shows that the property was worth from $10,000 to $12,000. Inadequacy of consideration is a circumstance that may be considered. . . .

It will also be noted that under the terms of the agreement it was provided that the defendant would hold the title to the property for four months "in trust for the second party." This provision clearly did not, under the circumstances surrounding its use, create a true trust, nor did it make of the quitclaim deed a trust deed in the common usage of that term whereby a grantor conveys property to a trustee to secure an obligation which the grantor owes to a third party. But even trust deeds of that nature are in fact mortgages and not absolute conveyances. . . . The use of the term "in trust" is inconsistent with the idea that an absolute estate was intended to be granted. . . .

The deed and agreement when taken together clearly establish a transaction whereby the land was hypothecated to the defendant as security for the sum which he advanced to redeem from the fore-

closure and for future advances that he might make and constituted
a mortgage. The right of redemption has not been terminated and
is still available to the plaintiff. . . .

[Judgment for plaintiff affirmed, holding transaction a mortgage.]

Batten v. Jurist
306 Pa. 64, 158 A. 557 (1932)

Jurist mortgaged certain land to Freeman to secure a debt of $13,000.
Jurist subsequently mortgaged the same property to Sutro to secure payment of $5,000 and "future advances." Thereafter, the Northwestern Na-
tional Bank & Trust Co., believing the property to be mortgaged for only
$18,000, extended credit to Jurist from time to time until the indebtedness
amounted to more than $41,000. The Freeman mortgage was assigned to
Batten, who brought suit against Jurist to foreclose the mortgage. After
payment of the Freeman debt, there remained $16,339.76 in the hands of
the sheriff. Sutro, who had advanced an additional $15,000 to Jurist,
claimed this money. The Northwestern National Bank & Trust Co. contended that Sutro was entitled only to the amount specifically set out in
the mortgage, $5,000, and interest. From a judgment in favor of Sutro
with respect to the additional $15,000, the bank appealed.

MAXEY, J. . . . A mortgage to secure a specific sum and also further
advances unlimited as to time and amount is . . . valid against
subsequent lien creditors. . . .

"It is also established that when such a contract obligates the
mortgagee either to make advances or assume future responsibilities
on behalf of the mortgagor, this lends a sufficient consideration to the
mortgage and the lien of payments made under such an agreement
relates back to the date of the mortgage; furthermore, this is true
even though the advances or liquidation of assumed responsibilities
occur after the date of a subsequent or junior encumbrance placed
upon the mortgaged premises."

. . . A mortgagee cannot make voluntary additional advances after
knowledge of an intervening claim and then have priority as to such
advances. "Actual notice to the mortgagee will cut off his priority as
to all optional future advances thereafter made." . . . However the
rule thus variously stated had no application . . . here.

There is much logic in the argument that the judicial recognition
accorded mortgages for unlimited future advances offends the spirit
of our modern recording acts. For example, the Act of April 29,
1909, . . . provides that the recorder shall deliver at stated intervals
to the board of revision of taxes or other officials charged with the
assessment of state tax a list of the mortgages recorded, assignments,
etc., with the names and residences of the mortgagees, assignees, or
persons entitled to interest, with the amount and date of the mort-

gages, etc. A mortgage given for future advances would put the recorder to the trouble of ascertaining the amount of such advances, and this information might be withheld from him. However, the act quoted would not in itself justify us in departing from the judicial precedents long established in cases like this and in cases of cognate character. . . . If public policy is to condemn such mortgages, it must find statutory expression, as it has in Maryland and New Hampshire. . . .

[Judgment in favor of Sutro sustained.]

Dampier v. Polk
214 Miss. 65, 58 So.2d 44 (1952)

Dampier mortgaged land to the Federal Land Bank. The mortgage agreement required him to pay the taxes on the land. He failed to do so, and the land was sold by the state for taxes. Dampier purchased the land at the tax sale in 1936 and remained in possession of the land. The mortgage was assigned to Polk who sought to enforce it. Dampier claimed ownership of the land free of the mortgage.

HOLMES, J. . . . It is contended that Plato Dampier, following the issuance to him of the patent from the State in 1936, has continued to occupy the property in question, claiming the ownership thereof, and that he has acquired title thereto by adverse possession. We do not concur in this contention. Plato's action in obtaining from the State the forfeited tax land patent amounted only to a redemption of the land for the benefit of the mortgagee in the deed of trust. The obligation to pay the taxes was his obligation. It was likewise his obligation to redeem the land from the tax sales. Having failed to pay the taxes or redeem the land from the tax sales, his purchase thereafter from the State inured to the benefit of the mortgagee, the Federal Land Bank, and could not be asserted against the bank or its assignee. It is well settled that the purchase of a tax title at a sale by the mortgagor who is under a duty to pay the taxes operates simply as a payment of the taxes so far as affects the interest of the mortgagee or those claiming under him. Likewise, where the mortgagor purchases from the State the land which was sold to the State for the nonpayment of the taxes and not redeemed, his action amounts merely to a redemption from the tax sale and inures to the benefit of the mortgagee. . . .

[Judgment for defendants affirmed.]

Gelfert v. National City Bank
313 U.S. 221 (1941)

The National City Bank, which held a mortgage on property owned by Gelfert, foreclosed the mortgage and purchased the property at the foreclosure sale. At the time that the mortgage had been executed, the law of the state provided that a mortgagee was entitled to a deficiency judgment against the mortgagor for the balance of the mortgage debt remaining unsatisfied after the mortgagor was credited with the net proceeds of the foreclosure sale. At the time that the mortgage was foreclosed, the state law provided that the court in fixing the amount of the deficiency judgment should "determine, upon affidavit or otherwise as it shall direct, the fair and reasonable market value of the mortgaged premises" and should deduct from the amount of the debt the "market value as determined by the court or the sale price of the property whichever shall be higher. . . ." The mortgagee objected to the application of the latter statute in determining the amount of his deficiency judgment on the ground that it impaired the obligation of the mortgage contract. From a judgment for the mortgagor on this point, the mortgagee appealed.

DOUGLAS, J. . . . We are concerned here solely with the application of this statute to a situation where the mortgagee purchases the property at foreclosure sale. We intimate no opinion of its constitutionality as applied to the case where the mortgagee is not the purchaser. . . .

The formula which a legislature may adopt for determining the amount of a deficiency judgment is not fixed and invariable. That which exists at the date of the execution of the mortgage does not become so imbedded in the contract between the parties that it cannot be constitutionally altered.

The control of judicial sales of realty by courts of equity and by legislatures in order to prevent sacrificial prices has a long history. . . . For about two centuries there has been a rather continuous effort . . . to prevent the machinery of judicial sales from becoming an instrument of oppression. . . . Numerous devices have been employed to safeguard mortgagors from sales which will or may result in mortgagees collecting more than their due. . . . Underlying that change has been the realization that the price which property commands at a forced sale may be hardly even a rough measure of its value. The paralysis of real estate markets during periods of depression, the wide discrepancy between the money value of property to the mortgagee and the cash price [received at such a] sale . . . reflect the considerations which have motivated departures from the theory that competitive bidding in this field amply protects the debtor.

Mortgagees are constitutionally entitled to no more than payment in full. . . . They cannot be heard to complain on constitutional grounds if the legislature takes steps to see to it that they get no more than that. . . . There is no constitutional reason why in lieu of the more restricted control by a court of equity the legislature cannot substitute a uniform comprehensive rule designed to reduce or to avoid in the run of cases the chance that the mortgagee will be paid more than once. . . . Certainly under this statute it cannot be said that more than that was attempted. The "fair and reasonable market value" of the property has an obvious and direct relevancy to a determination of the amount of the mortgagee's prospective loss. . . . The fact that men will differ in opinion as to the adequacy of any particular yardstick of value emphasizes that the appropriateness of any one formula is peculiarly a matter for legislative determination. . . . The fact that an emergency was not declared to exist when this statute was passed does not bring [the mortgage] within the protective scope of the contract clause. . . .

Respondent [mortgagee] points out that earlier decisions of this court have struck down under the contract clause, as respect contracts previously made, a state statute requiring judicial sale to bring two thirds of the amount of the appraised value of the property. . . . We cannot permit the broad language which those early decisions employed to force legislatures to be blind to the lessons which another century has taught.

[Judgment for mortgagor affirmed.]

Questions and Case Problems

1. What is the objective of each of the following rules of law?
    (a) A mortgage need not be restricted to a specific debt but may specify that it will secure all future advances which may be made at later dates.
    (b) A purchaser's wife is not required to sign a purchase-money mortgage.

2. Brooks owned an orange grove that was subject to a mortgage held by Adams. Adams went into possession as mortgagee upon the mortgagor's default. Later, Brooks brought an action to compel Adams to account for the profits collected by him while in possession. In his account, Adams deducted 10 per cent of the gross receipts as compensation for himself for caretaking and managing. Was he entitled to do so? (Brooks v. Adams, [Fla.] 115 So.2d 578)

3. Bradham and others, trustees of the Mount Olivet Church, brought an action to cancel a mortgage on the church property that had been executed by Davis and others as trustees of the church and given to Robinson as mortgagee. It was found by the court that Davis and the others, who had acted in executing the mortgage, were not lawful trustees of the church and had no authority to execute the mortgage. Furthermore, the court found that the church was not indebted to the mortgagee for any

amount. Should the mortgage have been canceled? (Bradham v. Robinson, 236 N.C. 589, 73 S.E.2d 555)

4. Taulblee borrowed money from the First National Bank of Jackson and executed to it a mortgage to secure the repayment of the debt. The mortgage recited that "This mortgage shall also secure any additional sum or sums of money advanced or loaned by the [mortgagee] to the [mortgagor] and shall also secure any other indebtedness of the [mortgagor] that may come in possession of the [mortgagee] not to exceed the aggregate sum of $2,000. . . ." Taulblee, acting as surety, signed a note as comaker for his brother to whom the bank loaned money. Taulblee later claimed that the mortgage did not cover this note because (a) he was merely a surety on the note and (b) the making of additional loans was optional under the mortgage. Decide. (Taulblee v. First National Bank of Jackson, 279 Ky. 153, 130 S.W.2d 48)

5. Howe purchased a house under construction from McGregor Gardens by an unrecorded contract executed on July 30, 1958. Unknown to Howe, McGregor Gardens applied for a loan from the Lee County Bank to be secured by a mortgage on Howe's future house. On November 20, a representative of the bank examined the property and was told by workmen completing the house that they were employed by McGregor Gardens. The representative informed the Lee County Bank that the house was unoccupied. On November 23, the Howe's moved into the house and lived there continuously. On November 24, the mortgage to the Lee County Bank was executed. McGregor Gardens delivered the deed to Howe on January 31, 1959. Thereafter Howe mortgaged his house to Knight who assigned that mortgage to the Metropolitan Life Insurance Co. Lee County Bank brought an action to foreclose the McGregor mortgage on Howe's house. Metropolitan claimed that the mortgage of the bank was not binding. Decide. (Lee County Bank v. Metropolitan Life Insurance Co., [Fla.] 126 So.2d 589)

6. Garland and Evans owned a tract of land subject to a mortgage given to the Federal Land Bank. The mortgage authorized the bank to pay taxes on the land if the owners failed to do so and to add such taxes to the mortgage debt. As a disabled war veteran, Garland was entitled to a tax exemption. Through a clerical error the township carried the real estate on its books as belonging to Evans, who did not have a tax exemption, and charged the property for the full amount of the taxes. The owners did not bring any action to correct this mistake, and the Federal Land Bank was never notified of it. At the end of five years the township put up the property for sale for unpaid taxes. The Federal Land Bank was notified of the sale and paid the taxes and interest to prevent the sale. Thereafter, the bank foreclosed the mortgage and added to its claim the taxes and interest it had paid. Garland brought an action to enjoin the bank from foreclosing on the ground that the adding of the taxes was improper because the taxes had been improperly charged as he had a tax exemption. Was Garland entitled to the injunction? (Garland v. Federal Land Bank of Springfield, [N.H.] 140 A.2d 568)

PART X
INSURANCE

CHAPTER 58

Nature of Insurance

At first, insurance was used primarily by merchants as a means of securing themselves against marine or sea loss. In the course of time a new branch of law relating to insurance developed as part of the law merchant. Toward the end of the Eighteenth Century the law of insurance was absorbed by the common law. Gradually, also, the security device of insurance was extended so that today it affords protection against practically every known kind of risk.

Sec. 58-A. Definitions. *Insurance* is a contract by which a promise is made to pay another a sum of money if the latter sustains a specified loss. Insurance is basically a plan of security against risk by charging losses against a fund created by the *premiums* or payments made by many individuals. (See p. 843, Barr's Estate) The promisor is called the *insurer,* sometimes the underwriter. The person to whom the promise is made is the *insured,* the assured, or the policyholder. The promise of the insurer is generally set forth in a contract called a *policy.*

Sometimes the risk involved is too great for one insurer. Several insurers may then divide the risk among them as *multiple or concurrent insurers,* or one insurer may reinsure in other companies against the risk of paying the loss on the policy.

Sec. 58-B. The Parties. As the result of statutory regulation virtually all insurance policies are today written by corporations, fraternal or benefit societies, and national or state governments.

The insured must have the capacity to make a contract. If a minor makes a contract of insurance, the policy is generally regarded as voidable.[1]

Sec. 58-C. Insurable Interest. The insured must have an insurable interest in the subject matter insured. This concept of insurable interest has been extended to all forms of insurance. The nature of the interest varies with the kind of policy.

(1) Insurable Interest in Property. A person has an insurable interest in property whenever he has any right or interest in the property so that its destruction or damage will cause him a direct pecuniary or money loss. It is immaterial whether the insured is the owner of the legal or equitable title, a lienholder, or a person in possession of the property. A person does not have an insurable interest in property if his only right is based upon a contract that is void or unenforceable.

In the case of property insurance the insurable interest must exist at the time the loss occurs. Except when expressly required by statute, it is not necessary that the interest exist at the time when the policy or contract of insurance was made.

A relaxation of the requirement of an insurable interest is made under a personal property or *floater policy* which covers property owned not only by the insured but also by members of his household, domicile, or family group.

(2) Insurable Interest in Life. Every person has an insurable interest in his own life and may therefore insure his own life and name anyone he chooses as beneficiary.

A person has an insurable interest in the life of another if he can expect to receive pecuniary gain from the continued life of the other person and, conversely, would suffer financial loss from the latter's death. Thus it is held that a creditor has an insurable interest in the life of his debtor since the death of the debtor may mean that the creditor will not be paid the amount owed him. The creditor may take out insurance in excess of the amount of the debt but, if the amount of the insurance is unreasonably greater than the debt, the policy will generally be void. In some cases the creditor is limited to recovering from the insurer the amount which is due him by the debtor plus the amount of the premiums paid on the policy and interest on those premiums.

A partnership has an insurable interest in the life of each of the partners, for the death of any one of them will dissolve the firm and cause some degree of loss to the partnership. A business enterprise has an insurable interest in the life of an executive or a key employee

---

[1] See p. 59.

because his death would inflict a financial loss upon the business to the extent that he could not be replaced or could not readily be replaced without a period of long training. No insurable interest exists when the employee is not a key employee or is merely a servant. (See p. 844, Gerard v. Metropolitan Life Insurance Co.)

There is uncertainty as to whether a person has an insurable interest in the life of another merely because of relationship. If there is a relationship of marriage or close blood relationship, it is generally found that there is an insurable interest. The majority of the cases, however, do not base the decision on the fact of that relationship alone. They hold that in view of the relationship it is proper to conclude that, had the deceased person continued in life, the other person could have expected to receive a pecuniary benefit or gain, of which he is defeated by death. Some recent decisions abandon this presumption of benefit and find an insurable interest solely on the basis of relationship. These courts, however, do not extend this principle to relationships by marriage beyond that of husband and wife.

In the case of life insurance the insurable interest must exist at the time the policy is obtained. It is immaterial that the interest no longer exists when the loss is actually sustained.

Sec. 58-D. The Insurance Contract. By statute it is now commonly provided that an insurance policy must be written. In order to avoid deception, many statutes also specify the content of certain policies, in whole or in part, and some even specify the size and style of type to be used in printing them. When a statute sets a standard, provisions in a policy in conflict with the statute are generally void. Most states now require that the forms of policies and endorsements be approved by a state insurance commissioner or other official.

An insurance policy specifies the term or period of time it covers. Often the nature of the risk against which insurance is sought determines the period or life of the policy. If an outdoor athletic event or concert is to be held, it is possible to obtain insurance against loss from rain falling on that day so as to prevent the holding of the scheduled event. Such a policy covers only the term or period of that day. Property insurance policies are usually written for one, three, or five years. A life insurance policy may cover a specified number of years or the balance of the insured's life.

(1) Formation. When a person applies for insurance, he ordinarily make an offer to the insurance company, which the company may accept or reject. Until the insurance company accepts the offer of the applicant, there is no contract of insurance.[2]

---

[2] As to the effect of delay by the insurer in acting upon an application, see Sec. 6-A (4), p. 84.

Under some circumstances, the offer of insurance may be made by the insurer, in which case the contract of insurance is binding when the applicant mails his signed application to the insurer. (See p. 845, Metts v. Central Standard Life Insurance Co.) A contract of insurance to protect against the hazards of a particular trip, as in the case of air travel insurance, is binding when the insured gives the application and premium to the representative of the insurer or places it in the vending machine provided for that purpose.

(2) When the Insurance Contract Is Effective. An applicant for insurance may or may not be protected by insurance before a formal written policy is issued to him. Four situations may arise:

(a) When the applicant tells a broker to obtain insurance, the applicant is merely making the broker his agent. If the broker procures a policy, the customer is insured. If the broker fails to do so, the customer does not have any insurance. But the broker may be personally liable to the customer for the loss.

(b) The person seeking insurance and the insurer or its agent may orally agree that the applicant will be protected by insurance during the interval between the time the application is received and the time when the insurer either rejects the application, or accepts it and issues a written policy. This agreement to protect the applicant by insurance during such an interval is binding even though it is oral. Generally, however, when such a preliminary contract is made, the agent will sign a memorandum stating the essential terms of the policy to be executed. This memorandum is called a *binder.*

If loss occurs during the binder period, the insurer is liable to the insured just as though a formal policy had been issued. If the details of the policy had not been specified in the binder agreement, the binder confers the same rights and is subject to the same limitations as the policy which would have been issued later.

(c) The parties may agree that at a later time a policy will be issued and delivered. In that case the insurance contract is not in effect until the policy is delivered or sent to the applicant. Accordingly, loss sustained after the transaction between the applicant and the insurance agent but before the delivery of the policy is not covered by the policy thereafter delivered. The stipulation that the insurance shall not be binding until the policy is issued is more likely to be found in life insurance because the applicant may be required to pass a physical examination before the insurer will issue a policy.

Regardless of whether the policy has been issued, it may be agreed by the parties that the insurance shall not become effective until the first premium is paid. Generally, however, the agreement of the parties is that the policy shall become effective immediately and the the first premium will be paid upon the delivery of the policy.

Most property and liability policies contain no provision with respect to the payment of premiums. These policies become effective according to the agreement of the parties, without regard to whether any premium has been paid.

(d) The parties may agree that a policy of life insurance shall be binding upon the payment of the first premium even though the applicant has not been examined, provided he thereafter passes an examination. Under such an agreement the applicant is ordinarily covered by insurance when he dies before the examination, if it can be shown that he would have passed a fair examination.

(3) Modification of Contract Form. In order to make changes or corrections to the policy, it may not be necessary to issue a new policy. An *endorsement* on the policy or the execution of a separate *rider* is effective for the purpose of changing the policy. It is not essential that the rider be attached to the policy.

Sec. 58-E. Premiums. Statutes commonly prohibit insurance companies from making premium discriminations among members of the same risk class and from making rebates or refunds to particular individuals only.

(1) Method of Payment of Premiums. Premiums may be paid in legal tender or by check. The latter form of payment is, of course, conditional upon the instrument being properly honored. If the check is not paid, the instrument loses its character as payment. This in itself does not immediately forfeit or terminate the policy of insurance. If the premiums are not paid thereafter, however, the policy will ordinarily lapse because of nonpayment of the premiums, subject to antilapse statutes or provisions.

(2) Return of Premiums. After the policy has become binding, the insured cannot ordinarily recover the premiums paid to the insurer. In a few instances, however, the insured may recover them as, for example, when the payments were made under a mistake of fact or when they were induced by fraud on the part of an agent of the insurer. If the insurer wrongfully terminates the policy, most courts allow the insured to recover the premiums paid by him. Most states also give the insured a right of action for breach of contract or for specific performance.

(3) Nonforfeiture and Antilapse Provisions. As to the payment of premiums due on life insurance policies subsequent to the first premium, the policies now in general use provide or a statute may specify that the policy shall not automatically lapse upon the date the next premium is due if payment is not then made. By policy pro-

vision or statute, the insured is also allowed a *grace period,* generally 30 or 31 days, in which to make payment of the premium due. In some jurisdictions the company is required to issue a paid-up policy in a smaller amount when there is a default in the payment of a premium by the insured.

Sec. 58-F. Defenses of the Insurer. The insurer may raise any defense that would be valid in an action upon a contract. Some defenses that do not apply to an action on an ordinary contract may also be raised.

(1) Violation of Statute. Statutes commonly specify that insurance policies shall have certain clauses or must not have certain prohibited clauses. If suit is brought to enforce an illegal provision of the policy, it is generally held that the provision is void because it is contrary to the statute.

Sometimes the violation of the statute is based not on the provisions of the policy but on the way the corporation or insurer does business. Generally it is held that an insurance company cannot profit by its own wrong and therefore cannot claim that it is not liable on its policy because it has conducted its business illegally. Thus a foreign (out-of-state) insurance corporation that violated the law by engaging in business without first obtaining a local license and filing local reports was liable on its policy.

(2) Ultra Vires. If a corporation issues a policy of insurance that it has no authority to issue, most states hold that the insurance company cannot raise the defense of ultra vires. A minority hold that the policy is void.

(3) Contrary to Public Policy. Insurance policies frequently provide that the policy shall not be effective if loss is sustained while the insured is engaged in violating the law. In some states a life insurance policy payable in the event of suicide is void if it provides for payment even though the person committing suicide was sane at the time.

(4) Lack of Insurable Interest. If the requirement of an insurable interest is not satisfied, the contract of insurance cannot be enforced.

(5) False Representations. In addition to rescission for fraud, the insurer may set aside a policy whenever the applicant in giving the insurer necessary information has made a *false representation,* that is, a misstatement, whether oral or written, as to a material fact without regard to whether the applicant intended to deceive.

Modern life insurance policies customarily provide that the policy is not avoided when the insured misstates his age but that the amount payable "shall be that sum which the premium paid would have provided for had the age been correctly stated."

(6) False Warranties. The insurer may generally insist that the applicant agree in the policy that the statements of fact or promises of the applicant shall be *warranties* so that if the facts prove not to be as stated or if the promise is not fulfilled, the policy can be avoided by the insurer.

A warranty differs from a representation in several respects. A warranty is part of the final contract of insurance made between the parties, and its terms therefore appear in the policy itself or are incorporated in it by reference. In contrast, the representation is merely a collateral or separate matter which leads up to or induces the execution of the contract. As the representation is not part of the policy itself, it may consist of oral statements or it may be included in a separate writing.

A breach of a warranty or a false warranty makes the insurance contract voidable without regard to whether the matter is material, while a representation does not affect the contract unless the matter is material. A warranty must be literally true or strictly performed, while a representation need only be substantially true.

Because of these considerations and a general reluctance to enforce forfeiture, the courts will, whenever possible, construe statements as representations rather than warranties; and even when they are held to be warranties, they will be construed strictly against the insurer in order to favor the insured. In addition, a number of states have adopted statutes which abolish the characteristics of warranties and provide that a warranty has no greater effect than a representation and that in the absence of proof of materiality or intention to defraud, a warranty, though broken, does not avoid the policy.

(7) Concealment. When an applicant for insurance withholds or conceals information as to material facts with the intent to deceive the insurer, the policy may ordinarily be avoided by the insurer for fraud. (See p. 846, Great American Insurance Co. of New York v. Clayton) In the case of marine insurance, withholding of material information amounts to concealment even though there is no fraudulent intent.

A fact is deemed material if it significantly increases the risk or loss. It is also held that any fact is material when the insurer specifically inquires about it. If the applicant refuses to answer a specific question or gives an answer that is obviously incomplete, there is no concealment in law.

(8) Breach of Condition. Just as in the case of an ordinary contract, a policy of insurance may contain conditions which, if not satisfied, bar recovery on the policy. Thus the failure to give notice to the insurer of a loss within the period specified in the policy is a breach of a condition subsequent and discharges the insurer from liability.

Sec. 58-G. Counterdefenses. In some instances the defenses of the insurer may be set aside by counterdefenses that are raised by the insured or the beneficiary.

(1) Waiver. As a general proposition, the insurer may waive any provision in the policy that was intended for its benefit unless the court deems that the waiver is against public policy.

(2) Estoppel. The insurer may be estopped from claiming the benefit of the violation of a provision of the policy by the insured. An estoppel arises whenever the insurer has by his words or acts led the insured to a certain conclusion on which the latter relies and would therefore suffer harm if the insurer were permitted to show that the conclusion was not true. If a company issues a receipt for a premium, for example, it is estopped from later denying that payment was made according to the terms of the insurance contract.

Estoppel may also apply to the insured.

Sec. 58-H. Subrogation. In property insurance, when the loss to the insured has been caused by the wrongful act of a third person, the insured has a right to sue that person for the damages caused him. If meanwhile the insurer has paid the insured for those damages, it would be unjust to permit the insured to recover damages from the wrongdoer also. The law accordingly holds that the insurer has the right to assert the insured's claim and to sue the third person for the damages which he caused the insured. This right is known as *subrogation.*

Ordinarily the principle of subrogation is not applicable to life insurance policies but is limited to those policies which are contracts of indemnity. By statute it is sometimes provided that an employer who is required to make workmen's compensation payments to an injured employee or the survivor of a deceased employee is subrogated to the claim against the third person who injured or killed the employee.

Cases for Chapter 58

Barr's Estate

104 Cal.App.2d 506, 231 P.2d 876 (1951)

Barr obtained a retirement income bond from the Pacific Mutual Life Insurance Co. under the terms of which she was to pay to the company annual premiums until she reached 65, from which time the company would pay her $100 a month. Barr died at the age of 66. The insurance company paid approximately $9,000 to the beneficiary of the policy. The inheritance tax was charged against this payment. The beneficiary objected on the ground that the money she received was "insurance" and was therefore exempt from taxes. The lower court held that the payment was exempt.

WILSON, J. . . . For a contract to be one of insurance it is essential that there be hazard and a shifting of the incidence. If there is no risk or if there be one and it is not shifted to another or others, there can be no insurance. . . . "Basically, insurance is a device which furnishes protection against a risk of loss by distributing the losses of the few among the many who are subject to the same risk. . . . An annuity is not insurance. Both insurance and annuity contracts are, it is true, gambles against the contingency of death. They are dissimilar, however, in that under an annuity the company's obligation is not to indemnify on the happening of a contingent event causing loss. From the viewpoint of risk, a life insurance policy and an annuity contract are, in fact, diametrically different. Under the former the company will lose in the event of the insured's premature death; under the latter the company will gain. The only risk of the company issuing an annuity, except for the possibility that the annuitant may outlive his expectancy, is the investment risk that the capital may shrink in value or that the return may be less than the amounts payable to the annuitant.". . .

"A life insurance policy is a contract whereby the insurance company agrees to insure or indemnify the beneficiary against the death of the insured; it is a contract by which the insured protects the beneficiary against loss accruing by the early or premature death of the insured. The refund annuity contract, such as we are here considering, is very different. By it the insurance company agrees to repay to the annuitant, in installments during his life, the amount paid in by him to the company and if at his death there be a balance unpaid to him, to pay that balance to the person designated by the annuitant to receive the same. It is a contract by which the annuitant protects himself, during his life, by making an investment which will assure the receipt by himself, of an adequate or desired annual sum during his life, with the further assurance that if he should die prematurely, his estate or those whom he desires to receive distribution thereof will not suffer the loss of the repayment he has himself not yet received. . . . This is not a life insurance policy.

In the instant case the retirement income bond was taken out by decedent in 1930, at which time she paid the annual premium of $590.40. She paid the annual premium until 1948 when, at age 65, she was entitled to receive $100 a month for life. From the schedule of death benefits attached to the policy it is evident that the insurance company did not assume any risk of loss on her death. The first year she paid a premium of $590.40 and was guaranteed in case of death $520. The second year the paid premiums totaled $1,180.80 and the death benefits slightly exceeded the amount of premiums paid but they would not exceed the amount contributed by decedent plus the income thereon. What the beneficiary received is that portion of decedent's money which had not been repaid to her, and whatever risk the insurance company assumed was an investment risk and not an insurance risk. . . .

[Judgment exempting payment from tax reversed. Since the policy was not "insurance," the payment made to the beneficiary was not exempt under the statute which exempted payments made under insurance policies.]

Gerard v. Metropolitan Life Insurance Co.
167 Miss. 207, 149 So. 793 (1933)

Gerard brought suit to recover the value of a policy of insurance for $400 issued in her favor by the Metropolitan Life Insurance Co. on the life of her servant, Jones. The insurance company contended that the policy was not enforceable because there was a lack of insurable interest. From a decree dismissing the bill, the complainant appealed.

ANDERSON, J. . . . There was no relation of consanguinity or affinity existing between appellant [plaintiff] and the insured. The bill alleged that Fannie Jones was appellant's . . . servant and had been for a long time; that . . . appellant looked after and handled her business, giving a considerable amount of her time and attention to her. An insurable interest in the life of another means that there must be a reasonable ground based on the relation of the parties to each other, either pecuniary, blood, or affinity, to expect some advantage from the continuance of the life of the insured; otherwise the contract is a mere wager. The beneficiary in such a contract has more reason to desire the death of the insured than the continuance of life. "Such policies have a tendency to create a desire for the event. They are, therefore, independently of any statute on the subject, condemned as being against public policy."

[In] National Life & Accident Insurance Co. v. Ball, 157 Miss. 163, 127 So. 268, . . . a policy was taken out and the premiums paid by the son-in-law of the insured, who showed no reasonable expectation of any such benefit in the continuance of the life of the insured as the law regards as an insurable interest. The insured was without substantial property; to a large extent she was dependent upon others and was not a member of the household of her son-in-law. The court held that the latter had no insurable interest in the life of the mother-in-law, and that therefore the policy was void.

An allegation of appellant's bill touching insurable interest, fairly interpreted, means that the insured, Fannie Jones, had more interest in the continuance of appellant's life than appellant had in continuance of her life. It is true that the bill states that Fannie Jones was appellant's servant and that appellant had a personal and pecuniary interest in her, but there is an entire lack of any substantial allegation as to what constituted the pecuniary interest. Of course, merely personal interest is not an insurable interest. As we view it, the Ball Case is decisive of the question involved against appellant. . . .

[Judgment for defendant affirmed.]

Metts v. Central Standard Life Insurance Co.

142 Cal.App.2d 445, 298 P.2d 621 (1956)

Metts filled out a printed application form for polio insurance distributed by the Central Standard Life Insurance Co. He mailed the application to the company on May 15. It was received by the company on May 23. On May 21, Metts' son stricken with polio, of which the insurer was notified on May 28. The company refused to pay on the ground that it had not accepted the application. Metts sued the insurer. From a judgment in his favor, the insurer appealed.

BRAY, J. . . . The application form, on its reverse side, stated: "Infantile Paralysis. Immediate First Day Coverage Automatically Covers Entire Family." "No Waiting Period." "Pays from *First Day* that poliomyelitis manifests itself and thereafter, as provided. . . ."

Plaintiff contends that the application form itself was an offer to contract which was accepted by him; that the above mentioned wording on the back of the form caused him to believe that when he mailed the completed form and premium payment, the contract was then in effect and that he was immediately covered.

Defendant contends that there was no representation that the policy would take effect as of the date of the application, and that the application was an offer by the insured not accepted until a policy was issued. . . .

"Because contracts of insurance are not the result of negotiation and are generally drawn by the insurer, any uncertainties or ambiguities therein are resolved most strongly in favor of the insured. . . ."

Our first task is to determine, then, whether there is any uncertainty or ambiguity in the language of the application. . . . The only language [of the application form] important here is that above quoted appearing on the reverse side: *"Immediate* First Day Coverage *Automatically* Covers Entire Family." (Emphasis added.) The use of the words "immediate" and "automatically" in these phrases is difficult to explain as having any meaning other than that the coverage commences from the date of the application. At least, a reasonable conclusion is, that did these phrases apply to the first day of sickness rather than the first day of coverage, there would be no need for the words "immediate" and "automatically." The policy when issued would state that it covered illness from the first day of illness and covered the entire family. The form further states: "Pays from *First Day* that poliomyelitis manifests itself. . . ." In view of that statement, what is the meaning of the words "immediate First Day Coverage" if not coverage immediately upon signing?

Under the rules above mentioned such words are fairly capable of an interpretation which would afford the greater measure of protection to the insured. A layman could hardly be expected to give any other interpretation. . . . We are therefore required to hold that the application form constituted an offer by defendant of coverage to take effect immediately upon the signing and posting of the application. . . .

[Judgment affirmed.]

Great American Insurance Co. of New York v. Clayton
247 Ky. 612, 57 S.W.2d 467 (1932)

As a result of a disagreement between Clayton, a mine physician at the plant of the Southern Mining Co., and certain miners, who were dissatisfied with a contract under which the doctor's pay was deducted by the company from their wages, it was alleged that the miners had made threats against the doctor. Thereafter, without informing the Great American Insurance Co. as to the conditions existing at the mine or as to the threats, Clayton procured a renewal of one policy and two new policies of insurance on his personal property. In an action on the policies, the company set up as a defense the concealment of material facts. From a judgment for the plaintiff, the defendant appealed.

REES, J. . . . To avoid the policy, the concealment must be of a matter material to the risk; and it must not only appear that the insured knew, or that the circumstances were such that an ordinarily prudent person would know, that the fact concealed was material to the risk, but also that it was intentionally and fraudulently concealed. . . . Fraudulent concealment exists where the insured has knowledge of a fact material to the risk which honesty and fair dealing require that he should communicate to the insurer but which he intentionally withholds, although no inquiries were made. . . .

Here the [insurer has] defended on the ground that Dr. Clayton concealed material facts . . . in obtaining the policies. He knew and recognized that the facts within his knowledge were material because he stated that it was on account of the threats and conditions existing at the mining camp where the property was located that he procured the additional insurance. It is conceded that he did not disclose these facts . . . when he applied for the insurance. By his own admission his fear of danger to the property was the moving cause of procuring the insurance, and the facts producing this fear should have been disclosed to the insurer. The facts were such as to cause a reasonable apprehension by him of the danger to his property, and the danger itself was of such a nature as would enhance the risk in the mind of an ordinarily prudent and intelligent man. Ordinarily the materiality of the facts concealed is a question for the jury, but here there is no dispute as to materiality. It was shown without contradiction that an insurer acting reasonably and naturally in accordance with the practice usual among fire insurance companies under similar circumstances would not have insured the property if the facts had been disclosed. . . .

[Judgment for plaintiff reversed.]

Questions and Case Problems

1. What is the objective of each of the following rules of law?
    (a) In the case of property insurance the insured must have an insurable interest at the time of the loss.
    (b) An insurer who pays a property loss claim is subrogated to the claim of the insured against the third person causing the harm.

2. Lisle applied for life insurance with the Federal Life & Casualty Co. Both Lisle and his wife made false, fraudulent statements to the insurer in connection with the application. The insurer's physician examined Lisle twice but did not ascertain anything that revealed the falsity of those statements. After the insured's death about a year later, the insurer denied liability on the ground of fraud. Lisle's widow claimed that the insurer could not raise the question of fraud since it had examined the insured before accepting his application. Was the insurer liable? (Federal Life & Casualty Co. v. Lisle, [Ohio] 172 N.E.2d 919)

3. Einhorn held warehouse receipts as collateral security for a loan that he had made to the prior holder of the receipts. Einhorn obtained a fire insurance policy from the Firemen's Insurance Co., which insured him against loss of the property by fire to the extent of his interest in the collateral. The property represented by the receipts was destroyed by fire. Einhorn assigned his claim on the policy to Flint Frozen Foods, which then

sued the insurer. Was the policy obtained by Einhorn valid? (Flint Frozen Foods v. Firemen's Insurance Co., 8 N.J. 606, 86 A.2d 673)

4. Members of the Greenfield Mutual Burial Association made contributions to a common fund from which a specified sum was paid for funeral expenses upon the death of any member. The State of Indiana claimed that the association was engaged in the insurance business and brought an action against its representative, Willett, for failing to comply with the applicable insurance laws. Decide. (Indiana v. Willett, 171 Ind. 296, 86 N.E. 68)

5. Moore's wife applied to the Palmetto State Life Insurance Co. for accident insurance on her husband. She paid the premium due. Unknown to the wife, the application was rejected sixteen days later. However, when she inquired of the agent thereafter as to the status of the application, the agent said that he had had no word. When she inquired some time later, the agent said he thought that the policy had come in and, if it had not, she would be notified in a few days. She heard nothing from the company. Two weeks later her husband was killed accidentally. After his death the insurance company informed her that the application had been rejected. She sued the insurance company. Decide. (Moore v. Palmetto State Life Insurance Co., 222 S.C. 492, 73 S.E.2d 688)

6. Hicks obtained an automobile collision policy from the Alabama Farm Bureau Mutual Casualty Insurance Co. The policy provided that there was no coverage of loss during the period between the expiration of the term of the policy and the date of the actual payment of a renewal premium. Hicks did not pay the renewal premium until several months after the expiration of the policy. During the noncovered period, he was in a collision. When he paid the renewal premium to the agent-manager at the insurer's local office, he informed him of this collision. He then filed a proof of loss for the damage sustained in the collision. The insurer retained the renewal premium but denied liability for the collision. Hicks sued the insurer. Decide. (Alabama Farm Bureau Mutual Cas. Ins. Co. v. Hicks, [Ala.App.] 133 So.2d 217)

7. Bondurant obtained a public liability insurance policy from the United States Fidelity and Guarantee Co. Johnson sustained an injury that came within the coverage of the policy and brought suit against Bondurant and U.S.F.&G. Co. While the action was pending, Bondurant was declared a bankrupt and received his discharge in bankruptcy. Because of such discharge, Johnson could not hold Bondurant liable. U.S.F.&G. Co. thereupon claimed that since Bondurant was not liable to Johnson, it was not liable either since its liability was no greater than that of its insured. Decide. (Johnson v. Bondurant, [Kan.] 359 P.2d 861)

CHAPTER 59

Kinds of Insurance

Today many different kinds of insurance are available. They tend, however, to group themselves into a few categories in terms of the nature of the interest protected.

Fire Insurance

A *fire insurance policy* is a contract to indemnify the insured for destruction of or damage to property caused by fire. In almost every state the New York standard fire insurance form (1943) has been adopted as the standard policy.

Sec. 59-A. Risk Assumed. There must be an actual flame or burning which is accidental or which has escaped from its proper confines, that is, a *hostile fire.* (See p. 858, Youse v. Employers Fire Insurance Co.) Damage from heat alone is not covered, but damage from heat or smoke caused by a hostile fire is covered.

The fire must be the immediate or proximate cause of the loss. When there is a reasonable connection between a fire and the ultimate loss sustained, the insurer is liable for the loss.

In the absence of a stipulation to the contrary, the fire insurance policy also covers various forms of harm that are reasonably foreseeable as incidental to a fire. The policy thus covers loss caused by water used in extinguishing a fire, loss arising from the necessary removal of the property from the scene of the fire, loss due to theft of goods during the fire when the insured was not negligent in protecting them from theft, and loss due to explosions caused by the fire.

The New York standard form of fire insurance policy excludes loss or damage caused directly or indirectly by enemy attack by armed forces, invasion, insurrection, rebellion, revolution, civil war, or usurped power, or by order of any civil authority; or by neglect of the insured to use all reasonable means to save and preserve the property at and after a fire or when the property is endangered by fire in neighboring premises; or by theft.

Damage by explosion is also excluded unless fire follows and then the insurer is liable only for that part of the damage caused by the fire. The standard form of fire insurance policy includes protection from lightning damage even though no fire is caused thereby.

Sec. 59-B. Notice and Proof of Loss. Fire insurance policies commonly provide that the insured must give the insurer notice of his loss and file a detailed statement of the loss within a certain period and in a certain manner. If proof of loss is not furnished within the time specified by the statute or policy, the insurer generally is not liable.

Sec. 59-C. Insurer's Liability. Basically the insurer is liable for the actual amount of the loss sustained. This liability is limited, however, by the maximum amount stated in the policy or the amount of damages sustained by total destruction of the property, whichever is less. That is, the recovery can never be greater than the damages which would be sustained in the case of a total destruction, and this in turn cannot exceed the maximum amount stated in the policy.

The amount of the loss, in the absence of statute or agreement to the contrary, is the actual cash value at the time of the loss. A *total loss* does not necessarily mean that the property has been completely destroyed. The loss is regarded as being total if the unconsumed portion is of no value for the purposes for which the property was utilized at the time of the insurance.

Frequently the insurer will stipulate in the policy that it has the right to replace or restore the property to its former condition in lieu of paying the insured the cash value of the loss.

Sec. 59-D. Assignment of Fire Insurance Policy. Fire insurance is a personal contract, and in the absence of statute or contractual authorization it cannot be assigned before a loss is sustained without the consent of the insurer. In addition, it is commonly provided that the policy shall be voided if an assignment to give a purchaser of the property the protection of the policy is attempted. Such a forfeiture clause applies only when the insured attempts to transfer his entire interest in the policy. It is held not to apply to equitable assignments. Likewise, a mortgagee who assigns his mortgage may assign his rights under a fire insurance policy.

Sec. 59-E. Mortgage Clause. Either or both the mortgagor and mortgagee may take out policies of fire insurance to protect their respective interests in property. In the absence of a contrary stipulation, the policy taken out by either covers only his own interest. When one policy protects both parties as their respective interests may appear, it is generally provided that the insurance of the mortgagee shall not be affected by any act of the mortgagor.

Sec. 59-F. Extended Coverage. In the case of fire insurance policies to protect homes and buildings, it is common to include extended coverage by which the property is insured against hazards in addition to that of fire. The term "extended coverage" generally refers to protection against loss from windstorm, hail, explosion other than those within steam boilers on the premises, riot, civil commotion, aircraft damage, vehicle damage, and smoke damage.

Sec. 59-G. Other Provisions. Fire insurance policies commonly prohibit the insured from doing certain acts that will or may increase the hazard or risk involved and provide that the policy is void if the insured commits the prohibited acts.

It is commonly provided that false statements made by the insured when they are known to be false shall avoid the policy. Under such a provision it is held that a fraudulent misstatement of the value of the property avoids the policy.

The insured may take out more than one policy on the same property, in the absence of a provision in any of the policies to the contrary; but in the event of loss he cannot recover more than the total loss he sustains. Such a loss is pro-rated among the insurers.

An insurer is not liable when the damage or destruction of the property is intentionally caused by the insured. The fact that the insured negligently caused a fire is not a defense to the insurer, even when there is a stipulation that the insured shall not change or increase the hazard insured against.

Sec. 59-H. Cancellation. In the absence of a provision in the fire insurance policy or a statute authorizing the cancellation by the act of one party, the agreement of both parties, the insurer and the insured, is essential. It is common, however, to provide by statute or by the terms of the policy that under certain circumstances the policy may be terminated or canceled by the act of one party alone. When this is done, the provisions of the statute and the policy must be strictly followed in order to make the cancellation effective.

Automobile Insurance

Commonly, two types of motor vehicle insurance are available. One type compensates the owner or operator for his own loss or damages from fire, theft, and collision or upset, while another type protects the owner from the claims of other persons for damage caused by him to them or their property. The latter type is generally called liability insurance. In addition, many policies include an extended coverage to cover liability for injuries sustained in connection with any kind of accident.

Associations of insurers, such as the National Bureau of Casualty Underwriters and the National Automobile Underwriters Association, have proposed standard forms of policies that have been approved by their members in virtually all the states.

Sec. 59-I. Financial Responsibility Laws. By state law drivers are required to carry liability insurance in order to obtain or maintain the right to operate an automobile. In practically all states, the law does not apply until the driver is involved in an automobile accident, when he is required to furnish proof of financial responsibility before he can drive again. One of the ways of proving financial responsibility under the statutes is to show that liability insurance in an amount stated by the statute is maintained by the operator. This type of statute is called a *financial responsibility law*. It is open to the criticism that it applies only after a driver has had his first accident, which is little consolation to the victim of the first accident.

Sec. 59-J. Liability Insurance. The owner or operator of a motor vehicle may obtain *liability insurance* to protect himself from claims made by third persons for damage to their property (property damage liability) or person (bodily injury liability) arising from the use or operation of an automobile. When the insurer pays under such a policy, it makes the payment directly to the third person and is liable to pay him the same amount and for the same items as the insured would be required to pay if sued by the third person, although it is not required to pay more than the maximum stated in the policy.

If the insurer is liable for the damage caused a third person or his property, it is likewise liable for cost of repairs, destruction of property, loss of services, and other items of damages for which the insured himself would be liable.

The liability of the insured is not affected by the fact that he is insured. The fact that he is legally liable although insured means that if for any reason his policy does not cover the full loss or if the insurance company is not solvent or in business at that time, he is liable for any amount not paid, assuming that he would be liable in the absence of insurance.

(1) Person Operating. Liability policies ordinarily protect the owner of the auto from liability when it is operated by another person

with the permission of the insured, as in the case of an employee or agent of the owner.

Liability insurance may also protect an insured individual or his spouse against liability incurred while operating another person's automobile. This is referred to as *D.O.C.* (drive-other-car) *coverage.*

(2) Exclusions. In liability insurance the insurer may protect itself by excluding damage claims arising out of certain types of causes. Such policies may exclude claims of employees of the owner or claims under the workmen's compensation laws, or liability for claims when the insured admits to the injured third person that the insured is liable and agrees to pay his claim.

The fact that the owner or operator is violating a speed law does not free the insurer from liability in the absence of an express provision to that effect.

In the case of commercial vehicles the insurer may stipulate that it shall only be bound by the policy "provided: (a) the regular and frequent use of the automobile is confined to the area within a fifty mile radius of the limits of the city or town where the automobile is principally garaged . . . , (b) no regular or frequent trips are made by the automobile to any locations beyond such radius."

(3) Notice and Cooperation. A liability policy generally provides that the insurer is not liable unless the insured (a) gives the insurer prompt notice of any serious accident or claim or lawsuit brought against him, (b) furnishes the insurance company with all details of the occurrence, and (c) cooperates with the insurer in the preparation of the defense against a lawsuit brought on the policy and participates at the trial. Notice and cooperation under such a policy are conditions precedent to the liability of the insurer.

Sec. 59-K. Collision or Upset Insurance. Liability insurance does not indemnify the owner for damage to his own automobile. In order to obtain this protection, the owner of the auto must obtain property insurance.

Such a policy commonly provides that the insurer is not liable when the automobile is used by a person engaged in violating the law. It may also be stipulated that liability is avoided if the auto is subject to a lien or encumbrance that has not been disclosed. It is common to exclude damages, resulting from collision, for the loss of the use of the auto, depreciation, or for loss of personal property in the auto.

Automobile collision insurance policies frequently contain a deductible clause and are known as "$50 deductible" or "$100 deductible" policies. The effect of such a clause is that for each accident the insurer is liable only for the loss in excess of the amount stated to be deductible.

As in the case of liability insurance, the auto owner is under a duty to give notice, to inform, and to cooperate with the insurer. He must also give the insurer an opportunity to examine the automobile to determine the extent of damage before making repairs.

Sec. 59-L. Theft Insurance. The owner of an automobile can secure theft insurance, which will protect him from loss through the theft of the auto (see p. 859, Cox v. World Fire and Marine Insurance Co.) and from damage to the auto caused by a theft. The standard form of policy covers loss from larceny, robbery, and pilferage as well as theft. In addition, statutes in some states provide that a "theft" occurs within the meaning of a theft policy whenever there is any taking or use of the automobile not authorized by the owner.

It is common to exclude liability for the loss sustained while a passenger auto is used for commercial transportation or is rented to another. Such exclusions are, of course, not found in policies covering vehicles used for commercial purposes or for renting to others.

An automobile theft policy does not necessarily protect against loss of contents. It is common to exclude liability for equipment or personal property taken from the auto, but additional insurance protecting from such theft can be secured.

Sec. 59-M. Fire, Lightning, and Transportation Insurance. In this type of insurance the insurer agrees to pay for any loss arising out of damage to or the destruction of a motor vehicle or its equipment caused by fire originating in any manner, by lightning, or by the stranding, sinking, burning, collision, or derailment of any conveyance in or upon which the automobile or the truck is being transported.

This type of policy is commonly combined with a policy against theft and pilferage and is usually subject to the same exclusions. Loss while used in violation of the law may be excluded.

Sec. 59-N. Comprehensive Insurance. In many automobile insurance policies comprehensive material damage coverage, which protects the policyholder against virtually all such risks except collision or upset, replaces fire and theft insurance. The exclusions for this kind of insurance include wear and tear, freezing, mechanical breakdown, and loss of personal effects.

Life Insurance

A contract of *life insurance* requires the insurer to pay a stipulated sum of money upon the death of the insured. It is not a contract of indemnity since the insurer does not undertake to indemnify the beneficiary for the financial loss sustained as the result of the death of the insured.

Sec. 59-O. Kinds of Life Insurance Policies. Life insurance is commonly classified in three groups: (1) ordinary life insurance, (2) group insurance, and (3) industrial insurance. Ordinary life insurance in turn may be subclassified as (a) *straight life insurance*, which requires payments of premiums throughout the life of the insured; (b) *limited payment insurance*, requiring the payment of premiums during a limited period, such as ten, twenty, or thirty years, or until the death of the insured if that should occur before the end of the specified period; (c) *endowment insurance*, under which the insurer undertakes to pay a stipulated sum when the insured reaches a specified age, or upon his death if that occurs earlier; and (d) *term insurance*, under which the insurer undertakes to pay a stipulated sum only in the event of the death of the insured during a specified period, such as one, two, five, or ten years.

Somewhat similar to policies of endowment insurance are *annuity policies* and *retirement income insurance* under which the insured either pays a lump sum to the insurer and thereafter receives fixed annual payments, or pays periodic premiums to the insurer until a certain date and then receives fixed annual payments.

Group life insurance is an insurance of the lives of employees in a particular business or profession. Such policies are usually either term policies or ordinary policies. A medical examination is usually not required.

Industrial insurance is in substance ordinary life insurance written for a small amount, usually from $100 to $500. Premiums are generally paid weekly or monthly and are collected from door to door by the agent of the insured. No physical examination is required for industrial insurance. The industrial policy may be either term, straight life, limited payment, or endowment.

Life insurance policies may provide for *double indemnity* if death is caused by an accident and occurs within ninety days after the accident; for the making of payments to the insured in the event of his total permanent disability; and for reinstatement upon lapse of the policy for nonpayment of premiums.

Disability is usually defined in a life insurance policy as any "incapacity resulting from bodily injury or disease to engage in any occupation for remuneration or profit." The policy generally provides that a disability which has continued for a stated minimum period, such as four to six months, will be regarded as a *total permanent disability*. The policy may also provide that during such a period of disability, the payment of premiums will be waived. The waiver of

premium payments during disability may be included in a policy
without a provision for payments to the insured for his disability.

Sec. 59-P. The Beneficiary. The person to whom the proceeds of a
life insurance policy are payable upon the death of the insured is
called the *beneficiary*. He may be a third person, or the beneficiary
may be the estate of the insured. There may be more than one beneficiary. When the policy is payable directly to a named beneficiary,
the proceeds of the policy are generally not subject to the debts of
the insured.

The customary policy provides that the insured reserves the right
to change the beneficiary without the latter's consent. When the policy
contains such a provision, the beneficiary cannot object to a change
that destroys all rights which he had under the policy and which
names another as beneficiary in his place. (See p. 861, Metropolitan
Life Insurance Co. v. Sandstrand)

In industrial policies it is also customary for the policy to contain
a "facility-of-payment clause" under which the insurer is given the
option of selecting from a designated class or group anyone whom
the insurer deems equitably entitled to receive payment and to make
payment to that person. Such a clause enables the insurer to pay the
amount of the insurance proceeds directly to any person who pays the
debts of the decedent, such as his funeral bills, rather than to a named
beneficiary who has not expended any money or behalf of the decedent
or his estate.

Sec. 59-Q. Risks Assumed by the Insured. Policies frequently provide that death shall not be within the protection of the policy or
that a double indemnity provision shall not be applicable when death
is due to or caused by (1) suicide, (2) narcotics, (3) violation of the
law, (4) execution for crime, (5) war activities, or (6) operation of
aircraft.

Sec. 59-R. Incontestable Clause. Statutes commonly provide, and
many life insurance companies regardless of statutes provide, for
the inclusion of an incontestable clause in life insurance policies.
Ordinarily this clause states that after the lapse of two years the
policy cannot be contested by the insurance company. The insurer is
free to contest the validity of the policy at any time during the con-
testable period; but once that period has expired, it must pay the
stipulated sum upon the death of the insured and cannot claim that
in obtaining the policy the insured had been guilty of misrepresentation, fraud, or any other conduct that would exempt it from liability.

The incontestable clause does not bar matters of defense that arise
subsequent to the sustaining of loss. Generally the incontestable

clause is not applicable to double indemnity or disability provisions of the policy.

Sec. 59-S. Assignment by Insured. In the absence of a stipulation in the policy or a provision of a statute to the contrary, a policy of life insurance may be assigned before it matures or before the right of the insured becomes vested in it. In itself, an assignment does not change the beneficiary.

The assignment of a life insurance policy is frequently governed by statute. It is commonly provided that the assignment must be in writing, and in some states the right to make an assignment is restricted when the beneficiary is a wife or child of the insured.

Sec. 59-T. Loans and Surrender of Policy. The insured may to a certain extent obtain a loan on a policy (see p. 862, Schwartz' Estate), or surrender it for its cash surrender value or in return for a paid-up policy or extended insurance.

(1) Paid-Up Policy. The insured may, under modern statutes or common forms of policies, request the insured to issue to him a new policy of paid-up insurance. Instead of losing the reserve value that he has built up by the payment of his premiums, the insured in effect takes out a new paid-up policy of insurance for a smaller amount of protection and pays for that policy through the transfer of the reserve value of the old policy.

In some states it is provided that when a policy lapses for nonpayment of premiums, the insurer must automatically issue a paid-up policy on the basis of the reserve value of the lapsed policy.

(2) Extended Insurance. Instead of taking a paid-up policy for a smaller amount, it is generally possible under modern statutes and policies to obtain term insurance giving the same amount of protection. This remains effective until the reserve value of the original policy has been consumed.

Sec. 59-U. Rights of Creditors. If the insured makes the policy payable to his estate, the proceeds become part of the general assets of his estate upon his death and, in the absence of statute, are subject to the claims of his creditors. If the insured makes the policy on his own life payable to another person and if the insured is at all times solvent when he pays the premiums, his creditors cannot reach the policy in any way, and the beneficiary is entitled to the proceeds of the policy.

Between these two extremes are a variety of situations. The insured may have been insolvent during part or all of the life of the policy; or the obtaining of the insurance policy or the assignment of it or the changing of the beneficiary may have been done in fraud of creditors.

If the policy is originally payable to the estate of the insured, an assignment by the insured of his interest when made in fraud of creditors will not defeat the right of the creditors.

If the policy is made payable to a third person as beneficiary but the insured is insolvent, courts differ as to the rights of the insured's creditors.

Cases for Chapter 59

Youse v. Employers Fire Insurance Co.

172 Kan. 111, 238 P.2d 472 (1951)

Youse owned a ring that was insured with the Employers Fire Insurance Co. against loss, including "all direct loss or damage by fire." The ring was accidentally thrown by Youse into a trash burner and was damaged when the trash was burned. He sued the insurer. From a judgment for the plaintiff, the defendant appealed.

PRICE, J. . . . The company contends . . . that the quoted insuring clause of the policy, "against all direct loss or damage by fire" covers only loss or damage resulting from a hostile fire as distinguished from a friendly fire; that here the fire, being intentionally lighted in and confined to a place or receptacle where it was intended to be, was not a hostile fire within the usual and well-established meaning of the term and therefore no recovery can be had.

The insured argues that he purchased and paid for *fire insurance* —not just for fire insurance to cover loss resulting only from so-called hostile fires; that the direct loss and damage to the ring by fire is undisputed; that the company would have the court write into the policy an unauthorized and unreasonable restriction; that there is no ambiguity in the terms of the policy and therefore it should be enforced according to its literal terms; and that even though there were some uncertainty as to its meaning, the court is bound to construe the policy strictly against the company and favorably to the insured. . . .

"The distinction most commonly made by courts in considering contracts of fire insurance is that drawn between hostile and friendly fires. If the fire burns in a place where it (is) intended to burn, although damages may have resulted where none were intended, the fire is a friendly fire and the insurer is not liable for damages flowing therefrom. A friendly fire refers to one which remains confined within the place intended and refers to a fire in a furnace, stove, or other usual place. A hostile fire, on the other hand, means one not confined to the place intended or one not intentionally started; and it is generally considered to refer to such a fire which, if it had pursued its natural course, would have resulted in a total or partial destruction of the insured property. When a friendly fire escapes from the place it ought to be to some place where it ought not to be, causing damage, it becomes a hostile fire for which the insurer is liable.

"In order to recover for damages sustained, the insured must show that the fire was a hostile, rather than a friendly, fire. . . ."

. . . The very great weight of authority appears to be that fires, within the meaning of standard insuring clauses in fire insurance policies, are classified as friendly or hostile in nature, notwithstanding that such distinction is not made in the language of the policy itself. . . .

We think it cannot be denied that in common parlance and everyday usage one has not "had a fire" so long as it has burned only in the place where it was intended to burn, [as] . . . a fire in [a] furnace, cookstove, or fireplace. . . .

In our opinion there can be no question but that the fire which damaged or destroyed the sapphire ring was what in law is known as a friendly fire. It was intentionally lighted, was for the usual and ordinary purpose of burning trash, and was at all times confined to the place where it was intended, and did not escape.

[Judgment for plaintiff reversed.]

Cox v. World Fire and Marine Insurance Co.

239 S.W.2d 538 (Mo.App., 1951)

Cox sold his automobile to Maguire, who paid him with a cashier's check. The check later proved to be a forgery. Cox, unable to trace his auto, sued the insurance company from which he had obtained a theft policy. From a judgment for the plaintiff, the defendant appealed.

WOLFE, C. . . . In construing a contract of insurance its words must be given the ordinary meaning that they carry in common usage. . . .

The word "theft" is defined in the Merriam-Webster New International Dictionary, Second Edition, as "Act of stealing; specif., the felonious taking and removing of personal property, with intent to deprive the rightful owner of it; larceny." It is defined in 3 Bouv. Law Dictionary, Rawles Third Edition, p. 3267, as "A popular term for larceny. It is a wider term than larceny and includes other forms of wrongful deprivation of property of another. . . . Acts constituting embezzlement or swindling may be properly so called." The word is generally one of popular, rather than of legal, use, and it is held to embrace within its meaning, or to be equivalent to, the word "larceny." . . . Larceny has been extended in many states to include such offenses as obtaining property by trick or device and even to the unauthorized use of a motor vehicle. . . .

The defendant asserts that since Maguire obtained the automobile from Cox by presenting to him a forged check, and since Cox not only gave possession of the car but did so with the intent to pass title, no larceny was committed. . . .

"The law is well settled in [Missouri] that, where the owner of property through the influence of fraud, artifice, or trickery delivers the possession of his property without intending to part with the title thereto, and there is a preconceived design on the part of the taker of the property to convert it to his own use when obtained, the offense in such case is larceny. The law is equally well settled that, where the owner of the property delivers it with the intention of parting with it altogether, that is, by giving the title as well as the possession, the offense is that of false pretenses, and not larceny.". . .

Pronouncements of like import may be found in [Alabama, California, Iowa, Kentucky, New York, and Ohio]. . . .

The converse [is] to be found, and the Supreme Court of Kansas holds: "The prevailing rule is that any scheme, whether involving false pretenses or other fraudulent trick or device, whereby an owner of property is swindled out of it with the preconceived intent of the swindler not to pay for it, is classed as larceny and is punished accordingly.". . .

The Supreme Court of Rhode Island reached the same conclusion. . . .

It is apparent that the cases favoring the construction urged by the defendant arise in states where, as in Missouri, the common-law definition of larceny prevails, or in states, as in New York, where the term larceny has been extended to embrace offenses other than those contemplated by common law, [but] the courts hold that such larceny is not "theft" within the popular meaning of the word. . . .

It is difficult to say what meaning is embraced within the words as they are commonly used. As the larceny statutes in states are extended to embrace many types of crime including such as that committed here, people read and hear of convictions under such statutes and their conception of the words' meaning extends with their use. In forming their conception they do not resort to statutory definitions of crimes in the state where the policy is issued, but upon their own observation of how the words are used in common speech. We have concluded, however, that the common meaning of the words "theft" and "larceny" still carry with them some element of trespass and that neither [was] meant to apply where the owner gives the property to a malefactor with the intention of passing title. . . .

This appears to be the interpretation that we must adopt; for if we declare that the act here constituted theft under the terms of the policy, we would be extending it to include any number of fraudulent transactions by which the insured might lose his automobile when such coverage was not in the contemplation of the parties at the time the contract was entered into.

[Judgment for plaintiff reversed.]

Metropolitan Life Insurance Co. v. Sandstrand

78 R.I. 457, 82 A.2d 863 (1951)

Miller insured his life with the Metropolitan Life Insurance Co. and named his daughter, Elsie Sandstrand, with whom he was living, as his beneficiary. Because of differences between them he left to live with his other daughter, Esther. Elsie refused to return Miller's policy, which she had been keeping for him. On his death Elsie claimed the proceeds of the policy as beneficiary. Esther claimed that she had been substituted as beneficiary. From a judgment for Esther, Elsie appealed.

FLYNN, C.J. . . . It is clear that under a policy wherein the right to change the beneficiary is expressly reserved to the insured, as here, a beneficiary for the time being acquires no vested interest therein which would deprive the insured of the right to change the beneficiary in accordance with the terms of the policy. . . . Moreover the requirements that a change of beneficiary be filed at the home office and be endorsed upon the policy itself in order to make such change effective are conditions solely for the benefit of the insurer. . . .

By . . . raising no objection in its own behalf and offering to pay the proceeds to either claimant who is found to be entitled thereto, the insurer has waived any question as to completing the change of beneficiary in accordance with the strict terms of the policy. Furthermore, in circumstances where the insured is prevented from obtaining the policy, as here, it has been held that a substantial compliance by the insured with the terms of the policy is sufficient to effectuate a change of beneficiary. However, in our judgment such compliance requires that an insured must intend and personally or through an authorized agent send a change of beneficiary to the insurance company. In other words, he must do all that he reasonably could be expected to do in the circumstances in order to effectuate his intention to change the beneficiary in the policy. If an insured meets such requirement in a proper case, his action is given effect even though such a change had not reached the home office of the insurer before the death of the insured. . . .

In the instant case the insured made reasonable efforts to obtain the policy but was unsuccessful because of Elsie's attitude. He engaged attorneys and instructed them to obtain the policy and to make a change of beneficiary thereunder to Esther. Between July and October there was reasonable expectation that the policy would be obtained through either the attorneys' efforts or his own visits to Elsie. Nowhere is there any indication that he instructed the attorneys to withhold sending the change of beneficiary, and there is no evidence that he changed his original intent or instructions to them. On the contrary he directed Esther as late as October 22 to go to the attorneys and find out whether they had been successful in carrying out his instructions. When informed by Esther on her return that the intended change of beneficiary was mailed that day by his attorneys, he expressed himself in language that reasonably implied confirmation of what had been done in his behalf. . . .

We do not agree with Elsie's contention that the evidence showed only a desire on the part of the father to designate a new beneficiary or that the trial justice found merely that the father *desired* such a change without effecting it. In our opinion the decision shows that the trial justice found not only a desire on the father's part to change the beneficiary to Esther but also found that in view of Elsie's unlawful withholding of the policy and the other steps taken by the father and his attorneys, he had done all he reasonably could be expected to do by way of substantial performance to effectuate the change.

[Judgment for Esther affirmed.]

Schwartz' Estate
369 Pa. 574, 87 A.2d 270 (1952)

Schwartz obtained several policies of life insurance and named Kaufman and others as his beneficiaries. During his lifetime Schwartz obtained loans on the policies from the insurance company. At his death, the company paid the beneficiaries the amount of the policies less the loans. Kaufman claimed that the amount of the loans should be repaid by Schwartz's estate so that the beneficiaries would receive the full amount of the policies. From a judgment for the estate, Kaufman appealed.

STEARNE, J. . . . Courts . . . unanimously agree that a "loan" granted pursuant to a policy right does not create a debtor-creditor relationship. The nature of such a "policy loan" has recently been discussed in Fidelity Union Trust Co. v. Phillips, 5 N.J.Super. 529, 68 A.2d 574. It is said at page 575 of 68 A.2d: "A clear distinction is drawn between a loan made by an insurance company to an insured against a life policy, and a collateral loan made by a third party secured by an assignment or pledge of the policy on the life of the borrower. The former 'is not a loan in the strict technical sense, for there is no obligation of repayment on the insured but rather an advancement on the cash value of the policy, the repayment of which will reinstate the depleted insurance without the issuance of a new policy and the submission of evidence of insurability. A "loan" by the insurer in such circumstances does not give rise to the relationship of debtor and creditor.' . . . Mr. Justice Holmes declared in Board of Assessors v. New York Life Insurance Co., . . . 216 U.S. 517, . . . 'This is called a loan. It is represented by what is called a note, which contains a promise to pay the money. But as the plaintiff (insurance company) never advances more than it already is absolutely bound for under the policy, it has no interest in creating a personal liability and therefore the contract on the face of the note goes on to provide that if the note is not paid when due, it shall be extinguished automatically by the counter credit for what we have called the reserve value of the policy. In short, the claim of the policyholder on the one side and of the company on the other are brought into an account current by the very act that creates the latter. The so-called liability of the policyholder never exists as a personal liability, it never is a debt, but is merely a deduction in account from the sum that the plaintiff ultimately must pay.' Therefore, when an insurance company advances to an insured a sum of money against his policy and upon the death of the insured retains the amount required to satisfy the 'loan' or advance, the beneficiary named in the policy is not entitled to recover from the estate of the insured the amount by which the insurance had been depleted by borrowings by the insured upon the policy.". . .

[Judgment for estate affirmed.]

Questions and Case Problems

1. What is the objective of each of the following rules of law?
   (a) In a policy which insures the interest of the mortgagor and mortgagee as their interests appear, it may be provided that the rights of the mortgagee in the policy will not be affected by the acts of the mortgagor.
   (b) A policy of life insurance may be assigned without the consent of the insurer.

2. Marshall Produce Co. insured its milk and egg processing plant against fire with the St. Paul Fire & Marine Insurance Co. Smoke from a fire near its plant was absorbed by its egg powder. Cans of the powder delivered to the United States Government were rejected as contaminated. Marshall Produce sued the insurance company for a total loss. The insurer contended that there had been no fire involving the insured property and no total loss. Decide. (Marshall Produce Co. v. St. Paul Fire & Marine Insurance Co., [Minn.] 98 N.W.2d 280)

3. Harrison obtained a life insurance policy from the Occidental Life Insurance Co., on which his mother was the beneficiary. Harrison delivered the policy to his mother, and thereafter she paid the premiums on the policy until his death. Meanwhile, Harrison had changed the beneficiary of the

policy, under the power reserved in the policy, from his mother to his estate and then later to his wife. When the insurance company had requested the mother to surrender the policy so that the change of beneficiary could be endorsed thereon, she had refused to do so, but the insurer had changed the beneficiary on its records. After Harrison's death, his mother insisted that she was the beneficiary on the policy, or that at least she had a lien on the policy for the premium payments made by her. Harrison's widow sued Mattie Winstead, the now remarried mother, and the insurance company, claiming that she was the beneficiary. Who was entitled to the insurance money? (Harrison v. Winstead, [S.C.] 110 S.E.2d 903)

4. Walker obtained a policy of life insurance from the National Life and Accident Insurance Co. The policy reserved the right to change the beneficiary. Walker named his wife as beneficiary, and she paid the premiums on the policy. Later Walker's wife sued the insurance company and claimed that the insured could not change the beneficiary because she had paid the premiums on the policy. Decide. (National Life and Accident Insurance Co. v. Walker, [Ky.] 246 S.W.2d 139)

5. The Connecticut Mutual Life Insurance Co. issued to Pinkham a policy of life insurance payable in the event of death to the estate of the insured. Pinkham assigned the policy to his brother, Darius, who later assigned the policy to Tucker, as security for a loan. Upon the death of Pinkham, the proceeds of the policy were claimed by both Darius and Tucker. The insurance company brought an action of interpleader against the claimants to determine to whom the money should be paid. Could Darius object to Tucker's claim on the ground that the assignment to him had not been indorsed on the policy as required by its terms? (Connecticut Mutual Life Insurance Co. v. Tucker, 27 R.I. 170, 61 A. 142)

6. The Glens Falls Insurance Co. issued to Johnson a policy of insurance against loss to his automobile resulting from fire, lightning, or, while being transported in any conveyance, the stranding, sinking, collision, burning, or derailing of such conveyance. One morning Johnson placed the car on a ferry for transportation over a river. The automobile, for some unaccountable reason, suddenly started and ran off the ferry, which was then in the middle of the stream. Johnson brought an action to recover on the policy. Was he entitled to judgment? (Johnson v. Glens Falls Insurance Co., 131 S.C. 253, 127 S.E. 14)

7. The Great Eastern Casualty Co. issued to Solinsky a policy of insurance against loss to an automobile caused solely by collision with another object, either moving or stationary. While driving at a rate of 30 to 35 miles an hour, the insured, responding to what was thought to be a signal light at a railroad crossing, suddenly applied the brakes. The machine skidded, swerved, and reversed position during which time the right wheel collapsed. Solinsky brought an action against the insurer to recover on the policy. Was she entitled to judgment? (The Great Eastern Casualty Co. v. Solinsky, 150 Tenn. 206, 263 S.W. 71)

CHAPTER 60

Trust Estates

In addition to absolute transfers of property to a person for his own use, the law recognizes transfers made to one person for the use and benefit of another person.

Sec. 60-A. Definitions. A transfer of property to one person with the understanding that he will hold the property for the benefit or use of another person is a *trust* or a trust relationship. It is an express trust because the trust duty arises from the express statement by the original owner who transferred the property in trust. A trust may also be created when the owner of property makes a declaration that he holds the property in trust for the beneficiary.

The owner who creates the trust is the *settlor,* the word being taken from the old legal language of "settling the property in trust." He is sometimes called the donor. The person to whom the property is transferred in trust is the *trustee.* The person for whose benefit the trustee holds the property is the *beneficiary* or *cestui que trust.*

Property held in trust is sometimes called the *trust corpus, trust fund, trust estate,* or *trust res.* A distinction is made between the *principal,* or the property in trust, and the *income* which is earned by the principal and distributed by the trustee.

Sec. 60-B. Kinds of Trusts. If the trust is created to take effect within the lifetime of the settlor, it is an *inter vivos trust* or a living trust. If the trust is provided for in the settlor's will and is to become effective only when his will takes effect after his death, the trust is called a *testamentary trust.*

A trust created for the benefit of private individuals is termed a *private trust.* One created for the benefit of the public or certain classes of the public is known as a *charitable trust.*

Sec. 60-C. Creation of Trusts.

(1) Consideration. Since a trust is a transfer of property, consideration is not required, although the absence of consideration may show that the trust is a voidable transfer in fraud of creditors.

(2) Legality. A trust may be created for any lawful purpose, although in a few states statutes limit the purposes.

A trust is invalid when it is for an unlawful purpose or can be set aside if it is in fraud of creditors. A trust may also be void in whole or in part for violating the *rule against perpetuities.* This rule prohibits a person from creating by any transfer, whether in trust or not, a "floating" interest in property that will not become definite or vested until a date further away than twenty-one years after the death of persons alive at the time the owner of the property attempts to create the interest. For example, the owner of property who has no children cannot create a trust for the children (not yet born) of his own children (not yet born). The law is opposed to tying up property for such long periods because no one would know who was the owner of the property until all the grandchildren were born.

In varying degrees some states likewise prevent a settlor from directing that income be accumulated until a special event occurs, instead of paying it to the beneficiaries as it accrues.

(3) Capacity of Parties. Anyone having capacity to make an outright transfer of property can transfer it in trust, and any person having capacity to own the property in question may receive that property in trust. The capacity of the beneficiary of the trust to hold property or to contract is immaterial, and many trusts are created because the beneficiary lacks legal or actual capacity to manage the property for himself.

(4) Formality. In creating a trust, it is common practice to execute a writing, called a *trust agreement* or *deed of trust.* No particular form of language is necessary to create a trust so long as the property, the trust purpose, and the beneficiaries are designated. (See p. 872, Wyse v. Puchner) If an inter vivos trust relates to an interest in land, the Statute of Frauds requires that the trust be evidenced by a writing setting forth the details of the trust. When the

trust depends upon a transfer of title to land, there must be a valid transfer of the title to the trustee in addition to a writing establishing the trust. Ordinarily the two will be combined in one instrument so that the deed which transfers title will also specify the trust duties.

If a trust is created by the will of the settlor, there must be a writing which meets the requirements of a will.

(5) Intention. An intention to impose a duty on the trustee with respect to specific property must be expressed. It is not necessary, however, that the word "trust" or "trustee" be used. The settlor will ordinarily name a trustee, but his failure to do so is not fatal to the trust.

(6) Active Duty. A trust does not exist unless an active duty is placed upon the trustee to manage the property in some manner or to exercise discretion or judgment. A bare direction to hold the property in trust without any direction as to its use or distribution is not a sufficient duty.

(7) Identity of Beneficiary. Every trust must have a beneficiary. In a private trust the beneficiaries must be identified by name, description, or designation of the class to which the beneficiaries belong. In a charitable trust it is sufficient that the beneficiaries be members of the public at large or a general class of the public.

Trusts for religious masses, for the maintenance of grave monuments, or for the care of particular animals are technically invalid but are nevertheless enforced because of the social interests involved.

(8) Acceptance of Trust. As the performance of a trust imposes burdens upon the trustee, he cannot be required to serve as trustee against his wishes. He may therefore renounce or reject the trust. A renunciation, however, does not affect the validity of the trust because equity will appoint a substitute trustee if the settlor does not do so.

It is also said that it is necessary that the beneficiary accept the trust, but this is modified by the rule that the beneficiary's consent will be presumed in the absence of disclaimer.

(9) Bond of Trustee. Local statutes govern whether a trustee must file a bond for the faithful performance of his duties. Such a bond is generally required of a nonresident, and it may also be required of a resident by the court when it believes that the trustee may be guilty of misconduct that will harm the trust estate. The settlor may ordinarily declare that no bond shall be required of his trustee.

Sec. 60-D. Nature of Beneficiary's Interest. The effect of a transfer in trust is to divide the property so that the legal title is given to the trustee and the beneficial interest or *equitable title* is given to the beneficiary. The beneficiary may ordinarily transfer or assign his interest in the trust, and his creditors may reach his interest in satisfaction of their claims. An exception arises when the settlor has restricted the trust in such a way that the beneficiary cannot assign nor his creditors reach his interest, resulting in what is commonly called a *spendthrift trust*.

Sec. 60-E. Powers of Trustee. A trustee can exercise only those powers that are expressly given to him or those which the court will construe as being impliedly given. Modern trusts commonly give the trustee discretion to make decisions on matters that could not be foreseen by the settlor. For example, the trustee may be authorized to expend principal as well as income when in the trustee's opinion it is necessary for the education of a beneficiary.

Sec. 60-F. Duties of Trustee.

(1) Performance. A trustee is under the duty to carry out the trust according to its terms. When he fails to do so, he is personally liable for any loss sustained unless he can justify his failure. A trustee cannot delegate the performance of his personal duties.

(2) Due Care. The trustee is under a duty to use reasonable skill, prudence, and diligence in the performance of his trust duties. More simply stated, he must use due care. He is not an insurer against loss and is not liable if he has exercised the degree of care which a reasonable man would exercise under the circumstances. (See p. 873, Parks' Trust) A trustee is protected in making decisions if he has relied on the advice of an attorney, at least when there is no circumstance which would make a reasonable man believe that he should not follow the attorney's advice.

(3) Loyalty. A trustee is not permitted to profit personally from his position as trustee, other than to receive the compensation allowed him by contract or by law. An executive officer of a corporate trustee, though not personally a trustee, must not profit from the trust in any way that would not be proper for a trustee.

(4) Taking Possession and Preserving Trust Property. The trustee is under a duty to take possession of trust property and to preserve it from loss or damage. If the property includes accounts receivable or outstanding debts, he is under the duty to collect them.

(5) Defense of Trust. The trustee is under a legal duty to defend the trust when its validity is disputed in court. Conversely, he cannot attack its validity.

(6) Production of Income. Either by express or implied direction, the trustee is required to invest the money or property in enterprises or transactions that will yield an income to the estate. By statute he is generally limited as to the nature of investments that he may make. Most states now permit him to invest in corporate stocks. Court approval is generally required of all transactions relating to real estate held by the trust.

The device of the *common trust fund* has been legalized in a number of states. Under this plan the trustee, often a bank which is a trustee for a number of small trusts, pools the assets of all the trusts into a common trust fund. Each trust is given certificates in the fund proportionate to the size of its contribution. The fund is then invested in such investments as mortgages on large buildings and factories, in which the individual trust funds could not have been invested directly because of their small size.

(7) Accounting and Information. A trustee must keep accurate records so that it can be determined whether he has properly administered the trust. Upon request by the beneficiary, the trustee must furnish information with respect to the trust. Periodically, or at certain times, as determined by the law in each state, he must file an account in court, at which time the court passes upon his stewardship of the trust.

Sec. 60-G. Compensation of Trustee. A trustee is entitled to compensation. In some states a statute or a court rule prescribes the amount or percentage of compensation. In modern trust instruments it is common to specify that the trustee shall receive specific compensation expressed in terms of percentages of the principal or income amounts administered by him. In the absence of any controlling provision, the court in which the trustee files his account will award him such compensation as the court determines reasonable for the services rendered by him.

Sec. 60-H. Remedies for Breach of Trust. A breach of trust may occur in a variety of ways, which in turn affect the remedies available. These remedies include:

(1) Money judgment against trustee for loss caused by him.

(2) Injunction or order to compel the trustee to do or refrain from doing an act.

(3) Criminal prosecution of the trustee for his misconduct.

(4) Tracing and recovery of trust property which has been converted by the trustee, unless the property has been acquired by a bona fide purchaser who gives value and purchases without notice of the breach of trust.

(5) Judgment against surety on trustee's bond for loss caused the trust by the trustee's default.

(6) Removal of trustee for misconduct.

(7) Suit against third persons who participated in a breach of trust. (See p. 875, Cross v. Cross)

Sec. 60-I. Termination of Trust. A trust may be terminated (1) in accordance with its terms; (2) because of the impossibility of attaining the object of the trust; (3) by revocation by the settlor, when allowed by the terms of the trust; (4) by merger of interests of all beneficiaries in the same person; and (5) upon the request of all the beneficiaries when there is no express purpose that requires the continuation of the trust.

Sec. 60-J. Tentative Trusts. The law has developed a peculiar trust theory to govern a bank deposit made by *A* of his own money in an account marked "*A, in trust for B.*" If this were a true trust, *A* could not withdraw the money for his own use or revoke the trust, and the creditors of *A* could not reach the deposit unless they could show that the creation of the trust was in fraud of them. The law recognizes that many persons make such a deposit without actually intending to create a formal trust. It is therefore held that in the absence of any evidence showing an intention to create a formal trust by this method of deposit, a true trust is not created. Such a deposit is regarded as creating a *tentative trust* in which the depositor and his creditors are permitted to treat the deposit as though there were no trust; but if the depositor dies, any money that remains in the account after creditors are paid belongs to the person named as the beneficiary.

Sec. 60-K. Charitable Trusts.

(1) Purpose. Charitable trusts may be created for any purpose that advances the public welfare. These include trusts to: (a) maintain or propagate religion, religious education, and missionary work; (b) further health and relieve human suffering by establishing institutions or by direct aid of food, clothing, shelter, and medical care to the needy; (c) found or maintain educational institutions, museums, libraries, or aid individual students or teachers; (d) care for and maintain public cemeteries; (e) erect monuments to public men or national heroes; (f) construct and maintain public buildings or improvements, such as an irrigation system or a playground; (g) further patriotism; and (h) prevent cruelty to animals.

The mere fact that the purpose of a trust is to give money to others does not make it a charitable trust.

In the absence of a contrary provision in the trust agreement, the law will not permit a charitable trust to end even though the original purpose has been accomplished or can no longer be achieved, or because the beneficiary no longer exists. In such a case the courts apply the *cy-pres doctrine,* an abbreviation of the Norman French words "cy pres comme possible" or "as near as possible." By this doctrine the court directs that the trust fund be held for another purpose that will be as near as possible to that intended by the settlor. (See p. 876, Pierce's Petition) If, however, it is clear that he intended the trust to be performed exactly as he has indicated or not at all, the trust fails when it is not possible to follow his direction. In such a case the cy-pres doctrine will not be applied.

(2) Limitations. In most aspects a charitable trust is the same as a private trust. In some states additional limitations are imposed. Thus a maximum amount may be set on the property that a charitable corporation may own. In some states a decedent is limited as to the amount of his property which he can leave to charity when he is survived by near relatives.

In many states a gift to charity or for a charitable trust is void if the donor dies within a minimum period, such as thirty days, after making the gift. In those states it is also generally provided that a clause in a will making such a gift is void if the decedent dies within thirty days after making the will.

Sec. 60-L. Implied Trusts. In certain instances trusts are implied in order to carry out the presumed intention of the parties or to protect the former owner from the fraud of the present owner. When the court implies a trust to carry out the presumed intent of the parties, the trust is called a *resulting trust;* when it implies a trust to right a wrong, it is called a *constructive trust.*

(1) Purchase-Money Resulting Trust. The most common resulting trust arises when a person pays for the purchase of property but title to the property is taken in the name of another person. It is then presumed that the titleholder was intended to hold as trustee for the benefit of the person paying the money. To give effect to this presumption, a resulting trust is generally imposed upon the property and the titleholder. This means that the titleholder cannot use the property as his own but must use it or dispose of it as directed by the person paying the money. This presumption is not conclusive and may be overcome by evidence showing that it was the intention of the person paying the money to lend the money to the person taking title or to make a gift of the property to him. If the person paying the money is the husband or parent of the person taking title, there is a presumption that the payment was made as a gift, in which case

a resulting trust does not arise unless the presumption of a gift is overcome by contrary evidence.

(2) Constructive Trust of Improperly Acquired Property. When a person has acquired title to property by unlawful or unfair means or in breach of his duty as an agent or trustee, equity will make him hold it as constructive trustee for the person whom he has unjustly deprived of the property. Thus, if an agent purchases for himself in his own name property that he was instructed to purchase for his principal, the latter may hold the agent as constructive trustee.

Cases for Chapter 60

Wyse v. Puchner

260 Wis. 365, 51 N.W.2d 38 (1952)

C. Wyse brought an action to enforce an alleged trust declared by Elsie Wyse, deceased, for the benefit of her husband's children by a former marriage. It was claimed that the trust had been created in several letters written by Elsie. From a judgment for the plaintiff, the defendant appealed.

FAIRCHILD, J. . . . . That a trust fund in favor of the children of Elsie Wyse's husband was created is evidenced by the following declarations in her letters. . . .

"I have been thinking the matter over and have come to the conclusion that the right thing for me to do would be to set up a fund of $5,000, the income and principal to be used toward the expenses of the children's educations. . . . Please handle it directly with Mrs. Wyse, and do it in the least expensive way possible.

"During 1946 and 1947, I have sent Mrs. Wyse and the children approximately $500 each year. However, I think it will be better at this time to clean up the entire matter by putting aside a lump sum of $5,000 so Mrs. Wyse will know exactly what she has to spend towards the children's education and support. I would like this trust to become effective as of January, 1948."

On March 17, 1948, Elsie S. Wyse wrote the petitioner the following letter:

"Your air-mail letter just arrived with the wonderful news about Frank's scholarship—I am so thrilled and happy and proud—

"It was good of you to write me so promptly and I appreciate your thoughtfulness—

"Several months ago, when you first wrote me about Frank's college education, I had an opportunity to sell Mother's cooperative apartment in New York and I took $5,000 of the sales price and put it to one side marked 'Trust Fund for Frank and Kindy Wyse's education and maintenance—' The principal and income are to be used for this purpose—At that time I wrote my attorney in Milwaukee—Irving A. Puchner, Bankers Bldg.—and asked him to establish the fund at the proper time so you would know you had this amount to depend on—" . . .

Elsie S. Wyse . . . segregated and set apart the sum of $5,000 from the sales price received from the sale of an apartment building in New York as a trust fund for the education and maintenance of the said children, the principal and income of said fund to be used for that purpose. . . . Elsie Wyse died September 13, 1949, leaving a will. A claim for said trust fund . . . was duly filed in the estate.

Upon the foregoing facts, the court determined: "Elsie S. Wyse, in October, 1947, created a binding and enforceable self-declared trust in and to the sum of $5,000, the principal and income of which is for the education and maintenance of Frank O. Wyse and Clarinda C. Wyse, wards of petitioner in this action. . . ."

The evidence on which the trial court made its findings and conclusions is of acts which will admit or no other interpretation than that the settlor of the trust retained no legal rights other than the rights as trustee over the property. There was no reservation of power to revoke. While the existence of a trust need not be declared in express terms, this trust was established by proper written evidence—letters in writing, disclosing facts which created a fiduciary relation. . . .

It is considered that a trust was created. . . .

[Judgment for plaintiff affirmed.]

Parks' Trust

39 Wash.2d 763, 238 P.2d 1205 (1951)

James and Cora Parks created a trust for William Parks and others. James and Cora were the original trustees. Upon their deaths the Seattle First National Bank was made trustee. The trust assets were principally minority holdings of stock in businesses owned by members of the Parks family. These businesses and others owned by the family were actively managed by Harold Parks. Wilson and other beneficiaries claimed the trustee was negligent because it had not taken adequate steps to see that Harold Parks was not running the businesses in such a way as to prejudice those in which the trust had an interest. From a judgment for the trustee on this point, the beneficiaries appealed.

DONWORTH, J. . . . We have defined a trustee's duty of care, skill, and diligence to be that degree . . . that would be exercised by an ordinarily prudent man engaged in similar affairs. . . .

The [basis] of the objections is that respondent [trustee] failed to investigate the management and interrelationships of those family businesses in which the trust had interests and those in which it had none. Appellants [beneficiaries] assert that it was the duty of respondent to make a detailed investigation of the management of all the family ventures so as to ascertain and indicate in its final report and account whether the ventures in which the trust was interested were receiving a fair share of the income or whether income, properly receivable to those ventures, was being siphoned off by the other ventures through improper allocation of expenses and improper use of equipment.

In administering the trust, respondent relied on audits of the businesses in which the trust had a proprietary interest. The trust officer of respondent bank testified that these audits were prepared by a reputable firm of certified public accountants and were of the type known as "spot check" audits. They were not detailed audits of the operation of the businesses in which the accountant certifies that he has examined every single transaction appearing on the company's books. . . . He also testified that the "spot check" type of audit is the type commonly used for most business purposes and that detailed audits are very rare. It was his opinion that the cost to the trust of detailed audits would have been many thousands of dollars, so high as to be prohibitive considering that the trust owned minority interests only. The audits relied upon by respondent were of the same type and prepared by the same firm of certified public accountants as those that had been relied on by . . . the settlors of the trust during their respective tenures as trustee.

The trust officer testified that there was nothing in the "spot check" audits which would arouse any suspicion of mismanagement or unfair treatment in respect to the businesses in which the trust had interests. He further testified that Harold M. Parks was a competent manager and that, on the basis of the admittedly limited investigation made by the witness into the interrelationships of the ventures, it appeared to him that Mr. Parks had "leaned over backwards" in according fair treatment to the businesses in which the trust was interested.

It is undisputed that at the commencement of the three-year period encompassing respondent's stewardship of the trust, the total book value of the trust's interests in the businesses was $81,000 and that during that period the businesses earned for the trust, after corporate taxes, $167,000. The total cost of management to the trust during that period was only $6,000, or $3\frac{1}{2}$ per cent of the total income, which the trust officer considered to be very reasonable. It was his opinion that the ratio of earnings to capital and the low cost of management indicated excellent management. . . .

Decisions in cases of this type must rest entirely on the facts of each particular case. What might be patent neglect of duty in one case may be entirely reasonable in another.

. . . It appears to us wholly reasonable that the trustee made no further investigation than it did. . . .

[Judgment for trustee affirmed on this question.]

Cross v. Cross

363 Mo. 1098, 246 S.W.2d 801 (1952)

Clay Cross bequeathed a sum of money to his brother, Sam Cross, to hold in trust for himself for life; and upon his death, to Marvin Cross to hold in trust for himself for life; and upon his death, to be divided among Clay's brothers and sisters. Sam mixed the money with his own and used it to purchase a home for himself and his wife, Maggie. At the time, she knew the purchase money was partly trust funds. When Sam died, Marvin and others sued Maggie to obtain a judgment for the amount of the trust fund and to enforce a lien upon the land. From a judgment for the plaintiffs, the defendant appealed.

HYDE, J. . . . The trial court found . . . that Sam Cross commingled the trust fund with his own property; that Maggie had no separate property going into this commingled property; and that the whole was eventually placed in their joint names so that at Sam's death Maggie got the whole title. In this situation she was in the position of a donee of trust property because all the property she received was the product of the commingled trust fund and Sam's own property. . . . "It is a well-established rule that when . . . the trustee by wrongfully disposing of trust property acquires other property, the beneficiary can follow the trust property into its product and can enforce a constructive trust or equitable lien upon the product." . . .

As donee of trust property, by thus receiving her title without consideration, Maggie does not hold the property free from the trust. . . . If a donee without knowledge of the breach, she would only become personally liable for the value of the fund by a refusal to restore the property after she had knowledge of the breach of trust (which liability would be for its value with interest thereon from the time of refusal) ; or by making a transfer of the trust property after knowledge of the breach of trust.

. . . She did take the property with knowledge of its trust character. . . . To fix personal liability on her, it was not necessary that she should have participated in the original receipt of tne fund or in commingling it with other property during Sam's lifetime. It may be conceded that she was not personally liable when he died. However, she became liable personally for the value of the fund after his death because she knew of Sam's breach of trust in commingling the trust fund with his property and placing the title to all of it so that it would all go to her, leaving nothing in his estate to restore the fund and because knowing that she had acquired title to all of his property, including the trust fund, she refused to restore it to the beneficiaries after his death.

Thus plaintiffs were entitled to a personal judgment against Maggie and were entitled to an equitable lien upon the property she received from Sam and had not disposed of at the time of the suit . . . or upon the proceeds of such property if she had disposed of any of it. . . .

[Judgment for plaintiffs affirmed.]

Pierce's Petition

153 Maine 180, 136 A.2d 510 (1957)

By his will dated 1870, Joseph How bequeathed his residuary estate in trust to pay the income therefrom to certain persons for their respective lives and upon their deaths to be used by his trustee to found a "home for indigent seamen." Joseph had been the master and the captain of Ellen Stevens, a three-masted sailing vessel. At the time of his death his estate was valued at $1,500. Thereafter certain investments that Joseph had made which were regarded as worthless increased in value to more than $300,000 and income of $100,000 was received by the trustee. A petition was then filed with the court for instructions as to how this fund should be expended under the will. From the decision directing certain uses of the money, an appeal was taken.

DUBORD, J. . . . The doctrine of cy-pres does not apply to private trusts. . . .

Before the cy-pres doctrine will be applied, three prerequisites must be met. First, the court must find that the gift creates a valid charitable trust. Second; it must be established that it is to some degree impossible or impractical to carry out the specific purpose of the trust, for the cy-pres doctrine is inapplicable when the particular purpose of the settlor can be effectively carried out. The third prerequisite is the requirement of a general charitable intention. . . .

. . . The bequest in the How will is in terms a good charitable bequest.

Passing now to the second prerequisite, that it must be established that it is to some degree impossible or impractical to carry out the specific purpose of the trust, we find . . . that while the number of indigent seamen of the class seemingly intended by the testator has become substantially reduced, it has not entirely disappeared. Moreover, the record clearly indicates that there are still indigent seamen in existence, even of the class to which the testator belonged. Consequently, the trust has not entirely failed. However, it is also clear that the trust fund now available is in an amount too large to permit its application for the relief of indigent seamen of the class to which the testator belonged. . . .

The important issue, therefore, for determination is whether or not the testator expressed in his will a general charitable intent. If so, then the application of the cy-pres doctrine would be in order and the scope of the beneficiaries seemingly covered in the trust can be broadened and enlarged. In other words, seamen of a type different from that to which the testator belonged can be included as beneficiaries.

We give our attention, therefore, to the issue of determining whether or not Captain How manifested a general charitable intention when he created the trust which is now before us for consideration.

Legal authors describe this general charitable intention as a desire to give to charity generally, rather than to any one party, object, or institution. . . .

While . . . it seems to have been assumed by all interested parties that the beneficiaries of the trust created by Captain How were indigent seamen of the class to which he belonged, we are not thoroughly convinced that this is so. At times much earlier than the year when Captain How's will was executed, our Court had described crewmen of other types of vessels as seamen. . . .

If we endeavor to project ourselves into the past and contemplate upon the intention of Captain How, we may well suppose that while he was perhaps primarily interested in crewmen of ships such as he was master of, he nevertheless had in mind that wider group of men whose major means of livelihood was gained from the sea. . . .

It is, therefore, our opinion that the scope of the beneficiaries of this kindly gift should be widened and enlarged. We reach this conclusion not necessarily through the application of the cy-pres doctrine, but rather through an interpretation of the intention of the testator at the time he executed his will. . . .

The trustee is, therefore, authorized to use and employ the income for the benefit of indigent seamen not only of the class to which Captain How belonged, but to other classes, by way of illustration and not of limitation, such as crewmen of merchant vessels, oil tankers, and fishing vessels. . . .

[Cause remanded.]

Questions and Case Problems

   1. What is the objective of each of the following rules of law?

    (a) The law recognizes and enforces as a trust a transfer to one person made for the use of another.

    (b) The capacity of the beneficiary of a trust to hold property or to make a binding contract is immaterial.

   2. The Pioneer Trust and Savings Bank was trustee of certain land for the benefit of Harmon. Under the terms of the trust, Harmon could require the trustee to sell the land as he directed. Schneider wrote Pioneer Trust offering to buy the land. Harmon made a written notation on the letter that he accepted the offer and sent it back to Schneider. Schneider withdrew his offer and claimed that there was no contract. Harmon claimed that Schneider was bound by a contract. Decide. (Schneider v. Pioneer Trust and Savings Bank, [Ill.] 168 N.E.2d 808)

   3. William and Walter Asher were trustees under the will of J. M. Asher, deceased. As trustees, they loaned money to themselves at a low rate of interest, without security, and paid commissions to themselves from principal. Morrison, a beneficiary of the trust, brought an action to have them removed as trustees. Decide. (Morrison v. Asher, [Mo.App.] 361 S.W.2d 844)

   4. Nielsen held shares of stock of the Washington Realty Co. as trustee for Brecker and others. The beneficiaries brought an action to compel the realty company to permit them to inspect the corporate books because of their interest in the stock of the corporation. They asserted that they were afraid the corporation was not being operated to their best advantage and that their assets were being diverted. Were they entitled to an inspection? (Brecker v. Nielsen, 21 Conn. 33, 143 A.2d 463)

   5. Lorraine and Paul Perry, husband and wife, owned a tract of land as tenants by the entireties. Lorraine murdered Paul and was convicted of second degree murder. In the proceedings in the dead husband's estate, there was a total of $1,091.53 representing rents that had been collected from the tenant in possession of the property. Lorraine claimed this money as the surviving tenant by entirety. The guardian of Sylvia, the minor daughter of the Perry's, claimed the money. Who was entitled to such rents? (Perry's Estate, [N.C.] 123 S.E.2d 99)

   6. Bucklin's will created a trust for his son. The income was to be paid to the son "quarterly or yearly as may seem best to the trustees." At their discretion the trustees could pay him any part of the fund held in trust. The will further provided that no other person could acquire any interest in the fund and that if the son assigned any of his rights, the trustees had the discretion to exclude him from the trust although they could reinstate him later. What kind of trust was created? (Bucklin's Estate, 243 Iowa 312, 51 N.W.2d 412)

   7. Symonds bequeathed a legacy to the City of Keene to pay for and maintain a set of chimes on the public library or some other city building. Was this provision valid? (City of Keene v. Martin, 96 N.H. 504, 79 A. 2d 13)

CHAPTER 61

Decedents' Estates

After all of the debts of a decedent are paid, distribution is made of the balance of his estate, if any, to those entitled to receive it. If the decedent made a valid will, it determines which persons are entitled to receive the property. If the decedent did not make a valid will, the distribution is determined by the intestate law.

Wills

Sec. 61-A. Definitions. *Testate distribution* describes the distribution that is made when the decedent leaves a valid will. A person who makes a will is called a *testator* or, if a woman, a *testatrix*. A *will* is ordinarily a writing that provides for a distribution of property upon the death of the writer but which confers no rights prior to that time. Prior to his death, the testator may destroy or cancel the will.

The person to whom property is left by a will is called the *beneficiary*. A gift of personal property by will is called a *legacy* or *bequest,* in which case the beneficiary may also be called a *legatee*. A gift of real property by will is a *devise,* in which case the beneficiary may be called a *devisee*.

Sec. 61-B. Requirements of a Will. A will must satisfy requirements as to (1) capacity of parties, (2) intention, (3) formality, and (4) witnesses when necessary.

(1) Capacity of Parties.

(a) TESTATOR. Generally the right to make a will is limited to persons over 21. In some states the age qualification is lowered to 18 years. In a few states a girl of 12 years or over, or a boy of 14 years or over, may make a will disposing of personal property.

The testator must also have *testamentary capacity*. According to the decisions, this is not the same as the capacity to make a contract but is apparently a lower standard. The testator must have sufficient mental capacity at the time of executing his will to know the natural objects of his bounty, to understand the kind and extent of his property, to understand what he is doing when he makes a will, and to have the ability to dispose of the property according to a plan formed by him. Eccentricities of the decedent or peculiarities of his will do not establish that he lacked mental capacity sufficient to make a will. The fact that he does not have sufficient capacity to conduct business affairs does not mean that he necessarily lacks capacity to make a will.

An insane person lacks capacity to make a will. If the testator is insane but has lucid intervals, his will can be sustained when it is shown that the testator executed the will during a lucid interval. When a person is otherwise sane but suffers from an insane delusion, his will is invalid if it is affected by the insane delusion.

(b) BENEFICIARY. Generally there is no restriction with respect to the capacity of the beneficiary of a will. In some instances, as in the case of charitable corporations, a statute may set a maximum upon the amount of property that it may own. Such a limitation may prevent the corporation from receiving an additional gift by will.

By decision, and in many states by statute, a beneficiary who murders the testator is not entitled to receive a bequest made in the testator's will to the murderer.

(2) Intention. There cannot be a will unless the testator manifests an intention to make a provision that will be effective only upon his death. This is called a *testamentary intent.*

A contract to make a will is not effective as a will, although the estate of the decedent may generally be sued for breach of the contract.

(3) Formality. Generally a will must be written and must be signed by the decedent at the end. As is customary in the law, writing includes printing and typewriting. The signing must ordinarily be written by the decedent himself, although merely making an "X" is sufficient when illiteracy or illness makes any other signing impossible. There is a conflict of authority whether the signing must be at the physical or the logical end of the will. There is generally no requirement that a will be dated although some states so require when the will is written completely in the handwriting of the decedent.

(4) Witnesses. In some states no witnesses are required for a will. In others, two or three witnesses are required to subscribe the will under an *attestation clause* stating that they witnessed its execution by the decedent. It is commonly provided that attestation be made by the witnesses in the presence of the testator and of each other. *Publication* is the act of the testator in informing the attesting witnesses that the document which he is signing before them is his will. The law varies between states as to the necessity of publication.

Sec. 61-C. Revocation.

(1) Revocation by Act of Testator. A will is revoked when the testator destroys, burns, or tears the will, or crosses out the provisions of the will with the intention to revoke it. The revocation may be in whole or in part.

A will is also revoked by the execution of a later will which either expressly declares the prior will revoked or which displaces the prior will by disposing of all the property of the testator. In many states a will may also be revoked by a later writing executed with the same formality as a will which merely declares that the will is revoked. Such a writing is effective although it does not itself make any disposition of the property of the testator. In any case, a revocation that does not comply with the formal requirements of the Statute of Wills is not effective. (See p. 889, Fletcher Trust Co. v. Morse)

Since a revocation is effective only if made with the intent to revoke, a testator must have the same degree of mental capacity when he revokes his will as is required when he makes a will.

(2) Revocation by Operation of Law. In certain instances statutes provide that a change of circumstances shall have the effect of a revocation. Thus it may be provided that when a person marries after executing his will, the will is revoked in whole or in part or is presumed revoked unless it was made in contemplation of marriage or unless it provided for the future spouse. In some states the revocation is not total but only to the extent of allowing the spouse to take such share of the estate as that to which she would have been entitled had there been no will.

It is also commonly provided that the birth or adoption of a child after the execution of a will works a revocation or partial revocation as to that child. In some states both the marriage and birth of a child are necessary to revoke the decedent's will by operation of law.

The divorce of the testator does not in itself work a revocation; but the majority of courts hold that if a property settlement is carried out on the basis of the divorce, a prior will of the testator is revoked, at least to the extent of the legacy given to the divorced spouse.

Sec. 61-D. Modification of Will.
A will may be modified by executing a codicil. A *codicil* is a separate writing that amends a will. The will, except as changed by the codicil, remains the same. A codicil must be executed with all the formality of a will.

A will cannot be modified merely by crossing out a clause of the will and writing in what the testator wishes. Such an interlineation is not operative unless it is executed with the same formality required of a will, or in some states unless the will is republished in its interlineated form.

Sec. 61-E. Revival. *Revival* is the act of giving new validity to a will that has been revoked. This may be done by executing a codicil which specifically refers to the revoked will and indicates that it is to be effective. The will may also be revived by the direct procedure of re-executing the will. Beyond these two clear rules, there is great conflict of authority among the states as to whether any other conduct, such as merely republishing but not re-executing a revoked will, can revive it.

Sec. 61-F. Probate and Contest of Will. *Probate* is the act by which the proper court or official accepts a will and declares that the instrument satisfies the statutory requirements as the will of the testator. Until a will is probated, it has no legal effect.

Any person wishing to object to the probate of the will on the ground that it is not a proper will may appear before the official or court prior to the entry of the decree of probate, or he may petition after probate to have the probate of the will set aside.

The probate of a will may be refused or set aside on the ground that the will is not the free expression of the intention of the testator. It may be attacked on the ground of (1) lack of mental capacity to execute a will, (2) undue influence, duress, fraud, or mistake inducing the execution of the will, or (3) forgery of the testator's signature. With the exception of mental capacity, these concepts mean substantially the same as they do in contract law.

Sec. 61-G. Special Types of Wills.

(1) Holographic Wills. A *holographic will* is one that is written by the testator entirely in his own handwriting. In many states no distinction is made between a holographic and other wills. In other states the general body of the law of wills applies, but certain variations are established.

(2) Nuncupative Wills. A *nuncupative will* is an oral will made and declared by the testator in the presence of witnesses to be his will. Generally it can be made only during the last illness of the testator and can take effect only with respect to personal property.

(3) Soldiers' and Seamen's Wills. It is generally provided that soldiers and seamen may make an oral or a written will of their personal estate without complying with the formalities required of other wills. It is sufficient that testamentary intent be shown. Such a will remains in force even though the testator returns to civilian life, and it must be revoked in the same manner as any other will.

(4) Conditional or Contingent Will. A *conditional* or *contingent will* is one that the testator intends to be effective only upon the

occurrence or satisfaction of a condition or contingency specified in the will. For example, a will is conditional if the testator writes, "If I should not return from my trip, I bequeath my house to John."

Sec. 61-H. Interpretation and Distribution Under the Will. If the decedent dies testate, the last phase of the administration of his estate by his personal representative is the distribution of his property remaining after the payment of all debts and taxes, in accordance with the terms of his will. If the court can ascertain the intention of the testator, it will give that intention effect unless the testator intended a disposition which the law regards as illegal. The fact that the will does not conform to what the court believes would be a just disposition does not make it invalid.

There is no particular form that a will must follow, and there can be as many different forms as there are testators. Actually wills tend to follow a common pattern. The testator may bequeath to named persons certain sums of money, called *general legacies* because no particular money is specified, or identified property, called *specific legacies* or *devises*. Thus he may say, "$1,000 to *A*; $1,000 to *B*; my auto to *C*." The first two bequests are general, the third is specific. After he has made such legacies, he may make a bequest of everything remaining, called a *residuary bequest, devise,* or *legacy,* such as "the balance of my estate to *D*." A testator may also make a *demonstrative bequest,* such as "$1,000 to be paid from the money in my office safe."

(1) Abatement of Legacies. If the estate is insufficient to pay all legacies in full, they *abate* or bear loss in the following order: (a) residuary, (b) general, (c) specific. The law also holds that legatees of the same class abate proportionately. A demonstrative legacy is only affected by the insufficiency of the fund from which it is to be paid.

(2) Ademption of Property. When specifically bequeathed property is sold, given away, or destroyed by the testator before his death, the specific legacy is adeemed and the specific legatee is not entitled to receive any property or money. *Ademption* has the same consequence as though the testator had formally canceled the bequest.

No ademption takes place when specifically bequeathed property has been changed in form but preserves its basic identity. For example, a specific bequest of shares of stock is effective as a bequest of shares given in exchange for those shares in the course of a corporate reorganization, or additional shares issued on a stock split-up.

(3) Death of Legatee. If a legatee dies before the testator, the interest given him by the will usually lapses or is inoperative. In a number of states, however, antilapse statutes have been adopted. They provide that when the deceased legatee bears a certain family relation-

ship to the testator, the gift to him shall not lapse but may be claimed by his children. Such statutes are common when the deceased legatee is a descendant of the testator and to a lesser extent when the legatee is a brother or sister of the testator.

(4) Election to Take Against the Will. In order to protect the husband or wife of a testator from unfair treatment, it is generally provided that the surviving spouse may ignore the provisions of the will and elect to take against the will. In such a case the surviving spouse receives the share of the estate which that spouse would have received had the testator died without leaving a will, or a fractional share specified by statute.

The right to take against the will is generally barred by certain specified kinds of misconduct of the surviving spouse. Thus, if the spouse is guilty of such desertion or nonsupport as would have justified the decedent in obtaining a divorce, it is usually provided that the surviving spouse cannot elect to take against the will.

(5) Intestate Distribution. If the will is void for any reason, the decent's estate is distributed as though there had been no will. When the will fails as to part of the estate, the share passes to the residuary legatee, if there is one.

(6) Disinheritance. With two exceptions, any person may be disinherited or excluded from sharing in the estate of a decedent. A person who would inherit if there were no will is excluded from receiving any part of a decedent's estate if the decedent has left a will by which he gives all of his estate to other persons. It is not necessary that the decedent expressly declare in his will that the disinherited person is to receive nothing, nor is it necessary to bequeath him a nominal sum of money, such as a dollar, although there is a general erroneous belief to the contrary. The exceptions to this rule are based (a) upon the election of a spouse to take against the will and (b) in certain cases upon the partial revocation of a will by subsequent marriage, birth, or adoption.

(7) Tax Liability. A gift made by will may be subject to a state inheritance tax, and state and federal estate taxes. In making distribution, the personal representative must charge such taxes against the proper legatees or funds and if he fails to do so, he will generally be personally liable for the amount of the taxes.

Intestacy

If the decedent does not effectively dispose of his property by will or if he does not have a will, his property will be distributed by *intestate succession* to certain persons related to him.

Sec. 61-I. Plan of Intestate Distribution. Although wide variations exist among the statutory provisions of the states, they generally provide for distribution to the surviving spouse and children and *lineal* (or blood) *descendants;* and if this does not exhaust the estate, then to parents and to *collateral heirs.* The latter are not descendants of the decedent but are related to him through a common ancestor. Under some statutes a degree of relationship is specified, and no person more remotely related to the decedent is permitted to share in the estate. If the entire estate is not distributed within the permitted degree of relationship, the property that has not been distributed is given to the state government. This right of the state to take the property is the *right of escheat.* Under some statutes the right of escheat arises only when there is no relative of the decedent, however remotely related, to take his property.

It must be remembered that the above outline presents a composite picture. Within a particular state, qualification may be required in terms of homestead, dower and curtesy rights, or a modern statutory equivalent of such rights, in addition to changes in the actual pattern of distribution.

(1) Distribution Per Capita and Per Stirpes. The fact that different generations of distributees may be entitled to receive the estate creates a problem of determining the proportions in which distribution is to be made. When all the distributees stand in the same degree of relationship to the decedent, distribution is made per capita, each receiving the same share.

If the distributees stand in different degrees of relationship, distribution is made in as many equal parts as there are family lines or stirpes represented in the nearest generation. Parents take to the exclusion of their children or subsequent descendants; and when members of the nearest generation have died, descendants of such deceased members take by way of representation. This is called *stirpital distribution* or *distribution per stirpes.*

(2) Nature of Relation. A person not related to the decedent by marriage may inherit only if he has a blood relationship. "In-law" relations do not share under the intestate statutes.

Intestate statutes providing for the distribution of part of the decedent's estate to children, whether of the decedent or of other persons, are interpreted as applying to natural legitimate children. Modern statutes quite commonly extend this definition to include adopted children and treat them the same as natural children. By statute, illegitimate children are treated as legitimate children with respect to inheritance from or through their mother or members of her family, but are ignored in distribution with respect to the father or his family. If the paternity of the illegitimate children has been acknowledged or legally established, however, such children will inherit from the father.

(3) Murder of Decedent. The trend of intestate legislation is to provide that a person who murders the decedent cannot inherit from him by intestacy. In the absence of such a statute a majority of courts hold that such inheritance cannot be denied, while a minority refuse to allow inheritance under such circumstances.

(4) Death of Distributee After Decedent. The person entitled to distribution of a decedent's estate are determined as of the date of his death. If a distributee dies thereafter, his rights are not extinguished but pass to his own estate to be distributed either to his heirs or in accordance with the terms of his will.

Administration of Decedents' Estates

A decedent's estate consists of the assets that a person owns at the time of his death and which survive him. It must be determined who is entitled to receive that property. If the decedent died owing debts, those debts must be paid first. After that, any balance remaining is to be distributed according to the terms of his will, if he left a will, or by the intestate law, if he did not leave a will.

Sec. 61-J. Definitions. The decedent has the privilege of naming in his will the person to administer his estate. If he does so, the person is called an *executor*. If the person so named is a woman, the title is *executrix*. If the decedent failed to name an executor in his will or if he did not leave a will, the law permits another person, usually a close relative, to obtain the appointment of someone to wind up the estate. The latter person is an *administrator* or *administratrix*. Administrators and executors are often referred to generally as *personal representatives* of the decedent since they represent the decedent or stand in his place.

Sec. 61-K. When Administration Is Not Necessary. No administration is required when the decedent did not own any property at the time of his death or when all the property he owned was jointly owned with another person who acquired the decedent's interest by right of survivorship upon his death.

In some states special statutes have been adopted providing for a shortened procedure of administration when the decedent leaves only a small estate, commonly under $1,000. In many states, if all of the parties in interest, creditors and relatives of the decedent, can agree on what shares or amounts each one is to receive, it is possible for a *settlement agreement* to be made by which the estate is divided without any formal court proceedings.

Sec. 61-L. Appointment of Personal Representative. An executor or administrator is appointed by a court or officer by granting *letters testamentary*, in the case of an executor, or *letters of administration*, in the case of an administrator. For the appointment of a personal representative, an application or petition is filed with the court or officer setting forth the details of the decedent's death, stating that the decedent, if a resident of the state, lived within the county or, if a nonresident, that property of the decedent is within the county, and reciting the facts which justify the appointment of the personal representative.

(1) Person Entitled to Act as Personal Representative. If the decedent has named an executor in his will, that person has the right to act as personal representative or to decline to do so. If he refuses to act, or if no executor has been named, an administrator is appointed. Statutes generally give the right to act as administrator to the surviving spouse or near relatives of the decedent and his creditors, in that order. If there is no one in any of these classes who is willing to serve, provision is made for the appointment of "any fit person" to act as administrator. (See p. 890, Beach's Estate)

(2) Oath and Bond. When a personal representative is appointed, he is required to take an oath and file a bond that he will properly administer the estate according to law. In some states an executor is not required to furnish a bond if he is a resident of the state and in sound financial condition or if the testator has expressly directed in his will that no bond be required.

Sec. 61-M. Proof of Claims Against the Estate.

(1) Procedure. In very general terms the statutes provide for some form of public notice of the grant of letters, as by advertisement. Creditors are then required to give notice of their claims within a period specified either by statute or a court order, as within six months. In most states the failure to present the claim within the specified time bars the claim. In other states the creditor may assert a late claim with respect to any assets of the estate in the hands of the representative at the time that he asserts his claim.

(2) Nature of Claims. Generally any debt or liability of the decedent existing at the time of his death may be asserted against the estate. An exception is made to this rule in the case of those causes of action which are regarded as being so personal that the

cause of action dies with the death of a party to it. In addition to those claims that were the personal obligations of the decedent, his estate is also liable for reasonable funeral expenses, the expense of administering his estate, a statutory allowance given to the family to help tide them over the period of adjustment following the death, and estate taxes.

(3) Priority of Claims. When the estate of a decedent is insolvent, that is, when it is not sufficiently large to pay all debts and taxes, the law generally provides that certain claims shall be paid first. Although there is great variation of detail, the common pattern of priority provides for the payment of claims against the estate in the following order: (a) funeral expenses; (b) administration expenses; (c) family allowance; (d) claims due the United States; [1] (e) expenses of the last illness; (f) debts due the state, county, and city governments; (g) claims for wages; (h) lien claims; (i) all other debts.

If there are several claimants within a particular class, but not enough money to pay each in full, they share proportionately the balance remaining and creditors in lower priorities receive nothing.

Sec. 61-N. Powers and Duties of Personal Representative. Apart from special powers or duties that a decedent may confer or impose upon his executor, the powers of an executor and administrator are the same. A personal representative is in substance the same as a trustee with respect to performance of his duties, the use of due care, and the observance of loyalty. His right to compensation and the remedies for the breach of his duties are likewise the same as in the case of a trustee. Statutes also impose upon him various duties peculiar to the winding up of a decedent's estate, such as filing inventories showing the assets of the estate and the payment of estate taxes.

Unlike the trustee whose duty is in general to preserve and manage the trust fund, the personal representative's duty is to distribute the entire estate. He must use reasonable diligence to determine the proper persons to whom distribution is to be made (see p. 890, Stofft v. O'Shaughnessy), and to make distribution to them. He must pay the creditors, recognizing their priorities in the case of an insolvent estate, and distribute the balance remaining after the payment of debts to those persons entitled to it. In some states it may be necessary to obtain approval of the court or an official to the distribution to be made.

Sec. 61-O. Termination of Authority of Personal Representative. Ordinarily the authority of a personal representative ends by his being

---

[1] 31 United States Code, Sec. 191.

discharged officially upon the completion of his duties. His authority may also be terminated by the revocation of his letters of appointment because they were improperly granted, by his removal because of misconduct, or by his resignation or death.

Cases for Chapter 61

Fletcher Trust Co. v. Morse
230 Ind. 44, 101 N.E.2d 658 (1951)

By his original will, Heath bequeathed one third of his estate to Morse. When the will was probated, it was found that the bequest to Morse had been crossed out and at the bottom of the will was a typewritten statement "Under no condition do I wish . . . Morse . . . to be included in this will." Both the will and the final addition were signed by Heath. The will was witnessed and acknowledged, but the addition was not. There was no evidence as to when or under what circumstances any of the changes had been made to the will. There was no evidence as to where the will had been kept at any time. The Fletcher Trust Co. brought an action against Morse to obtain a declaratory judgment to determine what interest he had under the will. From a judgment in favor of Morse, the trust company appealed.

GILKINSON, J. . . . There is no evidence that the will was in testator's possession at any time from the date of its execution until the date it was offered for probate. . . . Hence there is nothing in the record showing that the act of obliterating the name of appellee [Morse] as a beneficiary in the will was the act of the testator, unless this is sufficiently shown by Exhibit B [the addition to the will]. . . . In this state the revocation of a will in whole or in part is wholly governed by statute. . . . This statute provides that a written will may not be revoked in whole or in part except in one of two ways mentioned: (1) "unless the testator, or some other person in his presence and by his direction, with intent to revoke, shall destroy or mutilate the same;" (2) "or such testator shall execute another writing for that purpose, signed, subscribed, and attested. . . ."

Exhibit B was not attested by two witnesses as required. . . . For the reason it was not so attested, it did not revoke the will in whole or in part, or otherwise affect it. . . .

There is not sufficient evidence in the record indicating that the testator ever had an intention to revoke his will in whole or in part. The mere fact that appellee's name as a beneficiary in the will had been inked out or otherwise mutilated when the will was probated is not sufficient in itself to make a prima facie showing of such intention on the part of the testator, nor is such fact, in itself, sufficient to make a prima facie showing that mutilation was done by testator to effect his intention to revoke the will either in whole or in part. Indeed there is no evidence in the record indicating that this mutilation was done by the testator, or by another "person in his presence and by his direction." . . .

[Judgment affirmed.]

Beach's Estate
206 Okla. 81, 241 P.2d 390 (1952)

Upon the death of Daisey Beach, her husband, Bernard, elected to take against her will. The executor named in the will had died, and Bernard petitioned for the appointment of Comstock, his attorney, as administrator of his wife's estate. When Comstock was appointed, other persons interested in the estate appealed.

GIBBSON, J. . . . Appellants urge that the appointment was improper for the reason that Mr. Comstock is one of the attorneys for the husband of deceased and is hostile to the will and will not seek to uphold that instrument. . . .

Appellants contend that the appointment of Comstock was improper, not because he was an incompetent person, but because he was one of the attorneys for the husband who stands in the position of being hostile to the will. . . . He was not hostile in praying that the will be admitted to probate. He is the husband of deceased and is named as a legatee in the will. . . .

Title 58 O.S. 1951, Section 122, authorizes the granting of letters of administration to some person therein named and sets forth the order in which they are respectively entitled to appointment. Under this section the surviving husband, or his nominee, is the person first named in the order of persons entitled to the appointment. . . . Section 221 of the probate code, 58 O.S. 1951, provides that in the event of death or incompetency of the executor or administrator, the court must issue letters of administration with the will annexed in the same order as is directed in relation to original letters of administration.

If, following his appointment, the executor or administrator by his acts or conduct shall waste, embezzle, mismanage, commit fraud on the estate, or is incompetent or has neglected the estate, he is subject to having his powers to act suspended. . . .

[Appointment of administrator confirmed.]

Stofft v. O'Shaughnessy
107 N.E.2d 643 (Ohio Probate, 1952)

O'Shaughnessy was appointed the administrator of Walsh's estate. He was in the process of administering it and had not yet made any distribution of the assets when a petition was filed by Mary Stofft requesting that the court determine who were Walsh's heirs. She filed the petition under the state law which provided that "whenever it shall be necessary for any

. . . person to determine who are the heirs at law of a deceased person, on the petition of any interested party, . . . the court may make a determination thereof." The administrator claimed that there was no necessity for making such a determination because he would do so as part of his administration.

McCLELLAND, J. . . . When an administrator is appointed, he assumes the duty under the law not only to properly administer the estate but also the duty to distribute the property of the decedent to the persons entitled thereto according to law. . . .

Since this responsibility rests solely with the administrator, he should be permitted to assume the responsibility. In most cases the administrator knows who the heirs of his decedent are and distributes the estate accordingly; he does not deem it necessary for his own protection to bring a suit to determine heirs. In fact, if there is no question in his mind as to who the heirs are, he would fail in his duty to the heirs if he brought such a suit and burdened them with the additional expense of such a suit. . . .

On the other hand, there are other cases where the administrator, at the time of his appointment, is not sure who are the heirs of the decedent. However, after research on his part and after considering the proof submitted to him, he may become entirely satisfied, before the time for distribution arrives, that his list of heirs is complete and does not deem it necessary to file a suit to determine heirs.

This brings us to the question of whether . . . an heir may force the hand of an administrator and compel him to submit to a suit to determine the heirs of the estate he is administering. It may be, before the estate is ready for distribution, that the administrator is satisfied that the heir bringing the suit is actually the heir he claims to be. . . .

Of course, if an administrator is not sure who the heirs of the estate are or that he has a complete list of them, for his own protection, he will file a suit to determine heirs. . . . But an administrator, if he does what is expected of him by virtue of his appointment, will prepare his list of heirs as meticulously as he knows how and will procure the necessary proof of relationship before he submits the matter to the Probate Court for a final determination of heirship. This of course takes time, and he will be deprived of this necessary time if an heir is permitted to enforce him into a suit to determine heirs before the period arrives when he may be forced to make a distribution. . . .

If this plaintiff is not permitted to bring this suit, it may then be asked: "What else can she do to protect her interest in the estate?" She has already protected herself by notifying the administrator that she claims to be a sister of the decedent. The administrator, being responsible under the law for a proper distribution of the estate, if he has any doubt about the authenticity of the claim of the plaintiff, is neither going to ignore or recognize her claim without submitting the matter to the Probate Court. If he ignores the plaintiff as an heir and distributes the estate to the other heirs, the plaintiff could attack the account of the administrator and procure a judgment against him and his bondsman. . . . It may be that after the administrator has been able to investigate the claim of the plaintiff and has procured proof of relationship that to him appears to be authentic, he may not deem it necessary for his protection to file a suit to determine heirs.

Again a suit to determine heirs is not the only procedure to which the administrator may resort for his own protection. He may, instead, choose to file an application for an order of distribution. . . . At the hearing on his application the court determines the persons entitled to distribution and makes an order of distribution accordingly. Such order of distribution protects the administrator the same as he is protected upon the settlement of his account. . . .

If nine months have expired after the appointment of the administrator and distribution has not been made, and if no proceeding has been brought by the administrator for a determination of the persons entitled to the estate, the plaintiff then may apply to the Probate Court for an order requiring the administrator to distribute the assets of the estate, in which proceeding she is afforded an opportunity to set up her claim. . . .

Since the petition does not allege facts showing that it is necessary for the plaintiff to determine who are the heirs-at-law of the decedent, it is our conclusion that the petition does not state facts sufficient to constitute a cause of action. . . .

[Judgment entered for the defendant administrator.]

Questions and Case Problems

1. What is the objective of each of the following rules of law?
   (a) When specifically bequeathed property is sold, given away, or destroyed by the testator before his death, the specific legacy is adeemed and the specific legatee is not entitled to receive any property or money.
   (b) When the estate of a decedent is insolvent and therefore all debts cannot be paid in full, the law generally provides for the payment of claims against the estate in a particular order.

2. Freeman executed a will. The Kansas statute required that a person's will "shall be attested and subscribed in the presence of such party by two or more competent witnesses, who saw the testator subscribe or heard him acknowledge the same." Freeman had two witnesses sign his will after in-

forming them that he had executed it, but they did not see him sign the will. After his death the will was offered for probate by Wallace but was opposed by Humphrey. Decide. (Humphrey v. Wallace, 169 Kan. 58, 216 P.2d 781)

3. Jahnke died intestate in 1935. His heirs were his uncles and aunts. Anna Selle was an aunt who had died in 1934. The heirs of Anna claimed that they were entitled to receive the share from Jahnke's estate which Anna would have received if she were alive. Were they correct? (Jahnke v. Selle, 368 Ill. 268, 13 N.E.2d 980)

4. Julia Kirkpatrick was the administratrix of her husband's estate. He had owned an automobile valued at $2,150.00, which was subject to a loan of $1,347.15. In order to prevent the loss of the auto, she personally borrowed $802.85 which she paid on the loan and refinanced the debt. At the audit of her account she claimed credit for making the payment of $802.85. Objection was made to the claim on the ground that no verified statement of the claim had been presented and court approval for the refinancing transaction had not been obtained. Decide. (Kirkpatrick's Estate, 109 Cal.App.2d 709, 241 P.2d 555)

5. R. Walker died. His entire estate was to go to his brother, W. Walker. This brother selected the Southern Trust Co. as administrator, and letters of administration were granted to it. An aunt and first cousin of the decedent petitioned to vacate the appointment and to appoint the first cousin as administrator. The applicable Tennessee statute provided that administration should be granted to the widow of a decedent or if none, then to the "next of kin." Who was entitled to administer the estate? (Tudor v. Southern Trust Co., 193 Tenn. 331, 246 S.W.2d 33)

6. Field executed a will. Upon her death the will was found in her safe deposit box, but the part of the will containing the fifth bequest was torn from the will. This torn fragment was also found in the box. There was no evidence that anyone other than Field had ever opened the box. A proceeding was brought by Flora against Hughes to determine whether the will was entitled to be probated. Decide. (Flora v. Hughes, 312 Ky. 478, 228 S.W.2d 27)

7. Rand executed his will. In it he stated, "I give to my five grandchildren . . . $50 each." Actually there were six grandchildren at the time and upon his death. The six grandchildren then brought an action against Case, the executor under the will of Rand, claiming that no provision was made for them under the will. If true, this would entitle them to a special statutory share under the Arkansas statute. The executor contended that the six children were provided for by the will. Decide. (Walker v. Case, 211 Ark. 1091, 204 S.W.2d 543)

8. Ewing died intestate. One of his brothers arranged for his funeral with the Lilly Funeral Home. The Home presented its bill to the estate, but the estate refused to pay it. (1) Was the estate liable for the bill in view of the fact that the funeral had not been ordered by the estate? (2) Was the estate liable if it did not prove that the funeral bill was unreasonable? Decide. (Ewing's Estate, 234 Iowa 950, 14 N.W.2d 663)

9. DeArmond opposed the probate of the will of Vivian Lingenfelter. It was shown that the testatrix was sick, highly nervous, and extremely jealous and that she committed suicide a week after executing the will. In support of the will, it was shown that she understood the will when she discussed it with an attorney; that her husband was seriously ill when she wrote the will; that he died the following day; and that she grieved his death. Was the will entitled to probate? (Lingenfelter's Estate, 38 Cal. 2d 571, 241 P.2d 990)

10. A Montana statute permits any interested party to contest a will. Hill was named executor by Thompson's will. Rees was named executor by a codicil to the will. Rees offered the will and codicil for probate. Hill contested the probate of the codicil. Was he entitled to do so? (Montana ex rel. Hill v. District Court, 126 Mont. 1, 242 P.2d 850)

11. Copenhaver wrote a will in ink. At her death it was found with her other papers in a locked closet in her bedroom. Pencil lines had been drawn through every provision of the will and the signature. There was no evidence as to the circumstances under which this had been done. Was the will entitled to probate? (Franklin v. MacLean, 192 Va. 684, 66 S.E.2d 504)

12. After Livingston's death, his will was offered for probate. The objection was made that when he made the will, he was old and his memory was failing. Should the will be probated? (Livingston's Will, 5 N.J. 65, 73 A.2d 916)

13. Todd conveyed to his daughter, Lenah, a tract of land to hold for herself "during her natural life, then to her heirs." In 1933 Lenah and her husband adopted Woods. In 1939 Lenah died. Crump and other persons who were blood relations of Lenah claimed that they were her heirs and that Woods was not entitled to share the land as one of her heirs. Decide. (Woods v. Crump, 283 Ky. 675, 142 S.W.2d 280)

14. Paradis executed a will. Three witnesses attested the will, but two of them paid no attention as to whether he was of sound mind at the time. Was the will entitled to probate? (Paradis' Will, 147 Maine 347, 87 A.2d 512)

15. By a will dated 1931, Munson created a trust. In 1940 he wrote a "last will and testament," which he signed but which was not witnessed in the manner required by the Statute of Wills. The trust provisions of the 1931 will were omitted from the 1940 will. After his death the 1931 will was admitted to probate, and the executor began to carry out its trust provisions. Objection was made that those provisions had been revoked by their omission from the 1940 will. Decide. (Munson's Estate, 238 Minn. 358, 57 N.W.2d 22)

16. The last paragraph of the will of English provided: "What money there is left to go to Crhist Home, Warminster Bucks Co. Pa." The testatrix did not dispose of building and loan stock and real property owned by her. The testatrix was clearly untutored, and the will contained many errors. It was claimed that by the gift of the "money" which remained, she intended to bequeath everything she had left, including the stock and the real property. Decide. (Crhist's Home v. William Mattson, 140 N.J.Eq. 433, 55 A.2d 14)

CHAPTER 62

Bankruptcy

Bankruptcy and insolvency laws provide a means by which the debtor may yield or be compelled to yield to a court the property he has so that he will be relieved of all unpaid debts and can start economic life anew. State insolvency laws have only a limited sphere of operation today because the federal bankruptcy laws have superseded them to a large degree, but state statutes relating to voluntary assignments made by a debtor for the benefit of all of his creditors may still be in force. Proceedings under the federal law are brought in the federal district courts.

Sec. 62-A. Classification of Bankrupts.

(1) Voluntary Bankrupts. A *voluntary bankrupt* is one who subjects himself to the bankruptcy law. Any person, and in most instances any corporation or an association, may become a voluntary bankrupt. The filing of a voluntary petition automatically operates as an *adjudication* or determination that the petitioner is bankrupt.

Municipal, railroad, insurance, and banking corporations, and savings and loan associations cannot be voluntary bankrupts.[1] Ordinarily it is unimportant why the debtor chooses to go into bankruptcy so long as the facts exist that bring the debtor within the scope of the bankruptcy act.

(2) Involuntary Bankrupts. An *involuntary bankrupt* is one who has been subjected to the bankruptcy law upon the petition of his creditors. Under the prescribed circumstances, most natural persons, partnerships, and corporations owing debts that amount to the sum of

---

[1] 11 United States Code, Sec. 22 (a).

$1,000 or more may be forced by creditors into bankruptcy. Wage earners [2] and farmers; municipal, railroad, insurance, and banking corporations; and savings and loan associations cannot be adjudicated involuntary bankrupts.[3]

Sec. 62-B. Involuntary Proceedings.

If there are twelve or more creditors, three or more of them must join in the petition. If there are less than twelve creditors, it is permissible for one of them to file the petition.[4]

The petitioning creditors must have provable claims [5] against the debtor that amount in the aggregate to $500 or more. In case one creditor files the petition, he must have a provable claim amounting to that sum or more. The amount of the claims must be in excess of the value of pledged securities, if any, held by the creditors.

The debtor against whom the petition is filed may appear and oppose the petition.[6] If the debtor should allege that there are more than eleven creditors when only one filed the petition, the creditors who have not joined in the petition are given an opportunity to be heard. If the statutory number of creditors do not join in the petition, it will be dismissed.[7]

Sec. 62-C. Acts of Bankruptcy.

An involuntary petition may not be filed unless the debtor has committed an act of bankruptcy within four months prior to the filing of the petition.[8]

A debtor commits an act of bankruptcy (1) by conveying, transferring, concealing, removing, or permitting to be concealed or removed, any part of his property with intent to hinder, delay, or defraud his creditors, or any of them; (2) by transferring, while insolvent, any portion of his property to one or more of his creditors with intent to prefer such creditor or creditors over his other creditors; (3) by suffering, or permitting, while insolvent, any creditor to obtain a lien upon any of his property through legal proceedings and not having vacated or discharged such lien within thirty days from date thereof or at least five days before the date set for any sale or other disposition of such property; (4) by making a general assignment for the benefit of his creditors; (5) while insolvent, by permitting or being forced

---

[2] A "wage earner" for this purpose is defined as an individual who works for wages, salary, or hire, and whose compensation does not exceed $1,500 a year. 11 USC Sec. 1(32).

[3] Special statutory provision is made for the reorganization and liquidation of such corporations because of the nature of the enterprise and in order to protect the public.

[4] USC Sec. 95(b).

[5] See p. 898. A claim may be unliquidated as to amount provided that it is not contingent as to liability, although the unliquidated claim may be disqualified if a maximum value cannot be estimated. Sec. 95(b).

[6] 11 USC Sec. 41(b).

[7] Sec. 95(d).

[8] Sec. 21(b).

to put a receiver or a trustee in charge of his property; or (6) by admitting in writing his inability to pay his debts and his willingness to be adjudged a bankrupt.[9]

Insolvency is a necessary element of the second, third, and fifth acts of bankruptcy, but not of the others. The Bankruptcy Act declares that a person is deemed to be *insolvent* under the provisions of the statute "whenever the aggregate of his property, exclusive of any property which he may have conveyed, transferred, concealed, removed, or permitted to be concealed or removed, with intent to defraud, hinder, or delay his creditors, shall not at a fair valuation, be sufficient in amount to pay his debts." [10]

Sec. 62-D. Bankruptcy Officials. The actual bankruptcy proceeding, apart from that which takes place in court, is under the control of certain officials:

(1) Receiver. On the petition of creditors who fear that the assets of the debtor will be lost, a *receiver* may be appointed as custodian to preserve the assets [11] and turn them over to the trustee when appointed.

(2) Trustee. The creditors of the debtor elect—or if they fail to do so, the court appoints—a trustee. The *trustee* has a double role in that he automatically by operation of law becomes the owner of the property of the debtor not otherwise exempt (see p. 902, New York Terminal Warehouse Company Case), and he acquires the rights that a most favored creditor would have to set aside past transactions of the debtor that are harmful to his creditors. Specifically he is authorized to avoid certain preferences gained by a judgment against the bankrupt or by a transfer of property, of which recording or registering is required, within four months prior to the filing of the petition or after the filing thereof and before adjudication. He is required by the terms of the Bankruptcy Act to recover for the benefit of the creditors any of the bankrupt's property that has been transferred within four months prior to the filing of the petition, with the intent to hinder, delay, or defraud any creditors, or that is in the hands of a person under a transfer that is void by the laws of any state.[12]

(3) Referee. A referee is appointed for a six-year term to hear the evidence in bankruptcy cases and to submit his findings to the court. He acts in the nature of a special bankruptcy court.

---

[9] The filing of a voluntary petition in bankruptcy is in itself an act of bankruptcy since the debtor admits in writing his inability to pay his debts and his willingness to be adjudged a bankrupt.

[10] 11 USC Sec. 1(19).

[11] Sec. 11(3).

[12] Sec. 107(d).

Sec. 62-E.   Administration of the Bankrupt's Estate.

(1) Meetings of Creditors. At various times in the administration of the bankruptcy, a meeting of the creditors is held, such as the initial meeting to appoint a trustee, subsequent meetings to pass on particular matters authorized by the Bankruptcy Act, and a final meeting when the estate is to be closed.[13]

The creditors pass upon matters submitted to them by a majority in number and in the amount of claims of all creditors whose claims have been allowed. Creditors who have priority or security are not entitled to vote, nor are their claims counted in computing the number of creditors or the amounts of their claims, unless the amounts of their claims exceed the values of such priorities or securities, and then only for such excess.[14]

(2) Examination of Persons. Provision is made for the examination of the bankrupt and other persons as to his property and his conduct relating thereto. The wife of the bankrupt may be examined only in respect to business transacted by her or to which she is a party, and to determine whether she has transacted or has been a party to any business of her husband.[15]

(3) Sale of Bankrupt's Assets. In order to pay the debts of the bankrupt, it is necessary to convert his assets into cash and the trustee is accordingly authorized to sell his property. The sale in general may be made in any manner that is in the best interests of the estate. Such sales are under the supervision of the bankruptcy court; and if any property is sold for less than 75 per cent of its value, confirmation by the court is necessary.

(4) Proof and Allowance of Claims. Each creditor is required to file a sworn statement setting forth his claim and the basis thereof. These claims are ordinarily passed upon by the referee, although in some instances they may be considered initially by the court. The claim is then allowed or disallowed as in any other lawsuit. A claim must ordinarily be disallowed if not presented until more than six months after the first meeting of creditors.[16] A creditor who received some preferential payment or transfer of property within four months prior to the filing of the petition in bankruptcy cannot prove his claim unless he surrenders such payment or transfer.[17] If the claim of a creditor is secured, he is also barred from proving his claim except as to that part of his claim in excess of the security.

---

[13] Sec. 91(d),(e).
[14] Sec. 92 (a),(b).
[15] Sec. 44(a).
[16] Sec. 93 (n).
[17] Secs. 93(g), 96(b),107.

(5) Claims That Are Provable. Not all claims may be proven, that is, be permitted to share in the distribution of the assets of the bankrupt debtor. The claims that may be proved are: (1) a debt evidenced by a judgment or an instrument in writing, absolutely owing at the time of the filing of the petition by or against the bankrupt, whether then payable or not; (2) a debt due as costs against an involuntary bankrupt who was, at the time of the filing of the petition against him, the plaintiff in an action that would pass to the trustee and that the trustee, upon notice thereof, declines to prosecute; (3) a debt founded upon a claim for costs, incurred in good faith by a creditor before the filing of the petition, in an action to recover a provable debt; (4) a debt based upon a open account, or upon a contract expressed or implied; (5) a debt based upon a provable debt reduced to judgment after the filing of the petition and before the consideration of the bankrupt's application for a discharge, less costs and interest after the filing of the petition; (6) an award of workmen's compensation; (7) a right to damages for negligence; (8) contingent debts and contingent contractual liabilities; and (9) claims for anticipatory breach of contract.[18]

In respect to an *unliquidated claim* of a creditor, that is, a claim for an uncertain or disputed amount, the Bankruptcy Act provides that upon application to the court of bankruptcy, such a claim shall be liquidated or estimated in such a manner as the court shall direct. If possible to liquidate or estimate the claim within a reasonable time, the claim may be allowed against the estate.[19]

(6) Distribution of Estate. After all of the bankrupt's debts are determined, the assets that have been collected by the trustee are distributed first to those creditors with priorities; then to the general creditors without priorities; and, should any balance remain after all creditors have been paid, the balance to the bankrupt. These payments, called *dividends*, are made in installments.

The Bankruptcy Act confers a prior right of payment to (a) costs of administration and expenses necessary to preserve the estate, filing fees paid by creditors in involuntary proceedings, expenses of creditors in recovering property transferred or concealed by the bankrupt, and the reasonable expenses of creditors in opposing a composition that is refused or set aside; (b) wages due to workmen, clerks, traveling or city salesmen, or servants, earned within three months preceding the petition, not to exceed $600 to each person (see p. 903, In re Pacific Oil & Meal Co.); (c) expenses of creditors in opposing an arrangement or a plan for the discharge of a bankrupt, or in convicting a person of violating the bankruptcy law; (d) taxes owed by the bank-

---

[18] Sec. 103(a).
[19] Secs. 93(d),103(d).

rupt, except taxes against real estate over and above the value of the interest of the bankrupt therein; and (e) debts owed persons, including corporations, the United States, states, and territories, who by law are entitled to priority.

Sec. 62-F. Rights and Duties of Bankrupt. The Bankruptcy Act confers certain rights upon and imposes certain duties on the bankrupt.[20] If the debtor fails to cooperate or if he deceives the court as by the concealment of property which he hopes to save for himself, the law provides adequate penalties, in addition to denying the bankrupt the benefits of the statute.

(1) Rights. The debtor has the right to request a discharge in bankruptcy and to object to being declared or adjudicated a bankrupt. He is also protected generally from arrest on civil process while within the court district on matters relating to the bankruptcy proceeding. The debtor is given an immunity from criminal prosecution based on his testimony at meetings other than at the hearing on his discharge and other than in a prosecution for perjury.

(2) Duties. The debtor is required to file statements showing the property he possesses, any claim to an exemption, and the names of his creditors, with detailed information as to their claims. He must also attend meetings of creditors and hearings before the referee and court, and answer all proper questions relating to his estate. He must examine the proofs of claim filed against him to see if he disputes them, and he must obey orders of the bankruptcy court. (See p. 904, In re Hines)

Sec. 62-G. Discharge in Bankruptcy.

(1) Application for Discharge. The adjudication of any individual to be a bankrupt operates automatically as an application for a discharge in bankruptcy. A corporation may file an application for a discharge within six months after it is adjudged to be a bankrupt.[21]

The application for discharge will be denied if the bankrupt has: (a) committed certain offenses punishable by imprisonment as provided in the act; (b) unjustifiably destroyed, mutilated, falsified, concealed, or failed to keep books of account or records from which his financial status and business transactions might be ascertained; (c) obtained property or credit by a false representation in writing concerning his financial condition; (d) permitted others, within a year previous to the filing of the petition, to remove, transfer, conceal, or destroy any of his property, with the intent to hinder, delay, or de-

[20] Sec. 25.
[21] Sec. 32 (a).

fraud creditors, or has been guilty of this himself; (e) been granted a discharge in bankruptcy within six years; (f) refused, during the proceedings, to answer any material question approved by the court, or to obey any lawful order of the court; or (g) failed to explain satisfactorily the loss of any assets, or the deficiency of his assets to pay his debts.[22]

(2) Effect of Discharge. A discharge in bankruptcy releases the bankrupt from all his provable debts, except debts that: [23] (a) are due as taxes; (b) are liabilities (1) for obtaining property by false pretenses or false representation, (2) for willful and malicious injuries to the person or the property of another, (3) for alimony for the support of a wife or a child, (4) for seduction of an unmarried female, (5) for breach of promise accompanied by seduction, and (6) for criminal conversation; (c) have not been listed by the bankrupt in time to be proved, unless the creditor had notice or actual knowledge of the proceedings; (d) are created by the bankrupt's fraud, embezzlement, misappropriation, or defalcation while acting as an officer or in any fiduciary position; (e) are wages due to workmen, clerks, salesmen, or servants, which have been earned within three months preceding the petition; or (f) are due for moneys of an employee received or retained by the bankrupt to secure the faithful performance by such employee of the provisions of the contract of employment.

Sec. 62-H. Compositions. The National Bankruptcy Act as amended in 1938 provides several plans for debtors that are in the nature of compositions or agreements by all parties to adjust the debt structure of the debtor. These plans are known as corporate reorganizations, arrangements, real property arrangements by persons other than corporations, and wage earners' plans.

The provisions for corporate reorganizations [24] permit a corporation, an indenture trustee, or three or more creditors of the corporation with certain claims that amount in the aggregate to $5,000 or over to file a petition for a reorganization. The petition must show among other things that the corporation is insolvent or is unable to pay its debts as they mature and that relief is necessary under this plan. It also must include the proposed scheme of reorganization. The statute directs the court to confirm a plan of reorganization provided that it is fair, equitable, and feasible; that it has been proposed and accepted in good faith; and that all payments made or promised are approved as reasonable.

---

[22] Sec. 32 (c).
[23] Sec. 35.
[24] 10 USC Secs. 501 to 676, inclusive.

Cases for Chapter 62

New York Terminal Warehouse Co. v. Bullington

213 F.2d 340 (C.A. 5th, 1954)

The Denton Peanut Co. stored peanuts with the New York Terminal Warehouse Co. for which the latter issued negotiable warehouse receipts. These receipts were given as security for a loan from the Commodity Credit Corporation. Later Denton became bankrupt, and Bullington was appointed its trustee in bankruptcy. The bankruptcy court required the Commodity Credit Corporation to surrender the warehouse receipts to Bullington before it would be allowed to prove the full amount of its claim in the bankruptcy court. Bullington then presented the warehouse receipts to the New York Terminal. Terminal refused to deliver any peanuts on the ground that it had already delivered the full quantity to Denton without requiring the production and surrender of the negotiable warehouse receipts. Bullington sued New York Terminal. From a judgment in his favor, Terminal appealed.

Rives, C.J. . . . Under the bankruptcy act, the trustee succeeds to the title of the bankrupt, and he has certain rights in addition to those possessed by the bankrupt. He has the status of a lien or execution creditor. . . . However, the trustee does not occupy the position of a bona fide purchaser for value without notice of any equity. . . .

We entertain no doubt of the authority of the bankruptcy court to direct the Commodity Credit Corporation to assign its security to the Trustee as a condition precedent to approving its claim. . . .

It does not follow, however, that the Trustee thereby attained the status theretofore occupied by Commodity Credit Corporation of a holder in due course of the negotiable warehouse receipts. To the contrary we think that the rights and title of the trustee are to be measured by the same principles as apply to other property of the bankrupt estate. The rule protecting one holding through a holder in due course . . . "does not apply to cases where the payee or a holder of paper, being so circumstanced at the start that he cannot recover thereon, transfers it to an innocent third party for value, and subsequently purchases it back for value." While the bankruptcy court had authority to require the Commodity Credit Corporation to surrender possession of the warehouse receipts before approving its unsecured claim with priority, the appellant warehouse company . . . had a right to show upon present trial that equity and justice do not require that the Trustee be subrogated to the position of an innocent holder for value of the warehouse receipts formerly held by Commodity Credit Corporation, absolved of all defenses and equities to which the bankrupt would have been subject. Certainly if the bankrupt has had the benefit of the peanuts once, equity does not require a second realization on the same asset by the Trustee. . . .

[Judgment reversed.]

In re Pacific Oil & Meal Co.

24 F.Supp. 767 (D.C. S.D. Cal., 1938)

A proceeding was pending for the reorganization of the Pacific Oil & Meal Co., a debtor corporation, under the provisions of the Bankruptcy Act. Hart filed a claim for $1,556.81. He contended that he was entitled to priority of payment to the extent of $600 on the ground that such sum was earned as a clerk within three months prior to the commencement of the proceedings. One of the creditors filed an objection to the allowance of the priority of payment.

JENNEY, D.J. . . . It is the contention of the claimant that he is a clerk, . . . that his title of Secretary and Treasurer was only a nominal one, and that his services were really those of a clerk and not those of a corporate officer; therefore he is entitled to priority to the extent provided in the act. . . .

The term "workmen, servants, clerks, or traveling or city salesmen," as used in the statute, should be given their common meaning. Priority of payment under the act was intended for the benefit only of those who are dependent upon their wages for a living and who, having lost their employment by the bankruptcy, would be in need of such protection. . . . Thus, while even the higher-salaried officer of a corporation may be its servant or clerk, he is not entitled to priority in bankruptcy distribution because that type of worker is not intended to be protected under the act. . . . But . . . "it is the nature of the actual work done by the employee, and not the mere title of the position held by him, which determines his right to a preference." . . . Of course, were claimant merely a nominal officer or director of the bankrupt corporation, such official position would not in itself preclude him from establishing a prior right if, as an actual matter of fact, he had been employed and earned wages as a clerk. . . . On the other hand, merely incidental work as a clerk will not be enough of itself to give him priority. . . .

It is not always easy to determine whether the services as performed by claimants are rendered as an officer or as a mere workman, clerk, servant, or salesman. . . . If a claimant has been hired to perform services usually associated with an officer or has been expressly hired as an officer, he is not entitled to priority under the act merely because a large part of the service actually rendered might well have been performed by a clerk. . . .

In the instant case Hart appears to have been employed as Secretary and Treasurer and not as a clerk. He was one of the active officers of debtor and was a director and stockholder. Even though some of Hart's services could just as well have been performed by a clerk, nevertheless he was not hired to perform them as such but as Secretary and Treasurer. No attempt has been made to segregate those services which he performed as Secretary and Treasurer from those which he rendered only as a clerk. . . . The bulk of his duties were those of an officer. The evidence shows clearly that the contract of employment provided for a single indivisible compensation. Under such circumstances wages due for his services would not be entitled to priority of payment. . . .

In re Hines

69 F.2d 52 (C.C.A. 2d, 1934)

John and Michael Hines, individually and as copartners, were adjudged bankrupts. Brower, as trustee in bankruptcy, asked the referee for an order directing the bankrupts to execute and deliver to the trustee an order requesting the State Tax Commission of New York to deliver to the trustee certified copies of all income tax returns filed for the years 1927 to 1931, inclusive. The referee made the order. The bankrupts contended that the trustee in bankruptcy was not entitled under the state statute to obtain such information. From an order of the District Judge reversing the order of the referee, the trustee appealed.

MANTON, C.J. . . . The state statute does not impose absolute secrecy upon the returns filed, nor does it make them in any way so privileged. . . .

The scheme of the state statute seems to be to provide for an interchange between state and federal governments for information on file with each, and it is apparent that information contained in the taxpayer's return is available to both governments. . . .

We do not hold that the state tax commission must recognize such an order when the bankrupt makes it. . . . The commission is not before us, and we cannot prejudge the issue; but a court of bankruptcy . . . may direct the bankrupt to assist a trustee, his legal representative, in administering the affairs of the bankrupt in every way, so as to gather into the estate all assets. . . . The trustee is the representative or successor in interest of the bankrupt. . . . While acting as trustee, he is vested with all the rights, title, and powers as of the date of adjudication, which the bankrupt had . . . and is therefore his legal representative.

Regardless of whether a request or order, signed by the bankrupt at the direction of the court of bankruptcy, would authorize the tax commission to give the certified copy . . . it is enough that the commission might recognize it, or the state courts might compel it to do so. That possibility will support an order requiring the bankrupt so to assist the trustee. Section 70a(1) of the Bankruptcy Act vests in the trustee, by operation of law, title to documents relating to his property. Any instrument in writing to which the bankrupt is entitled would be such a document. . . . A bankrupt must execute and deliver such papers as shall be ordered by the court . . . so as to vest title in the trustee. And the court has jurisdiction to "make such orders, issue such process, and enter such judgments in addition to those specifically provided for as may be necessary for the enforcement of the provisions of this title.". . .

With the power given to the court by this act, the court may direct the bankrupt to facilitate and aid the trustee in procuring helpful documents which will assist in bringing assets to the bankrupt's estate. Such documents as the tax returns, disclosed by the petition, would be helpful to the trustee. There is no reason for secrecy as against the trustee of the bankrupt. He should be fully advised of all the business affairs and conditions of the business of the bankrupt, particularly information given by the bankrupt to the taxing authorities. . . . The bankrupt [is] plainly in a position to assist the trustee . . . by signing the order of direction to the tax commissioner to deliver certified copies to the trustee. The referee properly granted the order, and the court below erred in reversing it.

[Judgment in favor of the trustee in bankruptcy.]

Questions and Case Problems

1. What is the objective of each of the following rules of law?
   (a) A creditor's claim is allowable in bankruptcy only as to the amount of the claim in excess of security held by the creditor.
   (b) An involuntary petition in bankruptcy may not be filed unless the debtor has committed an act of bankruptcy within four months prior to the filing of the petition.

2. De Shazo owed the Household Finance Corporation $349.02. In order to borrow additional money, he submitted a false statement to Household as to the total amount of his debts. Household, relying on this false statement, loaned him $150.98 more and had him sign one note for $500, representing both the unpaid balance of the old loan and the total amount of the new loan. Thereafter De Shazo was discharged in bankruptcy. What effect did the discharge have on the note held by Household Finance and listed in the bankrupt's schedule of indebtedness? (Household Finance Corp. of Seattle v. De Shazo, [Wash.] 359 P.2d 1044)

3. A Utah statute provides for the revocation of an operator's license if he fails to pay a judgment entered against him because of his negligent operation of an automobile. Kesler's license was revoked under this statute. He thereafter went into bankruptcy and the judgment was discharged. He then claimed that his state license should be restored. The Utah Department of Public Safety refused to restore the license because the Utah

statute expressly provides that the revocation of the license shall not be affected by a subsequent discharge in bankruptcy. Kesler claimed that the Utah statute was unconstitutional on the theory that it conflicted with the bankruptcy power of the national government. Decide. (Kesler v. Department of Public Safety, 369 U.S. 153)

4. Putman, as executrix of the estate of Fred Putman, obtained a judgment for $10,000 against the Ocean Shore Railway Co. for negligently causing the death of Putman. She and two others filed a petition in bankruptcy against Folger, who had a statutory liability for the debts of the railway corporation. In opposing the petition, he contended that the claim of Mrs. Putman was not a provable debt in bankruptcy. Do you agree? (In re Putman, [D.C. N.D. Cal.] 193 F. 464)

5. Three creditors filed a petition in bankruptcy against Larkin. It was alleged and proved that within four months preceding the filing of the petition, Larkin had conveyed and transferred the greater part of his assets without a present consideration to two persons with the intent to hinder, delay, or defraud his creditors. In opposing the petition, it was contended that Larkin had not committed an act of bankruptcy because he had not been insolvent at the time of the conveyance. Do you agree? (In re Larkin, [D.C. N.D. N.Y.] 168 F. 100)

6. An involuntary petition in bankruptcy was filed against a merchant doing business in a building leased from Abbot. On the same day a receiver was appointed, and he took possession of the store and the stock of goods. In an action brought by Abbot upon a claim connected with the possession of the building by the receiver, a question arose as to whether the receiver was vested with title to the bankrupt's assets. What is your opinion? (In re Rubel, [D.C. E.D. Wis.] 166 F. 131)

7. At the instigation of Perry, trustee in bankruptcy of Martin, the court directed a referee to decide the validity of claims made by several claimants to a gas and oil leasehold in which the bankrupt had some interest. Chandler and other claimants opposed the proceeding on the ground that the referee did not have power to hear and decide such a question and that it was for a bankruptcy court to decide. Was this contention sound? (Chandler v. Perry, [C.C.A. 5th] 74 F.2d 371)

8. Certain creditors filed a petition in bankruptcy against the Percy Ford Co. An adjudication of bankruptcy followed. At the time of the filing of the petition, the National Shawmut Bank held four notes upon which the bankrupt was absolutely liable, but the notes were not then due and payable. The bank contended that the notes constituted provable debts. Do you agree? (In re Percy Ford Co. [D.C.D. Mass.] 199 F. 334)

PART XII

GOVERNMENT and BUSINESS

CHAPTER 63

Government Regulation of Business

The states by virtue of their police power may regulate business in all of its aspects so long as they do not impose an unreasonable burden on interstate commerce or any activity of the federal government. The federal government may impose any regulation upon any phase of business that is required by "the economic needs of the nation." [1]

The regulations imposed by governments are subject to various limitations. Neither state nor federal government may impose a regulation that deprives any person of life, liberty, or property without due process of law, nor may it take property except for a public purpose or without paying just compensation. A state may not impair the obligation of contracts nor deprive any person of the equal protection of the laws, nor abridge the privileges and immunities of citizens of the United States. These constitutional limitations have been so liberally interpreted within recent decades that they do not in actual practice impose much of a restriction on governments in their regulation of business. [2]

---

[1] American Power & Light Co. v. S.E.C., 329 U.S. 90.

[2] See generally, Ronald A. Anderson, *Government and Business* (2d ed.; Cincinnati: South-Western Publishing Company, 1960).

Sec. 63-A. Regulation of Employment. Basically the parties are free to make an employment contract on any terms they wish, but by statute employment is subject to certain limitations.[3] Thus persons under a certain age and women cannot be employed at certain kinds of labor. Statutes commonly specify minimum wages and maximum hours which the employer must observe, and they require employers to provide many safety devices. A state may also require employers to pay employees' wages for the time that they are away from work for the purpose of voting.

(1) Fair Labor Standards Act. By this statute, which is popularly known as the Wage and Hour Act, Congress provides that, subject to certain exceptions, persons working in interstate commerce or in an industry producing goods for interstate commerce must be paid not less than $1.25 an hour (effective September, 1963) ; and they cannot be employed for more than 40 hours a week unless they are paid time and a half for overtime. The act prohibits the employment of children under the age of 14 years. It permits the employment of children between of ages of 14 and 16 years in all industries, except mining and manufacturing, under certain prescribed conditions. This act has been followed by a number of states in regulating those phases of industry not within the reach of the federal statute.

(2) Hours of Service Act. Congress provides in this act that no employee of a common carrier engaged in moving trains should work longer than 16 consecutive hours, or within 10 hours thereafter, or within 8 hours after 16 hours of labor within any 24 hours. Employees whose duties are to transmit orders by telephone or telegraph for moving trains are limited to 9 and 13 hours according to the specified circumstances. In case of emergency, however, the hours of work may be extended.

(3) Public Contracts Act. Whenever a contract to manufacture or furnish materials, supplies, and equipment for the United States exceeds $10,000 in amount, the Walsh-Healy Act requires that the contract specify that the contractor shall pay minimum wages and overtime pay, shall not employ child labor, and shall observe standards set by the act or by the Secretary of Labor of the United States.

(4) Public Works Contracts Act. When a building is constructed for the United States for more than $2,000, the Davis-Bacon Act requires that the contractor agree to pay his laborers and mechanics not less than the prevailing rate of wages as determined by the Department

---

[3] As to workmen's compensation laws, See Ch. 41. As to labor-management relations laws, see Ch. 64.

of Labor. By the Copeland Act it is made a federal crime for an employer, or an employee with power to hire and fire, to require any employee on public works construction to return or "kickback" to him any part of the employee's wages.

(5) *Fair Employment Practices Acts.* A number of states have enacted laws that are designed to eliminate discriminatory practices by employers, employment offices, and labor unions. Employers are forbidden to discriminate in privileges, terms, and conditions of employment against any person because of his race, religious creed, or national origin. Some of these statutes are compulsory; others may be classified as voluntary or educational because they provide no means for enforcement. Several municipalities, especially in Ohio and Pennsylvania, have adopted ordinances with similar provisions.

Two other kinds of discrimination are sometimes prohibited. Some states forbid discrimination between sexes in rates of pay. A few states prohibit discrimination on the basis of age.

(6) *Federal Social Security.* The Federal Social Security Act establishes a system of old-age, survivors, and disability insurance; unemployment compensation insurance; old age assistance; aid to the needy blind, to dependent children, and to persons permanently and totally disabled; maternal and child-health services; and services for child welfare and crippled children. Only the first of these categories— (OASDI) the old-age, survivors, and disability insurance—is operated directly by the United States government. The balance of the program is operated by the individual states with the national government cooperating and contributing to the cost when the state operates on a plan approved by the national government.

(7) *State Legislation.* The states also have statutory plans of assistance for the unemployed, aged, and disabled. There is a wide variety of detail among the statutes of the various states, although they tend to follow a common pattern in order to comply with the federal requirements for federal aid.

These state plans typically establish an administrative board or agency with which a claim for assistance is filed by a person coming within the category to be benefited by the statute. If the board approves the claim, assistance is given to the applicant in the amount specified by the statute for the number of weeks or other period of time designated by the statute.

State unemployment compensation laws generally deny the payment of benefits when the employee was discharged for good cause; when he abandoned the work without cause, or failed or refused to seek or accept an offer of other suitable employment; or when the unemployment was the result of a labor dispute.

Sec. 63-B. Regulation of Production, Distribution, and Financing.
In order to protect the public from harm, government may establish
health and purity standards for food, drugs, and cosmetics, and protect
consumers from false advertising and labeling.[4] Without regard to the
nature of the product, government may regulate business with respect
to what materials may be used, the quantity of a product that may be
produced or grown, and the price at which the finished product is to
be sold. Government may also engage in competition with private
enterprises or own and operate an industry. Ordinarily these powers
have only been exercised in case of emergency, as illustrated by the
establishment of prices in time of war, or when governmental ownership of the property or enterprise is of great importance to the public,
as illustrated by the national ownership of fissionable material.

Under its commerce power the federal government may regulate
all methods of interstate transportation and communication, and a
like power is exercised by each state as to its intrastate traffic. The
financing of business is directly affected by the national government
in creating a national currency and in maintaining a federal reserve
bank system. State and other national laws may also affect financing
by regulating the contracts and documents used in financing, such as
bills of lading and negotiable instruments.

Sec. 63-C. Regulation of Competition. The federal government, and
the states in varying degrees, prohibit unfair methods of competition.[5]
Frequently a commission is established to determine, subject to review
by the courts, whether a given practice comes within the general class
of unfair methods of competition. In other instances the statute specifically defines the practice that is condemned.

The Congress has declared "unlawful" all "unfair methods of competition" and has created a Federal Trade Commission to administer
the law. The commission has held that it is unfair to use certain
schemes to obtain patronage, such as making gifts to employees for
their influence, making gifts to customers, offering so-called "free"
articles or services, offering benefits of memberships in a fictitious
society or a fictitious membership in a given society, offering pretended
guaranties, offering pretended "free trial" offers, offering pretended
"valuable" premiums, making offers without intention to supply the
goods, making fake demonstrations, securing signatures by trick, and
lotteries.

---

[4] Federal legislation is particularly important because of the predominance of inter-
state business. The federal statutes include such acts as the Pure Food, Drug, and
Cosmetics Act, as amended; the Fur Labeling Act of 1921; the Textile Fibre Products
Identification Act of 1958; the Color Additive Acts of 1958 and 1962; the Hazardous
Substances Labeling Act of 1960; the Flammable Fabrics Act of 1953; and the Drug
Industry Act of 1962.

[5] Independently of statute, unfair competition may be an actionable tort. See p. 940.

The commission has also condemned the practice of using harassing tactics, such as coercion by refusing to sell, boycotting, discrimination, disparagement of a competitor or his products, enforcing payment wrongfully, cutting off or restricting the market, securing and using confidential information, spying on competitors, and inducing breach of customer contracts. Another form of unfair competition that has been condemned is misrepresentation by appropriating business or corporate names, simulating trade or corporate names, appropriating trade-marks, simulating the appearance of a competitor's goods, simulating a competitor's advertising, using deceptive brands or labels, and using false and misleading advertising.

In more than one third of the states, statutes prevent price wars by prohibiting the sale below cost of goods generally or of particular kinds of goods. (See p. 915, Flank Oil Co. Case)

Sec. 63-D. Price Discrimination. The federal Clayton Act of 1914, applicable to interstate and foreign commerce, prohibits price discrimination between different buyers of commodities "where the effect of such discrimination may be substantially to lessen competition or tend to create a monopoly in any line of commerce." Discrimination is expressly permitted when it can be justified on the basis of: (1) difference in grade, quality, or quantity involved; (2) the cost of the transportation involved in making the sale; or (3) when the sale is made in good faith in order to meet competition.

The Robinson-Patman Act of 1936 permits price differentials based on differences in the cost of manufacturing, selling, and delivery that are caused by differences in methods or quantities. Price differentials are also permitted because of the deterioration of goods or when the seller in good faith is making a close-out sale of a particular line of goods. The Robinson-Patman Act reaffirms the right of a seller to select his customers and to refuse to deal with anyone he chooses so long as he acts in good faith and not for the purpose of restraining trade.

The federal law prohibits the furnishing of advertising or other services that, when rendered to one purchaser but not another, will have the effect of granting the former a price discrimination or lower rate. It is made illegal for a seller to accept any fee or commission in connection with the sale except for services actually rendered and unless his services are equally available to all on the same terms. The act makes either the giving or the receiving of any illegal price discrimination a criminal offense.

Sec. 63-E. Prevention of Monopolies and Combinations. To protect the public from monopolies and combinations in restraint of trade, almost all of the states have enacted antitrust statutes.

The federal antitrust act, known as the Sherman Act [6] is applicable to both sellers and buyers. (See p. 916, Mandeville Island Farms Case) It provides: [Sec. 1] "Every contract, combination in the form of a trust or otherwise, or conspiracy, in restraint of trade or commerce among the several states, or with foreign nations, is declared to be illegal. [Sec. 2] Every person who shall monopolize, or attempt to monopolize, or combine or conspire with any other person or persons to monopolize any part of the trade or commerce among the several states, or with foreign nations, shall be deemed guilty of a misdemeanor." [7]

The punishment fixed for the violation of either of these provisions is a fine not exceeding $5,000, or imprisonment not exceeding one year, or both. In addition to this criminal penalty, the act provides for an injunction to stop the unlawful practice and permits the victim of such practices to sue the wrongdoers and recover from them three times the damages that he has sustained.

(1) The Rule of Reason and Industrial Giants. The general approach of the Supreme Court of the United States to the trust problem has been that an agreement is not automatically or per se to be condemned as a restraint of interstate commerce merely because it creates a power or a potential to monopolize interstate commerce. It is only when the restraint actually imposed on interstate commerce is unreasonable that the practice is unlawful.

Under Section 2 of the Act one man or corporation may violate the law if he or it monopolizes or attempts to monopolize interstate commerce. Some decisions indicated that a single enterprise violated the antitrust law when it held such a position of leadership that by its own act it could change the prices in the industry if it chose. It was apparently indicated that it was illegal to be so big that one could control prices in the industry for an improper purpose if one so desired even though this power had not been exercised. In other words, a giant, even though a sleeping giant, was bad. After seventy odd years of litigation, the question as to whether bigness, unattended by unlawful acts or purposes, is a violation of the antitrust law remains unanswered.

To some extent the question of bigness, at least when it results from merger, has been met by Congress by amending Section 7 of the Clayton Act to provide that a merger of corporations doing interstate business shall be illegal when the effect of the acquisition by one corporation of all or any part of the assets of the other "may be substantially to lessen competition, or tend to create a monopoly." [8]

---

6 This act has been amended by the Clayton Act, the Federal Trade Commission Act, the Shipping Act, and other legislation.
7 15 United States Code, Ch. 1, Secs. 1, 2.
8 15 USC Sec. 18.

(2) Price-Fixing. *Horizontal price-fixing,* that is, agreements between persons performing similar economic functions, such as agreements between manufacturers or between distributors, is illegal under the federal law without regard to whether the price so fixed is reasonable or fair. *Vertical resale price agreements,* that is, agreements made between a manufacturer and his distributor, a distributor and his dealer, and so on, are generally valid.[9]

(3) Delivered Pricing. In order to meet the problem of maintaining price stability when a geographic distribution of markets is involved, there developed a basing-point system of establishing a fixed price for the goods of all manufacturers within a given line of production. Thus, from 1900 to 1926, the steel industry used the *single basing-point plan* or the "Pittsburgh-Plus Plan" under which the price of steel of any producer to any purchaser anywhere in the United States was quoted as the price of steel at Pittsburgh, plus freight from Pittsburgh to the point of delivery, regardless of the route over which the producer actually shipped the steel. This single basing-point system was later replaced by a *multiple basing-point system* in which, instead of all deliveries being priced at Pittsburgh plus, the country was zoned so that each purchaser would pay the price at a certain city within his zone plus the cost of transportation as though the shipment had come from that city.

Both single and multiple basing-point systems have been condemned by the Supreme Court as illegal whenever they are based upon collusion between producers. The exact extent to which they are to be regarded as collusive is not clear. Because of this uncertainty, a number of leading manufacturers have abandoned the basing-point system and have adopted a sales price based on f.o.b. the manufacturer's location.

(4) Stock and Director Control. The federal Clayton Act prohibits the purchase by a corporation of the stock of another corporation engaged in interstate or foreign commerce when the effect is to lessen competition substantially, or when it restrains commerce or tends to create a monopoly. (See p. 919, DuPont Case) The act does not prohibit purchase merely for the purpose of investment or purchase when there is no lessening of competition. It does not prohibit the creation of a subsidiary corporation; the merger of competing corporations; the acquisition by one corporation of the physical facilities, as distinguished from the stock, of a competing corporation; nor the acquisition of stock in another company which, though manufacturing or selling the same or a similar article, does not sell within the same price range or within the same geographic market. Because of these qualifications, the provisions of the act have had little practical effect.

---

[9] See p. 143.

The Clayton Act does not prohibit the holding of stock in competing corporations by the same person. Although it prohibits the director of one corporation from being a director of another competing corporation engaged in commerce, this prohibition is not effective in checking the monopoly potential of interlocking private stockholding.

(5) Tie-in Sales and Exclusive Dealer Agreements. The federal Clayton Act of 1914, applicable to interstate and foreign commerce, prohibits the *tie-in sale* or *tie-in lease* by which the person buying or renting goods agrees that he will only use with such goods other material sold or leased by the other party. The act also prohibits *exclusive dealer agreements* by which a dealer agrees not to handle a competitor's articles. These tie-in and exclusive dealer arrangements are not absolutely prohibited, but only when their effect "may be to substantially lessen competition or tend to create a monopoly in any line of commerce." By virtue of this qualification, a provision that a person leasing machinery shall use only the materials furnished by the lessor is a lawful restriction if the nature of the materials and the machine are such that the machine will not operate with the materials produced or offered by any other person. When the materials furnished by any other competitor would be equally satisfactory, however, the agreement is illegal. Thus an agreement that the lessee of office machinery should use only the paper sold by the lessor for that type of office machine was illegal when it was shown that any other seller could supply paper of suitable quality.

The partial prohibition of the tie-in and the exclusive dealer agreements is expressly stated by the statute to be limited by the right of any seller to "select his own customers in bona fide transactions and not in restraint of trade." There has also been a judicial trend to approve such agreements when the seller did not hold a dominant position in the market.

(6) Exceptions to the Antitrust Law. By statute, associations of exporters, marine insurance associations, and farmers' and dairymen's cooperatives are exempt from the Sherman Antitrust Act. By decision, labor unions have been given an exemption. Under certain circumstances a minimum resale price maintenance agreement is also exempt. Congress has also authorized freight pooling and revenue division agreements between railroad carriers, provided the approval of the Interstate Commerce Commission is obtained.

By virtue of statutory exemptions, traffic and trust agreements otherwise prohibited by the antitrust law may be made by ocean carriers, and interstate railroads and telegraph companies may consolidate upon obtaining the approval of the government commission having jurisdiction over them.

Cases for Chapter 63

Flank Oil Co. v. Tennessee Gas Transmission Co.

141 Colo. 554, 349 P.2d 1005 (1960)

The Colorado Unfair Practice Act declared that it was unlawful to sell goods below cost for the purpose of injuring competitors and destroying competition. The Flank Oil Company brought suit against the Tennessee Company and others claiming that they were selling gas below cost for the purpose of harming competition. The defendants claimed that the statute was unconstitutional. From a decision in favor of the defendants, the plaintiff appealed.

DOYLE, J. . . . The term cost is defined as including cost of raw materials, labor, and all overhead expenses of the producer; as applied to distribution, cost is defined as the invoice or replacement cost, whichever is lower, plus the "cost of doing business" by the distributor and vendor. The "cost of doing business" or "overhead expense" is defined as all cost of doing business incurred in the conduct of such business. The Act declares that this item must include without limitation: labor, including salaries of executives and officers; rent, interest on borrowed capital, depreciation, selling cost, maintenance of equipment, delivery costs, credit losses, all types of licenses, taxes, insurance, and advertising. . . .

Defendants contend that the term "cost" contained in Section 3 of the Act, which prohibits selling of goods at less than cost for the purpose of injuring competitors and destroying competition, is so vague and indefinite that men of common intelligence must of necessity guess at its meaning and differ as to its application. They argue that this arises from the complexity of the petroleum industry involving as it does discovery of oil, its production and transportation, as well as the manufacture of gasoline. They say that there is a multitude of costs, including those which arise from the acquisition of crude oil, those incident to the refining of crude oil, including the production of numerous by-products, cost of items which must be purchased and mixed with refined products, cost of transportation, and the cost of sales at retail of not only petroleum products but other automobile items. They say that it is impossible to allocate the cost of processing crude oil to the many by-products which result from the processing. Shall it be on the basis of the price of each product or on the basis of the intrinsic value of each item? They point out that some residual products have little or no market value. They pose the question whether a portion of overhead must be applied to them.

Defendants also point out that the Act requires that overhead costs of production be taken into account and that "cost of doing business" incident to distribution be considered. They point out also that the statute is silent as to how this allocation or apportionment shall be made. . . .

". . . In the absence of provisions to the contrary, we must presume that the legislature did not intend to prescribe that the cost must be absolutely exact, and that it must be based upon the precise method of accounting which any one merchant might adopt, but meant, by 'cost,' what businessmen generally mean, namely, the approximate cost arrived at by a reasonable rule. Hence, if a particular method adopted by a merchant cannot, under the facts disclosed, be said to be unreasonable, and does not disclose an intentional evasion of the law, the method so adopted should be accepted as correct. In other words, all that a man is required to do under the statute is to act in good faith. . . ."

The conclusion as set out above . . . is at variance with the assumption of defendants that the evidence which seeks to establish "cost" and "cost of doing business" must be sufficient to establish these facts with mathematical precision and exactness. . . .   The proof need not exist to that high degree of certainty. . . .

It is also contended . . . that this particular statute is not in harmony with the present economic climate; . . . and that it is no longer suited to present-day economic problems. We can only say that it is not for the courts to determine questions of economic policy. The Legislature has concluded that the method adopted is a proper one for combating predatory competition and it is not our function to substitute our judgment for that of the General Assembly. The conclusion of the Legislature that predatory price wars are contrary to the interests of the public and that temporary public price advantages will ultimately lead to monopoly and prices uncontrolled by the forces of competition is not so ill founded as to be contrary to the law or the constitution. . . .

[Statute held constitutional.]

Mandeville Island Farms v. American Crystal Sugar Co.

334 U.S. 219 (1948)

Three California sugar refiners agreed among themselves to pay California sugar-beet farmers a uniform price for their crops. The refined sugar would be sold by the refiners in interstate markets. Mandeville Island Farms, a sugar-beet farmer, sued American Crystal Sugar Co., one of the refiners, for treble damages under the Sherman Act. From a judgment for Mandeville, the sugar company appealed.

RUTLEDGE, J. . . . Petitioner's farms are located in northern California. . . . The only practical market available to beet farmers in that area was sale to one of three refiners. Respondent was one of these. Each season growers contract with one of the refiners to grow beets and to sell their entire crops to the refiner under standard form contracts drawn by it. Since prior to 1939 petitioners have thus contracted with respondent.

The refiners control the supply of sugar-beet seed. Both by virtue of this fact and by the terms of the contracts, the farmers are required to buy seed from the refiner. The seed can be planted only on land specifically covered by the contract. Any excess must be returned to the refiner in good order at the end of the planting season.

The standard contract gives the refiner the right to supervise the planting, cultivation, irrigation, and harvesting of the beets, including the right to ascertain quality during growing and harvesting seasons by sampling and polarizing. Before delivering beets to the company the farmers must make preliminary preparations for processing them into raw sugar.

. . . Some time before the 1939 season the three refiners entered into an agreement to pay uniform prices for sugar beets. . . . The refiners adopted identical form contracts and began to compute beet prices on the basis of the average net returns of all three rather than the separate returns of the purchasing refiner.

. . . Since the refiners controlled the seed supply and the only practical market for beets grown in northern California, when the new contracts were offered to the farmers, they had the choice of either signing or abandoning sugar-beet farming. . . . Because beet prices were determined for the three seasons with reference to the combined returns of the three refiners, the prices received by petitioners for those seasons were lower than if respondent, the most efficient of the three, had based its prices on separate returns. . . .

[The respondent claimed that the growing, purchasing, and refining of sugar beets were local activities and not within the reach of the Sherman Act, which applied only to transactions in interstate commerce, and that no illegal practice occurred in the subsequent interstate distribution of the refined sugar.]

. . . The broad form of respondent's argument cannot be accepted. It is a reversion to conceptions formerly held but no longer effective to restrict either Congress' power . . . or the scope of the Sherman Act's coverage. The artificial and mechanical separation of "production" and "manufacturing" from "commerce," without regard to their economic continuity, the effects of the former two upon the latter, and the varying methods by which the several processes are organized, related, and carried on in different industries, or indeed within a single industry, no longer suffices to put either production or manufacturing and refining processes beyond reach of Congress' authority or of the statute. . . .

. . . The inquiry whether the restraint occurs in one phase or another, interstate or intrastate, of the total economic process is now merely a preliminary step. . . . For, given a restraint of the type forbidden by the act, though arising in the course of intrastate or local activities, and a showing of actual or threatened effect upon interstate commerce, the vital question becomes whether the effect is sufficiently substantial and adverse to Congress' paramount policy declared in the act's terms to constitute a forbidden consequence. If so, the restraint must fall; and the injuries it inflicts upon others become remediable under the act's prescribed methods, including the treble damage provision.

. . . It is clear that the agreement is the sort of combination condemned by the act, even though the price-fixing was by purchasers and the persons specially injured under the treble damage claim are sellers, not customers or consumers. And even if it is assumed that the final aim of the conspiracy was control of the local sugar-beet market, it does not follow that it is outside the scope of the Sherman Act. For monopolization of local business, when achieved by restraining interstate commerce, is condemned by the act. . . . And a conspiracy with the ultimate object of fixing local retail prices is within the act if the means adopted for its accomplishment reach beyond the boundaries of one state.

. . . The statute does not confine its protection to consumers, or to purchasers, or to competitors, or to sellers. Nor does it immunize the outlawed acts because they are done by any of these. . . . The act is comprehensive in its terms and coverage, protecting all who are made victims of the forbidden practices by whomever they may be perpetrated. . . .

Nor is the amount of the nation's sugar industry which the California refiners control relevant, so long as control is exercised effectively in the area concerned.

. . . Under the facts characterizing this industry's operation and the tightening of controls in this producing area by the new agreements and understandings, there can be no question that their restrictive consequences were projected substantially into the interstate distribution of the sugar. . . .

Even without the uniform price provision and with full competition among the three refiners, their position is a dominating one. The growers' only competitive outlet is the one which exists when the refiners compete among themselves. There is no other market. The farmers' only alternative to dealing with one of the three refiners is to stop growing beets. They can neither plant nor sell except at the refiners' pleasure and on their terms. The refiners thus effectively control the quantity of beets grown, harvested, and marketed, and consequently, of sugar sold from the area in interstate commerce, even when they compete with each other. They dominate the entire industry. And their dominant position, together with obstacles created by the necessity for large capital investment and the time required to make it productive, makes outlet through new competition practically impossible. . . . A tighter or more all-inclusive monopolistic position hardly can be conceived. . . .

Those monopolistic effects not only deprived the beet growers of any competitive opportunity for disposing of their crops by the immediate operation of the uniform price provision; they also tended to increase control over the quantity of sugar sold interstate; and finally by the tie-in provision they interlaced those interstate effects with the price paid for the beets.

These restrictive and monopolistic effects, resulting necessarily from the practices allegedly intended to produce them, fall squarely within the Sherman Act's prohibitions. . . .

[Judgment for Mandeville Island Farms affirmed.]

United States v. E. I. du Pont De Nemours & Company

353 U.S. 586 (1957)

In 1917 to 1919, du Pont acquired a 23 per cent stock interest in General Motors. During the following years, General Motors bought all its automotive finishes and fabrics from du Pont. In 1949, the United States claimed the effect of the stock acquisition had been to lessen competition in interstate commerce on the theory that the sales to General Motors had not been the result of successful competition but were the result of the stock ownership, and therefore such stock ownership violated the Clayton Act. The United States brought an action against du Pont, General Motors, and others. From a decision in their favor, the United States appealed.

BRENNAN, J. . . . The primary issue is whether du Pont's commanding position as General Motor's supplier of automotive finishes and fabrics was achieved on competitive merit alone, or because its acquisition of the General Motors' stock, and the consequent close intercompany relationship, led to the insulation of most of the General Motors' market from free competition, with the resultant likelihood, at the time of suit, of the creation of a monopoly of a line of commerce [contrary to § 7 of the Clayton Act]. . . .

Section 7 is designed to arrest in its incipiency not only the substantial lessening of competition from the acquisition by one corporation of the whole or any part of the stock of a competing corporation, but also to arrest in their incipiency restraints or monopolies in a relevant market which, as a reasonable probability, appear at the time of suit likely to result from the acquisition by one corporation of all or any part of the stock of any other corporation. The section is violated whether or not actual restraints or monopolies, or the substantial lessening of competition, have occurred or are intended. Acquisitions solely for investment are excepted, but only if, and so long as, the stock is not used by voting or otherwise to bring about, or in attempting to bring about, the substantial lessening of competition. . . .

The first paragraph of § 7 plainly is framed to reach not only the corporate acquisition of stock of a competing corporation, where the effect may be substantially to lessen competition between them, but also the corporate acquisition of stock of any corporation, competitor or not, where the effect may be either (1) to restrain commerce in any section or community, or (2) tend to create a monopoly of any line of commerce. . . .

We hold that any acquisition by one corporation of all or any part of the stock of another corporation, competitor or not, is within the reach of the section whenever the reasonable likelihood appears that the acquisition will result in a restraint of commerce or in the creation of a monopoly of any line of commerce. Thus, although du Pont and General Motors are not competitors, a violation of the section has occurred if, as a result of the acquisition, there was at the time of suit a reasonable likelihood of a monopoly of any line of commerce. . . .

Appellees argue that there exists no basis for a finding of a probable restraint or monopoly within the meaning of § 7 because the total General Motors market for finishes and fabrics constituted only a negligible percentage of the total market for these materials for all uses, including automotive uses. It is stated in the General Motors brief that in 1947 du Pont's finish sales to General Motors constituted 3.5 per cent of all sales of finishes to industrial users, and that its fabrics sales to General Motors comprised 1.6 per cent of the total market for the type of fabric used by the automobile industry.

Determination of the relevant market is a necessary predicate to a finding of a violation of the Clayton Act because the threatened monopoly must be one which will substantially lessen competition "within the area of effective competition." Substantiality can be determined only in terms of the market affected. The record shows that automotive finishes and fabrics have sufficient peculiar characteristics and uses to constitute them products sufficiently distinct from all other finishes and fabrics to make them a "line of commerce" within the meaning of the Clayton Act. . . . Thus, the bounds of the relevant market for the purposes of this case are not coextensive with the total market for finishes and fabrics, but are coextensive with the automobile industry, the relevant market for automotive finishes and fabrics.

The market affected must be substantial. . . . Moreover, in order to establish a violation of § 7 the Government must prove a likelihood that competition may be "foreclosed in a substantial share of . . . [that market]." Both requirements are satisfied in this case. The substantiality of a relevant market comprising the automobile industry is undisputed. The substantiality of General Motors' share of that market is fully established in the evidence.

General Motors . . . accounts annually for upwards of two-fifths of the total sales of automotive vehicles in the Nation. . . . Du Pont supplied 67 per cent of General Motors' requirements for finishes in 1946 and 68 per cent in 1947. In fabrics du Pont supplied 52.3 per cent of requirements in 1946, and 38.5 per cent in 1947. Because General Motors accounts for almost one-half of the automobile industry's annual sales, its requirements for automotive finishes and fabrics must represent approximately one-half of the relevant market for these materials. Because the record clearly shows that quantitatively and percentagewise du Pont supplies the largest part of General Motors' requirements, we must conclude that du Pont has a substantial share of the relevant market.

The appellees argue that the Government could not maintain this action in 1949 because § 7 is applicable only to the acquisition of stock and not to the holding or subsequent use of the stock. This argument misconceives the objective toward which § 7 is directed. The Clayton Act was intended to supplement the Sherman Act. Its aim was primarily to arrest apprehended consequences of intercorporate relationships before those relationships could work their evil, which may be at or any time after the acquisition, depending upon the circumstances of the particular case. . . . The Government may proceed at any time that an acquisition may be said with reasonable probability to contain a threat that it may lead to a restraint of commerce or tend to create a monopoly of a line of commerce. . . .

We agree with the trial court that considerations of price, quality, and service were not overlooked by either du Pont or General Motors. Pride in its products and its high financial stake in General Motors' success would naturally lead du Pont to try to supply the best. But the wisdom of this business judgment cannot obscure the fact, plainly revealed by the record, that du Pont purposely employed its stock to pry open the General Motors market to entrench itself as the primary supplier of General Motors' requirements for automotive finishes and fabrics.

Similarly, the fact that all concerned in high executive posts in both companies acted honorably and fairly, each in the honest conviction that his actions were in the best interests of his own company and without any design to overreach anyone, including du Pont's competitors, does not defeat the Government's right to relief. It is not requisite to the proof of a violation of § 7 to show that restraint or monopoly was intended.

The statutory policy of fostering free competition is obviously furthered when no supplier has an advantage over his competitors from an acquisition of his customer's stock likely to have the effects condemned by the statute. We repeat, that the test of a violation of § 7 is whether, at the time of suit, there is a reasonable probability that the acquisition is likely to result in the condemned restraints. The conclusion upon this record is inescapable that such likelihood was proved as to this acquisition. . . .

[Judgment reversed.]

Questions and Case Problems

1. What is the objective of each of the following rules of law?

    (a) Horizontal price-fixing is illegal under the federal law without regard to whether the price fixed is fair and reasonable.

    (b) Farmers' and dairymen's cooperatives are exempt by statute from the operation of the Sherman Antitrust Act.

2. The Winstead Hosiery Co. labeled mixed wool articles as "natural wool," "Australian wool," and other similar terms that did not indicate the mixed nature of the article. The Federal Trade Commission ordered the company to stop the practice of using a "wool" label to describe a mixed article on the ground that it was an unfair trade practice. The company defended on the ground that all other manufacturers understood that the label was not to be taken as true and that the competitors of the company were not deceived. Was this a valid defense? (Federal Trade Commission v. Winstead Hosiery Company, 258 U.S. 483)

3. The Delco Cleaners and Dyers did business in Delaware County. The name Delco was a contraction of the name of the county. A suit was brought to enjoin the use of the name "Delco" by another local concern calling itself the "Delco Valet Service." Decide. (Berberian v. Ferm, 166 Pa.Super. 108, 70 A.2d 394)

4. Moore ran a bakery in Santa Rosa, New Mexico His business was wholly intrastate. His competitor, Mead's Fine Bread Co., which was one of several corporations held under interlocking ownership and management, engaged in an interstate business. Mead cut the price of bread in half in Santa Rosa but made no price cut in any other place in New Mexico or any other state. As the result of this price cutting, Moore was driven out of business. He then sued Mead for damages for violation of the Clayton and Robinson-Patman acts. Mead claimed that the price cutting was purely intrastate and therefore did not constitute a violation of the federal statutes. Decide. (Moore v. Mead's Fine Bread Co., 348 U.S. 115)

5. In 1903, Congress adopted a law requiring the use of automatic couplers and safety brakes on all trains operating in interstate commerce. The Southern Railway ran certain intrastate trains on the same tracks used by the interstate trains. The coupling devices on one of the intrastate trains did not conform to the federal standards. The railroad was sued for violating the federal law. It defended on the ground that the federal law could apply only to interstate trains. Decide. (Southern Railway v. United States, 222 U.S. 20)

CHAPTER 64

Labor Law

Sec. 64-A. Labor Representation. Employees are today generally recognized as having the right to form a union and to require their employer to deal with their union as their bargaining representative.[1]

Although the federal law makes it the duty of both the union and the employer to bargain collectively, there is no duty on either to reach an agreement. (See p. 929, N.L.R.B. v. Insurance Agents' International Union) The federal act provides that in the case of industry-wide collective bargaining, the duty to bargain collectively shall also mean that neither party to the contract shall terminate or modify the contract without giving the other party sixty days' notice, and the parties must then meet to negotiate a new contract while both sides continue in operation during the sixty-day period.[2]

(1) Machinery to Enforce Collective Bargaining. To protect the rights of workers to unionize and bargain collectively, the federal government created the National Labor Relations Board. The board determines the proper collective bargaining unit and who is the representative to bargain on behalf of the workers; and it eliminates unfair practices by which the employer might interfere with unionization and collective bargaining by the employees.

---

[1] Taft-Hartley Act, Sec. 7. In 1935 the Federal Congress adopted the Wagner Act or National Labor Relations Act. A number of states then adopted similar statutes or "Little Wagner" acts as they were nicknamed. In 1947 the Federal Congress adopted the Taft-Hartley Act or the National Labor Management Relations Act. A number of states then amended their laws to match these changes. The student should therefore bear in mind that wherever it is stated in the text that the federal act of 1935 or 1947 made a particular provision, it is probable that a number of states also copied that provision. In the interest of brevity this observation will not be repeated. In general terms the federal law applies when the employment involved is in interstate commerce or in an industry producing goods for interstate commerce, while a state law applies with respect to local or intrastate production. In addition, the Federal Railway Labor Act contains many provisions similar to the other federal labor relations statutes.

[2] Sec. 8(d).

(2) Equal Representation of All Employees. Whatever union or person is selected by the majority of the workers within the unit becomes "the exclusive representative (s) of all employees in such unit for the purposes of collective bargaining in respect to rates of pay, wages, hours of employment, or other conditions of employment." [3] Whether all the workers are members of the representative union or not is immaterial, for in any case this union is the exclusive representative of every employee.[4] It is unlawful for an employee, whether a member of the union or not, to attempt to make a contract with the employer. Except as to grievances, every worker must act through the representative union with respect to his contract of employment. At the same time the union is required to represent all workers fairly, nonmembers as well as members. It is unlawful for the union, in bargaining with the employer, to discriminate in any way against any of the employees. The union cannot use its position as representative of all the workers to further its interests as a union.

Sec. 64-B.   Union Security. The *yellow-dog contract* by which the employer specified that an employee would be discharged if he joined any union is now invalid. In addition, the federal law now prohibits a contract by which an employee must belong to a particular union, except to the extent that a union shop is legalized.[5]

(1) Closed and Union Shops. A *closed shop* in which the employer agrees with a particular union that he will not employ anyone who is not a member of that union was expressly authorized by the 1935 Wagner Act.[6]

A number of statutes and state constitutional amendments were adopted in the late 40's outlawing the closed shop and declaring the right of the nonunion man to work. The Taft-Hartley Act prohibits a closed shop and permits only a *union shop*, when agreed to by the employer and the union. Under this plan the employer is free to hire whomever he pleases but, after a trial period of not more than thirty days, the new employee cannot keep his job unless he joins a union.

It is left to local state law to determine whether an *agency shop* is valid, that is, a union contract provision which requires that non-union men pay to the union a sum of money equal to union dues in order to retain their employment. (See p. 931, Higgins v. Cardinal Manufacturing Co.)

(2) Make-Work Practices. A union may try to make sure that there is enough work for all of its members by refusing to admit new

---

[3] Sec. 9(a).
[4] Sec. 9(a).
[5] Sec. 8(a)(3).
[6] Sec. 8(a)(3).

members to the union or by making it very difficult to join, as by a quota system or by the imposition of high initiation fees and dues; by restricting the amount of work which any union man is permitted to do in an hour or a day; by insisting that an employer hire additional or unnecessary men.

At times the policy of one union is in conflict with the policy of another union. This occurs in the case of the *jurisdictional dispute* when two or more unions claim the right to do a particular kind of work. For example the carpenter's union claims the right to install metal doors because the metal doors replace wooden doors, which were installed by carpenters. The metal workers' union points out that the metal workers and not the carpenters work with metal.

Sec. 64-C. Unfair Labor Practices. The Taft-Hartley Act declares certain practices to be unfair and authorizes the National Labor Relations Board to conduct proceedings to stop such practices.

(1) Unfair Employer Practices. The federal law declares that it is an unfair labor practice for an employer to interfere with unionization or to discriminate against any employee because of his union activities, or to refuse to bargain collectively.[7]

The Taft-Hartley Act preserves for the employer the right of fair comment. It provides that "the expression of any views, arguments, or opinion, or the dissemination thereof, whether in written, printed, graphic, or visual form, shall not constitute or be evidence of an unfair labor practice under any of the provisions of this act, if such expression contains no threat of reprisal or force or promise of benefit."[8]

(2) Unfair Union Practices. The federal law declares it to be an unfair labor practice for a union to interfere with employees in forming their unions or refraining from joining a union; to cause an employer to discriminate against an employee because he belongs to another union or no union; to refuse to bargain collectively; and under certain circumstances to stop work or to refuse to work on materials or to persuade others to stop work or refuse to so work.[9]

Although a strike is deemed an unfair labor practice under certain circumstances, the act does not outlaw strikes generally but provides that "nothing in this Act, except as specifically provided herein, shall be construed so as either to interfere with or impede or diminish in any way the right to strike, or to affect the limitations or qualifications on the right."[10] This protection is not extended to government em-

----

[7] Sec. 8(a).
[8] Sec. 8(c).
[9] Sec. 8(b).
[10] Sec. 13.

ployees. It is declared unlawful for them to strike. If they do so, they are to be discharged immediately, and shall forfeit any civil service status, and cannot be re-employed by the government for three years.[11]

The Labor-Management Reporting and Disclosure Act of 1959 expands the definition of unfair labor practices. The Act prohibits and makes criminal picketing conducted to extort money and makes it an unfair labor practice to picket for recognition when a rival union is lawfully recognized and no representation issue can be raised. Agreements between unions and employers that the latter shall not use non-union materials (hot cargo agreements) are made void and an unfair labor practice, except in the construction and garment industries. Secondary boycotts and the coercion of neutral employers thereby are made unfair labor practices, with exception to some extent of the garment industry. Neither the limitation of picketing nor the prohibition of secondary boycotts limits the union's right to publicize a labor dispute provided pressure is not exerted thereby on neutral employers nor their employees induced to refuse to work.

(3) Procedure for Enforcement. Under the federal act, whenever it is claimed that an unfair labor practice has been committed, the board issues a complaint. The complaint informs the party of the charges made against him and notifies him to appear at a hearing. The board makes findings of fact and conclusions of law and either dismisses the complaint or enters an order against the party to stop the unfair labor practice "and to take such affirmative action including reinstatement of employees with or without back pay, as will effectuate the policy of this Act; provided, that where an order directs reinstatment of an employee, back pay may be required of the employer or labor organization, as the case may be, responsible for the discrimination suffered by him. . . ." (See p. 934, Phelps Dodge Corp. v. N.L.R.B.) An employee can neither be reinstated nor awarded back pay if he was discharged for cause.[12]

Provision is made for appeals to the court of appeals and for the issuance of court orders to compel obedience by the parties.

Apart from the proceedings under the federal statutes, whenever the unfair labor practice is also a civil wrong or a crime under state law, the wrongdoer may be sued and prosecuted under the state law.

Sec. 64-D. Union Organization and Management. In order to insure the honest and democratic administration of unions, Congress adopted the Labor-Management Reporting and Disclosure Act of 1959 regulating unions operating in or affecting interstate commerce. Under it, such unions must adopt constitutions and bylaws, and file copies of

---

[11] Sec. 305.
[12] Sec. 10(c).

them together with detailed reports on administrative and financial matters. Each officer and key employee is required to file a report that sets forth any interest he or a member of his family has which conflicts with his duties to the union. Reports are required of labor relations consultants, and employers must report payments to union officers. The grounds on which a national union may exercise control or trusteeship power over a local union or its funds are specified to prevent abuse of that power.

The Act protects rights of union members within their unions by guaranteeing equality, the right to vote on specified matters, and information on union matters and contracts, and it protects members from interference with the enjoyment of these rights. The terms of office and the process of election are regulated to provide democratic elections by secret ballot by members in good standing. Communists and persons convicted of major crimes are barred as officers or employees of unions until a specified period of time has elapsed since termination of membership or conviction.

Union assets are protected from misappropriation by requiring those handling them to be bonded, imposing upon them a trustee's duty, making them criminally liable for theft or embezzlement, giving union members the right to sue them if the union fails to do so, and providing that the union cannot agree to release them from liability. Union assets are also protected by limiting loans to officers or employees and by prohibiting the union from paying fines imposed on officers or employees.

Sec. 64-E. Labor Disputes.

(1) Labor's Methods. The most common of the labor techniques are the strike, the boycott, and picketing. The *strike* is a concerted stopping of work as distinguished from individual workers deciding to quit. A *boycott* is the persuasion of others to stop patronizing or working for a particular person. *Picketing* is ordinarily placing persons outside a place of employment or distribution so that by words or banners they can inform others that a labor dispute is in existence. To these may be added the more recent innovations of the *slowdown,* a concerted slowing down of production, and the *sitdown strike,* in which the employees seize the plant and refuse to allow the employer to operate it.

In addition to distinguishing these various techniques, it is also necessary to consider the area of operation. Thus, if employees having a dispute with their employer picket his plant, it is called *primary picketing.* If they picket the plant of another manufacturer who uses the products made by their employer, it is called *secondary picketing.* If the employees picket the stores that sell the finished commodity or the customers who purchase them, it may be called *tertiary picketing,* although commonly any picketing that is not primary is called secondary. The purpose of secondary activity is to bring indirect pressure to bear on the employer and thus force him to agree in the dispute. A boycott is similarly called secondary or tertiary when it affects persons other than the employer.

Labor activity is more likely to be held legal when it relates to hours, wages, or working conditions. Likewise labor activity is more likely to be held lawful when it is engaged in by employees against their own employer with whom they have the dispute.

(2) Employers' Methods. The weapons of the employer have been primarily the *lockout* or the closing of the factory, the *blacklist* or the circulation among employers of a list of persons who should not be employed, and the traditional remedies of the injunction and antitrust prosecution.

(a) INJUNCTIONS. The right of the employer to obtain an injunction has been limited by the Federal Norris-LaGuardia Act and by many state statutes so that an injunction cannot be obtained in a labor dispute when no physical damage to property is involved. A limited right to obtain an injunction is conferred upon the National Labor Relations Board in order to stop certain unfair labor practices, and an injunction may be obtained upon the direction of the President of the United States to postpone for 80 days a strike in a national industry when national health or safety is threatened.

(b) ANTITRUST LAWS. The Sherman Antitrust law is now not applicable to ordinary activity of labor unions as long as they do not conspire with nonlabor groups. The Taft-Hartley law of 1947, however, subjects unions to a civil suit for damages for certain strikes and secondary boycotts that might in themselves be regarded as illegal conspiracies, and extortion picketing is made a crime by the Labor-Management Reporting and Disclosure Act of 1959.

Sec. 64-F. Settlement of Labor Disputes. A number of special procedures have been devised for the settlement of labor disputes. These include the grievance settlement; conciliation and mediation; arbitration; strike votes; strike notices and cooling off periods; injunctions, under some state laws, against strikes in the case of public utilities, and under the Taft-Hartley law, in the case of a national strike or lockout imperiling national health or safety; and government seizure of a plant in which production has stopped.

Although the procedures have been successful in many instances, there is no certainty that any of them will be effective in a given case. In the last analysis both the avoidance and the settlement of labor disputes depend in general upon the ability and willingness of management and labor to find a basis of cooperation.

Cases for Chapter 64

N.L.R.B. v. Insurance Agents' International Union

361 U.S. 477 (1960)

Insurance salesmen of the Prudential Insurance Co. were members of the Insurance Agents' International Union. The contract between the union and the company was about to expire, and negotiations were being conducted for a new contract. The agents engaged in certain work practices designed to force the company to reach an agreement. The National Labor Relations Board held that such activity was an unfair labor practice and ordered the union to stop. On appeal this order was set aside by the court of appeals, and the case was then appealed to the United States Supreme Court.

BRENNAN, J. . . . . The precise question is whether the Board may find that a union, which confers with an employer with the desire of reaching agreement on contract terms, has nevertheless refused to bargain collectively, thus violating that provision, solely and simply because during the negotiations it seeks to put economic pressure on the employer to yield to its bargaining demands by sponsoring on-the-job conduct designed to interfere with the carrying on of the employer's business. . . .

It was developed . . . that the union's harassing tactics involved activities by the member agents such as these: refusal for a time to solicit new business, and refusal (after the writing of new business was resumed) to comply with the company's reporting procedures; refusal to participate in the company's "May Policyholders' Month Campaign"; reporting late at district offices the days the agents were scheduled to attend them, and refusing to perform customary duties at the offices, instead engaging there in "sit-in-mornings," "doing what comes naturally" and leaving at noon as a group; absenting themselves from special business conferences arranged by the company; picketing and distributing leaflets outside the various offices of the company on specified days and hours as directed by the union; distributing leaflets each day to policyholders and others and soliciting policyholders' signatures on petitions directed to the company; and presenting the signed policyholders' petitions to the company at its home office while simultaneously engaging in mass demonstrations there. . . .

Collective bargaining . . . is not simply an occasion for purely formal meetings between management and labor, while each maintains an attitude of "take it or leave it"; it presupposes a desire to reach ultimate agreement, to enter into a collective bargaining contract. . . .

But at the same time, Congress was generally not concerned with the substantive terms on which the parties contracted. . . .

Section [8 (d) of the Taft-Hartley Act] defines collective bargaining as follows:

"For the purposes of this section, to bargain collectively is the performance of the mutual obligation of the employer and the representative of the employees to meet at reasonable times and confer in good faith with respect to wages, hours, and other terms and conditions of employment, or the negotiation of an agreement, or any question arising thereunder, and the execution of a written contract incorporating any agreement reached if requested by either party, but such obligation does not compel either party to agree to a proposal or require the making of a concession. . . ."

It is apparent from the legislative history of the whole Act that the policy of Congress is to impose a mutual duty upon the parties to confer in good faith with a desire to reach an agreement, in the belief that such an approach from both sides of the table promotes the overall design of achieving industrial peace. . . . Discussion conducted under that standard of good faith may narrow the issues, making the real demands of the parties clearer to each other, and perhaps to themselves, and may encourage an attitude of settlement through give and take. The mainstream of cases before the Board and in the courts reviewing its orders, under the provisions fixing the duty to bargain collectively, is concerned with insuring that the parties approach the bargaining table with this attitude. But apart from this essential standard of conduct, Congress intended that the parties should have wide latitude in their negotiations, unrestricted by any governmental power to regulate the substantive solution of their differences. . . .

It must be realized that collective bargaining, under a system where the Government does not attempt to control the results of negotiations, cannot be equated with an academic collective search for truth—or even with what might be thought to be the ideal of one. The parties—even granting the modification of views that may come from a realization of economic interdependence—still proceed from contrary, and to an extent antagonistic viewpoints and concepts of self-interest. The system has not reached the ideal of the philosophic notion that perfect understanding among people would lead to perfect agreement among them on values. The presence of economic weapons in reserve, and their actual exercise on occasion by the parties, is part and parcel of the system that the Wagner and Taft-Hartley Acts have recognized. Abstract logical analysis might find inconsistency between the command of the statute to negotiate toward an agreement in good faith and the legitimacy of the use of economic weapons, frequently having the most serious effect upon individual workers and productive enterprises, to induce one party to come to the terms desired by the other. But the truth of the matter is that at the present statutory stage of our national labor relations policy, the two factors—necessity for good-faith bargaining between parties, and the availability of economic pressure devices to each to make the other party incline to agree on one's terms—exist side by side. One writer recognizes this by describing economic force as "a prime motive power for agreements in free collective bargaining." Doubtless one factor influences the other; there may be less need to apply economic pressure if the areas of controversy have been defined through discussion; and at the same time, negotiation positions are apt to be weak or strong in accordance with the degree of economic power the parties possess. . . .

The scope of § 8(b)(3) and the limitations on Board power which were the design of § 8 (d) are exceeded, we hold, by inferring a lack of good faith not from any deficiencies of the union's performance at the bargaining table by reason of its attempted use of economic pressure, but solely and simply because tactics designed to exert economic pressure were employed during the course of the good faith negotiations. Thus the Board in the guise of determining good or bad faith in negotiations could regulate what economic weapons a party might summon to its aid. And if the Board could regulate the choice of economic weapons that may be used as a part of collective bargaining, it would be in a position to exercise considerable influence upon the substantive terms on which the parties contract. . . . Our labor policy is not presently erected on a foundation of government control of the results of negotiations. . . . Nor does it contain a charter for the National Labor Relations Board to act at large in equalizing disparities of bargaining power between employer and union.

The use of economic pressure . . . is of itself not at all inconsistent with the duty of bargaining in good faith. . . .

Congress has been rather specific when it has come to outlaw particular economic weapons on the part of unions. . . . But the activities here involved have never been specifically outlawed by Congress. . . .

It is suggested here that the time has come for a re-evaluation of the basic content of collective bargaining as contemplated by the federal legislation. But that is for Congress. . . .

[Judgment affirmed.]

Higgins v. Cardinal Manufacturing Co.

188 Kan. 11, 360 P.2d 456 (1961)

Higgins and others were nonunion employees of Cardinal Manufacturing Co. Under the union contract with Cardinal, nonunion employees were required to pay to the union an amount equal to the dues and assessments paid to it by the union members. Higgins and the nonunion employers claimed that this "agency shop" provision was prohibited by the "right-to-work" amendment to the Kansas constitution, and brought suit against Cardinal and the union. From a decision against the plaintiffs, they appealed.

SCHROEDER, J. . . . The issue of union security presented by this case brings into focus a conflict between two firmly-held American beliefs: The belief that a worker should not be required to support an organization which he may oppose, and the belief that a worker should not be a "free rider" who takes advantage of benefits secured by a union without contributing his share to its support. That issue has been the subject of legislation at both the state and national levels. . . .

Under Section 14 (b) of the Labor Management Relations Act, 1947, . . . Congress yielded to the states the authority to ban union shop agreements by providing: "Nothing in this [act] shall be construed as authorizing the execution or application of agreements requiring membership in a labor organization as a condition of employment in any State or Territory in which such execution or application is prohibited by State or Territorial law." It is by virtue of this provision that states are permitted to enact so-called "right-to-work laws," which escape federal pre-emption under the Labor Management Relations Act, 1947, even though interstate commerce is affected. . . .

The Constitution of . . . Kansas, . . . Article 15, Section 12, . . . reads: "No person shall be denied the opportunity to obtain or retain employment because of membership or nonmembership in any labor organization, nor shall the state or any subdivision thereof, or any individual, corporation, or any kind of association enter into any agreement, written or oral, which excludes any person from employment or continuation of employment because of membership or nonmembership in any labor organization." . . .

The basic issue upon which the campaign was conducted prior to the adoption of the constitutional amendment by the people of Kansas was whether or not the worker should be a "free rider" who takes advantage of benefits secured by a union without contributing his share to its support. Those supporting adoption of the amendment contended the worker should not be required to support a labor organization which he may oppose. Without question the people felt by adopting the amendment the decision would prevent the payment of forced tribute to any labor organization by any worker within the boundaries of this state. . . .

The appellees [employer and union] contend Kansas was one of the last states to enact the so-called "right-to-work law." They argue approximately nineteen of the states enacted "right-to-work laws" prior to the adoption of the Kansas constitutional amendment; that ten prohibited the collection of fees or charges without the employees' consent; and that nine did not so provide, among these being the State of Kansas. It is argued that inasmuch as the state legislators' attention had already been directed to the broader type of restraining law (In 1951 Senate Bill No. 116, incorporating the more restrictive language failed to pass), and since there were in existence these two types of legislation dealing with this subject matter, known to the legislature at the time the particular constitutional amendment was suggested, it must be considered conclusive the legislature did not see fit to incorporate in the specific statute the more restrictive language. . . .

The natural and logical interpretation of the Kansas constitutional amendment, prohibiting compulsory membership in a labor organization as a condition of employment or continued employment, includes by necessary implication a prohibition against forced payment of initiation fees, union dues and assessments, or the equivalent, by a worker to a labor organization as a condition of employment or continued employment. . . .

We hold the so-called "agency shop" provision in the contract here under attack violates Article 15, Section 12, of the Kansas Constitution. . . .

Wholly aside from the reasons heretofore assigned for our conclusion, the legislature must have recognized in 1951 the laws of Kansas already included legislation adopted in 1943. . . . It provides: "Employees shall have the right to self-organization, to form, join, or assist labor organizations, to bargain collectively through representatives of their own choosing, and to engage in concerted activities, for the purpose of collective bargaining or other mutual aid or protection, and such employees shall also have the right to refrain from any or all such activities." The foregoing statutory language is identical to Section 7 of the Taft-Hartley Act (29 U.S.C.A. § 157), omitting the exception authorized in section 8 (a) (3) of the act. . . .

The right of employees guaranteed in the foregoing statute to refrain from assisting labor organizations includes the right to refrain from giving financial assistance as well as personal assistance. In other words, [the statute] prohibits forced payment of union dues and fees by employees to labor organizations. It is therefore logical to assume the legislature in 1951 may have considered it unnecessary to submit a constitutional amendment on the same subject for referendum. . . .

It is immaterial to our decision herein that the agency shop provision of the contract here under attack labels the charge to employees, as a condition of continued employment, *"an amount of money equal to* that paid by other employees in the bargaining unit who are members of the Union, which shall be limited to *an amount of money equal in* the Union's regular and usual initiation fees, and its regular and usual dues and its general and uniform assessments." . . . This is nothing more than camouflage and is in substance a charge for union dues and fees within the meaning of section 8 (a) (3) (B) of the Taft-Hartley Act. . . .

[The legislative history of the Taft-Hartley Act shows an] intent of Congress to leave the states free to prevent all forms of compulsory

unionism, and taking into consideration many other states which have
adopted detailed statutes, and many states such as Kansas which have
adopted the broader use of constitutional amendments designed to
accomplish the same purpose, there is little question that Congress and
many state legislatures have construed the words "membership in a
labor organization as a condition of employment" as embracing and
including forced payments to unions of dues, fees and other charges
regardless of the appellation applied thereto. . . .

Does a state court have jurisdiction to grant the injunctive relief
requested by the appellants or is this matter within the exclusive
domain of the National Labor Relations Board under the federal pre-
emption doctrine? . . .

As we construe the decisions of the United States Supreme Court,
the question presented by the instant case is not whether the union
or the employer might be guilty of unfair labor practices under the
Taft-Hartley Act in executing the labor relations agreement in controversy containing the agency shop provision, or in its application. In
yielding to the states permission to enact "right-to-work" laws by section
14 (b) , Congress granted authority to the state courts to process violations of such laws. There would be little point in permitting the states
to enact such laws if they could not be enforced by the states. . . .

[Judgment reversed.]

Phelps Dodge Corp. v. N.L.R.B.

313 U.S. 177 (1941)

The Phelps Dodge Corp. refused to hire Curtis because he belonged to
a labor union. Curtis was unable to find any work for some time. He
complained that the Phelps Dodge Corporation was guilty of an unfair
labor practice. The National Labor Relations Board ordered the corporation to employ Curtis and to pay him the wages he would have received
had he not been improperly denied employment. The corporation appealed.

FRANKFURTER, J. . . . It is no longer disputed that workers cannot
be dismissed from employment because of their union affiliations. Is
the national interest in industrial peace less affected by discrimination
against union activity when men are hired? . . . Discrimination against
union labor in the hiring of men is a dam to self-organization at the
source of supply. The effect of such discrimination is not confined
to the actual denial of employment; it inevitably operates against the
whole idea of the legitimacy of organization. In a word, it undermines
the principle which, as we have seen, is recognized as basic to the
attainment of industrial peace. . . .

Reinstatement is the conventional correction for discriminatory
discharges. Experience having demonstrated that discrimination in

hiring is twin to discrimination in firing, it would indeed be surprising if Congress gave a remedy for the one which it denied for the other. The powers of the Board as well as the restrictions upon it must be drawn from Section 10 (c), which directs the Board "to take such affirmative action, including reinstatement of employees with or without back pay, as will effectuate the policies of this Act." It could not be seriously denied that to require discrimination in hiring or firing to be "neutralized," . . . by requiring the discrimination to cease not abstractly but in the concrete victimizing instances, is an "affirmative action" which "will effectuate the policies of this Act." Therefore, if Section 10 (c) had empowered the Board to "take such affirmative action as will effectuate the policies of this Act," the right to restore to a man employment which was wrongfully denied him could hardly be doubted. Even without such a mandate from Congress this Court compelled reinstatement to enforce the legislative policy against discrimination represented by the Railway Labor Act. . . . To differentiate between discrimination in denying employment and in terminating it, would be a differentiation not only without substance but in defiance of that against which the prohibition of discrimination is directed.

As part of its remedial action against the unfair labor practices, the Board ordered that workers who had been denied employment be made whole for their loss of pay. In specific terms, the Board ordered payment to the men of a sum equal to what they normally would have earned from the date of the discrimination to the time of employment less their earnings during this period. The court below added a further deduction of amounts which the workers "failed without excuse to earn," and the Board here challenges this modification.

Making the workers whole for losses suffered on account of an unfair labor practice is part of the vindication of the public policy which the Board enforces. Since only actual losses should be made good, it seems fair that deductions should be made not only for actual earnings by the worker but also for losses which he willfully incurred. To this the Board counters that to apply this abstractly just doctrine of mitigation of damages to the situations before it, often involving substantial numbers of workmen, would put on the Board details too burdensome for effective administration. Simplicity of administration is thus the justification for deducting only actual earnings and for avoiding the domain of controversy as to wages that might have been earned.

But the advantages of a simple rule must be balanced against the importance of taking fair account, in a civilized legal system, of every socially desirable factor in the final judgment. The Board, we believe, overestimates administrative difficulties and underestimates its administrative resourcefulness. . . .

The Board has a wide discretion to keep the present matter within reasonable bounds through flexible procedural devices. The Board will thus have it within its power to avoid delays and difficulties incident to passing on remote and speculative claims by employees, while at the same time it may give appropriate weight to a clearly unjustifiable refusal to take desirable new employment. By leaving such an adjustment to the administrative process, we have in mind not so much the minimization of damages as the healthy policy of promoting production and employment. . . .

[Judgment for employee modified.]

Questions and Case Problems

1. What is the objective of the following rule of law? Although the federal law makes it the duty of both the union and the employer to bargain collectively, there is no duty on either to reach an agreement.

2. The J. I. Case Co. had standard individual contracts of employment with its employees. A union then petitioned for certification as the bargaining representative of the employees. The employer claimed that the existence of the individual contracts with the individual employees prevented him from bargaining with the union until the expiration of the individual contracts. Decide. (J. I. Case Co. v. N.L.R.B., 321 U.S. 332)

3. The Brotherhood of Railroad Firemen was selected as the collective bargaining representative for the employees of the Louisville & Nashville Railway Co. The union made a contract with the employer under the terms of which those employees who were not members of the union were given less favorable rights than union members. Steele, a nonunion worker, brought a proceeding before the Railway Labor Board claiming that this was an unfair practice. Decide. (Steele v. Louisville & Nashville Railway Co., 323 U.S. 192)

4. Persons who were not employees of the Babcock & Wilcox Co. began distributing union literature on parking lots that were owned by the company. The plant was located near a small well-settled community where most of the employees of the company lived, and they could be reached by telephone, mail, or door-to-door contact. The company prohibited the distribution of the union literature by the nonemployees. They complained to the N.L.R.B. Decide. (N.L.R.B. v. Babcock & Wilcox Co., 351 U.S. 105)

CHAPTER 65

Business Security

Security from Torts

Sec. 65-A. Fraud. A person is entitled to be protected from fraud and is entitled to recover damages for the harm caused by fraud. For the purpose of tort law fraud has the same scope and meaning as fraud for the purpose of avoiding a contract,[1] with the important exception that in tort law damages must be sustained by the plaintiff in addition to his reliance on the false statement.

Sec. 65-B. Slander. Liability for slander is imposed to provide security of reputation. Reputation is injured by *defamation,* which is a publication tending to cause one to lose the esteem of the community.[2] *Slander* is a form of actionable defamation consisting of the publication or communication to another of false spoken words or gestures.[3]

(1) Damages. Whether the plaintiff must actually prove that he was injured by the slander depends upon the nature of the defamatory matter. Words that charge another with the commission of a crime involving moral turpitude and infamous punishment; that impute a disease at the present time that will exclude one from society; or that have a tendency to injure one in his business, profession, or occupation [4] are regarded by the law as *actionable per se* because from common experience it is known that damages occur as a natural consequence of the publication of such words. If defamatory matter is actionable per se, the plaintiff is not required to prove actual damage sustained in consequence of the slander. Otherwise he must do so and, if he cannot prove injury, he is not entitled to recover damages.

---

[1] See p. 98.
[2] Restatement of the Law of Torts, Sec. 559.
[3] Sec. 568(2).
[4] Sec. 570.

(2) Privilege. Under certain circumstances, no liability arises when false statements are published and cause damage:

(a) An *absolute privilege* exists in the case of public officers who, in the performance of their duties, should have no fear of possible liability for damages.[5]

(b) Other circumstances may afford a *conditional privilege.*[6] A communication made in good faith upon a subject in which the party communicating has an interest, or in reference to which he has a right, is privileged if made to a person having a corresponding interest or right, although it contains criminatory matter which, without this privilege, would be slanderous. Thus a person, in protecting his interests, may in good faith charge another with the theft of his watch. A mercantile agency's credit report is privileged when made to an interested subscriber in good faith in the regular course of its business. (See p. 943, Petition of Retailers Commercial Agency, Inc.)

(3) Malice. It is frequently said that there must be "malice" in order to constitute slander. This is not, however, malice in fact, but merely malice in law, which exists when the speaker is not privileged to make his defamatory statements.

Sec. 65-C. Libel. Another wrong against the security of business relations takes the form of written defamation. This is known as *libel.* Although usually in writing, it may be in print, picture, or in any other permanent, visual form.[7] For example, to construct a gallows in front of another's residence is libelous.

The elements necessary to maintain an action for libel are the same as for slander. In the case of libel, however, it is not necessary, as a general rule, to allege and prove damages because damages will be presumed.[8] In other words, all forms of libel are actionable per se.

There is a conflict of authority as to the classification of defamatory statements made over the radio or television. Some courts treat such statements as libelous when read from a written script and slanderous when not. Other courts regard the broadcasting as slander without regard to whether there was a script.

Sec. 65-D. Disparagement of Goods and Slander of Title. In the transaction of business one is entitled to be free from interference by means of malicious false claims or statements in respect to the quality or the title of his property.[9]

---

[5] Secs. 585 to 592.
[6] Secs. 593 to 598.
[7] Sec. 568(1).
[8] Sec. 569.
[9] Secs. 624 and 626.

Actual damages must be alleged and proved to have proximately resulted from the false communication to a third person. The plaintiff must show that in consequence thereof the third person has refrained from dealing with the plaintiff.

Sec. 65-E. Infringement of Trademarks. A *trademark* is a name, device, or symbol used by a manufacturer or seller to distinguish his goods from those of other persons. When the trademark of a particular person is used or substantially copied by another, it is said that the trademark is infringed. The owner of the trademark may then sue for damages and may enjoin its further wrongful use.[10]

Geographical and descriptive names cannot ordinarily be adopted as trademarks. To illustrate, "liquid glue" is not a proper trademark. Such names may, however, be used when they do not denote origin, style, or quality. Thus "a geographical name, when not used in a geographical sense, that is, when it does not denote the location of origin, but is used in a fictitious sense merely to indicate ownership and origin independent of location, may be a good trade-mark. For example, 'Liverpool' for cloth made at Riedersfield." [11] It is possible, however, through the continued usage of a geographic or descriptive name for a number of years that such a name has acquired a secondary meaning so as to become identified in the mind of the public with a particular product or manufacturer or dealer. In such case the name is protected as a trademark.

A person who by fraudulent statements obtains the registration of a trademark in the Federal Patent Office is liable for the damages which such false registration causes anyone.

Sec. 65-F. Infringement of Patents. A grant of a *patent* entitles the patentee to prevent others for a period of 17 years from making, using, or selling the particular invention. Anyone so doing without the patentee's permission is guilty of a patent infringement.

An infringement exists, even though all the parts or features of an invention are not copied, if there is a substantial identity of means, operation, and result between the original and new devices. In the case of a process, however, all successive steps or their equivalent must be taken. In the case of a combination of ingredients, the use of the same ingredients with others constitutes an infringement, except when effecting a compound essentially different in nature.

Sec. 65-G. Infringement of Copyrights. A wrong similar to the infringement of a patent is the infringement of a copyright. A *copyright*

10 Secs. 744 and 745.
11 *Drake Medicine Co.* v. *Glessner*, 68 Ohio 337, 67 N.E. 722.

is the right given by statute to prevent others for a limited time from printing, copying, or publishing a production resulting from intellectual labor. The right exists for a period of 28 years, and it can be renewed for an additional period of 28 years.

Infringement of copyright in general consists of copying the form of expression of ideas or conceptions. There is no copyright in the idea or conception itself, but only in the particular way in which it is expressed. In order to constitute an infringement, the production need not be entirely reproduced or be exact. Substantial reproduction, although paraphrased or otherwise altered, of some part of the original constitutes an infringement. Although appropriation of a word or of a line is insufficient, an appropriation of all of or even a substantial part of the production is unnecessary to amount to an infringement.

One guilty of infringement of copyright is liable to the owner for damages and profits, or only damages, which are to be determined by the court. The owner is also entitled to an injunction to restrain further infringement.

Sec. 65-H. Unfair Competition. Unfair competition is unlawful and the person injured thereby may sue for damages or for an injunction to stop the practice, or he may report the matter to a trade commission or other agency.[12]

A form of unfair competition whereby one is able to fraudulently dispose of his wares is the imitation of signs, store fronts, advertisements, and packaging of goods.[13] Thus, when one adopts a box of distinctive size, shape, and color in which to market candy, and another appropriates the same style, form, and dress of the package, the latter may be enjoined from its use and in some cases may be liable for damages.

Sec. 65-I. Wrongful Interference with Business Relations. One of the primary rights of an individual is to earn his living by selling his labor or by engaging in trade or business. A wrongful interference with this liberty is a tort for which damages may be recovered and which, in some cases, may be restrained by an injunction.

The right to conduct one's business is, nevertheless, subject to the rights of others. Hence the injuries suffered by one in business through legitimate competition give no right of redress.[14] It has been considered wrongful interference, however, if one destroys the business of another for a malicious purpose, even though legal means are used.[15]

---

12 See p. 910.
13 R., Sec. 741.
14 Sec. 708.
15 Sec. 709.

Sec. 65-J. Inducing Breach of Contract. When a person intentionally and without reasonable justification or excuse induces a party to a contract to refuse to perform according to its terms, he is liable to the other party to the contract for the damages which he sustains from the breach of contract. The fact that the person injured by the breach may sue the defaulting party for breaking the contract does not bar suing the person who induced the breach.

Sec. 65-K. Combinations to Divert Trade. Business relations may be disturbed by a combination to keep third persons from dealing with another who is the object of attack. Such a combination, resulting in injury, constitutes an actionable wrong known as *conspiracy* if the object is unlawful, or if a lawful object is procured by unlawful means.

If the object of a combination is to further lawful interests of the association, no actionable wrong exists so long as lawful means are employed. For example, when employees are united in a strike, they may peacefully persuade others to withhold their patronage from the employer. On the other hand, all combinations to drive or keep away customers or prospective employees by violence, force, threats, or intimidation are actionable wrongs. To illustrate, a combination is usually treated as an unlawful conspiracy for which damages may be recovered when the customers are threatened and for this reason withdraw their patronage.

Labor laws make some combinations unfair labor practices,[16] while other combinations to divert trade are condemned as illegal trusts.[17]

Security from Crimes

The crimes that affect business, particularly statutory crimes, are so numerous that it will only be possible to discuss the more common offenses.

Sec. 65-L. Obtaining Goods by False Pretenses. In almost all of the states, statutes are directed against obtaining money or goods by means of false pretenses. These statutes vary in detail and scope. Sometimes the statutes are directed against particular forms of deception, such as the use of bad checks. (See p. 945, Kaufman v. Maryland)

Sec. 65-M. False Weights, Measures, and Labels. Cheating, defrauding, or misleading the public by the use of false, improper, or inadequate weights, measures, and labels is a crime. Numerous federal and state regulations have been adopted on this subject.[18]

---

16 See p. 925.
17 See p. 911.
18 See p. 910.

Sec. 65-N. Swindles and Confidence Games. The act of a person who, intending to cheat and defraud, obtains money or property by trick, deception, fraud, or other device, is an offense known as a *swindle* or *confidence game*. False or bogus checks and spurious coins are frequently employed in swindling operations directed toward the man engaged in business.

Sec. 65-O. False Coins and Currency. It is a federal crime to make, to possess with intent to pass, or to pass counterfeit coins, bank notes, or obligations or other securities of the United States. Legislation has also been enacted against the passing of counterfeit foreign securities or notes of foreign banks.

The various states also have statutes preventing the making and passing of counterfeit coins and bank notes. These statutes often provide, as does the federal statute, a punishment for the mutilation of bank notes or the lightening or mutilation of coins.

Sec. 65-P. Use of Mails to Promote Fraud. Congress has made it a crime to use the mails to further any scheme or artifice to defraud. To constitute the offense, there must be (1) a contemplated or organized scheme or artifice to defraud or to obtain money or property by false pretenses, and (2) the mailing or the causing of another to mail a letter, writing, or pamphlet for the purpose of executing or attempting to execute such scheme or artifice. Illustrations of schemes or artifices that come within the statute are false statements to secure credit, circulars announcing false cures for sale, false statements to sell stock in a corporation, and false statements as to the origin of a fire and the value of the destroyed goods for the purpose of securing indemnity from an insurance company.

Sec. 65-Q. Forgery. *Forgery* consists of the fraudulent making or material altering of an instrument, which apparently creates or changes a legal liability of another. The instrument must have some apparent legal efficacy to constitute forgery.

Ordinarily forgery consists of signing another's name with intent to defraud. It may also consist of the making of an entire instrument or the alteration of an existing one. It may result from signing a fictitious name or the offender's own name with the intent to defraud.

Sec. 65-R. Criminal Libel. A person who falsely defames another without legal excuse or justification may be subject to criminal liability as well as civil liability. *Criminal libel* is based upon its tendency to cause a breach of the peace. Under some statutes, however, the offense appears to be based upon the tendency to injure another.

No publication or communication to third persons is required in the case of criminal libel. The offense is committed when the defendant communicates the libel directly to tha person libeled as well as when he makes it known to third persons.

The truth of the statement is now generally a defense in both criminal and civil libel. A few states require that a proper motive on the part of the accused be shown as well as the fact that the statement was true.

In a number of states, slander generally or particular kinds of slander have been made criminal offenses by statute.

Sec. 65-S. Lotteries. There are three elements to a lottery: (1) a payment of money or something of value for the opportunity to win (2) a prize (3) by lot or chance. If these elements appear, it is immaterial that the transaction appears to be a legitimate form of business, or advertising, or that the transaction is called by some name other than a lottery.

Cases for Chapter 65

Petition of Retailers Commercial Agency, Inc.

174 N.E.2d 376 (Mass., 1961)

Shore, doing business under the name of Mortgage Service Bureau, inquired whether Modern Funding Corporation could use his services as a mortgage broker. Modern asked Retailer's Commercial Agency, which was under a standing contract to furnish credit reports to Modern, to furnish a report on Shore. The agency gave a report which falsely stated that Shore's net worth and income were at a fraction of their actual amounts, that he had failed in business or had gone through bankruptcy, that there were many inquiries and complaints about his unethical practices, and that he was a common and notorious thief. Some time later, a second report was furnished that was substantially true and radically different than the first. When Shore learned of the first false report, he sued Retailers Commercial Agency for libel. From a judgment in favor of the plaintiff, the defendant filed a petition to review the judgment.

SPALDING, J. . . . By the great weight of authority a report made by a mercantile agency to a particular subscriber whose business interest is involved is conditionally privileged. . . .

Those about to engage in a commercial transaction like to know something about the persons with whom they are dealing. Often they are unable to get that information themselves and must obtain it through mercantile agencies. In furnishing such information, the agencies are supplying a legitimate business need and ought to have the protection of the privilege. Without such protection few would undertake to furnish the information and the cost would be high if not prohibitive. . . . We are not to be understood as holding that there is a privilege where information is published by the agency generally to subscribers having no particular interest in the report. . . .

A conditional privilege is destroyed if abused. On this issue the burden is on the plaintiff. . . . The defendant contends that the privilege could only be abused by actual or express malice, and having failed to present any evidence of such malice, the plaintiff cannot recover. . . . It is well established that proof of actual or express malice will destroy a qualified privilege. See Galvin v. New York, N.H. & H.R.R., 168 N.E.2d at page 265, and cases cited. . . . There was no evidence that would warrant a finding of actual or express malice. But, as noted in the Galvin case, there may be an abuse of a qualified privilege even though no actual malice or ill will is shown. In that case it was held that a conditional privilege can be abused by an "unnecessary, unreasonable or excessive publication of the defamatory matter." . . .

It has long been recognized that an absence of good faith may tend to prove ill will and thus actual malice. . . . But whether the lack of good faith is said to be symptomatic of ill will, or an abuse in itself, it is clear that there is no reason to protect such communications. A lack of good faith may be shown by recklessness. . . . "Malice in uttering false statements may consist either in a direct intention to injure another, or in a reckless disregard of his rights and of the consequences that may result to him." . . . Moreover, if a defendant makes a report which he asserts to be true . . . , when he has no reasonable grounds or probable cause for so doing, it could be found that he has not acted in good faith, and has abused the privilege. . . . There is no social utility in reports that are made recklessly or without reasonable grounds. The injury to the subject of the report can be great and the person receiving the report gains nothing.

The plaintiff argues that the real test should be whether the defendant has used reasonable care. That negligence may destroy the privilege finds some support in the authorities. . . . This view, although having something to commend it, has not generally been accepted by the courts, and with good reason, for it would place undue limitations on communications which the law seeks to protect. . . . The conduct which would destroy a qualified privilege must be "more than mere negligence or want of sound judgment" and there must be "more than hasty or mistaken action." The facts that these communications are confidential and that great speed may be required in their preparation militate against a rule that would destroy the privilege by proof of ordinary negligence.

In the light of these principles, a finding for the defendant was not required. It has been already noted that there were substantial differences between the first and second reports. And, contrary to both reports, there was evidence that the plaintiff had never failed in business or gone through bankruptcy. The estimates of his earnings and net worth were much less than those later reported. There was evidence that the statement of the plaintiff's court and business records was inaccurate and misleading. The facts as to the plaintiff's bankruptcy and criminal record were susceptible of precise check. We need not decide the effect of the misreporting in other respects, for as to these verifiable matters we are of the opinion that the finder of fact could in any event conclude that the defendant made the first report recklessly, without reasonable grounds for believing it was true. If this was the case (and the trier of fact could so find) the privilege was lost. . . .

[Judgment against defendant reversed on other grounds and action remanded.]

Kaufman v. Maryland

199 Md. 35, 85 A.2d 446 (1952)

Kaufman purchased merchandise from Carrick and paid for it with a worthless check. He was prosecuted for violating the Maryland Worthless Check Act. He was convicted, and then he appealed.

DELAPLAINE, J. . . . At common law it was an indictable offense from time immemorial to cheat any person of his money or chattels by using false weights or false measures. By the Statute of 33 Henry VIII, ch. 1, passed long before the American Revolution, cheating by means of false tokens was also made an indictable offense. Even after the passage of this statute, the fraud, in order to be a crime, must have been public in its nature by being calculated to deceive or injure the public in general, or by affecting the public trade or revenue or the public health, or being in fraud of public justice. . . .

In the course of time it was found that the law was inadequate to prevent the perpetration of many flagrant frauds. Obtaining property by a false representation of fact was not a criminal offense at common law. It was held that a person who fraudulently obtained money or goods by means of a worthless check drawn on a bank in which he had no funds could not be prosecuted for cheating, as the check was not a false token. . . .

The Maryland Worthless Check Act, which was first enacted by the Legislature in 1914, and finally re-enacted in 1941, provides that any person who, with intent to cheat and defraud another, shall obtain money, credit, goods, or anything of value by means of a check drawn upon any bank not indebted to the drawer, or where the drawer shall not have provided for the payment, and the same be not paid upon presentation, shall be deemed to have obtained such money, credit, goods, or things of value by means of a false pretense. The statute expressly declares that the giving of such a check shall be prima facie evidence of intent to cheat or defraud; provided that if such person shall be a bona fide resident of the State of Maryland and shall deposit with the drawee of the check within ten days thereafter funds sufficient to meet the same, with all costs and interest which may have accrued, he shall not be prosecuted under this section. . . .

The purpose of this act is to facilitate commerce and banking by averting the inconvenience and expense of handling worthless checks through banking channels and the difficulty of collecting bills from those who give worthless checks, as well as to reduce the hazard of the loss of merchandise obtained by such checks. . . .

By express terms of our statute, the existence of fraudulent intent is an essential element of the crime of obtaining money or property by false pretenses. It is because of the frequent difficulty in proving the intent to defraud that the Worthless Check Act contains the provision for the prima facie presumption of intent to defraud from the fact of giving a check which is dishonored. In a prosecution under this act the defendant has the burden of proving that he had no intent to defraud. . . . This presumption is rebuttable by proof of proper facts negativing a fraudulent intent. Thus it has been held that the drawer of a check may not be convicted where he shows that he had reasonable expectation that the check would be paid as a result of some arrangement or understanding with his bank. . . . It is also essential to a conviction for this offense that the person who received the worthless check must have relied upon the defendant's representations, and thereby was fraudulently induced to part with his money or property. . . .

[The court then discussed the evidence and concluded that it showed the defendant was guilty.]

[Judgment of conviction affirmed.]

Questions and Case Problems

1. What is the objective of the following rule of law? Geographical and descriptive names cannot ordinarily be adopted as trademarks.

2. When Taylor, a driver for Jones Bros. Bakery, was fired, he asked the reason for his discharge. The vice-president of the bakery told Taylor that he was discharged for shorting merchants in loaves of bread delivered and that the route supervisor had evidence to prove the charge. Taylor sued the bakery for slander. Did the company have any defense? (Taylor v. Jones Bros. Bakery, 234 N.C. 660, 68 S.E.2d 313)

3. The Gruen Watch Co. made an agreement with Lester Cowan Productions that certain Gruen advertising material would be used as part of the sets of a motion picture which was to be produced. Later Cowan changed the sets so that the name Bulova appeared in place of Gruen.

Gruen sued Artists Alliance, Cowan, and Bulova, claiming that Bulova maliciously interferred with its contract rights with Cowan. If Gruen could prove the charge, was Bulova liable for damages? (Gruen Watch Co. v. Artists Alliance, [C.C.A. 9th] 191 F.2d 700)

4. Ebersole brought an action for slander of title. He alleged that Fields falsely and maliciously impugned his title to certain lands, thereby causing him to be greatly worried, vexed, and harassed. Fields entered a demurrer, contending that Ebersole had failed to state a cause of action. Was the demurrer sustained? (Ebersole v. Fields, 181 Ala. 421, 62 So. 73)

5. Bullard purchased a house from Fausett, who was in the business of buying and selling houses. At the time, Fausett was living in the house. Before making the sale, Bullard asked him what the conditions were underneath the house. Fausett said that his crew of workmen had been under the house and it was in excellent condition. In reliance on this statement Bullard purchased the house He then discovered that much repair was needed and that Fausett's statement was false. He sued Fausett for damages. The seller defended on the ground that Bullard could have ascertained the true situation for himself. Decide. (Fausett & Co. v. Bullard, [Ark.] 229 S.W.2d 450)

6. Butts brought an action against Long and another to recover damages resulting from a false claim of title made by the defendant in respect to the plaintiff's property. During the trial the defendant proved that their claim had been made in good faith. Was this a valid defense? (Butts v. Long, 106 Mo.App. 313, 80 S.W. 312)

7. The Peerless Pattern Co. and the Pictorial Review Co. were both engaged in selling paper patterns. The Peerless Pattern Co. had contracts with certain storekeepers for periodical shipments of patterns at an agreed price. These contracts provided for cancellation by either party upon thirty days' notice. An agent of the Pictorial Review Co. sent to its rival's customers letters in which it advised them to cancel the foregoing contracts and made unfounded statements respecting the insolvency of the Peerless Pattern Co. Assuming some of the customers broke their contracts with the Peerless Pattern Co., was the Pictorial Review Co. liable for damages? (Peerless Pattern Co. v. Pictorial Review Co., 147 App.Div. 715, 132 N.Y.S. 37)

8. A subscriber to Stone's Mercantile Agency requested credit information on Susie Watwood. The agency supplied information which indicated that she was an unmarried mother. She sued the agency for slander and proved that (a) she was married, though she conducted business under her maiden name, and that (b) she had no children. Was the agency liable? (Watwood v. Stone's Mercantile Agency, [C.A. D.C.] 194 F.2d 160)

9. Morse was convicted of forging the name "Hillyard Motors" as the drawer of a check. He appealed on the ground that signing such a name had no legal effect, and that therefore he was not guilty of forgery. Decide. (Washington v. Morse, 38 Wash.2d 927, 234 P.2d 478)

APPENDIX

Law and Its Enforcement

The following discussion is a supplement to Chapter 3.

Classes and Sources of Law

Essential to an understanding of the law is a knowledge of its forms, classifications, and sources.

Sec. A. Forms of the Law. *Constitutional law* includes the constitutions in force in the particular area or territory. In each state, two constitutions are in force, the state and the national constitutions.

Statutory law includes statutes adopted by the lawmakers. Each state has its own legislature and the United States has the Congress, both of which enact laws. In addition, every city, county, or other subdivision has some power to adopt ordinances or local statutes.

Of rapidly increasing importance are the *administrative regulations* for business, such as rules of the Securities and Exchange Commission and the National Labor Relations Board. The regulations promulgated by national and state administrative agencies generally have the force of statute and are therefore part of the law.

Law also includes principles that are expressed for the first time in court decisions. This is *case law*. For example, when a court must decide a new question or problem, its decision becomes a *precedent* and stands as the law for that particular problem in the future. This rule that a court decision becomes a precedent to be followed in similar cases is the *doctrine of stare decisis*.

In England, common or community law developed in the centuries following the Norman Conquest in 1066. This *common law* was a body of unwritten principles that were based on customs and usages of the community. These principles were recognized and enforced by the courts. By the time the colonies were founded in America, the English common law had become a definite, established body of principles and was brought over to the New World to become the basis for the law of the colonies and of virtually all of the states of the United States.

Law also includes treaties made by the United States, and proclamations and orders by the President of the United States or by other public officials.

Sec. B. Classifications of Law.

(1) Classification Based upon Subject Matter. Law is classified for convenience in terms of the subject matter involved. Thus the area of law relating to contracts is contract law and the area relating to corporations is corporation law.

(2) Substantive and Procedural Law. Law is sometimes classified in terms of its character as *substantive law*, which defines the substance of legal rights and liabilities, and as *procedural* or *adjective law*, which specifies the procedure that must be followed in enforcing those rights and liabilities.

(3) Classification Based upon Nature of the Law. The great body of our law is *declaratory*, that is, it declares that a person has particular rights; if those rights are violated, the law specifies the procedures by which the injured party can enforce those rights or obtain damages for their breach. Some laws are *mandatory*, requiring the performance of an act, such as labeling drugs with a statement of their chemical composition and directions for use. Other laws are *prohibitive*, such as one prohibiting conspiracies and combinations in restraint of trade. Still other laws are *permissive*, such as a statute that permits proper persons to form a corporation.

(4) Public and Private Law. Law is classified as *public law* when it deals with the organization of government or with the relation of government to the individual. It includes, for example, *administrative law*, which deals with the mechanics by which government carries out its functions. Law which deals with the rights and liabilities between private persons, corporations, partnerships, and other organizations is called *private law*.

(5) Law and Equity. Law is frequently classified as being "law" or "equity." During the early centuries following the Norman Conquest, it was common for subjects of the English Crown to present to the King petitions requesting that particular favors or relief that could not be obtained in the ordinary courts of law be granted. The extraordinary or special relief granted by the chancellor, to whom the King referred such matters, was of such a nature as was dictated by principles of justice and equity. This body of principles was called *equity*. Today equity principles are administered by either a separate equity court or by a law court administering both "law" and "equity."

(6) Classification Based upon Historical Sources. Law is sometimes classified in terms of its source as the *civil law*, which comes from the Roman civil law, and the *common law*, which is based upon the English common law or the common law that has developed in the states of the United States. The *ecclesiastical law*, which was the law enforced by the church courts, and the *law merchant*, which was the body of principles recognized by early English merchants, have been absorbed to a large extent by the common law.

During the centuries that the common law was developing in England, merchants of different nations, trading in all parts of the world, developed their own sets of rules to govern their business transactions. In many countries local authorities would permit the merchants to set up their own temporary courts to settle disputes. In the course of time the law courts of the various countries of Europe recognized and applied the same principles that the merchants followed. In England these laws of the merchants, constituting what came to be known as the law merchant, were accepted and enforced by the law courts in the Eighteenth Century.

Much of our modern business law relating to negotiable instruments, insurance, credit transactions, and partnerships originally developed in the law merchant. To the common law we owe most of our business law relating to contracts, agency, property, bailments, carriers, torts, and crimes.

Sec. C. How to Find the Law. In order to determine what the law on a particular question or issue is, it may be necessary to examine the following:

(1) Compilations. In the consideration of a legal problem in business it is necessary to determine whether the matter is affected or controlled by the Constitution, national or state; by a national treaty; by an act of Congress or a state legislature, or by a city ordinance; by a decree or proclamation of the President of the United States, a governor, or a mayor; or by a regulation of a federal, state, or local administrative agency.

Each body or person that makes laws, regulations, or ordinances usually will compile and publish at the end of each year or session all of the matter that it has adopted. In addition to the periodical or annual volumes, it is common to compile all the treaties, statutes, regulations, or ordinances in separate volumes. To illustrate, the federal Anti-Injunction Act may be cited as the Act of March 23, 1932, 47 Stat. 70, 29 U.S.C. Sections 101 et seq. This means that this law was enacted on March 23, 1932, and that this law can be found at page 70 in Volume 47 of the reports that contain all of the statutes adopted by the Congress.

The second part of the citation, 29 U.S.C. Sections 101 et seq., means that in the collection of all of the federal statutes, which is known as the United States Code, the full text of the statute can be found in the sections of the 29th volume beginning with Section 101.

(2) Court Decisions. For complicated or important legal cases or when an appeal is to be taken, a court will generally write an *opinion*, which explains why the court made the decision. Appellate courts as a rule write opinions. The great majority of these decisions, particularly in the case of the appellate courts, are collected and printed.

The reference "Pennoyer v. Neff, 95 U.S. 714, 24 L.Ed. 565," includes two citations. The first, 95 U.S. 714, means that the opinion which the court filed in the case of Pennoyer and Neff may be found on page 714 of the 95th volume of a series of books in which are printed officially the opinions of the United States Supreme Court. Sometimes the same opinion is printed in two different sets of volumes. In the example, 24 L.Ed. 565 means that in the 24th volume of another set of books, called *Lawyers' Edition*, of the United States Supreme Court Reports, the same opinion begins on page 565.

In opinions by a state court there are also generally two citations, as in the case of "Morrow v. Corbin, 122 Tex. 553, 62 S.W.2d 641." This means that the opinion in the lawsuit between Morrow and Corbin may be found in the 122d volume of the reports of the highest court of Texas, beginning on page 553; and also in Volume 62 of the *Southwestern Reporter*, Second Series, at page 641.

The West Publishing Company publishes a set of sectional reporters covering the entire United States. They are called sectional because each reporter, instead of being limited to a particular court or a particular state, covers the decisions of the courts of a particular section of the country. Because of the large number of decisions involved, generally only the opinions of the state appellate courts are printed. A number of states have discontinued the official publication of the opinions of their courts, and those opinions are now found only in the West reporters.

The reason for the "Second Series" in the Southwestern citation is that when there were 300 volumes in the original series, instead of calling the next volume 301, the publisher called it Volume 1, Second Series. Thus 62 S.W.2d Series really means the 362d volume of the *Southwestern Reporter*. Six to eight volumes appear in a year for each geographic section.

The reports published by the West Publishing Company and Lawyers Co-operative Publishing Company are unofficial reports, while those bearing the name or abbreviation of the United States or of a state, such as "95 U.S. 714" or "122 Tex. 553" are official reports.

Court opinions are part of the public domain and not subject to any copyright or similar restriction.

(3) Digests of Opinions. The reports of court decisions are useful only if one has the citation, that is, the name of the book and the page number of the opinion he is seeking. For this reason, digests of the decisions have been prepared. These digests organize the entire field of law under major headings, which are then arranged in alphabetic order. A master outline is thus created on the subject.

(4) Treatises and Restatements. Very helpful in finding a case or a statute are the treatises on the law. These may be special books, each written by an author on a particular subject, such as *Williston on Contracts, Bogert on Trusts, Fletcher on Corporations,* or they may be general encyclopedias, as in the case of *American Jurisprudence, Corpus Juris,* and *Corpus Juris Secundum.*

A new type of treatise is found in the restatements of the law prepared by the American Law Institute. Each restatement consists of one or more volumes devoted to a particular phase of the law, such as the *Restatement of the Law of Contracts, Restatement of the Law of Agency,* and *Restatement of the Law of Property.* In each restatement the American Law Institute, acting through special committees of judges, lawyers, and professors of law, has set forth what the law is; and in many areas where there is no law or the present rule is regarded as unsatisfactory, the restatement specifies what the Institute deems to be the desirable rule.

(5) Loose-Leaf Services. A number of private publishers, notably Commerce Clearing House and Prentice-Hall, publish loose-leaf books devoted to particular branches of the law. Every one, two, or four weeks, the publisher sends to the purchaser of such books a number of pages that are to be inserted in the books. These pages set forth any decision, regulation, or statute made or adopted since the prior set of pages was prepared.

The Court System

A *court* is a tribunal established by government to hear and decide matters properly brought before it, giving redress to the injured or enforcing punishment against wrongdoers, and to prevent wrongs. A *court of record* is one whose proceedings are preserved in an official record. A *court not of record* has limited judicial powers; its proceedings are not recorded, at least, not officially.

Each court has inherent power to establish rules necessary to preserve order in the court or to transact the business of the court.

An infraction of these rules or the disobedience to any other lawful order, as well as a willful act contrary to the dignity of the court or tending to pervert or obstruct justice, may be punished as *contempt of court*.

The jurisdiction and organization of courts are regulated by constitutional and statutory provision. The procedure to be followed in a court may be regulated by constitution, statute, case law, or court rule.

Sec. D. Jurisdiction of Courts. A court may have original or appellate jurisdiction, or both. A court with *original jurisdiction* has the authority to hear a controversy when it is first brought into court. A court having *appellate jurisdiction*, on the other hand, has authority to review the judgment of an inferior court.

The jurisdiction of a court may be general as distinguished from limited or special. A court having *general jurisdiction* has power to hear and decide all controversies involving legal rights and duties. A court of *limited* or special *jurisdiction* has authority to hear and decide only those cases that fall within a particular class, or only certain cases within a class, such as cases in which the amounts involved are below a specified sum.

Courts are frequently classified in terms of the nature of their jurisdiction. A *criminal court* is one that is established for the trial of cases involving offenses against the public. A *civil court*, on the other hand, is authorized to hear and decide issues involving private rights and duties. In like manner, courts are classified into equity courts, juvenile courts, probate courts, and courts of domestic relations upon the basis of their limited jurisdiction.

Sec. E. Officers of the Court. The *judge* is the primary officer of the court. He is either elected or appointed. *Attorneys* or counselors at law are also officers of the court. They are usually selected by the parties to the controversy—but in some cases by the judge—to present to the court the issues of a case.

The *clerk* of the court is appointed in some of the higher courts, but he is usually elected to office in the lower courts. His principal duties are to enter cases upon the court calendar, to keep an accurate record of the proceedings, to attest the same, and, in some instances, to approve bonds and to compute the amount of costs involved.

The *sheriff* is the chief executive of a county. In addition to the duty of maintaining peace and order within the territorial limits of a county, he has many other duties in connection with the administration of justice in county courts of record. His principal duties consist of summoning witnesses, taking charge of the jury, preserving order in court, serving writs, carrying out judicial sales, and executing judgments. The *marshals* of the United States perform these duties in the federal courts. In county courts not of record, such as the courts of justices of the peace, these duties, when appropriate, are performed by a *constable*. Some of the duties of the sheriff are now performed by persons known as *court criers*, or by deputy sheriffs, known as *bailiffs*.

Sec. F. The Jury. The *jury* is a body of citizens sworn by a court to try to determine by verdict the issues of fact submitted to them. A trial jury consists of not more than twelve persons. The first step in forming a jury is to make a *jury list*. This step consists of the preparation by the proper officers or board of a list of qualified persons from which a jury panel may be drawn. The statutes usually exempt from jury service persons in certain classes, such as attorneys, doctors, ministers, firemen, and public officers.

A certain number of persons drawn from the jury list constitute the *jury panel*. The number drawn and the procedure are usually prescribed by statutes. Selection of the jury panel is generally made by an impartial means, such as by wheel or by drawing names from a box. A trial jury is selected from members of the panel.

Sec. G. Federal Courts. The federal system of courts includes the following:

(1) Supreme Court of the United States. The Supreme Court is the only federal court expressly established by the Constitution. Congress is authorized by the Constitution to create such other federal courts as are deemed necessary.

The Supreme Court has original jurisdiction in all cases affecting ambassadors, other public ministers, and consuls, and in those cases in which a state is a party. Except as regulated by Congress, it has appellate jurisdiction in all cases that may be brought into the federal courts in accordance with the terms of the Constitution. The Supreme Court also has appellate jurisdiction of certain cases that have been decided by the supreme courts of the states.

(2) Courts of Appeals. The United States, including the District of Columbia, is divided into 11 judicial circuits. Each of the circuits has a court of appeals. These courts are courts of record.

A court of appeals has appellate jurisdiction only and is empowered to review the final decisions of the district courts, except in cases that may be taken directly to the Supreme Court. The decision of the circuit court is final in almost all criminal cases, in controversies between a citizen of this country and a citizen of another country or between citizens of different states, and in cases involving amounts of not more than $1,000. The same is true in cases arising out of the Bankruptcy Act and other federal acts, such as the Safety Appliance Act, as well as out of the trade-mark, copyright, and patent laws. As a general rule, however, the Supreme Court may review such cases upon petition of a party or upon certification by the lower court of a question of law for decision by the Supreme Court.

(3) District Courts. The United States, including the District of Columbia, is divided into a number of judicial districts. Some states form a single district, whereas others are divided into two or more districts. District courts are also located in the territories.

The district courts have original jurisdiction in practically all cases that may be maintained in the federal courts. They are the trial courts for criminal as well as for civil cases. Illustrations of civil cases that may be brought in these courts are (a) civil suits brought by the United States; (b) actions brought by citizens of different states claiming land under grants by different states; (c) proceedings under the bankruptcy, internal revenue, postal, copyright, and patent laws; (d) civil cases of admiralty and maritime jurisdiction; (e) actions against national banking associations; and (f) cases involving $10,000 or more that arise under the federal Constitution, or laws and treaties made thereunder, between citizens of different states or between citizens of one state and of a foreign state.

The Supreme Court, the courts of appeals, and the district courts are known as *constitutional courts* because they have been created and organized under Article III of the Constitution. The federal court system also includes the following *legislative courts*, which have been created by Congress to determine other matters.

(4) United States Customs Court. This court has the duty of making decisions with respect to the law and facts concerning the classification of imported goods, the rate of duty for each class, and the rules and regulations governing the collection of revenues.

(5) Court of Customs and Patent Appeals. The function of this court of record is to review decisions of the Customs Court on classifications and duties upon imported merchandise, decisions of the Patent Office on patents and trade-marks, and legal questions in the findings of the Tariff Commission pertaining to unfair practices in import trade.

(6) Court of Claims. Subject to certain exceptions, this court has jurisdiction over claims of individuals against the United States Government. Its judgments are payable only upon an appropriation by Congress.

(7) Tax Court. The Tax Court of the United States tries controversies that involve deficiencies in or overpayments of federal taxes. Most of the decisions of the court are subject to review by the appropriate court of appeals.

(8) United States Court of Military Appeals. This is a judicially independent, final appellate tribunal in courtmartial convictions.

Sec. H. State Courts. The systems of courts in the various states are organized along similar lines, although differing in details, such as the number of courts, their names, and jurisdiction.

(1) State Supreme Court. The highest court in most states is known as the Supreme Court, although in a few states it may have a different name, as "Court of Appeals" in New York. The jurisdiction of a supreme court is ordinarily appellate, although in a few instances it is original. In some states the supreme court is required to render an opinion on certain questions that may be referred to it by the legislature or by the chief executive of the state. The decision of the state supreme court is final in all cases not involving the federal Constitution, laws, and treaties.

(2) Intermediate Courts. In some states intermediate courts have original jurisdiction in a few cases but, in the main, they have appellate jurisdiction of cases removed for review from the county or district courts. They are known as superior, circuit, or district appellate courts. As a general rule their decisions may be reviewed by the highest state court.

(3) County and District Courts. These courts or record have appellate jurisdiction of cases tried in the justice and police courts, as well as general original jurisdiction of criminal and civil cases. They also have jurisdiction of testamentary and guardianship matters, except when, as in some states, the jurisdiction of such cases has been given to special orphans', surrogate, or probate courts.

(4) Justice of Peace Courts. These courts, presided over by justices of the peace, are ordinarily not courts of record. Their jurisdiction extends usually to the preliminary examination of persons accused of felonies and to the trial of misdemeanors and civil cases that involve relatively small amounts of money. In some parts of certain states justice courts have been supplanted by city or municipal courts. There are also courts in almost all cities, called *police courts,* for the trial of misdemeanors.

(5) Small Claims Courts. In a number of states, chiefly in the larger cities, special courts have been created to handle small claims

in the interest of reducing the cost and delay that litigation ordinarily involves. Some states have adopted an alternative of compulsory arbitration of small claims, subject to the right of appeal to a court of law.

(6) Traffic Courts. Special courts limited to violations of motor vehicle laws have been created in most metropolitan areas to relieve the regular courts of the great number of such cases that have accompanied the rise in the use of the automobile.

Court Procedure

Detailed laws specify how, when, and where a legal dispute can be brought to court. These rules of procedure are necessary in order to achieve an orderly, fair determination of litigation and in order to obtain, as far as is humanly possible, the same decisions on the same facts.

Sec. I. Steps in a Lawsuit.

(1) Parties. In a lawsuit the person suing is the *plaintiff*, and the person against whom he makes his claim is the *defendant*. There may be more than one plaintiff or more than one defendant. If *A* and *B* jointly own an automobile which is damaged by *C*, both *A* and *B* must join in an action against *C*. It is improper for either *A* or *B* to sue alone since it is "their" and not "his" car.

(2) Proper Court. When a person desires to go to court to enforce a right, his attorney must bring the action in the proper court. A decision by the court on a case not within its jurisdiction has no legal effect.

(3) Form of Action. The plaintiff's lawyer determines the form of action to bring. Under the old common law this was frequently a difficult problem because there were many forms of action and the plaintiff would lose his case if his attorney selected the wrong form.

A little more than a century ago, many states attempted to overhaul their procedure and reduced the number of forms of action. Accordingly a number of states thus provided that an *ejectment* should be brought for the recovery of all interests in land, a *replevin* for the recovery of any personal property, an *action of assumpsit* for any contract claim, and an *action of trespass* for any tort claim. There were still special actions, such as *mandamus* to compel a public or corporate officer to do certain kinds of acts and *quo warranto* to question the authority of a public or corporate officer to do an act or the authority of a corporation to exercise a particular power. And there were still separate criminal and equity courts. In a number of states a separate court with jurisdiction over wills, decedent's estates, and trusts began to appear.

Other states combined the forms of action and provided that all actions at law should be brought under the name of "a civil action" or "a civil action for damages" without regard to the original common-law name. Some states even abolished the distinction between actions at law and actions in equity so that the "civil action" included all noncriminal proceedings.

(4) Commencement of Action. In the old common-law courts an action was commenced by filing an order with the keeper of the court records to issue a writ to the sheriff. This writ of summons ordered the sheriff to inform the defendant to appear before the court on a particular date. This method of commencing an action is still followed in many states.

By way of contrast, an action in a court of equity was begun when the plaintiff filed with the court a *complaint* in which he stated the facts about which he complained. No writ was issued, but a copy of the complaint was served on the defendant. In many states and in the federal courts, the reform of recent years has extended this equity practice to all legal actions. These actions are today commenced by the filing of the plaintiff's complaint. Some states still preserve the former distinction between law and equity, while others give the plaintiff the option of commencing the action by either method.

(5) Service of Process. The defendant must be served with process (a writ, notice, or summons; or the complaint itself) to inform him that the action is pending against him and to subject him to the power of the court.

(6) Pleadings. After process has been served on the defendant, the plaintiff is ready to proceed. If he has not filed with the clerk of the court a written statement of his claim or complaint, he will now do so. After the complaint is filed, a copy is served on the defendant. The defendant must make some reply, generally within 15 or 20 days. If he does not, the plaintiff ordinarily wins the case by default and a judgment is entered in his favor.

Before answering the plaintiff's complaint, the defendant may make certain preliminary objections. He may assert, for example, that the action was brought in the wrong court, or that he had not been properly served. If the objection is sustained, the case may be ended, depending upon the nature of the objection, or the plaintiff may be allowed to correct his mistake. The defendant may also raise the objection, sometimes called a *motion to dismiss* or *demurrer,* that even if the plaintiff's complaint is accepted as true, he is still not entitled to any relief.

If the defendant loses on his objection, he must file an *answer,* which either admits or denies some or all of the facts averred by the plaintiff. For example, if the plaintiff declared that the defendant made a contract on a certain date, the defendant may either admit that he made the contract or deny that he did so. The fact that he admits making the contract does not end the case, for the defendant may then plead that at a later date the plaintiff and the defendant agreed to set it aside.

Without regard to whether he pleads such new matter, the defendant may generally assert a *counterclaim* or *cross complaint* against the plaintiff. Thus he may contend that the plaintiff owes him money or damages and that this liability should be offset against any claim which the plaintiff may have.

After the defendant files his answer, the plaintiff may generally file preliminary objections to the answer. Just as the defendant could raise objections, the plaintiff may, in certain instances, argue that the counterclaim cannot be asserted in the court in which the case is pending, that the answer is fatally defective in form, or that it is not a legally sufficient answer. Again the court must pass upon the preliminary objections. When these are disposed of, the pleading stage is ordinarily over.

Generally, all of the pleadings in an action may raise only a few or perhaps one question of law, or a question of fact, or both. Thus the whole case may depend on whether a letter admittedly written by the defendant amounted to an acceptance of the plaintiff's offer, thereby constituting a contract. If this question of law is answered in favor of the plaintiff, a judgment will be entered for the plaintiff: otherwise, for the defendant. By way of contrast, it may be admitted that a certain letter would be an acceptance if it had been written; but the defendant may deny that he ever wrote it. Here the question is one of fact, and the judgment is entered for the plaintiff if it is determined that the fact happened as he claimed. Otherwise the judgment is entered for the defendant.

If the only questions involved are questions of law, the court will decide the case on the pleadings alone since there is no need for a trial to determine the facts. If questions of fact are involved, then there must be a trial to determine what the facts really were.

(7) Pretrial Procedure. Many states and the federal courts have adopted other procedural steps that may be employed before the trial, with the general objective of either eliminating the need for a trial, simplifying the issues to be tried, or giving the parties information needed for preparation for trial.

(a) MOTION FOR JUDGMENT ON THE PLEADINGS. After the pleadings are closed, many states permit either party to move for a *judgment on the pleadings*. When such a motion is made, the court examines the record and may then enter a judgment according to the merits of the case as shown by the record.

(b) MOTION FOR SUMMARY JUDGMENT. In some states a party may shorten a lawsuit by bringing into court sworn statements and affidavits which show that a claim or defense is false or a sham. This procedure cannot be used when there is substantial dispute of fact concerning the matters to be proved by the use of the affidavits.

(c) PRETRIAL CONFERENCE. In many states either party may request the court to call a *pretrial conference*, or the court may take the initiative in doing so. This conference is in substance a round-table discussion by a judge of the court and the attorneys in the case. The object of the conference is to eliminate matters that are not in dispute and to determine what issues remain for litigation.

The pretrial conference is not intended as a procedure to compel the parties to settle their case. It not infrequently results, however, that when the attorneys discuss the matter with the court, they recognize that the differences between the conflicting parties are not so great as contemplated or that one side has less merit than was at first believed; in consequence, a settlement of the case is agreed upon.

(d) DISCOVERY. The Federal Rules of Civil Procedure and similar rules in a large number of states now permit one party to inquire of the adverse party and of all witnesses about anything relating to the action. This includes asking the adverse party the names of witnesses; asking the adverse party and the witnesses what they know about the case; examining, inspecting, and photographing books, records, buildings, and machines; and making an examination of the physical or mental condition of a party when it has a bearing on the action. These procedures are classed as *discovery*.

Under the prior practice, except for the relatively unusual situation in which a party could obtain information before trial by filing a bill for discovery in equity, a party never knew what witnesses would appear in court for the adverse party or what they would say, or what documentary evidence would be produced.

(e) DEPOSITIONS. Ordinarily a witness testifies in court at the time of the trial. In some instances it may be necessary or desirable to take his testimony out of court before the time of the trial. It may be that he is aged or infirm or is about to leave the state or country and will not be present when the trial of the action is held. In such a case the interested party is permitted to have the testimony, called a *deposition*, of the witness taken outside of the court.

The taking of the deposition is accomplished by having the witness appear before an officer authorized to administer oaths who places the witness under oath to tell the truth. Questions are then asked the witness as at a regular trial. The answers are recorded, generally by a stenographer, and a transcript is made of the answers. These are ordinarily read by the witness, signed by him, and the questions and answers are sent by the officer in charge of the taking of the deposition to the court in which the action is pending.

(8) *Determination of Facts.*

(a) THE TRIER OF FACTS. If the legal controversy is one which in the common-law days would have been tried by a jury, either party to the action has the constitutional right today to demand that the action be tried before a jury. If all parties agree, however, the case may be tried by the court or judge alone without a jury, and in some instances referred to a *master* or a *referee* appointed by the court to hear the matter.

In equity, although there is no constitutional right to a jury trial, the chancellor or equity judge may submit questions to a jury. There is the basic difference that in such cases the verdict or decision of the jury is only advisory to the chancellor; that is, he seeks it for his own information but is free to ignore it if he wants to do so. In contrast, the verdict of a jury in an action at law is binding on the court unless a basic error is present.

When new causes of action are created by statute, such as the right of an employee to obtain workmen's compensation for an injury arising in the course of his employment without regard to whether the employer is negligent, there is no constitutional right to a trial by jury. The trier of facts may accordingly be a judge without a jury, or a special administrative board or agency, such as a Workmen's Compensation Board.

(b) BASIS FOR DECISION. The trier of fact, whether a jury, a judge, a referee, or a board, can only decide questions of fact on the basis of evidence presented before it. Each party offers evidence in support of his claim. The evidence usually consists of the answers of persons to questions in court. Their answers are called *testimony.* The evidence may also include some *real evidence,* that is tangible things, such as papers, books, and records. In some cases, such as a damage action for improper construction of a building, the trier of fact may be taken to view the building so that a better understanding can be obtained.

The witness who testifies in court is usually a person who had some direct contact with the facts in the case, such as a person who saw the events occur or who heard one of the parties say something.

In some instances it is also proper to offer the testimony of persons who have no connection with the case when they have expert knowledge and their opinions as experts are desired.

A witness who refuses to appear in court may be ordered to do so by a *subpoena*. He may also be compelled to bring relevant papers with him to court by a *subpoena duces tecum*. If he fails to obey the subpoena, the witness may be arrested for contempt of court. In some states the names of the order upon the witness and the procedure for contempt have been changed, but the substance remains the same.

(9) Conduct of the Trial. The conduct of a trial will be discussed in terms of a jury trial. Generally a case is one of several assigned for trial on a certain day or during a certain trial period. When the turn of the case is called, the opposing counsel seat themselves at tables in front of the judge and the jury is drawn. After the jury is sworn, the attorneys usually make *opening addresses* to the jury. Details vary in different jurisdictions, but the general pattern is that each attorney tells the jury what he intends to prove. When this step has been completed, the presentation of the evidence begins.

The attorney for the plaintiff starts with his first witness and asks him all the questions that he desires and that are proper. This is called the *direct examination* of the witness since it is made by the attorney calling his own witness. After the direct examination has been finished, the opposing counsel asks the same witness such questions as he desires in an effort to disprove his story. This is called *cross-examination*. Sometimes the opposing counsel may call other witnesses to impeach the credibility of the witness.

After the cross-examination has been completed, the attorney for the plaintiff may ask the same witness other questions to overcome the effect of the cross-examination. This is called *redirect examination*. This step in turn may be followed by further examination by the defendant's attorney, called *recross-examination*.

After the examination of the plaintiff's first witness has been concluded, the plaintiff's second witness takes the witness stand and is subjected to an examination in the same way as the first. This continues until all of the plaintiff's witnesses have been called. Then the plaintiff rests his case, and the defendant calls his first witness. The pattern of examination of witnesses is repeated, except that now the defendant is calling his own witnesses and his attorney conducts the direct and redirect examination, while the questioning by the plaintiff's attorney is cross- or recross-examination.

After the witnesses of both parties have been examined and all the evidence has been presented, each attorney makes another address, a *summation*, to the jury in which he sums up what he has

proved and suggests to the jury that it reach a decision in favor of
his client.

(10) Charge to the Jury and the Verdict. The summation by the
attorneys is followed by the *charge* of the judge to the jury. This
charge is a résumé of what has happened at the trial and an explanation of the applicable law. At its conclusion, the judge instructs the
jury to retire and study the case in the light of his charge and then
return a *verdict.* By his instructions, the judge leaves to the jury the
problem of determining the facts but states the law that they must
apply to such facts as they may find. The jury then retires to secret
deliberation in the jury room.

(11) Taking the Case from the Jury and Attacking the Verdict.
At several points during the trial or immediately after, a party may
take a step to end the case or to set aside the verdict.

(a) VOLUNTARY NONSUIT. If the plaintiff is dissatisfied with
the progress of his case, he may wish to stop the trial and begin
again at a later date. In most jurisdictions he can do so by taking
a *voluntary nonsuit.*

(b) COMPULSORY NONSUIT. After the plaintiff has presented
the testimony of all his witnesses, the defendant may request the court
to enter a nonsuit on the ground that the case presented by the plaintiff does not entitle him to recover.

(c) DIRECTED VERDICT. After the presentation of all the evidence at the trial, either party may request the court to direct the jury
to return a verdict in his favor. When the plaintiff would not be
entitled to recover even though all the testimony in the plaintiff's
favor were believed, the defendant is entitled to have the court direct
the jury to return a verdict for the defendant. The plaintiff is entitled
to a verdict in his favor when, even if all the evidence on behalf of
the defendant were believed, the jury would still be required to find
for the plaintiff. In some states the defendant may make such a motion
at the close of the plaintiff's proof.

(d) NEW TRIAL. After the verdict has been returned by the
jury, a party may move for a new trial if he is not satisfied with the
verdict or with the amount of damages that has been awarded. If
it is clear that the jury has made a mistake or if material evidence
that could not have been discovered sooner is available, the court
will award a new trial and the case will be tried again before another
jury.

(e) JUDGMENT N.O.V. If the verdict returned by the jury
is clearly wrong as a matter of law, the court may set aside the

verdict and enter a judgment contrary to the verdict. This in some states is called a *judgment non obstante veredicto*, or as it is abbreviated, a judgment n.o.v.

(12) Judgment and Costs. If a new trial is not granted or if a judgment n.o.v. is not entered, the court enters a judgment following the verdict. Generally whoever is the winning party will also be awarded costs in the action. In equity actions or those that had their origin in equity, and in certain statutory proceedings, the court has discretion to award costs to the winner, to divide them between the parties, or to have each party bear his own expense.

Costs ordinarily include the costs of filing papers with the court, the cost of having the sheriff or other officers of the court take official action, the statutory fees paid to the witnesses, the cost of a jury fee, if any, and the cost of printing the record when this is required on appeal. They do not include compensation for the time spent by the party in preparing his case or in being present at the trial, the expense in going to his attorney or to the court, the time lost from work because of the case, or the fee paid by him to his attorney. Sometimes when a special statutory action is brought, the statute authorizes recovery of a small attorney's fee. Thus, a mechanic's lien statute may authorize the recovery of an attorney's fee of 10 per cent of the amount recovered, or a "reasonable attorney's fee." As a general rule, the costs that a party recovers represent only a part of the total expenses actually sustained in the litigation.

(13) Appeal. After a judgment has been entered, the party who is aggrieved thereby may appeal. This means that a party who wins the judgment but is not awarded as much as he hoped, as well as a party who loses the case, may take an appeal.

The appellate court does not hear witnesses. It examines the record of the proceedings before the lower court, that is, the file of the case containing all the pleadings, the testimony of witnesses, and the judge's charge, to see if there was error of law. To assist the court, the attorneys for the parties file arguments or briefs and generally make an argument orally before the court.

If the appellate court does not agree with the application of the law made by the lower court, it generally sets aside or modifies the action of the lower court and enters such judgment as it concludes the lower court should have entered. It may set aside the action of the lower court and send the case back to the lower court with directions to hold a new trial or with directions to enter a new judgment in accordance with the opinion that is filed by the appellate court.

(14) Execution. After a judgment has been entered or after an appeal has been decided, the losing party generally will comply with

the judgment of the court. If he refuses to do so, the winning party may then take steps to execute or carry out the judgment.

If the judgment is for the payment of a sum of money, the plaintiff may direct the sheriff or other judicial officer to sell as much of the property of the defendant as is necessary to pay the plaintiff's judgment and the costs of the proceedings and of the execution. Acting under this authorization, the sheriff may make a public sale of the defendant's property and apply the proceeds to the payment of the plaintiff's judgment. In most states the defendant is allowed an exemption of several hundred dollars and certain articles, such as personal clothing and tools of his trade.

If the judgment is for the recovery of specific property, the judgment will direct the sheriff to deliver the property to the plaintiff.

If the judgment directs the defendant to do or to refrain from doing an act, it is commonly provided that his failure to obey the order is a contempt of court punishable by fine or imprisonment.

GLOSSARY

A

abandon: give up or leave employment; relinquish possession of personal property with intent to disclaim title.

abate: put a stop to a nuisance; reduce or cancel a legacy because the estate of the testator is insufficient to make payment in full.

ab initio: from the beginning.

abrogate: recall or repeal; make void or inoperative.

absolute liability: liability for an act that causes harm even though the actor was not at fault.

absolute privilege: protection from liability for slander or libel given under certain circumstances to statements regardless of the fact that they are false or maliciously made.

abstract of title: history of the transfers of title to a given piece of land, briefly stating the parties to and the effect of all deeds, wills, and judicial proceedings relating to the land.

acceleration clause: provision in a contract or any legal instrument that upon a certain event the time for the performance of specified obligations shall be advanced; for example, a provision making the balance due upon debtor's default.

acceptance: unqualified assent to the act or proposal of another; as the acceptance of a bill of exchange, of an offer to make a contract, of goods delivered by the seller, or of a gift or a deed.

accession: acquisition of title to property by a person by virtue of the fact that it has been attached to property that he already owned or was the offspring of an animal he owned.

accessory after the fact: one who after the commission of a felony knowingly assists the felon.

accessory before the fact: one who is absent at the commission of the crime but who aided and abetted its commission.

accident: an event that occurs even though a reasonable man would not have foreseen its occurrence, because of which the law holds no one legally responsible for the harm caused.

accommodation party: a person who signs a negotiable instrument to lend credit to another.

accord and satisfaction: an agreement to substitute a different performance for that called for in the contract and the performance of that substitute agreement.

accretion: the acquisition of title to additional land when the owner's land is built up by gradual deposits made by the natural action of water.

acknowledgment: an admission or confirmation, generally of an instrument and usually made before a person authorized to administer oaths, as a notary public; the purpose being to declare that the instrument was executed by the person making the instrument, or that it was his free act, or that he desires that it be recorded.

action: a proceeding brought to enforce any right.

action in personam: an action brought to impose a personal liability upon a person, such as a money judgment.

action in rem: an action brought to declare the status of a thing, such as an action to declare the title to property to be forfeited because of its illegal use.

action of assumpsit: an action brought to recover damages for breach of a contract or a quasi-contract.

action of ejectment: an action brought to recover the possession of land.

action of mandamus: an action brought to compel the performance of a ministerial or clerical act by an officer.

action of quo warranto: an action brought to challenge the authority of an officer to act or to hold office.

action of replevin: an action brought to recover the possession of personal property.

action of trespass: an action brought to recover damages for a tort.

act of bankruptcy: any of the acts specified by the national bankruptcy law which, when committed by the debtor within the four months preceding the filing of the petition in bankruptcy, is proper ground for declaring the debtor a bankrupt if the other requirements are met.

act of God: a natural phenomenon or act of nature that is not reasonably foreseeable.

administrative agency: a governmental commission or board given authority by statute to regulate particular matters.

administrator—administratrix: the person (man—woman) appointed to wind up and settle the estate of a person who has died without a will.

adverse possession: the hostile possession of real estate, which when actual, visible, notorious, exclusive, and continued for the required number of years, will vest the title to the land in the person in such adverse possession.

advisory opinion: an opinion that may be rendered in a few states when there is no actual controversy before the court and the matter is submitted by private persons, or in some instances by the governor of the state, to obtain the court's opinion.

affidavit: a statement of facts set forth in written form and supported by the oath or affirmation of the person making the statement, setting forth that such facts are true to his knowledge or to his information and belief. The affidavit is executed before a notary public or other person authorized to administer oaths.

affinity: the relationship that exists by virtue of marriage.

affirmation: a solemn statement or declaration made by a person in lieu of taking an oath when his religious scruples do not permit him to take an oath.

affirmative covenant: an express undertaking or promise in a deed to do an act.

agency: the relationship that exists between a person identified as a principal and another by virtue of which the latter may make contracts with third persons on behalf of the principal. (Parties—principal, agent, third person)

agency coupled with an interest in the authority: an agency in which the agent has given a consideration or has paid for the right to exercise the authority granted to him.

agency coupled with an interest in the subject matter: an agency in which for a consideration the agent is given an interest in the property with which he is dealing.

agent: one who is authorized by the principal or by operation of law to make contracts with third persons on behalf of the principal.

allonge: a paper securely fastened to a negotiable instrument in order to provide additional space for indorsements.

alluvion: the additions made to land by accretion.

alteration: any material change of the terms of a writing made by a party thereto.

ambulatory: not effective and therefore may be changed, as in the case of a will that is not final until the testator has died.

amicable action: an action that all parties agree should be brought and which is begun by the filing of such an agreement, rather than by serving the adverse parties with process. Although the parties agree to litigate, the dispute is real, and the decision is not an advisory opinion.

amicus curiae: literally, a friend of the court; one who is appointed by the court to take part in litigation and to assist the court by furnishing his opinion in the matter.

annexation: attachment of personal property to realty in such a way as to make it become real property and part of the realty.

annuity: a contract by which the insured pays a lump sum to the insurer and later receives fixed annual payments.

anomalous indorser: a person who signs a negotiable instrument but is not otherwise a party to the instrument.

anticipatory breach: the repudiation by a promisor of the contract prior to the time he is required to perform when such repudiation is accepted by the promisee as a breach of the contract.

anti-injunction acts: statutes prohibiting the use of injunctions in labor disputes except under exceptional circumstances; notably the Federal Norris-La Guardia Act of 1932.

Anti-Petrillo Act: a federal statute that makes it a crime to compel a radio broadcasting station to hire musicians not needed, to pay for services not performed, or to refrain from broadcasting music of school children or from foreign countries.

antitrust acts: statutes prohibiting combinations and contracts in restraint of trade, notably the Federal Sherman Antitrust Act of 1890, now generally inapplicable to labor union activity.

appeal: taking the case to a reviewing court to determine whether the judgment of the lower court or administrative agency was correct. (Parties —appellant, appellee)

appellate jurisdiction: the power of a court to hear and decide a given class of cases on appeal from another court or administrative agency.

arbitration: the settlement of disputed questions, whether of law or fact, by one or more arbitrators by whose decision the parties agree to be bound. Increasingly used as a procedure for labor dispute settlement.

assignment: transfer of a right. Generally used in connection with personal property rights, as rights under a contract, a negotiable instrument, an insurance policy, a mortgage, or a chattel real or lease. (Parties—assignor, assignee)

assumption of risk: the common-law rule that an employee could not sue the employer for injuries caused by the ordinary risks of employment on the theory that he had assumed such risks by undertaking the work. The rule has been abolished in those areas governed by workmen's compensation laws and most employers' liability statutes.

attachment: the seizure of property of, or a debt owed to, the debtor by the service of process upon a third person who is in possession of the property or who owes a debt to the debtor.

attractive nuisance doctrine: a rule imposing liability on a landowner for injuries sustained by small children playing on his land when the landowner permits a condition to exist or maintains equipment that he should realize would attract small children who could not realize the danger. The rule does not apply if an unreasonable burden would be imposed on the landowner in taking steps to protect the children.

authenticate: make or establish as genuine, official, or final, as by signing, countersigning, sealing, or any other act indicating approval.

B

bad check laws: laws making it a criminal offense to issue a bad check with intent to defraud.

baggage: such articles of necessity or personal convenience as are usually carried for personal use by passengers of common carriers.

bail: variously used in connection with the release of a person or property from the custody of the law, referring (a) to the act of releasing or bailing (b) to the persons who assume liability in the event that the released person does not appear or it is held that the property should not be released, and (c) to the bond or sum of money that such persons furnish the court or other official as indemnity for nonperformance of the obligation.

bailee's lien: a specific, possessory lien of the bailee on the goods for work done to them. Commonly extended by statute to any bailee's claim for compensation and eliminating the necessity of retention of possession.

bailment: the relation that exists when personal property is delivered into the possession of another under an agreement, express or implied, that the identical property will be returned or will be delivered in accordance with the agreement. (Parties—bailor, bailee)

bankruptcy: a procedure by which one unable to pay his debts may be declared a bankrupt, after which all his assets in excess of his exemption claim are surrendered to the court for administration and distribution to his creditors, and the debtor is given a discharge that releases him from the unpaid balance due on most debts.

bearer: the person in physical possession of a negotiable instrument payable to bearer.

beneficiary: the person to whom the proceeds of a life insurance policy are payable, a person for whose benefit property is held in trust, or a person given property by a will.

bequest: a gift of personal property by will.

bill of exchange (draft): an unconditional order in writing by one person upon another, signed by the person giving it, and ordering the person to whom it is directed to pay or deliver on demand or at a definite time a sum certain in money to order or to bearer.

bill of lading: a document issued by a carrier reciting the receipt of goods and the terms of the contract of transportation. Regulated by the Uniform Bills of Lading Act, the Federal Bills of Lading Act, or the Uniform Commercial Code.

bill of sale: a writing signed by the seller reciting that he has sold to the buyer the personal property therein described.

binder: a memorandum delivered to the insured stating the essential terms of a policy to be executed in the future when it is agreed that the contract of insurance is to be effective before the written policy is executed.

blank indorsement: an indorsement that does not state to whom the instrument is to be paid.

blue-sky laws: state statutes designed to protect the public from the sale of worthless stocks and bonds.

boardinghouse keeper: one regularly engaged in the business of offering living accommodations to permanent lodgers or boarders as distinguished from transient guests.

bona fide: in good faith; without any fraud or deceit.

bond: an obligation or promise in writing and sealed, generally of corporations, personal representatives, trustees; fidelity bonds.

boycott: a combination of two or more persons to cause harm to another by refraining from patronizing or dealing with such other person in any way or inducing others to so refrain; commonly an incident of labor disputes.

bulk sales acts: statutes to protect creditors of a bulk seller by preventing him from obtaining cash for his goods and then leaving the state. Notice must be given creditors, and the bulk sale buyer is liable to the seller's creditors if the statute is not satisfied. Expanded to "bulk transfers" under the Code.

business trust: a form of business organization in which the owners of the property to be devoted to the business transfer the title of the property to trustees with full power to operate the business.

C

cancellation: a crossing out of a part of an instrument or a destruction of all legal effect of the instrument, whether by act of party, upon breach by the other party, or pursuant to agreement or decree of court.

capital: net assets of a corporation.

capital stock: the declared money value of the outstanding stock of the corporation.

cash surrender value: the sum that will be paid the insured if he surrenders his policy to the insurer.

cause of action: the right to damages or other judicial relief when a legally protected right of the plaintiff is violated by an unlawful act of the defendant.

caveat emptor: let the buyer beware. This maxim is subject to modification by warranties.

certificate of protest: a written statement by a notary public setting forth the fact that the holder had presented the negotiable instrument to the primary party on the due date and that the latter had failed to make payment.

cestui que trust: the beneficiary or person for whose benefit the property is held in trust.

charter: the grant of authority from a government to exist as a corporation. Generally replaced today by a certificate approving the articles of incorporation.

chattel mortgage: a security device by which the owner of personal property transfers the title to a creditor as security for the debt owed by the owner to the creditor. Replaced under the Uniform Commercial Code by a secured transaction. (Parties—chattel mortgagor, chattel mortgagee)

chattels personal: tangible personal property.

chattels real: leases of land and buildings.

check: an order by a depositor on his bank to pay a sum of money to a payee; also defined as a bill of exchange drawn on a bank and payable on demand.

chose in action: intangible personal property in the nature of claims against another, such as a claim for accounts receivable or wages.

chose in possession: tangible personal property.

circumstantial evidence: relates to circumstances surrounding the facts in dispute from which the trier of fact may deduce what had happened.

civil action: in many states a simplified form of action combining all or many of the former common-law actions.

civil court: a court with jurisdiction to hear and determine controversies relating to private rights and duties.

closed shop: a place of employment in which only union members may be employed. Now generally prohibited by unfair labor practice statutes.

C

codicil: a writing by one who has made a will which is executed with all the formality of a will and is treated as an addition to or modification of the will.

coinsurance: a clause requiring the insured to maintain insurance on his property up to a stated amount and providing that to the extent that he fails to do so the insured is to be deemed a coinsurer with the insurer so that the latter is liable only for its proportionate share of the amount of insurance required to be carried.

collateral note: a note accompanied by collateral security.

collective bargaining: the process by which the terms of employment are agreed upon through negotiations between the employer or employers within a given industry or industrial area and the union or the bargaining representative of the employees.

collective bargaining unit: the employment area within which employees are by statute authorized to select a bargaining representative, who is then to represent all the employees in bargaining collectively with the employer.

collusion: an agreement between two or more persons to defraud the government or the courts, as by obtaining a divorce by collusion when no grounds for a divorce exist, or to defraud third persons of their rights.

color of title: circumstances that make a person appear to be the owner when he in fact is not the owner, as the existence of a deed appearing to convey the property to a given person gives him color of title although the deed is worthless because it was executed by one who was not the owner of the property.

commission merchant: a bailee to whom goods are consigned for sale.

common carrier: a carrier that holds out its facilities to serve the general public for compensation without discrimination.

common law: the body of unwritten principles originally based on the usages and customs of the community which were recognized and enforced by the courts.

common stock: stock that has no right or priority over any other stock of the corporation as to dividends or distribution of assets upon dissolution.

common trust fund: a plan by which the assets of small trust estates are pooled into a common fund, each trust being given certificates representing its proportionate ownership of the fund, and the pooled fund is then invested in investments of large size.

community property: the cotenancy held by husband and wife in property acquired during their marriage under the law of some of the states, principally in the southwestern United States.

complaint: the initial pleading filed by the plaintiff in many actions which in many states may be served as original process to acquire jurisdiction over the defendant.

composition of creditors: an agreement among creditors that each shall accept a part payment as full payment in consideration of the other creditors doing the same.

concealment: the failure to volunteer information not requested.

conditional estate: an estate that will come into being upon the satisfaction of a condition precedent or that will be terminated upon the satisfaction of a condition subsequent, provided in the latter case that the grantor or his heirs re-enter and retake possession of the land.

conditional sale: a credit transaction by which the buyer purchases on credit and promises to pay the purchase price in installments, while the seller retains the title to the goods, together with the right of repossession upon default, until the condition of payment in full has been satisfied. The conditional sale is replaced under the Uniform Commercial Code by a secured transaction.

confidential relationship: a relationship in which, because of the legal status of the parties or their respective physical or mental conditions or knowledge, one party places full confidence and trust in the other and relies upon him entirely for guidance.

conflict of laws: the body of law that determines the law of which state is to apply when two or more states are involved in the facts of a given case.

confusion of goods: the mixing of goods of different owners that under certain circumstances results in one of the owners becoming the owner of all the goods.

consanguinity: relationship by blood.

consideration: the promise or performance by the other party that the promisor demands as the price of his promise.

consignment: a bailment made for the purpose of sale by the bailee. (Parties—consignor, consignee)

consolidation of corporations: a combining of two or more corporations in which the corporate existence of each one ceases and a new corporation is created.

constructive: an adjective employed to indicate that the noun which is modified by it does not exist but the law disposes of the matter as though it did; as a constructive bailment or a constructive trust.

contingent beneficiary: the person to whom the proceeds of a life insurance policy are payable in the event that the primary beneficiary dies before the insured.

contract: a binding agreement based upon the genuine assent of the parties, made for a lawful object, between competent parties, in the form re-

quired by law, and generally supported by consideration.

contract carrier: a carrier who transports on the basis of individual contracts that it makes with each shipper.

contract to sell: a contract to make a transfer of title in the future as contrasted with a present sale.

contribution: the right of a cosurety who has paid more than his proportionate share of the loss to demand that the other surety pay him the amount of the excess payment he has made.

contributory negligence: negligence of the plaintiff that contributes to his injury and at common law bars him from recovery from the defendant although the defendant may have been more negligent than the plaintiff.

conveyance: a transfer of an interest in land, ordinarily by the execution and delivery of a deed.

cooling-off period: a procedure designed to avoid strikes by requiring a specified period of delay before the strike may begin during which negotiations for a settlement must continue.

cooperative: a group of two or more persons or enterprises that act through a common agent with respect to a common objective, as buying or selling.

copyright: a grant to an author of an exclusive right to publish and sell his work for a period of 28 years, renewable for a second period of 28 years.

corporation: an artificial legal person or being created by government grant, which for many purposes is treated as a natural person.

cost plus: a method of determining the purchase price or contract price by providing for the payment of an amount equal to the costs of the seller or the contractor to which is added a stated percentage as his profit.

costs: the expenses of suing or being sued, recoverable in some actions by the successful party, and in others, subject to allocation by the court. Ordinarily they do not include attorney's fees or compensation for loss of time.

counterclaim: a claim that the defendant in an action may make against the plaintiff.

covenants of title: covenants of the grantor contained in a deed that guarantee such matters as his right to make the conveyance, his ownership of the property, the freedom of the property from encumbrances, or that the grantee will not be disturbed in the quiet enjoyment of the land.

crime: a violation of the law that is punished as an offense against the state or government.

cross complaint: a claim that the defendant may make against the plaintiff.

cross-examination: the examination made of a witness by the attorney for the adverse party.

cumulative voting: a system of voting for directors in which each stockholder has as many votes as the number of voting shares he owns multiplied by the number of directors to be elected, which votes he can distribute for the various candidates as he desires.

cy-pres doctrine: the rule under which a charitable trust will be carried out as nearly as possible in the way the settlor desired, when for any reason it cannot be carried out exactly in the way or for the purposes he had expressed.

D

damages: a sum of money recovered to redress or make amends for the legal wrong or injury done.

damnum absque injuria: loss or damage without the violation of a legal right, or the mere fact that a person sustains a loss does not mean that his legal rights have been violated or that he is entitled to sue someone.

declaratory judgment: a procedure for obtaining the decision of a court on a question before any action has been taken or loss sustained. It differs from an advisory opinion in that there must be an actual, imminent controversy.

dedication: acquisition by the public or a government of title to land when it is given over by its owner to use by the public and such gift is accepted.

deed: an instrument by which the grantor (owner of land) conveys or transfers the title to a grantee.

de facto: existing in fact as distinguished from as of right, as in the case of an officer or a corporation purporting to act as such without being elected to the office or having been properly incorporated.

deficiency judgment: a personal judgment for the amount still remaining due the mortgagee after foreclosure, which is entered against any person liable on the mortgage bond. Statutes generally require the mortgagee to credit the fair value of the property against the balance due when the mortgagee has purchased the property.

del credere agent: an agent who sells goods for the principal and who guarantees to the principal that the buyer will pay for the goods.

delegation: the transfer of the power to do an act for another.

de minimis non curat lex: a maxim that the law is not concerned with trifles. Not always applied, as in the case of the encroachment of a building over the property line in which case the law will protect the landowner regardless of the extent of the encroachment.

demonstrative evidence: evidence that consists of visible, physical objects, as a sample taken from the wheat in controversy or a photograph of the subject matter involved.

demonstrative legacy: a legacy to be paid or distributed from a specified fund or property.

demurrage: a charge made by the carrier for the unreasonable detention of cars by the consignor or consignee.

demurrer: a pleading that may be filed to attack the sufficiency of the adverse party's pleading as not stating a cause of action or a defense.

dependent relative revocation: the doctrine recognized in some states that if a testator revokes or cancels a will in order to replace it with a later will, the earlier will is to be deemed revived if for any reason the later will does not take effect or no later will is executed.

deposition: the testimony of a witness taken out of court before a person authorized to administer oaths.

devise: a gift of real estate made by will.

directed verdict: a direction by the trial judge to the jury to return a verdict in favor of a specified party to the action.

directors: the persons vested with control of the corporation, subject to the elective power of the shareholders.

discharge in bankruptcy: an order of the bankruptcy court discharging the bankrupt debtor from the unpaid balance of most of the claims against him.

discharge of contract: termination of a contract by performance, agreement, impossibility, acceptance of breach, or operation of law.

discovery: procedures for ascertaining facts prior to the time of trial in order to eliminate the element of surprise in litigation.

dishonor by nonacceptance: the refusal of the drawee to accept a bill of exchange.

dishonor by nonpayment: the refusal to pay a negotiable instrument when properly presented for payment.

dismiss: a procedure to terminate an action by moving to dismiss on the ground that the plaintiff has not pleaded a cause of action entitling him to relief.

disparagement of goods: the making of malicious, false statements as to the quality of the goods of another.

distress for rent: the common-law right of the lessor to enter the premises when he was not paid the rent and to seize all personal property found on the premises. Statutes have modified or abolished this right in many states.

distributive share: the proportionate part of the estate of the decedent that will be distributed to an heir or legatee, and also as devisee in those jurisdictions in which real estate is administered as part of the decedent's estate.

documentary evidence: evidence consisting of writings and papers of any nature or character.

domestic corporation: a corporation that has been incorporated by the state as opposed to incorporation by another state.

domicile: the home of a person or the state of incorporation of a corporation, to be distinguished from a place where a person lives but which he does not regard as his home, or a state in which a corporation does business but in which it was not incorporated.

dominant tenement: the tract of land that is benefited by an easement to which another tract, or servient tenement, is subject.

double indemnity: a provision for payment of double the amount specified by the insurance contract if death is caused by an accident and occurs under specified circumstances.

D

double jeopardy: the principle that a person who has once been placed in jeopardy by being brought to trial at which the proceedings progressed at least as far as having the jury sworn cannot thereafter be tried a second time for the same offense.

draft: see bill of exchange.

due care: the degree of care that a reasonable man would exercise to prevent the realization of harm, which under all the circumstances was reasonably forseeable in the event that such care were not taken.

due process of law: the guarantee by the 5th and 14th amendments of the federal Constitution and of many state constitutions that no person shall be deprived of life, liberty, or property without due process of law. As presently interpreted, this prohibits any law either state or federal that sets up an unfair procedure or the substance of which is arbitrary or capricious.

duress: conduct that deprives the victim of his own free will and which generally gives the victim the right to set aside any transaction entered into under such circumstances.

E

easement: a permanent right that one has in the land of another, as the right to cross another's land or easement of way.

eleemosynary corporation: a corporation organized for a charitable or benevolent purpose.

embezzlement: a statutory offense consisting of the unlawful conversion of property entrusted to the wrongdoer with respect to which he owes the owner a fiduciary duty.

eminent domain: the power of a government and certain kinds of corporations to take private property against the objection of the owner, provided the taking is for a public purpose and just compensation is made therefor.

encumbrance: a right held by a third person in or a lien or charge against property, as a mortgage or judgment lien on land.

equity: the body of principles that originally developed because of the inadequacy of the rules then applied by the common-law courts of England.

erosion: the loss of land through a gradual washing away by tides or currents, with the owner losing title to the lost land.

escheat: the transfer to the state of the title to a decedent's property when he dies intestate not survived by anyone capable of taking the property as his heir.

escrow: a conditional delivery of property or of a deed to a custodian or escrow holder, who in turn makes final delivery to the grantee or transferee when a specified condition has been satisfied.

estate: the extent and nature of one's interest in land. Also the assets constituting the decedent's property at the time of his death.

estate in fee simple: the largest estate possible in which the owner has the absolute and entire property in the land.

estoppel: the principle by which a person is barred from pursuing a certain course of action or of disputing the truth of certain matters when his conduct has been such that it would be unjust to permit him to do so.

evidence: that which is presented to the trier of fact as the basis on which the trier is to determine what had happened.

exception: an objection, as an exception to the admission of evidence on the ground that it was hearsy; the exclusion of particular property from the operation of a deed.

ex contractu: a claim or matter that is founded upon or arises out of a contract.

ex delicto: a claim or matter that is founded upon or arises out of a tort.

execution: the carrying out of a judgment of a court, generally directing that property owned by the defendant be sold and the proceeds first used to pay the execution or judgment creditor.

exemplary damages: damages in excess of the amount needed to compensate for the plaintiff's injury, which are awarded in order to punish the defendant for his malicious or wanton conduct so as to make an example of him.

exoneration: an agreement or provision in an agreement that one party shall not be held liable for loss; the right of the surety to demand that those primarily liable pay the claim for which the surety is secondarily liable.

expert witness: one who has acquired special knowledge in a particular field through practical experience, or study, or both, which gives him a superior knowledge so that his opinion is admissible as an aid to the trier of fact.

ex post facto law: a law making criminal an act that was lawful when done or that increases the penalty for an act which was subject to a lesser penalty when done. Such laws are generally prohibited by constitutional provisions.

extinguishment of debt: the discharge of a claim as by payment, as contrasted with a mere bar to its enforcement as by the running of the Statute of Limitations.

extraordinary bailment: a bailment in which the bailee is subject to unusual duties and liabilities, as a hotelkeeper or common carrier.

F

facility-of-payment clause: a provision commonly found in an industrial policy permitting the insurer to make payment to any member of a designated class or to any person the insurer believes equitably entitled thereto.

factor: a bailee to whom goods are consigned for sale.

factors' acts: statutes protecting persons who buy in good faith for value from a factor although the goods had not been delivered to the factor with the consent or authorization of their owner.

fair employment practice acts: statutes designed to eliminate discrimination in employment in terms of race, religion, natural origin, or sex.

fair labor standards acts: statutes, particularly the federal statute designed to prevent excessive hours of employment and low pay, the employment of young children, and other unsound practices.

fair trade acts: statutes that authorize the making of resale price maintenance agreements as to trade-mark and brand name articles, and generally provide that all persons in the industry are bound by such an agreement whether they have signed it or not.

featherbedding: the exaction of money for services not performed or not to be performed, which is made an unfair labor practice generally and a criminal offense in connection with radio broadcasting.

Federal Securities Act: a statute designed to protect the public from fraudulent securities.

Federal Securities Exchange Act: a statute prohibiting improper practices at and regulating security exchanges.

Federal Trade Commission Act: a statute prohibiting unfair methods of competition in interstate commerce.

fellow-servant rule: a common-law defense of the employer that barred an employee from suing an employer for injuries caused by a fellow employee.

felony: a criminal offense that is punishable by confinement in prison or by death, or that is expressly stated by statute to be a felony.

financial responsibility laws: statutes that require a driver involved in an automobile accident to prove his financial responsibility in order to retain his license, which responsibility may be shown by procuring public liability insurance in a specified minimum amount.

financing factor: one who lends money to manufacturers on the security of goods to be manufactured thereafter.

firm offer: an offer stated to be held open for a specified time, which must be so held in some states even in the absence of an option contract, or under the Code, with respect to merchants.

fixture: personal property that has become so attached to or adapted to real estate that it has lost its character as personal property and is part of the real estate.

Food, Drug, and Cosmetic Act: a federal statute prohibiting the interstate shipment of misbranded or adulterated foods, drugs, cosmetics, and therapeutic devices.

forbearance: refraining from doing an act.

foreclosure: procedure for enforcing a mortgage resulting in the public sale of the mortgaged property and less commonly in merely barring the right of the mortgagor to redeem the property from the mortgage.

foreign bill of exchange: a bill of exchange made in one nation and payable in another.

foreign corporation: a corporation incorporated under the laws of another state.

forgery: the fraudulent making or altering of an instrument that apparently creates or alters a legal liability of another.

fraud: the making of a false statement of a past or existing fact with knowledge of its falsity or with reckless indifference as to its truth with the intent to cause another to rely thereon, and he does rely thereon to his injury.

freight forwarder: one who contracts to have goods transported and, in turn, contracts with carriers for such transportation.

fructus industriales: crops that are annually planted and raised.

fructus naturales: fruits from trees, bushes, and grasses growing from perennial roots.

fungible goods: goods of a homogenous nature of which any unit is the equivalent of any other unit or is treated as such by mercantile usage.

future advance mortgage: a mortgage given to secure additional loans to be made in the future as well as an original loan.

G

garnishment: the name given in some states to attachment proceedings.

general creditor: a creditor who has a claim against the debtor but does not have any lien on any of the debtor's property, whether as security for his debt or by way of a judgment or execution upon a judgment.

general damages: damages that in the ordinary course of events follow naturally and probably from the injury caused by the defendant.

general legacy: a legacy to be paid out of the assets generally of the testator without specifying any particular fund or source from which the payment is to be made.

general partnership: a partnership in which the partners conduct as co-owners a business for profit, and each partner has a right to take part in the management of the business and has unlimited liability.

gift causa mortis: a gift made by the donor because he believed he faced immediate and impending death, which gift is revoked or is revocable under certain circumstances.

grace period: a period generally of 30 or 31 days after the due date of a premium of life insurance in which the premium may be paid.

grand jury: a jury not exceeding 23 in number that considers evidence of the commission of crime and prepares indictments to bring offenders to trial before a petty jury.

grant: convey real property; an instrument by which such property has been conveyed, particularly in the case of a government.

gratuitous bailment: a bailment in which the bailee does not receive any compensation or advantage.

grievance settlement: the adjustment of disputes relating to the administration or application of existing contracts as compared with disputes over new terms of employment.

guarantor: one who undertakes the obligation of guaranty.

guaranty: an undertaking to pay the debt of another if the creditor first sues the debtor and is unable to recover the debt from the debtor or principal. (In some instances the liability is primary, in which case it is the same as suretyship.)

H

hearsay evidence: statements made out of court which are offered in court as proof of the information contained in the statements, which, subject to many exceptions, are not admissible in evidence.

hedging: the making of simultaneous contracts to purchase and to sell a particular commodity at a future date with the intention that the loss on one transaction will be offset by the gain on the other.

heirs: those persons specified by statute to receive the estate of a decedent that he has not disposed by will.

holder: the person in possession of a negotiable instrument payable to him as payee or indorsee, or the person in possession of a negotiable instrument payable to bearer.

holder in due course: the holder of a negotiable instrument under such circumstances that he is treated as favored and is given an immunity from certain defenses.

holder through a holder in due course: a person who is not himself a holder in due course but is a holder of the instrument after it was held by some prior party who was a holder in due course, and who is given the same rights as a holder in due course.

holographic will: a will written by the testator in his own hand.

hotelkeeper: one regularly engaged in the business of offering living accommodations to all transient persons.

hung jury: a petty jury that has been unable to agree upon a verdict.

I

ignorantia legis non excusat: ignorance of the law is not an excuse.

implied contract: a contract expressed by conduct or implied or deduced from the facts. Also used to refer to a quasi-contract.

imputed: vicariously attributed to or charged to another, as the knowledge of an agent obtained while acting in the scope of his authority is imputed to his principal.

incidental authority: authority of an agent that is reasonably necessary to execute his express authority.

incontestable clause: a provision that after the lapse of a specified time the insurer cannot dispute the policy on the ground of misrepresentation or fraud of the insured or similar wrongful conduct.

in custodia legis: in the custody of the law.

indemnity: the right of a person secondarily liable to require that a person primarily liable pay him for his loss when the secondary party discharges the obligation which the primary party should have discharged; the right of an agent to be paid the amount of any loss or damage sustained by him without his fault because of his obedience to the principal's instructions; an undertaking by one person for a consideration to pay another person a sum of money to indemnify him when he incurs a specified loss.

independent contractor: a contractor who undertakes to perform a specified task according to the terms of a contract but over whom the other contracting party has no control except as provided for by the contract.

indictment: a formal accusation of crime made by a grand jury which accusation is then tried by a petty or trial jury.

inheritance: the estate which passes from the decedent to his heirs.

injunction: an order of a court of equity to refrain from doing (negative injunction) or to do (affirmative or mandatory injunction) a specified act. Its use in labor disputes has been greatly restricted by statute.

inland bill of exchange: a bill of exchange drawn and payable in the same nation.

in pari delicto: equally guilty; used in reference to a transaction as to which relief will not be granted to either party because both are equally guilty of wrongdoing.

insolvency: an excess of debts and liabilities over assets.

insurable interest: an interest in the nonoccurrence of the risk insured against, generally because such occurrence would cause financial loss, although sometimes merely because of the close relationship between the insured and the beneficiary.

insurance: a plan of security against risks by charging the loss against a fund created by the payments made by policyholders.

intangible personal property: an interest in an enterprise, such as an interest in a partnership or stock of a corporation, and claims against other persons, whether based on contract or tort.

interlineation: a writing between the lines or adding to the provisions of a document, the effect thereof depending upon the nature of the document.

interlocutory: an intermediate step or proceeding that does not make a final disposition of the action and from which ordinarily no appeal may be taken.

interpleader: a form of action or proceeding by which a person against whom conflicting claims are made may bring the claimants into court to litigate their claims between themselves, as in the case of a bailor when two persons each claim to be the owner of the bailed property, or an insurer when two persons each claim to be the beneficiary of the insurance policy.

inter se: among or between themselves, as the rights of partners inter se or as between themselves.

inter vivos: any transaction which takes place between living persons and creates rights prior to the death of any of them.

intestate: the condition of dying without a will as to any property.

intestate succession: the distribution made as directed by statute of property owned by the decedent of which he did not effectively dispose by will.

ipso facto: by the very act or fact in itself without any further action by any one.

irrebuttable presumption: a presumption which cannot be rebutted by proving that the facts are to the contrary; not a true presumption but merely a rule of law described in terms of a presumption.

irreparable injury to property: an injury that would be of such a nature or inflicted upon such an interest that it would not be reasonably possible to compensate the injured party by the payment of money damages because the property in question could not be purchased in the open market with the money damages which the defendant could be required to pay.

J

joint and several contract: a contract in which two or more persons are jointly and severally obligated or are jointly and severally entitled to recover.

joint contract: a contract in which two or more persons are jointly liable or jointly entitled to performance under the contract.

joint stock company: an association in which the shares of the members are transferable and control is delegated to a group or board.

joint tenancy: the estate held by two or more jointly with the right of survivorship as between them, unless modified by statute.

joint venture: a relationship in which two or more persons combine their labor or property for a single undertaking and share profits and losses equally unless otherwise agreed.

judgment: the final sentence, order, or decision entered into at the conclusion of the action.

judgment note: a promissory note containing a clause authorizing the holder of the note to enter judgment against the maker of the note if it is not paid when due. Also called cognovit note.

judgment n.o.v.: a judgment which may be entered after verdict upon the motion of the losing party on the ground that the verdict is so wrong that a judgment should be entered the opposite of the verdict, or non obstante veredicto (notwithstanding the verdict).

judgment on the pleadings: a judgment which may be entered after all the pleadings are filed when it is clear from the pleadings that a particular party is entitled to win the action without proceeding any further.

judicial sale: a sale made under order of court by an officer appointed to make the sale or by an officer having such authority as incident to his office. The sale may have the effect of divesting liens on the property.

jurisdiction: the power of a court to hear and determine a given class of cases; the power to act over a particular defendant.

jurisdictional dispute: a dispute between rival labor unions which may take the form of each claiming that particular work should be assigned to it.

justifiable abandonment by employee: the right of an employee to abandon his employment because of nonpayment of wages, wrongful assault, the demand for the performance of services not contemplated, or injurious working conditions.

justifiable discharge of employee: the right of an employer to discharge an employee for nonperformance of duties, fraud, disobedience, disloyalty, or incompetence.

L

laches: the rule that the enforcement of equitable rights will be denied when the party has delayed so long that rights of third persons have intervened or the death or disappearance of witnesses would prejudice any party through the loss of evidence.

J-L

land: earth, including all things imbedded in or attached thereto, whether naturally or by act of man.

last clear chance: the rule that if the defendant had the last clear chance to have avoided injuring the plaintiff, he is liable even though the plaintiff had also been contributorily negligent. In some states also called the humanitarian doctrine.

law of the case: matters decided in the course of litigation which are binding on the parties in the subsequent phases of the litigation.

leading questions: questions which suggest the desired answer to the witness, or assume the existence of a fact which is in dispute.

lease: an agreement between the owner of property and a tenant by which the former agrees to give possession of the property to the latter in consideration of the payment of rent. (Parties—landlord or lessor, tenant or lessee)

leasehold: the estate or interest which the tenant has in land rented to him.

legacy: a gift of personal property made by will.

legal tender: such form of money as the law recognizes as lawful and declares that a tender thereof in the proper amount is a proper tender which the creditor cannot refuse.

letters of administration: the written authorization given to an administrator as evidence of his appointment and authority.

letters testamentary: the written authorization given to an executor as evidence of his appointment and authority.

levy: a seizure of property by an officer of the court in execution of a judgment of the court, although in many states it is sufficient if the officer is physically in the presence of the property and announces the fact that he is "seizing" it, although he then allows the property to remain where he found it.

lex loci: the law of the place where the material facts occurred as governing the rights and liabilities of the parties.

lex loci contractus: the law of the place where the contract was made as governing the rights and liability of the parties to a contract with respect to certain matters.

lex loci fori: the law of the state in which the action is brought as determining the rules of procedure applicable to the action.

lex loci sitae rei: the law of the place where land is located as determining the validity of acts done relating thereto.

libel: the defamation of another without legal justification.

license: a personal privilege to do some act or series of acts upon the land of another not amounting to an easement or a right of possession, as the placing of a sign thereon.

lien: a claim or right against property existing by virtue of the entry of a judgment against its owner or by the entry of a judgment and a levy thereunder on the property, or because of the relationship of the claimant to the particular property, such as an unpaid seller.

life estate: an estate for the duration of a life.

limited jurisdiction: a court with power to hear and determine cases within certain restricted categories.

limited liability: loss of contributed capital as maximum liability.

limited partnership: a partnership in which at least one partner has a liability limited to the loss of the capital contribution that he has made to the partnership, and such a partner neither takes part in the management of the partnership nor appears to the public to be a partner.

lineal consanguinity: the relationship that exists when one person is a direct descendant from the other.

liquidated damages: a provision stipulating the amount of damages to be paid in event of default or breach of contract.

liquidation: the process of converting property into money whether of particular items of property or all the assets of a business.

lis pendens: the doctrine that certain types of pending actions are notice to everyone so that if any right is acquired from a party to that action, the transferee takes that right subject to the outcome of the pending action.

lobbying contract: a contract by which one party agrees to attempt to influence the action of a legislature or Congress, or any members thereof, by the use of improper means.

lottery: any plan by which a consideration is given for a chance to win a prize.

lucri causa: with the motive of obtaining gain or pecuniary advantage.

M

majority: of age, as contrasted with being a minor; more than half of any group, as a majority of stockholders.

malice in fact: an intention to injure or cause harm.

malice in law: a presumed intention to injure or cause harm when there is no privilege or right to do the act in question, which presumption cannot be contradicted or rebutted.

maliciously inducing breach of contract: the wrong of inducing an employee to break his contract with his employer or inducing the breach of any other kind of contract with knowledge of its existence and without justification.

malum in se: an offense that is criminal because contrary to the fundamental sense of a civilized community, as murder.

malum prohibitum: an offense that is criminal not because inherently wrong but is prohibited for the convenience of society, as overtime parking.

marshalling assets: the distribution of a debtor's assets in such a way as to give the greatest benefit to all of his creditors.

martial law: government exercised by a military commander over property and persons not in the armed forces, as contrasted with military law which governs the military personnel.

mechanics' lien: protection afforded by statute to various types of laborers and persons supplying materials, by giving them a lien on the building and land that has been improved or added to by them.

mens rea: the mental state that must accompany an act to make the act a crime. Sometimes described as the "guilty mind," although appreciation of guilt is not required.

merger by judgment: the discharge of a contract through being merged into a judgment which is entered in a suit on the contract.

merger of corporations: a combining of corporations by which one absorbs the other and continues to exist, preserving its original charter and identity while the other corporation ceases to exist.

mesne: intermediate, intervening, as mesne profits, which are the fruits or income from the land received in between the time that the true owner was wrongfully dispossessed and the time that he recovers the land.

misdemeanor: a criminal offense which is neither treason nor a felony.

misrepresentation: a false statement of fact although made innocently without any intent to deceive.

mobilia sequuntur personam: the maxim that personal property follows the owner and in the eyes of the law is located at the owner's domicile.

M

moratorium: a temporary suspension by statute of the enforcement of debts or the foreclosure of mortgages.

mortgage: an interest in land given by the owner to his creditor as security for the payment to the creditor of a debt, the nature of the interest depending upon the law of the state where the land is located. (Parties— mortgagor, mortgagee)

multiple insurers: insurers who agree to divide a risk so that each is only liable for a specified portion.

N

National Labor Management Relations Act: the federal statute, also known as the Taft-Hartley Act, designed to protect the organizational rights of labor and to prevent unfair labor practices by management or labor.

natural and probable consequences: those ordinary consequences of an act which a reasonable man would foresee.

negative covenant: an undertaking in a deed to refrain from doing an act.

negligence: the failure to exercise due care under the circumstances in consequence of which harm is proximately caused to one to whom the defendant owed a duty to exercise due care.

negligence per se: an action which is regarded as so improper that it is declared by law to be negligent in itself without regard to whether due care was otherwise exercised.

negotiable instruments: bills of exchange, promissory notes, checks, and certificates of deposit in such form that greater rights may be acquired thereunder than by taking an assignment of a contract right.

negotiation: the transfer of a negotiable instrument by indorsement and delivery by the person to whom then payable in the case of order paper,

and by physical transfer in the case of bearer paper.

nominal damages: a nominal sum awarded the plaintiff in order to establish that his legal rights have been violated although he in fact has not sustanied any actual loss or damages.

nominal partner: a person who in fact is not a partner but who holds himself out as a partner or permits others to do so.

Norris-LaGuardia Anti-Injunction Act: a federal statute prohibiting the use of the injunction in labor disputes, except in particular cases.

notice of dishonor: notice given to parties secondarily liable that the primary party to the instrument has refused to accept the instrument or to make payment when it was properly presented for that purpose.

novation: the discharge of a contract between two parties by their agreeing with a third person that such third person shall be substituted for one of the original parties to the contract, who shall thereupon be released.

nudum pactum: a mere promise for which there is no consideration given and which therefore is ordinarily not enforceable.

nuisance: any conduct that harms or prejudices another in the use of his land or which harms or prejudices the public.

nuisance per se: an activity which is in itself a nuisance regardless of the time and place involved.

nuncupative will: an oral will made and declared by the testator in the presence of witnesses to be his will and generally made during the testator's last illness.

O

obiter dictum: that which is said in the opinion of a court in passing or by the way, but which is not necessary to the determination of the case and is therefore not regarded as authoritative as though it were actually involved in the decision.

obliteration: any erasing, writing upon, or crossing out that makes all or part of a will impossible to read, and which has the effect of revoking such part when done by the testator with the intent of effecting a revocation.

occupation: taking and holding possession of property; a method of acquiring title to personal property which has been abandoned.

open-end mortgage: a mortgage given to secure additional loans to be made in the future as well as the original loan.

operation of law: the attaching of certain consequences to certain facts because of legal principles that operate automatically, as contrasted with consequences which arise because of the voluntary action of a party designed to create those consequences.

opinion evidence: evidence not of what the witness himself observed but the conclusion which he draws from what he observed, or in the case of an expert witness, also from what he is asked or what he has heard at the trial.

option contract: a contract to hold an offer to make a contract open for a fixed period of time.

P

paper title: the title of a person evidenced only by deeds or matter appearing of record under the recording statutes.

parol evidence rule: the rule that prohibits the introduction in evidence of oral or written statements made prior to or contemporaneously with the execution of a complete written contract, deed, or instrument, in the absence of clear proof of fraud, accident, or mis-

take causing the omission of the statement in question.

passive trust: a trust that is created without imposing any duty to be performed by the trustee and is therefore treated as an absolute transfer of the title to the trust beneficiary.

past consideration: something that has been performed in the past and which therefore cannot be consideration for a promise made in the present.

patent: the grant to an inventor of an exclusive right to make and sell his invention for a nonrenewable period of 17 years; a deed to land given by a government to a private person.

pawn: a pledge of tangible personal property rather than of documents representing property rights.

pecuniary legacy: a general legacy of a specified amount of money without indicating the source from which payment is to be made.

per autre vie: limitation of an estate. An estate held by *A* during the lifetime of *B*, is an estate of *A* per autre vie.

per curiam opinion: an opinion written "by the court" rather than by a named judge when all the judges of the court are so agreed on the matter that it is not deemed to merit any discussion and may be simply disposed of.

perpetual succession: a phrase describing the continuing life of the corporation unaffected by the death of any stockholder or the transfer by stockholders of their stock.

perpetuities, rule against: a rule of law that prohibits the creation of an interest in property which will not become definite or vested until a date further away than 21 years after the death of persons alive at the time the owner of the property attempts to create the interest.

per se: in, through, or by itself

person: a term that includes both natural persons, or living people, and artificial persons, as corporations which are created by act of government.

personal defenses: certain defenses that cannot be asserted by the defendant against a holder in due course or a holder through a holder in due course. This term is not expressly used in the Uniform Commercial Code.

per stirpes: according to the root or by way of representation. Distribution among heirs related to the decedent in different degrees, the property being divided into lines of descent from the decedent and the share of each line then divided within the line by way of representation.

petty jury: the trial jury of twelve. Also petit jury.

picketing: the placing of persons outside of places of employment or distribution so that by words or banners they may inform the public of the existence of a labor dispute.

pleadings: the papers filed by the parties in an action in order to set forth the facts and frame the issues to be tried, although under some systems, the pleadings merely give notice or a general indication of the nature of the issues.

pledge: a bailment given as security for the payment of a debt or the performance of an obligation owed to the pledgee. (Parties—pledgor, pledgee)

police power: the power to govern; the power to adopt laws for the protection of the public health, welfare, safety, and morals.

policy: the paper evidencing the contract of insurance.

polling the jury: the process of inquiring of each juror individually in open court as to whether the verdict announced by the foreman of the jury was agreed to by him.

possession: exclusive domain and control of property.

possessory lien: a right to retain possession of property of another as security

for some debt or obligation owed the lienor which right continues only as long as possession is retained.

possibility of reverter: the nature of the interest held by the grantor after conveying land outright but subject to a condition or provision that may cause the grantee's interest to become forfeited and the interest to revert to the grantor of his heirs.

postdate: to insert or place a later date on an instrument than the actual date on which it was executed.

power of appointment: a power given to another, commonly a beneficiary of a trust, to designate or appoint who shall be beneficiary or receive the fund upon his death.

power of attorney: a written authorization to an agent by the principal.

precatory words: words indicating merely a desire or a wish that another use property for a particular purpose but which in law will not be enforced in the absence of an express declaration that the property shall be used for the specified purpose.

pre-emptive offer of shares: the right, subject to many exceptions, that each shareholder has that whenever the capital stock of the corporation is increased he will be allowed to subscribe to such a percentage of the new shares as his old shares bore to the former total capital stock.

preferred creditor: a creditor who by some statute is given the right to be paid first or before other creditors.

preferred stock: stock that has a priority or preference as to payment of dividends or upon liquidation, or both.

preponderance of evidence: the degree or quantum of evidence in favor of the existence of a certain fact when from a review of all the evidence it appears more probable that the fact exists than that it does not. The actual number of witnesses involved is not material nor is the fact that the margin of probability is very slight.

prescription: the acquisition of a right to use the land of another, as an easement, through the making of hostile, visible and notorious use of the land, continuing for the period specified by the local law.

presumption: a rule of proof which permits the existence of a fact to be assumed from the proof that another fact exists when there is a logical relationship between the two or when the means of disproving the assumed fact are more readily within the control or knowledge of the adverse party against whom the presumption operates.

presumption of death: the rebuttable presumption which arises that a person has died when he has been continuously absent and unheard of for a period of 7 years.

presumption of innocence: the presumption of fact that a person accused of crime is innocent until it is shown that he in fact is guilty of the offense charged.

presumption of payment: a rebuttable presumption that one performing continuing services which would normally be paid periodically, as weekly or monthly, has in fact been paid when a number of years have passed without any objection or demand for payment having been made.

presumptive heir: a person who would be the heir if the ancestor should die at that moment.

pretrial conference: a conference held prior to the trial at which the court and the attorneys seek to simplify the issues in controversy and eliminate matters not in dispute.

price: the consideration for a sale of goods.

prima facie: such evidence as by itself would establish the claim or defense of the party if the evidence were believed.

primary beneficiary: the person designated as the first one to receive the proceeds of a life insurance policy, as distinguished from a contingent beneficiary who will receive the proceeds only if the primary beneficiary dies before the insured.

primary liability: the liability of a person whose act or omission gave rise to the cause of action and who in all fairness should therefore be the one to pay the victim of his wrong, even though others may also be liable for his misconduct.

principal: one who employs an agent to act on his behalf; the person who as between himself and the surety is primarily liable to the third person or creditor.

principal in the first degree: one who actually engages in the commission or perpetration of a crime.

principal in the second degree: one who is actually or constructively present at the commission of the crime and who aids and abets in its commission.

private carrier: a carrier owned by the shipper, such as a company's own fleet of trucks.

privileged communication: information which the witness may refuse to testify to because of the relationship with the person furnishing the information, as husband-wife, attorney-client.

privilege from arrest: the immunity from arrest of parties, witnesses, and attorneys while present within the jurisdiction for the purpose of taking part in other litigation.

privity: a succession or chain of relationship to the same thing or right, as a privity of contract, privity of estate, privity of possession.

probate: the procedure for formally establishing or proving that a given writing is the last will and testament of the person purporting to have signed it.

P

process: a writ or order of court generally used as a means of acquiring jurisdiction over the person of the defendant by serving him with process.

profit à prendre: the right to take a part of the soil or produce of the land of another, such as to take timber or water.

promissory estoppel: the doctrine that a promise will be enforced although not supported by consideration when the promisor should have reasonably expected that his promise would induce action or forebearance of a definite and substantial character on the part of the promisee, and injustice can only be avoided by enforcement of the promise.

promissory note: an unconditional promise in writing made by one person to another, signed by the maker, engaging to pay on demand, or at a definite time, a sum certain in money to order or to bearer. (Parties—maker, payee)

promissory representation: a representation made by the applicant to the insurer as to what is to occur in the future.

promissory warranty: a representation made by the applicant to the insurer as to what is to occur in the future which the applicant warrants will occur.

promoters: the persons who plan the formation of the corporation and sell or promote the idea to others.

proof: the probative effect of the evidence; the conclusion drawn from the evidence as to the existence of particular facts.

property: the rights and interests one has in anything subject to ownership.

pro rata: proportionately, or divided according to a rate or standard.

protest: the formal certification by a notary public or other authorized person that proper presentment of a negotiable instrument was made to the primary party and that he defaulted, the certificate commonly also including a recital that notice was given to secondary parties.

proximate cause: the act which is the natural and reasonably foreseeable cause of the harm or event which occurs and injures the plaintiff.

proximate damages: damages which in the ordinary course of events are the natural and reasonably foreseeable result of the defendant's violation of the plaintiff's rights.

proxy: a written authorization by a stockholder to another person to vote the stock owned by the stockholder; the person who is the holder of such a written authorization.

public charge: a person who because of a personal disability or lack of means of support is dependent upon public charity or relief for sustenance.

public domain: public or government owned lands.

public easement: a right of way for use by members of the public at large.

public policy: certain objectives relating to health, morals, and integrity of government that the law seeks to advance by declaring invalid any contract which conflicts with those objectives even though there is no statute expressly declaring such contract illegal.

punitive damages: damages in excess of those required to compensate the plaintiff for the wrong done, which are imposed in order to punish the defendant because of the particularly wanton or willful character of his wrongdoing.

purchase-money mortgage: a mortgage given by the purchaser of land to the seller to secure the seller for the payment of the unpaid balance of the purchase price, which the seller purports to lend the purchaser.

purchaser in good faith: a person who purchases without any notice or knowledge of any defect of title, misconduct, or defense.

Q

qualified acceptance: an acceptance of a bill of exchange which varies in some way the order of the bill.

qualified indorsement: an indorsement that includes words such as "without recourse" evidencing the intent of the indorser that he shall not be held liable for the failure of the primary party to pay the instrument.

quantum meruit: an action brought for the value of the services rendered the defendant when there was no express contract as to the payment to be made.

quantum valebant: an action brought for the value of goods sold the defendant when there was no express contract as to the purchase price.

quasi: as if, as though it were, having the characteristics of; a modifier employed to indicate that the subject is to be treated as though it were in fact the noun which follows the word "quasi:" as in quasi contract, quasi corporation, quasi public corporation.

quid pro quo: literally "what for what." An early form of the concept of consideration by which an action for debt could not be brought unless the defendant had obtained something in return for his obligation.

quitclaim deed: a deed by which the grantor purports only to give up whatever right or title he may have in the property without specifying or warranting that he is transferring any particular interest.

quorum: the minimum number of persons, shares represented, or directors who must be present at a meeting in order that business may be lawfully transacted.

R

ratification by minor: the approval of a contract given by a minor after attaining majority.

ratification of agency: the approval of the unauthorized act of an agent or of a person who is not an agent for any purpose after the act has been done, which has the same effect as though the act had been authorized before it was done.

ratio decidendi: the reason or basis for deciding the case in a particular way.

ratio legis: the reason for a principle or rule of law.

real defenses: certain defenses that are available against any holder of a negotiable instrument regardless of his character, although this term is not expressly used by the Uniform Commercial Code.

real evidence: tangible objects that are presented in the courtroom for the observation of the trier of fact as proof of the facts in dispute or in support of the theory of a party.

real property: land and all rights in land.

reasonable care: the degree of care that a reasonable man would take under all the circumstances then known.

rebate: a refund made by the seller or the carrier of part of the purchase price or freight bill. Generally illegal as an unfair method of competition.

rebuttable presumption: a presumption which may be overcome or rebutted by proof that the actual facts were different than those presumed.

receiver: an impartial person appointed by a court to take possession of and manage property for the protection of all concerned.

recognizance: an obligation entered into before a court to do some act, such as to appear at a later date for a hearing. Also called a contract of record.

Q-R

redemption: the buying back of one's property, which has been sold because of a default, upon paying the amount which had been originally due together with interest and costs.

referee: an impartial person selected by the parties or appointed by a court to determine facts or decide matters in dispute.

referee in bankruptcy: a referee appointed by a bankruptcy court to hear and determine various matters relating to bankruptcy proceedings.

reformation: a remedy by which a written instrument is corrected when it fails to express the actual intent of both parties because of fraud, accident, or mistake.

registration of titles: a system generally known as the Torrens system of permanent registration of title to all land within the state.

reimbursement: the right of one paying money on behalf of another which such other person should have himself paid to recover the amount of the payment from him.

release of liens: an agreement or instrument by which the holder of a lien on property, such as a mortgage lien, releases the property from the lien although the debt itself is not released.

remedy: the action or procedure that is followed in order to enforce a right or to obtain damages for injury to a right.

remote damages: damages which were in fact caused by the defendant's act but the possibility that such damages should occur seemed so improbable and unlikely to a reasonable man that the law does not impose liability for such damages.

renunciation of duty: the repudiation of one's contractual duty in advance of the time for performance, which repudiation may be accepted by the adverse party as an anticipatory breach.

renunciation of right: the surrender of a right or privilege as the right to act as administrator or the right to receive a legacy under the will of a decedent.

reorganization of corporation: procedure devised to restore insolvent corporations to financial stability through readjustment of debt and capital structure either under the supervision of a court of equity or of bankruptcy.

repossession: any taking again of possession although generally used in connection with the act of a conditional vendor in taking back the property upon the default of the conditional vendee.

representations: statements, whether oral or written, made to give the insurer the information which it needs in writing the insurance, and which if false and relating to a material fact will entitle the insurer to avoid the contract.

representative capacity: action taken by one not on his own behalf but on behalf of another, as an executor acting on behalf of the decedent's estate, or action taken both on one's behalf and on behalf of others, as a stockholder bringing a representative action.

resale price maintenance agreement: an agreement that the buyer will not resell a trademark or brand name article below a stated minimum price which agreement, by virtue of fair trade laws, is valid not only as between the contracting parties but may also bind other persons in the trade who know of the agreement although they did not sign it.

rescission upon agreement: the setting aside of a contract by the action of the parties as though the contract had never been made.

rescission upon breach: the action of one party to a contract to set the contract aside when the other party is guilty of a breach of the contract.

reservation: the creation by the grantor of a right that did not exist before, which he reserves or keeps for himself upon making a conveyance of property.

residuary estate: the balance of the testator's estate available for distribution after all administrative expenses, exemptions, debts, taxes, and specific, pecuniary, and demonstrative legacies have been paid.

res inter alios acta: the rule that transactions and declarations between strangers having no connection with the pending action are not admissible in evidence.

res ipsa loquitur: the rebuttable presumption that the thing speaks for itself when the circumstances are such that ordinarily the plaintiff could not have been injured had the defendant not been at fault.

res judicata: the principle that once a final judgment is entered in an action between the parties, it is binding upon them and the matters cannot be litigated again by bringing a second action.

respondeat superior: the doctrine that the principal or employer is vicariously liable for the unauthorized torts committed by his agent or employee while acting with the scope of his agency or the course of his employment, respectively.

restraints on alienation: limitations on the ability of the owner to convey freely as he chooses. Such limitations are generally regarded as invalid.

restrictive covenants: covenants in a deed by which the grantee agrees to refrain from doing specified acts.

restrictive indorsement: an indorsement that prohibits the further transfer, constitutes the indorsee the agent of the indorser, vests the title in the indorsee in trust for or to the use of some other person, is conditional, or is for collection or deposit.

resulting trust: a trust that is created by implication of law when the purpose of the original trust fails or is fully performed and the cy pres doctrine is inapplicable, the effect of the resulting trust being to revert the remaining property to the settlor or his heirs.

retaliatory statute: a statute that provides that when a corporation of another state enters the state it shall be subject to the same taxes and restrictions as would be imposed upon a corporation from the retaliating state if it had entered the other state. Also called reciprocity statutes.

reversible error: an error or defect in court proceedings of so serious a nature that on appeal the appellate court will set aside the proceedings of the lower court.

reversionary interest: the interest that a lessor has in property which is subject to an outstanding lease.

revival of judgment: the taking of appropriate action to preserve a judgment, in most instances to continue the lien of the judgment that would otherwise expire after a specified number of years.

revival of will: the restoration by the testator of a will which he had previously revoked.

rider: a slip of paper executed by the insurer and intended to be attached to the insurance policy for the purpose of changing it in some respect.

riparian rights: the right of a person through whose land runs a natural watercourse to use the water free from unreasonable pollution or diversion by the upper riparian owners and from blocking by lower riparian owners.

risk: the peril or contingency against which the insured is protected by the contract of insurance.

Robinson-Patman Act: a federal statute designed to eliminate price discrimination in interstate commerce.

R

run with the land: the concept that certain covenants in a deed to land are deemed to "run" or pass with the land so that whoever owns the land is bound by or entitled to the benefit of the covenants.

S

sale or return: a sale in which the title to the property passes to the buyer at the time of the transaction but he is given the option of returning the property and restoring the title to the seller.

scienter: knowledge, referring to those wrongs or crimes which require a knowledge of wrong in order to constitute the offense.

scope of employment: the area within which the employee is authorized to act with the consequence that a tort committed while so acting imposes liability upon the employer.

seal: at common law an impression on wax or other tenacious material attached to the instrument. Under modern law, any mark not ordinarily part of the signature is a seal when so intended, including the letters "L. S." and the word "seal," or a pictorial representation of a seal, without regard to whether they had been printed or typed on the instrument before its signing.

sealed verdict: a verdict that is rendered when the jury returns to the courtroom during an adjournment of the court, the verdict then being written down and sealed and later affirmed before the court when the court is in session.

seaman's will: an oral or informal written will made by a seaman to dispose of his personal property.

secondary evidence: copies of original writings or testimony as to the contents of such writings which are admissible when the original cannot be produced and the inability to do so is reasonably explained.

secret partner: a partner who takes an active part in the management of the partnership but is not known to the public as a partner.

servient tenement: the land which is subject to an easement or other right held by another.

settlor: one who settles property in trust or creates a trust estate.

severable contract: a contract the terms of which are such that one part may be separated or severed from the other, so that a default as to one part is not necessarily a default as to the entire contract.

several contracts: separate or independent contracts made by different persons undertaking to perform the same obligation.

severalty: sole ownership of property by one person.

severed realty: real property that has been cut off and made moveable, as by cutting down a tree, and which thereby loses its character as real property and becomes personal property.

shareholder's action: an action brought by one or more shareholders on behalf of the shareholders generally and of the corporation to enforce a cause of action of the corporation against third persons.

sheriff's deed: the deed executed and delivered by the sheriff to the purchaser at a sale conducted by the sheriff in his official capacity.

Sherman Antitrust Act: a federal statute prohibiting combinations and contracts in restraint of interstate trade, now generally inapplicable to labor union activity.

shop right: the right of an employer to use in his business without charge an invention discovered by an employee during working hours and with the employer's material and equipment.

sight draft: a bill of exchange payable on sight or when presented for payment.

silent partner: a partner who takes no active part in the business without regard to whether he is known to the public as a partner.

sitdown strike: a strike in which the employees remain in the plant and refuse to allow the employer to operate it.

slander: defamation of character by spoken words or gestures.

slander of title: the malicious making of false statements as to a seller's title.

slander per se: certain words deemed slanderous without requiring proof of damages to the victim, as words charging a crime involving moral turpitude and an infamous punishment, a disease which would exclude from society, or which tend to injure the victim in his business, profession, or occupation.

slowdown: a slowing down of production by employees without actual stopping of work.

social security acts: statutes providing for assistance for the aged, blind, unemployed, and similar classes of persons in need.

soldier's will: an oral or informal written will made by a soldier to dispose of his personal estate.

special agent: an agent authorized to transact a specific transaction or to do a specific act.

special damages: damages that do not necessarily result from the injury to the plaintiff but at the same time are not so remote that the defendant should not be held liable therefore provided that the claim for special damages is properly made in the action.

special indorsement: an indorsement that specifies the person to whom the instrument is indorsed.

special jurisdiction: a court with power to hear and determine cases within certain restricted categories.

specific goods: goods which are so identified to the contract that no other goods may be delivered in performance of the contract.

specific lien: the right of a creditor to hold particular property or assert a lien on any particular property of the debtor because of the creditor's having done work on or having some other association with the property, as distinguished from having a lien generally against the assets of the debtor merely because the debtor is indebted to him.

specific performance: an action brought to compel the adverse party to perform his contract on the theory that merely suing him for damages for its breach will not be an adequate remedy.

spendthrift trust: a trust, which to varying degrees, provides that creditors of the beneficiary shall not be able to reach the principal of income held by the trustee and that the beneficiary shall not be able to assign his interest in the trust.

spoliation: an alteration or change made to a written instrument by a person who has no relationship to or interest in the writing. It has no effect as long as the terms of the instrument can still be ascertained.

stare decisis: the principle that the decision of a court should serve as a guide or precedent and control the decision of a similar case in the future.

status quo: the requirement that before a contract may be rescinded, the status quo must be restored, that is, the parties must be placed in their original positions prior to the making of the contract.

Statute of Frauds: a statute, which in order to prevent fraud through the use of perjured testimony, requires that certain types of transactions be evidenced in writing in order to be binding or enforceable.

S

Statute of Limitations: a statute that restricts the period of time within which an action may be brought.

stoppage in transitu: the right of the unpaid seller to stop goods being shipped to the buyer while they are still in transit and to recover them when the buyer becomes insolvent.

stop payment: an order by a depositor to his bank to refuse to make payment of his check when presented for payment.

sublease: a transfer of the premises by the lessee to a third person, the sublessee or subtenant, for a period less than the term of the original lease.

subpoena: a court order directing a person to appear as a witness. In some states also it is the original process that is to be served on the defendant in order to give the court jurisdiction over his person.

subpoena duces tecum: a court order directing a person to appear as a witness and to bring with him specified relevant papers.

subrogation: the right of a party secondarily liable to stand in the place of the creditor after he has made payment to the creditor and to enforce the creditor's right against the party primarily liable in order to obtain indemnity from him.

subsidiary corporation: a corporation that is controlled by another corporation through the ownership by the latter of a controlling amount of the voting stock of the former.

subsidiary term: a provision of a contract that is not fundamental or does not go to the root of the contract.

substantial performance: the equitable doctrine that a contractor substantially performing a contract in good faith is entitled to recover the contract price less damages for noncompletion or defective work.

substantive law: the law that defines rights and liabilities.

substitution: discharge of contracts by substituting another in its place.

subtenant: one who rents the leased premises from the original tenant for a period of time less than the balance of the lease to the original tenant.

sui generis: in a class by itself, or its own kind.

sui juris: legally competent, possessing capacity.

summary judgment: a judgment entered by the court when no substantial dispute of fact is present, the court acting on the basis of affidavits which show that the claim or defense of a party is a sham.

summons: a writ by which an action was commenced under the common law.

superior servant rule: an exception to the fellow-servant rule that is made when the injured servant is under the control of the servant whose conduct caused him injury.

supersedeas: a stay of proceedings pending the taking of an appeal or an order entered for the purpose of effecting such a stay.

surcharge: a money judgment entered against a fiduciary for the amount of loss which his negligence or misconduct has caused the estate under his control.

suretyship: an undertaking to pay the debt or be liable for the default of another.

surrender: the yielding up of the tenant's leasehold estate to the lessor in consequence of which the lease terminates.

survival acts: statutes which provide that causes of action shall not terminate on death but shall survive and may be enforced by or against a decedent's estate.

survivorship: the right by which a surviving joint tenant or tenant by the entireties acquires the interest of the predeceasing tenant automatically upon his death.

symbolic delivery: the delivery of goods by delivery of the means of control, as a key, or relevant document of title, as a negotiable bill of lading.

syndicate: an association of individuals formed to conduct a particular business transaction, generally of a financial nature.

T

tacking: the adding together of successive periods of adverse possession of persons in privity with each other in order to constitute a sufficient period of continuous adverse possession to vest title thereby.

Taft-Hartley Act: popular name for the National Labor Management Relations Act of 1947.

tenancy at sufferance: the holding over by a tenant after his lease has expired of the rented land without the permission of the landlord and prior to the time that the landlord has elected to treat him as a trespasser or a tenant.

tenancy at will: the holding of land for an indefinite period that may be terminated at any time by the landlord or by the landlord and tenant acting together.

tenancy for years: a tenancy for a fixed period of time, even though the time is less than a year.

tenancy from year to year: a tenancy which continues indefinitely from year to year until terminated.

tenancy in common: the relation that exists when two or more persons own undivided interests in property.

tenancy in partnership: the ownership relation that exists between partners under the Uniform Partnership Act.

tender of payment: an unconditional offer to pay the exact amount of money due at the time and place specified by the contract.

tender of performance: an unconditional offer to perform at the time and in the manner specified by the contract.

tentative trust: a trust which arises when money is deposited in a bank account in the name of the depositor "in trust for" a named person.

terminable estate: an estate that terminates upon the happening of a contingency without any entry by the grantor or his heirs, as a conveyance for "so long as" the land is used for a specified purpose.

testamentary: designed to take effect at death, as by disposing of property or appointing an executor.

testate: the condition of leaving a will upon death.

testate succession: the distribution of an estate in accordance with the will of the decedent.

testator—testatrix: a man—woman who makes a will.

testimonium clause: a concluding paragraph in a deed, contract, or other instrument, reciting that the instrument has been executed on a specified date by the parties.

testimony: the answers of witnesses under oath to questions given at the time of the trial in the presence of the trier of fact.

theory of the case: the rule that when a case is tried on the basis of one theory, the appellant in taking an appeal cannot argue a different theory to the appellate court.

third-party beneficiary: a third person whom the parties to a contract intend to benefit by the making of the contract and to confer upon him the right to sue for breach of the contract.

tie-in sale: the requirement imposed by the seller that the buyer of particular goods or equipment also purchase certain other goods from the seller in order to obtain the original property desired.

T

time draft: a bill of exchange payable at a stated time after sight or a stated time after a certain date.

title insurance: a form of insurance by which the insurer insures the buyer of real property against the risk of loss should the title acquired from the seller be defective in any way.

toll the statute: stop the running of the period of the Statute of Limitations by the doing of some act by the debtor.

Torrens System: see registration of titles.

tort: a private injury or wrong arising from a breach of a duty created by law.

trade acceptance: a draft or bill of exchange drawn by the seller of goods on the purchaser at the time of sale and accepted by the purchaser.

trade fixtures: articles of personal property which have been attached to the freehold by a tenant and which are used for or are necessary to the carrying on of the tenant's trade.

trade-mark: a name, device, or symbol used by a manufacturer or seller to distinguish his goods from those of other persons.

trade name: a name under which a business is carried on and, if fictitious, it must be registered.

trade secrets: secrets of any character peculiar and important to the business of the employer that have been communicated to the employee in the course of confidential employment.

treason: an attempt to overthrow or betray the government to which one owes allegiance.

treasury stock: stock of the corporation which the corporation has reacquired.

trier of fact: in most cases a jury, although it may be the judge alone in certain classes of cases, as in equity, or in any case when jury trial is waived, or an administrative agency or commission.

trust: a transfer of property by one person to another with the understanding or declaration that such property be held for the benefit of another, or the holding of property by the owner in trust for another, upon his declaration of trust, without a transfer to another person. (Parties —settlor, trustee, beneficiary.)

trust corpus: the fund or property that is transferred to the trustee as the body or subject matter of the trust.

trust deed: a form of deed which transfers the trust property to the trustee for the purposes therein stated, particularly used as a form of mortgage when the trustee is to hold the title to the mortgagor's land in trust for the benefit of the mortgage bondholders.

trustee de son tort: a person who is not a trustee but who has wrongly intermeddled with property of another and rather than proceed against him for the tort, the law will require him to account for the property as though he were such a trustee.

trustee in bankruptcy: an impartial person elected to administer the bankrupt's estate.

trust receipt: a credit security device under which the wholesale buyer executes a receipt stating that he holds the purchased goods in trust for the person financing the purchase by lending him money. The trust receipt is replaced by the secured transaction under the Uniform Commercial Code.

U

uberrima fides: utmost good faith, a duty to exercise the utmost good faith which arises in certain relationships, as that between an insurer and the applicant for insurance.

ultra vires: an act or contract which the corporation does not have authority to do or make.

underwriter: an insurer.

undisclosed principal: a principal on whose behalf an agent acts without disclosing to the third person the fact that he is an agent nor the identity of the principal.

undue influence: the influence that is asserted upon another person by one who dominates that person.

unfair competition: the wrong of employing competitive methods that have been declared unfair by statute or an administrative agency.

unfair labor practice acts: statutes that prohibit certain labor practices and declare them to be unfair labor practices.

unincorporated association: a combination of two or more persons for the furtherance of a common nonprofit purpose.

union contract: a contract between a labor union and an employer or group of employers prescribing the general terms of employment of workers by the latter.

union shop: under present unfair labor practice statutes, a place of employment where nonunion men may be employed for a trial period of not more than 30 days after which the nonunion worker must join the union or be discharged.

universal agent: an agent authorized by the principal to do all acts that can lawfully be delegated to a representative.

usury: the lending of money at greater than the maximum rate allowed by law.

V

vacation of judgment: the setting aside of a judgment.

valid: legal.

verdict: the decision of the trial or petty jury.

vice-principal rule: the rule that persons performing supervisory functions or acting as vice employers are not to be regarded as fellow servants of those under their authority for the purpose of determining the liability of the employer for the injuries of the employee at common law.

void: no legal effect and not binding on anyone.

voidable: a transaction that may be set aside by one party thereto because of fraud or similar reason but which is binding on the other party until the injured party elects to avoid the contract.

voidable preference: a preference given by the bankrupt to one of his creditors, but which may be set aside by the trustee in bankruptcy.

voir dire examination: the preliminary examination of a juror or a witness to ascertain that he is qualified to act as such.

volenti non fit injuria: the maxim that the defendant's act cannot constitute a tort if the plaintiff had consented thereto.

voluntary nonsuit: a means of the plaintiff's stopping a trial at any time by moving for a voluntary nonsuit.

voting trust: the transfer by two or more persons of their shares of stock of a corporation to a trustee who is to vote the shares and act for such shareholders.

W

waiver: the release or relinquishment of a known right or objection.

warehouse receipt: a receipt issued by the warehouseman for goods stored with him. Regulated generally by the Uniform Warehouse Receipts Act or the Uniform Commercial Code, which clothe the receipt with some degree of negotiability.

warehouseman: a person regularly engaged in the business of storing the goods of others for compensation. If he holds himself out to serve the public without discrimination, he is a public warehouseman.

warranties of indorser of negotiable instrument: the implied covenants made by an indorser of a negotiable instrument distinct from any undertaking to pay upon the default of the primary party.

warranties of insured: statements or promises made by the applicant for insurance which he guarantees to be as stated and which if false will entitle the insurer to avoid the contract of insurance in many jurisdictions.

warranties of seller of goods: warranties consisting of express warranties that relate to matters forming part of the basis of the bargain; warranties as to title and right to sell; and the implied warranties which the law adds to a sale depending upon the nature of the transaction.

warranty deed: a deed by which the grantor conveys a specific estate or interest to the grantee and covenants that he has transferred the estate or interest by making one or more of the covenants of title.

warranty of authority: an implied warranty of an agent that he has the authority which he purports to possess.

warranty of principal: an implied warranty of an agent that he is acting for an existing principal who has capacity to contract.

watered stock: stock issued by a corporation as fully paid when in fact it is not.

way: an easement to pass over the land of another.

will: an instrument executed with the formality required by law, by which a person makes a disposition of his property to take effect upon his death or appoints an executor.

willful: intentional as distinguished from accidental or involuntary. In penal statutes, with evil intent or legal malice, or without reasonable ground for believing one's act to be lawful.

witness: a person who has observed the facts to which he testifies or an expert witness who may testify on the basis of observation, the testimony presented in the court, or hypothetical questions put to him by the attorneys in the case.

Wool Products Labeling Act: a federal statute prohibiting the misbranding of woolen fabrics.

workmen's compensation: a system providing for payments to workmen because they have been injured from a risk arising out of the course of their employment while they were employed at their employment or have contracted an occupational disease in that manner, payment being made without consideration of the negligence of any party.

works of charity: in connection with Sunday laws, acts involved in religious worship or aiding persons in distress.

works of necessity: in connection with Sunday laws, acts that must be done at the particular time in order to be effective in saving life, health, or property.

Y

year and a day: the common-law requirement that death result within a year and a day in order to impose criminal liability for homicide.

Z

zoning restrictions: restrictions imposed by government on the use of property for the advancement of the general welfare.

INDEX OF CASES

---

* Decided under the Uniform Commercial Code.
† Uniform Commercial Code Comment added to case.

_____

* Decided under the Uniform Commercial Code.
† Uniform Commercial Code Comment added to case.

* Decided under the Uniform Commercial Code.
† Uniform Commercial Code Comment added to case.

---

* Decided under the Uniform Commercial Code.
† Uniform Commercial Code Comment added to case.

* Page references for definitions are indicated by italic type.